Revision Checklist

Considering Your Whole Essay—Chapter 4

Using the <u>FACT</u> acronym, ask yourself these questions:

- ❑ Does my essay <u>F</u>IT together, presenting a central point for a specific audience? Does my thesis statement accurately reflect the content of my essay, or have I included material that has no bearing on the main point?
- ❑ Have I included all the material my reader will need to grasp my meaning, or do I need to <u>A</u>DD information or examples?
- ❑ Have I included material that fits the thesis but needs to be <u>C</u>UT because it is uninteresting, uninformative, or repetitious?
- ❑ Does a <u>T</u>EST of my organization show that the writing flows smoothly, with clear transitions between the various ideas?

Strengthening Paragraph Structure and Development—Chapter 5

- ❑ Does each paragraph have only one central idea?
- ❑ Is the idea stated in a topic sentence or clearly implied?
- ❑ Does the topic sentence help to develop the thesis statement?
- ❑ Does each paragraph contain enough supporting detail?
- ❑ Is each paragraph appropriately organized?
- ❑ Is the relationship between successive sentences clear?
- ❑ Is each paragraph clearly and smoothly related to those that precede and follow it?
- ❑ Does the introduction arouse interest and set the appropriate tone?
- ❑ Does the conclusion reflect the content of the essay and provide a sense of completeness?

Sharpening Sentences and Words—Chapters 6 and 7

- ❑ Are my sentences clearly and effectively constructed?
- ❑ Have I varied the pattern and length of my sentences?
- ❑ Do I know the meanings of the words I use?
- ❑ Do I explain meanings my reader may not know?
- ❑ Have I used the appropriate tone and level of diction?
- ❑ Does/would figurative language enhance my style?
- ❑ Have I avoided wordiness, euphemisms, cliches, mixed metaphors, and sexist language?

Editing the Draft—Handbook

- ❑ Have I inspected my writing for the types of errors listed in the editing symbols on the last page of the book?

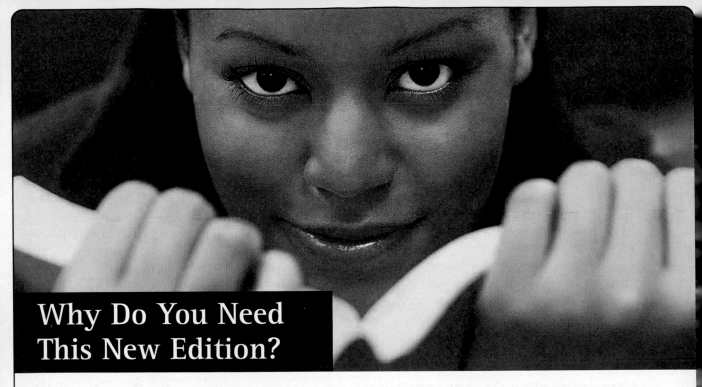

Why Do You Need This New Edition?

If you're wondering why you should buy this new edition of *Strategies for Successful Writing*, here are a few great reasons!

1. Chapter 3 on planning and drafting and Chapter 4 on revising and editing have been revised around a single, new, and stronger student example to make the writing process easier for students to follow.

2. The chapters on paragraphs, sentences, and diction, tone, and style now appear earlier in the book as Chapters 5, 6, and 7, placing all material on developing texts before the analysis of types of strategies.

3. The material in Chapter 3 on writing a thesis statement has been strengthened and includes additional exercises.

4. In chapters 4 and 5, a greater emphasis has been placed on developing a draft by making it more complete for the subsequent reader.

5. New exercises have been added on summarizing and paraphrasing.

6. New and updated writing suggestions appear throughout.

7. Six new student examples have been added, drawing on samples from classrooms around the country.

8. Short examples throughout the text have been updated.

9. New reading selections appear for Process Analysis, Cause and Effect, Definition, Argumentation, and Mixed Strategies that were selected to be appropriate to current student interests and within the range of student writing ability while allowing for the discussion of themes across the course.

10. Other updates and additions, too numerous to mention individually, appear throughout the text.

ANNOTATED INSTRUCTOR'S EDITION

NINTH EDITION

Strategies for Successful Writing

A Rhetoric, Research Guide, Reader, and Handbook

James A. Reinking

Robert von der Osten

Prentice Hall

Boston   Columbus   Indianapolis   New York   San Francisco   Upper Saddle River
Amsterdam   Cape Town   Dubai   London   Madrid   Milan   Munich   Paris   Montreal   Toronto
Delhi   Mexico City   Sao Paulo   Sydney   Hong Kong   Seoul   Singapore   Taipei   Tokyo

Senior Acquisitions Editor: Brad Potthoff
Senior Marketing Manager: Sandra McGuire
Project Manager, Editorial: Jessica A. Kupetz
Senior Media Product: Stefanie Liebman
**Project Coordination, Text Design, and Electronic
Page Makup:** GGS Higher Education Resources/PMG
Art Director: Anne Nieglos
Cover Designer: Ilze Lemesis
Image Permission Coordinator: Kathy Gavilanes
Photo Researcher: Pearson Image Resource Center/Beth Brenzel
Operations Specialist: Mary Ann Gloriande
Printer and Binder: Courier Companies/Kendallville
Cover Printer: Coral Graphic Service, Inc.

For permission to use copyrighted material, grateful acknowledgment is made to the copyright holders on page 741, which are hereby made part of this copyright page.

Prentice Hall
is an imprint of

www.pearsonhighered.com

1 2 3 4 5 6 7 8 9 10—CRK—12 11 10 09
AIE ISBN-13: 978-0-205-68945-3
ISBN-10:   0-205-68945-0
Student Edition ISBN 13: 978-0-205-68944-6
ISBN 10:   0-205-68944-2

Contents

Reader

Rhetorical Table of Contents

Contemporary Issues

Women's Issues

Diversity in Our Lives

American Borders

Language Use and Abuse

Struggling with Ethical Issues

Handbook

Preface

The ninth edition of *Strategies for Successful Writing: A Rhetoric, Research Guide, Reader, and Handbook* is a comprehensive textbook that offers ample material for a full-year composition course. Instructors teaching a one-term course can make selections from Chapters 1–17, from whatever types of specialized writing suit the needs of their students, and from appropriate essays in the Reader.

Because we strongly believe that an effective composition textbook should address the student directly, we have aimed for a style that is conversational yet clear and concise. We believe that our style invites students into the book, lessens their apprehensions about writing, and provides a model for their own prose. This style complements our strong student-based approach to writing, and together they help create a text that genuinely meets student needs.

Changes in the Ninth Edition

The enthusiastic response to the eight previous editions both by teachers and students has been very gratifying. The ninth edition retains the many popular features of the previous editions and incorporates a number of improvements suggested by users and reviewers that should considerably enhance the utility of the text. Among the changes the following are noteworthy.

- Chapters 3 and 4 have been revised around a single, new, and stronger student example to make the writing process easier for students to follow.
- Chapters 15, 16, and 17 have been moved earlier and are now Chapters 5, 6, and 7, placing all material on developing texts before the analysis of types of strategies.
- The material on writing a thesis statement has been strengthened and includes additional exercises.
- A greater emphasis has been placed in Chapters 4 and 5 on developing a draft by making it more complete for the subsequent reader.
- New exercises have been added on summarizing and paraphrasing.
- Writing suggestions have been updated.
- Six new student examples have been added, drawing on samples from classrooms around the country.

- Short examples throughout the text have been updated.
- There are several new selections in the reader.
- There are new reading selections for Process Analysis, Cause and Effect, Definition, Argumentation, and Mixed Strategies that were selected to be appropriate to current student interests and within the range of student writing ability while allowing for the discussion of themes across the course.
- Expanded Chapter: Business Letters and Résumés. This chapter, now enhanced with fourteen new case-based scenarios, is hosted online after the index in *Strategies for Successful Writing*, Ninth Edition, e-Book version of MyCompLab. Instructors please contact your Pearson representative for details and to package access to MyCompLab with this text, or visit www.mycomplab.com.

Assorted updates and additions throughout the text, too numerous to mention individually, should help make the text even more effective.

The Rhetoric

In addition to these improvements, the text offers many other noteworthy features. The Rhetoric consists of nineteen chapters, grouped into four parts. The first part includes four chapters. Chapter 1 introduces students to the purposes of writing; the need for audience awareness, which includes a discussion of discourse communities; and the qualities of good writing. Chapter 2 offers suggestions for effective reading. Chapter 3 looks at the planning and drafting stages. Chapter 4 takes students through the various revision stages, starting with a systematic procedure for revising the whole essay and then moving to pointers for revising its component parts. Sets of checklists pose key questions for students to consider. Chapters 3 and 4 are unified by an unfolding case history that includes the first draft of a student paper, the initial revision marked with changes, and the final version. Notes in the margin highlight key features of the finished paper. Students can relate the sequence of events to their own projects as they work through the various stages. Both chapters offer suggestions for using word-processing programs, and Chapter 4 explains peer evaluation of drafts, collaborative writing, and maintaining and reviewing a portfolio.

In the second part, we shift from full-length essays to the elements that make them up. Chapter 5 first discusses paragraph unity; it then takes up the topic sentence, adequate development, organization, coherence, and finally introductory, transitional, and concluding paragraphs. Throughout this chapter, as elsewhere, carefully selected examples and exercises form an integral part of the instruction.

Chapter 6 focuses on various strategies for creating effective sentences. Such strategies as coordinating and subordinating ideas and using parallelism help students to increase the versatility of their writing. The concluding section offers practical advice on crafting and arranging sentences so that they work together harmoniously. Some instructors may wish to discuss the chapters on paragraphs and sentences in connection with revision.

Chapter 7, designed to help students improve their writing style, deals with words and their effects. We distinguish between abstract and concrete words as well as between specific and general terms, and we also discuss the dictionary and thesaurus. Levels of diction—formal, informal, and technical—and how to use them are explained, as are tone, various types of figurative language, and irony. The chapter concludes by pointing out how to recognize and avoid wordiness, euphemisms, clichés, mixed metaphors, and sexist language.

The ten chapters in the third part (Chapters 8–14) feature the various strategies, or modes, used to develop papers. These strategies, which follow a general progression from less to more complex, are presented as natural ways of thinking, as problem-solving strategies, and therefore as effective ways of organizing writing. One chapter is devoted to each strategy. This part concludes with a chapter on mixing the writing strategies, which explains and shows that writers frequently use these patterns in assorted combinations for various purposes. Planning and writing guidelines are presented for problem/solution and evaluation reports, two common types that rely on a combination of strategies.

Except for Chapter 17, the discussion in each chapter follows a similar approach, first explaining the key elements of the strategy; next pointing out typical classroom and on-the-job applications to show students its practicality; and then providing specific planning, drafting, and revising guidelines. Practical heuristic questions are also posed. A complete student essay, accompanied by questions, follows the discussion section. These essays represent realistic, achievable goals and spur student confidence, while the questions reinforce the general principles of good writing and underscore the points we make in our discussions. Twenty carefully chosen writing suggestions follow the questions in most chapters. All chapters conclude with a section entitled "Critical Edge." These sections, intended for above-average students, explain and illustrate how they can advance their writing purpose by synthesizing material from various sources. Synthesis, of course, helps students develop and hone their critical reading and thinking skills. Furthermore, the *Annotated Instructor's Edition* includes suggestions for using the Reader essays and writing strategies to build assignments around themes.

The fourth and final part of the Rhetoric concentrates on three specialized types of college and on-the-job writing. Chapter 18 offers practical advice on studying for exams, assessing test questions, and writing essay answers. To facilitate student comprehension, we analyze both good and poor answers to the same exam question and provide an exercise that requires students to perform similar analyses.

Chapter 19 uses Stephen Crane's "The Bride Comes to Yellow Sky" as a springboard for its discussion. The chapter focuses on plot, point of view, character, setting, symbols, irony, and theme—the elements students will most likely be asked to write about. For each element, we first present basic features and then offer writing guidelines. Diverse examples illustrate these elements. The chapter ends with sections that detail the development of a student paper and explain how to include the views of others when writing about literature.

An expanded chapter on Business Writing is now available in the e-Book at www.mycomplab.com.

The Research Guide

The Research Guide consists of three chapters. Chapter 20 is a thorough and practical guide to writing library research papers. A sample pacing schedule not only encourages students to plan their work and meet their deadlines but also enables them to track their progress. As in Chapters 2 and 3, a progressive case history gradually evolves into an annotated student paper, which includes the results of a personal interview, thus demonstrating that primary research can reinforce secondary research.

Chapter 21 details and illustrates the correct formats for bibliographical references and in-text citations for both the MLA and APA systems of documentation. Guidelines are based on the 2009 edition of the *Publication Manual of the American Psychological Association* and current online updates as well as the 2009 edition of *The MLA Style Manual*. The chapter also explains how to handle the various types of quotations and how to avoid plagiarism. Our detailed treatment in the e-Chapter and Chapter 21 should make supplemental handouts or a separate research-paper guide unnecessary.

Chapter 22 offers an in-depth discussion of interview, questionnaire, and direct-observation reports. After pointing out the nature, usefulness, and requirements of primary research, we explain how to plan and write each report, concluding with an annotated student model that illustrates the guidelines.

The Reader

The Reader, sequenced to follow the order of the strategies presented in the Rhetoric, expands the utility of the text by providing a collection of forty-two carefully selected professional models that illustrate the various writing strategies and display a wide variety of style, tone, and subject matter. These essays, together with the nine student models that accompany the various strategy chapters, should make a separate reader unnecessary.

Supplementing the chapter on reading strategies, the Reader comes with reading suggestions for each strategy that detail how to read the essays of a given type, how to read essays critically, and how to read the essays as a writer.

Each essay clearly illustrates the designated pattern, each has been thoroughly class-tested for student interest, and each provides a springboard for a stimulating discussion. In making our selections we have aimed for balance and variety:

1. Some are popular classics by acknowledged prose masters; some, anthologized for the first time, are by fresh, new writers.
2. Some are straightforward and simple, some challenging and complex.
3. Some adopt a humorous, lighthearted approach; some a serious, thoughtful one.
4. Some take a liberal stance, some a conservative one; and some address ethnic, gender, and cultural diversity.
5. A few are rather lengthy; most are relatively brief.

The first essay in each strategy section is annotated in the margin to show which features of the strategy are included. These annotations not only facilitate student understanding but also help link the Rhetoric and Reader into an organic whole. A brief biographical note about the author precedes each selection, and stimulating questions designed to enhance student understanding of structure and strategy follow it. In addition, a segment entitled "Toward Key Insights" poses one or more broad-based questions prompted by the essay's content. Answering these questions, either in discussion or writing, should help students gain a deeper understanding of important issues. Finally, we include a writing assignment suggested by the essay's topic.

The Handbook

The comprehensive Handbook, which features tab indexing on each page for easy access to all material, consists of five parts: "Sentence Elements," "Editing to Correct Sentence Errors," "Editing to Correct Faulty Punctuation and Mechanics," "Spelling," and "Glossary of Word Usage." Explanations skirt unneeded grammatical terminology and are reinforced by sets of sentence exercises in the first three sections. The section on "Sentence Elements" explains how students can use these elements to improve their writing skills. We also include connected-discourse exercises—unfolding narratives that engage and retain student interest and therefore facilitate learning—in the "Sentence Errors" and "Punctuation and Mechanics" sections. Extra sets of twenty-item exercises that parallel those in the Handbook are available upon request to instructors who adopt the book. The "Spelling" unit presents four useful spelling rules and an extensive list of commonly misspelled words. The "Glossary of Word Usage" offers similarly comprehensive coverage of troublesome usages. Instructors can use the Handbook either as a reference guide or as a basis for class discussion.

Supplementary Material for Instructors and Students

The *Annotated Instructor's Edition* (978-0-205-68945-3) consists of the entire student edition as well as strong instructional support. The material in the margins of the text consists of background information on particular aspects of writing; key insights into how students view writing projects and why they experience difficulties; case studies that raise ethical issues for student discussion; answers to all discussion questions and to appropriate exercises in the text; supplementary exercises; teaching strategies and classroom activities that instructors may want to consider; and Reader/Theme strategies that show how to use the Reader to build writing assignments based on themes.

The *Teaching Composition with Strategies for Successful Writing*, Ninth Edition (978-0-205-76903-2), supplement offers various suggestions for teaching first-year composition, a sample syllabus for a sequence of two fifteen-week semesters, numerous guidelines for responding to student writing, and a detailed set of grading standards. In addition, it contains an extra set of twenty-item exercises that parallel those in the Handbook section of *Strategies*. The exercises can be used either in the classroom or as assignments.

MyCompLab empowers student writers and facilitates writing instruction by uniquely integrating a composing space and assessment tools with market-leading instruction, multimedia tutorials, and exercises for writing, grammar and research.

Students can use MyCompLab on their own, benefiting from self-paced diagnostics and a personal study plan that recommends the instruction and practice each student needs to improve her writing skills. The composing space and its integrated resources, tools, and services (such as online tutoring) are also available to each student as he writes.

MyCompLab is an eminently flexible application that instructors can use in ways that best complement their course and teaching style. They can recommend it to students for self-study, set up courses to track student progress, or leverage the power of administrative features to be more effective and save time. The assignment builder and commenting tools, developed specifically for writing instruction, bring instructors closer to their student writers, make managing assignments and evaluating papers more efficient, and put powerful assessment within reach. Students receive feedback within the context of their own writing, which encourages critical thinking and revision and helps them to develop skills based on their individual needs.

Learn more at www.mycomplab.com.

The *Interactive Pearson eText,* Ninth Edition (ISBN 978-0-205-76904-9) an e-book version of *Strategies for Successful Writing,* is also available in MyCompLab. This dynamic, online version of the text is integrated throughout MyCompLab to create an enriched, interactive learning experience for writing students.

Acknowledgments

Like all textbook writers, we are indebted to many people. Our colleagues at Ferris State University and elsewhere, too numerous to mention, have assisted us in several ways: critiquing the manuscript; testing approaches, essays, and exercises in their classrooms; and suggesting writing models for the text.

We would like to thank all those faculty members who forwarded student work to be considered for the 9th edition. There was a wide range of excellent student essays to consider. In the end we selected works that represented the strategies clearly and that represented the wide variety of skill levels of the students who use this text. These essays are powerful evidence of the effective teaching of all of the contributors and their tremendous impact on student lives. David Burlingame, Heald College; Sandra Cusak, Heald College & Reedley

College; Ruth Dalton, Montgomery College; Linda Gary, Tyler Junior College; Vicki Holmes, University of Nevada Las Vegas; Theresa Mlinarcik, Macomb Community College; Emily Moorer, Hinds Community College; Carol Osborne, Coastal Carolina University; Roseann Shansky, Ferris State University; Efstathia Siegel, Montgomery College; Geraldine Yap, Cosumnes River College.

In addition, we thank our reviewers, whose many suggestions have greatly improved our text: Betty Bettacchi, Collin College; Maria Christian, Oklahoma State University–Okmulgee; Cathie Cline, East Arkansas Community College; Sandra J. Cusak, Heald College; Linda Gary, Tyler Junior College; Mark Hall, Central Carolina Community College; Vicki L. Holmes, UNLV; Samuel Iniguez, Cosumnes River College; Michael Keathley, Ivy Tech Community College; Alissia J.R. Lingaur, Oakland Community College; Joyce Marie Miller, Collin College; Ricki Miller, Santiago Canyon College; Bryan Moore, Arkansas State University; Emily Moorer, Hinds Community College; Betty Moss, San Antonio College; Todd Neuman, Pensacola Junior College; Nancy M. Risch, Caldwell Community College; Kenny Rowlette, Liberty University; Barbara Rusher, Central Carolina Community College; Joyce Whitaker Russell, Rockingham Community College; Elena Solomon, UNLV; Shannon C. Stewart, Coastal Carolina University; Ann Stotts, Gateway Technical College and Michael Tucker, Western Oklahoma State College.

Special thanks are also due to the outstanding team at Pearson, whose editorial expertise, genial guidance, and promotional efforts have been vital to this project: Phil Miller, former President of Humanities and Social Sciences Division, who first saw the potential in our approach, proposed the Annotated Instructor's Edition, and suggested and supported many other improvements; Joe Opiela, Editorial Director for English, and Brad Potthoff, Senior Acquisitions Editor, whose efficiency, knowledge, and understanding of authors' concerns have enhanced our pleasure in preparing this edition; Kelly Keeler, our Production Editor; and Sandra McGuire, whose marketing expertise will help our book find its way.

J.A.R.
R.v.d.O.

To the Student

No matter what career you choose, your ability to communicate clearly and effectively will directly affect your success. In the classroom, your instructor will often evaluate your mastery of a subject by the papers and examinations you write. Prospective employers will make judgments about your qualifications and decide whether to offer you an interview on the basis of your job application letter and résumé. On the job, you will be expected to write clear, accurate reports, memorandums, and letters.

There is nothing mysterious about successful writing. It does not require a special talent, nor does it depend on inspiration. It is simply a skill, and like any other skill, it involves procedures that can be learned. Once you understand them and the more you practice, the easier writing becomes.

Strategies for Successful Writing will help you become a successful writer. And after you graduate it can serve as a useful on-the-job reference if writing problems occur. The first, third, and fourth chapters explore the fundamentals of writing and the general steps in planning, drafting, and revising papers. The next ten explain the basic writing strategies as well as papers that mix them. The following three chapters zero in on paragraphs, sentences, and writing style, and the final six turn to specialized writing—essay examinations, papers about literature, library research papers, and papers based on your own original research results. The book concludes with a Reader and, if you are using the complete version of the text, a Handbook.

From time to time you have probably had the unpleasant experience of using textbooks that seemed to be written for instructors rather than students. In preparing this book, we have tried never to forget that you are buying, reading, and using it. As a result, we have written the text with your needs in mind. The book uses simple, everyday language and presents directions in an easy-to-follow format. The chapters on writing strategies provide examples of student essays that supplement the professional essays in the Reader. These student examples represent realistic, achievable goals. When you compare them to the professional examples, you'll see that students can indeed do excellent work. We are confident that by learning to apply the principles in this text, you will write well too.

Here's wishing you success!

Strategies for
Successful Writing

Rhetoric

CHAPTER 1

Writing: A First Look

Why write? Aren't e-mail, voice mail, cellular phones fast dooming ordinary writing? Not long ago, some people thought and said so, but events haven't supported those predictions. In fact, much electronic media, such as Blogging, have increased the amount of writing people do. Although devices such as cell phones have made some writing unnecessary, the written word still flourishes both on campus and in the world of work.

Writing offers very real advantages to both writers and readers:

1. It gives writers time to reflect on and research what they want to communicate and then lets them shape and reshape the material to their satisfaction.
2. It makes communication more precise and effective.
3. It provides a permanent record of thoughts, actions, and decisions.
4. It saves the reader's time; we absorb information more swiftly when we read it than when we hear it.

Many people will expect you to write for them. College instructors ask you to write reports, research papers, and essay exams. Job hunting usually requires you to write application letters. And once you're hired, writing will probably figure in your duties. You might be asked to discuss the capabilities of new computer equipment, report on a conference you attended, or explain the advantages of new safety procedures to supervisors or staff. Perhaps you'll propose that your organization install a new security system, conduct a market survey, or develop an alternative traffic flow pattern. The ability to write will help you earn better grades, land the job you want, and advance in your career.

PERSPECTIVE
Students seldom recognize how writing ability will influence their careers. Your course will be more likely to engage student interest if its practical value is readily apparent. To demonstrate this value, you might reproduce the following quotation as a class handout or on the board. We have found that it primes students for the upcoming term. They begin to sense the usefulness of writing in the "real" world and become more receptive to the instruction that will follow.

As soon as you move one step up from the bottom, your effectiveness depends on your ability to reach others through the spoken or written word. And the further away your job is from manual work, the larger the organization of which you are an employee, the more important it will be that you know how to convey your thoughts in writing or speaking. In the very large organizations, whether it is the government, the large business corporation, or the Army, this ability to express oneself is perhaps the most

important of all the skills a person can possess.
Peter Drucker, "How to Be an Employee"

TEACHING STRATEGY
Have students interview either working professionals or their advisors on the importance of writing and then share their findings with the class. The interview could double as the first writing assignment.

CLASSROOM ACTIVITIES
1. Pair students and have them orally exchange a brief personal history. Next time the class meets, have students write down what they remember of their partner's history. They will quickly see the importance of an accurate written record.
2. Bring in copies or overheads of a week's worth of interoffice memos to demonstrate the variety of situations that require writing.
3. Have each student identify some personal situations (beyond those listed in the text) that require writing. This type of activity, along with the previous two, helps set the stage for a writing course.

Furthermore, writing ability yields personal benefits. You might need to defend a medical reimbursement claim that you filed with your health insurer, request clarification of an inadequate or ambiguous set of directions, or document a demand for replacement of a faulty product. Skill in writing will help you handle these matters.

As you can see, we usually write in response to a situation. This situation often determines the purpose and audience of our writing as well as its content, style, and organization. We don't, then, write in isolation but rather to communicate with others who have an interest in our message. To do an effective job, you will need to understand the different situations that can prompt a piece of writing and respond accordingly.

The Purposes of Writing

Whenever you write, some clear purpose should guide your efforts. If you don't know why you're writing, neither will your reader. Fulfilling an assignment doesn't qualify as a real writing purpose, although it may well be what sends you to your desk. Faced with a close deadline for a research paper or report, you may tell yourself, "I'm doing this because I have to." An authentic purpose, however, requires you to answer this question: What do I want this piece of writing to do for both my reader and me?

Purpose, as you might expect, grows out of the writing situation. You explore the consequences of the greenhouse effect in a report for your science instructor. You write an editorial for the college newspaper to air your frustration over inadequate campus parking. You propose that your organization replace an outdated piece of equipment with a state-of-the-art model. Clearly, your purpose stems from the writing situation.

Here are four common *general writing purposes*, two or more of which often join forces in a single piece:

To Inform   Presenting information is one of the most common writing purposes. The boating enthusiast who tells landlubber classmates how to handle a skiff plays the role of teacher, as does the researcher who summarizes the results of an investigation for coworkers. Some professional writers carve careers out of writing articles and books that fill gaps in the public's knowledge of timely topics. Instructors often ask you to write exams and papers so that they can gauge how well you have mastered the course material.

To Persuade   You probably have strong views on many issues, and these feelings may sometimes impel you to try swaying your reader. In a letter to the editor, you might attack a proposal to establish a nearby chemical waste dump. Or, alarmed by a sharp jump in state unemployment, you might write to your state senator and argue for a new job-training program.

To Express Yourself   Creative writing includes personal essays, fiction, plays, and poetry, as well as journals and diaries. But self-expression has a place in other kinds of writing too. Almost everything you write offers you a chance to display your mastery of words and to enliven your prose with vivid images and fresh turns of phrase.

To Entertain Some writing merely entertains; some writing couples entertainment with a more serious purpose. A lighthearted approach can help your reader absorb dull or difficult material. Satire lets you expose the shortcomings of individuals, ideas, and institutions by poking fun at them. An intention to entertain can add savor to many kinds of writing.

More Specific Purposes

Besides having one or more *general purposes*, each writing project has its own *specific purpose*. Consider the difference in the papers you could write about solar homes. You might explain how readers could build one, argue that readers should buy one, express the advantages of solar homes to urge Congress to enact a tax credit for them, or satirize the solar home craze so that readers might reevaluate their plans to buy one.

Having a specific purpose assists you at every stage of the writing process. It helps you define your audience; select the details, language, and approach that best suit their needs; and avoid going off in directions that won't interest them. The following example from the newspaper *USA Today* has a clear and specific purpose.

We'll Trash *USA Today*, Too

J. Winston Porter

1   What will you do with *USA Today* after you finish reading it? If you're like most of us, you'll put the paper out with the garbage and it'll end up buried in a landfill. Over 80% of all household and commercial garbage ends up this way, and this is a problem.

2   The USA is relentlessly producing more and more trash, and we are rapidly running out of landfill space. At the same time, new landfills and incinerators are encountering local opposition. Before we are truly wallowing in waste, we need to declare a war on garbage.

3   The first battle we need to win is for public acceptance of a strategy that includes reducing the amount of waste generated and increasing the amount recycled. EPA is pushing a national goal of recycling 25% of all garbage within the next four years. But waste reduction and recycling aren't enough to stem the tide of trash that threatens to engulf us. We will continue to need safe landfilling of some garbage and incineration, preferably with energy recovery, as another option. EPA and the states are working to strengthen environmental controls on these facilities. The appropriate mix of waste reduction and recycling, landfilling and incineration should be "custom designed" by states and localities.

4   How can we all do our part? To begin with, we must recognize that we all contribute to the garbage problem. Next, we should cooperate in efforts to reduce the amount of trash requiring disposal. Finally, we must adopt new attitudes about disposal, because there will always be trash to be handled. This means that instead of simply opposing any new disposal facilities, citizens should assist in choosing the best options.

5   Recycling is the cornerstone of a sound waste-management strategy. We all have special responsibilities to make recycling work. Individuals must be willing to participate in local programs. Local governments should plan programs and operate

a writing project if its purpose were to (a) tell stories that make friends laugh; (b) explain to high school students how to prepare for college; or (c) explain to college professors why students have difficulty adjusting. The class will see that different purposes require different approaches.

SUGGESTED INSTRUCTOR READINGS
Flower, L. "The Construction of Purpose in Writing and Reading." College English 50 (1988): 528–50. Provides insights into how writers and readers work with purposes and explains how inexperienced and experienced writers "frame" their purposes differently.
Kinneavy, J. "The Basic Aims of Discourse." College Composition and Communication 20 (1969): 297–304. A briefer version of A Theory of Discourse, this article classifies types of discourse and how they relate to purpose.

TEACHING STRATEGY
Many students have trouble finding things to say, and as a result they believe they have no purpose for writing except to fulfill the assignment. You could have them list or freewrite things they

would like to tell people but haven't or can't: personal experiences that others might not initially understand, activities they

required facilities. States should do statewide planning and enforce their own laws and regulations. Industry should step up its recycling efforts. The federal government should provide national leadership, research and information-sharing as well as develop certain underlying regulations.

6   No one segment of society can, alone, lead us to victory in the war on garbage. Instead, we need a coordinated national effort to confront the solid-waste issue head-on.

From *USA Today*

Porter hints at his purpose in the first paragraph by noting that the disposal of garbage in landfills poses a problem. The last sentence of paragraph 2 states the purpose clearly. The remaining paragraphs name the strategies that he recommends to wage war on garbage and explain how individuals, government, and industry can all contribute. Everything Porter has written relates to his purpose.

Now examine the next paragraph, which does *not* have a firmly fixed specific purpose:

> Community is a sea in which people swim unconsciously, like fish. We fail to recognize our neighbors as fellow humans, and they show the same lack of fellow feeling for us. A complete lack of concern for one another is evident in today's complex society. What is community? Is it a plant? A building? A place? A state of being? Knowing what it is, we can see if such a place exists. To know community, one must realize who he or she is. Identity of a person is the first step in establishing a community.

This student writer can't decide what aspect of community to tackle. The opening sentence attempts a definition, but the next two veer onto the shortcomings of the modern community. Notice how aimlessly the thoughts drift. The vague leadoff sentence asserts "Community is a sea . . . ," but the later question "What is community?" contradicts this opening. Also, if community is a plant, a building, or a place, why must we realize who we are in order to know it? This contradictory and illogical paragraph reveals a writer groping for a purpose.

The paragraph, however, isn't a wasted effort. These musings offer several possibilities. By developing the first sentence, the writer might show some interesting similarities between community and a sea so that instead of taking community for granted, readers can see it in a new light. By pursuing the idea in the second and third sentences, the writer might show the callous nature of modern society to encourage readers to act more humanely. The last two sentences might lead to a statement on the relationship between individual and community in order to overcome the common view that the two are in conflict. A specific purpose can sometimes emerge from preliminary jottings.

The Audience for Your Writing

Everything you write is aimed at some audience—a person or group you want to reach. The ultimate purpose of all writing is to have an effect on a reader (even if that reader is you), and therefore purpose and audience are closely linked. Our discussion on pages 4–5 makes this point clear by noting that your purpose can be to inform *someone* of something, to persuade *someone* to believe or do something, to express feelings or insights to *someone,* or to entertain *someone.* Any of these objectives requires that you *be able to define* that someone, the audience for your writing.

Writing operates on a delayed-action fuse, detonating its ideas in the readers' minds at a later time and place. Sometimes problems follow. In face-to-face conversations, you can observe your listeners' reactions, and whenever you note signs of hostility, boredom, or puzzlement, you can alter your tone, offer some examples, or ask a question. You can also use gestures and facial expressions to emphasize what you're saying. When you write, however, the words on the page carry your message. Once written work has left your hands, it's on its own. You can't call it back to clear up a misunderstanding or satisfy a disgruntled reader.

Establishing rapport with your audience is easy when you're writing for your friends or someone else you know a great deal about. You can then judge the likely response to what you say. Often, though, you'll be writing for people you know only casually or not at all: employers, customers, fellow townsfolk, and the like. In such situations, you'll need to assess your audience before starting to write and/or later in the writing process.

A good way to size up your readers is to develop an audience profile. This profile will emerge gradually as you answer the following questions:

1. What are the educational level, age, social class, and economic status of the audience I want to reach?
2. Why will this audience read my writing? To gain information? Learn my views on a controversial issue? Enjoy my creative flair? Be entertained?
3. What attitudes, needs, and expectations do they have?
4. How are they likely to respond to what I say? Can I expect them to be neutral? Opposed? Friendly?
5. How much do they know about my topic? (Your answer here will help you gauge whether you're saying too little or too much.)
6. What kind of language will communicate with them most effectively? (See "Level of Diction" in Chapter 7.)

College writing assignments sometimes ask you to envision a reader who is intelligent but lacking specialized knowledge, receptive but unwilling to put up with boring or trite material. Or perhaps you'll be assigned, or choose, to write for a certain age group or one with particular interests. At other times, you'll be asked to write for a specialized audience—one with some expertise in your topic. This difference will affect what you say to each audience and how you say it.

The Effect of Audience on Your Writing

Let's see how audience can shape a paper. Suppose you are explaining how to take a certain type of X-ray. If your audience is a group of lay readers who have never had an X-ray, you might note at the outset that taking one is much like taking an ordinary photograph. Then you might explain the basic process,

believe they can do better than others, and the like. Such beginnings can often lead to a specific purpose.

PERSPECTIVE
Audience is a difficult concept for students since they are most familiar with writing that is aimed exclusively at their instructor. The classroom situation often ties them to that assumption. You might attempt therefore to broaden their sense of audience. Students should understand that assorted readers with a variety of characteristics will receive and react to their writing and that reader response must be anticipated.

TEACHING STRATEGIES
1. Have students write to actual readers who might supply a response. They could complain about a defective product, request a free product, or write to a state representative.
2. Have students identify the needs, attitudes, and expectations they have as readers and how these factors influence their response.
3. To show your class that an audience can be other than the instructor, you might specify an assumed audience for a paper and then respond to student efforts as if you belonged to that audience.
4. Have students develop an audience profile for their papers and indicate how it will affect their planning.

CLASSROOM ACTIVITIES
1. Bring in writing samples aimed at a nonstudent audience. Have students identify how they respond and why.
2. Bring in samples of communication that are clearly inappropriate to their audience. Any faculty member's mailbox is full of examples. Have students identify the problems and suggest changes.
3. Bring in samples of sales literature and have students identify the assumptions being made about audience and how they have influenced the writing.
4. Bring in a writing example that has no clear sense of audience. Have students identify the problems they have with it and suggest needed changes. An excellent example appears in Flower's article cited below.

SUGGESTED INSTRUCTOR READINGS
Flower, L., "Writer-Based Prose: A Cognitive Basis for Problems in Writing." College English 41 (1979): 19–37. Shows how students can go from writer-oriented prose to reader-oriented prose and supplies excellent examples.
Harris, J. "The Idea of Community in the Study of Writing." College Composition and Communication 40 (1989): 11–21. A pivotal essay in the debate over the role of audience and the place of student

including the positioning of the patient and the equipment, comment on the safety and reliability of the procedure, and note how much time it takes. You probably would use few technical terms. If, however, you were writing for radiology students, you might emphasize exposure factors, film size, and required views. This audience would understand technical terms and want a detailed explanation of the procedure. You could speak to these readers as colleagues who appreciate precise information.

Audience shapes all types of writing in similar fashion, even your personal writing. Assume you've recently become engaged, and to share your news you write two letters: one to your minister, the other to your best friend back home. You can imagine the differences in details, language, and general tone of each letter. Further, think how inappropriate it would be if you accidentally sent the letter intended for one to the other. Without doubt, different readers call for different approaches.

Discourse Communities

Professionals often write as members of specific communities. For example, biologists with similar interests often exchange information about their research. The members of a community share goals, values, concerns, background information, and expectations, and this fact in turn affects how they write. Because such writing is closely tied to the interests of the community, professional articles often start with a section linking their content to previous research projects and articles. Often, too, custom dictates what information must be included, the pattern of organization, and the style the paper should follow. Throughout college, you will discover that part of learning to write is becoming familiar with the values and customs of different discourse communities. To do this, you'll need to read carefully in your major field, acquainting yourself with its current issues and concerns and learning how to write about them. As you start reading in any professional area, ask yourself these questions:

1. What are the major concerns and questions in this field?
2. What seems to be common knowledge?
3. To what works do writers regularly refer?
4. How do those in the field go about answering questions?
5. What methods do they follow?
6. Which kinds of knowledge are acceptable? Which are not?
7. What values seem to guide the field?
8. What kinds of information must writers include in papers?
9. How are different writing projects organized?
10. What conventions do writers follow?

We all, of course, belong to many different communities. Furthermore, a community can involve competing groups, conflicting values, differing kinds of writing projects, and varying approaches to writing. But as part of your growth as a writer and professional, you'll need to understand the goals and rules of any community you enter.

The following three excerpts deal with the same subject—antigens—but each explanation is geared to a different audience. Read the passages carefully; then answer the following questions:

1. What audience does each author address? How do you know?
2. Identify ways in which each author appeals to a specific audience.

1. The human body is quick to recognize foreign chemicals that enter it. "Foes" must be attacked or otherwise got rid of. The most common of these foes are chemical materials from viruses, bacteria, and other microscopic organisms. Such chemicals, when recognized by the body, are called *antigens*. To combat them, the body produces its own chemicals, protein molecules called *antibodies*. Each kind of antigen causes the production of a specific kind of antibody. Antibodies appear in the body fluids such as blood and lymph and in the body's cells.

L. D. Hamilton, "Antibodies and Antigens," The New Book of Knowledge

2. [An] *antigen* [is a] foreign substance that, when introduced into the body, is capable of inducing the formation of antibodies and of reacting specifically in a detectable manner with the induced antibodies. For each antigen there is a specific antibody, the physical and chemical structure of which is produced in response to the physical and chemical structure of the antigen. Antigens comprise virtually all proteins that are foreign to the host, including those contained in bacteria, viruses, protozoa, helminths, foods, snake venoms, egg white, serum components, red blood cells, and other cells and tissues of various species, including man. Polysaccharides and lipids may also act as antigens when coupled to proteins.

"Antigen," Encyclopaedia Britannica

3. The substance which stimulates the body to produce antibodies is designated antigen (antibody stimulator) . . .

   Most complete antigens are protein molecules containing aromatic amino acids, and are large in molecular weight and size. However, it has been demonstrated that other macromolecules, such as pure polysaccharides, polynucleotides, and lipids, may serve as complete antigens.

   However, certain other materials, incapable of stimulating antibody formation by themselves can, in association with a protein or other carrier, stimulate antibody formation and are the antigenic determinants. These determinants are referred to as *incomplete antigens* or *haptens* and they are able to react with antibodies which were produced by the determinant–protein complex.

   However, before an antigen can stimulate the production of antibodies, it must be soluble in the body fluids, must reach certain tissues in an unaltered form, and must be, in general, foreign to the body tissues. Protein taken by mouth loses its specific foreign-protein characteristics when digested in the alimentary tract. It reaches the tissues of the body as amino acids or other altered digested products of protein. Consequently, it no longer meets the requirements for antigenic behavior.

Orville Wyss and Curtis Eklund, Microorganisms and Man

writers in so-called discourse communities.

Lunsford, A. A., and L. Ede. "Representing Audience: 'Successful' Discourse and Disciplinary Critique." College Composition and Communication 47(1996): 167–80. Provides a critical review of the concept of audience.

Maimon, E. P. "Talking to Strangers." College Composition and Communication 30 (1979): 364–69. Indicates how important it is for students to recognize that they are addressing strangers who will not necessarily share their experiences or their present context.

TEACHING STRATEGIES

1. Ask students to list their expectations of the discourse communities they plan to enter. After discussing these expectations in class, assign students to read some of the professional literature in their chosen fields. Have them answer questions 1–10 on page 8 to the best of their abilities.

2. Perhaps discuss the composition classroom as a discourse community. Have students individually list what they think are its goals, values, assumed knowledge, rules, and nature. Then discuss and compare students' expectations with yours.

Just as you would not dial a telephone number at random and then expect to carry on a meaningful conversation, so you should not expect to communicate effectively without a specific audience in mind.

One other note: As you shape your paper, it is important that the writing please you as well as your audience—that it satisfy your sense of what good writing is and what the writing task requires. You are, after all, your own first reader.

The Qualities of Good Writing

Good writing is essential if you want your ideas to be taken seriously. Just as you would have trouble listening to someone with his shirt on backwards and wearing two different kinds of shoes, most readers dismiss out of hand writing that is disorganized, poorly worded, or marred by errors in grammar and spelling. In a world where most people are drowning under an information overload, few have the time or inclination to hunt through bad writing to search for quality ideas. Employers discard job seekers with poorly worded cover letters, badly written proposals are rejected, and few bother to read poorly written articles.

Three qualities—fresh thinking; a sense of style including the use of correct grammar and punctuations; and effective organization—help to ensure that a piece of prose will meet your reader's expectations.

Fresh Thinking   You don't have to astound your readers with something never before discussed in print. Genuinely unique ideas and information are rare. You can, however, freshen your writing by exploring personal insights and perceptions. Using your own special slant, you might show a connection between seemingly unrelated items, as does a writer who likens office "paper pushers" to different kinds of animals. Keep the expression of your ideas credible, however; far-fetched notions spawn skepticism.

Sense of Style   Readers don't expect you to display the stylistic flair of Maya Angelou or E. B. White. Indeed, such writing would impair the neutral tone needed in certain kinds of writing, such as technical reports and legal documents. Readers do, however, expect you to write in a clear style. And if you strengthen it with vivid, forceful words, readers will absorb your points with even greater interest. Readers also expect you to use standard grammar, spelling, and punctuation. The chapters ahead show you how to use language in ways that project your views and personality. Chapters 6 and 7, in particular, will help you develop a sense of style, as will the many readings throughout the book and the Handbook.

Effective Organization   All writing should be organized so it is easy to follow. A paper should have a beginning, a middle, and an end, that is, an introduction, a body, and a conclusion. The introduction sparks interest and acquaints the reader with what is to come. The body delivers the main message and exhibits a clear connection between ideas so that the reader can easily follow your thoughts. The conclusion ends the discussion so the reader feels satisfied rather than suddenly cut off. Overall, your paper should follow a pattern that is suited to its content and will guide the reader. Organizational patterns, or strategies of development, are the subject of Chapters 8–17. Pages 93–96 discuss introductions and conclusions.

Freshness, style, and organization are weighted differently in different kinds of writing. A writer who drafts a proposal to pave a city's streets will probably attach less importance to fresh thinking than to clear writing and careful organization. On the other hand, fresh thinking can be very important in a description of an autumn forest scene. You will learn more about these qualities throughout this book.

Writing and Ethics

Think for a minute about how you would react to the following situation. You decide to vacation at a resort after reading a brochure that stressed its white-sand beach, scenic trails, fine dining, and peaceful atmosphere. When you arrive, you find the beach overgrown with weeds, the trails littered and the view unappealing, and the restaurant a greasy-spoon cafeteria. Worse, whenever you go outside, swarms of vicious black flies attack you. Wouldn't you feel cheated? Closer to home, think how you'd react if you decided to attend a college because of its distinguished faculty members only to discover upon arrival that they rarely teach on campus. The college counts on their reputations to attract students even though they are usually unavailable. Hasn't the college done something unethical?

As these examples show, good writing is also ethical writing. Like you, readers expect that what they read will be dependable information. Few if any would bother with a piece of writing that they realized was intended to deceive. A good test of the ethics of your writing is whether you would read your own work and act on the basis of it. Would you feel comfortable with it, or would you feel cheated, manipulated, deceived, or harmed in some way? By learning and practicing the principles of ethical writing, you will help ensure that your writing meets the standards your readers expect.

The Principles of Ethical Writing

- **Truthful** Writing perceived as truthful should *be* truthful. Granted, a writer may use humorous exaggeration to make us laugh, and some sales pitches may stretch the truth a bit in order to entice buyers. ("Try Nu-Glo toothpaste and add sparkle to your life.") But most readers recognize and discount such embellishments which, unlike major distortions, harm nobody. Deliberate, serious falsehoods, however, may harm not only the reader but sometimes the writer as well. Angered by the misrepresentations in the vacation brochure, you would certainly warn your friends against the resort and might even take some legal action against it.
- **Complete** Writing meant to be perceived as truthful should tell the whole truth, omitting nothing the reader needs to know in order to make informed decisions. The text should not be deliberately

as tedious and pompous. Good writing instruction helps students to understand that our sense of good writing is not arbitrary but stems from how readers receive writing.

CLASSROOM ACTIVITIES

1. Bring in a newspaper article, magazine article, and professional essay on the same topic. Have students identify textual differences, account for them, and identify what is common to the texts. Suggest that the common qualities are features of good writing; also suggest the qualities that are specific to particular writing situations.

2. Have students rank three versions of a paper or memo. One version might be vague and general, another ineffectively organized, and the third a clear example of good writing. Compare student rankings and discuss the reasons for their decisions.

SUGGESTED INSTRUCTOR READINGS

Appleman, D., and D. E. Green. "Mapping the Elusive Boundary Between High School and College Writing." College Composition and Communication 44 (1993): 191–99. Provides a concise account of the trade-offs involved in establishing what constitutes good college writing.

Booth, W. C. "The Rhetorical Stance."

College Composition and Communication 14 (1963): 139–45. Defines the quality of writing as a balance among subject, object, and the writer's persona.

Carter, M. "The Idea of Expertise: An Exploration of Cognitive and Social Dimensions of Writing." College Composition and Communication 41 (1990): 265–86. Offers a useful perspective on the skills instructors may need to develop in students.

Lawson, B., S. S. Ryan, and W. R. Winterowd, eds. Encountering Student Texts: Interpretive Issues in Reading Student Writing. Urbana, IL: NCTE, 1990. Offers a good overview of the issues involved in how teachers read student writing.

TEACHING STRATEGY
Ethical issues can make for lively class discussion. Each writing strategy chapter as well as the chapters on writing about literature, the library research paper, and primary research strategies contains an "Ethical Issues" section and accompanying "Teaching Strategies." You can use these teaching strategies to help students understand the ethical implications involved in each kind of writing.

incomplete so as to mislead. Suppose that a university's recruitment brochures stress that 97 percent of its students get jobs upon graduation. What the brochures don't say is that only 55 percent of the jobs are in the graduates' chosen fields despite strong employer demand for graduates in those areas. Clearly these brochures are deceptive, perhaps attracting students who would otherwise choose schools with better placement records.

- **Clear**   Writing should be clear to the reader. All of us know the frustration of trying to read a crucial regulation that is impossible to comprehend. A person who writes instructions so unclear that they result in harmful mistakes is partially responsible for the consequences. Readers have a right to expect understandable, accurate information. Thus, it would be deceptive for a group of state legislators to call a proposed bill the Public Education Enhancement Act when it would in fact bar teachers from belonging to unions.

- **No Harm**   Writing should not be intended to harm the reader. Certainly it is fair to point out the advantages of a product or service that readers might not need. Most people understand the nature of this type of advertising. But think how unethical it would be for a writer to encourage readers to follow a diet that the writer knew was not only ineffective but harmful. Think of the harm a writer might cause by attempting, deliberately, to persuade readers to try crack cocaine.

Plagiarism

Pivotal to ethics in writing is avoiding plagiarism. When you turn in a piece of writing, you designate it as your own work in your own words. If you have taken material from sources (including the Internet) without using the proper documentation discussed in Chapter 21, even if it is in your own words, it is plagiarism, an unacceptable practice for any writer. If you use another writer's language, even in part, without using quotation marks, you are also engaged in plagiarism. Most faculty members check carefully for plagiarism and many automatically fail a paper for academic dishonesty. Some even give the student an F for the entire course.

Why is this an important issue?

1. Other people have worked hard to develop ideas, do research, and write effectively. They deserve credit for their work when someone else uses it; it is their property. The authors of this text, for example, pay fees to use the essays of others. You would probably not like it if others used material from your papers without giving you credit.

2. Proper documentation strengthens your work since the source, often written by an expert, can add credibility to your claims if properly recognized.

3. If you take some material from a source and use it in your paper without documentation or quotation, you are falsely presenting another writer's

work as your own. It is not much different from cheating and simply presenting an entire paper purchased from the Internet as your own work.

4. You are in the process of being trained in college to be professionals. Professionals need to be ethical. You wouldn't want someone to take credit for the computer program you wrote, charge you for repairs they didn't make, or write you a ticket for a traffic violation you didn't commit. Journalists have been fired, politicians have lost elections, and companies have been sued because they have been involved in plagiarism.

5. You certainly cannot develop as a writer if your writing isn't mostly your own work.

How can you avoid plagiarism and the failing grade that often comes with it?

1. Be committed to honesty. You should make certain your writing is your own work.

2. If an assignment does not ask you to use sources but you believe information from sources would be useful, talk to your teacher. There may be a reason that you are not asked to use sources. If sources are acceptable, you may be asked to follow a specific procedure for that assignment such as turning in copies of your sources.

3. If sources are required for an assignment or seem reasonable and acceptable, carefully review Chapter 21, including the section on plagiarism. Be meticulous in documenting your sources, even if the material is in your own words, and in quoting and documenting any language that comes from another writer, even if it is only part of a sentence.

4. Carefully double-check to make certain that all the content in your text is your own and that if you used a source at all, it is documented.

5. Carefully double-check to make certain that all of your text uses your own language and that if you did use another writer's language, you used quotation marks.

6. If you are not sure about whether documentation or quotation marks are necessary, check with your teacher.

You must make a conscious effort to avoid plagiarism. Ignorance and carelessness are rarely accepted as an excuse by professors trying hard to make certain that students are graded fairly and no one gets credit for work that is not their own. If you follow the guidelines in this text and ask your teacher for help when you are confused, you will easily avoid the embarrassment and the often dire consequences of being accused of plagiarism.

A First Look at Your Writing

Know your discourse community.

- What are shared questions?
- What counts as knowledge?
- What conventions do they follow?

Know your purpose.

- Are you going to inform, persuade, express yourself, entertain?
- What specific purpose do you want to accomplish?

Know your audience.

- What do they already know?
- Why will they read my writing?
- How are they likely to respond?
- How can I best reach them?

Apply principles of good writing.

- Write with fresh thinking that offers your own slant.
- Use a clear style in your own voice.
- Use effective organization.

Make certain your writing is ethical!

- Is your writing truthful, unslanted, complete, clear, helpful rather than harmful?
- Is your writing your own? Have you carefully avoided plagiarism?

CHAPTER 2

Strategies for Successful Reading

Effective reading is not the passive process that many people imagine. On the contrary, it requires the ongoing interaction of your mind and the printed page. Bringing your knowledge and experience to bear on a piece of writing can help you assess its events, ideas, and conclusions. For example, an understanding of marriage, love, and conflict, as well as experience with divorce, can help readers comprehend an essay that explores divorce. As you read, you must also understand each point that's made, consider how the various parts fit together, and try to anticipate the direction the writing will take. Successful reading requires work. Fortunately, you can follow specific strategies to help yourself read better.

Orienting Your Reading

Different purposes require different approaches to reading. When reading for pleasure, you can relax and proceed at your own pace, slowing down to savor a section you especially enjoy, speeding up when you encounter less interesting material, and breaking off when you wish. Reading for information, for solid understanding, or to critique the writing calls for a more methodical approach. Even so there are some questions you should ask:

- **Why am I reading this material?** Is it for long-term use, as a reference for a project, as a building block to understanding more material?

- **How well do I need to know the material in the article?**   Can you look back to the article as a reference? Is there only one main point you need to know? Are you going to be tested on much of the material in depth?
- **Is some material in the article more important to me than other material?** Sometimes in doing research you may be looking for a specific bit of information that is only a paragraph in a long article. If so, you can skim for the information. In most things you read, some sections are more important than others. Often you can read to get the main points of the article and not focus on all the details. Sometimes, of course, you need to know the material in depth.
- **What will I need to do with the material from the article?**   If you are looking for ideas for your own writing, you might read quickly. If you will be responsible for writing a critique of the article, you will need to read carefully and critically.
- **What kind of reading does the material suggest?**   The significance, the difficulty, and the nature of the writing all can influence how you read. An easy humorous narrative can be read in a more leisurely fashion. A careful argument on an important issue merits careful attention to the main points and the evidence and may even require you to outline the argument.

ACTIVITY ANSWER
Several answers are possible. If students read the essay for pleasure, they may read it quickly and stop reading if it becomes uninteresting. Students may read the essay as part of a larger research project on models of being "male." In this case,

Look briefly at "The Appeal of the Androgynous Man" on page 23. Identify three purposes you could have for reading this essay. Identify how these purposes would affect how you would read the essay and what you would look for in the essay.

they would want to take careful notes on Gross's definition and on specific examples. If students are reading to write a critique, they may read with careful attention to possible objections to Amy Gross's argument.

ACTIVITY ANSWERS
Student answers may vary.

1. Since Amy Gross has a degree in sociology, she has some of the tools to examine the topic; but she is not an expert in psychology so her views may not be solid. Given

A First Reading

You don't just jump in your car and take off. Usually you take a few minutes to think about where you want to go. Sometimes you even have to check your route. The same is true of effective reading. Because of the challenging nature of most college-level reading assignments, you should plan on more than one reading. A good first reading should orient you to the material.

Orient Yourself to the Background of the Essay   Before you begin, scan any accompanying biographical sketch and try to determine the writer's expertise and views on the topic. Henry Jenkins' background as a university professor and director of the Comparative Media Studies graduate program at MIT along with his numerous publications on popular culture give additional weight to his article on video games "Art Form for the Digital Age" (pages 539–542). Sometimes there is material by the author or the editor on the writing of the essay. Professional essays often start with an abstract that provides a brief summary of the article. At this point you may want to judge the credibility of the source, a topic discussed in depth on pages 258–262.

Use the Title as a Clue   Most titles identify the topic and often the viewpoint as well. Thus "The Sweet Smell of Success Isn't All That Sweet" (pages 559–561) suggests that the author isn't overly impressed with the conventional attitudes toward success. Some titles signal the writer's primary strategy, whether it is a comparison, definition, or argument.

Skim to Get the Gist of the Article   Sometimes you can just read the introductory and concluding paragraphs and the topic sentences (often the first or last sentences of paragraphs). Other times you will need to read the whole essay quickly. Try to gain an idea of the essay's main thrust, the key ideas that support it, and the ways that they are organized. In your first reading, you can skim the more difficult sections without trying to understand them fully.

Make Connections with What You Have Read   When you've finished skimming the essay, and before you reread the essay, think about what you've learned and then, either by saying it to yourself or jotting it down, express it *in your own words.* You can hardly be said to understand what you've read, and you will be less likely to remember it, until you can state its essence in your own words. Go back and underline the thesis statement or, if one is not included, try to formulate one in your own words. Try to identify the strategy used by the writer. Also stop and identify what you already know about the topic and your connection to the issue. You will read more effectively if you can connect what you read to your own knowledge and interests. Jot down questions that the first reading has raised in your mind.

Reading Activities

1. Identify what you can about the background of the article "The Appeal of the Androgynous Man" (page 23) from the statement about the author.
2. Write what you expect based on the title.
3. Skim the essay and then write down what you identify as the main points of the essay. Identify the essay's thesis. Jot down at least two questions you have.

the kinds of women's magazines for which she has written, it is likely that she will write from a woman's perspective but not necessarily with a strongly feminist slant.

2. Clearly the essay is going to define a type of man, in this case one who is both male and female. The focus is also going to be on identifying ways that this type of man appeals to Amy Gross.

3. Amy Gross compares the macho male who sticks to clichéd male roles with the androgynous male who is willing to tackle male and female aspects of life. She believes the androgynous male is more creative, more sensitive, and a better companion. Her thesis seems unclear but it seems to be that the androgynous man has the characteristics of both male and female and as a result is a better companion for women. Much of her essay seems to be a comparison between the all-man and the androgynous man. A fundamental question or objection is whether she is exaggerating and stereotyping.

Additional Readings

If the material was difficult or you need to know it well, a second or even third reading may be necessary. On the second reading, which will take more time than the first, you carefully absorb the writer's ideas.

Read Carefully and Actively   Read at a pace suitable to the material. Underline significant topic sentences as well as other key sentences and ideas or facts that you find important, but keep in mind that underlining in itself doesn't ensure comprehension. Restating the ideas in your own words is more effective. Depending on your purposes, you may want to write down the main points in your own words or jot down the ideas in the margins. As you proceed, examine the supporting sentences to see how well they back up the main idea. Keep an eye out for how the essay fits together.

ACTIVITY ANSWERS
Student answers may vary.

1. (p. 24) All-male = imperialistic, superhuman; androgynous man not as imperialistic. Why should that be so? Can't women be imperialistic? Can't androgynous males?
(p. 24) All-males are hard to talk to since they have different interests. But can't a woman cultivate

wider interests? Can't a woman be androgynous?

2. Thesis: Androgynous males, not hermaphrodites, are more than all-males by including the characteristics of men and women. As a result, they are "appealing" for women.

Androgynous male

Doesn't resist the feminine and engages in such activities

Less imperialistic and doesn't act superhuman

Broader interests than the all-male

Creative males score higher on femininity, which indicates an openness to feeling and emotion

Supports welfare of other, group harmony, but also supports his position

Shares and invites, doesn't conquer

All-male

Has no interest in non-male activities such as shopping and has no taste in the arts, books, movies, etc.; resists anything feminine

Even when educated and well mannered can be imperialistic and act superhuman

Interests tend to be exclusively male and different from the author's interests

Less creative and imaginative and less intelligent, confirmed by a Stanford psychology professor's study

Studies show them less supportive and less able to "express warmth, playfulness, and concern"

Treats female partners as competition and opportunity to perform

Consider Reading as a Kind of Conversation with the Text   Develop the habit of asking questions about facts, reasons, ideas—practically anything in the essay. Jot your queries and their answers in the margins. (On page 23 you can see how a student interacted with the first page of Amy Gross's essay "The Appeal of the Androgynous Man.") Good writers anticipate your questions and answer them; and because you have posed the questions yourself, you are more likely to see the connections in the text. If the author hasn't answered your questions, there may be problems with the work. It can help to keep a reading log in a notebook or as a computer file where you jot down your ideas as you are reading.

Master Unfamiliar Words   At times, unfamiliar words can hinder your grasp of the material. Whenever you encounter a new word, circle it, use context to help gauge its meaning, check the dictionary for the exact meaning, and then record it in the margins or some other convenient place. If the writing is peppered with words you don't know, you may have to read the whole piece to figure out its general drift, then look up key words, and finally reread the material.

Take Conscious Steps to Understand Difficult Material   When the ideas of a single section prove difficult, restate the points of those sections you do understand. Then experiment by stating in your own words different interpretations of the problem section and see which one best fits the writing as a whole.

Sometimes large sections or entire texts are extremely difficult. There are several strategies you can use to help yourself.

- State the ideas that are easier for you to understand and use them as keys to unlock meanings that are difficult but not unintelligible. Save the most difficult sections until last. Don't think you have to understand everything completely. Some works take a lifetime to fully understand.
- Discuss a difficult essay with others who are reading it.
- Read simpler material on the topic.
- Go to your teacher for help. He or she may help you find background material that will make the selection easier.

Pull the Entire Essay Together   Whenever you finish a major section of a lengthy essay, express your sense of what it means. Speak it out loud or write it down. If you have trouble seeing the connections between ideas, try visually representing them. You might make an outline that states the main points followed by subpoints (see pages 43–44 for how to outline). For a comparison, you might create a table with the main points of the comparison side by side. You can make a drawing connecting the main ideas in a network, list the steps in an instruction, or write out the main facts.

To strengthen your grasp of material you'll need to remember for some time, try restating its main points a couple of days after the second reading. Sometimes it is helpful to explain the material to a sympathetic listener. If anything has become hazy or slipped your mind, reread the appropriate section(s). If you really must know the material, try making up your own test and giving it to yourself.

Mastering Reading Problems

Master the Problems That Interfere with Reading Many factors are important to effective reading. If your environment is too noisy, you are too tired, or you have something on your mind, you can have trouble reading. Do your reading at the time of day when you are most alert. Be sure you are in an environment that lets you concentrate and that is well lit. Try to be rested and comfortable. If you get tired, take a break for a specific time period; perhaps go for a short walk. If something else is bothering you, try to resolve the distraction or put it out of your mind. If you find the material uninteresting, try to find a connection between the topic and your interests and goals; read more actively.

If you have extensive problems reading for college, you can get help. Most colleges have courses in reading and tutors. College often requires a lot of reading, so take the steps necessary to be the most effective reader possible.

Reading Activities

1. Read "The Appeal of the Androgynous Man" a second time, continuing to write your own questions and notes in the margin.
2. Create a table with two columns comparing the all-man and the androgynous man.
3. Identify three words that you might find relatively new and find their definitions from the context and a dictionary.
4. Try explaining the article to a friend or your roommate.

Reading to Critique

In college you usually read not only to understand but also to evaluate what you read. Your instructors will want to know what you think about what you've read. Often you'll be asked whether you agree or disagree with a piece of writing. Sometimes you will be asked to write an explicit critique of what you read.

Merely because information and ideas are in print does not mean that they are true or acceptable. An essay, for example, might include faulty logic, unreasonable ideas, suspect facts, or unreliable authorities. Don't hesitate to dispute the writer's information.

- Does it match your experience?
- Do the pieces of evidence support the claim?
- Do the ideas appear reasonable?
- Are there other pieces of evidence or other works that contradict these claims?
- Do the ideas connect in a logical way?

5. The author seems to be involved in an either/or fallacy. She casts men as either all-male or androgynous. Clearly most real men are complex mixtures of many ways of acting in many different situations.

Knowledge of the principles of argumentation and various reasoning fallacies can help you critique a piece of writing. These issues are discussed in the chapter on argumentation, pages 256–291.

EXERCISE

Reading Activities

Prepare your critique of "The Appeal of the Androgynous Man" by doing the following:

1. Identify where and how the claims don't match your experience.
2. Indicate where the evidence does not support the claims.
3. Indicate at least a few places where the ideas do not appear reasonable.
4. Identify any evidence that seems to contradict the author's claims.
5. Evaluate whether the ideas connect in a logical way.

Reading Assignments Carefully

Many students could get better grades by simply reading their assignments more carefully. In assignments, professors often indicate possible topics, suggest readers, identify the kinds of information that should and **should not** be included, set expectations on style and format, and establish procedures for the assignment such as the due date. You should read the assignment several times. Carefully note any specifications on topic, audience, organizational strategy, or style and format. Be sure to jot down procedures, such as due dates, in an assignment log or your calendar. Do not make assumptions. If you are not clear about a part of the assignment, ask your instructor.

Below is a very specific assignment; read it over carefully to determine what it requires.

Objective Description Short Assignment (50 points)

Typed final draft following the class format guide is due in class September 12. This assignment page should be turned in with your completed description:

The corner of Perry and State Street, near the Starr building has been the scene of a terrible accident. The insurance company has asked you to write a brief objective description (approximately 2 pages double spaced) of the intersection for a report for possible use in court. Your description should not try to take a position about the relative danger of the intersection but rather provide as clear a picture as possible of the situation. The description should include the arrangement of the streets including the number of lanes, the businesses located immediately around the intersection, traffic and pedestrian flow, and the timing of the lights and the effect of that timing on traffic.

Checklist:

The description should:

1. Provide the general location of the intersection.
2. Indicate their traffic function—i.e., major route from 131 into downtown Big Rapids.
3. Describe the actual roads.
4. Identify the businesses and their locations.
5. Describe traffic and pedestrian flow.
6. Detail the timing of the lights.
7. Maintain objective language.
8. Use clear, nontechnical language.

The assignment specifies the topic (a specific intersection), an audience (a court of law and an insurance company), key elements that are required as part of the description, a general style of writing (objective without taking a stance), and procedures including a deadline and format constraints. Clearly a short paper about the accident would not be acceptable since the assigned topic is the actual structure of the intersection. A style of writing that stressed the "horribly short lights that force students to scurry across like mice in front of a cat" would lose points since it takes a position and is not objective. Any description that left out any of the required elements (such as the timing of the lights) would also lose points.

Reading as a Writer

All of us who write can use reading as a springboard for improving our writing. You can do several things to make your reading especially useful.

As you read, the views of others, the experiences they relate, and the information they present often deepen your understanding of yourself, your relationships, and your surroundings. In turn, this broadened perspective can supply you with writing ideas. When possibilities surface, be sure to record them. Some writers keep a reading journal in which they summarize what they've read and jot down writing ideas that come to mind. In addition, you can take down specific ideas, facts, and perhaps even a few particularly telling quotations that you discover. You may want to incorporate this material into your writing at a later time. Carefully record the source so that you can document it properly in order to avoid plagiarism (see pages 434–436).

When you read various sources that explore the same topic or related topics, you may notice connections among their ideas. Since these connections can be fertile ground for a paper of your own, don't neglect to record them. Once you have jotted down these ideas, circle and label related thoughts. You can also draw a line linking the different thoughts to one another and to the main point that relates them. Express as a thesis statement your view of how these ideas fit together. Interacting with various sources and using their ideas to advance the purpose of your writing is a form of synthesis (see pages 149–150). When you proceed in this fashion, as in writing any paper, review your information, determine the points you want to make, and experiment until you find the order that works best. As you write, use the material from your sources as you would any support; be careful, however, to credit the authors properly in order to avoid plagiarism.

Let's see how you might use synthesis in writing an actual essay. Suppose, for example, you've read Amy Gross's "The Appeal of the Androgynous Man" (pages 23–25), Martin Gottfried's "Rambos of the Road" (pages 500–501), and Ellen Goodman's "The Company Man" (pages 507–508). You've noticed several connections among these essays. Gross describes "all-man" men who are insensitive in their treatment of women; Gottfried shows how some men need to assert their masculinity by driving aggressively; and Goodman characterizes a man who works himself to death. You might start your essay with Gross's definition of the "all-man" male and then cite some of her examples along with some of your own that identify how such a man would act. Next, you could stress that this particular concept of masculinity includes aggressiveness, then develop this point by using some illustrations from Gottfried's essay and from your own experience. Finally, you might conclude that being enslaved by such a narrow masculine role can have serious consequences and then support your view with material from Goodman's essay and your own observations. All of these ideas and examples could help you build an essay that points out how men can sometimes become desensitized or trapped, even victimized, by living according to stereotypes of masculinity. If you will be writing a paper that synthesizes material from various sources, review pages 407–431 on how to document your sources properly.

Because writers solve problems, you'll want to pay attention to the techniques and strategies that other writers use. If you find an introduction, an organizational pattern, a transition, a certain description or comparison unusually engaging, study the writer's technique. Perhaps you can use it yourself. Similarly, observe when a piece of writing fails and try to determine why.

EXERCISE

Reading Activities

1. Identify at least two strategies that the author used that you would find useful.

2. Identify at least two phrases that you found effective.

3. Identify at least two ideas that could spark your own writing.

AMY GROSS

both male and female in one

The Appeal of the (Androgynous) Man

Amy Gross, a native of Brooklyn, New York, earned a sociology degree at Connecticut College. Upon graduation, she entered the world of fashion publishing and has held writing or editorial positions at various magazines, including Talk, Mademoiselle, Good Housekeeping, Elle, *and* Mirabella. *She is the newly appointed editor-in-chief of* O, *the* Oprah Magazine. *In our selection, which first appeared in* Mademoiselle, *Gross compares androgynous men favorably to macho "all-men."*

1   James Dean was my first androgynous man.[1] I figured I could talk to him. He was anguished and I was 12, so we had a lot in common. With only a few exceptions, all the men I have liked or loved have been a certain kind of man: a kind who doesn't play football or watch the games on Sunday, who doesn't tell dirty jokes featuring broads or chicks, who is not contemptuous of conversations that are philosophically speculative, introspective, or otherwise foolish according to the other kind of man. He is more self-amused, less inflated, more quirky, vulnerable and responsive than the other sort (the other sort, I'm visualizing as the guys on TV who advertise deodorant in the locker room). He is more like me than the other sort. He is what social scientists and feminists would call androgynous: having the characteristics of both male and female.

2   Now the first thing I want you to know about the androgynous man is that he is neither effeminate nor (hermaphroditic.) All his primary and secondary sexual characteristics are in order and I would say he's all-man, but that is just what he is not. He is more than all-man.   *both male and female sex organs*

3   The merely all-man man, for one thing, never walks to the grocery store unless the little woman is away visiting her mother with the kids, or is in the hospital having a kid, or there is no little woman. All-men men don't know how to shop in a grocery store unless it is to buy a 6-pack and some pretzels. Their ideas of nutrition expand beyond a 6-pack and pretzels only to take in steak, potatoes, scotch or rye whiskey, and maybe a wad of cake or apple pie. All-men men have absolutely no taste in food, art, books, movies, theatre, dance, how to live, what are good questions, what is funny, or anything else I care about. It's not exactly that the all-man's man is an uncouth illiterate. He may be educated, well-mannered, and on a first-name basis with fine wines. One all-man man I knew was a handsome individual who gave the impression of being gentle, affectionate, and sensitive. He sat and ate dinner one night while I was doing something endearingly feminine at the sink. At one point, he mutely held up his glass to indicate in a primitive, even ape-like, way his need for a refill. This was in 1967, before Women's Liberation. Even so, I was disturbed. Not enough to break the glass over his handsome head, not even enough to mutely indicate the whereabouts of the refrigerator, but enough to remember that moment in all its revelatory clarity. No androgynous man would ever brutishly expect to be waited on without even a "please." (With a "please," maybe.)

4   The brute happened to be a doctor—not a hard hat—and, to all appearances, couth. But he had bought the whole superman package, complete with that fragile beast, the male ego. The androgynous man arrives with a male ego

[1]James Dean (1931–1955) was a 1950s film star who gained fame for his portrayals of restless, defiant young men.

Marginal annotations:

2. "I like polarity myself, but the poles have to be within earshot." I didn't think writing could be humorous while making a serious point. "If your image of the creative male accessorizes him with a beret, smock, and artist's palette, you will not believe the all-man man has been seriously short-changed." I like the way the use of detail really makes the sentence vivid.

3. There are a lot of ideas here: how men treat women on dates, whether men and women live in different universes, what it takes to be creative.

Does she favor androgynous men? What kind of appeal?

She will give a woman's perspective. She writes for and edits women's magazines.

Seems like she is going to talk about the advantages of androgynous men as compared to other men. Sees them as better.

Attempt to counter stereotype? Can't androgynous men also be effeminate?

Suggests "All-men" men reject behaviors and interests they consider feminine, but isn't she stereotyping? Are all these men like this? She seems to be exaggerating.

CLASSROOM ACTIVITY
Ask students to review a controversial essay in small groups. Have them identify the writer's main claims and their support, note any weakness in either, and list possible objections to the views expressed. The whole class can then discuss whether the writer's position is valid.

TEACHING STRATEGY
You might have students interact with the remaining pages of Gross's essay in a fashion similar to the student reactions on the first page.

CLASSROOM ACTIVITY
As a follow-up to the teaching strategy above, divide students into small groups and ask them to compare their reactions to the essay. A short writing assignment could follow.

SUGGESTED INSTRUCTOR READING
Spellmeyer, K. "A Common Ground: The Essay in the Academy." College English 51 (1989): 262–75. Offers an excellent defense of the importance of having students read essays critically.

too, but his is not as imperialistic. It doesn't invade every area of his life and person. Most activities and thoughts have nothing to do with masculinity or femininity. The androgynous man knows this. The all-man man doesn't. He must keep a constant guard against anything even vaguely feminine (i.e., "sissy") rising up in him. It must be a terrible strain.

5   Male chauvinism is an irritation, but the real problem I have with the all-man man is that it's hard for me to talk to him. He's alien to me, and for this I'm at least half to blame. As his interests have not carried him into the sissy, mine have never taken me very far into the typically masculine terrains of sports, business and finance, politics, cars, boats and machines. But blame or no blame, the reality is that it is almost as difficult for me to connect with him as it would be to link up with an Arab shepherd or Bolivian sandalmaker. There's a similar culture gap.

6   It seems to me that the most masculine men usually end up with the most feminine women. Maybe they like extreme polarity. I like polarity myself, but the poles have to be within earshot. As I've implied, I'm very big on talking. I fall in love for at least three hours with anyone who engages me in a real conversation. I'd rather a man point out a paragraph in a book—wanting to share it with me—than bring me flowers. I'd rather a man ask what I think than tell me I look pretty. (Women who are very pretty and accustomed to hearing that they are pretty may feel differently.) My experience is that all-men men read books I don't want to see paragraphs of, and don't really give a damn what I or any woman would think about most issues so long as she looks pretty. They have a very limited use for women. I suspect they don't really like us. The androgynous man likes women as much or as little as he likes anyone.

7   Another difference between the all-man man and the androgynous man is that the first is not a star in the creativity department. If your image of the creative male accessorizes him with a beret, smock and artist's palette, you will not believe the all-man man has been seriously short-changed. But if you allow as how creativity is a talent for freedom, associated with imagination, wit, empathy, unpredictability, and receptivity to new impressions and connections, then you will certainly pity the dull, thick-skinned, rigid fellow in whom creativity sets no fires.

8   Nor is the all-man man so hot when it comes to sensitivity. He may be true-blue in the trenches, but if you are troubled, you'd be wasting your time trying to milk comfort from the all-man man.

9   This is not blind prejudice. It is enlightened prejudice. My biases were confirmed recently by a psychologist named Sandra Lipsetz Bem, a professor at Stanford University. She brought to attention the fact that high masculinity in males (and high femininity in females) has been "consistently correlated with lower overall intelligence and lower creativity." Another psychologist, Donald W. MacKinnon, director of the Institute of Personality Assessment and Research at the University of California in Berkeley, found that "creative males give more expression to the feminine side of their nature than do less creative men. . . . [They] score relatively high on femininity, and this despite the fact that, as a group, they do not present an effeminate appearance or give evidence of increased homosexual interests or experiences. Their elevated scores on femininity indicate rather an openness to their feelings and emotions, a sensitive intellect and understanding self-awareness and wide-ranging interests including many which in the American culture are thought of as more feminine. . . ."

10   Dr. Bem ran a series of experiments on college students who had been categorized as masculine, feminine, or androgynous. In three tests of the degree of nurturance—warmth and caring—the masculine men scored painfully low

(painfully for anyone stuck with a masculine man, that is). In one of those experiments, all the students were asked to listen to a "troubled talker"—a person who was not neurotic but simply lonely, supposedly new in town and feeling like an outsider. The masculine men were the least supportive, responsive or humane. "They lacked the ability to express warmth, playfulness and concern," Bem concluded. (She's giving them the benefit of the doubt. It's possible the masculine men didn't express those qualities because they didn't possess them.)

11   The androgynous man, on the other hand, having been run through the same carnival of tests, "performs spectacularly. He shuns no behavior just because our culture happens to label it as female and his competence crosses both the instrumental [getting the job done, the problem solved] and the expressive [showing a concern for the welfare of others, the harmony of the group] domains. Thus, he stands firm in his opinion, he cuddles kittens and bounces babies and he has a sympathetic ear for someone in distress."

12   Well, a great mind, a sensitive and warm personality are fine in their place, but you are perhaps skeptical of the gut appeal of the androgynous man. As a friend, maybe, you'd like an androgynous man. For a sexual partner, though, you'd prefer a jock. There's no arguing chemistry, but consider the jock for a moment. He competes on the field, whatever his field is, and bed is just one more field to him: another opportunity to perform, another fray. Sensuality is for him candy to be doled out as lure. It is a ration whose flow is cut off at the exact point when it has served its purpose—namely, to elicit your willingness to work out on the field with him.

13   Highly masculine men need to believe their sexual appetite is far greater than a woman's (than a nice woman's). To them, females must be seduced: Seduction is a euphemism for a power play, a con job. It pits man against woman (or woman against man). The jock believes he must win you over, incite your body to rebel against your better judgment: in other words—conquer you.

14   The androgynous man is not your opponent but your teammate. He does not seduce: he invites. Sensuality is a pleasure for him. He's not quite so goal-oriented. And to conclude, I think I need only remind you here of his greater imagination, his wit and empathy, his unpredictability, and his receptivity to new impressions and connections.

Writing About What You Read

Often in college you will be asked to write about what you read. This culminates in the Research Paper, which is discussed in Chapters 20 and 21. However, sometimes you will have to write shorter summaries and critiques.

Writing a Summary

A summary states the main points of an essay in *your own words*. A good summary lets someone who hasn't read the essay understand what it says. A summary can be one or more paragraphs. It should

- provide a context for the essay,
- introduce the author of the essay,
- and state the thesis, (these first three elements often form the introduction of a multiparagraph summary)

- then state the main points of the essay (sometimes but not always based on the topic sentences),
- and conclude by pulling the essay together.

To prepare to write a summary, follow the steps in effective reading. A brief outline of the main points will make it easy to write a summary. Be careful to avoid using the author's exact wording without using quotation marks. You may want to review the section on plagiarism on page 000. Also, don't interject your views. A summary should reflect only the author's words.

A Sample Single Paragraph Summary of "The Appeal of the Androgynous Man"

What kind of man should appeal to women? According to Amy Gross, the editor-in-chief of *O* magazine, in "The Appeal of the Androgynous Man," her ideal is and the ideal of women should be the "androgynous man," a man who shares the personality characteristics of both male and female. To make her point, Amy Gross contrasts the all-man man and the androgynous man. She believes that the all-man man does not share in activities like shopping, has no taste in the arts, is imperialistic, resists anything feminine, and is interested in only exclusively male topics. Worse, she points to studies that show that more masculine men are less creative. Further, she argues that the all-man tends to see women as something to conquer rather than as partners. The androgynous man, by comparison, is very different. He does not resist things that are feminine and so shares in domestic activities, is comfortable with the arts, and can share interests with women. He is shown by studies to be more creative. Further, according to Gross, "The androgynous man is not your opponent but your teammate." As a result, she concludes that the androgynous man has the qualities that women should really look for in a man.

Writing a Critique

Often you will be asked to give your views on an essay, indicating where you agree and disagree with the author's position. Remember you can always agree with part of what a person says and disagree with other parts. A critique combines a summary of the article with your thoughtful reaction. Most critiques consist of several paragraphs. A critique usually includes

- a context for the essay
- an introduction to the author
- a statement of the essay's thesis
- the thesis for your critique
- a summary of the essay
- a statement of the points with which you agree
- a statement with reasons and evidence for your disagreement
- a conclusion

You are well prepared to write a critique if you follow the steps for reading effectively and reading critically.

A Sample Multiparagraph Critique of
"The Appeal of the Androgynous Man"

1   What kind of man should appeal to women? According to Amy Gross, the editor-in-chief of O magazine, in "The Appeal of the Androgynous Man," her ideal is and the ideal of women should be the "androgynous man," a man who shares the personality characteristics of both male and female. But matters are not so simple. Amy Gross falsely divides men into two stereotyped categories. In fact, real men are much more complex.

2   To make her point, Amy Gross contrasts the all-man man and the androgynous man. She believes that the all-man man does not share in activities like shopping, has no taste in the arts, is imperialistic, resists anything feminine, and is interested in only exclusively male topics. Worse, she points to studies that show that more masculine men are less creative. Further, she argues that the all-man tends to see women as something to conquer rather than as partners. The androgynous man, by comparison, is very different. He does not resist things that are feminine and so shares in domestic activities, is comfortable with the arts, and can share interests with women. He is shown by studies to be more creative. Further, according to Gross, "The androgynous man is not your opponent but your teammate." As a result, she concludes that the androgynous man has the qualities that women should really look for in a man.

3   She is right that if the all-man male was like she said, he would truly be undesirable. No woman should want a partner who takes her for granted, doesn't share her interests, or treats her simply as someone to conquer. But is that really what men are like? My brother plays football and loves to watch it on television. He also hunts and fishes. But that isn't all he does. He plays with kittens, loves to cook, plays the guitar and sings, and secretly likes "chick flicks." As far as I can tell, he treats his girlfriend well. He seems genuinely concerned about her, will spend hours shopping with her, goes to events that interest her, and generally seems sensitive to her needs. Is he an "all-man" or an "androgynous man"? Equally a man can write poetry, love Jane Austen, cook gourmet meals, and still take women for granted. From what I have read, Pablo Picasso treated women dreadfully, even if he was a great artist. Was he an "all-man" man or an "androgynous man"?

4   Ms. Gross seems to present evidence from psychological studies that show that more masculine men are less creative than more feminine

men. Maybe so, but she doesn't give us the evidence we need to make up our own minds. How did they actually measure masculinity and femininity? How many people were tested? What did they count as creativity? Personally I have my doubts. Writers such as Ernest Hemingway and Norman Mailer were pretty masculine men and yet were still very creative. I know a lot of men who have feminine characteristics who aren't any more creative than the average person.

5   The mistake Ms. Gross makes is that she believes that women should select types of men. They shouldn't. Women date, love, and marry individual men. As a result, a woman should really be concerned about whether the man shares her interests, treats her well, has qualities she can love, and will be faithful. Where the man fits on Ms. Gross's little chart is far less important than the kind of man he is, regardless of whether he is "androgynous."

Successful Reading

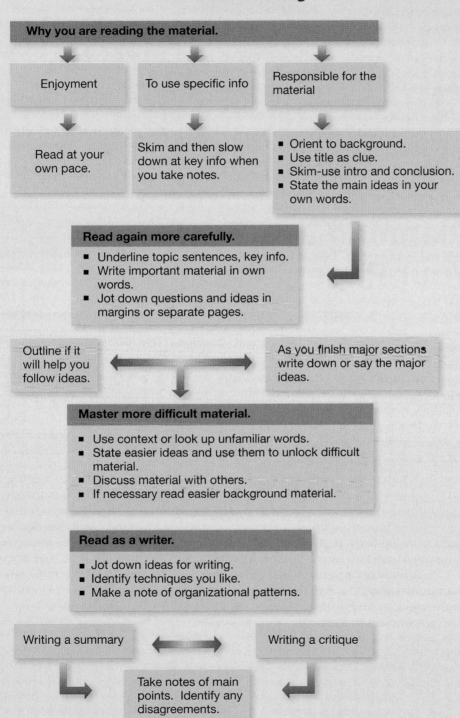

Why you are reading the material.

- Enjoyment
- To use specific info
- Responsible for the material

Enjoyment → Read at your own pace.

To use specific info → Skim and then slow down at key info when you take notes.

Responsible for the material →
- Orient to background.
- Use title as clue.
- Skim-use intro and conclusion.
- State the main ideas in your own words.

Read again more carefully.

- Underline topic sentences, key info.
- Write important material in own words.
- Jot down questions and ideas in margins or separate pages.

Outline if it will help you follow ideas. ↔ As you finish major sections write down or say the major ideas.

Master more difficult material.

- Use context or look up unfamiliar words.
- State easier ideas and use them to unlock difficult material.
- Discuss material with others.
- If necessary read easier background material.

Read as a writer.

- Jot down ideas for writing.
- Identify techniques you like.
- Make a note of organizational patterns.

Writing a summary ↔ Writing a critique

Take notes of main points. Identify any disagreements.

Planning and Drafting Your Paper

Many students believe that good essays are dashed off in a burst of inspiration by born writers. Students themselves often boast that they cranked out their top-notch papers in an hour. Perhaps. But for most of us, writing is a process that takes time and work.

Writing is a flexible process. No one approach works for every writer. Some writers establish their purpose and draft a plan for carrying it out at the start of every project. Others begin with a tentative purpose or plan and discover their final direction as they write. As a project proceeds, the writer is likely to leapfrog backward and forward one or more times rather than to proceed in an orderly, straightforward sequence. Partway through a first draft, for instance, a writer may think of a new point to present, then pause and jot down the details needed to develop it. Similarly, part of the conclusion may come to mind as the writer is gathering the details for supporting a key idea.

Regardless of how it unfolds, the writing process consists of the following stages. Advancing through each stage will guide you if you have no plan or if you've run into snags with your approach. Once you're familiar with these stages, you can combine or rearrange them as needed.

Understanding the assignment
Zeroing in on a topic
Gathering information
Organizing the information
Developing a thesis statement
Writing the first draft

Types of Writers

Planners	Explorers
Start with a focused idea. Usually have a clear plan. Tend to develop existing plan.	Discover ideas while writing. Often follow out inspirations. Can develop tangents. Usually write more than final.
Can write like an outline. May tend to underdevelop. Can miss possible ideas.	Can go off on tangents. May initially lack obvious organization. Usually have more than needed.
Can benefit from additional brainstorming. May need additional development. May need to explore ideas outside plan.	May need to plan after drafting. Might need several revisions. Might need to refocus and cut.

revising to increase their flexibility. Over-writers may have to be taught how to limit themselves and under-writers given extra practice in gathering information.

Understanding the Assignment

Instructors differ in making writing assignments. Some specify the topic; some give you several topics to choose from; and still others offer you a free choice. Likewise, some instructors dictate the length and format of the essay, whereas others don't. Whatever the case, be sure you understand the assignment before you go any further. (See Chapter 2 on reading an assignment.)

Think of it this way: If your boss asked you to report on ways of improving the working conditions in your office and you turned in a report on improving worker benefits, would you expect the boss's approval? Following directions is crucial, so if you have any questions about the assignment, ask your instructor to clear them up right then. Don't be timid; it's much better to ask for directions than to receive a low grade for failing to follow them.

Once you understand the assignment, consider the project *yours*. If you are asked to describe a favorite vacation spot for a local newspaper, here is your

TEACHING STRATEGIES
1. Have students keep logs recording how, when, and where they write and the problems they have. Review the logs and offer suggestions for correcting problems.
2. Research shows that most students do little planning when they write. You might spend in-class time on the various stages of the writing process and supervise student writing efforts.

chance to inform others about a place special to you. By asking yourself what the assignment allows you to accomplish, you can find your own purpose.

Zeroing In on a Topic

A subject is a broad discussion area: sports, college life, culture, and the like. A topic is one small segment of a subject, for example, testing athletes for drug use, Nirvana College's academic probation policy, the Web-surfing phenomenon. If you choose your own topic, pick one narrow enough so that you can develop it properly within any length limitation. Avoid sprawling, slippery issues that lead to a string of trite generalities.

In addition, choose a familiar topic or one you can learn enough about in the time available. Avoid overworked topics such as arguments about the death penalty or the legal drinking age, which generally repeat the same old points. Instead, select a topic that lets you draw upon your unique experiences and insights and offer a fresh perspective to your reader.

Strategies for Finding a Topic

Whenever your instructor assigns a general subject, you'll need to stake out a limited topic suitable for your paper. If you're lucky, the right one will come to mind immediately. More often, though, you'll need to resort to some special strategy. Here are six proven strategies that many writers use. Not all of them will work for everyone, so experiment to find those that produce a topic for you.

Tapping Your Personal Resources   Personal experience furnishes a rich storehouse of writing material. Over the years, you've packed your mind with memories of family gatherings, school activities, movies, concerts, plays, parties, jobs, books you've read, TV programs, dates, discussions, arguments, and so on. All these experiences can provide suitable topics. Suppose you've been asked to write about some aspect of education. Recalling the difficulties you had last term at registration, you might argue for better registration procedures. Or if you're a hopeless TV addict who must write on some advertising topic, why not analyze video advertising techniques?

Anything you've read in magazines or journals, newspapers, novels, short stories, or textbooks can also trigger a topic. Dan Greenburg's "Sound and Fury" (pages 461–463), in which a potentially explosive situation is defused, might suggest a paper on some dangerous encounter in your past. An article reviewing the career of a well-known politician might stir thoughts of a friend's experience in running for the student council.

Select five of the subjects listed below. Tapping your personal resources, name one topic suggested by each. For each topic, list three questions that you might answer in a paper.

Life on a city street
A particular field of work
Some branch of the federal bureaucracy
Concern for some aspect of the environment
Saving money
Home ownership
Schools in your town
Leisure activities
Trends in technology
A best-selling book

Some aspect of nature
Contemporary forms of dancing
Youth gangs
Fashions in clothing
Trendiness
Human rights
Public transportation
Childhood fears
A new scientific discovery
A religious experience

Keeping a Journal Many writers, not comfortable relying on their memories, record their experiences in a journal—a private gathering of entries accumulated over time. Journal keeping provides an abundance of possible writing topics as well as valuable writing practice.

The hallmark of the journal entry is the freedom to explore thoughts, feelings, responses, attitudes, and beliefs without reservation and without concern for "doing it right." *You* control the content and length of the entry. Furthermore, depending on your instructor's preference, you usually don't have to worry about correct spelling or grammar. Journal writing does not represent a finished product but rather an exploration.

A few simple guidelines ensure effective journal entries:

1. Write in any kind of notebook that appeals to you; the content, not the package, is the important thing.
2. Write on a regular basis—at least five times a week, if possible. In any event don't write by fits and starts, cramming two weeks' entries into one sitting.
3. Write for ten to twenty minutes, longer if you have more to say. Don't aim for uniform entry length, for example, three paragraphs or a page and a half. Simply explore your reactions to the happenings in your life or to what you have read, heard in class, or seen on television. The length will take care of itself.

Let's examine a typical journal entry by Sam, a first-year composition student.

Last week went back to my hometown for the first time since my family moved away and while there dropped by the street where I spent my first twelve years. Visit left me feeling very depressed. Family home still there, but its paint peeling and front porch sagging. Sign next to the porch said house now occupied by Acme Realtors. While we lived there, front yard lush green and bordered by beds of irises. Now an oil-spattered parking lot. All

of general and specific assignments.

Good writing assignments should allow students to draw upon their backgrounds and interests; have a genuine, clearly evident purpose and be aimed at a real audience; provide a learning experience for students; tailor any research requirements to the ability of students; gradually increase in difficulty as the course progresses; be clear about what students must do to develop the paper; stem from reading and discussions.

TEACHING STRATEGY
It often helps to have students read about and discuss a subject that can serve as a seedbed for a variety of topics. For example, the influence of television on viewers' lives might lead to papers about its influence on our buying habits, dating practices, views of minorities, attitudes toward violence, and health concerns.

CLASSROOM ACTIVITY
Students often pick overly broad topics because they fear they can say very little about narrow topics. To correct this notion, you could have the class orally brainstorm some seemingly insignificant item, perhaps a particular kind of ballpoint pen, and write each observation on the blackboard. Such a listing should clearly demonstrate the rich possibilities of narrow topics.

PERSPECTIVE
Students often mistakenly
believe that they have no
personal resources to tap or
that their own experiences
are invalid for a paper. To
overcome this perception,
have each student
brainstorm or freewrite
about some personal
experience and then
present the results to the
class. The ensuing
discussion can help
students see that they may
indeed have legitimate
things to say about a variety
of experiences, even
though some research
might be necessary.

**TEACHING
STRATEGIES**
1. At the beginning of the
term, you might have stu-
dents fill out a personal
interest inventory, indicating favorite activities,
movies seen, books read,
and the like. Then use
these inventories to for-
mulate in-class examples
for discussion and to help
students who are having
trouble finding topics.
2. To help students convert personal experiences
into topics, have them
write about some concern,
such as problems they
have had in school, and
then formulate a series of
topics related to the problems. Possibilities include
registration difficulties,
coping with on- or off-
campus life, studying
effectively, and overcom-
ing homesickness.

PERSPECTIVE
Unless students
understand just what their
journals are meant to
accomplish, they aren't

*the other houses on our side of the street gone, replaced
by a row of dumpy buildings housing dry cleaner, bowling
alley, hamburger joint, shoe repair shop, laundromat. All of
them dingy and rundown looking, even though only a few
years old.*

*Other side of the street in no better shape. Directly across
from our house a used-car dealership with rows of junky
looking cars. No trace left of the Little League park that
used to be there. Had lots of fun playing baseball and learned
meaning of sportsmanship. To left of the dealership my old grade
school, now boarded and abandoned. Wonder about my fifth-grade
teacher Mrs. Wynick. Is she still teaching? Still able to make
learning a game, not a chore? Other side of dealership the
worst sight of all. Grimy looking plant of some sort pouring foul
smelling smoke into the air from a discolored stack. Smoke made
me cough.*

Don't think I'll revisit my old street again.

This journal entry could spawn several essays. Sam might explore the causes of
residential deterioration, define sportsmanship, explain how Mrs. Wynick made
learning a game, or argue for stricter pollution control laws.

*Write journal entries over the next week or two for some of the
following items that interest you. If you have trouble finding a
suitable topic for a paper, review the entries for possibilities.*

Encounters with technology   Developing relationships
Single or married life   Parents
Financial or occupational considerations   Ideas gained through reading

Sorting Out a Subject   All of us sort things. We do it whenever we tackle the
laundry, clear away a sinkful of dishes, or tidy up a basement or garage. Sorting
out a subject is similar. First, we break our broad subject into categories and subcategories, then allow our minds to roam over the different items and see what
topics we can turn up. The chart on page 36 shows what one student found when
she explored the general topic of public transportation.

As you'll discover for yourself, some subjects yield more topics than others; some, no topics at all.

Select two of the following subjects, then subdivide those two into five topics.

Advertising   Movies   The space program
Dwellings   Occupations   Sports
Fashions   Popular music   Television programs
Magazines   Social classes   Vacations

Asking Questions   Often, working your way through these basic questions will lead you to a manageable topic:

1. Can I define my subject?
2. Does it break into categories?
3. If so, what comparisons can I make among these categories?
4. If my subject is divided into parts, how do they work together?
5. Does my subject have uses? What are they?
6. What are some examples of my subject?
7. What are the causes or origins of my subject?
8. What impact has my subject had?

Let's convert these general questions into specific questions about telescopes, a broad general subject:

1. What is a telescope?
2. What are the different kinds of telescopes?
3. How are they alike? How do they differ?
4. What are the parts of each kind of telescope, and how do they work together?
5. What are telescopes used for?
6. What are some well-known telescopes?
7. Who invented the telescope?
8. What impact have telescopes had on human life and knowledge?

Each of these questions offers a starting point for a suitably focused essay. Question 3 might launch a paper comparing reflecting and refracting

likely to use them properly. Several kinds of journals are possible. *Personal response* allows students to record stray thoughts and ideas as well as interesting experiences. Beyond having students write a certain amount each day, instructors impose no restrictions. *Focused response* features a collection of responses to topics set by the instructor and is tailored toward future writing assignments or specific skills being introduced. Thus students who will write comparison and description essays may be asked to write a page or two contrasting two family members or describing a fellow student. *Reading log* allows students to summarize reading assignments, possibly connect readings to their own experience, compare different readings, or record their thoughts while reading. Such a log helps prepare for a paper based on readings.

TEACHING STRATEGIES

1. Students are likely to confuse journals with diaries and jot down diary-type entries. To counter this tendency, show them examples of what you'll expect and specify the purpose of journal assignments. Focused responses avoid this problem.

2. Many students are likely to write as little as possible and dash off all their entries at the last minute. It is therefore a good idea to review journals frequently.

Results of Sorting Out the Subject Public Transportation

Land			Water		Air	
Buses	Taxis	Trains	Seagoing	Lake, River	Airplanes	Helicopters
County bus services for the handicapped	Rights of passengers	The Orient Express, the Twentieth Century Limited	The Titanic	Barge Cruises	Airline deregulation	Air taxis
Bus tours	Preventing Crimes against drivers	Monorails	Luxury liners		Overbooking flights	Cargo
Jitney buses		Preventing subway crimes	Theme Cruises		Making air travel safer	
Improving bus terminals		Guardian Angels	Modern sea pirates		Coping with hijacking	
Designing buses to accommodate the handicapped		Amtrak	Traveling by freighter		Causes and prevention of jet lag	
		Japan's high-speed trains	The impact of overseas flights on ship travel		Development of the stealth bomber	
		Deterioration of railroad track beds			Noise pollution around airports	

telescopes; question 6 might be answered in a paper about the Hubble Space Telescope and the problems with it.

EXERCISE

Select two of the following subjects. Create general questions, then convert them into specific questions. Finally, suggest two essay topics for each of your two subjects.

Astrology	Games	Shopping malls
Books	Microorganisms	Stars
Colleges	Plays	Television
Emotions	Religions	Warships

Freewriting   The freewriting strategy snares thoughts as they race through your mind, yielding a set of sentences that you then look over for writing ideas. To begin, turn your pen loose and write for about five minutes on your general subject. Put down everything that comes into your head, without worrying about grammar, spelling, or punctuation. What you produce is for your eyes alone. If the thought flow becomes blocked, write "I'm stuck, I'm stuck . . ." until you break the mental logjam. When your writing time is up, go through your sentences one by one and extract potential topic material. If you draw a blank, write for another five minutes and look again.

The following example shows the product of one freewriting session. Drew's instructor had assigned a two- or three-page paper on technology; and since Drew is a business major, he considers a more personal technology with which he has experience, the cell phone.

> Technology, huh. What do I know about technology? Cell phones are technology? What about them? There are so many kinds. Razors, Blacberries. I love my new i-phone. It does everything, plays music, lets me text, check out U-tube, e-mail, take pictures and store them. They change people lives. But how? Well, we are always on them talking to friends, to anybody, and parents and teachers never get it. But why do we talk on them so much. Stuck, stuck, stuck. Well, I keep in touch with friends. Some are way at college. My girlfriend is always calling me. We also get lots of stuff done, like checking out my stupid bills.

This example suggests at least three papers. For people shopping for a new cell phone, Drew could identify the advantages of different types. He could write to people considering buying an i-phone about the features of the phone. He could write to those perplexed by student behavior to explain why students use cell phones so extensively.

to thought. It often helps to have students translate topics into questions and then develop a set of related questions.

PERSPECTIVE
Freewriting was heralded by Peter Elbow, who initially used it as a strategy to help MIT engineers whose writing anxiety blocked their writing. A useful way to unlock the mind and bring up interesting and new associations, it can be used at any point in the writing process to help students develop new approaches to papers in progress. Don't expect splendid results every time: Students who think trite thoughts produce trite freewriting. And like any activity, freewriting becomes more effective with repeated use. It can be unfocused, with students writing whatever comes into their heads, or focused on some subject or topic.

TEACHING STRATEGIES
1. Have students freewrite on anything, circle sentences that interest them, and then freewrite on those sentences. Ask them to repeat the process until a potential topic emerges.
2. To ingrain the habit of freewriting, ask students to freewrite for five minutes at the beginning of the class, perhaps during the first couple of weeks of the term. You might also have students freewrite before class discussions in order to develop things to say.

Brainstorming   Brainstorming, a close cousin of freewriting, captures fleeting ideas in words, fragments, and sometimes sentences, rather than in a series of sentences. Brainstorming garners ideas faster than the other strategies do. But unless you move immediately to the next stage of writing, you may lose track of what some of your fragmentary jottings mean.

To compare the results of freewriting and brainstorming a topic, we've converted our freewriting example into this list, which typifies the results of brainstorming:

Types of cell phones	stores pictures
Razors	text message
Blackberries	e-mails
i-phones	why people use e-mail
plays music	to coordinate life
view u-tube	to get things done
takes pictures	to keep in touch

Return to the five subjects you selected for the exercise on page 32. Freewrite or brainstorm for five minutes on each one; then choose a topic suitable for a two- or three-page essay. State your topic, intended audience, and purpose.

Narrowing a familiar subject may yield not only a topic but also the main divisions for a paper on it. Drew's freewriting session uncovered several possible cell phone topics as well as a way of approaching each: classifying types of cell phones and writing about the strengths and weaknesses of each or identifying the different features of an i-phone and describing each feature and how it works or explaining each of the reasons college students use cell phones so frequently. Ordinarily, though, the main divisions will emerge only after you have gathered material to develop your topic. Drew, on considering his options, decides he doesn't know enough about types of cell phones and might get carried away when writing about the i-phone. He decides to write about the reasons college students are so attached to their cell phones.

Identifying Your Audience and Purpose

You can identify your purpose and audience at several stages in the writing process. Sometimes both are set by the assignment and guide your selection of a topic. For example, you might be asked to write the college president to recommend improvements in the school's registration system. At other times, you may have to write a draft before you can determine either. Usually, though, the selection of audience and purpose goes hand in hand with determining a topic. Think of the different types of information Drew would gather if he wrote for

(1) college students to break them of their cell phone habits, (2) college professors and parents to make cell phone use seem less peculiar, (3) a sociology professor to demonstrate how common behaviors can be explained through sociological theories.

Gathering Information

Once you have a topic, you'll need things to say about it. This supporting material can include facts, ideas, examples, observations, sensory impressions, memories, and the like. Without the proper backup, papers lack force, vividness, and interest and may confuse or mislead readers. The more support you can gather, the easier it will be for you to write a draft. Time spent gathering information is never wasted.

Strategies for Gathering Information

If you are writing on a familiar topic, much of your supporting material may come from your own head. Brainstorming is the best way to retrieve it. With unfamiliar topics, brainstorming won't work. Instead, you'll have to do some background reading. Whatever the topic, familiar or unfamiliar, talking with friends, parents, neighbors, or people knowledgeable about the topic can also produce useful ideas.

Brainstorming   Brainstorming a topic, like brainstorming a subject, yields a set of words, fragments, and occasionally sentences that will furnish ideas for the paper. Drew has decided that he wants to demonstrate to professors and parents that there are good reasons for student cell phone use. He generated the following list through brainstorming.

students open cell phones after class
coordinating life
meeting friends for study sessions
arranging a lunch date
getting a ride
coordinating a team project
getting things done
resolving bill disputes
scheduling car repairs
finding babysitters

weather updates
sending e-mails
sending pictures by e-mail
holding up a phone at a concert
calling when something funny happens
keeping in touch
old friends in different colleges
boyfriends or girlfriends
text messaging
playing music

You can see how some thoughts have led to others. For example, the first jotting, "arranging a lunch date" leads naturally to the next one, "getting a ride." and "keeping in touch" leads to "old friends in different colleges."

3. Some students can't believe that the instructor doesn't want perfect writing; others view the activity as a waste of time since it doesn't immediately result in a finished paper. Explain the rationale for freewriting and distribute far-from-perfect samples. You could freewrite with the class and share your results.

4. Other students might see freewriting as a green light to produce essays that are merely tidied up freewriting. Maintain a clear distinction between freewriting designed to uncover topics, the drafts that are increasingly audience oriented, and the final draft—developed, organized, and polished.

SUGGESTED INSTRUCTOR READINGS
Elbow, P. Writing Without Teachers. New York: Oxford UP, 1973. The classic account of the rationale for freewriting and how to use it effectively to develop a draft.
Jensen, G. H., and J. K. DiTiberio. Personality and the Teaching of Composition. Norwood, NJ: Ablex, 1989. Discusses the different personalities that students and teachers bring to the classroom and how these personalities influence student writing.
Vipond, D., and R. A. Hunt. "The Strange

PERSPECTIVE
Students are surprised to learn that brainstorming, both by individuals and groups, is widely used in corporations to generate ideas, especially for advertisements.

TEACHING STRATEGIES
1. Brainstorming and freewriting can be combined. A student can brainstorm, select an item from the resulting list, freewrite about it, and then brainstorm an item from the freewriting sample.
2. Following the practice of business, have the class brainstorm a subject as a group, write their responses on the board, weed out ideas inappropriate for papers, then brainstorm some more.
3. Some students claim to be stuck after listing just two or three ideas. Nudge them into jotting down *any* ideas, no matter how absurd they seem. They can always be deleted later.

PERSPECTIVE
Lack of supporting material is one of the most evident weaknesses in student writing. Even when you point out that they must support their ideas,

Branching is a helpful and convenient extension of brainstorming that allows you to add details to any item in your list. Here's how you might use this technique to approach "cell phone use":

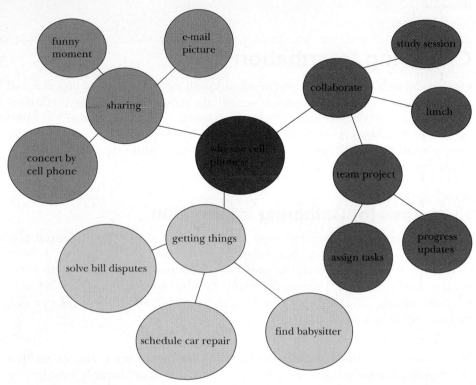

Don't worry if your brainstorming notes look chaotic and if some seem irrelevant. Sometimes the most unlikely material turns out to be the freshest and most interesting. As you organize and write your paper, you'll probably combine, modify, and omit some of the notes, as well as add others. Drew decides from his brainstorming that "playing music," "sending e-mails," and "getting weather updates" are too specific to only a few kinds of cell phones and should not be part of his paper.

Prepare a brainstorming sheet of supporting details for one of the topics you developed for the exercise on page 34.

Reading   When you have to grapple with an unfamiliar topic, look in the library for material to develop it. Before going there, however, see Chapter 20, "The Research Paper," and review the guidelines under the headings "Computerized Card Catalog" and "Periodical and Database Indexes." These sections tell you how to unearth promising references to investigate. Once you have a list of references, start searching for the books or articles. Look through each one you find and jot down information that looks useful, either as direct quotations or in your own words.

Whenever you use a direct quotation or rephrased material in your paper, you must give proper credit to the source. If you don't, you are guilty of plagiarism, a serious offense that can result in a failing grade for the course or even expulsion from college. See "Handling Quotations" and "Avoiding Plagiarism" in Chapter 21.

Talking with Others   You can expand the pool of ideas gained through brainstorming or reading by talking with some of the people around you. Imagine you're writing a paper about a taxpayers' revolt in your state. After checking the leading state newspapers at the library, you find that most of the discontent centers on property taxes. You then decide to supplement what you've read by asking questions about the tax situation in your town.

Your parents and neighbors tell you that property taxes have jumped 50 percent in the last two years. The local tax assessor tells you that assessed valuations have risen sharply and that state law requires property taxes to keep pace. She also notes that this situation is causing some people on fixed incomes to lose their homes. A city council member explains that part of the added revenue is being used to repair city streets, build a new library wing, and buy more fire-fighting equipment. The rest is going to the schools. School officials tell you they're using their extra funds to offer more vocational courses and to expand the program for learning-disabled students. As you can see, asking questions can broaden your perspective and provide information that will help you to write a more worthwhile paper.

Organizing the Information

If you have ever listened to a rambling speaker spill out ideas in no particular order, you probably found it hard to pay attention to the speech, let alone make sense of it. So, too, with disorganized writing. A garbled listing of ideas serves no one; an orderly presentation highlights your ideas and helps communication succeed.

Your topic determines the approach you take. In narrating a personal experience, such as a mishap-riddled vacation, you'd probably trace the events in the order they occurred. In describing a process, say caulking a bathtub, you'd take the reader step by step through the procedure. To describe a hillside view near your home, you might work from left to right. Or you could first paint a word picture of some striking central feature and then fan out in either direction. Other topics dictate other patterns, such as comparison and contrast, cause and effect, and illustration. Chapters 5–13 describe the basic patterns in detail.

You can best organize long pieces of writing, such as library research papers, by following a formal outline. (See "Organizing and Outlining," in Chapter 20.) For shorter papers, however, a simple, informal system of *flexible notes* will do nicely.

many students don't know how, particularly when they dash off a paper the night before it is due. Some think that support consists only of library research. Students should understand that a four-page paper can be the crystallization of eight pages of notes. The problem for them is to get those eight pages. You might allot time in your syllabus and also classroom time for gathering support. Students need to know not only the expectation of support but also the process of gathering it.

TEACHING STRATEGY
After initial brainstorming or freewriting, ask students to develop a list of questions they want their paper to answer and then propose how they will address these questions—perhaps by further brainstorming, talking, observing, or reading. You might ask them to propose a timetable for gathering this information.

CLASSROOM ACTIVITIES
1. Introduce a possible topic for a paper, perhaps student attitudes toward writing, and have students, working in small groups, suggest various ways to obtain information for a paper. A classroom discussion could then ensue.
2. You might allow students to talk in small groups about their developing papers. Peer questions

and opinions help them formulate their own ideas and discover where they need more information.

SUGGESTED INSTRUCTOR READING
Reither, J. A. "Writing and Knowing: Toward Redefining the Writing Process." College English 47 (1985): 620–28. Argues that we err in expecting students to create papers entirely by techniques such as brainstorming and that we should have them write as a result of primary or library research.

READER/THEME STRATEGIES
Students should understand that they can also glean ideas from their reading. If you are building your course around one theme, you might assign a Reader essay, such as "Sound and Fury," and have students jot down any ideas or personal experiences that the essay triggers. If students draw a blank, first discuss the essay's theme; then ask the class to freewrite how it relates to their experience. This exercise can also help students become more interactive readers.

PERSPECTIVE
Writers organize differently. Some allow their pattern to evolve over several drafts. Such an approach lets the structure of the paper

The Flexible Notes System

To create a set of flexible notes, write each of your key points at the top of a separate sheet of paper. If you have a thesis statement (see page 44), refer to it for your key points. Next, list under each heading the supporting details that go with that heading. Drop details that don't fit and expand points that need more support. When your sheets are finished, arrange them in the order you expect to follow in your essay. Drew's notes for the cell phone paper look like this:

Coordinating Activities

Meeting friends for a study session
Arranging a lunch date
Getting a ride
Coordinating a team project

Getting Things Done

Resolving bill disputes
Scheduling car repairs
Finding babysitters

Sharing

Sending pictures by e-mail
Holding up phone at concert
Call about something funny happening

Keeping in Touch

Old friends in different colleges
Boyfriends and girlfriends
Text messaging

Since coordinating activities, getting things done, sharing, and keeping in touch are equivalent reasons, this listing arranges them according to their probable importance—starting with the most important reason from the point of view of the audience.

Now you're ready to draft a plan showing how many paragraphs you'll have in each part of the essay and what each paragraph will cover. Sometimes the number of details will suggest one paragraph; other times you'll need a paragraph block—two or more paragraphs. Here's a plan for Drew's cell phone essay:

Coordinating Activities

Meeting for study session
Arranging a lunch date
Getting a ride
Corrdinating a team project

Getting Things Done

Resolving bill disputes
Scheduling car repairs
Finding a babysitter

Sharing

Sending pictures by e-mail
Holding up phone at concert
Calling about a funny event

Keeping in Touch

Old friends in different colleges ⎫
Boyfriends and girlfriends   ⎬ By voice
Text messaging   ⎫ By text

These groupings suggest one paragraph about coordinating activities, one about getting things done, one about sharing, and two about keeping in touch.

Organize into flexible notes the supporting details that you prepared for the exercise on page 40. Arrange your note pages in a logical sequence and draft a plan showing the number and content of the paragraphs in each section.

Creating an Outline

With longer essays or if it fits your organizational style, it can be helpful to develop an outline. An outline can show you how to organize and develop your paragraphs. In an outline, you organize your essay into major units using Roman numerals (I, II, III), letters (A, B, C), and numbers to show the structure you will use in the paper. Introductions and conclusions are not usually included in the outline. There are two kinds of outlines. A topic outline simply states the main topic to be addressed in a section.

    I. Coordinating Activities
        A. Meeting friends for study sessions
           1. Setting the time
           2. Making certain everyone gets there
        B. Arranging a lunch date
           1. Deciding where everyone is meeting
           2. Arranging a ride to lunch

develop with the ideas. Others prepare an outline prior to the first draft. An early plan lets the writer see immediately whether the topic is workable and where more information is needed. It also shows the importance of the overall structure of the paper rather than merely the sentence-to-sentence flow.

TEACHING STRATEGY
After students have written a draft, have them check it against their plan to see if, where, and why they have strayed. Then ask them to make the necessary changes or to appropriately revise their plan to match the new ideas of the draft.

CLASSROOM ACTIVITIES
1. Ask students to break a sample essay, perhaps from the Reader, into a set of flexible notes or an outline. This exercise helps students see that even professional writers develop their work from basic, ordered information.

2. Have students, working in small groups, develop two alternative organization plans for the tennis essay and then explain their rationale.

3. Discuss with the class when to follow and when to revise a plan. Give students a premature plan and have them determine whether the writer should follow it or bypass it and start drafting to discover new ideas and possible structures. What are the consequences in each case? While plans can be useful, students need to understand that they aren't engraved on marble.

CLASSROOM ACTIVITIES
1. Have the class brainstorm a topic, formulate several possible thesis statements, evaluate them against the requirements of a good thesis statement, and select the best one.
2. Have students review one another's thesis statements, write down any questions about their scope and adequacy, then return the responses to their authors. This exercise can help students redefine and redirect their efforts.

TEACHING STRATEGIES
1. Students often have trouble focusing on and then narrowing a thesis statement. You might have them freewrite what they want to say in the paper, boil that writing down to

one or two sentences, check to see whether those sentences say what's wanted, and then make necessary modifications in the thesis statement. Further, have them question each term of the thesis to see if it is clear and conveys the right message. Have them check off in their planning notes what does and does not fit under the thesis.
2. If some students develop their thesis statements before gathering

II. Getting Things Done
   A. Coordinating a team project
      1. Assign tasks
      2. Monitor progress
   B. Resolving bill disputes
      1. Call during business hours

Topic outlines will quickly let you know if you have enough information for a paragraph. If under one major heading, you only have one letter or under a letter only one number as in II B you may need to do more brainstorming.

In a sentence outline, you make full statements or sentences that can often be used in your paper. A sentence outline makes you think about what you really want to say.

   I. Cell phones can be used to coordinate activities that would be otherwise difficult to coordinate given students' busy schedules.
      A. Cell phones can help students find out where a study session is being held.
      B. Often there is a complex schedule of classes, work, meals, and meetings to organize.
      C. Cell phones can let members of a team project keep the project on track.

For a more complete example of a sentence outline, check the example on pages 381–383 in Chapter 20.

To develop your outline, you take your brainstorming or notes and mark the major units as I, II, III based on the main ideas they demonstrate. Then start to develop your outline, identifying the major points for each major heading (I, II . . .) and the next major points (A, B, C). You can use your outline as a goad to additional planning as you see the holes. You should rarely have an A without a B or a 1 without a 2.

Developing a Thesis Statement

A thesis statement presents the main idea of a piece of writing, usually in one sentence. The thesis statement points you in a specific direction, helping you to stay on track and out of tempting byways. In addition, it tells your reader what to expect.

Thesis statements can emerge at several points in the writing process. If an instructor assigns a controversial topic on which you hold strong views, the statement may pop into your head right away. At other times it may develop as you narrow a subject to a topic. Occasionally, you even have to write a preliminary draft to determine your main idea. Usually, though, the thesis statement emerges after you've gathered and examined your supporting information.

As you examine your information, search for the central point and the key points that back it up; then use these to develop your thesis statement. Converting the topic to a question may help you to uncover backup ideas and write a thesis statement.

For example:

> *Topic:* The commercial advantages of computerized data storage systems.
>
> *Question:* What advantages do computerized data storage systems offer business?
>
> *Thesis statement:* Computerized data storage systems offer business enormous storage capacity, cheap, instant data transmission almost anywhere, and significantly increased profits.

The thesis statement stems from the specifics the student unearthed while answering the question.

Below are some key strategies that can help you develop a thesis statement.

- Identify your main topic.
- Review your notes or research and identify the specific, major claims you want to make about your topic.
- Select those claims that will be the focus and organizational structure of the paper. You may need to outline first.
- Combine the major claim or claims with the topic in a statement that represents the main point of your paper.

Requirements of a Good Thesis Statement

Unless intended for a lengthy paper, a thesis statement *focuses on just one central point or issue.* Suppose you prepare the following thesis statement for a two- or three-page paper:

> Centerville College should reexamine its policies on open admissions, vocational programs, and aid to students.

This sprawling statement would commit you to grapple with three separate issues. At best, you could make only a few general remarks about each one.

To correct matters, consider each issue carefully in light of how much it interests you and how much you know about it. Then make your choice and draft a narrower statement. The following thesis statement would do nicely for a brief paper. It shows clearly that the writer will focus on *just one issue:*

> Because of the rising demand among high school graduates for job-related training, Centerville College should expand its vocational offerings.

A good thesis statement also *tailors the scope of the issue to the length of the paper.* No writer could deal adequately with "Many first-year college students face crucial adjustment problems" in two or three pages. The idea is too broad to yield more than a smattering of poorly supported general statements. Paring it down to "Free time is a responsibility that challenges many first-year college students," however, results in an idea that could probably be developed adequately.

support, have them write down what information they will need in the papers. This exercise helps launch the drafting stage.

3. Some students can become fixated on the thesis statement, constantly reworking it as though it were a replacement for the draft. Others will never get beyond the most general restatement of a topic. In both cases, encourage students to write a preliminary draft before formulating a thesis statement.

4. Other students resist modifications to their thesis because changes require additional effort. You might show them how one of your thesis statements evolved as new information surfaced or ideas developed.

5. A thesis statement, of course, does not have to be a single sentence but could actually encompass two or more sentences. Give students writing samples that contain such thesis statements and have them discuss why more than one sentence is needed and how effective the choice is.

SUGGESTED INSTRUCTOR READING
Wallace, D. L. "From Intentions to Text: Articulating Initial Intentions for Writing." Research in the Teaching of English 30 (1996): 182–220. Explains the impact of how students frame their intention for writing.

EXERCISE ANSWERS

2a. This statement is not precise. It could mean that the writer will discuss (a) the causes of absenteeism; (b) the effects of absenteeism; (c) the efforts industry is making to reduce absenteeism. Any attempt to discuss these aspects adequately would require far more than two or three pages.

2b. This thesis statement is satisfactory. Its topic is narrow enough to be covered adequately in two or three pages, and it signals the organization of the paper.

2c. This thesis statement offers no clue to why Acme College is not well run. Does the writer mean that (a) the administrators are doing a poor job? (b) the faculty is underpaid and poorly motivated? (c) the course offerings are inadequate? (d) the school doesn't provide adequate recreational facilities? Furthermore, by saying "Although I don't know much about running a college," the student undermines his or her credibility.

2d. This thesis statement fails on two counts. First, it makes two separate assertions—about school construction and worker training. Second, each assertion is too complex to be discussed adequately in a short paper.

2e. This is a good thesis statement. It could be explained in two or three pages, and the phrase "wanting simpler and slower-paced lives" signals that the writer might contrast the two types of jobs

A good thesis statement further provides *an accurate forecast of what's to come.* If you plan to discuss the effects of overeating, don't say, "Overeating stems from deep-seated psychological factors and the easy availability of convenience foods." Such a statement, incorrectly suggesting that the paper will focus on causes, would only mislead and confuse your reader. On the other hand, "Overeating leads to obesity, which can cause or complicate several serious health problems" accurately represents what's to follow.

Finally, a good thesis statement is *precise, often previewing the organization of the paper.* Assertions built on fuzzy, catchall words like *fascinating, bad, meaningful,* and *interesting,* or statements like "My paper is about . . ." tell neither writer nor reader what's going on. To illustrate:

- New York is a fascinating city.
- My paper is about no-fault divorce.

These examples raise a host of questions. Why does the writer find New York fascinating? Because of its skyscrapers? Its night life? Its theaters? Its restaurants? Its museums? Its shops? Its inhabitants? And what about no-fault divorce? Will the writer attack it, defend it, trace its history, suggest ways of improving it? To find out, we must journey through the paper, hoping to find our way without a road-map sentence.

Now look at the rewritten versions of those faulty thesis statements:

- New York's art museums offer visitors an opportunity to view a wide variety of great paintings.
- Compared to traditional divorce, no-fault divorce is less expensive, promotes fairer settlements, and reflects a more realistic view of the causes of marital breakdown.

These statements tell the reader not only what points the writer will make but also the order they will follow.

In brief, your thesis statement should

- focus on just one central point or issue.
- narrow the scope of the issue to what is manageable.
- provide an accurate forecast of what is to come.
- often preview the organization of the paper.

Your thesis statement should **not**

- be too vague or general.
- include more than you can reasonably manage in a paper.
- suggest a different focus or organization than you follow in your paper.
- use clichéd and excess wording like "In this paper I will discuss . . ."

Omission of Thesis Statement

Not all papers have explicit thesis statements. Narratives and descriptions, for example, sometimes merely support some point that is unstated but nevertheless clear, and professional writers sometimes imply their thesis rather than state it openly. Nonetheless, a core idea underlies and controls all effective writing. Usually it is best to state that core idea in a thesis statement.

Changing Your Thesis Statement

Before your paper is in final form, you may need to change your thesis statement several times. If you draft the thesis statement during the narrowing stage, you might change it to reflect what you uncovered while gathering information. Or you might amend it after writing the first draft so that it reflects your additions and deletions. Drew in his first rough draft thought "In the end this cell phone mania is a necessary part of college life" was an adequate thesis statement. In revising his draft, however, he realized that it was not precise enough to direct his readers. He added a more precise statement that identified the main reasons addressed in his paper to serve as his thesis: "They use cell phones to coordinate the day's activitites, to get some business done, to share life's events, and to keep in touch."

Tentative or final, formulated early or late, the thesis statement serves as a beacon that spotlights your purpose.

1. **Write a thesis statement for the flexible notes that you developed for the exercise on page 43.**
2. **Reread "Requirements of a Good Thesis Statement"; then explain why each of the following does or does not qualify as an effective thesis statement for a two- or three-page essay.**
   a. My paper discusses the problem of employee absenteeism in American industry.
   b. Living on a small island offers three advantages: isolation from city problems, the opportunity to know your neighbors, and the chance to go fishing whenever you want.
   c. Although I don't know much about running a college, I know that Acme College is not run well.
   d. Increasing federal outlays for education will help us construct needed school buildings and create a better-trained workforce.
   e. Many people, wanting simpler and slower-paced lives, have abandoned highpaying executive positions for lower-paying, less stressful jobs.
   f. Vacationing in Britain is a nice way to spend a summer.
   g. Extending Middletown's intracity transit system will save consumers money, reduce pollution, and increase city revenues.
   h. Most cable TV companies provide subscribers with several specialized-program channels.
3. **Revise the following five weak thesis statements.**
   a. The first year of college can be hard.
   b. FaceBook offers lots of features.
   c. My paper discusses the importance of writing for college students.
   d. Global warming is changing the weather.
   e. In this paper I will talk about how wireless phones do more than ever.

and discuss the rewards of the latter type.

2f. This thesis statement, like c, is far too imprecise. Vacationing in Britain might be nice for several reasons, including the opportunity to (a) meet and mingle with the British people; (b) enjoy London's theaters and nightlife; (c) tour the nation's historic cities and shrines; (d) enroll in a summer program at Oxford or Cambridge. A better thesis statement might be "Vacationing in Britain offers the traveler a chance to visit the birthplaces of some of the world's foremost literary figures."

2g. This thesis statement commits the writer to deal with three separate issues, any one of which would require two or three pages. The discussion needs narrowing to just one issue.

2h. Another good thesis statement, this one restricts the writer to a topic that suits the length limitations. The paper might include paragraphs about channels devoted to sports, religion, movies, and children's programs.

3. a. Students in their first year of college are challenged by a greater than expected academic workload.

b. FaceBook offers users the ability to connect to a number of virtual friends, list interests, post pictures, write blogs that let friends know what they are doing, and even schedule group activities.

c. Good writing skills are essential for students to be successful in their coursework and in their future careers.

d. Global warming is increasing the number of extreme storms in the United States.

e. Wireless phones have combined the traditional phone with a PDA to provide a devise that lets users maintain a schedule, play music, take photos, receive and send e-mails, browse the Internet, and more.

PERSPECTIVE
Reiterate that a first draft is not a final draft, might not be anything like a final draft, can be subject to massive change, might be thrown out entirely, and is an experiment. Despite these caveats, many students will attempt to get it right on the first try in order to save time. You might jokingly label this version the zero draft, fertilizer draft, or overhaul draft. Students approach drafting differently. Some use notes and plans to build a more organized draft; others merely refer to notes and then experiment with getting ideas on paper, well aware that the draft will probably need reorganization and more information.

TEACHING STRATEGIES
1. If you have basic students, you might show them how *you* write a draft, perhaps using an overhead. Students are amazed to discover that even teachers write in a series of fits and starts and change direction.

Writing the First Draft

Now on to the first draft of your essay. The writing should go rather quickly. After all, you have a topic you're qualified to write about, a thesis statement that indicates your purpose, enough information to develop it, and a written plan to follow. But sometimes when you sit down to write, the words won't come; and all you can do is doodle or stare at the blank page. Perhaps the introduction is the problem. Many writers are terrified by the thought of the opening paragraph. They want to get off to a good start but can't figure out how to begin. If this happens to you, additional brainstorming or freewriting can make you more comfortable and may suggest an opening. Keep in mind that any lead-in you write now can be changed later. If these suggestions don't solve your problem, skip the introduction for the time being. Once you have drafted the body of the paper, an effective opening should come more easily.

Here are some general suggestions for writing a first draft:

1. Stack your thesis statement, flexible notes, and written plan in front of you. They will start you thinking.
2. Skip every other line (double-space) and leave wide margins. Then you'll have room to revise later.
3. Write quickly; capture the drift of your thoughts. Concentrate on content and organization. Get your main points and supporting details on paper in the right sequence. Don't spend time correcting grammatical or punctuation errors, improving your language, or making the writing flow smoothly. You might lose your train of thought and end up doodling or staring again.
4. Take breaks at logical dividing points, for example, when you finish discussing a key point. Before you start to write again, scan what you've written.

Now for some specific suggestions that will help you with the actual writing:

1. Rewrite your thesis statement at the top of your first page to break the ice and build momentum.
2. Write your first paragraph, introducing your essay and stating your thesis. If you get stuck here, move on to the rest of the paper.
3. Follow your plan as you write. Begin with your first main point and work on each section in turn.
4. Look over the supporting details listed under the first heading in your flexible notes. Write a topic sentence stating the central idea of the paragraph.
5. Turn the details into sentences; use one or more sentences to explain each one. Add other related details, facts, or examples if they occur to you.
6. When you move from one paragraph to the next, try to provide a transitional word or sentence that connects each paragraph.
7. Write your last paragraph, ending your essay in an appropriate fashion. If you get stuck, set your conclusion aside and return to it later.

Writing a draft isn't always so systematic. If you are inspired, you may want to abandon your plans and simply use your first draft to explore ideas. You can always revise, so don't be overly concerned if you get off track. You might uncover some of your best material during this type of search.

Using the plan you prepared for the exercise on page 43, write the first draft of an essay.

Drew now uses his thesis statement and paragraph-by-paragraph plan to write the following draft. Notice that Drew, like many writers, gets off track. That is a common occurrence at this stage and can even be a step in generating new ideas. It isn't something to reject. Drew knows even as he writes that he will need to make significant revisions. We will focus on the revision process and Drew's revisions in the next chapter.

CASE HISTORY
Cell Phone Use
Rough Draft

Students open their cell phones almost before they are out of the room. It confuses professors and parents. My parents complain that young people are so wrapped up in their cell conversations that they completely miss the world around them. Why are students such non-stop cell phone users? It looks ridiculous when large numbers of college students wander around talking into their phones, ignoring the people around them. In the end this cell phone mania is a necessary part of college life.

It is hard to imagine how people managed their lives without cell phones since there seems to be so much to get done. Weren't friends going to meet after class for a study session? Where is everybody? Life in College can be crazy. We juggle complex schedules, work, meals. A quick phone call can organize it all. We arrange study sessions, confirm a lunch date, get a ride, coordinate a team project for class, and maybe even make time for a date.

Students, like everyone else, need to call about possible jobs, resolve disputes over bills, arrange to have theirs car fixed, find out the results of medical tests, and even, in some cases, find babysitters. Sometimes walking back to the dorm from a night class, students are on the phone simply to feel safer so that if anything happens they can let someone else know and perhaps get help. Cell phones let them get all this done.

Cell phones let us be together at the same time, even if we are in different places. Part of the reason for such widespread cell phone use is that instead of having to wait. A quick phone call has one person getting out of bed while another is getting out of class. Two friends seated at different ends of a stadium can enjoy the blow by blow of the action at the same time.

Continued on next page

---

2. Have basic writers prepare a draft in class. If you see them repeatedly making corrections at the sentence and word level, encourage them to move on with their ideas and reassure them that they can work on mechanics later.

3. If students get stuck, have them write about what they want to say in the paper, then use the results along with their written plan to develop a draft. Many who are stuck need to consider whether they have enough information.

SUGGESTED INSTRUCTOR READINGS

Perl, S. "The Composing Processes of Unskilled College Writers." Research in the Teaching of English 13 (1978): 317–36. A good case study of why and how students have trouble developing drafts.

Pianko, S. "Reflection: A Critical Component of the Composing Process." College Composition and Communication, 30 (1979): 275–78. Discusses how students need to reflect when writing and how instructors can encourage such reflection.

PERSPECTIVE

Several kinds of computer programs—including those that focus on interactive planning, outlining, and mechanics—are available to help students. The word-processing program, however, is the most useful because it makes planning, drafting, and revising so much easier. Various programs that differ in power and complexity are available. If your class is scheduled for a word-processing lab, review the promotional material and available programs with the lab director and select the one that best suits the needs of your class.

TEACHING STRATEGIES
1. Rather than relying only on the manual to teach students how to use the word processor, develop simple handouts that build computer skills step by step. It helps if you are in the lab while students learn the program and draft a brief practice paper. Students need to become familiar with the functions of the computer before being assigned a longer paper.
2. If students plan and draft using their own word processor, ask them to print out the different stages of their work so that

you can review them and offer pointers. Often students view a computer as an electronic hot rod and speed prematurely into a draft.

TEACHING STRATEGIES
1. Because changes can be made so easily, some students become compulsive about reworking words and sentences and therefore lose any sense of the overall paper.

(Continued from previous page)

Everyone likes to share. Cell phones let people share. Many phones even let you take a picture and send it by e-mail to a friend. It is because of this practice that cell phones are banned in some locker rooms and why it is dangerous to be caught in an embarrassing situation at a party. You never know what can be e-mailed to your friends or even posted to the Internet. At concerts some in the audience call up friends and then hold up the phone so that they can hear part of a concert. When something really funny is happening, anyone can with a quick call share it with someone else who would appreciate the moment. L.O.L. Cell phones allow an instant connection, a voice instant messenger.

Cell phone calls let people reach out and touch each other. Most phone calls are very short. "Hey, what's up"? "What are you doing"? "How are you"? Little information is exchanged. "Nothing much," in fact, is a common answer. What do such phone calls accomplish? They let people keep in touch with each other.

Text messaging is really a very handy way to keep in touch. Even if you can't reach the other person, you can leave a message to let you know that you are thinking about them. Other people keep in touch through MySpace or Face Book which lets friends know what is going on with each others lives, even long lost friends. Face Book can even be a great space for sharing since you can post pictures, blog your ideas, identify your favorite group or more. If anything, college students of today can be considered the in touch generation.

It must have been weird to wait an entire day before bragging to friends and family about getting the only A on a Chemistry test. It is almost impossible that students managed the complex schedule of their days before cell phones. It should not be surprising that students talk on their cell phones over nothing.

Planning and Drafting with a Computer

Using a computer with word-processing software allows you to compose, save what you write, insert new material, delete unwanted material, move sections around, and when you are ready, print copies.

Prewriting

When you are using your computer to generate ideas for your paper, do not be lulled into treating your work as a draft. If the spell and grammar check slow you down, turn them off and then turn them on again when you are writing an actual draft or proofreading. There are many ways to use your computer to generate ideas. Since you are not writing a draft but getting ideas, do not be afraid of being messy.

- Generate a list of ideas or key points you may want to make and then go back and add whatever details or ideas come to mind about those points.
- Freewrite, pull out the best ideas, and then either on the same page by inserting material or as part of different files freewrite about those ideas and repeat as necessary.
- If you are approaching a topic through the set of questions on page 35, convert them into specific questions related to the broad subject area, and then enter them and your responses to the question into either the same page or different files for each question, depending how much material you might have.
- Keep a file or two for jotting down ideas for papers, observations about a topic, and even sentences that come to mind.
- Create a table of the main points you want to consider, such as a table for a comparison or argument, and then fill in the table with the details and ideas you will want to include in your paper.
- Use other approaches to get ideas. Some writers get ideas by discussing issues in a chat room, writing e-mails, or participating in listservs. Remember that if you take ideas from a source, you need to document the information following the method explained in Chapter 21, even if it is something you discovered in a chat room or on a listserv.

Encourage them to push forward.

2. Other students, seeing their ideas first on screen and then in print, prematurely conclude that their work is finished. Remind them that typed doesn't necessarily mean finished.

3. Still other students find that words and ideas flow so readily that they forget to edit or limit their work. Remind these students to make choices.

4. Dogs may not have eaten student homework, but far too often computers do. Students need frequent reminders to save. It's helpful if they keep a printed copy, the saved original, and a backup disk of major work.

Of course, you will want to find your own techniques that work best with your style. Don't be wedded to your computer. Word-processing programs are organized in very specific text-based ways. If you are visually oriented or benefit from clustering, use regular paper and leave the computer for drafting.

Planning

Computers are excellent tools for organization. However, you should use the computer in a way that suits your own writing style. If you need to write a very rough draft without a preestablished program, let it rip. Recognize that the computer will make it easier to revise later. However, if you do benefit from a plan, you can easily create a plan on your computer and experiment with it by deleting, adding, and moving material until you have your points in the order that makes the most sense for you. You can build your draft by inserting material in the appropriate section of your plan. Some individuals who prefer formal outlines create an outline using the outline view of their program and then fill it in later. If you have created multiple files or sections as you generated ideas and made notes, you can label those sections and from this see how the ideas fit together to form a pattern.

Drafting

Do not let the final look on the screen fool you into being overly meticulous. When you are writing a draft, you know you will revise later, so you can afford to experiment. If you are writing and want to come back to a section later to develop an idea or try a different approach, mark it with an asterisk and then continue to write. You can leave gaps you fill in later. If you have more than one idea for a section, write down the other approaches, either bracketed on the same page or as a separate file. Always save each draft in a separate file, if not in a hard copy. You may want to use parts of an early draft in a later version.

Planning and Drafting Your Paper

Understand the assignment.

- Understand the topic.
- Identify key expectations.
- Make the project yours.

Find your topic.

- Talk with others.
- Keep a journal.
- Sort out the subject into categories.
- Brainstorm.

Identify audience, purpose.

Develop details.

Read, talk to others, and brainstorm.

Organize the information.

- Create labeled flexible notes.
- Develop a rough plan—a list of points in order.
- Write a quick draft to find your focus and pattern.

Develop a focused thesis.

- Focus on just one central point or issue.
- Provide an accurate forecast of what is to come.

Draft to capture your thoughts—expect to revise.

CHAPTER 4

Revising and Editing Your Paper

All of us at one time or another have said something careless to a friend, date, or partner and then spent the rest of the night regretting our words. In contrast, when we write we can make sure we say exactly what we mean. Good writers don't express themselves perfectly on the first try, but they do work hard at revising their initial efforts.

Just what is revision? Don't confuse it with proofreading or editing, the final stage of the writing process, where you carefully inspect your word choice, spelling, grammar, and punctuation. Revision is much more drastic, often involving an upheaval of your draft as you change its content and organization in order to communicate more effectively.

Most of what you read, including this book, has been considerably altered and improved as the writers progressed through early drafts. This fact shouldn't surprise you. After all, a rough copy is merely a first attempt to jot down some ideas in essay form. No matter how well you gather and organize your material, you can't predict the outcome until you've prepared a draft. Sometimes only touch-up changes are required. More often though, despite your efforts, this version will be incomplete, unclear in places, possibly disorganized. You might even discover an entirely different idea, focus, or approach buried within it. During revision you keep changing things—your focus, approach to the topic, support-ing material, and thesis statement—until the results satisfy you.

Inexperienced writers often mistakenly view initial drafts as nearly finished products rather than as experiments to alter, or even scrap, if need be. As a result, they often approach revision with the wrong attitude. To revise successfully, you need to control your ego and your fear and become your own first critical reader. Set aside natural feelings of accomplishment ("After all, I've put a great deal of thought into this") and dread ("Actually, I'm afraid of what I'll find if I look too closely"). Instead, recognize that revision offers an opportunity to upgrade your strong features and strengthen your weak ones.

Preparing to Revise

To distance yourself from your writing and sharpen your critical eye, set your first draft aside for at least a half day, longer if time permits. When you return to it, gear up for revision by jotting down your intended purpose and audience before you read your paper. These notations will help keep your changes on track. In addition, note any further ideas that have occurred to you.

The right attitude is vital to effective revision. Far too many students hastily skim their essays to reassure themselves that "Everything sounds O.K." Avoid such a quick-fix approach. If your draft appears fine on first reading, probe it again with a more critical eye. Try putting yourself in your reader's place. Will your description of a favorite getaway spot be clear to someone who has never seen it? Will your letter home asking for money really convince parents who might think they've already given you too much? Remember: If you aren't critical now, anticipating confusion and objections, your reader certainly will be later.

Read your essay at least three times, once for each of these reasons:

To improve the development of the essay as a whole

To strengthen paragraph structure and development

To sharpen sentences and words

When you finish reading your paper for content, make a final, meticulous sweep to search for errors and problems that mar your writing. Use the Personal Revision Checklist on the inside back cover of this book to note your own special weaknesses, perhaps some problem with punctuation or a failure to provide specific support. Later chapters discuss paragraphs, sentences, and words in detail. Check these chapters for more information about the points introduced here.

Considering the Whole Essay

If you inspect your draft only sentence by sentence, you can easily overlook alternative directions for your work, gaps in the text, or how the parts work together. A better approach is to step back and view the overall essay rather than its separate parts, asking questions such as "Is there any entirely new direction to take the paper, perhaps following up on a section that works especially well?" "Does the beginning mesh with the end?" "Does the essay wander?" "Has anything been left out?" In this way you can find new approaches and gauge how part and whole relate.

Use the acronym *FACT* to guide this stage of your revision.

F. Ask yourself first whether the whole essay *FITS* together, presenting a central point for a specific audience. Have you delivered what the

---

2. Students benefit greatly when you *show* them how to revise. You might use an overhead to make and explain revision decisions or to present several drafts of a paper, identifying the changes that were made. If you have the computer in the classroom, you can actually revise the document in front of the students, demonstrating effective revision practices. The best drafts are those closest to the types of writing students will actually do.

CLASSROOM ACTIVITY
You might give students useful metaphors for the writing process. Writing could be described as working with clay, where one shapes and reshapes a figure; as gardening, where constant weeding, watering, and waiting are required; as a relationship, where people meet, slowly get to know each other, and kiss only after they are comfortable. The more plastic the metaphor, the better. Ask students to jot down their metaphors for writing (often very punitive) and discuss their features, making it clear that writing is not a straight line from first idea to final draft.

thesis statement promises? First drafts often include paragraphs, or even large sections, that have little bearing on the main point. Some drafts contain the kernels of several different essays. Furthermore, one section of a draft might be geared to one audience (parents, for example) and another section to an entirely different audience (students, perhaps). As you read each part, verify its connection to your purpose and audience. Don't hesitate to chop out sections that don't fit, redo stray parts so they accord with your central idea, or alter your thesis statement to reflect better your supporting material. Occasionally, you might even expand one small, fertile section of your draft into an entirely new essay.

A. Whenever we write first drafts, we unwittingly leave out essential material. We often produce text based on our own knowledge and assume far too much, leaving large holes, "writer-based prose." We need to revise these drafts to produce much more complete texts that meet the needs of our readers, "reader-based prose." As we revise, we need to identify and fill these inevitable gaps. Ask yourself: "Where will the reader need more information or examples to understand my message?" "Where do I need to explain things more fully?" "What major ideas have I left out?" It can be helpful to reread your notes or do some additional brainstorming. *ADD* the appropriate sentences, paragraphs, or even pages.

C. First drafts often contain material that fits the thesis but doesn't contribute to the essay. Writing quickly, we tend to repeat ourselves, include uninteresting or uninformative examples, and crank out whole paragraphs when one clear sentence would suffice. As you revise, *CUT* away this clutter with a free hand. Such paring can be painful, especially if you're left with a skimpy text, but your message will emerge with much greater clarity. As you've probably guessed, revising a draft often requires both adding and cutting.

T. Carefully *TEST* the organization of your essay. The text should flow smoothly from point to point with clear transitions between the various ideas. Test the organization by outlining your major and minor points, then checking the results for logic and completeness. Alternatively, read the draft and note its progression. Look for spots where you can clarify connections between words and thus help your readers.

Chapters 8–16 explain nine different writing strategies, each concluding with revision questions geared specifically to that strategy. Use these questions, together with the *FACT* of revision, to help you revise more effectively.

Drew carefully reconsiders his rough draft, which you read on pages 49–50. As we indicated there, the draft needs extensive work.

FIT. While most of Drew's paper fits his audience and thesis, the material concerning the misuses of the cell phone to e-mail pictures and instant messenger slang like L.O.L. don't match his audience or purpose. It is offtrack, raises unnecessary suspicion about cell phone use, and is too informal for the audience.

ADD. If Drew really wishes to convince a skeptical audience that student cell phone use is necessary, he needs to make his examples more detailed. The material on using cell phones to be together at the same time and keeping in touch are especially scanty, but each paragraph could be more fully explained with more detailed examples.

CUT. The paragraph on text messaging may fit the topic but it is different in kind from voice communication. Cutting that paragraph will allow the paper to be more focused on a single type of cell phone use.

TEST. If the paper is going to be organized according to the order of importance to the audience, it would make sense to put a paragraph on sharing after "getting business done" and "keeping in touch" before "together at the same time." A careful review of the flow of the paragraphs shows that the third paragraph lacks a clear transitional topic sentence.

It is crucial that you view revision not as a hasty touch-up job or as a quick sweep through your draft just prior to handing it in. Instead, revision should be an ongoing process that often involves an upheaval of major sections as you see your draft through your reader's eyes and strive to write as well as you can.

As you read your own essay, note on a separate sheet of paper problems to solve, ideas to add, and changes to try. When you mark the actual essay, make your job easier by using these simple techniques:

1. To delete something, cross it out lightly; you may decide to resurrect it later.
2. To add a section of text, place a letter (*A, B, C, D*) at the appropriate spot and write the new material on a separate sheet, keyed to the letter. Make changes within sections by crossing out what you don't want and writing the replacement above it or nearby.
3. To rearrange the organization, draw arrows showing where you want things to go, or cut up your draft and rearrange the sections by taping them on new sheets of paper. Use whatever method works best for you.

When you finish revising your draft, you might want to team up with one or more classmates and read one another's work critically. The fresh eye you bring to the task can uncover shortcomings that would otherwise go unnoticed. Pages 66–72 discuss peer editing in detail.

needed changes in their drafts. In any case, encourage the class not to merely respond "yes" or "no" to questions, but to identify precisely what is causing problems and why. You could collect these sheets with the final drafts.

2. Students often identify problems and then do nothing about them. Require your students to suggest, and then carry out, a plan for making changes in their drafts.

3. Students find it easy to learn from acronyms. The editors of *Fortune*, noted for quality reporting and superb prose, encourage their writers to think about DARK (Don't Assume the Reader Knows) and AGO (Acute Grasp of the Obvious) when preparing an article. These acronyms can also alert students to the common problems of inadequate support and trite information.

4. Generally it is best to strike a balance between supplying the responses students need in order to develop, on the one hand, and increasing their responsibility over their

EXERCISE

1. *List Drew's other options for revising this draft; then indicate the necessary changes if he had decided to write for fellow college students.*
2. *Use the FACT acronym to revise the draft you prepared for the exercise on page 49.*

Here Lies A Writing Project That Kept Getting Better ...and Better ...and Better own work, on the other. To achieve this goal, you could have students revise a draft before they receive any feedback.

CLASSROOM ACTIVITIES

1. You might take the lead and show students how to mark up a draft while revising.

2. Before students revise their own drafts, have the class apply revision guidelines to sample drafts similar to the ones students will write.

CLASSROOM ACTIVITIES

1. Before students begin to read the *FACT* analysis of this essay, you might have them complete their own *FACT* sheet. Then have the class (perhaps in small groups) compare their analyses to the text analysis.

2. Have students candidly state their feelings about all the changes this draft is undergoing. Many will be discouraged by all the work, but they should recognize that if this draft can be salvaged, almost anyone's writing can be improved (one of the reasons we use this realistic example).

EXERCISE ANSWER

Drew has several options for revision. He could remove material focused on the confusion of parents and teachers and focus more on students understanding their own behavior. Since students may know many of his reasons for cell phone use already, he might want to

CASE HISTORY   Cell Phone Use
Rough Draft Marked up

At the end of their class,
Students open their cell phones almost before they are out of the room. It con-
flip   *are greatly confused by this practice and*
fuses professors and parents. ~~My parents~~ complain that young people are so
    Some
wrapped up in their cell conversations that they completely miss the world
    Most wonder   *are compulsive*
around them. ~~why~~ students such ~~non-stop cell~~ phone users? It ~~looks~~
    The
~~ridiculous when~~ large numbers of college students wander around talking
    ing
    may seem ridiculous to
into their phones, ignoring the people around them. In the end this cell phone
outsiders. However,
mania is a necessary part of college life.

There are many reasons students wander around campus talking into the air. They use cell phones to coordinate the day's activities, to get some business done, to share life's events, and to keep in touch.

It is hard to imagine how people managed their lives without cell phones since there seems to be so much to get done. Weren't friends going to meet
    Add Ⓐ
after class for a study session? Where is everybody? Life in College can be
hectic as students   *of classes*   *and a social life.*
~~crazy.~~ We juggle complex schedules, work, ~~meals.~~ A quick phone call can organize it all. We arrange study sessions, confirm a lunch date, get a ride, coordinate a team project for class, and maybe even make time for a date.
Add Ⓑ
Students, like everyone else, need to call about possible jobs, resolve dis-
            q   *s*
putes over bills, arrange to have theirs car fixed, find out the results of med-
There is often a lot to get done that has to be squeezed into a busy day.
ical tests, and even, in some cases, find babysitters. Sometimes walking back to the dorm from a night class, students are on the phone simply to feel safer so that if anything happens they can let someone else know and perhaps get help. Cell phones let them get all this done, *in the time between classes or even while walking back to their dorm, leaving them with more time for other things like studying or going out with friends.*

~~Cell phones let us be together at the same time, even if we are in different places.~~ Part of the reason for such widespread cell phone use is that instead
    We can be part of the immediate now.
of having to wait. A quick phone call has one person getting out of bed while another is getting out of class. Two friends seated at different ends of a
Anyone can know what almost anyone else their call list is doing at any moment.
stadium can enjoy the blow by blow of the action at the same time.

Everyone likes to share. Cell phones let people share. Many phones even *moments of delight, success, and even failures with others who care.* let you take a picture and send it by e-mail to a friend. ~~It is because of this~~ *When a baby is expected, the soon to be grandparents* ~~practice that cell phones are banned in some locker rooms and why it is dan-~~ *can't wait for the call.* ~~gerous to be caught in an embarrassing situation at a party. You never know~~ ~~what can be e-mailed to your friends or even posted to the internet.~~ At con-

certs some in the audience call up friends and then hold up the phone so that

they can hear part of a concert. When something really funny is happening,

anyone can with a quick call share it with someone else who would appreci-

ate the moment. L.O.L. Cell phones allow an instant connection, *to let people experience what you* ~~a voice~~ *are experiencing, whether it is excitement over a success, an idea, the finals of* ~~instant messenger.~~ *a sporting event, or a newscast.* *Add Ⓒ*

Cell phone calls let people reach out and touch each other. Most phone

calls are very short. "Hey, what's up?" "What are you doing?" "How are you?"

Little information is exchanged. "Nothing much," in fact, is a common answer.

What do such phone calls accomplish? They let people keep in touch with

each other.

Text Messaging is really a very handy way to keep in touch. Even if you

can't reach the other person, you can leave a message to let you know that you

are thinking about them. Other people keep in touch through MySpace or Face

Book which lets friends know what is going on with each others lives, even

long lost friends. Face Book can even be a great space for sharing since you

can post pictures, blog your ideas, identify your favorite group or more. If any-

thing, college students of today can be considered the in touch generation.

It must have been weird to wait an entire day before bragging to friends and

family about getting the only A on a Chemistry test. It is almost *incomprehensible* ~~impossible~~

that students managed the complex schedule of their days before cell phones.

snap open   *at the* It should not be surprising that students ~~talk~~ on their cell phones ~~over nothing~~.

drop of almost anything. The surprise would be if they kept their cell phones in *their pockets and waited. ↗ Add Ⓓ*

What did a student do if a ride didn't show up? How did a couple share the *excitement of a concert in the moment or a good joke if they had to wait days?* *Earlier generations who seem puzzled by the cell phone fever that has hit college* *campuses might wonder how they might have felt without a phone, having to wait* *for weeks for the mail or longer for a visit.*

Continued on next page

focus in more detail on the less familiar explanations. He might think about his purpose. If he wanted to make students feel better about their cell phone use, he could focus more on the actual advantages of their pattern of use. He could structure the paper as arming them to answer their parents' criticisms.

TEACHING STRATEGY

You may encounter a few students who become so involved in revising that they fail to complete a final draft. Probably they are confused about the nature of revision or subconsciously fear having their draft evaluated. Show them the gravestone and caption on page 57, which we saw many years ago and never forgot.

Continued from previous page

A.   A quick cell phone call to a friend reveals that the study session was moved to the student center. Does everyone have his or her part ready for the presentation speech class at 3:00 p.m.? A flurry of cell phone calls makes certain everyone is ready. Will Collin be able to meet his girlfriend this afternoon? He needs to call to see if she is still free. Where is Jennifer since she said she was picking me up in front of the Science Building?

B.   Sometimes cell phone calls get important business done. Heather needs to convince her parents that she really, really needs more money to cover the cost of books. Tim needs to contact his advisor so he can schedule for the next semester.

C.   If you got an A on a paper that you thought would get an F, you can quickly spread the celebration to anyone who would echo your joy while the feeling was still hot. Sometimes a cell phone call can make the sharing very concrete, getting someone to go outside to look at a spectacular meteor shower, getting a friend to change channels so they can see an interview with a favorite rock star, or letting family know about a terrible earthquake in China.

D.   Contact is what helps keep people close. Parents like their children to visit. Couples need to make time for each other. When people keep in touch, it lets them know that others care, lets them keep each other as important parts of their lives. Some students call their parents every day keeping the family ties tight, getting the emotional reassurance of those loving connections. Sometimes it seems like couples seem to be holding electronic hands as they walk across campus, with little room for some interloper to break up their relationships. Friends may not be able to see each other since they are going to different colleges, but a simple cell phone lets them each know the others are still friends.

 CASE HISTORY   **Cell Phone Use**
Second Draft

> Clarified classroom
> by adding class.

        At the end of their class, students flip open their cell phones almost before they are out of the room. Professors and parents are confused by this practice. Some complain that young people are so wrapped up in their cell conversations that they completely miss the world around them. Most wonder why students are compulsive cell phone users. There are many reasons students wander around campus talking into the air. They use cell phones to coordinate the day's activities, to get some business done, to share life's events, and to keep in touch. The large number of college students wandering around talking into their phones, ignoring the people around them, may seem ridiculous to outsider. However, in the end this cell phone mania is a necessary part of college life.

It is hard to imagine how people managed their life without cell phones since there is so much to coordinate. Weren't friends going to meet after class for a study session? Where is everybody? A quick cell phone call to a friend reveals that the study session was moved to the student center. Does everyone have his or her part ready for the presentation in Speech class at 3:00 p.m.? A flurry of cell phone calls makes certain everyone is ready. Will Collin be able to meet his girlfriend this afternoon? He needs to call to see if she is still free. Where is Jennifer since she said she was picking me up in front of the Science Building? Life in College can be hectic as students juggle complex schedules of classes, work, meal times, and a social life. A quick phone call can organize it all; arrange study sessions, confirm a lunch date, arrange a ride, coordinate a team project for class, and maybe even make time for a date.

Sometimes cell phone calls get important business done. Heather needs to convince her parents that she really, really needs more money to cover the cost of books. Tim needs to contact his advisor since he needs to lift his holds so he can schedule for the next semester. Students, like everyone else, need to call about possible jobs, resolve disputes over bills, arrange to have their car fixed, find out the results of medical tests, and even, in some cases, find babysitters. There is often a lot to get done that has to be squeezed into a busy day. Sometimes walking back to the dorm from a night class, students are on the phone simply to feel safer so that if anything happens they can let someone else know and perhaps get help. Cell phones let them get all this done in the time between classes or even while walking back to their dorm, leaving them with more time for other things like studying or going out with friends.

Everyone likes to share moments of delight, success, and even failure with others who care. When a baby is expected, the soon to be grandparents can't wait for the call. Cell phones let people share. Many phones even let you take a picture and send it by e-mail to a friend. At concerts some in the audience call up friends and then hold up the phone so that they can hear part of a concert. When something really funny is happening, anyone can with a quick call share it with someone else who would appreciate the moment. If you got an A on a paper that you thought would get an F, you can quickly spread the celebration

Continued on next page

Added thesis statement that outlines paper order.

Provided more detailed account of cell phone use helped.
Placed academic material first for audience.

Clarified what was complex.

Added a transitional thesis statement.
Added more specific examples to appeal to audience.

Added context that relates to understanding of reader. Moved sharing paragraph up to make order of material. Cut material on inappropriate use of phone picture that might offend audience. Added more concrete examples appropriate to target audience.

to anyone who would echo your joy while the feeling was still hot. Sometimes a cell phone call can make the sharing very concrete, getting someone to go outside to look at a spectacular meteor shower, getting a friend to change channels so they can see an interview with a favorite rock star, or letting family know about a terrible earthquake in China. Cell phones allow an immediate connection to let people experience what you are experiencing, whether it is excitement over a success, an idea, the finals of a sporting event, or a news event.

Adds more detailed examples appropriate to target audience.

Cell phone calls let people stay in touch with each other. Most phone calls are very short, over before students have gotten from the classroom to the door of the building. "Hey, what's up?" "What are you doing?" "How are you?" Little information is exchanged and little is really shared. "Nothing much," in fact, is a common response. What do such phone calls accomplish? They let people keep in touch with each other. Contact is what helps keep people close. Parents like their children to visit. Couples need to make time for each other. When people keep in touch, it lets them know that others care, lets them keep each other as important parts of their lives. Some students call their parents every day keeping the family ties tight, getting the emotional reassurance of those loving connections. Sometimes it seems like couples seem to be holding electronic hands as they walk across campus, with little room for some interloper to break up their relationships. Friends may not be able to see each other since they are going to different colleges, but a simple cell phone lets them each know the others still are friends.

Cut paragraph on text messages.

This paragraph still needs improvement.

Part of the reason for such widespread cell phone use is that instead of having to wait, we can be part of the immediate now. A quick phone call has one person getting out of bed while another is getting out of class. Two friends seated at different ends of a stadium can enjoy the blow by blow of the action at the same time. Anyone can know what almost anyone else in their call list is doing at any moment.

It must have been lonely to wait an entire day before bragging to friends and family about getting the only A on a Chemistry test. It is almost incomprehensible that students managed the complex schedule of their days before cell phones. What did a student do if a ride didn't show up? How did people share the excitement of a concert in the moment or a good joke if they had to wait days? Earlier generations who seem puzzled by the cell phone fever that has hit college campuses might wonder how they might have felt without a phone, having to wait for weeks for the mail or longer for a visit. It should not be surprising that students snap open their cell phones at the drop of almost anything. The surprise would be if they kept their cell phones in their pockets and waited.

Strengthening Paragraph Structure and Development

Once you finish considering the essay as a whole, examine your paragraphs one by one, applying the *FACT* approach that you used for the whole paper. Make sure each paragraph *FITS* the paper's major focus and develops a single central idea. If a paragraph needs more support or examples, *ADD* whatever is necessary. If a paragraph contains ineffective or unhelpful material, *CUT* it. *TEST* the flow of ideas from paragraph to paragraph and clarify connections, both between and within paragraphs, as necessary. Ask the basic questions in the checklist that follows about each paragraph, and make any needed revisions.

REVISION CHECKLIST FOR PARAGRAPHS

- Does the paragraph have one, and only one, central idea?
- Does the central idea help to develop the thesis statement?
- Does each statement within the paragraph help to develop the central idea?
- Does the paragraph need additional explanations, examples, or supporting details?
- Would cutting some material make the paragraph stronger?
- Would reorganization make the ideas easier to follow?
- Can the connections between successive sentences be improved?
- Is each paragraph clearly and smoothly related to those that precede and follow it?

Don't expect to escape making changes. Certain paragraphs may be stripped down or deleted, others beefed up, still others reorganized or repositioned. Chapter 5 contains more information on writing effective paragraphs.

EXERCISE

Here are three sample student paragraphs. Evaluate each according to the Revision Checklist for Paragraphs and suggest any necessary changes.

1. I can remember so many times when my father had said that he was coming to pick me up for a day or two. I was excited as a young boy could be at the thought of seeing my father. With all the excitement and anticipation raging inside of me, I would wait on the front porch. Minutes would seem like hours as I would wait impatiently.

2. Going to high school for the first time, I couldn't decide if I should try out for the cheerleading team or wait a year. Since I had time and had been on other

---

SUGGESTED INSTRUCTOR READING
Prior, P. "Tracing Authoritative and Internally Persuasive Discourses: A Case Study of Response, Revision, and Disciplinary Enculturation." <u>Research in the Teaching of English</u> 29 (1995): 288–326. Offers a critical perspective on how students revise according to teachers' comments.

PERSPECTIVE
Students often don't know how to revise systematically. Having them first focus on the text as a whole and then on the individual paragraphs ensures that they direct their attention to different elements of the text. Revising paragraphs demonstrates that good paragraphs don't just happen but result from extensive work. Students need to be reminded, however, not to become so engrossed in paragraph revision that they lose sight of the essay's overall thrust.

EXERCISE ANSWERS
1. This paragraph has only one central idea (waiting for Father) but clearly lacks the detail needed to convey the boy's feeling of anticipation. Also, it isn't clear whether the father ever picks up the young boy.

Possible Revision
Time and again my father would call and announce that he would

arrive in an hour to pick me up for a day or two stay at his place. I was as excited as any young boy could be at the thought of seeing my father and always raced out to the front porch where I could sit and gaze at the road. There I would wait with all the anticipation imaginable, excited about the two of us watching a football game together or perhaps fishing at the lake. Every now and then a car would cruise down the road, leaving behind it a trail of dust, but none ever turned in. Minutes would tick by like hours, and hours drag past like

squads, I decided "why not?" I had nothing to lose but a lot to gain. Tryouts were not as hard as I thought, but I just knew I had to be on the squad. The tryout consisted of learning the routine they made up, making up your own routine, doing splits, and making a chant. Yet although these things were not that hard, I still was not sure whether I would make the team or not. The time came for the judges to make their decisions on who made the squad. Totaling the votes, they handed the results to the coach. She gave her speech that all coaches give. We were all good, but only a few could be picked for the team. As she started to read the names, I got hot. When she called my name, I was more than happy.

3. For hours we had been waiting under the overhang of an abandoned hut. None of us had thought to bring ponchos on our short hike through the woods. Soon it would be dark. Earlier in the day it had been a perfectly clear day. We all agreed that we didn't want to stand here all night in the dark, so we decided to make a dash for it.

days. When it grew dark, at last I would go inside, my hope extinguished.

2. This paragraph, touching briefly on several different ideas, is in reality the skeleton of a short paper that needs fleshing out with more details. The writer should explain the reasons for her indecision, tell what she had to gain by joining the team, add a more descriptive account of the tryouts and selection process, and redo the conclusion. What did she do when her name was finally read? What did she feel? "More than happy" doesn't say much. What would being selected have meant to her?

3. This paragraph seems to have one basic idea (the hikers making a dash for "it"), but the sentences are not clearly connected. For example, "Earlier in the day it had been a

Sharpening Sentences and Words

Next, turn your attention to sentences and words. You can improve your writing considerably by finding and correcting sentences that convey the wrong meaning or are stylistically deficient in some way. Consider, for example, the following sentences:

Just Mary was picked to write the report.
Mary was just picked to write the report.
Mary was picked to write just the report.

The first sentence says that no one except Mary will write the report; the second says that she was recently picked for the job; and the third says that she will write nothing else. Clearly, each of these sentences expresses a different meaning.

Now let's look at a second set of sentences:

Personally, I am of the opinion that the results of our membership drive will prove to be pleasing to all of us.

I believe the results of our membership drive will please all of us.

The wordiness of the first sentence slows the reader's pace and makes it harder to grasp the writer's meaning. The second sentence, by contrast, is much easier to grasp.

Like your sentences, your words should convey your thoughts precisely and clearly. Words are, after all, your chief means of communicating with your reader. Examine the first draft and revised version of the following paragraph, which describe the early morning actions of the writer's roommate. The underlined words identify points of revision.

First Draft

Coffee cup in hand, she <u>moves</u> toward the bathroom. The coffee spills <u>noisily</u> on the tile floor as she <u>reaches</u> for the light switch and <u>turns</u> it on. After <u>looking</u> briefly at the face in the mirror, she <u>walks</u> toward the bathtub.

Revised Version

Coffee cup in hand, she <u>stumbles</u> toward the bathroom. <u>Spilled</u> coffee <u>slaps</u> on the tile floor as she <u>gropes</u> for the light switch and <u>flips</u> it on. After <u>squinting</u> briefly at the face in the mirror, she <u>shuffles</u> toward the bathtub.

Note that the words in the first draft are general and imprecise. Exactly how does she move? With a limp? With a strut? With a spring in her step? And what does "noisily" mean? A thud? A roar? A sharp crack? The reader has no way of knowing. Recognizing this fact, the student revised her paragraph, substituting vivid, specific words. As a result, the reader can visualize the actions more sharply.

Don't confuse vivid, specific words with "jawbreaker words"—those that are complex and pretentious. Words should promote communication, not block it.

Reading your draft aloud will force you to slow down, and you will often hear yourself stumble over problem sections. You'll be more likely to uncover errors such as missing words, excessive repetition, clumsy sentences, and sentence fragments. Be honest in your evaluation; don't read in virtues that aren't there or that exaggerate the writing quality.

REVISION CHECKLIST FOR SENTENCES

- What sentences are not clearly expressed or logically constructed?
- What sentences seem awkward, excessively convoluted, or lacking in punch?
- What words require explanation or substitution because the reader may not know them?
- Where does my writing become wordy or use vague terms?
- Where have I carelessly omitted words or mistakenly used the wrong word?

Chapters 6 and 7 discuss sentences and words in detail.

Reread exercise paragraph 1 on page 63 and revise the sentence structure and word choice to create a more effective paragraph.

perfectly clear day" is out of logical order. Furthermore, additional information about the rainstorm, which is implied but never discussed, is obviously needed.

Possible Revision

For hours we had been waiting under the overhang of an abandoned hut while the rain poured down. Earlier in the day it had been perfectly clear, so none of us had brought ponchos on our short hike through the woods. The downpour had caught us unprepared. We had thought it would let up as sudden storms usually do, but no relief was in sight. Worse, it would soon be dark. None of us wanted to stand there all night, so we didn't have much choice. Even if we were going to get thoroughly soaked, we had to make a dash for the car.

PERSPECTIVE

Many students think sentences and words are revised only to correct errors. They should understand that their sentence structure and word choice can usually be improved to increase the impact on readers. On the other hand, students must keep this level of revision in its place—as a type of polish applied after the body work of major revision has been completed.

TEACHING STRATEGIES
1. If you take up the different sentence strategies discussed in Chapter 16. you might have students select several sentences from their text and rewrite them using the different strategies.
2. Because students have different abilities, some

Writing the Introduction and Conclusion

If you've put off writing your introduction, do it now. Generally, short papers begin with a single paragraph that includes the previously drafted thesis statement, which sometimes needs to be rephrased so that it meshes smoothly with the rest of the paragraph. The introduction acquaints the reader with your topic; it should clearly signal your intention as well as spark the reader's interest. Pages 93–96 discuss and illustrate effective introductions.

The conclusion wraps up your discussion. Generally a single paragraph in short papers, a good ending summarizes or supports the paper's main idea. Pages 96–98 discuss and illustrate effective conclusions.

teachers prefer to identify each one's problems on his or her draft rather than addressing such matters in the classroom.

CLASSROOM ACTIVITIES
1. Have students exchange papers and circle sentences that seem ineffective. The writer could then prepare several improved versions of each.
2. Have students circle vague or ineffective words in their own drafts or those of others and then develop a list of possible substitutes.
3. Use examples from your own writing to demonstrate how you might revise a sentence.

Selecting a Title

Most essays require titles. Unless a good title unexpectedly surfaces while you are writing, wait until you finish the paper before choosing one. Since the reader must see the connection between what the title promises and what the essay delivers, a good title must be both accurate and specific.

Titling the essay "Cell Phone Use" would mislead the reader since this would seem to suggest that the essay is on how to use a cell phone. A specific title suggests the essay's focus rather than just its topic. For example, "The Reasons for College Cell Phone Fever" is clearer and more precise than simply "Cell Phone Use." The essay is about why cell phones are so extensively used, not about how they are to be used.

To engage your reader's interest, you might try your hand at a clever or catchy title, but don't get so carried away with creativity that you forget to relate the title to the paper's content. Here are some examples of common and clever titles:

Common	"Handling a Hangover"
Clever	"The Mourning After"
Common	"Selecting the Proper Neckwear"
Clever:	"How to Ring Your Neck"

Use a clever title only if its wit or humor doesn't clash with the overall purpose and tone of the paper.

Put the changes on the board and explain why each was made.
4. Provide students with several versions of the same sentence. Have them rank the sentences according to effectiveness and explain their decisions.

Peer Evaluation of Drafts

At various points in the writing process, your instructor may ask you and your classmates to read and respond to one another's papers. Peer response often proves useful because even the best writers cannot always predict how their readers will react to their writing. For example, magazine articles designed to reduce the fear of AIDS have, in some cases, increased anxiety about the disease. Furthermore, we often have difficulty seeing the problems with our own drafts because so much hard work has gone into them. What seems clear and effective to us can be confusing or boring to our readers. Comments from our peers can frequently launch a more effective essay.

Just as the responses of others help you, so will your responses help them. You don't have the close, involved relationship with your peers' writing that you do with your own. Therefore, you can gauge their drafts objectively. This type of critical evaluation will eventually heighten your awareness of your own writing strengths and weaknesses. And knowing how to read your own work critically is one of the most important writing skills you can develop.

Responding to Your Peers' Drafts

Responding to someone else's writing is easier than you might imagine. It's not your job to spell out how to make the draft more effective, how to organize it, what to include, and what language to use. The writer must make these decisions. Your job is to *identify* problems, not *solve* them. You can do that best by responding honestly to the draft.

Some responses are more helpful than others. You don't help the writer by casually observing that the draft "looks O.K." Such a response doesn't point to problem areas; rather it suggests that you didn't read the paper carefully and critically. Wouldn't you inform a friend who was wearing clothes that looked terrible *why* they looked terrible? The same attitude should prevail about writing, something that makes a statement just as clothes do. Nor is a vague comment such as "The introduction is uninteresting" helpful. Point out *why* it is uninteresting. For instance, you might note that "The introduction doesn't interest me in the paper because it is very technical, and I get lost. I ask myself why I should read on." Here are two more examples of ineffective responses and their more effective counterparts.

Ineffective

The paper was confusing.

Effective

Paragraphs 2, 3, and 4 confused me. You jumped around too much. First you wrote about your experience on the first day of college, then you went on to how much you enjoyed junior high school, and finally you wrote about what you want to do for a career. I don't see how these ideas relate or why they are in the order that they are.

Ineffective

More examples would help.

Effective

When you indicate that college is a scary place. I get no real idea of why or how. What are the things that you think make college scary? I would like some examples.

Here are some steps to follow when responding to someone else's draft. First, read the essay from beginning to end without interruption. On a separate sheet of paper, indicate what you consider to be the main idea. The writer can entranced with the block-move command often move chunks of text without integrating them into the body of the draft, thus creating a very disjointed essay. Other students add or delete material without adjusting the surrounding material. Some students keep backspacing and reworking sentences until these sentences become incoherent. Sometimes previous sections are integrated with revised sections, or notes are left in the draft. In some cases it is evident that the scope of the revision equals the amount of material that fills the screen at any given time.

TEACHING STRATEGIES

1. Ask students to perform at least the final revision on a printout.

2. If your school has a computer lab, show students how to use the word-processing program for revision. Many students have limited knowledge of this operation. Direct them to open a new file for one of their paragraphs, draft several versions, and then reinsert the best one into their draft.

3. In the lab you can enter your comments directly onto the student's disk. Some programs allow you to create a margin for your comments. With others, you simply insert the comments into the text. These practices make your comments rather difficult to ignore.

4. If you collect drafts with the final paper, insist

then see whether the intended message has come through. Next, identify the biggest problem and the biggest strength. Writers need both negative and positive comments. Finally, reread the paper and write either specific responses to each paragraph or your responses to general questions such as the ones that follow. In either case, don't comment on spelling or grammar unless it really inhibits your reading.

PEER RESPONSE CHECKLIST

- What is the main point of this essay?
- What is the biggest problem?
- What is the biggest strength?
- What material doesn't seem to fit the main point or the audience?
- What questions has the author not answered?
- Where should more details or examples be added? Why?
- At what point does the paper fail to hold my interest? Why?
- Where is the organization confusing?
- Where is the writing unclear or vague?

As you learn the various strategies for successful writing, new concerns will arise. Questions geared to these concerns appear in the revision section that concludes the discussion of each strategy.

An Example of Peer Response in Response to "Cell Phone Use."

What is the main point of this essay?

There are many reasons students use cell phones so extensively, including to coordinate activities, get business done, share with others, keep in touch.

What is the biggest problem?

I didn't really know what was meant by this idea of the immediate now. Where did this idea come from? In what ways do we share the same now. Is this different from keeping in touch?

What is the biggest strength?

The reasons in the paper ring true to my experience, especially with the examples that are used.

What doesn't seem to fit the main point or the audience?

The material on the babysitter doesn't seem to fit or seem likely for most college students. Is walking back to *the dorm getting something done? How many students really do that? Doesn't it make you even more vulnerable?*

Where should more details or examples be added? Why?

The introduction is kind of boring. An example would make it more real. Also, more details about the now paragraph would make it clearer. Isn't the paper missing something about a really important reason which is simply that everyone is doing it?

Where is the writing unclear or vague?

The writing is pretty clear. But some places could be clearer in the intro. Which "some" and "most" do you mean? Some sentences could be tightened up like "Tim needs to contact his advisor..." Your pronouns jump around. Sometimes you use "we" and sometimes "students" and "they."

Acting on Your Peers' Responses

Sometimes you need strong nerves to act on a peer response. You can easily become defensive or discount your reader's comments as foolish. Remember, however, that as a writer you are trying to communicate with your readers, and that means taking seriously the problems they identify. Of course, you decide which responses are appropriate, but even an inappropriate criticism sometimes sets off a train of thought that leads to good ideas for revision.

As you read the final version of Drew's paper on cell phones, carefully examine the margin notes, which highlight key features of the revision. Drew added an example to the introduction to make it more interesting, added a section on how the common use of cell phones has an impact, and clarified the paragraph on "the now." He has cut the material on babysitters and walking across campus that his readers found inappropriate. He has tightened his language by sharpening his sentences and his word choice in a few places and using more consistent pronouns.

in advance that students using a word processor print out copies of early drafts. Otherwise, early drafts will vanish as students make their changes.

PERSPECTIVE
Peer groups can accomplish several important things. First, submitting their work to readers other than the instructor helps students understand that what they produce are public documents—not private letters to their instructors. Furthermore, it is gratifying for students to learn that they can communicate. When peers identify problems, writers see that such matters are not simply instructor concerns but actually affect communication. For those acting as peer readers, a critical response to another person's paper helps develop the kind of eye they can eventually apply to their own writing. Often students detect a problem in someone else's paper and then recognize that they have the same problem. Peer groups can

 CASE HISTORY   **The Reasons for College Cell Phone Fever Final Draft**

Changed title to make it more focused.

At the end of their college classes, students flip open their cell phones almost before they are out of the room.

"Hey, just got out of English."

"What ya goin' to do?"

"Get some coffee and study before Biology. You?"

" Got Intro to Business in ten minutes."

"Well, see ya."

Added short conversation to make more interesting.

Continued on next page

Added sentence with more active verbs to capture scene.

Clarified the "some."

Added trend that is a later paragraph.

Clarified the word necessary by expanding idea.

Simplifies language since calls are obvious cell phones. Through out, changes language so consistently student and they, not we.

Changed language to tighten life in college to college life.

Tightened sentence by cutting wordiness.

Tightened language.

Cut the line about walking across campus at night.

Changed pronouns to be consistent.

Continued from previous page

These conversations seem far from necessary. Yet students plow their way from class to class with their cell phones glued to their ears. Professors and parents are confused by this practice. Some parents complain that young people are so wrapped up in their cell conversations that they completely miss the world around them. Many wonder why students are compulsive cell phone users. There are many reasons students wander around campus talking into the air. They use cell phones to coordinate the day's activities, to get business done, to share life's events, and to keep in touch. Part of this trend, undeniably, is that many others are also doing it. The large number of college students who wander around talking into their phones, ignoring the people around them, may seem ridiculous to outsider. However, in the end this cell phone mania is a reasonable, pleasurable, and vital part of college life.

It is hard to imagine how people managed their lives without cell phones since there is so much to coordinate. Weren't friends going to meet after class for a study session? Where is everybody? A quick call reveals that the study session was moved to the student center. Does everyone have his or her part ready for the presentation in Speech class at 3:00 p.m.? A flurry of calls makes certain everyone is ready. Will Collin be able to meet his girlfriend this afternoon? He needs to call to see if she is still free. Where is Jennifer since she said she was picking me up in front of the Science Building? College life can be hectic as students juggle classes, work, meal times, and a social life. A quick phone call can organize it all: arrange study sessions, confirm a lunch date, arrange a ride, coordinate a team project for class, and maybe even make time for a date.

Sometimes cell phone calls get important business done. Heather needs to convince her parents that she really, really needs more money to cover the cost of books. Tim needs to ask his adviser to lift his holds so he can schedule next semester's classes. Students, like everyone else, need to call about possible jobs, resolve bill disputes, arrange to have theirs car repaired, and find out medical test results. Cell phones let them get all this done in the time between classes or while walking back to their dorms, leaving them with more time for other things like studying or going out with friends.

Everyone likes to share moments of delight, success, and even failure with others who care. When a baby is expected, the expectant grandparents can't wait for the call. Cell phones let people share. At concerts, some in the audience call up friends and then hold up the phone so that they can hear part of a concert. When something really funny is happening, anyone can with a quick call share it with someone else who would appreciate the moment. If students get an unexpected A, they can quickly spread the celebration to those who would echo their joy. Sometimes a cell phone call can make the sharing very concrete, getting someone to go outside to look at a spectacular meteor shower, getting a friend to change channels to see an interview with a favorite rock star, or letting family know about a terrible earthquake in China. Cell phones allow an immediate connection to let people experience what callers are experiencing, whether it is excitement over a success, a great idea, the finals of a sporting event, or a news event.

Cut unnecessary phrase "while the feeling was still hot."

Changed from any idea to a great idea, more likely to be shared.

Cell phone calls can let people stay in touch with each other. Most phone calls are very short, over before students have gotten from the classroom to the door of the building. "Hey, what's up?" "What are you doing?" "How are you?" Little information is exchanged and little is really shared. "Nothing much," in fact, is a common answer. What do such phone calls accomplish? They let people keep in touch with each other. Contact is what helps keep people close. Parents like their children to visit. Couples need to make time for each other. When people keep in touch, it lets them know that others care, lets them keep each other as important parts of their lives. Some students call their parents every day to maintain family ties while getting the emotional reassurance of those loving connections. Couples hold electronic hands as they walk across campus. Friends may not be able to see each other since they are going to different colleges, but a simple cell phone confirms their continued friendship.

"Answer" is chosen as a better word than "response."

Provided a context for the paragraph. Reworded to be clearer.

A sociology professor told her class that she thought that the cell phone "created a virtual society of now." Cell phones create a feeling that all are in it together at the same time, even if in different places. Instead of having to wait to find out what might be happening, students can be part of the same now. A quick phone call has one person getting out of bed while another is getting out of class. Two friends seated at different ends of a stadium can enjoy the blow by blow of the action at the same time. Anyone can know what almost anyone else in their call list is doing at any moment. A clip from a news story on television about cosmetic surgery conveyed this perfectly. A woman is talking on her cell phone while she is undergoing liposuction. "Yeh," she declares, "I am undergoing surgery right now. No, I don't feel much, maybe just a tickle." It is hard to get more immediate than that.

Added a very specific example to make the idea clearer.

All of this is made possible because others are doing it. Teenagers are notorious for doing what others are doing. Parents ask, "If your friends jumped

Added section on how everyone is doing this has an impact in response to peers.

Continued on next page

Continued from previous page

off a bridge, would you do it too?" The answer is an embarrassing "yes," especially if the jumpers were attached to bungee cords. It would be embarrassing not to have a cell phone, ideally a razor or an iPhone or whatever is the latest trend. Everyone else seems to be talking while walking. So using cell phones right after class, between classes, during lunch, or at a concert just seems to be normal behavior—and most people want to be normal. Besides, if students are lucky enough to have good friends, their friends are probably calling them; and if friends are calling, it is important to call them back.

It must have been lonely to wait an entire day before bragging to friends and family about getting the only A on a Chemistry test. It is almost incomprehensible that students managed their complex schedules before cell phones. What did a student do if a ride didn't show up? How did people share the excitement of a concert in the moment or a good joke if they had to wait days? Earlier generations who seem puzzled by the cell phone fever that has hit college campuses might wonder how they might have felt without a phone, having to wait for weeks for the mail or longer for a visit. It should not be surprising that students snap open their cell phones at the end of class. The surprise would be if they kept their cell phones in their pockets and waited.

Added a phrase to be memorable.

Added specific idea to explain concept.

be a helpful teaching tool, but they won't work brilliantly on the first attempt. It will take several papers for students to acclimate. Peer groups can be used throughout the revision process. In the first stages of drafting, they can provide sympathetic readers for writers trying to figure out what they want to say and also help writers chart their course. Once a rough draft is finished, peer groups can identify its strengths and problems.

TEACHING STRATEGIES

1. For peer groups to work, students must know how to evaluate papers. You might first demonstrate on a sample draft, focusing on how a reader would honestly respond. Next, ask students to respond individually to a sample draft and then discuss their comments. Finally, have peer groups judge samples and discuss these judgments in class.

2. You can set up peer groups in different ways.

Of course, you decide which responses are appropriate, but even an inappropriate criticism sometimes sets off a train of thought that leads to good ideas for revisions.

ACTING ON PEER RESPONSE CHECKLIST

■ Did the readers understand my main point? If not, how can I make it clearer?

■ What did they see as the main problem? Can I solve it?

■ What strengths did they identify that I can keep?

■ What didn't fit that I need to cut or make clearer?

■ Which reader's questions should I answer more completely?

■ Where should I add details or examples?

■ How could I make sections that lose my reader's interest more engaging or should I cut those sections?

■ Why did my readers find some sections confusing? How could I reorganize those sections?

■ Where could I rewrite sections to make them clearer?

Proofreading Your Draft

After revising your draft, proofread or edit it to correct errors in grammar, punctuation, and spelling. Effective proofreading is essential since even a few errors quickly detract from the credibility of your work. Since we often overlook our own errors simply because we know what we meant, proofreading can be difficult. Even after you have checked your paper using spell and grammar check, inch through your draft deliberately, moving your finger along slowly under every word. Repeat this procedure several times, looking first for errors in grammar, then for sentence errors and problems in punctuation and mechanics, and finally for mistakes in spelling. Be especially alert for problems that have plagued your writing in the past.

Effective proofreading calls for you to assume a detective role and probe for errors that weaken your writing. If you accept the challenge, you will certainly improve the quality of your finished work.

If students form their own groups, those of like ability might join together, as might friends, who could be reluctant to respond critically to each other's papers. Alternatively, you could organize the groups so that different levels of ability are represented, making sure that every strong writer is matched with another strong writer who can provide effective responses. Groups of three to five participants are best.

Revising with a Computer

Many writers prefer the advantages of revising on a computer. All word-processing programs allow you to write over unwanted sections of your draft, add new information, delete useless material, and move parts of the text around. Learn all the commands of your particular program and experiment to see exactly what your options are. The following practical tips will improve your efficiency:

1. Always keep a backup copy of everything. Accidentally erasing a file or losing your work to an electrical power surge is not uncommon. In addition, save copies of your earlier drafts, either as printouts or on disk; selected parts may prove useful later, and new papers sometimes sprout from old drafts. You can either save each draft under variations of your file name—"COPY A," "COPY B," "COPY C"—or keep deleted sections in specially labeled files.

2. Jot down helpful ideas or comments in your text as you revise. Enclose them with a special symbol, such as < >, and either save them in a separate file or delete them later if they serve no purpose.

3. If you struggle with a section of the text, write two or three versions and then pick your favorite. You might even open a new file, experiment freely, and then use the best version in your draft.

4. Don't allow the program to control how you revise. Don't be tempted to do what the commands make easiest: fiddle endlessly with sentences and words, never develop the essay as a whole, and move blocks of writing around indiscriminately. Avoid being electronically bewitched and make only those additions and changes that improve your writing.

5. Usually revise using a printout. If you use just the computer, you are limited to only one full screen at a time. A printed page has a different look. In addition, a printout allows you to compare several pages at once: You

3. You can direct groups to respond in different ways. Some instructors prefer to have the writer read the paper aloud and "readers" respond orally. Oral responses, however, often cause student minds to wander, and most writers forget the comments. Another alternative is to have students exchange papers and respond in writing. This procedure reinforces the importance of written communication, allows students more time to reflect on their response, provides more responses, and establishes a written record of the responses.

4. Just as you can guide students to respond generally to a draft, you can also guide peer responses by posing a set of specific questions, similar to the revision questions in each chapter, which are keyed to particular features of the assignment.

5. To prevent students from ignoring peer

responses, have all writers review the comments they receive, prepare a written plan that incorporates them, and turn in peer responses along with their revised draft.

6. You may have to speak to students who are not making an effort to provide quality peer responses.

SUGGESTED INSTRUCTOR READINGS

Bruffee, K. "Peer Tutoring and the Conversation of Mankind." <u>Writing Center</u>. Ed. Gary Olsen. Urbana, IL: NCTE, 1984, 3–15. Argues that peer tutors can, in some cases, be more effective than the instructor.

Holt, M. "The Value of Written Peer Criticism." <u>College Composition and Communication</u> 43 (1992): 384–93. Defends the use of peer criticism.

TEACHING STRATEGY
You might want to assign one large collaborative project each semester. Students could begin it early in the term and then continue it while they do other assignments. For example, they could prepare a guide to the campus or the community for new students or even do a research paper on an issue currently affecting the campus. Each individual in the group could assume responsibility for a

can see, for example, how the second paragraph might be more effective if repositioned as paragraph 5.

6. When you finish revising, check the coherence of your draft. The writing must flow smoothly at the points where you have added, deleted, or moved sections of text. In addition, altered sentences must be clearly written and logically constructed. You can best check the essay's flow with a printout.

7. While every writer should run a spell and grammar check program before turning in work, proofreading with a word processor does have certain limitations. For example, a spelling check function can't judge whether you used the wrong word (*form* instead of *from*) or confused identical sounding but differently spelled words (*their, there, they're*). Furthermore, the unit will sometimes flag words that are not misspelled but are simply not in the computer's list. While the programs to check grammar or punctuation can offer you useful suggestions, they are intended only to give you options. **You** are still the ultimate proofreader.

8. Some programs, such as Microsoft Word (under *View, Toolbar, Reviewing*), have options to Track Changes, which let you make revisions, which then appear in color with the record of changes noted in the margin. Later you can go back and accept or reject the changes. This feature can be especially useful if you are getting peer feedback or working on a collaborative writing project.

Collaborative Writing

In many careers you'll have to work as part of a group to produce a single document. Recognizing this fact, many instructors assign collaborative writing projects. Writing as part of a group offers some advantages and poses some challenges. You can draw on many different perspectives and areas of expertise, split up the work, and enjoy the feedback of a built-in peer group. On the other hand, you must also coordinate several efforts, resolve conflicts over the direction of the project, deal with people who may not do their fair share, and integrate different styles of writing.

Even though you write as part of a group, the final product should read as though it were written by one person. Therefore, take great pains to ensure that the paper doesn't resemble a patchwork quilt. You can help achieve this goal by following the principles of good writing discussed throughout this book. Here are some suggestions for successful collaborative work:

1. Select a leader with strong organizational skills.
2. Make sure each person has every other group member's phone number and e-mail address.
3. Analyze the project and develop a work plan with clearly stated deadlines for each step of the project.
4. Assign tasks on the basis of people's interests and expertise.
5. Schedule regular meetings to gauge each person's progress.
6. Encourage ideas and feedback from all members at each meeting.

7. If each member will develop a part of the paper, submit each one's contribution to the other members of the group for peer evaluation. This can be done electronically.

8. To ensure that the finished product is written in one style and fits together as a whole, give each member's draft to one person and ask him or her to write a complete draft.

9. Allow plenty of time to review the draft so necessary changes can be made.

Collaborative writing provides an opportunity to learn a great deal from other students. Problems can arise, however, if one or more group members don't do their work or skip meetings entirely. This irresponsibility compromises everyone's grade. The group should insist that all members participate, and the leader should immediately contact anyone who misses a meeting. If a serious problem develops despite these efforts, contact your instructor.

Collaboration Using E-Mail, Instant Messenger, or Chat Rooms

Many college students use electronic communication to collaborate on writing projects. This allows you to exchange material and comments at every stage of the writing process. To illustrate, you can share

1. brainstorming ideas developed during the search for a writing topic
2. brainstorming ideas developed during the search for supporting information
3. tentative thesis statements or any general statement that will shape the document
4. individual sections of the writing project
5. copies of the entire original draft.

Whenever you use e-mail for collaborative writing, it's a good idea to designate a project leader who will ensure that all members participate and who will receive and distribute all materials. Your instructor may request copies of the e-mail exchanges in order to follow your work.

Maintaining and Reviewing a Portfolio

A portfolio is an organized collection of your writing, usually kept in a three-ring binder or folder. It's a good idea to retain all your work for each class, including the assignment sheet, your prewriting, and all your drafts. Organize this material either in the order the papers were completed or by type of assignment.

Why assemble a portfolio? Not only can a portfolio be a source of ideas for future writing, but it also allows you to review the progress of your current papers. In addition, should any confusion arise about a grade or an assignment, the contents of your portfolio can quickly clarify matters.

---

different segment of the project. You would probably want to ensure that the members of the group coordinate tasks and adhere to due dates as well as supply you with regular progress reports. As an alternative, students could do a collaborative project near the end of the term, perhaps evaluating your writing class.

SUGGESTED INSTRUCTOR READING

Dale, Helen. <u>Co-Authoring in the Classroom</u>. Urbana, IL: NCTE, 1997. Offers several practical suggestions on how to make collaborative writing work.

TEACHING STRATEGIES

1. Having students use e-mail to draft a shorter piece of writing such as a class-attendance policy can teach them to work cooperatively and respond seriously to peer comments. Because many students have e-mail addresses, collaboration should present no problem. If you ask students to furnish copies of their e-mail exchanges, you should gain good insight into their collaborative processes.

2. After students participate in an e-mail collaboration project, ask them to discuss how it is similar to and different from face-to-face collaboration. What are some of the strengths and weaknesses of e-mail collaboration?

TEACHING STRATEGY
Many instructors require students to keep an organized portfolio. The portfolio simplifies the task of evaluating an entire term's work and allows you to review assignments. It's a good idea to have students evaluate themselves halfway through the term and also at the end. They should be able to identify their progress and their areas of weakness. You can help them assume responsibility for improving their writing.

TEACHING STRATEGIES
1. Students often find it difficult to respond to papers because they mistakenly believe that they must respond as instructors. You could point out that the text examples are not "instructor"-style comments but honest responses.
2. Many students experience difficulty using peer (or instructor) comments in revision. To confront this problem, have students write down their sense of their readers' concerns as well as their own plans for addressing those concerns during revision.

Some instructors will require you to maintain a portfolio. They will probably specify both what is to be included and how it is to be organized. They may use the portfolio to help you gain a better understanding of your strengths and weaknesses. Furthermore, portfolios give your instructor a complete picture of your work. Some departments collect student portfolios to assess their writing program; by reviewing student progress, instructors can determine what adjustments will make the program even more effective. Increasingly colleges may have you maintain a portfolio using a Web-based program. If your school has you maintain an electronic portfolio, you will receive clear instructions about the process. Do not be afraid to ask questions about this process.

You can review your own portfolio to gain a better understanding of your writing capabilities. Answer these questions as you look over your materials:

1. With what assignments or topics was I most successful? Why?
2. What assignments or topics gave me the most problems? Why?
3. How has my prewriting changed? How can I make it more effective?
4. How has my planning changed? How can I make it more effective?
5. What makes my best writing good? How does this writing differ from my other work?
6. What are the problem areas in my weakest writing? How does this writing differ from my other work?
7. Did I use the checklists in the front of this text to revise my papers? Do I make significant changes on my own, in response to peer evaluation, or in response to my instructor's comments? If not, why not? What kinds of changes do I make? What changes would improve the quality of my work?
8. What organizational patterns have I used? Which ones have been effective? Why? Which ones have given me trouble? Why?
9. What kinds of introductions have I used? What other options do I have?
10. What kinds of grammar or spelling errors mar my writing? (Focus on these errors in future proofreading.)

Revising Your Paper

Prepare to revise.

- Distance yourself from your writing.
- Jot down your initial plans for your writing and ideas that came to mind.
- Talk about your paper with others.
- Read peer response and judge what makes sense.

Revise your whole essay.

- To discover new directions.
- Find what *FITS* and doesn't.
- *ADD* to develop and clarify.
- *CUT* what doesn't help.
- *TEST* the organization and restructure and add transitions.

Revise your paragraphs.

Read out loud if it is helpful. Pay attention to where you stumble and what doesn't sound good. Slow down your reading to revise so you don't skim.

- Fit the thesis.
- Focus on central idea.
- Add detail as necessary.
- Cut what doesn't fit.
- Reorganize for easier flow.

Strengthen words and sentences.

- Use more precise and vivid words.
- Make sure sentences mean what you want.
- Cut excess wordiness.

Repeat entire process or parts as needed.

Now proofread your paper.

CHAPTER 5

Paragraphs

SUGGESTED INSTRUCTOR READINGS

Larson, R. "Structure and Form in Non-Narrative Prose." <u>Teaching Composition: Twelve Bibliographic Essays.</u> Ed. G. Tate. Fort Worth: Texas Christian UP, 1987, 39–82. Discusses contemporary paragraph theory, including Larson's own theory.

Shaughnessy, M. P. <u>Errors and Expectations: A Guide for the Teacher of Basic Writing.</u> New York: Oxford UP, 1977. While this book is best known for its helpful discussion of how to deal with grammatical errors, the chapter "Beyond the Sentence" provides practical advice on helping basic writers understand the paragraph.

Imagine the difficulty of reading a magazine article or book if you were faced with one solid block of text. How could you sort its ideas or know the best places to pause for thought? Paragraphs help guide readers through longer pieces of writing. Some break lengthy discussions of one idea into segments of different emphasis, thus providing rest stops for readers. Others consolidate several briefly developed ideas. Yet others begin or end pieces of writing or link major segments together. Most paragraphs, though, include a number of sentences that develop and clarify one idea. Throughout a piece of writing, paragraphs relate to one another and reflect a controlling purpose. To make paragraphs fit together smoothly, you can't just sit down and dash them off. Instead, you first need to reflect on the entire essay, then channel your thoughts toward its different segments. Often you'll have to revise your paragraphs after you've written a draft.

Characteristics of Effective Paragraphs

Unity

A paragraph with unity develops one, and only one, key controlling idea. To ensure unity, edit out any stray ideas that don't belong and fight the urge to take interesting but irrelevant side trips; they only create confusion about your destination.

The following paragraph *lacks unity:*

> The Montessori Method for teaching math in the earliest grades builds on the child's natural link to physical objects and concrete learning. Spelling and reading is also taught with special materials. It was the

psychologist Piaget who recognized that there were different kinds of cognition from the concrete to the more abstract. Maria Montessori was a pioneer in applying insights into how children actually think to the classroom.

What exactly is this writer trying to say? We can't tell. Each sentence expresses a different, undeveloped idea:

1. The use of concrete materials to teach math.
2. The use of special materials to teach spelling and reading.
3. Piaget's contribution in identifying levels of intelligence.
4. Maria Montessori's contribution to education.

In contrast, the following paragraph develops and clarifies only one central idea, the Montessori Method's use of concrete materials to teach math:

> The Montessori Method for teaching math in the earliest grades builds on the child's natural link to physical objects and concrete learning. Children count out unit beads. When they reach ten unit beads, they can exchange them for a ten-bar, a line of ten linked beads. Ten ten-bars can be exchanged for one one-hundred square. By physically placing unit beads, ten-lines, and hundred-squares on a mat, children quickly learn about the units, tens, and hundreds place and how to carry. These concrete tools can also help children learn addition and subtraction. Children lay out a number like two hundred thirty six on a mat as well as the number one hundred sixty five. They add them together, counting up the five and the six to get eleven and exchanging ten unit-beads for the ten bar leaving one unit bead, adding up the now ten ten-bars and exchanging them for a hundred-square and then reading out the resulting number of four hundred and one. While the description of the procedure may sound complicated, the actual process of using these concrete materials to understand addition and carrying is easy for children to grasp.
>
> Diane Honegger

Because no unrelated ideas sidetrack the discussion, the paragraph has unity. To check your paragraphs for unity, ask yourself what each one aims to do and whether each sentence helps that aim.

EXERCISE

After reading the next two paragraphs, answer the questions that follow.

1. The legend—in Africa—that all elephants over a large geographical area go to a common "graveyard" when they sense death is approaching led many hunters

TEACHING STRATEGIES

1. Select several kinds of essay, perhaps from the Reader, and have students examine the unity in various paragraphs to determine how each sentence relates to the controlling idea and to identify any sentences that seem out of place.

2. Students could review their own essays, testing the unity of each paragraph. Revising those that are faulty helps create an awareness of unified writing.

to treat them with special cruelty. Ivory hunters, believing the myth and trying to locate such graveyards, often intentionally wounded an elephant in the hopes of following the suffering beast as it made its way to the place where it wanted to die. The idea was to wound the elephant seriously enough so that it thought it was going to die but not so seriously that it died in a very short time. All too often, the process resulted in a single elephant being shot or speared many times and relentlessly pursued until it either fell dead or was killed when it finally turned and charged its attackers. In any case, no wounded elephant ever led its pursuers to the mythical graveyard with its hoped-for booty of ivory tusks.

Kris Hurrell

EXERCISE ANSWERS

1. This paragraph is unified. The first sentence is the topic sentence, and the rest develop the point that many hunters treated elephants cruelly in hopes of locating the elephants' "graveyard."

2. The paragraph is mostly unified in explaining how buyers find downloading convenient and easy and so are less likely to buy CDs in stores, hurting traditional CD sales. Toward the end of the paragraph, the writer goes off track in addressing the advantages of this trend, which seems to be a different topic entirely.

PERSPECTIVE

Alexander Bain (English Composition and Rhetoric, 1866) was the first person to offer a systematic theory of the paragraph. Among other things, he stressed the essential role of the topic sentence. More recently, some researchers have questioned whether topic sentences are as crucial or prevalent as traditional paragraph theory suggests. While it is true that in some writing topic sentences are noticeably absent, it's probably best if students guide their paragraphs with clearly stated topic sentences, at least initially. Later they can advance to implied topic sentences. Writing topic sentences isn't

2. It is not surprising that the sale figures for CDs keep slumping since it is easier and more convenient to download the music buyers want from the Internet. The online music stores, such as i-tunes, are very easy to use with simple instructions for searching for music and making purchases. Music fans can quickly find the performers or albums of their choice, even obscure works, from the convenience of their living room without having to drive from store to store. Then they can buy either the songs or entire albums that interest them. Once downloaded they can either burn a CD to play on more traditional stereos or copy the music to an mp3 player of some kind. The effects have been devastating on the music retail industry. Major stores such as Tower Records went out of business. Barnes and Noble has cut back on the number of CDs that the chain sells. The shift to online distribution of music has had the added advantage of allowing alternative groups to present their music that they would have had trouble getting made into CDs and distributed through major chains. This also ends the potential impact of major chains such as Wal-Mart on what music is sold.

Annonymous

1. Which of these paragraphs lacks unity? Refer to the paragraphs when answering.
2. How would you improve the paragraph that lacks unity?

The Topic Sentence

The topic sentence states the main idea of the paragraph. Think of the topic sentence as a rallying point, with all supporting sentences developing the idea it expresses. A good topic sentence helps you gauge what information belongs in a paragraph, thus ensuring unity. At the same time, it informs your reader about the point you're making.

Placement of the topic sentence varies from paragraph to paragraph, as the following examples show. As you read each, note how supporting information develops the topic sentence, which is italicized.

Topic Sentence Stated First Many paragraphs open with the topic sentence. The writer reveals the central idea immediately and then builds from a solid base.

Starting about one million years ago, the fossil record shows an accelerating growth of the human brain. It expanded at first at the rate of one cubic inch of additional gray matter every hundred thousand years; then the growth rate doubled; it doubled again; and finally it doubled once more. Five hundred thousand years ago the rate of growth hit its peak. At that time, the brain was expanding at the phenomenal rate of ten cubic inches every hundred thousand years. No other organ in the history of life is known to have grown as fast as this.

Robert Jastrow, *Until the Sun Dies*

Topic Sentence Stated Last   In order to emphasize the support and build gradually to a conclusion, a topic sentence can end the paragraph. This position creates suspense as the reader anticipates the summarizing remark.

An experience of my own comes handily to mind. Some years ago, when the Restaurant de la Pyramide in Vienne was without question one of the best half-dozen restaurants in the world, I visited it for the first time. After I had ordered my meal, the sommelier[wine steward] appeared to set before me a wine list of surpassing amplitude and excellence. But as I cast my eyes down this unbelievable offering of the world's most tantalizing wines, the sommelier bent over me and pointed out a wine of which I had never heard, ticketed at a price one-fifth that of its illustrious neighbors. "Monsieur," said the sommelier, "I would suggest this one. It is a local wine, a very good wine. It is not a great wine, but after all, monsieur, you are likely to pass this way only once. The great wines you will find everywhere; this wine you will find only in Vienne. I would like you to try it, while you have the opportunity." *This, to my mind, was true sophistication—on the part of M. Point for having the wine and on the part of the waiter for offering it.*

Stephen White, "The New Sophistication: Defining the Terms"

Topic Sentence Stated First and Last   Some paragraphs lead with the main idea and then restate it, usually in different words, at the end. This technique allows the writer to repeat an especially important idea.

Everything is changing. . . . This is a prediction I can make with absolute certainty. As human beings, we are constantly in a state of change. Our bodies change every day. Our attitudes are constantly evolving. Something that we swore by five years ago is now almost impossible for us to imagine ourselves believing. The clothes we wore a few years ago now look strange to us in old photographs. The things we take for granted as absolutes, impervious to change, are, in fact, constantly doing just that. Granite boulders become sand in time. Beaches erode and shape new shorelines. Our buildings become outdated and are replaced with modern structures that also will be torn down. Even those things which last thousands of years, such as the Pyramids and the Acropolis, also are changing. This simple insight is very important to grasp if you want to be a no-limit person, and are desirous of raising no-limit children. *Everything you feel, think, see, and touch is constantly changing.*

Wayne Dyer, *What Do You Really Want for Your Children?*

Topic Sentence Stated in the Middle   On occasion, the topic sentence falls between one set of sentences that provides background information and a follow-up set that develops the central idea. This arrangement allows the writer to shift the emphasis and at the same time preserve close ties between the two sets.

Over the centuries, China has often been the subject of Western fantasy. In their own way, a number of scholars, journalists, and other travelers have perpetuated this

always a conscious act. During the drafting stage, students may automatically create them for many paragraphs as they try to achieve unity. The remaining topic sentences are then deliberately added during revision as students check for paragraphs that lack them.

TEACHING STRATEGIES

1. Ask students to review several kinds of writing, including essays in the Reader, business essays, magazine articles, and textbooks, to determine where topic sentences tend to be located. Some paragraphs, of course, will contain no topic sentence.

2. Students could follow the same procedure as they review their own writing.

CLASSROOM ACTIVITIES

1. You might rewrite a short essay so that the topic sentences are removed or reworded so as not to function as topic sentences. Have students identify where they have trouble reading the essay and why, develop topic sentences for the paragraphs, and then compare these sentences with those in the original essay.

2. Have students revise several of the sample paragraphs, reposition the topic sentence, and then evaluate the results. This activity shows that placement of the topic sentence can influence the effect, and even the meaning, of the paragraph.

tradition in recent years, rushing to rediscover the country after its long period of isolation. Some of these visitors, justifiably impressed by the Communists' achievements in eliminating the exploitative aspects of pre-1949 mandarin society, propagated the view that the revolution, after its initial successes, had continued to "serve the people," and that China was "the wave of the future"—a compelling alternative to the disorder and materialism of contemporary Western society. Human rights were not at issue, they argued, because such Western concepts were inapplicable to China. *In the past year, however, the Chinese have begun to speak for themselves, and they are conveying quite a different picture.* In the view of many of its own people, China is a backward and repressive nation. "China is Asia's Gulag Archipelago," an elderly Chinese scholar said to me shortly after I had arrived in China last spring. "I was in Germany right after the Second World War, and I saw the horrors of Buchenwald and other concentration camps. In a way—in its destruction of the human spirit these past two decades—China has been even worse."

David Finkelstein, "When the Snow Thaws"

Topic Sentence Implied
Some paragraphs, particularly in narrative and descriptive writing, have no topic sentence. Rather, all sentences point toward a main idea that readers must grasp for themselves.

[Captain Robert Barclay] once went out at 5 in the morning to do a little grouse shooting. He walked at least 30 miles while he potted away, and then after dinner set out on a walk of 60 miles that he accomplished in 11 hours without a halt. Barclay did not sleep after this but went through the following day as if nothing had happened until the afternoon, when he walked 16 miles to a ball. He danced all night, and then in early morning walked home and spent a day partridge shooting. Finally he did get to bed—but only after a period of two nights and nearly three days had elapsed and he had walked 130 miles.

John Lovesey, "A Myth Is As Good As a Mile"

The details in this paragraph collectively suggest a clear central idea: that Barclay had incredible physical endurance. But writing effective paragraphs without topic sentences challenges even the best writers. Therefore, control most of your paragraphs with clearly expressed topic sentences.

EXERCISE

Identify the topic sentences in each of the following paragraphs and explain how you arrived at your decisions. If the topic sentence is implied, state the central idea in your own words.

1. Last winter, while leafing through the <u>Guinness Book of World Records</u>, I came across an item stating that the tallest sunflower ever had been grown by G. E. Hocking, an Englishman. Fired by a competitive urge, I planted a half acre of sunflower seeds. That half acre is now a magnificent 22,000 square feet of green and gold flowers. From the elevated rear deck of my apartment, I can look out over the swaying mass of thick, hairy green stalks and see each stalk thrusting up through the darker heart-shaped leaves below and supporting

SUGGESTED INSTRUCTOR READINGS

Braddock, R. "The Frequency and Placement of Topic Sentences in Expository Prose." <u>Research in the Teaching of English</u> (Winter 1974): 287–302. Braddock reports that in the professional writing he examined, topic sentences were used less than 15% of the time but that "percentages vary greatly among individual writers."

D'Angelo, F. "The Topic Sentence Revisited." <u>College English</u> 37 (1986): 431–41. Answering critics, D'Angelo argues that we should teach topic sentences since they enhance readability.

EXERCISE ANSWERS
1. The topic sentence is the third sentence of the paragraph. The first two sentences explain why the writer started to grow sunflowers. The four sentences following the topic sentence develop the idea that the plot is magnificent. The last two sentences talk about the writer's plans for next season.
2. The topic sentence is the last sentence in the paragraph. The preceding sentences deal with two things Susskind's mother never

an ever-bobbing imitation of the sun. In this dwarf forest, some of the flower heads measure almost a foot in diameter. Though almost all my plants are now blooming, none will top the sixteen feet, two inches reached by Hocking's plant. My tallest is just thirteen feet even, but I don't think that's too bad for the first attempt. Next year, however, will be another matter. I plan to have an automatic watering system to feed my babies.

Joseph Wheeler

2.   What my mother never told me was how fast time passes in adult life. I remember, when I was little, thinking I would live to be at least as old as my grandmother, who was dynamic even at ninety-two, the age at which she died. Now I see those ninety-two years hurtling by me. And my mother never told me how much fun sex could be, or what a discovery it is. Of course, I'm of an age when mothers really didn't tell you much about anything. My mother never told me the facts of life.

Joyce Susskind, "Surprises in a Woman's Life"

3.   The UN's International Labor Organization estimates that as many as 200 million children go to work rather than to school. They are in developing nations throughout the world, making everything from clothing and shoes to handbags and carpets. These children are the dark side of the new global economy, an international underclass working 12 or more hours a day, six or seven days a week. In the carpet factories of India, they are often separated from their families for years at a time. In the leather-handbag plants of Thailand, children report being forced to ingest amphetamines just to keep up their strength. In the charcoal industry of Brazil, tens of thousands of children work in a soot-drenched hell producing ingredients for steel alloys used in the manufacture of American cars. Child laborers everywhere develop arthritis and carpal tunnel syndrome from the repetitive work; their respiratory systems are damaged by inhaling toxic chemicals in poorly ventilated workshops; their posture is permanently altered by the long hours in cramped conditions. And the products they make are in homes across America, serving as a bitterly ironic commentary on what we consider a child's right to a carefree youth.

Mark Schapiro, "Children of a Lesser God"

4.   The first hostage to be brought off the plane was a dark little man with a bald head and a moustache so thick and black that it obliterated his mouth. Four of the masked terrorists were guarding him closely, each with a heavy rifle held ready for fire. When the group was about fifty feet from the plane, a second hostage, a young woman in flowered slacks and a red blouse, was brought out in clear view by a single terrorist, who held a pistol against the side of her head. Then the first four pushed the dark little man from them and instructed him to kneel on the pavement. They looked at him as they might an insect. But he sat there on his knees, seemingly as indifferent as if he had already taken leave of his body. The shots from the four rifles sounded faintly at the far end of the field where a group of horrified spectators watched the grisly proceedings.

Bradley Willis

told her: that time flies and sex can be fun. These sentences provide specific examples that support the general point made in the final sentence.

3. The first sentence is the topic sentence. The remaining sentences provide supporting details.

4. This paragraph has an implied topic sentence. A suitable topic sentence might be "The terrorists, ignoring all efforts to negotiate the release of the passengers, began carrying out their threat to execute hostages."

PERSPECTIVE
The amount of development needed varies according to the situation. Students, for various reasons, consistently underdevelop their paragraphs. Students simply may not take the time to gather the necessary information. Or they may be afraid of going into too much detail "for fear of boring the reader." (The short, pithy paragraphs of the popular press and of advertising reinforce this tendency.) Finally, some students just don't know how to develop their paragraphs. How to address the problem depends of course on its cause.

1. Develop one of the ideas below into a topic sentence. Then write a unified paragraph that is built around it.

   a. The career (or job or profession) I want is _____ .
   b. The one quality most necessary in my chosen field is _____.
   c. The most difficult aspect of my chosen field is _____.
   d. One good example of the American tendency to waste is _____.
   e. The best (or worst) thing about fast-food restaurants is _____.
   f. The college course I find most useful (or interesting) is _____.
   g. Concentration (or substitute your own term here) is an important part of a successful golf game (or substitute your own sport) _____.
   h. The one place where I feel most at home is _____.
   i. More than anything else, owning a pet (or growing a garden) involves _____.

2. Write a topic sentence that would control a paragraph on each of the following:

   a. Preparations for traveling away from home
   b. Advantages of having your own room
   c. Some landmark of the community in which you live
   d. The price of long-distance telephone calls
   e. Registering for college courses
   f. A cherished memento or souvenir
   g. High school graduation
   h. New Year's resolutions

TEACHING STRATEGY
Since students are often most familiar with newspapers and magazines, they sometimes write short, even single-sentence, paragraphs. Have them review several kinds of writing to determine how, and how extensively, each author develops paragraphs and what writing situations require greater development. They will probably find that most paragraphs are developed by elaboration and that when the writing is directed to a more professional audience, paragraphs tend to be longer and more internally complex.

Adequate Development

Students often ask for guidelines on paragraph length: "Should I aim for fifty to sixty words? Seven to ten sentences? About one-fourth of a page?" The questions are natural, but the approach is wrong. Instead of targeting a particular length, ask yourself what the reader needs to know. Then supply enough information to make your point clearly. Developing a paragraph inadequately is like inviting guests to a party but failing to tell them when and where it will be held. Skimpy paragraphs force readers to fill in the gaps for themselves, a task that can both irritate and stump them. On the other hand, a paragraph stuffed with useless padding dilutes the main idea. In all cases, the reader, the information being presented, and the publication medium determine the proper amount of detail. A newspaper might feature short paragraphs including only key facts, whereas a scientific journal might have lengthy paragraphs that offer detailed development of facts.

The details you supply can include facts, figures, thoughts, observations, steps, lists, examples, and personal experiences. Individually, these bits of information may mean little, but together they clearly illustrate your point. Keep in mind, however, that development isn't an end in itself but instead advances the purpose of the entire essay. Still, less experienced writers often produce underdeveloped paragraphs. Look for places where you can specifically add a clarifying explanation, a detailed example, or a more complete account of an already provided example. You might want to take weak paragraphs and brainstorm for additional details.

Here are two versions of a paragraph, the first inadequately developed:

Underdeveloped Paragraph

Most of the delegates to the Constitutional Convention of 1787 feared too much democracy. As a result, they drafted the Constitution as a document outlining a limited democracy. Indeed, some of the provisions were simply undemocratic. But despite reflecting the delegates' distrust of popular rule, the Constitution did provide a framework in which democracy could evolve.

Adequately Developed Paragraph

Most of the delegates to the Constitutional Convention of 1787 feared too much democracy. As a result, they drafted the Constitution as a document outlining a limited democracy. Indeed, some of the provisions were simply undemocratic: *universal suffrage was denied; voting qualifications were left to the states; and women, blacks, and persons without property were denied the federal franchise. Until the passage of the Seventeenth Amendment in 1913, senators were not popularly elected but were chosen by state legislators.* But despite reflecting the delegates' distrust of popular rule, the Constitution did provide a framework in which democracy could evolve.

The first paragraph lacks examples of undemocratic provisions, whereas the second one provides the needed information.

Readability also helps set paragraph length. Within a paper, paragraphs signal natural dividing places, allowing the reader to pause and absorb the material presented up to that point. Too little paragraphing overwhelms the reader with long blocks of material. Too much creates a choppy effect that may seem simplistic, even irritating. To counter these problems, writers sometimes use several paragraphs for an idea that needs extended development, or they combine several short paragraphs into one.

EXERCISE

1. Indicate where the ideas in this long block of material divide logically; explain your choices.

During the summer following graduation from high school, I could hardly wait to get to college and "be on my own." In my first weeks at State University, however, I found that independence can be tough and painful. I had expected raucous good times and a carefree collegiate life, the sort depicted in old beach movies and suggested by the selective memories of sentimental alumni. Instead, all I felt at first was the burden of increasing responsibilities and the loneliness of "a man without a country." I discovered that being independent of parents who kept at me to do my homework and expected me to accomplish certain household chores did not mean I was free to do as I pleased. On the contrary, living on my own meant that I had to perform for myself all the tasks that the family used to share. Studying

CLASSROOM ACTIVITY
Bring in copies of retyped essays with all indentations removed. Have students, working in small groups, break the essay into paragraphs. Then discuss the differing ways of paragraphing, their effects, and the rationale for each way. Compare student decisions with those of the author and discuss differences and similarities. You might also point out how different ways of paragraphing influence meaning and emphasis.

EXERCISE ANSWERS
1. This material can be divided logically into three paragraphs. The introductory paragraph ends with sentence 4, "Instead, all I felt at first. . . ." which serves as the main idea sentence of the writing and charts the course it will follow. The second paragraph focuses on the responsibilities of the writer and concludes with the sentence "Studying became a full-time occupation. . . ." The remaining material constitutes the final paragraph and deals with the writer's sense of being alone.
2. Possible details to use in expanding inadequately developed paragraphs. Paragraph 1: Strangers smile, say "hello"; Neighbors are friendly, visit back and forth, have block parties, baby-sit one another's children, borrow household items;

Salesclerks and waiters are cheerful and helpful, as are public servants such as police officers and trash collectors. Paragraph 2: Strangers never smile or speak; Neighbors keep to themselves, almost never talk; Often neighbors' names are not known; Salesclerks and waiters are impersonal, often discourteous; Public servants also are impersonal or discourteous.

became a full-time occupation rather than a nightly duty to be accomplished in an hour or two, and my college instructors made it clear that they would have little sympathy for negligence or even for my inability to do an assignment. But what was more troubling about my early college life than having to do laundry, prepare meals, and complete stacks of homework was the terrifying sense of being entirely alone. I was independent, no longer a part of the world that had seemed to confine me, but I soon realized that confinement had also meant security. I never liked the feeling that people were watching over me, but I knew that my family and friends were also watching out for me—and that's a good feeling to have. At the university no one seemed particularly to be watching, though professors constantly evaluated the quality of my work. I felt estranged from people in those first weeks of college life, desperately needing a confidant but fearful that the new and tenuous friendships I had made would be damaged if I were to confess my fears and problems. It was simply too early for me to feel a part of the university. So there I was, independent in the fullest sense, and thus "a man without a country."

2. **The following short, choppy units are inadequately developed. List some details you could use to expand one of them into a good paragraph.**

   I like living in a small town because the people are so friendly. In addition, I can always get the latest gossip from the local busybody.

   In a big city, people are afraid to get too friendly. Everything is very private, and nobody knows anything about anybody else.

3. **Scan the compositions you have written in other classes for paragraphs that are over- or underdeveloped. Revise any you find.**

Organization

An effective paragraph unfolds in a clear pattern of organization so that the reader can easily follow the flow of ideas. Usually when you write your first draft, your attempt to organize your thoughts will also organize your paragraphs. Writers do not ordinarily stop to decide on a strategy for each paragraph. But when you revise or are stuck, it's useful to understand the available choices. Here are some options:

1. The strategies discussed in Chapters 8–16
2. Order of climax

The choice you make depends upon your material and purpose in writing.

Writing Strategies   These include all of the following patterns:

Time sequence (narration)

Space sequence (description)

PERSPECTIVE
The wide array of strategies for organizing paragraphs can be daunting. Nevertheless, it is important for students to study and understand the possibilities, as this awareness will help them revise their paragraphs more effectively.

TEACHING STRATEGIES
1. Have students evaluate the organizational strategies used in several types of paragraph. They could determine how the type of writing, purpose, and audience sophistication affect these strategies.
2. Have students review their own writing, identify the strategies used, and determine why they used such strategies.

Process analysis

Illustration

Classification

Comparison

Cause and effect

Definition

Argument

Four example paragraphs follow. The first, organized by *time sequence*, traces the final years of the Model T Ford, concluding with a topic sentence that sums up its impact.

In 1917 the Model T lost much of its attraction when its exterior appearance was drastically altered. The famous flat-sided brass radiator disappeared and the new style featured (in the words of the catalogue) "The stream-lined hood, large radiator and enclosed fan, crown fenders, black finish and nickel trimmings" ("crown fenders" would be described in England as domed mud-guards). Electric lighting and starting followed in 1919, and the model then continued with little alteration until 1927, when it was finally withdrawn. After a considerable pause it was replaced by the Model A, a very conventional machine with wire wheels, three-speed gearbox and four-wheel brakes (the "T" had never made this concession to progress and continued to the last with two minute brake drums on the back wheels only). While it was in preparation, others had taken the lead and the "A" never replaced the immortal "T" in the public fancy. Indeed, the "Tin Lizzy" or "Flivver" had become almost a national characteristic, and at the end of its eighteen years in production the total number sold was fifteen million.

Cecil Clutton and John Stanford, *The Vintage Motor-Car*

The next paragraph, organized by *space sequence*, describes a ceramic elf, starting from the bottom and working up to the top. Other common spatial arrangements include top to bottom, left to right, right to left, nearby to far away, far away to nearby, clockwise, and counterclockwise.

The ceramic elf in our family room is quite a character. His reddish-brown slippers, which hang over the mantel shelf, taper to a slender point. Pudgy, yellow-stockinged legs disappear into a wrinkled tunic-style, olive-green jacket, gathered at the waist with a thick, brown belt that fits snugly around his roly-poly belly. His short, meaty arms hang comfortably, one hand resting on the knapsack at his side and the other clutching the bowl of an old black pipe. An unkempt, snow-white beard, dotted by occasional snarls, trails patriarch-fashion from his lower lip to his belt line. A button nose capped with a smudge of gold dust, mischievous black eyes, and an unruly snatch of hair peeking out from under his burnt-orange stocking cap complete Bartholomew's appearance.

Maria Sanchez

To explain subordination, you might use the following sentence from Lewis Thomas's Lives of a Cell: Notes of a Biology-Watcher as an example:

1. The microorganisms that seem to have it in for us in the worst way . . . turn out on close examination to be rather more like bystanders, strays, strangers in from the cold.
2. They will invade and replicate if given the choice . . . but it is our response to their presence that makes the disease.
3. Our arsenals for fighting off bacteria are so powerful, and involve so many different defense mechanisms, that we are in more danger from them than from the invaders.
4. We live in the midst of explosive devices: We are mined.

Point out that each supporting sentence refers to and throws light on the preceding sentence. Thus, *they* and *their* in the second sentence refer to *microorganisms* in the first sentence; *arsenals for fighting off bacteria* and *defense mechanisms* in the third sentence are linked to *response to their presence* in the second; and *explosive devices* and *mined* in the final sentence tie in with *danger* in the third.

Although descriptive paragraphs, like those developed by narration, often lack topic sentences, our example leads off with the central idea.

Here is a paragraph showing *process* development.

> Making beer nuts is a quick, simple procedure that provides a delicious evening snack. You'll need six cups of raw peanuts, three cups of sugar, and one-and-one-half cups of water. To begin, combine the sugar and water in a two-quart saucepan and stir to dissolve the sugar. Next, add the peanuts and stir again until all of the peanuts are covered by the sugar-water solution. Leave the pan, uncovered, on a burner set at medium-high heat for ten to twelve minutes, until the sugar crystallizes and coats the peanuts thoroughly. Stay at the stove during the heating process and stir the mixture every two or three minutes to ensure even coating of the nuts. When the peanuts are thoroughly coated, pour them onto an ungreased cookie sheet and bake at 350 degrees for about thirty minutes, stirring and lightly salting at ten-minute intervals. Serve your beer nuts fresh out of the oven or eat them at room temperature.
>
> Kimberlee Walters

Again, the topic sentence comes first.

The final example illustrates development by *comparison* and also proceeds from an opening topic sentence.

> There is an essential difference between a news story, as understood by a newspaperman or a wire-service writer, and the newsmagazine story. The chief purpose of the conventional news story is to tell what happened. It starts with the most important information and continues into increasingly inconsequential details, not only because the reader may not read beyond the first paragraph but because an editor working on galley proofs a few minutes before press time likes to be able to cut freely from the end of the story. A newsmagazine is very different. It is written to be read consecutively from beginning to end, and each of its stories is designed, following the critical theories of Edgar Allan Poe, to create one emotional effect. The news, what happened that week, may be told in the beginning, the middle, or the end; for the purpose is not to throw information at the reader but to seduce him into reading the whole story, and into accepting the dramatic (and often political) point being made.
>
> Otto Friedrich, "There Are 00 Trees in Russia"

Order of Climax Climactic order creates a crescendo pattern, starting with the least emphatic detail and progressing to the most emphatic. The topic sentence can begin or end the paragraph, or it can remain implied. This pattern holds the reader's interest by building suspense. On occasion, writers reverse the order, landing the heaviest punch first; but such paragraphs can trail off, leaving the reader dissatisfied.

Here is a paragraph illustrating climactic order:

> The speaking errors I hear affect me to different degrees. I'm so conditioned to hearing "It don't make any difference" and "There's three ways to solve the problem" that I've almost accepted such usage. However, errors such as "Just between you and I, Arnold loves Edna" and "I'm going back to my room to lay down" still offend my sensibility. When hearing them, I usually just chuckle to myself and walk away. The "Twin I's"—<u>irrevelant</u> and <u>irregardless</u>—are another matter. More than any other errors, they really grate on my ear. Whenever I hear "that may be true, but it's irrevelant" or "Irregardless of how much I study, I still get C's," I have the urge to correct the speaker. It's really surprising that more people don't clean up their language act.
>
> Valerie Sonntag

From a magazine or newspaper article, select four paragraphs that illustrate different patterns of organization. Identify the topic sentence in each case; or if it is implied, state it in your own words. Point out the organization of each paragraph.

Coherence

Coherent writing flows smoothly and easily from one sentence and paragraph to another, clarifying the relationships among ideas and thus allowing the reader to grasp connections. Because incoherent writing fails to do this, it confuses, and sometimes even irritates, the reader.

Here is a paragraph that lacks coherence:

> I woke up late. I had been so tired the night before that I had forgotten to set the alarm. All I could think of was the report I had stayed up until 3 a.m. typing, and how I could possibly get twenty copies ready for next morning's 9 o'clock sales meeting. I panicked and ran out the door. My bus was so crowded I had to stand. Jumping off the bus, I raced back up the street. The meeting was already under way. Mr. Jackson gestured for me to come into the conference room. Inserting the first page of the report into the copier, I set the dial for twenty copies and pressed the print button. The sign started flashing CALL KEY OPERATOR. The machine was out of order. Mr. Jackson asked whether the report was ready. I pointed to the flashing red words. Mr. Jackson nodded grimly without saying anything. He left me alone with the broken machine.

This paragraph has some degree of unity: most of its sentences relate to the writer's disastrous experience with the sales report. Unfortunately, though, its many gaps in logic create rather than answer questions, and in very bumpy prose, at that. Note the gap between the third and fourth sentences. Did the writer jump out of bed and rush right out the door? Of course not, but the reader has no real clue to the actual sequence of events. Another gap occurs between the next two sentences, leaving the reader to wonder why the writer had populace is often a diet soft drink. The populace, after all, is comprised of lost cows in a meadow. Further, the populace is comprised of wolves baying at the moon. With these definitions of the populace, we have to doubt their will and go off willynilly to our own picnic.

TEACHING STRATEGIES
1. As they study coherence in individual paragraphs, you might remind students that body paragraphs are interconnected units developed in relation to some overall essay purpose, not a string of discrete units that exist in a vacuum.
2. Many students probably use most of these transitions in their paragraphs. You can help them diversify by having them review their writing, identify these techniques, and circle those they repeat excessively.
3. Advise students to deal with coherence problems primarily during the revision stage. They should read their drafts as a stranger would, particularly noting places where someone might be confused.
4. All of us have encountered students who have problems with coherence. In some cases, the material in each paragraph seems linked by free association rather than logic. Problems can occur because students are anxious or depressed about the thought of writing or because they simply lack

to race up the street upon leaving the bus. And who is Mr. Jackson? The paragraph never tells, but the reader will want to know.

Now read this rewritten version, additions italicized:

> I woke up late *because* I had been so tired the night before that I had forgotten to set the alarm. All I could think of was the report I had stayed up until 3 a.m. typing, and how I could possibly get twenty copies ready for next morning's 9 o'clock sales meeting. *When I realized it was 8:30, I panicked. Jumping out of bed, I threw on some clothes, grabbed the report*, and ran out the door. My bus was so crowded I had to stand *and could not see out the window. Two blocks beyond my stop, I realized I should have gotten off.* "Stop!" I cried and, jumping off the bus, raced back up the street. *When I reached the office, it was 9:15, and* the meeting was already under way. Mr. Jackson, *the sales manager,* saw me and gestured for me to come into the conference room. *"One moment," I said as calmly as I could and hurried to the copier.* Inserting the first page of the report into it, I set the dial for twenty copies and pressed the print button. *Immediately,* the sign started flashing CALL KEY OPERATOR. The machine was out of order. *The next thing I knew,* Mr. Jackson *was at my side* asking whether the report was ready. I pointed to the flashing red words, *and* Mr. Jackson nodded grimly without saying anything. *Turning on his heel,* he *walked away and* left me alone with the broken machine.

As this example shows, correcting an incoherent paragraph may call for anything from a single word to a whole sentence or more.

Coherence derives from a sufficient supply of supporting details and your firm sense of the way your ideas go together. If you brainstorm your topic thoroughly and think carefully about the relationships between sentences, incoherence isn't likely to haunt your paragraphs.

As you write, and especially when you revise, signal connections to the reader by using *transitions*—devices that link sentences to one another. These are the most common transitional devices:

1. Connecting words and phrases
2. Repeated key words
3. Pronouns and demonstrative adjectives
4. Parallelism

You can use them to furnish links both within and between paragraphs.

Connecting Words and Phrases   Connectors clarify relationships between sentences. The following list groups them according to function:

Showing similarity: in like manner, likewise, moreover, similarly

Showing contrast: at the same time, but, even so, however, in contrast, instead, nevertheless, still, on the contrary, on the other hand, otherwise, yet

Showing results or effects: accordingly, as a result, because, consequently, hence, since, therefore, thus

Adding ideas together: also, besides, first (second, third . . .), furthermore, in addition, in the first place, likewise, moreover, similarly, too

Drawing conclusions: as a result, finally, in brief, in conclusion, in short, to summarize

Pointing out examples: for example, for instance, to illustrate

Showing emphasis and clarity: above all, after all, again, as a matter of fact, besides, in fact, in other words, indeed, nonetheless, that is

Indicating time: at times, after, afterward, from then on, immediately, later, meanwhile, next, now, once, previously, subsequently, then, until, while

Conceding a point: granted that, of course, to be sure, admittedly

Don't overload your paper with connectors. In well-planned prose, your message flows clearly with only an occasional assist from them.

In the following excerpt, which clarifies the difference between workers and workaholics, the connectors are italicized:

> My efforts to define workaholism and to distinguish workaholics from other hard workers proved difficult. *While* workaholics do work hard, not all hard workers are workaholics. Moonlighters, *for example*, may work 16 hours a day to make ends meet, but most of them will stop working when their financial circumstances permit. Accountants, *too*, seem to work non-stop, but many slow down after the April 15 tax deadline. Workaholics, *on the other hand*, always devote more time and thought to their work than their situation demands. Even in the absence of deadlines to meet, mortgages to pay, promotions to earn, or bosses to please, workaholics still work hard. What sets them apart is their attitude toward work, not the number of hours they work.
>
> Marilyn Machlowitz, "Workaholism: What's Wrong with Being Married to Your Work?"

Discussion Questions

1. What ideas do each of the italicized words and phrases connect?
2. What relationship does each show?

Repeated Key Words   Repeating key words, especially those that help convey a paragraph's central idea, can smooth the reader's path. The words may appear in different forms, but their presence keeps the main issues before the reader. In the following paragraph, the repetition of *majority, minority,* and *will* aids coherence, as does the more limited repetition of *government* and *interests.*

> Whatever fine-spun theories we may devise to resolve or obscure the difficulty, there is no use blinking the fact that the *will* of the *majority* is not the same thing as the *will* of all. *Majority* rule works well only so long as the *minority* is *willing* to accept the *will* of the *majority* as the *will* of the *nation* and let it go at that. Generally speaking, the *minority* will be *willing* to let it go at that so long as it feels that its essential *interests* and rights are not fundamentally different from those of the current *majority*, and so long as it can, in any case, look forward with confidence to mustering enough votes within four or six years to become itself the *majority* and so redress the balance. But if it comes to pass that a large *minority* feels that it has no such chance, that it is a fixed and permanent *minority* and that another group or class with rights and *interests* fundamentally hostile to its own is in permanent control, then *government* by *majority* vote ceases in any sense to be *government* by the *will* of the people for the good of all, and becomes *government* by the *will* of some of the people for their own *interests* at the expense of the others.
>
> Carl Becker, *Freedom and Responsibility in the American Way of Life*

experience with any logical discipline. Such problems need to be addressed in an individual conference. In some cases, students may need to change topics. In others, they may need practice with exercises that require them to arrange preselected sentences under appropriate topic headings and discard those that don't fit.

CLASSROOM ACTIVITY
Bring in several paragraphs that lack coherence. Have students identify the reasons for the incoherence and suggest ways to correct the problem.

SUGGESTED INSTRUCTOR READINGS
Bamberg, B. "What Makes a Text Coherent?" College English 34 (1983): 417–30. Elaborates on the role meaning plays in determining coherence.
Fleckenstein, K. S. "An Appetite for Coherence: Arousing and Fulfilling Desires." College Composition and Communication 43 (1992): 81–87. Offers some practical suggestions for helping students achieve greater coherence.
Laib, N. "Conciseness and Amplification." College Composition and Communication 41 (1990): 443–59. Because

most students have trouble balancing conciseness and development, this article is especially useful. A noteworthy feature is its contemporary look at paragraphs. Markels, R. B. *A New Perspective on Cohesion in Expository Paragraphs.* Carbondale, IL: Southern Illinois UP, 1984. Details both the semantic and syntactic considerations that produce cohesion.

DISCUSSION QUESTIONS
In this paragraph, *while* picks up the contrast suggested in the first sentence and provides a link to the specific contrast in the sentence in which it appears. *For example* links the illustration presented in its sentence with the general idea stated in the second. *Too* in the fourth sentence indicates that the writer is adding another example to illustrate her point. *On the other hand* in the fifth sentence sets up the contrast between hard workers and workaholics that is at the heart of the paragraph.

EXERCISE

Write a paragraph using one of the following sentences as your topic sentence. Insert the missing key word and then repeat it in your paragraph to help link your sentences.

1. _____ is my favorite relative.
2. I wish I had (a, an, some, more) _____.
3. _____ changed my life.
4. _____ is more trouble than it's worth.
5. A visit to _____ always depresses me.
6. Eating _____ is a challenge.
7. I admire _____.

Pronouns and Demonstrative Adjectives   Pronouns stand in for nouns that appear earlier in the sentence or in previous sentences. Mixing pronouns and their nouns throughout the paragraph prevents monotony and promotes clarity. We have italicized the pronouns in the following excerpt from an article about the writer's first visit to a gambling casino.

There are three of *us* on this trip, two veterans of Atlantic City and *I*, a neophyte, all celebrating the fact that *we* have recently become grandmothers. One of *my* companions is the canny shopper in *our* crowd; as a bargain-hunter *she* knows the ways of the world. *I* have followed *her* through discount shops and outlet stores from Manhattan's Lower East Side to the Secaucus, New Jersey, malls. . . . Without saying a word, *she* hands *me* a plastic container of the kind that might hold two pounds of potato salad, and takes one *herself*. *She* drags *me* off to the change booth, where *she* exchanges bills for tubes of silver, careful not to let *me* see just how much. *I* do the same. Then *she* leads *me* to a clattering corner, where a neon sign winks on and off, *Quartermania.* "Let's try to find a couple of machines that only have handles," *she* says. . . .

Eileen Herbert Jordan, "My Affair with the One-Armed Bandit"

All the pronouns in the excerpt refer to the writer, her bargain-hunting friend, or the whole group.

Four demonstrative adjectives—*this, that, these,* and *those*—also help hook ideas together. Demonstratives are special adjectives that identify or point out nouns rather than describe them. Here is an example from the Declaration of Independence:

We hold *these* truths to be self-evident, that all men are created equal, that they are endowed by their Creator with certain unalienable Rights, that among *these* are Life, Liberty, and the pursuit of Happiness. That to secure *these* rights, Governments are instituted among Men, deriving their just powers from the consent of the governed. That whenever any Form of Government becomes destructive of *these* ends, it is the Right of the People to alter or to abolish it, and to institute new Government, laying its foundation on such principles and organizing its power in such form, as to them shall seem most likely to effect their Safety and Happiness.

In a magazine, newspaper, textbook, or some other written source, find two paragraphs that use pronouns and demonstrative adjectives to increase coherence. Copy the paragraphs, underline the pronouns and demonstrative adjectives, and explain what each refers to.

Parallelism   Parallelism uses repetition of grammatical form to express a series of equivalent ideas. Besides giving continuity, the repetition adds rhythm and balance to the writing. Note how the following italicized constructions tie together the unfolding definition of poverty:

> *Poverty is staying* up all night on cold nights to watch the fire, knowing one spark on the newspaper covering the walls means your sleeping children die in flames. In summer *poverty is watching* gnats and flies devour your baby's tears when he cries. The screens are torn and you pay so little rent you know they will never be fixed. *Poverty means* insects in your food, in your nose, in your eyes, and crawling over you when you sleep. *Poverty is hoping* it never rains because diapers won't dry when it rains and soon you are using newspapers. *Poverty is seeing* your children forever with runny noses. Paper handkerchiefs cost money and all your rags you need for other things. Even more costly are antihistamines. *Poverty is cooking* without food and cleaning without soap.
>
> Jo Goodwin Parker, "What Is Poverty?"

Paragraphs with Special Functions

Special-function paragraphs include introductions, transitional paragraphs, and conclusions. One-paragraph introductions and conclusions appear in short, multi-paragraph essays. Transitional paragraphs occur primarily in long compositions.

Introductions

A good introduction acquaints and coaxes. It announces the essay's topic and may directly state the thesis. In addition, it sets the tone—somber, lighthearted, angry—of what will follow. An amusing anecdote would not be an appropriate opening for a paper about political torture.

With essays, as with people, first impressions are important. If your opening rouses interest, it will draw the reader into the essay and pave the way for your ideas. If, instead, you'd like to try your hand at turning the reader away, search for a beginning that is mechanical, plodding, and dull. Your success will astonish you. Here are some bad openings:

In this paper I intend to . . .

Wars have always afflicted humankind.

As you may know, having too little time is a problem for many of us.

In the modern world of today . . .

How would you respond to these openings? Ask yourself that same question about every opening you write.

TEACHING STRATEGIES

1. Have students review the introductions, conclusions, and transitions used in a variety of essays. They might note how type of writing, purpose, and audience influence the choice.

2. Many students tend to use the first opening and closing paragraphs that come to mind. To counter this tendency, have students use the techniques in this chapter to write at least three different introductions and conclusions for an essay in progress.

3. Students might submit their introductions and conclusions to the class for evaluation.

SUGGESTED
INSTRUCTOR
READING
Hilbert, B. S. "It Was A
Dark and Nasty Night It
Was A Dark and You
Would Not Believe How
Dark It Was A Hard
Beginning." College
Composition and
Communication 43
(1992): 75–80. Offers an
entertaining and
thoughtful look at how
to help students with
introductions.

Gear the length of the introduction to that of the essay. Although longer papers sometimes begin with two or more introductory paragraphs, generally the lead-in for a short essay is a single paragraph. Here are some possibilities for starting an essay. The type you select depends on your purpose, subject, audience, and personality.

A Directly Stated Thesis   This is a common type of opening, orienting the reader to what will follow. After providing some general background, the writer of our example narrows her scope to a thesis that previews the upcoming sections of her essay.

> An increasing number of midlife women are reentering the workforce, pursuing college degrees, and getting more involved in the public arena. Several labels besides "midlife" have been attached to this type of person: the mature woman, the older woman, and, more recently, the re-entry woman. By definition, she is between thirty-five and fifty-five years old and has been away from the business or academic scene anywhere from fifteen to thirty years. The academic community, the media, marketing people, and employers are giving her close scrutiny, and it is apparent that she is having a greater impact on our society than she realizes.
>
> Jo Ann Harris

A Definition   This kind of introduction works particularly well in a paper that acquaints the reader with an unfamiliar topic.

> You are completely alone in a large open space and are struck by a terrifying, unreasoning fear. You sweat, your heart beats, you cannot breathe. You fear you may die of a heart attack, although you do not have heart disease. Suppose you decide you will never get yourself in this helpless situation again. You go home and refuse to leave its secure confines. Your family has to support you. You have agoraphobia— a disabling terror of open spaces.
>
> "Controlling Phobias Through Behavior Modification"

A Quotation   A beginning quotation, particularly from an authority in the field, can be an effective springboard for the ideas that follow. Make sure any quote you use relates clearly to your topic.

> The director of the census made a dramatic announcement in 1890. The Nation's unsettled area, he revealed, "has been so broken into by isolated bodies of settlement that there can hardly be said to be a frontier line." These words sounded the close of one period of America's history. For three centuries before, men had marched westward, seeking in the forests and plains that lay beyond the settled areas a chance to begin anew. For three centuries they had driven back the wilderness as their conquest of the continent went on. Now, in 1890, they were told that a frontier line separating the settled and unsettled portions of the United States no longer existed. The west was won, and the expansion that had been the most distinctive feature of the country's past was at an end.
>
> Ray Allen Billington, "The Frontier Disappears"

An Anecdote or Personal Experience   A well-told personal anecdote or experience can lure readers into the rest of the paper. Like other introductions, this kind should bear on what comes afterward. Engle's anecdote, like the stories she reviews, demonstrates that "women also have dark hearts."

> My mother used to have a little china cream and sugar set that was given to her by a woman who later killed her children with an axe. It sat cheerfully in the china cabinet, as inadequate a symbol as I have ever seen of the dark mysteries within us. Yet at least it was there to remind us that no matter how much Jesus wanted us for a sunbeam, we would still have some day to cope with a deeper reality than common sense could explain. It stood for strange cars not to get into, running shoes to wear when you were out alone at night and the backs of Chinese restaurants you were not supposed to go into.
> Marian Engle, review of *The Goddess and Other Women* by Joyce Carol Oates.

An Arresting Statement   Sometimes you can jolt the reader into attention, using content, language, or both, particularly if your essay develops an unusual or extreme position.

> It's like Pearl Harbor. The Japanese have invaded, and the U.S. has been caught short. Not on guns and tanks and battleships—those are yesterday's weapons—but on mental might. In a high-tech age where nations increasingly compete on brainpower, American schools are producing an army of illiterates. Companies that cannot hire enough skilled workers now realize they must do something to save the public schools. Not to be charitable, not to promote good public relations, but to survive.
> Nancy Perry, "Saving the Schools: How Business Can Help"

Interesting Details   These details pique curiosity and draw the reader into the paper.

> It is Friday night at any of the ten thousand watering holes of the small towns and crossroads hamlets of the South. The room is a cacophony of the ping-pong-ding-ding ding of the pinball machine, the pop-fizz of another round of Pabst, the refrain of "Red Necks, White Socks and Blue Ribbon Beer" on the juke box, the insolent roar of a souped-up engine outside and, above it all, the sound of easy laughter. The good ole boys have gathered for their fraternal ritual—the aimless diversion that they have elevated into a life-style.
> Bonnie Angelo, "Those Good Ole Boys"

A Question   A provocative question can entice the reader into the essay to find the answer.

> When you leave your apartment or house, do you begin to feel better? If you leave for a week-long trip, do you find your head clears, your migraine disappears, dizziness stops, your aches and pains subside, depression fades away, and your entire attitude is better? If so, chemical pollution of the atmosphere in your home may be making you ill.
> Marshall Mandell, "Are You Allergic to Your House?"

1. Explain why each of the preceding introductions interests or does not interest you. Does your response stem from the topic or the way the author introduces it?
2. Find magazine articles with effective introductory paragraphs illustrating at least three different techniques. Write a paragraph explaining why each impresses you.

Transitional Paragraphs

In the midst of a lengthy essay, you may need a short paragraph that announces a shift from one group of ideas to another. Transitional paragraphs summarize previously explained ideas, repeat the thesis, or point to ideas that follow. In our example, Bruno Bettelheim has been discussing a young boy named Joey who has turned into a kind of human machine. After describing Joey's assorted delusions, Bettelheim signals his switch from the delusions to the fears that caused them.

> What deep-seated fears and needs underlay Joey's delusional system? We were long in finding out, for Joey's preventions effectively concealed the secret of his autistic behavior. In the meantime we dealt with his peripheral problems one by one.
>
> Bruno Bettelheim, "Joey: 'A Mechanical Boy'"

The following transitional paragraph looks back as well as ahead:

> Certainly these three factors—exercise, economy, convenience of shortcuts—help explain the popularity of bicycling today. But a fourth attraction sometimes overrides the others: the lure of the open road.
>
> Mike Bernstein

Conclusions

A conclusion rounds out a paper and signals that the discussion has been completed. Not all papers require a separate conclusion; narratives and descriptions, for example, generally end when the writer finishes the story or concludes the impression. But many essays benefit from a conclusion that drives the point home a final time. To be effective, a conclusion must mesh logically and stylistically with what comes earlier. A long, complex paper often ends with a summary of the main points, but any of several other options may be used for shorter papers with easy-to-grasp ideas. Most short essays have single-paragraph conclusions; longer papers may require two or three paragraphs.

Here are some cautions about writing your conclusion:

1. Don't introduce new material. Draw together, round out, but don't take off in a new direction.
2. Don't tack on an ending in desperation when the hour is late and the paper is due tomorrow—the so-called midnight special. Your reader deserves better than "All in all, skiing is a great sport" or "Thus we can see that motorcycle racing isn't for everyone."

TEACHING STRATEGIES
1. Students experience difficulty writing conclusions. Part of the reason is that they believe they have nothing more to say. You might reassure them that it is acceptable, even useful, to repeat their main point in new language.
2. When students are working on a paper, have them freewrite on the kind of final impression they want to leave with the reader. Then they could try writing several conclusions until one meets their objectives.
3. You might have students try to write different conclusions to some of the essays in the Reader to note the effect that the new endings have on the impact of the work. Encourage students to stick as closely as possible to the style of the author.

3. Don't apologize. Saying that you could have done a better job makes a reader wonder why you didn't.
4. Don't moralize. A preachy conclusion can undermine the position you have established in the rest of your composition.

The following examples illustrate several common types of conclusion.

Restatement of the Thesis   The following conclusion reasserts Jordan's thesis that "a mood of antisocial negativism is creeping through the structure of American life, corroding our ideals, and suffocating the hopes of poor people and minorities."

> There is room for honest differences about each of these key issues, but the new negativism's overt greed and the implicit racism of its loud "No" to minority aspirations indicate that this is a poisonous movement that denies the moral ideals and human values that characterize the best in America's heritage.
>
> Vernon E. Jordan, Jr., "The New Negativism"

A Summary   A summary draws together and reinforces the main points of a paper.

> There are, of course, many other arguments against capital punishment, including its high cost and its failure to deter crime. But I believe the most important points against the death penalty are the possibility of executing an innocent man, the discriminatory manner in which it is applied, and the barbaric methods of carrying it out. In my opinion, capital punishment is, in effect, premeditated murder by society as a whole. As the old saying goes, two wrongs don't make a right.
>
> Diane Trathen

A Question   The paragraph below concludes an argument that running should not be elevated to a religion, that its other benefits are sufficient. A final question often prompts the reader to think further on the topic. If your essay is meant to be persuasive, be sure to phrase a concluding question so that the way a reasonable person would answer emphasizes your point of view.

> Aren't those gifts enough? Why ask running for benefits that are plainly beyond its capacity to bestow?
>
> James Fixx, "What Running Can't Do for You"

A Quotation   A quotation can capture the essence of your thought and end the essay with authority.

> "We had no idea of the emotional involvement and the commitment of these women," Richard says. "Suddenly a constituency arose. Suddenly there are thousands and thousands of women who don't care about your moral position or mine—they want a baby."
>
> David Zimmerman, "Are Test-Tube Babies the Answer for the Childless?"

Ironic Twist or Surprising Observation   These approaches prompt the reader to think further about a paper's topic. The following paragraph points out the ironic refusal of the government to confront poverty that exists a mere ten blocks away from its offices:

> Thus, a stark contrast exists between the two cultures of 14th Street, which appears to be like an earthworm with half of its body crushed by poverty but the other half still alive, wriggling in wealth. The two are alike only in that each communicates little with the other because of the wide disparity between the lives of the people and the conditions of the environments. The devastating irony of the situation on 14th Street lies in the fact that only ten blocks away sit the very government institutions that could alleviate the poverty—the Senate, the House of Representatives, and the White House.
>
> Student Unknown

Clever or Lighthearted Ending   In our example, the writer, capitalizing on the essay's topic, ends by exaggerating the fault being criticized.

> Because using clichés is as easy as falling off a log, it goes without saying that it would be duck soup to continue in this vein till hell freezes over. However, since that would be carrying coals to Newcastle, let's ring down the curtain and bid adieu to the fair topic of the cliché. (No use beating a dead horse.)
>
> Student Unknown

Personal Challenge   A challenge often prompts the reader to take some action.

> And therein lies the challenge. You can't merely puff hard for a few days and then revert to the La-Z-Boy recliner, smugly thinking that you're "in shape." You must sweat and strain and puff regularly, week in and week out. They're your muscles, your lungs, your heart. The only care-taker they have is you.
>
> Monica Duvall

Hope or Recommendation   Both a hope and a recommendation may restate points already made in the essay or suggest actions to take in order to arrive at a solution.

> Periodically my pilot and I climb into our aircraft and head out over the Minnesota wilderness, following a succession of electronic beeps that lead to some of the last remaining wolves in the lower 48 states. We hope that the data we collect will provide a better understanding of the wolf. We especially hope that our work

will help guide authorities into a management program that will insure the perpetuation of the species in the last vestiges of its former range.

L. David Mech, "Where Can the Wolves Survive?"

   I who am blind can give one hint to those who can see—one admonition to those who would make full use of the gift of sight: Use your eyes as if tomorrow you would be stricken blind. And the same method can be applied to the other senses. Hear the music of voices, the song of the bird, the mighty strains of an orchestra, as if you would be stricken deaf tomorrow. Touch each object you want to touch as if tomorrow your tactile sense would fail. Smell the perfume of flowers, taste with relish each morsel, as if tomorrow you could never smell and taste again. Make the most of every sense; glory in all the facets of pleasure and beauty which the world reveals to you through the several means of contact which Nature provides. But of all the senses, I am sure that sight must be the most delightful.

Helen Keller, "Three Days to See"

EXERCISE

1. Explain why each of the foregoing conclusions does or does not interest you. Does your response stem from the topic or from the author's handling of it?
2. Copy effective concluding paragraphs, illustrating at least three different techniques, from magazine articles. Then write a paragraph explaining why each impresses you.

Effective Sentences

Sentences take many forms, some straightforward and unadorned, others intricate and ornate, each with its own stylistic strengths. Becoming familiar with these forms and their uses gives you the option to

- emphasize or de-emphasize an idea
- combine ideas into one sentence or keep them separate in more than one sentence
- make sentences sound formal or informal
- emphasize the actor or the action
- achieve rhythm, variety, and contrast.

Effective sentences bring both exactness and flair to your writing. You may wish to read the Handbook section for review if you are not familiar with the sentence elements or how to identify and correct sentence errors effectively.

Sentence Strategies

Effective sentences are not an accident; they require work. There are several strategies you can employ, including avoiding unnecessary wordiness; varying sentence length, complexity, and word order; building a rhythm for your reader; and selecting the right verb voice. Usually it's best to work on these different strategies as you revise rather than pausing to refine each sentence after you write it.

Avoiding Unnecessary Wordiness

Sometimes in first drafts we write flabby sentences.

- It is my considered opinion that you will make an excellent employee.
- Joan will give a presentation on our latest sales figures to the CEO.
- Mr. Headly, who was my seventh-grade biology teacher, recently was honored for the research he had done over the years with his classes.
- My neighbor's Subaru that was old and rusty still could navigate the winter streets better than most other cars.

Although there may be stylistic reasons for these sentences, such as creating variety or adding a particular emphasis, a writer could sharpen them by reordering the sentence structure and eliminating unnecessary words.

- You will make an excellent employee. (The fact that you write it makes it clear that it is your opinion.)
- Joan will present our latest sales figures to the CEO. (Many times we use verbs as nouns with a filler verb—"have a meeting," "give a talk," "go running." Change these nouns back to verbs and dragging sentences can be energized.)
- Mr. Headly, my seventh-grade biology teacher, recently was honored for the research he had done over the years with his classes. (The rules of English let you delete some redundant phrases, even repeated subjects, to tighten your language.)
- My neighbor's rusty, old Subaru still could navigate the winter streets better than most other cars. (Changing a relative clause to simple adjectives makes this sentence crisper. Often you can change word order to produce more emphatic sentences.)

The actual rules for tightening sentences are discussed in the Handbook. How do most writers do it? Cut out words that seem unnecessary, organize sentences different ways, let verbs bear the brunt of the burden.

Rewrite the sentences to avoid unnecessary wordiness.

1. The principal will give a talk to the parents at the PTA meeting about how important it is for their children to get to school on time.
2. I would like to say that no playwright has ever used language as effectively as Shakespeare.
3. Mozart, who was a musical prodigy, is best known for his operas.
4. The jewelry store sold me a watch that was stolen.
5. The meeting that was scheduled for 3 P.M. was cancelled because Mr. Rushton, the consultant who was giving the presentation about the results on our computer security, was arrested for creating computer viruses that were very destructive.

might, to students, seem a sentence, while "He is trying" might not because the missing pronoun reference makes the sentence seem incomplete.

TEACHING STRATEGY
Students who experience difficulty with the sentence elements mentioned here could review the appropriate sections of the Handbook.

EXERCISE ANSWERS
1. The principal will talk to the parents at the PTA meeting about how important it is for their children to get to school on time or The principal will talk at the PTA meeting about the importance of getting children to school on time.
2. No playwright has ever used language as effectively as Shakespeare.
3. Mozart, a musical prodigy, is best known for his operas.
4. The jewelry store sold me a stolen watch.
5. The 3 P.M. meeting was cancelled because Mr. Rushton, the consultant presenting the results on our computer security, was arrested for creating very destructive computer viruses.

ADDITIONAL SENTENCE-COMBINING EXERCISES
1. It had rained for four days. All the snow had melted.
   The dog sled race had to be cancelled.

Because it had rained for four days, all the snow had melted and the dog sled race had to be cancelled.

2. Mr. James is the accountant for our company. He vanished mysteriously.

The auditors discovered an accounting fraud. The fraud was in excess of a million dollars.

Mr. James, the accountant for our company, vanished mysteriously before the auditors discovered an accounting fraud that was in excess of a million dollars.

3. Jason said he didn't believe in ghosts. He refused to walk past the Karnes mansion. Many people believe the mansion is haunted.

Though Jason said he didn't believe in ghosts, he refused to walk past the Karnes mansion, which many people believe is haunted.

4. Amy looks forward to her third class in economics. Economics is her best subject. Other students say the class is extremely difficult.

Amy looks forward to her third class in economics, which is her best subject, even though other students say the class is extremely difficult.

5. Travis had worked as a police officer for many years. He was used to investigating murder scenes. This scene was particularly hard to take. The murdered man was his best friend.

Travis, who had worked as a police officer for many years, was used to investigating murder scenes; but this one was particularly hard to take since the murdered man was his best friend.

Varying Sentence Complexity and Length

Sentences that are all the same length yield a repetitive, tedious prose.

> Janice hated pain. She had her nose pierced. She had her bellybutton pierced. She had her tongue pierced. She wanted to be different. She ended up just like her friends.

This string of simple sentences unnecessarily repeats word phrases and gives the reader a bumpy ride. Combining these sentences results in a smoother and more varied prose style.

> Although Janice hated pain, she had her nose, bellybutton, and tongue pierced in order to be different. She ended up, however, just like her friends.

Simple sentences of one subject and predicate—"The audience was young"—can be combined through coordinate and subordinate conjunctions, as well as the use of relative clause structures and other techniques. The result is not only a smoother style but a combination that more effectively shows the relationship of your ideas.

Coordination

Discussed more fully in the Handbook, coordinating conjunctions include *and, but, or, nor, for, yet, so,* and can combine clauses or phrases in a way that makes them equal.

- The audience was young, friendly, *and* responsive; *so* it cheered for each speaker.
- *Either* we hang together *or* we hang separately.
- A tornado ripped through our town *but* fortunately it spared our house.

Subordination

Subordinate conjunctions such as *because, since, while, before, during, after,* and *instead of* can link dependent clauses to the main independent clause in a way that shows logical relationship.

- Millicent swam 400 laps today **because** *she was feeling unusually strong.*
- Arthur collapsed on the sofa **after** *the dance was over.*
- **Once** *they had reached the lakeshore,* the campers found a level spot **where** *they could pitch their tent.*

Relative Clauses

Nouns can often be modified by relative clauses, which use a **relative pronoun** that substitutes for a noun and binds ideas together.

- Students **who** *work hard* usually succeed.
- The books on the history of Crete **that** *you ordered* have finally arrived.

There are certainly other ways to combine sentences and vary sentence length, including the use of prepositional phrases, participle phrases, and infinitive phrases.

- The crook raced **around** *the corner,* **down** *the alley,* **into** *the arms* **of** *the waiting police officers.* (prepositional phrases)
- Some people handle a crisis by avoiding it, **ignoring** *the problem until someone else solves it.* (participle phrase)
- The early settlers moved west **to escape** *an unsavory or difficult past,* **to forge** *a new life,* **to realize** *dreams.* (infinitive phrases)

The point is to find ways to vary your sentences to increase interest and rhythm.

Intentional Fragments

A fragment is a part of a sentence that is capitalized and punctuated as if it were a complete sentence.

Although fragments are seldom used in formal prose, they form the backbone of most conversations. Here's how a typical bit of dialogue might go:

"Where are you going tonight?" (*sentence*)
"To Woodland Mall." (*fragment*)
"What for?" (*fragment*)
"To buy some shoes." (*fragment*)
"Alone?" (*fragment*)
"No, with Maisie Perkins." (*fragment*)
"Can I come too?" (*sentence*)
"Sure." (*fragment*)

As with most conversations, the sprinkling of complete sentences makes the fragments clear.

Writers of nonfiction use fragments to create special effects. In the following passage, the fragment emphasizes the importance of the question it asks and varies the pace of the writing:

> Before kidney transplants, people had an ethical unease about renal dialysis—the artificial kidney machine. Unquestionably it was a great technical advance making it possible to treat kidney dysfunctions from which thousands die. But the machine was, and is, expensive and involves intensive care of the patient by doctors and nurses. For whom the machine? In the United States the dilemma was evaded but not solved by having lay panels, like juries, making life-or-death choices. In Britain, where the National Health Service entitles everyone, rich or poor, to have access to any necessary treatment, the responsibility rests on the medical staff. It was (and still is) a difficult decision.
>
> Lord Ritchie-Calder, "The Doctor's Dilemma"

Once in a while, as in the following example, a writer will use a whole series of fragments. In the following paragraph, they create a kaleidoscopic effect that mirrors the kaleidoscopic impressions offered by the Jazz Age itself.

> The Jazz Age offers a kaleidoscope of shifting impressions. Of novelties quickly embraced and quickly discarded. Of flappers flaunting bobbed hair and short skirts. Of hip flasks and bootleg whisky, fast cars and coonskin coats, jazz and dancing till dawn. And overall a sense of futility, an uneasy conviction that all the gods were dead.
>
> Elliott L. Smith and Andrew W. Hart,
> *The Short Story: A Contemporary Looking Glass*

PERSPECTIVE
Coordination and subordination are not merely important ways of structuring sentences. Encouraging students to coordinate or subordinate helps them understand the logical relationships among their ideas. Sentence combining is an effective way of exposing students to more mature syntax. Although sentence-combining texts are available, exercises are easy to prepare: Simply break any more complicated sentence into basic simple sentences. Two cautions, however, need mentioning. First, sentence combining can result in excessively cumbersome sentences; students should always evaluate the quality of those they produce in light of clarity and stylistic effectiveness. Second, students who attempt more complex structures probably will commit the errors associated with them. Reassure students that these errors stem from the attempt to grow and are only temporary.

TEACHING STRATEGY
Using sentence-combining techniques, start with simple sentences that have a relationship that can be demonstrated through coordination and subordination. Ask the class to determine ways of establishing the relationship, and then introduce the structure you wish to teach. For example, "The dance was over. Arthur collapsed on the sofa." might become "After

the dance was over, Arthur collapsed on the sofa." Have students try to explain what is gained conceptually and stylistically by the new sentence.

SUGGESTED INSTRUCTOR READING
O'Hare, F. Sentence-Combining: Improving Student Writing Without Formal Grammar Instruction. Urbana, IL: NCTE, 1973. Perhaps the most effective introduction to the sentence-combining technique.

PERSPECTIVE
Because students encounter fragments in professional as well as informal and artistic writing, any attempt to forbid them on the grounds of "standard practice" soon crashes into reality. Whether fragments are acceptable is a complex matter involving the type of writing and kind of fragments. Generally, fragments are more acceptable in informal writing but even then only if they are extremely clear. Whether to allow "intentional" fragments in student writing depends, of course, on your attitude and your class. Overall, it may be best to acknowledge the use of fragments but caution against them until students first master complete sentences.

TEACHING STRATEGIES
1. You could open the discussion of fragments with a statement such as "If you want to get a good grade

Before using any fragment in your own writing, think carefully about your intended effect and explore other ways of achieving it. Unless only a fragment will serve your needs, don't use one; fragments are likely to be viewed as unintentional—and thus errors—in the work of inexperienced writers.

The following passage includes one or more fragments. Identify each and explain its function.

He [Richard Wagner] wrote operas; and no sooner did he have the synopsis of a story, but he would invite—or rather summon—a crowd of his friends to his house and read it aloud to them. Not for criticism. For applause. When the complete poem was written, the friends had to come again, and hear *that* read aloud. Then he would publish the poem, sometimes years before the music that went with it was written. He played the piano like a composer, in the worst sense of what that implies, and he would sit down at the piano before parties that included some of the finest pianists of his time, and play for them, by the hour, his own music, needless to say. He had a composer's voice. And he would invite eminent vocalists to his house, and sing them his operas, taking all the parts.

Deems Taylor, "The Monster"

Working together, these techniques provide varied sentences that create interest. In the following paragraph, the sentences differ considerably in length.

To protest that some fairly improbable people, some people who could not possibly respect themselves, seem to sleep easily enough is to miss the point entirely, as surely as those people miss it who think that self-respect has necessarily to do with not having safety pins in one's underwear. There is a common superstition that "self-respect" is a kind of charm against snakes, something that keeps those who have it locked in some unblighted Eden, out of strange beds, ambivalent conversations, and trouble in general. It does not at all. It has nothing to do with the face of things, but concerns instead a separate peace, a private reconciliation.

Joan Didion, "On Self-Respect"

Much of the appealing rhythm of this passage stems from varied sentence length. The first two rather long sentences (forty-nine and thirty-six words) are followed by the very brief "It does not at all," which gains emphasis by its position. The last sentence adds variety by means of its moderate length (nineteen words), quite apart from its interesting observation on the real nature of self-respect.

Varying sentence length can help you emphasize a key idea. If a key point is submerged in a long sentence, highlight it as a separate thought, giving it the recognition it deserves.

Original Version

Employers find mature women to be valuable members of their organizations. They are conscientious, have excellent attendance records, and stay calm when things go awry, *but unfortunately many employers exploit them.* Despite their desirable qualities, most remain mired in clerical, sales, and elementary teaching positions. On the average they earn two-thirds as much as men.

Revised Version

    Employers find mature women to be valuable members of their organizations. They are conscientious, have excellent attendance records, and stay calm when things go awry. *Unfortunately, many employers exploit them.* Despite their desirable qualities, most remain mired in clerical, sales, and elementary teaching positions. On the average they earn two-thirds as much as men.

Using coordination and subordination, rewrite the following passages to reduce words and/or improve smoothness.

1. He played the piano. He played the organ. He played the French horn. He did not play the viola.
2. The weather was icy cold and windy. Lee was wearing only a T-shirt and athletic shorts.
3. Life on Venus may be possible. It will not be the kind of life we know on Earth. Life on Mars may be possible. It will not be the kind of life we know on Earth.
4. He felt his classmates were laughing at his error. He ran out of the room. He vowed never to return to that class.
5. Albert lay in bed. He stared at the ceiling. Albert thought about the previous afternoon. He had asked Kathy to go to dinner with him. She is a pretty, blond-haired woman. She sits at the desk next to his. They work at Hemphill's. She had refused.
6. I went to the store to buy a box of detergent. I saw Bill there, and we talked about last night's game.
7. Tim went to the newsstand. He bought a magazine there. While he was on the way home, he lost it. He had nothing to read.

Varying Word Order

What other tools do you have to create more interesting prose? One powerful technique is to vary word order in a sentence.

Word Order in Independent Clauses

Most independent clauses follow a similar arrangement. First comes the subject, then the verb, and finally any other element needed to convey the main message.

    Barney blushed. (*subject, verb*)

    They built the dog a kennel. (*subject, verb, indirect object, direct object*)

    Samantha is an architect. (*subject, verb, subject complement*)

This arrangement puts the emphasis on the subject, right where it's usually wanted.

    But the pattern doesn't work in every situation. Occasionally, a writer wants to emphasize some element that follows the verb, create an artistic effect, or give the subject unusual emphasis. Enter inverted order and the expletive construction.

on the final exam" and then stop. Puzzled looks will, of course, abound. When someone asks for the missing information, acknowledge the fragment and tell the class that written fragments often create the same confusion as your oral one just did.

2. Have students check textbooks, newspaper and magazine articles, and advertisements for fragments. Where do they occur most frequently? Why are they used? Are they effective?

3. Break a formal text, such as a piece of business correspondence, into fragments and have students read the result and assess the competence of the author. Then provide them with the original and ask for a reassessment.

EXERCISE ANSWERS
The fragments are "Not for criticism. For applause." These fragments give added emphasis to why Wagner summoned his friends and also highlight his egotism.

SUGGESTED INSTRUCTOR READING
Kline, C. R., Jr., and W. D. Memering. "Formal Fragments: The English Minor Sentence." <u>Research in the Teaching of English</u> 11 (1977): 97–110. Provides a useful catalog of the conditions under which fragments are effectively used.

Inverted Order   To invert a sentence, move to the front the element you want to emphasize. Sometimes the rest of the sentence follows in regular subject-then-verb order; sometimes the verb precedes the subject.

Lovable he isn't. (*subject complement, subject, verb*)
This I just don't understand. (*direct object, subject, verb*)
Tall grow the pines in the mountains. (*subject complement, verb, subject*)

Sentences that ask questions typically follow an inverted pattern.

Is this your coat? (*verb, subject, subject complement*)
Will you let the cat out? (*verb, subject, verb, direct object*)

Most of your sentences should follow normal order: Readers expect it and read most easily through it. Furthermore, don't invert a sentence if the result would sound strained and unnatural. A sentence like "Fools were Brett and Amanda for quitting college" will only hinder communication.

Expletives   An expletive fills a vacancy in a sentence without contributing to the meaning. English has two common expletives, *there* and *it*. Ordinarily, *there* functions as an adverb, *it* as a pronoun, and either can appear anywhere in a sentence. As expletives, however, they alter normal sentence order by beginning sentences and anticipating the real subjects or objects.

Expletives are often used unnecessarily, as in the following example:

There were twenty persons attending the sales meeting.

This sentence errs on two counts: Its subject needs no extra emphasis, and it is very clumsy. Notice the improvement without the expletive and the unneeded words:

Twenty persons attended the sales meeting.

When the subject or object needs highlighting, leading off with an expletive will, by altering normal order, call it more forcefully to the reader's attention.

Normal order: A fly is in my soup.
He seeks her happiness.

Expletive construction: There is a fly in my soup. (*expletive anticipating subject*)
It is her happiness he seeks. (*expletive anticipating object*)

Once in a while you'll find that something just can't be said unless you use an expletive.

There is no reason for such foolishness.

No other construction can express exactly the same thought.

Indicate which of these sentences follow normal order, which are inverted, and which have expletive constructions. Rewrite so that all will be in normal order.

1. Dick Lewis is a true friend.
2. It was her car in the ditch.
3. An intelligent person is she.
4. May I go to the movie with you?
5. A sadder but wiser man he became.
6. There are many dead fish on the beach.
7. The instructor gave the class a long reading assignment.
8. The Willetts have bought a new house.
9. It is Marianne's aim to become a lawyer.
10. Harry works at a supermarket.

Positioning of Movable Modifiers

Movable modifiers can appear on either side of the main statement or within it.

Modifiers after Main Statement   Sentences that follow this arrangement, frequently called *loose sentences*, occur more commonly than either of the others. They mirror conversation, in which a speaker first makes a statement and then adds further thoughts. Often, the main statement has just one modifier.

> Our company will have to file for bankruptcy *because of this year's huge losses*. (*phrase as modifier*)

Or it can head up a whole train of modifiers.

> He burst suddenly into the party, *loud, angry, obscene*. (*words as modifiers*)

> The family used to gather around the hearth, *doing such chores as polishing shoes, mending ripped clothing, reading, chatting, always warmed by one another's presence as much as by the flames*. (*words and phrases as modifiers*)

A sentence may contain several layers of modifiers. In the following example, we've indented and numbered to show the different layers.

1. The men struggled to the top of the hill,
   2. thirsty,
   2. drenched in sweat,
   2. and cursing in pain
      3. as their knapsack straps cut into their raw, chafed shoulders
         4. with every step.

In this sentence, the items numbered 2 refer to *men* in the item numbered 1. Item 3 is linked to *cursing* in the preceding item 2, and item 4 is linked to *cut* in item 3.

The modifiers-last arrangement works well for injecting descriptive details into narratives and also for qualifying, explaining, and presenting lists in other kinds of writing.

Modifiers before Main Statement   Sentences that delay the main point until the end are called *periodic*. In contrast to loose sentences, they lend a formal note to what is said, slowing its pace, adding cadence, and making it more serious.

even when all have similar skills, some students will improve slowly, while the sentences of others will quickly start showing more variety and flexibility.

TEACHING STRATEGIES
1. You can teach any of these sentence strategy sections as a separate unit. If you choose this option, don't be surprised by the results. Sometimes when students are introduced to sentence structure, they make more errors as they try to understand new options. Furthermore, some students, baffled by an abstract account of what they have done unconsciously, will simply ignore your instruction.
2. Have students review several types of writing to see what word order predominates. They will probably discover that academic writing tends to include many expletives, and poetic writing contains more inverted-order sentences than do other types. Otherwise, standard subject–verb–object patterns predominate.
3. To demonstrate the importance of word order in English, you might select a paragraph, scramble the word order in several of its sentences, then have students read the paragraph and indicate why they are having problems understanding it. Students could then try to reconstruct the scrambled sentences and note how their changes improve clarity.

If you can keep your head when everyone around you is panicking, you probably don't understand the situation. (*clauses as modifiers*)

The danger of sideswiping another vehicle, the knowledge that a hidden bump or hole could throw me from the dune buggy, both of these things added to the thrill of the race. (*noun plus phrase and noun plus clause as modifiers*)

1. *When the public protests,*
2. *confronted with some obvious evidence of the damaging results of pesticide applications,* it is fed little tranquilizing pills of half truth. (*clause and phrase as modifiers*)

Rachel Carson, *Silent Spring*

As shown in the Carson example, periodic sentences can also have layers of modifiers.

Positioning the modifiers before the main point throws the emphasis to the end of the sentence, adding force to the main point. The delay also lets the writer create sentences that, like the first example, carry stings, ironic or humorous, in their tails.

Modifiers within Main Statement   Inserting one or more modifiers into a main statement creates a sentence with *interrupted order*. The material may come between the subject and the verb or between the verb and the rest of the predicate.

The young girl, *wearing a tattered dress and looking anything but well-off herself*, gave the beggar a ten-dollar bill. (*phrases between subject and verb*)

The evolutionists, *piercing beneath the show of momentary stability*, discovered, *hidden in rudimentary organs*, the discarded rubbish of the past. (*one phrase between subject and verb, another between verb and rest of predicate*)

By stretching out the main idea, inserted modifiers slow the forward pace of the sentence, giving it some of the formality and force of a periodic sentence.

EXERCISE

Identify each sentence as loose, periodic, or interrupted. Rewrite each as one of the other kinds.

1. Victoria, rejected by family and friends, uncertain where to turn next, finally decided to start a new life in Chicago.
2. When told that she had to have her spleen removed, the woman gasped.
3. The first graders stood in line, talking and giggling, pushing at one another's caps and pencil boxes and kicking one another's shins, unmindful of the drudgery that awaited them within the old schoolhouse.
4. Good health, warm friends, a beautiful summer evening—the best things cannot be purchased.
5. A customer, angry and perspiring, stormed up to the claims desk.
6. Stopping just short of the tunnel entrance, the freight train avoided a collision with the crowded commuter train stalled inside.
7. The new kid hammered away at the fading champ, determination in his eyes and glory in his fists.
8. The new tract house sparkled in the sunlight, pink and trim, its lawn immaculate, its two bushes and newly planted crab apple tree, by their very tininess, making the yard look vaster than its actual size.

Building Rhythm

Effective sentences have patterns of organization that help convey meaning while assisting the readers in following the text. Poor organization, even if grammatical, is usually awkward.

Using Parallelism

Parallelism presents equivalent ideas in grammatically equivalent form. Dressing them in the same grammatical garb calls attention to their kinship and adds smoothness and polish. The following sentence pairs demonstrate the improvement that parallelism brings:

Nonparallel:	James's outfit was *wrinkled, mismatched,* and *he needed to wash it.* (*words and independent clause*)
Parallel:	James's outfit was *wrinkled, mismatched,* and *dirty.* (*words*)
Nonparallel:	Oscar likes *reading books, attending plays,* and *to search for antiques.* (*different kinds of phrases*)
Parallel:	Oscar likes *reading books, attending plays,* and *searching for antiques.* (*same kind of phrases*)
Nonparallel:	Beth performs her tasks *quickly, willingly,* and *with accuracy.* (*words and phrase*)
Parallel:	Beth performs her tasks *quickly, willingly,* and *accurately* (*words*)

As the examples show, revising nonparallel sentences smooths out bumpiness, binds the ideas together more closely, and lends them a more finished look.

Parallelism doesn't always stop with a single sentence. Writers sometimes use it in a series of sentences:

He had never lost his childlike innocence. He had never lost his sense of wonder. He had never lost his sense of joy in nature's simplest gifts.

For an example of parallelism that extends over much of a paragraph, see page 93.

Balance, a special form of parallelism, positions two grammatically equivalent ideas on opposite sides of some pivot point, such as a word or punctuation mark.

Hope for the best, and prepare for the worst.

Many are called, but few are chosen.

When I'm right, nobody ever notices; when I'm wrong, nobody ever forgets.

The sheep are in the meadow, and the cows are in the corn.

Like regular parallel sentences, balanced sentences sometimes come in series:

The tension in this city is not between white people and Negro people. The tension is, at bottom, between justice and injustice, between the forces of light and the forces of darkness. And if there is a victory, it will be a victory not merely for fifty thousand Negroes, but a victory for justice and the forces of light.

Martin Luther King, Jr., "Pilgrimage to Nonviolence"

environmentalists. Harry Travis, _____, signed a three-year contract with the Boston Celtics.

SUGGESTED INSTRUCTOR READING

Christensen, F. "A Generative Rhetoric of the Sentence." College Composition and Communication 14 (1963): 155–61.

EXERCISE ANSWERS
1. Interrupted order. Rewritten as a periodic sentence: Rejected by family and friends, uncertain where to turn next, Victoria finally decided to start a new life in Chicago.
2. Periodic. Rewritten as a loose sentence: The woman gasped when told that she had to have her spleen removed.
3. Loose. Rewritten as a periodic sentence: Talking and giggling, pushing at one another's caps and pencil boxes, kicking one another's shins, unmindful of the drudgery that awaited them within the old schoolhouse, the first graders stood in line.
4. Periodic. Rewritten in interrupted order: The best things—good health, warm friends, a beautiful summer evening—cannot be purchased.
5. Interrupted. Rewritten as a periodic sentence: Angry and perspiring, a customer stormed up to the claims desk.
6. Periodic. Rewritten in interrupted order: The freight train, stopping just short of the tunnel entrance, avoided a collision with the crowded

commuter train stalled inside.

7. Loose. Rewritten as a periodic sentence: Determination in his eyes and glory in his fists, the new kid hammered away at the fading champ.

8. Loose. Rewritten as a periodic sentence: Pink and trim, its lawn immaculate, its two bushes and newly planted crab apple tree making by their very tininess the yard look vaster than its actual size, the new tract house sparkled in the sunlight.

PERSPECTIVE
The attempt to produce parallel structures can prompt students to ask a rhetorical "What else?" and expand one modifier into a parallel series. As a result, "He cleared the table" can become "He cleared the table, washed the dishes, then put his daughter to bed." In attempting to achieve parallelism, however, students can strain syntax and verb forms. Encourage them to check parallel structures for other faults.

TEACHING STRATEGY
You can encourage students to generate parallel sentences by providing them with fill-in-the-blank exercises like the following: _____ and _____ are essential to every college student. To gain victory our team will _____, _____, and even _____ . Today we celebrate our victories, but tomorrow _____.

Balance works especially well for pitting contrasting or clashing ideas against each other. It sharpens the difference between them while achieving compactness and lending an air of insight to what is said.

Identify each sentence as nonparallel, parallel, or balanced; then rewrite each nonparallel sentence to make it parallel.

1. Professor Bartlett enjoys helping students, counseling advisees, and participation in faculty meetings.
2. I can still see Aunt Alva striding into the corral, cornering a cow against a fencepost, try to balance herself on a one-legged milking stool, and butt her head into the cow's belly.
3. The city plans on building a new fishing pier and on dredging the channel of the river.
4. Elton plans on vacationing in New York, but Noreen wants to raft down the Colorado River.
5. Being half drunk and because he was already late for work, Tom called his boss and said he was too ill to come in that day.
6. The novel's chief character peers through a tangle of long hair, slouches along in a shambling gait, and gets into trouble constantly.
7. You can take the boy out of the country, but you can't take the country out of the boy.
8. Joe's problem is not that he earns too little money but spending it foolishly.
9. The room was dark, gloomy, and everything was dusty.
10. The apparition glided through the wall, across the room, and up the fireplace chimney.

Choosing the Right Verb Voice

A sentence's verb voice derives from the relationship between the subject and the action. A sentence in the *active voice* has a subject that does something plus a verb that shows action.

> The boy hit the target.
>
> The girl painted the garage.

This pattern keeps the key information in the key part of the sentence, making it strong and vigorous and giving the reader a close-up look at the action.

The *passive voice* reverses the subject–action relationship by having the subject receive, rather than perform, the action. It is built around a form of the verb *to be*, for example, *is, are, was, were*. Some sentences identify the actor by using a prepositional phrase; others don't mention the actor at all.

> The target was hit by the boy. (*actor identified*)
>
> The federal debt limit is to be increased. (*actor unidentified*)

Demoting or banishing the actor dilutes the force of the sentence, puts greater distance between the action and the reader, and almost always adds extra words to the message.

Most writers who overuse the passive voice simply don't realize its effects on their writing. Read the following paragraph, written mainly in the passive voice:

> Graft becomes possible when gifts are given to police officers or favors are done for them by persons who expect preferential treatment in return. Gifts of many kinds may be received by officers. Often free meals are given to them by the owners of restaurants on their beats. During the Christmas season, they may be given liquor, food, or theater tickets by merchants. If favored treatment is not received by the donors, no great harm is done. But if traffic offenses, safety code violations, and other infractions are overlooked by the officers, corruption results. When such corruption is exposed by the newspapers, faith is lost in law enforcement agencies.

This impersonal, wordy passage plods across the page and therefore lacks any real, persuasive impact. Now note the livelier, more forceful tone of this rewritten version.

> Graft becomes possible when police officers accept gifts or favors from persons who expect preferential treatment in return. Officers may receive gifts of many kinds. Restaurant owners often provide free meals for officers on the beat. During the Christmas season, merchants may give them liquor, food, or theater tickets. If donors do not receive favored treatment, no great harm is done. But if officers overlook traffic offenses, safety code violations, and other infractions, corruption results. When the newspapers expose such corruption, citizens lose faith in law enforcement agencies.

Don't misunderstand: The passive voice does have its uses. It can mask identities—or at least try to. A child may try to dodge responsibility by saying, "Mother, while you were out, the living room lamp got broken." Less manipulatively, reporters may use it to conceal the identity of a source.

Technical and scientific writing customarily uses the passive voice to explain processes.

> In the production of steel, iron ore is first converted into pig iron by combining it with limestone and coke and then heating the mixture in a blast furnace. Pig iron, however, contains too many impurities to be useful to industry, and as a result must be refined and converted to steel. In the refining process, manganese, silicon, and aluminum are heated with the pig iron in order to degas it, that is, to remove excess oxygen and impurities from it. The manganese, silicon, and aluminum are vaporized while the iron remains in the liquid state and the impurities are carried away by the vapors. Once this step has been completed, the molten steel is poured into ingots and allowed to cool. The steel is now ready for further processing.

Putting such writing in the passive voice provides a desirable objective tone and puts the emphasis where it's most important: on the action, not the actor. On occasion, everyday writing also uses the passive voice.

> The garbage is collected once a week, on Monday.
> These caves were formed about 10 million years ago.

In the first case, there's no need to tell who collects the garbage; obviously, garbage collectors do. In the second, the writer may not know what caused the formation, and saying "Something formed these caves about 10 million years ago" would sound ridiculous. In both situations, the action, not the actor, is paramount.

EXERCISE ANSWERS
1. Nonparallel. Professor Bartlett enjoys helping students, counseling advisees, and participating in faculty meetings.
2. Nonparallel. I can still see Aunt Alva striding into the corral, cornering a cow against a fencepost, trying to balance herself on a one-legged milking stool, and butting her head into the cow's belly.
3. Parallel.
4. Balanced.
5. Nonparallel. Because he was half drunk and because he was already late for work, Tom called his boss and said he was too ill to come in that day.
6. Parallel.
7. Balanced.
8. Nonparallel. Joe's problem is not that he earns too little money but that he spends it foolishly. *Or* Joe's problem is not earning too little money but spending it foolishly.
9. Nonparallel. The room was dark, gloomy, and dusty.
10. Parallel.

PERSPECTIVE
Sometimes the passive voice is not only acceptable but preferred. It is used extensively in scientific, legal, and administrative writing where the doer is often irrelevant or difficult to identify. Because much of what college students read makes extensive use of the passive voice, it seems to them the mark of more advanced writers. No wonder they become confused when we encourage them to write more effective prose but at the same time chide them about using the passive voice.

Unless special circumstances call for the passive voice, however, use the active voice.

After determining whether each sentence below is in active or passive voice, rewrite the passive sentences as active ones.

1. Mary's parents gave her a sports car for her sixteenth birthday.
2. Fires were left burning by negligent campers.
3. The new ice arena will be opened by the city in about two weeks.
4. Harry left the open toolbox out in the rain.
5. Corn was introduced to the Pilgrims by friendly American Indians.
6. Maude took a trip to Sante Fe, New Mexico.
7. We have just installed a new computer in our main office.
8. The club president awarded Tompkins the Order of the Golden Mace.
9. The sound of war drums was heard by the missionaries as they floated down the river.
10. Objections were raised by some members of the legislature to the ratification of the proposed amendment.

Beyond the Single Sentence

What makes a team successful? Skilled players, to be sure, but teamwork as well. Likewise, your sentences need to work together to produce the desired effect. Your content and purpose will guide you in determining how your sentences will work together. You will need to vary sentence length, word order, and rhythms to produce your desired effect; but in a way that is not obvious or clumsy. This takes work. A good place to start is by studying the essays in the Reader to see what kinds of combinations they use—a series of questions that are then answered; long sentences with modifiers that lead to a short sentence that gains emphasis; a series of fragments followed by a long sentence. In your own writing, keep an eye on what kind of sentences you are creating and how those sentences create a pattern. Once you have finished a draft of your paper, read it over, see how its rhythms strike your inner ear, and put check marks by sections that "sound" wrong. Play with your sentences to get the results that you want.

Revise the following passages to improve their style.

1. Andrew Carnegie came to America from Scotland. He worked as a factory hand, a telegrapher, and a railway clerk to support himself. His savings from these jobs were invested in oil and later in the largest steel works in the country. Historians do not agree in their assessments of Carnegie. Some have considered him a cruel taskmaster and others a benevolent benefactor. His contributions to American

society, however, cannot be denied. He established public libraries all across the country and spent much time in promoting peace. Good or bad, he ranks as one of our most noteworthy nineteenth-century immigrants.

2. She went to the seashore. She found some seashells. She picked up the seashells. She put the seashells into a basket. She had a whole basketful of seashells. She went home with the basket. She took the shells out of the basket. She put the shells on a dinette table. She brought jeweler's tools to the table. She pierced holes in the shells. She strung the shells on small chains. The chains were gold and silver. She made twenty necklaces. The selling price of the necklaces was $10 apiece. She earned $175 profit. She used her profits to go to the shore again. She could afford to stay for a week this time.

lished all across the country and his efforts in promoting peace, cannot be denied. Good or bad, he ranks as one of our country's most noteworthy nineteenth-century immigrants.

2. She went to the seashore to hunt for seashells. Whenever she found one, she picked it up and placed it in the basket she carried with her. As soon as she had a whole basketful of shells, she hurried home. Dumping her burden on a dinette table, she grabbed her jeweler's tools and began piercing holes in each of the shells. Then, when all the shells were pierced, she strung them on small gold and silver chains. Eventually she had twenty small necklaces, which she was able to sell for $10 apiece. With the $175 profit she netted, she went off to the shore again. This time she was able to stay for a week.

CHAPTER 7

Diction, Tone, Style

Your decisions about words and sentences set the tone and style of your writing. Not only do you choose sentence strategies for correctness and effectiveness, but you also choose words for accuracy and effect. Sentences must be clear and effective; so must words. Diction deals broadly with words, not in isolation but as parts of sentences, paragraphs, and essays. Every time you write and revise, diction comes into play.

Toward Clear Diction

Clear diction stems from choosing words with the right meanings, using abstract and concrete words appropriately, and picking terms that are neither too specific nor too general. Dictionaries and thesauruses can guide your choices.

Word Meanings

Make sure the words you use mean what you think they do, so that inaccurate words will not distort your message. Sound-alike word pairs often trip up unwary writers. Take *accept* and *except* for example. *Accept* means "to approve." *Except*, when used as a verb, means "to exclude or omit." If you want to indicate approval but you say, "The following new courses were *excepted* by the committee," think of the obvious consequences. Likewise, consider the distinction between *continual* (frequently or regularly repeated) and *continuous* (uninterrupted). If you illustrate your popularity by saying "My phone rings *continuously*," your reader will wonder why you never answer it and how you ever sleep.

114

Concrete and Abstract Words

A concrete word names or describes something that we can perceive with one or more of our five senses. A thing is concrete if we can weigh it, measure it, hold it in our hands, photograph it, taste it, sniff it, add salt to it, drop it, smash into it, or borrow it from a neighbor. If it's abstract, we can't do any of these things. *Eric Clapton* is a concrete term, as are *Swiss cheese, petroleum, maple syrup,* and *Dallas*. On the other hand, *jealousy, power, conservatism, size,* and *sadness* are abstract terms.

Concrete words evoke precise, vivid mental images and thus help convey a message. The images that abstract terms create differ from person to person. Try this test: Ask several of your friends to describe what comes to mind when they think of *joy, hatred, fear,* or some other abstract term. To illustrate, the word *hatred* might call up images of a person with cold, slitted eyes, and a grimly set jaw, for one person and another image for a different person. As you can see, concrete terms help us specify what we mean and thus enhance communication.

In the following passage, the concrete diction is italicized:

> To do without self-respect . . . is to be an unwilling *audience of one* to an interminable *documentary* that details one's failings, both real and imagined, with *fresh footage spliced* in for every *screening*. There's *the glass you broke* in anger, there's *the hurt on X's face; watch now, this next scene, the night Y came back from Houston,* see how you muff this one. To live without self-respect is to *lie awake some night,* beyond the reach of *warm milk, phenobarbital,* and *the sleeping hand on the coverlet,* counting up the sins of commission and omission, the trusts betrayed, the promises subtly broken, the gifts irrevocably wasted through sloth or cowardice or carelessness. However long we postpone it, we eventually lie down alone in that notoriously *uncomfortable bed,* the one we make ourselves. Whether or not we sleep in it depends, of course, on whether or not we respect ourselves.
>
> Joan Didion, "On Self-Respect"

Now note how vague and colorless the passage becomes without the concrete diction:

> To do without self-respect is to be continuously aware of your failings, both real and imagined. Incidents stay in your mind long after they are over. To live without self-respect means being bothered by intentional or unintentional failings, trusts betrayed, promises subtly broken, and gifts irrevocably wasted through sloth or cowardice or carelessness. However long we postpone it, we eventually must come to terms with who we are. How we respond to this situation depends, of course, on whether or not we respect ourselves.

Underline the concrete terms in the following passage:

The fog which rises from the river has no color, no texture, no taste, smell, or sound. It is sheer vision, a vision of purity, a slow, mesmeric, inexorable erasure of the slate. You see fog mushrooming along the river's course. Gently, it obliterates the alders tangled on the banks, wipes out the road. Buildings without foundations,

out of context but not explain, (3) understand and explain, (4) use productively. We should encourage students to learn new words and help them understand the nuances and appropriate contexts of those they already know.

TEACHING STRATEGIES

1. Have students review their essays, circle any words that are improperly used, and then make appropriate substitutions.

2. Ask students to record in their journals new words they encounter, along with their contexts and definitions.

3. Pages 719–740 list and explain commonly confused words. If your students are using the version of this book that includes a Handbook, suggest that they refer to this list as they revise and use a dictionary if they have any doubt about meaning.

SUGGESTED INSTRUCTOR READINGS

Halliday, M. A. K. <u>Learning How to Mean: Explorations in the Development of Language.</u> London: Arnold, 1975. A seminal account of how we acquire mastery over language.

Smith, F. <u>Writing and the Writer.</u> Mahwah, NJ: L. Erlbaum Assoc., 1994. Provides a good psycholinguistic account of the writing process. Chapters 4 and 5 concentrate on the nature of language and language learning.

trees without trunks, hang in the air like mirages. Sun may be shining brightly on them, or rain drenching them, or stars twinkling above or among them. Slowly the fog reaches higher and spreads. Ridgepoles, small topmost branches, and your own dooryard vanish. There is nothing left now but shining mist. It is all, and you float on it, utterly alone, as one imagines he might in empty space if flung off by earth; as the mind does, drifting into sleep; as the spirit does, having escaped its mortal frame.

Gladys Hasty Carroll, *Sing Out the Glory*

Specific and General Terms

One concrete term can be more specific or more general than another. As we move from *Lassie* to *collie* to *dog* to *mammal* and finally to *animal*, we become less and less specific, ending with a term that encompasses every animal on earth. With each step we retain only those features that fit the more general term. Thus, when we move from *collie* to *dog*, we leave out everything that makes collies different from terriers, greyhounds, and other breeds.

The more specific the term, the less difference among the images it calls to mind. If you say *animal* to a group of friends, one may think of a dog, another of a horse, and a third of a gorilla. *Collie,* on the other hand, triggers images of a large, long-haired, brown and white dog with a pointed muzzle.

Ask yourself how specific you need to be and then act accordingly. Often, the more specific term will be the better choice. If, for instance, you're describing a wealthy jet-setter, noting that he drives a Ferrari, not just a car, helps establish his character. But if you're writing a narrative about your flight to New Orleans and your experience at Mardi Gras, nothing is gained by naming the make of car you rented and used uneventfully during your stay.

EXERCISE

1. **Arrange each set of words from less specific to more specific.**

    a. man, ex-President, human being, Bill Clinton, American
    b. Forest Hills Apartments, building, structure, condominium, dwelling
2. **Expand each of the following words into a series of four or more that become progressively more specific. Use 1a or 1b as a pattern.**

    a. activity
    b. event
    c. political party
    d. institution
    e. device
    f. reading matter

Dictionaries and Thesauruses

Get the dictionary habit and learn to use a thesaurus. These will increase your vocabulary as well as your skill at using words you already know.

Dictionaries Dictionaries are storehouses of word meanings. In general, dictionary makers do not try to dictate how words should be used. Instead, they note current and past meanings. When a word gains or loses a meaning or a newly minted word enjoys wide circulation, dictionary makers observe and record. Most users, however, regard dictionaries as authorities on correctness.

Dictionaries supply much more than word meanings. Figure 7.1, an annotated entry from a college-level dictionary, shows what they can provide. Some dictionary entries include idioms, irregular forms of words, usage labels, and supplementary information, as well.

Idioms Idioms express meanings that differ from those of the words that make them up. Here are two examples.

I won't *put up with* any foolishness.

The dowager *gave me the cold shoulder.*

Put up with means "tolerate"; *gave me the cold shoulder* means "snubbed me." Looking up the most prominent word of an unfamiliar idiom may lead you to a listing and a definition.

Irregular Forms Any irregular forms are indicated. In *Webster's New World Dictionary,* the entry for the verb *spring* notes that the other forms are *sprang, sprung,* and *springing.* This information helps you use correct forms in your writing.

Usage Labels Usage labels help you determine whether a word suits the circumstances of your writing. Here are the most common labels:

Label	Meaning
Colloquial	Characteristic of informal writing and speaking; should not be considered nonstandard.
Slang	Informal, newly coined words and expressions or old expressions with new meanings.
Obsolete	No longer in use but found in past writing.
Archaic	Still finds restricted use, for example, in legal documents; otherwise not appropriate.
Poetic	Used only in poetry and in prose with a poetic tone.
Dialect	Used regularly only in a particular geographical location such as the southeastern United States or the Scottish Lowlands.

Supplementary Information While focusing primarily on individual words, college-level dictionaries often provide several other kinds of information. They may include a history of the language, lists of standard abbreviations and of colleges and universities, biographical notes on distinguished individuals, and geographical notes on important locations.

2. Have students attempt to define an abstract term like *self-respect,* perhaps by determining its relation to other abstract terms or providing a list of abstract characteristics associated with it. They might, for example, consider the relation of self-respect to self-love and self-awareness.

EXERCISE ANSWER

The *fog* which rises from the *river* has no color, no texture, no taste, smell, or sound. It is sheer vision, a vision of purity, a slow mesmeric, inexorable erasure of the *slate.* You see *fog* mushrooming along the *river's course.* Gently, it obliterates the *alders* tangled on the *banks,* wipes out the *road. Buildings* without *foundations, trees* without *trunks,* hang in the *air* like *mirages. Sun* may be shining brightly on them, or *rain* drenching them, or *stars* twinkling above or among them. Slowly the *fog* reaches higher and spreads. *Ridgepoles,* small topmost *branches,* and your own *dooryard* vanish. There is nothing left now but shining *mist.* It is all, and you float on it, utterly alone, as one imagines he might in empty space if flung off by *earth*; as the mind does, drifting into sleep; as the spirit does, having escaped its mortal *frame.*

EXERCISE ANSWERS

1 a. Human being, man, American, ex-President, Bill Clinton

b. Structure, building, dwelling, condominium, Forest Hills Apartments

2 a. activity, sport, skiing, water skiing

b. event, meeting, stock-holders' meeting, GM stockholders' meeting

c. organization, political party, British political party, Labour Party

d. institution, school, college, Kendall College

e. thing, device, TV, Sony TV

f. reading matter, book, novel, *From Here to Eternity*

PERSPECTIVE

We give students the right message if we require them to purchase and use a dictionary. When they misuse a word in their writing, refer them to the dictionary rather than supply the appropriate definition.

TEACHING STRATEGIES

1. Have students create dictionary entries for modern slang expressions not yet included in most dictionaries (retro, diss). Students will have to familiarize themselves with actual dictionary entries before they compile their own.

2. Few students know the versatility of dictionaries. Have them examine the origins of words in order to gain new insights into their meaning. Or have students use the *OED* to trace the changes in the usage of words like *husband*. Then ask them to suggest possible reasons for the changes.

3. Many students regard dictionary entries as unchanging and absolute. To dispel this notion, have students compare how different dictionaries define the same word, especially

Spelling, Syllabication. When a word has variant spellings, some dictionaries indicate a preferred version. Alphabetically close variants appear in the same entry. Dots or hyphens separate syllables and tell where to divide a word written on two lines.

Pronunciation. Dictionaries indicate preferred as well as secondary pronunciations. Accent marks (´) show which syllable gets the primary stress and which the secondary stress, if any. To determine the pronunciation, follow the key at the bottom of the page.

Parts of Speech. Each word is classified by grammatical function. Usually, abbreviations such as *n* (noun), *adj.* (adjective), and *vt.* (transitive verb) identify the part of speech.

Etymology. This term means the origin and development of words. Most college dictionaries limit the entry to the root (original) word and an abbreviation for the original language. The abbreviation key near the front of the dictionary identifies the language.

man·i·fold (man´ ə fōld´) *adj.* [ME. see MANY & -FOLD] 1. having many and various forms, features, parts, etc. *[manifold wisdom]* 2. of many sorts; many and varied; multifarious: used with a plural noun *[manifold duties.]* 3. being such in many and various ways or for many reasons *[a manifold villain]* 4. comprising, consisting of, or operating several units or parts of one kind: said of certain devices —*n.* 1. something that is manifold 2. a pipe with one inlet and several outlets or with one outlet and several inlets, for connecting with other pipes, as, in an automobile, for conducting exhausts from each cylinder into a single exhaust pipe —*vt.* 1. to make manifold; multiply 2. to make more than one copy of *[to manifold a letter with carbon paper]* —*SYN.* see MANY —**man´i·fold´er** *n.* —**man´i·fold´ly** *adv.* —**man´i·fold´ness** *n.*

[< OE. *manigfeald:*]

MANIFOLD
(A. manifold; B. cylinders)

Additional Word Formations. These are words derived from the one being defined. Their parts of speech are also indicated. Because they have the same basic meaning as the parent word, definitions are omitted.

Meanings. Meanings are grouped by parts of speech. Sometimes usage is briefly illustrated (*manifold* duties). Some dictionaries list meanings in historical order, others according to frequency of use. The front part of the dictionary specifies the arrangement.

Synonyms. These are words close in meaning to the one being defined. Although no synonym carries exactly the same meaning as the original, the two may be interchangeable in some situations.

Figure 7.1 From *Webster's New World Dictionary of the American Language,* Third College Edition

Any dictionary is better than none, but some clearly outrank others in usefulness. A pocket dictionary is handy but not as comprehensive as a desk dictionary. Excellent desk-sized dictionaries include the following:

The American Heritage Dictionary
Funk and Wagnall's Standard College Dictionary

The Random House Dictionary of the English Language
Merriam-Webster's Collegiate Dictionary
Webster's New World Dictionary of the American Language

Unabridged (complete) dictionaries such as *Webster's Third New International Dictionary* and the *Oxford English Dictionary* can be found in college and public libraries. There you'll also find a variety of specialized dictionaries. Your librarian can direct you to dictionaries that list terms in particular fields.

Use a good desk dictionary to look up the specified information for each of the following lists of words:

1. Variant spellings:

airplane	aesthete	gray	tornadoes
color	gaily	theater	usable

2. Syllabication and the syllable that receives the main stress:

anacrusis	cadenza	harbinger	misanthrope
baccalaureate	exclamation	ionize	sequester

3. Parts of speech:

before	fair	separate	to
deep	here	then	where

4. Etymology:

carnival	Icarian	phenomenon	supercilious
fiduciary	lethargy	sabotage	tawdry

5. Idiomatic phrases:

beat	get	jump	put
eat	high	make	set

6. Synonyms:

attack	ghastly	mercy	plot
distress	keep	object	range

Thesauruses   Thesauruses list synonyms for words but omit the other elements in dictionary entries. Figure 7.2 shows a typical entry. Note that the items are grouped according to parts of speech, and some are cross-indexed.

A thesaurus will help you find a word with just the right shade of meaning or a synonym when you want to avoid repetition. But synonyms are never exactly equal, nor are they always interchangeable. To illustrate, *old* means "in existence or use for a long time"; *antiquated* conveys the notion that something is old-fashioned or outdated. Therefore, use the thesaurus along with the dictionary. Only then can you tell which synonym fits a specific sentence.

Excellent guides to synonyms include the following:

Roget's International Thesaurus
Webster's New Dictionary of Synonyms
Modern Guide to Synonyms and Related Words

one likely to generate controversy, such as *communist* or *feminist*. Similarly, students could trace the changes in the definition of such a word through successive editions of the same dictionary. They will come to appreciate the role of history and individual perceptions in shaping word definitions.

EXERCISE ANSWERS

1. Variant spellings: aeroplane, colour, esthete, gayly, grey, theatre, tornados, useable

2. Syllabication and the syllable that receives the main stress: an-a-*cru*-sis, bac-ca-*lau*-re-ate, ca-*den*-za, ex-cla-*ma*-tion, *har*-bin-ger, *i*-on-ize, *mis*-an-thrope, se-*ques*-ter

3. Parts of speech:

■ *before* (adverb, preposition, conjunction)

■ *deep* (adjective, noun, adverb)

■ *fair* (adjective, adverb, noun)

■ *here* (adverb, interjection, noun)

■ *separate* (verb, adjective, noun)

■ *then* (adverb, adjective, noun)

■ *to* (preposition, adverb); also serves as sign of infinitive (*to* run)

■ *where* (adverb, conjunction, pronoun)

4. Etymology:

■ *carnival*—based on the French *carnaval* or Italian *carnevale*, which in turn are derived from the Middle Latin *carnelevarium*, meaning "to remove meat."

■ *fiduciary*—based on the Latin *fiducarius*, which is derived from the Latin *fiducia*, meaning "trust" and "thing held in trust." *Fiducia* in turn derives from the Latin *fidere*, meaning "to trust."

- *Icarian*—based on the Latin *Icarus*, which is derived from the Greek *Ikaros*.

- *lethargy*—based on the Middle English *litarge*, which is derived from the late Latin *lethargia*. This term in turn derives from the Greek *lethargos*, meaning "forgetful."

- *phenomenon*—based on the late Latin *phaenomenon*, which is derived from the Greek *phainesthai*, meaning "to appear." The latter word is related to the Greek *phainein*, meaning "fantasy."

- *sabotage*—based on the French word *sabot*, which designates a kind of wooden shoe. In the past, workers used sabots to damage machines during

247. FORMLESSNESS

.1 NOUNS **formlessness, shapelessness;** amorphousness, amorphism, amorphia; **chaos,** confusion, messiness, orderlessness; disorder 62; entropy; anarchy 740.2; **indeterminateness, indefiniteness,** indecisiveness, vagueness, mistiness, haziness, fuzziness, blurriness, unclearness, obscurity.

.2 unlicked cub, diamond in the rough.

.3 VERBS **deform, distort** 249.5; unform, unshape; disorder, jumble, mess up, muddle, confuse; obfuscate, obscure, fog up, blur.

.4 ADJS **formless, shapeless,** featureless, characterless, nondescript, inchoate, lumpen, blobby *or* baggy [both informal], inform: amorphous, amorphic, amorph(o)-: **chaotic, orderless,** disorderly 62.13, unordered, unorganized, confused, anarchic 740.6; kaleidoscopic; **indeterminate, indefinite,** undefined, indecisive, vague, misty, hazy, fuzzy, blurred *or* blurry, unclear, obscure.

.5 **unformed, unshaped,** unshapen, unfashioned, unlicked; uncut, unhewn.

Figure 7.2   From *Roget's International Thesaurus*, 5th edition, Peter Mark Roget. Copyright © 1992 by HarperCollins Publishers, Inc. Reprinted by permission of HarperCollins Publishers, Inc.

---

times of labor strife, hence the present meaning of *sabotage*.

- *supercilious*—based on the Latin *supercilium*, meaning "eyebrow." The term refers to the raised eyebrows of someone who is prideful or contemptuous of others.

- *tawdry*—based on the name St. Audrey, with special reference to the cheap laces sold at St. Audrey's fair in Norwich, England.

5. Idiomatic phrases:

- *beat*: beat (about, back, down, it, off, out, up [on], the band, on the beat)

- *ear*: be all ears, bend an ear, fall on deaf ears, lend an ear, keep an ear to the ground, have someone's ear, in one ear and out the

Toward Rhetorical Effect

Rhetorical effect refers to the response that the manner of writing, not the message, generates in the reader. Successful writers create a desired response through the level of their diction and the tone of their writing.

Level of Diction

What level of diction is best? The answer depends on the writer's audience and purpose. Think about a safety engineer who investigates a serious industrial accident on which she must write two reports, one for the safety director of the company, who represents a technical audience, and another for the local newspaper, read by a general audience. Although the two accounts would deal with the same matter, clearly they would use very different language: specialized and formal in the first case, everyday and more relaxed in the second. In each case, the language would reflect the background of the audience. As you write, always choose language suited to your audience and purpose.

Edited American English follows the familiar grammatical rules maintained in most formal and academic writing. Generally, everything you write for college courses or on the job should be in edited American English. *Nonstandard English* refers to any version of the language that deviates from these rules.

Here is an example from Mark Twain's famous novel *The Adventures of Huckleberry Finn:*

> You don't know about me without you have read a book by the name of *The Adventures of Tom Sawyer,* but that ain't no matter. That book was made by Mr. Mark Twain, and he told the truth, mainly. There was things which he stretched, but mainly he told the truth. That is nothing. I never seen anybody but lied one time or another, without it was Aunt Polly, or the widow, or maybe Mary. Aunt Polly—Tom's Aunt Polly, she is—and Mary, and the Widow Douglas is all told about in that book, which is mostly a true book, with some stretchers, as I said before.

Nonstandard English does have a place in writing. Fiction writers use it to narrate the talk of characters who, if real, would speak that way. Journalists use it to report eyewitness reactions to accidents and crimes, and people who compile oral histories use it to record the recollections of people they interview.

Edited American English includes four levels of usage: formal, informal, formal–informal, and technical. Another commonly recognized category is colloquial language and slang.

Formal Level

Formal Level   The formal level, dignified and serious, is suitable for important political, business, and academic occasions. Its vocabulary is marked by many abstract and multisyllabic words but no slang or contractions. Long sentences and deliberately varied sentence patterns help give it a strong, rhythmic flow. Sentences are often periodic, and many have parallel or balanced structures. (See pages 109–110.) Overall, formal prose impresses the reader as authoritative, stately, and graceful.

The following excerpts from John F. Kennedy's inaugural address illustrate the formal level:

> Now the trumpet summons us again—not as a call to bear arms, though arms we need; not as a call to battle, though embattled we are; but a call to bear the burden of a long twilight struggle, year in and year out, "rejoicing in hope, patient in tribulation," a struggle against the common enemies of man: tyranny, poverty, disease, and war itself.
>
> In the long history of the world, only a few generations have been granted the role of defending freedom in its hour of maximum danger. I do not shrink from this responsibility; I welcome it. I do not believe that any of us would exchange places with any other people or any other generation. The energy, the faith, the devotion which we bring to this endeavor will light our country and all who serve it, and the glow from that fire can truly light the world.
>
> And so, my fellow Americans, ask not what your country can do for you; ask what you can do for your country.

The first sentence opens with parallelism to show contrast: "not as a call to bear arms, though arms we need" and "not as a call to battle, though embattled we are." In the second paragraph, parallelism in the second sentence shows contrast; in the last sentence it does not. Except for the second sentence in paragraph 2, all of the sentences are periodic rather than loose. Thus, not until the end of the opening sentence do we learn the nature of the "long twilight struggle"

other, play (it) by ear, set on its ear, turn a deaf ear

- *get:* get (about, across, after, along, around, around to, at, to, away, away with, back at, behind, by, down [to, from], in, together, it, nowhere, off, on with, out of, over, through, up)

- *high:* high and dry, high and low, high and mighty, high on, high, wide, and handsome, on high

- *jump:* jump (a claim, at, bail, in with both feet, off, on [all over], the track, get the jump on)

- *make:* make (a fool of, a meal on, as if, away with, believe, do, it, like, off [with], or break, out, over, up, up to, with, on the make)

- *put:* put (about, across, ahead, aside, away, back, down, forth, forward, in [for], in on, over [on], it there, off, on [to], out, through, up, upon, up with)

- *set:* set (about, against, apart, aside, back, down, forth, in, off, out, straight, to, up, upon, all set)

6. Synonyms:
- *attack* (assail, assault, beset, bombard, storm)
- *distress* (agony, anguish, suffering)
- *ghastly* (grim, grisly, gruesome, horrible, macabre, terrible)
- *keep* (reserve, retain, withhold)
- *mercy* (charity, clemency, kindness, leniency)
- *object* (demur, expostulate, protest, demonstrate)
- *plot* (cabal, conspiracy, intrigue, machination, scheme)
- *range* (compass, gamut, reach, scope, spectrum)

to which "the trumpet summons us." Time and again Kennedy uses elevated diction—polysyllabic words like *embattled, rejoicing, tribulation, tyranny, poverty, generations, devotion,* and *endeavor,* along with shorter abstract words like *hope, freedom,* and *faith.* These carefully controlled sentence patterns, along with this wording, lend rhythmical dignity to the whole passage.

Informal Level   Informal writing resembles orderly, intelligent conversation. Earmarked by relatively ordinary words, loose sentences, and numerous shorter, less varied sentence structures than formal prose, informal writing may include contractions or even slang, and it is more likely than formal writing to use the pronouns *I, me, my, you,* and *yours.* Casual and familiar rather than dignified and rhythmic, informal writing does not usually call attention to itself. Nevertheless, the language is precise and effective. Here is an example:

> There was a distressing story in the paper a few months ago. I wish I'd clipped it out and saved it. As it is, I can only hope I remember it fairly accurately. There was a group of people who wanted a particular dictionary removed from the shelves of the local library because it contained a lot of obscenity. I think they said there were sixty-five or so dirty words in it. Some poor woman who was acting as a spokesman for the group had a list of offending words, which she started to read aloud at a hearing. She managed to read about twenty of them before she started sobbing uncontrollably and couldn't continue.
>
> Thomas H. Middleton, "The Magic Power of Words"

Unlike the Kennedy excerpt, this one has relatively uncomplicated sentences. Three of them—the fourth, sixth, and seventh—are loose rather than periodic. The passage includes two contractions, *I'd* and *couldn't,* one casual expression, *a lot of,* and the pronoun *I.* Most of the words are very short, and none would be out of place in an ordinary conversation.

Formal–Informal Level   As life has become less formal, informal diction has become increasingly widespread. Today many articles and books, even ones on relatively serious topics, mix informal and formal elements. Here is an example:

> . . . faith in sports has been vigorously promoted by industry, the military, government, the media. The value of the arena and the locker room has been imposed on our national life. Coaches and sportswriters are speaking for generals and businessmen, too, when they tell us that a man must be physically and psychologically "tough" to succeed, that he must be clean and punctual and honest, that he must bear pain, bad luck, and defeat without whimpering or making excuses. A man must prove his faith in sports and the American Way by whipping himself into shape, playing by the rules, being part of the team, and putting out all the way. If his faith is strong, he will triumph. It's his own fault if he loses, fails, remains poor.
>
> Robert Lipsyte, *Sports World*

All these sentences except the next to last are loose. Two are quite long, four quite short, and only two have parallel phrases or clauses. Although a few expressions—"bear," "the American Way," "triumph"—echo formal diction, most of the words have an informal ring, and two expressions, "whipping himself into shape" and "putting out all the way," skirt the edges of slang.

Technical Level   A specialist writing for others in the same field or for sophisticated nonspecialists writes on the technical level, a cousin to the formal level. Technical language uses specialized words that may be unfamiliar to a general audience. Its sentences tend to be long and complex, but unlike formal diction it doesn't lean toward periodic sentences, parallelism, and balance. Read this example from the field of entomology, the study of insects:

> The light organs of fireflies are complex structures, and recent studies using the electron microscope show them to be even more complex than once supposed. Each is composed of three layers: an outer "window," simply a transparent portion of the body wall; the light organ proper; and an inner layer of opaque, whitish cells filled with granules of uric acid, the so-called "reflector." The light organ proper contains large, slablike light cells, each of them filled with large granules and much smaller, dark granules, the latter tending to be concentrated around the numerous air tubes and nerves penetrating the light organ. These smaller granules were once assumed by some persons to be luminous bacteria, but we now know that they are mitochondria, the source of ATP [adenosine triphosphate] and therefore of the energy of light production. The much larger granules that fill most of the light cells are still of unknown function; perhaps they serve as the source of luciferin.
>
> Howard Ensign Evans, Life on a Little-Known Planet

Note the specialized vocabulary—*granules, uric acid, mitochondria,* and *luciferin*—as well as the length and complexity of the sentences. Five sentences make up the passage, the shortest having twenty-four words. None is periodic, and none has a parallel or balanced structure.

Every field has *jargon,* specialized terms or inside talk that provides a convenient shorthand for communication among its members. For an audience of biologists, you may write that two organisms have a *symbiotic relationship,* meaning "mutually beneficial"; for psychology majors, you might use *catalepsy* instead of "a temporary loss of consciousness and feeling, often accompanied by muscular rigidity." As a general rule, use technical terms only if your audience will know their meanings. If you must use unfamiliar words when writing for a general audience, define them the first time they appear.

Colloquial Language and Slang   *Colloquial* originally meant "the language of ordinary conversation between people of a particular region." *Slang,* according to *Webster's Tenth New Collegiate Dictionary,* is "an informal nonstandard vocabulary composed typically of coinages, arbitrarily changed words, and extravagant, forced, or facetious figures of speech." These two categories shade into each other, and even authorities sometimes disagree on whether to label a term *colloquial* or *slang.* The word *bender,* meaning "a drinking spree," seems firmly in the colloquial camp, and *bummer,* a term once used by young people to mean "a bad time," is just as clearly slang. *Break a leg* is theater slang used to wish a performer success. But what about *guy* and *kid?* Once they were slang, but so many people have used them for so long that they have now become colloquial.

Regardless of their labels, colloquial and slang terms are almost never appropriate in formal writing. They sometimes serve a useful purpose in informal writing by creating a special effect or increasing audience appeal. Even so, careful writers use them sparingly. Some readers may not understand some colloquial

is the dialect used in school and business, students must master it to compete effectively. Sometimes it's helpful to have students mimic the speech of an instructor. Another good approach is to compare the rules that govern edited American English and nonstandard English. In especially difficult cases, students can benefit from reading a passage in edited American English and deliberately stressing the constructions that differ from those in their dialect.

TEACHING STRATEGY
Have students write different versions of one short assignment, directing them at different audiences and using different levels of diction. If they write about some college problem, one version (informal and colloquial) might be directed to friends at home, a second (informal) to their parents, and a third (formal) to the college president.

EXERCISE ANSWERS

1. This is technical diction. The writing is directed at sophisticated nonspecialists rather than physicists specializing in the matter of relativity. The passage uses words that a general audience would probably have difficulty understanding: *recapitulate, topography, simultaneity,* and *temporal*. For the most part, the expressions are abstract, and there are no contractions or slang. The sentences are long and their patterns varied, but only one of them, the next-to-the-last sentence, is periodic, and only the last one uses parallelism: "for one observer"—"for another observer."

2. This is formal–informal diction. Informal elements include loose sentences that, except for sentences 6 and 9, are relatively short; the use of the pronouns *I, me,* and *my;* and the colloquial expressions *yells* and *tough*. Formal elements include parallelism ("I am" in sentences 1–3, and "I have" in sentences 5 and 7–9) and the absence of contractions.

3. This is informal diction. The language is casual, familiar, and frantic rather than stately and serious. The passage includes two original and highly figurative examples of slang— "short-circuiting themselves into hot little twitching death balls" and "charred-in-the-flankers"—as well as such less flamboyant slang and colloquial expressions as "gets them queer," "hot-in-the-pants," "God knows where else," and "winds up." The first and third

language, and slang usually becomes dated quickly. The following paragraph uses colloquial and slang expressions successfully:

> . . . When I was just a kid on Eighth Avenue in knee pants [Big Bill] was trying to get himself killed. He was always in some fight with a knife. He was always cutting or trying to cut somebody's throat. He was always getting cut or getting shot. Every Saturday night that he was out there, something happened. If you heard on Sunday morning that somebody had gotten shot or stabbed, you didn't usually ask who did it. You'd ask if Big Bill did it. If he did it, no one paid much attention to it, because he was always doing something like that. They'd say, "Yeah, man. That cat is crazy."
>
> Claude Brown, *Manchild in the Promised Land*

Kid, yeah, and *cat* reflect the speech of Brown's characters and thus add authenticity to his account. Despite the informal diction, Brown uses parallelism in the second, third, and fourth sentences; repetition of "he was always" emphasizes the single-minded self-destructiveness of Big Bill's behavior.

Identify the level of diction in each of the following passages. Support your answers with examples from the passages. Point out slang or colloquial expressions.

1. We may now recapitulate the reasons which have made it necessary to substitute "space-time" for space and time. The old separation of space and time rested upon the belief that there was no ambiguity in saying that two events in distant places happened at the same time; consequently it was thought that we could describe the topography of the universe at a given instant in purely spatial terms. But now that simultaneity has become relative to a particular observer, this is no longer possible. What is, for one observer, a description of the state of the world at a given instant, is, for another observer, a series of events at various different times, whose relations are not merely spatial but also temporal.

Bertrand Russell, *The ABC of Relativity*

2. In some ways I am an exceptionally privileged woman of thirty-seven. I am in the room of a private, legal abortion hospital, where a surgeon, a friend of many years, is waiting for me in the operating room. I am only five weeks pregnant. Last week I walked out of another hospital, unaborted, because I had suddenly changed my mind. I have a husband who cares for me. He yells because my indecisiveness makes him anxious, but basically he has permitted the final choice to rest in my hands: "It would be very tough, especially for you, and it is absolutely insane, but yes, we could have another baby." I have a mother who cares. I have two young sons, whose small faces are the most moving arguments I have against going through with this abortion. I have a doctorate in psychology, which among other advantages, assures me of the professional courtesy of special passes in hospitals, passes that at this moment enable my husband and my mother to stand in my room at a nonvisiting hour and yell at each other over my head while I sob.

Magda Denes, *In Necessity and Sorrow: Life and Death in an Abortion Hospital*

3. I have just spent two days with Edward T. Hall, an anthropologist, watching thousands of my fellow New Yorkers short-circuiting themselves into hot little twitching death balls with jolts of their own adrenalin. Dr. Hall says it is overcrowding that does it.

Overcrowding gets the adrenalin going, and the adrenalin gets them queer, autistic, sadistic, barren, batty, sloppy, hot-in-the-pants, charred-in-the-flankers, leering, puling, numb—the usual in New York, in other words, and God knows where else. Dr. Hall has the theory that overcrowding has already thrown New York into a state of behavioral sink. Behavioral sink is a term from ethology, which is the study of how animals relate to their environment. Among animals, the sink winds up with a "population collapse" or "massive die-off." O rotten Gotham.

Tom Wolfe, *The Pump House Gang*

Tone

Tone reveals the author's attitude toward the topic and the reader. Every piece of writing has a tone, intended or otherwise, that stems from the meanings and connotations of words, the sentence patterns, and the rhythm of the prose.

Denotation and Connotation The denotation of a word is its direct, essential meaning: what the word always stands for. The word *book*, for example, denotes "a set of printed or blank sheets bound together along one edge to form a volume." This definition is objective and neutral. It does not assign any special value or convey any particular attitude toward the word or what the word stands for. Connotations are the values and emotional associations that accompany a word. When the self-made man snorts "book learnin'" at his better-educated junior partner, he assigns a value and an attitude—that he ranks experience higher than the knowledge gained from books.

Some words—*death*, for instance—almost always carry strong connotations or emotional associations. *Webster's Tenth New Collegiate Dictionary* defines it as "a permanent cessation of all vital functions" or "the end of life," but it means much more. All of us have hopes, fears, and memories about death, feelings that color our responses whenever we hear or read the word. Likewise, we have personal responses to words like *sexy, cheap, radical, politician*, and *mother*. Experience, to a considerable extent, conditions how we think and feel about a word. To an Olympic swimmer who has won a gold medal, *swimming* may stir pleasant memories of the victory and the plaudits that went with it. The victim of a near-drowning, however, might react to the same word with something approaching horror.

Nonetheless, cultural connotations are more important than personal ones. Cultural connotations develop the way individual ones do, but on a much larger scale, growing out of the common experiences of many speakers and writers and changing with usage and circumstances.

Context, the parts of a passage that precede and follow a word, also affects connotation. Note, for instance, the different associations of *dog* in these sentences:

That movie is a real dog.

I sure am putting on the dog!

It's a dog-eat-dog world.

Your dog-in-the-manger attitude makes you very unpopular.

Denotation is sometimes called the language of science and technology, connotation, the language of art. But we need both to communicate effectively.

sentences are long, but the remaining five are relatively short. All are loose rather than periodic, and none of them shows parallelism or balanced construction. Although Wolfe uses one term, *ethology*, which even a sophisticated audience might not know, he defines it for his readers.

PERSPECTIVE
Students often have trouble mastering tone. Sensitivity to tone requires social awareness, an extensive vocabulary, and a flexible syntax. Students struggling to develop their ideas, express them in appropriate language, and present them in some coherent order often find tone one burden too many. Nevertheless, students should be encouraged to use a tone appropriate to their writing topics, the image they wish to project, and to their audience.

TEACHING STRATEGY
Have students change the wording of several neutral sentences so that their denotations are preserved but their connotations altered. **Samples:** The police officer arrested the suspected felon. The gentleman embraced his young lady friend. Our two nations are engaged in armed conflict.

TEACHING STRATEGIES
1. Bring in several samples of writing—letters to the editor or junk mail sales pitches—in which the tone is inappropriate;

then have the class discuss their tonal shortcomings.
2. Assign short pieces of writing that call for different tones. Students might write a brief argument in an objective tone and then recast it as a strongly emotional plea.
3. Ask students to read the sample paragraphs in the chapter and indicate in writing how the tone influences the image they have of each author. Then have students read over their assessments and examine the image they have projected, altering it if necessary.

CLASSROOM ACTIVITY
Have students, working in small groups, change the tone of some campus newspaper editorial or story about a school event. One group might strive for an objective tone, another for the tone of a furious participant, and a third group for the tone of someone who finds the whole matter ridiculous.

Denotation allows us to convey precise, essential meanings. Connotation adds richness, warmth, and bite. Without these qualities our language would be bland and sterile, our lives bleak and mechanical.

Objective Tone   An objective tone keeps the writer's personality and opinions out of the message. Here is an example:

> Myopia is a condition of the eye that makes distant vision blurry. In brief, the myopic individual is nearsighted. When the eye is normal, rays of light pass through it and come to focus on the retina, located at the back of the eye. In the myopic eye, however, the rays of light come together a little in front of the retina. As a result, the distant image is not seen clearly. Myopia may result from the eye itself being too long or the lens of the eye being too flat. In either case, the rays converge in front of the retina, and the nearsighted individual is likely to have difficulty making out distant objects.
>
> Janine Neumann

This tone suits a popular explanation of a medical condition. The prose is businesslike and authoritative, the sentence patterns uncomplicated, and nothing reveals the person behind the words.

Other Attitudes   Sometimes you write merely to inform, sometimes to persuade. In persuasive writing, let your attitude toward your topic set the tone. Decide how subtle, flamboyant, or formal your writing should be and what special tone—satiric, cynical, serious, mock pompous, bawdy, playful—will win your reader over.

Every essay has combined characteristics that give it a special tone. The following excerpts illustrate some of tone's many dimensions:

> Unless you have led an abnormally isolated adulthood, the chances are excellent that you know many people who have at one time or another committed an act, or consorted with someone who was committing an act, for which they might have been sent to prison. We do not consider most of these people, or ourselves, criminals; the act is one thing, the criminality of it quite something else. Homicide, for example, is in our law not a crime; murder only is proscribed. The difference between the two is the intention, or to be more accurate, society's decision about the nature of that intention.
>
> Bruce Jackson, "Who Goes to Prison: Caste and Careerism in Crime"

Here we have a sophisticated and rather formal tone. Terms like *consorted* and *proscribed*, while exactly suited to Jackson's meaning, do not form part of most people's word kits. The complexity of the first sentence and the varied patterns of the others add to the air of sophistication. The emphatic *quite*, meaning "entirely," is cultivated usage; and along with *society's decision*, it lends the tone a wry touch.

> Cans. Beer cans. Glinting on the verges of a million miles of roadways, lying in scrub, grass, dirt, leaves, sand, mud, but never hidden. Piels, Rheingold, Ballantine, Schaeffer, Schlitz, shining in the sun or picked by moon or the beams of headlights at night; washed by rain or flattened by wheels, but never dulled, never buried, never destroyed. Here is the mark of savages, the testament of wasters, the stain of prosperity.

Who are these men who defile the grassy borders of our roads and lanes, who pollute our ponds, who spoil the purity of our ocean beaches with the empty vessels of their thirst? Who are the men who make these vessels in millions and then say, "Drink and discard"? What society is this that can afford to cast away a million tons of metal and to make a wild and fruitful land a garbage heap?

Marya Mannes, "Wasteland"

Rhythm and word choice contribute equally to the tone of this passage. The excerpt opens with imagistic sentence fragments that create a panoramic word picture of our littered roadways. Then complete sentences and somber commentary follow. Words and patterns are repeated, mixing the dignified language of epic and religion with common derogatory terms—*testament, purity, vessels,* and *fruitful* set against *savages, wasters, defile,* and *garbage heap*—to convey the contradictions Mannes deplores. The rhetorical questions, used instead of accusations, add a sense of loftiness to her outrage, helping create a tone both majestic and disdainful.

Erethizon dorsatus, an antisocial character of the Northern U.S. and Canadian forest, commonly called a porcupine, looks like an uncombed head, has a grumpy personality, fights with his tail, hides his head when he's in trouble, attacks backing up, retreats going ahead, and eats toilet seats as if they were Post Toasties. It's a sad commentary on his personality that people are always trying to do him in.

R. T. Allen, "The Porcupine"

The tone of this passage is affectionately humorous. Allen sets this tone by noting the porcupine's tousled appearance, testy personality, and peculiar habits, such as eating outdoor toilet seats (for their salt content, as Allen later explains). The net effect is to personify porcupines, making them seem like the eccentric reprobate human that others regard with amused toleration.

The final passage begins by referring to a "promissory note": the Constitution and the promise of life, liberty, and the pursuit of happiness spelled out in the Declaration of Independence.

It is obvious today that America has defaulted on this promissory note in so far as her citizens of color are concerned. Instead of honoring this sacred obligation, America has given the Negro people a bad check; a check which has come back marked "insufficient funds." But we refuse to believe that the bank of justice is bankrupt. We refuse to believe that there are insufficient funds in the great vaults of opportunity of this nation. And so we've come to cash this check, a check that will give us upon demand the riches of freedom and the security of justice.

We have also come to this hallowed spot to remind America of the fierce urgency of now. This is no time to engage in the luxury of cooling off or to take the tranquilizing drug of gradualism. Now is the time to make real the promises of democracy; now is the time to rise from the dark and desolate valley of segregation to the sunlit path of racial justice; now is the time to lift our nation from the quicksands of racial injustice to the solid rock of brotherhood; now is the time to make justice a reality for all of God's children.

Martin Luther King, Jr., "I Have a Dream"

This writing speaks passionately for freedom and justice. Its most obvious rhetorical strategy is metaphor, first the extended one of the promissory note, then brief separate metaphors that make the same point. The repetition of *now* sharpens the

EXERCISE ANSWERS

1. This passage is elegiac but undespairing. Eiseley establishes his elegiac tone by first likening the glade in which the drama is played out to a cathedral and by calling the raven "the black bird at the heart of life." This tone is sustained by the strongly rhythmic and repetitious pattern of the sentences ("It was then I saw the judgment. It was the judgment of life against death. I will never see it again so forcefully presented. I will never hear it again in notes so tragically prolonged."). Much of the impact of the passage stems from its allegorical character: Like Eiseley's sparrows, all of us exist "under the brooding shadow of the raven" and, again like them, have no choice except to sing in the shadow of death.

2. The tone here is one of deeply felt anger at people who produce the shoddy goods. The anger comes through strongly in the expressions "schlock," "shoddy goods," and, most notable of all, "the sanitary-fill schlock heaps that are the feces of our Gross (and how!) National Product."

3. This passage conveys a strong sense of excitement and adulation, aroused in the opening short, pithy sentences with their stars, capitalized words, and exclamation points. Durocher then sustains this tone by invoking the carnival atmosphere of the games in which Ruth played and by his behavior when he got a hit. The language is highly informal—short sentences, slang and colloquialisms, and contractions—and adds to the excitement of the passage.

PERSPECTIVE
While stylistic techniques create more memorable prose, they also convey meaning that cannot be captured in a more literal fashion. Metaphors help us draw connections between apparently dissimilar ideas and establish a link between abstract ideas and our physical contact with the world. Modern physicists who talk of light as a wave or space as curved speak metaphorically. Overstatement and understatement are bound to our fundamental notion of character; the British traditional understatement and emphasis on a "stiff upper lip" are examples. Irony establishes an outlook that distrusts

insistent tone. Eloquence comes through parallelism, repetition, and words like *sacred* and *hallowed*, vividness through figures of speech like "vaults of opportunity" and "sunlit path of racial justice." Like George Orwell, Mark Twain, Joseph Conrad, and other masters of tonal effects whose work appears in this book, King uses both rhythm and diction to create a tone that infuses and invigorates his message.

Characterize the tone of each of the following paragraphs. Point out how word choice, sentence structure, rhythm, and other elements contribute to it.

1. When I awoke, dimly aware of some commotion and outcry in the clearing, the light was slanting down through the pines in such a way that the glade was lit like some vast cathedral. I could see the dust motes of wood pollen in the long shaft of light, and there on the extended branch sat an enormous raven with a red and squirming nestling in its beak.

   The sound that awoke me was the outraged cries of the nestling's parents, who flew helplessly in circles around the clearing. And he, the murderer, the black bird at the heart of life, sat there, glistening in the common light, formidable, unperturbed, untouchable. The sighing died. It was then I saw the judgment. It was the judgment of life against death. I will never see it again so forcefully presented. I will never hear it again in notes so tragically prolonged. For in the midst of protest, they forgot the violence. There, in that clearing, the crystal note of a song sparrow lifted hesitantly in the hush. And, finally, after painful fluttering, another took the song, and then another, the song passing from one bird to another, doubtfully at first, as though some evil thing was being slowly forgotten. Till suddenly they took heart and sang from many throats joyously together as birds are known to sing. They sang under the brooding shadow of the raven. In simple truth they had forgotten the raven, for they were the singers of life, and not of death.

   Loren Eiseley, "The Judgment of the Birds"

2. America, which leads the world in almost every economic category, leads it above all in the production of schlock. Christmas toys broken before New Year's, wash-n-wear suits that neither wash well nor wear well, appliances that expire a month after the guarantee, Barbie dolls, frozen pizza—these are but a few of the shoddy goods whose main contribution to our civilization, apart from a momentary satisfaction to the purchaser, is to swell the sanitary-fill schlock heaps that are the feces of our Gross (and how!) National Product.

   Robert Claiborne, "Future Schlock"

3. Babe Ruth was *** The Sultan of Swat ***
   Babe Ruth was *** THE BAMBINO ***
   Babe Ruth was what you came to see!!!!

   It was like going to a carnival, with Babe as both the star performer and the side-show attraction. Hell, that's what we called him: "You big ape." He was what a home-run hitter was supposed to look like. Wide, flat nose. Big feet. Little ankles. Belly hanging over his belt. All he had to do was walk on to the field and everybody would applaud. The air became charged with electricity. You just felt that something great was going to happen.

He'd twirl that big 48-ounce bat around in little circles up at the plate as if he were cranking it up for the Biggest Home Run Ever Hit—*you felt that*—and when he'd hit one he would hit it like nobody has hit it before or since. A mile high and a mile out. I can see him now, as I did so many times, just look up, drop the bat and start to trot, the little pitter-patter pigeon-toed, high-bellied trot that seemed to say, I've done it before and I'll do it again, but this one was for you.

Leo Durocher, *Nice Guys Finish Last*

appearances and envisions a world fraught with contradictions.

TEACHING STRATEGIES
1. Have students record the metaphors and similes

Special Stylistic Techniques

The style of a piece of writing is its character or personality. Like people, writing can be many things: dull, stuffy, discordant, sedate, lively, flamboyant, eccentric, and so on. Figurative language and irony can contribute to your own distinctive writing style.

Figurative Language

Figurative language uses concrete words in a nonliteral way to create sharply etched sensory images that catch and hold the reader's attention. Besides energizing the writing, figurative language strengthens the reader's grip on the ideas. Five figurative devices are especially important: simile, metaphor, personification, overstatement, and understatement.

Simile and Metaphor   A *simile* directly compares two unlike things by the use of *like* or *as*. "Todd is as restless as an aspen leaf in a breeze" and "Her smile flicked on and off like a sunbeam flashing momentarily through a cloud bank" are similes. A *metaphor* also compares unlike things, but without using *like* or *as*. Some metaphors include a linking verb (*is, are, were,* and so on); others do not. "The moon was a wind-tossed bark" and "The curtain of darkness fell over the land" are both metaphors. Here is an excerpt that contains similes and metaphors:

The field is a sea of deep, dark green, a sea made up of millions of small blades of grass blended together as one. Each blade is a dark green spear, broad at the bottom and narrowing to a needle point at the tip. Its full length is arched so that, viewed from one end, it looks like a shallow trough with paper-thin sides. On the inner side of this trough, small ridges and shallow valleys run from base to tip. To a finger rubbed across them, they feel like short, bristly hairs.

Daniel Kinney

they use daily. They should discover that, like most of us, they often think in terms of metaphors and similes without deliberately trying to create them.

2. Students sometimes mistakenly believe that metaphors and similes belong exclusively to more literary writing. To correct this impression, have students review scientific and technical writing for examples of metaphors and then determine whether they were employed for stylistic effect or to help present an idea.

3. Students can be spurred to write effective metaphors and similes by completing unfinished statements, then evaluating the results in terms of stylistic effectiveness and the insights provided. For example: Education today is _____ . My life _____ (action verb) like _____ (concrete but correlated object). Time _____ our days. Love _____ like a _____ in us. His voice _____ .

Discussion Questions

1. Locate the similes in this passage and explain how they help the reader.
2. Locate the metaphors and point out how each heightens the sensory impact of the writing.

Writers too often snatch hastily at the first similes and metaphors that come to mind and end up strewing their pages with overused and enfeebled speci-mens. Johnny is "as blind as a bat," Mary runs around "like a chicken with its head cut off"—and the writing slips into trite gear. Other comparisons link items that are too dissimilar. For example, "The wind whistled through the trees like a herd of galloping horses" would only puzzle a reader.

Personification   This is a special sort of metaphor that assigns human qualities or traits to something nonhuman: a plant, an abstraction, a nonliving thing. Here are some examples:

The vine clung stubbornly to the trunk of the tree.

May fortune smile upon you.

The waves lapped sullenly against the base of the cliff.

Each of these sentences assigns its subject a different emotional quality—stubbornness, friendliness, gloom—each figurative rather than literal: Vines aren't stubborn, fortune doesn't smile, and waves aren't sullen.

Personification sometimes extends beyond a single sentence. To illustrate, the following passage carries a single image through two paragraphs:

> "I figured when my legislative program passed the Congress," [Lyndon] Johnson said in 1971, "that the Great Society had a real chance to grow into a beautiful woman. And I figured her growth and development would be as natural and inevitable as any small child's. In the first year, as we got the laws on the books, she'd begin to crawl. Then in the second year, as we got more laws on the books, she'd begin to walk, and the year after that, she'd be off and running, all the time growing bigger and healthier and fatter. And when she grew up, I figured she'd be so big and beautiful that the American people couldn't help but fall in love with her, and once they did, they'd want to keep her around forever, making her a permanent part of American life, more permanent than the New Deal.
>
> "But now Nixon has come along and everything I've worked for is ruined. There's a story in the paper every day about him slashing another one of my Great Society programs. I can just see him waking up in the morning, making that victory sign of his and deciding which program to kill. It's a terrible thing for me to sit by and watch someone else starve my Great Society to death. She's getting thinner and thinner and uglier and uglier all the time; now her bones are beginning to stick out and her wrinkles are beginning to show. Soon she'll be so ugly that the American people will refuse to look at her; they'll stick her in a closet to hide her away and there she'll die. And when she dies, I too will die."
>
> Doris Kearns, "Who *Was* Lyndon Baines Johnson?"

Through personification, Johnson expresses affection for his social program, dis-approval of Nixon's policies, and sorrow over the coming demise of the "child" he has so carefully nurtured.

Personification works best when it is used in moderation and doesn't make outrageous comparisons. Dishes don't run away with spoons except in nursery rhymes.

Overstatement Overstatement, sometimes called hyperbole, deliberately and drastically exaggerates in order to make a point. An example is "Wilfred is the world's biggest fool."

One of the best examples of sustained overstatement is Mark Twain's essay "Fenimore Cooper's Literary Offences." In it, Twain claims, "In one place in *Deerslayer*, and in the restricted space of two-thirds of a page, Cooper has scored 114 offences against literary art out of a possible 115." Twain also asserts, "There have been daring people in the world who claimed that Cooper could write English, but they are all dead now. " Through such exaggerations, Twain mocks the shortcomings of Cooper's novels.

Used sparingly, overstatement is emphatic, adding real force to an event or situation. Writers who consistently exaggerate, however, risk losing their credibility.

Understatement Understatement makes an assertion in a humble manner without giving something its due, as when a sportscaster calls a team's 23–2 record "pretty fair." By drawing attention to the thing it appears to slight, this soft-spoken approach offers writers an effective strategy. Here is an example:

> To assume that Heidi Mansfield lacks the qualifications for this position is not unwarranted.

Without ever actually calling Mansfield unqualified, the statement suggests that she is. Similarly, when a meat company executive says, "It is not unlikely that beef prices will jump ten cents a pound in the next two months," we might as well count on spending another dime. As these statements show, understatement not infrequently has an ulterior motive.

EXERCISE

Identify the similes, metaphors, personifications, overstatements, or understatements in these sentences.

1. The old table greedily sucked up the linseed oil.
2. Russia's social and economic system is a giant staircase that leads nowhere.
3. Stanley has the bile of human meanness by the quart in every vein.
4. Their music sounds like the drumming of an infant's fists against the sides of a crib.
5. The foundations of our divorce are as strong as ever.
6. It is not unlike Muriel to be late.
7. You're the world's biggest liar!
8. "Fashion, though folly's child, and guide of fools, Rules e'en the wisest, and in learning rules."
9. Einstein's theories have had some impact on modern science.
10. I'm as tired as a farm horse at sunset.

Irony

Irony occurs when a writer intentionally states one thing but actually means something different or even opposite. A certain point is thus highlighted. The sportswriter who refers to the "ideal conditions" for a tennis tournament when

sympathies by drawing a parallel between human life and the life of Johnson's Great Society program, based on their shared traits of growth and decay.

3. To help students learn to create effective personifications, have them list a number of traits that people might share with education, the night, winter, or a stream, and then construct several personifications, each based on one of the traits.

SUGGESTED INSTRUCTOR READINGS

Lakoff, G., and M. Johnson. Metaphors We Live By. Chicago: U of Chicago Press, 1981. Demonstrates how and why metaphors underlie most of our everyday language.

Ortony, A., ed. Metaphor and Thought. Cambridge, England: Cambridge University Press, 1993. Includes some interesting theoretical accounts of the ways we think metaphorically.

TEACHING STRATEGIES

1. Fed a steady diet of media hype that discovers a crisis in even modest events, many students overstate, not for any particular effect but because they don't realize how shrill they sound. Have them read newspapers for examples of overstatements and then discuss the effects on readers.

2. Have students review their own writing for instances of overstatement and tone down any inappropriate examples they find.

3. Have students attempt to turn the following statements into effective overstatements: Students have some mechanical errors in their papers; It can be difficult to register for the class you want; Dorms may be noisy in the evening; Dorm food can occasionally be unappetizing.

TEACHING STRATEGY
Have students attempt to turn the following statements into effective understatements: College can be extremely expensive; This class will be terribly difficult; A serious illness will result in extensive medical bills.

EXERCISE ANSWERS
1. Personification.
2. Metaphor.
3. Overstatement.
4. Simile.
5. Metaphor.
6. Understatement.
7. Overstatement.
8. Personification.
9. Understatement.
10. Simile.

TEACHING STRATEGIES
1. Because students often fail to recognize that they use irony, you might provide them with relevant examples. "Oh, it was a wonderful date. He fascinated me hour after hour with a detailed account of his high school exploits. He was so interesting I never had to say a thing. And what a big spender; he treated me to dinner at McDonald's." Have students record examples of irony they have heard or inadvertently produced themselves.

rain has drenched the courts and forced cancellation of matches speaks ironically. Here is a longer example of the same sort of irony:

> The baron, though a small man, had a large soul, and it swelled with satisfaction at the consciousness of being the greatest man in the little world about him. He loved to tell long stories about the dark old warriors whose portraits looked grimly down from the walls around, and he found no listeners equal to those that fed at his expense. He was much given to the marvellous, and a firm believer in all those supernatural tales with which every mountain and valley in Germany abounds. The faith of his guests exceeded even his own; they listened to every tale of wonder with open eyes and mouths, and never failed to be astonished, even though repeated for the hundredth time. Thus lived the Baron Von Landshort, the oracle of his table, the absolute monarch of his little territory, and happy, above all things, in the persuasion that he was the wisest man of the age.
>
> Washington Irving, "The Spectre Bridegroom"

Irving never directly states the baron's shortcomings. Rather, suggestive details such as the swelling of the baron's soul, his belief in the supernatural, and his deception by the sponging guests portray one who, far from being "the wisest man of the age," is pompous, superstitious, and gullible.

Eliminating Flawed Diction

Diction flaws include wordiness, euphemisms, clichés, mixed metaphors, and sexist language. As you revise, stay alert for these culprits and eliminate any that you find.

Wordiness

Wordiness has more than one cause. Some writers overnourish their prose to make it sound more impressive, some to pad an assignment, and some simply because they don't realize they're doing it. Whatever the reason, the results are the same: ponderous, slow-moving papers that lack punch. To inject vigor, cut out every word that doesn't serve a purpose. If five words are doing the work of one, drop four.

The two major forms of wordiness, deadwood and gobbledygook, often occur together. *Deadwood*, which does nothing but take up space and clutter the writing, is bracketed in the following sentence:

> Responsible parents [of today] neither allow their children [to have] absolute freedom [to do as they please] nor severely restrict their children's activities.

Now read the sentence without the deadwood:

> Responsible parents neither allow their children absolute freedom nor severely restrict their children's activities.

Careful revision has increased the clarity and reduced the words from twenty-three to fourteen.

Gobbledygook consists of long, abstract, or technical words that help create unnecessarily long and complex sentences. Some people who write it mistakenly believe it "dignifies" their thoughts. Others want to conceal their meanings by clouding their statements. And some naively think that long words are better than short ones. All of these writers use gobbledygook, but none of their readers appreciates it. Here are some samples of gobbledygook followed by revised versions in plain English:

Original Version	Revised Version
The fish exhibited a 100 percent mortality response.	All the fish died.
We have been made cognizant of the fact that the experiment will be terminated in the near future.	We have learned that the experiment will end soon.

Euphemisms

Euphemisms take the sting out of something unpleasant or add stature to something humble. Familiar expressions include *pass away* for *die*, *preowned* for *used*, and *sanitation engineer* for *garbage collector*.

In most cases, the writer simply intends to cushion reality. But euphemisms also have grisly uses. Mobsters don't *beat up* merchants who refuse *protection* (itself a euphemism); they *lean on* them. Hitler didn't talk about *exterminating the Jews* but about *the final solution to the Jewish problem*. These euphemisms don't just blur reality; they blot out images of horror. Of merchants with broken limbs and bloodied faces. Of cattle cars crammed with men, women, and children en route to death camps. Of barbed wire and gas ovens and starved corpses in the millions.

Any euphemism, however well-intentioned, probably obscures an issue. On occasion you may need one in order to protect the sensitive reader, but usually you will serve readers best by using direct expressions that present reality, not a tidied-up version.

Clichés and Mixed Metaphors

Clichés   Clichés are expressions that have become stale from overuse. Rather than respond to experience with their own perceptions, writers sometimes resort to oft-repeated words or phrases that stem from patterned thinking. Dullness follows. Daily conversation abounds with stale expressions because talk is unplanned, but writing allows you time to find invigorating and effective language. Your individual response is what draws the reader's interest, and only fresh thinking will produce that response. The following list of clichés barely "scratches the surface":

acid test	burn the midnight oil	green with envy
almighty dollar	chip off the old block	last but not least
beat a hasty retreat	clear as a bell	nipped in the bud
better late than never	cool as a cucumber	rears its ugly head
black sheep	easier said than done	set the world on fire
blind as a bat	goes without saying	sick as a dog

Mixed Metaphors   Clichéd writing often suffers as well from mixed metaphors—inappropriate combinations that startle or amuse the reader. How would you respond if you came across this example?

> When he opened that can of worms, he bit off more than he could chew.

Can you visualize someone chewing a mouthful of worms? The point is obvious.

Sexist Language

Sexist language can assume several guises. Sometimes it appears as unneeded information that dilutes or even demeans someone's accomplishments. It can occur when the writer uses gender-exclusive pronouns like *he* and *she* inappropriately. And it may attach arbitrary gender labels to persons and groups. All U.S. government agencies, most businesses, and most academic publications prohibit sexist language. Deliberate or accidental, such language has no place in your writing. These guidelines will help you avoid it.

1. Don't unnecessarily mention a person's appearance, spouse, or family.

    Sexist: The cute new loan officer at the Godfather Finance Company is a real hit with customers.

    Sexist: Craig Helmond, husband of nationally known cardiologist Dr. Jennifer Helmond, won election to the Beal City Board of Education.

    Sexist: After eight years of attending college part time, Angelica Denham, a three-time grandmother, was awarded a bachelor of science degree.

    Nonsexist: The efficient new loan officer at the Godfather Finance Company is a real hit with customers.

    Nonsexist: Craig Helmond, an accountant at Oakwood Growth Enterprise, won election to the Beal City Board of Education.

    Nonsexist: After eight years of attending college part time, Angelica Denham was awarded a bachelor of science degree.

    Note how, in each case, the sentence has been rewritten to include only relevant information.

2. Use the pronouns *he, him, his,* and *himself* only when referring to antecedents that are clearly masculine and *she, her, hers,* or *herself* only when their antecedents are clearly feminine.

    Sexist: Each tourist must carry his passport with *him* at all times.

    Sexist: If a collector wishes to find an out-of-print book, she should try http://www.bibliofind.com on the Web.

    Correct this type of error by substituting plural antecedents and pronouns for the singular ones or by rewriting the sentence to eliminate the pronouns.

    Nonsexist: Tourists must carry their passports with *them* at all times.

    Nonsexist: Any collector wishing to find an out-of-print book should try http://www.bibliofind.com on the Web.

3. Don't use occupational labels that imply the positions are held only by one sex.

Sexist	Nonsexist
chairwoman	chair
draftsman	drafter
fireman	fire fighter
policeman	police officer
postman	letter carrier
weatherman	weather reporter

A word of caution here. To avoid sexism, some writers substitute the suffix *-person* for *-man* in many job titles (such as *handyperson* for someone who does odd jobs). Such attempts, however, often create awkward expressions that you should avoid.

EXERCISE

The following sentences are flawed by wordiness, euphemisms, clichés, mixed metaphors, and sexist language. When you have identified the faults, revise the sentences.

1. The American eagle will never, in the face of foreign threats, pull in its horns or draw back into its shell.
2. Last summer, I was engaged in the repair of automobiles.
3. You're looking as bright as a button this morning.
4. My mother was called to her heavenly reward last winter.
5. Any student wishing to attend summer school at Burns State College must pay his tuition one week before registration day.
6. My brother is in the process of pursuing a curriculum of industrial chemistry.
7. The ball's in your court, and if you strike out, don't expect me to pick up the pieces.
8. The beautiful, sultry-voiced clerk quickly filled the order.
9. Winning first prize for her essay was a real feather in Peggy's cap.
10. Our company plans to confer retirement on 200 employees by year's end.

2. Have students review their own writing to identify sexist language, then make the appropriate revisions.

3. If your students are using the version of this book that includes a Handbook, refer them to pages 662–664 for additional information on eliminating sexist language.

EXERCISE ANSWERS
1. Mixed metaphor. The American eagle (*or* America) will never back down in the face of foreign threats.
2. Wordiness. Last summer, I repaired automobiles.
3. Cliché. You're looking exceptionally bright (very perky, radiant) this morning.
4. Euphemism. My mother died last winter.
5. Sexist language. Students wishing to attend summer school at Burns State College must pay their tuition one week before registration day.
6. Wordiness. My brother is majoring in industrial chemistry.
7. Mixed metaphor. The ball is in your court (or The matter is in your hands), and if you fail to handle things properly, don't expect any help from me.
8. Sexist language. The efficient clerk quickly filled the order.
9. Cliché. Winning first prize for her essay was a real accomplishment for Peggy.
10. Wordiness. Our company plans to retire 200 employees by year's end.

CHAPTER 8

TEACHING SUGGESTION
Have the students examine the picture and discuss elements of a narrative. Where might be she located, why would she be there, why is she draped in a blanket, who is she, what is she thinking about? What might have happened before this scene? What is likely to happen right after this scene? Use this to discuss the aspects of a narration including setting, character, conflict, point of view, and resolution.

SUGGESTED WRITING ASSIGNMENT
After discussing the image have students write a one-to two-page narrative that can account for the scene. They may include dialogue and imagine what comes before or after this picture, but they need to include the scene of this picture in their narrative.

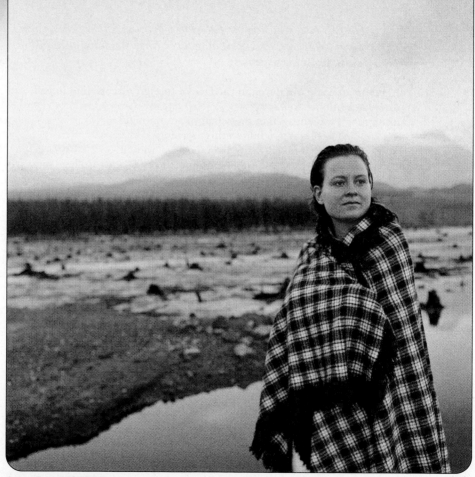

© Ant Strack/CORBIS

Narration: Relating Events

Clicking off the evening news and padding toward bed, Heloise suddenly glimpsed, out of the corner of her eye, a shadow stretching across the living room floor from under the drawn curtains.

"Wh—who's there?"

No response.

Edging backward toward the phone, her eyes riveted on the shadow, she stammered, "I–I don't have any money."

Still no answer.

Reaching the phone, she gripped the receiver and started to lift it from its cradle. Just then . . .

Just now you've glimpsed the start of a *narrative*. A narrative relates a series of events. The events may be real—as in histories, biographies, or news stories—or imaginary, as in short stories and novels. The narrative urge stirs in all of us, and like everyone else, you have responded almost from the time you began to talk. As a child, you probably swapped many stories with your friends, recounting an exciting visit to a circus or amusement park or an unusually funny experience with your pet. Today you may tell a friend about the odd happening in your biology laboratory or on the job.

Many classroom and on-the-job writing occasions call for narratives. Your English instructor might want you to trace the development of some literary character. Your history instructor might have you recap the events leading to a major war, your sociology instructor have you relate your unfolding relations with a stepparent or someone else, your psychology instructor ask you to report on society's changing attitudes toward the treatment of insanity. At work, a police officer may record the events leading to an arrest, a scientist recount the development of a research project, a nurse report on a patient's changing attitudes toward surgery, and a department manager prepare a brief history of an employee's work problems.

PERSPECTIVE
Narratives provide a convenient launch point for many writing courses since most students find it relatively easy to tell stories about their lives. The confidence they gain can help lessen apprehension about later assignments.

TEACHING STRATEGIES
1. Have each student bring to class an example of a narrative.

2. You might generate a class discussion that attempts to answer exactly what we gain when we exchange stories about ourselves with others. Some possible answers: (a) the story helps us pull our life into a pattern; (b) hearing about someone else's life gives us perspective on our own; (c) narratives help us understand how other people live; (d) swapping narratives binds us together as a community.

3. To prepare students for writing a narrative, ask

them to freewrite in their journals about memorable events in their lives. Emphasize that they include as much detail as possible. These journal entries can become background material for the narrative assignment.

4. You could progress from narratives to types of expository writing. For example, students could write a narrative about what it means to grow up. Then they might write a process essay on the stages of adolescence or a cause-and-effect essay on the problems of growing up.

Purpose

A narrative, like any other kind of writing, makes a point or has a purpose. The point can either be stated or left unstated, but it always shapes the writing.

Some narratives simply tell what happened or establish an interesting or useful fact. The reporter who writes about a heated city council meeting or a lively congressional committee hearing usually wants only to set facts before the public.

Most narratives, however, go beyond merely reciting events. Writers of history and biography delve into the motives underlying the events and lives they portray, while narratives of personal experience offer lessons and insights. In the following conclusion to a narrative about an encounter with a would-be mugger, the writer offers an observation on self-respect.

> I kept my self-respect, even at the cost of dirtying my fists with violence, and I feel that I understand the Irish and the Cypriots, the Israelis and the Palestinians, all those who seem to us to fight senseless wars for senseless reasons, better than before. For what respect does one keep for oneself if one isn't in the last resort ready to fight and say, "You punk!"?

Harry Fairlie, "A Victim Fights Back"

5. Some students have trouble writing personal narratives because they feel uncomfortable writing about themselves. A number of alternative narrative assignments can work well for such students. They can interview and report on the life of someone else, investigate and trace the development of some professional's career, or narrate a campus or community event.

TEACHING STRATEGY
Have students read a narrative and outline the events, list the motives, and circle places where the author offers observations on the action.

TEACHING STRATEGIES
1. Have students keep a weekend log of actions that could be part of a narrative; then discuss

Action

Action plays a central role in any narrative. Other writing often only suggests action, leaving readers to imagine it for themselves:

> A hundred thousand people were killed by the atomic bomb, and these six were among the survivors. They still wonder why they lived when so many others died. Each of them counts many small items of chance or volition—a step taken in time, a decision to go indoors, catching one streetcar instead of the next—that spared him. And now each knows that in the act of survival he lived a dozen lives and saw more death than he ever thought he would see. At the time, none of them knew anything.

John Hersey, *Hiroshima*

This passage suggests a great deal of action—the flash of an exploding bomb, the collapse of buildings, screaming people fleeing the scorching devastation—but *it does not present the action*. Narration, however, re-creates action:

> When I pulled the trigger I did not hear the bang or feel the kick—one never does when a shot goes home—but I heard the devilish roar of glee that went up from the crowd. In that instant, in too short a time, one would have thought, even for the bullet to get there, a mysterious, terrible change had come over the elephant. He neither stirred nor fell, but every line of his body had altered. He looked suddenly stricken, shrunken, immensely old, as though the frightful impact of the bullet had paralyzed him without knocking him down. At last, after what seemed a long time—it might have been five seconds, I dare say—he sagged flabbily to his knees. His mouth slobbered. An enormous senility seemed to have settled upon him. One could have imagined him thousands of years old. I fired again into the same spot. At the second shot he did not collapse but climbed with desperate slowness to his feet and stood weakly upright, with legs sagging and head drooping. I fired a third time. That was the shot that did it for him. You could see the agony of

it jolt his whole body and knock the last remnant of strength from his legs. But in falling he seemed for a moment to rise, for as his hind legs collapsed beneath him he seemed to tower upward like a huge rock toppling, his trunk reaching skywards like a tree. He trumpeted, for the first and only time. And then down he came, his belly towards me, with a crash that seemed to shake the ground even where I lay.

George Orwell, "Shooting an Elephant"

Orwell's account offers a stark, vivid replay of the slaying, leaving nothing significant for the reader to infer.

A few words of caution are in order here. Action entails not only exotic events such as the theft of mass-destruction weapons, then the ransom demand, then the recovery of the weapons and the pursuit of the villains. A wide variety of more normal events also qualify as action: a long, patient wait that comes to nothing, an unexpected kiss after some friendly assistance, a disappointing gift that signals a failed relationship. Furthermore, the narrative action must all relate to the main point—not merely chronicle a series of events.

Conflict

The events in our lives and our world are often shaped by conflicts that need to be resolved. It should not be surprising then that conflict and its resolution, if any, are crucial to a narrative since they motivate and often structure the action. Some conflicts pit one individual against another or against a group, such as a union, company, or religious body. In others, the conflict may involve either an individual and nature or two clashing impulses in one person's head. Read the following student paragraph and note how common sense and fear struggle within the writer, who has experienced a sharp, stabbing pain in his side:

> Common sense and fear waged war in my mind. The first argued that a pain so intense was nothing to fool with, that it might indicate a serious or even life-threatening condition. Dr. Montz would be able to identify the problem and deal with it before it worsened. But what if it was already serious? What if I needed emergency surgery? I didn't want anyone cutting into me. "Now wait a minute," I said. "It's probably nothing serious. Most aches and pains aren't. I'll see the doctor, maybe get some pills, and the problem will clear up overnight. But what if he finds something major, and I have to spend the night in the hospital getting ready for surgery or recovering from it? I think I'll just ignore the pain."
>
> Luis Rodriguez

Point of View

Narrative writers may adopt either a first-person or third-person point of view. In first-person narratives, one of the participants tells what happened, whereas with third-person narration the storyteller stays completely out of the tale. Narratives

how these events might function in a narrative.

2. Examine sample narratives to see how the basic action of the plot fits together. Students are often surprised at how little plot action many professional narratives contain.

CLASSROOM ACTIVITY
Take this simple action: "John finally kissed her. He waited on the step. Mary turned to watch him leave." Have students, working in small groups or individually, see how they might detail the action to show what happened. Discuss the alternative versions produced.

PERSPECTIVE
Conflict is also a feature of human lives, generating many of our actions. You might point out how conflict applies to students.

TEACHING STRATEGIES
1. Have students list key conflicts they have had, what led up to them, the actions they took, and how each conflict was resolved.

2. When you assign narrative essays, have students identify the key conflicts, then determine how the conflicts relate to the action in the narrative. This exercise helps students see how narrative events fit around the conflict.

3. You might center class discussion, and even

writing assignments, on more general conflicts such as (a) the problems teenagers have with their parents; (b) the kinds of difficult choices college students have to make; (c) the conflicts students have with teachers. Such conflict-oriented prompts often produce interesting class discussions in which students swap stories and begin to develop ideas. When given as part of writing assignments, these prompts help ensure that student narratives have a point and reasonable momentum.

you write about yourself use the first person, as do autobiographies. Biographies and histories use the third person, and fiction embraces both points of view.

In first-person narration, pronouns such as *I, me, mine, we,* and *ours* identify the storyteller. With the third person, the narrator remains unmentioned, and the characters are identified by nouns and such pronouns as *he, she, him,* and *her.* These two paragraphs illustrate the difference:

First-Person Narration

We would go to the well and wash in the ice-cold, clear water, grease our legs with equally cold stiff Vaseline, then tiptoe into the house. We wiped the dust from our toes and settled down for schoolwork, cornbread, clabbered milk, prayers and bed, always in that order. Momma was famous for pulling the quilts off after we had fallen asleep to examine our feet. If they weren't clean enough for her, she took the switch . . . and woke up the offender with a few aptly placed burning reminders.

Maya Angelou, "Momma's Encounter"

CLASSROOM ACTIVITY
Students often have an exaggerated sense of what conflict entails. Introduce a simple conflict, such as confronting an unruly computer, and show how it can lead to a narrative. Have students then list, in small groups or as an entire class, the kinds of conflicts people encounter.

As this example shows, first-person narrators may refer to other characters in the narrative by using nouns and third-person pronouns:

Third-Person Narration

In the depths of the city walk the assorted human creatures who do not suspect the fate that hangs over them. A young woman sweeps happily from store to store, pushing a baby carriage along. Businessmen stride purposefully into their office buildings. A young black sulks down the sidewalks of his tenement, and an old woman tugs her shopping basket across a busy thoroughfare. The old woman is not happy: she has seen better days. Days of parks and fountains, of roses and grass, still stir in her memory. Reaching the other side, she stops and strains her neck upward, past the doorways, past the rows and rows of mirror glass, until her eyes rest on the brilliant blue sky so far away. She looks intently at the sky for a few minutes, noting every cloud that rolls past. And the jet plane. She follows the plane with her deep-socketed eyes and for some unexplainable reason suspects danger. She brings her gaze back to earth and walks away as the jet releases a large cloud of brownish-yellow gas. The gas hangs ominously in the air for a while, as if wanting to give humankind just a few more seconds. Then the cloud slowly descends to the surface, dissipating as it goes. By the time it reaches the glittering megalopolis, it is a colorless, odorless blanket of death.

Richard Latta

PERSPECTIVE
Point of view can be a complex matter to discuss. The first-person narrator, of course, need not be the author, or even the main character, of a narrative. Third-person narrators can possess various degrees of omniscience. With a capable class you might examine different points of view and their effects on a narrative.

EXERCISE ANSWERS
1. This excerpt illustrates third-person narration.
2. This excerpt illustrates first-person narration.

Identify the point of view in each of the following excerpts:

1. The bus screeched to a stop, and Pat stepped out of it and onto the sidewalk. Night enveloped the city, and a slight drizzle fell around her as she made her way to Al's office. Turning the corner, she stepped into the dark entryway. The receptionist had gone home, so she proceeded directly to the office. She knocked on the door and entered. Al, standing behind his desk and looking out the window, turned toward her with a startled look on his face.

    Jennifer Webber

2. It had really begun back in the Charlestown Prison, when Bimbi first made me feel envy of his store of knowledge. Bimbi had always taken charge of any conversation he was in, and I had tried to emulate him. But every book I picked up had few sentences which didn't contain anywhere from one to nearly all of the words that might as well have been in Chinese. When I just skipped those words, of course, I really ended up with little idea of what the book said. So I had come to the Norfolk Prison Colony still going through only book-reading motions. Pretty soon, I would have quit even these motions, unless I had received the motivation that I did.

    Malcolm X, *The Autobiography of Malcolm X*

Key Events

Any narrative includes many separate events, enough to swamp your narrative boat if you try to pack them all in. Suppose you wish to write about your recent attack of appendicitis in order to make a point about heeding early warnings of an oncoming illness. Your list of events might look like this:

Awakened	Ate lunch	Entered building
Showered	Ate breakfast	Greeted fellow
Experienced acute	Opened garage door	employees
but passing pain	Started car	Began morning's work
in abdomen	Drove to work	Felt nauseated
Dressed	Parked in employee	Met with boss
Took coffee break	lot	Underwent diagnostic
Visited bathroom	Returned to work	tests
Experienced more	Began afternoon's	Had emergency
prolonged pain	work	operation
in abdomen	Collapsed at work	
Walked to cafeteria	Was rushed to hospital	

A narrative that included all, or even most, of these events would be bloated and ineffective. To avoid this outcome, identify and build your narrative around its key events—those that bear directly on your purpose. Include just enough secondary events to keep the narrative flowing smoothly, but treat them in sketchy

ALTERNATIVE EXERCISES

1. Have students collect a variety of narratives, bring them to class, identify their points of view, and suggest reasons for these choices.

2. Have students rewrite these examples, or segments from essays in the Reader, changing the point of view. Then discuss the effects of these changes in class.

3. Ask students to write about someone else's life from the first-person point of view. If nothing else, this exercise builds empathy.

TEACHING STRATEGIES

1. Many students have difficulty selecting key events. Often they have no idea of where to begin and end. You might suggest that they identify the narrative's major conflict or focal point, then select the events relevant to it.

2. Other students have trouble because they aren't skilled in using transitions. They might recognize that the appendicitis narrative doesn't need to include opening the garage door, but they simply don't know how to move the narrative from home to office. Introduce transition devices that will allow them to skip extraneous material. They could say, "After that brief attack, everything seemed fine. I even made it to work a little early that morning, as if nothing had happened."

3. Have students identify the key events in some of

the essays in the Reader and discuss why they were used. Discuss how the writers handled transitions to avoid unwanted details.

4. Ask students to identify a central event in their lives that might be the basis for a narrative, list all the events related to it, and then select the key events.

TEACHING STRATEGY
Students often have trouble going from events to ideas. After they outline an important event, have them freewrite or brainstorm their reasons

for the action and any thoughts they have about what happened.

TEACHING STRATEGIES
1. To introduce students to effective dialogue techniques, you might have them review the narrative essays in the Reader in light of directed questions such as "How do various authors indicate who is speaking?"
2. Have students record an interesting conversation as best they can remember and then transform it into effective dialogue. Ask them to observe the changes they needed to make.

TEACHING STRATEGY
You might want to discuss the following case with your students.
  Frank, a social worker, must write narrative reports about each contact with clients. While visiting one family, he

fashion. The pain and nausea certainly qualify as key events. Here's how you might present the first attack of pain:

> My first sign of trouble came shortly after I stepped out of the shower. I had just finished toweling when a sharp pain in my lower right side sent me staggering into the bedroom, where I collapsed onto an easy chair in the corner. Biting my lip to hide my groans, I sat twisting in agony as the pain gradually ebbed, leaving me gray faced, sweat drenched, and shaken. What, I asked myself, had been the trouble? Was it ulcers? Was it a gallbladder attack? Did I have stomach cancer?

This passage convinces, not just tells, the reader that an attack has occurred. Its details vividly convey the nature of the attack as well as the reactions of the victim. As in any good narrative, the reader shares the experience of the writer, and the two communicate.

Dialogue

Dialogue, or conversation, animates many narratives, livening the action and helping draw the reader into the story. Written conversation, however, doesn't duplicate real talk. In speaking with friends, we repeat ourselves, throw in irrelevant comments, use slang, lose our train of thought, and overuse expressions like *you know*, *uh*, and *well*. Dialogue that reproduced real talk would weaken any narrative.

Good dialogue resembles real conversation without copying it. It features simple words and short sentences while avoiding the over-repetition of phrases like *she said* and *he replied*. If the conversation unfolds smoothly, the speaker's identity will be clear. To heighten the sense of reality, the writer may use an occasional sentence fragment, slang expression, pause, and the like, as in this passage:

> Mom was waiting for me when I entered the house.
>
> "Your friends. They've been talking to you again. Trying to persuade you to change your mind about not going into baseball. Honey, I wish you'd listen to them. You're a terrific ballplayer. Just look at all the trophies and awards you've . . ." She paused. "Joe's mother called me this morning and asked if you were playing in the game on Saturday. Davey, I wish you would. You haven't played for two weeks. Please. I want you to. For me. It would be so good for you to go and—and do what you've always . . ."
>
> "O.K., Mom, I'll play," I said. "But remember, it's just for you."
>
> Diane Pickett

Note the mother's use of the slang expression "terrific" and of sentence fragments like "your friends" and "for me" as well as the shift in her train of thought and the repetition of "and." These strategies lend an air of realism to the mother's words.

Besides making your dialogue realistic, be sure that you punctuate it correctly. Here are some key guidelines: Each shift from one speaker to another requires a new paragraph. When an expression like *he said* interrupts a single quoted sentence, set it off with commas. When such an expression comes between two complete quoted sentences, put a period after the expression and capitalize the first word of the second sentence. Position commas and periods that come at the end of direct quotations inside the quotation marks. Our example illustrates most of these guidelines.

Ethical Issues

Think how you'd react to a supervisor who wrote a narrative about the development of a new product which exaggerated his role and minimized your crucial contribution to the result. The report might cost you the opportunity for a promotion. Think of your response if you were surfing the Internet and came across a narrative about your first date that used your actual name and cast you in an unfavorable light. At the very least you would find it embarrassing. As you mull over any narrative you write, you'll want to think about several ethical issues, especially if you're depicting an actual event.

- Have I provided a truthful account that participants will recognize and accept? Deliberate falsification of someone's behavior that tarnishes that person's reputation is libel and could result in legal action.
- Would the narrative expose any participants to possible danger if it became public? Do I need to change any names in order to protect people from potential harm? Say your narrative includes someone who cooperates behind the scenes with authorities to help solve a case of cyber-vandalism. You should probably give that person a fictitious name.
- Does the narrative encourage unethical or illegal behavior? For example, extolling the delights of smoking marijuana for a teenage audience is clearly unethical.

These guidelines don't rule out exaggerated, humorous, or painfully truthful narratives. As with any kind of writing, however, narratives can impact the lives of people; as ethical writers we need to consider the possible consequences of our work.

Writing a Narrative

Planning and Drafting the Narrative

Most of the narratives you write for your composition class will relate a personal experience and therefore use the first person. On occasion, though, you may write about someone else and therefore use the third person. In either case make sure the experience you pick illustrates some point. A paper that indicates only how you violated a friend's confidence may meander along to little purpose. But if that paper is shaped by some point you wish to make—for instance, that you

witnesses a loud argument between the father and his nine-year-old son, during which the father threatens to kill the son. Frank has grown to like and respect this family and has never observed any sign of violence. He is sure the father issued his threat because he was upset.

Frank knows that reporting the incident could lead to an investigation and cause the family problems. Should he report it? Why or why not?

TEACHING STRATEGY
How responsible is a writer for the content of a narrative? Is it acceptable to extol the virtues of, for instance, a destructive rampage or racist activities? To explore this matter, have students role-play, some representing the writer, some potential readers, some actual readers whose lives were influenced by the narrative. On the other hand, is it deceptive to present a fictional narrative as though it were factual? Take, for instance, the fictional biographies and endorsements common in advertising. What

responsibility does the company have to indicate the basis of the ad accurately? Again, have students role-play and represent the various positions.

PERSPECTIVE
While writing a narrative seems like a straightforward activity, the process can be difficult for some students. They don't believe that there is anything in their lives worth writing about, and they find it hard to link their events to a purpose.

TEACHING STRATEGY
To prepare students for writing a narrative, you might focus class discussion, and even journal writing, around a common theme such as "What does it really take to be a friend?" Such preparation often convinces students that they have something to say and provides a purpose for their papers.

READER/THEME STRATEGIES
Many essays in the Reader can lead to interesting narrative topics. Selections such as "Momma's Encounter," "What Are Friends For?," "The Men We Carry in Our Minds," "Then and Now," "Why we Flirt," "Supermarket Pastoral," or "Why Marriages Fail." could prompt students to discuss occasions when they judged others or were judged and the ensuing results. Students could then develop narratives based on their experiences.

gained insight into the obligations of friendship—the topic can be worthwhile. To get started, do some guided brainstorming, asking yourself these questions:

- What experience in my life or that of someone I know would be worth narrating?
- What point does this experience illustrate? (Try to state the point in one or two sentences.)
- What people were involved and what parts did they play?

When you have pinpointed a topic, use further brainstorming to garner supporting material. Here are some helpful questions:

- What background information is necessary to understand the events?
- What action should I include?
- What is the nature of the conflict? Was it resolved? If so, how?
- Which events play key roles, which are secondary, and which should go unmentioned?
- Is any dialogue necessary?

Before you start to write, develop a plot outline showing the significant events in your narrative. For each one, jot down what you saw, heard, or did, and what you thought or felt.

Use the opening of your paper to set the stage for what follows. You might tell when and where the action occurred, provide helpful background information, note the incident that activated the chain of events, or identify the problem from which the action grew. If you state your main point directly, do it here or in the conclusion.

The body of the narrative should move the action forward until a turning point is about to be reached. Build the body around your key events. To avoid stranding your reader, use time signals whenever the development of the action might be unclear. Words, phrases, and clauses like *now, next, finally, after an hour,* and *when I returned* help the reader understand the sequence of events. Don't get carried away, though; a paper loaded with time signals makes the sequence seem more important than the events themselves. Finally, think about how you can best use conflict and dialogue to heighten narrative interest.

The conclusion should tie up any loose ends, settle any unresolved conflicts, and lend an air of completion to the narrative. Effective strategies to think about include introducing a surprise twist, offering a reflective summary of the events, noting your reaction to them, and discussing the aftermath of the affair.

Revising the Narrative

As you revise, follow the guidelines in Chapter 4, and in addition ask yourself these questions:

Have I made the point, stated or unstated, that I intended?

Does all of the action relate to the main point?

Is the conflict handled appropriately?

Have I included all of the key events that relate to my purpose? Given each the right emphasis? Used time indicators where needed?

Is my point of view appropriate?

Does my dialogue ring true?

Have I considered appropriate ethical issues?

SAMPLE STUDENT ESSAY OF **NARRATION**

Joy Through the Tears

Brittany Coggin

Tyler Junior College

Faculty Member: Dr. Linda Gary

1   When I was growing up, there was a plaque in my grandmother's kitchen that read, "Don't get too busy making a living that you forget to make a life." My grandmother certainly followed this precept. Family was the most important thing in the world to her, and my family and I knew that we were loved.

2   As a child, I spent most days with my grandmommy while my mother was finishing school. My days were filled with baking cookies, playing games, reading stories, and making our famous mud pies. Grandmommy made time for all of this while working and taking care of all the daily chores around the house. When my mother would arrive to pick me up, it was no surprise for her to walk into the house and see Grandmommy and me prancing through the house banging pans while singing "Jingle Bells," with bright red buckets on our heads. We even called ourselves the "bucket heads."

3   My grandmother was a remarkable woman. I have always thought of her as the "center" of my family because she was. Grandmommy held high standards for her children and grandchildren, but she held even higher standards for herself. There was never a time that we did not know where she stood on an issue or where we stood with her. She had a way of holding us accountable while still leaving us in no doubt of her love for us. Although I can recall many times that I disappointed her, there was never a time that my grandmother ever disappointed me. If I thought I was in trouble and might get spanked, I usually was and did. If I thought she would be proud of me, she was. Honesty and integrity were very important to her, and she had both in abundance.

Continued on next page

SUGGESTED INSTRUCTOR READINGS

Beach, R. "Differences in Autobiographical Narratives of English Teachers, College Freshmen, and Seventh Graders." College Composition and Communication 38 (1987): 56–69. Discusses the differences in the three groups' self-concepts and knowledge of literary conventions.

Bret, C. "Remedial Writers and Fictive Techniques." College Composition and Communication 39 (1988): 27–30. Shows less experienced writers how to use such techniques as plot, characterization, and dialogue to develop a personal narrative.

Campbell, J. "Stepping Through a Mirror: The Historical Narrative Assignment." College Composition and Communication 38 (1987): 95–97. Historical narratives in which students present the events through the personas of historical figures can provide a research-oriented alternative to the personal narrative.

Crew, L. "Rhetorical Beginnings: Professional and Amateur." College Composition and Communication 38 (1987): 346–49. Reviews the opening paragraphs of a number of essays and concludes that professional writers often begin their essays with narrative while students

Continued from previous page

4   Tragedy usually strikes when we least expect it. Nothing could have prepared me for what happened with my grandmother. She was the larger-than-life force who kept our family focused. If ever there was a problem, we took it to Grandmommy, knowing she would be able to point us in the right direction.

5   The first sign that there was a problem was when she began having excruciating pain in her legs. Her doctor thought it could be neuropathy or nerve damage because she had shingles when she was young. The doctor then sent her to a specialist, who could find nothing wrong. The following months were filled with specialist after specialist who prescribed pain medication after pain medication but could never diagnose the problem. The second clue that there was actually more to the story began when my grandmother complained that every time she ate, it felt as if her chest was on fire, and she would experience a lot of pressure in her chest. Once again, specialist after specialist could find nothing wrong. By this point, my grandmother's weight went from 125 pounds to 85 pounds. Despite the weight loss, our family doctor told her that he could find nothing wrong with her. He told her to take Tylenol and to "go home and live her life."

6   Two weeks later, she was so weak that she fell down the porch steps of our family's farmhouse. We rushed her to the hospital in Henderson, Texas. She had broken her ankle, wrist, and both of her hips when she fell. While in the hospital, the doctor ordered a "swallow study" to be completed. My aunt, who is a speech pathologist, knew the speech pathologist doing the study. She asked her to go down lower into the esophagus and to use contrast. That was when we found out that my grandmother's esophagus had completely closed and the opening into the stomach was blocked. Everything she swallowed, including any medication that was prescribed, had gathered at the end of her esophagus. By this time, she was much too weak to have the procedure to open the esophagus. Her doctor sent her to Tyler to have a procedure to remove all of the material in her esophagus and to try alternatives to surgery. During this time, the doctor finally ordered a scan, which revealed that she had lung cancer and that the cancer had metastasized to the bone.

7   This news was shocking to all of us. I had the surreal feeling that I was dreaming and that at any moment, I would wake up and my world would be as it had always been. Instead, the reality was that my world would never be the same again. Grandmommy was devastated but ready to fight.

My mom stayed with her the first night in the hospital because she had to have three rounds of chemotherapy the first night. Mom said that after each round, she and Grandmommy "high-fived." That's my Grandmommy!

8   During this time, amazingly, it was my grandmother who gave us the strength to handle each day. Mom started graduate school that summer, so I would stay with Grandmommy while she was at school. Each day, Grandmommy seemed to lose the use of something. I found that I could handle more than I ever thought possible. I had to learn how to feed her and administer medication through a feeding tube. All I could think about was how I could not possibly do this. It was just too much and too hard. After a while, it became second nature. I can remember putting her false teeth in without thinking twice about it. When she lost all of her hair, we would play with hats and headbands. I would give her a makeover every time she had a doctor's appointment. Even when she began to lose the use of her hands, she cooked dinner for my mother. Grandmommy was disappointed with how it came out, but my mom said those were the best salmon patties she had ever eaten. That dinner was a labor of love because every step in the process involved immense pain.

9   While this was a time of loss, it was also a time of happiness. The time I was able to spend with my grandmother drew us closer. Each moment I spent with her seemed suspended in time. Every word, facial expression, and hug became an everlasting memory. Sometimes it seemed that my whole family was in so much pain, and no one could reach out to help each other. My grandmother loved each of us so much, so she reached out to help each family member. Her love enveloped each of us, and it kept us believing that she would get better. I know that love is not tangible, but during this time, Grandmommy could look at me, and I could feel how much she loved me. In the midst of her suffering, she gave me love and comfort. In a sense, she helped prepare me for what was to come.

10   In December 2005, my grandfather was taking Grandmommy to her doctor's appointment. After getting in the car, she collapsed and then became unconscious. I rushed to meet my family at the emergency room. When I got there, Grandmommy had regained consciousness but was not getting enough oxygen. My mother explained to her that she had pneumonia, and the doctors wanted to put her on a breathing machine until she got over it. Mom asked her to squeeze her hand if that was okay.

Continued on next page

frequently begin with rhetorical questions. Schreffler, P. "Where All the Children Are Above Average: Garrison Keillor As a Model for Personal Narrative Assignments." College Composition and Communication 40 (1989): 82–85. Shows how to use Keillor's stories as a prompt for narrative assignments.

DISCUSSION QUESTIONS

1. The narrative was written from the first-person point of view, as indicated by the use of "I" and "my." The first-person point of view here allows the writer to reflect more personally about her relationship with her grandmother, the key point of the narrative.

2. The context captures the positive relationship between the writer and her grandmother before the illness. It establishes a relationship before the illness so that we could better understand why the illness was so important to the writer.

3. Many details were effective: "making our famous mud pies," "prancing through the house . . . with bright red buckets on our heads," "after each round, she and Grandmommy 'high-fived,'" "she cooked dinner for my mother." These details were effective because they were very concrete and distinctive.

4. This narrative could have been more focused. Despite the conclusion, the focus of the paper seems to be how a remarkable woman faced death

in a way that continued to demonstrate her commitment to her family. The writer could have focused more on how her grandmother lived a life that needed no apology by focusing on an event where her grandmother was expected to conform but didn't. She could have written about the painful decision about whether to honor a loved one's wishes to not suffer or try to cling to them through medical technology by focusing on making that difficult decision. There are many other possible focuses available.

5. Dialogue could have focused a few scenes. A dialogue between the writer and the grandmother could have helped capture the relationship more precisely. The conversation with the doctor about the final choices about her care would have highlighted the difficulty of the choices. She might have better demonstrated by dialogue how her grandmother gave her the strength to face the difficult situation of dealing with her grandmother's poor health.

Continued from previous page

Though Grandmommy could not speak, she squeezed my mom's hand to tell her to let the doctors go ahead with the procedure. She then went into a coma that lasted a week.

11   When she awoke, she was terrified. The doctors said that she had a severe staph infection. This scared her because her father died of a staph infection. Doctors told us she would not be able to live without the breathing machine. Grandmommy had signed an advance directive requesting that she not be allowed to live with such suffering. The days following were miserable. I did not want to lose the one person who truly understood me, but we could not let her suffer. Even without the use of her body, her mind remained alert. We would stand around the bed in her room, and she would look past us with the most beautiful smile on her face. She mouthed that she was tired, and we knew it was time. The following morning, the doctor took her off the breathing machine, and she died with her family around her.

12   My grandmother lost her battle with cancer in December 2005. While I still mourn her loss, I feel honored to have known her. Grandmommy's life will always serve as an example of how to live a life that needs no apology. She taught me that love is everlasting and that people are more important than material things. Because of her, I am stronger than I ever thought possible. I am blessed to have had this remarkable woman as my grandmother.

Discussion Questions

1. Identify the point of view of the narrative. Why is that choice of point of view important to this particular narrative?
2. What context did the writer provide before the central conflict of her grandmother's illness? What was the role of this context information?
3. Narratives depend on very specific details. What details best helped develop the character of the writer's grandmother? Why were those details effective?
4. What is the main point of this narrative? What other possible conflicts or themes might the reader have focused on? How would the narrative have to be rewritten to make that point?
5. This narrative uses very little dialogue. Would the narrative have been improved by dialogue? Where could dialogue have been added effectively?

Suggestions for Writing

1. Write a personal narrative about an experience that

   a. altered either your opinion of a friend or acquaintance or your views about some important matter;

b. taught you a lesson or something about human nature;

c. acquainted you with some previously unrecognized facet of your character or personality;

d. brought about a significant change in your way of life.

Keep in mind all the key narrative elements: purpose, action, conflict, point of view, key events, and dialogue.

2. A *maxim* is a concise statement of a generally recognized truth. Noting the key elements above, write a first-person or third-person narrative that illustrates one of the following maxims or another that your instructor approves:

   a. A little learning is a dangerous thing.

   b. The more things change, the more they stay the same.

   c. Don't judge a book by its cover.

   d. The road to hell is paved with good intentions.

   e. Pride goeth before a fall.

   f. Sometimes too much of a good thing can be wonderful.

   g. Sometimes good intentions have unexpected consequences.

3. Write a third-person narrative based on the following activities:

   a. Interview someone who works in a career area that interests you. Ask them about how they got involved in that area and write a narrative reporting the results.

   b. Find out about the history of a place that you know well and write a narrative about how the place changed.

   c. Interview someone in your class about an important event that made them who they are and write a narrative about that person.

   d. Talk to a small business owner in your area or a leader of a nonprofit group to find out how it got started in your area and write a narrative about that business or group.

CRITICAL EDGE

Sometimes writers create narratives by weaving together information from different sources. When developing a narrative about some childhood experience, you might supplement your own recollections by asking relatives and friends to supply details that you've forgotten or clear up points that have become hazy. A police officer investigating an accident questions witnesses, examines physical evidence, and uses the findings to draft an accurate report. A historian writing a biography draws upon public documents, newspaper accounts, diaries, notes of other investigators, and—depending on when the subject lived—other material such as newsreels, TV clips, and interviews in order to create a balanced portrait.

Integrating material from several sources into a coherent piece of writing is called *synthesis*. When you synthesize, you reflect on ideas you have found in various sources, establish on your own the connections among those ideas,

Continued on next page

SUGGESTED INSTRUCTOR READINGS
Beach, R. "Differences in Autobiographical Narratives of English Teachers, College Freshmen, and Seventh Graders." <u>College Composition and Communication</u> 38 (1987): 56–69. Discusses the differences in the three groups' self-concepts and knowledge of literary conventions.

Bret, C. "Remedial Writers and Fictive Techniques." College Composition and Communication 39 (1988): 27–30. Shows less experienced writers how to use such techniques as plot, characterization, and dialogue to develop a personal narrative.

Campbell, J. "Stepping Through a Mirror: The Historical Narrative Assignment." College Composition and Communication 38 (1987): 95–97. Historical narratives in which students present the events through the personas of historical figures can provide a research-oriented alternative to the personal narrative.

Crew, L. "Rhetorical Beginnings: Professional and Amateur." College Composition and Communication 38 (1987): 346–49. Reviews the opening paragraphs of a number of essays and concludes that professional writers often begin their essays with narrative while students frequently begin with rhetorical questions.

Schreffler, P. "Where All the Children Are Above Average: Garrison Keillor As a Model for Personal Narrative Assignments." College Composition and Communication 40 (1989): 82–85. Shows how to use Keillor's stories as a prompt for narrative assignments.

Continued from previous page

and then determine how the ideas and connections can advance the purpose of your writing. Thus, synthesis features independent thinking in which *you* evaluate, select, and use the material of others—which, of course, must be properly documented—to further your own purpose. Although synthesis can be challenging and does call for judgment on your part, following an effective procedure can help ensure success. Start by jotting down the main points of information from your sources and identifying where those points agree. Sometimes accounts of the same event differ. A friend's memory of your childhood experience may differ markedly from your own. A police officer may find that two witnesses disagree about how an accident happened. A historian may discover that public documents and newspapers offer different motives for an action by a biographical subject. When you encounter this type of contradiction, you'll need to weigh each position carefully in order to determine the most believable account. Then, as in developing any narrative, arrange your material in a pattern that helps make your point.

Let's say, for example, that you're narrating the history of a suburban housing development for low-income families built on land that was formerly owned by a nearby chemical plant and later was found to be contaminated by toxic chemicals. Company officials admit that wastes were buried there but insist that the chemicals were properly contained and posed absolutely no health threat. After stating the company's position, you present the findings of government investigators who analyzed soil samples from the site. These findings revealed that the containers were corroded and leaking and that the wastes included chemicals that attack the nervous system, as well as highly toxic herbicides designed for chemical warfare operations. You conclude that the company is responsible for the serious health problems that now plague the people living in the housing development. Note how the strategy of presenting the company's position early in the narrative lends added force to the point that shapes your writing—company accountability for the health of the housing development's residents.[1]

Suggestions for Writing

1. Review a number of articles in your school or local newspaper to develop a sense of journalistic style. Then interview several people about a recent event on campus or at the place you live and write a narrative that reports the event and draws on the interviews.
2. Read "Momma's Encounter" (page 464) and then write a narrative that relates a particular minority experience and incorporates material from any of the three essays.
3. Takes notes from several newspaper accounts of an important or controversial event and write an account of the event that includes your notes.

[1]Because synthesis involves using several sources, including information from published ones, it is important to read the sections on card catalogs and periodical indexes in Chapter 20 and those on handling quotations and avoiding plagiarism in Chapter 21. As always, follow your instructor's guidelines for documenting sources.

Writing a Narrative

Plan the narrative.

- Identify part of topic if assigned or brainstorm personal experiences or observations for ideas.
- Talk to others to get ideas, more information, and for new perspectives.
- Read for information if needed (see Chapter 21 on documentation).

Write out main points you want to make.

Brainstorm details.

- Background information
- Actions—key conflicts
- Those involved and details
- Any dialogue

Organize narrative with plot outline.

- Let main point guide you.
- Identify the key conflict.
- List sequence of events (plot outline).
- Identify point of view: first or third.
- Identify needed context.

Revise.

Did you make your main point?
Does the action fit the main point?
Are any key events missing?
Is the point of view appropriate?
Does the dialogue ring true?
Is the narrative ethical?

Write a rough draft.

- Intro sets context, provides background, initiates action, may state main point.

- Body develops action in sequence of key event—signals transitions in time.

- Conclusion pulls together narrative, may state main point.

Proofread.

CHAPTER 9

TEACHING SUGGESTIONS

1. Discuss the differences between writing a description and taking a photograph. Explore how are they different and what can writing do that the photograph cannot. For example, the written description focuses the reader's attention to the details important to the meaning, will necessarily interpret the scene, can include more of the context, but cannot as completely and exactly provide the image.

2. Have students work in small groups to determine what details they would want to include in a description of this scene and then identify how they would organize the resulting description.

SUGGESTED WRITING ASSIGNMENT

After discussing how to write a description of this scene, have students write a one- or two-page description. Afterwards, you might want to have students compare their descriptions to contrast their subject matter and effectiveness.

Description: Presenting Impressions

The sound of hot dogs sizzling on a grease-spattered grill gave way to the whirling buzz of a cotton-candy machine. Fascinated, we watched as the white cardboard cone was slowly transformed into a pink, fluffy cloud. Despite their fiberglass appearance, the sticky puffs dissolved on my tongue into a sugar-like sweetness. Soon our faces and hands were gummed with a sticky mess.

You are there. Seeing, hearing, touching, tasting. This is one student writer's *description* of a small segment of a county fair. Effective description creates sharply etched word pictures of objects, persons, scenes, events, or situations. Sensory impressions—reflecting sight, sound, taste, smell, and touch—form the backbone of descriptive writing. Often, they build toward one dominant impression that the writer wants to evoke.

The human mind is not merely a logical thinking machine. Because of our emotional makeup, we react with shock to a photo of a battered victim of child abuse. We feel stirrings of nostalgia upon hearing a song from our past. We smile with satisfaction when quenching our summer thirst with tart sips from a tall, frosted drink.

Many occasions call for description. Your chemistry instructor might ask you to characterize the appearance and odor of a series of substances prepared in the laboratory; your art instructor might want you to describe a painting; your hospitality management instructor might have you portray an appealing banquet room. On the job, a realtor might write a glowing advertisement to sell a house, a nurse describe the postoperative status of a surgical incision, and a journalist describe the eruption of a volcano. All are attempts to capture the world through description.

Purpose

Sometimes description stands alone; sometimes it enriches other writing. It appears in histories and biographies, fiction and poetry, journalism and advertising, and even in technical writing. Some descriptions merely create images and

TEACHING STRATEGY
To show students how the writer's perspective affects observation and description, you might have several students, or the entire class, describe one campus feature. Then have students read the descriptions out loud and discuss why the descriptions varied.

SUGGESTED INSTRUCTOR READING
Berthoff, A. E. and J. Stephens. Forming, Thinking, Writing: The Contemporary Imagination. Portsmouth, NH: Boynton Cook, 1988. Explores relationships among observing, thinking, and writing and provides several interesting activities to help students become self-conscious observers and thinkers.

PERSPECTIVE
Students should recognize that purpose dictates how we observe and describe. While an advertising

153

copywriter might search for dramatic embellishments, a scientist writing a lab report will try to remain objective. Students often have difficulty with description because they lose sight of their purpose.

mood, as when a writer paints a word picture of a boggy, fog-shrouded moor. But description can also stimulate understanding or lead to action. A historian may juxtapose the splendor of French court life with the wretchedness of a Paris slum to help explain the French Revolution. And everyone knows the persuasive power of advertising's descriptive enticements.

Description will provide effective backup for the writing you do in your composition classes, helping you to drive home your points vividly.

Sensory Impressions

Precise sensory impressions begin with close observation. If you can reexamine your subject, do it. If not, recall it to mind; then capture its features with appropriate words. When you can't find the right words, try a comparison. Ask yourself what your subject (or part of it) might be likened to. Does it smell like a rotten egg? A ripe cantaloupe? Burning rubber? Does it sound like a high sigh? A soft rustle? To come across, the comparison must be accurate and familiar. If the reader has never smelled a rotten egg, the point is lost.

Here is a passage marked by particularly vivid sight impressions:

> After our meal we went for a stroll across the plateau. The day was already drawing to a close as we sat down upon a ledge of rock near the lip of the western precipice. From where we sat, as though perched high upon a cloud, we looked out into a gigantic void. Far below, the stream we had crossed that afternoon was a pencil-thin trickle of silver barely visible in the gloaming. Across it, on the other side, the red hills rose one upon another in gentle folds, fading into the distance where the purple thumblike mountains of Adua and Yeha stretched against the sky like a twisting serpent. As we sat, the sun sank fast, and the heavens in the western sky began to glow. It was a coppery fire at first, the orange streaked with aquamarine; but rapidly the firmament expanded into an explosion of red and orange that burst across the sky sending tongues of flame through the feathery clouds to the very limits of the heavens. When the flames had reached their zenith, a great quantity of storks came flying from the south. They circled above us once, their slender bodies sleek and black against the orange sky. Then, gathering together, they flew off into the setting sun, leaving us alone in peace to contemplate. One of the monks who sat with us, hushed by the intensity of the moment, muttered a prayer. The sun died beyond the hills; and the fire withdrew.
>
> Robert Dick-Read, *Sanamu: Adventures in Search of African Art*

At first, the western sky glows with "a coppery fire," which then expands into "an explosion of red and orange" that sends "tongues of flame" heavenward and then withdraws as the sun disappears. Comparisons strengthen the visual impression: the "pencil-thin" stream, the "thumblike" mountains stretching across the sky "like a twisting serpent." The familiar pencil, thumb, and serpent help us to visualize the unfamiliar landscape.

Most descriptions blend several sense impressions rather than focusing on just one. In the following excerpt, Mark Twain, reminiscing about his uncle's farm, includes all five. As you read it, note which impressions are most effective.

> As I have said, I spent some part of every year at the farm until I was twelve or thirteen years old. The life which I led there with my cousins was full of charm, and so is the memory of it yet. I can call back the solemn twilight and mystery of the

deep woods, the earthy smells, the faint odors of the wild flowers, the sheen of rain-washed foliage, the rattling clatter of drops when the wind shook the trees, the far-off hammering of woodpeckers and the muffled drumming of wood pheasants in the remoteness of the forest, the snapshot glimpses of disturbed wild creatures scurrying through the grass—I can call it all back and make it as real as it ever was, and as blessed. I can call back the prairie, and its loneliness and peace, and a vast hawk hanging motionless in the sky, with his wings spread wide and the blue of the vault showing through the fringe of their end feathers. I can see the woods in their autumn dress, the oaks purple, the hickories washed with gold, the maples and the sumachs luminous with crimson fires, and I can hear the rustle made by the fallen leaves as we plowed through them. I can see the blue clusters of wild grapes hanging among the foliage of the saplings, and I remember the taste of them and the smell. I know how the wild blackberries looked, and how they tasted, and the same with the pawpaws, the hazelnuts, and the persimmons; and I can feel the thumping rain, upon my head, of hickory nuts and walnuts when we were out in the frosty dawn to scramble for them with the pigs, and the gusts of wind loosed them and sent them down. I know the stain of blackberries, and how pretty it is, and I know the stain of walnut hulls, and how little it minds soap and water, also what grudged experience it had of either of them. I know the taste of maple sap, and when to gather it, and how to arrange the troughs and the delivery tubes, and how to boil down the juice, and how to hook the sugar after it is made, also how much better hooked sugar tastes than any that is honestly come by, let bigots say what they will.

Mark Twain, *Autobiography*

Spend some time in an environment such as one of the following. Concentrate on one sense at a time. Begin by observing what you see; then jot down the precise impressions you receive. Now do the same for impressions of touch, taste, smell, and sound.

1. The woods in the early morning
2. A city intersection
3. A restaurant or cafeteria
4. A scenic spot under a full moon
5. A storm
6. A pool or other recreation area
7. A crowded classroom or hallway
8. A construction site
9. A park or playground
10. A holiday gathering

CLASSROOM ACTIVITIES

Because students are likely to be vague in their descriptions, you might have them do some in-class activities before attempting the exercises. Encourage students to gather an excess of sensory impressions and then eliminate inappropriate ones. This practice makes writing easier. Here are some possible activities to consider.

1. Form small groups and have students list various words that describe such things as different kinds of rain, voices, hair colors, walking. List the responses on the board. This may be a good time to introduce students to the thesaurus.

2. Have students, working in small groups, list the distinctive features of the day. Encourage them to look closely at the kinds of light, types of clouds, atmospheric conditions, and the like.

3. Have students jot down their precise impressions of the classroom using one sense at a time; then have them compare results.

4. Senses other than sight can, of course, be difficult to convey because our vocabulary is more limited. Have the class bring in devices such as bells or whistles that create distinctive sounds; then work with students on how to describe the sounds they make, paying close attention to how we formulate useful comparisons.

Dominant Impression

Skillful writers select and express sensory perceptions in order to create a *dominant impression*—an overall mood or feeling such as joy, anger, terror, or distaste. This impression may be identified or left unnamed for the reader to deduce. Whatever the choice, a verbal picture of a storm about to strike, for example, might be crafted to evoke feelings of fear by describing sinister masses of clouds, cannon salvos of thunder, blinding lightning flashes, and viciously swirling wind-caught dust.

The following paragraph establishes a sense of security as the dominant impression:

> A marvelous stillness pervaded the world, and the stars together with the serenity of their rays seemed to shed upon the earth the assurance of everlasting security. The young moon recurved, and shining low in the west, was like a slender shaving thrown up from a bar of gold, and the Arabian Sea, smooth and cool to the eye like a sheet of ice, extended its perfect level to the perfect circle of a dark horizon. The propeller turned without a check, as though its beat had been part of the scheme of a safe universe; and on each side of the *Patna* two folds of water, permanent and sombre on the unwrinkled shimmer, enclosed within their straight and diverging ridges a few white swirls of foam bursting in a low hiss, a few wavelets, a few ripples, a few undulations that, left behind, agitated the surface of the sea for an instant after the passage of the ship, subsided splashing gently, calmed down at last into the circular stillness of water and sky with the black speck of the moving hull remaining everlastingly in its centre.
>
> Joseph Conrad, *Lord Jim*

The first sentence directly identifies the impression, "security," to which the "stillness" and the "serenity" contribute. Other details also do their part: the "smooth" sea, the "perfect circle" of the horizon, the "safe universe," the quick calming of the water, and the moving hull "everlastingly" in the center of water and sky.

Select one of the following topics and write a paragraph that evokes a dominant impression. Omit details that run counter to your aim.

1. A multi-alarm fire
2. A repair facility (automobile, appliance, and so on)
3. A laboratory
4. Some aspect of summer in a particular place
5. A religious service
6. A doctor's or dentist's office
7. A dark street
8. A parade or other celebration
9. Some landmark on your college campus
10. A municipal night court or small-claims court

Vantage Point

You may write a description from either a fixed or a moving vantage point. A fixed observer remains in one place and reports only what can be perceived from there. Here is how Marilyn Kluger describes the Thanksgiving morning sounds she remembers hearing from her bed as a child:

> On the last Thursday in November, I could stay in bed only until the night chill left the house, hearing first the clash of the heavy grates in the huge black iron

range, with its flowery scrolls and nickled decorations, as Mother shook down the ashes. Then, in their proper sequence, came the sounds of the fire being made— the rustle of newspaper, the snap of kindling, the rush of smoke up the chimney when Mother opened the damper, slid the regulator wide open, and struck a match to the kerosene-soaked corncobs that started a quick hot fire. I listened for the bang of the cast-iron lid dropping back into place and for the tick of the stovepipes as fierce flames sent up their heat, then the sound of the lid being lifted again as Mother fed more dry wood and lumps of coal to the greedy new fire. The duties of the kitchen on Thanksgiving were a thousand-fold, and I could tell that Mother was bustling about with a quicker step than usual.

Marilyn Kluger, "A Time of Plenty"

A moving observer views things from a number of positions, signaling changes in location with phrases such as "moving through the turnstile" and "as I walked around the corner." Below, H. L. Mencken takes us with him as he observes from a moving express train.

On a Winter day some years ago, coming out of Pittsburgh on one of the expresses of the Pennsylvania Railroad, I rolled eastward for an hour through the coal and steel towns of Westmoreland county. It was familiar ground; boy and man, I had been through it often before. But somehow I had never quite sensed its appalling desolation. Here was the very heart of industrial America, the center of its most lucrative and characteristic activity, the boast and pride of the richest and grandest nation ever seen on earth—and here was a scene so dreadfully hideous, so intolerably bleak and forlorn that it reduced the whole aspiration of man to a macabre and depressing joke. Here was wealth beyond computation, almost beyond imagination—and here were human habitations so abominable that they would have disgraced a race of alley cats.

I am not speaking of mere filth. One expects steel towns to be dirty. What I allude to is the unbroken and agonizing ugliness, the sheer revolting monstrousness, of every house in sight. From East Liberty to Greensburg, a distance of twenty-five miles, there was not one in sight from the train that did not insult and lacerate the eye. Some were so bad, and they were among the most pretentious—churches, stores, warehouses, and the like—that they were downright startling; one blinked before them as one blinks before a man with his face shot away. A few linger in memory, horrible even there: a crazy little church just west of Jeannette, set like a dormer-window on the side of a bare, leprous hill; the headquarters of the Veterans of Foreign Wars at another forlorn town, a steel stadium like a huge rat-trap somewhere further down the line. But most of all I recall the general effect—of hideousness without a break. There was not a single decent house within eye-range from the Pittsburgh suburbs to the Greensburg yards. There was not one that was not mis-shapen, and there was not one that was not shabby.

H. L. Mencken, "The Libido for the Ugly"

The phrase "on one of the expresses of the Pennsylvania Railroad" signals that Mencken will be a moving observer, and "From East Liberty to Greensburg" pinpoints the extent of his journey. "West of Jeannette," "another forlorn town," and "somewhere further down the line" specify the positions from which he views the church, the headquarters of the veterans' organization, and the stadium.

Whatever your vantage point, fixed or moving, report only what would be apparent to someone on the scene. If you describe how a distant mountain looks from a balcony, don't suddenly leap to a description of a mountain flower; you couldn't see it from your vantage point.

1. **Writing as a fixed observer, describe in a paragraph your impressions of one of the following. Be sure to indicate your vantage point.**

   a. A post office lobby two weeks before Christmas
   b. The scene following a traffic accident
   c. A classroom when the bell rings
   d. A campus lounge
   e. An office
   f. The entrance to some building

2. **Writing as a moving observer, describe in a paragraph or two your impressions as you do one of the following things. Clearly signal your movements to the reader.**

   a. Walk from one class to another
   b. Shop in a supermarket or clothing store
   c. Walk from your home to the corner
   d. Cross a long bridge
   e. Water-ski
   f. Go through a ticket line and enter a theater, auditorium, or sports arena

ALTERNATIVE EXERCISE
Have students describe the same object or scene from several vantage points and then write a brief account of the differences and the impact on the description.

Selection of Details

CLASSROOM ACTIVITY
Have students list the details in the classroom and then as a group determine which ones they would use for different effects.

Effective description depends as much on exclusion as on inclusion. Don't try to pack every possible detail into your paper by providing an inventory of, for example, a room's contents or a natural setting's elements. Such an approach shows only that you can see, not write. Instead, select details that deliberately point toward the mood or feeling you intend to create. Read the following student description:

> At night, a restful stillness falls over the suburbs. . . . Everyone has vanished inside the carefully maintained homes that line the winding streets. The children have gone to bed, leaving the occasional motionless wagon or tricycle in the driveway. A light gleams in some bedroom windows. TV sets silently flicker a tranquil blue in a few living rooms. The street lamps curve protectively over the empty streets and sidewalks. The stillness is only disturbed by the brief, familiar bark of a neighbor's dog, quickly hushed, intensifying in its wake the silence that holds sway with the dark.
>
> Kim Granger

This writer evokes a sense of stillness by noting "the occasional motionless wagon or tricycle," that "TV sets silently flicker a tranquil blue," that "The street lamps curve protectively," that the dog is "quickly hushed." She ignores the car that cruises homeward, stereo booming; the husband and wife screaming at each other; the caterwauling cat fight. Mentioning these things would detract from the desired mood.

Arrangement of Details

Description, like any other writing, must have a clear pattern of organization to guide the reader and help you fulfill your purpose. Often some spatial arrangement works nicely. You might, for example, move systematically from top to bottom, left to right, front to back, nearby to far away, or the reverse of these patterns. To describe Saturday afternoon at the football game, you might start with the crowded parking lot; move into the bustling stadium; and finally zoom in on the sights, sounds, and smells of the playing field. Or if you wanted to highlight the surroundings rather than the central event, the order could be reversed. Going another route, you might start with some striking central feature and then branch out to the things around it. To capture the center of a mall, you might first describe its ornate fountain illuminated with flashing, multicolored lights, shift to the reflection of the lights on the skylight above, and end by portraying the surrounding store fronts.

Sometimes a description follows a time sequence. A writer might, for example, portray the changes in a woodland setting as winter gives way to spring and spring, in turn, yields to summer.

Ethical Issues

Imagine a police description of an auto accident that misstated the length of a car's skid marks or failed to note the icy patches of road at the scene. It might cost a blameless driver a heavy fine and a steep increase in auto insurance premiums. Imagine your disappointment and anger if you booked a weekend at a distant resort only to find it situated on an algae-covered pond instead of the beautiful lake described in the brochure. Imagine your irritation if a going-out-of-business sale described as "fabulous" turned out to offer only 10 percent price reductions. Clearly, inaccurate descriptions can create a wide range of undesirable consequences. Ask and answer these questions about your description.

- Would readers find my writing credible if they were at the scene?
- Are readers given adequate clues so that they will recognize any deliberate exaggeration?
- Will the description deceive readers in a harmful way?

You have an ethical obligation to present a reasonably accurate portrayal of your topic.

Writing a Description

Planning and Drafting the Description

If you're choosing your own topic, always select one that is familiar. Don't describe the inside of a restaurant kitchen or Old Faithful geyser in Yellowstone National Park if you've never seen either one. Instead, opt for some place where

TEACHING STRATEGIES

Here are two cases you might want to discuss with your class.

1. Tom placed a personal ad in a newspaper stating that he was tall and muscular when in reality he is short and somewhat flabby. Angie responded to the ad. On their first date she laughed at Tom's false description but found his personality attractive and started dating him. Tom explained that he was merely taking artistic license with his description. Did he act ethically? Explain.

2. In advertising a certain property, Ace Realtors decided to alter the description. Since much of the property was swampy, they described it as adjacent to wetlands; while there were only a few scrubby bushes, they called it a wooded lot; though it was half a mile to a nearby river, they identified the parcel as having "a river view." One client who traveled four hundred miles to examine the property felt cheated and expressed outrage. The company claimed that it used standard real estate exaggeration. Did the company act ethically? Explain.

you've actually worked or a locale you've recently visited. If you keep a journal, thumb through it for possible leads.

For each potential topic that surfaces, ask yourself the following questions.

What do I want to accomplish by writing this description? Create one or more impressions? Help the reader understand something? Persuade the reader to act?

Who is my audience and why would this topic interest them?

What dominant impression will I develop?

To help gather and organize support for your topic, pose these additional questions:

What details should I include?

What sensory impressions are associated with each detail? (Jot down any words that you feel will best convey the impressions.)

How does each detail contribute to the dominant impression?

What sequence should I follow in presenting my impressions? (Map out the sequence, setting up a 1-2-3 listing or possibly a paragraph-by-paragraph plan.)

After brainstorming a list of potential details, you might use branching (below) to start accumulating sensory impressions. This illustrates how student writer Kim Swiger used branching to obtain and group the sensory impressions for a paragraph describing the sounds of her kitchen at breakfast time. Note that her grouping provided Swiger with the pattern used to organize her paragraph. Thus, the paragraph begins with stove-related sounds, moves to sounds associated with coffee-making and cooking, and ends with the sounds of mixing orange juice.

Begin your paper with an introduction that eases the reader into your topic. You might, for example, provide a historical overview, ask a provocative question, or snare the reader's attention with an arresting statement.

Develop each major feature in one or more paragraphs. Present each feature in the order you've mapped out. To ensure that the reader follows your thoughts, clearly signal any shifts in vantage point or time. As you write, aim for vivid, original language. We've all encountered writers who tell us that raindrops "pitter-patter," clouds are "fleecy white," and the sun is "a ball of fire." Such stale, worn-out language does nothing to sharpen our vision of the rain, the clouds, or the sun. The Swiger paragraph avoids this pitfall.

> Sure signs of a new day are the sounds in the kitchen as breakfast is prepared. The high sigh of the gas just before it whooshes into flame and settles into a whispering hum blends with the gurgling of the water for the morning coffee. Soon the gloop, gloop, gloop of the coffee sets up a perky beat. Then in mingles the crackle of creamy butter on a hot skillet and the shush of an egg added to the pan. Ribbons of bacon start to sizzle in the spitting grease. The soft rustle of plastic as bread is removed from its wrapper contributes to the medley. The can opener whirs, and the orange juice concentrate drops with a splat into the blender, which whizzes together the orange cylinder and splashed-in water. For minutes after the blender stops, bubbles of various sizes fizz.
>
> Kim Burson Swiger

You are there in the kitchen, hearing the carefully selected and freshly described sounds.

A word of caution about making your writing vivid. Some students are tempted to enhance their descriptions by stringing together a chain of adjectives without considering the effect on a reader. Think how you'd react if told that

> A dented, cylindrical, silver-gray, foul-smelling, overloaded trash can sat in the alley.

As you can see, more than the garbage can is overloaded here. Resist the temptation to inject similar sentences into your description. Carefully examine your adjectives and eliminate those that don't advance your purpose.

End your paper by pulling your material together in some way. If you've created an impression or mood, you might offer your reaction to it. If you want your reader to understand something, you might spell your message out. If you wish to persuade, you might urge some action.

Revising the Description

As you revise, apply the guidelines in Chapter 4 and ask the following questions:

Have I written with a clear sense of purpose and audience in mind?

Have I conveyed how my topic looks, sounds, feels, tastes, or smells?

    Would comparisons or more precise descriptive terms help convey my perceptions?

READER/THEME STRATEGIES

A descriptive essay could emerge from the exploration of a theme. For the theme "Life's Changes," students might read such essays as "Once More to the Lake," "Momma's Encounter," and "Grant and Lee: A Study in Contrasts" and discuss how the places where people reside help shape their identities. The class could then write essays describing places important to their development. For the theme "Who We Are," students might read such essays as "Once More to the Lake" and "The Men We Carry in Our Minds," then discuss how place or position affects who we are, and finally write essays describing places important to their development. A natural topic for a description essay is "Our Relationship to Nature." Students could read such essays as "When the Full Moon Shines Its Magic over Monument Valley," "Let's Get Vertical!" and "Taking Carl Down," and then write essays describing encounters they had with nature.

TEACHING STRATEGIES

1. Since students usually under-write descriptions, you might have them freewrite additional sensory details for key parts of their papers and then incorporate the best material into their drafts.

2. Peer responses can reveal under-written or

misplaced description, especially if peers are asked to write down their questions and identify vague passages.
3. Have students circle their key descriptive terms and brainstorm possible substitutes.

Have I evoked one dominant impression? Can I strengthen this impression by adding certain selected details? By eliminating details that detract from the impression?

Have I used an appropriate vantage point? If the observer is moving, have I signaled changes in location? Have I included only details that would be visible to the observer?

Have I arranged my details in an order appropriate to the topic?

Have I considered appropriate ethical issues?

SAMPLE

SAMPLE STUDENT ESSAY OF **DESCRIPTION**

My Serenity

Rachel Harvey

Ferris State University

Faculty Member: RoseAnn Shansky

1   The building blends in with the landscape, its faint yellow tinsiding disguising it from passersby on the road. As the icicles split-splop from the entryway overhang, one devious droplet sneaks into my shirt to roll down my neck. As I step into the barn, I am bombarded with the musty smell of clay dirt, sawdust, and sweet hay. The air here is more inviting than outside; it beckons me as an old friend would. I know my welcoming committee is in full swing when I hear a faint meow and a series of whinnies rising up out of the stalls. A large black-and-white barn cat, appropriately named Sylvester for his markings and ability to catch birds, stares at me with his intense yellow eyes. My boots sink into the soft dirt as I wade my way over to the worn, wooden stalls and stoop to pet the oversized feline. I stop at Dynamite Kid's stall to pay him a visit.

2   Kid stands a beautiful five feet two inches tall, with his white blond mane and tail and sleek white coat dappled with gray. As I approach him, he starts to dance, or at least a horse's version of dancing. His front legs splayed wide and rocking his weight from side to side, he resembles a flagpole in a gusty storm. I find myself giggling because he thinks I'm going to feed him; he always dances for his food. I slip into his stall and his petal-soft lips scour my hand for his treat. His teeth sound as if they're cutting bolts as he pulverizes the pea-green pellet into bits. I nuzzle up to his soft neck and inhale his aroma. The musk of a horse is unforgettable

because it's natural but so unique. This scent brings some of my most treasured memories back. Here I can forget about my ten-page paper that's due Friday and about the fight my significant other and I just had.

3   Everything seeps away from my mind as I snatch a stiff-bristled brush and start grooming him, plumes of dust rising off his back. Here it's only Kid, me, and the rustles and sighs of the other horses in their stalls. Twenty minutes later, once I've lunged and tied him, I head to the tack room to find Kid's equipment. I step into a room full of worn leather, colorful nylon, and jangling metal. I sort out his equipment: a burgundy leather bridle with a jointed bit, matching reins, and chocolate saddle trimmed with burgundy suede. The feel of chafed leather in my hand is a familiar one, both comforting and exciting. I slip the bridle over Kid's head and force the bit between his teeth. He mauls it, trying to get comfortable with the feel and taste of the harsh metal. I heft the heavy woolen saddle blanket and awkward saddle over his back to his withers and cinch it down. After some fine tuning and other adjustments, I'm sitting five foot two taller and making my way out toward the woods.

4   On top of Kid, I feel as if nothing can touch me. The rich smell of wet, rotting wood and melting snow waft over me as I pick my way through the trees. The dull colors of the landscape contrast with the white snow that is slowly but surely disappearing. The first robins are back: I can't see them, but their fluttering voices reveal their presence. Red squirrels are starting to venture out to harvest their stores of nuts, their red fur a sharp distinction from their surroundings. I steer Kid through a small depression. His feet squish into the ground, and I realize a small creek has revived. As I breathe deeply, I inhale the spring breeze picking its way over the fields. Here, spring is a timid but gay being; she will take her time in showing herself, but what she shows is wonderful and can enrapture the most stubborn of souls. I stop and close my eyes.

5   Surrounded by the countryside, I have a sense of peace and tranquility. I try my hardest to stow away this emotion, this feeling of completeness. Nature has always been able to capture my mind and whisk it away from my problems, giving me a temporary relief from the pressures of life. Kid snorts impatiently underneath me. He's eager to continue exploring, but I'm content to just stay here. After a few minutes of serenity, my cell

Continued on next page

DISCUSSION QUESTIONS

1. *Sound* "icicles split-splop," "faint meow and a series of whinnies," "teeth sound cutting bolts," "jangling metal," "fluttering voices," "cell phone blares."

   Smell "bombarded with the musty smell." "musk of a horse," "The rich smell of wet, rotting wood,"

   Feel "roll down my neck," "boots sink into the soft dirt," "lips scour my hand," "feel of chafed leather," "squish into the ground."

   Sight As with much description, most is visual. "large black and white barn cat," "intense yellow eyes," "white blond mane and tail and sleek white coat dappled with gray," "front legs splayed wide . . . resembles a flag-pole in a gusty storm," "plumes of dust," "worn leather, colorful nylon," "a burgundy leather bridle with a joined bit, matching reins, and chocolate saddle trimmed with burgundy suede," "dull colors of the landscape . . . white snow," "Red squirrels."

   The dominant impression of the essay is of calm and of a different time and space, partially because of the careful pace of the descriptions and the description of very quiet scenes.

2. The essay moves forward in time and space. The person steps into the barn, enters a stall, describes the horse, describes the tack-room, prepares the horse for a ride, moves into a woods. This is contrasted with the harsh

phone call and the sudden end of the ride. This patient description that comes to an abrupt end meets the purpose of capturing a space for serenity that is only temporary.

3. The reader uses careful transitions for the movement in time and space. "As I stepped into the barn," "I stop at Dynamite Kid's stall," "As I approach him," "Twenty minutes later," "I head for the tack room," "I'm sitting," "I pick my way through trees," As a result of these transitions, readers always know where they stand.

4. The description of the phone call makes a sharp distinction by using harsh language: "blares," "searing intrusion, "violently ripped." The fact that the phone call ends the essay helps make it a strong contrast to the rest of the scene. However, earlier language that is abrupt make the contrast less forceful: "bombarded, "cutting bolts," "pulverizes," "jangling metal."

SUGGESTED INSTRUCTOR READINGS

Brand, J. "Descriptive Experiment." School Arts 12 (1979): 44–45. Provides a provocative and imaginative assignment that uses description.

Taylor, M. "Draw: A Heuristic for Expressive Writing." Journal of Teaching Writing 4 (1985): 210–14. Demonstrates how a form of creative description can help students to develop ideas for expressive writing.

Continued from previous page

phone blares out an excerpt of a song from George Strait, its noise a searing intrusion, and my head is violently ripped from its retreat. It's my boyfriend. I choose not to answer, trying to prolong my escape, but the spell is broken. I turn Kid back toward the barn and reality.

Discussion Questions

1. Identify details that appeal to each of the senses. Describe the dominant impression these details produce.
2. How is this description organized? Given the purpose of the essay, how effective is this pattern?
3. Where does the writer indicate movement in time and space? Does she keep the reader clearly located?
4. How effectively does the description of the phone call in the conclusion contrast with the rest of the description?

Suggestions for Writing

Choose one of the following topics or another that your instructor approves for a properly focused essay of description. Create a dominant impression by using carefully chosen, well-organized details observed from an appropriate vantage point. Try to write so that the reader actually experiences your description.

1. Holiday shopping
2. A concert of some type
3. An exercise class
4. A crafts class
5. An amusement park, a miniature or full-sized golf course, or some other type of recreational facility
6. A juice bar or coffee shop
7. A pet store or zoo
8. The lobby of a theater
9. A professional wrestling performance
10. A shopping center or minimart
11. A fast-food restaurant
12. Some type of party
13. An outdoor place of special importance to you
14. A Thanksgiving dinner
15. A reunion of some type
16. A NASCAR race
17. A video game arcade
18. An advertisement
19. A scene of environmental damage
20. A historical building or site

Most of us know that any two people are likely to see and describe the same object, place, or event differently. A motorist whose car broke down in the desert would note the impossible distances, the barrenness, the absence of human life, the blazing sun. A biologist who was well-supplied with food and water would see a rich ecosystem with a wide variety of plant life and an interesting population of insects and animals. Each would produce a different description that served a different purpose. The motorist would emphasize the grueling heat and desolation to establish the danger of the situation. The biologist would provide a detailed description of the plants, insects, and animals to advance scientific understanding of the area.

As a writer, you may occasionally need to synthesize (see pages 149–150) information supplied by others when creating your own description. Suppose that you're writing a paper about the old growth forests of Oregon. You may read a naturalist's description of the ancient, rare species of trees and how the forest provides a habitat for much unique wildlife. You might also read a lumber industry study indicating that the trees are an important economic resource. You might even uncover an account by an early explorer that captures the emotions aroused by the discovery of the forest.

Armed with these and other descriptions, you could create a composite picture that captures all the different perspectives. You might start by offering the views of the Native American forest dwellers, then detail the towering majesty of the trees and the abundance of game as reported by early explorers. Next, you might turn to the accounts of early farmers, who regarded the forest as an obstacle to be cleared away, and continue by presenting the view of the forest as a lumber resource, perhaps including a description of a depleted lumbering site. To end the paper, you might note how contemporary conservationists view what remains of the forest. Collectively, this information would offer a stark portrayal of the near-total destruction of a splendid natural resource and by implication argue for preserving what is left. While this kind of writing task seems daunting, you can simplify it if you take up one perspective at a time.

Because different people are likely to see and describe the same object, place, or event differently, it's important to look critically at any description you consider for your paper. When you finish reading, ask yourself what features might have been omitted and what another slant on the material might have yielded. To illustrate, in "Once More to the Lake" E. B. White describes early morning fishing as follows: "We went fishing the first morning. I felt the same damp moss covering the worms in the bait can, and saw the dragonfly alight on the tip of my rod as it hovered a few inches from the surface of the water." (See paragraph 5, page 479.) If White had found fishing repugnant, he could just as easily have described the worms squiggling in the can as if they were afraid of the hook, the slimy feel of his hands after baiting the hook, the swarm of mosquitoes around his face, and the tangle in his line. Clearly, description demands choices. Different impressions and varying emphases can be selected. And like any other writer, you should carefully consider the details and slant of any description you write[1].

Suggestions for Writing

1. Select a famous U.S. landmark, such as the Grand Canyon, and read several writers' descriptions of it. After taking notes, write a description that includes their differing perspectives.
2. Rewrite a shortened version of an essay such as "Once More to the Lake" by building on the original details to create a different emphasis.
3. Interview several students to learn their impressions of your campus and weave those impressions into a descriptive essay.

---

[1]Because this type of paper includes information from published sources, it is important to read the sections on card catalogs and periodical indexes in Chapter 20 and those on handling quotations and avoiding plagiarism in Chapter 21. As always, follow your instructor's guidelines for documenting sources.

Writing a Description

Plan the description.

- Read assignment and select familiar topic.
- Identify your purpose for your description.
- Identify audience and analyze.

Brainstorm details perhaps using branching.

- Reobserve subject of paper if possible.
- Identify dominant impression.
- Select the relevant details for description.

Develop organizational strategy.

Establish **organizational strategy** and rough plan possibly ordering by space, importance, or time.

Write draft.

Intro establishes context and identifies object and reason; paragraphs of body detail major features, conclusions.

Revision often calls for additional brainstorming and possibly new observations.

Revise.

Read description critically, collect reader response, reobserve if possible.
- Be consistent with impression.
- Add details as needed.
- Cut details that don't fit.
- Test organization, and make consistent with transitions.

Proofread.

CHAPTER 10

TEACHING SUGGESTION

The picture represents one step in part of forming a pot. Have students work in small groups to carefully describe from the picture what seem to be the elements of this process of forming the feature of the mouth of the pottery. They should note that the clay has been moistened so that it can be manipulated, that the clay is being lightly pinched on thin and lift it, and that it is done gently with the hands. Have students working in small groups identify what they believe than to be some of the principles or processes of pottery.

SUGGESTED WRITING ASSIGNMENTS

1. After the small group have reported their results to the class, have each student write a detailed account of the steps evident in the picture.

2. Have students individually write a paper about how to do some aspect of an art with which they are familiar whether it is taking an effective picture, mixing paint, or performing a dance step.

© Image Source/Corbis

168

Process Analysis: Explaining How

"Hey Bill, I'd like you to take a look at Mr. Gorgerise's car. He's really fuming. Says the engine's burning too much oil, running rough, and getting poor mileage. Check it out and see what you can find."

Bill begins by removing the spark plugs, hooking a remote-control starter to the starter in the car, and grounding the ignition to prevent the car's starting accidentally. Next, he fits a compression pressure gauge into the spark plug hole by cylinder number one, starts the engine, and reads and records the pressure; then he does the same for each of the other cylinders. Finally, he compares the readings with one another and the automaker's engine specs. The verdict? An excessively worn engine that needs rebuilding. Bill has carried out a *process*, just one among many that fill his workdays.

As we pursue our affairs, we perform processes almost constantly, ranging from such daily rituals as brewing a pot of coffee and flossing our teeth to taking a picture, burning a compact disc, preparing for a date, or replacing a light switch. Often we share our special technique for doing something—for example, making chicken cacciatore—by passing it on to a friend.

Many popular publications feature process analyses that help readers to sew zippers in garments, build catamarans, live within their means, and improve their wok technique. Process analysis also frequently helps you meet the writing demands of your courses. A political science instructor may ask you to explain how your state's governor won nomination, or a biology instructor may want an explanation of how bees find their way back to the hive. Another instructor may call for directions relating to some process in your field—for example, analyzing a chemical compound, taking fingerprints, or obtaining a blood sample.

On the job, a greenhouse crew leader may provide summer employees with directions for planting various kinds of shrubs and flowers. A technical writer may prepare a list of steps for workers to follow when unloading a particular solvent from a tank car. A sanitation department technician may write a brochure telling city residents how to get paper, glass, and metal trash ready for recycling.

As these examples show, a process can be nontechnical, historical, scientific, natural, or technical.

PERSPECTIVE
Explaining a process helps students develop some of the key qualities of good writing. They learn to be complete in their information, precise in their statements, and careful about their organization as well as to consider the background knowledge of their intended audience, especially when preparing instructions. Finally, in writing about a process students assume the role of an authority, a role essential to better writing.

TEACHING STRATEGIES
1. Have students review their assignments, exams, or lecture notes from other classes to see where process analysis would be useful.
2. To prepare students for the research demands of later courses, assign each to research the use of a different library reference tool and write a paper incorporating the explanation. These papers could then be bound

169

together and distributed as a resource.

3. Because so many "how to" articles appear in the popular press, students find it tempting to plagiarize. How, after all, is the teacher to know that the explanation of how to change oil came from an obscure car magazine? To counter this problem, you might have students write about some unique procedure at your school or on topics that are less likely to be readily available in print, such as how to break a date or patch up a quarrel with a friend.

TEACHING STRATEGIES
1. Ask students to evaluate the two kinds of process writing in the Reader. "Fast Track to Perfection" offers directions for readers who will perform the process; "Taking Carbon Down" is aimed at nonperformers. Have students identify the different purposes of these essays and how they influence the form of address, material included, and organization.
2. In some high school English classes, students have been warned endlessly not to use *you* in their writing. You might reassure them that *you* can be appropriate, identify works that follow the "*you* approach," but also establish where *you* is not appropriate.

Kinds of Process Analysis Papers

Process papers fall into two categories: those intended for readers who will perform the process and those intended to explain the process for nonperformers. Papers in either category can range from highly technical and sophisticated to nonspecialized and simple.

Processes for Readers Who Will Perform Them
The audience for these papers may be technical and professional personnel who need the information to carry out a work-related task or individuals who want to perform the process for themselves.

A how-to-do-it paper must include everything the reader needs to know in order to ensure a successful outcome. Its directions take the form of polite commands, often addressing readers directly as "you." This approach helps involve readers in the explanation and emphasizes that the directions must, not merely should, be followed. Here is an illustration:

> To prepare a bacterial smear for staining, first use an inoculating loop to place a drop of distilled water on a clean glass microscope slide. Next, pass the loop and the opening of the tube containing the bacterial culture to be examined through a Bunsen burner flame to sterilize them. From the tube, remove a small bit of culture with the loop, and rub the loop in the drop of water on the slide until the water covers an area one and one-half inches long and approximately the width of the slide. Next, reflame the opening of the culture tube to prevent contamination of the culture, and then plug it shut. Allow the smear to air dry, and then pass the slide, smear side up, through the flame of the burner until it is warm to the touch. The dried smear should have a cloudy, milky-white appearance.
>
> Darryl Williams

Often each separate step is represented as a step in a numbered list to make it easier for the reader to see the separate actions that need to be completed.

Processes for Readers Who Won't Perform Them
These papers may tell how some process is or was performed or how it occurs or occurred. A paper might, for instance, detail the stages of grief, the procedure involved in an operation, the role of speech in the development of children's thinking, or the sequence involved in shutting down a nuclear reactor. These papers serve many purposes—for example, to satisfy popular curiosity; to point out the importance, difficulty, or danger of a process; or to cast a process in a favorable or unfavorable light. Even though the writers of such papers often explain their topic in considerable detail, they do not intend to provide enough information for readers to carry out the process.

Papers of this sort present the needed information without using polite commands. Sometimes a noun, a pronoun like *I, we, he, she,* or *it,* or a noun–pronoun combination identifies the performer(s). At other times, the performer remains unidentified. Three examples follow.

Pronouns Identify Performer

Thus, when I now approach a stack of three two-inch cinder blocks to attempt a breaking feat, I do not set myself to "try hard," or to summon up all my strength. Instead I relax, sinking my awareness into my belly and legs, feeling my connection with the ground. I breathe deeply, mentally directing the breath through my torso, legs, and arms. . . . When I make my final approach to the bricks, if I regard them at all they seem light, airy, and friendly; they do not have the insistent inner drive in them that I do.

Don Ethan Miller, "A State of Grace: Understanding the Martial Arts"

Noun–Pronoun Combination Identifies Performers

Termites are even more extraordinary in the way they seem to accumulate intelligence as they gather together. Two or three termites in a chamber will begin to pick up pellets and move them from place to place, but nothing comes of it; nothing is built. As more join in, they seem to reach a critical mass, a quorum, and the thinking begins. They place pellets atop pellets, then throw up columns and beautiful, curving, symmetrical arches, and the crystalline architecture of vaulted chambers is created.

Lewis Thomas, "Societies as Organisms"

Performer Unidentified

The analyzer was adjusted so the scale read zero and was connected to the short sampling tube, which had previously been inserted into the smokestack. The sample was taken by depressing the bulb the requisite number of times, and the results were then read and recorded. The procedure was repeated, this time using the long sampling tube and sampling through the fire door.

Charles Finnie

EXERCISE

1. Examine your favorite newspaper or magazine for examples of process analysis. Bring them to class for group discussion of which kind each represents and the writer's purpose.
2. Examine science textbooks and professional journals for more complex examples of process analysis. Bring your examples to class and discuss how they differ from simple instructions.

Ethical Issues

Unclear, misleading, incomplete, or erroneous instructions written for someone to follow can spawn a wide range of unwanted consequences. Often frustration and lost time are the only results. Sometimes, though, the fallout is more serious, as in the case of a lab explosion. And in extreme cases, the outcome can be catastrophic, as when an accident occurs in a nuclear power plant. As writers, we have an ethical obligation to write clear and complete instructions. To help you do this, ask and answer the following questions when you're writing a process that the reader will perform.

- Have I used clear and unambiguous language so that the reader will not encounter unnecessary frustration and inconvenience?
- Have I clearly indicated any requirements such as time needed or additional supplies that will have to be purchased?
- Have I clearly warned readers about any possible harm they could face?

Writing a Process Analysis

Planning and Drafting the Process Analysis

As always, when the choice is yours, select a familiar topic. If you're not the outdoor type and prefer a Holiday Inn to the north woods, don't try to explain how to plan a campout. Muddled, inaccurate, and inadequate information will result. On the other hand, if you've pitched many a tent, you might want to share your technique with your readers.

Finding a suitable topic should be easy. But if you do hit a snag, turn to the strategies on pages 32–38. In any event, answer the following questions for each potential choice:

Will the reader find the process important, interesting, or useful?

Should I provide directions for the reader to follow, explain how the process takes place, or explain how others perform it?

Can I explain the process adequately within the assigned length?

Processes for Readers Who Will Perform Them   If you will develop a process for readers to follow, ponder this second set of questions to help you accumulate the details you'll need:

What separate actions make up the process? (Be especially careful not to omit any action that is obvious to you but wouldn't be to your reader. Such an oversight can ruin your reader's chances of success.)

What is the reason for each action?

What warnings will the reader need in order to perform the process properly and safely?

When you have your answers, record them in a chart similar to this one:

Action	Reason for Action	Warning
First action	First reason	First warning
Second action	Second reason	Second warning

Sometimes a reason will be so obvious no mention is necessary, and many actions won't require warnings. When you've completed the chart, review it carefully and supply any missing information. If necessary, make a revised chart.

Once you've listed the actions, group related ones to form steps, the major subdivisions of the procedure. The following actions constitute the first step—getting the fire going—of a paper explaining how to grill hamburgers:

remove grill rack   light briquets
stack charcoal briquets   spread out briquets

1. **Develop a complete list of the actions involved in one of the following processes; then arrange them in an appropriate order.**

   a. Baking bread
   b. Assembling or repairing some common household device
   c. Carrying out a process related to sports
   d. Breaking a bad habit
   e. Building a fire in a fireplace
   f. Accessing the Internet

2. **Examine your favorite newspaper or magazine for examples of process analysis. Bring them to class for group discussion of how they illustrate step-by-step directions.**

Start your paper by identifying the process and arousing your reader's interest. You might, for example, note the importance of the process, its usefulness, or the ease of carrying it out. Include a list of the items needed to do the work, and note any special conditions required for a successful outcome. The paper explaining how to grill hamburgers might begin as follows:

Grilling hamburgers on an outdoor charcoal grill is a simple process that almost anyone can master. Before starting, you will need a clean grill, charcoal briquets, charcoal lighter fluid and matches, hamburger meat, a plate, a spatula, and some water to put out any flames caused by fat drippings. The sizzling, tasty patties you will have when you finish are a treat that almost everyone will enjoy.

Discussion Question

How does the writer try to induce the reader to perform the process?

Use the body of the paper to describe the process in detail, presenting each step in one or more paragraphs so that each is distinct and easily grasped.

- Present each step clearly, accurately, and fully.
- Include everything the reader needs to know.
- Note the reason for every action unless the reason is obvious.
- Flag with a cautionary warning any difficult or dangerous step or one that will result in undesirable consequences if not carried out.

TEACHING STRATEGIES
1. Ask students to examine some of the essays in the Reader and list their apparent assumptions about an audience. Or bring to class some instructions that don't assume the reader's limited background knowledge, perhaps instructions for installing or operating electronic equipment or computers.

2. To help students see how a process is developed, break down a finished essay, such as "Fast Track to Perfection," into a chart similar to the one in this section.

3. To help students understand process writing, you could have them break down a complex process from one of their textbooks into its component parts. Alternatively, ask them to become knowledgeable about some procedure, such as how to use a library tool, change majors, or gain certification in some occupation. They might conduct interviews (see pp. 440–443) as part of the assignment.

4. To demonstrate the consequences of imprecise instructions, point out that the official review of the Three Mile Island incident cited ambiguity in the operating manual as one of the causes of the disaster.

PERSPECTIVE
When writing process papers, students often assume the reader is somewhat familiar with

- If two steps must be performed simultaneously, tell the reader at the start of the first one.
- In some places, tell readers what to expect if they have completed the instructions properly. Feedback lets readers know they are on track or that they need to redo something.

Let's see how the first step of the hamburger-grilling paper might unfold:

> The first step is to get the fire going. Remove the grill rack and stack about twenty charcoal briquets in a pyramid shape in the center of the grill. Stacking allows the briquets to burn off one another and thus produces a hotter fire. Next, squirt charcoal lighter fluid over the briquets. Wait about five minutes so that the fluid has time to soak into the charcoal. Then toss in a lighted match. The flame will burn for a few minutes before it goes out. When this happens, allow the briquets to sit for another fifteen minutes so that the charcoal can start to burn. Once the burning starts, do not squirt on any more lighter fluid. A flame could quickly follow the stream back into the can, causing it to explode. As the briquets begin to turn from pitch black to ash white, spread them out with a stick so that they barely touch one another. Air can then circulate and produce a hot, even fire, the type that makes grilling a success.

Discussion Questions

1. At what points has the writer provided reasons for doing things?
2. Where has the writer included a warning?

Some processes can unfold in *only one order*. When you shoot a free throw in basketball, for example, you step up to the line and receive the ball before lining up the shot, and you line up the shot before releasing the ball. Other processes can be carried out in an *order of choice*. When you grill hamburgers, you can make the patties either before or after you light the charcoal. If you have an option, use the order that has worked best for you.

End your paper with a few brief remarks that provide some perspective on the process. A summary of the steps often works best for longer, multistep processes. Other popular choices include evaluating the results of the process or discussing its importance. The paper on hamburger grilling notes the results.

> Once the patties are cooked the way you like them, remove them from the grill and place them on buns. Now you are ready to enjoy a mouthwatering treat that you will long remember.

E. M. Pryzblyo

Processes for Readers Who Won't Perform Them   Like how-to-do-it processes, those intended for nondoers require you to determine the steps, or for natural processes the stages, that are involved and the function of each before you start to write. In addition, since this type of essay will not enable readers to perform the process, think carefully about why you're presenting the information and let that purpose guide your writing. If, for instance, you're trying to persuade readers that the use of rabbits in tests of the effects of cosmetics should be discontinued, the choices you make in developing your steps should reflect that purpose.

To arouse your reader's interest, you might, among other possible options, begin with a historical overview or a brief summary of the whole process, or you could note its importance. The following introduction to an essay on the aging of stars provides a brief historical perspective:

> Peering through their still-crude telescopes, eighteenth-century astronomers discovered a new kind of object in the night sky that appeared neither as the pin-prick of light from a distant star nor as the clearly defined disk of a planet but rather as a mottled, cloudy disk. They christened these objects planetary nebulas, or planetary clouds. . . . Modern astronomers recognize planetary nebulas as the fossil wreckage of dying stars ripped apart by powerful winds. . . .

Because the reader will not perform the process, supply only enough details in the body of the paper to provide an intelligent idea of what the procedure entails. Make sure the reader knows the function of each step or stage and how it fits into the overall process. Present each in one or more paragraphs with clear transitions between the steps or stages. The following excerpt points out the changes that occur as a young star, a red giant, begins the aging process:

> As the bloated star ages, this extended outer atmosphere cools and contracts, then soaks up more energy from the star and again puffs out: with each successive cycle of expansion and contraction the atmosphere puffs out a little farther. Like a massive piston, these pulsations drive the red giant's atmosphere into space in a dense wind that blows with speeds up to 15 miles per second. In as little as 10,000 years some red giants lose an entire sun's worth of matter this way. Eventually this slow wind strips the star down close to its fusion core.

As with processes aimed at performers, end your paper with a few remarks that offer some perspective. You might, for example, evaluate the results of the process, assess its importance, or point out future consequences. The ending of the essay on star aging illustrates the last option:

> The cloud of unanswered questions surrounding planetaries should not obscure the real insight astronomers have recently gained into the extraordinary death of ordinary stars. In a particularly happy marriage of theory and observation, astronomers have discovered our own sun's fate. With the interacting stellar winds model, they can confidently predict the weather about 5 billion years from now; very hot, with *really* strong gusts from the east.
>
> Adam Frank, "Winds of Change"

TEACHING
STRATEGIES
1. Students should know
that they can revise their
process papers effectively
by following the instruc-
tions and seeing if everything works.
2. If the assignment
allows it, have students
exchange essays and then
attempt to follow each
other's instructions,
reporting on any failures.
If this exchange isn't possible, peer response works
especially well with
process papers since the
peer is more likely than
the writer to identify
omissions and point out
other problems.

Revising the Process Analysis

To revise, follow the guidelines in Chapter 4 and pose these questions:

> Have I written consistently for someone who will perform the process or someone who will merely understand it?
>
> If my paper is intended for performers, have I included every necessary action? Explained any purpose that is unclear? Warned about any steps that are dangerous or might be performed improperly?
>
> Are my steps presented in an appropriate order? Developed in sufficient detail?
>
> Have I considered appropriate ethical issues?

SAMPLE

STUDENT ESSAY OF **PROCESS ANALYSIS**

Basic Songwriting Techniques

Hannah Hill

Tyler Junior College

Faculty Member: Dr. Linda Gary

1 When listening to a song, one always wonders where the idea of the song comes from. What was the singer thinking, and what provoked him or her to write such a song? Songwriting is a simple technique that anyone can do if they put their hearts into it. Songs are stories put to music through the process of emotion, thought, and rhythm.

2 Emotional feelings are important when composing a good song. Start by finding a comfortable place to relax and to think freely. Perhaps a favorite room or an outdoor getaway could rid the mind of distractions. Once settled and comfortable, begin jotting down notes. Focus on feel-ings and emotions that are current to life or thoughts from the past that weigh heavily on the mind. For example, express how a certain situation feels or affects day-to-day life. Make it either dominantly positive or neg-ative, but avoid mixing the emotions. Allow the mysterious secrets to flow freely. Do not be afraid to let go. Expression of the heart and mind is the most coveted form of music because it is so real. "To take an emotion and make it mean something, take other people into the feeling" is famous country singer/songwriter Kenny Chesney's initial form of song-writing ("Kenny Chesney" 1). He puts his true life on the line to create

TEACHING STRATEGY
You might have students
identify the warnings and
feedback that accompany
the actual steps. Suggest
that they reread the
directions, omit these
elements, and note the
effectiveness of the essay
with and without the
omissions.

amazing music for country fans to enjoy. Ultimately, personal experience will always draw the listener in with the passion that comes from loving to write and listen to music.

3   After putting feelings into words, a clear thought process helps to organize and put these emotions into a clear composition. Don't worry about rhyme scheme yet until all the ideas are put down and arranged. Processing through the jotted notes of life will add organization. This assembling will, in turn, add clarity of understanding for the listener. Add description and detail that brings insight of the writer out to the listener. Although life experience is the best writing utensil, it is not the only one. Add fantasy or exaggeration to liven up and add spice. Be overly emotional in certain and pertinent areas. The most important situation should show the most drama to the listener. It is common for depressing lyrics to be favored over upbeat ones. For instance, twists and turns are always more interesting than perfectly happy endings. Always remember, less is more. Take out the unnecessary, so there's not an overload of information. Leave mystery to be interpreted by the listener.

4   After modifying thoughts and before moving onto rhyme, put all information in an organized structure. Assembling begins with determining the order of the writing. Pick out the writing and separate it into sections. The first paragraph part becomes the introduction or verse one. Next is the chorus, which will repeat in between each verse. Add the second section, which becomes verse two, and repeat the chorus. If necessary, add a bridge, which is the part that intertwines but differs from the rest of the song. Then repeat the chorus one more time. Organization puts an intellectual tweak on mainstream emotions on which the song is based.

5   Finally, thoughts and feelings are translated into a potential rhythmic pattern. This is where the mainstream thinking turns into a complete thought. The story is then formed into a poetic framework. Manipulate words and sentences to contrast the feelings in the most exciting way. Be sure to avoid clichés, but add interest and uniqueness. Determine a pattern of rhyme as one would in poetry. Rhyming every other line is the most popular style of rhyme, but this is where the exotic twist of the writer can step in. However, avoid overrhyming and nonsense rhyming. Make certain that the rhyme has a reasonable flow. Form the song

Continued on next page

Continued from previous page

around individuality. This distinguishing and poetic step perfects the complete thought and finishes the writing step of song formation.

6   Writing songs can be a subtle attempt to make a statement. Songwriting is an emotional release that can be personal to both writer and listener for many different reasons. Writing of any kind should be emotionally sincere and can be very therapeutic for both writer and reader. Honest writing is always the easiest and best procedure. A passionate realization can openly interpret thoughts and feelings in an indescribable way. So get out there, write, and discover the hidden truth.

Work Cited

"Kenny Chesney: Here Comes His Life." *Cincinnati Post* 8 July 2004: T14. Infotrac Newspapers. Web. 20 Sept. 2007.

DISCUSSION QUESTIONS

1. As the final sentence of the paper reveals, the paper intends to encourage people to write music. For that reason, the writer works to make the process seem easy.

2. While there are many details to the process, there are key steps offered by the writer:

■ Make notes about a dominant feeling.

■ Add details and description to feeling notes.

■ Organize the material into an order with verse, chorus, verse.

■ Translate thoughts and feelings into rhythmic pattern and rhyme.

3. "avoid mixing of emotion," "remember, less is more," "Be sure to avoid cliché," "avoid over-rhyming and nonsense rhyming."

4. This approach may not be consistent with how everyone writes songs. Some might find this approach overly formulaic. However, it also gives beginner song writers a way to start, and it is easy to follow.

5. There are a few things that could make this essay more effective. Specific examples would make the process more vivid. It would be helpful if the reader used sharp, precise words to capture the process and rehearse that process to make it more memorable.

Discussion Questions

1. What is the purpose of this process essay? How does this purpose influence how the process is explained?
2. Identify the key steps the writer recommends for writing a song.
3. Identify places where the writer offers clear warnings.
4. There are many possible ways to write a song, yet the writer only suggests one approach. What are the advantages and disadvantages of this approach?
5. What changes could the writer provide to make this essay even more effective?

Suggestions for Writing

Write a process analysis on one of the topics below or one approved by your instructor. The paper may provide instructions for the reader to follow, tell how a process is performed, or describe how a process develops. Prepare a complete list of steps, arrange them in an appropriate order, and follow them as you write the body of your essay.

1. A natural process, such as erosion, that you observe or research
2. Overcoming some particular phobia
3. The stages in a technical process such as paper production
4. The stages in a student's adjustment to college
5. Creating a FaceBook page
6. Preparing for a romantic picnic in the park, on the beach, or some other place
7. Using a particular computer program
8. Registering for classes online
9. Carrying out a process related to your hobby
10. Placing an item for sale on e-Bay or bidding on e-Bay

11. Studying for an examination
12. Performing a process required by your job
13. Performing a process required by one of your classes
14. Breaking a bad habit
15. Performing a weight-training program
16. Throwing a successful party
17. The stages in some type of storm
18. The stages in a developing friendship
19. The steps in pledging a fraternity or sorority
20. The stages in becoming independent

CRITICAL EDGE

Is there only one way to study effectively, develop a marketing campaign, or cope with a demanding supervisor? No, of course not. As you've already learned, not all processes unfold in a single, predetermined order. The writing process itself illustrates this point.

If you were to think about how you write and talk with other students about their writing processes, you would learn that different writing occasions call for different approaches. When you write a letter to a good friend, you probably spend little or no time on preliminaries but start putting your thoughts on paper as they occur to you. By contrast, other kinds of correspondence, such as inquiry and claim letters, require careful planning, drafting, and perhaps rewriting.

Sometimes the same writing occasion may allow for differing procedures. If you're writing an essay for your English class, you might brainstorm for ideas, develop a detailed outline, rough out a bare-bones draft, and add details as you revise. In talking to other students with the same assignment, you might find that they prefer to write a much longer draft and then whittle it down. Still other students might do very little brainstorming or outlining but a great deal of revising, often making major changes in several drafts. Research papers present a more complex challenge, requiring that the student find and read source material, take notes, and document sources properly. Here again variations are possible: One student might prepare the list of works cited before writing the final draft, while another might perform this task last.

If you decided to synthesize (see pages 149–150) your findings about student writing practices, you would, of course, need to organize your material in some fashion. Perhaps you might focus on the differences that distinguish one writing occasion from another. You could develop each occasion in a separate section by presenting the practices followed by most students while ignoring variations. A second possibility would be to report different practices used for the same writing occasion, first considering the most common practice and then describing the variations. The result might be likened to a cookbook that gives different recipes for the same dish.

SUGGESTED INSTRUCTOR READINGS

Berman, N. "Language, Process, and Tinkertoys." College Composition and Communication 26 (1975): 390–92. To help students develop language skills, Berman suggests that they construct something with Tinkertoys and then write instructions so others can duplicate their product.

Kroll, B. "Explaining How to Play a Game: The Development of Informative Writing Skills." Written Communication 3 (1986): 195–218. To show how students develop as writers, Kroll uses an assignment in which they are taught to play a game and then asked to write instructions for it.

Some important processes have been disputed in print, and if you wanted to investigate them you would need to consult written sources rather than talk to others. Informed disagreements exist about how the human species originated, how language developed, and how children mature. Police officers debate the best way to handle drunks, management experts the best way to motivate employees. When you investigate such controversies, determine which view is supported by the best evidence and seems most reasonable. Then, as a writer, you can present the accounts in an appropriate order and perhaps indicate which one you think merits acceptance.[1]

Suggestions for Writing

1. Interview several students about the stages they experienced in a developing friendship and write a paper that discusses these stages. Note any discrepancies in the accounts provided by different students.

2. Research the writing process as presented in several first-year composition textbooks; after pointing out how they differ, indicate which process you prefer and why.

3. Research a controversial process, such as the extinction of the dinosaurs. After presenting different theories about the process, explain which one seems most plausible and why.

---

[1]If you'll rely on information obtained through interviews, read pages 440–443 in Chapter 22. If you'll rely on published sources, read the sections on card catalogs and periodical indexes in Chapter 20 and those on handling quotations and avoiding plagiarism in Chapter 21. As always, follow your instructor's guidelines for documenting sources.

Writing a Process Analysis

Plan.

- Select a topic you know well.
- Brainstorm a list of any materials, all steps, any reasons for the steps, any warnings, and any useful feedback.
- Write out a sequence of steps in their order and double-check them for accuracy.

Writing a **draft** for readers who will perform the action.

Writing a **draft** for readers who will not perform the action.

Use polite implied "you" command.

Use pronouns, identified performer, or performer unidentified.

- Provide an intro that explains context for process.
- Identify necessary materials.
- Provide steps in sequence with reasons.
- Offer warnings where needed.
- Give periodic feedback so reader knows if work is successful.

- Provide an intro that engages readers.
- Provide steps in process and reasons that they happen.
- Let the reader know the function of each step and stage and how it fits the overall process.

Revise.

- Recheck each step, get peer feedback, and revise until satisfactory.
- Have you written consistently for whether the person is performing the action or just understanding it?
- Have you explained all steps, purpose, and any dangers?
- Are your steps in the appropriate order?
- Have you considered appropriate ethical issues?

Proofread.

CHAPTER 11

© Ariel Skelley/Corbis RF

TEACHING SUGGESTION

Images such as this one were used by newspapers to illustrate the housing crisis specifically and the financial crisis more generally. Have students in small groups identify what they believe the image illustrates and why. As a large group discuss whether this image effectively illustrates the housing crisis and the financial crisis and why? List other things that might be used to illustrate both and compare the effectiveness of the illustration. You might also have students bring in from newspapers or other media pictures that have been used as an illustration of a general trend.

SUGGESTED WRITING ASSIGNMENTS

1. Have students write a brief illustration paragraph that identifies a key concept and then in a description of either the picture from the text or a picture of their own choice demonstrate how the picture illustrates that concept.

2. Have students investigate how pictures are used

182

Illustration: Making Yourself Clear

"It doesn't pay to fight City Hall. For example, my friend Josie . . ."

"Many intelligent people lack common sense. Take Dr. Brandon . . ."

"Predicting the weather is far from an exact science. Two winters ago, a surprise snowstorm . . ."

Have you ever noticed how often people use *illustrations* (examples) to clarify general statements?

Ordinary conversations teem with "for example . . ." and "for instance . . .," often in response to a puzzled look. A local character, Hank Cassidy, might serve as the perfect example of a "good old boy" or Chicago's Water Tower Place illustrate a vertical shopping mall. But illustration is not limited to concrete items. Teachers, researchers, and writers often present an abstract principle or natural law, then supply concrete examples that bring it down to earth. An economics instructor might illustrate compound interest by an example showing how much $100 earning 5 percent interest would appreciate in ten years. Examples can also persuade, as when advertisers trot out typical satisfied users of their products to induce us to buy.

Many classroom writing assignments can benefit from the use of illustration. A business student writing a paper on effective management can provide a better grasp of the topic by including examples of successful managers and how they operate. A paper defining democracy for a political science course will be more effective if it offers examples of several democratic governments. An explanation of irony for a literature course will gain force and clarity through examples taken from stories and poems. Illustration plays a similarly important role in work-related writing. A teacher wanting a bigger student-counseling staff might cite students who need help but can't get it. An advertising copywriter urging that new copiers be bought might mention different instances of copier breakdown and the resulting delays in customer service. A union steward wanting a better company safety program might call attention to several recent accidents.

in various news media to illustrate a key concept and then have students write a paper illustrating their main point about this usage with examples they have identified.

PERSPECTIVE
Illustration isn't merely a writing strategy. Often we understand a general assertion only when we connect it to one or more specific examples. Illustration is therefore the cornerstone of all writing that deals with ideas and of all the writing strategies discussed in this book. Students should understand the importance of connecting general ideas to specific examples and the pivotal role that illustration will play in much of their college and on-the-job writing.

TEACHING STRATEGIES
1. Have students review their textbooks and lecture notes to determine where illustration is used

effectively to clarify and where it is either missing or badly used. Ask students to evaluate commu-

The old saying that a picture is worth a thousand words best explains the popularity of illustration. The concrete is always easier to grasp than the abstract, and examples add flavor and clarity to what might otherwise be flat and vague.

Selecting Appropriate Examples

nication effectiveness with and without illustration.

2. Writers often support their illustrations with narration and description. If you've already covered these strategies, you might ask students to examine the illustration essays in the Reader, point out any instances where narration and description are used, and explain why.

3. Have students list communication situations in their lives, other classes, or careers where illustration would be either helpful or essential.

CLASSROOM ACTIVITY

Ask students to bring in different examples of illustration and then in either small or large

Make sure that your examples stay on target, that is, actually support your general statement and do not veer off into an intriguing side issue. For instance, if you're making the point that the lyrics in a rock group's latest album are not in good taste, don't inject comments on the fast lifestyle of one of its members. Instead, provide examples of lyrics that support your claim, chosen from different songs in the album to head off objections that your examples aren't representative.

Furthermore, see that your examples display all the chief features of whatever you're illustrating. Don't offer a country as an example of a democracy if, though an election is held, there is only one party on the ballot and the results are all rigged. Consider the following appropriate student example of someone suffering from depression.

> Carl wasn't just sad. Nothing really bad had happened in his life. But he had lost all interest in his past favorite activities. His skateboard had been discarded in a corner of his room. He no longer bothered to play his video games. Simple things like getting tickets to a rock concert seemed to be too much effort for him. Some days he stayed in bed and missed his classes. Often he irritably snapped at anyone who talked with him. Friends could easily see the difference in him when he shuffled to the dining room, his head down. Without a doubt, Carl was depressed.

> This short example meets many of the key characteristics of depression: a lack of interest in normal activities, a sense that ordinary things aren't worth the effort, inability to attend to ordinary responsibilities, irritability.

Number of Examples

groups compare them to determine the different types, their purposes, their relative effectiveness, and any problems.

TEACHING STRATEGIES

1. You might have students examine the essays in the Reader and then evaluate the appropriateness, number, and organization of the examples.

2. Examples can, of course, be selected to make specific points. Discuss what

How many examples will you need? One long one, several fairly brief ones, or a large number of very short ones? Look to your topic for the answer. To illustrate the point that a good nurse must be compassionate, conscientious, and competent, your best bet would probably be one example, since one person must possess all these traits.

When dealing with trends, however, you'll need several examples. To show that parents have been raising children more and more permissively over the last half century, at least three examples are called for: one family from around 1955, a second from about 1980, and a third from the present time. Sometimes topics that do not involve trends require more than one example, as when you demonstrate the sharp differences between Japanese and American attitudes toward work.

Finally, some topics require a whole series of examples. If you were contending that many everyday expressions have their origins in the world of gambling, you'd need many examples to demonstrate your point.

EXERCISE

1. **Choose one of the following topic sentences. Select an appropriate example and write the rest of the paragraph.**

   a. Sometimes a minor incident drastically changes a person's life.
   b. _____'s name exactly suits (her/his) personality.
   c. I still get embarrassed when I remember_____ .
   d. Not all education goes on in the classroom.
   e. I learned the value of _____ the hard way.

2. **Explain why you would use one extended illustration, several shorter ones, or a whole series of examples to develop each of the following statements. Suggest appropriate illustrations.**

   a. Many parents I know think for their children.
   b. The hamburger isn't what it used to be.
   c. The ideal pet is small, quiet, and affectionate.
   d. Different college students view their responsibilities differently.
   e. The hotels in Gotham City run the gamut from sumptuous to seedy.
   f. Modern English includes any number of words taken directly from foreign languages.

examples might be used to create a positive impression of hackers or how the description of Bob Shaw could be rewritten to make a positive point.

3. Discuss the different possible effects on a specific essay if it was developed with different numbers and lengths of examples.

EXERCISE ANSWERS 2

a. One illustration would work if the parent tried to run every important aspect of the child's life: dating, diet, recreation, friends, and the like. This

Organizing the Examples

A single extended example often assumes the narrative form, presenting a series of events in time sequence. One person's unfolding experience might show that "doing your thing" doesn't always work out for the best. Sets of examples that trace trends also rely on time sequence, moving either forward or backward. This arrangement would work well for a paper on the growing permissiveness in child rearing.

On the other hand, a paper showing that different individuals exhibit some characteristic to different extents would logically be organized by order of climax (from the least to the greatest extent) or perhaps the reverse order. To demonstrate how salesclerks differ in their attitudes toward customers, you might first describe a hostile clerk, then a pleasant one, and finally an outstandingly courteous and helpful one.

Sometimes any arrangement will work equally well. Suppose you're showing that Americans are taking various precautions to ward off heart attacks. Although you might move from a person who exercises to one who diets and finally to one who practices relaxation techniques, no special order is preferable.

Large numbers of examples might first be grouped into categories and the categories then arranged in a suitable order. For example, the expressions from the world of gambling could be grouped according to types of gambling: cards, dice, horse racing, and the like. Depending upon the specific categories, one arrangement may or may not be preferable to another.

paper could also present several examples of parents, all of whom tried to control one aspect of their children's lives.

b. At least two examples would be needed. The first might describe hamburgers the writer could buy ten years ago at a since-vanished neighborhood hamburger shop; the second might describe a typical hamburger from Burger King or McDonald's.

c. One example is needed here: that of a small animal, probably a cat or dog, that has the characteristics mentioned in the statement.

d. At least two examples would be required. The

Ethical Issues

In writing an illustration, we try to show readers something truthful about our understanding of the world. They wouldn't read what we've written if they suspected we were unusually careless in our thinking or knew we were trying to

writer could provide one illustration of an irresponsible student and another of a responsible student.

A third example could be added—of a student who is responsible part of the time (or about some things) and irresponsible part of the time (or about other things).

e. "Run the gamut" suggests perhaps a paper with three illustrations: one of a luxury hotel, another of a hotel serving a middle-class clientele, and the third of a run-down hotel.

f. This statement would require a whole series of examples—for instance, *kimono, bungalow, saboteur,* and *kindergarten.*

deceive them. Deception may stem from prejudice, which causes people to distort examples. For instance, parents trying to talk their teenager out of a career in acting will probably cite only examples of failed or struggling performers who have miserable lives, and they will fail to mention many successful performers. Such a distortion isn't fair to the acting profession or the teenager. Some distortions can be outright lies. In the past debate about welfare, some commentators wrote about people who lived like millionaires while on welfare. It turned out the examples were falsified, and no real instances of such massive abuse could be found. To avoid ethical pitfalls, ask and answer the following questions.

- Have I given adequate thought to the point I'll make and the examples I'll use?
- Are the examples supporting my point truthful, or are they slanted to deceive the reader?
- Could my illustrations have harmful consequences? Do they stereotype an individual or group? Harm someone's reputation unjustly?
- Will my examples promote desirable or undesirable behavior?

Writing an Illustration

Planning and Drafting the Illustration

Assertions, unfamiliar topics, abstract principles, natural laws—as we've seen, all of these can form the foundation for your paper. If you have a choice, you should experience little difficulty finding something suitable. After all, you've observed and experienced many things—for example, how people can be TV junkies and the ways students manage the stresses of college life. As always, the strategies on pages 31–38 can help generate some possibilities, which you can then evaluate by asking these questions:

Exactly what point am I trying to make? (Write it down in precise terms.)

Why do I want to make this point? To show how bad something is? To encourage something? To scare people into or away from something?

Who is my prospective audience?

Should I use one extended example, or will I need more? Why?

Once you've picked your topic, ask yourself, "What example(s) will work best with my audience?" Then brainstorm each one for supporting details. Use a chart patterned after the one below to help you.

Example 1	Example 2	Example 3
First supporting detail	First supporting detail	First supporting detail
Second supporting detail	Second supporting detail	Second supporting detail

Review your details carefully and add any new ones you think of; then make a new chart and re-enter the details into it, arranged in the order you intend to present them.

Your introduction should identify your topic and draw your reader into the paper. If you're illustrating a personal belief, you might indicate how you developed it. If you're trying to scare the reader into or away from something, you might open with an arresting statement.

Present your examples in the body of your paper, keeping your purpose firmly in mind as you plan your organization. If you have many brief examples, perhaps group them into related categories for discussion. The paper on expressions from gambling, for instance, might devote one paragraph each to terms from the worlds of cards, dice, and horse racing. If you're dealing with a few relatively brief examples—say to show a trend—put each in its own paragraph. For a single extended example, use the entire body of the paper, suitably paragraphed. Thus, an extended example of someone with an eccentric lifestyle might include paragraphs on mode of dress, living accommodations, and public behavior.

Conclude in whatever way seems most appropriate. You might express a hope or recommendation that the reader implement or avoid something, or you might issue a personal challenge that grows out of the point you've illustrated.

Revising the Illustration

Think about the following questions and the general guidelines in Chapter 4 as you revise your paper:

Exactly what idea am I trying to put across? Have I used the examples that best typify it?

Do my examples illuminate my idea without introducing irrelevant material?

Are my examples interesting?

Have I used an appropriate number of examples?

Have I organized my paper effectively?

Have I considered appropriate ethical issues?

SAMPLE

STUDENT ESSAY OF **ILLUSTRATION**

If It Is Worth Doing . . .
Janice Carlton

1   Everyone should keep a slogan in his or her back pocket to pull out at difficult times. Mine may seem a bit ridiculous, but I have found it to be a life saver: "If it is worth doing, it is worth doing badly." This slogan turns my parent's phrase—If it is worth doing, it is worth doing well—completely upside down. To be clear, I am not suggesting that anyone should deliberately do things badly. No one wants to be operated on by

Continued on next page

Similarly, is it appropriate to use as an example of a distasteful person someone the readers might know? A class discussion could ensue.

TEACHING STRATEGY
Students often believe that simply stating an example is sufficient; they are not likely to provide adequate supporting details. Even though the brainstorming chart will help, you might caution them about the problems caused by vague writing.

READER/THEME STRATEGIES
Because almost all writing relies on examples, an illustration paper might follow your discussion of a theme. If you're dealing with the theme "Life's Changes," you might assign "The Perfect Picture," "The Company Man," and "Private Language, Public Language." Drawing upon their observations of themselves and others, students might then write papers that explain and illustrate how we respond to the different stages of life. If you'd like to take up "Women's Issues," students could read "Barbie Doesn't Live Here Anymore," "The Men We Carry in Our Minds," "Why Marriages Fail," "When Is It Rape?," and "The Appeal of the Androgynous Man," discuss the ways males and females interact, and then write essays presenting their conclusions about such interactions. The natural theme for

illustration is "Who We Are." Students could read such essays as "Rambos of the Road," "The Company Man," "Going for Broke," and "Binge Drinking," discuss them, and then write essays illustrating distinctive characteristics of Americans or the American lifestyle.

Continued from previous page

a surgeon whose hand shakes. Hopefully, accountants know their subject and offer sound advice. Still, some activities are so worth doing that the fact that we might do them badly is no reason not to take up the task. Far too often we are tempted to give up art because our paintings are bad, avoid writing because our spelling is poor, or avoid helping a friend build a pole barn because we might make mistakes. My slogan reminds me that my possible failure is no reason to avoid a worthwhile project.

2   Consider singing for a moment. Singing can be tremendous fun. A good song can lift the heart. Singing with others can offer a delightful sense of sharing. My only problem is that I have a terrible voice. It cracks, soars when it should sink, and rises when it should drop. Usually, I hit the right pitch, but sometimes I have to wiggle into it as though it were a pair of excessively tight jeans. My more musically gifted friends usually cringe when they hear me sing and mutter something under their breath about "the tone deaf." Should I stop singing just because I do it badly? To me, I sound like a great rock singer, at least when I sing in the shower. Sometimes I sing while I walk from class to class, and I feel, as a result, that I am in an exciting musical. I can even sing with my friends, who only insist that I sing a little more quietly and try, try, try to stay on tune. Probably it would be unfair of me to log in hours at a karaoke bar, and I usually keep from singing around those who tend to stuff their fingers in their ears. But with some reasonable precautions, the fact that I sing badly should not prevent me from enjoying the obvious pleasures of singing.

3   Writing poetry is another practice that is worth doing even if we do it badly. What makes poetry worth writing? Writing poetry involves taking time out of the rush of life to reflect on what you're feeling, to perceive more clearly, to hunt for the right word. When it works, you feel like everything in your life has come together.

> As I raced through the forest,
> I stopped to smell a flower,
> a violet, perhaps, a purple pause
> Between home and grandmother's house.
> The flower didn't have any smell,
> But that didn't matter any.
> For a moment, I contemplated
> The breath of a flower,
> And avoided, in the process,
> Meeting any unexpected wolves.

4   This poem isn't very good, I admit. No one would want to publish it. Most readers may not understand how, feeling like Little Red Riding Hood, I rush from place to place to avoid meeting stray wolves. None of that is the point. When writing the poem, I felt in touch with my life while savoring a creative joy. There is no reason to let anything get in the way of such a delight, not even the poor quality of the resulting poem.

5   Of course, it is easy to sing in the shower and write poetry no one ever sees, even if the results, to put it mildly, stink. What about where others are involved? Imagine my predicament when my big brother called and asked me if I would help him put up a pole barn. "Me," I pleaded, "I'm all thumbs." And I meant it, but somehow he needed my help, so despite my complete lack of construction experience, I chanted my mantra three times and said "yes." For a day I held up beams, sawed boards (sometimes off the measured line), and hammered in nails (bending more than a few). But I did help my brother. He said that he couldn't have done it without me; and while he probably could have built the barn without me, it would have been harder for him. Besides, working side by side for a day, we got to reconnect in ways that I hadn't thought possible. I also learned some construction skills. Without being willing to help badly, I would have missed a tremendous opportunity.

6   There are times when doing something badly is significantly better than doing nothing at all. Our local newspaper featured a story about a hiker who was miles from anywhere on the trail when he came across another hiker who was choking on his lunch. What could he do? He couldn't run for help. He was out of his cell phone region. And he didn't know CPR. What he did know was that the man in front of him was starting to turn blue. He pounded the man on the back, but that didn't work. Finally, in desperation he pushed down underneath the man's rib cage. The pressure popped something out of his windpipe and he started breathing again. The point of the article was the importance of learning CPR, the Heimlich maneuver, and other lifesaving skills. The hiker, of course, knew none of those skills and could have done tremendous damage, perhaps breaking the victim's ribs. Clearly, it would be worthwhile to be expert at lifesaving skills. But what should the hiker have done? If he had just stood there paralyzed by his lack of expertise, the man would have choked to death. Fortunately, he seems to have believed in my slogan and did what was worth doing, saving a life, even if he did it badly.

Continued on next page

Continued from previous page

7   There are lots of pressure in our culture to "leave it to the experts." We can listen to CDs instead of sing ourselves. We can call towing services that are glad to change our flats for us. We can watch soccer instead of play it. With so many skilled people, it is easy to be embarrassed by our own lack of expertise and abandon everything except what we do well. Unfortunately, our lives would be significantly poorer for such a surrender. Instead, we would be better off adapting the adage that "if it is worth doing, it is worth doing badly" and step up to the plate at a softball game, grab a sketch pad and draw what we see, write a poem, sing, cook a meal for a friend. In the end, we have nothing to lose but our false pride.

DISCUSSION QUESTIONS
1. The writer is trying to illustrate the importance of a slogan, "If it is worth doing, it is worth doing badly." But she is extending this illustration to apply to an attitude about life and a way of acting.
2. The illustration is developed by a series of examples that show the advantage of doing something badly.

3. The poem is a specific example that may indeed be done badly but clearly was worth doing, if only to the writer.

4. The CPR section demonstrates that this principle does not simply apply to private activities such as singing and writing poetry but actually has a broader application.

5. The author seems to use the pronoun "we" to invite the reader to adopt this attitude. That is why at the end of the conclusion the writer stresses the kinds of things all of us could do.

Discussion Questions

1. What is the writer trying to illustrate?
2. How is this particular illustration developed?
3. Why did the writer include a poem in her essay?
4. What does the paragraph on the use of CPR add to the essay?
5. In the last paragraph, why does the writer use the pronoun "we"?

Suggestions for Writing

Use one of the following ideas or another that your instructor approves for your illustration essay. Select appropriate examples, determine how many you will use, and decide how you will organize them.

1. "I don't have enough time" is a common complaint of many people today.
2. Many people appear obsessed with exercise (or diet).
3. Incivility has become quite common in public places.
4. New communication technologies help keep friends in close touch.
5. Dedication is the secret of success for many athletes (or use any other field or occupation).
6. Video games can take over people's lives.
7. Sometimes actions can have unintended consequences.
8. A good nurse must be compassionate, conscientious, and competent (or use another occupation with appropriate characteristics).
9. Campus gambling assumes various forms.
10. Many intelligent people lack common sense.
11. Sleep deprivation is causing problems for many young people.
12. Talk show hosts often leave much to be desired (or stimulate listeners to think).

13. "Doing your own thing" does not always work out for the best.
14. _____ is the most (or least) effective teacher I have ever had.
15. Not to decide is to decide.
16. How we react to circumstances, not the circumstances themselves, often makes us unhappy.
17. Today's college student is _____ .
18. Sometimes we need to take risks.
19. Wanting more than we need can be destructive.
20. Many people become obsessed with appearance.

CRITICAL EDGE

When we write an illustration paper, we don't always draw our examples from personal experience. As we reflect on a topic, we may talk with other people and read various source materials to broaden our understanding. We explore differing perspectives and determine the connections between them en route to arriving at our own views and insights. Take, for instance, the topic of racism in America. "The Scholarship Jacket" (page 468), "Momma's Encounter" (page 464), and "I Have a Dream" (page 586) offer poignant illustrations of how racism affects people's personal lives. Reading these essays, drawing upon your own observations, and perhaps questioning other students could lead you to an important insight: for example, that racism can have personal effects that are very different from the more widely discussed kinds of institutional discrimination. You might then synthesize (see pages 149–150) others' illustrations and your own to produce a paper that presents this insight.

Sometimes illustrations don't reflect reality. An author trying to make the point that many college students are irresponsible might offer examples of students who skip classes, fail to hand in assignments, and party constantly. These examples, however, overlook the many students who hold part-time jobs while taking a full load of classes, participate in professional organizations, and function successfully as spouses, and even parents, while earning good grades. Because published material can paint an inaccurate picture, develop the habit of judging the examples you read in the light of what your knowledge, further investigation, and other sources reveal. Critical thinking is one of the most important skills a writer can cultivate.[1]

---

[1]Because this type of paper draws upon published information, it is important to read the sections on card catalogs and periodical indexes in Chapter 20 and those on handling quotations and avoiding plagiarism in Chapter 21. As always, follow your instructor's guidelines for documenting sources.

Suggestions for Writing

1. Examine the Reader essays on racism cited above. Then, drawing upon examples from the essays and perhaps the observations of minority students you know, write a paper presenting your own conclusions about the personal effects of racism.

2. Read several issues of a magazine such as *Sports Illustrated* or *Working Woman* and determine what the articles suggest about American life. Then write an essay that illustrates your conclusions and incorporates relevant material from the articles.

3. Martin Gottfried, author of "Rambos of the Road," concludes by noting, "It seems to me that it is a new America we see on the road now. It has the mentality of a hoodlum and the backbone of a coward" (page 501). Write an essay that includes both your own illustrations and one or more of Gottfried's and that agrees or disagrees with his assessment.

Writing an Illustration

Plan.

- Identify and write key concept or observation to illustrate by reading, talking to others, or jotting down your own observations.
- Identify your purpose.
- Identify your audience.

Brainstorm examples and details of examples.

- Decide how many examples you need.
- Select the best examples.

Determine pattern of organization.

- Categories, order of importance, time.
- Create a rough plan.
- Go back and brainstorm if needed.

Write a rough draft.

- Intro engages reader and establishes topic.
- Body provides examples with detail.
- Conclusion reestablishes main point.

Return to earlier stages as needed.

Revise: Collect and use peer responses.

- Check fit to the main point.
- Add examples or details.
- Cut what doesn't work.
- Test organization.
- Test for ethics.

Proofread.

CHAPTER 12

TEACHING STRATEGY
Have the students look closely at the picture. Have them identify the classification patterns used in this shelf display. They will note that the yogurts are classified by brand, by size, and by type with the drinkable yogurts on the top. Notice that the snack packs are lowest at the height of children. Discuss why the store chose this pattern of classification. Discuss other possible patterns of classification.

© image100/Corbis.

SUGGESTED WRITING ASSIGNMENT
After discussing the picture, have students visit a local supermarket to study the organization of the cereal aisle, or some other part of the supermarket, and write a paper explaining the classification system and the reason for that classification system.

Classification: Grouping into Categories

Help Wanted, Situations Wanted, Real Estate, Personal. Do these terms look familiar? They do if you've ever scanned the classified ads of the newspaper. Ads are grouped into categories, and each category is then subdivided. The people who assemble this layout are *classifying.* Figure 12.1 (see page 196) shows the main divisions of a typical classified ad section and a further breakdown of one of them.

As this figure indicates, grouping allows the people who handle ads to divide entries according to a logical scheme and helps readers find what they are looking for. Imagine the difficulty of checking the real estate ads if all the entries were run in the order the ads were placed.

Our minds naturally sort information into categories. Within a few weeks after their birth, infants can tell the faces of family members from those of outsiders. Toddlers learn to distinguish between cats, dogs, and rabbits. In both cases the classification rests solely on physical differences. As we mature we start classifying in more abstract ways, and by adulthood we are constantly sorting things into categories: dates or mates, eating places, oddballs, friends, investments, jobs, political views.

Classification also helps writers and readers come to grips with large or complex topics. It breaks a broad topic into categories according to some specific principle, presents the distinctive features of each category, and shows how the features vary among categories. Segmenting the topic simplifies the discussion by presenting the information in small, neatly sorted piles rather than in one jumbled and confusing heap.

Furthermore, classification helps people make choices. Identifying which groups of consumers—students, accountants, small-business owners—are most likely to buy some new product allows the manufacturer to advertise in appropriate media. Knowing the engine size, maneuverability, seating capacity, and gas mileage of typical subcompact, compact, and intermediate-size cars helps customers decide which one to buy. Examining the features of term, whole-life, and endowment insurance enables prospective buyers to select the policy that best suits their needs.

195

have a coat, or finding a radio station that plays their kind of music.

2. Have students go to a local grocery store and see whether they can determine how the merchandise is classified. For example, some stores display health and beauty products together; some display them separately. Students could develop a list of the different categories, noting examples of the items in each one.

3. Have students examine popular writing and note any classifications that the writers use. Possibilities include types of parents, stereo systems, or food groups.

4. Classification can be a useful learning tool. Have students identify where direct or implied classification is used in their other courses. You might help them chart the classification system.

TEACHING STRATEGIES
1. Charting a classification system helps students organize and test it. Such a chart helps ensure that everything is connected, stresses the hierarchical nature of classification, and allows students to determine whether all relevant items have an appropriate place. Encourage students to verify their classification systems.

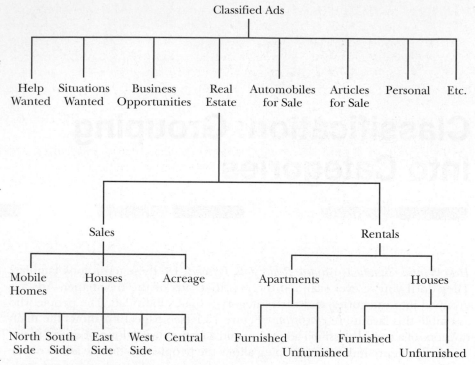

Figure 12.1

Because classification plays such an important part in our lives, it is a useful writing tool in many situations. Your accounting instructor may ask you to categorize accounting procedures for retail businesses. In a computer class, you may classify computer languages and then specify appropriate applications for each grouping. For an industrial hygiene class, you might categorize types of respiratory protective equipment and indicate when each type is used. On the job, a state health department employee may prepare a brochure grouping illegal drugs into categories based on their effects. The communications director of an investment firm might write a customer letter categorizing investments according to their degree of risk. An employee of a textbook publisher might prepare a catalog grouping new books by field of study.

Selecting Categories

2. A helpful way to think of categories is as mail slots grouped according to zip code; each and every item would have one, and only one, place.

People classify in different ways for different purposes, which generally reflect their interests. A clothing designer might classify people according to their fashion sense, a representative of the National Organization for Women according to their views on women's rights, and the Secretary of Labor according to their occupations. A college's director of housing might classify students according to their type of residence, the dean of students according to their behavior problems, and the financial aid officer according to their sources of income.

When you write a classification paper, choose a principle of classification that's suited not only to your purpose but also to your audience. To illustrate, if you're writing for students, don't classify instructors according to their manner of dress, body build, or cars they drive. These breakdowns probably wouldn't interest most students and certainly wouldn't serve their needs. Instead, develop a more useful principle of classification—perhaps by teaching styles, concern for students, or grading policies.

Sometimes it's helpful or necessary to divide one or more categories into subcategories. If you do, use just one principle of classification for each level. Both levels in Figure 12.2 meet this test because each reflects a single principle: place of origin for the first, number of cylinders for the second.

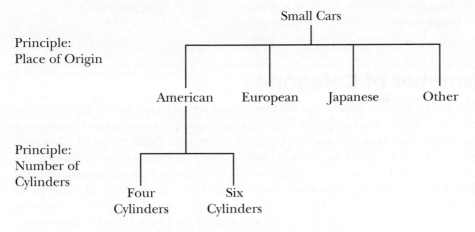

Figure 12.2 Proper Classification of Small Cars

Now examine Figure 12.3. This classification is *improper* because it groups cars in two ways—by place of origin and by kind—making it possible for one car to end up in two categories. For example, the German Porsche is both a European car and a sports car. When categories overlap in this way, confusion reigns and nothing is clarified.

Figure 12.3 Improper Classification of Small Cars

3. Although students often confuse classification with comparison, it is probably better not to introduce the distinction. If the question does come up, however, you might point out that classification always shows the relationships among categories of things, while comparison shows how specific things are similar and/or different. To illustrate, comparison would be used to evaluate the performance of two instructors, classification to present the characteristics of good and bad instructors. If a good instructor is fired and a bad one becomes a dean, the two classification categories remain intact.

PERSPECTIVE
Students tend to see classification systems as immutable and without alternatives. They should understand that these systems are human creations designed to serve particular purposes but are sometimes modified or even rejected when they are not appropriate.

CLASSROOM ACTIVITIES
1. Ask students to list how they (as students) might be classified by (a) the administration, (b) financial aid, (c) housing, (d) the instructor in a particular class, (e) fraternities or sororities. Have them point out how the different purposes for classification yield different categories.

2. Have students, working in groups, establish what classification systems would be helpful for marketing several new products or services to the student population. Possible services or products include a new tutoring service, pizza or newspaper delivery, research assistance, perfume, minirefrigerators, stereo equipment.

EXERCISE ANSWERS

1. Classifying the families in Anytown, USA:

   a. The Roman Catholic bishop would probably

1. **How would each of the following people be most likely to classify the families in Anytown, USA?**

   a. The bishop of the Roman Catholic diocese in which the city is located
   b. The state senator who represents the city
   c. A field worker for the NAACP
   d. The director of the local credit bureau

2. **The following lists contain overlapping categories. Identify the inconsistent item in each list and explain why it is faulty.**

Nurses	Pictures	Electorate in Midville
Surgical nurses	Oil paintings	Republicans
Psychiatric nurses	Magazine illustrations	Democrats
Emergency room nurses	Lithographs	Nonvoters
Terminal care nurses	Watercolors	Independents
Night nurses	Etchings	

classify the families by religious preference: Catholic, Protestant, Jewish, Muslim, no religion.

b. The state senator would probably categorize the families by political preference: Democratic, Republican, Libertarian, independent.

c. The NAACP representative would probably categorize them by

Number of Categories

Some classification papers discuss every category included in the topic. Others discuss only selected categories. Circumstances and purpose dictate the scope of the discussion. Suppose you work for the commerce department of your state and are asked to write a report that classifies the major nonservice industries in a certain city and assesses their strengths and weaknesses. Your investigation shows that food processing, furniture making, and the production of auto parts account for more than 95 percent of nonservice jobs. Two minor industries, printing and toy making, provide the rest of the jobs. Given these circumstances, you'd probably focus on the first three industries, mentioning the others only in passing. But if printing and toy making were significant industries, they too would require detailed discussion.

race: caucasian, black, Asian.

d. The director of the local credit bureau would probably categorize them by their credit ratings: good credit risks, questionable credit risks, poor credit risks. You might remind students that in all cases the same group of people is being

Developing Categories

Develop every category you include with specific, informative details that provide a clear picture of each one and help the reader grasp the distinctions and relationships among them.

Consider the student example on video games at the end of this chapter. The student does not just identify interactive simulation games as a type of games. She explains how these games are distinctive and provides a detailed example of how the games must be played. "One of the earliest of these games was an arcade game called *Dance Dance Revolution*. It requires players to match on a dance pad the moves they are instructed to do on the screen. . . . The success of this game prompted many others like *Karaoke Revolution* in which players sing popular songs into a microphone for points and *Guitar Hero* and *Donkey Konga* where players play on controllers that emulate a guitar and a set of bongos." By developing the paragraph with different examples of how interactive games are played, she builds a better understanding of that distinctive kind of game.

Ethical Issues

Classification can seem quite innocent, and yet it can cause great harm. In India, an entire group numbering millions of people was once classified as "untouchables" and so was denied the jobs and rights of other citizens. Although political progress has considerably improved the lot of these people, discrimination still hobbles their lives. In this country, many high school students have suffered the sting of being classified as "nerds" or "geeks." Clearly you'll have to evaluate the appropriateness and consequences of your classification scheme. To avoid problems, ask and answer these questions:

- Is my classification called for by the situation? It may be appropriate to classify students in a school environment according to their reading skills, but classifying factory workers in this fashion may well be inappropriate and unfair to the people involved.
- Have I avoided the use of damaging classifications? We resent stereotyping because it unjustly reduces us to some distorted general idea. No one is simply a "hillbilly" or a "jock."
- Have I applied my classification without resorting to overgeneralization? In a paper classifying student drinkers, it would be a mistake, and even harmful, to imply that all college students drink excessively.
- Could my classification promote harmful behavior? When classifying the behavior patterns of young urban dwellers, it would be unethical to present favorably the lifestyle of a group that uses hard drugs and engages in disruptive behavior at sporting events.

We are ethically responsible for the classification systems that we use in our writing. Always examine the one you use for suitability, fairness, and potential harm.

Writing a Classification

Planning and Drafting the Classification

Many topics that interest you are potential candidates for classification. If you're selecting your own topic, you might explain different kinds of rock music to novices, take a humorous look at types of teachers, or, in a more serious vein, identify types of discrimination. As always, use one or more of the narrowing strategies on pages 31–38 to stimulate your thinking. As possibilities come to mind, examine each one in light of these questions:

What purpose will this classification serve?

Who is my audience and what will interest them?

What are the categories of this topic?

What features distinguish my categories from one another?

categorized. An individual might be a Catholic, a Republican, a black, and a good credit risk. In addition, these groupings might be expanded. The population of Anytown might include Buddhists, socialists, Native Americans, and people who have no credit rating of any sort.

2. Identifying the overlapping category:
- *Nurses:* The overlapping category is "night nurses"; these might work as surgical nurses, emergency room nurses, etc.
- *Pictures:* The overlapping category is "magazine illustrations"; the illustration may be an oil painting, a lithograph, etc.
- *Electorate in Midville:* The overlapping category is "nonvoters"; these people may favor Republicans or Democrats or they may take a neutral position.

TEACHING STRATEGIES
1. You might point out that specific details help writers avoid stereotyping, particularly when the essay features types of people.
2. Have students visit a bookstore and note what classification schemes were used to organize the books. Then have them examine some of the titles in each section and use their findings as the basis of a writing assignment.

TEACHING STRATEGIES
You might want to discuss these two cases with your class.
1. Eliot wrote a paper classifying the women in his class by their sexual characteristics. Clearly he showed bad taste, but was he unethical? How would the classification affect women students if they read it?
2. A large company administered a well-known psychological test to its employees, used the results to classify them according to psychological type, and entered the results into their personal files. These classifications were then used in job assignments and promotions. Did the company act ethically? Explain.

TEACHING STRATEGY
Students often view writing a classification as a formal activity without a real purpose or audience. To correct this mistaken belief, you might specify both or guide students to do so. For example, students could classify the types of sororities or fraternities for those thinking of pledging. A more challenging assignment is to have them research the categories of jobs in their chosen fields (what are the different kinds of medical technicians or accountants?) in order to help others in the field select a specialty.

READER/THEME STRATEGIES
The discussion of a theme could lead to a

Next, determine whether you'll discuss every category or only selected ones, and then set up a classification chart similar to the one following.

Category 1	**Category 2**	**Category 3**
First distinguishing feature	First distinguishing feature	First distinguishing feature
Second distinguishing feature	Second distinguishing feature	Second distinguishing feature

Such a chart helps you see the relationships among categories and provides a starting point for developing your specific details. Proceed by jotting down the details that come to mind for each distinguishing feature of every category. Then prepare a second chart with the distinguishing features and details arranged in the order you want to present them.

Begin your paper by identifying your topic and capturing your reader's attention in some way. A paper classifying hair dyes might point out their growing popularity among both men and women. One classifying snobs might offer an anecdote showing how far snobbery can go. Or you could cite a personal experience that relates to your topic. As always, circumstances dictate your choice.

In the body discuss your categories in whatever order best suits your purpose. Order of climax—least important, more important, most important—often works well. Or perhaps your topic will suggest arranging the categories by behavior, income, education, or physical characteristics. Whatever your arrangement, signal it clearly to your reader. Don't merely start the discussions of your categories by saying first . . . , second . . . , another . . . , next . . . , and the like. These words offer no hint of the rationale behind your order.

In addition, make sure the arrangement of material within the categories follows a consistent pattern. In classifying restrooms, after noting where the restroom can be found, the writer could discuss its floor, walls, and lighting, move to the furniture, and end by discussing the lavatories, soap, and toweling for each category of restroom.

The strategies for ending a classification paper are as varied as those for starting it. A paper on hair dyes might conclude by predicting their continued popularity. One on snobs might end with your recommendations for dealing with them. In other cases, you might express a hope of some kind or advise your reader to do something.

Revising the Classification

Revise your paper by following the guidelines in Chapter 4 as well as by pondering these questions:

Does my classification have a clear sense of purpose and audience?

Does my principle of classification accord with my purpose?

Do any of my categories overlap?

Have I chosen an appropriate number of categories?

Are these categories developed with sufficient details?

Are the categories and details arranged in an effective order?

Have I considered appropriate ethical issues?

classification. If you'd like to explore the theme "Who We Are," students might read such essays as "Gender Gap in Cyberspace," "The Company Man," "Assembly Line Adventure," "The Men We Carry in Our Minds," "The Sweet Smell of Success Isn't All That Sweet," and "The Appeal of the Androgynous Man." These readings could launch a discussion that explores the different ways of categorizing people. Students might then write papers classifying the attitudes people display toward such matters as dating, sports, or success. If you prefer the theme "Health," the class could read such essays as "Sound and Fury," "Going for Broke," "Yes, Don't Impede Medical Progress," "The Company Man," and "Binge Drinking," and then, after discussion, write papers classifying various attitudes toward health or the health profession.

SAMPLE
STUDENT ESSAY FOR **CLASSIFICATION**

Types of Video Games for Children
Kyra Glass

1   Gift-giving for children and grandchildren has been getting increasingly difficult as the number of options increase. Today dolls and toy cars and board games just aren't going to cut it. Many children are used to interactive toys and toys with electronic components. Most children don't think of Monopoly or tag when they hear the word *game*; to them games are played on a television or a computer screen. Indeed, video game consoles in homes with children have become almost as ubiquitous household appliances as televisions. Most parents and grandparents are familiar with demands for *the* hot new game, but buying video games for their loved ones can be overwhelming. Many adults never had video games growing up, or if they did, video games meant *Pac Man*, *Donkey Kong*, or two plumbers named Mario and Luigi. Although these gaming icons are still available, many parents and grandparents are concerned that they are far out numbered by extremely violent or gruesome video games that they don't want their children playing. Those buying for young gamers may feel that they are stuck, that they will either be unable to buy a game or will end up with a hack-and-slash game that is too violent for younger children. In reality, there is a wide variety of fun and family-friendly games that parents or grandparents can feel good about buying for their young gaming enthusiasts. The easiest way to pick safe games is to check the ratings printed on them; anything that is rated E (for everyone) is safe for children of any age to play; anything rated E 10+ may have some mild cartoon violence but is usually acceptable for most families as well. Games that are rated Teen (T) or Mature (M) are

Continued on next page

Continued from previous page

not a good bet for younger children, and parents should research these games before giving them to their children. But checking the ratings is only the first step. There are many different categories of games with options that are appropriate for younger players: interactive simulation games, adventure/role-playing games, party games, and sports games.

2   One of the most common types of games for children or adults is adventure/role-playing games. In these games, players take on the persona of a character (or several characters) and work their way through a narrative as that character. Although there are many games of this type that aren't appropriate for younger children, a number of age-appropriate games do fall into this category. The key to finding adventure/role-playing games that are appropriate for younger players is in looking at what story the game tells and who the main characters are. A large number of games in this category are based on characters with which children are already familiar. Some of these are based on both live-action and animated children's movies. *A Series of Unfortunate Events* and *The Incredibles* inspired games of the same name, and a whole series of games based on the popular Harry Potter books and movies have been produced. Many of these games based on movies let the players go through an enhanced version of the plot of the movies or books, letting children interact with their favorite stories. Other games are based on TV cartoons like *Jimmy Neutron*, *Kim Possible*, and *SpongeBob SquarePants*, to name only a few. These games often retain the characters and themes of the shows while inventing a new narrative for players to go through in the game. Many of these games, including *Kingdom Hearts* for Play Station 2 or *Nicktoons Unite!* for GameCube, combine many characters owned by the same company such as Disney or Nickelodeon. However, there are also adventure/role-playing games with well-known and beloved characters from other children's video games. The familiar kid-friendly Mario has a role-playing game called *Paper Mario* and an adventure game called *Super Mario Sunshine*, while older children might enjoy *Sonic the Hedgehog*'s cousin in the adventure game *Shadow the Hedgehog*. When trying to choose an adventure or simulation game for a child, often the best place

to start is by picking one of the child's favorite stories or characters from movies, cartoons, and games and seeing if there is a game that features them. It is surprising how often the answer is "yes."

3   In general, the category of sports games is a pretty safe choice when picking games for children. Sports games emulate a version of a sports competition or event for the player's participation. Many different types of games fall into this category: racing games are included here, as are games based on team sports like basketball or football, extreme sports like skateboarding or motorbike racing, and individual sports like skiing or golf. Although there are some sports games that aren't appropriate for children, shoppers can usually find a game rated E for everyone in nearly any category of sports. However, although most sports games are appropriate for children, there are also, on every platform, sports games that are made especially for children to play. These games, like the adventure/role-playing games, keep the best aspects of their genre but draw on characters and environments that are familiar to children. Disney's *Extreme Skate Adventure*, on all three platforms, is a skateboarding game that allows children to create their own character or play as a familiar Disney character. They can then skate in environments from *Toy Story 2*, *The Lion King*, and *Tarzan*. Because this game is tailored to children, it allows them to pick objects such as mirrors or frying pans as well as skateboards. This is part of a series of Disney sports games including *Soccer*, *Football*, and *Basketball*, all on GameCube, and *Golf*, on Playstation 2. The ever-present Mario also has his own series of sports games for children, including *Mario Kart* racing games; *Super Mario Strikers*, a racing game; and games based on baseball, tennis, and golf. These sports franchises might be good for younger players because they are often easier to play and use familiar characters, while *Madden*, *Fifa*, or *NBA* sports games from Electronic Arts may be better choices for older children.

4   Interactive simulation games are an excellent choice for families because they are capable of getting children off the couch, something that many parents worry about with TV and video games. Interactive simulation games give players a hands-on experience that is as close as possible to what their character is doing in the game. One of the

Continued on next page

Continued from previous page

earliest of these games was an arcade game called *Dance Dance Revolution*. It requires players to match on a dance pad the moves they are instructed to do on the screen. Versions of this game are now available on the three main game consoles: X-Box, Playstation 2, and GameCube. The success of this game prompted many others like *Karaoke Revolution*, in which players sing popular songs into a microphone for points, and *Guitar Hero* and *Donkey Konga*, where players play on controllers that emulate a guitar or set of bongos. Most interactive simulation games require special controllers or accessories to play, and one of these accessories, the Eye Toy for Playstation 2, might change the way children think about "sitting" in front of the TV and playing video games. Eye Toy uses a USB camera so the player's body becomes the controller. Games using Eye Toy respond to the movement of the player's body to interact with the game play on screen. Eye Toy was originally packaged with the game *Play*, which featured 12 mini games that used this body motion for everything from dancing to kung fu. Since then, Eye Toy has come out with a variety of interactive games including *Play 2*, *Operation Spy*, and *AntiGrav*, as well as workout-minded games such as *Eye Toy Groove* and *Kinetic*. Interactive simulation games are the perfect choice for parents and grandparents who want to see their children physically active while having a good time.

5   Along with the concern that children spend too much time in front of the TV or on the couch, another common complaint parents have about video games is that unlike board games, they don't always encourage siblings or families to play together. That is why party games are such a great option for parents who want to be able to play along with their children and are interested in making video game time part of family time. Party games usually involve up to four players in competition and are short enough to play a round in one sitting. Most of them are made up of a series of many mini-games (short and simple games or puzzles) that are easy to learn. Most, although not all,

of these party games are styled after board games and are turn-based. A few, like *Monopoly Party*, are exactly like popular board games in video game form. Like adventure games, most party games are based on well-known children's characters. Some of these family-friendly party games are *Disney Party*, *Nickelodeon Party Blast*, *Muppets Party Cruise*, *Shrek*, *Super Party*, and *Wario Ware Inc*. These games range across a variety of console platforms, and all feature well-known characters from movies, television, and children's games. However, perhaps the best-known game in this category is the *Mario Party* series; for Game Cube, there are *Mario Parties 4 through 7*. All these games are different and feature an extensive number of levels and mini-games for families to play together.

6   There are clearly many options for parents and grandparents who want to allow their children to enjoy the same electronic entertainment as their peers while still making sure that they are playing games that are appropriate for them. Buyers can choose from a variety of sports and adventure games that allow children to play as their favorite cartoon characters from movies like Harry Potter to video game icons like Mario or Sonic. Sports games in general are usually good choices for children, but Disney and Mario series can be easier and more fun for younger children. Interactive simulation games get children on their feet dancing, singing, and moving their body to win the game. Party games allow family members to play together in board-game-like formats filled with mini-games. This account of video games is, of course, not all-inclusive, and there are other categories of games, including puzzle games, arcade games, and strategy games, that can be appropriate for children as well. The most important thing for any parent or grandparent to realize is that not all video games are the same. Becoming active in how children spend their play time and helping them choose the games that are appropriate for their age and their personality can help to make sure that they are playing games that are both fun for them and good for the family.

Discussion Questions

1. This classification paper is written to help parents or grandparents select video games for children. How do the purpose and audience of the paper influence how it was written?
2. How does the writer organize each classification section? Is this approach effective?
3. Why does the writer point out the advantage of each kind of video game? Is this appropriate for a classification?
4. In the concluding paragraph the writer indicates that there are other kinds of video games that are not discussed in the paper. How does this affect the credibility and overall effectiveness of the paper?
5. Transitions can be a difficult part of any classification. How would you evaluate the effectiveness of this writer's transitions?

Suggestions for Writing

Write a classification paper on one of the topics below or one approved by your instructor. Determine your purpose and audience, select appropriate categories, decide how many you'll discuss, develop them with specific details, and arrange them in an effective order.

1. College teachers (or college pressures)
2. Pet owners (or types of pets)
3. Herbal remedies
4. Kinds of extreme sports
5. Action movies (or romantic comedies)
6. Video games
7. Dancing
8. Reasons for surfing the Internet
9. Talk show hosts
10. Sports announcers (or fans)
11. Television reality shows (or sitcoms)
12. Alternative medicines
13. Bottled water
14. Careers in your field of interest
15. Friends
16. Dates
17. Web pages
18. Advertisements
19. Cheating (or lies)
20. Leaders

CRITICAL EDGE

Classification provides an effective tool for organizing material into categories. But you won't always rely exclusively on your own knowledge or experience to determine or develop categories. At times you'll supplement what you bring to a writing assignment with information gained through outside reading.

Suppose that for an introductory business course, you're asked to prepare a paper that explores major types of investments. You realize that some research will be necessary. After consulting a number of books and magazines, you conclude that stocks, bonds, and real estate represent the three main categories of investments and that each category can be divided into several subcategories. Bonds, for example, can be grouped according to issuer: corporate, municipal, and U.S. Treasury securities.

At this point, you recognize that the strategy of classification would work well for this assignment. Reading further, you learn about the financial risks, rewards, and tax consequences associated with ownership. For example, U.S. Treasury securities offer the greatest safety, while corporate and municipal bonds, as well as stocks and real estate, entail varying degrees of risk depending on the financial condition of the issuer and the state of the economy. Similarly, the income from the different categories and subcategories of investments is subject to different kinds and levels of taxation. Thus, income from municipal bonds is generally tax free, income from U.S. Treasury securities is exempt from state and local taxes, and income from other kinds of investments does not enjoy such exemptions.

After assimilating the information you've gathered, you could synthesize (see pages 149–150) the views expressed in your sources as well as your own ideas about investments. You might organize your categories and subcategories according to probable degree of risk, starting with the least risky investment and ending with the most risky. For your conclusion you might offer purchase recommendations for different groups of investors such as young workers, wealthy older investors, and retirees.

Before using the material of others in your writing, examine its merits. Do some sources seem more convincing than others? Why? Do any recommendations stem from self-interest? For example, a writer who seems overly enthusiastic about one type of investment may be associated with an organization that markets it. Are any sources overloaded with material irrelevant to your purpose? Which sources offer the most detail? Asking and answering questions such as these will help you write a more informed paper.[1]

is important to indicate those additional categories so that the reader recognizes that you are familiar with the other options but have deliberately focused on a select set of categories. This can actually help sustain the credibility of the essay.

5. This essay employs effective transitions. The transitions are varied enough so that the essay does not seem stiff or overly formulaic. Yet, the transitions still follow enough of a pattern so that the reader finds the shift to a new category familiar. Each transition quickly identifies by name the new category of game under consideration and the distinctive and defining characteristic of that game.

SUGGESTED INSTRUCTOR READING

Laruccia, J. A. "Stories Out of Eden: Reorganizing Naming as Rhetorical Strategy." College English 39 (1978): 979–84. An important approach to teaching the significance of classification is to have students experiment with the consequences of renaming.

---

[1]Because you'll rely on published sources, it is important to read the sections on card catalogs and periodical indexes in Chapter 20 and those on handling quotations and avoiding plagiarism in Chapter 21 before you start to write. As always, follow your instructor's guidelines for documenting sources.

Suggestions for Writing

1. Examine the Reader essays on women's issues or health and then write a paper that draws upon these sources and classifies their content.
2. Read several authors' views on success and then write a paper that draws on these sources and classifies their content.
3. Reflect on the Reader essays that you've studied and then write a paper that presents an appropriate classification system for them, perhaps based on the writers' levels of diction, tone, or reliance on authorities.

Writing a Classification

Plan.

- Identify subject for classification.
- Establish purpose for classification.
- Identify audience.

Determine categories.

- List key categories appropriate to purpose.
- Create a table of categories and brainstorm distinguishing features and details.
- If multiple levels of categories, create a category tree.
- Test categories to make certain they are complete and not overlapping.

Consider order of categories.

- From most important to least
- From least to most important
- By key topic
- Use the table to organize

Create a rough draft.

- Intro: engage reader, identify reason for classification, establish topic.
- Body: explain and exemplify each category in order.
- Conclusion: vary.

Revise.

Gather peer feedback; test hard to see if a category is missing; try other categories.

- Does classification fit purpose?
- Do categories overlap?
- Add necessary details or categories.
- Cut categories that don't fit or help.
- Test the organization.
- Test for ethics.

Proofread.

CHAPTER **13**

**TEACHING
SUGGESTION**
Have students work in
small groups to identify the
similarities and differences
in the two pictures of the
same woman. Have them
also identify what they
seem to see as a fundamental difference in the two
personalities or charac-
teristics represented in
the picture. They would
probably identify that the
woman on the left is
wearing a more brightly
colored dress that seems
more traditional, has her
legs covered, has more
traditional jewelry on her
arm, and what seems a
more stylized stance, and
as a result seems more
traditionally a part of her
culture; the woman on the
left, by contrast, is wearing
what seems to be a western
style dress, her legs are
exposed, her pose seems
less formal and more
emotional and as a result
she seems more modern
and freer. Discuss with the
class why the picture is
called originally "Woman
with her Alter Ego." You
might discuss with students

© Fly Fernandez/Zefa/Corbis

210

Comparison: Showing Relationships

Which candidate for senator should get my vote, Ken Conwell or Jerry Mander?

Let me know whether this new shipment of nylon thread meets specs.

Doesn't this tune remind you of an Anne Murray song?

How does high school in Australia stack up against high school in this country?

Everyone makes *comparisons*, not just once in a while but day after day. When we compare, we examine two or more items for likenesses, differences, or both.

Comparison often helps us choose between alternatives. Some issues are trivial: whether to play World of Warcraft or Warhammer, whether to order pizza or a sub sandwich. But comparison also influences our more important decisions. We weigh majoring in chemistry against majoring in physics, buying against renting, working for Microsoft against working for IBM. An instructor may ask us to write a paper comparing the features of two word-processing systems. An employer may have us weigh two proposals for decreasing employee absenteeism and write a report recommending one of them.

Comparison also acquaints us with unfamiliar things. To help American readers understand the English sport of rugby, a sportswriter might compare its field, team, rules, and scoring system with those for football. To teach students about France's government, a political science textbook might discuss the makeup and election of its parliament and the method of picking its president and premier, using our own government as a backdrop.

Both your classes and your job will call for comparison writing. Your humanities instructor may ask you to compare baroque and classical music and their contributions to later musical developments. Your psychology instructor may want you to compare two types of psychosis and assess the legal and medical ramifications of each. Your biology instructor may have you consider how the features of two kinds of body cell enable them to perform their functions. Comparisons in the workplace are common because they help people make decisions. An office manager may compare several phone systems to determine which one the company should install, a nurse assesses the condition of a patient

in what ways people do or don't change when they shift from their traditional culture to influences of western culture.

SUGGESTED WRITING ASSIGNMENTS
1. Have students write a detailed comparison of the two presentations of this woman. They may speculate about the attitudes reflected by her stance.
2. Have students investigate how a culture might be modernizing, such as India, and write a comparison of some focused aspect of traditional culture and the modern change. They could compare traditional architecture and modern buildings, traditional transportation and modern transportation, or traditional dating practices and modern dating practices.

PERSPECTIVE
Some philosophers and psychologists have argued that comparison is fundamental to all perception and knowledge. For example, to identify a friend in the distance

involves distinguishing that person from others while matching his or her features with the image we carry in our head. Because comparisons underlie so much of our daily lives, students are familiar with the act of comparing. They often see a written comparison, however, as simply a kind of paper with a given form, not a strategy that is utilized in a particular writing situation for a specific purpose. You might help them to view comparison in the proper perspective.

TEACHING STRATEGIES

1. Ask students to keep a one-week log of situations where they compare and then have them identify why—perhaps to make a decision, help understand something, or reaffirm an item's distinctiveness.

2. Have students bring in writing examples that feature comparisons and then try to identify the purpose of each comparison.

CLASSROOM ACTIVITY

First in small groups and then as a whole class, students could discuss writing situations where comparison would be useful. Some of the better suggestions could be used as writing assignments.

PERSPECTIVE

Purpose dictates the items selected for a comparison and also how they are developed. It is therefore crucial that students start and proceed with a clear purpose in mind.

"WE'D LIKE TO TAKE YOU UPSTAIRS AND SHOW YOU THE REAL GRACIOUSNESS OF FRATERNITY LIFE, BUT IT'S SORT OF A RULE AROUND HERE TO WAIT UNTIL THE 'RUSHEE' IS PLEDGED."

Richard Bibler, Worthal College Cartoon. Reprinted by permission.

before and after a new medicine is given, an insurance agent points out the features of two insurance policies to highlight the advantages of one.

Selecting Items for Comparison

Any items you compare must share some common ground. For example, you could compare two golfers on driving ability, putting ability, and sand play, or two cars on appearance, gas mileage, and warranty; but you can't meaningfully compare a golfer with a car, any more than you could compare guacamole with Guadalajara or chicken with charcoal. There's simply no basis for comparison.

Any valid comparison, on the other hand, presents many possibilities. Suppose you head the music department of a large store and have two excellent salespeople working for you. The manager of the store asks you to prepare a one- or two-page report that compares their qualifications for managing the music department in a new branch store. Assessing their abilities becomes the guiding purpose that motivates and controls the writing. On the spot you can rule out points such as eye color, hair style, and religion, which have no bearing on job performance. Instead, you must decide what managerial traits the job will require and the extent to which each candidate possesses them. Your thinking might result in a list like this:

Points of Similarity or Difference	Pat	Mike
1. Ability to deal with customers, sales skills	Excellent	Excellent
2. Effort: regular attendance, hard work on the job	Excellent	Excellent
3. Leadership qualities	Excellent	Good
4. Knowledge of ordering and accounting procedures	Good	Fair
5. Musical knowledge	Excellent	Good

This list tells you which points to emphasize and suggests Pat as the candidate to recommend. You might briefly mention similarities (points 1 and 2) in an introductory paragraph, but the report would focus on differences (points 3, 4, and 5), since you're distinguishing between two employees.

Say you want to compare two good restaurants in order to recommend one of them. List the points of similarity and difference that you might discuss. Differences should predominate because you will base your decision on them.

Developing a Comparison

Successful comparisons rest upon ample, well-chosen details that show just how the items under consideration are alike and different. Such support helps the reader grasp your meaning. Read the following two student paragraphs and note how the concrete details convey the striking differences between south and north 14th Street:

> On 14th Street running south from P Street are opulent department stores, such as Woodward and Lothrop and Julius Garfinkle, and small but expensive clothing stores with richly dressed mannequins in the windows. Modern skyscraping office buildings harbor banks and travel bureaus on the ground floors and insurance companies and corporation headquarters in the upper stories. Dotting the concretescape are high-priced movie theaters, gourmet restaurants, multilevel parking garages, bookstores, and candy-novelty-gift shops, all catering to the prosperous population of the city. This section of 14th Street is relatively clean: The city maintenance crews must clean up after only a nine-to-five populace and the Saturday crowds of shoppers. The pervading mood of the area is one of bustling wealth during the day and, in the night, calm.

> Crossing P Street toward the north, one notes a gradual but disturbing change in the scenery of 14th Street. Two architectural features assault the eyes and automatically register as tokens of trouble: the floodlights that leave no alley or doorway in shadows and the riot screens that cage in the store windows. The buildings are old, condemned,

PERSPECTIVE
Student comparisons are often marked by skimpy detail. To avoid this shortcoming, remind students that ample details are necessary to assist readers. Point out that a comparison is sometimes developed by drawing on other writing strategies. A comparison of two building sites might require description, the ways of life in two cultures might employ narration, and many kinds of comparisons depend on illustration.

decaying monoliths, each occupying an entire city block. Liquor stores, drugstores, dusty television repair shops, seedy pornographic bookstores that display photographs of naked bodies with the genital areas blacked out by strips of tape, discount stores smelling perpetually of stale chocolate and cold popcorn, and cluttered pawnshops—businesses such as these occupy the street level. Each is separated from the adjoining stores by a littered entranceway that leads up a decaying wooden stairway to the next two floors. All the buildings are three stories tall; all have most of their windows broken and blocked with boards or newspapers; and all reek of liquor, urine, and unidentifiable rot. And so the general atmosphere of this end of 14th Street is one of poverty and decay.

Student Unknown

Vivid details depict with stark clarity the economic differences between the two areas.

TEACHING STRATEGY
Have students analyze the supporting details in some of the essays in the Reader and identify the purposes that these details serve.

Organizing a Comparison

You can use either of two basic patterns to organize a comparison paper: block or alternating. The paper may deal with similarities, differences, or some combination of them.

CLASSROOM ACTIVITY
Have students, working in small groups, brainstorm for details they might need to compare two jobs, two types of parents, or some other appropriate topic. Encourage them to consider the purpose of the details.

The Block Pattern   The block pattern first presents all of the points of comparison for one item and then all of the points of comparison for the other. Here is the comparison of the two salespeople, Pat and Mike, outlined according to the block pattern:

PERSPECTIVE
While we usually find it easy to organize a comparison effectively, some students may not. They have difficulty juggling similarities and differences while maintaining a consistent pattern of organization. Reviewing student outlines can help overcome this difficulty.

   I. Introduction: mentions similarities in sales skills and effort but recommends Pat for promotion.
  II. Specific points about Mike
      A. Leadership qualities
      B. Knowledge of ordering and accounting procedures
      C. Musical knowledge
 III. Specific points about Pat
      A. Leadership qualities
      B. Knowledge of ordering and accounting procedures
      C. Musical knowledge
  IV. Conclusion: reasserts that Pat should be promoted.

The block pattern works best with short papers or ones that include only a few points of comparison. The reader can easily remember all the points in the first block while reading the second.

TEACHING STRATEGY
Transitions are important in comparisons. Therefore,

The Alternating Pattern   The alternating pattern presents a point about one item, then follows immediately with a corresponding point about the other. Organized in this way, the Pat-and-Mike paper would look like this:

I. Introduction: mentions similarities in sales skills and effort but recommends Pat for promotion.
II. Leadership qualities
   A. Mike's qualities
   B. Pat's qualities
III. Knowledge of ordering and accounting procedures
   A. Mike's knowledge
   B. Pat's knowledge
IV. Musical knowledge
   A. Mike's knowledge
   B. Pat's knowledge
V. Conclusion: reasserts that Pat should be promoted.

For longer papers that include many points of comparison, use the alternating method. Discussing each point in one place highlights similarities and differences; your reader doesn't have to pause and reread in order to grasp them. The alternating plan also works well for short papers.

Once you select your pattern, arrange your points of comparison in an appropriate order. Take up closely related points one after the other. Depending on your purpose, you might work from similarities to differences or the reverse. Often, a good writing strategy is to move from the least significant to the most significant point so that you conclude with punch.

EXERCISE

Using the points of comparison you selected for the exercise on page 213, prepare outlines for a paper organized according to the block and then the alternating pattern.

Using Analogy

An *analogy*, a special type of comparison, calls attention to one or more similarities underlying two kinds of an item that seem to have nothing in common. While some analogies stand alone, most clarify concepts in other kinds of writing. Whatever their role, they follow the same organizational pattern as ordinary comparisons.

An analogy often explains something unfamiliar by likening it to something familiar. Here is an example:

> The atmosphere of Earth acts like any window in serving two very important functions. It lets light in, and it permits us to look out. It also serves as a shield to keep out dangerous or uncomfortable things. A normal glazed window lets us keep our houses warm by keeping out cold air, and it prevents rain, dirt, and unwelcome insects and animals from coming in. . . . Earth's atmospheric window also helps to keep our planet at a comfortable temperature by holding back radiated heat and protecting us from dangerous levels of ultraviolet light.
>
> Lester del Ray, *The Mysterious Sky*

Conversely, an analogy sometimes highlights the unfamiliar in order to help illuminate the familiar. The following paragraph discusses the qualities and

VI. Prices
   A. Restaurant A
   B. Restaurant B
VII. Conclusion: recommends one of the restaurants.

PERSPECTIVE
Analogy can be seen as a key to creativity and effective problem solving. Insights often come from seeing the connections between two seemingly different things. And because an analogy shows a relationship between the familiar and unfamiliar, it is a powerful tool for explaining things.

TEACHING STRATEGIES
1. Have students jot down over a week's time the analogies they observe in writing or speech and determine whether they were or were not effective, and why.

2. Have students identify difficult concepts from another class and attempt to work out an analogy that might facilitate understanding.

CLASSROOM ACTIVITY
Have students complete, with something concrete and physical, sentences such as "Writing is like _____" or "Education is like _____." Then the class can discuss and modify the analogies. This activity shows students that an analogy requires careful thinking and that there are many ways of viewing writing and education.

obligations of an unfamiliar person, the mountain guide, to shed light on a familiar practice—teaching:

> The mountain guide, like the true teacher, has a quiet authority. He or she engenders trust and confidence so that one is willing to join the endeavor. The guide accepts his leadership role, yet recognizes that success (measured by the heights that are scaled) depends upon the close cooperation and active participation of each member of the group. He has crossed the terrain before and is familiar with the landmarks, but each trip is new and generates its own anxiety and excitement. Essential skills must be mastered; if they are lacking, disaster looms. The situation demands keen focus and rapt attention: slackness, misjudgment, or laziness can abort the venture.
>
> Nancy K. Hill, "Scaling the Heights: The Teacher as Mountaineer"

When you develop an analogy, keep these points in mind:

1. Your readers must be well acquainted with the familiar item. If they aren't, the point is lost.
2. The items must indeed have significant similarities. You could develop a meaningful analogy between a kidney and a filter or between cancer and anarchy but not between a fiddle and a flapjack or a laser and limburger cheese.
3. The analogy must truly illuminate. Overly obvious analogies, such as one comparing a battle to an argument, offer few or no revealing insights.
4. Overextended analogies can tax the reader's endurance. A multipage analogy between a heart and a pump would likely overwhelm the reader with all its talk of valves, hoses, pressures, and pumping.

Ethical Issues

Although an old adage declares that "comparisons are odious," most people embrace comparisons except when they are unfair. Unfortunately, this situation occurs all too often. For example, advertisers commonly magnify trivial drawbacks in competitive products while exaggerating the benefits of their own merchandise. Politicians run attack ads that distort their opponents' views and demean the opponents' character. And when scientific theories clash, supporters of one view have been known to alter their findings in order to undermine the other position. Your readers expect any comparison to meet certain ethical standards. Ask and answer these questions to help ensure that those you write measure up.

- Have I avoided skewing one or both of my items in order to ensure a particular outcome?
- Are the items I'm comparing properly matched? It would be unethical to compare a student essay to a professional one in order to demonstrate the inadequacy of the former.
- If I'm using an analogy, is it appropriate? Comparing immigration officials to Nazi storm troopers is ethically odious: It trivializes the suffering and deaths of millions of Nazi victims and taints the officials with a terrible label.

Writing a Comparison

Planning and Drafting the Comparison

Don't write merely to fulfill an assignment; if you do, your paper will likely ramble aimlessly and fail to deliver a specific message. Instead, build your paper around a clear sense of purpose. Do you want to show the superiority of one product or method over another? Do you want to show how sitcoms today differ from those twenty years ago? Purpose governs the details you choose and the organization you follow.

Whether you select your own topic or write on an assigned one, answer these questions:

What purpose will my comparison serve?

Who will be my audience and why will they want to read the essay?

What points of similarity or difference will I discuss?

To develop the comparison, draw up a chart similar to this one.

Item A	Item B
First point of comparison	First point of comparison
Second point of comparison	Second point of comparison

Next, brainstorm each point in turn, recording appropriate supporting details. When you finish, stand back and ask these questions:

Do all the details relate to my purpose?

Do any new details come to mind?

In what order should I organize the details?

When you decide upon an order, copy the points of comparison and the details, arranged in the order you will follow, into a chart like the one below.

Item A	Item B
First point of comparison	First point of comparison
First detail	First detail
Second detail	Second detail
Second point of comparison	Second point of comparison

Use the introduction to identify your topic and arouse the reader's interest. If you intend to establish the superiority of one item over the other, you might call attention to your position. If you're comparing something unfamiliar with something familiar, you might explain the importance of understanding the unfamiliar item.

Organize the body of your paper according to whichever pattern—block or alternating—suits its length and the number of points you're planning to take the theme "Our Relationship to Nature," the essay "Taking Down Carbon" could lead to a discussion and then to papers about how environment change has altered our rapport with nature. Depending on your class, you might help students learn to write from sources by having them compare essays in various ways. For instance, the class might discuss the ways people can relate to places and then, using examples from "Once More to the Lake" and "When the Full Moon . . . ," compare how E. B. White and John V. Young do so. As another option, students might read "The Company Man," "The Sweet Smell of Success . . . ," and Richard Tomkins's "Old Father Time Becomes a Terror" and then compare the authors' views of our success-driven society. Assignments like these will require that you help students identify, use, and document key ideas in a source. Such assignments, while admittedly difficult, will make the writing of longer research papers less intimidating and help students handle future comparisons.

up. If you explain something familiar by comparing it with something unfamiliar, start with the familiar item. If you try to show the superiority of one item over another, proceed from the less to the more desirable one. Note that both of the Pat-and-Mike outlines (pages 214–215) put Mike ahead of Pat, the superior candidate.

Write whatever kind of conclusion will round off your discussion effectively. Many comparison papers end with a recommendation or a prediction. A paper comparing two brands of stereo receivers might recommend purchasing one of them. A paper comparing a familiar sport, such as football, with an unfamiliar one, such as rugby, might predict the future popularity of the latter. Unless you've written a lengthy paper, don't summarize the likenesses and differences you've presented. If you've done a proper writing job, your reader already has them clearly in mind.

Revising the Comparison

Revise your paper in light of the general guidelines in Chapter 4 and the questions that follow:

Have I accomplished my purpose, whether to choose between alternatives or acquaint the reader with something unfamiliar?

For something unfamiliar, have I shown clearly just how it is like and unlike the familiar item?

Have I consistently written with my audience in mind?

Have I considered all points of similarity and difference that relate to my purpose?

Have I included appropriate supporting details?

Are my comparisons arranged effectively?

Have I considered appropriate ethical issues?

SAMPLE

STUDENT ESSAY OF **COMPARISON**

Differences between Korean and English

Sunho Lee

University of Nevada Las Vegas

Director: Vicki Homes

1   As the world undergoes globalization, English is given a great deal of weight as an official language; as a result, many people have been trying to learn English. The Korean people have also been making efforts to acquire the language; however, learning is troublesome for Korean students because English and Korean have a lot of differences. Three major differences between English and Korean give people from Korea special difficulty in learning English: accent, tense, and articles.

2   Accent is one of the obvious differences that frustrate Korean people who try to become skilled at English. For instance, *impact* can be a noun or a verb, depending on how it is stressed. When people who speak English emphasize the first syllable, *impact* is a noun. If people who use English stress the second syllable, *impact* is a verb. The Korean tongue does not use accents in this way and spells noun and verb forms completely differently. Thus distinguishing parts of speech by accent is not something familiar to Korean learners.

3   The second difference is tense, especially the present perfect tense. The present perfect tense describes actions or states that begin in the past, continue into the present, and might continue into the future. This kind of tense does not exist in Korean grammar. For example, the meanings of "I worked out" and "I have worked out" are slightly dissimilar. Of course, Korean students can interpret both meanings, yet when people who are used to speaking Korean use the present perfect tense in English, they have trouble because past and present perfect are not distinguished in the Korean language.

4   The last noticeable difference between Korean and English is the use of articles: definite and indefinite. "Ducks like to swim," "There is a duck in my bathtub," and "The duck quacked all night" are good examples. Each *ducks* or *duck* is different in these examples, but a Korean learner cannot easily see the difference between the usages. One English instructor said, "When I speak English, a bird flies to me and gives me some tips about what article I should use in this situation." This means that even native English speakers cannot define exactly how to use articles. To be sure, English grammar has some rules about how to use articles, but the number of exceptions is more than the regulations. The Korean language does not have articles; in addition, before Korean students learn English, they do not know what an article is exactly. Accordingly, for someone learning English using articles precisely is very complicated.

5   All languages have differences. Thus for a second language learner, studying English is very hard, and it is challenging to overcome the variations between the two languages. It is especially difficult because of the differences in stress, the present perfect tense, and articles. Although these features of English are not easy to understand and use, if Koreans who struggle to use English fluently study constantly, they can finally conquer English.

DISCUSSION QUESTIONS
1. Point by point is the right choice here. It leads the reader to focus on very distinctive differences between the languages. Since the differences are not closely related in kind, a block approach would have been confusing.

2. Since the writer recognizes that most of the readers will not know Korean, examples in Korean would more likely than not confuse the situation. Instead the writer chose a broader description of how Korean functions that most readers should be able to follow. This was the right decision.

3. The audience here is clearly native speakers of English, especially those who teach English to nonnative speakers. The essay is especially intended to help the readers understand why speakers of Korean might have difficulty with some features of English. It achieves its purpose but might have been stronger if it had also provided examples of some common errors by Koreans learning English.

4. The writer signals in the introduction the main points of comparison to be examined, clearly introduces each point of comparison, and follows the same pattern of first discussing the English features and then the Korean language quality. The last is especially appropriate since readers are likely to know the features of English but not know how Korean works.

Discussion Questions

1. This writer decided to use a point-by-point rather than a block comparison. Was this the right decision? Why?
2. While the writer provides clear examples in English, there are no matching examples in Korean. Is this the right choice for this communication situation? Why or why not?
3. What is the audience and purpose for this essay? Does it achieve its purpose?
4. What are some of the effective organizational strategies of this essay?
5. What are the advantages and disadvantages that would result if the writer had looked at additional differences between English and Korean?

Suggestions for Writing

1. Write a properly focused comparison essay on one of the topics below or another that your instructor approves. Determine the points you will discuss and how you will develop and arrange them. Emphasize similarities, differences, or both.

   a. The representation of women, fathers, teenagers, or some other group in a 1950s or '60s sitcom and in a similar contemporary sitcom
   b. The physical or mental demands of two jobs
   c. Male and female styles of conversation
   d. Online and brick-and-morter shopping
   e. A print and an online newspaper
   f. The playing styles of two NBA or WNBA superstars
   g. Two Web servers such as AOL and Earthlink
   h. A high-pressure and a no-pressure salesperson
   i. Online and traditional dating
   j. The business or residential districts of two cities or a wealthy and a working-class residential district in the same city
   k. A favorite social spot during the day and during the evening
   l. Film and digital photography
   m. The effectiveness of two pieces of writing
   n. Traditional and extreme sports
   o. Two or more college or business Web pages
   p. Two musical groups or musical styles
   q. Two managers (or styles of managing)
   r. Authoritarian vs. permissive parenting
   s. Two or more products being considered for purchase
   t. Two or more video games

2. Develop an analogy based on one of the following sets of items or another set that your instructor approves. Proceed as you would for any other comparison.

   a. The offerings in a college catalog and a restaurant
   b. A conquering army and a swarm of locusts

c. Driving on certain highways and gambling

d. A heart and a pump

e. Writing and gardening

f. A teacher and a merchant

g. Cancer and anarchy

h. A parent and a farmer

i. A brain and a computer

j. Developing an idea and building a house

k. Succeeding at school and winning a military campaign

l. A workaholic and an alcoholic

m. A mob and a storm

n. A kidney and a filter

o. A cluttered attic and a disorderly mind

p. Reading a book and exploring a new place

q. A rock concert and a circus

r. A party and a circus

s. Casinos and robbery

t. Contemporary America and an amusement park

5. The comparison of more points of difference would have made the paper much more thorough and helpful to a very informed reader, such as an English as a Second Language instructor. However, for most other readers by focusing on a few points of difference the writer has made the main point without adding too much confusing, and perhaps less interesting, details.

CRITICAL EDGE

Although you rely on your own knowledge or findings to develop many comparisons, in some cases you'll synthesize (see pages 149–150) material from other sources.

Let's say that your business management instructor has asked you to prepare a report on the management styles of two high-profile chief executive officers (CEOs) at Fortune 500 companies that manufacture the same kinds of products. You realize that you'll need to do some reading in business periodicals like *Forbes, Fortune,* and the *Wall Street Journal* in order to complete this assignment. Your sources reveal that the first CEO favors a highly centralized managerial structure with strict limits on what can be done by all employees except top executives. The company has pursued foreign markets by establishing factories overseas and has aggressively attempted to merge with or acquire its domestic competitors. The second CEO has established a decentralized managerial structure that allows managers at various levels of the company to make key decisions. The company has also established a strong foreign presence, but it has done so primarily by entering into joint ventures with foreign firms. Most of its domestic expansion has resulted from the construction of new plants rather than from mergers or takeovers. Both CEOs have borrowed heavily to finance their companies' expansion. These three differences and one similarity are your points of comparison, which you can organize using either the block or alternating pattern. You might conclude by indicating why you prefer one of the two management styles.

After you've read the views expressed by your sources, examine them critically. Does any of the information about the two CEOs seem slanted so that it appears to misrepresent their management styles? For example, do any of the writers seem to exaggerate the positive or negative features of centralized or decentralized management? Do appropriate examples support the writers' contentions? Does any relevant information appear to be missing? Does any source contain material that isn't related to your purpose? Judging the works of others in this fashion will help you write a better report.[1]

Suggestions for Writing

1. Read "The Case for Amnesty" (pages 595–599) and "Not Amnesty but Attrition" (pages 600–604) and then compare the views of these two writers.
2. Read several reviews of the same movie and then compare what the critics have written.
3. Write a criticism of a comparison you recently read that you thought was unreasonable.

[1]Because you'll rely on published sources, it is important to read the sections on card catalogs and periodical indexes in Chapter 20 and those on handling quotations and avoiding plagiarism in Chapter 21 before you start to write. As always, follow your instructor's guidelines for documenting sources.

Writing a Comparison

Plan.

- Identify items for comparison.
- Establish purpose for comparison.
- Identify and analyze audience.

Brainstorm key points of comparison.

- Brainstorm details for each comparison
- Make observations of items if possible

Test whether:
  Points are complete.
  Points are not
    skewed.
  Points meet purposes.

Create rough plan or table.

- Create table laying out points of comparison and details.
- Determine pattern: block or point by point.

Create a rough draft.

- Introduction establishes purpose for comparison and main point.
- Body develops each point of comparison with detail using pattern.
- Conclusions vary but reaffirm main point.

Revise: Gather peer responses, talk over topic, reexamine items.

- Re-brainstorm points of comparison.
- Does everything fit the purpose?
- Add additional similarities or differences as needed.
- Cut points that don't fit.
- Test organization, especially transitions that are critical.

Proofread.

CHAPTER 14

TEACHING SUGGESTION

Have students work in small groups to create a list of causes that could have resulted in the situation in the picture. Discuss with the class what factors might have been relevant and those factors that were not relevant. For example, since it is clearly winter, the rear window might have been iced over and the road surface slippery, which might have been relevant factors. The man looking at the accident probably came later and was not likely a factor.

SUGGESTED WRITING ASSIGNMENT

Have students write a short cause-and-effect paper that explains what might have happened to produce the situation pictured, including a description of the resulting situation.

Cause and Effect: Explaining Why

Cause and effect, like the two sides of a coin, are inseparably linked and together make up *causation*. Cause probes the reasons why actions, events, attitudes, and conditions exist. Effect examines their consequences. Causation is important to us because it can explain historical events, natural happenings, and the actions and attitudes of individuals and groups. It can help us anticipate the consequences of personal actions, natural phenomena, or government policies.

Everyone asks and answers questions of causation. Scott wonders why Sue *really* broke off their relationship, and Jennifer speculates on the consequences of changing her major. People wonder why child abuse and homelessness are on the rise, and millions worry about the effects of corporate cost cutting and violence in our schools.

Inevitably, therefore, you will need to write papers and reports that employ causation. Your instructors might ask you to write on topics such as the causes of the American Revolution, the consequences of white-collar crime, the reasons why so many couples are divorcing, or the effects of different fertilizers on plant growth. An employer may want a report on why a certain product malfunctions, what might happen if a community redesigns its traffic pattern, or how a school closing might affect business.

Patterns in Causal Analysis

Several organizational patterns are possible for a causal analysis. Sometimes, a single cause produces several effects. For instance, poor language skills prevent college students from keeping up with required reading, taking adequate notes, and writing competent papers and essay exams. To explore such a single cause–multiple effect relationship, construct outlines similar to the following two:

I. Introduction: identifies cause   I. Poor language skills
II. Body   II. Body
     A. Effect number 1   A. Can't keep up with required reading

225

4. You might help students gain experience in causal thinking by having them read about and discuss some familiar events or problems, such as the high dropout rate in the public schools or students' poor showing on standardized science and math tests. This type of exercise often helps students select writing topics.

TEACHING STRATEGIES

1. Students can better understand causal patterns if they have experience breaking down the articles they read into causes and effects. Ask students to note especially the connection between cause(s) and effect(s) and the patterns the writers followed in presenting them.

2. Have students plot the pattern of cause and effect in common, everyday events. Examples might include the causes of being late for class or the effects of doing poorly on a test. These examples make excellent journal entries.

CLASSROOM ACTIVITIES

1. As with comparison, have students approach writing problems through a class discussion (possibly starting with small group projects) that helps establish the causes of a well-known problem—bad study habits, environmental pollution, or high absenteeism. Once these causes, and possibly the associated effects, are placed on the board, students can begin to

B. Effect number 2
C. Effect number 3
III. Conclusion

B. Can't take adequate notes
C. Can't write competent papers or exams
III. Conclusion

Alternatively, you might discuss the cause after the effects are presented.

On the other hand, several causes may join forces to produce one effect. Zinc production in the United States, for example, has decreased over the last few years because it can be produced more cheaply abroad than it can here, it is being replaced on cars by plastics and lighter metals, and it cannot be recycled. Here's how you might organize a typical multiple cause–single effect paper:

I. Introduction: identifies effect
II. Body
   A. Cause number 1
   B. Cause number 2
   C. Cause number 3
III. Conclusion

I. Decrease in U.S. zinc production
II. Body
   A. Produced more cheaply abroad
   B. Replaced on cars by plastics, lighter metals
   C. Cannot be recycled
III. Conclusion

Sometimes discussion of the effect follows the presentation of causes.

At times a set of events forms a causal chain, with each event the effect of the preceding one and the cause of the following one. For example, a student sleeps late and so misses breakfast and ends up hungry and distracted, which in turn results in a poor performance on an exam. Interrupting the chain at any point halts the sequence. Such chains can be likened to a row of upright dominoes that fall one after the other when the first one is pushed. Belief in a domino theory, which held that if one nation in Southeast Asia fell to the communists all would, one after the other, helped bring about U.S. entry into the Vietnam War. Causal chains can also help explain how devices function and some social changes proceed. The following outlines typify the arrangement of a paper explaining a causal chain:

I. Introduction
II. Body
   A. Cause
   B. Effect
   C. Cause
   D. Effect
III. Conclusion

I. Introduction
II. Body
   A. Sleep late
   B. Miss breakfast
   C. Become hungry and distracted
   D. Perform poorly on exam
III. Conclusion

Papers of this kind resemble process analyses, but process is concerned with *how* the events occur, cause and effect with *why*.

In many situations the sequence of causes and effects is too complex to fit the image of a chain. Suppose you are driving to a movie on a rainy night. You approach an intersection screened by bushes and, because you have the right-of-way, start across. Suddenly a car with unlit headlights looms directly in your path. You hit the brakes but skid on the slippery pavement and crash into the other car, crumpling its left fender and damaging your own bumper. Later, as you think about the episode, you begin to sense its complexities.

Obviously, the *immediate cause* of the accident was the other driver's failure to heed the stop sign. But other causes also played roles: the bushes and unlit headlights that kept you from seeing the other car sooner; the starts and stops, speedups and slowdowns that brought the two cars to the intersection at the same time; the wet pavement you skidded on; and the movie that brought you out in the first place.

You also realize that the effects of the accident go beyond the fender and bumper damage. After the accident, a police officer ticketed the other driver. As a result of the delay, you missed the movie. Further, the accident unnerved you so badly that you couldn't attend classes the next day and therefore missed an important writing assignment. Because of a bad driving record, the other driver lost his license for sixty days. Clearly, the effects of this accident rival the causes in complexity.

Here's how you might organize a multiple cause–multiple effect essay:

Introduction	The accident
Body	Body
I. Causes	I. Causes of the accident
A. Cause number 1	A. Driver ran stop sign
B. Cause number 2	B. Bushes and unlit headlights
C. Cause number 3	impaired vision
II. Effects	C. Wet pavement caused skidding
A. Effect number 1	II. Effects of the accident
B. Effect number 2	A. Missed the movie
C. Effect number 3	B. Unnerved so missed classes
Conclusion	next day
	C. Other driver lost license
	Conclusion

In some situations, however, you might first present the effects, then turn to the causes.

EXERCISE

1. **Read the following selection and then arrange the events in a causal chain:**

Although some folk societies still exist today, similar human groups began the slow process of evolving into more complex societies many millennia ago, through settlement in villages and through advances in technology and organizational structure. This gave rise to the second level of organization: civilized preindustrial, or "feudal," society. Here there is a surplus of food because of the selective cultivation of grains—and also because of the practice of animal husbandry. The food surplus permits both the specialization of labor and the kind of class structure that can, for instance, provide the leadership and command the

---

determine the most coherent pattern to use. Similarly, such an activity could concentrate on the effects of an action or trend—raising the entrance requirements at a college, establishing or eliminating a class attendance policy, marrying later in life.

2. For an especially good class, you might note that causes fall into three categories: necessary causes, which must be present for an event to occur but may not be solely responsible for it; contributory causes, which help bring about, but cannot by themselves produce, an effect, which may also occur independently; and sufficient causes, which can bring about effects all by themselves. To illustrate the first type, you might point out that watering a houseplant is necessary because it would otherwise die. For survival, though, the plant also needs proper sunlight, drainage, nutrients, and temperature. To illustrate a contributory cause, you could note that high winds may intensify but can't start a brush fire and also that the fire might occur without wind. To illustrate a sufficient cause, you could point out that a dose of potassium cyanide by itself will kill a person. Indicate that the great majority of causes are either necessary or contributory.

EXERCISE ANSWERS
1. Folk → *Settlement in*
societies   *villages, technological and organizational advances (effect)*

Tech- → *Surplus of food*
nological *(effect)*
and organi-
zational
advances
(cause)

Feudal → *Specialization of*
society, *labor, improved*
surplus of *class structure*
food *(effect)*
(cause)

Speciali- → *Irrigation sys-*
zation of *tems, greater*

labor, *surplus of food*
improved *(effect)*
class struc-
ture (cause)

2. a. You might complain
to the manager,
become ill and have to
cancel a shopping trip,
scream and leave the
restaurant, or remove
the worm from the leaf
and eat the salad.

b. You might have to
leave school for the
remainder of the term;
drop out of some kind
of athletic competition;
suffer complications
that cause you to lose
use of the arm; or, if
the break is a simple
one, merely miss a
day's classes.

c. You might lose your
job, fail to find another
one that pays as well,
and have to settle for a
less comfortable and
desirable lifestyle; your
boss might impose a
two-week layoff without
pay, forcing you to
postpone or cancel the
purchase of some
household item; or you
might convince your
boss that the tardiness
was unavoidable.

manpower to develop and maintain extensive irrigation systems (which in turn makes possible further increases in the food supply). . . .

Gideon Sjöberg, "The Origin and Development of Cities"

2. **Trace the possible effects of the following occurrences:**

   a. You pick out a salad at the cafeteria and sit down to eat. Suddenly you notice a large green worm on one of the lettuce leaves.

   b. As you leave your composition classroom, you trip and break your arm.

   c. Your boss has warned you not to be late to work again. You are driving to work with ten minutes to spare when you get a flat tire.

Reasoning Errors in Causal Analysis

Ignoring Multiple Causes

An effect rarely stems from a single cause. The person who believes that permissive parents have caused the present upsurge of venereal disease or the one who blames television violence for the climbing numbers of emotionally disturbed children oversimplifies the situation. Permissiveness and violence perhaps did contribute to these conditions. Without much doubt, however, numerous other factors also played important parts.

Mistaking Chronology for Causation

Don't assume that just because one event followed another that the first necessarily caused the second. This kind of faulty thinking feeds many popular superstitions. Horace walks under a ladder, later stubs his toe, and thinks that his path caused his pain. Sue breaks a mirror just before Al breaks their engagement; then she blames the cracked mirror. Many people once believed that the election of Herbert Hoover as president in 1928 brought on the Great Depression in 1929. Today some people believe that the testing of atomic weapons has altered our weather patterns. Don't misunderstand: One event *may* cause the next; but before you go on record with your conclusion, make sure that you're not dealing with mere chronology.

Confusing Causes with Effects

Young children sometimes declare that the moving trees make the wind blow. Similarly, some adults may think that Pam and Paul married because they fell in love, when in reality economic necessity mandated the vows, and love came later. Scan your evidence carefully in order to avoid such faulty assertions.

1. **Which of the following statements point toward papers that will focus on causes? Which point toward papers focusing on effects? Explain your answers.**

   a. Most of the problems that plague newly married couples are the direct outgrowth of timidity and pride.

b. The Marshall Plan was designed to aid the economic recovery of Europe after World War II.

c. The smoke from burning poison ivy can bring on a skin rash and lung irritation.

d. Popularity in high school stems largely from good looks, a pleasing personality, participation in school activities, the right friends, and frequent dates.

2. **Identify which of the following paragraphs deals with causes, which with effects. List the causes and effects.**

a.   Color filters offer three advantages in black-and-white photography. First, a particular color will be lightened by a filter of the same color. For example, in a photograph of a red rose in a dark blue vase, both will appear almost the same shade of gray if no filter is used. However, when photographed through a red filter, the rose will appear much lighter than the vase; and through a blue filter the vase will appear much lighter than the rose. This effect can be useful in emphasizing or muting certain objects in a photograph. Second, a particular color filter will darken its complementary color in the scene. Consequently, any orange object will appear darker than normal if a blue filter is used. Finally, color filters can reduce or increase atmospheric haze. For example, in a distant aerial shot there will often be so much haze that distant detail is obscured. To eliminate haze almost entirely, the photographer can use a deep red filter. On the other hand, if more haze is desired in order to achieve an artistic effect, varying shades of blue filters can be used.

Timothy Kelly

b.   Overeating, which has become a national pastime for millions of Americans, has several roots. For example, parents who are concerned that their children get enough to eat during the growing years overfeed them and thereby establish a lifetime overeating habit. The child who is constantly praised for cleaning up his plate experiences a sort of gratification later on as he cleans up all too many plates. The easy availability of so much food is a constant temptation for many people, especially the types of food served at fast-food restaurants and merchandised in the frozen food departments of supermarkets. Equally tempting are all the snack foods constantly advertised on TV. But many people don't need temptation from the outside; their overeating arises from such psychological factors as nervousness, boredom, loneliness, insecurity, an overall discontent with life, or an aversion to exercise. Thus, overeating can actually be a symptom of psychological surrender to, or withdrawal from, the complexities and competition of modern life.

Kenneth Reichow

EXERCISE ANSWERS

1. a. The phrasing "are the direct outgrowth of" identifies timidity and pride as causes of marital discord.

b. The phrasing "was designed to aid" denotes a paper that will deal with *effects*, concentrating on the ways in which the Marshall Plan aided European recovery.

c. The phrasing "can bring on" denotes that a skin rash and lung irritation are the *effects* of exposure to burning poison ivy.

d. This paper would explain the *causes* of high school popularity.

2. a. This paragraph deals with effects. These effects include making a color lighter by using a filter of the same color; making a color darker by using a filter of a complementary color; and reducing or increasing atmospheric haze by the appropriate filter.

b. This paragraph deals with causes. The causes include the overfeeding of children by their parents; the availability of fast foods; the advertising of snack foods on TV; and psychological factors such as nervousness, boredom, loneliness, insecurity, discontent with life, and indolence.

Ethical Issues

Causation is not immune from abuse, either accidental or deliberate. Imagine the consequences of an article that touts a new herbal remedy but fails to mention several potentially serious side effects that could harm many users. Think about the possible strain on your relationship with a friend if she unjustly suspected you of starting a vicious rumor about her. Writing cause-and-effect papers creates an ethical responsibility. Asking and answering these questions will help you meet that obligation.

- Have I tried to uncover all of the causes that might result in a particular outcome? A report blaming poor instruction alone for a high student failure rate in a certain town's public schools almost certainly overlooks such factors as oversized classes, inadequate facilities, and poor home environments.
- Have I carefully weighed the importance of the causes I've uncovered? If a few, but not most, of the classes in the school system with problems are oversized, then the report should not stress their significance.
- Have I tried to uncover and discuss every important effect, even one that might damage a case I'm trying to make? A report emphasizing the beneficial effects of jogging would be dangerously negligent if it failed to note the potential for injury.
- What would be the consequences if people act on my analysis?

Careful evaluation of causes and effects not only fulfills your writing obligation but also your ethical one.

Writing a Causal Analysis

Planning and Drafting the Causal Analysis

Because you have probably speculated about the causes and effects of several campus, local, state, or national problems, writing this type of paper should pose no great difficulty. If you choose your own topic, perhaps your personal experience will suggest something promising. Topics such as "Why I Dislike (or Like) Foreign Cars" and "How My Father's (or Someone Else's) Death Has Changed My Life" might work well. Nonpersonal topics also offer writing possibilities. For instance, "What's Behind Teenage Suicides?" and "The Impact of Global Markets on American jobs" would allow you to draw on library resources.

The strategies on pages 31–39 can also help you find several topics. Answer these questions about each candidate:

What purpose will guide this writing?

Who is my audience? Will the topic interest them? Why or why not?

Shall I focus on causes, effects, or both?

Brainstorming your topic for supporting details should be easy. If you're dealing with causes, pose these questions about each one:

How significant is this cause?

Could it have brought about the effect by itself?

TEACHING STRATEGY
Ask students to record examples of faulty causal analysis that they find in their academic and personal lives. Have them write a short paper identifying such errors, explaining why they are errors, and examining the consequences.

PERSPECTIVE
A vast amount of faulty thinking stems from inept causal analysis. It's rather alarming to hear students reason that since they did better on a test when they didn't study, why bother in the future? As part of our responsibility to teach students how to think about causes, we should help them identify such errors.

TEACHING STRATEGIES
You might want to discuss the following cases with your class.
1. A preliminary research study found some correlation between the use of certain yard insecticides and childhood learning disabilities. The study stressed that the findings were preliminary and did not rule out other causes. Tom, a local newspaper writer, obtained a copy of the study and wrote an article urging parents to avoid using the insecticides. Did Tom act ethically? Why or why not?
2. A school district adopted a policy requiring all teachers to minimize the number of D's and F's

Does it form part of a chain?

Precisely how does it contribute to the effect?

For papers dealing with effects, substitute the following questions for the ones above:

How important is this effect?

What evidence will establish its importance?

Charting your results can help you prepare for writing the paper. To tabulate causes, use an arrangement like this one:

Cause	Contribution to Effect
First cause	Specific contribution
Second cause	Specific contribution

For effects, use this chart:

Effect	Importance
First effect	Why important
Second effect	Why important

Once your items are tabulated, examine them carefully for completeness. Perhaps you've overlooked a cause or effect or have slighted the significance of one you've already mentioned. Think about the order in which you'd like to discuss your items and prepare a revised chart that reflects your decision.

Use the opening of your paper to identify your topic and indicate whether you plan to discuss causes, effects, or both. You can signal your intention in a number of ways. To prepare for a focus on causes, you might use the words *cause, reason,* or *stem from,* or you might ask why something has occurred. To signal a paper on effects, you might use *effect, fallout,* or *impact,* or you might ask what has happened since something took place. Read these examples:

Signals causes: Midville's recent decrease in street crime stems primarily from its expanded educational program, growing job opportunities for young people, and falling rate of drug addiction.

Signals effects: Since my marriage to Rita, how has my social life changed?

At times you may choose some dramatic attention-getter. For a paper on the effects of radon, a toxic radioactive gas present in many homes, you might note that "Although almost everyone now knows about the hazards associated with smoking, eating high-cholesterol foods, and drinking excessively, few people are aware that just going home could be hazardous to one's health." If you use an arresting statement, be sure the content of your paper warrants it.

How you organize the body of the paper depends on your topic. Close scrutiny may reveal that one cause was indispensable; the rest merely played supporting roles. If so, discuss the main cause first. In analyzing your automobile

they handed out. What possible reasons might the district have for implementing this policy? Is it ethically justified? Why or why not? What undesirable consequences might result from the policy?

TEACHING STRATEGIES

1. Spending class time on interesting issues can help students find a topic. You might assign the cause-and-effect essays in the Reader and then have the class discuss the ways people are affected by time pressure or how they perceive others, or discuss the causes of divorce. Most students can relate to and write about these topics. Such discussions can also be personalized. For example, students might list, and then determine the underlying causes of, the time pressures in their lives.

2. Reinforce the notion of the writing purpose. It's one thing to write the school board, showing the negative effects of a certain school policy; it's quite another to objectively review the effects for an impartial judge.

3. Encourage students to write a short paragraph explaining why their target audience would be interested and what it would want to know.

4. Even after students analyze causes and effects, they often under-write their papers. Show students how to describe cause and effect and how to establish that one resulted from the other. It isn't enough to state that bad study habits affect grades. The writer must describe what these habits are and then show how they result in poor grasp of the material, poor test answers, and ultimately poor test scores.

READER/THEME STRATEGIES

If you would like to take up the theme "Life's Changes," you could explore the factors that contribute to a person's identity. Students, after reading and discussing any of the essays included under this category, could write themes that deal with the ways that their experiences and surroundings have shaped them. As another possibility, students could read and talk about "The Sweet Smell of Success Isn't All That Sweet," then write papers that explain why they picked their majors. If you prefer the theme "Contemporary Issues," essays such as "Why Marriages Fail," "Binge Drinking," "Has Canada Got the Cure?," "The Problem with Single-Payer Plans," "The Case for Amnesty," and "Not Amnesty but Attrition" can provide the starting point for a detailed discussion of an important problem facing the country and to papers about its causes and effects. Depending on your class, you might even have students do short research papers that build on one of the essays. They might explore the racial attitudes that

mishap, which fits this situation, start with the failure of the other driver to yield the right-of-way; then fan out to any other causes that merit mentioning. Sometimes you'll find that no single cause was essential but that all of them helped matters along. Combinations of this kind lie at the heart of many social and economic concerns: inflation, depression, and urban crime rates, to name just a few. Weigh each cause carefully and rank them in importance. If your topic and purpose will profit from building suspense, work from the least important cause to the most important. Otherwise, reverse the order. For analyzing causal chains, chronological order works effectively.

If space won't permit you to deal adequately with every cause, pick out the two or three you consider most important and limit your discussion to them. To avoid giving your reader an oversimplified impression, note that other causes exist. Even if length poses no problem, don't attempt to trace every cause to some more remote cause and then to a still more remote one. Instead, determine some sensible cutoff point that accords with your purpose, and don't go beyond it.

Treat effects as carefully as you do causes. Keep in mind that effects often travel in packs, and try to arrange them in some logical order. If they occur together, consider order of climax. If one follows the other in a chainlike sequence, present them in that fashion. If space considerations dictate, limit your discussion to the most interesting or significant effects. Whatever order you choose for your paper, don't jump helter-skelter from cause to effect to cause in a way that leaves your reader bewildered.

As you write, don't restrict yourself to a bare-bones discussion of causes and effects. If, for instance, you're exploring the student parking problem on your campus, you might describe the jammed lots or point out that students often miss class because they have to drive around and look for spots. Similarly, don't simply assert that the administration's insensitivity contributes to the problem. Instead, cite examples of the college's refusal to answer letters about the situation or to discuss it. To provide statistical evidence of the problem's seriousness, you might note the small number of lots, the limited spaces in each, and the approximate number of student cars on campus.

It's important to remember, however, that you're not just listing causes and effects; you're showing the reader their connection. Let's see how one student handled this connection. After you've read "Why Students Drop Out of College," the student essay that follows in this chapter, carefully reexamine paragraph 3. Note how the sentence beginning "In many schools" and the two following it show precisely how poor study habits develop. Note further how the sentence beginning "This laxity produces" and the three following it show precisely how such poor habits result in "a flood of low grades and failure." Armed with this information, readers are better able to avoid poor study habits and their consequences.

Causal analyses can end in several ways. A paper discussing the effects of acid rain on America's lakes and streams might specify the grave consequences of failing to deal with the problem or express the hope that something will be done. Frequently, writers use their conclusions to evaluate the relative importance of their causes or effects.

Revising the Causal Analysis

Follow the guidelines in Chapter 4 and answer these questions as you revise your causal analysis:

Have I made the right decision in electing to focus on causes, effects, or both?

Have I ferreted out all important causes and effects? Mistakenly labeled something as an effect merely because it follows something else? Confused causes with effects?

Am I dealing with a causal chain? An immediate cause and several supporting causes? Multiple causes and effects?

Have I presented my causes and effects in an appropriate order?

Have I supported my discussion with sufficient details?

Have I considered appropriate ethical issues?

underlie the conflict in "Momma's Encounter" or examine, after reading "The Company Man," the social and financial costs of workaholism. Finally, they might read "Momma's Encounter," and "The Scholarship Jacket" and then look into the effects of various kinds of stereotyping.

SAMPLE

STUDENT ESSAY OF **CAUSE AND EFFECT**

Why Students Drop Out of College

Diann Fisher

1   Each fall a new crop of first-year college students, wavering between high hopes for the future and intense anxiety about their new status, scan college maps searching for their classrooms. They have been told repeatedly that college is the key to a well-paying job, and they certainly don't want to support themselves by flipping hamburgers or working at some other dead-end job. So, notebooks at the ready, they await what college has in store. Unfortunately many of them—indeed, over 30 percent—will not return after the first year. Why do so many students leave? There are several reasons. Some find the academic program too hard, some lack the proper study habits or motivation, others fall victim to the temptations of the college environment, and a large group leave for personal reasons.

2   Not surprisingly, the academic shortcomings of college students have strong links to high school. In the past, a high school student who lacked the ability or desire to take a college-preparatory course could settle for a diploma in general studies and afterward find a job with

Continued on next page

Continued from previous page

decent pay. Now that possibility scarcely exists, so many poorly pre-pared students feel compelled to try college. Getting accepted by some schools isn't difficult. Once in, though, the student who has taken noth-ing beyond general mathematics, English, and science faces serious trouble when confronted with college algebra, first-year composition, and biological or physical science. Most colleges do offer remedial courses and other assistance that may help some weaker students to survive. In spite of everything, however, many others find themselves facing ever-worsening grade-point averages and either fail or just give up.

3   Like academic shortcomings, poor study habits have their roots in high school, where even average students can often breeze through with a minimum of effort. In many schools, outside assignments are rare and so easy that they require little time or thought to complete. To accommo-date slower students, teachers frequently repeat material so many times that slightly better students can grasp it without opening their books. And when papers are late, teachers often don't mark them down. This laxity produces students who can't or don't want to study, students totally unprepared for the rigorous demands of college. There, courses may require several hours of study each week in order to be passed with even a C. In many programs, outside assignments are commonplace and demanding. Instructors expect students to grasp material after one explanation, and many won't accept late papers at all. Students who don't quickly develop disciplined study habits face a flood of low grades and failure.

4   Poor student motivation aggravates faulty study habits. Students who thought high school was boring find even less allure in the more challenging college offerings. Lacking any commitment to do well, they shrug off assigned papers, skip classes, and avoid doing required reading. Over time, classes gradually shrink as more and more students stay away. With final exams upon them, some return in a last-ditch effort to salvage a passing grade, but by then it is too late. Eventually, repetition of this scenario forces the students out.

5   The wide range of freedoms offered by the college environment can overwhelm even well-prepared newcomers. While students are in high school, parents are on hand to make them study, push them off to class, and send them to bed at a reasonable hour. Once away from home and parents, however, far too many students become caught up in a constant round of parties, dates, bull sessions, and other distractions that seem more fascinating than schoolwork. Again, if such behavior persists, poor grades and failure result.

6   Personal reasons also take a heavy toll on students who might otherwise complete their programs successfully. Often money problems are at fault. For example, a student may lose a scholarship or grant, fail to obtain needed work, or find that the family can no longer afford to help out. Some students succumb to homesickness; some are forced out by an illness, injury, or death in the family; and yet others become ill or injure themselves and leave to recuperate. Finally, a considerable number become disillusioned with their programs or the size, location, or atmosphere of their schools and decide not to return.

7   What happens to the students who drop out? Some re-enroll in college later, often in less demanding two- and four-year schools that offer a better chance of academic success. Of the remainder, the great bulk find civilian jobs or enlist in the armed forces. Most, whatever their choice, go on to lead productive, useful lives. In the meantime, campus newcomers need to know about the dangers that tripped up so many of their predecessors and make every effort to avoid them.

Discussion Questions

1. Identify the thesis statement in this essay.
2. Trace the causal chain that makes up paragraph 2.
3. What is the function of the first sentence in paragraph 3?
4. In which paragraphs does the writer discuss causes? Effects?

Suggestions for Writing

Use one of the following topics, or another that your instructor approves, to develop a causal analysis. Determine which causes and/or effects to consider. Scrutinize your analysis for errors in reasoning, settle on an organization, and write the essay.

1. Reasons that relationships fail
2. The effect of some friend, acquaintance, public figure, or writer on your life
3. Effects of talking on cell phones while driving
4. Effects of divorce on children
5. Why you are a _____ major
6. Causes, effects, or both of the popularity of FaceBook
7. Causes of school violence
8. Causes or effects of the popularity of casino gambling
9. Causes, effects, or both of widespread cell phone use
10. Reasons that you have a particular habit or participate in a particular sport
11. Causes or effects of sleep deprivation
12. Reasons that _____ is a popular celebrity
13. Effects of some recent Supreme Court decision or change in public policy
14. The effects of environmental concerns on our way of life
15. Causes, effects, or both of our hunger for heroes
16. Causes, effects, or both of the high cost of gasoline
17. Causes, effects, or both of drinking on college students
18. Causes of procrastination
19. Reasons that some students drop out of high school
20. Causes and effects of violence at sporting events

CRITICAL EDGE

Although nearly everyone recognizes the role of causation in human affairs, differences of opinion often surface about the causes and effects of important matters. What lies behind the widespread incivility in the United States today? Why are women more likely than men to leave management jobs? How do video games affect children? What impact does the high divorce rate have on American society? Obviously such questions lack simple answers; and as a result investigators, even when they agree on the causes and effects involved, often debate their relative importance.

Suppose your women's studies instructor has asked you to investigate the departure of women from managerial positions. A library search reveals several articles on this topic as well as a number of reasons for resigning.

Some women leave because they find it harder to advance than men do, and as a result they seldom attain senior positions. Others leave because they receive lower salaries than their male counterparts. Still others leave because of the stifling effects of corporate rigidity, unrealistic expectations, the demands of raising a family, or possibly diminished chances of marriage. Although most articles cite these causes, their relative importance is debatable. One writer, for example, emphasizes family concerns by discussing them last and at greatest length. Another puts the chief blame on obstacles to upward mobility—the existence of a "glass ceiling" that blocks women from upper-level positions along with an "old-boy network" of entrenched executives that parcels out jobs among its members.

Once you've finished your research, you're ready to synthesize (see pages 149–150) the views of your sources as well as your own views. Before you start to write, though, take some time to consider carefully each cause and effect you've uncovered. Obviously you should ground your paper on well-supported and widely acknowledged causes and effects, but you might also include more speculative ones as long as you clearly indicate their secondary nature. To illustrate, one writer, while mentioning corporate rigidity as a reason that women leave management jobs, clearly labels this explanation as a theory and backs it with a single example. As you examine your material, ask yourself these critical questions as well as any others that occur to you: Does any writer exhibit obvious bias? Do the studies cited include a sufficient number of examples to be meaningful? Do the statistics appear reliable, or are some out of date, irrelevant, or skimpy? Have the writers avoided the reasoning errors discussed on page 228–229 Whenever you find a flaw, note where the problem lies so that you can discuss it in your writing if you choose. Such discussions often clear up common misconceptions. There are various possibilities for organizing your paper. If your sources substantially agree on the most important cause, you might begin with that one and then take up the others. A second possibility, the order-of-climax arrangement, reverses the procedure by starting with secondary causes and ending with the most significant one. You can use the same options for organizing effects. When no clear consensus exists about the relative importance of the different causes and effects, there is no best arrangement of the material.[1]

[1]Because this type of paper draws upon published information, it is important to read the sections on card catalogs and periodical indexes in Chapter 20 and those on handling quotations and avoiding plagiarism in Chapter 21 before you start to write. As always, follow your instructor's guidelines for documenting sources.

1. The thesis statement is the final two sentences of paragraph 1. Your better students may recognize that thesis statements sometimes consist of more than one sentence. You might point out that the second of these sentences forecasts the reasons for dropping out that the essay will discuss.

2. The causal chain is as follows: Failure of college-bound high school students to take appropriate preparatory courses - difficulties of these students when faced with college courses - worsening grade-point average - final failure or decision to leave college.

3. This sentence, the topic sentence of the paragraph, links both the first and second reasons for students dropping out of college.

4. Paragraphs 3–6 discuss causes, and paragraph 7 discusses effects.

SUGGESTED INSTRUCTOR READING

Buchan, U. "Why and Because Method Really Works." Improving College and University Teaching 21 (1973): 273–74. Explains how a basic why-and-because question–answer strategy can be an effective teaching tool.

Suggestions for Writing

1. Read three articles on the causes of a major social problem such as domestic violence and incorporate those causes and your own views in a paper.
2. Read two articles that disagree about the effects of a proposed government program such as oil and gas drilling on public land and write a paper that incorporates the writers' views and presents your own conclusions.
3. Write an essay that corrects a common misconception about the causes or effects of a matter about which you feel strongly. Possibilities might include the causes of homelessness or the impact of capital punishment on murder rates in different states.

Writing a Causal Analysis

Plan.

- Identify key topic based on assignment or personal interest.
- Identify audience and purpose.
- Decide if you are more interested in causes or effects.

Brainstorm and take notes on causes and effects.

- Read and conduct research.
- Observe.
- Talk with others for ideas.

Test causes and effects.

Are you
- missing causes or effects?
- ignoring multiple causes?
- mistaking correlation for causation?
- confusing causes and effects?

Do you have good evidence to claim something a cause or effect?

Identify most appropriate pattern.
Effects of a single cause, of a single event, a chain of effects or causes, and effects of an event.

Create a table that organizes causes or effects and provides details.

Decide on focus.

Create a rough **outline** or **plan** of pattern of cause and effect.

Write a rough draft.

- **Intro** introduces topic, reasons for analysis, focus on cause or effect.
- **Body** provides causes or effects with details and reasons, shows connections, follows pattern.
- **Conclusion** may specify consequences, warn readers, evaluate importance of cause or effect.

Revise.

Gather peer response, test analysis carefully, read more if needed, talk over with others.

- Does focus on cause or effect fit purpose and facts?
- Add missing cause or effect, detail, or evidence.
- Cut parts that don't fit.
- Evaluate accuracy of account and pattern.
- Test organization to make it clear to reader.
- Test for ethics.

Proofread.

CHAPTER 15

TEACHING SUGGESTIONS

Recently there has been an extensive debate about what is or is not a planet. If Pluto is included, why shouldn't other objects be included that are similar? Have students research by a web search the recent debate by astronomers about what should be the definition of a planet. Discuss in class what they think should or should not be a factor in counting an object as a planet. Where there are unintended consequences, such as defining a planet as a round object in orbit around the sun also includes our moon, help them see the consequences. Keep track of the discussion and then determine what processes needed to be included to reach a decision about a definition.

WRITING SUGGESTION

After class discussion, have students write a definition about what should or shouldn't count as a planet. As part of that definition, they should discuss whether large asteroids would fulfill the definition. They might address whether in

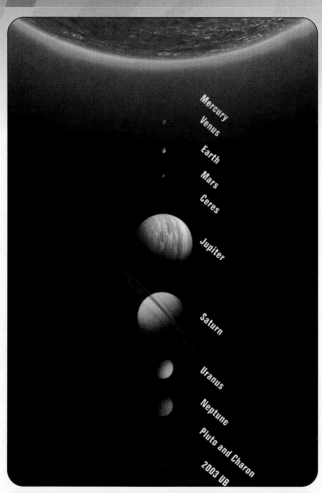

Mercury
Venus
Earth
Mars
Ceres
Jupiter
Saturn
Uranus
Neptune
Pluto and Charon
2003 UB

© IAU/Martin Kommesser/Handout/epa/Corbis

Definition: Establishing Boundaries

That movie was egregious.

Once the bandage is off the wound, swab the proud flesh with the disinfectant.

Speaking on statewide television, Governor Blaine called his opponent a left-winger.

Do you have questions? You're not alone. Many people would question the sentences above: "What does *egregious* mean?" "How can flesh be *proud?*" "What does the governor mean by *left-winger?* What specific policies does the opponent support that warrant this label?" To avoid puzzling and provoking your own readers, you'll often need to explain the meaning of some term. The term may be unfamiliar (*egregious*), used in an unfamiliar sense (*proud flesh*), or mean different things to different people (*left-winger*). Whenever you clarify the meaning of some term, you are *defining*.

Humans are instinctively curious. We start asking about meanings as soon as we can talk, and we continue to seek, as well as supply, definitions all through life. In school, instructors expect us to explain all sorts of literary, historical, scientific, technical, and social terms. On the job, a member of a company's human resources department might prepare a brochure that explains the meaning of such terms as *corporate responsibility* and *product stewardship* for new employees. An accountant might define *statistical sampling inventory* in a report calling for a change in the inventory system. A special education teacher might write a memo explaining *learning disabled* to the rest of the staff.

When you define, you identify the features that distinguish a term, thereby putting a fence around it, establishing its boundaries, and separating it from all others. Knowing these features enables both you and your reader to use the term appropriately.

Sometimes a word, phrase, or sentence will settle a definition question. To clear up the mystery of "proud flesh," all you'd need to do is insert the parenthetical phrase "(excessively swollen and grainy)" after the word *proud*. But when you're dealing with new terms—*information superhighway* and *virtual reality* are

another solar system two planets could have one in rotation around the other. This writing assignment could be done with or without additional research on the part of students.

PERSPECTIVE
It's no accident that definition precedes argument since no rational argument, scientific theory, or philosophical position is possible without a precise definition of the terms involved. For Plato, knowledge is attained only when humans recognize the true nature of virtue or the good; his pursuit of wisdom was a search for definition. On the other hand, where there is confusion about the meaning of key terms, such as the often-disputed idea of "free elections," then communication, and even international negotiations, can break down. Many students, however, regard definitions as merely the subject matter of

241

dictionaries to be used only in moments of complete bewilderment. Besides knowing how to write definitions, students need to understand their relevance to thought and communication.

TEACHING STRATEGIES

1. Ask students where they have observed confusion or conflicts triggered by differing perceptions of what a term means. For a short assignment, they could write a report that names the term involved, identifies thedifferent definitions, and describes the resulting difficulties.

2. Have students identify several key terms in their major field and report on their meaning and significance. This exercise demonstrates the practical importance of precise definitions in every occupation.

3. To demonstrate that words change meaning and can have several meanings, have students use the *Oxford English Dictionary* and report on the evolution of a particular word.

CLASSROOM ACTIVITIES

1. To help students appreciate that precise definitions are essential to effective communication, write several abstract terms on the board (*freedom, love, success*) and have the class jot down, and then compare, their own definitions. They will see how

examples—brief definitions won't provide the reader with enough information for proper understanding.

Abstract terms—those standing for things we can't see, touch, or otherwise detect with our five senses—often require extended definitions, too. It's impossible to capture the essence of *democracy* or *hatred* or *bravery* in a single sentence: The terms are too complex, and people have too many differing ideas about what they mean. The same holds true for some concrete terms—those standing for actions and things we can perceive with our five senses. Some people, for instance, limit the term *drug pusher* to full-time sellers of hard drugs like cocaine and heroin. Others, at the opposite extreme, extend the term to full- and part-time sellers of any illegal drug. Writing an argument recommending life sentences for convicted drug pushers would require you to tell just what you mean by the term so that the reader would have solid grounds for judging your position.

Types of Definitions

Three types of definition—synonyms, essential definitions, and extended definitions—serve writers' needs. Although the first two seldom require more than a word or a sentence, an extended definition can run to several pages. The three types, however, are related. Synonyms and essential definitions share space between the covers of dictionaries, and both furnish starting points for extended definitions.

Synonyms

Synonyms are words with very nearly the same meanings. *Lissome* is synonymous with *lithe* or *nimble*, and *condign* is a synonym of *worthy* and *suitable*. Synonyms let writers clarify meanings of unfamiliar words without using cumbersome explanations. To clarify the term *expostulation* in a quoted passage, all you'd have to do is add the word *objection*, in brackets, after it. Because synonyms are not identical twins, using them puts a slightly different shade of meaning on a message. For example, to "protest" and to "object" are certainly similar in many ways. Yet the claim that we "object" to the establishment of a nuclear waste site in our area fails to capture the active and sustained commitment implied in our willingness to "protest" against such a site. Still, synonyms provide a convenient means of breaking communications logjams.

Essential Definitions

An essential definition does three things: (1) names the item being defined, (2) places it in a broad category, and (3) distinguishes it from other items in that category. Here are three examples:

Item Being Defined	Broad Category	Distinguishing Features
A howdah	is a covered seat	for riding on the back of an elephant or camel.
A voiceprint	is a graphical record	of a person's voice characteristics.
To parboil	is to boil meat, vegetables, or fruits	until they are partially cooked.

Writing a good essential definition requires careful thought. Suppose your instructor has asked you to write an essential definition of one of the terms listed in an exercise, and you choose vacuum cleaner. Coming up with a broad category presents no problem: A vacuum cleaner is a household appliance. The hard part is pinpointing the distinguishing features. The purpose of a vacuum cleaner is to clean floors, carpets, and upholstery. You soon realize, however, that these features alone do not separate vacuum cleaners from other appliances. After all, carpet sweepers also clean floors, and whisk brooms clean upholstery. What then does distinguish vacuum cleaners? After a little thought, you realize that, unlike the other items, a vacuum cleaner works by suction. You then write the following definition:

> A vacuum cleaner is a household appliance that uses suction to clean floors, carpets, and upholstery.

The same careful attention is necessary to establish the distinguishing features of any essential definition.

Limitations of Essential Definitions   Essential definitions have certain built-in limitations. Because of their brevity, they often can't do full justice to abstract terms such as *cowardice, love, jealousy, power.* Problems also arise with terms that have several settled meanings. To explain *jam* adequately, you'd need at least three essential definitions: (1) a closely packed crowd, (2) preserves, and (3) a difficult situation. But despite these limitations, an essential definition can be useful by itself or as part of a longer definition. Writers often build an extended definition around an essential definition.

Pitfalls in Preparing Essential Definitions   When you prepare an essential definition, guard against these flaws:

Circular definition. Don't define a term by repeating it or changing its form slightly. Saying that a psychiatrist is "a physician who practices psychiatry" will only frustrate someone who's never heard of psychiatry. Repress circularity and provide the proper insight by choosing terms the reader can relate to, for example, "A psychiatrist is a physician who diagnoses and treats mental disorders."

Overly broad definition. Shy away from definitions that embrace too much territory. If you define a skunk as "an animal that has a bushy tail and black fur with white markings," your definition is not precise. Many cats and dogs also fit this description. But if you add "and that ejects a foul-smelling secretion when threatened," you will clear the air—of any misconceptions at least.

Overly narrow definition. Don't hem in your definition too closely, either. "A kitchen blender is a bladed electrical appliance used to chop foods" illustrates this error. Blenders perform other operations, too. To correct the error, add the missing information: "A kitchen blender is a bladed electrical appliance used to chop, mix, whip, liquefy, or otherwise process foods."

Omission of main category. Avoid using "is where" or "is when" instead of naming the main category. Here are examples of this error: "A bistro is where food and wine are served" and "An ordination is when a person is formally recognized as a minister, priest, or rabbi." The reader will not know exactly what sort of thing (a bar? a party?) a *bistro* is and may think that *ordination* means a time. Note the

differing attitudes can lead people to crosspurposes.

2. Have the class, working in small groups, list terms that they use but their parents do not, and then develop definitions aimed at the parents.

TEACHING STRATEGY
Have students, using dictionaries or thesauruses, select several synonyms for terms you provide and then determine contexts in which each synonym would be suitable. This activity offers an opportunity to distinguish between denotation and connotation.

PERSPECTIVE
The structure of essential definitions dates back to the Greeks and particularly to Plato, who developed it most fully. Approaching ideas by fitting them into general categories and noting their distinguishing features is fundamental to Western analytic thought. Although most obvious in the sciences, this approach is crucial in every other field. Thus filmmakers use it to distinguish camera shots and bankers to categorize mortgages. Because nearly every idea they encounter will involve one or more essential definitions, students should appreciate the power of these definitions to organize the conceptual world.

TEACHING STRATEGIES
1. You might point out that this chapter functions as an extended definition by providing several

distinguishing features of the strategy it discusses.

2. Students often believe that dictionary definitions are completely objective and unchanging. You might point out that dictionaries are compiled on the basis of common usage. It is interesting to compare the definitions of controversial words—*rebel*, for instance—in dictionaries from several historical periods. Students might also examine several definitions to determine any latent, and possibly questionable, assumptions. Those, for example, who have faith in astrology would dispute a definition calling it "a pseudoscience claiming that the relative positions of the stars, planets, sun, and moon can be used to foretell the future."

EXERCISE ANSWERS
1. Key: broad category// distinguishing traits

a. Gangue is useless rock//accompanying valuable minerals in a deposit.

b. A catbird is a small American songbird// with a slate-colored body, a black cap, and a catlike cry.

c. A soldier is a man or woman//serving in an army.

d. Myelin is a white, fatty substance//that forms a sheath around some nerve fibers.

e. A gargoyle is a waterspout//carved in the likeness of a grotesque animal or imaginary creature and projecting from the gutter of a building.

improvement when the broad categories are named: "A bistro is a small restaurant where both food and wine are served" and "An ordination is a ceremony at which a person is formally recognized as a minister, priest, or rabbi."

 EXERCISE

1. Identify the broad category and the distinguishing traits in each of these essential definitions:

a. Gangue is useless rock accompanying valuable minerals in a deposit.

b. A catbird is a small American songbird with a slate-colored body, a black cap, and a catlike cry.

c. A soldier is a man or woman serving in an army.

d. Myelin is a white, fatty substance that forms a sheath around some nerve fibers.

e. A gargoyle is a waterspout carved in the likeness of a grotesque animal or imaginary creature and projecting from the gutter of a building.

f. A magnum is a wine bottle that holds about two-fifths of a gallon.

2. Indicate which of the following statements are acceptable essential definitions. Explain what is wrong with those that are not. Correct them.

a. A scalpel is a small knife that has a sharp blade used for surgery and anatomical dissections.

b. A puritan is a person with puritanical beliefs.

c. A kraal is where South African tribes keep large domestic animals.

d. A rifle is a firearm that has a grooved barrel and is used for hunting large game.

e. A motorcycle is a two-wheeled vehicle used mainly for human transportation.

f. Fainting is when a person loses consciousness owing to inadequate flow of blood to the brain.

3. Write an essential definition for each of the following terms:

a. groupie	**c.** hit man	**e.** pushover
b. happy hour	**d.** jock	**f.** hard grader

Extended Definitions

Sometimes it's necessary to go beyond an essential definition and write a paragraph or whole paper explaining a term. New technical, social, and economic terms often require extended definitions. To illustrate, a computer scientist might need to define *data integrity* so that computer operators understand the importance of maintaining it. Terms with differing meanings also frequently require extended definitions. To let voters know just what he means by *left-winger*, Governor Blaine might detail the kinds of legislation his opponent favors and opposes. Furthermore, extended definition is crucial to interpretation of the law, as we see when courts clarify the meaning of concepts such as obscenity.

Extended definitions are not merely academic exercises; they are fundamental to your career and your life. A police officer needs to have a clear understanding of what counts as *reasonable grounds for search and seizure;* an engineer must comprehend the meaning of *stress;* a nuclear medical technologist had better have a solid grasp of *radiation*. And all of us are concerned with the definition of our basic rights as citizens.

Extended definitions are montages of other methods of development—narration, description, process analysis, illustration, classification, comparison, and cause and effect. Often, they also define by negation: explaining what a term *does not* mean. The following paragraphs show how one writer handled an extended definition of *sudden infant death syndrome*. The student began by presenting a case history (illustration), which also incorporated an essential definition and two synonyms.

> Jane and Dick Smith were proud, new parents of an eight-pound, ten-ounce baby girl named Jenny. One summer night, Jane put Jenny to bed at 8:00. When she went to check on her at 3:00 A.M., Jane found Jenny dead. The baby had given no cry of pain, shown no sign of trouble. Even the doctor did not know why she had died, for she was healthy and strong. The autopsy report confirmed the doctor's suspicion—the infant was a victim of "sudden infant death syndrome," also known as SIDS or crib death. SIDS is the sudden and unexplainable death of an apparently healthy, sleeping infant. It is the number-one cause of death in infants after the first week of life and as a result has been the subject of numerous research studies.

Discussion Questions

1. What synonyms does the writer use?
2. Which sentence presents an essential definition?

In the next paragraph, the writer turned to negation, pointing out some of the things that researchers have ruled out about SIDS.

> Although researchers do not know what SIDS is, they do know what it is *not*. They know it cannot be predicted; it strikes like a thief in the night. Crib deaths occur in seconds, with no sound of pain, and they always happen when the child is sleeping. Suffocation is *not* the cause, nor is aspiration or regurgitation. Researchers have found no correlation between the incidence of SIDS and the mother's use of birth control pills or tobacco or the presence of fluoride in water. Since it is not hereditary or contagious, only a slim chance exists that SIDS will strike twice in the same family.

Finally, the student explored several proposed causes of SIDS as well as how parents may react to the loss of their child.

> As might be expected, researchers have offered many theories concerning the cause of crib death. Dr. R. C. Reisinger, a National Cancer

f. A magnum is a wine bottle//that holds about two-fifths of a gallon.

2. **a.** This definition is good.

b. This is a circular definition. A person who didn't know the meaning of puritan would not know the meaning of puritanical. Change to "A puritan is a person with strict moral and religious views."

c. This definition does not name a broad category. Change to "A kraal is a fenced enclosure where South African tribes keep large domestic animals."

d. This definition is too narrow; rifles are used for other purposes besides hunting. Change to "A rifle is a firearm that has a grooved barrel and is used primarily for hunting large game and as a military weapon."

e. This definition is too broad; bicycles also fit the definition. Change to "A motorcycle is a two-wheeled vehicle powered by a gasoline engine and used mainly for human transportation."

f. This definition does not name a broad category. Change to "Fainting is a condition in which a person loses consciousness due to an inadequate flow of blood to the brain."

3. Writing essential definitions:

a. A groupie is a young fan who follows after rock bands or celebrities in the hope of forming a close attachment.

b. A happy hour is a period of time, usually from late afternoon to early evening, when a bar or restaurant sells alcoholic drinks at reduced prices.

c. A hit man is a criminal who specializes in paid murder.

d. A jock is a man or woman who is dedicated to athletic participation.

e. A pushover is a person who is easily swindled, defeated, or persuaded. OR a pushover is anything that can be accomplished without significant effort.

f. A hard grader is an instructor who sets especially high standards for his or her students.

TEACHING STRATEGY
A common problem in student and professional writing is purposeful or accidental equivocation, that is, subtly changing the meaning of a term. In opposing the legalization of drugs, a writer might start by using *drugs* to refer to heroin, cocaine, and the like, but later, after establishing the danger of these drugs, shift the term so that it also covers marijuana. The arguments against

Institute scientist, has linked crib deaths to the growth of a common bacterium, *E. coli*, in the intestines of newborn babies. The organisms multiply in the intestines, manufacturing a toxin that is absorbed by the intestinal wall and passes into the bloodstream. Breast milk stops the growth of the organism, whereas cow's milk permits it. Therefore, Dr. Reisinger believes, bottle-fed babies run a higher risk of crib death than other babies. . . .

The loss of a child through crib death is an especially traumatic experience. Parents often develop feelings of guilt and depression, thinking they somehow caused the child's death. To alleviate such feelings, organizations have been established to help parents accept the fact that they did not cause the death.

Trudy Stelter

Ethical Issues

How we define can have devastating consequences. For centuries, the practice of defining Africans as "subhuman" helped justify the slave trade and slavery. During the 1930s and early 1940s, labeling Jews as "vermin" was used to fuel the attempt to exterminate them both in Nazi Germany and much of Western Europe. Even in the absence of malice, definition can have far-reaching effects, both good and bad. For instance, a change in the federal definition of "poverty" can increase or decrease by millions the number of individuals and households eligible for benefits such as Medicaid. Although the consequences of your writing won't approach those of the above examples, you'll nevertheless need to think about possible ethical implications. Addressing the following questions will help you do this.

- Have I carefully evaluated all of the features of my definition? In clarifying what constitutes "excessive force" by the police, it would be unfair to include the reasonable means necessary to subdue a highly dangerous suspect.
- Have I slanted my definition to reflect some prejudice? Let's say a writer opposed to casino gambling is defining "gambling addicts." The paper should focus on those who spend an excessive amount of time in casinos, bet and often lose large sums of money, and in so doing neglect family, financial, and personal obligations. It would be unfair to include those who visit casinos occasionally and strictly limit their losses.
- Have I avoided unnecessary connotations that might be harmful? A definition of teenagers that overemphasized their swift changes in mood might be unfair, perhaps even harmful, since it may influence the reactions of readers.

Writing an Extended Definition

Planning and Drafting the Extended Definition

If you choose your own topic, pick an abstract term or one that is concrete but unfamiliar to your reader. Why, for instance, define *table* when the discussion would likely bore the reader? On the other hand, a paper explaining *computer virus* might well prove interesting and informative. Use one of the strategies on pages 31–39 to unearth promising topics. Then answer these questions about them:

> Which topic holds the most promise? Why?
>
> What purpose will guide my writing? To clarify a technical or specialized concept? To show what the term means to me? To persuade the reader to adopt my attitude toward it? To discuss some neglected facet of it?
>
> For what audience should I write?

Here's a helpful process to follow as you think your definition through. First, select a clear example that illustrates what you wish to define: the United States could exemplify *democracy*. Then brainstorm to uncover major identifying characteristics. For democracy your list might include majority rule, free elections, a separately elected chief executive, and basic human rights. Next, test these characteristics against other legitimate examples and retain only the characteristics that apply. Britain is clearly a democracy but doesn't have a separately elected chief executive. Finally, test the unfolding definition against a clear counter-example, perhaps the People's Republic of China. If the definition fits the example, something is wrong.

Now evaluate what methods you might use to develop your definition. Each method has its own set of special strengths, as the following list shows:

Narration. Tracing the history of a new development or the changing meaning of a term: the birth of the Internet

Description. Pointing out interesting or important features of a device, an event, or an individual: a blizzard

Process. Explaining what a device does or how it is used, how a procedure is carried out, or how a natural event takes place: an earthquake

Illustration. Tracing changes in meaning and defining abstract terms by providing examples: tyranny

Classification. Pointing out the different categories into which an item or an event can be grouped: types of romantic comedies

Comparison. Distinguishing between an unfamiliar and a familiar item: terrorist distinguished from soldier

Cause and effect. Explaining the origins and consequences of events, conditions, problems, and attitudes: disease defined by cause

Negation. Placing limitations on conditions and events and correcting popular misconceptions: why liberty isn't anarchy

Examine your topic in light of this listing and select the methods of development that seem most promising. Don't hesitate to use a method for some purpose not

legalizing marijuana then become the same as those directed against the harder drugs, even though the real differences between marijuana and the others mandate different reasons for keeping it illegal. You could ask students to look for instances of equivocation in their own, and even professional, writing, or bring in illustrative examples yourself.

DISCUSSION QUESTIONS
1. The writer uses the synonym *crib death* for *sudden infant death syndrome.*
2. The next-to-the-last one.

TEACHING STRATEGY
Have students develop a list of words whose definitions might present sensitivity problems. Possibilities might include *slow learner, minority, gay, feminist, masculine, illiterate.* Establish and discuss the consequences of some possible definitions and connotations for the terms. You might also take up the controversy over political correctness and the consequences of using such terms as *handicapped, disabled,* and *physically challenged.* What ethical concerns might help determine which one to use?

TEACHING STRATEGIES
Below are two cases you might want to discuss with your class.
1. In an op ed piece he wrote for a local paper,

Shawn defined *feminism* as an attempt to completely overturn a male-dominated society and insinuated a link between feminism and lesbianism. Discuss the ethics of his article.

2. Here is a fictional case. To promote a policy that would lift the embargo on Cuba, a Senator introduced a bill making it illegal for the United States to withhold trade from any democracy. He defined democracy as any system where leaders are elected by a vote of the people. What he didn't indicate was that this definition would apply to one-party systems where only certain people could be elected. He hoped to argue that Cuba, if it held a single-party election, was a democracy and the embargo should therefore be lifted. Discuss the ethics of this definition.

PERSPECTIVE
As with all writing, having a clear purpose and a definite audience helps ensure the success of student definition papers. In addition, students need to spend considerable time evaluating their particular concepts of terms—reading what others have written, discussing aspects with peers, and doing ample brainstorming. Students often assume that because of their general familiarity with terms such as *friendship, stubbornness, greed,* or *stress,* they can crank out papers defining them off the tops of their heads. Not so.

mentioned here. If you think that a comparison will help your reader understand some abstract term, use it.

Chart the methods of development you'll use, and then brainstorm each method in turn to gather the details that will inform the reader. When you've finished, look everything over, rearrange the details as necessary, add any new ones you think of, and prepare a revised chart. The example that follows is for a paper using four methods of development.

Narration	Classification	Process	Negation
Beginning American Democracy	Types of democracy	Election process	Not democracies
First supporting detail	First supporting detail	First supporting detail	First supporting detail
Forming a constitutional committee	Parliamentary democracy: England	Initial exploration	Single party states: Old Soviet Union
Second supporting detail	Second supporting detail	Second supporting detail	Second supporting detail
Drafting a constitution	Independent presidency: U.S.	Fund raising	Controlled elections: Egypt

Definition papers can begin in various ways. If you're defining a term with no agreed-upon meaning (for example, *conservatism*), you might note some differing views of it and then state your own. If the term reflects some new social, political, economic, or technological development (such as the *wireless Internet*), you might mention the events that brought it into being. A colloquial or slang term often lends itself nicely to an attention-getting opener. A paper defining *chutzpah* might begin by illustrating the brash behavior of someone with this trait. Often an introduction includes a short definition, perhaps taken from a dictionary. If you do include a dictionary definition, use the full name of the dictionary (*Webster's New World Dictionary* says . . .). Several dictionary titles include the word *Webster*, and unless you use the full name your reader won't know which one you mean. Draw on a dictionary definition, however, only as a last resort.

In writing the body of the paper, present the methods of development in whatever order seems most appropriate. A paper defining *drag racing* might first describe the hectic scene as the cars line up for a race, then classify the different categories of vehicles, and finally explain the steps in a race. One defining *intellectual* might start by showing the differences between intellectuals and scholars, then name several prominent intellectuals and note how their insights have altered our thinking, and conclude by trying to explain why many Americans hold intellectuals in low regard.

Definition papers can end, as well as begin, in a number of ways. If you're defining some undesirable condition or event (such as *sudden infant death syndrome*), you might express hope for a speedy solution. If you're reporting on some new development (like *information superhighway*), you might predict its economic or social impact. Often, a summary of your main points is effective. Choose whichever type of ending best supports your main idea.

Revising the Extended Definition

Use the general guidelines in Chapter 4 and these specific questions as you revise your extended definition:

Are my purpose and audience clear and appropriate?

If I've used an essential definition, does it do what it should and avoid the common pitfalls?

Are the methods of development suitable for the topic?

Is the paper organized effectively?

Are there other factors or examples I need to consider?

Have I considered appropriate ethical issues?

SAMPLE

STUDENT ESSAY OF **DEFINITION**

Rediscovering Patriotism

Peter Wing

1   After the horrifying events of September 11, 2001, when terrorists flew jet planes into the World Trade Center and the Pentagon, killing thousands of Americans, there was a surge of patriotism. America was under attack, and as we frequently do when our nation is threatened, we rallied around the flag. Flags were pasted in the back windows of cars and the front windows of homes. So many Americans bought flags that stores were quickly sold out. It was a rare car that didn't have a United We Stand bumper sticker. Rock groups that had built their image around cynicism gleefully participated in patriotic concerts. In short, it became fashionable once again to be a flag-waving, "Star Spangled Banner"-singing, country-loving patriot.

2   These results were good, but there was also an alarming side to this newfound patriotism. Those who even suggested that American foreign policy might have contributed to the attack were branded *traitor* and were effectively silenced. People, including members of Congress, who criticized the way the war on terrorism was being conducted were

Continued on next page

TEACHING STRATEGY
You might have students identify issues or situations requiring definitions. Perhaps one student is disgusted with the misuse of the phrase *peer pressure* by parents while another, who is studying computers, might find that lay readers are confused about the nature of a *database*. Students should then indicate what they want to accomplish by writing their papers. Because students often concentrate on technique and shortchange purpose, have them draft a brief statement of purpose. Next, have them draft an audience profile detailing what the audience does and doesn't know about the concept. Only at this point are students ready to consider the appropriate strategies to use in developing their papers.

CLASSROOM ACTIVITY
Since most students will be interested in the personal characteristics addressed in the Reader—success and honesty—you could lead a class discussion that explores these subjects. More controversial issues could also be introduced, such as ascertaining limitations on freedom of speech or determining whether assault rifles are included under our right to bear arms.

READER/THEME STRATEGIES
If you elect to deal with the theme "Who We Are," many reading selections could lead to a definition paper. Students might

read and discuss such essays as "The Company Man," "The Sweet Smell of Success Isn't All That Sweet," and "Why We Flirt" and then write definitions of such personal characteristics as charisma, cuteness, aggressiveness, assertiveness, or dedication, or of such personal accomplishments as success and happiness. Depending on your class, you could develop an assignment that calls for writing from sources. Students could compare implicit and explicit definitions of success in "The Company Man," and "The Sweet Smell of Success Isn't All That Sweet," the differing conceptions of masculinity in "Rambos of the Road" and "The Appeal of the Androgynous Man," or the ways racism is manifested in "Momma's Encounter" and "The Scholarship Jacket" Here too is an opportunity for students to discuss and define successful writing.

TEACHING STRATEGY
Given the difficult and often slippery nature of extended definitions, caution students to revise not only the form but also the substance of their drafts with great care. They could write out a revision plan that details appropriate questions they've asked and answered.

Continued from previous page

lambasted as unpatriotic. In my neighborhood, those who didn't fly flags, who didn't have patriotic bumper stickers, who didn't seethe with righteous anger at America's enemy were labeled un-American. All of this raises an obvious question: What is patriotism?

3 The obvious answer is that patriotism is love for one's country. But clearly that answer is too broad. Someone could easily love the skyscrapers of Manhattan, the gorgeous vistas of the Grand Canyon, and even the cornfields of Iowa and still sell military secrets to an enemy of America, a far-from-patriotic act. Timothy McVeigh would probably have said that he loved his country, but it would be troubling to consider his attack on the Alfred P. Murrah Federal Building a patriotic act. Certainly patriotism can include an intense love for the land, an appreciation for the people that make up our nation, and a pride in the accomplishments of our country. Part of the heart-swelling quality of patriotism is the recognition of all that is great and good about our nation: the valiant role of our soldiers in World War II; the innovative spirit that forged new technologies, cured diseases, and allowed Americans to journey to the moon. However, that pride would be incomplete without an appreciation for and dedication to the core principles that define this nation.

4 In the end, what is most essential to America is not our industrial wealth, our military power, or artistic works. America is defined by its initial vision, the commitment to democracy, to basic political equality for all Americans, to liberty, to the rights of the individual. Consider how odd it would be if someone's claim to patriotism were a desire for a military coup that toppled democracy to establish a more powerful military. Surely we would find someone seriously misguided who loved American industry but wanted to discard the Constitution and have only the heads of corporations serve in Congress. While there may be many aspects to patriotism, the core of American patriotism would have to be a solid commitment to the core values of the Constitution.

5 What is it, then, to have a love for and commitment to the core values of a nation? It is easy to confuse patriotism with the symbols of patriotism, the flag waving and anthem singing. Just as a husband who gives his wife a love poem and a diamond ring and then rushes out to cheat on her isn't really the best husband, someone who proudly flies a flag

but never votes, refuses to serve on juries, and actively discriminates is not the best patriot. Serving in the military is rightly considered one of the most distinguished acts of patriotism, and properly so. Soldiers don't just say they love their country; they risk their lives to protect the people and the principles of their nation, to preserve liberty. Just as love for a spouse isn't simply a matter of gushy greeting cards but rather concerted day-to-day action, including listening patiently to the other's problems, so patriotism lives and breathes through actions. That doesn't have to be military action but can be participation in anything that preserves and strengthens what is best about a nation. Patriotism then means voting in elections, actively participating in campaigns, writing to legislators, serving on juries, volunteering for schools, building homes for the poor, obeying laws, honoring those who serve, and criticizing things that are wrong.

6   One of the paradoxes of this notion of patriotism is that it makes it essential to criticize and even protest against government policy. It would be a poor friend who let a buddy slide into alcoholism without comment. It would be a poor patriot who would let America move away from the best it can be without action. To really love one's country is to struggle to help make that country realize its best ideals. Those who protested against segregation in America were patriots, recalling America to the fundamental commitment to equality. Many who marched against the Vietnam War were patriotic since they believed that the war violated America's commitment to justice. So too were those who felt the Vietnam War was necessary to American security, for they only wanted to protect America from a perceived communist threat. Those who objected to the way the war against terrorism was being conducted also, then, could be considered patriotic, for they too, out of a love for their country, were participating in the democratic process, raising their voice so that America would choose the best course of action. Patriotism doesn't reside in being on one side or the other of a political debate; it exists in the honest struggle to realize the best ideals of the country. Given this view, in a democracy, no group has a monopoly on patriotism.

7   That is why some of the bitter slogans of supposed patriotism—*My Country Right or Wrong* or *America: Love It or Leave It*—are just plain

Continued on next page

Continued from previous page

wrong. While it is true that patriotism would suggest that we not disown our country when it takes what we consider a misguided direction, it would surely not be patriotic to defend and support a direction we thought wrong. Those who are alarmed by the policies of the government or are deeply dissatisfied with some injustice, such as the horrible conditions of many inner-city schools, are not lacking in patriotism and have no obligation to leave. Those who complain, carp, protest, point out shortcomings are acting out of a profound patriotism. Because of their love for their country, they struggle to move the country to realize its best ideals. If there were any bumper sticker I would want to see for patriotism, it would be *Our Country: Make It the Best It Can Be.*

8   It is heartening to see the revival of patriotism. Hopefully, that patriotism will go beyond simple flag waving and dig deeper to the core meaning of patriotism where Americans together struggle to preserve and develop American ideals. Patriotism will really have taken root in America when citizens become involved in the political process, eagerly serve on juries, work to improve the lives of fellow citizens, and, surprisingly enough, raise their voices in criticism when we, as a government and a people, fall short of the very best we can become.

Discussion Questions

DISCUSSION QUESTIONS
1. The author identifies patriotism with "love of country" but American patriotism more specifically with the valuing of the Constitution's core values.

2. The writer starts the essay by identifying the importance of patriotism as a theme, the need to examine the issue, and the more superficial concept of patriotism against which he will contrast his own definition.

3. The writer develops his concept of patriotism by

1. Identify the essay's essential definition.
2. What purpose do the first two paragraphs serve?
3. How does the writer develop his definition?
4. What do the first three sentences of paragraph 6 accomplish?
5. Why might the writer have decided to discuss bumper sticker slogans in the next to the last paragraph?

Suggestions for Writing

Write a properly focused extended definition using one of the following suggestions or one approved by your instructor. The term you define may be new, misused, or misunderstood or may have a disputed meaning. Develop the essay by any combination of writing strategies.

1. Integrity
2. Green technologies

3. Depression
4. School violence
5. Stress
6. Human genome
7. Extreme sports
8. Alternative rock
9. Breaking as a dance form
10. Cybervandals
11. Campus security
12. Feminist
13. Hate crimes
14. Family values
15. Some term from your field
16. Online class
17. Addiction
18. The Internet
19. The Christian Right
20. Rap music

contrasting it against other concepts, analyzing the core concepts, and providing examples.

4. The writer introduces an unusual extension of his definition but tries to make this claim plausible by connecting it with an analogy with which most readers would agree.

5. Often concepts such as patriotism are made into bumper sticker slogans. Here, the writer can identify the common clichéd slogans and then remind readers of his definition by offering a contrasting slogan.

CRITICAL EDGE

Definitions are always social creations. The way various people and communities understand and use any word determines its definition. As a result, writers who use complex words such as *justice, love,* and *charisma* to convey a message may need to consult a number of sources to determine how others have used the words. With their findings of this research in mind, the writers can stake out their own meanings of those words.

If you were writing a paper defining *dance* for a humanities class, you would probably find several conflicting meanings of the term. Frank Thiess, writing in *The Dance as an Artwork,* defines dance as the use of the body for expressive gesture. But as you mull over that definition, you realize that it is both too broad and too narrow. While some forms of dance, such as ballet, feature expressive gesture, so does pantomime or even a shaken fist; and neither of these qualifies as dance. A square dance clearly qualifies, but does it represent expressive gesture? Susanne Langer, in *Philosophy in a New Key,* defines dance as "a play of Powers made visible," pointing to the way dancers seem to be moved by forces beyond themselves. You recognize that this definition may apply to religious dance forms, that dancers sometimes appear swept away by the music, and that you yourself have experienced a feeling of power when dancing. Nevertheless, upon reflection you decide that often it's the dancer's skill that attracts us, and rarely do we dance to reveal invisible powers. Finally, you discover that Francis Sparshott, in *The Theory of the Arts,* defines dance as a rhythmical, patterned motion that transforms people's sense of their own existence according to the dance they do. As you evaluate Sparshott's contention, you decide that it has considerable merit, although you aren't convinced that every dance transforms our sense of existence. When you think about the kinds of dance you know and the various definitions you have uncovered, you conclude that each of these writers, like the blind men who felt different parts of an elephant and tried to describe it, is only partly correct. For your humanities paper, you decide to synthesize (see pages 149–150) the different definitions. You might explain that all dance involves a rhythmical, patterned movement of the body for its own sake. Sometimes such movement can transform our sense of existence, as in trance dances or even waltzes. Other dances, such as story ballets, use rhythmical movements as expressive gestures that tell stories or convey emotions. Still other dances may suggest the manifestation of powers beyond the dances themselves. You proceed to explain each of these features with details drawn from both your sources and personal experience.

Carrying out this type of project requires you to look critically at the definitions of others. Do they accurately reflect the examples you know about? Do they describe examples that do not fit the definition? Are any parts of the definition questionable? Once you've answered these questions, you can then draw on the appropriate elements of the definitions to formulate your own. You might organize such a paper by developing each definition in a separate section, first presenting it in detail and then pointing out its strengths and weaknesses. In the final section, you could offer your own definition and support it with your reasoning and suitable examples.[1]

Suggestions for Writing

1. Read the essay "Supermarket Pastoral" (pages 605–608) as well as several others on organic food that you find in the library. Reflect on the different definitions of "organic" then, drawing on your reading, offer your own definition.
2. Read "The Sweet Smell of Success . . ." (pages 559–560) and "I Have a Dream" (pages 586–588). Then write your own definition of success, taking into account the views expressed in these essays.
3. Do some reading about an abstract term like *bravery, democracy,* or *hatred* in at least three sources. Use the sources to develop your own definition of the term.

---

[1]Because you'll draw upon published sources, it is important to read the sections on card catalogs and periodical indexes in Chapter 20 and those on handling quotations and avoiding plagiarism in Chapter 21 before you start to write. As always, follow your instructor's guidelines for documenting sources.

Writing a Definition

Plan.

Identify your topic, establish audience, identify purpose.

Brainstorm distinguishing characteristics, examples, examples and characteristics excluded; read, talk to others about the term, observe its use.

 Test your defining features against ordinary usage; Is it too broad or too narrow?

Create a table or chart of your definition with key characteristics, examples, and exclusions.

 Identify useful strategies: description, narration, process, illustration, classification, comparison, cause-effect, and negation.

Create a plan of organization or organize your table: organization may reflect strategies used or be by key defining characteristics.

Develop rough draft.

- **Intro** introduces term, reason for definition, dominant characteristic.
- **Body** presents distinctive defining characteristics.
- **Conclusion** may summarize main point, call for action, predict an outcome, stress Importance.

Revise.

Gather reader responses; discuss with others; test definition against many examples; check for too general, too narrow, or circular definitions.

- Do defining characteristics fit?
- Add needed traits or examples.
- Cut unneeded elements.
- Test to make certain definition is complete and follows clear pattern.
- Test for ethics.

Proofread.

255

CHAPTER 16

TEACHING SUGGESTIONS

Discuss whether the picture is or is not an argument and why slogans cannot really function as arguments. Have students in small groups identify possible arguments for and against the idea that silence can be equaled to death. The original image was about AIDS but the slogan could be applied to child abuse, dangerous conditions in a mine, bad policies leading to war, or even knowledge about an illness.

SUGGESTED WRITING ASSIGNMENT

After the small-group project and a subsequent large-group discussion, have students write a short argument paper taking a position on whether silence does or does not equal death. The students should be able to select the issue to which they want to apply the expression.

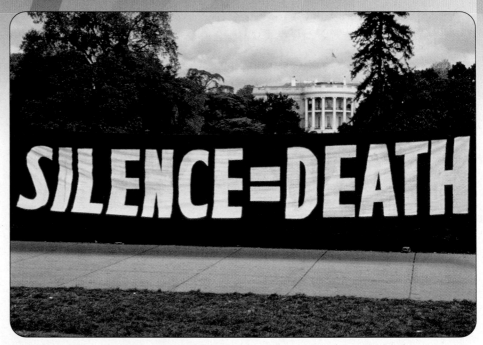

Argument: Convincing Others

"What did you think of that movie?"

"Great!"

"What do you mean, *great*? I thought the acting was wooden and the story completely unbelievable."

"That's about what I'd expect from you. You wouldn't know a good movie if it walked up and bit you."

"Oh yeah? What makes you think you're such a great . . . ?"

Argument or quarrel? Many people would ask, "What's the difference?" To them, the two terms convey the same meaning, both calling to mind two angry people, shouting, trading insults, and sometimes slugging it out. In writing, however, *argument* stands for something quite different: a paper, grounded on logical, structured evidence, that attempts to convince the reader to accept an opinion, take some action, or do both. Argument is also a process during which you explore an issue fully, considering different perspectives, assumptions, reasons, and evidence to reach your own informed position.

The ability to argue effectively will help you succeed both in class and on the job. A business instructor may ask students to defend a particular management style. A political science instructor may want you to support or oppose limiting the number of terms that members of a legislature can serve. A special education instructor may have students make a written case for increased funding for exceptional students. In the workplace, a computer programmer may argue that the company should change its account-keeping program, an automotive service manager call for new diagnostic equipment, and a union president make a case that a company's employees merit raises.

Arguments don't always involve conflicts. Some simply support a previously established decision or course of action, as when a department manager sends her boss a memo justifying some new procedure that she implemented. Others try to establish some common ground, just as you might do when you and your date weigh the pros and cons of two films and pick one to see.

PERSPECTIVE

The idea of argument poses a dilemma for some students. Used to being tested on factual matters, they often view an argumentative position as either completely justified or completely unjustified. Students need to understand that such is rarely the case, that justification is a matter of degree, with some positions more justified than others. This knowledge can in turn create further confusion, for if there is some justification for both of two opposing positions, isn't any final judgment of their merits arbitrary? At times such confusion can become emotionally distressing to students. Who are they, after all, to reach a conclusion, and won't someone attack their position? For these students, argument is a problem because it presents an unfamiliar situation that forces them to deal with matters that are not cut-and-dried.

257

When preparing to write an argument, you need to be aware that certain kinds of topics just aren't arguable. There's no point, for instance, in trying to tackle questions of personal preference or taste (Is red prettier than blue?). Such contests quickly turn into "it is," "it isn't" exchanges that establish nothing except the silliness of the contenders. Questions of simple fact (Was Eisenhower first elected president in 1952?) don't qualify either. Bickering will never settle these issues; reference books quickly will. We turn to argument when there is room for disagreement.

When you write an argument, you don't simply sit down and dash off your views as though they came prefabricated. Instead, argument represents an opportunity to think things through, to gradually, and often tentatively, come to some conclusions, and then, in stages, begin to draft your position with the support you have discovered. You should try to keep an open mind as you formulate and then express your views. And remember, you rarely start from scratch. Instead, you join a conversation where ideas and evidence have already been exchanged. As a result, you need to be thoughtful and informed.

The most successful arguments rest on a firm foundation of solid, logical support. In addition, many arguments include emotion because it can play an important part in swaying reader opinion. Furthermore, writers often make ethical appeals by projecting favorable images of themselves since readers form conclusions based on their judgments of the writer.

The Rational Appeal

In society, and certainly in professional circles, you are usually expected to reach your conclusions on the basis of good reasons and appropriate evidence. Reasons are the key points or general ideas you'll use to defend your conclusions. If, for instance, you support the needle-exchange program for intravenous drug users, one reason might be the considerable reduction in AIDS-related deaths that could result. If you oppose the program, one reason may be the drug dependency that will continue.

To convince readers, your reasons must be substantiated by evidence. If you favor needle exchange, you could cite figures that project the number of deaths that will be prevented. If you're against the program, you might quote a respected authority who verifies that dependency will become entrenched.

When you appeal to reason in an argument, then, you present your reasons and evidence in such a way that if your readers are also reasonable they will likely agree with you, or at least see your position as plausible. That assumes, of course, that you and your readers start from some common ground about the principles you share and what you count as evidence. Evidence falls into several categories: established truths, opinions of authorities, primary source information, statistical findings, and personal experience. The strongest arguments usually combine several kinds of evidence.

Established Truths

These are facts that no one can seriously dispute. Here are some examples:

Historical fact: The First Amendment to the United States Constitution prohibits Congress from abridging freedom of the press.

Scientific fact: The layer of ozone in the earth's upper atmosphere protects us from the sun's harmful ultraviolet radiation.

Geographical fact: The western part of the United States has tremendous reserves of coal.

Established truths aren't arguable themselves but do provide strong backup for argumentative propositions. For example, citing the abundant coal supply in the western regions could support an argument that the United States should return to coal to supply its energy needs.

Some established truths, the result of careful observations and thinking over many years, basically amount to enlightened common sense. The notion that everyone possesses a unique combination of interests, abilities, and personality characteristics illustrates this kind of truth. Few people would seriously question it.

Opinions of Authorities

An authority is a recognized expert in some field. Authoritative opinions—the only kind to use—play a powerful role in winning readers over to your side. The views of metropolitan police chiefs and criminologists could support your position on ways to control urban crime. Researchers who have investigated the effects of air pollution could help you argue for stricter smog-control laws. Whatever your argument, don't settle for less than heavyweight authorities, and, when possible, indicate their credentials to your reader. This information makes their statements more persuasive. For example, "Ann Marie Forsythe, a certified public accountant and vice-president of North American operations for Touche Ross Accounting, believes that the president's tax cut proposal will actually result in a tax increase for most Americans." You should, of course, also cite the source of your information. Follow your instructor's guidelines.

The following paragraph, from an article arguing that extra-high-voltage electric transmission lines pose a health hazard, illustrates the use of authority:

> Robert Becker, a physician and director of the Orthopedic–Biophysics Laboratory at the Syracuse, New York, Veterans Administration Hospital–Upstate Medical Center, has been researching the effects of low-frequency electric fields (60 Hz) for fifteen years. Testifying at health and safety hearings for proposed lines in New York, he said that exposure to the fields can produce physiological and functional changes in humans—anything from increased irritability and fatigue to raised cholesterol levels, hypertension and ulcers. Studies of rats exposed to low-level electric fields showed tumor growths and abnormalities in development. Dr. Becker believes we are performing unauthorized medical experiments by exposing people to the electromagnetic fields surrounding the transmission lines.
>
> Kelly Davis, "Health and High Voltage: 765 KV Lines"

justified position based on available evidence is the best anyone can reasonably expect.

CLASSROOM ACTIVITY
Have students, working in small groups, review an article to identify claims supported and not supported by evidence. When claims are supported, students could evaluate the adequacy of the evidence.

TEACHING STRATEGY
Some students quickly assume that a statement is an established truth when in fact it is merely opinion or easily contested. You might discuss the criteria that an established truth must meet. One technique is to envision how someone could legitimately object to the claim. If the objection seems reasonable, the student might reconsider the "truth." Or students might develop their own lists of established truths on a given topic and verify them.

CLASSROOM ACTIVITY
You could list so-called established truths on the board and have students discuss which ones qualify. Or students might develop their own list on a given topic, which could be discussed in class.

CLASSROOM ACTIVITY
You might present students with the names, and brief biographies, of authorities who might

Beware of biased opinions. The agribusiness executive who favors farm price supports or the labor leader who opposes any restrictions on picketing may be writing merely to guard old privileges or garner new ones. Unless the opinion can stand especially close scrutiny, don't put it in your paper; it will just weaken your case with perceptive readers.

Because authorities don't always see eye to eye, their views lack the finality of established truths. Furthermore, their opinions will convince only if the audience accepts the authority *as* authoritative. Although advertisers successfully present football stars as authorities on shaving cream and credit cards, most people would not accept their views on the safety of nuclear energy.

Primary Source Information

You'll need to support certain types of argument with primary source information—documents or other materials produced by individuals directly involved with the issue or conclusions you reached by carrying out an investigation yourself. To argue whether the United States should have dropped the atom bomb on Japan to end World War II, for example, you would want to examine the autobiographies of those involved in making the decision and perhaps even the documents that prompted it. To take a position on the violence mentioned in some gangster rap, you would want to analyze the actual lyrics in a number of songs. To make a claim about the press coverage of the first Persian Gulf War, you would want to read the newspaper and magazine accounts of correspondents who were on the scene. To convince readers to adopt your solution for the homeless problem, you might want to visit a homeless shelter or interview (in a safe place) some homeless people. This type of information can help you reach sound conclusions and build strong support for your position. Most college libraries contain a significant amount of primary source materials. Document the sources you use according to your instructor's guidelines.

Statistical Findings

Statistics—data showing how much, how many, or how often—can also buttress your argument. Most statistics come from books, magazines, newspapers, handbooks, encyclopedias, and reports, but you can use data from your own investigations as well. *Statistical Abstract of the United States* is a good source of authoritative statistics on many topics.

Because statistics are often misused, many people distrust them, so any you offer must be reliable. First, make sure your sample isn't too small. Don't use a one-day traffic count to argue for a traffic light at a certain intersection. City Hall might counter by contending that the results are atypical. To make your case, you'd need to count traffic for perhaps two or three weeks. Take care not to push statistical claims too far. You may know that two-thirds of Tarrytown's factories pollute the air excessively, but don't argue that the same figures probably apply to your town. There's simply no carryover. Keep alert for biased statistics; they can cause as serious a credibility gap as biased opinions. Generally, recent data are better than old data, but either must come from a reliable source. Older information from the *New York Times* would probably be more accurate than current data from some publication that trades on sensationalism. Note how the following writer uses statistics in discussing America's aging population and its impact on the federal budget:

> . . . In 1955 defense spending and veterans benefits accounted for almost 70 percent of federal outlays. By 1995 their share was 19 percent. In the same period social security and Medicare (which didn't exist until 1965) went from 6 percent to 34 percent of the budget. Under present trends, their share would rise to 39 percent by 2005, projects the Congressional Budget Office. . . . Between 2010 and 2020, the older-than-65 population will rise by about a third; in the next decade, it will rise almost another third. Today, about one in eight Americans is older than 65; by 2030, the proportion is projected to be one in five. The older-than-85 population will rise even faster.
>
> Robert J. Samuelson, "Getting Serious"

Again, follow your instructor's guidelines when documenting your sources.

Personal Experience

Sometimes personal experience can deliver an argumentative message more forcefully than any other kind of evidence. Suppose that two years ago a speeder ran into your car and almost killed you. Today you're arguing for stiffer laws against speeding. Chances are you'll rely mainly on expert opinions and on statistics showing the number of people killed and injured each year in speeding accidents. However, describing the crash, the slow, pain-filled weeks in the hospital, and the months spent hobbling around on crutches may well provide the persuasive nudge that wins your reader over.

Often the experiences and observations of others, gathered from books, magazines, or interviews, can support your position. If you argue against chemical waste dumps, the personal stories of people who lived near them and suffered the consequences—filthy ooze in the basement, children with birth defects, family members who developed a rare form of cancer—can sway your reader.

Despite its usefulness, personal experience generally reinforces but does not replace other kinds of evidence. Unless it has other support, readers may reject it as atypical or trivial.

Evaluation of Evidence

Once you have gathered the appropriate type(s) of evidence, certain standards govern the evaluation and use of that evidence. That a piece of information is in some way connected to your topic does not make it good evidence or qualify it for inclusion in your paper. Readers won't be convinced that trains are dangerous merely because you were in a train wreck. You should not reach a conclusion based on such flimsy evidence either. In order to reach a reasonable conclusion and defend a position with suitable evidence, you should apply the following principles.

Evaluation Criteria	Explanation
How credible are the sources of the information? How reliable is the evidence?	Not all sources are created equal. U.S. Census data about population change is more credible than a local newspaper's estimate, though both may be more valid than your own estimate.
How much confirming evidence is there?	With evidence, more is better. One scientific study on the efficacy of high-protein diets would be good, but several would be better. One authority who claims that global warming is a reality becomes more credible when confirmed by several other authorities.
How much contradictory evidence is there?	If several scientific studies or authorities point to the efficacy of high-protein diets and several other studies find such diets harmful, clearly you would need to weigh the evidence more carefully.
How well established is the evidence?	Extremely established evidence, such as the evidence for atoms, becomes the basis for textbooks and is assumed in most other research. This evidence is usually unquestionable, although it also can be overturned.
How well does the evidence actually support or fit the claim?	The fact that most Americans are immigrants or descendents of immigrants has no bearing on whether the country is admitting too many or too few immigrants. To make a case for or against some policy on immigration, the evidence would have to focus on its good or bad results.
What does the evidence actually allow you to conclude?	The evidence shouldn't lead you to reach an exaggerated conclusion. Studies showing that TV violence causes children to play more aggressively do not warrant the conclusion that it causes children to kill others.

Sometimes unwarranted conclusions result because a writer fails to take competing claims and evidence into consideration. For example, evidence shows that children in Head Start programs do better than others during the first three years of school. Other evidence, however, shows that in later years these students do not do significantly better. Yet other evidence shows that they are more likely to stay in school and less likely to get into trouble. Clearly, you shouldn't argue that Head Start ensures continuing success at all grade levels. You would need to weigh the credibility, quantity, reliability, and applicability of the available evidence to reach and defend a more limited conclusion.

Reasoning Strategies

An argument, then, consists of a conclusion you want to support, your reasons for that conclusion, and the evidence that supports your reasons. But how are reasons and evidence fitted together? Rational appeals include three reasoning strategies: induction, deduction, and analogy.

Induction

An argument from induction occurs when a general claim is supported by specific evidence, whether direct observations, statistical data, or scientific studies. Most of our conclusions are supported inductively. When we conclude that a movie is worth watching because our friends liked it, when we decide a college program is effective because most students in it get jobs, or even when we support a scientific hypothesis based on formal experimentation, we are basing a conclusion on bits of evidence. We need to be thoughtful in reaching such conclusions. Are our friends like us and trustworthy? Are the jobs students get good jobs? All the principles for evaluating evidence apply.

Induction makes our conclusions probable but rarely proves them. To prove something by induction, we must check every bit of evidence and often that's just not practical or possible. The greater the number of observations and the larger the populations surveyed, the more strongly the conclusion is supported. Obviously then, just a few observations makes the evidence very weak. If you ask ten of fifteen thousand students whether they like the meal plan, you cannot conclude much if eight of the students liked the plan. These students may just be atypical.

All inductive evidence only makes supported conclusions likely. It is important to measure the strength of the supporting evidence.

You have several options for organizing an inductive argument. You might begin by posing some direct or indirect question in order to snare your reader's interest, or you might simply state the position you will argue. The body of the paper provides the supporting evidence. In the conclusion you could reaffirm your position or suggest the consequences of that position. You can also raise a general question, evaluate the evidence, and then come to a conclusion.

The following short example illustrates inductive argument:

> Systematic phonics, the method of reading instruction that shows children how to sound out letters, is an effective method of teaching word reading in the first three grades. A large study, sponsored by the federal government in the 1970s, compared how effective different instructional methods were in helping disadvantaged children. The direct instruction program resulted in children, otherwise expected to fall below the norm, to meet or be close to the national standard for reading (Stebbins, et al., 1977). Another study compared the effect of the whole-language instruction, embedded phonics, and direct code instruction on 285 students in a

district with a high risk of reading failure. The university researchers found that the children taught by direct instruction improved in word reading much faster than students in the other groups. In fact, most taught with the whole-language approach had no measurable gains in word reading, even if they did have a more positive attitude towards reading (Stahl et al., 1994). While these studies may not fully demonstrate that systematic phonics is the best method for teaching reading, the fact that in experiments students taught with direct code instruction demonstrated greater gains in word reading than those taught by other methods at least shows that systematic phonics can help students make gains in word reading.

Marjorie Hawkins

When writing an induction argument, in addition to presenting the available evidence, there are two other important things you should do. It is helpful to demonstrate the credibility of your evidence. Here the student writer identified that the first study was large and sponsored by the federal government and gave the exact number of subjects in the second study, as well as the information that the researchers were from a university.

Also, if possible, try to show how the evidence fits the conclusion you want to reach. The author, above, made certain her claims were not overstated by being clear about what she was not stating and then directly tied the research studies to her conclusion.

Deduction

Deduction is a process of argumentation that demonstrates how a specific conclusion follows logically from some initial premises about which people might agree. For example, to convince a friend to study harder, you begin with the assumption that a profitable career requires a good education; proceed to argue that for a good education students must study diligently; and conclude that, as a result, your friend should spend more time with the books. Politicians who assert that we all want to act in ways beneficial to future generations, then point out how the policies they favor will ensure that outcome, argue deductively.

As with induction, you have several options when organizing a deductive argument. You might begin with the position you intend to prove, with a question that will be answered by the argument, or with a synopsis of the argument. The body of the paper works out the implications of your assumption. In the conclusion you could directly state (or restate, in different words) your position, suggest the consequences of adopting or not adopting that position, or pose a question that is easily answered after reading the argument. Here is a short example of deductive argument:

> The recent spot-checks of our rooms by the dorm's head advisor are an unacceptable invasion of privacy. This practice should stop immediately.

The United States Constitution prohibits searches by police officers unless these officers have adequate reason. That is why the police need a search warrant before they can search any home. If they fail to obtain one, a case that ends up in court will likely be thrown out. Our right to privacy, then, can't be violated without due cause.

If the police can't search our homes without good reason, why should our head advisor spot-check our rooms for signs of wrongdoing?

Sammy Borchardt

engineers opposed the launch, arguing deductively about how the O-ring materials should behave in cold weather. Unfortunately, the engineers were correct.

When arguing from deduction, you need to make clear how your conclusions do actually follow from the agreed-upon premises. Those premises may also be questionable and need support, whether by induction or by demonstrating their deductive relationship to other strongly held ideas.

Reductio ad Absurdum   A common and powerful form of deduction called *reductio ad absurdum* ("to reduce to absurdity") is used to question a position by showing that its consequences are problematic if carried to their logical end. To counter the position that the government should impose no restrictions on the public's right to bear arms, you might point out that, carried to its logical extreme, such a policy would allow individuals to own bazookas, cannons, and nuclear bombs. This absurd result makes it clear that certain restrictions should apply to our right to bear arms. The question then becomes where we should draw the ownership line.

Syllogism   Sometimes a deductive argument is built around a categorical syllogism, a set of three statements that follow a fixed pattern to ensure sound reasoning. The first statement, called the *major premise,* names a category of things and says that all or none of them shares a certain characteristic. The *minor premise* notes that a thing or group of things belongs to that category. The *conclusion* states that the thing or group shares the characteristics of the category. Here are two examples:

Major premise:	All persons are mortal.
Minor premise:	Sue Davis is a person.
Conclusion:	Therefore, Sue Davis is mortal.
Major premise:	No dogs have feathers.
Minor premise:	Spot is a dog.
Conclusion:	Therefore, Spot does not have feathers.

Note that in each case both major and minor premises are true and the conclusion follows logically.

Syllogisms frequently appear in stripped-down form, with one of the premises or the conclusion omitted. The following example omits the major premise: "Because Wilma is a civil engineer, she has a strong background in mathematics." Obviously the missing major premise is as follows: "All civil engineers have strong backgrounds in mathematics."

TEACHING STRATEGIES
1. Some students tend to use shaky assumptions in their major premises and then move rather haphazardly to a conclusion. Caution against these flaws.
2. You could discuss the extent to which syllogisms are used in arguments, and why. Bring in and discuss syllogisms with a missing premise, a very common occurrence.
3. Have students record where they or others have argued deductively. Students could write down the major and minor premises, the conclusions, and the connections between them. Have them test the truth and validity of the syllogism.

CLASSROOM ACTIVITY
You might present the class with views that some students hold ("Since I'm paying for this class, I'm entitled to determine when I'll attend.") and then discuss what absurd consequences could follow.

Syllogistic Argument at Work   A syllogism can occur anywhere in an essay: in the introduction to set the stage for the evidence, at various places in the body, even in the conclusion in order to pull the argument together. Here is an example that uses a syllogism in the introduction:

> In 1966, when the Astrodome was completed in Houston, Texas, the managers concluded that it would be impossible to grow grass indoors. To solve their problem, they decided to install a ruglike synthetic playing surface that was fittingly called Astroturf. In the ensuing years, many other sports facilities have installed synthetic turf. Unfortunately, this development has been accompanied by a sharp rise in the number and severity of injuries suffered by athletes—a rise clearly linked to the surface they play upon. *Obviously, anything that poses a threat to player safety is undesirable. Because synthetic turf does this, it is undesirable and should be replaced by grass.*
>
> Denny Witham

To support his position, the writer then notes that turf, unlike grass, often becomes excessively hot, tiring players and increasing their chances of injury; that seams can open up between sections of turf and lead to tripping and falling; that players can run faster on artificial turf and thus collide more violently; and that the extreme hardness of the turf leads to torn ligaments and tissues when players slam their toes into it.

Avoiding Misuse of Syllogisms   Two cautions are in order. *First,* make sure any syllogism you use follows the proper logical order. The writer of the following passage has ignored this caution:

> And that's not all. Newton has stated openly that he favors federally funded abortions for the poor. Just the other day, the American Socialist party took this same stand. In my book, Newton's position puts him squarely in the Socialist camp. I strongly urge anyone supporting this man's candidacy to reconsider. . . .

Restated in syllogistic form, the writer's argument goes like this:

Socialists favor federally funded abortions for the poor.

Newton favors federally funded abortions for the poor.

Therefore, Newton is a Socialist.

The last two statements reverse the proper logical relationship, and as a result the syllogism proves nothing about Newton's politics: he may or may not be "in the Socialist camp."

Second, make sure the major premise of your syllogism is in fact true. Note this example:

All conservatives are opposed to environmental protection.

Mary is a conservative.

Therefore, Mary is opposed to environmental protection.

But is every conservative an environmental Jack the Ripper? In some communities, political conservatives have led fights against air and water pollution, and most conservatives agree that at least some controls are worthwhile. Mary's sympathies, then, may well lie with those who want to heal, rather than hurt, the environment.

Which of these syllogisms is satisfactory, which have false major premises, and which is faulty because the last two statements reverse the proper order?

1. All singers are happy people.
   Mary Harper is a singer.
   Therefore, Mary Harper is a happy person.

2. All cowards fear danger.
   "Chicken" Cacciatore is a coward.
   Therefore, "Chicken" Cacciatore fears danger.

3. All cats like meat.
   Towser likes meat.
   Therefore, Towser is a cat.

4. No salesperson would ever misrepresent a product to a customer.
   Sabrina is a salesperson.
   Therefore, Sabrina would never misrepresent a product to a customer.

Analogy in Argument

An analogy compares two unlike situations or things. Arguers often use analogies to contend that because two items share one or more likenesses, they are also alike in other ways. Familiar analogies assume that humans respond to chemicals as rats do and that success in school predicts success on the job. You have used analogy if you ever pressed your parents for more adult privileges, such as a later curfew, by arguing that you were like an adult in many ways.

Because its conclusions about one thing rest upon observations about some different thing, analogy is the weakest form of rational appeal. Analogies never prove anything. But they often help explain and show probability and therefore are quite persuasive.

For an analogy to be useful, it must feature significant similarities that bear directly on the issue. In addition, it must account for any significant differences between the two items. It is often helpful to test an analogy by listing the similarities and differences. Here's an effective analogy, used to back an argument that a liberal education is the best kind to help us cope successfully with life:

> Suppose it were perfectly certain that the life and fortune of every one of us would, one day or other, depend upon his winning or losing a game of chess. Don't you think that we should all consider it to be a primary duty to learn at least the names and the moves of the pieces; to have a notion of a gambit, and a keen eye for all the

EXERCISE ANSWERS

1. Syllogism is faulty because its initial statement is untrue: Singers are not necessarily happy.

2. Syllogism is satisfactory.

3. Syllogism is faulty because the final two statements reverse the proper order.

4. Syllogism is faulty because its initial statement is untrue: Salespeople sometimes misrepresent the products they sell.

PERSPECTIVE
While an argument from analogy is never totally conclusive, it is extraordinarily common and, in some ways, unavoidable. We can't always do medical research on humans; and even when we do, it is often in controlled situations dissimilar to daily life. If we learn lessons from history, it can only be on the basis of analogy since historical situations are rarely identical. Economists, political scientists, and sociologists all regularly

attempt to reach conclusions and make predictions on the basis of analogy. Indeed, any attempt to work from a scientific model implicitly relies on an analogy since few scientists confuse the model with the real world. More practically, when business executives review the potential for a marketing strategy based on the performance of other plans, they are probably drawing on an implicit analogy. For these reasons, students should understand, work with, and evaluate arguments from analogy.

TEACHING STRATEGY

Ask students to review their textbooks and several newspaper editorials to observe where and how appropriately arguments from analogy were used.

CLASSROOM ACTIVITY

Choose a current controversy—for example,

the legalization of drugs, the death penalty, surrogate mothers—and have the class determine what analogies, if any, would be helpful in thinking through the issue. Are the current laws against marijuana similar to Prohibition? Is the execution of criminals murder? Is receiving money to have a baby for others the same as prostitution? Have students carefully test the analogies by listing the points of similarity and dissimilarity.

means of giving and getting out of check? Do you not think that we should look with a disapprobation amounting to scorn, upon the father who allowed his son, or the state which allowed its members, to grow up without knowing a pawn from a knight?

Yet it is a very plain and elementary truth, that the life, the fortune, and the happiness of every one of us, and, more or less, of those who are connected with us, do depend upon our knowing something of the rules of a game infinitely more difficult and complicated than chess. It is a game which has been played for untold ages, every man and woman of us being one of the two players in a game of his or her own. The chessboard is the world, the pieces are the phenomena of the universe, the rules of the game are what we call the laws of Nature. The player on the other side is hidden from us. We know that his play is always fair, just, and patient. But also we know, to our cost, that he never overlooks a mistake, or makes the smallest allowance for ignorance. To the man who plays well, the highest stakes are paid, with that sort of overflowing generosity with which the strong shows delight in strength. And one who plays ill is checkmated—without haste, but without remorse. . . .

Well, what I mean by Education is learning the rules of this mighty game. In other words, education is the instruction of the intellect in the law of Nature, under which name I include not merely things and their forces, but men and their ways; and the fashioning of the affections and of the will into an earnest and loving desire to move in harmony with those laws. For me, education means neither more nor less than this. Anything which professes to call itself education must be tried by this standard, and if it fails to stand the test, I will not call it education, whatever may be the force of authority, or of numbers, upon the other side.

Thomas Henry Huxley, "A Liberal Education and Where to Find It"

To develop an argument by analogy, brainstorm the two items being compared for significant similarities and prepare a chart that matches them up. The greater the number and closeness of these similarities, the better the argument by analogy.

The Emotional Appeal

Although effective argument relies mainly on reason, an emotional appeal can lend powerful reinforcement. Indeed, emotion can win the hearts and the help of people who would otherwise passively accept a logical argument but take no action. Each Christmas, newspapers raise money for local charities by running stark case histories of destitute families. Organizations raise funds to fight famine by displaying brochures that feature skeletal, swollen-bellied children. Still other groups use emotion-charged stories and pictures to solicit support for environmental protection, to combat various diseases, and so on. Advertisers use emotion to play upon our hopes, fears, and vanities in order to sell mouthwash, cars, clothes, and other products. Politicians paint themselves as God-fearing, honest toilers for the public good while lambasting their opponents as the uncaring tools of special interests. In evaluating or writing an argument, ask yourself whether the facts warrant the emotion. Is the condition of the destitute family truly cause for pity? Is any politician unwaveringly good, any other irredeemably bad?

The following passage, from a student argument favoring assisted suicide for the terminally ill, represents an appropriate use of emotion:

> When I visited Grandpa for the last time, he seemed imprinted on the hospital bed, a motionless, skeleton-like figure tethered by an array of tubes to the droning, beeping machine at his bedside. The eyes that had once sparkled with delight as he bounced grandchildren on his knee now stared blankly at the ceiling, seemingly ready to burst from their sockets. His mouth, frozen in an open grimace, emitted raspy, irregular noises as he fought to breathe. Spittle leaked from one corner of his mouth and dribbled onto the sheet. A ripe stench from the diaper around his middle hung about the bedside, masking the medicinal sickroom smells. As I stood by the bedside, my mind flashed back to the irrepressible man I once knew, and tears flooded my eyes. Bending forward, I planted a soft kiss on his forehead, whispered "I love you, Gramps," and walked slowly away.

> Dylan Brandt Chafin

To develop an effective emotional appeal, identify the stories, scenes, or events of the topic that arouse the strongest emotional response within you. Do some thinking about the types of words that will best convey the emotion you feel. Then write the section so that it builds to the kind of emotional conclusion that will help your argument.

The Ethical Appeal

Before logic can do its work, the audience must be willing to consider the argument. If a writer's tone offends the audience, perhaps by being arrogant or mean-spirited, the reasoning will fail to penetrate. But if the writer comes across as pleasant, fair-minded, and decent, gaining reader support is much easier. The image that the writer projects is called the *ethical appeal.*

If you write with a genuine concern for your topic, a commitment to the truth, and a sincere respect for others, you will probably come across reasonably well. When you finish writing, check to see that an occasional snide comment or bitter remark didn't slip unnoticed onto the page. In the following introductory paragraph, from an essay arguing that many universities violate the Constitution by imposing campus rules that restrict freedom of speech, the student establishes an appealing ethical image:

> Most of us would agree that educated people should not indulge in name-calling and stereotyping in their speaking and writing. To do so is an essential mark of irrational prejudice. Nevertheless, such speaking and writing are protected by the United States Constitution, which

prohibits anyone from abridging freedom of expression. Today, many colleges and universities, in a well-meaning attempt to shield particular groups from unwelcome or insensitive words, are subverting this prohibition. Former Supreme Court Justice William Brennan, noted for his liberal views, has stated, "If there is a bedrock principle underlying the First Amendment, it is that the government may not prohibit the expression of an idea simply because society finds the idea offensive or disagreeable."

Linda Kimrey

The writer opposes on constitutional grounds any attempts to ban the expression of two forms of "irrational prejudice." Nevertheless, she characterizes these attempts as "well-meaning" and acknowledges that they are prompted by worthy motives. As a result, she emerges as fair-minded, decent, sensitive, and concerned, an image she maintains throughout the essay.

Ferreting Out Fallacies

Fallacies are lapses in logic that reflect upon your ability to think clearly, and therefore they weaken your argument. The fallacies described below are among the most common. Correct any you find in your own arguments, and call attention to those used by the opposition.

Hasty Generalization

Hasty generalization results when someone bases a conclusion on too little evidence. The student who tries to see an instructor during one of her office hours, finds her out, and goes away muttering, "She's never there when she should be" is guilty of hasty generalization. Perhaps the instructor was delayed by another student, attended a special department meeting, or went home ill. Even if she merely went shopping, that's not a good reason for saying she always shirks her responsibility. Several more unsuccessful office visits would be needed to make such a charge stick.

Non Sequitur

From the Latin "It does not follow," the *non sequitur* fallacy draws unwarranted conclusions from seemingly ample evidence. Consider this example: "Bill's been out almost every night for the last two weeks. Who is she?" These evening excursions, however numerous, point to no particular conclusion. Bill may be studying in the library, participating in campus organizations, taking night classes, or walking. Of course, he *could* be charmed by a new date, but that conclusion requires other evidence.

Stereotyping

A person who commits this fallacy attaches one or more supposed characteristics to a group or one of its members. Typical stereotypes include "Latins make better lovers," "Blondes have more fun," and "Teenagers are lousy drivers." Stereotyping racial, religious, ethnic, or nationality groups can destroy an argument. The images are often malicious and always offensive to fair-minded readers.

CLASSROOM ACTIVITY
Bring in advertisements or political speeches and have students identify the fallacies and their intended effect on the reader. This exercise makes an excellent short writing assignment.

Card Stacking

In card stacking, the writer presents only part of the available evidence on a topic, deliberately omitting essential information that would alter the picture considerably. For instance: "College students have a very easy life; they attend classes for only twelve to sixteen hours a week." This statement ignores the many hours that students must spend studying, doing homework and/or research, writing papers, and the like.

Either/Or Fallacy

The either/or fallacy asserts that only two choices exist when, in fact, several options are possible. A salesperson who wants you to buy snow tires may claim, "Either buy these tires or plan on getting stuck a lot this winter." But are you really that boxed in? You might drive only on main roads that are plowed immediately after every snow-storm. You could use public transportation when it snows. You could buy radial tires for year-round use. If very little snow falls, you might not need special tires at all.

Not all either/or statements are fallacies. The instructor who checks a student's record and then issues a warning, "Make at least a *C* on your final or you'll fail the course," is not guilty of a reasoning error. No other alternatives exist. Most situations, however, offer more than two choices.

Begging the Question

A person who begs the question asserts the truth of some unproved statement. Here is an example: "Vitamin A is harmful to your health, and all bottles should carry a warning label. If enough of us write the Food and Drug Administration, we can get the labeling we need." But how do we know vitamin A does harm users? No evidence is offered. People lacking principles often use this fallacy to hit opponents below the belt: "We shouldn't allow a right-wing sympathizer like Mary Dailey to represent us in Congress." Despite a lack of suitable evidence, voters often accept such faulty logic and vote for the other candidate.

Circular Argument

Circular argument, a first cousin to begging the question, supports a position merely by restating it. "Pauline is a good manager because she runs the company effectively" says, in effect, that "something is because something is." Repetition replaces evidence.

1. A hasty generalization. Nancy has reached her conclusion after slicing just one orange. Such a conclusion would be justified only after she had tried a number of oranges and found all or most of them rotten.

2. The either/or fallacy. Failure of the federal government to help poverty-stricken people would not necessarily cause starvation for all of them. Some might receive help from relatives or private charities, or state and local governments might provide financial assistance.

3. The *post hoc, ergo propter hoc* fallacy. The wife might have been unfaithful not because she had attended the X-rated movie but because she was angry with her husband or infatuated with the person with whom she was unfaithful.

4. Stereotyping and hasty generalization. The speaker has condemned all motor cycle riders because of the behavior of just two of them.

5. A *non sequitur*. Bill may love to eat, but we can't conclude that he will have a serious weight problem someday. He may be a person who never puts on weight regardless of his food intake, or he may alter his eating habits.

6. Begging the question. The statement assumes, without any supporting evidence, that no-fault divorce has caused the divorce rate to jump sharply.

7. A circular argument. The statement that the picture is "much more attractive than the others"

Arguing off the Point

The writer who argues off the point, which is sometimes called "ignoring the question" or "a red herring," sidetracks an issue by introducing irrelevant information. To illustrate: "The Ford Thunderbolt is a much better value than the Honda Harmony. Anyway, far too many foreign cars are coming into the country. As a result, thousands of auto workers have lost their jobs and had to take lower-paying jobs. Many Americans strongly oppose this state of affairs." The writer sets out to convince us that the American car is superior in value but then abruptly shifts to the plight of downsized auto workers—a trend that has no bearing on the argument.

The Argument ad Hominem

The Latin term "to the man" designates an argument that attacks an individual rather than that individual's opinions or qualifications. Note this example: "Sam Bernhard doesn't deserve promotion to personnel manager. His divorce was a disgrace, and he's always writing letters to the editor. The company should find someone more suitable." This attack completely skirts the real issue—whether Sam's job performance entitles him to the promotion. Unless his personal conduct has caused his work to suffer, it should not enter into the decision.

Appeal to the Crowd

An appeal of this sort arouses an emotional response by playing on the irrational fears and prejudices of the audience. Terms like *communists*, *fascists*, *bleeding hearts*, *right-winger*, *welfare chiselers*, and *law and order* are tossed about freely to sway the audience for or against something. Consider:

The streets of our country are in turmoil. The universities are filled with students rebelling and rioting. Communists are seeking to destroy our country. Russia is threatening us with her might, and the public is in danger. Yes, danger from within and without. We need law and order. Yes, without law and order our nation cannot survive. Elect us, and we shall by law and order be respected among the nations of the world. Without law and order our republic shall fall.

Tapping the emotions of the crowd can sway large groups and win acceptance for positions that rational thinking would reject. Think what Adolf Hitler, the author of the foregoing excerpt, brought about in Germany.

Guilt by Association

This fallacy points out some similarity or connection between one person or group and another. It tags the first with the sins, real or imagined, of the second. The following excerpt from a letter protesting a speaker at a lecture series illustrates this technique:

The next slated speaker, Dr. Sylvester Crampton, was for years a member of the Economic Information Committee. This foundation has very strong ties with other ultraright-wing groups, some of which have been labeled fascistic. When he speaks next Thursday, whose brand of Americanism will he be selling?

Post Hoc, ergo Propter Hoc

The Latin meaning, "after this, therefore because of this," refers to the fallacy of assuming that because one event follows another, the first caused the second. Such shoddy thinking underlies many popular superstitions ("If a black cat crosses your path, you'll have bad luck") and many connections that cannot be substantiated ("I always catch cold during spring break"). Sometimes one event does cause another: A sudden thunderclap might startle a person into dropping a dish. At other times, coincidence is the only connection. Careful thinking will usually lay far-fetched causal notions to rest.

Faulty Analogy

This is the error of assuming that two circumstances or things are similar in all important respects, when in fact they are not. Here's an example: Harvey Thompson, high school football coach, tells his players, "Vince Lombardi won two Super Bowls by insisting on perfect execution of plays and enforcing strict disciplinary measures. We're going to win the conference championship by following the same methods." Thompson assumes that because he and Lombardi are coaches, he can duplicate Lombardi's achievements by using Lombardi's methods. Several important differences, however, mark the two situations:

1. Lombardi had very talented players, obtained through the player draft or trades; Thompson can choose only from the students in his high school.
2. Lombardi's players were paid professionals who very likely were motivated, at least in part, by the financial rewards that came from winning the Super Bowl; Thompson's players are amateurs.
3. "Perfect execution of plays" is probably easier to attain on the professional level than in high school because of the players' experience.
4. Despite Lombardi's rigid disciplinary measures, very few of his players quit, perhaps because they were under contract. Could Thompson expect his players, essentially volunteers, to accept the kind of verbal and physical rigors Lombardi was famous for?

essentially repeats the statement "This is the best-looking picture in the exhibit."

8. Argument *ad hominem.* Instead of attacking McAndrews's position on the bill, this critic attacks McAndrews's personality, which would seem irrelevant. Unless the critic can show that McAndrews's personality has led him to sponsor a faulty proposal (a task that would appear impossible), personality should not be mentioned.

9. Appeal to the crowd. This statement attempts to sway its readers by playing upon their dislike of "wooly-brained do-gooders" and "big-spending, pie-in-the-sky welfare programs," as well as upon their favorable attitudes toward our free enterprise system.

10. Arguing off the point and also begging the question. The writer sets out to argue against the ban on public smoking and then abruptly shifts to his own health—an entirely different matter. Furthermore, he asserts that his health won't suffer but cites no evidence.

11. Card stacking. The writer ignores such past hardships as higher disease and death rates, more difficult working conditions, poorly heated and lighted houses without the appliances now taken for granted, and the great social isolation of most people.

EXERCISE

Identify and explain the fallacies in the following examples. Remember that understanding the faulty reasoning is more important than merely naming the fallacy.

1. After slicing a Golden Glow orange, Nancy discovers that it is rotten. "I'll never buy another Golden Glow product," she declares emphatically.
2. A campaigning politician states that unless the federal government appropriates funds to help people living in poverty, they will all starve.

3. A husband and wife see an X-rated movie called *Swinging Wives*. A week later the husband discovers that his wife, while supposedly attending an evening class, has been unfaithful to him. He blames the movie for her infidelity.

4. "Look at those two motorcycle riders trying to pick a fight. All those cycle bums are troublemakers."

5. "Bill really loves to eat. Some day he'll have a serious weight problem."

6. "Because no-fault divorce is responsible for today's skyrocketing divorce rate, it should be abolished."

7. "This is the best-looking picture in the exhibit; it's so much more attractive than the others."

8. "I do not support this school millage proposal. It's sponsored by James McAndrews, who's about the most ill-tempered, quarrelsome person I've ever met. I'd never favor anything he supports."

9. "My position on social and economic issues is easy to state. I am against wooly-brained do-gooders and big-spending, pie-in-the-sky social programs that have brought us to the brink of social disaster. I stand foursquare behind our free-enterprise system, which has given us a standard of living the whole world envies; and if elected, I will defend it with everything at my command."

10. "I am against the proposed ban on smoking in public places. As long as I don't inhale and I limit my habit to ten cigarettes a day, my health won't suffer."

11. "Life today has become far too frenzied and stressful. It was much better a century ago."

ETHICAL ISSUES
Is it ethical to fabricate a character or ethical credentials that are not yours? What if such fabrication is for the public good?

TEACHING STRATEGY
Are there circumstances when it is ethical to deliberately (1) engage in card stacking, i.e., emphasize all the positive edvidence and completely ignore any other? (2) exaggerate or fabricate evidence to support a position? (3) use a fallacy to trick unwary readers? (4) misrepresent an opponent's position in order to refute it more easily?

Ethical Issues

When writing an argument we attempt to alter attitudes or spark some action. These objectives create an ethical responsibility for both the quality and the possible consequences of our arguments. Suppose a doctor writing a nationally syndicated advice column recommends an over-the-counter herbal product but fails to disclose that it may cause a serious reaction in users who also take a certain prescription drug. Clearly this writer has acted irresponsibly and risks legal action if some readers suffer harm. Asking and answering the following questions will help you avoid any breach of ethics.

- Have I carefully considered the issue I'm arguing and the stance I'm taking? Since you're trying to convince readers to adopt your views, you'll need either to make sure they are credible or make very clear that your position is tentative or dependent on certain conditions.

- Am I fair to other positions on the issue? Careless or deliberate distortion of opposing views is ethically dishonest and could raise questions about your credibility.

- Are my reasons and evidence legitimate? Presenting flawed reasons as if they were credible or falsifying evidence are attempts to deceive the reader.

- Do I use fallacies or other types of faulty thinking to manipulate the reader unfairly?

- What consequences could follow if readers adopt my position? Say a writer strongly opposes genetically modified foods and advocates disrupting installations that help develop them. If some who agree act on the recommendation, innocent people could be injured.

Writing an Argument

Planning and Drafting the Argument

Some instructors assign argumentative topics, and some leave the choice of topic to you. If you will be choosing, many options are available. Interesting issues— some local, some of broader importance—crowd our newspapers, magazines, and TV airways, vying for attention. Because several of them have probably piqued your interest, there's a good chance you won't have to rely on the strategies on pages 31–39 for help in choosing your topic.

Focusing Your Question

As you explore your topic you should be prepared to focus your question. You may begin to examine whether you should support or oppose gun control, but you will soon begin to discover there are hundreds of related, narrower questions. Does the right to carry concealed weapons reduce crime? How should the Second Amendment be interpreted? Should guns be registered? Does the Brady Bill work? Do background checks deter criminals from purchasing guns? Should there be a ban on automatic and semiautomatic weapons? You may discover that one of your related questions is more than enough of a subject.

> Some students approach an argument with such strong attitudes that they ignore evidence that contradicts their thinking. Don't make this mistake. Instead, maintain an open mind as you research your issue, and then, after careful thought, choose the position you'll take. Often, several possible positions exist. On the question of whether individuals should have the right to carry handguns, the positions might include (1) banning the right to carry handguns by anyone except law officers and military personnel, (2) allowing anyone who legitimately owns a handgun to carry that weapon without a permit, (3) allowing citizens to carry concealed weapons but only with a permit granted after training and a background check. Even if you don't shift your position, knowing the opposition's strengths allows you to counter or neutralize it, and thus enhance your argument. Suppose you favor the first position. You need to know that several state constitutions grant citizens the right to carry handguns without those states collapsing into Wild West shoot-outs. Unless you acknowledge and somehow counter this fact, your case will suffer and perhaps even founder.

Exploring Your Topic

You never really start an argument with a blank page. There is almost always an ongoing conversation about the issue. Before you enter a conversation, it helps to be informed. You can do research by reading. If your paper is based on sources, you may want to review Chapters 20 and 21 for ideas and information about proper documentation. You may want to talk to others to get their views on the matter. Or you might make your own formal or informal observations; if so, you may be helped by Chapter 22 about additional research strategies.

different positions and consider potential objections to each. A few might need special attention as they confront a particularly difficult issue.

Some find it useful to create a table like the following to sort out the different positions.

Ban Concealed Handguns	Right to Carry Handguns by all Owners	Allow Right to Carry Handguns but Registered and for Justified Purposes
■ People have the right to be protected from potential harm from others.	■ Right to self-protection. ■ Broad interpretation of Second Amendment.	■ Commonly register cars and other significant property that people then use according to the law.
■ Handguns result in accidental shootings. ■ Could cause increase in emotional killings. ■ Could create increased risk to public safety.	■ Persons could protect self and others. ■ Could reduce crime. ■ People have a constitutional right.	■ A combination of the reasons from the first two. ■ Gun owners need to be held responsible. ■ Guns should not be carried by unstable or dangerous people. ■ The evidence on the first two.
■ Statistics and examples of accidental shootings. ■ Statistics on states with right-to-carry laws. ■ Examples of emotional uses of hand guns.	■ Statistics on overall crime rates. ■ Examples of when guns prevented crimes. ■ Statistics comparing right-to-carry states with other states. ■ Authoritative material on the Second Amendment.	■ Examples and statistics on handguns used in crimes. ■ Examples and statistics on how such restrictions would have had a positive consequence.
■ Is the position unconstitutional? ■ Don't criminals carry guns anyway? ■ How often are legitimately owned and carried guns misused?	■ Aren't there other interpretations of the Second Amendment? ■ Why do police groups often oppose this position?	■ Who should really get to say who should have handguns? ■ Can't a registration process be misused? ■ Can't criminals or others find illegal ways to get guns and carry them?

Obviously, this table is far from complete, and the writer would need to supply the actual evidence and flesh out the reasons. Still, such a table can be a useful device in sorting out and organizing an argument.

As you investigate the various positions, ask and answer the following questions about each:

What are the reasons for the various positions?

What values are at stake, and what conclusions do they imply?

What shared ideas do we accept, and what can be deduced from those ideas?

What kinds of evidence support the position?

If the evidence includes statistics and authoritative opinions, are they reliable or flawed for some reason?

What are the objections to each position, and how can they be countered?

If the issue involves taking some action, what might be its consequences?

Another effective technique for developing an argument is to write a dialogue between two or more people that explores the various sides of an issue without trying to arrive at a conclusion. The beginning of such a dialogue on the right to carry handguns might look like the following:

Joe: If people have a right to own a gun for self-protection, they should have a right to carry that gun. How can they use the gun for self-protection if it isn't with them? Besides allowing them to carry a handgun could act to make criminals think twice. It could surely deter crime.

Doug: It could also lead to public shoot-outs where innocent people could be killed. The United States has the highest murder rate in the industrialized world and the largest number of people owning guns. This is no coincidence. A handgun makes it easy to kill people. Letting people carry a concealed weapon would only make it easier for emotional people to kill each other. Imagine a bar fight with guns.

Leslie: People who legitimately carry concealed weapons don't go around having public shoot-outs. Just owning and carrying a gun doesn't make someone kill. Most legitimate handgun owners who carry a concealed weapon will never use their guns on another human being. Many criminals do, however, kill with illegal weapons, including already banned semiautomatic weapons.

Kyra: Do states where people have a right-to-carry law actually have lower crime rates? I don't think so.

Joe: I didn't say it would always reduce the crime rate. For me the most important issue is that the right-to-carry is the obvious consequence of the Second Amendment.

Writing such a dialogue can help start your mental juices flowing, help you see the issue from many sides, and help you develop effective material for your paper.

Arguments for Different Purposes

As you contemplate your position and evidence, consider the purpose of your argument and how that might affect the strategies you choose to employ. Arguments are written for several purposes, each requiring a different approach. Some arguments *try to establish that something is a fact*—nursing is hard work, dormitories are poor study places, bologna is an unhealthy food. This type of paper usually relies on assorted evidence, perhaps some combination of statistics, authoritative opinion, and personal experience. To prove that nursing is quite demanding, you might narrate and describe some of the strenuous activities in a typical nursing day, cite hospital nursing supervisors who verify the rigors of the job, and perhaps give statistics on nurses who quit the profession because of stress.

Other arguments *defend or oppose some policy*—for example, whether first-year students should be allowed cars on campus or a company should begin drug-testing its employees—or *support or oppose some action or project,* such as the construction of a study lounge for students or the addition of computer equipment with Internet links to more classrooms. In this type of paper, you usually discuss the need for the policy or action, how it can best be met, the cost or feasibility of your recommendation, and the benefits that will result. For instance, if you believe your college needs more computer-equipped classrooms, you might indicate how computers are currently used in some classrooms (to show PowerPoint presentations, offer clips from DVDs, demonstrate how to use computer applications, link to the Web to provide important illustrations), compare the number of classrooms equipped with the number not equipped, indicate the costs of equipping classrooms with computers and projectors, calculate the number of classes that would be able to use the new equipment, and demonstrate the ways teachers and students would benefit.

Still other arguments *assert the greater value of someone or something,* as when a supervisor ranks one candidate for promotion ahead of another. To write this type of paper, generally you would indicate what you're trying to prove; identify the points on which the items will be evaluated; and then, using reasons along with details, examples, or statistics, demonstrate that one of the items has greater worth than the other. Often such an argument will be deductive as you show how your conclusions follow from agreed-upon values.

Directing Arguments to Readers

With an argument, as with any essay, purpose and audience are closely linked. For example, imagine that your audience is a group of readers who are neutral or opposed to your position; there's no point in preaching to the converted. Take a little time to analyze these readers so that you can tailor your arguments appropriately. Pose these questions as you proceed:

What are the readers' interests, expectations, and needs concerning this issue?

What evidence is most likely to convince them?

What objections and consequences would probably weigh most heavily with them?

How can I answer the objections?

To convince an audience of farmers that the federal school lunch program needs expanding, you might stress the added income they would gain. For nutritionists, you might note the health benefits that would result, and for school officials, the improved class performance of the students. Even though you are unlikely to convince everyone, it is best to adopt the attitude that most readers are willing to be convinced if your approach is appealing and your evidence is sound.

Rogerian Arguments

If you're arguing an emotionally charged issue such as gun control or federally funded abortions for the poor, you may want to use *Rogerian argument*. Named for psychologist Carl Rogers, this type of argument attempts to reduce the antagonism that people with opposing views might feel toward your position. To succeed, you must show that you understand and respect the opposing position as well as acknowledge its good points. You try to establish some common point of agreement, then show how the conclusion you want really follows from the reader's own values and assumptions without compromising your own. For example, if you want stricter gun-control laws, you might begin by acknowledging that the Constitution grants citizens the right to bear arms and that you believe anyone with legitimate uses for guns—hunters, target shooters, and the like—should have access to them. Moving on, you might point out that gun owners and those who agree with the Second Amendment support the proper, safe use of firearms and are concerned about firearm abuse. You might then possibly agree with the premise that people, rather than guns themselves, kill people, and for that reason, no one wants criminals to have guns. Finally, you might demonstrate that requiring computer background checks before issuing handgun permits would deprive criminals of such weapons while protecting the constitutional right to bear arms.

Exploratory Argument

You do not always have to write an argument to forcefully convince someone. You can also write to share with your reader how you came to your conclusion. This form of discussion allows you to indicate your doubts about your own position, explain why certain reasons and evidence have weight for you, include personal reasons that influenced you, and address alternative positions and arguments that may tempt you. The goal in such an argument is really to provide the readers with your thinking on the matter; if they are convinced along the way, so much the better. Below is a short excerpt of what a section of an answer to an argument against a ban on semi-automatic weapons might look like.

> While the authors of the Bill of Rights may have intended the Second Amendment to allow all citizens the right to bear arms, the amendment was drafted in a very different period of our history. We had just won a revolutionary war that had depended on a citizen army. Americans faced real threats from the native population and other armed groups. Their weapons were different as well. Citizens mostly owned a muzzle-loading musket that was slow and cumbersome to use, as well as inaccurate. It would seem that understanding the intent of these authors would require us to understand the historical period shaping their vision, a period when a well-ordered militia seemed essential. What would they make, then, of our current situation where the threat we face is almost always from fellow citizens and the power of today's guns would have been unimaginable?

and "Why We Keep Stuff" provide a starting point for discussions and papers that address a variety of issues such as whether stereotyping is still a barrier, whether marriage is an important social institution, or even whether we have too much clutter in our lives. If the theme is "Our Relationship to Nature," essays such as "When the Moon Shines Its Magic over Monument Valley," "Taking the Carbon Down," and "Supermarket Pastoral" can lead to arguments about controlling pollution, global warming, whether the wilderness is worth saving, and whether we have responsibilities as consumers. Whatever the topic, you might wish to require some library or Internet research and a paper that includes outside source material.

Exploratory essays do not need to be informal or personal. An academic paper that considers the political influences on TV programming may make little use of the personal pronoun and yet still explain tentative ideas and show connections in an exploratory rather than strictly argumentative fashion. Sometimes it can be useful to write out an exploratory essay to find your position before you craft a more focused argument.

Drafting the Argument

CLASSROOM ACTIVITY
You might ask students, working in small groups, to discuss their tentative propositions and supporting evidence. Peers should adopt a critic's role and prompt any necessary re-evaluation. Students could also be shown how to act on peer criticism by refuting it in an argument.

When you have a good grasp on your position, reasons, evidence, and the approach you want to take, you're ready to draft your paper. A typical introduction arouses the reader's interest and may also present the proposition—a special thesis statement that names the issue and indicates which position the writer will take. It can declare that something is a fact, support a policy, call for a certain action, or assert that something has greater value than something else. Here are examples:

1. Carron College does not provide adequate recreational facilities for its students. *(Declares something is fact.)*
2. Our company's policy of randomly testing employees for drug use has proved effective and should be continued. *(Supports policy.)*
3. Because the present building is overcrowded and unsafe, the people of Midville should vote funds for a new junior high school. *(Calls for action.)*
4. The new Ford Fire-Eater is superior to the Honda Harmony in performance and economy. *(Asserts value.)*

TEACHING STRATEGY
Many students will benefit if they are guided through the stages of writing an argument. You might want to schedule conferences to help students deal with the challenge of this assignment.

Any of the techniques on pages 93–96 can launch your paper. For example, in arguing for stepped-up AIDS education, you might jolt your reader by describing a dying victim. If your issue involves unfamiliar terms, you might define them up front; and if the essay will be long, you could preview its main points.

Introductions can also take other tacks. In a Rogerian argument, you may want to start by affirming the reader's core values or beliefs on which you build your argument. In an exploratory essay, you might raise the core question you will discuss without taking position.

After the introduction comes the evidence, arranged in whatever order you think will work best. If one of your points is likely to arouse resistance, hold it back and begin by making points your reader can more easily accept. Argument always goes more smoothly if you first establish some common ground of agreement that recognizes the values of your reader. Where strong resistance is not a factor, you could begin or end with your most compelling piece of evidence.

The strategies discussed in earlier chapters can help you develop an argument. Some papers incorporate one strategy, while others rely on several. Let's see how you might combine several in an argument against legalized casino gambling. You might open with a brief *description* of the frantic way an all-too-typical gambling addict keeps pulling the lever of a slot machine, his eyes riveted on the spinning dials, his palms sweating, as flashing lights and wailing sirens announce winners at other machines. Next, you could offer a brief *definition* of gambling fever so that the writer and reader are on common ground, and, to show the dimensions of the problem, *classify* the groups of people who are especially addicted. Then, after detailing the negative *effects* of the addiction, you might end by *comparing* gambling addiction with drug addiction, noting that both provide a "high" and both kinds of addict know their habits hurt them.

Whatever strategies you use, make sure that substantiating evidence is embedded in them. Strategies by themselves won't convince. To illustrate, in discussing the negative effects of gambling, you might cite statistics that show the extent and nature of the problem. An expert opinion might validate your classification of addicts. Or you might use personal experience to verify gambling's addictive effects.

Besides presenting evidence, use this part of your paper to refute, that is, to point out weaknesses or errors in the opposing position. You might try the following:

- **Point out any evidence that undermines that position.** If one viewpoint holds that drug testing violates cherished privacy rights, you might note that employers already monitor phone calls, check employees' desks, and violate privacy in other ways.
- **Identify faulty assumptions and indicate how they are faulty: they don't lead to the implied conclusion, they lack the effectiveness of an alternative, or they are false or unsupported.** If you oppose drug testing, you could point out problems in the assumption that such tests are necessary to protect the public. Closer supervision of work performance might be a better protection; after all, fatigue, stress, negligence, and alcohol abuse can all result in serious problems, and they are not detected by drug tests.
- **Identify problems in the logic of the argument.** Are there missing premises, faulty connections between reasons, or conclusions that don't follow from the premises? The argument against drug testing usually proceeds by asserting that privacy is a fundamental right, that drug testing violates privacy, and that therefore drug testing should not be allowed. There is a missing premise, however: that because privacy is a fundamental right it should never be violated. This premise is, in fact, at the heart of the dispute and therefore cannot be accepted as a reason to disallow drug testing.

You can place refutations throughout the body of the paper or group them together just ahead of the conclusion. Whatever you decide, don't adopt a gloating or sarcastic tone that will alienate a fair-minded reader. Resist the urge to engage in *straw man* tactics—calling attention to imaginary or trivial weaknesses of the opposing side so that you can demolish them. Shrewd readers easily spot such ploys. Finally, don't be afraid to concede secondary or insignificant points to the opposition. Arguments have two or more sides; you can't have all the ammunition on your side. (If you discover you must concede major points, however, consider switching sides.) Here is a sample refutation from a student paper:

Not everyone agrees with workplace drug testing for employees in public transportation companies, electric utilities, nuclear power plants, and other industries involving public safety. Critics assert that such tests invade privacy and therefore violate one of our cherished freedoms. While the examination of one's urine does entail inspection of something private, such a test is a reasonable exception because it helps ensure public safety and calm public fears. Individuals have a right to be protected from the harm that could be caused by an employee who abuses drugs. An airline pilot's right to privacy should not supersede the security of hundreds of people who could be injured or killed in a drug-induced accident. Thus the individual's privacy should be tempered by concern for the community—a concern that benefits all of us.

Annie Louise Griffith

Conclude in a manner that will sway the reader to your side. Depending on the argument, you might restate your position, summarize your main points, predict the consequences if your position does or doesn't prevail, or make an emotional appeal for support or action.

There can be more than one pattern for an argument. Below are three examples.

Example 1	Example 2	Example 3
Introduction	Introduction	Introduction
Definition of the issue (optional)	Definition of the issue (optional)	Definition of the issue (optional)
Your reasons and evidence (can be a large number of paragraphs)	Alternative positions and reasons for those positions Objections and contrary evidence and reasons to those positions (can be several paragraphs)	Common objections or questions and answers to both
Objections or questions and answers to both (can be several paragraphs)	Restatement of your position and reasons and evidence for that position. Objections or questions and answers to both	Your reasons and evidence
Conclusion	Conclusion	Conclusion

You are not limited to these patterns. Alternative positions and objections can be discussed and answered within the context of presenting your own reasons. An argument can be built around answering common questions. A Rogerian argument starts by affirming the reader's core values and beliefs and then shows deductively and by supporting evidence how those values and beliefs yield the conclusion you hope to support.

Revising the Argument

Review the guidelines in Chapter 4 and ponder these questions as you revise your argument paper:

Is my topic controversial? Have I examined all of the main positions?
  Assessed the evidence supporting each one? Considered the objections

to each position and how they can be countered? Weighed the consequences if a position involves taking some action?

Is the paper aimed at the audience I want to reach? Have I tailored my argument to appeal to that audience?

Is my evidence sound, adequate, and appropriate to the argument? Are my authorities qualified? Have I established their expertise? Are they biased? Will my audience accept them as authorities? Do my statistics adequately support my position? Have I pushed my statistical claims too far?

If I've used analogy, are my points of comparison pertinent to the issue? Have I noted any significant differences between the items being compared?

If I've included an emotional appeal, does it center on those emotions most likely to sway the reader?

Have I made a conscious effort to present myself in a favorable light?

Is my proposition clearly evident and of the appropriate type—that is, one of fact, policy, action, or value? If the proposition takes the form of a syllogism, is it sound? If faulty, have I started with a faulty premise? Reversed the last two statements of the syllogism?

Is my evidence effectively structured? Have I adequately refuted opposing arguments? Developed my position with one or more writing strategies?

Is my argument free of fallacies?

Have I considered appropriate ethical issues?

SAMPLE

STUDENT ESSAY OF **ARGUMENT**

Bottled Troubled Water

Scott Lemanski

Macomb Community College

Faculty Member: Theresa Mlinarcik

1   A disease has swept over our nation. It's called consumeritis, and its symptoms, among many others, include sluggishness, chronic apathy, alienation, obesity, and a constant, nagging feeling that there is something missing from our lives. We temporarily relieve these symptoms, or at least distract ourselves from them, by seeing or hearing an advertisement, label, or slogan that convinces us that we absolutely need some useless product, then call a toll-free number to place an order or drive over to the local megamart to buy it, along with a few other superfluous items we feel that we just can't do without. Perhaps the most senseless product with

Continued on next page

Continued from previous page

which we've been treating our consumeritis in recent years is that clear, cool, tasteless drink that comes in a plastic container—bottled water. It comes in many attractive shapes and sizes from mountain springs and glaciers all over the world, promising us better health and a convenient way to attain it. The thought of drinking tap water for some people today is simply ridiculous because of the commonly held belief that it's just not pure enough. But do we really know how pure our beloved bottled water is? How often do we think about the impact our obsession with bottled water is having on the world or how much we actually benefit from such a product? The harm done to our environment, the waste of our resources, and the potential health risks caused by bottled water's mass production, distribution, and consumption far outweigh its possible benefits.

2   Our thirst for bottled water has become seemingly unquenchable, and as it grows, so does its impact on our environment. According to Tony Azios in his article "The Battle over Bottled vs. Tap Water," over 25 billion plastic water bottles per year are sold in the United States (3). Since 2002, production has increased an average of 9% per year; and since 2003, water has become the highest-selling commercial drink, second only to soft drinks (Azios 1). In "Bottled Water: Pure Drink or Pure Hype?" the National Resources Defense Council (NRDC) reports that "in 2006, the equivalent of 2 billion half-liter bottles of water were shipped to U.S. ports, creating thousands of tons of global-warming pollution and other air pollution" (par. 7). The transport of bottled water that year from eastern Europe to New York con- tributed approximately 3,800 tons of global-warming pollution to the atmosphere, while the shipping of 18 million gallons of bottled water from Fiji to California produced about 2,500 tons of such pollution (par. 7).

3   Given the virtually incomprehensible quantities of bottled water manufactured, transported, bought, and sold, it is no surprise that the waste from it amounts to alarmingly large numbers. In some U.S. states, we are required by law to pay a small deposit when purchasing plastic soda bottles, which works quite well as an incentive to bring them back for recycling. The same is not true for bottled water, although the bottles are recyclable. The NDRC notes that, "only about 13% of the bottles we use get recycled. In 2005, 2 million tons of plastic water bottles ended up clogging up landfills" (par. 7). Oil, however ultimately damaging to the future of our world it may be, is an ever-increasingly precious resource,

now perhaps more than ever, and we're wasting that on bottled water, too. Azios points out that in 2006, "more than 17 million barrels of oil (not including fuel for transportation) were used in plastic bottle production" (3). Even water, arguably our most precious resource, is used in copious amounts in the production. Water is necessary to cool machinery in power plants and molds that form plastic parts, so when taking into account the huge volume of plastic water bottles made every year, it's no wonder that "it takes about 3 liters of water to produce 1 liter of bottled water" (3). It's also no wonder, with all the energy and resources wasted, that we end up paying 2,000 times more for a liter of bottled water than we would a liter of tap water (2).

4   While it's obvious we are willing to pay entirely too much money for it, are we also willing to gamble our health on bottled water? Since so many different brands of bottled water have words on their labels such as *pure* or *natural*, we are led to believe that drinking bottled water is a choice that will be a benefit to our health. It would be prudent, then, to become educated on some of the risks involved. According to Janet Jemmott in "Bottled Water vs. Tap Water," most of the bottles are made of a plastic called polyethylene terepthalate, or PET, which is suppose to be generally safe, but if heated, the plastic could leach chemicals into the water (3). There are hazards linked to these chemicals, but "the exact health risks are unknown" (3). Consequently, we are taking a chance with our health if we, for example, leave a bottle in a hot car all day long and later return to drink it. Though a consensus hasn't been reached on the risks of PET chemicals, Jemmott notes that some findings may be unsettling.

5   In the meantime, experts have raised a warning flag about a few specific chemicals. Antimony is a potentially toxic material used in making PET. Last year, scientists in Germany found that the longer a bottle of water sits around (in a store, in your home), the more antimony it develops. High concentrations of antimony can cause nausea, vomiting, and diarrhea. In the study, levels found were below those set as safe by the EPA, but it's a topic that needs more research (Jemmott 3).

6   Many of us are willing to take our chances with the possible health risks associated with bottled water because, if nothing else, we see it as such a convenient way to obtain the water we need to drink every day.

Continued on next page

Continued from previous page

Is it really more convenient to go to the store and spend entirely too much money on a bottle of water than it is to simply fill a glass at home at the faucet? If we want to take it with us while we're out, there are plenty of containers that we can purchase for just such a purpose. Advertisers have cleverly convinced us that somehow it's more convenient to go out of our way to buy what they're selling than it is to take a moment and think about whether we truly need it or not. Do we really need to buy a product such as bottled water?

7   Many of us cite the most compelling reason to drink bottled water, besides convenience, is the concern over impurities in the water that comes out of our faucets and drinking fountains. It is a legitimate concern but one that doesn't necessarily have to result in the automatic response of reaching for the bottle. In "Water Quality: Bottled Water," the Cornell University Cooperative Extension says that tap water can and often does contain contaminants in varying concentrations, such as microorganisms, including pathogens, and sulfur compounds, including metals and metal-loids, such as arsenic, lead and iron, just to name a few. However, the regulation of tap water is somewhat more reliable and transparent:

> Tap water from municipal drinking water treatment plant is regulated by the U.S. Environmental Protection Agency (EPA) . . . for close to a hundred chemicals and characteristics, [while] bottled water sold across state lines is regulated by the U.S. Food and Drug Administration (FDA). Your supplier must notify the community if there are problems with the water supply. Municipal plants are generally subject to much more frequent testing and inspection and must report test results to the public. (Cornell)

Furthermore, since more than 25% of the bottled water comes from a municipal source (Jemmott 4), there is a sizable chance that the water in the bottles from which we drink is just as contaminated as the water that comes out of the faucet in our kitchen sink.

8   The fluoridation of tap water is another positive health benefit. Most of us have seen enough television toothpaste commercials go uncontested for long enough to be reasonably confident in fluoride's ability to help prevent tooth decay. Tap water is generally fluoridated, while most bottled water is not, and since many children are drinking more bottled

water than tap water, this could explain the current rise in tooth decay among children (Jemmott 5).

9   Recently in the *USA Today* article "AP: Drugs Show Up in Americans' Water," it has been reported that quite a few pharmaceuticals, "including antibiotics, anti-convulsants, mood stabilizers and sex hormones have been found in the water supply of at least 41 million Americans" (Donn, Mendoza, and Prichard). Though utilities say their water is safe and that the levels of the drugs found are measured in parts per billion or trillion, "far below the levels of a medical dose . . . [their presence is] heightening worries among scientists of long-term consequences to human health" (Donn, Mendoza, and Pritchard). Though these concerns are certainly valid, they still don't warrant turning to bottled water as the solution to the problem. Going back to the point Cornell University made about water regulation, it follows that it is unlikely that bottled water companies are doing the sort of rigorous testing of their water for substances such as pharmaceuticals that could ease our concerns on this matter; and even if they were, would they report it to the public? Also, if over 25% of bottled water comes from municipal sources, what percentage of that percentage might contain such pharmaceuticals?

10   "In general, toxins in drinking water don't exceed EPA limits" (Jemmott 5). However, there are steps we can take to inform ourselves of and reduce the risks of tap water contamination. A water quality or consumer confidence report is generally sent out to all customers of local water companies once a year, and it will show if any contaminants have gone over the maximum allowable levels (5). We can also have our water tested by a state-certified lab (5). There are also many varieties of tap-water filters we can buy to purify the water coming out of our taps, but in order to ensure their effectiveness, they should be "approved by NSF, Underwriters Laboratories, or the Water Quality Association" (5). If after taking all this information into account, you still feel it necessary to replace tap water with bottled water, you can at least look for a brand that comes from a local source, so as to at least limit the environmental impact and waste or resources caused by long-distance mass transport. Also, look for brands with "NSF certification or [those that] belong to the IBWA. Check out the lists at NSF.org or bottledwater.org, or look at the bottle itself" for the NSF logo (5).

Continued on next page

Continued from previous page

11   In our consumerist society, where so many things are available to us and convenience often seems to be of the greatest importance, it's easy to forget that everything we do in our personal lives has a direct or indirct effect on the rest of the world and our planet. If we go on ignoring growing environmental threats and the resources we're wasting, the consequences will affect us all. No absolute cure has been found for consumeritis, but we can take steps to minimize its impact by taking a little time out from our overly busy lives and trying to think rationally about the implications of something so seemingly harmless as drinking bottled water. The convenience and minimal, if any, health benefits we receive from drinking bottled water don't come close to justifying the harm it causes the earth and perhaps ourselves.

Works Cited

Azios, Tony. "The Battle over Bottled vs. Tap Water." *Christian Science Monitor.* 17 Jan. 2008. Web. 17 Mar. 2008.

Cornell University Cooperative Extension. "Water Quality: Bottled Water." *Cornell University Cooperative Extension.* 13 Feb. 2008. Web. 20 Mar. 2008.

Donn, Jeff, Martha Mendoza, and Justin Prichard. "AP: Drugs Show Up in Americans' Water." *USAToday.com* 9 Mar. 2008. Web. 20 Mar. 2008.

Jemmott, Janet Majeski. "Rethink What You Drink : Growing Thirst." *Reader's Digest.* 10 Jan. 2008. Web. 17 Mar. 2008

"National Resources Defense Council: Bottled Water FAQ." *NRDC: The Earth's Best Defense.* 12 Sept. 2007. Web. 17 Mar. 2008.

DISCUSSION QUESTIONS

1. The writer uses "we" rather than "you," which has the effect of making it seem the writer is identifying with the reader. The writer acknowledges that the reader may have what seems like good reasons

Discussion Questions

1. This essay tries to convince many readers to give up a common habit. Often readers can be sensitive about such an approach. How does this writer lessen the possible negative impact of his criticism?
2. How does this author's argument appeal to his readers' concerns and values, assuming that many who drink bottled water are concerned about the environment and are health conscious?
3. What types of evidence does the writer use in his argument?

4. Why does the writer in paragraph 10 offer some suggestions for buying bottled water when the entire paper is dedicated to discouraging the practice?

5. In the introduction and the conclusion the writer links buying bottled water with something he calls "consumeritis." Is this strategy effective? Why or why not?

Suggestions for Writing

Write a properly focused argument on some topic you feel strongly about. Study all sides of the issue so you can argue effectively and appeal to a particular audience. Support your proposition with logical evidence. Here are some possibilities to consider if your instructor gives you a free choice:

1. Compulsory composition classes in college
2. Requiring safety locks on firearm triggers
3. Prohibiting development of private property to save endangered species
4. Prayer in public schools
5. English as the official language of the United States
6. Filters on Internet stations at public libraries
7. Increasing federal support of developing alternative energy such as solar power
8. Gay marriage
9. Universal health care
10. Bilingual instruction in schools
11. The effectiveness of some kind of alternative medicine (or some particular diet)
12. Allowing or prohibiting guns on college campuses
13. Taxpayer funding for professional athletic facilities
14. Use of animals for research
15. A campus, local, or state issue
16. Immigration reform
17. Providing federal funding to support religious charities
18. Publicly funded private school vouchers
19. Monitoring U.S. citizens' phone conversations to detect potential terrorist threats
20. Virtual universities where all classes are conducted on the Internet

CRITICAL EDGE

A successful argument, by its very nature, requires critical thinking. This chapter has given you the tools you'll need to test the logic and evaluate the evidence offered in support of argumentative positions. After all, rarely will you generate an idea on your own and then argue for it. Instead, because most important issues have already been debated in print, you'll enter a discussion that's already under way. Sometimes it's on a topic of national interest, such as the desirability of politically correct speech and writing or the need to limit the number of terms elected officials can serve. At other times, the topic may be more localized: Should your state outlaw teacher strikes, your company install new equipment to control air pollution, or your college reduce its sports programs? On any of these issues you begin to form your own view as you read and assess the arguments of other writers.

for their behavior. The writer avoids directly condemning the reader for his or her behavior.

2. Those who drink bottled water are often concerned about the environment and health conscious. The writer demonstrates how drinking bottled water harms the environment, something likely to be of concern to many readers. He also shows the reader that bottled water doesn't have the health benefits some might think by providing facts that contradict those assumptions.

3. Much of the writer's evidence is statistical evidence such as the amount of global warming pollution generated by shipping bottles. He also reports on scientific findings such as the levels and impact of antimony. The strength of this evidence is that much of it is verifiable by using multiple sources. Little of the evidence rests on authority, though the author does use sources to build credibility.

4. The reader's goal is to reduce the negative impact of people drinking bottled water. Since some readers may not avoid bottled water, he provides an additional option to obtain his long-term goal. However, this section has another effect which is to make the writer seem less absolute and more reasonable, giving greater credibility to the rest of his argument. It positively affects the ethical appeal of this particular writer and gives to him an increased air of reasonableness and understanding.

5. The introduction and conclusion pose a risk. By tying the problem of bottled water to the larger issue of consumerism, the writer could make readers who would in general oppose being a blind consumer to think twice. Few want to see themselves as suffering from "consumeritis," so readers might, therefore, see drinking bottled water more negatively. However, this approach may alienate readers who think they drink bottled water for good reasons and who would find the "consumeritis" label as extreme, undercutting the credibility of the writer and the writer's argument.

A good way to take stock of conflicting opinions is to make a chart that summarizes key reasons and evidence on each side of the argument. Here is a segment of a chart that presents opposing viewpoints on whether industrial air pollution poses a significant threat of global warming:

Pro-threat side	No-threat side
Industrial emissions of carbon dioxide, methane, and chlorofluorocarbons let sun's rays in but keep heat from escaping. Andrew C. Revkin	Natural sources account for almost 50 percent of all carbon dioxide production. Dixy Lee Ray
Atmospheric levels of carbon dioxide are now 25 percent higher than in 1860. Computer models indicate a continuing rise will cause a temperature increase of 3–9°F. Revkin	The computer models are inaccurate, don't agree with each other, and fail to account for the warming effects of the oceans. H. E. Landsberg

Even though you investigate the reasons and evidence of others, deciding what position to take and how to support it—that is, establishing your place in the debate—is the real work of synthesis. (See pages 149–150.) Therefore, after evaluating your sources, outline the main points you want to make. You can then incorporate material that supports your argument. Let's say that you're considering the issue of global warming. After examining the differing viewpoints, you might conclude that although those who believe that global warming is occurring sometimes overstate their case, those who disagree tend to dismiss important scientific evidence. Because global warming is a serious possibility if not a certainty, you decide to argue for immediate environmental action. You might begin your paper by pointing out the dire consequences that will ensue if global warming becomes a reality, then offer evidence supporting this possibility, acknowledge and answer key opposing viewpoints, and finally offer your recommendations for averting a crisis.[1]

Suggestions for Writing

1. Read several sources that explore the cost of health care and write an argument that incorporates the views expressed in the sources and suggests the extent of the problem.
2. Read several sources that take different positions on the question of whether the United States should be "the world's police officer" and write an argument that draws on those sources.
3. Read several sources that explore the issue of children suing parents or guardians for physical or sexual abuse and then write an argument that incorporates the views expressed in those sources.

[1]Before starting to write this type of paper, it is important to read the sections on card catalogs and periodical indexes in Chapter 20 and those on handling quotations and avoiding plagiarism in Chapter 21. As always, follow your instructor's guidelines for documenting sources.

Writing an Argument

Plan.

- Identify question or topic you want to explore.
- Read about issue.
- Talk to others.
- Take notes and keep references clear.

Brainstorm.

Brainstorm and perhaps create a table of reasons and evidence for and against the position.

Evaluate evidence.

- Credibility of source.
- Confirming evidence.
- Contradictory evidence.
- Strength of evidence.
- Evidence support for claims.

Plan.

- Establish your position and draft thesis statement.
- Establish purpose.
- Identify audience—what key beliefs and attitudes do readers have you can build on?

Establish approaches to argument.

- Rational—what key reasons and evidence—how much induction, deduction, reductio ad absurdum, Rogerian?
- Emotional appeal.
- Ethical appeal.

Identify terms to define and draft definition.

Option for organization.

- Definition of issue.
- Your reasons and evidence.
- Objections or questions and answers.

Option for organization.

- Definition of issue.
- Other positions and reasons for those positions.
- Objections and contrary evidence for positions.
- Your position.
- Reasons and evidence.
- Objections to your view.
- Answer to objections.

- Create a **rough plan** or even **outline** of major argument.
- Gather reader responses, test argument against.

Create a **rough draft.** Be sure to document any info from source.

Option for organization.

- Definition of issue.
- Common objections and questions.
- Answers.
- Your position.
- Your reasons and evidence.

Revise argument.

Gather peer responses; read critically as if you oppose your own position. Talk it over with others, check to see if there is another position that makes more sense.

- Do arguments fit audience?
- Add any additional reasons or evidence; answer any outstanding objections.
- Cut reasons, evidence that seem invalid, that doesn't work.
- Test reason and evidence to be sure valid.
- Test tone to be sure seems reasonable.
- Test organization so easy to follow with clear transitions.
- Test for ethics.

Proofread.

CHAPTER 17

TEACHING SUGGESTIONS

Discuss this picture with students, indicating how it is organized, how the different sections can be contrasted, how it would compare to the image if it were only of one unaltered person, and possible processes, the effects the approach has on the viewer. Identify the different strategies that were used to make sense of the picture.

SUGGESTED WRITING ASSIGNMENT

Have students write a paper examining the relative effectiveness of this image. In the paper, they will need to describe the image, contrast the different parts, compare the image to a standard image, explore the processes used to create the image, and discuss the effects it has on them as viewers.

© Royalty-Free/CORBIS.

Mixing the Writing Strategies

Why and How to Mix Strategies

Writing strategies seldom occur in pure form. Writers nearly always mix them in assorted combinations for various purposes, not just in papers of definition and argument, as we've noted in Chapters 15 and 16, but also in papers of narration, description, process analysis, illustration, classification, comparison, and cause and effect. An essay that is primarily narration might contain descriptive passages or note an effect. A comparison might include illustrations or carry an implied argument. The purpose, audience, and occasion of the individual essay dictate the mixture, which can't be predetermined. Your best bet is to familiarize yourself with the individual strategies and use them as needed.

Assignments in other classes and on the job will also require you to mix the writing strategies. Your political science professor might ask for a paper that evaluates the advantages of a democratic state over a totalitarian one. You could open with contrasting *definitions* of the two forms of government and then, to make them more concrete, offer XYZ as an *illustration* of a typical democracy, ABC as a typical totalitarian state. After *describing* the key characteristics of each type, you might *compare* their social, economic, and religious effects on their citizens.

At work, a sales manager might have to write a year-end analysis that *compares* sales trends in the first and second quarters of the year, suggests the *causes* of any areas of weakness, and *classifies* the regions with superior potential in the upcoming year. And almost any employee could be asked to compose a report that *defines* and *illustrates* a problem, examines its *causes*, and *argues* for a particular solution.

When tackling a multistrategy writing assignment, break the project into separate stages. Determine first what you need to accomplish, then which strategies will serve your purpose, and finally how best to implement and organize them. It also helps to list all the strategies before you start reflecting on which ones to use. After a brief consideration of ethical issues, let's apply these guidelines to the writing of a problem/solution report and then to an evaluation report, two common projects that rely on a mix of writing strategies.

PERSPECTIVE
One of our goals is to offer students a variety of conceptual and writing tools that they can use to handle more complex writing projects. Students should understand that using the proper combination of strategies offers a way of approaching many writing situations, including the research paper assignment. When students discover that they have already blended various strategies in earlier papers and that complex writing tasks can be broken into segments, any apprehension they may have about mixing the strategies should be lessened considerably.

TEACHING STRATEGIES
1. Have students go over their previous essays to determine and annotate where they used more than one strategy. They might find that in an earlier narrative, for example,

293

they implicitly referred to a cause and explicitly used description.

2. Ask students to review a number of professional pieces of writing (perhaps even a proposal or a business report), establish the writers' purposes, and then determine what strategies were used and why. This could also be a classroom activity with the material presented on an overhead.

Ethical Issues

As you might guess, when your writing includes several strategies, the ethical issues pertinent to each apply. You may, however, need to consider additional issues with problem/solution and evaluation reports.

> *Problem/Solution.* What consequences might follow if my recommendation is adopted? If a college with a grade inflation problem implements a policy that instructors grant no more than 10 percent A's and 20 percent B's, some students who do excellent work could be denied the grades they deserve.
>
> *Evaluation.* Are my evaluation criteria fair? When evaluating the job performance of the clerks in a bookstore, it would seem unfair and discriminatory to include their ability to do heavy lifting if a number of them are older employees.

TEACHING STRATEGY
You might want to discuss the following case with your students.

Tom Hasty reviews movies for a local paper. Halfway through a new action movie, he left but then wrote an extremely critical review without mentioning his early exit. Has he acted ethically? Why or why not?

PERSPECTIVE
Problem/solution and evaluation reports can introduce students to more complex writing tasks that, because of their highly organized nature, students are capable of doing. These reports also allow students to adopt the voice of an authority, a stance crucial to their growth as writers. Furthermore, such assignments provide an opportunity to write for actual readers, not "just for my composition teacher." Still, given the complexity of these reports, students will often have to be guided through their various stages.

Problem/Solution Report

Suppose many students have experienced serious delays in getting to use the computers in your college library and you want to report the situation to the administration. Your goal is to eliminate the problem. After a little thought, you realize that you must first demonstrate that a problem exists and that it warrants action.

Before you can write such a report, you need to investigate the extent of the problem (does it really need solving?), look for its causes (possibly hidden causes), and determine the possible effects. Almost always these are your first steps before you decide on any solutions. Often you can find effective solutions by addressing the causes of the problem, but you might also explore new ways of improving the situation. You'll want to consider carefully whether your solution will work. After you review your options, you decide to use illustration and description to demonstrate the problem, and then to examine the effects and their causes.

Here's how you might proceed as you write the report. Your introduction states the problem. Then you portray a typical evening with long lines of students waiting to use the computers, while others mill around, grumble, and sometimes leave in disgust. Next, you take up effects, noting a number of occasions when both you and your friends have turned in late papers due to unavailable computers and received low grades. Turning to causes, you report your findings. Perhaps the library lacks funds to buy more computers. Perhaps it has limited hours, or instructors tend to schedule research projects at the same times.

The solution you recommend will, of course, depend on the cause(s). If extending the library hours would solve the problem, then purchasing more computers would just waste funds. The best solution may consist of several actions: buying a few computers, extending the library hours, and persuading instructors to stagger their research assignments. In some cases, you may have to explain the process of implementing your solution and/or defend (argue) its feasibility by showing that it will not have unacceptable consequences. For instance, in our computer example, you would need to consider the costs of keeping the library open and staffed for longer hours.

Evaluation Report

Imagine that your school has been experimenting with metal whiteboards that use markers instead of chalk. The administration has asked you to assess how effectively these boards serve student and instructor needs and to present your findings in an evaluation report.

As you think the project through, you realize that you first need to determine the key criteria for evaluation, which you decide are glare, the quality of the writing left by the markers, and the effectiveness of erasing. Because these boards compete with conventional blackboards, you decide that you need a comparison of the two that includes a description of the whiteboards and illustrations supporting your observations. You also decide that a discussion of the effects the boards have on students would be in order.

After drawing your conclusions, you begin your report by indicating why it's being written, providing a definition and description of the whiteboards, and noting the criteria you will use. Following this introduction, you discuss each criterion in turn, describing with illustrative examples how well the whiteboard measures up in comparison to conventional blackboards. You also note the effects of any shortcomings on students. In your conclusion, you argue that the irregular performance of the markers, the glare of the whiteboard surfaces, and the difficulty of erasing the marking frustrate students and make classes more difficult for instructors to conduct. You recommend that the college discontinue using whiteboards except in computer classrooms where chalk dust damages the units.

Suggest what combination of writing strategies you might use in each of the situations below.

1. The company you work for, school you attend, or club you belong to has a serious morale problem. You have been asked to evaluate its various dimensions, propose feasible solutions, and then make a recommendation to the appropriate person.

2. Your company, school, or club is about to purchase some specific type of new equipment. You have been asked to write a report examining the available brands and recommending one.

3. Your local newspaper has asked you to write about your college major or occupation and how you regard it. The article will help high school students decide whether this major or occupation would be appropriate for them.

4. Your general science instructor has asked you to study and report on some industrial chemical. The report must answer typical questions a layperson would likely ask about the chemical.

The margin notes on the following essay show the interplay of several writing strategies.

2. Students often experience considerable difficulty identifying evaluation criteria. You might want to spend class time explaining these criteria and helping students distinguish between criteria and subjective responses.

3. Evaluations serve different purposes and come in different forms. Have students compare movie reviews from *USA Today* to determine the different purposes, styles, and organization.

CLASSROOM ACTIVITY

Have students work in small groups to prepare an evaluation of a common object, perhaps this textbook. They should develop, define, and apply the criteria and then support their conclusions with specific examples.

Illustration in narrative form

Definition

Description

Effect

Step in process

SAMPLE

ESSAY **USING SEVERAL WRITING STRATEGIES**

BRUCE JAY FRIEDMAN

Eating Alone in Restaurants

Bruce Jay Friedman (born 1930) is a native of New York City and a 1951 graduate of the University of Missouri, where he majored in journalism. Between 1951 and 1953, he served in the U.S. Air Force and for the next decade was editorial director of a magazine management company. He now freelances. A versatile writer, Friedman has produced novels, plays, short stories, and nonfiction, earning critical acclaim as a humorist. In our selection, taken from The Lonely Guy's Book of Life *(1979), he offers the urban male who must dine out alone witty advice on coping with the situation.*

1   Hunched over, trying to be as inconspicuous as possible, a solitary diner slips into a midtown Manhattan steakhouse. No sooner does he check his coat than the voice of the headwaiter comes booming across the restaurant.

2   "Alone again, eh?"

3   As all eyes are raised, the bartender, with enormous good cheer, chimes in: "That's because they all left him high and dry."

4   And then, just in case there is a customer in the restaurant who isn't yet aware of the situation, a waiter shouts out from the buffet table: "Well, we'll take care of him anyway, won't we fellas!"

5   *Haw, haw, haw,* and a lot of sly winks and pokes in the ribs.

6   Eating alone in a restaurant is one of the most terrifying experiences in America.

7   Sniffed at by headwaiters, an object of scorn and amusement to couples, the solitary diner is the unwanted and unloved child of Restaurant Row. No sooner does he make his appearance than he is whisked out of sight and seated at a thin sliver of a table with barely enough room on it for an hors d'oeuvre. Wedged between busboy stations, a hair's breadth from the men's room, there he sits, feet lodged in a railing as if he were in Pilgrim stocks, wondering where he went wrong in life.

8   Rather than face this grim scenario, most Lonely Guys would prefer to nibble away at a tuna fish sandwich in the relative safety of their high-rise apartments.

9   What can be done to ease the pain of this not only starving but silent minority—to make dining alone in restaurants a rewarding experience? Absolutely nothing. But some small strategies *do* exist for making the experience bearable.

Before You Get There

10   Once the Lonely Guy has decided to dine alone at a restaurant, a sense of terror and foreboding will begin to build throughout the day. All the more reason for him to get there as quickly as possible so that the experience can

soon be forgotten and he can resume his normal life. Clothing should be light and loose-fitting, especially around the neck—on the off chance of a fainting attack during the appetizer. It is best to dress modestly, avoiding both the funeral-director-style suit as well as the bold, eye-arresting costume of the gaucho. A single cocktail should suffice; little sympathy will be given to the Lonely Guy who tumbles in, stewed to the gills. (The fellow who stoops to putting morphine in his toes for courage does not belong in this discussion.) En route to the restaurant, it is best to play down dramatics, such as swinging the arms pluckily and humming the theme from *The Bridge on the River Kwai.*

| | Description |

Once You Arrive

11   The way your entrance comes off is of critical importance. Do not skulk in, slipping along the walls as if you are carrying some dirty little secret. There is no need, on the other hand, to fling your coat arrogantly at the hatcheck girl, slap the headwaiter across the cheeks with your gloves and demand to be seated immediately. Simply walk in with a brisk rubbing of the hands and approach the headwaiter. When asked how many are in your party, avoid cute responses such as "Jes lil ol' me." Tell him you are a party of one; the Lonely Guy who does not trust his voice can simply lift a finger. Do not launch into a story about how tired you are of taking out fashion models, night after night, and what a pleasure it is going to be to dine alone.

| | Step in process |

| | Comparsion |

12   It is best to arrive with no reservation. Asked to set aside a table for one, the restaurant owner will suspect either a prank on the part of an ex-waiter, or a terrorist plot, in which case windows will be boarded up and the kitchen bomb-swept. An advantage of the "no reservation" approach is that you will appear to have just stepped off the plane from Des Moines, your first night in years away from Marge and the kids.

13   All eyes will be upon you when you make the promenade to your table. Stay as close as possible to the headwaiter, trying to match him step for step. This will reduce your visibility and fool some diners into thinking you are a member of the staff. If you hear a generalized snickering throughout the restaurant, do not assume automatically that you are being laughed at. The other diners may all have just recalled an amusing moment in a Feydeau farce.

| | Effect |

14   If your table is unsatisfactory, do not demand imperiously that one for eight people be cleared immediately so that you can dine in solitary grandeur. Glance around discreetly and see if there are other possibilities. The ideal table will allow you to keep your back to the wall so that you can see if anyone is laughing at you. Try to get one close to another couple so that if you lean over at a 45-degree angle it will appear that you are a swinging member of their group. Sitting opposite a mirror can be useful; after a drink or two, you will begin to feel that there are a few of you.

15   Once you have been seated, and it becomes clear to the staff that you are alone, there will follow The Single Most Heartbreaking Moment in Dining Out Alone—when the second setting is whisked away and yours is spread out a bit to make the table look busier. This will be done with great ceremony by the waiter—angered in advance at being tipped for only one dinner. At this point, you may be tempted to smack your forehead against the table and curse the fates that brought you to this desolate position in life. A wiser course is to grit

| | Definition |

Continued on next page

Continued from previous page

your teeth, order a drink and use this opportunity to make contact with other Lonely Guys sprinkled around the room. A menu or a leafy stalk of celery can be used as a shield for peering out at them. Do not expect a hearty greeting or a cry of "huzzah" from these frightened and browbeaten people. Too much excitement may cause them to slump over, curtains. Smile gently and be content if you receive a pale wave of the hand in return. It is unfair to imply that you have come to help them throw off their chains.

Effect 16   When the headwaiter arrives to take your order, do not be bullied into ordering the last of the gazelle haunches unless you really want them. Thrilled to be offered anything at all, many Lonely Guys will say "Get them right out here" and wolf them down. Restaurants take unfair advantage of Lonely Guys, using them to get rid of anything from withered liver to old heels of roast beef. Order anything you like, although it is good to keep to the light and simple in case of a sudden attack of violent stomach cramps.

Some Proven Strategies

Step in process 17   Once the meal is under way, a certain pressure will begin to build as couples snuggle together, the women clucking sympathetically in your direction. Warmth and conviviality will pervade the room, none of it encompassing you. At this point, many Lonely Guys will keep their eyes riveted to the restaurant paintings of early Milan or bury themselves in a paperback anthology they have no wish to read.

Effect

Classification 18   Here are some ploys designed to confuse other diners and make them feel less sorry for you:

19   ■ After each bite of food, lift your head, smack your lips thoughtfully, swallow and make a notation in a pad. Diners will assume you are a restaurant critic.

20   ■ Between courses, pull out a walkie-talkie and whisper a message into it. This will lead everyone to believe you are part of a police stake-out team, about to bust the salad man as an international dope dealer.

21   ■ Pretend you are a foreigner. This is done by pointing to items on the menu with an alert smile and saying to the headwaiter: "Is good, no?"

22   ■ When the main course arrives, brush the restaurant silverware off the table and pull some of your own out of a breastpocket. People will think you are a wealthy eccentric.

23   ■ Keep glancing at the door, and make occasional trips to look out at the street, as if you are waiting for a beautiful woman. Half-way through the meal, shrug in a world-weary manner and begin to eat with gusto. The world is full of women! Why tolerate bad manners! Life is too short.

The Right Way

Step in process 24   One other course is open to the Lonely Guy, an audacious one, full of perils, but all the more satisfying if you can bring it off. That is to take off your dark glasses, sit erectly, smile broadly at anyone who looks in your direction, wave off inferior wines, and begin to eat with heartiness and enormous

Implied Argument

confidence. As outrageous as the thought may be—enjoy your own company. Suddenly, titters and sly winks will tail off, the headwaiter's disdain will fade, and friction will build among couples who will turn out to be not as tightly cemented as they appear. The heads of other Lonely Guys will lift with hope as you become the attractive center of the room.

25   If that doesn't work, you still have your fainting option.[1]

CRITICAL EDGE

Most writing, including writing that draws on outside sources, uses a mixture of several strategies. As you determine which strategies will help you present your ideas, you can draw upon the principles of critical thinking that you used with each individual strategy. You can, for example, evaluate the merits of different writers' opinions, look for evidence of bias, weigh the type and amount of support backing each assertion, and select the key points you'll include in your paper.

Let's say that you're taking an elementary education class and are asked to write a paper evaluating the effectiveness of computers as an educational tool in elementary schools. Obviously, this assignment would require you to synthesize (see pages 149–150) the results of your outside reading and very likely the conclusions drawn from one or more observations of computer use in classrooms. It would, in short, require both secondary (that is, library) research and direct observations (see pages 451–454), a form of primary research.

You might begin your paper by describing a typical morning's activities in a computer-equipped classroom, noting particularly the students' responses to computer instruction. Next, you might classify the different uses of computers in the classroom and provide a brief history of the movement toward this type of instruction. You could proceed by citing the positive effects of computers in the classroom, as noted by those who advocate their use, and then evaluate whether these claims are exaggerated or reflect any bias. For example, you might notice some kind of bias in a comparison of classrooms with and without computers and then suggest how to make such a comparison so as to eliminate the bias. Finally, you might also critically examine the objections of those who oppose computer instruction. After you've completed this research and analysis, you could argue for or against the use of computers as an educational tool. Even though this type of assignment may seem overwhelming, you can meet the challenge if you tackle the project one stage at a time.[2]

EXERCISE ANSWERS
Here are *possible* approaches to the writing situations:

1. You'd probably begin by *defining* the problem and offering a few *illustrations* of it. Then you might suggest its *causes* and *effects*, *compare* the alternative solutions, and *argue* for (recommend) implementing one of them.

2. You might begin by examining the reasons why (*causes*) the old equipment is obsolete and projecting the beneficial *effects* if new equipment is purchased. After *comparing* the features of several competing brands, you could review the *process* of operation for one of them and then *argue* for (recommend) its purchase.

3. For starters, you might mention the reasons (*causes*) that led to your choice. Next, you could *classify* your duties, *narrate* a typical work day, and finally move to *effects* by noting how your occupation benefits the public. You might enhance your account with plenty of enticing *descriptive* details.

4. A layperson would most probably want to know the following: What does the chemical look like? How is it made? What is it used for? Is it harmful in any way? The paper should therefore include a brief physical *description* of the compound, analyze the *process* by which it's made, *classify* its uses, and note any *effects* it can have on the environment or those working with it.

---

[1]From *The Lonely Guy's Book of Life* by Bruce Jay Friedman. Copyright © 1979 by McGraw-Hill, Inc. Reproduced with permission.
[2]Because you'll need to consult library sources, it is important to read the sections on card catalogs and periodical indexes in Chapter 20 and those on handling quotations and avoiding plagiarism in Chapter 21 before you start to write. As always, follow your instructor's guidelines for documenting sources.

READER/THEME
STRATEGIES
Any of the themes
explored in the Reader
could lead to a mixed-
strategy paper. Because of
student apprehension
about such a complex
assignment, it might help
to provide specific
guidance. Students could,
for example, consider the
cause of some contem-
porary issue, problem, or
crisis and recommend a
solution. The pattern we
suggest for the computer
paper—illustration, description, effects, causes, and
then a recommendation—
might provide a model. If
you prefer the theme "Who
We Are," the class could
discuss and write on the
different behaviors
displayed by restaurant
employees toward different
types of customers. These
essays could classify the
customers, describe and
compare the treatment
received by each group,
speculate on the causes of
the difference, and
consider the effects on the
customers.

After finishing this part
of the book, you might
wish to have students
discuss and establish anew
the criteria for good
writing. They could then
examine two Reader essays
on the same general topic
or two samples of their
own writing and judge
which meets the criteria
better.

Suggestions for Writing

1. Using a combination of strategies, write a paper that investigates and assesses the placement of students with mental and emotional handicaps in "main-stream" rather than special classes. You might visit classrooms with and without handicapped students.

2. Examine several sources that favor or oppose the use of community tax revenues to modernize an existing sports stadium or construct a new one. Then use a combination of strategies to write a paper that presents and assesses your findings.

3. Investigate using outside sources a current national phenomenon such as the upsurge in sensationalist television programming, the popularity of diet and exercising, or the increase in antismoking sentiment. Then use a combination of strategies to write a paper that presents and assesses these findings.

4. Identify what you consider a problem with some social policy of your college. Discuss this problem with several responsible students and also examine any available printed material that addresses this policy. Then use a combination of strategies to write a paper that identifies the problem and proposes a reasonable solution.

5. Identify what you consider a problem with some local, state, or national law. Perhaps you see it as unjust, unfairly applied, outdated, or the like. Examine several sources that discuss this law and then use a combination of strategies to write a paper that identifies the problem and proposes a reasonable solution.

CHAPTER 18

The Essay Examination

Instructors use essay examinations to gauge your grasp of ideas, noting how well you apply, analyze, challenge, compare, or otherwise handle them. Facts and figures, on the other hand, are more often tested by objective examinations. Writing essay answers under pressure and with minimal time to rethink and revise differs from writing at home. Instructors expect reasonably complete and coherent answers but not models of style or neatness. They do expect legibility. An effective presentation increases your chances for success; the skills learned in composition class can help you achieve it. A plan, a thesis, specific support, staying on track, and the pointers presented in this chapter—all are grade boosters.

Studying for the Examination

Here are some pointers for studying:

1. Allow adequate preparation time. For a comprehensive test, start reviewing several days in advance. For one that covers a small segment of the course, a day or two should be enough.

2. Reread the key points you've marked in your class notes and textbook. Use them to develop a set of basic concepts.

3. Make up a set of sample questions related to these concepts and do some freewriting to answer them. Even if none of the questions appears on the test, your efforts will ease pretest jitters and supply insights that apply to other questions.

4. Answer your questions by drawing on your concepts and supplying details from your notes and textbook.

TEACHING STRATEGY
You might teach this unit before midterm exams. Students could then interview instructors briefly about why they give essay exams, what they expect of students, and how they evaluate the results. Findings could be discussed orally or submitted in writing, bound, and distributed to the class as a resource.

TEACHING STRATEGY
To help students develop good study habits, have them maintain a study log in which they record when, where, and how long they study; how they go about doing it; and the problems they have. When reading the logs, you will probably find that many

Types of Test Questions

Some instructors favor narrow, highly focused test questions with detailed answering instructions. Others like broad items, perhaps with simple directions such as "Write for twenty minutes." The sample questions below range from very broad to very narrow. Note how when answering them you can often use the writing strategies discussed in Chapters 5–13.

1. Analyze the *influences* of the industrial revolution on European society.
2. Discuss the most important *causes* of the Spanish–American War.
3. *Compare and contrast* the David statues of Michelangelo and Bernini.
4. Select three different camera shots used in the movie *Titanic*. Identify at least one scene that *illustrates* each shot; then explain how each shot functions by *describing* the relationship between the shot and the action or dialogue.
5. Discuss the stock market plunge of October 27, 1997. Consider the major *factors* involved, such as the liberal lending practices of international banks, the growth in global manufacturing capacity, the severe recessions and monetary turmoil in Pacific Rim countries like Thailand and Malaysia, the concerns of Wall Street, and how these *factors* interacted. Use a thesis statement that signals the points you will discuss.

A highly focused question such as item 5 suggests how to organize and develop the essay. If you know the answer, you can begin writing quickly. In contrast, item 1 forces you to focus and narrow the subject before you respond. Answering this type of item requires careful planning.

Preparing to Write

You can't get from Pocatello to Poughkeepsie without knowing and following an appropriate route. The same principle applies to exam writing. Often students fail to read general directions or to answer what is asked. Low grades follow. To avoid penalizing yourself, scan the test items, noting how many must be answered and which ones, if any, are optional. When you have a choice, select the questions you can answer most thoroughly. Pay attention to any suggestions or requirements concerning length (one paragraph, two pages) or relative weight (25 points, 30 minutes, 40 percent), and budget your time accordingly.

The first requirement for most essay tests is to read the question for *key words*. Does the instructor want you to analyze, compare, criticize, defend, describe, discuss, evaluate, illustrate, explain, justify, trace, or summarize? If you are asked to explain how Darwin's theory of evolution affected nineteenth-century thinking, do just that; you won't like your grade if, instead, you summarize the theory. Merely putting ideas on paper, even perceptive ideas, does not substitute for addressing the question.

EXERCISE

Indicate what each of the following questions calls for. What is required? By what methods—arguing, describing, or the like—would you develop the answer?

1. Distinguish between mild depression and severe depression. You might focus on the nature, the symptoms, or the potential treatments of each condition.
2. Support or refute the following statement: Because waste incineration generates stack gases and ash that contain high levels of toxic substances, it is not an acceptable solution to waste-disposal problems.
3. Explain how to pressure test a rediator.
4. Briefly relate the events in the Book of Job and then explain the significance of the tale. Could the tale be called symbolic? Why or why not?

When you have the essay question clearly in mind, don't immediately start writing. Instead, take a few moments to plan your answer. Following these steps will help you do this:

1. Jot down specific supporting information from your reading lecture notes.
2. Make a rough outline that sketches the main points you'll cover and an effective order for presenting them.
3. Prepare a thesis statement that responds to the question and will control your answer.

Writing an essay exam, like writing an essay, is a front-end-loaded process. Much of the brain work occurs before you put your answer on paper. You won't get to Poughkeepsie just by starting to drive.

EXERCISE ANSWERS
1. This question calls for a comparison that might, like any other comparison, be organized by either the block or the alternating method.
2. This question calls for the use of argument. Because of the nature of the topic, the writer will probably need to use statistics and supporting illustrations.
3. This question calls for a process explanation.
4. This answer would begin with a narrative ("relate the events"), move to an analysis ("explain the significance"), and end with an argument.

Writing the Examination Answer

Here are some guidelines that will help you write a successful exam:

1. Position your thesis statement at the beginning of your answer. Make sure each paragraph is controlled by a topic sentence tied to the thesis statement.
2. Don't become excessively concerned about your wording. Focus on content and, if time permits, make stylistic changes later.
3. Fight the impulse to jot down everything you know about the general subject. The grader doesn't want to plow through verbiage to arrive at your answer.

The following essay illustrates these guidelines:

> *Question:*   Discuss the various appeals described by classical rhetoric that an orator can use. Give a brief example of each kind of appeal.

PERSPECTIVE
Some students are victims of test anxiety, a psychological problem few instructors are prepared to treat. They may ask repeatedly and nervously about an upcoming test, expressing fears that they will do poorly. During the actual test they may sweat excessively, look nervously about, even become ill. If you notice these symptoms, ask whether the student has had past problems and if so, suggest a counselor.

TEACHING STRATEGY
Have students bring in previously written exams and revise them as necessary according to the suggestions in this section. If students have no sample exams, you could follow the same practice with one you hand out.

Answer:
Thesis statement previews focus and order of answer

Classical rhetoric defines three major appeals—logical, emotional, and ethical—that orators may use to win support from their audience.

Topic sentence:

Most rhetoricians agree that any argument must be based on logic; that is, it must appeal to the intellect of the listeners. Unless it does,

Example 1:

the orator will fail to convince them. For example, a speaker who is urging the election of a candidate and presents the candidate's voting record is appealing to logic, asking the audience to understand that the voting record predicts how the candidate will continue to vote if

Example 2:

elected. Likewise, a candidate for public office who describes how a tax cut will stimulate the economy and create new jobs is using a logical appeal.

Topic sentence:

In addition to logic, emotional appeals are a powerful means of swaying people, especially groups. Though emotional appeals work along with logical appeals, they are quite different because they are directed at the listener's hopes,

Example 1:

fears, and sympathies. The presidential candidate who indicates that a vote for an opponent is a vote to increase government spending and risk a financial crisis is making an emotional

Example 2:

appeal. So, too, is the gubernatorial candidate who asserts that her state's industry can be revitalized and serve as a model for all other states.

Topic sentence:

The ethical appeal is more subtle than either of the other two but probably just as important. The orator must strike the audience as a sensible, good person if they are to believe the

Example 1:

message. Sometimes the speaker's logic and also the tone—moderate, sensible, or wise—

Example 2:

will convey sufficient ethical appeal. At other times, a speaker will use statements that are deliberately intended to create ethical appeal. "In developing this program, I will work closely with both houses of the legislature, including the members of both political parties" and "Despite our differences, I believe my opponent to be a decent, honest person" are examples of such statements.

Restatement of thesis:

In any speech, all these appeals—logical, emotional, and ethical—work together to convince an audience.

Student Unknown

In contrast, the next two responses to the same question illustrate common faults of examination essays.

Answer A

1   There are three basic appeals that a speaker can make to captivate an audience. These are the ethical appeal, the logical appeal, and the emotional appeal.

2   The first of these—the ethical appeal—includes all the speaker's efforts to be viewed as rational, wise, good, and generous. Needless to say, the ethical appeal is very important. Without it, no one would pay attention to the speaker's argument.

3   The second appeal—logical—is also extremely important. It carries the burden of the argument from speaker to listener and appeals to the intellect of the audience.

4   Emotional appeal—the third and final one—is made to the passions and feelings of the listeners. The significance of such an appeal is obvious.

5   A speaker often uses all three appeals to win an audience over.

Answer *A* starts with a thesis statement and includes brief definitions of the three appeals; however, it omits any concrete examples and includes no specific details. As a result, the significance of the emotional appeal is not "obvious," as paragraph 4 claims, nor does the answer offer any hints as to why the other appeals are important. This response resembles an outline more than an answer and suggests the student lacked the knowledge to do a good job.

Answer B

1   Orators may make three different kinds of appeals to win favor from an audience: emotional appeal, logical appeal, and ethical appeal.

2   Let's start with emotional appeal because this is the one that is not essential to a speech. Logical and ethical appeals are always included; emotional appeal may be used to help sway an audience, but without logical and ethical appeals no argument is accepted. This simply makes sense: If there is no logic, there is no argument; and if the speaker doesn't come across as an ethical person—someone to be relied upon—then no one will accept the message. But emotional appeal is different. Unemotional arguments may be accepted.

3   Nevertheless, emotional appeal is important. It includes whatever a speaker does to move the feelings of the audience. The speaker asks, "Don't you want to protect your families?" Such an appeal is emotional. A speaker may appeal to the prejudices or biases of listeners. Someone at a Ku Klux Klan rally does that. So does a minister who exhorts people to be "saved." Both speakers address the emotions of the groups they talk to.

4   There is a very fine use of emotional appeal in the "Letter from Birmingham Jail" by Martin Luther King, Jr. At one point King asks his audience of white clergy how they would feel if, like blacks, they had to deny their children treats such as amusement parks and had to fear for the lives of their families, and so on. He also describes the bombings and burnings that blacks are subjected to. All the details move readers emotionally, so that they come to sympathize with blacks who live in fear.

5   Logical appeal, as noted earlier, is crucial. The speaker must seem to have an intelligent plan. The listeners want the plan to meet their needs.

6   The other appeal is the ethical one. It is made when speakers make themselves seem generous, good, and wise.

7   All three appeals can be used in one speech, although the logical and ethical appeals are essential to it.

ANSWER TO EXAM QUESTION
The student is asked to (1) distinguish between eukaryotic and prokaryotic cells and (2) tell where each is found. The response notes (1) that the first type has a true nucleus containing its genetic material while the second has no nucleus and dispersed genetic material and (2) that the first type is found in all life forms except bacteria and blue-green algae, which have the second type. Thus the student has addressed both parts of the question.

ANSWER TO EXAM QUESTIONS

a. The student uses the importance of setting as a springboard for her discussion. After noting the power of imagination to control one's perception of reality and the form the poem takes, she turns her attention to the setting, the lime-tree bower "prison" in which the speaker finds himself. Paragraph 3 discusses his reactions to the bower, which lead to imaginative participation in his friends' walk, while paragraph 4 notes his newfound appreciation of the bower itself. Setting has triggered his imaginative faculties and transformed his perception of the setting itself.

b. Indirectly, the answer suggests that the speaker's mind is a sort of setting in which he walks imaginatively with his friends. Reality is defined as being not just what we perceive with our eyes but what we imagine and how we regard our circumstances. Although the answer does not explain *how* friendship triggers the insights revealed in the poem, it does suggest that friendship plays a role in stimulating the imagination: It's unlikely that one could as easily participate imaginatively in the activities of strangers or casual acquaintances.

c. The thesis statement is the first sentence in the answer. Everything that follows supports its contention that imagination shapes reality and is itself a sort of reality. Paragraph 3 notes that imagination allows the speaker to share

Although the writer opens with an acceptable thesis statement, this answer shows little evidence of advance planning. Does it make sense to begin in paragraph 2 with an appeal tagged "not essential"? And note how the paragraph drifts from the emotional appeal to the other two types, despite its topic sentence. Paragraphs 3 and 4 do focus on the emotional appeal and ironically, through specific examples, make a good case for its importance. Paragraphs 5 and 6 shortchange logical and ethical appeals by saying next to nothing about them. The essay contradicts itself: If logical and ethical appeals are the essential ones and emotional appeals "not essential," why is more than half of the essay about emotional appeal?

Read the examination questions and answers below. Then respond to the questions that follow the answers.

A. Question

Living organisms are composed of cells. On the basis of structure, biologists categorize cells into two groups: the prokaryotic cells and the eukaryotic cells. What are the major differences between prokaryotic cells and eukaryotic cells, and in which living organisms are these cells found?

Answer

1 Eukaryotic cells have a true nucleus and their genetic material, the DNA-containing chromosomes, is located within this nucleus, which is surrounded by a nuclear membrane. Prokaryotic cells lack a true nucleus, and their genetic material lies free in the cytoplasm of the cell.

2 Eukaryotic cells are also much more complex than prokaryotic cells. Eukaryotic cells commonly contain organelles such as mitochondria, a Golgi complex, lysosomes, an endoplasmic reticulum, and in photosynthetic cells, chloroplasts. These organelles are typically lacking in the simpler prokaryotic cells.

3 Prokaryotic cells make up the structure of all bacteria and the blue-green algae. These are the simplest of all known cellular organisms. All other cellular organisms, including humans, are composed of eukaryotic cells.

Scott Wybolt

a. Does the response answer the question that was asked? Discuss.

B. Question

Analyze the significant relationships between imagination and reality in Coleridge's "This Lime-Tree Bower My Prison." In your answer, you might consider some of the following questions: What is the importance of setting in the poem? Is the speaker's mind a form of setting? How is reality implicitly defined in the poem? How, and through what agencies, can reality be transmitted? What relationship is finally perceived between the spiritual and the concrete? How does friendship or fellow feeling trigger the essential insights revealed in the poem?

Answer

1   Coleridge's "This Lime-Tree Bower My Prison" shows imagination to be a powerful force that can control one's perception of reality and that is, in itself, a kind of reality—perhaps the most important reality. Thus, imagination and reality are more intimately linked and more similar in Coleridge's poem than they are ordinarily thought to be.

2   The relationship between imagination and reality is revealed by the speaker of "Lime-Tree Bower," although he doesn't openly state it. The technique for revelation is dramatic monologue, with the speaker seemingly talking spontaneously as his situation gives rise to a series of thoughts.

3   As the poem begins, the speaker finds himself "trapped" at home in his lime-tree bower, while his friends go on a walk he had hoped to take with them. This situation at first bothers the speaker, causing him to feel imprisoned. As the poem progresses, however, the speaker begins to imagine all the places his friends are visiting on their walk. Though he laments not being with them, he shows excitement as he describes the scenes his friends are viewing: the "roaring dell," the sea, and so on. Thus the speaker recognizes that he is able to participate imaginatively in the walk and, in doing so, to escape his "prison" reality and enter the reality of his friends.

4   The moment of recognition occurs at the beginning of stanza three: "A delight/ Comes sudden on my heart, and I am glad/As I myself was there!" Interestingly, however, this point marks a turn in the speaker's thoughts. Once again he realizes where he actually is—the lime-tree bower. But now he appreciates its beauties. The natural beauties he imagined have taught him to appreciate the beauties of nature right before him. He has learned that there is "No plot so narrow, be but Nature there." The lime-tree bower is no longer a prison but a rich and beautiful, if somewhat small, world.

5   Imagination has again shaped the speaker's perceptions of reality. It controls the perception of circumstances—whether one views a place as a prison or a microcosm of a larger world, with beauties and possibilities in its own right. The use of imagination can teach one about reality, as it has Coleridge's speaker. And, if one surrenders to it completely—as the speaker does when he envisions the world of the walkers—imagination is a delightful reality, as valid as the reality of the place in which one sits.

6   Imagination and reality are merged in "This Lime-Tree Bower My Prison," and though this identification is apparently temporary, one may learn through imagination how to cope with and enjoy reality. Thus, imagination is intimately involved in shaping the perception of reality.

Lori McCue

his friends' reality. Paragraph 4 points out that imagination transforms the speaker's perceptions of his surroundings, and paragraph 5 shows that the reality of imagination is as valid as the reality of one's actual location.

d. The answer begins with a thesis sentence that indicates what the writer will discuss and in what order. Then she explains her first point and her second point, using an inductive organization: First she discusses a specific situation and set of reactions, then draws general conclusions. The conclusion reiterates the two points stated in the thesis.

e. Paragraph 3 supports the statement that "the speaker begins to imagine all the places his friends are visiting. . . ." The speaker "shows excitement" in describing the scenery viewed by his friends: a "roaring dell" and "the sea." The two quotations cited in paragraph 4 support the student's comments about the relationship between imagination and reality.

a. Which of the possible approaches suggested in the question does the student select?

b. Which of the other questions does she indirectly answer? Which ones are not addressed?

c. Identify the thesis statement and explain how it controls the answer.

d. Show how the answer demonstrates careful planning.

e. Point out some effective supporting details.

Writing About Literature

Teachers of literature generally expect you to write about what you've read. Typically they might ask you to

- show how an author handled one element of a short story, play, or poem
- compare how two different works treat a particular element
- weigh several elements and then determine the writer's intention
- air your reactions to some work.

Writing about literature offers several benefits. Weighing and recording your thoughts on the different elements sharpen your critical thinking ability. Literary papers also pay artistic dividends, as careful reading and subsequent writing deepen your appreciation of the writer's craft or themes. Furthermore, you'll feel a sense of accomplishment as you coherently express your perceptions. Finally, writing a literature paper offers yet another opportunity to apply the writing guidelines discussed in Chapters 1–4. Focusing, gathering information, organizing, writing, revising, and editing—the old familiar trail leads to success here too.

The Elements of Literature

Most writing assignments on literature will probably feature one or more of the following elements:

Plot	Symbols
Point of view	Irony
Character	Theme
Setting	

Depending on the work, some of these will be more important than others. Read the following story by Stephen Crane, "The Bride Comes to Yellow Sky." The discussions that follow it point out the basic features of each element and offer useful writing suggestions.

The Bride Comes to Yellow Sky

Stephen Crane

I

The great Pullman was whirling onward with such dignity of motion that a glance from the window seemed simply to prove that the plains of Texas were pouring eastward. Vast flats of green grass, dull-hued spaces of mesquit and cactus, little groups of frame houses, woods of light and tender trees, all were sweeping into the east, sweeping over the horizon, a precipice.

A newly married pair had boarded this coach at San Antonio. The man's face was reddened from many days in the wind and sun, and a direct result of his new black clothes was that his brick-colored hands were constantly performing in a most conscious fashion. From time to time he looked down respectfully at his attire. He sat with a hand on each knee, like a man waiting in a barber's shop. The glances he devoted to other passengers were furtive and shy.

The bride was not pretty, nor was she very young. She wore a dress of blue cashmere, with small reservations of velvet here and there, and with steel buttons abounding. She continually twisted her head to regard her puff sleeves, very stiff, straight, and high. They embarrassed her. It was quite apparent that she had cooked, and that she expected to cook, dutifully. The blushes caused by the careless scrutiny of some passengers as she had entered the car were strange to see upon this plain, under-class countenance, which was drawn in placid, almost emotionless lines.

They were evidently very happy. "Ever been in a parlor-car before?" he asked, smiling with delight.

"No," she answered; "I never was. It's fine, ain't it?"

"Great! And then after a while we'll go forward to the diner, and get a big layout. Finest meal in the world. Charge a dollar."

"Oh, do they?" cried the bride. "Charge a dollar? Why, that's too much—for us—ain't it, Jack?"

"Not this trip, anyhow," he answered bravely. "We're going to go the whole thing."

Later he explained to her about the trains. "You see, it's a thousand miles from one end of Texas to the other; and this train runs right across it and never stops but four times." He had the pride of an owner. He pointed out to her the dazzling fittings of the coach; and in truth her eyes opened wider as she contemplated the sea-green figured velvet, the shining brass, silver, and glass, the wood that gleamed as darkly brilliant as the surface of a pool of oil. At one end a bronze figure sturdily held a support for a separated chamber, and at convenient places on the ceiling were frescos in olive and silver.

To the minds of the pair, their surroundings reflected the glory of their marriage that morning in San Antonio; this was the environment of their new estate; and the man's face in particular beamed with an elation that made him appear ridiculous to the negro porter. This individual at times surveyed them from afar with an amused and superior grin. On other occasions he bullied them with skill in ways that did not make it exactly plain to them that they were being bullied. He subtly used all the manners of the most unconquerable kind of snobbery. He oppressed them; but of this oppression they had small knowledge, and they speedily forgot

---

informally explore various reactions to a work—their feelings about the plot or understanding of the setting, for example. A directed journal features a more structured response to specific questions such as "In what ways did the main character change and why?"

2. A class discussion can help prepare students for the content of a literary work. To illustrate, before reading "The Bride Comes to Yellow Sky," students might discuss the nature of the Wild West, what a sheriff and gunslinger were like, and so on.

TEACHING STRATEGIES

1. Encourage students to jot down their reflections about the story in the margin of their text, perhaps showing them how you've done the same with your copy. This type of running commentary can prepare students for quizzes and class discussions as well as provide raw material for papers.

2. After students have read the story once, you could have them do some freewriting about particular elements, perhaps their reactions to Scratchy Wilson or the parlor car. Students thus begin to articulate their experiences with the story.

CLASSROOM ACTIVITIES

You can pose several types of questions to help students respond to literature. In general, it's best to ask open-ended questions that can't be

answered simply by "yes"
or "no."

1. You might start with a
general question such as
"What point was the
author trying to make in
this story?" As students
respond, follow with additional questions that ask
them to defend their views
with evidence from the
story. "Why do you think
that is important?" "How
does Scratchy Wilson fit
into this view?" Such an
approach shows students
that the details of the story
must support their views.

2. You could start with a
more provocative question
that relates to the interpretation of the story: "Was it
fair of Potter to bring a
bride to Yellow Sky?" "Do
you think the old Yellow
Sky was a better place than
the one yet to come? Why?"

3. Perhaps start with a
general question that leads
to a particular insight into
the story: "Why do you
think Scratchy Wilson
backed down?" Student
responses can be followed
by questions that ask for
more detail: "In what ways
does this action seem consistent or inconsistent with
his character?" "What
clues in the text led to
your conclusion?"

4. Ask students to identify
or explain specific fea-
tures. For example: "The
drummer is calmed by
gazing at 'various zinc and
copper fittings that bore a
resemblance to armor-
plate.' What do you think
these fittings symbolize?"

5. Some instructors prefer
to ask imaginative ques-
tions that call for speculation about what happens
after the ending. You

that infrequently a number of travelers covered them with stares of derisive enjoyment. Historically there was supposed to be something infinitely humorous in their situation.

"We are due in Yellow Sky at 3:42," he said, looking tenderly into her eyes.

"Oh, are we?" she said, as if she had not been aware of it. To evince surprise at her husband's statement was part of her wifely amiability. She took from a pocket a little silver watch; and as she held it before her, and stared at it with a frown of atten-tion, the new husband's face shone.

"I bought it in San Anton' from a friend of mine," he told her gleefully.

"It's seventeen minutes past twelve," she said, looking up at him with a kind of shy and clumsy coquetry. A passenger, noting this play, grew excessively sardonic, and winked at himself in one of the numerous mirrors.

At last they went to the dining car. Two rows of negro waiters, in glowing white suits, surveyed their entrance with the interest, and also the equanimity, of men who had been forewarned. The pair fell to the lot of a waiter who happened to feel pleasure in steering them through their meal. He viewed them with the manner of a fatherly pilot, his countenance radiant with benevolence. The patronage, entwined with the ordinary deference, was not plain to them. And yet, as they returned to their coach, they showed in their faces a sense of escape.

To the left, miles down a long purple slope, was a little ribbon of mist where moved the keening Rio Grande. The train was approaching it at an angle, and the apex was Yellow Sky. Presently it was apparent that, as the distance from Yellow Sky grew shorter, the husband became commensurately restless. His brick-red hands were more insistent in their prominence. Occasionally he was even rather absent-minded and far-away when the bride leaned forward and addressed him.

As a matter of truth, Jack Potter was beginning to find the shadow of a deed weigh upon him like a leaden slab. He, the town marshal of Yellow Sky, a man known, liked, and feared in his corner, a prominent person, had gone to San Antonio to meet a girl he believed he loved, and there, after the usual prayers, had actually induced her to marry him, without consulting Yellow Sky for any part of the transaction. He was now bringing his bride before an innocent and unsuspecting community.

Of course people in Yellow Sky married as it pleased them, in accordance with a general custom; but such was Potter's thought of his duty to his friends, or of their idea of his duty, or of an unspoken form which does not control men in these mat-ters, that he felt he was heinous. He had committed an extraordinary crime. Face to face with this girl in San Antonio, and spurred by his sharp impulse, he had gone headlong over all the social hedges. At San Antonio he was like a man hidden in the dark. A knife to sever any friendly duty, any form, was easy to his hand in that remote city. But the hour of Yellow Sky—the hour of daylight—was approaching.

He knew full well that his marriage was an important thing to his town. It could only be exceeded by the burning of the new hotel. His friends could not forgive him. Frequently he had reflected on the advisability of telling them by telegraph, but a new cowardice had been upon him. He feared to do it. And now the train was hurrying him toward a scene of amazement, glee, and reproach. He glanced out of the window at the line of haze swinging slowly in toward the train.

Yellow Sky had a kind of brass band, which played painfully, to the delight of the populace. He laughed without heart as he thought of it. If the citizens could dream of his prospective arrival with his bride, they would parade the band at the station and escort them, amid cheers and laughing congratulations, to his adobe home.

He resolved that he would use all the devices of speed and plainscraft in making the journey from the station to his house. Once within that safe citadel, he could issue some sort of vocal bulletin, and then not go among the citizens until they had time to wear off a little of their enthusiasm.

The bride looked anxiously at him. "What's worrying you, Jack?"

He laughed again. "I'm not worrying, girl; I'm only thinking of Yellow Sky." She flushed in comprehension.

A sense of mutual guilt invaded their minds and developed a finer tenderness. They looked at each other, with eyes softly aglow. But Potter often laughed the same nervous laugh; the flush upon the bride's face seemed quite permanent.

The traitor to the feelings of Yellow Sky narrowly watched the speeding landscape. "We're nearly there," he said.

Presently the porter came and announced the proximity of Potter's home. He held a brush in his hand, and, with all his airy superiority gone, he brushed Potter's new clothes as the latter slowly turned this way and that way. Potter tumbled out a coin and gave it to the porter, as he had seen others do. It was a heavy and muscle-bound business, as that of a man shoeing his first horse.

The porter took their bag, and as the train began to slow they moved forward to the hooded platform of the car. Presently the two engines and their long string of coaches rushed into the station of Yellow Sky.

"They have to take water here," said Potter, from a constricted throat and in mournful cadence, as one announcing death. Before the train stopped his eye had swept the length of the platform, and he was glad and astonished to see there was none upon it but the station-agent, who, with a slightly hurried and anxious air, was walking toward the water-tanks. When the train had halted, the porter alighted first, and placed in position a little temporary step.

"Come on, girl," said Potter, hoarsely. As he helped her down they each laughed on a false note. He took the bag from the negro, and bade his wife cling to his arm. As they slunk rapidly away, his hang-dog glance perceived that they were unloading the two trunks, and also that the station-agent, far ahead near the baggage-car, had turned and was running toward him, making gestures. He laughed, and groaned as he laughed, when he noted the first effect of his marital bliss upon Yellow Sky. He gripped his wife's arm firmly to his side, and they fled. Behind them the porter stood, chuckling fatuously.

II

The California express on the Southern Railway was due at Yellow Sky in twenty-one minutes. There were six men at the bar of the Weary Gentleman saloon. One was a drummer[1] who talked a great deal and rapidly; three were Texans who did not care to talk at that time; and two were Mexican sheepherders, who did not talk as a general practice in the Weary Gentleman saloon. The barkeeper's dog lay on the boardwalk that crossed in front of the door. His head was on his paws, and he glanced drowsily here and there with the constant vigilance of a dog that is kicked on occasion. Across the sandy street were some vivid green grass-plots, so wonderful in appearance, amid the sands that burned near them in a blazing sun, that they caused a doubt in the mind. They exactly resembled the grass mats used to represent lawns on the stage. At the cooler end of the railway station, a man without a coat sat in a tilted chair and smoked his pipe. The fresh-cut bank of the Rio Grande circled near the town, and there could be seen beyond it a great plum-colored plain of mesquit.

might ask students what they think the future holds for Scratchy Wilson and Potter. After they respond, ask what clues in the story led to their conclusion or how their views fit the themes of the story.

---

[1] Traveling salesman

Save for the busy drummer and his companions in the saloon, Yellow Sky was dozing. The new-comer leaned gracefully upon the bar, and recited many tales with the confidence of a bard who has come upon a new field.

"—and at the moment that the old man fell downstairs with the bureau in his arms, the old woman was coming up with two scuttles of coal, and of course—"

The drummer's tale was interrupted by a young man who suddenly appeared in the open door. He cried: "Scratchy Wilson's drunk, and has turned loose with both hands." The two Mexicans at once set down their glasses and faded out of the rear entrance of the saloon.

The drummer, innocent and jocular, answered: "All right, old man. S'pose he has? Come in and have a drink, anyhow."

But the information had made such an obvious cleft in every skull in the room that the drummer was obliged to see its importance. All had become instantly solemn. "Say," said he, mystified, "what is this?" His three companions made the introductory gesture of eloquent speech; but the young man at the door forestalled them.

"It means, my friend," he answered, as he came into the saloon, "that for the next two hours this town won't be a health resort."

The barkeeper went to the door, and locked and barred it; reaching out of the window, he pulled in heavy wooden shutters, and barred them. Immediately a solemn, chapel-like gloom was upon the place. The drummer was looking from one to another.

"But say," he cried, "what is this, anyhow? You don't mean there is going to be a gun-fight?"

"Don't know whether there'll be a fight or not," answered one man, grimly; "but there'll be some shootin'—some good shootin'."

The young man who had warned them waved his hand. "Oh, there'll be a fight fast enough, if any one wants it. Anybody can get a fight out there in the street. There's a fight just waiting."

The drummer seemed to be swayed between the interest of a foreigner and a perception of personal danger.

"What did you say his name was?" he asked.

"Scratchy Wilson," they answered in chorus.

"And will he kill anybody? What are you going to do? Does this happen often? Does he rampage around like this once a week or so? Can he break in that door?"

"No; he can't break down that door," replied the barkeeper. "He's tried it three times. But when he comes you'd better lay down on the floor, stranger. He's dead sure to shoot at it, and a bullet may come through."

Thereafter the drummer kept a strict eye upon the door. The time had not yet been called for him to hug the floor, but, as a minor precaution, he sidled near to the wall. "Will he kill anybody?" he said again.

The men laughed low and scornfully at the question.

"He's out to shoot, and he's out for trouble. Don't see any good in experimentin' with him."

"But what do you do in a case like this? What do you do?"

A man responded: "Why, he and Jack Potter—"

"But," in chorus the other men interrupted, "Jack Potter's in San Anton'."

"Well, who is he? What's he got to do with it?"

"Oh, he's the town marshal. He goes out and fights Scratchy when he gets on one of these tears."

"Wow!" said the drummer, mopping his brow. "Nice job he's got."

The voices had toned away to mere whisperings. The drummer wished to ask further questions, which were born of an increasing anxiety and bewilderment; but when he attempted them, the men merely looked at him in irritation and motioned him to remain silent. A tense waiting hush was upon them. In the deep shadows of the room their eyes shone as they listened for sounds from the street. One man made three gestures at the barkeeper; and the latter, moving like a ghost, handed him a glass and a bottle. The man poured a full glass of whisky, and set down the bottle noiselessly. He gulped the whisky in a swallow, and turned again toward the door in immovable silence. The drummer saw that the barkeeper, without a sound, had taken a Winchester from beneath the bar. Later he saw this individual beckoning to him, so he tiptoed across the room.

"You better come with me back of the bar."

"No, thanks," said the drummer, perspiring: "I'd rather be where I can make a break for the back door."

Whereupon the man of bottles made a kindly but peremptory gesture. The drummer obeyed it, and, finding himself seated on a box with his head below the level of the bar, balm was laid upon his soul at sight of various zinc and copper fittings that bore a resemblance to armorplate. The barkeeper took a seat comfortably upon an adjacent box.

"You see," he whispered, "this here Scratchy Wilson is a wonder with a gun—a perfect wonder; and when he goes on the wartrail, we hunt our holes—naturally. He's about the last one of the old gang that used to hang out along the river here. He's a terror when he's drunk. When he's sober he's all right—kind of simple—wouldn't hurt a fly—nicest fellow in town. But when he's drunk—whoo!"

There were periods of stillness. "I wish Jack Potter was back from San Anton'," said the barkeeper. "He shot Wilson up once—in the leg—and he would sail in and pull out the kinks in this thing."

Presently they heard from a distance the sound of a shot, followed by three wild yowls. It instantly removed a bond from the men in the darkened saloon. There was a shuffling of feet. They looked at each other. "Here he comes," they said.

III

A man in a maroon-colored flannel shirt, which had been purchased for purposes of decoration, and made principally by some Jewish women on the East Side of New York, rounded a corner and walked into the middle of the main street of Yellow Sky. In either hand the man held a long, heavy, blue-black revolver. Often he yelled, and these cries rang through a semblance of a deserted village, shrilly flying over the roofs in a volume that seemed to have no relation to the ordinary vocal strength of a man. It was as if the surrounding stillness formed the arch of a tomb over him. These cries of ferocious challenge rang against walls of silence. And his boots had red tops with gilded imprints, of the kind beloved in winter by little sledding boys on the hillsides of New England.

The man's face flamed in a rage begot of whisky. His eyes, rolling, and yet keen for ambush, hunted the still doorways and windows. He walked with the creeping movement of the midnight cat. As it occurred to him, he roared menacing information. The long revolvers in his hands were as easy as straws; they were moved with an electric swiftness. The little fingers of each hand played sometimes in a musician's way. Plain from the low collar of the shirt, the cords of his neck straightened and sank, straightened and sank, as passion moved him. The only sounds were his terrible invitations. The calm adobes preserved their demeanor at the passing of this small thing in the middle of the street.

There was no offer of fight—no offer of fight. The man called to the sky. There were no attractions. He bellowed and fumed and swayed his revolvers here and everywhere.

The dog of the barkeeper of the Weary Gentleman saloon had not appreciated the advance of events. He yet lay dozing in front of his master's door. At sight of the dog, the man paused and raised his revolver humorously. At sight of the man, the dog sprang up and walked diagonally away, with a sullen head, and growling. The man yelled, and the dog broke into a gallop. As it was about to enter an alley, there was a loud noise, a whistling, and something spat the ground directly before it. The dog screamed, and, wheeling in terror, galloped headlong in a new direction. Again there was a noise, a whistling, and sand was kicked viciously before it. Fear-stricken, the dog turned and flurried like an animal in a pen. The man stood laughing, his weapons at his hips.

Ultimately the man was attracted by the closed door of the Weary Gentleman saloon. He went to it and, hammering with a revolver, demanded drink.

The door remaining imperturbable, he picked a bit of paper from the walk, and nailed it to the framework with a knife. He then turned his back contemptuously upon this popular resort and, walking to the opposite side of the street and spinning there on his heel quickly and lithely, fired at the bit of paper. He missed it by a half-inch. He swore at himself, and went away. Later he comfortably fusilladed the windows of his most intimate friend. The man was playing with this town: it was a toy for him.

But still there was no offer of fight. The name of Jack Potter, his ancient antagonist, entered his mind, and he concluded that it would be a glad thing if he should go to Potter's house, and by bombardment induce him to come out and fight. He moved in the direction of his desire, chanting Apache scalp-music.

When he arrived at it, Potter's house presented the same still front as had the other adobes. Taking up a strategic position, the man howled a challenge. But this house regarded him as might a great stone god. It gave no sign. After a decent wait, the man howled further challenges, mingling with them wonderful epithets.

Presently there came the spectacle of a man churning himself into deepest rage over the immobility of a house. He fumed at it as the winter wind attacks a prairie cabin in the North. To the distance there should have gone the sound of a tumult like the fighting of two hundred Mexicans. As necessity bade him, he paused for breath or to reload his revolvers.

IV

Potter and his bride walked sheepishly and with speed. Sometimes they laughed together shamefacedly and low.

"Next corner, dear," he said finally.

They put forth the efforts of a pair walking bowed against a strong wind. Potter was about to raise a finger to point the first appearance of the new home when, as they circled the corner, they came face to face with a man in a maroon-colored shirt, who was feverishly pushing cartridges into a large revolver. Upon the instant the man dropped his revolver to the ground and, like lightning, whipped another from its holster. The second weapon was aimed at the bridegroom's chest.

There was a silence. Potter's mouth seemed to be merely a grave for his tongue. He exhibited an instinct to at once loosen his arm from the woman's grip, and he dropped the bag to the sand. As for the bride, her face had gone as yellow as old cloth. She was a slave to hideous rites, gazing at the apparitional snake.

The two men faced each other at a distance of three paces. He of the revolver smiled with a new and quiet ferocity.

"Tried to sneak up on me," he said. "Tried to sneak up on me!" His eyes grew more baleful. As Potter made a slight movement, the man thrust his revolver venomously forward. "No; don't you do it, Jack Potter. Don't you move a finger toward a gun just yet. Don't you move an eyelash. The time has come for me to settle with you, and I'm goin' to do it my own way, and loaf along with no interferin'. So if you don't want a gun bent on you, just mind what I tell you."

Potter looked at his enemy. "I ain't got a gun on me, Scratchy," he said. "Honest, I ain't." He was stiffening and steadying, but yet somewhere at the back of his mind a vision of the Pullman floated: the sea-green figured velvet, the shining brass, silver, and glass, the wood that gleamed as darkly brilliant as the surface of a pool of oil—all the glory of the marriage, the environment of the new estate. "You know I fight when it comes to fighting, Scratchy Wilson; but I ain't got a gun on me. You'll have to do all the shootin' yourself."

His enemy's face went livid. He stepped forward, and lashed his weapon to and fro before Potter's chest. "Don't tell me you ain't got no gun on you, you whelp. Don't tell me no lie like that. There ain't a man in Texas ever seen you without no gun. Don't take me for no kid." His eyes blazed with light, and his throat worked like a pump.

"I ain't takin' you for no kid," answered Potter. His heels had not moved an inch backward. "I'm takin' you for a damn fool. I tell you I ain't got a gun, and I ain't. If you're goin' to shoot me up, you better begin now; you'll never get a chance like this again."

So much enforced reasoning had told on Wilson's rage; he was calmer. "If you ain't got a gun, why ain't you got a gun?" he sneered. "Been to Sunday-school?"

"I ain't got a gun because I've just come from San Anton' with my wife. I'm married," said Potter. "And if I'd thought there was going to be any galoots like you prowling around when I brought my wife home, I'd had a gun, and don't you forget it."

"Married!" said Scratchy, not at all comprehending.

"Yes, married. I'm married." said Potter, distinctly.

"Married?" said Scratchy. Seemingly for the first time, he saw the drooping, drowning woman at the other man's side. "No!" he said. He was like a creature allowed a glimpse of another world. He moved a pace backward, and his arm, with the revolver, dropped to his side. "Is this the lady?" he asked.

"Yes; this is the lady," answered Potter.

There was another period of silence.

"Well," said Wilson at last, slowly, "I s'pose it's all off now."

"It's all off if you say so, Scratchy. You know I didn't make the trouble." Potter lifted his valise.

"Well, I 'low it's off, Jack," said Wilson. He was looking at the ground. "Married!" He was not a student of chivalry; it was merely that in the presence of this foreign condition he was a simple child of the earlier plains. He picked up his starboard revolver, and, placing both weapons in their holsters, he went away. His feet made funnel-shaped tracks in the heavy sand.

Plot

Plot Factors   Plot is the series of events that moves a narrative along. The opening of a story with a conventional plot introduces important characters and sets the stage for what happens. Then one or more conflicts develop, some pitting person against person, others setting characters against society, nature, fate, or themselves. Action gradually builds to a climax, where events take a decisive turn. The ending can do a number of things—clear up unanswered questions, hint at the future, state a theme, or reestablish some sort of relationship between

TEACHING STRATEGIES
1. To help students appreciate the importance of plot, have them discuss how the story would change if key plot elements were altered. What would have happened if Potter had arrived an hour earlier? If the men in

the saloon had come to watch the showdown?

2. To help students appreciate the different devices of plot organization, have them discuss the effects if significant changes were made in plot structure. For example, how would the story differ if it were told as a flashback from the time Potter confronts Scratchy Wilson?

two foes. In "The Bride," Potter experiences two conflicts: one with Scratchy Wilson and the other within himself over his marriage. The climax comes when Potter and Scratchy meet face to face, and Scratchy learns about his old adversary's marriage. As Scratchy walks away, we sense that the two old foes have had their last confrontation, that Potter's marriage has altered forever the relationship between them.

To organize plots, writers use a number of techniques. In foreshadowing, for example, the writer hints at later developments, thus creating interest and building suspense. In H. H. Munro's short story "The Open Window," a visitor to a country house observes that "An undefinable something about the room seemed to suggest masculine habitation." Yet he accepts the story of a young girl that her uncle, the man of the house, had lost his life in a bog three years before. Because he ignores his observation and accepts the girl's story at face value, the visitor is terrified by the sudden appearance of the uncle, who seems to be a ghost. The careful reader, however, senses what's coming and enjoys the trick more for having been in on it.

When using a flashback, another organizational technique, the writer interrupts the flow of events to relate one or more happenings that occurred before the point at which the story opened, then resumes the narrative at or near the point of interruption. Ernest Hemingway's short story "The Short Happy Life of Francis Macomber" provides an illustration. As the story opens, we meet characters who hint that Macomber displayed cowardice by running from, rather than shooting, a charging, wounded lion. A bit later the story flashes back to detail the actual incident. Flashbacks supply essential information and either create or resolve suspense.

Not every plot unfolds in clear stages. Many modern stories lack distinct plot divisions and focus on psychological, not physical, conflicts. In extreme cases, writers may abandon the traditional plot structure and present events in a disorganized sequence that helps accomplish some literary purpose, such as reflecting a character's disturbed state of mind. Joyce Carol Oates's short story "How I Contemplated the World from the Detroit House of Correction and Began My Life Over Again" fits this mold. To dramatize her chief character's mental turmoil, Oates presents the story as a series of notes for an English composition. These notes, labeled "Events," "Characters," "Sioux Drive," "Detroit," and "That Night," are internally disorganized and arranged in a jumbled sequence.

A poem sometimes includes a series of actions and events, as Edwin Arlington Robinson's "The Miller's Wife" illustrates:

> The miller's wife had waited long,
>   The tea was cold, the fire was dead;
> And there might yet be nothing wrong
>   In how he went and what he said:
> "There are no millers any more,"
>   Was all that she had heard him say:
> And he had lingered at the door
>   So long that it seemed yesterday.
>
> Sick with a fear that had no form
>   She knew that she was there at last;

And in the mill there was a warm
    And mealy fragrance of the past.
What else there was would only seem
    To say again what he had meant;
And what was hanging from a beam
    Would not have heeded where she went.

And if she thought it followed her,
    She may have reasoned in the dark
That one way of the few there were
    Would hide her and would leave no mark;
Black water, smooth above the weir
    Like starry velvet in the night,
Though ruffled once, would soon appear
    The same as ever to the sight.

Most poems, however, present a series of images, building statements that make a philosophical point rather than tell a conventionally plotted story.

Writing About Plot   Unless your instructor asks for a plot summary, don't merely repeat what happens in the story. Instead, help your reader understand what's special about the plot and how it functions. Does it build suspense, mirror a character's confusion, shape a conflict, show how different lives can intersect, or help reveal a theme?

Before starting to write, answer the following questions:

What are the key events of the story? Do they unfold in conventional
    fashion or deviate from it in some way?

Does the writer use foreshadowing or flashback? If so, for what purpose?

Is the plot believable and effective, or does it display weakness of some sort?

Does it include any unique features?

Is it similar to the plot of another story or some type of story?

What plot features could I write about? What examples from the story
    would support my contentions?

As you prepare your analysis, determine the important events and how they relate to your topic. If the story is disjointed or incoherent, arrange the events so that they make sense and ask yourself why the writer chose that sequence. To mirror the main character's disordered state of mind? To show that life is chaotic and difficult to understand? Similarly, assess the reason for any use of foreshadowing or flashback. Does it build, create, or resolve suspense?

Not all plots are successful. A character's actions may not fit his or her personality or the situation. The plot might be too hard to follow or fail to produce the desired effect, as in a mystery where the clues are too obvious to create suspense. Or a writer might rely on chance or coincidence to resolve a conflict or problem: It's unacceptable to have the cavalry charge in gallantly out of nowhere and rescue the hero.

If there's something unique about the plot—perhaps a surprise event that works well—describe it and tell how it functions in the story, or perhaps you can

TEACHING STRATEGY
You might ask students to answer, perhaps as short journal assignments, some of the plot questions posed in the text. This exercise helps them develop an understanding of plot and ingrains the habit of specific textual support.

compare the plot with one in another story in order to show how both develop some key insight.

The organization of a paper on plot is simple: You'll either present a thesis and then support it with examples taken from the text, or you'll write a comparison. Writing about "The Bride Comes to Yellow Sky," you could show how foreshadowing moves the story toward an inevitable showdown. As support, you could cite the deliberate, forward motion of the train, the repeated emphasis on clocks and time, the repeated suggestions of Potter's anxiousness, and Scratchy's ongoing conflict with Potter. As a more ambitious project, you might compare the plot of "The Bride" to that of a conventional western showdown, noting any important differences and what they accomplish. A more critical approach would be to argue that the plot is implausible, citing Potter's unplanned marriage and the coincidence of his return to Yellow Sky precisely when Scratchy Wilson was drunk and shooting up the town.

In a short story with a strong plot line, identify conflicts and climax and tell what the ending accomplishes. Point out any use of foreshadowing or flashback.

Point of View

Point-of-View Factors   The point of view is the vantage point from which the writer of a literary work views its events. A writer may adopt either a first-person or a third-person point of view. In *first-person* narration, someone in the work tells what happens and is identified by words like *I, me, mine,* and *my.* A *third-person* narrator stays completely out of the story and is never mentioned in any way. "The Bride Comes to Yellow Sky" illustrates third-person narration.

The most common form of first-person narration features a narrator who takes part in the action. This technique puts the readers directly on the scene and is excellent for tracing the growth or deterioration of a character. Instead of participating in the action, the narrator may view it from the sideline, an approach that preserves on-the-scene directness and allows the narrator to comment on the characters and issues. The narrator, however, cannot enter the mind and reveal the unspoken thoughts of anyone else.

Third-person narrators don't participate in the action but can survey the whole literary landscape and directly report events that first-person narrators would know only by hearsay. Most third-person narrators reveal the thoughts of just one character. Others, with *limited omniscience,* can enter the heads of several characters, while still others display *full omniscience* and know everything in the literary work, including all thoughts and feelings of all characters. Omniscience allows the narrator to contrast two or more sets of thoughts and feelings and draw general conclusions from them. The narrator of Stephen Crane's "The Open Boat" is fully omniscient. The story is about four shipwrecked sailors adrift in a lifeboat, and the narrator, knowing what they all think, traces their developing awareness that nature is completely indifferent to their plight.

TEACHING STRATEGIES
1. Have students record the different vantage points from which they observe events and what differences result. This activity can lead to a class discussion that establishes point of view as not just a literary device but essential to every observation and account of events.
2. After students understand the third-person point of view, have them discuss how the story would differ if the point of view were changed. What would change if the point of view were restricted to third-person limited? How would the plot have to change if the story were told in the first person? How would the story differ if it were told exclusively from Scratchy Wilson's point of view? Such questions usually prompt interesting discussions that help students appreciate the impact point of view has on an entire story.

Yet another type of third-person narration, *dramatic,* has emerged in contemporary fiction. A dramatic narrator, like a motion-picture camera, moves about recording the characters' actions and words but without revealing anyone's thoughts. Stories with surprise endings often use this technique.

Writing About Point of View   For a paper about point of view, ask and answer these questions:

> What point of view is used? Why is it used?
>
> Is it suitable for the situation? Why or why not?
>
> If the story uses first-person narration, is the narrator reliable? What textual evidence supports my answer?
>
> What focus would produce an effective paper? What textual evidence could support its discussion?

Various reasons might prompt the choice of a particular point of view. For example, an author might use the first person to show a character's mental deterioration. A third-person narrator might enter two minds to contrast opposing attitudes toward some incident or enter no minds at all to heighten the emotional impact of a story's climax.

If a point of view seems unsuitable, say so and suggest why. Suppose a man is planning an elopement that will create a surprising ending. A point of view that revealed the man's thoughts would give away that ending.

First-person narrators are sometimes unreliable; that is, they offer the reader a warped view of things. To gauge reliability, compare the narrator's version of the facts with what the work otherwise reveals. The narrator may come off as stupid, psychologically warped, or too biased to view events fairly. If so, speculate on the reasons. A mentally unreliable narrator may be meant, for example, to heighten the horror of events.

Although organization can vary, papers on point of view basically follow a cause-and-effect format, first identifying the point of view used and then demonstrating, with examples, its effect on the story and reader. In "The Bride," the third-person point of view allows Crane to shift from Potter and his new wife to the men in the saloon to the rampaging Scratchy and then to Potter and Scratchy as they confront each other. Shifting scenes in this way builds a sense of impending conflict, which would be difficult to produce with a first-person narrator, who could not move about in this fashion.

Read the following two excerpts and answer the questions that follow them:

Max shook his head no at the mugger, his mouth in a regretful pout.

The teenager lunged at Max's chest with the blade. Instinctively, Max moved one step to his right. He didn't shift far enough. The knife sank into him. Max

TEACHING STRATEGIES
1. To ensure that students have a firm grasp of their purpose, you might discuss the various options in writing about point of view.
2. Students typically accept the narrator's account of events. To counter this tendency, have them read a story with a decidedly unreliable narrator. Poe's "The Tell-Tale Heart" is excellent in this regard. Have students reconstruct the underlying "actual" events and compare them with the narrator's account.

EXERCISE ANSWERS
1. Yglesias enters Max's mind, noting both his attitude toward the mugger and toward his own seemingly imminent death. We learn about the mugger's mental state from his

stunned look, sagging mouth, frightened eyes, and flight.

2. The first-person approach in this excerpt from a novel by a contemporary Native American allows the reader to enter the mind of the protagonist, a young Native American girl who is competing in a rodeo, and experience her thoughts and emotions as her bucking mount unseats her. A third-person narrative could have told the reader what she thought and felt, but presenting these reactions directly strengthens their impact on the reader.

lowered his head and watched as the metal disappeared into his arm and chest. He felt nothing. With the blade all the way in, the teenager's face was only inches from Max's; he stared at the point of entry, stunned, his mouth sagging open. The mugger's eyes were small and frightened. Max didn't like him. He put his hand on the kid's chest and pushed him away. He didn't want to die looking into scared eyes.

The mugger stumbled back, tripped over his feet and fell. . . . Max felt the point of the blade in his armpit. He realized he wasn't cut. The stupid kid had stuck the knife in the space below Max's armpit, the gap between his arm and chest. He had torn Max's polo shirt, but missed everything else. For a moment the knife hung there, caught by the fabric. Max raised his arm and the switchblade fell to the ground.

The teenager jumped to his feet and ran away, heading uptown.

Rafael Yglesias, *Fearless*

"Now!" I cry, aloud or to myself I don't know. Everything has boiled down to this instant. There's nothing in the world except the hand of the gate judge, lowering in slow motion to the catch that contains us. I see each of his fingers clearly, separately, as they fold around the lever, I see the muscles in his forearm harden as he begins to push down.

Wheeling and spinning, tilting and beating, my breath the song, the horse the dance. Time is gone. All the ordinary ways of things, the gettings from here to there, the one and twos, forgot. The crowd is color, the whirl of a spun top. The noises blend into a waving band that flies around us like a ribbon on a string. Beneath me four feet dance, pounding and leaping and turning and stomping. My legs flap like wings. I sail above, first to one side, then the other, remembering more than feeling the slaps of our bodies together. Things happen faster than understanding, faster than ideas. I'm a bird coasting, shot free into the music, spiraling into a place without bones or weight.

Michael Dorris, *A Yellow Boat in Blue Water*

1. In this third-person excerpt, Yglesias depicts the climax of an unsuccessful mugging, entering one character's mind but not the other's. Whose mind does he enter, and how does he convey the other person's mental state?
2. What does Dorris accomplish by using the first-person point of view?

Character

Character Factors The characters in a literary work function in various ways. Some are centers of physical and mental action. Others furnish humor, act as narrators, provide needed information, act as *foils* who highlight more important characters by contrast, serve as symbols, or simply populate the landscape. In "The Bride," the drummer helps funnel information to the reader. He asks questions, the bartender answers them, and the reader learns all about Scratchy.

Writers present characters in several ways. Some tell the reader point-blank that a person is brave, stupid, self-serving, or the like. But most authors take an indirect approach by indicating how their characters look and act, what they think and say, how they live, and how other characters regard them.

Beware of uncritically accepting Character X's assessment of Character Y. X may be prejudiced, simpleminded, a deliberate liar, or too emotionally involved or disturbed to be objective. To illustrate, Scratchy Wilson, despite the bartender's fearful comments, proves to be something less than a real terror. He makes no real attempt to break down any doors and toys with, rather than shoots, the dog and Potter.

In picturing Potter, Crane first notes his appearance and self-conscious behavior, then delves into his mind to show the turmoil his marriage has stirred. Somewhat later, the bartender adds his brush strokes to Potter's portrait. At the confrontation, we again observe Potter's thoughts and behavior, as well as what he says to Scratchy. From all this, Potter emerges not as a mere one-dimensional lawman but as someone with a recognizably lifelike personality.

Some characters remain static; others mature, gain insight, or deteriorate in some telling way. Potter changes. As the story unfolds he abandons his doubts about the course he's charted and ends up fully committed to "the environment of the new estate." Scratchy, on the other hand, ends just as he started, "a simple child of the earlier plains."

Writing About Character

Start the process by asking yourself these questions:

What characters offer the potential for a paper?

What are their most important features, and where in the story are these features revealed?

Do the characters undergo any changes? If so, how and why do the changes occur?

Are the characters believable, true to life? If not, why?

What focus would produce an effective paper?

What textual evidence could support the discussion?

Usually, you'll write about the main character, but at times you might choose the chief adversary or some minor character. For a lesser character, point out how that person interacts with the main one.

Most main characters change; most lesser ones do not. But sometimes a main character remains frozen, allowing the writer to make an important point. To show that a certain social group suffers from paralysis of the will, an author might create a main character who begins and ends weak and ineffectual. Whatever the situation, when you determine what purpose your character serves, tell the reader.

Think hard about your character's credibility. Ask yourself if he or she is true to life. Cruel stepmothers, brilliant but eccentric detectives, mad scientists, masked seekers after justice—these and other stereotyped figures don't square with real-life people, who are complex mixtures of many traits. Inconsistent acts or unexplained and unmotivated personality changes don't ring true: Most people behave the same in similar situations and change only when properly motivated. Not every character needs to be a full-dress creation, but all require enough development to justify their roles.

Start your paper by identifying your character's role or personality; then back your contention with illustrations that support it, possibly following the sequence in which the writer presents them. If a character changes, say so, tell why, and indicate the results of the change, again using supporting examples.

Such a paper is usually a cause-and-effect analysis. Papers that evaluate two characters are essentially comparisons.

For an example of a paper analyzing a character, see pages 333–334.

EXERCISE ANSWER
The speaker is vindictive, cunning, and without conscience. He's irrevocably committed to revenge, clever and calculating in plotting it, and shows no remorse over his impending act.

Write a paragraph describing the personality of the character in the following passage:

The thousand injuries of Fortunato I had borne as I best could, but when he ventured upon insult, I vowed revenge. You, who so well know the nature of my soul, will not suppose, however, that I gave utterance to a threat. *At length* I would be avenged; this was a point definitely settled—but the very definiteness with which it was resolved precluded the idea of risk. I must not only punish, but punish with impunity. A wrong is unredressed when retribution overtakes its redresser. It is equally unredressed when the avenger fails to make himself felt as such to the one who has done the wrong.

Edgar Allan Poe, "The Cask of Amontillado"

TEACHING STRATEGY
You can help students appreciate the role of setting in stories such as "The Bride" because the symbolic, thematic, and plot implications are very clear. Have students list characteristics of the setting, then indicate what these characteristics suggest.

Setting

Setting Factors
Setting locates characters in a time, place, and culture so they can think, feel, and act against this background. Writers can generate feelings and moods by describing settings. Sunny spring landscapes signal hope or happiness, dark alleys are foreboding, and thunderstorms suggest violent possibilities. Poetry, especially, uses setting to create mood. In "Cannery Town in August," Lorna Dee Cervantes combines images of tired, work-stained employees, a noisy workplace, and dismal streets to evoke an unpleasant setting.

> All night it humps the air.
> Speechless, the steam rises
> from the cannery columns. I hear
> the night bird rave about work
> or lunch, or sing the swing shift
> home. I listen, while bodyless
> uniforms and spinach specked shoes
> drift in monochrome down the dark
> moon-possessed streets. Women
> who smell of whiskey and tomatoes,
> peach fuzz reddening their lips and eyes—
> I imagine them not speaking, dumbed
> by the can's clamor and drop
> to the trucks that wait, grunting
> in their headlights below.
> They spotlight those who walk
> like a dream, with no one
> waiting in the shadows
> to palm them back to living.

Setting can also help reveal a character's personality. In this excerpt from Amy Tan's novel *The Joy Luck Club,* the size and contents of the wealthy merchant Wu Tsing's house reflect the owner's love of wealthy display:

> As soon as we walked into that big house, I became lost with too many things to see; a curved staircase that wound up and up, a ceiling with faces in every corner, then hallways twisting and turning into one room then another. To my right was a large room, larger than I had ever seen, and it was filled with stiff teakwood furniture: sofas and tables and chairs. And at the other end of this long, long room, I could see doors leading into more rooms, more furniture, then more doors. To my left was a darker room, another sitting room, this one filled with foreign furniture: dark green leather sofas, paintings with hunting dogs, armchairs, and mahogany desks. And as I glanced in these rooms I would see different people. . . .

Settings sometimes function as symbols, reinforcing the workings of the other elements. A broad, slowly flowing river may stand for time or fate, a craggy cliff for strength of character, a blizzard-swept plain for the overwhelming power of nature. The following section, a discussion of symbols, points out some symbolic settings in "The Bride."

At times, setting provides a clue to some observation about life. At one point in Stephen Crane's story "The Open Boat," the men spot a nearby flock of seagulls sitting comfortably on the turbulent waves. Juxtaposing the complacent gulls and the imperiled men suggests the philosophical point of the story: that the universe is indifferent to human aspirations and struggles.

Shifts in setting often trigger shifts in a character's emotional or psychological state. Jack Potter, typically calm and assured in Yellow Sky, displays great awkwardness and embarrassment in the unfamiliar environment of the Pullman car.

Writing About Setting Begin your search for a topic by identifying the settings in the story and then asking these questions about each one:

What are its key features?

What does it accomplish? Does it create a mood? Reveal a character? Serve as a symbol? Reinforce the story's point? How does it accomplish these things?

In what ways does it support or interfere with the story?

Does the setting seem realistic? If not, why not?

What focus would produce an effective paper? What textual evidence would support it?

Check the impact of setting on mood by seeing how well the two match up for each setting. Sometimes, as in "The Bride," the two bear little or no relationship to each other. In other cases, the two intertwine throughout the work.

Try to establish connections between settings and characters. If an emotionally barren individual always appears against backdrops of gloomy furnished rooms, cheerless restaurants, and decaying slums, you can assume that the writer is using setting to convey character. Look for links between changes in characters and changes in settings. If the setting remains the same, point out any shifts in the way the character views it.

Occasionally, a writer drums home settings so insistently that they overpower the characters and story line. A novel about the super rich may linger so lovingly over their extravagant surroundings that the plot lacks force and the characters seem mere puppets. If the setting hobbles the other elements, identify this flaw in your analysis.

When you write about setting, describe it and discuss its impact on the story's other elements, supporting your claims with specific examples. In writing about "The Bride," you might argue that Crane used as his chief setting a pulp fiction cliché of a western town in order to heighten the atypical nature of the showdown. As support, you could cite such stock features as the train station, saloon, dog, and dusty streets, all of which point toward an actual shootout rather than Scratchy Wilson's backdown.

What mood does the following description of a room generate? What does it suggest about the situation of the room's inhabitants, two women in an Old Ladies' Home?

EXERCISE ANSWER
The description of the small, dark, closed-in, wet-smelling and overcrowded room generates a gloomy mood. The room bears a strong resemblance to a jail cell, and the description suggests that its inhabitants are, like prisoners in a jail, hopelessly trapped creatures.

    Marian stood enclosed by a bed, a washstand, and a chair; the tiny room had altogether too much furniture. Everything smelled wet—even the bare floor. She held onto the back of the chair, which was wicker and felt soft and damp. . . . How dark it was! The window shade was down, and the only door was shut. Marian looked at the ceiling. . . . It was like being caught in a robbers' cave . . .

Eudora Welty, "A Visit of Charity"

Symbols

Symbol Factors   To strengthen and deepen their messages, writers use symbols: names, persons, objects, places, colors, or actions that have a significance beyond their surface meaning. A symbol may be very obvious—as a name like Mr. Grimm, suggesting the person's character—or quite subtle, as an object representing a universal human emotion.

Some symbols are private and others conventional. A private symbol has special significance within a literary work but not outside it. Conventional symbols are deeply rooted in our culture, and almost everyone knows what they represent. We associate crosses with Christianity and limousines with wealth and power. In "The Bride," the plains pouring eastward past the Pullman windows, Scratchy's eastern clothing, and the mirage-like grass plots in front of the saloon are all private symbols that stand for the passing of the Old West. Because people of Crane's time associated Pullman cars with an urbane, eastern lifestyle, the Pullman is a conventional symbol that represents the new order of things. Like the Pullman, a symbol may appear more than once in a literary work.

Whether or not a recurring item is a symbol depends upon its associations. In Ernest Hemingway's novel *A Farewell to Arms,* rain may fairly be said to symbolize

TEACHING STRATEGIES
1. It helps to start your discussion with common symbols known to all students. The school mascot often provides a good, and sometimes humorous, example. Once students understand the array of symbols in their world, you could turn to literary symbols.
2. To help students begin to think about literary symbols, have them draw a

doom because it consistently accompanies disasters, and one of the main characters says that she has visions of herself lying dead in the rain. But if rain is randomly associated with a rundown lakeside resort, a spirited business meeting, a cozy weekend, and the twentieth-anniversary celebration of a happy marriage, the writer probably intends no symbolism.

Writing About Symbols   When you examine the symbols in a literary work, think about these questions:

What symbols are used and where do they appear?

Are they private or conventional?

What do they appear to mean?

Do any of them undergo a change in meaning? If so, how and why?

Which symbol(s) could I discuss effectively?

What textual evidence would support my interpretation?

To locate symbols, read the literary work carefully, looking for items that seem to have an extended meaning. You might, for example, discover that the cracked walls of a crumbling mansion symbolize some character's disordered mental state or that a voyage symbolizes the human journey from birth to death. Several symbols often mean the same thing; writers frequently use them in sets. In "Bartleby the Scrivener," for instance, Herman Melville uses windows that look upon walls, a folding screen, and a prison to symbolize Bartleby's alienated condition, that is, his mental separation from those around him. Determining whether each symbol is private or conventional can provide clues to its meaning.

Sometimes a symbol changes meaning during the course of a work. A woman who regards her lover's large, strong hands as symbols of passion may, following an illness that leaves him a dangerous madman, view them as symbols of danger and brute strength. Note any changes you discover, and suggest what they signify.

A word of caution: Don't let symbol hunting become an obsession. Before you assert that something has a different and deeper meaning than its surface application, make sure the evidence in the work backs your claim.

For each symbol you discuss, state what you think it means and then support your position with appropriate textual evidence. You could argue, for example, that the Pullman car in "The Bride" symbolizes the Eastern civilization that is encroaching on the West, offering as evidence the car's "figured velvet . . . shining brass, silver, and glass" and darkly gleaming wood appointments.

EXERCISE

Read the following poem and answer the questions that follow:

Heritage

Margaret Abbott

We were building there together,
Two children playing blocks,
And I debated whether
To copy your cautious scheme
That would withstand the knocks
Of a careless hand or try
My own impracticable plan
Of block on block until a high
Column, random and unsure, would stand
Memento to my dream.
I looked at you and planned
My tower. Each block fanned
My zeal. The shaft rose higher
And higher, like a spire
To my joy. I knew it could not last at all,
And yet—yet, when I saw it fall,
Some nameless hope came tumbling, too.
I crept, forlornly, close to you
And laid a finger on your solid square
And wished my heart would learn to care
For safety. Then, within that selfsame hour,
My traitor hands began another tower.

1. What does the "high / Column, random and unsure" symbolize? The "solid square"?
2. What is the significance of the final statement?

Irony

Irony Factors   Irony features some discrepancy, some difference between appearance and reality, expectation and outcome. Sometimes a character says one thing but means something else. The critic who, tongue in cheek, says that a clumsy dancer is "poetry in motion" speaks ironically.

Irony also results when the reader or a character recognizes something as important, but another character does not. In "The Bride" this situation occurs when Potter, not knowing that Scratchy is on a rampage, flees the station agent, who tries to let him know. A character's behavior sometimes offers ironic contrasts, too. There's high irony in the contrast between Potter's unflinching face-off with Scratchy and his fear of telling the townsfolk about his marriage.

At times the ending of a work doesn't square with what the reader expects: the confrontation between Potter and Scratchy ends not in a fusillade of bullets but a flurry of words. To add to the irony, Potter wins because he is armed with a new and unfamiliar weapon—his wife. The emotional impact of an ironic ending depends upon the circumstances of plot and character. As Scratchy walks off, we're likely to view matters with amusement. In other cases, we might register joy, horror, gloom, or almost anything else.

Writing About Irony   Start by answering these questions:

Where does irony occur?

What does it accomplish?

What could my thesis be, and how could I support it?

In probing for irony, check for statements that say one thing and mean something else, situations in which one character knows something that another doesn't, and contrasts between the ways characters should and do behave. Review the plot to see whether the outcome matches the expectations.

To prove that irony is intended, examine the context in which the words are spoken or the events occur. Also, tell the reader what the irony accomplishes. In "The Bride," it is ironic that someone as wild as Scratchy Wilson would be awed by, and retreat from, Potter's wife; yet this irony is central to the idea that the Old West, despite its violence, was no match for the civilizing forces of the East.

EXERCISE

Discuss the irony in this poem:

Yet Do I Marvel

Countee Cullen

I doubt not God is good, well-meaning, kind,
And did He stoop to quibble could tell why
The little buried mole continues blind,
Why flesh that mirrors Him must some day die,
Make plain the reason tortured Tantalus[2]
Is baited by the fickle fruit, declare
If merely brute caprice dooms Slsyphus[3]
To struggle up a never-ending stair.
Inscrutable His ways are, and immune
To catechism by a mind too strewn
With petty cares to slightly understand
What awful brain compels His awful hand.
Yet do I marvel at this curious thing:
To make a poet black, and bid him sing!

Theme

Theme Factors   The theme of a literary work is its controlling idea, some observation or insight about life or the conditions and terms of living, such as the prevalence of evil, the foolishness of pride, or the healing power of love.

[2]In Greek mythology, a king confined to hell who is teased by water and fruit trees forever beyond his reach.
[3]In Greek mythology, a king confined to hell who must continually roll a heavy rock up a hill and then see it roll back down.

actually proves to be warm and deeply concerned about students. You could discuss examples in class, first identifying one or two discrepancies yourself and then gradually having students point out those in the remaining examples.

TEACHING STRATEGY
Like symbols, irony is usually discussed in connection with a character or theme rather than as the primary emphasis in a literary paper.

EXERCISE ANSWER
1. Cullen makes two ironic points in this poem. First, he draws a contrast between the goodness of God and the physical shortcomings, suffering, and death in God's world. Then, racism clearly in mind, he notes the irony of expecting song from a black poet like himself. The phrase "marvel at this curious thing" strongly suggests that he finds the second irony harder to accept than the first.

PERSPECTIVE
Since we read literature not simply as an art form but also for insights into life, much of the writing about literature is about theme. Students, however, experience problems

when approaching this element. First, many of them see works as having only one theme. Instead, of course, it is the endless suggestiveness that allows us to go back to the best works repeatedly. Second, students tend to reduce theme to a simple generalization rather than recognize that it emerges from the actual dynamics of the story and how it is developed.

Many literary works suggest several themes: sometimes one primary motif and several related ones, sometimes a number of unrelated motifs. Theme is central to a work of literature; frequently all of the other elements help develop and support it.

On occasion, the writer or a character states the theme directly. Mrs. Alving, the main character in Henrik Ibsen's play *Ghosts,* notes that the dead past plays a powerful and evil role in shaping human lives:

> . . . I am half inclined to think that we are all ghosts, Mr. Manders. It is not only what we have inherited from our fathers and mothers that exists again in us, but all sorts of old dead ideas and all kinds of old dead beliefs and things of that kind. They are not actually alive in us; but there they are dormant, all the same, and we can never be rid of them.

Ordinarily, though, the theme remains unstated and must be deduced by examining the other elements of the literary work.

Writing About Theme   Before you begin writing, ask and answer these questions:

What are the themes of this work? Which of these should I write about? Are they stated or unstated?

If stated, what elements support them?

If unstated, what elements create them?

What, if any, thematic weaknesses are present?

TEACHING STRATEGIES
1. Have students explain in a journal or as a class how the story either confirmed or changed their view of the world. Then have them articulate how that attitude might be a theme and, in turn, how it is realized in the text.
2. After students have identified a theme, have them list some of the associated themes and identify how these themes are developed in the text. Students tend to suppress the conflicts and contradictions in a theme in order to reduce it to the simplest form. Encourage them to note any conflicts and where they are resolved. For example, in "The Bride," there is a clear conflict between eastern society and the Wild West.

Check the comments of the characters and the narrator to see whether they state the themes directly. If they don't, assess the interaction of characters, events, settings, symbols, and other elements to determine them.

Let's see how the elements of Nathaniel Hawthorne's short story "Young Goodman Brown" work together to yield the primary theme. The story has four characters—Goodman Brown; his wife, Faith; Deacon Gookin; and Goody Cloyse—whose names symbolically suggest that they are completely good. Another symbol, Faith's pink hair ribbon, at first suggests innocence and later its loss. The story relates Brown's nighttime journey into a forest at the edge of a Puritan village and subsequent attendance at a baptismal ceremony for new converts to the Devil. He proceeds into the forest, suggestive of mystery and lawlessness, during a dark night, suggestive of evil, where he meets his guide, the Devil in the guise of his grandfather. As he proceeds, Brown vacillates between reluctance to join the Devil's party and fascination with it. Innocent and ignorant, he is horrified when he finds that the deacon and Goody Cloyse seem to be in league with the Devil. Brown tries to preserve his pure image of his wife, Faith, but her pink ribbon falls out of a tumultuous sky seemingly filled with demons, and Brown sees her at the baptismal ceremony. He shrieks out to her to "resist the wicked one" and is suddenly alone in the woods, not knowing whether she obeyed. The end of the story finds Brown back in his village, unable to view his wife and neighbors as anything but totally evil.

In light of these happenings, it's probably safe to say that the primary theme of the story is somewhat as follows:

Human beings are a mixture of good and evil, but some individuals can't accept this fact. Once they realize that "good" people are susceptible to sin, they decide that everyone is evil, and they become embittered for life.

Point out any thematic weakness that you find. Including a completely innocent major character in a story written to show that people are mixtures of good and evil would contradict the writer's intention.

A paper on theme is basically an argument, first presenting your interpretation and then supporting it with textual evidence. You might argue that the primary theme of "The Bride" is the demise of the Old West under the civilizing influence of the East. You could cite the luxurious Pullman car in contrast to the drab town, Potter's uncomfortable submission to the waiter and porter, and Scratchy Wilson's retreat at the story's end. In addition, you could suggest a related theme: People out of their element often founder—sometimes even appear ridiculous. As support, you might point to Potter's behavior on the train, the drummer's subdued attitude when Scratchy's arrival is imminent, and Scratchy's reaction when told about Potter's wife.

EXERCISE

State the controlling idea of this poem by Emily Dickinson:

'Twas like a Maelstrom, with a notch,
That nearer, every Day,
Kept narrowing its boiling Wheel
Until the Agony

Toyed coolly with the final inch
Of your delirious Hem—
And you dropt, lost,
When something broke—
And let you from a Dream—

As if a Goblin with a Gauge—
Kept measuring the Hours—
Until you felt your Second
Weigh, helpless, in his Paws—
And not a Sinew—stirred—could help,
And sense was setting numb—
When God—remembered—and the Fiend
Let go, then, Overcome—

As if your Sentence stood—pronounced—
And you were frozen led
From Dungeon's luxury of Doubt
To Gibbets, and the Dead—

And when the Film had stitched your eyes
A Creature gasped "Reprieve"!
Which Anguish was the utterest—then—
To perish, or to live?

EXERCISE ANSWER
Dickinson's controlling idea, which is presented in the last stanza and stated in the form of a question, might be expressed as follows: The anguish of an individual who suffers but survives an excruciating ordeal perhaps exceeds the anguish of an ordeal that ends in death.

Ethical Issues

TEACHING STRATEGIES
1. You might want to discuss these two cases with your class.
2. John Linsom writes reviews for his local paper. He has long had mixed feelings about fantasy fiction, so when he reviewed *Harry Potter and the Goblet of Fire,* a children's book, he compared it with several great works of literature and reached the conclusion that *Harry* was useless nonsense. Was his review ethical? Why or why not?
3. Joan Findley analyzed the theme of Jack

When you write about literature, you'll need to be aware of certain ethical considerations. Imagine someone reading only part of a short story and then writing a scathing analysis that suggests he has read the entire work. Imagine a thematic analysis of a novel that deliberately ignores large sections of the text in order to develop a twisted interpretation about the evils of capitalism. Imagine citing atypical quotations from the heroine of a play that deliberately create a distorted impression of her character. To help fulfill your ethical responsibility, ask and answer the following questions.

- Have I read the entire work carefully?
- Is my interpretation supported by the preponderance of textual evidence? Does it avoid deliberate distortion? A student who emphasizes a story's passing description of the pleasant feelings that accompany cocaine use while downplaying the drug's progressive effects that destroy a character could send a dangerous message.
- Have I avoided using quotations that are atypical or taken out of context?
- Is my interpretation fair to the text and the author rather than distorting events to promote an agenda?

Writing a Paper on Literature

The Writing Procedure

Kerouac's *On the Road* for her college writing class. She saw the novel as a work about personal liberation and spontaneity that depends on defying society's norms. Her paper praised the search for complete freedom. She liked the paper so much that she later used it, without comment, when teaching a tenth-grade class. Was it ethical to use the paper as she did? Why or why not?

PERSPECTIVE
You can help students write a paper about literature by giving them some sense of purpose and audience. If a class discussion of some work has raised questions of interest to your students, clearly the purpose of their writing should be to share their insights. In general, students will write

Focusing, gathering information, organizing, writing, revising, and editing—the same procedure leads to success in a literature paper as in any other type.

First, make sure you *understand the assignment*. Let's assume you have been asked to do the following:

Write a 750-word essay that analyzes one of the elements in Stephen Crane's "The Bride Comes to Yellow Sky." Take into account all the pertinent factors of whatever element you choose.

For this assignment you could focus on plot, point of view, character, setting, symbols, irony, or theme.

Next, *decide on a suitable topic*. For papers on literature, your best approach is to reread the work carefully and then reflect on it. As you do this for the assignment on "The Bride," you rule out a paper centering on plot, setting, irony, point of view, or theme. Because your class has discussed the first three so thoroughly, you doubt you can offer anything more. The matter of the narrator stumps you; you can understand why Crane uses a third-person narrator who airs Potter's thoughts, but you can't see what's accomplished by the brief looks into other characters' minds. Regarding theme, you doubt you can do justice to the topic in 750 words. As you mentally mine character and symbolism for possible topics, your thoughts turn to the many gunfighters you've watched in the movies and read about in western fiction. Because gunfighters have always fascinated you and Scratchy Wilson seems an intriguing example of the breed, you decide to analyze his character.

To complete the next stage, *gathering information*, reread the story again and as you do, list all pertinent information about Scratchy that might help develop a character analysis. Your efforts might yield these results:

1. Scratchy "a wonder with a gun."
2. "about the last one of the old gang that used to hang out along the river here."
3. "He's a terror when he's drunk," the opposite otherwise.
4. Potter "goes out and fights Scratchy when he gets on one of these tears."
5. Has shot Scratchy once, in the leg.
6. Does nothing to stop "tears" from happening.
7. On street, Scratchy "in a rage begot of whisky." Neck works angrily.
8. Utters "Cries of ferocious challenge."
9. Moves with "the creeping movement of the midnight cat."
10. Guns move "with an electric swiftness."
11. Clothes—maroon shirt, gilded red-topped boots—not adult western garb.
12. Doesn't shoot dog.
13. Doesn't try breaking down doors.
14. Warns Potter not to go for gun rather than shooting him.
15. Says he'll hit Potter with gun, not shoot him, if Potter doesn't "mind what I tell you."
16. Only sneers when Potter calls him "damn fool," and when Potter says, "If you're goin' to shoot me up, you better begin now; you'll never get a chance like this again."
17. Backs down and walks away when confronted with Potter's marriage.

List in hand, you are now ready to *organize your information*. As you examine your items and answer the questions about character on page 321, you start to realize that Scratchy is not merely a one-dimensional gunslinging menace. To reflect your discovery, you prepare a formal topic outline.

I. Bartender's assessment
   A. Evidence that Scratchy is a menace
      1. A wonder with a gun
      2. Former outlaw gang member
      3. A terror when drunk
   B. Contradictory evidence
      1. Mild when sober
      2. Only one actual shootout with Potter

II. Scratchy's behavior
   A. Evidence that Scratchy is a menace
      1. Rage
      2. Wary movements
      3. Skillful handling of guns

better if they see themselves helping an actual reader gain a new perspective on a work of literature.

TEACHING STRATEGY
An interesting discussion of the work can establish the context for writing assignments. Furthermore, students benefit if you discuss the range of papers they might possibly write and the ways they could approach them. Finished papers might be copied or exchanged as a way of carrying on the discussion.

B. Contradictory evidence
  1. Mode of dress
  2. Failure to shoot dog
  3. Failure to try breaking down doors
  4. Behavior during confrontation
  5. Final retreat

The next stage, *developing a thesis statement,* presents few difficulties. After examining the outline and thinking about its contents, you draft the following sentence:

A close look at Scratchy Wilson shows that he has much more depth than his pulp fiction counterparts.

Drawing on your notes and following your outline, you now *write a first draft* of your essay, and then follow up with the necessary revising and editing. In addition, you review the story and verify your interpretation.

As you *prepare your final draft,* follow these guidelines.

Handling Quotations   Like aspirin, quotations should be used when necessary, but not to excess. Cite brief, relevant passages to support key ideas, but fight the urge to quote huge blocks of material. Place short quotations, fewer than five lines, within quotation marks and run them into the text. For longer passages, omit the quotation marks and indent the material ten spaces from the left-hand margin. When quoting poetry, use a slash mark (/) to show the shift from one line to the other in the original: "A honey tongue, a heart of gall, / Is fancy's spring, but sorrow's fall." Pages 432–434 provide added information on handling quotations.

Documentation   Document ideas and quotations from outside sources by following the guidelines on pages 451–456.

If your instructor wants you to document quotations from the work you're writing about, include the information within parentheses following the quotations. For fiction, cite the page number on which the quotation appeared: (83). For poetry, cite the word "line" or "lines" and the appropriate numbers: (lines 23–24). For plays, cite act, scene, and line numbers, separated by periods: (1.3.18–19). When discussing a work of fiction not in your textbook, identify the book you used as your source. Your instructor can then easily check your information. In short papers like the following student essay, internal documentation is often omitted.

Tense   Write your essay in the present rather than the past tense. Say "In *The Sound and the Fury,* William Faulkner uses four narrators, each of whom provides a different perspective on the events that take place," not ". . . William Faulkner used four narrators, each of whom provided a different perspective on the events that took place."

SAMPLE STUDENT ESSAY ON **LITERATURE**

Scratchy Wilson: No Cardboard Character
Wendell Stone

Stephen Crane's short story "The Bride Comes to Yellow Sky" is artful on several counts. For one thing, the story is rich in irony. It makes use of an elaborate set of symbols to get its point across. It is filled with vivid language, and in Jack Potter and Scratchy Wilson it offers its readers two very unusual characters. Potter's actions and thoughts clearly show that he is a complex person. In fact, his complexity is so conspicuous that it becomes easy to regard Scratchy as nothing more than a one-dimensional badman. But this judgment is mistaken. A close look at Scratchy shows that he, like Potter, has much more depth than his pulp fiction counterparts.

Nothing in what the bartender says about Scratchy hints that there is anything unusual about the old outlaw. We learn that Scratchy is "a wonder with a gun," that he is "about the last one of the old gang that used to hang out along the river here," and that "He's a terror when he's drunk" but mild-mannered and pleasant at other times. One thing may strike the careful reader as a little odd, though. Although Potter "goes out and fights Scratchy when he gets on one of these tears," he has wounded Scratchy just once, and then only in the leg. Apparently, Potter has been able to talk the supposed terror out of a shootout each of the other times. Nor has Potter apparently tried doing anything to stop Scratchy's "tears."

As he steps onto the main street of Yellow Sky, Scratchy seems every bit as menacing as the bartender has described him. His face flames "in a rage begot of whisky," the cords in his neck throb and bulge with anger, and he hurls "cries of ferocious challenge" at the barricaded buildings. Scratchy is clearly no stranger to either weapons or shootouts. He walks with "the creeping movement of the midnight cat," moves his revolvers with "an electric swiftness," and keeps constantly on the alert for an ambush.

Nevertheless, Scratchy comes across as less than totally menacing. For one thing, his maroon shirt and gilded, red-topped boots make him look not like a westerner but like some child's notion of one. When he sees the dog, he deliberately shoots to frighten rather than to kill it. And in spite of all his

Continued on next page

Continued from previous page

bluster, he makes no real attempt to break down any doors and get at the people hiding behind them. Scratchy's clothing shows that eastern ways have touched even this "child of the earlier plains." But one could easily argue that eastern gentleness has had some slight softening influence on him, too. Be that as it may, it seems evident that Scratchy, perhaps without quite realizing it himself, is mainly play-acting when he goes on his rampages and that Potter knows this.

During the whole final confrontation, Scratchy seems more of an actor than a gunman wanting revenge against his "ancient antagonist." Instead of shooting when Potter makes a slight movement, Scratchy warns him not to go for a gun and says that he intends to take his time settling accounts, to "loaf along with no interferin'." Significantly, he threatens to hit Potter with a gun, not shoot him, if the marshal does not "mind what I tell you." Even when Potter, recovered from his brief fright, calls Scratchy a "damn fool" and says "If you're goin' to shoot me up, you better begin now: you'll never get a chance like this again," Scratchy does nothing except sneer. This confrontation, like all but one of the others, ends with no shots fired. But one thing is different. Potter's marriage has forced Scratchy to realize that something unstoppable is changing the Old West forever. When he drops his revolver to his side, stands silent for a while, and then says, "I s'pose it's all off now," we sense that he means not just this episode but any future clashes as well.

Scratchy is not a cardboard creation. His behavior is by no means as easily explainable as it at first seems, and he is capable of some degree of insight. Nonetheless, Scratchy remains very much a creature of the past, something that time has passed by. As he leaves, his feet make "funnel-shaped tracks," reminiscent of hourglasses, in the sand. Soon these tracks, along with Scratchy and his way of life, will disappear.

EXERCISE ANSWER
The student should note that Campion presents a highly idealized image of the woman he writes about. Shakespeare presents a much more realistic assessment of his mistress, yet asserts, in the final two lines of the poem, that his love ("mistress") is every bit as precious as any woman ("she") lied about ("belied") through false comparison.

Including the Views of Others

Obviously you are not the first one to write about an established piece of literature. To help deepen your understanding, your instructor may ask you to draw upon various sources that analyze the work you are discussing.

As you read these secondary sources, jot down any insights you find helpful. Be sure to record the name of the author and the source so that you can document appropriately and therefore avoid plagiarism. (For an explanation of plagiarism and when you need to document a source, see "Avoiding Plagiarism" in Chapter 21.) Keep track of where you disagree or have a different insight. Some students keep a reading journal in which they record useful quotes or information about both the piece of literature and the secondary source.

When you write the paper, you can synthesize (see pages 149–150) the views of the critics you've read and offer them as additional support for your view. Alternatively, you might summarize the conclusions, or perhaps the conflicting views, of critics and then offer your own observations along with appropriate support. Think of writing in response to others' views as entering a conversation with friends about a good book; they have their opinions, but your insights will add something to the discussion.

Using the guidelines offered in this chapter, write a short essay comparing and contrasting the two writers' assessments of the women in the following poems. (You might find it helpful to review pages 210–218 on comparison.) Limit your focus and back any general statements you make with appropriate support from the poems.

There Is a Garden in Her Face

Thomas Campion (1617)

There is a garden in her face,
Where roses and white lilies grow;
A heavenly paradise is that place,
Wherein all pleasant fruits do flow.
There cherries grow which none may buy
Till "Cherry ripe" themselves do cry.

Those cherries fairly do inclose
Of orient pearl a double row,
Which when her lovely laughter shows,
They look like rosebuds filled with snow;
Yet them nor peer nor prince can buy,
Till "Cherry ripe" themselves do cry.

Her eyes like angels watch them still;
Her brows like bended bows do stand.
Threat'ning with piercing frowns to kill
All that attempt with eye or hand
Those sacred cherries to come nigh,
Till "Cherry ripe" themselves do cry.

SUGGESTED INSTRUCTOR READINGS

Biatt, G. T., and L. M. Rosen. "The Writing Response to Literature." The Journal of Reading 28 (1984): 8–12. Reviews how writing can serve as an important vehicle for understanding literature.

Lodge, D., ed. 20th-Century Criticism. London: Longman, 1972. Contains many of the key twentieth-century essays on literary criticism. While no substitute for reading Richards, Empson, Brooks, and others, it provides an effective overview of many of the key issues in contemporary criticism.

Moran, C. "Teaching Writing/Teaching Literature." College Composition and Communication 32 (1981): 21–29. Gives helpful suggestions for effectively combining the teaching of writing and the teaching of literature.

Rosenblatt, L. The Reader, The Text, The Poem: The Transactional Theory of the Literary Work. Carbondale, IL: Southern Illinois UP, 1994. Provides helpful insights into how students read literature and experience the literary work.

Scott, P. G. "Flowers in the Path of Science: Teaching Composition Through Traditional High Literature."

College English 42
(1980): 1–9. Reviews the
reasons that literature
can sometimes be an
important ingredient
for a successful
composition class.

Sonnet 130

William Shakespeare (1609)

My mistress' eyes are nothing like the sun;
Coral is far more red than her lips red;
If snow be white, why then her breasts are dun;
If hairs be wires, black wires grow on her head.
I have seen roses damask'd, red and white,
But no such roses see I in her cheeks;
And in some perfumes there is more delight
Than in the breath that from my mistress reeks.
I love to hear her speak, yet well I know
That music hath a far more pleasing sound;
I grant I never saw a goddess go;
My mistress, when she walks, treads on the ground.
And yet, by heaven, I think my love as rare
As any she belied with false compare.

Research Guide

Much of your college and workplace writing will require some type of research—obtaining information from one or more sources to help achieve your writing purpose. The nature of your writing task and the demands of the situation determine the format you use and the way you document your sources.

This section of the text explores in detail the research tools and procedures you will use to develop various types of papers and reports. Sometimes you'll draw upon books, magazines, newspapers, and other printed sources, as well as electronic sources, in order to prepare a longer library research paper; at other times you'll do the same for shorter papers. Still other situations call for using primary research—the type in which you develop the information you use—to accomplish your purpose. The three chapters in this section will help you to meet these writing demands.

Chapter 20 explains how to choose a suitable library research topic and then focuses on carrying out the necessary steps to write a research paper. The chapter includes a continuing case history that leads to a finished paper complete with margin notes that will provide guidance as you prepare your own paper.

Chapter 21 shows how to prepare correct references for your paper's bibliography. It also shows the correct formats for references within the body of the paper, explains how to handle quotations, and offers guidelines for avoiding plagiarism.

Chapter 22 explains and illustrates the most common primary research strategies—interviews, questionnaires, and direct observations. In each case, student models, annotated with margin notes, embody the key features of that strategy.

Together, the material in these three chapters should provide all the information you'll need to complete writing assignments that require research.

CHAPTER 20

The Research Paper

Scene: A dark, sinister-looking laboratory. In the center of the stage stands a large laboratory bench crowded with an array of mysterious chemistry apparatus. Tall, cadaverous, and foreboding, Dr. Frankenslime leers as he pours the contents of a tube through a funnel and into a bubbling flask. A short, hunched-over figure looks on with interest. Suddenly the doctor spreads his arms wide and flashes a sardonic smile.

Frankenslime: Igor! At last! At last I've got it! With this fluid, I can control . . .

Research yes. But not all researchers are mad scientists, or scientists, or even mad. You might not be any of these things, but no doubt you'll be asked to prepare a *library research paper* for your composition class. This assignment calls for you to gather information from a variety of sources and then to focus, organize, and present it in a formal paper that documents your sources. The procedure will familiarize you with the mechanics of documentation, and when you finish you'll have a solid grasp of your topic and pride in your accomplishment. In addition, the experience will help you learn how to meet the research demands of other courses and your job.

For many students, the thought of writing a research paper triggers feelings of anxiety and fears of drudgery. Some feel overwhelmed by the amount of material in a college library and the need to make a lengthy search for useful information. Others doubt that they could have anything more to say about any topic they might choose: What's the point of simply rehashing what experts have already said much better? Still others are daunted by how much there might actually be to say about their topic.

But writing a research paper really isn't so formidable. You can acquaint yourself with the various library resources that will provide easy access to the

PERSPECTIVE
The reports of the research paper's demise have been, of course, greatly exaggerated; the research paper is still the key assignment in many courses. Furthermore, many professionals do on-the-job research-report writing: Business people detail new production methods, social workers explore the effects of a new law, and hospital pharmacists relate developments in their field. To advance in many fields, students must be able to research, synthesize, and report on published information that affects their occupation.

TEACHING STRATEGY
Students often believe that research papers are busywork. To counter this notion, have them interview faculty or working professionals in their fields to determine the role of research writing and then report back to the class. If this is too impractical, you could have students review publications in their fields to determine what kinds of reports are written and why.

information you need. Reading what others have written on a topic will give you a chance to draw your own conclusions. And as a writer you can limit your topic so that it doesn't balloon out of control.

Research writing is common both in the classroom and on the job. A history professor might require a long report on the causes of the Vietnam War. A business instructor might ask you to trace the history of a company, evaluate an advertising campaign, or review the latest styles of management. A building trades instructor might call for a short report that compares the effectiveness of several new insulating materials. At work, a marketing analyst might report on the development costs, sales potential, and competition for a product the company is considering introducing. An engineer might write a journal article that summarizes recent developments in plastic fabrication. A physical therapist might prepare a seminar paper that evaluates different exercise programs to follow arthroscopic surgery.

Whatever the writing project, let your purpose guide your research and determine the information you elect to use. When you write, the conclusions you have reached from thinking about what you have read and your purpose in communicating, not your notes, should dictate what you say.

PERSPECTIVE
Students often know little about researching in the library. Some don't understand how to use a card catalog. Most are unfamiliar with periodical indexes. Hardly any know how to use the more specialized indexes and resources. And yet the ability to find essential information is important, even crucial, to their academic, professional, and personal lives. Rather than regarding libraries as academic torture chambers, students should see them as useful resources that provide information they'll need in order to complete college and on-the-job writing assignments and resolve personal problems such as getting a landlord to make repairs.

Learning About Your Library

Before starting a library research paper, take time to familiarize yourself with your library. Many college libraries offer guided tours, and almost all of them display floor plans that show where and how the books are grouped. If your library doesn't have tours, browse through it on your own and scan its contents. As you do, note the following features:

Card Catalog: The card catalog indexes the library's books and often most of its other holdings as well. Most colleges now have computerized card catalogs. Pages 350–354 discuss computerized catalogs.

Computerized Databases: These databases, like printed periodical indexes, provide listings of articles in magazines and newspapers, and some even provide the full text of the article. Information may be on compact discs or transmitted to the library by wire from another location. Pages 355–362 discuss databases.

Computers with Internet Access: These computers connect users to a worldwide network of organizations and individuals, providing access to an almost endless variety of information. Pages 363–369 discuss the Internet.

Stacks: These are the bookshelves that hold books and bound periodicals (magazines and newspapers). Stacks are either open or closed. Open stacks allow you to go directly to the books you want, take them off the shelf, and check them out. Closed stacks do not allow you direct access to shelved material. Instead, a staff member brings you what you want.

Periodical Area: Here you'll find current and recent issues of magazines and newspapers. If your topic calls for articles that have appeared within the last few months, you're likely to find them in this area.

Microfilm and Microfiche Files: Microfilm is a filmstrip bearing a series of photographically reduced printed pages. Microfiche is a small card with a set of photographically reduced pages mounted on it. Often, most of a library's magazine and newspaper collection is on film. Ask a librarian how to work the viewing machines. Once you can run them, you'll have access to many library resources.

Circulation Desk: Here's where you check materials in and out, renew books you want to keep longer, and pay overdue fines. If you can't find something you want, the desk clerk will tell you whether it's missing, on reserve, or checked out. If it's out, fill out a hold card, and the library will notify you when it is available.

Reserve Area: This area contains books that instructors have had removed from general circulation so students can use them for particular courses. Ordinarily, you can keep these books for only a few hours or overnight.

Reference Area: This area houses the library's collection of encyclopedias, periodical indexes, almanacs, handbooks, dictionaries, and other research tools that you'll use as you investigate your topic. You'll also find one or more reference guides—Eugene P. Sheehy's *Guide to Reference Books* (1996), for example—that direct you to useful reference tools. To ensure that these books are always available, they must be used in the library. Someone is usually on duty to answer questions.

TEACHING STRATEGY
You might develop an extensive library assignment that requires students to find a wide-ranging variety of information on such matters as the side effects of medication or the toxic waste sites located in their state. Depending on your students' abilities, you can specify the source and call numbers, just the source, the type of source, or provide no assistance at all. Students might be assigned to work in teams (since they will anyway). It's helpful to spend some time in the library with students when they are doing such assignments.

TEACHING STRATEGIES
1. Since few students are experienced in selecting suitable research topics, you might provide some guidelines. An assignment

Choosing a Topic

Instructors take different approaches to assigning library research papers. Some want explanatory papers, others want papers that address a two-sided question, and still others allow students a free choice. An explanatory paper takes no position but provides information that gives the reader a better grasp of the topic. For example, it may explain the key advantages of solar heating, thereby clearing up popular misconceptions. An argument paper, on the other hand, attempts to sway the reader toward one point of view—for instance, that solar heat is commercially feasible. Some instructors specify not only the type of paper but also the topic. Others restrict students to a general subject area, ask them to pick topics from lists, or give them free choice. If you have little to say in the selection, take a positive view: At least you won't have to wrestle with finding a topic.

Whatever the circumstances, it's a good idea to follow a schedule that establishes completion dates for the various stages of your paper. Such a timetable encourages you to plan your work, clarifies both your progress and the work remaining, and provides an overview of the project. You can use the following sample schedule as a guide, modifying the stages or adding other ones as necessary.

that specifies purpose and audience is often helpful. For instance, after discussing problems of concern to your state or local area, you could have each student write a research report for the governor or mayor, detailing one particular problem and arguing for some solution.

2. One way of teaching the research paper is to have everyone participate in a larger research project. The class might select a major problem, such as prison overcrowding, and then, after some initial reading, break this problem down

into smaller projects that individual students take up according to their interests. One student might explore the success of alternative punishment programs; another might consider whether we should spend funds on early prevention; a third could evaluate the effects of overcrowding on prisoners. When the project is finished, student reports could be bound into a document and used as a teaching tool for future classes.

3. A pacing schedule helps guard against the tendency of some students to procrastinate, especially on a project of this magnitude. Depending on your class, you could specify the dates or have students determine their own. The latter option teaches students to budget their time effectively. This type of schedule deters plagiarism, particularly if you inspect the work at each stage and ask students to revise according to your suggestions.

TEACHING STRATEGIES
1. To help students avoid dead-end topics, specify that papers must either recommend a solution to a problem or argue one side of a controversial issue. Significant problems and issues are rarely personal or found in a single source. More important, you instill the notion that students should use their sources for a purpose rather than merely collecting and displaying them.
2. You might show students how to generalize personal or recent topics and restrict broad ones.

Sample Schedule for a Library Research Paper

Activity	Targeted Completion Date
Topic Selection	_____
Working Bibliography	_____
Research Question and Tentative Thesis	_____
Note Taking	_____
Working Outline	_____
First Draft	_____
Revised Drafts	_____ _____ _____
Date Due:	_____

Topics to Avoid

If you have free rein to pick your topic, how should you proceed? To begin, rule out certain types of topic.

- Those based entirely on personal experience or opinion such as "The Thrills I Have Enjoyed Waterskiing" or "Colorado Has More [or Less] Scenic Beauty than New Mexico." Such topics can't be supported by library research. Don't hesitate, however, to include personal judgments and conclusions that emerge from your reading.
- Those fully explained in a single source. An explanation of a process, such as cardiopulmonary resuscitation, or the description of a place, such as the Gobi Desert, does not require coordination of materials from various sources. Although you may find several articles on such topics, basically they all contain the same information.
- Those that are brand new. Often it's impossible to find sufficient source material about such topics.
- Those that are overly broad. Don't try to tackle such elephant-sized topics as "The Causes of World War II" or "Recent Medical Advances." Instead, slim them down to something like "How Did Germany's Depression Contribute to the Rise of Hitler?" or "Eye Surgery with Laser Beams."
- Those that have been worked over and over, such as abortion and the legal drinking age. Why bore your reader with information and arguments that are all too familiar already?

EXERCISE

Using the advice on topics to avoid, explain why each of the following would or would not be suitable for a library research topic:

1. Genetic counseling
2. Neoconservatism

3. The fiber optics revolution
4. How last night's riot got started
5. Building a rock garden
6. A Third World hot spot as described on the evening news
7. Reforming the financing of presidential election campaigns

Drawing on Your Interests

Let your interests guide your choice. A long-standing interest in basketball might suggest a paper on the pros and cons of expanding the number of teams in the National Basketball Association. An instructor's lecture might spark your interest in a historical event or person, an economic crisis, a scientific development, a sociological trend, a medical milestone, a political scandal, or the influences on an author. An argument with a friend might spur you to investigate latch-key children. A television documentary might arouse your curiosity about a group of primitive people. A recent article or novel might inspire you to explore the occult or some taboo.

Be practical in selecting a topic. Why not get a head start on a particular aspect of your major field by researching it now? Some management, marketing, or advertising strategy; the beginnings of current contract law; medical ethics— all of these topics, and many others, qualify. Think about your audience, the availability of information, and whether you can fit it into the guidelines for your paper.

To develop a focus for your paper, it's often helpful to brainstorm, skim encyclopedia articles and other materials, and use the branching or clustering technique. If you're exploring the topic of child abuse, preparing a clustering diagram like the one in Figure 20.1 can help you decide how to narrow your topic as well as provide a rough map of areas to research. The more you brainstorm, the richer your map will be. Brainstorming often results in a series of questions, perhaps based on the writing strategies discussed in Chapters 8–16, that will help guide your research. Often it is helpful to state your main research question, followed by a series of related questions that elaborate on it. From our cluster example, a student wishing to explore the topic of psychological abuse might develop the following set of questions:

What can be done to help victims of psychological abuse?
    What is psychological abuse?
    What long-term and short-term effects does it have on a child?
    How can a child living at home be helped?
        Are there services to help limit the abuse?
        Is family therapy an option?
            What is family therapy, and what does it do?
    What psychological help is available for an adult who experienced
        childhood abuse?
        What therapies work best?
        What do they do?
        How effective are they?

While "How last night's riot got started" is obviously too current, it might be acceptable if recast as "What causes student riots at sporting events, and how can these riots be prevented?" While "The home computer revolution" is clearly too broad, it could be narrowed to "How do home computers serve the needs of those in their twenties?"

EXERCISE ANSWERS

1. Suitable. The topic is narrow enough to be discussed adequately, and material is available in periodicals, newspapers, and possibly books.

2. Unsuitable. The topic is too broad.

3. Unsuitable. The topic is too broad.

4. Unsuitable. The topic is too contemporary for sufficient source material to be available. Also, most riots lack sufficient significance to be suitable topics.

5. Unsuitable. This is a process paper, and any articles that might be found would probably repeat the same information.

6. Suitable. See item 1 for reasons. (If the place has become a hot spot *very recently*, it may not be a suitable topic because of lack of source material.)

7. Suitable. See item 1 for reasons.

PERSPECTIVE

Students often focus on their topic without considering their audience and purpose. Such a misplaced emphasis is one reason why many students write anemic papers: They are not writing to anyone but the teacher or for any reason except the grade.

TEACHING STRATEGIES

1. To show the range of potential audiences, give students specific topics, such as the effectiveness of different cancer treatments, and have them develop lists of possible audiences, such as physicians and families of cancer victims. Then have students indicate how the audience would influence the kind of research they would do and also the final report. Next, do the same thing with purpose. Will they be helping patients select a treatment? Trying to convince legislators to legalize a certain treatment? How would purpose influence the research and final report?

2. Encourage students to transform their topic ideas into questions. Questions call for responses, especially when related ones are clustered. Have students turn in sets of research questions for topics they have selected.

3. To keep students on track, you might require them to turn in an early prospectus. In it they should identify their topic, why it interests them, their potential audience and purpose, the initial research questions, what they know about the topic, and their next step in the project.

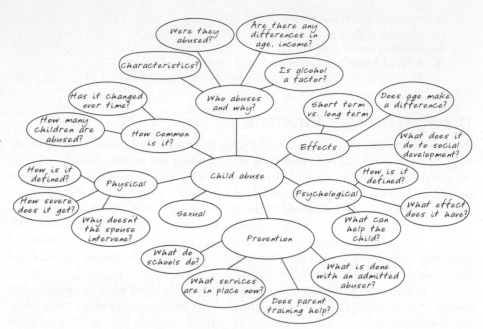

Figure 20.1 Clustering Diagram on Child Abuse

These questions make research easier. After all, the purpose of research is to answer questions. Later, as you examine source material, you will be seeking specific answers, not just randomly searching for information.

Encyclopedias are usually neither current enough nor sufficiently detailed to be major sources for a paper. They can, however, provide an overview of a topic's essential points and alert you to areas of controversy that you'll need to investigate in order to produce a thoughtful paper. You can consult both general and specialized encyclopedias, and other specialized publications are also available. If, for instance, you need material on a historical figure, you can check the *Dictionary of American Biography* for deceased American figures, the *Dictionary of National Biography* for deceased British figures, and the *McGraw-Hill Encyclopedia of World Biography*. Your librarian can suggest other useful resources. Once you've found your focus, the branching technique will allow you to expand the list of items obtained by brainstorming. Note that it may be tempting to turn to *Wikipedia*, an online encyclopedia, for background information. While you may find *Wikipedia* useful for getting an overview of your topic, you should note that most faculty consider *Wikipedia* a very unreliable source since anyone, regardless of their level of expertise, can add to or change a *Wikipedia* entry. Unless your instructor gives you permission, you should not use *Wikipedia* as a source for your paper and should confirm any *Wikipedia* information with more reliable, expert sources.

More often than not, things won't fall neatly into place as you probe for a topic and then a focus. Don't be discouraged by false starts and blind alleys. Think of yourself as an explorer who will gradually become well-versed in your chosen topic.

CASE HISTORY Keith Jacque was a first-year composition student majoring in criminal justice when he wrote the library research paper at the end of this chapter. The assignment was to write about a recent technological development or an innovative solution to a social problem. Intrigued by the possible solutions to the problem of prison overcrowding, Keith decided to explore several options: building more prisons, developing early release programs for the least dangerous criminals, setting up house-arrest programs verified by electronic monitoring systems, utilizing halfway houses, converting empty military bases into prisons, and reevaluating legal codes to determine which offenses should require incarceration. After a little thought, Keith realized that in order to develop his paper properly he would need to concentrate on only one option. Because he had recently watched a televised report on electronic monitoring and found it interesting, he decided to investigate this alternative.

To establish a focus for his paper, Keith drafted a series of questions suggested by the writing strategies discussed in Chapters 8–16. Here are the questions he developed:

Could I *narrate* a brief history of electronic monitoring?
Could I *describe* how a monitoring system works?
Could I *classify* monitoring systems?
Could I *compare* monitoring systems to anything?
Could I explain the *process* involved in monitoring?
What *causes* led to the development of monitoring?
What *effects* is monitoring likely to have?
What systems best *illustrate* the essence of monitoring?
Is there a widely accepted *definition* of electronic monitoring?
Could I *argue* for or against the expanded use of monitoring?

These writing strategies can often help you narrow a subject down to a manageable topic.

For background reading, Keith consulted two general encyclopedias: the *Encyclopedia Americana* and the *Encyclopaedia Britannica*. After preparing a list of possible entries that included "electronic monitoring," "electronic surveillance," "electronic incarceration," "home incarceration," and "house arrest," he began searching for those entries but found none of them. Next, he decided to look in more specialized publications. Not knowing how to proceed, he asked a reference librarian, who directed him to the latest editions of the *Encyclopedia of Crime and Justice* and the *McGraw-Hill Encyclopedia of Science and Technology*. These sources also contained no useful information.

At this point, drawing on what he had learned from his criminal justice instructor and the television report, Keith brainstormed in order to determine a possible focus for his paper. He came up with the following list:

1. Brief history of electronic monitoring
2. Technical problems in developing systems

Continued on next page

Continued from previous page

3. Types of monitoring systems
4. Benefits of monitoring
5. Problems associated with monitoring

Upon reflection, Keith eliminated the second item because it would require reading highly technical material, which he might not understand. The other items were interesting to him, and he believed that they would also interest his audience—fellow students at the vocationally oriented school he attended.

Next, Keith used branching to expand his list and guide his library search, concentrating on what he knew at this stage.

Benefits of monitoring
- reduces jail population
- less expensive than prison
- effective for non-violent offenders
- several systems available

Problems associated with monitoring
- signal interference problems
- legal concerns

CASE HISTORY Once Keith Jacque had selected a focus for his paper on electronic monitoring, he began compiling his working bibliography. First he turned to the computerized card catalog and began his search for books and government documents by typing in the subject entry "house arrest," but he found nothing. Next he tried "electronic monitoring of prisoners." This entry yielded a cross-reference directing him to the entries "punishment—United States" and "criminal statistics—analysis." These two entries yielded a list of seven books and eleven government documents. Further examination revealed that three of the books and four of the documents appeared promising.

Keith's search for periodical articles took him to the college's *InfoTrac* database. Using this system, he found three useful subject headings: "home detention," "electronic monitoring of prisoners," and "criminal statistics—analysis." A search of these subjects turned up twenty-four journal articles, all of which were available in the library. Eight looked as if they would be useful. Three newspaper articles seemed suitable, and a search of *NewsBank* revealed another promising newspaper article.

Since his library offered access to the Internet, Keith also searched the World Wide Web. He used the Lycos and Yahoo search engines and entered complete phrases such as "electronic incarceration," "home detention," "electronic monitoring," and "incarceration, electronic." Many of the Web sites he found were not relevant to his topic, but he persisted and finally found two that seemed promising. One, from an organization concerned with public policy, discussed the indirect costs of incarceration. The other, from the Probation Division of Georgia's Department of Corrections, discussed alternatives to jail sentences.

After completing his search for library and Internet sources, Keith sought and obtained his instructor's permission to conduct primary research on his topic. Unsure of how to proceed, he talked to his advisor in the criminal justice department. She suggested that he ask the director of Michigan's electronic surveillance program for a personal interview. (See pages 440–442). He was able to obtain the interview, which provided information on the scope, operation, and success rate of the program as well as the savings it has achieved.

Satisfied that ample information was available, Keith carefully evaluated the content of the articles and of pertinent sections of the books and government documents he had located. His instructor had suggested that one good way to approach a topic is to pose a question about it and then draft a *tentative* answer, if possible. Here's how Keith proceeded:

> *Q.* What benefits does electronic monitoring offer jurisdictions that adopt it?
>
> *A.* Electronic monitoring is less expensive than incarceration, presents no serious problems, and offers a choice among several systems.

This answer provided a *tentative thesis*, an informed opinion that guided Keith's later note taking, giving him a sense of direction and indicating what information would probably prove useful and what was likely to be useless. Tentative theses can be altered slightly or changed completely if necessary. If later reading indicated that electronic monitoring can sometimes be more expensive than incarceration, Keith could alter his thesis accordingly.

CASE HISTORY Working bibliography in hand, Keith Jacque prepared note cards. Most of his notes were summaries of the source material, but in a few cases he chose quotations because of the importance of the source or the significance of the material. For example, one quotation cited a former U.S. Attorney General who pointed out the disproportionate number of crimes committed by habitual violent offenders. Another quotation cited a key reason for the growing use of electronic monitoring: the high cost of prisons. Still another detailed various difficulties encountered in transmitting signals.

As Keith took notes, a plan for his paper began to emerge. The introduction would explain the reasons behind the growing use of electronic monitoring. The body would present a brief history of monitoring and then detail the different kinds of systems, examine the problems encountered when using them, and point out their effectiveness.

CASE HISTORY Sorting and re-sorting was challenging and at times frustrating for Keith. Since some of his material could be arranged in different ways, he found himself experimenting, evaluating, and rearranging as he tried various options. After much thought and some trial and error, the following *initial draft* of his outline emerged:

I. Reasons why monitoring used
   A. Serious crime problem and number of people in prisons
   B. High cost of prisons
II. Brief history of electronic monitoring
III. Types of monitoring systems
   A. Programmed-contact systems
   B. Continuous-contact systems
   C. Hybrid systems
IV. Problems with these systems
   A. Practical problems
      1. Offenders' problems
      2. Transmission difficulties
   B. Legal problems
      1. Do the systems violate constitutional rights?
      2. "Net-widening" effect
V. Effectiveness of electronic monitoring
   A. Effectiveness with low-risk offenders
   B. Cost effectiveness
VI. Expanded use of monitoring likely

This version is marked by nonparallel structure and inadequate attention to some points. Despite these weaknesses, it provided an adequate blueprint for the first draft of Keith's paper.

CASE HISTORY Using his outline and thesis statement as a guide, Keith prepared a first draft of his paper, following the MLA format required by his instructor. It didn't all come easily. In order to ensure an effective presentation, he checked his note cards carefully to determine which material would provide the strongest support for his conclusions. He was careful to use his own words except when he was quoting. To achieve smoothness, he tried to connect his major sections with transitions, aware that he could polish these connections when he revised the paper.

When he had completed the first draft, Keith set it aside for two days in order to distance himself from his writing. Then he returned to it and revised it carefully. Reading the paper from the perspective of a slightly skeptical critic, he looked for unsupported claims, questions that readers might have, sections that might be confusing or poorly organized, and weak transitions. Like most writers, Keith found sections that could be improved. Next, he revised his initial topic outline and followed it when drafting the sentence outline that appears on pages 381–383. Keith then prepared the final draft of the paper itself, which is on pages 384–395. Direct your attention to its noteworthy features, which include italicized notations next to the paper indicating where Keith used the writing strategies discussed earlier in the text.

Assembling a Working Bibliography

Once you have a topic, you're ready to see whether the library has the resources you'll need to complete the project. This step requires you to check additional reference tools and compile a working bibliography—a set of cards that list promising sources of information. This section discusses these reference tools and how to use them.

Encyclopedias

What They Are   Encyclopedias fall into two categories, general and specialized. General encyclopedias, the *Encyclopedia Americana* and the *Encyclopaedia Britannica*, for instance, offer articles on a wide range of subjects. Specialized encyclopedias cover one particular field, such as advertising or human behavior. Here's a sampling of specialized encyclopedias:

Encyclopedia of Advertising
Encyclopedia of Education
Encyclopedia of Environmental Science
Encyclopedia of Human Behavior: Psychology, Psychiatry, and Mental Health
Encyclopedia of Social Work
Encyclopedia of World Art
Harper's Encyclopedia of Science
International Encyclopedia of the Social Sciences
McGraw-Hill Encyclopedia of Science and Technology

How to Use Them   Encyclopedias are sometimes a convenient launching pad for your investigation because they provide an overview of the broad field your topic fits into. For a nonspecialized topic, like the impact of commercial television during the 1950s, check the articles on television in one or more general encyclopedias. For a specialized aspect of television, say the development of the picture tube, consult one or more specialized encyclopedias, such as *Harper's Encyclopedia of Science* and the *McGraw-Hill Encyclopedia of Science and Technology*, along with the general encyclopedias. During this search you'll re-encounter material you scanned while trying to focus on a topic.

they search for sources. Library holdings may be inadequate; periodical issues may have been stolen or articles torn out of magazines; books may be checked out or mis-shelved. Students can quickly become frustrated. Confront this problem in class by discussing the difficulties students are having and suggesting possible solutions. Could they check the local public library? Look for a nearby organization that would have the information? Ask a faculty member for help? Visit their own city library or another college library while home for the weekend? Obtain the material through inter-library loan?

Encourage students to assess the strengths of their college library and capitalize on them. If it has an inadequate selection of scholarly periodicals but a large collection of popular magazines, encourage students to consider current topics for their papers.

Some instructors allow you to acknowledge encyclopedias as a source; others prohibit their use; and still others allow material from specialized, but not general, encyclopedias. As always, follow your instructor's wishes.

If you will be using encyclopedia sources, jot down the following information for each note you take:

Title of article

Author(s) of article (Not always available. Sometimes only initials at the end of an article identify an author. In that case, check the list of contributors at the front of the first volume for the full name.)

Name of encyclopedia

Year of publication

For specialized encyclopedias, also include the number of volumes in the set, the encyclopedia editor, and the place of publication.

Most important, check for bibliographies at the ends of articles and copy down any reference that looks promising.

Computer-Based Encyclopedias

Today, a number of encyclopedias, both general and specialized, are available on computer compact discs or over the Internet. They are easy to search and often allow you to search for a key phrase such as "Greek architecture." The results will guide you not only to articles devoted to your topic but also to others that refer to it, even if only in a paragraph. If you use an electronic encyclopedia, write down, in addition to the other source information, the publication medium, the name of the vendor (Microsoft, for example, for a Microsoft product), and the name and date of the electronic publication.

When you've finished your exploratory reading in encyclopedias, turn to the card catalog and periodical indexes—the prime sources of information for library research papers.

Computerized Card Catalog

What It Is   A computerized card catalog lists all the books in the library, usually along with other holdings like magazines, newspapers, government documents, and electronic recordings. It may also provide additional information, such as whether a book has been checked out and, if so, the return date. Some catalogs even include the holdings of nearby libraries. Books are usually cataloged using Library of Congress call numbers, although some libraries use the Dewey decimal system.

Several catalog systems are available, all having similar terminals that consist essentially of a viewing screen and a keyboard on which to enter requests for information. Some terminals also have printers for copying material shown on the screen. To use the unit properly, read the instructions at the terminal or ask a librarian. Remember, a computer can't think. It can only match the string of letters you type to similar strings of letters in its database. If you misspell a word, you will not find any matches.

Figure 20.2   The Online Catalog's opening screen allows you to select the type of search.
Software of Innovative Interface, Inc. Screens presented by permission of Innovative Interfaces, Inc.

Most systems let you conduct searches by key terms (those appearing in book titles and descriptions), author, title, and subject (based on the Library of Congress's cataloging system). Most systems now let you select the kind of search by a menu or icons as in Figure 20.2. Older systems have you type in a code such as—A for "author" or KT for "key term" and then, in some cases, an equal sign and your specific search request. Searching may require you to view a series of screens having increasingly specific instructions, with the final screen providing information from a single book. Figure 20.3 illustrates a keyword search. Figure 20.4 shows the list of works discovered by the search, including the publication date; Figure 20.5 one specific work, including the call number to locate the book in your library stacks, an indication of the availability of the book, a brief description of the contents, and a list of subjects that could be used in additional searches. Most libraries have handouts and training programs that explain the different symbols and options of their specific symbols.

Often, a key term search (see Figure 20.5) can be the most helpful way to approach a topic. In this type of search, the computer checks the titles and descriptions of books for the key terms you enter and lists any that it finds. Different key terms will produce varying strings of articles, so it is a good idea to try different words or phrases for the same topic. For example, if you're searching for material on "electric cars," you might also try "electronic cars," "alternative fuels," and so on. Because such searches are very rapid, you can experiment with different combinations of terms to focus your search. If, for instance, you're asked to write a paper on some aspect of Japanese culture, you might investigate such combinations as "Japanese business," "Japan and education," and "Japanese feminists." Because key term searches allow you to use logical terms like *and, or, but,* and *not,* they are especially useful for narrowing a broad focus.

Figure 20.3   Keyword Search

Figure 20.4   Results Screen. Click on the blue underlined terms to display more information.

FerrisNet

ONLINE CATALOG

| Previous Record | Next Record | Return to Browse | Another Search | Modify Search | MARC Display | Save This Record | Place a Hold |

(Search History) ◆

| WORD ◆ | acquaintance rape | Ferris State University ◆ | Search |

Sorted by Date

Author   Wiehe, Vernon R.

Title   **Intimate betrayal : understanding and responding to the trauma of acquaintance rape /**
            Vernon R. Wiehe, Ann L. Richards.

Publisher   Thousand Oaks : Sage Publications, c1995.

LOCATION	CALL #	STATUS
FSU Main Stacks Lower LVL	HV6561 .W53 1995	AVAILABLE

Copy call numbers to find the book

Descript.   xv, 214 p. : ill. ; 24 cm.

Bibliog.   Includes bibliographical references (p. 193-200) and index.

Contents   The problem -- The victim and the perpetrator -- The assault -- Survivors' response to their assault
           -- The assault's impact on the survivor -- Marital rape -- Understanding acquaintance rape --
           The legal aspects of acquaintance rape -- The counselor in the recovery process -- The survivor
           in the recovery process -- Preventing acquaintance rape.

Subject   Acquaintance rape -- United States.

             Rape victims   *Related subject(s) to search,*
             United States   *if desired*

Alt author   Richards, Ann L.

ISBN   0803973608 (cl. : acid-free paper)

             0803973616 (pbk. : acid-free paper)

Details about the book

| Previous Record | Next Record | Return to Browse | Another Search | Modify Search | MARC Display | Save This Record | Place a Hold |

(Search History) ◆

Figure 20.5 Detailed Search Results

Obtaining the Books Most researchers start with a key term search. Following the instructions in the paragraph on page 351, type in one or several terms, using the appropriate logical terms. Advanced search functions will allow you to limit the dates of your search if you are only looking for more recent texts.

Successful key term and subject searches often turn up more book titles than a single screen can accommodate. In this case, using a key designated at the bottom of the screen will let you review the rest of the list. With especially long lists, you may need to narrow your focus and start a new search.

Sometimes it is useful to conduct a subject search because such a search can produce different works and often a more focused list. If you find a book under term search, the screen will suggest related subjects, as in Figure 20.5. If you found a promising title in an encyclopedia or another source, enter the title exactly using the "title" code. The resulting title screen will also show possible subject headings. Usually you will start a subject search based on headings suggested by a term or title search. There are also reference tools to help. If your library uses the Library of Congress system, turn to the *Library of Congress Subject Headings*. If it uses the Dewey decimal system, consult the *Sears List of Subject Headings*.

When you have found a promising title, entering its number, or a command and the number, will call up a screen with relevant information. This is illustrated in Figure 20.5. With some systems, this screen indicates whether the book is in the library or checked out and tells you how to proceed if you can't find it on the shelf. With other systems, you can get the information by entering a command. Some systems even allow you to reserve a book by entering the request into the computer.

If your terminal has a printer, use it to make a copy of each promising reference. Otherwise, record the following information on a 3 × 5-inch note card:

Author(s)

Title

Editor(s) and translator(s), as well as author(s) of any supplementary material

Total number of volumes (if more than one) and the number of the specific volume that you want to use

City of publication

Name of publisher

Date of publication

Also, copy the book's call number in the upper left corner of the card.

Next, scan the books themselves. If your library stacks are closed, give the librarian a list of your call numbers and ask to see the books. If you can enter the stacks, locate the general areas where your books are shelved. Once you find a number range that includes one of your call numbers, follow the trail of guides on the book spines until you find your book. Spend a few extra minutes browsing in the general area of each book; you may discover useful sources that you overlooked in the card catalog.

Skim each book's table of contents and any introductory material, such as a preface or introduction, to determine its scope and approach. Also check the index and note the pages with discussions that relate to your topic. Finally, thumb through portions that look promising. If the book won't help you, throw away the note card.

If a book is missing from the shelf and the computer hasn't indicated that someone has checked it out, then it's probably on reserve. Check at the circulation desk; if the book is on reserve, go to that section and examine it there. If someone has checked the book out and the due date is some time away, perhaps a library nearby will have a copy.

How to Use It   Follow the procedure given on pages 350–354 for computerized card catalogs, making any needed modifications.

EXERCISE

1. **Select five of the following subjects. Go to the online card catalog and find one book about or by each. List each book's call number, author, title, publisher, and date of publication. Because subject headings may vary, investigate related categories, if necessary, to find an entry. To illustrate, if you find nothing under "mountaineering," check "mountain climbing" or "backpacking."**

1. AIDS research	16. Home schooling
2. The American family	17. The Internet and business
3. The American workplace	18. The Internet and games
4. Campaign reform	19. Stephen King
5. Cancer research	20. Bobby Knight
6. Charter schools	21. Barbara Mandrell
7. Children and divorce	22. Mountaineering
8. Hillary Clinton	23. Colin Powell
9. Diets	24. Robots
10. Electric cars	25. Laura Schlessinger
11. Gloria Estefan	26. School vouchers
12. Bill Gates	27. Tupac Shakur
13. Genetic research	28. Telecommunication
14. Global warming	29. Andrew Weil
15. HMOs	30. Oprah Winfrey

2. **Provide your instructor with a list of the books you found that appear useful for developing your paper's topic. For each book, furnish the information specified in Exercise 1, along with a brief note indicating why you think the book will be useful.**

Periodical and Database Indexes

What They Are   Periodical indexes catalog articles in magazines and newspapers. Indexes may be in book form, on microfilm or microfiche, or computerized. Some are offered in two or more forms. Computerized indexes, called *databases,* are available to libraries through subscription. Depending upon the particular database, information may be furnished on compact discs or transmitted via wire from a mainframe computer to the library. The term *CD-ROM* (compact disc, read-only memory) designates the first type of system, and *online* designates the second type. Databases are accessed through terminals equipped with a keyboard and a viewing screen. Some have printers that can supply lists of references and even copies of articles.

Updated frequently, sometimes every week, periodical indexes provide access to information that hasn't yet found its way into books and perhaps never will. Their listings allow you to examine new topics, follow developments in older ones, and explore your topic in greater depth than you could by using books alone. In short, indexes help you avoid doing a superficial paper.

The *Readers' Guide to Periodical Literature,* available since 1900 in printed form, is now available online and on compact discs. The *Guide* indexes the material in more than 200 widely circulated magazines—*Harper's, Newsweek, Scientific American,* and the like. Articles are indexed by subject and author, and other categories are indexed by title and author. The *Guide* is especially useful for finding material on historical events (say the Persian Gulf War or the Iran-Contra hearings) and on social, political, and economic developments (for instance, the assisted-suicide movement and the drive to limit the terms of political officeholders). The *Guide* also includes scientific, technical, and even literary articles intended for a general audience rather than specialists, but such articles do not include all the available research.

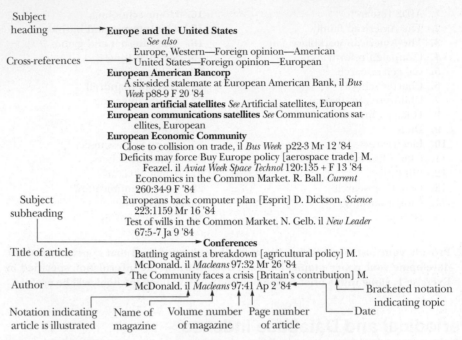

Figure 20.6 From *Readers' Guide to Periodical Literature,* May, 1984. Copyright © 1984 by the H. W. Wilson Company. Reproduced by permission.

The first pages in the printed version of the *Guide* identify the abbreviations used for the magazines indexed. Figure 20.6 shows the arrangement of the index and the "see also" cross-references that direct you to related subject headings.

The *Magazine Index,* available on microfilm or online, indexes some four hundred popular publications by author, title, and subject. Updated monthly, it covers a five-year period and includes references to articles no more than two weeks old. The viewing machines for units using microfilm resemble small television sets and have motorized controls that allow swift movement through the filmstrip. Accompanying the viewer are coded reels of microfilm containing the indexed articles, together with a reader/printer that allows you to read articles and obtain printed copies. Your librarian will demonstrate how these machines work. The producers of the index also publish a list of recent articles on twenty to thirty current topics.

The *National Newspaper Index* covers five national newspapers: the *Christian Science Monitor,* the *Los Angeles Times,* the *New York Times,* the *Wall Street Journal,* and the *Washington Post.* It is available on microfilm, on compact discs, and online. Each monthly issue covers two-and-one-half years of references, and back issues can be obtained on microfiche cards. Microfilm units have the same kind of viewer as the microfilm version of the *Magazine Index.*

The *New York Times Index* comes in printed and online form. It indexes, by subject, all news articles, book reviews, commentaries, and features that have appeared in the paper and briefly summarizes each listing. The index entries refer to the "late city edition" of the paper, the one most libraries have on microfilm.

If your library subscribes to a regional edition, an article may appear on another page or not at all.

NewsBank may be your best bet for a topic of regional interest. This CD-ROM database covers more than five hundred newspapers in all fifty states and Canada, indexing articles on politics, economics, business, the environment, and the entertainment world. It also offers the full text of many articles. A loose-leaf notebook version of *NewsBank,* accompanied by the articles on microfiche cards, is also available.

Database Indexes

Database indexes allow you to search quickly and effectively for articles in journals, magazines, and newspapers. Some databases such as *ERIC* (Educational Resources Information Center) and *Medline* (National Library of Medicine) give you access to citations of articles appearing in professional journals in a specific area. These articles, however, are usually aimed at a specialized audience and may be difficult to comprehend. Perhaps the best place to start a search is with a general periodical database such as *First Search* or *InfoTrac.* These databases provide access to listings of articles, arranged and subdivided by subject and key word, that have appeared in over a thousand magazines and newspapers, including the entries in various other indexes. Articles are sometimes accompanied by abstracts—brief summaries of the articles' main points—and increasingly the full articles are available on screen. *A word of caution: Don't mistake an abstract for the full article; an abstract is a*

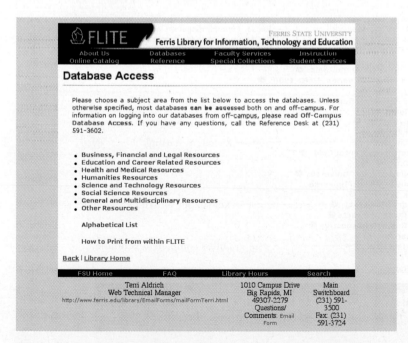

Figure 20.7 Initial Library Screen. From this list of database topics, choose the database that best matches the subject of your research.
Software by Innovative Interface, Inc.

200–300-word summary of a journal article and should not be used as a source. Always take notes on the full article. Also do not restrict your research to just articles available online. These databases are easy to operate. Your library probably has handouts that explain how to use your school's system and probably offers training sessions as well. Figure 20.7 as page 357 in an example of a database screen that allows the user to select a specific subject area which will make the databases for that area available. Unless you are prepared to use specialty information in an area, start by reviewing General and Multidisciplinary Resources.

Often the next screen offers you a choice of different databases. Many users find FirstSearch and Wilson Select Plus as useful places to start their research, but let your topic be your guide (Figure 20.8).

Subject Search   Because some periodical indexes, like *InfoTrac,* are organized around subject headings, it's a good idea to try a variety of subject terms because each will yield different articles. If your entry matches a subject heading or you are referred to a cross-reference, the computer will use a series of screens to direct you to a list of articles.

Figure 20.8   Second Library Screen. From this list of databases, you can choose those that are most likely to have resources you can use in your research papers.

Along the way, one of the screens may list subdivisions of the request being searched, as in the following example:

Acquaintance Rape, subdivisions of

—analysis
—cases
—investigation
—laws, regulations, etc.
—media coverage
—moral and ethical aspects
—personal narratives
—prevention
—psychological aspects
—research
—social aspects
—statistics
—studying and teaching
—usage

Such a list can uncover facets of your topic that you hadn't considered and that might enrich your final paper. For example, the subdivision "personal narratives" might contain an experience that would provide a powerful opening for the paper. Similarly, articles cataloged under "statistics" could provide information on the scope of the acquaintance rape problem.

Key Word Search   Most databases now allow you to search for a key term. Just follow the instructions for beginning the search and then enter your key term. If, for example, your topic is "teenage suicide," type "teenagers and suicide" onto the screen that's already showing and press the search or enter key. The computer will check titles and abstracts for the key terms and provide a list of the corresponding articles. Allow ample time to explore a number of possibilities. If you try several terms related to your topic, you will find a wider variety of articles that serve your purpose. Below is a sample database screen where users can indicate the term or terms they intend to search and, if desired, select limits on the search. You would be well served by not limiting your search initially unless your teacher has placed certain restrictions on the dates of sources (Figure 20.9).

Advanced Search   The final result of any search is a list of articles like the following one, obtained through General Reference Center Gold, for the search term "acquaintance rape":

Sometimes the result of a search may be formatted like the following list of magazine articles from an older version of Infotrac:

An open letter to a rape victim. Gail Elizabeth Wyatt. *Essence*, April 1992 v22 n12 p80(3). Mag. Coll.: 64B0749.
—Abstract Available—
Holdings: AS Magazine Collection

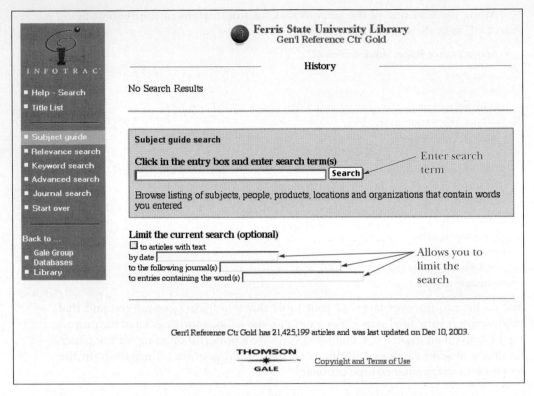

Figure 20.9 Search Screen for General Reference Center Gold.
Screens included by permission of Thomson Gale.

Between seduction and rape. (date rape) Kathy Dobie. *Vogue*, Dec 1991
v181 n12 p154(4). Mag. Coll.: 62G6035.
Abstract Available
Holdings: AS Magazine Collection

Rape on campus: is your daughter in danger? Kate Fillion. *Chatelaine*,
August 1991 v64 n8 p33(5). Mag. Coll.: 61A5794.
Holdings: AS Magazine Collection

The results for a search might look like the screen shot below. Notice that several
of the sources are available directly online by locating your cursor on the text
choice and clicking (Figure 20.10).

This list shows that all three magazines are available in the library and that two
articles are abstracted in the computer. (If the database provides the full text of an
article, the notation "full text available" will appear after the citation.) The coded
notation "Mag. Coll." indicates that the magazine is available on microfilm. The
first two numbers and the letter in the code identify the number of the microfilm
cassette. The remaining numbers indicate the microfilm page on which the article
starts. The exact listings of your system may be somewhat different from what's
shown here; the same kind of information, however, should be available.

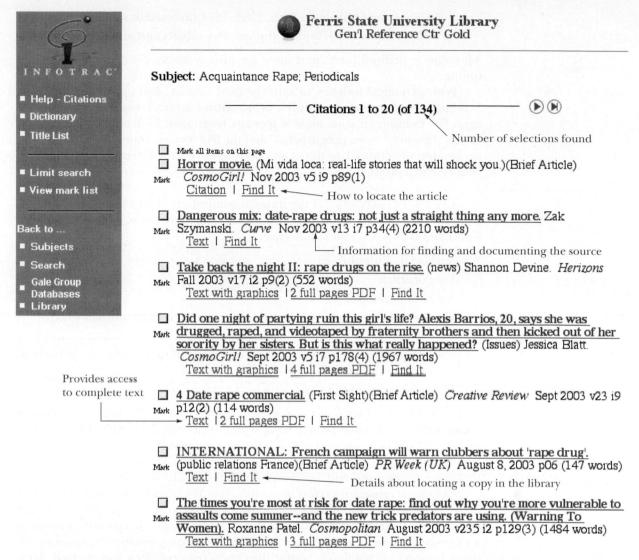

Figure 20.10 List of Results. Click on the blue underscored "Text" to see the complete article.

Besides the previously mentioned specialized indexes, many others are available that you could use to supplement your search of general indexes. Here is a brief sampling of them:

Applied Science and Technology Index, 1958–date (indexed by subject)

Education Index, 1929–date (indexed by subject and author)

Humanities Index, 1974–date (indexed by subject and author)

International Index to Periodicals, 1907–1964 (indexed by subject and author; titled *Social Sciences and Humanities Index,* 1965–1974, and then separated into the *Humanities Index* and the *Social Sciences Index*)

Social Sciences and Humanities Index, 1965–1974 (indexed by subject and author)

Social Sciences Index, 1975–date (indexed by subject and author)

All come in printed form, and most are also available on compact discs and online.

With periodical indexes, as with the card catalog, don't give up if a subject heading you're exploring yields few or no entries. Instead, explore related headings. For example, if your topic is teenage marriages, look also under "adolescence," "divorce," "teen pregnancies," and the like. Browse through the system and try a variety of options. Use this as an opportunity to gain different perspectives on your research project.

Obtaining the Articles   If the index is computerized and provides printouts, print a copy of each promising reference you find. Otherwise, copy the following information on a 3 × 5-inch note card.

Author(s), if identified

Title of article

Name of periodical

Volume or issue number (for professional and scholarly journals only)

Date of periodical

For newspapers, the edition name (city, metro) if more than one published, and section letter

The page range of the entire article

Obtain printouts of whatever articles you can and check the topic sentences of paragraphs for essential points. Also, scan any accompanying abstracts or summaries. If an article appears useful, check to see whether it has a bibliography, which might include additional useful sources. Keep the note cards for articles that seem promising—and any useful articles—and throw away the others.

Check the remaining references, including the ones from encyclopedia bibliographies, against the library's periodical catalog to see which periodicals are available and where they are located. Libraries frequently keep current issues in a periodical room or some other special section. Back issues of magazines are often kept on microfilm or bound into hardcover volumes and shelved. Most newspapers are on microfilm. Check the articles for which you don't have printouts in the same manner that you checked the others.

Select five of the following subjects and find one magazine article about each. Use at least three periodical indexes to locate the articles. List the author, if given; the title of the article; the name of the magazine; its date; the page range; and the name of the index used. Because subject categories may vary, investigate related categories, if necessary, to find an entry. To illustrate, if you find nothing under "bioengineered foods," check "genetically modified foods" or "bioaltered foods."

1. Animal rights
2. Bandwidth technology
3. Bioengineered foods
4. Black holes
5. Tony Blair
6. Campaign funds
7. Campus drinking
8. Cellular phones
9. Corporate mergers
10. DNA testing
11. Fiber optics
12. Alan Greenspan
13. Hedge funds
14. Laser surgery
15. NASDAQ stock exchange
16. National missile defense system
17. Rosie O'Donnell
18. Shaquille O'Neal
19. Oral history
20. Racial profiling
21. John Rocker
22. Sport utility vehicles
23. Telemarketing
24. Televangelism
25. Unemployment
26. Vegetarianism
27. Venus or Serena Williams
28. Wiretapping
29. X-ray astronomy
30. Yale University

The Internet

What It Is   The Internet is a worldwide network that links the computer systems of educational institutions, government agencies, businesses, professional organizations, and individuals. The Internet offers a number of services, including the World Wide Web, electronic mail (e-mail), newsgroups, and listservs. It allows you to check the holdings of college libraries; obtain information from online books, magazines, and newspapers; access research and government documents; gather viewpoints and information from numerous organizations and individuals; and communicate with people around the world or at the next computer station. This abundance of information and perspectives, sometimes not more than a day old, can greatly enhance your research. But remember that you'll still need to consult traditional sources in addition to using the Internet.

You can easily learn how to access the Internet and World Wide Web if you don't already know how. Your school may offer training sessions that you can attend. In addition, a number of excellent, easy-to-follow books are available. Whether enrolled in a training session or learning on your own, you'll need to obtain a log-on name, your own password, and an e-mail address if you plan to use your school's computers. If you encounter problems, personnel in the computer labs can probably answer many of your questions.

World Wide Web   During the 1990s the World Wide Web exploded into national prominence. The Web gained quick popularity because it is easy to use and offers visuals, including many sites dedicated to art, and hypertext, that is, text with color-coded words that can link you to other related sites. Web pages can include text, graphics, sound, video clips, entire computer programs, files that can be downloaded, and even animated images.

To use the World Wide Web, you need access to a computer with a Web browser such as *Netscape Navigator Microsoft Internet Explorer,* or Safari and an Internet service provider to connect you to the Web. The top of the screen on any browser features a tool bar that you can click on to save locations for future reference, stop the transfer of data, or initiate a search.

TEACHING STRATEGIES.

1. Most students know how to use the Internet. However, some may not be familiar with using it for more scholarly research. In our experience, the best way for students to learn how to use the Internet for academic research is to pair them in a lab setting and allow them to experiment with only minimal instruction. You may want to give them targeted subjects to research that you know well and which have a reasonable amount of professional material. You may need to demonstrate to students how to narrow and vary their search by using additional terms or by changing the key terms they are using in their search.

2. Your computer center may be able to help you set up a Web page for your class. Or your school may have commercial programs such as Blackboard and WebCT. You can have the syllabus and assignments online for students, especially if you are involved in distance learning. The computer center may also be able to set up a bulletin page for you so that students can respond to a prompt you establish, see the responses of other students, and also respond to student comments. This bulletin page allows you to engage students in a written discussion of a topic outside of class. You could ask them to print out a copy of the forum discussion and bring it to class for further analysis. A writing assignment could follow.

3. If you meet your class part of the time in a computer lab, programs such as *Daedalus, Commonspace,* Blackboard, and WebCT allow you to turn your class into a chat room—an interesting alternative way to involve students in a written discussion. Some instructors find that this method has several advantages: It allows more students to participate, results in more thoughtful responses, keeps an ongoing record of comments for instructors or students to consult, allows an instructor time to formulate a response or to further query a student response, and lets students print out the discussion for use in class or for a paper.

Each Web page has an address called a URL (uniform resource locator), which allows the browser to locate that page. Here is a sample address: http://www.whitehouse.gov

How to Use It   The Internet includes millions of computers and offers a stupendous amount of information. As a result, finding just the material you want can be quite difficult. To solve this problem, several indexes, or *search engines,* have been developed that can connect any search term or terms with potentially millions of sites that include the key words. The easiest way to connect with these search engines is to simply select the search command or its nearest equivalent on your browser or Internet service. This will connect you with a specific search engine but also give you a choice of several others. You can also enter the direct address (URL) in the address window. Figure 20.11 provides the addresses of several popular search engines. Because the various search engines often select differently and produce different results, it's a good idea to use several engines while conducting your search.

While each search engine works in a slightly different manner, they all provide similar sorts of information. When prompted by the key words you enter, the engine searches and returns lists of links to information containing these words. Such engines simplify the job of finding what you want on the Internet. Still, expect the job to require patience since search engines often provide information that isn't useful. For that reason, you'll often want to narrow your search when you begin. Single terms such as "health," "cancer," or "crime" could give you a million possible sites; instead, you may want to search for "ovarian cancer" or even "ovarian cancer cures." Most search engines also let you add key words that will further narrow what has already been found. Different words or phrases can produce different results, so try a variety of words for the same topic.

You can scroll through the list of sites the engine has found. The sites are usually accompanied by a short description that may help you decide whether they are useful. If you select any highlighted words, the search engine will transfer the data from that site and will connect you to the selected Web page.

Figures 20.12, 20.13, and 20.14 show the results of searching the subject "robotic advances." Figure 20.12 shows a search engine screen with the search

SUGGESTED INSTRUCTOR READINGS

Hawisher, G., and C. Selfe, eds. Literacy, Technology and Society: Confronting the Issues. NJ: Prentice-Hall, 1997, and Vitanza, V. J., ed. CyberReader. Boston: Allyn & Bacon, 1996. Collections of interesting readings on the Web and other Internet topics.

Search Engine	Address
Google	http://www.google.com
Yahoo	http://www.yahoo.com
WebCrawler	http://webcrawler.com
Alta Vista	http://www.altavista.com
Excite	http://www.excite.com

Figure 20.11   Popular Search Engines

Figure 20.12   Screen Showing Search Entry
Google, Inc. used by permission.

subject entered, Figure 20.13 shows some of the Web sites found during the search, and Figure 20.14 shows a Web page with potentially useful information.

When viewing a Web page, you may notice menus, highlighted words, or specially marked graphics. These features, called *hyperlinks*, will usually take you to a different location: another section within the original page, a different page within the same domain, or even a new page on a computer in a different country. Following these hyperlinks allows you to explore related information from a variety of sources. As you move from Web page to Web page, browsers provide an easy way to navigate, such as "back" and "forward" buttons. If you move back far enough, you will eventually get back to your main search site or even your home page. When you find an interesting site, you can print it out, or you can "bookmark" the site, allowing you easy future reference to the page. You'll need to keep track of site addresses that you use so you can include them in your bibliography.

Evaluating Internet Material   Because anyone can post virtually anything on the Internet, it is crucial that you check the accuracy and validity of information you obtain from it. A source that sounds like a research center, for example, the Institute for Social Justice, could be a political or even a cult organization giving out one-sided or false information for its own purposes. While articles for professional journals are reviewed by experts to ensure that the information is reliable, no such safeguard exists on the Internet. Carelessly researched or ethically questionable material can and does appear. Here are some guidelines for checking the validity of an Internet source:

1. Is the source identified as a reputable professional organization, such as the American Cancer Society, a university like MIT, or a government agency like the Department of Justice? Keep in mind that anyone can use a professional-sounding name, so be alert.

Figure 20.13   Search Screen Showing Results of Search

2. Is there an identified author whose credentials you can check and who speaks with some authority? If there is no e-mail contact listed or you can't find another way to verify the contents of the Web site, don't use it.

3. Is the tone of the site professional? Does it maintain an objective stance and support its position with credible evidence?

4. Is the information consistent with the other material you have found? If the site disagrees with the standard information, does it offer adequate support for its claims?

5. Does the site explain how the data were obtained?

6. Does the site appear to misuse any data? For instance, is the sample too small? Are the claims pushed too far? Are the statistics biased?

Look at the selected Web page. The address of this Web site in Figure 20.14 is normally at the bottom of the Web page (not shown here). This article has an author, which increases the credibility of the report. However, research shows that the author is founder and vice president of a robotics technology company, which though it demonstrates a clear expertise suggests a bias in favor of such technologies. A check of the home page shows that Appliance Manufacturer is an established organization promoting applied technologies. This group would have the professional expertise to make certain the article is credible. However, they might also have a slight bias to stress the effectiveness of such technologies rather than dwell on the negatives.

Sometimes, of course, you may want to check out pages that present the views of individuals or organizations with strong but slanted positions to gain a better understanding of their thinking, but don't consider such pages to be reliable sources. When using the Internet, "Reader beware" is a prudent attitude.

E-Mail   You probably have your own e-mail address. You may also have an address provided to you by your university. In some cases, your professor may be using a Web based instructional program that includes e-mail specific to your class. It is a good idea to jot down the e-mail addresses of other students in your class, making certain it is the one they actually are using, so that you can exchange ideas. Your professor, however, may prefer that you use the class or university e-mail.

You can also use e-mail to ask knowledgeable people about your research topic and get swift answers to your questions. Use this approach, however, as a last resort since busy people have limited time. If you must contact experts, don't bother them with questions that you could easily answer by reading background material. Reserve e-mail for specific queries that defy answer after extensive research. Most search engines have clearly identified directories that allow you to look up an e-mail address if you know a person's name. Sometimes you can find the name of an expert through the Web pages of major universities. If you do get a response to your query, evaluate it carefully; an overburdened expert may dash off a quick response while doing something else.

Newsgroups   A newsgroup is a group of people who discuss a common interest by posting their responses to a common address for everyone to read. These discussions can be informal and often are not monitored; as a result, they leave

TEACHING STRATEGIES
1. There are many interesting pedagogical uses of e-mail. If your goal is to increase fluency, you could have students find e-mail pen pals either at other colleges, at your school, in other English classes, or even in your own class. Students might be required to exchange ideas on a classroom topic each week and provide you with a printout or forward a copy of the messages to you.
2. Forming a distribution list of your students' e-mail addresses can be worthwhile. It allows you to remind students about assignments, give them things to think about, or even provide them with material you might teach in class by attaching a file. Either a large or small distribution list can help students exchange ideas, questions, drafts, and suggestions.

Software Breakthrough Advances Robotic Painting
Complex breakthrough makes automation simpler.

Albert L. Harlow, Jr.

Posted on: 06/01/2000

Listing of controllable spray painting or coating variables

Whether wet or powder, variables in spray painting that influence painting results, such as color and thickness, include many things. A list of the controllable or measurable variables in an ARTomation system is given below:

- Temperature:
  a. Coating / viscosity.
  b. Atmosphere.

- Humidity.

- Speed at which nozzle passes over the part's surface.

- Angle of inference relative to a surface, or part's position relative to the gun.

- Spray gun nozzle and cap.

- Fluid or powder's delivery rate.

- Spray gun settings:
  Wet: Atomization and Fan Air.
  Powder: Conveying Air and Fluidizing Air

Figure 20.14 Online Article

something to be desired as a source for research. Still, your university system will likely give you access to newsgroups, so ask your computer center for an instruction sheet. A word of caution: Many newsgroups are intolerant of uninformed people intruding upon their conversation. Common netiquette (the etiquette of the Internet) calls for you to read what has already been written and to think before you write.

Listservs A listserv consists of numerous e-mail addresses that make up a mailing list of people interested in a particular topic. Once you sign up, everything posted to that listserv will be sent to your e-mail address. People who subscribe to three or four listservs may receive thirty or forty e-mail messages every day. If you post a question on a listserv, you may get dozens of responses from professionals interested in the topic, and sorting out the validity of the different responses can be difficult. As with newsgroups, netiquette calls for you to acquire an understanding of your subject and follow the discussions on the listserv for some time before you post a question or a response. Your university computer professionals can probably supply you with instructions on how to find and sign up for a listserv. You can access a subject index of listservs at http://www.liszt.com.

FAQs Whenever you find a promising Web site, newsgroup, or listserv, you will often see a line for FAQs (frequently asked questions). It's a good idea to read the FAQs first since they may well answer your questions.

1. **Using an appropriate search engine, find information on each of the following topics:**
   a. the Vietnam War
   b. current crime statistics
   c. sexual harassment
   d. current government immigration policy

2. **Enter the name of a major university into a search engine and then search. You should find that university's home page. Try to access the university's library to find what books are available on a topic of your choice. You might try schools like Harvard, Duke, or Notre Dame.**

Primary Research Findings

Besides relying on library materials, you may wish to use information obtained by conducting primary research. Chapter 22 provides detailed instructions for interviewing specialists, sending out questionnaires, and making direct observations. Before doing any type of primary research, always get your instructor's permission.

Adjusting Your Topic

After finishing your search for sources, you may need to adjust the scope and emphasis of your topic. If you start with "America's First Nuclear-Powered Submarine" but fail to turn up enough sources, you might expand your emphasis to "America's First Nuclear-Powered Warships." On the other hand, if you're working with "America's First Nuclear-Powered Warships" and find yourself floundering in an ocean of sources, you might zero in on one type of vessel. Gathering evidence helps to develop your judgment about how many sources you need to do the job.

SUGGESTED INSTRUCTOR READING
Hawisher, G. E., and C. Moran. "Electronic Mail and the Writing Instructor." College English 55 (1993): 627–43. Explains why e-mail can and should be an important part of a writing class.

TEACHING STRATEGY
If you are building a course around a topic that has a listserv or a newsgroup, have students sign up with the listserv or regularly sign on to the newsgroup. Doing so will familiarize them with various points of view and perhaps also suggest an idea for a writing assignment. As students become more involved in the topic, they can begin to participate in the online conversation and in so doing learn about the real impact of the written word and community discourse.

TEACHING STRATEGIES
1. After students have examined their working bibliographies, ask them if they need to revise their research questions in light of their findings.

2. At this point students might write brief progress reports specifying problems they are having and outlining their plans for further research. Such reports allow you to provide helpful suggestions.

Taking Notes

To take notes, read your references carefully and record significant information. You might review or even expand your original research questions (page 345) so that you can read with a better sense of purpose. Notes are the raw materials for your finished product, so develop them accurately.

Evaluating Your Sources

Evaluate your sources by considering these factors.

The Expertise of the Author   Judge an author's expertise by examining his or her professional status. Say you're searching for information on some new cancer-treating drug. An article by the director of a national cancer research center would be a better bet than one by a staff writer for a magazine. Similarly, a historian's account of a national figure will probably have more balance and depth than a novelist's popularized account of that person's life. Gauging a writer's credentials is not difficult. Articles in periodicals often note authors' job titles along with their names. Some even supply thumbnail biographies. For a book, check its title page, preface, or introduction, and—if it's been left on—the dust jacket. Finally, notice whether the writer has other publications on this general subject. If your sources include two or more items by one person or if that person's name keeps cropping up as you take notes, you're probably dealing with an expert.

The Credibility of the Publication   A book's credibility hinges on its approach and its reception by reviewers. Cast a cautious eye on books that take a popular rather than a scholarly approach. For research papers, scholarly treatments provide more solid fare. Weigh what reviewers said when a book first appeared. Two publications excerpt selected reviews and provide references to others. The *Book Review Digest* (1905–date) deals mainly with nontechnical works, while the *Technical Book Review Index* (1935–date) covers technical and scientific books. Turn first to the volume for the year the book came out. If you don't find any reviews, scan the next year's index. Often books published in the fall are not reviewed until the following year.

Periodical articles can also take a scholarly or popular tack. Editors of specialized journals and of some wide-circulation magazines—for example, *Scientific American* and *The Atlantic Monthly*—publish only in-depth, accurate articles. Most newsstand publications, however, popularize to some extent, and some deliberately strive for sensationalism. Popularizing may result in broad, general statements, skimpy details, and a sensational tone.

Don't automatically reject a source because the writer lacks expertise or offers a popularized treatment. Often, especially when writing about a current topic, you'll need to use material that falls short in some way. Remember, though, that you undertake research to become more knowledgeable than general readers are about a topic. When information in popular periodicals provides less than adequate coverage, candidly acknowledge the shortcomings.

Mechanics of Note Taking

Generally your most effective approach to note taking is to use note cards. Copy each note on a 4 × 6-inch card to avoid confusion with the smaller bibliography cards. Record only one note per card, even when you take several notes from a single page; you may use the notes at different points. If you can't fit a note on a single card, continue the note on a second card and paper-clip or staple the two together. Cards allow you to test different arrangements of notes and use the best one to write the paper.

Before you take a note, indicate its source at the bottom of the card. You will then have all the details necessary for documenting the information if you use it in your paper. Usually, the author's last name and the page number suffice, since your bibliography card contains all other details. To distinguish between two authors with the same last name or between two works by the same author, add initials or partial titles. *Don't forget to include the page number or numbers for each note.* Otherwise, you'll have to waste time looking them up when you cite your sources in the paper.

Summarize briefly the contents of the note at the top of the card. Later, when you construct an outline, these notations will help you sort your cards into categories and subcategories.

TEACHING STRATEGY
Encourage students to include on their cards not only notes but also their personal reactions to them. Students must of course clearly distinguish between their borrowing and their commentary.

Responding to Notes

As you take notes, reflect on your topic and try to come up with new ideas, see connections to other notes, and anticipate future research. Think of yourself as having a conversation with your sources, and jot down your responses on the backs of your note cards. Ask yourself these questions: Does this information agree with what I have learned so far? Does it suggest any new avenues to explore? Does it leave me with questions about what's been said? Although it may take a few minutes to record your responses to a note, this type of analysis will help you write a paper that reflects *your* opinions, decisions, and evaluations, not one that smacks of notes merely patched together from different sources.

Types of Notes

A note can be a summary, paraphrase, or quotation. *Whenever you use any kind of note in your paper, give proper credit to your source. Failure to do so results in plagiarism— that is, literary theft—a serious offense even when committed unintentionally.* Pages 434–436 discuss plagiarism, and pages 407–434 explain proper documentation of sources.

Summary   A summary condenses original material, presenting its core ideas *in your own words*. In order to write an effective summary, you must have a good grasp of the information, and this comprehension ensures that you are ready to use the material in your paper. You may include brief quotations if you enclose them in quotation marks. A properly written summary presents the main points in their original order without distorting their emphasis or meaning, and it omits supporting details and repetition. Summaries, then, serve up the heart of the matter.

TEACHING STRATEGY
As an exercise, you might have students, working in groups, summarize all or part of one of the essays in the Reader. Then have them compare the summaries and prepare a final version.

Begin the summarizing process by asking yourself, "What points does the author make that have an important bearing on my topic and purpose?" To answer, note especially the topic sentences in the original, which often provide essential information. Copy the points in order; then condense and rewrite them in your own words. Figure 20.15 summarizes the Bertrand Russell passage that follows. We have underscored key points in the original.

Necessity for law

About a century and a half ago, there began a still-existing preference for impulsive actions over deliberate ones. Those responsible for this development believed that people are naturally good but institutions have perverted them. Actually, unfettered human nature breeds violence and brutality, and law is our only protection against anarchy. The law assumes the responsibility for revenge and settles disputes equitably. It frees people from the fear of being victimized by criminals and provides a means of catching them. Without it, civilization could not endure.

Russell, pp. 63-65

Figure 20.15 Summary

Under the influence of the romantic movement, a process began about a hundred and fifty years ago, which has continued ever since—_a process of revaluing the traditional virtues,_ placing some higher on the scale than before, and others lower. _The tendency has been to exalt impulse at the expense of deliberation._ The virtues that spring from the heart have come to be thought superior to those that are based upon reflection: a generous man is preferred to a man who is punctual in paying his debts. _Per contra,_ deliberate sins are thought worse than impulsive sins: a hypocrite is more harshly condemned than a murderer. The upshot is that we tend to estimate virtues, not by their capacity for providing human happiness, but by their power of inspiring a personal liking for the possessors, and we are not apt to include among the qualities for which we like people, a habit of reflecting before making an important decision.

The men who started this movement were, in the main, gentle sentimentalists who imagined that, when the fetters of custom and law were removed, the _heart would be free to display its natural_ goodness. _Human nature,_ they thought, is good, but institutions have corrupted it; remove the institutions and we shall all become angels. _Unfortunately, the matter is not so simple as they thought._ Men who follow their impulses establish governments based on pogroms, clamour for war with foreign countries, and murder pacifists and Negroes. _Human nature unrestrained by law is violent and cruel._ In the London Zoo, the male baboons fought over the females until all the females were torn to pieces; human beings, left to the ungoverned impulse, would be no better. In ages that have had recent experience of anarchy, this has been obvious. All the great writers of the middle ages were passionate in their admiration of the law; it was the Thirty Years' War that led Grotius to become the first advocate of international law. _Law, respected and enforced, is in the long run the only alternative to violent and predatory anarchy;_ and it is just as necessary to realize this now as it was in the time of Dante and Grotius.

What is the essence of law? On the one hand, it takes away from private citizens the right of revenge, which it confers upon the government. If a man steals your money, you must not steal it back, or thrash him, or shoot him; you must establish the facts before a neutral tribunal, which inflicts upon him such punishment as has seemed just to the disinterested legislators. On the other hand, _when two men have a dispute, the law provides a machinery for settling it,_ again on principles laid down in advance by neutrals. The advantages of law are many. It diminishes the amount of private violence, and settles disagreements in a manner more nearly just than that which would result if the disputants fought it out by private war. _It makes it possible for men to work without being perpetually on the watch against bandits. When a crime has been committed it provides a skilled machine for discovering the criminal._

Without law, the existence of civilized communities is impossible. In international law, there is as yet no effective law, for lack of an international police force capable of overpowering national armies, and it is daily becoming more evident that this defect must be remedied if civilization is to survive. Within single nations there is a dangerous tendency to think that moral indignation excuses the extra-legal punishment of criminals. In Germany an era of private murder (on the loftiest grounds) preceded and followed the victory of the Nazis. In fact, nine-tenths of what appeared as just indignation was sheer lust for cruelty; and this is equally true in other countries where mobs rob the law of its functions. In any civilized community, toleration of mob rule is the first step towards barbarism.

Bertrand Russell, "Respect for Law," _San Francisco Review,_ Winter 1958, 63–65.

EXERCISE

1. Select two passages that your instructor approves from an essay in the Reader and prepare summary note cards for them.
2. Submit summaries of three pieces of information that you plan to use in writing your paper; also submit complete versions of the original.

Paraphrase   To paraphrase is to restate material _in your own words_ without attempting to condense it. Unlike a summary, a paraphrase allows you to present an essentially complete version of the original material. A note of caution, however: Don't copy the original source nearly verbatim, changing only a word here and there. To do so is to plagiarize. To avoid this offense, follow a read, think, and write-without-looking-at-the-original strategy when you take notes so that you concentrate on recording the information in your own words. Then verify the accuracy of your notes by checking them against the original source. Here is a sample passage; Figure 20.16 is its paraphrase.

Over time, more and more of life has become subject to the controls of knowledge. However, this is never a one-way process. Scientific investigation is continually increasing our knowledge. But if we are to make good use of this knowledge, we

TEACHING STRATEGY
Put several paraphrases on the board and have students determine whether each is acceptable, and why or why not. Sample paraphrases of the first part of paragraph 2 of the Bertrand Russell passage:
Acceptable
The initiators of this movement were "sentimentalists" who believed that people, when no longer bound by social and legal constraints, would behave decently. People, they believed, were naturally decent but debased by institutions. Without institutions, everyone will behave justly.
Unacceptable
The men who began this movement were gentle sentimentalists who believed that when the restraints of custom and law were removed, the human heart would display its natural goodness. Human nature, they believed, is good; it is institutions that have corrupted it.

must not only rid our minds of old, superseded beliefs and fragments of magic, but also recognize new superstitions for what they are. Both are generated by our wishes, our fears, and our feelings of helplessness in difficult situations.

Margaret Mead, "New Superstitions for Old," *A Way of Seeing*, New York: McCall, 1970. 266.

Combatting Superstitions

As time has passed, knowledge has asserted its sway over larger and larger segments of human life. But the process cuts two ways. Science is forever adding to the storehouse of human knowledge. Before we can take proper advantage of its gifts, however, we must purge our minds of old and outmoded convictions, while recognizing the true nature of modern superstitions. Both stem from our desires, our apprehensions, and our sense of impotence under difficult circumstances.

Mead, p. 266

Figure 20.16 Paraphrase

Paraphrase a short passage from one of your textbooks. Submit a complete version of the passage with the assignment.

Quotation   A quotation is a copy of original material. Since your paper should demonstrate that you've mastered your sources, don't rely extensively on quotations. You need practice in expressing yourself. As a general rule, avoid quotations except when

- the original displays special elegance or force
- you really need support from an authority
- you need to back up your interpretation of a passage from a literary work.

Paraphrasing a passage as well-written as the one below would rob it of much of its force.

> Man is himself, like the universe he inhabits, like the demoniacal stirring of the ooze from which he sprang, a tale of desolation. He walks in his mind from birth to death the long resounding shores of endless disillusionment. Finally, the commitment to life departs or turns to bitterness. But out of such desolation emerges the awful freedom to choose beyond the narrowly circumscribed circle that delimits the rational being.
>
> Loren Eiseley, *The Unexpected Universe*

Special rules govern the use of quotations. If, for clarity, you need to add an explanation or substitute a proper name for a personal pronoun, enclose the addition in *brackets*.

> The Declaration of Independence asserts that "the history of the present King of Great Britain [George III] is a history of repeated injuries and unsurpations. . . ."

If your keyboard doesn't have brackets, insert them neatly with a dark pen.

Reproduce any grammatical or spelling errors in a source exactly as they appear in the original. To let your reader know that the original author, not you, made the mistake, insert the Latin word *sic* (meaning "thus") within brackets immediately after the error.

> As Wabash notes, "The threat to our enviroment [sic] comes from many directions."

If you're using the MLA documentation system and exclude an unneeded part of a quotation, show the omission with three spaced periods. Indicate omissions *within sentences* as follows:

> Writing in *The Age of Extremes,* Eric Hobsbawm observed, "What struck both the opponents of revolution and the revolutionists was that, after 1945, the primary form of revolutionary struggle . . . seemed to be guerilla warfare."

When an omission comes *at the end of a sentence* and what is actually quoted can also stand as a complete sentence, use an unspaced period followed by an ellipsis.

> In his second inaugural address, Lincoln voiced his hopes for the nation: "With malice toward none, with charity for all, with firmness in the right as God gives us to see the right, let us strive on to finish the work we are in. . . ."

Do the same when you drop *a whole sentence* within a quoted passage.

> According to newspaper columnist Grace Dunn, "Williamson's campaign will undoubtedly focus primarily on the legalized gambling issue because he hopes to capitalize on the strong opposition to it in his district. . . . Nonetheless, commentators all agree he faces an uphill fight in his attempt to unseat the incumbent."

Don't change or distort when you delete. Tampering like the following violates ethical standards:

Original passage: This film is poorly directed, and the acting uninspired; only the cameo appearance by Laurence Olivier makes it truly worth seeing.

Distorted version: This film is . . . truly worth seeing.

If the original passage you are quoting already includes ellipsis, place your own ellipsis in brackets [. . .] to distinguish your ellipsis from the one in the original. Some instructors may require you to enclose all ellipses in brackets. Follow your instructor's directions.

If you're using the APA documentation system, never enclose ellipsis within brackets.

You can summarize or paraphrase original material but retain a few words or phrases to add vividness or keep a precise shade of meaning. Simply use quotation marks but no ellipsis.

Presidential spokesperson Paula Plimption notes that because of the "passionate advocacy" of its supporters, the push to roll back property taxes has been gaining momentum across the country.

When you copy a quotation onto a note card, put quotation marks at the beginning and the end so you won't mistake it for a paraphrase or a summary when you write the paper. If the quoted material starts on one page and ends on the next, use a slash mark (/) to show exactly where the shift comes. Then if you use only part of the quotation in your paper, you'll know whether to use one page number or two.

Don't expect to find a bonanza on every page you read. Sometimes one page will yield several notes, another page nothing. If you can't immediately gauge the value of some material, take it down. Useless information can be discarded later. Place a rubber band around your growing stack of note cards. Store them in a large envelope closed with a snap or string and labeled with your name and address. Submit them with your completed paper if your instructor requests.

Organizing and Outlining

Next comes your formal outline, the blueprint that shows the divisions and subdivisions of your paper, the order of your ideas, and the relationships between ideas and supporting details. An outline is a tool that benefits both writer and reader.

A formal outline follows the pattern shown below:

```
I.
   A.
   B.
      1.
      2.
         a.
         b.
II.
```

You can see the significance of an item by its numeral, letter, or number designation and by its distance from the left margin; the farther it's indented, the less important it is. All items with the same designation have roughly the same importance.

Developing Your Outline

Developing an outline is no easy job. It involves arranging material from various sources in an appropriate manner. Sorting and re-sorting your note cards is a good way to proceed. First, determine the main divisions of your paper by checking the summarized notations at the tops of your cards, and then make one stack of cards for each division. Next, review each stack carefully to determine further subdivisions and sort it into smaller stacks. Finally, use the stacks to prepare your outline.

There are two types of formal outline: *topic* and *sentence*. A topic outline presents all entries as words, short phrases, or short clauses. A sentence outline presents them as complete sentences. To emphasize the relationships among elements, items of equal importance have parallel phrasing. Although neither is *the* preferred form, a sentence outline includes more details and also your attitude toward each idea. Many students first develop a topic outline, do additional research, and then polish and expand this version into a sentence outline. While it's easy to be sloppy in a topic outline, forming a sentence outline requires you to reach the kinds of conclusions that will be the backbone of your paper. The following segments of a topic and a sentence outline for a paper on tranquilizer dependence illustrate the difference between the two:

TEACHING STRATEGY
Before students construct a formal outline, you might have them draft a more general plan, perhaps just a list of questions to be answered or issues to be addressed. They can then add to or reorganize the plan as they build it into a formal outline.

Topic Outline

II. The tranquilizer abuse problem
    A. Reasons for the problem
      1. Overpromotion
      2. Overprescription
      3. Patient's misuse
        a. Dosage
        b. Length of usage
    B. Growth of the problem

Sentence Outline

II. Tranquilizers are widely abused.
    A. Several factors account for the abuse of tranquilizers.
      1. Drug companies overpromote their product.
      2. Doctors often unnecessarily prescribe tranquilizers.
      3. Patients often do not follow their doctors' instructions.
        a. Some patients take more than prescribed doses.
        b. Some continue to use tranquilizers beyond the prescribed time.
    B. The problem of tranquilizer abuse appears to be growing.

Note that the items in the sentence outline are followed by periods, but those in the topic outline are not.

Keying Your Note Cards to Your Outline

When your outline is finished, key your note cards to it by writing at the top of each card the letters and numbers—such as IIA or IIIB2—for the appropriate outline category. Now arrange the cards into one stack, following the order shown in the outline. Finally, start with the top card in the stack and number all of them consecutively. If they later fall off the table or slide out of place, you can easily put them in order again. You might have a few stragglers left over when you complete this keying. Some of these may be worked into your paper as you write or revise it.

Ethical Issues

When you present the information you've gathered from a variety of sources, you'll want to proceed in an ethically responsible way. Asking and answering the following questions will help you do just that.

- Have I carefully researched my topic so that my conclusions are well-founded? Imagine the consequences if slipshod testing by an auto company led to the erroneous conclusion that the steering mechanism on one of its models met current safety standards.
- Have I adequately acknowledged any evidence that runs counter to the conclusions I draw? A paper that stresses the advantages of charter schools but deliberately avoids mentioning their disadvantages could be a form of deception.
- Have I properly documented my sources? Using someone else's words or ideas without giving proper credit is a form of academic dishonesty (see pages 434–436).
- Have I honestly represented the authority of my sources? If you read an article touting almond extract as a cure for cancer that was written by a practicing foot doctor, it would be dishonest to suggest that the article was written by a "prominent research scientist." Refer to someone as an "expert" only when that person's credentials warrant the label.
- Could my information have an undersirable effect on readers? If so, how can I address their concerns? A report describing a new antibiotic-resistant strain of tuberculosis might alarm some readers, and therefore the writer could provide appropriate reassurances of the limited risk to most people.

Writing Your Research Paper

TEACHING STRATEGY
As students draft their papers, you might set aside class time to discuss problems they are experiencing. Since some students forget their initial audience and purpose, ask the class to redefine both. Sometimes the initial outline won't work, and changes are necessary.

Some students think of a library research paper as a series of quotations, paraphrases, and summaries, one following the other throughout the paper. Not so. Without question, you use the material of others, but *you* select and organize it according to *your purpose*. *You* develop insights, and *you* draw conclusions about what you've read. You can best express your conclusions by setting your notes aside, stepping back to gain some perspective, and then expressing your sense of what you've learned. Many students find it helpful to write two or three pages on which they summarize what they want to say as well as whom they want to reach with their message and why. Like all forms of writing, research papers are written for some purpose and aimed at some audience.

Writing the First Draft

Your final research results will be expressed in a thesis. You've already drafted a tentative thesis (see page 347), and now you'll probably refine or revise it to accommodate any changes in your perspective on the topic. Position the thesis in the introductory part of your paper unless you're analyzing a problem or recommending a solution; then you might hold back the thesis until later in the essay. If you do hold it back, state the problem clearly at the outset. Because of the paper's length, it's a good idea to reveal your organizational plan in your introductory section.

Write the paper section by section, following the divisions of your outline. But keep in mind that you're not locked into its pattern. If you see an opportunity to develop an important idea that you omitted from your outline, try it. If you discover that it might be better to introduce an item earlier than you intended, go ahead. Just be sure to check your organization later. As you write, think of yourself as supporting the conclusions you have reached with the appropriate material on your note cards, not just as stringing these cards together. You will then incorporate the material on your note cards with your own assessments and with transitional elements that clarify your information and orient the reader. As you proceed, here again you'll use the writing strategies presented earlier in the book.

Because of this paper's length, you will probably need to connect its major sections with transitional paragraphs that pull together the material already covered and prepare the reader for what follows. Don't fret if the style bumps along or connections aren't always clear. These problems can be smoothed out when you revise. You will, of course, need to know how to document your sources properly, handle quotations, and avoid plagiarism. Chapter 21 presents guidelines on these important subjects.

On occasion you may want to include supplementary information that would interrupt the flow of thought if you placed it in the paper. When this happens, use an explanatory note.[1] A typical explanatory note might clarify or elaborate on a point, discuss some side issue, or define a term used in a specialized way.

When you finish writing, let this version sit for a day or two. Then revise it, just as you would with a shorter essay. Keep track of all sources so that preparing the bibliography will go smoothly.

Preparing Your Finished Copy

Follow the revision guidelines in Chapter 4. In addition, verify that you have

- included all key information
- clearly organized your material
- not overloaded your paper with quotations
- worked in your own observations
- put in-text documentation and source information in proper form.

Prepare your final draft with a word-processing program. Be sure you have access to a laser or inkjet printer that produces dark, readable copy. Double-space throughout, including indented block quotations and the list of works you used to prepare the paper.

---

[1]This is an explanatory note. Position it at the bottom of the page, spaced four lines away from the main text. If more than one note occurs on a page, double-space between them. If the note carries over to the next page, separate it from your text with a solid, full-length line. Put two spaces above the line and two spaces below it.

TEACHING STRATEGY
After students have taken a fair number of notes, you might have them write an in-class "metadraft" while you check their notes. Ask them to define their audience and purpose, state their thesis, present their major conclusions in paragraph form, explain how they'd like to organize their materials, note any further research that appears necessary, and identify actual and potential problems. Such metadrafts provide students with an overview of what they want to accomplish before they begin drafting or even outlining, and they also help them reach their own conclusions and make the paper truly theirs. At the same time, metadrafts apprise you of students' progress and give you a chance to help them with their problems.

TEACHING STRATEGY
You might comment on student drafts in conference sessions. The scope of their projects often makes such sessions particularly helpful to students.

Two systems for formatting and documenting library research papers are in common use: the Modern Language Association (MLA) system, favored by many English and humanities instructors, and the American Psychological Association (APA) system, used by many social science and psychology instructors.

MLA System for Preparing Papers

- Number each page in the upper right corner, one-half inch from the top. Precede each page number with your last name.
- Starting one inch from the top of the first page, type your full name, the instructor's name, the course designation, and the date, all flush with the left margin.
- Double-space below the date, and center the title; then double-space before starting the first paragraph.
- Leave one-inch margins on all four sides except at the top of the first page. Indent the first line of each paragraph five spaces or one-half inch.
- The MLA system does not require a title page. If your instructor wants one, however, center (1) the title of the paper about two inches below the top of the sheet, (2) your name in the middle of the sheet, and (3) the instructor's name, course designation, and date about two inches from the bottom. Use capital and lowercase letters for everything. Repeat the title, again in capital and lowercase letters, on the first text page, centered about two inches from the top.
- Begin the bibliography on a new page that follows the text of the paper, and give it the heading "Works Cited," without quotation marks. Center the heading on the page.
- List each bibliographic entry alphabetically according to the author's last name or, if no author is given, by the first significant word in the title. For a work with more than one author, alphabetize by the name that comes first. If there's more than one entry for an author, substitute three unspaced hyphens, followed by a period and a double space, for the author's name in the second and subsequent entries.
- Begin the first line of each entry at the left margin and indent subsequent lines five spaces. In most word-processing programs, you can select "hanging indent" as a format option, under Format/Paragraph in *Word*, which will automatically provide the proper indentation for each entry.

APA System for Preparing Papers

- The APA system includes a brief abstract on the first main page of the article which summarizes the main argument concisely.
- The APA system requires a title page. Center (1) the title of the paper about four inches from the top and (2) your name, two spaces below the title. About three-fourths of the way from the top, provide the course designation, the name of your instructor, and the date, typed double-spaced and flush with the right margin. Two inches from the top of the

page, type the words "Running Head," without quotation marks, flush with the left margin; then type a colon and a word or phrase that identifies the paper's topic. Type the running head in capital letters; type everything else in capital and lowercase letters.

- Repeat the title of the paper on the first text page, centered about one-and-a-half inches from the top and typed in capital and lowercase letters.

- Number every page of the text in the upper right corner, starting with the title page. Put the running head (an abbreviated version of the paper's title) in the upper left corner, in all capital letters.

- Leave one-inch margins at the bottom and at both sides of each page. Indent the first line of each paragraph five spaces.

- Begin the bibliography on a new page that follows the text of the paper, and give it the heading "References," without quotation marks. Center this heading on the page. Follow the alphabetizing and positioning guidelines for the MLA system except that if the listing includes more than one entry for an author, repeat the author's name.

- Begin the first line of each entry at the left margin and indent subsequent lines five spaces. In most word-processing programs, you can select "hanging indent" as a format option, under Format/Paragraph in *Word*, which will automatically provide the proper indentation for each entry. Double-space all entries.

SAMPLE

MLA STUDENT RESEARCH PAPER

Sentence Outline

Thesis statement: House arrest offers a choice of several monitoring systems, presents no insurmountable problems, proves effective in controlling low-risk offenders, and costs less than incarceration.

    I. The use of house arrest stems from the country's serious crime problem.

        A. Violent crimes are committed by a small number of repeat offenders.

        B. These crimes have led to tougher crime-control legislation.

        C. This legislation has increased the country's prison population and the cost of incarceration.

Sentence outline: Note use of complete sentences throughout, use of periods following section and subsection markers, and the indentation arrangement.

   D. As a result, many jurisdictions have adopted house-
    arrest programs for low-risk offenders.

 II. Electronic monitoring has a short history.

   A. The idea first appeared in the comic *Spiderman*.

   B. A New Mexico judge asked computer companies to
    develop an electronic bracelet.

   C. Monitoring was first used in 1984 to control offenders,
    and the concept quickly spread across the country.

 III. Electronic monitoring devices fall into three categories.

   A. A programmed-contact system calls the offender's
    home during curfew periods and reports absences.

    1. A computer may simply record the offender's voice.

    2. A computer may compare the voice heard over the
     phone to a recording of the offender's voice.

    3. The offender may wear an encoded bracelet and insert
     it into a special telephone transmitter.

    4. A camera may transmit photos of the offender over tele-
     phone lines.

   B. A continuous-signal system requires the offender to
    wear a transmitter that sends uninterrupted electronic
    signals.

   C. A hybrid system combines programmed-contact and
    continuous-signal techniques.

    1. The programmed-contact component usually includes
     voice- and photo-transmission units.

    2. Jurisdictions can tailor systems to their needs.

 IV. Electronic systems have created practical and legal problems.

   A. Practical problems include both difficulties experi-
    enced by offenders and transmission difficulties.

    1. Encoded bracelets can cause offenders discomfort and
     embarrassment.

    2. Telephone lines and objects in the offender's home can
     interfere with signal pickup.

   B. Legal problems include possible constitutional
    infringements and the net-widening effect.

1. Charging surveillance fees and limiting surveillance to the least dangerous persons may infringe on offenders' equal-protection rights.
2. Monitoring may violate the right to privacy of others in offenders' homes.
3. Net-widening can result in an excessive number of individuals under house arrest.

V. Electronic monitoring has proved effective with low-risk offenders.
   A. The great majority of offenders successfully complete monitoring programs.
   B. Monitoring costs less than incarceration.

VI. The advantages of house arrest should increase its use.

Keith Jacque

Professor Reinking

English 250

May 4, 2001

House Arrest: An Attractive Alternative to Incarceration

Few of us would deny that crime is a serious national problem. Almost daily, newspapers and television screens offer accounts of "white-collar crimes" such as embezzlement and tax evasion and violent crimes such as aggravated assault, rape, and murder. Unlike nonviolent crimes, most violent ones are committed by chronic offenders. As former U.S. Attorney General William Barr notes, "Study after study shows that there is a tiny fraction of the population who . . . commit a disproportionate amount—a vast amount—of predatory violence in our society."

These violent crimes have hardened society's attitude toward criminals and brought about a demand for "get-tough" policies in dealing with all kinds of offenses. The result has been federal legislation like the Crime Control Act of 1984 and the Anti-Drug Abuse Act of 1986. The first of these makes incarceration mandatory for certain habitual offenders; the second does the same for persons convicted of specified drug offenses (United States, *Senate* 12). The introduction of mandatory sentencing guidelines, now common on the state as well as the federal level, provides consistent punishment for similar crimes. It has led, however, to an explosion in the number of prison inmates, which by mid-1999 totaled over 1.8 million, including a 4.4 percent increase between mid-1997 and mid-1998 (Gearan). Between 1980 and 1995, the nation's prison population grew 242 percent ("Inmate Populations" 10). Many of these inmates are guilty of nonviolent offenses. In 1997, three-fourths of all prisoners fell into the nonviolent category (Richey).

Marginal notes:

Title reflects main thrust of paper.

Paper is double-spaced throughout.

Opening paragraph cites *cause:* nonviolent and violent crimes.

Omission within sentence, ellipsis within brackets

Effect of nonviolent and violent crimes

Causal chain

Jacque 2

It is likely that the prison population will continue to grow. The National Council on Crime and Delinquency has estimated that the total number of prisoners might reach 1.4 million by the year 2000, a jump of 24 percent over the 1995 level ("Inmate Populations" 10). The Bureau of Prisons has projected construction costs of some four billion dollars for new federal prisons scheduled to open in the 1996-2006 decade and between ten billion and fourteen billion dollars for the new state prisons required to house the anticipated increase in prisoners (10).

Even these figures don't tell the whole story. Director of the Federal Bureau of Prisons J. Michael Quinlan comments that over the lifetime of a prison, "construction costs are only 5-7 percent of the total expense. This means that from 15-20 times the construction costs will have to be budgeted over the life of each prison now being built" (114). Underestimating operating costs can result in unused facilities as in Florida, where in 1992, two newly constructed 900-person prisons and a 336-person death-row facility remained empty because the state lacked the money to operate them (Katel).

Overcrowding and the high costs of prisons have seriously undermined state spending on public services and created a number of hidden expenses. In Michigan, for example, corrections spending increased over 300 percent between 1979 and 1989, as compared to a 98 percent increase in social services spending and a 40 percent increase in education spending (Baird 122). And these figures do not include hidden costs such as welfare payments to the families of imprisoned offenders and the loss of tax revenues from prisoners removed from the job market (Lynch).

Faced with the social and educational consequences of current policy, many state legislators have recommended using prison space only for violent offenders and developing, for nonviolent ones, low-cost alternatives that provide adequate public

---

Statistics, forecasts of prisoner increases, costs provide interest, depth

Author's name introduces short run-in quote within quotation marks; page number follows quote.

Effect of underestimating costs

Comparison of spending figures

Jacque 3

protection. At times, results have been mixed. In the early 1980s, for example, the state of Georgia attempted to relieve severe prison overcrowding by greatly expanding the use of closely supervised probation. While significant cost savings were realized, tremendous work overloads on the probation staff resulted, according to the Georgia Probation Division.

House arrest—a strategy that confines nonviolent offenders to their homes and monitors their compliance with electronic devices—avoids the drawbacks of other approaches. It offers a choice of several monitoring systems, presents no insurmountable problems, is effective in controlling low-risk offenders, and costs less than incarceration.

Electronic monitoring (sometimes called electronic tethering, electronic surveillance, electronic house arrest, or electronic incarceration) has curious roots—the comic *Spider-Man*. The idea first occurred in 1979 to New Mexico Judge Jack Love, who observed that Kingpin, Spider-Man's nemesis, used an electronic bracelet to control his crime-fighter enemy. Love asked computer companies to develop a similar device (Scaglione, "Jails" 32; Sullivan). The first house-arrest program using electronic monitoring was implemented in 1984, and five years later, programs had been established in over a hundred jurisdictions across more than thirty states (Peck 26; Scaglione, "You're Under Arrest" 26). By 1993, the number of offenders being electronically monitored totaled 65,650 nationwide (Carey and McLean).

The U.S. Department of Justice classifies electronic monitoring systems according to their signaling characteristics (1). Types include programmed contact, continuous signal, and hybrid systems—a combination of the first two.

With a programmed-contact system, a computer calls an offender's residence on a random basis during established curfew periods and reports any unauthorized absence to

---

Definition of term

Thesis statement reflects paper's content, previews organization.

Narrative relates brief history of monitoring.

Double citations show two sources with essentially identical information; shortened titles distinguish between separate articles by same author.

Classification of monitoring systems

Definition of system

Explanatory note

Jacque 4

correctional authorities. Various levels of sophistication are possible, depending on how much certainty is desired. In the simplest system, the computer merely records the offender's voice. Correctional authorities then review the taped responses the next day to determine any curfew violations. A variant approach uses a prerecording of the offender's voice, which the computer compares to the voice heard during random calls. If the two do not match, the computer can immediately notify authorities of a violation. Voice systems are comparatively inexpensive as no special equipment needs to be installed in the offender's home or worn by the individual (Hofer and Meierhoefer 36-37).

Comparison of systems

A more sophisticated means of checking on offenders makes use of an encoded bracelet worn by the offender. Again, a computer calls randomly during curfew. Instead of answering in the usual manner, however, the offender responds by inserting the bracelet into a special transmitter attached to the telephone. The bracelets can be made in such a way that unauthorized attempts to remove them will damage their transmitting ability (Hofer and Meierhoefer 36-37).

Visual verification probably offers the best assurance against curfew violation. A special camera that can transmit photographs over telephone lines is installed in the offender's home. During calls, the computer can request the monitored individual to provide a variety of poses to the camera. These photographs can then be stored in the computer for later review or compared immediately to a reference key for the individual (Hofer and Meierhoefer 37).

Process explained

Continuous-signal systems, unlike programmed-contact systems, require the offender to wear a transmitter that sends a continuous sequence of electronic signals, often several times a minute, to his or her home telephone. If a break in transmission occurs during a detention period, the monitoring

Comparison of systems; definition of system

Jacque 5

computer notifies authorities. The transmitters are relatively small and generally worn on a tamper-resistant strap around the ankle. Attempts to remove the strap could cause the unit to stop sending signals or could be detected during periodic inspections. These systems provide a greater degree of supervision than programmed-contact systems, which check on offenders only intermittently (Hofer and Meierhoefer 38-39).

Comparison of systems

Hybrid systems combine programmed-contact and continuous-signal techniques in order to realize the advantages of each (United States Dept. of Justice 1). Typically, the programmed-contact component includes both voice and video units. This component can function as a backup for continuous-signal monitoring or as a supplement to it. In the first case, the computer is programmed to call for voice-video identification whenever the offender's transmitter fails to send a continuous signal. In the second case, the computer randomly calls for voice-video verification as well as receives transmitter signals (Scaglione, "Jails" 36).

Jurisdictions can develop hybrid systems tailored to their individual needs. For example, a house-arrest program for drunk drivers could employ a continuous-signal transmitter supplemented by random telephone verification. Home monitoring equipment could even include a Breathalyzer to determine and transmit to the computer the offender's blood-alcohol level during telephone verification calls (Scaglione, "Jails" 36). A variation of this type of system is used in Annapolis, Maryland, where video cameras have been installed in the homes of some convicted drunk drivers. The offenders are called periodically and required to give themselves a blood-alcohol test in front of the camera (Peck 28).

Not surprisingly, electronic monitoring has resulted in some practical problems and legal concerns. Most problems arise with those who wear encoded verification bracelets or

Jacque 6

transmitters. These offenders complain that the devices cause physical discomfort or embarrassment. Correction officials can adjust the fit of the device or suggest that offenders wear a cut-off tube sock, tennis-type wrist band, or other type of padding under the strap. Wearers, however, must find their own ways of coping with embarrassment. In studying the electronic monitoring of federal parolees, Beck, Klein-Saffran, and Wooten found that offenders could be quite innovative in explaining why they were wearing units. When questioned by strangers, "the majority told the truth, while other parolees stated that [the unit] was a heart monitor, pager, battery charger for a video camera, or a fish caller" (29).

Transmitting difficulties have created other practical problems. In some areas, existing telephone lines may be inadequate or incompatible with the transmitting characteristics of certain monitoring systems. In other cases, the offender's home may cause difficulties. Ford and Schmidt, who conducted research for the National Institute of Justice, point out that

> The typical room has dead space in which the receiver cannot pick up the transmitter's signal. In particular, metal tends to limit the range of the transmitter; kitchens are therefore an especially difficult environment.

> Transmission breaks have also been attributed to metal furniture, faulty wiring, other electronic devices, bathroom fixtures, waterbeds, and even certain sleeping positions. Mobile homes constitute a problem for offenders trying to do yard chores: The range outside the building is as little as ten feet, as compared to as much as 200 feet from a mainframe building. (3)

Cites article with three authors; page number follows quotation

Brackets enclose explanatory words inserted into quotation.

Extended quotation indented ten spaces, without quotation marks, double- spaced.

Period precedes citation

Jacque 7

Other researchers have noted similar interference problems. In one situation, authorities suspected noncompliance when they discovered breaks in an offender's continuous signal transmissions. These breaks always occurred during the same time period and only on Sundays. Investigation revealed that a large rock and metal coffee table was blocking the signal from the transmitter on the offender's ankle while he was watching football on television (Beck, Klein-Saffran, and Wooten 27).

Most practical problems associated with electronic monitoring pose no serious challenge. Troublesome bracelets and transmitters can be adjusted or padded. Offenders often develop ingenious explanations for the units they wear. Difficulties in signal transmission can often be overcome by having trained technicians install equipment or by having offenders slightly modify their routine. Legal problems, on the other hand, pose a greater challenge.

Electronic surveillance programs necessarily involve some type of entry into offenders' homes. Therefore, they need careful examination to ensure that they don't violate the equal protection and right to privacy provisions of the Constitution. The American Civil Liberties Union is concerned that two common practices—charging a fee to cover surveillance costs and restricting surveillance to classes of offenders least likely to violate house arrest—may infringe on the equal protection clause of the Constitution. The first practice, the ACLU notes, can discriminate against young and indigent offenders by imprisoning them because they cannot pay their fees. The second, by singling out persons guilty only of property crimes and without serious criminal records or histories of drug abuse, may target disproportionately high numbers of white-collar offenders (Petersilia 3).

These concerns can be answered. Because electronic monitoring programs are always voluntary, participants essentially waive their right to privacy. By agreeing to a program in lieu

> Transition paragraph summarizes solutions to practical problems, looks ahead to legal problems.

Jacque 8

of prison, they have indicated their willingness to undergo surveillance. Still, as the Bureau of Justice Assistance notes, court rulings may uphold a convicted person's right to privacy if electronic surveillance "cannot be justified in terms of an articulated security interest, ability to deter future criminal conduct or ability to reduce the risk of flight" (United States, Dept. of Justice 5). Furthermore, electronic monitoring can invade the privacy of others in the offender's home. Family members who have not committed an offense and have not waived their right to privacy can accidentally be photographed or recorded. To prevent such intrusions, Kentucky, Nevada, and West Virginia have banned the use of equipment that might accidentally record extraneous sights and sounds. And because North Carolina prohibits photographing juveniles, visual verification cannot be used in that state (Scaglione, "Jails" 34).

> Quotation indicates precise conditions that justify monitoring.

Besides protecting an offender's constitutional rights, correction officials must try to avoid a "net-widening" effect when electronic monitoring is used. This effect occurs when a judge approves surveillance for offenders who would formerly have received probation but denies it to anyone who would formerly have gone to prison. The result is a "widening of the net of social control" to encompass more individuals. When such abuses take place, the system does not provide an option for those who would otherwise have gone to prison, and it serves as a new form of punishment for those who would otherwise have been placed on probation. Prison overcrowding is not reduced, and the costs of punishment actually rise because of the excess number of individuals under surveillance (Morris and Tonry 225). The net-widening effect has been avoided in some jurisdictions by establishing strict rules for the selection of participants. New Jersey, for instance, restricts alternative punishment programs to offenders who have already been sentenced to prison (Hofer and Meierhoefer 22).

> Definition of term

Jacque 9

Interview supplements
library research.

Classification of
offenders

Classification of
punishments

Arguments in favor of
monitoring

Comparison of costs

Independent
conclusion concerning
savings in prison costs

Richard N. Irrer, who supervises the Michigan Department of Corrections electronic monitoring program, has provided convincing evidence that monitoring works well in supervising low-risk prisoners. Monitoring began experimentally in 1986, and the following year, the program was expanded to include the entire state. Offenders monitored by the department include circuit-court probationers, prison parolees, and prisoners released from halfway houses. By mid-2000, some twenty-nine hundred offenders were being monitored.

The department uses the continuous-signal monitoring system exclusively. Before being fitted with bracelets, offenders are fully briefed on the operation of the system and must read and sign a set of rules and regulations that includes a list of possible penalties for violations. These preliminaries and the fact that the program includes only carefully screened offenders with minimum-security status have undoubtedly helped the program achieve its high success rate. For 2000, according to Irrer, only 2.2 percent of the offenders were arrested for new felonies, and just 6.7 percent disappeared. The penalty for program violators depends on the status of the violator and the nature of the crime. For example, parolees and probationers who commit serious violations may go to prison, while prisoners on furlough from halfway houses may be returned there. Minor violations could result in extended curfew hours.

The Michigan program has also been a financial success. Imprisoning offenders costs the state an average of $65 a day. In contrast, Irrer notes, electronic monitoring costs just $7.30 a day, and financially able offenders must reimburse the state. Those who can't pay must perform community service. Earlier findings reported by Hofer and Meierhoefer also reveal wide spreads between the costs of imprisoning and monitoring offenders (54-55). Clearly, electronic monitoring can significantly reduce the country's enormous prison costs.

Jacque 10

Electronic monitoring is not a cure-all for prison overcrowding. But it does offer a number of advantages that deserve serious consideration: Several systems are available, no insurmountable problems are evident, low-risk offenders are effectively controlled, and the costs are less than those for incarceration. As we move on into the twenty-first century, authorities in increasing numbers can be expected to establish house-arrest programs that monitor compliance with electronic devices.

Independent conclusion draws together and reinforces main points of paper; predicts future of house-arrest programs.

Works Cited

Baird, Christopher. "Building More Prisons Will Not Solve Prison Overcrowding." *America's Prisons: Opposing Viewpoints*. Ed. David Bender, Bruno Leone, and Stacey Tipp. San Diego: Greenhaven, 1991. 118-24. Print.

Barr, William. "Corraling the Hard-Core Criminal." *Detroit News and Free Press* 18 Oct. 1992, state ed.: B3. Print.

Beck, James L., Jody Klein-Saffran, and Harold B. Wooten. "Home Confinement and the Use of Electronic Monitoring with Federal Parolees." *Federal Probation* Dec. 1990: 22–31. Print.

Carey, Anne R., and Elys A. McLean. "Electronic Prison Bars." *USA Today* 30 Sept. 1993: A1. Print.

Ford, Daniel, and Annesley K. Schmidt. *Electronically Monitored Home Confinement*. United States. Natl. Inst. of Justice, Dept. of Justice. Washington: GPO, 1989. Print.

Gearan, Anne. "1.8M in U.S. Prisons, the Most Ever." *USA Today* 15 March 1999: A1. Print.

Georgia State. Probation Div. of the Georgia Dept. of Corrections. *Alternatives to Incarceration*. 1 July 1997. Web. 3 Feb. 1998.

Entry for collection containing several authors' contributions compiled by three editors

Entry for newspaper article

Entry for occupational journal article with three authors

Entry for newspaper item with two authors

Entry for government document, two authors given

Entry for Internet report, no author given

Jacque 11

Entry for book with two authors

Hofer, Paul J., and Barbara S. Meierhoefer. *Home Confinement: An Evolving Sanction in the Federal Criminal Justice System*. Washington: Federal Judicial Center, 1987. Print.

"Inmate Populations, Costs and Projection Models." *Corrections Compendium* Jan. 1997: 10-11. Print.

Entry for interview

Irrer, Richard N. Personal interview. 20 Feb. 2001.

Entry for popular magazine article with one author

Katel, Peter. "New Walls, No Inmates." *Newsweek* 18 May 1992: 63. Print.

Entry for Internet report, one author given

Lynch, Allen. *Cost Effectiveness of Incarceration*. 1994. Web. 1 July 1997.

Morris, Norval, and Michael Tonry. *Between Prison and Probation: Intermediate Punishments in a Rational Sentencing System*. New York: Oxford UP, 1990. Print.

Peck, Keenan. "High-Tech House Arrest." *Progressive* July 1988: 26-28. Print.

Entry for government document, one author given

Petersilia, Joan. *House Arrest*. United States. Natl. Inst. of Justice, Dept. of Justice. Washington: GPO, 1988. Print.

Quinlan, J. Michael. "Building More Prisons Will Solve Prison Overcrowding." *America's Prisons: Opposing Viewpoints*. Ed. David Bender, Bruno Leone, and Stacey Tipp. San Diego: Greenhaven, 1991. 112-16. Print.

Richey, Warren. "Bulging Cells Renew Debate over Prisons as Tools to Fight Crime." *Christian Science Monitor* 22 Jan. 1997: 3. Print.

Entry for occupational journal article with one author

Scaglione, Fred. "Jails without walls." *American City and County* Jan. 1989: 32-40. Print.

Jacque 12

---. "You're Under Arrest—at Home." *USA Today* magazine Nov. 1988:
26-28. Print.

Sullivan, Robert E. "Reach Out and Guard Someone: Using Phones
and Bracelets to Reduce Prison Overcrowding." *Rolling Stone*
29 Nov. 1990: 51. Print.

United States. Dept. of Justice. Bureau of Justice Assistance, Office of
Justice Programs. *Electronic Monitoring in Intensive Probation
and Parole Programs*. Washington: GPO, 1989.
Print.

United States. Senate. Subcommittee on Federal Spending, Budget,
and Accounting of the Committee on Governmental Affairs.
100th Cong., 1st sess. *Prison Projections: Can the United States
Keep Pace?* Washington: GPO, 1987. Print.

Using a Computer

Word-processor software programs can help you with the various stages
of library research. Several guidelines will enhance your efficiency as you
proceed.

Taking Notes

Students with laptop computers or notebooks sometimes take them into the
library and enter notes as they read their sources, despite the inconvenience that
often results. In most cases, though, you will find it works best to take notes on
cards, then afterward enter them and your bibliographical references into your
word processor. You can type notes into one central file and distribute them later
to separate files by topic or distribute them as you go along.

As you proceed, take great care to distinguish between your notes and your
thoughts about them. One good way to do this is to establish some system, such
as typing notes in boldface and putting brackets around your thoughts. To avoid
inadvertently using the exact words of others without giving proper credit, always

put quotation marks around directly quoted material. As an added safeguard you might also use different spacing for quotations. To identify the sources of your notes, you could number them to match the number of the source or end each note with the author's name. For an anonymous source use a shortened title. Finally, don't neglect to keep printouts of your notes and bibliography to guard against accidental erasure or a power surge.

Outlining

Many word-processing programs provide options that facilitate outlining. With some programs you can compare two arrangements side by side; others enable you to call up your stored and organized notes on one side of the screen and create your outline on the other side.

Don't let limitations of your software cramp your explorations of possibilities. If your program lets you compare two outlines but you'd like to check more, make a second and if necessary a third printout; then examine them side by side. Similarly, if an outline includes more items than a single screen can accommodate, continue on a second screen and use printouts to check the complete product.

Drafting

Students follow different approaches when drafting on a computer. Some follow the outline section by section, entering their notes and any thoughts that previously occurred to them, then go through everything again and add material. Others finish off one section before moving on to the next, some by focusing on their notes and then developing thoughts that elaborate on them, others by developing their thoughts and working in their notes afterward. Follow the procedure that works best for you.

When you write the paper, fight the urge simply to string your notes together. Such an approach results in a draft that lurches from one bit of information to another without consistent style or proper attention to the underlying thesis. If you find yourself merely typing in notes, stop, open a separate file, read each note carefully, and then enter your thoughts concerning it. When you've examined all the notes, begin the drafting process over again, integrating your notes and your thoughts in the new file.

As you compose, don't overfill any of your files; too many words leave little room for revision. You can avoid this problem by establishing a separate file for each section of your paper.

Revising and Formatting

Students often hesitate to revise research papers because of their length. A word processor gives you an edge. You can isolate sections and experiment with them; move large sections of the text around; or, if you used separate files for different sections, change transitions to reflect different orders. When you make such changes, check to see that you maintain the flow of the paper. An adjustment in one section must mesh logically and stylistically with what precedes and follows.

Reviewing a printout offers the best opportunity to check your paper's continuity. As you revise, always keep copies of earlier versions. Some part that seemed ineffective may fill a gap or take on a new look in view of your changes.

Finally, the formatting capabilities of word-processor software can be a powerful asset. Most programs will position page numbers, set margins properly, and add your name at the top of each page. Some programs will also indent bibliographic entries properly. Don't, however, neglect your instructor's specifications with regard to spacing, print style, and the like.

Using Images, Illustrations, and Graphs

Computer programs make it easy to import photographs, illustrations, and graphs into an essay and report. Visuals can be useful. An essay on different kinds of cats would be enhanced by pictures of cats. The best way to explain the bones in the skull is a labeled drawing. Complicated numbers can be presented best through the appropriate graphs or charts.

General Principles for Using Visuals

- **Use visuals only when they help.** Excess visuals detract from a text; visuals should be used when they are the best way of presenting the information. Clichéd clip art only detracts from important messages.
- **Visuals should fit the text.** Visuals shouldn't be just thrown in. Instead, they should have a connection to nearby text so that the meanings are related.
- **Visuals need to be explained.** Visuals don't always stand on their own. You need to explain to readers why they should look at the visual and direct their attention to what they should notice. With graphs and tables, it is helpful to explain first what to look for in the visual and then, after the visual, identify the major conclusion the readers could reach from the visual.
- **Visuals often need a title.** To direct the reader's attention, label all visuals. The title should tell the story of the visual.
- **Place visuals so they don't break up the text.** You want your page to be attractive but not distracting. Visuals need to be positioned so the page looks good but the flow of the text is not seriously interrupted.
- **Visuals should be honest.** It is important to represent the data fairly and not distort the image or graph to slant the information.

Pictures The use of a scanner or digital camera makes it easy to import pictures, which can spice up the text. If you use pictures, make certain they are clear and simple. Readers shouldn't have to spend time trying to decipher the picture.

Tables Including tables with columns and rows is an excellent way of comparing information such as the features of different computers, the quantity of sales, or even the quality of different employees. Make certain your table is clearly labeled. See Table 20.1 for an example.

Table 20.1 Use Different Classroom Media for Different Purposes			
Features	**Blackboard**	**Overhead**	**PowerPoint**
Class Time Used	Extensive; text written out in class	Minimal; prepared before class	Minimal; prepared before class
Equipment Required	Usually in every classroom	In most classrooms or easily obtained	Limited by limited number of computers and screens
Information Presented	Text and handdrawn images or low-resolution graphs	Text and images or graphs; variable resolutions	All text and visuals with good resolution
Flexibility in Classroom Environment	Plans can be easily changed; readily accepts new direction and student input	Limited flexibility: order can be varied between overheads; can write on blank overheads	Limited; hard to change order of presentation or enter new input

Pie Charts   Pie charts are an excellent way to present percentages or quantities of a whole. Figure 20.17 is a sample pie chart.

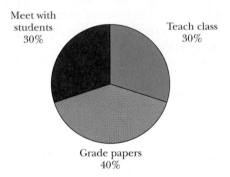

Figure 20.17   How Teachers Use Their Time

Bar Graphs   Bar graphs can help you present and compare data that isn't a continuous trend, as Figure 20.18 shows.

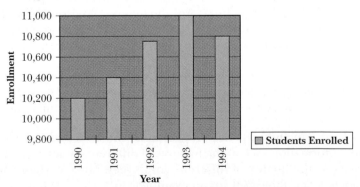

Figure 20.18   Student Enrollment Grows

Line Graphs   Line graphs are an excellent way to show data that are continuous over time and shows trends effectively. See Figure 20.19 for an example.

Figure 20.19   Temperatures at Noon Show Cold Spell

Headers, Numbered Lists, and Bullets

Information in longer reports is not always presented in an unbroken stream of text. You can use a number of devices to help readers.

- **Bold headings and subheadings can guide the reader to different sections of the text.** When the sections of a longer report, or even a shorter business memo, can be broken into distinct sections, it can be helpful to label those sections with bold words or phrases that will direct the reader's attention. This text uses headings and subheadings and so do some of the articles in the Reader.
- **Lists can be a useful way to present organized information.** Steps in a process, several recommendations, the identification of important qualities can all be well represented by an indented list. The discussion questions in this text are all presented as numbered lists.
- **Bullets are used when listed information shouldn't be numbered because there is no implied sequence.** The recommendations for using visuals in this section are presented as a bulleted list. Lists and bullets should use parallelism, the same grammatical form.

Writing Your Research Paper Checklist

Search Checklist

- Brainstorm to focus your topic.
- Get an overview by searching general references such as encyclopedias.
- Search your library for books.
     Use either key term or subject searches using a computer catalog.
     Copy or print out the call number that locates the book.
     Scan the books in your located section for unexpected finds.

- Search your periodical indexes and databases.

  Select an index or database that fits your topic.

  InfoTrac and Wilson Select are often useful starting indexes.

  Use either key term or subject searches.

  Use the headings you find to narrow or guide your search.

  Print or copy the title of the articles, the author, the magazine, the volume number, the page number, and the date.

  If you use a full text of an online article, be sure to copy the reference information.

  Find the hard copy, microfiche, or microfilm version of your article.

- Search the Internet.

  Use an appropriate search engine such as Google or Yahoo.

  Try several combinations of terms or modify them to narrow a search.

  Assess the credibility of all Internet sources based on the source for the site, author, quality of the Web pages, consistency with other credible information.

  Be sure to copy or print the URL, author (if any), and title (if any).

Taking Notes Checklist

- Evaluate your source by author's qualification, publication's credibility, and obvious bias.
- Take notes using cards, yellow pad, or computer file.

  Keep track of source and page number for each note.

  You may want to cross-reference notes with bibliography cards.

  Give a title to each note card that identifies the notes topic.

- Respond as you take notes with your own thoughts and observations.
- Consciously decide to summarize, paraphrase, or quote in your notes.

  If you paraphrase, it must be completely in your own words.

  If you quote, be sure to mark your quotes so you don't forget.

- Always consciously work to avoid plagiarism.

  Always carefully record your sources for notes.

  Do not simply change a few words in a paraphrase.

  Do not forget to mark quotes when you quote.

  Ask you teacher or a tutor if you are not sure of the rules.

Drafting Your Paper Checklist

- Take steps to integrate your information.

  Read over your notes.

  Possibly write a brief draft without looking at your notes.

- Write an outline.

  Determine the main divisions of your paper.

  Read note cards for subdivisions.

  Detail either a sentence or topic outline.

- Key your note cards to your outlines.
- Determine if you need to perform additional research.

- Draft your paper in sections.
  - Work to keep the paper in your own voice.
  - Don't get stuck on the introduction. Just write.
  - Use your notes to support your claims but don't just cut and paste.
  - Be sure to document as you write.
  - Avoid plagiarism.
  - Create deliberate transitions between sections.
  - Go back and rework the introduction and conclusion.
  - Carefully document using the material from the next chapter.

Revising Your Draft Checklist

- Do not be afraid to make extensive changes.
- Read and change the paper with an eye to your original purpose.
- Get feedback from other readers.
- Check for material that doesn't fit and needs to be cut.
- Check for holes that may require additional research and do it if needed.
- Check your notes to see that you didn't leave out something important.
- Check to see that the paper is easy to follow.
- Smooth your transitions and add transition paragraphs where needed.
- Make certain the draft is in a consistent voice.

SAMPLE

SAMPLE APA STUDENT RESEARCH PAPER

Running head: INSTANT COMMUNICATION   1

Instant Communication Does Not Ensure Good Communication

Bruce Gilchrist

Ferris State University

Abstract Page

INSTANT COMMUNICATION   2

Abstract

This review of the literature finds that increased rates of communication from voice mail, cellular phones, e-mail, and other sources results in increased levels of stress and decreased productivity. Technostress includes interruptions and the perceived demand for immediate response to the stress. Studies have found that the interruption negatively affects on productivity and even IQ. Defense mechanisms for instant communication need to be adopted as coping strategies.

Keywords: instant communication, e-mail, text messaging, technostress, productivity.

~~~~~~

Instant Communication Does Not Ensure Good Communication

The technological revolution ushered many new communications technologies and devices into the modern office over the past 25 years. "Every day brings yet another new communication device, software program, or piece of computer hardware that workers have to know, need to use, or must have to do their job" (Weil & Rosen, 1999, p. 56). The popularity of these devices at the office and declining costs eventually led to their acceptance for personal use outside the office. After all, who wouldn't want to take advantage of the benefits they offer? The fax machine reduces dependence on the postal system for moving paper documents. Voice mail, pagers, and cell phones make it possible to communicate with others even when they are away from their home or office telephones. Newer technologies such as e-mail and electronic text messaging allow individuals to remain connected with business associates, family, and friends on an almost perpetual basis.

Each new electronic communications gadget is hyped by its creator as yet another labor-and time-saving device. Marketing efforts and corporate management describe these devices almost as if they possess magical powers. Simply by using these devices, one is suddenly able to do more with less. Less time, less manual labor, lower costs, and so on. But are the users of these communications technologies really reaping the benefits that they were promised? Or have the negative aspects of these technologies been masked by clever marketing campaigns and corporate policies? Whether used professionally, personally, or both, many end users of these technologies are unaware of the negative effects to which they are subjecting themselves. Excessive or uncontrolled use of fax machines, voice mail, pagers, cellular phones, e-mail, and text messaging can lead to increased stress levels and decreased productivity.

INSTANT COMMUNICATION   4

Speaking in general terms, the first problem presented by instant communication technologies is that they contribute to a specialized form of stress known as technostress. The term was first defined in 1983 by clinical psychologist Craig Brod as "'a modern disease of adaptation caused by an inability to cope with the new computer technologies in a healthy manner'" (Genco, 2000, p. 1). Brod's original definition was primarily addressing the personal computer revolution and has since been modified to be more inclusive of newer forms of technology. In 1997, clinical psychologists Michelle Weil and Larry Rosen enhanced the definition of technostress to include "'any negative impact on attitudes, thoughts, behaviors, or body psychology caused directly or indirectly by technology'" (p. 1). Weil further explains technostress as "'our reaction to technology and how we are changing due to its influence'" (p. 1). Using these expanded definitions it is not difficult to conclude that instant communication technologies can indeed be a source of technostress.

The simplest form of technostress produced by instant communication technologies is the stream of constant interruptions they ultimately produce. As an information technology support specialist, I often find myself working on complex technical problems that require my full attention and mental concentration. Interruptions from pagers, cell phones, and text messaging are distracting, as they force me to break away from the task at hand to deal with the incoming communication. Not only do these distractions lengthen the time necessary to complete a task, but they can also introduce errors, as my attention is not fully focused on a single task.

Adding to this stress is the prevailing attitude that because these technologies provide for instant communication, one should receive an instant response to any messages they send. For me, having to interrupt the task at hand and respond to these incoming messages is indeed disruptive and can lower my productivity when the volume of messages becomes excessive. Personal interviews revealed that my views are shared by others as well. One interviewee stated his biggest complaint is that the constant stream of interruptions brought on by pagers, cell phones, and e-mail make it difficult for him to prioritize or sometimes even complete tasks (L. Murphy, personal communication, March 25, 2005). He further added that not only does everyone think their message is a top priority, they are also unaware of how many other messages the recipient already has waiting for a response. Another respondent criticizes overzealous management for adding to the problem. In a crisis situation, management frequently requests status updates via some form of instant communication. What they fail to realize is that every message they send requires the recipient to divert their focus away from the crisis situation and only lengthens the time it takes to resolve the problem (J. Tice, personal communication, March 25, 2005).

Newly published research supports these individuals' claims that the constant interruptions resulting from instant communications technologies are not only disruptive but detrimental to productivity. In one study, more than 1,000 individuals were subjected to persistent interruptions either through e-mail or text messaging. Monitoring and testing of the subjects allowed researchers to determine that such interruptions produce a temporary but measurable drop in intelligence (Burnett & Ortiz, 2005). *The Houston Chronicle* summarized the study by reporting, "Constant e-mailing and text messaging reduces mental ability by 10 IQ points, a more severe effect than smoking cannabis, by distracting the brain from other tasks" (Moore, 2005). By comparison, a sleepless night will produce the same effect while smoking marijuana only causes a 4 point reduction (Moore, 2005).

Even more troubling is that the disruptions produced by instant communications technologies extend outside the professional and laboratory environments as well. Because pagers and cell phones with text messaging are portable devices and most employees have Internet access to their corporate e-mail from home, their reach is extended far outside the office. These devices have invaded the home and are eating away at our personal time. Research indicates somewhere between one-half and three-quarters of office professionals use business-related communication technologies outside the office for up to 2 hours per day (Weil & Rosen, 2004). A recent article in *Today's Parent* discusses how time spent working outside of office hours is taken away from other activities

INSTANT COMMUNICATION   6

such as time parents should be spending with their families (Lopez-Pacheco, 2003).

Psychologists concur that all this electronic communication is contributing to a wide array of undesirable psychological changes and increasing personal stress levels. People are becoming more isolated as they choose to use electronic means of communicating over traditional interpersonal methods (Rizzo, 1999). It is becoming increasingly more difficult for people to define their personal space boundaries and separate their personal and professional lives. According to Terrie Hienrich Rizzo (1999), "This boundary breakdown leads to a feeling of never being able to get away and contributes to an inability to relax" (p. 1). That anyone may be watching TV or reading a good book when a pager or cell phone beckons with a work-related problem clearly demonstrates this lack of separation and its consequences.

I do not argue that instant communication technologies can offer benefits to the busy professional. However, the growing body of research supports my belief that these devices can elevate stress levels and reduce productivity when used inappropriately. I know from personal experience that I was a victim of the negative effects that these technologies can manifest. The experts call it technostress, multitasking mania, or information overload, but for me, the end result was career burnout regardless of what term is used to define how or why it happened. In fact, I am probably one of the statistics cited in an *Information Week* report stating that information technology professionals are burning out in ever-increasing numbers (Lally, 1997).

The reality is that not only are these electronic communication technologies a current problem we must deal with, but if left unchecked, the problem will only grow worse in the future. The number one recommendation of experts to reduce the stress manifested by instant communication devices and technologies is to limit their use. While this seems like an obvious solution, few people fail to put it into practice. Implementing some basic defense strategies to manage the interruptions of instant messages can go a long way toward reducing the stress they can produce (Rizzo, 1999). One is to disable notification

INSTANT COMMUNICATION   7

of new voice mail and e-mail so that users can check it on their own schedule rather than when it demands their attention. Another is for users to take regular time-out periods where they inform others that they will not be reachable via a pager or cell phone. This will ensure that today's professionals have some time available to redefine personal space boundaries, spend with their family, or just read a good book (Rizzo, 1999).

INSTANT COMMUNICATION

References

Burnett, J. H., & Ortiz, V. (2005, April 23). Does more IM = a lower IQ? *Milwaukee Journal Sentinel*, P. A3.

Genco, P. (2000, September/October). Technostress in our schools and lives. *Book Report*, pp. 42–43. Retrieved from WilsonSelectPlus database.

Lally, R. (1997, October 6). Managing techno-stress. *Getting Results—for the Hands-On Manager, 6,* 5–6. Retrieved from WilsonSelectPlus database.

Lopez-Pacheco, A. (2003, February). Baby, baby, don't get hooked on me. *Today's Parent*, pp. 110–112.

Moore, K. J. (2005, April 23). Constant e-mail harms intellect. [Electronic version.] *The Houston Chronicle*, p. B3.

Rizzo, T. H. (1999, November/December). Taming technostress. *IDEA Health & Fitness*. Retrieved from InfoTrac Onefile database.

Weil, M., & Rosen, L. (1999). Don't let technology enslave you. *Workforce, 78(2),* 56–60.

———. (2004). TechnoStress. Retrieved from http://www.technostress.com

CHAPTER 21

Documenting Sources

In order to acknowledge and handle sources, you must know how to (1) prepare proper bibliographical references, (2) document sources within your text, (3) handle quotations, and (4) avoid plagiarism.

The kind of information included in bibliographical references depends on the type of source and the documentation system. Two systems are in common use: the Modern Language Association (MLA) system and the American Psychological Association (APA) system. The entries that follow illustrate basic MLA and APA conventions. Both the MLA and APA systems use the hanging indent for entries in the reference list. Start the first line of each entry flush to the left margin and indent all subsequent lines five spaces.

For more information, consult the *MLA Handbook for Writers of Research Papers*, 7th ed., 2009, and the *Publication Manual of the American Psychological Association*, 6th ed., 2009. When documenting online sources, consult the Web site noted on page 421 to supplement the information in the *Manual*. **It is important to note two changes to the MLA style for bibliographic references.**

1. The MLA now uses italics instead of underlining for idependently published works such as books, periodicals, Web sites, and television and radio broadcasts. You still use quotation marks for shorter works such as articles or poems that appear in a larger publication.
2. At the end of each entry, the MLA style now has you indicate the medium through which you retrieved it. The categories are Print, Web, CD, Peformance, etc. An electronic version of a book retrieved online would be Web, and a copy of an article retrieved from a bound volume would be Print.

MLA

Preparing Proper MLA Bibliographic References

Books

■ A Book with One Author

Wilk, Max. *Every Day's a Matinée*. New York: Norton, 1975. Print.

■ A Book with Two Authors

Duncan, Dayton, and Ken Burns. *Lewis and Clark*. New York: Knopf, 1997. Print.

■ A Book with More than Three Authors

Alder, Roger William, et al. *Mechanisms in Organic Chemistry*. New York: Wiley,
        1971. Print.   The MLA system permits the use of "et al." for four or more
        authors or editors (listing all authors is also permitted).

■ A Book with a Title That Includes Another Title

Set off the title of the mentioned work with quotation marks.

Tanner, John. *Anxiety in Eden: A Kierkegaardian Reading of "Paradise Lost."*
        Oxford: Oxford UP, 1992. Print

■ A Book with Corporate or Association Authorship

United Nations. Public Administration Div. *Local Government Training*.
        New York: United Nations, 1968. Print.

■ An Edition Other than the First

Turabian, Kate L. *A Manual for Writers of Term Papers, Theses, and Dissertations*.
        6th ed. Chicago: U of Chicago P, 1996. Print.

■ A Book in Two or More Volumes

Bartram, Henry C. *The Cavalcade of America*. 2 vols. New York: Knopf,
        1959. Print.

2 **REPRESENTATIONS OF THE POST/HUMAN**

Monsters, aliens and others in popular culture

1 ELAINE L. GRAHAM

Rutgers University Press **4**
3 New Brunswick, New Jersey

1 Author—last name first
2 Title in italics
3 City of publication followed by a colon
4 Publisher
5 Date of publication
6 Medium

First published in the United States 2002 by Rutgers University Press, New Brunswick, New Jersey

First published in Great Britain 2002 by Manchester University Press Oxford Road, Manchester M13 9NR, UK www.manchesteruniversitypress.co.uk

ISBN 0-8135-3058-X (cloth)
ISBN 0-8135-3059-8 (paperback)

British Cataloging-in-Publication information is available from the British Library.

1 **2**
Graham, Elaine L. *Representations of the Post/Human: Monsters, Aliens and Others in Popular Culture. New Brunswick: Rutgers* **3** **4**
UP, 2002 Print.
4 **5** **6**

---

6 **3** **4** **5**
18   SCIENCE FICTION STUDIES, VOLUME 33 (2006)

1 **Robert Harding**

2 Manuel Castells's Technocultural Epoch in *The Information Age*

Manual Castells writes on economy and society in the age of postmodern capital in his sociological trilogy *The Information Age*, published in 1996–98. Aiming for a "grounded theory" (Kreisler 3)—a hybridized approach that synthesizes contemporary French thought with an American empirical tradition—Castells stresses that his work is based on direct observation rather than merely "playing with words" (Kreisler 3), an approach he associates with those who "deconstruct" and abstractly theorize. As he writes at the beginning of the second volume of the trilogy, *The Power of Identity*: "This is not a book about books" (2).

In this essay, I will trace the development of what Castells calls information society. My approach involves three overlapping tracks. First, I sketch what Castells calls network "flows"—of images, wealth, and power—in global information technology. Second, I evaluate social changes arising out of the network society and how they redefine identity in both global and local contexts. Finally, I read selected science fiction texts with a view to remarking on fictional parallels with Castells's theses on informationalism.

Castells is known for his cross-cultural approach, fusing research into the information-technology revolution in the San Francisco Bay area with quantitative and qualitative data drawn from Europe, Latin America, and the Asian-Pacific Rim. In Volume 1 of *The Information Age, The Rise of Network Society*, Castells demonstrates that an information-based future will materialize in the form of a new kind of urban space: the "new global economy and the emerging informational society have indeed a new spatial form, which develops in a variety of social and geographical contexts: megacities" (*Rise* 434). He then outlines how future urban development will assume new levels of power and influence: "mega-cities articulate the global economy, link up the informational networks, and concentrate the world's power" (*Rise* 434). Castells projects this mode of development by detailing a Chinese example, the emerging "Hong Kong—Shenzen—Canton—Peral River Delta—Macau—Zhuhai metropolitan regional system" (*Rise* 436), which constitutes a massive transformation of the social world for global marketing and informational purposes.

Like sociologist Max Weber, Castells seeks to define the spirit of the age. Where Weber studied the animating force of the industrial age in the Protestant work ethic, Castells sees the ethos of the information age in the *network*. In his essay "The New Weber," Chris Freeman writes that Castells "characterises the 'informational society' as essentially a capitalist system" (156). As Castells himself puts it:

1 **2**
Harding, Robert. "Manuel Castells's Technocultural Epoch in *The Information Age*." Science Fiction Studies 33 (2006): 18-38 Print.
2 **3** **4** **5** **6** **7** **8**

1 Author—last name first
2 Title of article in quotation marks with period inside quotation marks
3 Title of journal in italics
4 Volume number
5 Date of publication
6 First page number
7 Final page number on final page of article
8 Medium

What Was Jim Crow?

Jim Crow FERRIS STATE UNIVERSITY
MUSEUM OF RACIST MEMORABILIA

What Was Jim Crow?

Many Blacks resisted the indignities of Jim Crow, and, far too often, they paid for their bravery with their lives.
1
© Dr. David Pilgrim, Professor of Sociology Ferris State University
Sept., 2000 **4**

[1] Kennedy, Stetson. Jim Crow Guide: The Way It Was. Boca Raton: Florida Atlantic University Press, 1959/1990, pp.216–117.

[2] This list was derived from a larger list composed by the Martin Luther King, Jr., National Historic Site Interpretive Staff
6

http://www.ferris.edu/jimcrow/what.htm

1 Author—last name first
2 Title of article in quotation marks
3 Periodical or source location
4 Date the article was published
5 Page numbers of the article
6 Medium
7 Date it was retrieved

1 **2** **3**
Pilgrim, David. "What Was Jim Crow?" *Jim Crow Museum of Racist Memorabilia. Sept. 2000: 1-8. 20 Mar. 2006.* **4** *Web. 9.*
6 **4** **5** **7**

■ A Reprint of an Older Work

Matthiessen, F. O. *American Renaissance: Art and Expression in the Age of Emerson and Whitman.* 1941. New York: Oxford UP, 1970. Print.

■ A Book with an Editor Rather than an Author

Deetz, James, ed. *Man's Imprint from the Past: Readings in the Methods of Archaeology.* Boston: Little, 1971. Print.

■ A Book with Both an Author and an Editor

Melville, Herman. *The Confidence Man.* Ed. Hershel Parker. New York: Norton, 1971. Print.

■ A Translation

Beauvoir, Simone de. *All Said and Done.* Trans. Patrick O'Brian. New York: Putnam, 1974. Print.

■ An Essay or Chapter in a Collection of Works by One Author

Woolf, Virginia. "The Lives of the Obscure." *The Common Reader, First Series.* New York: Harcourt, 1925. 111-18. Print.

■ An Essay or Chapter in an Anthology

Angell, Roger. "On the Ball." *Subject and Strategy.* Ed. Paul Eschholz and Alfred Rosa. New York: St. Martin's, 1981. 34-41. Print.

Periodicals

Periodicals include newspapers, popular magazines, and specialized occupational and scholarly journals. The basic information for a periodical article includes the name of the article's author, the name of the periodical, the title of the article, the date of publication, the page range of the entire article, and, for scholarly journals, the volume number of the periodical. The MLA system capitalizes periodical titles; however, the MLA style omits an introductory *The* from these titles.

■ An Article in a Scholarly Journal Consecutively Paged through the Entire Volume

Pfennig, David. "Kinship and Cannibalism." *Bioscience* 47 (1997): 667–75. Print.

■ An Article in a Scholarly Journal That Pages Each Issue Separately

Block, Joel W. "Sodom and Gomorrah: A Volcanic Disaster." *Journal of Geological Education* 23.5 (1976): 74-77. Print.

■ An Unsigned Article in a Scholarly Journal

"Baby, It's Cold Inside." *Science* 276 (1997): 537-38. Print.

■ A Signed Article in an Occupational or Popular Magazine

Gopnik, Adam. "The Good Soldier." *New Yorker* 24 Nov. 1997: 106-14. Print.

■ An Unsigned Article in an Occupational or Popular Magazine

"Robot Productivity." *Production Engineering* May 1982: 52-55. Print.

■ A Signed Article in a Daily Newspaper

Wade, Nicholas. "Germ Weapons: Deadly but Hard to Use." *New York Times* 26 Nov. 1997, natl. ed.: A13+. Print.

■ An Unsigned Article in a Daily Newspaper

"The Arithmetic of Terrorism." *Washington Post* 14 Nov. 1997: A26. Print.

Encyclopedia Articles

When documenting familiar works, such as the *Encyclopedia Americana*, the basic information for the MLA system includes the name of the article's author if known, the title of the article, the name of the encyclopedia, and the date of the edition.

Sobieszek, Robert A. "Photography." *World Book Encyclopedia*. 1991 ed. Print.

The MLA system requires additional information when less familiar publications are documented.

Fears, J. Rufus. "Emperor's Cult." *Encyclopedia of Religion*. Ed. Mircea Eliade. 16 vols. New York: Macmillan, 1987. Print.

For an anonymous article, references begin with the article's title.

Government Documents

The basic information for a federal, state, or foreign government publication that is documented using the MLA system includes the name of the author; the title of the publication; the name of the government and the agency issuing the publication; the place of publication; the name of the printing group, if known; and the date. If no author is named, begin by identifying the government and then cite the government agency as the author.

Carpenter, Russell D. *Defects in Hardened Timber*. United States. Dept. of
    Agriculture, Forest Service. Washington: GPO, 1989. Print.

United States. Environmental Protection Agency, Consumer Products Safety
    Commission. *Asbestos in the Home*. Washington: GPO, 1989. Print.

United States. Cong. Office of Technology Assessment. *The Biology of Mental
    Disorders*. 102nd Cong., 2nd sess. Washington: GPO, 1992. Print.

Other Sources

■ Book Reviews

Koenig, Rhoda. "Billy the Kid." Rev. of *Billy Bathgate*, by E. L. Doctorow. *New York*
    20 Feb. 1989: 20-21. Print.

If the review is untitled, follow the above format but omit the missing element.

■ Published Interviews

Noriega, Manuel. "A Talk with Manuel Noriega." By Felipe Hernandez. *News
    Report* 20 Mar. 1997: 28-30. Print.

■ Personal Interviews

If you conducted the interview yourself and are using the MLA system, start with the name of the person interviewed and follow it with the kind of interview and the date conducted.

Newman, Paul. Personal interview. 18 May 2001.

■ Audiovisual Media

Frankenstein. Dir. James Whale. Perf. Boris Karloff, John Boles, Colin Clive, and
    Mae Clarke. Universal, 1931. Film.

If you are interested in the contribution of a particular person, start with that person's name. Use the same model for videocassette and DVD recordings, and add release dates and distributors.

Whale, James, dir. *Frankenstein*. Perf. Boris Karloff, John Boles, Colin Clive, and
    Mae Clarke. Universal, 1931. Film.

Whale, James, dir. *Frankenstein*. Perf. Boris Karloff, John Boles, Colin Clive, and
Mae Clarke. 1931. DVD. Universal, 1999. DVD.

■ Television and Radio Programs

Washington Week in Review. Prod. S. Ducat. PBS. WKAR, East Lansing. 6 Jan. 1995.
Television.

Use this format when additional information is pertinent:

Peril at End House. By Agatha Christie. Adapt. Clive Exton. Dir. Renny Rye. Prod.
Brian Eastman. Perf. David Suchet and Hugh Fraser. Mystery. Introd. Diana
Rigg. PBS. WKAR, East Lansing. 12 Aug. 1993. Television.

■ Music and Sound Recordings

Smith, Bessie. *The World's Greatest Blues Singer*. Columbia, 1948. LP.

Smith, Bessie. "Down Hearted Blues." *The World's Greatest Blues Singer*.
Columbia, 1948. LP.

■ CD-ROMs

Norman, J. L. "Barcelona." *Software Toolworks Multimedia Encyclopedia*. Disc 1.
Danbury: Grolier, 1996. CD.

Online Sources

Be sure to ask your instructor which format to follow, and then use that format
consistently. Often data from the Internet are incomplete, perhaps lacking an
author, a title, or page or paragraph number. Include all the available information, but omit the correct address.

■ Books

The basic information for a book documented by the MLA system includes the
name of the author, if known; the title of the book; the place and date of original
publication, if applicable; the electronic site, if named; the date of electronic
publication if the online version has never been published in print or if it is part
of a scholarly project; the sponsor of the site; the medium by which it was
retrieved; and the date the material was retrieved.

Chaney, Walter J., William J. Diehm, and Frank Seeley. *The Second 50 Years: A
Reference Manual for Senior Citizens*. Weed: London Circle, 1999. Web. 8
Aug. 2000.

Locke, John. *An Essay concerning Human Understanding*. London, 1690. Inst. of
Learning Technologies. 1995. Columbia U. Web. 24 June 2000.

■ Periodicals on the World Wide Web

Periodicals online include specialized occupational and scholarly journals, popular magazines, newspapers, and newsletters. The basic information for a periodical includes the author's name, if known; the title of the article; the title of the periodical; the volume and issue numbers, if applicable; the date the article was published; the article's page numbers (or n. *pag.* if none are given); the medium of the material; the date the material was retrieved; and the online address only when necessary to find the material.

Cervetti, Nancy. "In the Breeches, Petticoats, and Pleasures of Orlando." *Journal
of Modern Literature* 20.2 (1996): n. pag. Web. 8 Jan. 1998.

Navarro, Mireya. "Women in Sports Cultivating New Playing Fields." *New York
Times on the Web* 13 Feb. 2001. Web. 22 Feb. 2001.

"No Link Found in Violence, Videos." *Boston Globe Online* 8 Aug. 2000. Web. 27
Aug. 2000.

Oakes, Jeannie. "Promotion or Retention: Which One Is Social?" *Harvard Education
Letter*. Jan.-Feb. 1999: n. pag. Web. 8 Aug. 2000.

■ Periodicals Accessed through an Online Library Service or Large Network
Provider

Full-text articles are available online at libraries or at home through services such as LexisNexis, ProQuest Direct, and America Online. Cite the author's name, if known; the title of the article; the title of the periodical; the date the article was published; the page numbers for the article (if the service identifies only the initial page of the article, indicate the page followed by a plus sign, 132+; if no page is given, use *n. pag.*); the name of the database or Web site in italics; *Web* as the medium of publication; and the date the material was accessed.

Clemetson, Lynette. "A Ticket to Private School." *Newsweek* 27 Mar. 2000: n. pag.
LexisNexis. Web. 5 May 2000.

Mayo Clinic. "Lung Cancer." 21 Feb. 2000. *America Online*. Web. 10 June 2000.

■ Encyclopedia Articles

The basic information for an encyclopedia article accessed through the Web includes the author's name, if known; the title of the article; the name of the encyclopedia; the date of the edition; the vendor; the medium of publication; and the date of access.

Daniel, Ralph Thomas. "The History of Western Music." *Britannica Online: Macropaedia*. 1995. Encyclopaedia Britannica. Web. 14 June 1995.

■ Government Documents

The basic information for a government document includes the name of the author, if known; the title; the name of the government and agency issuing the document; the place of publication and printing group, if known; the date of publication; the medium of publication; the date the material was retrieved; and the online address only if necessary to find the material. If no author is given, begin by identifying the government and then give the government agency as the author.

Georgia State. Probation Div. of the Georgia Dept. of Corrections. *Alternatives to Incarceration*. 1 July 1997. Web. 3 Feb. 1998.

■ Personal Home Page

The basic information for a personal home page documented according to the MLA system includes the name of its originator, if known; the title of the site, if any (use *Home page* or other such description if no title is given); the date of the latest update, if given; the medium of publication; and the date the material was retrieved from the site.

Lanthrop, Olin. Home page. Web. 24 June 2000.

■ Newsgroups, Electronic Mailing Lists, and E-Mail

MLA gives guidelines for including newsgroups, electronic mailing lists (sometimes called Listservs), and e-mail within the Works Cited list.

Corelli, Aldo. "Colleges and Diversity." Dept. of English, U of Michigan, 20 Apr. 2003. Web. 25 Apr. 2003.

Nicholson, Brad. "Casino Gambling." Message to Jason Elridge. 2 Feb. 2001. E-mail.

Preparing Proper APA Bibliographic References

The APA has recently published its 6th edition. To better meet the challenges of online publications, APA style now recommends that the unique work you are referencing in print and electronic form be identified by the digital object identifier (DOI), a unique identification sequence assigned by the International DOI Foundation. The DOI can often be found near the copyright notices of electronic journal articles or in some cases at the top of the first page of the article. When the DOI is used, there is no need to indicate the URL of the reference.

■ Sample

Mesmer-Magnus, J. R., & DeChurch, L. A. (2009). Information sharing and team
performance: A meta-analysis. *Journal of Applied Psychology, 94*(2), 535–546.
doi:10.1037/a0013773

Consult with your faculty member on whether they wish you to employ the DOI with print and online sources when it is available.

Books

The APA system uses initials rather than first and middle names for authors, editors, and translators.

■ A Book with One Author

Wilk, M. (1975). *Every day's a matinée*. New York, NY: Norton.

■ A Book with Two Authors

Duncan, D., & Burns, K. (1997). *Lewis and Clark*. New York, NY: Knopf.

■ A Book with More than Three Authors

Alder, R. W., Finn, T., Bradley, M. A., and Li, A. W. (1971). *Mechanisms in organic
chemistry*. New York, NY: Wiley.

The APA system gives up to and including six author or editor names in the reference list. Substitute "et al." for the seventh or more.

■ A Book with a Title That Includes Another Title

Words that would be italicized on their own should be set roman as part of an itlicized title.

Tanner, J. (1992). *Anxiety in Eden: A Kierkegaardian reading of* Paradise Lost.
Oxford, England: Oxford University Press.

■ A Book with Corporate or Association Authorship

United Nations, Public Administration Division. (1968). *Local government training*.
New York, NY: Author.

When the author of the work is also the publisher, the APA system uses the word "Author" following the place of publication. If the work is published by another organization, its name replaces "Author."

■ An Edition Other than the First

Turabian, K. L. (1996). *A manual for writers of term papers, theses, and dissertations* (6th ed.). Chicago, IL: University of Chicago Press.

■ A Book in Two or More Volumes

Bartram, H. C. (1959). *The cavalcade of America* (Vols. 1–2). New York, NY: Knopf.

■ A Reprint of an Older Work

Matthiessen, F. O. (1970). *American renaissance: Art and expression in the age of Emerson and Whitman*. New York, NY: Oxford University Press. (Original work published 1941)

■ A Book with an Editor Rather than an Author

Deetz, J. (Ed.). (1971). *Man's imprint from the past: Readings in the methods of archaeology*. Boston, MA: Little, Brown.

■ A Book with Both an Author and an Editor

Melville, H. (1971). *The confidence man* (H. Parker, Ed.). New York, NY: Norton. (Original work published 1857)

■ A Translation

Beauvoir, S. de. (1974). *All said and done* (P. O'Brian, Trans.). New York, NY: Putnam. (Original work published 1972)

■ An Essay or Chapter in a Collection of Works by One Author

Woolf, V. (1925). The lives of the obscure. In *The common reader, first series* (pp. 111–118). New York, NY: Harcourt Brace.

■ An Essay or Chapter in an Anthology

Angell, R. (1981). On the ball. In P. Eschholz & A. Rosa (Eds.), *Subject and strategy* (pp. 34–41). New York, NY: St. Martin's Press.

Periodicals

Periodicals include newspapers, popular magazines, and specialized occupational and scholarly journals. The basic information for a periodical article includes the name of the article's author, the date of publication, the title of the article, the name of the periodical, the page range of the entire article, and, for scholarly journals, the volume number of the periodical.

APA

■ An Article in a Scholarly Journal Consecutively Paged through the Entire Volume

Pfennig, D. (1997). Kinship and cannibalism. *Bioscience, 47,* 667–675.

■ An Article in a Scholarly Journal That Pages Each Issue Separately

Block, J. W. (1976). Sodom and Gomorrah: A volcanic disaster. *Journal of Geological Education, 23*(5), 74–77.

■ An Unsigned Article in a Scholarly Journal

Baby, it's cold inside. (1997). *Science, 276,* 537–538.

■ A Signed Article in an Occupational or Popular Magazine

Gopnik, A. (1997, November 24). The good soldier. *The New Yorker, 73,* 106–114.

■ An Unsigned Article in an Occupational or Popular Magazine

Robot productivity. (1982, May). *Production Engineering, 29,* 52–55.

■ A Signed Article in a Daily Newspaper

Wade, N. (1997, November 26). Germ weapons: Deadly but hard to use. *The New York Times,* pp. A13, A15.

■ An Unsigned Article in a Daily Newspaper

The arithmetic of terrorism. (1997, November 14). *The Washington Post,* p. A26.

Encyclopedia Articles

The APA system requires publication information for all encyclopedia citations when documenting familiar works, such as the *Encyclopedia Americana.*

Fears, J. R. (1987). Emperor's cult. In *The encyclopedia of religion* (Vol. 5, pp. 101–102). New York, NY: Macmillan.

For an anonymous article, references for the APA system begin with the article's title. Position the publication date, within parentheses, after this title. The remaining format is identical to citations with an author.

Government Documents

The APA system includes the name of the author, the date of publication, and the place of publication and adds a cataloging code where one exists.

Carpenter, R. D. (1989). *Defects in hardened timber* (UCLC Puplication No. 20504424). U.S. Department of Agriculture, Forest Service. Washington, DC: Government Printing Office.

U.S. Environmental Protection Agency, Consumer Products Safety Commission. (1989). *Asbestos in the home* (SUDOCS Report No. Y3.C76/3:2/A51/989). Washington, DC: Government Printing Office.

U.S. Congress, Office of Technology Assessment. (1992). *The biology of mental disorders* (SUDOCS Report No. Y3.T22/2:2/B57/10). Washington, DC: Government Printing Office.

APA

Other Sources

■ Book Reviews

Koenig, R. (1989, February 20). Billy the Kid [Review of the book *Billy Bathgate*]. *New York, 21,* 20–21.

If the review is untitled, follow the above format but omit the missing element.

■ Published Interviews

Hernandez, F. (1997, March 20). A talk with Manuel Noriega. *News Report, 15,* 28–30.

If the interview is untitled, follow the example above, omitting mention of a title.

■ Personal Interviews

For the APA system, a personal interview is considered personal correspondence and is not included in the References list. Instead, use an in-text parenthetical citation. Include the name of the person interviewed, the notation "personal communication," and the date: (P. Newman, personal communication, May 18, 2001).

■ Audiovisual Media

In the APA format, the citation begins with an individual's name and his or her contribution to the *motion picture* (use this term, not *film*). The country of origin (where it was made and released) is now required.

Whale, J. (Director). (1931). *Frankenstein* [Motion picture]. United States: Universal.

■ Television and Radio Programs

Ducat, S. (Producer). (1995, January 6). *Washington week in review* [Television broadcast]. Washington, DC: Public Broadcasting Service.

Use the following format when additional information is pertinent:

Exton, C. (Writer), & Rye, R. (Director). (1993). Peril at End House [Television series episode]. In B. Eastman (Producer), *Mystery*. Washington, DC: Public Broadcasting Service.

With the APA system, the name of the scriptwriter appears in the author's position, followed by the director. Any in-text references begin with the first name in the bibliographical reference (for example, Exton, 1993).

■ Music and Sound Recordings

The APA format requires identification of all formats, including a CD.

Smith, B. (1997). *The essential Bessie Smith* [CD]. New York, NY: Columbia Records.

Smith, B. (1948). Down hearted blues. On *The world's greatest blues singer* [CD]. New York, NY: Columbia Records. (Original recording February 17, 1923)

Recording dates, if different from the copyright year, follow the entry, enclosed in parentheses, with no final period.

■ Computer Software

Data Desk (Version 6.0) [Computer software]. (1997). Ithaca, NY: Data Description.

In the APA system, only specialized software or computer programs are listed in the References. Standard commercial software and languages should be cited by their proper name and version in the text itself.

■ CD-ROMs and Other Databases

Norman, J. L. (1996). Barcelona. In *Software toolworks multimedia encyclopedia* [CD-ROM]. Boston, MA: Grolier.

The APA *Manual* (6th ed.) takes the view that all aggregated databases are the same type of source, regardless of the format or manner of access (CD-ROM, library or university server, or online Web supplier). Follow the model above when you need to cite an entire CD-ROM (not a document from it). In a reference to information taken from a database (even a CD-ROM), give a "retrieval statement" containing the date you retrieved the document, article, or piece of data, as well as the full, correct name of the database. When you retrieve information from an online database, end the entry with a correct and complete URL for the specific document or version. In this case, the name of the database is omitted, unless this information will help in retrieval from a large or complex site. (See online models in the next section.)

Online Sources

The most recent edition of the *Publication Manual of the American Psychological Association* provides the APA's newest guidelines for documenting online sources. You can also consult the association's Web site for its most up-to-date information about citing electronic sources:

http://www.apastyle.org/elecref.html

Be sure to ask your instructor which format to follow and then use that format consistently. Often data from the Internet are incomplete, perhaps lacking an author, a title, or page or paragraph numbers. Include all the available information. The recommendation from the APA is that you cite document locations rather than home pages and that the referenced address actually works for that file. Remember, your goal is to allow your reader to find the source. Note the use of the DOI explained at the beginning of the section on APA References.

■ Books

Follow the general guidelines for a printed book, and conclude with appropriate electronic source information, as modeled here, or use the DOI, if known.

Locke, J. (1995). *An essay concerning human understanding*. New York, NY: Columbia University. Retrieved from http://www.ilt.columbia.edu/projects/digitexts/locke/understanding/title.html (Original work published 1690)

When some of the basic information is not provided, use whatever is available.

Chaney, W. J., Diehm, W. J., & Seeley, F. (1999). *The second 50 years: A reference manual for senior citizens*. Weed, CA: London Circle. Retrieved from http://www.londoncircle.com/2d50.html

To cite part of an electronic book, place the part's title after the date of publication. The APA also cites a chapter or section identifier following the title of the complete document.

Trochim, W. M. K. (2001). Language of research. In *The research methods knowledge base* (Foundations sec.). Cincinnati, OH: Atomic Dog. Retrieved from http://www.trochim.human.cornell.edu/kb/language.html

■ Periodicals on the World Wide Web

The APA recommends using the models for print periodicals when document-ing online articles that do not vary from their printed versions. In such cases, add [Electronic version] after the title and before the period to complete the citation. When the electronic format alters the printed version (e.g., no pagina-tion, added data or links), then cite as an online document, using a retrieval statement and the name of the database and/or the URL. APA guidelines ask for the identification of the server or the Web site in a retrieval statement only when it would be helpful in finding the source; for example, it is not necessary to state "Retrieved from the World Wide Web" since it is the most common access point to the Internet. If the DOI is available, that should be used instead of retrival data.

Cervetti, N. (1996). In the breeches, petticoats, and pleasures of Orlando. *Journal of Modern Literature, 20*(2). Retrieved from http://www.indiana.edu/~iupress /journals/mod-art2.html

Navarro, M. (2001, February 13). Women in sports cultivating new playing fields. *The New York Times on the Web*. Retrieved from http://www.nytimes.com

No link found in violence, videos. (2000, August 8). *Boston Globe Online*, p. A14. Retrieved from http://www.boston.com/dailyglobe2/no_li_nk_found_in_ violence_videos+.shtml

Oakes, J. (1999, January/February). Promotion or retention: Which one is social? *Harvard Education Letter*. Retrieved from http://www.edletter.org/past /issues/1999-jf/promotion.shtml

■ Periodicals Accessed through an Online Library Service or Large Network Provider

Increasingly, full-text articles are available online at libraries or at home through services such as LexisNexis, ProQuest Direct, and America Online. These serv-ices may or may not provide an online address for accessed material. In the APA documentation system, cite the author's name, if known; the date the article was published; the title of the article; the title of the periodical; and the page num-bers for the article, if available. Do not include the name of database.

Clemetson, L. (2000, March 27). A ticket to private school. *Newsweek*. Retrieved, from http://www.newsweek/com.icl/83469

APA style prefers that the URL that leads directly to the document file be pro-vided, following the word *from*.

■ Encyclopedia Articles

The basic information for an encyclopedia article accessed through the World Wide Web includes the author's name, if known; the date of the edition; the title of the article; the name of the encyclopedia; and the online address.

Daniel, R. T. (1995). The history of western music. In *Britannica online: Macropaedia*.
Retrieved from http://www.eb.com:180/cgi-bin/g:DocF=macro/5004/45/0.html

■ Government Documents

The basic information for a government document includes the name of the author, if known; the date of publication; the title; a cataloging code if one is available; and the online address. If no author is given, begin by identifying the government agency as the author.

Probation Division of the Georgia Department of Corrections. (1997, July 1).
Alternatives to incarceration (CSP Document No. 239875). Retrieved from
http://www.harvard.edu/~innovat/aiga87.html

■ Personal Home Page

The APA *Manual* offers no specific guidelines for personal home pages. We suggest that you use the following pattern, which conforms to general APA practice. Note that the APA system includes the date of the latest Web page revision, if known, in parentheses.

Lanthrop, O. (2000, May 28). Home page. Retrieved from http://www.cognivis.com
/olin/photos.htm

■ Newsgroups, Electronic Mailing Lists, and E-Mail

The APA format treats e-mail as personal communications, which are cited in parentheses in the text only. Newsgroups, online forums, discussion groups, and electronic mailing lists that maintain archives can be cited in the References. With these electronic forms, indicate the author's full last name and initials (screen name if the name is not available), the exact posting date, the name of the thread or blog, a label in brackets describing the type of message, "Retrieved from" followed by the name of list if not in the URL; and the address for the archived message. Categories include Online forum comment (messages posted to newsgroups, online forums, or discussion group), Electronic mailing list message (a message on an electronic mailing List or Listserve), Web log message (for a blog post), and Video file (Video blog post).

Trehub, A. (2002, January 28). Re: The conscious access hypothesis [Online forum
comment]. Retrieved from University of Houston Psyche Discussion Forum:
http://listserv.uh.edu/cig-bin/wa?A2=psyche-b&F=&S=&P=2334

EXERCISE ANSWERS (MLA STYLE)

a. Dow Chemical Company. *Gas Conditioning Fact Book.* Midland: Dow, 1962. Print.

b. "Booze Plays a Big Role in Car Crashes." *Detroit News.* 28 Nov. 1997, state ed. C2. Print.

c. Mills, C. Wright. "The Competitive Personality." *Power, Politics, and People.* Ed. Irving Horowitz. New York: Ballantine, 1963. 263-73. Print.

d. "Global Warming Fears on Rise." *Newswatch.* 25 Oct. 1997: 29-31. Print.

e. Theroux, Paul. *The Kingdom by the Sea.* Boston: Houghton, 1983. Print.

f. Chopin, Kate. *The Awakening.* Ed. Margaret Culley. New York: Norton, 1976. Print.

g. Cooke, James E. "Alexander Hamilton." *World Book Encyclopedia,* 1996 ed. Print.

h. McBride, Sarah. "Young Deadbeats Pose Problems for Credit-Card Issuers." *Wall Street Journal* 28 Nov. 1997, Midwest ed: B1+. Print.

i. Dabrowski, Magdalena, and Rudolph Leopold. *Egon Schiele.* New Haven; Yale UP, 1997. Print.

j. Descola, Jean. *A History of Spain.* Trans. Elaine P. Halperin. New York: Knopf, 1962. Print.

k. Flanagan, John T., and Raymond I. Grimer. "Mexico in American Fiction to 1850." *Hispania* 23 (1940): 307-18. Print.

l. United States. Marine Fisheries Service Dept. of Commerce. Nat. *Marine Fisheries Review.* Washington: GPO, 1993. Print.

1. **Using the MLA or APA system, write a proper reference for each of the unstyled information sets that follow:**

   a. A book titled Gas Conditioning Fact Book. The book was published in 1962 by Dow Chemical Company in Midland, Michigan. No author is named.

   b. An unsigned article titled Booze Plays a Big Role in Car Crashes. The article was published in the November 28, 1997, state edition of the Detroit News. It appears on page 2 of section C.

   c. An essay written by C. Wright Mills and titled The Competitive Personality. The essay appeared in a collection of Mills's writings titled Power, Politics, and People. The collection was published in 1963 by Ballantine Books in New York. The book is edited and introduced by Irving Louis Horowitz. The essay appears on pages 263 through 273.

   d. An unsigned article titled Global Warming Fears on Rise. The article was published in the October 25, 1997, issue of Newswatch magazine. It appears on pages 29 to 31.

   e. A book written by Paul Theroux and titled The Kingdom by the Sea. The book was published in 1983 by the Houghton Mifflin Company in Boston.

   f. A book written by Kate Chopin and titled The Awakening. The book, edited by Margaret Culley, was published in 1976 by W. W. Norton and Company in New York.

   g. An article written by James E. Cooke and titled Alexander Hamilton. The article appears on pages 31 and 32 of the World Book Encyclopedia, Volume 9, published in 1996.

   h. An article written by Sarah McBride and titled Young Deadbeats Pose Problems for Credit-Card Issuers. The article was published in the November 28, 1997, midwest edition of the Wall Street Journal. It appears on pages 1 and 6 of section B.

   i. A book written by Magdalena Dabrowski and Rudolph Leopold and titled Egon Schiele. The book was published in 1997 by the Yale University Press in New Haven, Connecticut.

   j. A book written by Jean Descola and titled A History of Spain. The book, translated by Elaine P. Halperin, was published in 1962 by Alfred A. Knopf in New York.

   k. An article written by John T. Flanagan and Raymond L. Grimer and titled Mexico in American Fiction to 1850. The article was published in 1940 in a journal called Hispania. It appears on pages 307 through 318. The volume number is 23.

   l. A United States government document titled Marine Fisheries Review. It was published by the National Marine Fisheries Service of the U.S. Department of Commerce in 1993 and is available from the Government Printing Office. No author is given.

   m. A book written by David Kahn and titled The Codebreakers. The second edition of the book was published in 1996 by Scribner's in New York.

   n. A book written by Joseph Blotner and titled Faulkner: A Biography. The book was published in two volumes in 1974 by Random House in New York.

   o. An article written by Calvin Tompkins and titled The Importance of Being Elitist. The article was published in the November 24, 1997, issue of the New Yorker. It appears on pages 58 through 69.

   p. A book written by Thomas Beer and titled Stephen Crane: A Study in American Letters. The book was published in 1923 and reprinted in 1972 by Octagon Books in New York.

   q. A review of a book written by Jacques Barzun and titled The Culture We Deserve. The review, by Beth Winona, appeared in the March 1989 issue of American Issues magazine and was titled Barzun and Culture. It appeared on pages 46 through 50.

r. An interview of playwright Neil Simon. The interview was titled Neil Simon on the New York Theater and appeared in the September 3, 1997, issue of the Long Island News, on pages C4 and C5. The interviewer was Pearl Barnes.

s. A film titled Casablanca. The film was directed by Michael Curtiz and starred Humphrey Bogart, Ingrid Bergman, Claude Rains, and Paul Henreid. It was released in 1942 by Warner Brothers.

t. A television program titled Grizzly. It appeared on WNTR, New York, on February 3, 1997. The station is part of the CBS network.

u. An online article with no author titled Robert Frost: A Reader Response Perspective. The article appears on the online journal Off the Wall and had a location of <http://www.offthewall.com/articles/backdated_bin_RobertFrost_archive.html>. The article is listed with the date May 8, 2003, but you found it on January 4, 2004.

v. An article written by May Gottchalk and titled Reconsidering Dyslexia that you accessed through a database. The article was published in the May 24, 2002, issue of Education Matters, and you retrieved the article using Wilson Select on November 22, 2003, on the Ferris State University Library Web Database Access with the address http://library.ferris.edu/databaseframes.html.

w. A personal page by Randy Cordial titled My Best Science Fiction Movies Ever. You found the Web page on May 4, 2004, at http://www.cordial.com/bestscifi.htm.

2. **Prepare a proper MLA or APA reference for each of the works you plan to use in writing your paper.**

Handling In-Text Citations

Both the MLA and APA systems use notations that appear within the text and are set off by parentheses. The systems are illustrated by the following examples.

Basic Citation Form

For the MLA system, the citation consists of the last name of the author and the page number of the publication in which the material originally appeared. The APA system identifies the last name of the author or authors and the year of publication. A page number is provided in APA both with quotations and when the information is so specific that it is important to reference the specific page.

■ Bibliographic Reference (MLA)

Rothenberg, Randall. "Life in Cyburbia." *Esquire* Feb. 1996: 56-63. Print.

■ Passage and Citation

MLA

A mania for the Internet has invaded many important aspects of our culture.

Newspapers run stories on it, businesses have rushed to set up Web sites, and

---

In Text

m. Kahn, David. *The Code-breakers.* 2nd ed. New York: Scribner's, 1996. Print.

n. Blotner, Joseph. *Faulkner: A Biography.* 2 vols. New York: Random, 1974. Print.

o. Tompkins, Calvin. "The Importance of Being Elitist." *New Yorker* 24 Nov. 1997: 58-69. Print.

p. Beer, Thomas. *Stephen Crane: A Study in American Letters.* 1923. New York: Octagon, 1972. Print.

q. Winona, Beth. "Barzun and Culture." Rev. of *The Culture We Deserve*, by Jacques Barzun. *American Issues* Mar. 1989: 46-50. Print.

r. Simon, Neil. "Neil Simon on the New York Theater." By Pearl Barnes. *Long Island News* 3 Sept. 1997: C4-C5. Print.

s. *Casablanca.* Dir. Michael Curtiz. Perf. Humphrey Bogart, Ingrid Berman, Claude Rains, and Paul Henreid. Warner Brothers, 1942. Film.

t. *Grizzly.* CBS. WNTR. New York. 3 Feb. 1997. Television.

u. "Robert Frost: A Reader Response Perspective." *Off the Wall* 8 May 2003: n. pag. Web. 22 Jan. 2004.

v. Gottchalk, May. "Reconsidering Dyslexia." *Education Matters* 24 May 2002; n. pag. *Wilson Select.* Web. 22 Nov. 2003.

w. Cordial, Randy. *My Best Science Fiction Movies Ever.* Web. 4 May 2004. http://www.cordial.com/bestscifi.htm>.

the Speaker of the House of Representatives has stated that even our poorest children have a stake in the Internet (Rothenberg 59).

MLA

Rothenberg states that a mania for the Internet has invaded many important aspects of our culture. Newspapers run stories on it, businesses have rushed to set up Web sites, and the Speaker of the House of Representatives has stated that even our poorest children have a stake in the Internet (59).

APA

. . . our poorest children have a stake in the Internet (Rothenberg, 1996).

APA

Rothenberg (1996) states . . . have a stake in the Internet.

■ **Bibliographic Reference (MLA)**

Weider, Benjamin, and David Hapgood. *The Murder of Napoleon.* New York: Congdon, 1982. Print.

■ **Passage and Citation**

MLA

Four different autopsy reports were filed. All the reports agreed that there was a cancerous ulcer in Napoleon's stomach, but none of them declared that the cancer was the cause of death. Nevertheless, cancer has become accepted as the cause (Weider and Hapgood 72).

APA

. . . Nevertheless, cancer has become accepted as the cause (Weider & Hapgood, 1982).

If a source has more than three authors (more than five for the APA), use "et al.," meaning "and others," for all but the first-named one.

■ **Bibliographic Reference (MLA)**

Baugh, Albert C., et al. *A Literary History of England.* New York: Appleton, 1948. Print.

■ **Passage and Citation (MLA)**

MLA

Although no one knows for certain just when Francis Beaumont and John Fletcher started collaborating, by 1610 they were writing plays together (Baugh et al. 573).

APA

. . . writing plays together (Baugh et al., 1948).

Authors with the Same Last Name

If your citations include authors with the same last name, use the initials of their first names to distinguish them.

■ **Bibliographic References (MLA)**

Adler, Jerry. "Search for an Orange Thread." *Newsweek* 16 June 1980: 32-34. Print.

Adler, William L. "The Agent Orange Controversy." *Detroit Free Press* 18 Dec. 1979, state ed.: B2. Print.

■ **Passage and Citation**

MLA

As early as 1966, government studies showed that dioxin-contaminated 2,4,5-T caused birth defects in laboratory animals. Later studies also found that this herbicide was to blame for miscarriages, liver abscesses, and nerve damage (J. Adler 32).

APA

. . . miscarriages, liver abscesses, and nerve damage (J. Adler, 1980).

Separate Works by the Same Author

If your references include two or more works by the same author, add shortened forms of the titles to your in-text citation if you follow the MLA system. But shortened book titles in italics, and use quotation marks around article and essay titles. For the APA system, use the conventional name–date–page number format. (Note: Page numbers are not always needed.)

■ **Bibliographic References (MLA)**

Mullin, Dennis. "After U.S. Troops Pull Out of Grenada." *US News & World Report* 14 Nov. 1983: 22-25. Print.

In Text

l. U.S. Department of Commerce, National Marine Fisheries Service. (1993). *Machine fisheries. review.* Washington, DC: Government Printing Office.

m. Kahn, D. (1996). *The codebreakers* (2nd ed.). New York, NY: Scribner's.

n. Blotner, J. (1974). *Faulkner: A biography* (Vols. 1–2). New York, NY: Random House.

o. Tompkins, C. (1997, November 24). The importance of being elitist. *The New Yorker,* 58–69.

p. Beer, T. (1972). *Stephen Crane: A study in American letters.* New York, NY: Octagon Books. (Original work published 1923)

q. Winona, B. (1989, March). Barzun and culture [Review of the book *The Culture We Deserve*]. *American Issues,* 46–50.

r. Barnes, P. (1973, September 3). Neil Simon on the New York theater. *Long Island News,* pp. C4, C5.

s. Curtiz, M. (Director). (1942). *Casablanca* [Motion picture]. United States: Warner Brothers.

t. *Grizzly.* (1997, February 3). [Television broadcast]. New York, NY: Columbia Broadcasting System.

u. Robert Frost: A reader response perspective. (2003, May 8). *Off the Wall.* Retrieved from http://www.offthewall

.com/articles/backdated_
bin_RobertFrost_archive.
html.

v. Gottchalk, M. (2002,
May 24). Reconsidering
dyslexia *Educational
Matters*. Retrieved
http://library.ferris
.edu/databaseframes.html

w. Cordial, R. My best
science fiction movies
ever. Retrieved from
http://www.cordial.com/
bestscifi.htm.

_ _ _. "Why the Surprise Move in Grenada—and What Next." *US News & World
　　Report* 7 Nov. 1983: 31-34. Print.

■ Passage and Citation

MLA

As the rangers evacuated students, the marines launched another offensive
at Grand Mal Bay, then moved south to seize the capital and free the governor
(Mullin, "Why the Surprise" 33).

APA

. . . and free the governor (Mullin, 1983b).

As the APA example illustrates, if the two works appeared in the same year, put
an "a" or a "b," without quotes, after the date to identify whether you are referring to the first or second entry for that author in the bibliography, arranged
alphabetically by title.

Two Sources for the Same Citation

If two sources provide essentially the same information and you wish to mention
both in one parenthetical citation, alphabetize them according to their authors'
last names, list them with a semicolon between them, and position the citation as
you would any other citation. (Citations in MLA style do not need to be listed
alphabetically.)

■ Bibliographic References (MLA)

Bryce, Bonnie. "The Controversy over Funding Community Colleges." *Detroit Free
　　Press* 13 Nov. 1988, state ed.: A4. Print.

Warshow, Harry. "Community College Funding Hits a Snag." *Grand Rapids Press*
　　15 Nov. 1988, city ed.: A2. Print.

■ Passage and Citation

MLA

In contending that a 3% reduction in state funding for community colleges
would not significantly hamper their operations, the governor overlooked the
fact that community college enrollment was expected to jump by 15% during
the next year (Warshow A2; Bryce A4).

APA

. . . enrollment was expected to jump by 15% during the next year (Bryce,
1988; Warshow, 1988).

In Text

Unsigned References

When you use a source for which no author is given, the in-text citation consists of all or part of the title, the appropriate page numbers, and, for the APA system, the date.

■ Bibliographic Reference (MLA)

"Money and Classes." *Progressive* Oct. 1997: 10. Print.

■ Passage and Citation

MLA

According to the General Accounting Office, repairing the country's dilapidated school buildings would carry a price tag of over $110 billion. Furthermore, constructing the 6,000 buildings needed to end classroom overcrowding would cost many billions more ("Money and Classes" 10).

APA

. . . many billions more ("Money and Classes," 1997).

Citing Quotations

In Text

When the quotation is run into the text, position the citation as shown in the following examples.

■ Bibliographic Reference (MLA)

Schapiro, Mark. "Children of a Lesser God." *Harper's Bazaar* Apr. 1996: 205+.
     Print.

■ Passage and Citation

MLA

UN investigators who have studied the extent of child labor in Third World countries estimate that "as many as 200 million children go to work rather than to school . . . making everything from clothing and shoes to handbags and carpets" (Schapiro 205).

APA

". . . handbags and carpets" (Schapiro, 1996, p. 205).

With longer, indented quotations, skip one space after the end punctuation and type the reference in parentheses.

■ Bibliographic Reference (MLA)

Newhouse, John. "The Diplomatic Round: A Freemasonry of Terrorism." *New Yorker* 8 July 1985: 46-63. Print.

■ Passage and Citation

MLA

One commentator offers this assessment of why foreign terrorist groups don't operate in this country:

> The reason that America has been spared so far, apparently, is that it is less vulnerable than Europe, especially to Middle Eastern extremists. Moving in and out of most European countries isn't difficult for non-Europeans; border controls are negligible. But American customs and immigration authorities, being hyper-alert to drug traffic, tend to pay attention to even marginally doubtful people, and a would-be terrorist . . . could come under surveillance for the wrong reason. (Newhouse 63)

APA

. . . come under surveillance for the wrong reason. (Newhouse, 1985, p. 63)

Indirect Citations

In MLA style, if you use a quotation from person A that you obtained from a book or article written by person B, or you paraphrase such a quotation, put "qtd. in" before the name of the publication's author in the parenthetical reference. In APA style, name the original work in the text and, then give the secondary source in parentheses preceded by "as cited in" rather than "qtd. in."

■ Bibliographic Reference (MLA)

Klein, Joe. "Ready for Rudy." *New York* 6 Mar. 1989: 30-37. Print.

■ Passage and Citation

MLA

Rudolph Giuliani favors the death penalty for "the murder of a law-enforcement officer, mass murder, a particularly heinous killing" but would impose it only "when there is certainty of guilt well beyond a reasonable doubt" (qtd. in Klein 37).

APA

Rudolph Giuliani favors ". . . certainty of guilt well beyond a reasonable
doubt" (as cited in Klein, 1989, p. 37).

Authors Identified in Text

Sometimes you'll want to introduce a paraphrase, summary, or quotation with
the name of its author. In this case, the page number may be positioned immediately after the name or follow the material cited.

■ Bibliographic Reference (MLA)

Jacoby, Susan. "Waiting for the End: On Nursing Homes." *New York Times
Magazine* 31 Mar. 1974, city ed.: 80+. Print.

■ Passage and Citation

MLA

Susan Jacoby (80) sums up the grim outlook of patients in bad nursing
homes by noting that they are merely waiting to die.

Susan Jacoby sums up the grim outlook of patients in bad nursing homes by
noting that they are merely waiting to die (80).

APA

Susan Jacoby (1974, p. 80) sums up . . .

Susan Jacoby (1974) sums up . . . waiting to die (p. 80).

1. Depending on your instructor, *using either the MLA or APA system,
   write a proper in-text citation for exercise 1 on pages 424 and 425. The type
   of information (info only or quote) and page number in the original source
   are provided: a (info p. 222), and c (a quote p. 271), and g (info p. 31),
   i (info only p. 221), o (a partial quote on page 60, also use same author
   published a different year).*
   Assume that you have not used the author's name to introduce the material you cite. Where
   there are multiple pages in the reference, you can select the page or pages appropriate to your
   citation.
2. Depending on your instructor, *using either the MLA or APA system, write a proper
   in-text citation for each of the bibliographic references you prepared for part 2 on page 425.
   Assume that you have not used the author's name to introduce the material you cite. Where
   there are multiple pages in the reference, you can select the page or pages appropriate to your
   citation.*

In Text

Handling Quotations

Set off quotations fewer than five lines long for the MLA system (fewer than forty words long for the APA system) with quotation marks and run them into the text of the paper. For longer quotes, omit the quotation marks and indent the material ten spaces from the left margin for the MLA system (five spaces for the APA system). Double-space the typing. If you quote part or all of one paragraph, don't further indent the first line. If you quote two or more consecutive paragraphs, indent each one's first line three additional spaces for the MLA system (five for the APA system—except for the first paragraph in the quote which should not be additionally indented). Use single quotation marks for a quotation within a shorter quotation and double marks for a quotation within a longer, indented quotation. The following examples illustrate the handling of quotations. The documentation and indentation follow the MLA guidelines.

■ Short Quotation

Ellen Goodman offers this further observation about writers who peddle formulas for achieving success through selfishness: "They are all Doctor Feelgoods, offering placebo prescriptions instead of strong medicine. They give us a way to live with ourselves, perhaps, but not a way to live with each other" (16).

■ Quotation within Short Quotation

The report further stated, "All great writing styles have their wellsprings in the personality of the writer. As Buffon said, 'The style is the man'" (Duncan 49).

■ Quotation within Longer, Indented Quotation

Barbara Tuchman's *Proud Tower* presents a somewhat different view of the new conservative leaders:

> Besides riches, rank, broad acres, and ancient lineage, the new government also possessed, to the regret of the liberal opposition, and in the words of one of them, "an almost embarrassing wealth of talent and capacity." Secure in authority, resting comfortably on their electoral majority in the House of Commons and on a permanent majority in the House of Lords, of whom four-fifths were conservatives, they were in a position, admitted the same opponent, "of unassailable strength." (4)

Always provide some context for material that you quote. Various options exist. When you quote from a source for the first time, you might provide the author's full name and the source of the quotation, perhaps indicating the author's expertise as well. The passage just above omits the author's expertise; the passage below includes it.

Writing in *Newsweek* magazine, Riena Gross, chief psychiatric social worker at Illinois Medical Center in Chicago, said, "Kids have no real sense that they belong anywhere or to anyone as they did ten or fifteen years ago. Parents have loosened the reins, and kids are kind of floundering" (74).

Or you might note the event prompting the quotation and then the author's name.

Addressing a seminar at the University of Toronto, Dr. Joseph Pomeranz speculated that "acupuncture may work by activating a neural pain suppression mechanism in the brain" (324).

On other occasions, you might note only the author's full name and expertise.

Economist Richard M. Cybert, president of Carnegie Mellon University, offers the following sad prediction about the steel industry's future: "It will never be as large an industry as it has been. There are a lot of plants that will never come back and many laborers that will never be rehired" (43).

After first citing an author's full name, use only the last name for subsequent references.

In answering the objections of government agencies to the Freedom of Information Act, Wellford commented, "Increased citizen access should help citizens learn of governmental activities that weaken our First Amendment freedoms. Some administrative inconvenience isn't too large a price to pay for that" (137).

When quoting from a source with no author given, introduce the quotation with the name of the source.

Commenting on the problems that law enforcement personnel have in coping with computer crime, *Credit and Financial Management* magazine pointed out, "A computer crime can be committed in three hundredths of a second, and the criminal can be thousands of miles from the 'scene,' using a telephone" ("Computer Crime" 43).

Page numbers are not helpful when you cite passages from plays and poems, as these literary forms are available in many editions. When you quote from a play, identify the act, scene, and line numbers. Use Arabic numbers separated by periods. Here's how to cite Act 2, Scene 1, lines 295–300 of Shakespeare's *Othello*:

That Cassio loves her, I do well believe it;

That she loves him, 'tis apt, and of great credit:

The Moor, how be it that I endure him not,

Is of a constant, loving, noble nature;

And I dare think he'll prove to Desdemona

A most dear husband. (*Othello* 2.1.295–300)

PERSPECTIVE
The sad fact of plagiarism, intentional or otherwise, cannot be ignored. Advertisements in many school papers offer to sell term papers, students write them for a fee, and fraternities and sororities often keep "A" models on file. There are, however, several ways of coping with the problem.

TEACHING STRATEGIES
1. Have students bring in the appropriate original sources and proofread in class for instances of unintentional plagiarism in their papers. This activity reinforces the message that plagiarism is unacceptable and also gives students an opportunity to detect and redress problems.

2. Have students turn in the paper in stages—working bibliography, note cards, rough outline, different drafts, and the like. If students are asked to revise according to your responses, they can't simply turn in a prewritten paper. Refuse to accept a finished draft on an entirely new topic "because the old one just wasn't working out."

3. You might add unique requirements that serve as plagiarism fingerprints, such as including faculty interviews (on their topic) in the paper.

When quoting from a short poem, use "line" or "lines" and the line number(s).

> In "Dover Beach," Matthew Arnold offers this melancholy assessment of the state of religion:
>> The Sea of Faith
>>
>> Was once, too, at the full, and round earth's shore
>>
>> Lay like the folds of a bright girdle furl'd.
>>
>> But now I only hear
>>
>> Its melancholy, long, withdrawing roar. (lines 21-25)

In quoting poetry that has been run into the text, use a slash mark(/) with a space on each side to indicate the shift from one line to the next in the original:

> In his ode "To Autumn," Keats says that autumn is the "Season of mists and mellow fruitfulness, / Close bosom-friend of the maturing sun" (lines 1-2).

Avoiding Plagiarism

Plagiarism occurs when a writer uses another person's material without properly acknowledging the debt. Sometimes plagiarism is deliberate, but often it happens because students simply don't understand what must be acknowledged and documented. Deliberate or not, plagiarism is absolutely unacceptable. *Any summary, paraphrase, or quotation you include in your paper must be documented as must statistics and graphics.* The only types of information escaping this requirement are those listed below:

1. *Common knowledge.* Common knowledge is information that most educated people would know. For instance, there's no need to document a statement that the Disney theme parks in California and Florida attract thousands of visitors each year. However, if you include precise daily, monthly, or yearly figures, then documentation is necessary.

2. *Your own conclusions.* As you write your paper, you'll incorporate your own conclusions at various points. (See the margin notes accompanying Keith Jacque's library research paper, page 393, for examples.) Such comments require no documentation. The same holds true for your own research. If you polled students on a campus issue, simply present the findings as your own.

3. *Facts found in many sources.* Facts such as the year of Shakespeare's death, the size of the 2001 national budget surplus, and the location of the Taj Mahal need not be documented. However, where there may be disputes about the facts in question (such as the size of the 2003 deficit) or where there may be some need to enforce the credibility of your figures, provide the source for your facts. If you are not certain that something is common knowledge, indicate your source.

4. *Standard terms.* Terms widely used in a particular field require no documentation. Examples include such computer terms as *mouse, CD-ROM,* and *download.*

Any piece of information not set off with quotation marks must be in your own words. Otherwise, even though you name your source, you plagiarize by stealing the original phrasing.

The following passages illustrate the improper and proper use of source material.

Original Passage

> One might contend, of course, that our country's biological diversity is so great and the land is so developed—so criss-crossed with the works of man—that it will soon be hard to build a dam anywhere without endangering some species. But as we develop a national inventory of endangered species, we certainly can plan our *necessary* development so as to exterminate the smallest number possible.
>
> James L. Buckley, "Three Cheers for the Snail Darter," *National Review*, September 14, 1979: 1144–45. Print.

■ Plagiarism

> Our country's biological diversity is so great and the land is so developed that it will soon be hard to build a dam anywhere without endangering some species. But as we develop a national inventory of endangered species, we certainly can plan our necessary development so as to exterminate the smallest number possible.

This writer clearly plagiarizes. The absence of Buckley's name and the failure to enclose his words in quotation marks create the impression that this passage is the student's own work.

■ Plagiarism

> Given the extensive diversity of species in America, development such as the construction of dams is likely to endanger some species, whether it is a rare plant, a species of frog, or a rare variety of fish. By creating a database of endangered species, however, we can facilitate a planning process that will place the minimum number of species at risk.

Although this writer uses original language, the absence of documentation suggests that these ideas are the student's without any recognition of Buckley's contribution. Despite the paraphrase, this is still plagiarism.

■ Plagiarism

> Our country's biological diversity is so great and the land so developed that in the near future we may pose a threat to some creature whenever we construct a dam. By developing a national inventory of endangered species, however, we can plan necessary development so as to preserve as many species as possible (Buckley 1144).

insurance system that would foster reform would need to encourage changes in delivery and determine whether the changes resulted in improved quality. No one really knows the ideal for a health care delivery system. However, an improved system needs a structure to better coordinate health care services while enhancing how information is shared. This can only occur if there is a financial incentive for change (Emanuel 39).

QUOTE
Ezekiel Emanuel argues that an improved health care delivery system would require "an infrastructure that coordinates doctors, hospitals, home health care agencies, and other providers administratively, fiscally, and clinically" (39).

EXERCISE ANSWERS
1. This is not plagiarism. This is not specifically from text and common knowledge

2. This is plagiarism. Though the information is referenced, the sentence is followed too exactly with only a few word changes.

3. This is plagiarism. It is not a quote, but it is not common knowledge for most of us either.

4. This is not plagiarism. This does not use the author's words and is appropriately cited.

5. This is not plagiarism. This is an appropriate partial quote with documentation.

6. This is plagiarism. While appropriately quoted, it is not appropriately documented.

This version credits the ideas to Buckley, but the student has plagiarized by failing to put quotation marks around the phrasing (underlined here) that was copied from the original. As a result, readers will think that the passage represents the student's own wording.

■ Proper Use of Original

> America has so many kinds of plants and animals, and it is so built up, that in the near future we may pose a threat to some living thing just by damming some waterway. If, however, we knew which of our nation's plants and animals were threatened, we could use this information to preserve as many species as we can (Buckley 1144).

This student has identified the author and used her own words. As a result, no plagiarism occurs.

Plagiarism is a serious offense because it robs the original writer of recognition. Students caught plagiarizing risk failure in the course or perhaps suspension from school. Whenever you are unsure whether material requires documentation, supply a reference. And always handle direct quotations by following the guidelines beginning on page 434.

Avoiding plagiarism, from the article "The Problem with Single-Payer Plans," summarize paragraphs 11, 12, and 13; create a paraphrase of paragraph 11, and create an effective quote from material in paragraph 11. Use the original source The Hastings Center Report 38 no. 1 38-41 JA/F 2008, assuming that the material in question comes from page 39 of that report.

Indicate if each of the following statements used in a paper that drew on a reading of "The Problem with Single-Payer Plans" is plagiarism or not and why.

1. A single-payer is a system where only one party, most likely the government, pays health care costs instead of multiple private insurance companies.

2. Changes in the health care system need to consider problems with both the financing and delivery systems (Emanuel xxx).

3. One third of all doctor visits are to physicians with their own practice.

4. While the contemporary need is for chronic care, the delivery system is structured for acute care (Emanuel xxx).

5. One problem with our current finance system is that many tax payers contribute to systems like Medicaid and "yet are excluded from these programs" (Emanuel xxx).

6. The government fails to meet its responsibility for the current system since it doesn't "address key policy issues, fraud, and—for Medicaid—complex determinations of eligibility."

CHAPTER 22

Additional Research Strategies: Interviews, Questionnaires, Direct Observations

The library isn't the only source of information for research writing. Investigators also gather information through *primary research*, which includes such activities as consulting public records in local, state, and federal archives, performing experiments, conducting interviews, sending out questionnaires, and making direct observations of various kinds.

This chapter focuses on the latter three types, the most common primary research strategies.

The Value of Primary Research

What makes primary research so valuable? First, it allows individuals and organizations to collect recent information, often unavailable elsewhere, that precisely suits their needs. A company that has developed a new product can't turn to published data to estimate its sales prospects; such information simply doesn't exist. But polling test users with a well-crafted questionnaire could suggest some answers and perhaps also some tips for improving the product. Similarly, someone wanting to gauge the success of an ongoing clothing drive by a local charitable organization might interview its director.

PERSPECTIVE
Students should learn about primary research strategies because they will use these strategies frequently in their courses and careers. Furthermore, because this type of research involves a more active relationship with the actual data, students are forced to reach their own conclusions rather than parrot someone else's findings.

Even when published material exists, it may not contain desired information. Although numerous articles discuss student attitudes about required courses, you probably wouldn't find a report that explores student reaction to a new general-education requirement at your school. You could, however, assemble this information by distributing a questionnaire. The findings might even contradict, and therefore cause you to question, the conclusions of others.

Primary research can also yield unexpected and significant material. Suppose you're investigating adult illiteracy, and you interview a professor with a specialty in this area of study. She explains the reasons why people who can't read resist help and supplies several relevant examples. Such information might not appear anywhere in print. Certainly the resulting report would carry more weight and elicit more interest than one without such insights.

You can integrate primary research into a report that consists largely of *secondary research*, the kind that depends on library materials. The student who wrote the research paper on electronic monitoring (see pages 384–395) incorporated the results of a personal interview with the director of Michigan's electronic monitoring program. This interview provided information on the scope, operation, success rate, and cost advantage of the program. Often, however, writers detail the findings of primary research in separate reports. This would be the case if, for example, your employer asked you to interview users of a new computer system in order to determine their degree of satisfaction with it.

General Principles for Primary Research

Primary research, like all research, requires well-formulated questions. Such questions must be specifically focused, contain clearly defined terms, and be answerable by the actual research. A vague, general question such as "What attitudes do Americans have about their government?" lacks the necessary precision and therefore can't be resolved. What kind(s) of attitudes? What level or branch of government? Which Americans? How would you gather their opinions? A more realistic question might be "According to the Mason College faculty, how adequate is the new congressional proposal for funding academic research in this country?" You could easily develop and distribute to faculty members a questionnaire addressing the different provisions of the proposal. In addition, you can't resolve ethical or philosophical questions through primary research. While you could use a questionnaire to determine student attitudes about the police using sobriety check lanes, such information won't decide the ethical issue of whether the police should use such check lanes.

For valid results, conduct your primary research in an impartial manner. Always aim to determine facts rather than to justify some belief you hold. This means, first of all, that you must develop questions that have no built-in bias. If you poll other students and ask them to tell you "how core-course teachers on this campus marked their papers unreasonably hard," those responding might falsify their answers to give you what you want. Instead, use neutral phrasing such as "Do you believe core-course teachers on this campus mark your papers fairly or unfairly? Explain." Second, don't rely on atypical sources and situations for your data. If you investigate the adequacy of parking space on campus, don't deliberately observe the parking lots on a day when some special event has flooded the campus with visitors. Careful readers will see what you have done and reject your findings.

Just as you avoid bias when gathering information, so also do you report your results fairly. For one thing, don't use inaccurate interpretations of your findings to make them agree with the conclusions you're after. If you believe peer editing produces questionable results, don't claim that the students in a class you observed spent their time sneering at one another's work when in fact they offered constructive criticism. While such criticism can sometimes be straightforward, certainly most people wouldn't consider it sneering. Similarly, don't report conclusions that are unsupported by your actual research. If you observe a large number of violent acts while watching Saturday cartoons, don't leap to the conclusion that the violence in the cartoons causes violent behavior in children. You simply don't have the evidence to support that assertion. Finally, don't cover up results that you don't like. If your survey of teachers' marking practices shows that most of your respondents believe core-course instructors mark fairly, don't hide the fact because it doesn't match what you expected to discover. Instead, report your findings accurately and rethink your original position. The following section further explores ethical matters.

Ethical Issues

Today most people chuckle at an advertisement for a product recommended by "nine out of ten doctors." We recognize that the doctors were hand picked and don't represent an objective sample of adequate size. As a result, little harm occurs. With primary research, however, distorted investigating and reporting are sometimes hard to detect and can have significant consequences.

Say the officials of Anytown, USA, alarmed at a sharp rise in auto accidents caused by distracted drivers, schedule a special meeting attempting to ban cell phone calls by those driving within city limits. It would be unethical for a reporter opposed to the ban to write a supposedly objective feature article on the issue but include interviews only with people who share his views. Now suppose a presumably neutral group in the city of Lost Wages distributes a questionnaire to residents to gauge their reaction to a proposed gambling casino. It would be unethical to include a biased question such as "Should the city deprive its citizens of the revenue that a casino can provide?" Finally, imagine that a city manager, concerned by reports of motorists running the red light at a major intersection, gets the Department of Public Safety to investigate. A department employee conducts a twenty-minute observation, then writes a report concluding that surveillance cameras are not needed there. Clearly, the employee has acted unethically in drawing a conclusion after such a limited observation. To help ensure that your primary research reports are ethically responsible, ask and answer the following questions.

TEACHING STRATEGIES
You might want to discuss these two cases with your class.

1. Professor Robbins wants administrative approval for a Japanese Studies major. Proposals for new programs must include the results of a survey of potential participants. Robbins surveyed his Japanese literature class after talking to them at length about the advantages of the major. His report, however, made no mention of the talk but merely indicated that 75 percent of the students surveyed approved of the new major. Was it unethical of Robbins to omit mention of the talk? Why or why not?

2. Jenny Ellens, a novice reporter for a local paper, was having dinner with Chad Grayson, a college friend now working for the mayor's office. Chad, unaware that Jenny was a reporter, told her that a serious city budget crisis was developing. He hinted, but didn't directly state, that this was not public information. Jenny, sensing a scoop, wrote a feature article on the crisis, citing Chad's name several times. Discuss the ethics of this situation.

- Have I attempted to avoid bias in gathering and evaluating information?
- Are my data based on an adequate sample size? If not, have the limitations of the sample been clearly indicated?
- Is my information presented objectively and completely with no intentional effort to omit findings that run counter to my position?
- Are the people involved, whether I'm preparing an interview, questionnaire, or direct observation report, aware that they are part of a study and how the information will be used? Are they protected from harm that might result from their inclusion?
- Do I have permission to name in my report persons interviewed or observed?
- In an interview report, would the interviewee recognize and accept statements attributed to him or her?
- Have I noted any apparent bias in the interviewee?
- In a questionnaire report, have I avoided any biased questions?

Interviews

During an interview, questions are asked and answered. Some interviews amount to little more than brief, informal chats. Others, like those discussed here, may feature extended conversations, involve a series of questions, and require careful preparation. Interviewing an informed person provides you with firsthand answers to your queries, lets you ask follow-up questions, and gives you access to the most up-to-date thinking.

If you major in a business program, an instructor may require you to question a personnel manager about the company's employee relations program. If your field is social work, you might have to interview a case worker as part of your study of some kind of family problem. On the job, you might have to talk with prospective employees and then assess their suitability for a position in the company. Police officers routinely interview witnesses to accidents and crimes, and journalists do the same in pursuit of stories.

Choosing the Interviewee

Professional and technical personnel are a rich source of interview candidates. The faculty of any university can provide insights into a wide range of subjects. Doctors, pharmacists, and other health professionals can draw upon their expertise to help you, as can lawyers, engineers, researchers, corporation managers, and employees at every level of government—federal, state, and local.

Whom you interview depends, of course, on what you wish to know. For information on the safe disposal of high-level nuclear waste, you might consult a physics professor. If you want an expert view on the causes of homelessness, contact an authority such as a sociologist, who could provide objective information. If, however, you want to gain a sense of what it's like to be homeless, you might interview the manager of a shelter or (in a safe place) one or more homeless people.

Preparing for the Interview

If you don't relish the thought of phoning to request an interview, keep in mind that most interviewees are eager to discuss their areas of expertise and are often flattered by the opportunity. The worst that can happen is a turndown, and in that event you can always find someone else in the same field.

Before you phone, review your own upcoming commitments and try to determine which ones you could reschedule if necessary. You may need to make an adjustment to accommodate the schedule of a busy person. When you call, indicate who you are, that you are requesting an interview, the subject of the interview, and how much time you'd like.

If the person agrees to meet with you, then ask when it would be convenient. Carefully record the time, day, and place of the interview, and if for any reason you need to cancel be sure to call well in advance.

Before the interview, do as much background reading as possible. This reading will help you develop a list of key questions and avoid those with obvious and readily available answers. Write out your questions to help ensure that the interview will proceed smoothly.

Good questions permit elaboration and don't call for simple "yes" or "no" answers. To illustrate:

Poor: Is it difficult to work with adult illiterates? (The obvious answer is "yes.")

Better: What have you found most challenging about working with adult illiterates?

On the other hand, don't ask overly broad questions that can't be answered in a relatively brief interview.

Poor: What's wrong with primary-school education?

Better: Why do you think so many children have trouble learning to read?

Avoid questions that are biased and may insult the interviewee.

Poor: Why do you bother to work with adult illiterates?

Better: Why did you decide to work with adult illiterates?

Likewise, avoid questions that restrict the interviewee's options for answering.

Poor: What do you think accounts for the poor academic performance of so many American secondary-school students—too much TV watching or overly large classes?

Better: People often blame the poor academic performance of so many American students on too much TV watching or overly large classes. What importance do you attach to these factors? Do you think other factors contribute to the problem?

The number of questions you prepare depends on the length of the interview. It's a good idea to draft more questions than you think you'll have time to ask, then arrange them from most to least important. If the interviewee keeps to the schedule, you'll obtain your desired information. If the interviewee grants you extra time, your written follow-up will have even more substance.

TEACHING STRATEGIES

1. Because many students will be apprehensive about conducting interviews, you might set aside class time to talk about their concerns. You could explain that just as they have interests they are willing to discuss with others, so do interviewees.

2. Students often have trouble identifying appropriate interviewees. To help them, select several of the topics students are working on and have the class brainstorm for candidates. You could suggest that they examine a campus directory or phone book to pinpoint individuals. Some students may try taking the easy way out by proposing interviews with friends or relatives. Remind them that the candidate must have experience or expertise in the area of interest to the student.

3. Have students evaluate one another's interview questions, or if you prefer, evaluate them yourself. Students often overlook important questions or draft ones that exhibit the shortcomings mentioned in the text.

4. To help students interview properly, you might have select members of the class interview you. You could then follow up by critiquing their performance.

5. Some students will procrastinate on this assignment. To prevent stalling, you could, at intervals of a couple of days, ask which ones haven't scheduled their interviews and the reasons for the delay, and then provide extra assistance to those who need it.

Conducting the Interview

Naturally you'll want to arrive on time and to bring a notepad and a pen. Sometimes you can tape-record an interview but only if you ask permission first. Because most people warm up slowly, you might start with one or two brief, general questions that provide you with useful background. Possibilities include "What is the nature of your specialty?" and "How long have you been employed in this field?"

Proceed by asking your most important questions first. If you believe that a question hasn't been answered or that an answer is incomplete, don't hesitate to ask follow-up questions.

As the interview unfolds, take notes but don't attempt to copy everything that's said. Instead, jot down key phrases and ideas that will serve as memory prompts. If you want to capture an essential explanation or some other important material in the interviewee's own words, ask the person to go slowly while you copy them down. When the interview is over, thank the person for talking to you. You may also offer to supply a copy of the finished report. Write a personal note thanking the person for his or her time. With the answers to your questions fresh in your mind, expand on your notes by filling in details, supplying necessary connections between points that were made, and noting your reactions.

Writing About the Interview

The project you're working on determines how to handle your interview information. If you're preparing a library research paper, include the material, suitably presented, at the appropriate spot and document it according to whatever system, MLA or APA, you're using (see page 407).

Often, however, you'll be asked to prepare a separate report of the interview. Then, as with any other report, you'll need to organize and present the material in an effective order. Your topic, purpose, and audience will determine the arrangement you select. In any event, remember to establish the context for the report, identify the interviewee and his or her position, and present the information accurately.

TEACHING STRATEGY
When writing an interview report, students often will want to report their results by following the pattern of the interview. Point out the differences between speech and writing. If possible, pass out an interview transcript and ask students to identify why they experience difficulty reading it. To make their own reports more effective, have students identify the main points they want to make and the order that will facilitate their presentation.

SAMPLE

STUDENT INTERVIEW REPORT

Budget Cuts Affect State Police: An Interview Report with Officer Robert Timmons

Holly Swain

Paragraph 1: establishes context for interview

Confronted with a billion-dollar budget deficit, the state legislature and the governor have been forced to make sharp budget cuts. One of these cuts is the allocation to the state police. This decision has threatened the loss of some police jobs and aroused considerable controversy.

How, many ask, will the police, who were already on a tight budget, be able to provide the public with adequate protection when they have even less money and fewer personnel?

When Trooper Robert Timmons, a state police officer based in Marywood County, first heard that the governor might call for police cutbacks, he didn't believe they would become a reality. Timmons thought the governor was just making "political noise." Actually, the state police head did at first propose cutting 350 jobs, Timmons's among them, to help meet a $19 million cutback. This proposal was rejected in favor of one that combined demotions, pay cuts, and the elimination of special programs. In addition, the amounts allotted for other purposes were also cut.

All of these actions, Timmons says, have had an unfortunate effect on the operations of the state police. As an example, he mentions a sergeant who was demoted to "accident reconstructionist," a job requiring him to review severe accidents and reconstruct what happened for the court. This demotion, Timmons says, has taken an excellent police officer out of the field, where he's most needed, and put him behind a desk.

Timmons notes several bad effects of cuts in the allocation for gasoline. Because of these cuts, troopers are expected to drive just ninety miles a night. Timmons thinks this limitation has a "direct effect on the public." A motorist stranded on a freeway might not be spotted and aided by a trooper who is unable to make another run through that territory. Late-night accidents might go undiscovered, with serious or fatal consequences for those involved. Many more speeders and drunk drivers will escape being caught.

As of now, Timmons says, there are only 3,000 state police, about 400 fewer than needed. Each year, 100 to 200 officers retire. These vacancies need to be filled, but according to Timmons, the state academy has been closed for over a year. The personnel shortages that already exist and the cutbacks resulting from the state's budget troubles are making it harder and harder for the state police to do an adequate job of protecting the public.

Officer Timmons understands that the state government needs to control its spending. However, he believes that the present budget cutbacks for a department that is already understaffed are very unwise. "I feel the governor should have given the matter more thought," he says.

> Sentence 1, paragraph 2: identifies interviewee and his position

> Remainder of report: presents information provided by interviewee

Questionnaires

A questionnaire consists essentially of a series of statements or questions to which recipients are asked to respond. Questionnaires help individuals and organizations determine what select groups of people think about particular products, services, issues, and personal matters. You yourself have probably completed a variety of questionnaires, including teacher evaluations and market surveys.

Questionnaires are used extensively both on campus and in the workplace. A social science instructor might ask you to prepare a survey that explores community reaction to a recently implemented curfew for teenagers. A business instructor might want you to survey a test-market group to determine its response to some new product. In fact, some marketing classes focus on survey techniques. But even if marketing isn't your specialty, learning how to construct questionnaires can serve you well in your career. If you work in the hotel, restaurant, or health service field, you could use a questionnaire to gauge customer satisfaction. The same holds true if you manage or own a small repair service. As a landscape specialist, you might survey the people in your community to learn what planting and maintenance services they desire.

Developing the Questionnaire

When you develop a questionnaire, you need to target precisely what you want to know and what group you intend to survey. You could survey restaurant customers to determine their attitudes about the service and the quality of the food or to assess the types of food they prefer. Zero in on only one area of interest and then explore it with appropriate questions.

Begin the questionnaire with a clear explanation of what you intend to accomplish, and supply brief but clear instructions on how to respond to each part. Keep the questionnaire as short as possible, preferably no longer than a page or two. The longer the survey, the less likely that people will answer all the questions.

As you draw up your questions, take care to avoid these common errors:

1. Don't ask two questions in the same sentence. Their answers may be different.

   Unacceptable: Do you find that this year's Ford Taurus has better acceleration and fuel economy than last year's model?

   To correct this fault, use separate sentences.

   Better: Do you find that this year's Ford Taurus has better acceleration than last year's model?

   Better: Do you find that this year's Ford Taurus has better fuel economy than last year's model?

2. Don't include vague or ambiguous questions. Since people won't understand your intent, their answers may not reflect their beliefs.

Unacceptable: Is assisted suicide a good idea?

Better: Should assisted suicide be permitted for terminally ill patients?

3. **Avoid biased questions.** They might antagonize those who don't share your views and cause them not to complete the questionnaire.

Unacceptable: Should Century City taxpayers continue to waste money on renovating the North Park Bridge?

Better: Should Century City taxpayers spend an additional $100,000 to complete the North Park Bridge renovation?

Most questionnaire items fall into the categories that follow. The information you want determines which you choose. Often you'll need to include several or all of the categories in your questionnaire.

Two-Choice Items
Some items have two possible responses: yes/no, true/false, male/female.

Example: Do you plan to repaint your house during the summer months?

☐ yes
☐ no

Multiple-Choice Items
Often there are several possible responses to a questionnaire item. When you prepare this type of item, make sure that you include all significant choices and that the choices share some common ground. Don't ask if someone's primary vehicle is a subcompact, compact, full-size, or foreign car as size and place of manufacture are unrelated. To determine whether the vehicle is domestic or foreign, use a separate item.

Example: Check the income group that describes your combined family income.

☐ less than $9,999 a year
☐ $10,000–$19,999 a year
☐ $20,000–$29,999 a year
☐ $30,000–$39,999 a year
☐ $40,000–$50,000 a year
☐ over $50,000 a year

Checklists
Checklists allow respondents to mark more than one option. They can help you determine the range of factors that led to a decision.

Example: Please check any of the following factors that help explain why you decided not to re-enroll your child in Good Growth Private School:

☐ can no longer afford tuition
☐ moved
☐ dissatisfaction with child's progress
☐ disagree with school's educational approach

figures, the conclusions they reach from the responses to each topic. These conclusions might serve as the topic sentences of the paragraphs in the Results section.

5. Depending on your class, you may want to explain how surveys can be slanted, samples skewed, and statistics abused. This understanding is perhaps as important to the development of critical reasoning skills as a sound knowledge of argumentative fallacies.

CLASSROOM ACTIVITIES

1. List several biased and unbiased questions on the board. Have students identify those that are biased and rewrite them in an acceptable fashion. Here are two samples:

Biased: What types of disorderly student behavior occur during a class period in a typical, chaotic high school?

Acceptable: What types of student behavior occur during a class period in randomly selected high schools?

Biased: Given the problems associated with holding student attention during the last month of the school year, do you favor extending the school year from 180 to 220 days?

Acceptable: Do you favor extending the school year from 180 to 220 days?

2. You might suggest several different situations in which someone would gather data and then have students identify the possible bias. Here are some

examples: A person in a supermarket hands out food samples and then asks customers if they might buy the product. A professor has students complete a questionnaire on a new course after she enthusiastically supports the course. A principal observes a new teacher's class after giving the teacher two weeks' notice of the pending observation.

3. Students could bring in copies of articles relevant to their research papers. In small groups they might examine the articles for potentially biased reporting. Alternatively, you could bring in an article on a subject known to students, perhaps student behavior, that demonstrates clear-cut bias. Students could then evaluate the article and identify the bias.

☐ conflict with teacher
☐ conflict with other staff
☐ child unhappy with school
☐ child had conflict with other children

Ranking Lists   Sometimes you may need to ask people to rank their preferences. This information will help you select the most suitable option from among several possibilities.

Example: Designating your first choice as "1," please rank your preferences in music from 1 through 5.

☐ classical
☐ country and western
☐ jazz
☐ rock and roll
☐ heavy metal
☐ rap

Using the responses to this item, the manager of a local radio station could broadcast the type of music that listeners clearly prefer.

Scale Items   When you are trying to determine the extent to which members of a group support or oppose some issue, using a scale can be helpful. Be sure to have people respond to a statement, *not* a question.

Example: Please circle the response that best reflects your feelings about the statement below.

SA = strongly agree, A = agree, N = no opinion, D = disagree, SD = strongly disagree

Women should be allowed to fly combat aircraft in time of war.

SA   A   N   D   SD

Open-Ended Items   When you want to gather ideas from other people, you might turn to open-ended items—those that don't limit the reader's response. If you do, keep such items narrow enough to be manageable. You should know, however, that readers are less likely to complete open-ended items and that they are difficult to sort and tally.

Example: Please list the three improvements that you would most like to see in Lowden's high school curriculum.

_____

_____

_____

_____

_____

_____

SAMPLE

STUDENT QUESTIONNAIRE

Survey on Public Smoking

Please take a few minutes to fill out this questionnaire. Your responses will help Bartram College ensure that its smoking policies are sensitive to the smoking habits and attitudes toward public smoking of Bartram College male smokers.

1. Do you smoke cigarettes? (check one) yes/no item
   _____ yes (If you checked yes, please go on to the next question.)
   _____ no (If you checked *no*, please go on to question 4.)

   Multiple-choice item

2. If you smoke, indicate how many cigarettes each day. (check one)
   _____ less than half a pack
   _____ between a half and a whole pack
   _____ between one and two packs
   _____ more than two packs

3. If you smoke, what are you likely to do upon entering a public place with no posted smoking restrictions? (check one)
   _____ smoke freely
   _____ check to see whether your smoking is bothering others
   _____ ask others whether they would be bothered if you smoke
   _____ not smoke

4. Check the statements you believe are true.
   _____ My health is at risk only if I am a smoker.
   _____ Secondhand smoke contains the same ingredients as directly inhaled smoke.
   _____ Secondhand smoke poses no health risk to nonsmokers.
   _____ Secondhand smoke poses a health risk to nonsmokers.
   _____ Secondhand smoke poses less of a health risk than directly inhaled smoke.

   Checklist

5. Please rate each of the statements below, using the following scale:
   SA = strongly agree, A = agree, N = no opinion, D = disagree,
   SD = strongly disagree.

   Scale items

Continued on next page

Continued from previous page

_____ There should be no restrictions on public smoking.

_____ Smoking should be prohibited in stores, banks, offices, and workshops.

_____ Smoking and nonsmoking sections in restaurants should be separated by a barrier that smoke cannot penetrate.

_____ Smokers and nonsmokers should have separate workplace lounges.

_____ All public smoking should be prohibited.

6. Please add one or two comments you might have regarding public smoking.

_____

_____

_____

_____

Open-ended item

Testing and Administering the Questionnaire

When you have finished creating the questionnaire, ask several people to respond to the items and gauge their effectiveness. Are any items vague, ambiguous, biased, or otherwise faulty? If so, rewrite and retest them.

To ensure that you obtain an accurate assessment, make certain that you select an appropriate cross section of recipients. To illustrate, assume that you and many of your campus friends dislike early morning classes. You decide to draw up a questionnaire to sample the attitudes of other students. You suspect that many students share your dislike, and you plan to submit your findings to the college president for possible action. To obtain meaningful results, you'll have to sample a sizable group of students. Furthermore, this group will need to include representative numbers of first-year students, sophomores, juniors, and seniors because these classes may not share a uniform view. Failure to sample properly can call your results into question and cause the administration to disregard them. Proper sampling, on the other hand, pinpoints where dissatisfaction is greatest and suggests a possible response. Thus if first-year students and sophomores register the most objections, the administration might decide to reduce the number of 100- and 200-level classes meeting at 8 A.M.

Totaling the Responses

When the recipients have finished marking the questionnaire, you will need to total the responses. Even without computer scoring, this job is easier than you might think. Simply prepare a table that lists the questionnaire items and the possible responses to each; then go through the questionnaire and add up the number of times each response is marked.

When you finish, turn your numbers into percentages, which provide an easier-to-understand comparison of the responses. Simply divide the number of times each possible response is checked by the total number of questionnaires and then multiply the result by 100.

Writing the Questionnaire Report

When you write your report, don't merely fill it with numbers and responses to the questionnaire items. Instead, look for patterns in the responses and try to draw conclusions from them. Follow the logical order of the conclusions you want to stress.

Typically, a report consists of two or three sections. The first, "Purpose and Scope," explains why the survey was performed, how many questionnaires were distributed and returned, and how the recipients were contacted. The second section, "Results," reports the conclusions that were drawn. Finally, if appropriate, a "Recommendations" section offers responses that seem warranted based on the survey findings.

SAMPLE

STUDENT QUESTIONNAIRE REPORT

**Findings from Smoking Questionnaire Distributed
to Bartram College Students**

Kelly Reetz

Purpose and Scope of Survey

This survey was carried out to determine the smoking habits and attitudes toward public smoking of Bartram College's male students. The assignment was one of my requirements for completing Public Health 201. Each of the 240 male students in Crandall Hall received a copy of the questionnaire in his mailbox, and 72 completed questionnaires were returned. This latter number equals 10 percent of the college's male student population and therefore can be considered a representative sample. Of those responding, 37, or 51 percent, were cigarette smokers. Thirty-five, or 49 percent, were nonsmokers. Of the smokers, all but 11 percent smoked over a pack of cigarettes a day.

> Provides background details on project, profile of respondents

Continued on next page

Continued from previous page

<u>Results of Survey</u>

Discusses responses to
questionnaire item 3

Smokers seemed fairly considerate of nonsmokers in public places. Only 16 percent said they would smoke freely. In fact, 51 percent said they wouldn't smoke at all. The remaining 33 percent indicated they would either look around to see whether they were bothering others or ask others whether they objected to cigarette smoke.

Discusses responses to
questionnaire item 4

In general, respondents seemed aware that secondhand smoke poses a health risk. Seventy-six percent believe that such smoke contains the same ingredients as directly inhaled smoke, and an amazing 96 percent believe that anyone exposed to secondhand smoke may be at risk. Only 3 percent think no health risk is involved.

Discusses responses to
questionnaire item 5

Opinions were strongly divided on the matter of banning all public smoking, with 79 percent strongly opposed and 21 percent strongly in favor. As might be expected, all of the smokers fell in the first group, but a surprising 51 percent of the nonsmokers did too. A sharp division was equally apparent between supporters and opponents of restaurant barriers, with 81 percent for or strongly for them and 19 percent against or strongly against them. In contrast to the findings on a smoking ban, all of the smokers favored barriers. Respondents overwhelmingly endorsed, 90 percent to 10 percent, prohibiting smoking in stores and banks and providing separate workplace lounges. Nobody registered a "no opinion" vote on any of the statements under item 5.

Discusses patterns in
responses to items 3–5

Responses to items 3 through 5 reveal an awareness among smokers of the dangers posed by secondhand cigarette smoke, a concern for the well-being of nonsmokers, and a willingness to accept restrictions, though not an outright ban, on public smoking. This attitude was consistent for both light and heavy smokers. For their part, about half the nonsmokers showed a tolerant attitude by supporting smoking restrictions but rejecting an outright ban.

Discusses responses to
item 6

No smokers, but 71 percent of the nonsmokers, responded to the request to provide one or two additional comments. All of these comments dealt with how the respondents would act if bothered by someone else's smoke. Two-thirds said they would move to another spot, half of the remainder said they would ask the smoker to stop, and the other half said they would remain silent rather than risk an argument.

<u>Recommendations</u>

As noted previously, this survey included only male students. To determine how its results compare with those for females, the same questionnaire should be administered to a similar group of female students.

Direct Observations

Often direct observation is the most effective means of answering research questions. If you want to know the extent and nature of violence in children's TV cartoons, watching a number of shows will tell you. Similarly, a researcher who seeks information about living conditions in an inner-city area of some metropolis can obtain it by visiting that locale. Such observations furnish firsthand answers to our questions.

In college and on the job, you may need to report your own observations. If you're majoring in business, an instructor might require a report on the work habits of employees at a small local company. If your field is biology, you might need to assess and report on the environmental health of a marsh, riverbank, or other ecological area. On the job, a factory superintendent might observe and then discuss in writing the particulars of some problem-plagued operation. Police officers routinely investigate and report on accidents, and waste-management specialists inspect and report on potential disposal sites.

The following suggestions will help you make your observations, record them, and then write your report.

Preparing to Make the Observations

First, determine the purpose of your observations and keep the purpose firmly in mind as you proceed. Otherwise, you'll overlook important details and record less-than-helpful information. Obviously, observing a classroom to assess the interaction of students calls for a different set of notes than if you were observing the teacher's instructional style or the students' note-taking habits.

Next, establish the site or sites that will best supply you with the information you need. If you're trying to determine how college students interact in the classroom, then the time of day, kind of class, and types of students will all make a difference. You might have to visit more than one class in order to observe the different types of behavior.

If your observations will take place on private property or will involve an organized group such as a class or a legislative body, you'll need to obtain permission and to make an appointment. Also, you might want to supplement your observations

PERSPECTIVE
Students often find it easy to make personal observations as part of their library research projects. A student doing a paper on sexism in society could review supermarket magazines to find advertisements showing sexism. Another student, doing a paper on homelessness, might check the newspaper to determine the average rental price of advertised apartments and then compare it with the monthly income of a person making the minimum wage. These activities not only help students better understand how other writers reach their conclusions but also let students know that they too have the ability to answer their own questions.

TEACHING STRATEGIES
1. Using material from the Reader (or secondary sources that students are using in their research), have students identify which claims are based on

some form of direct observation. Have them write out the claim, the kinds of observations that were made, and their own evaluations of the observations.

2. Have students identify questions about college life or college students that they could answer by their own observations, then make those observations and report back to the class. This activity could lead to a paper.

3. Have students identify questions that are important to their library research proj-ects, then select which questions can and cannot be answered by direct observation. Students could outline their strategy for gaining the necessary information. If, for instance, a paper is on violence and television, the writer could observe children's programs to determine the extent and nature of any violence.

4. Many students will experience difficulty being objective and specific in reporting their results. You might want to compare more objective and less objective reports on the same data to help students see the difference. You could put a few student reports on the overhead projector and have the class offer suggestions for improvement.

with an interview. Ordinarily, the interview will take place after you make your observations so that you can ask about what you've seen. If technical information is needed in advance, the interview should precede the observations. However, you should have done research first so that you do not waste the expert's time and goodwill by asking about information that is reasonably available.

Because you'll probably be making a great many individual observations, try to develop a chart and a code for recording them. Suppose you're comparing the extent to which students interact with one another and with the instructor in remedial and nonremedial composition courses. After much thought, you might develop a chart like the one following:

Class Designation: Composition 100				
Minutes into observation when interaction occurred	Classroom location of interacting students	Number and sex of students	Subject of interaction	Length of interaction

With certain kinds of observations, using a chart will not be possible. In developing your code, you would undoubtedly use M = male and F = female to distinguish the sexes. To show the location of the interacting students, FC = front of class, MC = middle of class, and BC = back of class would probably work quite well. Coding the kinds of interaction presents a more difficult task. Here, after considering several possibilities, you might decide upon these symbols: CR = class related, SR = school related, SP = sports, D = dating, O = other matters. To save writing time, you'd probably want to use "min." for "minutes" and "sec." for "seconds" when recording the lengths of the interactions.

Making the Observations

If your visit involves a scheduled appointment, be sure to arrive on time and be ready to take notes. Select a location where you can observe without interfering. If you are observing people or animals, remember that they need to adjust to you before they will behave naturally.

Before you begin taking notes, record any pertinent general information. If you're observing a class, you might note the time it is meeting, its size, the name of the instructor, and whether he or she is present when you arrive. If you're observing an apartment, pertinent information would include the location and condition of the building, the time of the visit, and the general nature of the environment. Note also whether the landlord as well as the tenant knew you were coming: It is amazing how much cleanup landlords can carry out when they know an observer will soon arrive.

Don't feel as though you must take extensive notes. Do, however, record enough details to ensure that you won't forget any events, activities, or features that are important. If you have a chart and coding system, rely on it as much as possible when recording information. Refer to the chart on the next page for how the coded notes for part of a classroom visit might look.

If you haven't developed a chart, take enough notes so that you can produce a thorough report. Try to follow some note-taking pattern. When observing the condition of an apartment, you could proceed from room to room, jotting down observations such as "Front hallway, entranceway: paint peeling in large strips from wall, paint chips on floor. Hallway dark, bulb burned out. Linoleum curling up along sides. Cockroaches running along lower molding." Remain as objective as possible as you take notes. Record what you see, hear, and smell, and avoid loaded language. If you must record a subjective impression, identify it as such.

Ask questions if necessary, but rely primarily on what you observe, not what you're told. If the landlord of a run-down apartment you're visiting tells you that he's repainting the building but you see no signs that this is happening, ignore what he says or report it along with an appropriate cautionary comment. When you finish, thank the person(s) who made your observations possible or helped you in other ways.

When you leave the observation site, expand your notes by adding more details. Supply any needed connections and record your overall impressions. To illustrate, suppose you are expanding your notes on student interactions in a composition class. You might note that the greatest number of interactions occurred before and immediately after the instructor arrived, that all student–student interactions involved individuals seated together, that student–instructor interactions included students in all parts of the room, and that all the latter interactions were about subject-related matters. This information might stimulate interesting speculation concerning the student–student and student–teacher relationships in the class, causing you to conclude that the students were hesitant about having exchanges with the instructor. As you proceed, record only what you actually observed, not what you wanted or expected to observe.

Class Designation: Composition 100				
Minutes into observation when interaction occurred	Classroom location of interacting students	Number and sex of students	Subject of interaction	Length of interaction
0	FC	M-M	SP	1 min. 30 sec.
3	MC	F-F	D	
Instructor arrived				
5	FC, MC, BC	M-M-M-F-F	CR	3 min. 45 sec.
20	FC, MC	M-F-M	CR	1 min.

If upon reviewing your notes you find that you require more information, you may need to arrange a second or even a third visit to the observation site.

Writing the Report

Once your notes are in final form, you can start writing your report. On the job your employer may specify a certain form to follow. As a general rule, all such reports reflect their purposes, focus on relevant information, and remain objective.

Usually you begin by explaining the reason for the investigation, noting any preliminary arrangements that were made, and if appropriate, providing an overview of the observation site. Depending on the nature of the report, the primary means of organization may be as follows:

1. *Narration.* A report on the changing conduct of a child over a three-hour period in a day-care center would probably be organized by narration.
2. *Description.* A report assessing the tornado damage in a large urban area could present its details in spatial order.
3. *Classification.* A visit to a toxic-waste dump suspected of violating state regulations might produce a report classifying the types of waste improperly stored there.
4. *Point-by-point comparison.* If you're comparing two possible sites for a baseball stadium, shopping mall, or other structure, a point-by-point comparison will probably best suit your purpose.
5. *Cause and effect.* This pattern works well for reporting events whose effects are of special concern, such as the testing of a new siren intended to scare birds from an airport runway.
6. *Process.* This arrangement is indicated when readers will want to know step-by-step how some process—for example, a new test for determining the mineral content of water—is carried out.

Conclude the report by discussing the significance of the findings and making any other comments that seem justified.

SAMPLE

STUDENT OBSERVATION REPORT

Observations of an Inner-City Apartment Building
Caleb Thomas

Gives reason for visit, location of site

To fulfill part of the requirements for Social Service 321, I observed the housing conditions in an inner-city residential area. The building I selected is located in the city of Grand Mound, at the corner of Division Avenue and Hall Street, an area where most of the residents hold minimum-wage jobs or receive some form of public assistance.

Notes preliminary arrangements, provides overview of site location

I met the building supervisor, who had agreed to this visit, at 9:30 A.M. on Friday, April 13, 2001. The brick sides of the three-story apartment building appeared to be in good repair, but one second-story window was broken out and boarded up. Most windows had standard window shades, but a few were blocked with sheets or black plastic bags. Two had no coverings of any kind. Overall, the building's appearance was similar to that of several nearby apartment buildings.

Heavy traffic clogged Division Avenue at the time of my visit. Next to the apartment building stood three single-story wooden buildings housing an adult video store, a bar, and a novelty shop, all with boarded windows and peeling paint. Across the street, a single-story Goodwill store occupied the entire block. In front of it, three women in short skirts walked slowly back and forth, eyeing the cars that passed. Two men sat on crates, their backs to the building, drinking something out of paper bags.

> Continues overview of site location

The supervisor opened the unlocked metal door of the apartment building, and we went in. The hallway was lighted by a single dim bulb located on the wall toward the rear. Other bulbs along the wall and in two light fixtures hanging from the ceiling appeared burned out. Scraps of newspaper and chips of paint that had peeled from the ceiling and walls littered the floor. A strong urine-like smell pervaded the air.

> Describes building's hallway

Stating that he couldn't show me an occupied apartment because he "respected the privacy of the tenants," the supervisor took me to an unoccupied apartment on the first floor. He had trouble unlocking the wooden door; the key appeared to stick in the lock. The inside of the door had two bolt locks, one a few inches above the door handle and the other one near the floor. The door opened into a short hall with rooms off either side. Here, as in the building entrance, paint chips from the peeling walls and ceiling littered the floor. A battered socket on the wall held a single bulb, but when I flicked its switch, the bulb did not light. On the hall floor, linoleum curled at the edges. When I bent down to examine it more closely, several cockroaches scurried under the curl.

> Describes apartment hallway

The first door on the right-hand side of the hall led into a 10-by-12-foot room that the supervisor identified as the living room. Here the walls had been recently painted—by a former tenant, the supervisor said—and a strong paint smell was still apparent. However, nothing else had been done to the rest of the room. The radiator was unshielded, several nail heads protruded from

> Describes apartment living room

Continued on next page

Continued from previous page

the stained and uncovered wooden floor, and the sagging ceiling had several long cracks. Plaster chips dotted the floor.

Describes apartment kitchen

A small kitchen was situated behind the living room. Again, linoleum floor covering curled from the baseboard, and cockroaches scurried for cover. The kitchen was furnished with a battered-looking gas stove, but there was no refrigerator (the supervisor said one was on order). The surface of the sink was chipped and had many brownish stains. When I turned on the faucet, a rusty brown stream of water spurted out. I asked for a sample to be tested for lead content, but the supervisor refused.

Describes apartment bathroom

The bathroom, located at the end of the hall, had no radiator. Its floor tiles, broken in a number of places, exposed a foot-long section of rotted wood. The toilet, with seat missing, would not flush when I tried it but simply made a hissing noise. A brown stain spread over the bottom of the bathtub and a large portion of its sides. The wall tiles around the tub bulged outward and appeared ready to collapse into the tub. The supervisor offered the observation that there had been "some trouble with the plumbing."

Describes apartment bedrooms

Two small bedrooms opened off the left side of the hall. Like the living room, both had unprotected radiators, uncovered wooden floors, and cracked ceilings. Walls were papered rather than painted, but long strips of the wallpaper were missing. In one bedroom, a piece of plasterboard hung on the wall as if covering a hole. The windows in both bedrooms were covered with sheets tacked to the wall.

When I had finished looking at the bedrooms, the supervisor quickly escorted me from the apartment and the building, declaring that he was too busy to show me any other vacant apartments. He also said he had no time to answer any questions.

Discusses significance of findings

Clearly, the building I visited fails to meet city housing code: The living conditions are not what most people would consider acceptable. A careful investigation, including a test of the water and of the paint for lead content, seems called for to determine whether this apartment constitutes a health risk.

NARRATION ■■ ■ ■ ■ ■ ■ ■ ■ ■

Reading Strategies

1. Read the narrative rapidly to get a feel for the story and identify the main point.
2. Identify the main conflict that moves the story forward. Identify the major characters and what they may represent.
3. Read the narrative more slowly with the main point in mind. Keep an eye on how the narrative supports the main point.

Reading Critically

1. Consider if the narrative would seem different if told from another person's point of view. Consider that point of view.
2. Ask whether the narrative really supports the author's main point. Consider what other narratives could be told about the issue and determine whether they might undermine the writer's claims.

Reading As a Writer

1. Determine the setting, conflict, characters, and development of the narrative. You might want to outline the plot to determine how it was organized.
2. Notice any particularly effective movements in the plot. If you find a useful strategy, jot it down.
3. Observe how the writer used dialogue. Make a note of any especially effective uses.

JAMES ALEXANDER THOM

The Perfect Picture[1]

James Alexander Thom (born 1933) is a native of Gosport, Indiana, where his parents were physicians, and a graduate of Butler University. Before becoming a freelance writer in 1973, he worked as an editor for the Indianapolis Star *and the* Saturday Evening Post *and as a lecturer at Indiana University. He has authored one volume of essays and several historical novels, one of which,* Panther in the Sky, *earned the Best Novel Award from the Western Writers of America. His latest novel,* The Red Heart, *appeared in 1998. He is a contributor to many magazines. "The Perfect Picture" depicts an incident and an ethical dilemma that Thom experienced as a cub reporter.*

1   It was early in the spring about 15 years ago—a day of pale sunlight and trees just beginning to bud. I was a young police reporter, driving to a scene I didn't want to see. A man, the police-dispatcher's broadcast said, had accidentally backed his pickup truck over his baby granddaughter in the driveway of the family home. It was a fatality.

PERSPECTIVE
Dialogue is a prime way of developing conflict between and among individuals. Because this narrative focuses entirely on internal rather than external conflict, Thom uses almost no dialogue. You might point out that professional writers use narrative elements purposefully, not haphazardly.

OVERVIEW OF NARRATION ESSAYS
Two of the essays have unstated points and two (by Greenburg and Salinas) stated points. All have a serious tone. One essay (by Greenburg) contains some dialogue, two (by Angelou and Salinas) offer brief snatches of it, and one (by Thom) has only two brief comments by a single person. Three essays involve conflicts between persons, while one (by Thom) features an internal conflict. All essays are in the first person.

Introduction: notes time, locale, and cause of action; first-person point of view

---

[1]Reprinted with permission from the August 1976 *Reader's Digest.* Copyright © 1976 by The Reader's Digest Assn., Inc.

Body: paragraphs 2–12; action begins

2   As I parked among police cars and TV-news cruisers, I saw a stocky white-haired man in cotton work clothes standing near a pickup. Cameras were trained on him, and reporters were sticking microphones in his face. Looking totally bewildered, he was trying to answer their questions. Mostly he was only moving his lips, blinking and choking up.

Time signal
Key event

3   After a while the reporters gave up on him and followed the police into the small white house. I can still see in my mind's eye that devastated old man looking down at the place in the driveway where the child had been. Beside the house was a freshly spaded flower bed, and nearby a pile of dark, rich earth.

Dialogue

4   "I was just backing up there to spread that good dirt," he said to me, though I had not asked him anything. "I didn't even know she was outdoors." He stretched his hand toward the flower bed, then let it flop to his side. He lapsed back into his thoughts, and I, like a good reporter, went into the house to find someone who could provide a recent photo of the toddler.

Time signal
Secondary event

5   A few minutes later, with all the details in my notebook and a three-by-five studio portrait of the cherubic child tucked in my jacket pocket, I went toward the kitchen where the police had said the body was.

6   I had brought a camera in with me—the big, bulky Speed Graphic which used to be the newspaper reporter's trademark. Everybody had drifted back out of the house together—family, police, reporters and photographers. Entering the kitchen, I came upon this scene:

Key event

7   On a Formica-topped table, backlighted by a frilly curtained window, lay the tiny body, wrapped in a clean white sheet. Somehow the grandfather had managed to stay away from the crowd. He was sitting on a chair beside the table, in profile to me and unaware of my presence, looking uncomprehendingly at the swaddled corpse.

Time signal

8   The house was very quiet. A clock ticked. As I watched, the grandfather slowly leaned forward, curved his arms like parentheses around the head and feet of the little form, then pressed his face to the shroud and remained motionless.

9   In that hushed moment I recognized the makings of a prize-winning news photograph. I appraised the light, adjusted the lens setting and distance, locked a bulb in the flashgun, raised the camera and composed the scene in the viewfinder.

10   Every element of the picture was perfect: the grandfather in his plain work clothes, his white hair backlighted by sunshine, the child's form wrapped in the sheet, the atmosphere of the simple home suggested by black iron trivets and World's Fair souvenir plates on the walls flanking the window. Outside, the police could be seen inspecting the fatal rear wheel of the pickup while the child's mother and father leaned in each other's arms.

Conflict

11   I don't know how many seconds I stood there, unable to snap that shutter. I was keenly aware of the powerful story-telling value that photo would have, and my professional conscience told me to take it. Yet I couldn't make my hand fire that flashbulb and intrude on the poor man's island of grief.

Time signal
Action ends

12   At length I lowered the camera and crept away, shaken with doubt about my suitability for the journalistic profession. Of course I never told the city editor or any fellow reporters about that missed opportunity for a perfect news picture.

Conclusion: paragraphs 13 and 14; indirectly states point; notes writer's reaction

13   Every day on the newscasts and in the papers, we see pictures of people in extreme conditions of grief and despair. Human suffering has become a spectator sport. And sometimes, as I'm watching news film, I remember that day.

14   I still feel right about what I did.

Discussion Questions

1. Thom notes in his opening paragraph that he is "driving to a scene I didn't want to see." How does this statement help explain what happens later?
2. These details, while providing the makings of a perfect picture, also highlight the horror of what has happened and through their impact on his sensitivity help influence his decision.
3. Do you think that Thom made the right decision? Why or why not?

Toward Key Insights

How have the media affected our sense of privacy?
Is their influence good or bad?
To answer these questions, consider the role of the newspaper photographer in "The Perfect Picture," TV crews at disasters, and talk shows built around very personal revelations.

Suggestion for Writing

Write a personal narrative that features a conflict over a choice between an advantageous and a morally satisfying decision. State your point directly or indirectly, and use time signals and dialogue as necessary.

Dan Greenburg

Sound and Fury

Dan Greenburg is a native of Chicago who holds a bachelor of fine arts from the University of Illinois and a master of fine arts from UCLA. A prolific writer, he has authored over forty books, including such best sellers as How to Be a Jewish Mother, How to Make Yourself Miserable, How to Avoid Love and Marriage, *and a series of more than twenty-four children's books,* The Zack Files. *His articles have appeared in a wide and diverse range of popular magazines and been reprinted in many anthologies of humor and satire. He has been a guest on* The Today Show, Larry King Live, Late Night with David Letterman, *and other major TV talk shows. In this selection, Greenburg relates a situation in which soft words defused a potentially explosive situation.*

1   We carry around a lot of free-floating anger. What we do with it is what fascinates me.

2   My friend Lee Frank is a stand-up comedian who works regularly in New York comedy clubs. Not long ago I accompanied him to one of these places, where he was to be the late-night emcee and where I myself had once done a stand-up act in a gentler era.

3   The crowd that night was a typical weekend bunch—enthusiastic, hostile and drunk. A large contingent of inebriated young men from Long Island had decided that a comedian named Rusty who was currently on stage was the greatest

paragraph 30 and use this as an opportunity to explain your policy on students using fragments in their writing. We feel it's better to point out fragments before students call them to our attention.

thing since pop-top cans and began chanting his name after almost everything he said: "Rus-TEE! Rus-TEE!"

4   My friend Lee knew he had a tough act to follow.

5   Indeed, the moment Lee walked on stage, the inebriated young men from Long Island began chanting "Rus-TEE! Rus-TEE!" and didn't give him a chance. Poor Lee, the flop sweat running into his eyes, tried every trick he knew to win them over, and finally gave up.

6   When he left the stage I joined him at the bar in the back of the club to commiserate.

7   "You did the best you could," I told him.

8   "I don't know," he said, "I could have handled it better."

9   "How?"

10   "I don't know," he said.

11   As we spoke, the young men who'd given him such a tough time trickled into the bar area. One of them spotted Lee and observed to a companion that Lee might want to do something about their heckling.

12   Lee thought he heard the companion reply, "I'm down," a casual acknowledgment that he was willing to have a fistfight. Lee repeated their remarks to me and indicated that he, too, was "down."

13   Though slight of frame, Lee is a black belt in Tae Kwon Do, has had skirmishes with three-card monte con men in Times Square, and once even captured a robber-rapist. I am also slight of frame but have had no training in martial arts. I did have one fistfight in my adult life (with a movie producer), but as Lee's best friend, I assumed that I was "down" as well.

14   Considering that there were more than a dozen of them and only two of us, the period of time that might elapse between our being "down" and our being down seemed exceedingly brief.

15   The young man who'd made the remark drifted toward Lee.

16   The eyes of everyone in the bar shifted slightly and locked onto the two men like heat-seeking missiles. Fight-or-flight adrenaline and testosterone spurted into dozens of male cardiovascular systems. Safeties snapped off figurative weapons. Red warning lights lit up dozens of DEFCON systems; warheads were armed and aimed. In a moment this bar area might very well resemble a saloon in a B grade western.

17   "How ya doing?" said Lee, his voice flat as unleavened bread, trying to make up his mind whether to be friendly or hostile.

18   "Okay," said the guy, a pleasant-looking, clean-cut kid in his mid-20s.

19   I was fascinated by what was going on between the two of them, each feeling the other out in a neutral, unemotional, slightly bemused manner. I saw no hostility here, no xenophobic loathing, just two young males jockeying for position, going through the motions, doing the dance, willing to engage at the slightest provocation. I had seen my cat do this many times when a stranger strayed onto his turf.

20   And then I had a sudden flash of clarity: These guys could either rip each other's heads off now or they could share a beer, and both options would be equally acceptable to them.

21   I'd felt close to critical mass on many occasions myself. But here, feeling outside the action, I could see clearly that it had to do with the enormous reservoir of rage that we men carry around with us, rage that seethes just under the surface and is ready to be tapped in an instant, with or without just provocation.

22   "What're you in town for?" asked Lee casually.

23   The guy was watching Lee carefully, making minuscule adjustments on his sensing and triggering equipment.

24   "It's my birthday," said the guy.

25   Lee mulled over this information for a moment, still considering all his options. Then he made his decision.

26   "Happy birthday," said Lee finally, sticking out his hand.

27   The guy studied Lee's hand a moment. Then, deciding the gesture was sincere, he took the hand and shook it.

28   "Thanks," he said, and walked back to his buddies.

29   All over the room you could hear safeties snapping on, warheads being unarmed. The incident was over, and in a moment it was as if it had never happened.

30   I felt I had just witnessed in microcosm the mechanism that triggers most acts of aggression, from gang fights to international conflagrations. It was so simple: a minor act of provocation. A decision on how to interpret it. Whether or not to escalate. And, in this particular case, a peaceful outcome. What struck me was how absolutely arbitrarily it had all been decided.

Discussion Questions

1. Discuss the appropriateness of Greenburg's title.
2. Does this essay have a stated or an unstated point? If it is stated, indicate where. If it is unstated, express it in your own words.
3. The expression "our being down" occurs twice in paragraph 14. Explain what it means in each instance.
4. Discuss the effectiveness of the figurative language in paragraph 16.
5. In paragraph 21 Greenburg credits "feeling outside the action" for helping him understand the rage involved in this situation as well as in others. Explain what he means.
6. How often do you think that the "equally acceptable" options mentioned in paragraph 20 occur in confrontations?

Toward Key Insights

What reasons can you give for the "free-floating anger" that Greenburg mentions at the outset of the essay?

How frequently and in what ways is this anger manifested?

What are some effective strategies for coping with this anger?

Suggestion for Writing

Write a narrative about a small incident that turned into a serious confrontation. Possible incidents might include an improper or reckless action of another driver, a minor disagreement with a friend or spouse, or a retaliation for an action at a sporting event. The outcome can be peaceful or otherwise.

DISCUSSION QUESTIONS

1. The title echoes Shakespeare's soliloquy in which Macbeth likens life to "a tale / told by an idiot, full of sound and fury, / Signifying nothing." Similarly, Greenburg presents hecklers who act idiotically and a situation fraught with potential fury, but in the end it amounts to nothing. Thus the title is appropriate and effective. (Ironically, the confrontation signified a great deal to the narrator, providing him with an important insight.)

2. Paragraph 30 states the main point.

3. In the first instance it refers to the willingness to fight and in the second to the likelihood of being knocked down should a fight take place.

4. The figurative language dramatizes and highlights the confrontation by likening it to several much more serious situations and to a stereotypical Western movie scenario. We caution our students not to overuse figurative language, a tendency we have observed in our classes.

5. Because Greenburg is more an observer than a participant, he can offer a more objective assessment of the situation. You might want to discuss with your class how being an observer rather than a participant is likely to affect their narrative writing.

6. This question should prompt a stimulating discussion. A writing assignment could follow.

MAYA ANGELOU

Momma's Encounter[1]

Maya Angelou has earned a reputation as one of this country's foremost black writers. Born (1928) Marguerite Johnson in St. Louis, Missouri, she spent much of her childhood in Stamps, Arkansas, the locale of our selection, where her grandmother ran a general store. Angelou has written plays, poems, and a six-part autobiography that includes I Know Why the Caged Bird Sings *(1970), from which our selection is taken. She has acted in numerous plays and has served as a television narrator, interviewer, and poet. At the January 1993 inauguration of President William Clinton, she recited a poem, "On the Pulse of Morning," that she had written especially for the occasion. In our selection, Angelou tells about an encounter in which her grandmother, whom she calls Momma, tri-umphs over a pack of taunting neighborhood children.*

1   "Thou shall not be dirty" and "Thou shall not be impudent" were the two com-mandments of Grandmother Henderson upon which hung our total salvation.

2   Each night in the bitterest winter we were forced to wash faces, arms, necks, legs and feet before going to bed. She used to add, with a smirk that unprofane people can't control when venturing into profanity, "and wash as far as possible, then wash possible."

3   We would go to the well and wash in the ice-cold, clear water, grease our legs with the equally cold stiff Vaseline, then tiptoe into the house. We wiped the dust from our toes and settled down for schoolwork, cornbread, clabbered milk, prayers and bed, always in that order. Momma was famous for pulling the quilts off after we had fallen asleep to examine our feet. If they weren't clean enough for her, she took the switch (she kept one behind the bedroom door for emer-gencies) and woke up the offender with a few aptly placed burning reminders.

4   The area around the well at night was dark and slick, and boys told about how snakes love water, so that anyone who had to draw water at night and then stand there alone and wash knew that moccasins and rattlers, puff adders and boa constrictors were winding their way to the well and would arrive just as the person washing got soap in her eyes. But Momma convinced us that not only was cleanliness next to Godliness, dirtiness was the inventor of misery.

5   The impudent child was detested by God and a shame to its parents and could bring destruction to its house and line. All adults had to be addressed as Mister, Missus, Miss, Auntie, Cousin, Unk, Uncle, Buhbah, Sister, Brother and a thousand other appellations indicating familial relationship and the lowliness of the addressor.

6   Everyone I knew respected these customary laws, except for the powhite-trash children.

7   Some families of powhitetrash lived on Momma's farm land behind the school. Sometimes a gaggle of them came to the Store, filling the whole room, chasing out the air and even changing the well-known scents. The children crawled over the shelves and into the potato and onion bins, twanging all the time in their sharp voices like cigarbox guitars. They took liberties in my Store that I would never dare. Since Momma told us that the less you say to whitefolks (or even powhitetrash) the better, Bailey and I would stand, solemn, quiet, in the displaced air. But if one of the playful apparitions got close to us, I pinched it.

[1]Editors' title.

Partly out of angry frustration and partly because I didn't believe in its flesh reality.

8   They called my uncle by his first name and ordered him around the Store. He, to my crying shame, obeyed them in his limping dip-straight-dip fashion.

9   My grandmother, too followed their orders, except that she didn't seem to be servile because she anticipated their needs.

10   "Here's sugar, Miz Potter, and here's baking powder. You didn't buy soda last month, you'll probably be needing some."

11   Momma always directed her statements to the adults, but sometimes, Oh painful sometimes, the grimy, snotty-nosed girls would answer her.

12   "Naw, Annie . . ."—to Momma? Who owned the land they lived on? Who forgot more than they would ever learn? If there was any justice in the world, God should strike them dumb at once!—"Just give us some extry sody crackers, and some more mackerel."

13   At least they never looked in her face, or I never caught them doing so. Nobody with a smidgen of training, not even the worst roustabout, would look right in a grown person's face. It meant the person was trying to take the words out before they were formed. The dirty little children didn't do that, but they threw their orders around the Store like lashes from a cat-o'-nine tails.

14   When I was around ten years old, those scruffy children caused me the most painful and confusing experience I had ever had with my grandmother.

15   One summer morning, after I had swept the dirt yard of leaves, spearmint-gum wrappers and Vienna-sausage labels, I raked the yellow-red dirt, and made half-moons carefully, so that the design stood out clearly and mask-like. I put the rake behind the Store and came through the back of the house to find Grandmother on the front porch in her big, wide white apron. The apron was so stiff by virtue of the starch that it could have stood alone. Momma was admiring the yard, so I joined her. It truly looked like a flat redhead that had been raked with a big-toothed comb. Momma didn't say anything but I knew she liked it. She looked over toward the school principal's house and to the right at Mr. McElroy's. She was hoping one of those community pillars would see the design before the day's business wiped it out. Then she looked upward to the school. My head had swung with hers, so at just about the same time we saw a troop of the powhitetrash kids marching over the hill and down by the side of the school.

16   I looked to Momma for direction. She did an excellent job of sagging from her waist down, but from the waist up she seemed to be pulling for the top of the oak tree across the road. Then she began to moan a hymn. Maybe not to moan, but the tune was so slow and the meter so strange that she could have been moaning. She didn't look at me again. When the children reached halfway down the hill, halfway to the Store, she said without turning, "Sister, go on inside."

17   I wanted to beg her, "Momma, don't wait for them. Come on inside with me. If they come in the Store, you go to the bedroom and let me wait on them. They only frighten me if you're around. Alone I know how to handle them." But of course I couldn't say anything, so I went in and stood behind the screen door.

18   Before the girls got to the porch I heard their laughter crackling and popping like pine logs in a cooking stove. I suppose my lifelong paranoia was born in those cold, molasses-slow minutes. They came finally to stand on the ground in front of Momma. At first they pretended seriousness. Then one of them wrapped her right arm in the crook of her left, pushed out her mouth and started to hum. I realized that she was aping my grandmother. Another said, "Naw, Helen, you ain't standing like her. This here's it." Then she lifted her chest, folded her arms and mocked that strange carriage that was Annie

Angelou keeps the reader involved. When students write their own narratives, have them exchange papers within peer groups, get some feedback on the interest level, and then revise accordingly.

DISCUSSION QUESTIONS (p. 467)

1. This narrative has an unstated main point that might be rendered somewhat as follows: High standards of behavior are an important part of life, and one should not abandon them, even under severe provocation. By maintaining her dignity when confronted with the rudeness of the "powhitetrash" children, Momma triumphs over them. The whole episode has a classic Christian outcome, as Momma's triumph comes through acting humbly and turning the other cheek.

2. Angelou's strict upbringing stresses cleanliness and respect for elders. Each night, even during the winter, she and the other children must wash in the ice-cold water of the well, and all adults have to be addressed by some title. In contrast, the "powhitetrash" children are so dirty that they change "the well-known scents" of the store whenever they enter it. In the store they show disrespect by messing up the merchandise and treating the proprietors disrespectfully, behavior that foreshadows their later abuse of Momma.

3. Angelou is a prisoner of her sociological and

familial backgrounds. The first of these dictates deference to whites, and the second prohibits her from responding in kind to the taunts of her grandmother's tormenters. Like Angelou, the "powhite-trash" children are prisoners of their upbringing. Reared in a society that regards blacks as inferiors and lacking any sense of respect for adults, they behave in a manner that fully accords with their upbringing.

4. This dialogue marks the climax of the confrontation between Momma and her tormenters and points up her triumph over them. Having survived their insolent behavior with her dignity intact, she replies courteously to their final taunting "bye's" and in so doing signals their final defeat.

5. The pattern of concentric hearts pierced by an arrow suggests the love that the 10-year-old Angelou bears for her family and perhaps the wish for love to bind everyone together. Momma's "Glory, glory, hallelujah . . ." reflects both her recognition of the difficulty of maintaining her standards of behavior and her determination to do so as long as she lives.

6. At 10, Angelou, as paragraph 35 indicates, realizes that her grandmother has won the contest with the girls but does not understand why. At 18, the reason would have been clear, and Angelou would have recognized why the grandmother reacted as she did.

Henderson. Another laughed, "Naw, you can't do it. You mouth ain't pooched out enough. It's like this."

19 I thought about the rifle behind the door, but I knew I'd never be able to hold it straight, and the .410, our sawed-off shotgun, which stayed loaded and was fired every New Year's night, was locked in the trunk and Uncle Willie had the key on his chain. Through the fly-specked screen-door, I could see that the arms of Momma's apron jiggled from the vibrations of her humming. But her knees seemed to have locked as if they would never bend again.

20 She sang on. No louder than before, but no softer either. No slower or faster.

21 The dirt of the girls' cotton dresses continued on their legs, feet, arms and faces to make them all of a piece. Their greasy uncolored hair hung down, uncombed, with a grim finality. I knelt to see them better, to remember them for all time. The tears that had slipped down my dress left unsurprising dark spots, and made the front yard blurry and even more unreal. The world had taken a deep breath and was having doubts about continuing to revolve.

22 The girls had tired of mocking Momma and turned to other means of agitation. One crossed her eyes, stuck her thumbs in both sides of her mouth and said, "Look here, Annie." Grandmother hummed on and the apron strings trembled. I wanted to throw a handful of black pepper in their faces, to throw lye on them, to scream that they were dirty, scummy peckerwoods, but I knew I was as clearly imprisoned behind the scene as the actors outside were confined to their roles.

23 One of the smaller girls did a kind of puppet dance while her fellow clowns laughed at her. But the tall one, who was almost a woman, said something very quietly, which I couldn't hear. They all moved backward from the porch, still watching Momma. For an awful second I thought they were going to throw a rock at Momma, who seemed (except for the apron strings) to have turned into stone herself. But the big girl turned her back, bent down and put her hands flat on the ground—she didn't pick up anything. She simply shifted her weight and did a hand stand.

24 Her dirty bare feet and long legs went straight for the sky. Her dress fell down around her shoulders, and she had on no drawers. The slick pubic hair made a brown triangle where her legs came together. She hung in the vacuum of that lifeless morning for only a few seconds, then wavered and tumbled. The other girls clapped her on the back and slapped their hands.

25 Momma changed her song to "Bread of Heaven, bread of Heaven, feed me till I want no more."

26 I found that I was praying too. How long could Momma hold out? What new indignity would they think of to subject her to? Would I be able to stay out of it? What would Momma really like me to do?

27 Then they were moving out of the yard, on their way to town. They bobbed their heads and shook their slack behinds and turned, one at a time:

28 "'Bye, Annie."

29 "'Bye, Annie."

30 "'Bye, Annie."

31 Momma never turned her head or unfolded her arms, but she stopped singing and said, "'Bye, Miz Helen, 'bye, Miz Ruth, 'bye, Miz Eloise."

32 I burst. A firecracker July-the-Fourth burst. How could Momma call them Miz? The mean nasty things. Why couldn't she have come inside the sweet, cool store when we saw them breasting the hill? What did she prove? And then if they were dirty, mean and impudent, why did Momma have to call them Miz?

33 She stood another whole song through and then opened the screen door to look down on me crying in rage. She looked until I looked up. Her face was a brown moon that shone on me. She was beautiful. Something had happened out

there, which I couldn't completely understand, but I could see that she was happy. Then she bent down and touched me as mothers of the church "lay hands on the sick and afflicted" and I quieted.

34   "Go wash your face, Sister." And she went behind the candy counter and hummed, "Glory, glory, hallelujah, when I lay my burden down."

35   I threw the well water on my face and used the weekday handkerchief to blow my nose. Whatever the contest had been out front, I knew Momma had won.

36   I took the rake back to the front yard. The smudged footprints were easy to erase. I worked for a long time on my new design and laid the rake behind the wash pot. When I came back in the Store, I took Momma's hand and we both walked outside to look at the pattern.

37   It was a large heart with lots of hearts growing smaller inside, and piercing from the outside rim to the smallest heart was an arrow. Momma said, "Sister, that's right pretty." Then she turned back to the Store and resumed, "Glory, glory, hallelujah, when I lay my burden down."

Discussion Questions

1. Does this narrative have a stated or an unstated point? If it is stated, indicate where. If it is unstated, express it in your own words.
2. Point out the contrast between Angelou's upbringing and that of the "powhite-trash" children. How does this contrast prepare the reader for the events that follow?
3. Explain what Angelou means in paragraph 22 when she says ". . . but I knew I was as clearly imprisoned behind the scene as the actors outside were confined to their roles."
4. Discuss the significance of the dialogue in paragraphs 28–31.
5. Suggest the significance of the pattern of hearts that Angelou draws in the front yard. Of Momma singing "Glory, glory, hallelujah, when I lay my burden down."
6. Angelou recalls that she was "around ten years old" when the encounter took place. Explain why her age was significant. How would her perception have differed had she been, say, eighteen?
7. Angelou uses the first-person point of view. Explain why third-person narration would have been inappropriate for this narrative.

Toward Key Insights

Was Momma's strategy for enduring the children's taunts the most effective approach? Why or why not?

What else could she have done?

Has she really won?

Some argue that racism should always be actively confronted since passive endurance only perpetuates it. Do you agree? If not, when and how should racism be confronted and when should it be endured?

Suggestion for Writing

Write a narrative that illustrates how a friend, an acquaintance, or a family member achieved a personal triumph through turning the other cheek.

7. Third-person narration would have been inappropriate for two reasons. First, Angelou is telling about a personal experience. Second, third-person narration could not have captured so vividly the thoughts and feelings she experienced during the confrontation.

PRESPECTIVE

This essay provides an excellent example of how a writer can use a situation that may reflect their ethnically distinct experience to articulate a universal theme. While it is important that Marta is Mexican American, the conflict over social justice explored by this narrative applies to everyone. Students can be introduced here to how the writer used her own situation to build a universal theme by making the basis of the injustice social privilege rather than race and by including characters such as Mr. Schmidt who supported Marta while clearly not being Mexican American.

TEACHING STRATEGIES

1. Have students identify features of the narrative that reflect the writer's Mexican American heritage and those features that seem more universal. Discuss the ways the Mexican American elements affect the narrative.

2. Have students identify the points in the story where their expectations about the outcome might change, as when Marta's grandfather refused to pay the fifteen dollars. Let them plot the different possible routes the events could have taken.

3. Discuss paragraphs 4, 5, 6, 7, and 8 with students and explore the role the overheard conversation had in the development of the plot. Have the students identify why they did or did not find this approach effective.

4. Based on the brief dialogue from the different characters, have students list what they would conclude about each character. Have them identify what specifically in the dialogue made them reach those conclusions.

5. Have the students identify in paragraphs 9, 10, and 11 the behaviors the principal exhibits that show he is uncomfortable with what he is asked to do. Have them develop a short dialogue with inserted description of behavior that shows that the person is uncomfortable or even disagrees with what he or she is saying.

6. Have students identify situations where a policy may seem fair but be devised to have an unjust result. The use of the poll tax was one historical example. Some students may point out how grades that depend on the quality of a document may actually be rewarding students with a better printer and more developed software.

Marta Salinas

The Scholarship Jacket

Marta Salinas has published stories in the Los Angeles Herald *and in* California Living. *She is also an environmental activist.*

1   The small Texas school that I attended carried out a tradition every year during the eighth grade graduation; a beautiful gold and green jacket, the school colors, was awarded to the class valedictorian, the student who had maintained the highest grades for eight years. The scholarship jacket had a big gold S on the left front side and the winner's name was written in gold letters on the pocket.

2   My oldest sister Rosie had won the jacket a few years back and I fully expected to win also. I was fourteen and in the eighth grade. I had been a straight A student since the first grade, and the last year I had looked forward to owning the jacket. My father was a farm laborer who couldn't earn enough money to feed eight children, so when I was six I was given to my grandparents to raise. We couldn't participate in sports at school because there were registration fees, uniform costs, and trips out of town; so even though we were quite agile and athletic, there would never be a sports school jacket for us. This one, the scholarship jacket, was our only chance.

3   In May, close to graduation, spring fever struck, and no one paid any attention in class; instead we stared out the windows and at each other, wanting to speed up the last few weeks of school. I despaired every time I looked in the mirror. Pencil thin, not a curve anywhere, I was called "Beanpole" and "String Bean" and I knew that's what I looked like. A flat chest, no hips, and a brain, that's what I had. That really isn't much for a fourteen-year-old to work with, I thought, as I absentmindedly wandered from my history class to the gym. Another hour of sweating in basketball and displaying my toothpick legs was coming up. Then I remembered my P.E. shorts were still in a bag under my desk where I'd forgotten them. I had to walk all the way back and get them. Coach Thompson was a real bear if anyone wasn't dressed for P.E. She had said I was a good forward and once she even tried to talk Grandma into letting me join the team. Grandma, of course, said no.

4   I was almost back at my classroom's door when I heard angry voices and arguing. I stopped. I didn't mean to eavesdrop; I just hesitated, not knowing what to do. I needed those shorts and I was going to be late, but I didn't want to interrupt an argument between my teachers. I recognized the voices: Mr. Schmidt, my history teacher, and Mr. Boone, my math teacher. They seemed to be arguing about me. I couldn't believe it. I still remember the shock that rooted me flat against the wall as if I were trying to blend in with the graffiti written there.

5   "I refuse to do it! I don't care who her father is, her grades don't even begin to compare to Martha's. I won't lie or falsify records. Martha has a straight A plus average and you know it." That was Mr. Schmidt and he sounded very angry. Mr. Boone's voice sounded calm and quiet.

6   "Look, Joann's father is not only on the Board, he owns the only store in town; we could say it was a close tie and—"

7   The pounding in my ears drowned out the rest of the words, only a word here and there filtered through. ". . . Martha is Mexican . . . resign . . . won't do it. . . ." Mr. Schmidt came rushing out, and luckily for me went down the opposite way toward the auditorium, so he didn't see me. Shaking, I waited a few

minutes and then went in and grabbed my bag and fled from the room. Mr. Boone looked up when I came in but didn't say anything. To this day I don't remember if I got in trouble in P.E. for being late or how I made it through the rest of the afternoon. I went home very sad and cried into my pillow that night so Grandmother wouldn't hear me. It seemed a cruel coincidence that I had overheard that conversation.

8   The next day when the principal called me into his office, I knew what it would be about. He looked uncomfortable and unhappy. I decided I wasn't going to make it any easier for him so I looked him straight in the eye. He looked away and fidgeted with the papers on his desk.

9   "Martha," he said, "there's been a change in policy this year regarding the scholarship jacket. As you know, it has always been free." He cleared his throat and continued. "This year the Board decided to charge fifteen dollars—which still won't cover the complete cost of the jacket."

10   I stared at him in shock and a small sound of dismay escaped my throat. I hadn't expected this. He still avoided looking in my eyes.

11   "So if you are unable to pay the fifteen dollars for the jacket, it will be given to the next one in line."

12   Standing with all the dignity I could muster, I said, "I'll speak to my grandfather about it, sir, and let you know tomorrow." I cried on the walk home from the bus stop. The dirt road was a quarter of a mile from the highway, so by the time I got home, my eyes were red and puffy.

13   "Where's Grandpa?" I asked Grandma, looking down at the floor so she wouldn't ask me why I'd been crying. She was sewing on a quilt and didn't look up.

14   "I think he's out back working in the bean field."

15   I went outside and looked out at the fields. There he was. I could see him walking between the rows, his body bent over the little plants, hoe in hand. I walked slowly out to him, trying to think how I could best ask him for the money. There was a cool breeze blowing and a sweet smell of mesquite in the air, but I didn't appreciate it. I kicked at a dirt clod. I wanted that jacket so much. It was more than just being a valedictorian and giving a little thank you speech for the jacket on graduation night. It represented eight years of hard work and expectation. I knew I had to be honest with Grandpa; it was my only chance. He saw me and looked up.

16   He waited for me to speak. I cleared my throat nervously and clasped my hands behind my back so he wouldn't see them shaking. "Grandpa, I have a big favor to ask you," I said in Spanish, the only language he knew. He still waited silently. I tried again. "Grandpa, this year the principal said the scholarship jacket is not going to be free. It's going to cost fifteen dollars and I have to take the money in tomorrow, otherwise it'll be given to some else." The last words came out in an eager rush. Grandpa straightened up tiredly and leaned his chin on the hoe handle. He looked out over the field that was filled with the tiny green bean plants. I waited, desperately hoping he'd say I could have the money.

17   He turned to me and asked quietly, "What does a scholarship jacket mean?"

18   I answered quickly; maybe there was a chance. "It means you've earned it by having the highest grades for eight years and that's why they're giving it to you." Too late I realized the significance of my words. Grandpa knew that I understood it was not a matter of money. It wasn't that. He went back to hoeing the weeds that sprang up between the delicate little bean plants. It was a time consuming job; sometimes the small shoots were right next to each other. Finally he spoke again.

CLASSROOM ACTIVITIES

1. Have the students work in groups to develop an account of what this narrative would be like if the principal were telling the story.

2. Have the students work in small groups to determine how the meaning of the narrative would have changed if the grandfather had agreed to pay the money or the principal had followed the policy and awarded the jacket to Joann. Students could work to write an alternative ending or simply list the ways that these changes in plot would change the meaning of the narrative.

DISCUSSION QUESTIONS (p. 471)

1. The narrator is very explicit in paragraph 16. The scholarship jacket "represented eight years of hard work and expectation." It clearly means more than this, however. Her sister Rosie had won the jacket, so clearly there is some family competition at work. Marta sees the jacket as a measure of her worth as well as proof of the ability to earn success through merit. The scholarship jacket is a symbol of whether the society is just or not.

2. The key conflict is whether or not Marta will get the scholarship jacket. That major conflict is supported by other conflicts that move the narrative forward. Will the grandfather pay the fifteen dollars? How will the principal react to her grandfather's refusal to pay the money for the jacket?

3. The overheard conversation lets the reader know the key conflict over the jacket, the reasons for the conflict, and the different positions people take. While the device of having Marta return to the classroom for her gym shorts is awkward and contrived, it does let the writer inform the narrator and the reader of the basic conflict in a very compact manner.

4. The school could not simply give the jacket to Joann, despite her father's important position, because the bias would be too obvious. The expectation clearly was that Marta would not be able to pay the fifteen dollars and that this would allow them to legitimately give the jacket to Joann. This is pivotal to the theme since it demonstrates the way seemingly legitimate policies can be erected to gain unjust results.

5. By refusing to pay the fifteen dollars, Marta's grandfather rejects the new policy that would make the jacket no longer a just reward for the best academic performance but also a measure of the ability to pay.

6. Dialogue can tell us a lot about a character very economically. Mr. Boone's willingness to fudge the facts because of the role of Joann's father tells us about his lack of integrity. Mr. Schmidt's unwillingness to comply, and even the word "resign," lets us know that he places a high value on fairness and

19   "Then if you pay for it, Marta, it's not a scholarship jacket, is it? Tell your principal I will not pay the fifteen dollars."

20   I walked back to the house and locked myself in the bathroom for a long time. I was angry with Grandfather even though I knew he was right, and I was angry with the Board, whoever they were. Why did they have to change the rules just when it was my turn to win the jacket?

21   It was a very sad and withdrawn girl who dragged into the principal's office the next day. This time he did look me in the eyes.

22   "What did your grandfather say?"

23   I sat very straight in my chair.

24   "He said to tell you he won't pay the fifteen dollars."

25   The principal muttered something I couldn't understand under his breath, and walked over to the window. He stood looking out at something outside. He looked bigger than usual when he stood up; he was a tall gaunt man with gray hair, and I watched the back of his head while I waited for him to speak.

26   "Why?" he finally asked. "Your grandfather has the money. Doesn't he own a small bean farm?"

27   I looked at him, forcing my eyes to stay dry. "He said if I had to pay for it, then it wouldn't be a scholarship jacket," I said and stood up to leave. "I guess you'll just have to give it to Joann." I hadn't meant to say that; it had just slipped out. I was almost to the door when he stopped me.

28   "Martha—wait."

29   I turned and looked at him, waiting. What did he want now? I could feel my heart pounding. Something bitter and vile tasting was coming up in my mouth; I was afraid I was going to be sick. I didn't need any sympathy speeches. He sighed loudly and went back to his big desk. He looked at me, biting his lip, as if thinking.

30   "Okay, damn it. We'll make an exception in your case. I'll tell the Board, you'll get your jacket."

31   I could hardly believe it. I spoke in a trembling rush. "Oh, thank you, sir!" Suddenly I felt great. I didn't know about adrenaline in those days, but I knew something was pumping through me, making me feel as tall as the sky. I wanted to yell, jump, run the mile, do something. I ran out so I could cry in the hall where there was no one to see me. At the end of the day, Mr. Schmidt winked at me and said, "I hear you're getting a scholarship jacket this year."

32   His face looked as happy and innocent as a baby's, but I knew better. Without answering I gave him a quick hug and ran to the bus. I cried on the walk home again, but this time because I was so happy. I couldn't wait to tell Grandpa and ran straight to the field. I joined him in the row where he was working and without saying anything I crouched down and started pulling up the weeds with my hands. Grandpa worked alongside me for a few minutes, but he didn't ask what had happened. After I had a little pile of weeds between the rows, I stood up and faced him.

33   "The principal said he's making an exception for me, Grandpa, and I'm getting the jacket after all. That's after I told him what you said."

34   Grandpa didn't say anything, he just gave me a pat on the shoulder and a smile. He pulled out the crumpled red handkerchief that he always carried in his back pocket and wiped the sweat off his forehead.

35   "Better go see if your grandmother needs any help with supper."

36   I gave him a big grin. He didn't fool me. I skipped and ran back to the house whistling some silly tune.

Discussion Questions

1. Why is the scholarship jacket so important to Marta?
2. What are some of the key conflicts that are essential to the plot?
3. What is the importance of the overheard conversation in the development of the plot? How effective is it as a technique in this context?
4. Why did the school charge fifteen dollars for the scholarship jacket? How is this important to the developing theme of the narrative?
5. What is the significance of the grandfather's refusal to pay the fifteen dollars for the scholarship jacket?
6. How does the writer use very short pieces of dialogue to reveal the essential values of the characters and how they meet the situation?
7. Why doesn't the story end with the principal's statement that he will make an exception and she will get the jacket? What do the additional scenes with Mr. Schmidt and Martha's grandfather add to the narrative?
8. What is the significance of the fact that the principal calls the narrator "Martha" while her grandfather calls her "Marta"?

Toward Key Insights

Instead of simply giving the jacket to Joann in an outright act of discrimination, the school developed a policy that was likely to have the same result but seem reasonable. What policies or procedures have you observed that may seem reasonable on the surface but could simply serve to perpetuate an injustice?

The main character of this narrative is Mexican American. Is the suggestion that the scholarship jacket go to someone else based on race? Are there other social injustices that may be credited to race but have other causes?

Suggestion for Writing

Write a narrative about an injustice you experienced so that those involved in the situation could better understand what the event meant to you.

DESCRIPTION ■■ ■ ■ ■ ■ ■ ■

Reading Strategies

1. Identify a thesis statement (possibly first or last paragraph) and/or a statement of purpose. Read the essay with an anticipation of what the description is intended to accomplish.
2. Don't get lost in the details. Note, possibly write in the margins, the overall impression or mood the description is evoking.
3. Decide how much of the description you need to remember. If the description is intended to create a mood, you may read quickly. If you are reading a description of rock formations for a geology class, you might want to take notes that organize the key features you need to remember under the appropriate headings.
4. Note if there is a pattern to the organization of the description. Recognizing the organizational pattern can make even dense writing easier to read.

honesty. The principal's short phrase "Okay, damn it. We'll make an exception in your case. I'll tell the board, you'll get your jacket" indicates a man under pressure who had hoped for a compromise, such as her grandfather actually paying the fee, but faced with her grandfather's position will uncomfortably and with some anger do what seems to him the right and just thing.

7. The narrative could end with the principal's announcement that he would make sure she would

get the jacket, but that would make the principal's decision the most important feature of the story. More important still were Mr. Schmidt's and Marta's grandfather's unwillingness in different ways to surrender to the injustice of the situation. The ending allows the writer to confirm their

importance by allowing Marta to share her success with each of them in turn. The last two paragraphs also place the event in context. While this was an important success in Marta's life, life and family will continue to be important for a long time to come.

8. The fact that the principal and the grandfather use a slightly different name subtly shows that Marta actually inhabits two different cultures: the Spanish-speaking culture of her grandfather and the English-speaking culture of her school. She has to be able to respond to both.

Reading Critically

1. Identify the point of view of the description. The scene described might look very different from a different vantage point.
2. Look for how the details were selected. An emphasis on different details might have painted a very different picture.
3. Check to see if the conclusion of the essay really follows from the description. Just because a wilderness can be described as pristine doesn't mean that careful logging should be entirely banned.

Reading As a Writer

1. Identify and note down the organizational pattern if it is effective.
2. Jot down any phrases or sections that you find especially effective.
3. Examine the essay for word choice. Notice how the writer obtained the effects he or she did.

JOHN V. YOUNG

When the Full Moon Shines Its Magic over Monument Valley

John V. Young (1909–1999) was born in Oakland, California. After attending San Jose State Teachers College, he spent twelve years as a reporter and editor for several rural California newspapers, then held a series of personnel and public relations positions. In 1966, he became a full-time freelance writer, specializing in western travel pieces. His books include The Grand Canyon *(1969),* Ghost Towns of the Santa Cruz Mountains *(1979, 1984),* Hot Type and Pony Wire *(1980),* State Parks of New Mexico *(1984),* State Parks of Arizona *(1986), and* State Parks of Utah *(1989). His articles have appeared in the* New York Times *as well as in numerous travel publications. In the article that follows, he focuses on the sensations generated first by his surroundings and then by the moonrise.*

1   We were camped here in early spring, by one of those open-faced shelters that the Navajos have provided for tourists in this part of their vast tribal park on the Arizona–Utah border, 25 miles north of Kayenta. It was cool but pleasant, and we were alone, three men in a truck.

2   We were here for a purpose; to see the full moon rise over this most mysterious and lonely of scenic wonders, where fantastically eroded red and yellow sandstone shapes soar to the sky like a giant's chess pieces and where people—especially white strangers—come quickly to feel like pretty small change indeed.

3   Because all Navajo dwellings face east, our camp faced east—toward the rising sun and the rising moon and across a limitless expanse of tawny desert, that ancient sea, framed by the towering nearby twin pinnacles called The Mittens. We began to feel the magic even before the sun was fully down. It occurred when a diminutive wraith of a Navajo girl wearing a long, dark, velvet dress gleaming with silver ornaments drifted silently by, herding a flock of ghostly sheep to a waterhole somewhere. A bell on one of the rams tinkled faintly, and then its music was lost in the soft rustle of the night wind, leaving us with an impression that perhaps we had really seen nothing at all.

4   Just then, a large woolly dog appeared out of the gloom, seeming to materialize on the spot. It sat quietly on the edge of the glow from our campfire, its eyes shining like mirrors. It made no sound but when we offered food, it accepted the gift gravely and with much dignity. The dog then vanished again, probably to join the girl and her flock. We were not certain it was not part of the illusion.

> Time signal
> Sight impression
> Comparison

5   As the sun disappeared entirely, the evening afterglow brush tipped all the spires and cliffs with magenta, deepening to purple, and the sand ripples stood out like miniature ocean waves in darkening shades of orange. Off to the east on the edge of the desert, a pale saffron glow told us the moon was about to rise behind a thin layer of clouds, slashed by the white contrail of an invisible jet airplane miles away.

> Time signal
> Sight impressions
> Comparison
> Sight impressions

6   We had our cameras on tripods and were fussing with light meters, making casual bets as to the exact place where the moon would first appear, when it happened—instant enchantment. Precisely between the twin spires of The Mittens, the enormous globe loomed suddenly, seeming as big as the sun itself, behind a coppery curtain on the rim of creation.

> Sight impressions
> Comparison
> Vivid language

7   We were as totally unprepared for the great size of the moon as we were for its flaming color, nor could we have prepared ourselves for the improbable setting. We felt like the wizards of Stonehenge, commanding the planets to send their light through the magic orifices in line at the equinox. Had the Navajo medicine men contrived this for our benefit?

> Sight impressions

8   The massive disk of the moon seemed to rise very fast at first, an optical effect magnified by the crystalline air and the flatness of the landscape between us and the distant, ragged skyline. Then it seemed to pause for a moment, as if it were pinioned on one of the pinnacles or impaled on a sharply upthrusting rocky point. Its blazing light made inky shadows all around us, split by the brilliant wedge of the moon's path between the spires. The wind had stopped. There was not a sound anywhere, nor even a whisper. If a drum had sounded just then, it would not have been out of place, I suppose, but it would have frightened us half to death.

> Comparison
>
> Sight impressions
>
> Vivid language
>
> Absent sound
> Impression

9   Before the moon had cleared the tops of The Mittens, the show was over and the magic was gone. A thin veil of clouds spread over the sky, ending the spell as suddenly as it had come upon us. It was as if the gods had decided that we had seen enough for mere mortals on one spring night, and I must confess it was something of a relief to find ourselves back on mundane earth again, with sand in our shoes and a chill in the air.

> Conclusion: time signal; renames dominant impression
>
> Notes writer's reaction

Discussion Questions

1. How does the last sentence in paragraph 7 ("Had the Navajo medicine men contrived this for our benefit?") relate to the purpose of the essay?
2. This description takes the form of a narrative. Where does the climax occur, and how does it affect the viewers?

> Touch impression
>
> **DISCUSSION QUESTIONS**
> 1. This question suggests that the whole episode is a piece of magic deliberately created by the medicine men.

Toward Key Insights

What makes certain experiences seem magical?

How important are such magical experiences, and how might they shape our perceptions of the everyday world?

2. The climax occurs in the last sentence of paragraph 6, when the moon suddenly looms between the twin spires of the mountain called "The Mittens." The men are awestruck, and they liken their reactions to those of the ancient wizards at Stonehenge, in England, "commanding the planets to send their light through the magic orifices in line at the equinox."

PERSPECTIVE

Economic forecasters have correctly noted that the service sector, not manufacturing, is the new engine driving America's economy. Nevertheless, manufacturing, particularly the automotive industry, is far from a spent force. Our selection speaks to the vitality of this industry by describing the on-the-job reality of auto production.

TEACHING STRATEGIES

1. Hazleton uses a number of sentence fragments at various places in her essay. You might want to call attention to them and explain professional license. You could also use this opportunity to explain your policy on students using "intentional" fragments in their writing.

2. Ask students what audience Hazleton has in mind and what evidence in the essay supports their answers.

3. Ask students to characterize Hazleton's style and support their contentions with references to the essay.

Suggestion for Writing

Select a place you know well and describe it by conveying some dominant impression that emerges during daylight hours. Settle on an appropriate vantage point and either identify the impression or allow readers to determine it for themselves.

LESLEY HAZLETON

Assembly Line Adventure[1]

Lesley Hazleton (born 1945) is a native of England who earned a B.A. degree from Manchester University and an MA degree from the Hebrew University of Jerusalem before emigrating to the United States in 1979. Hazleton is a nationally known automotive journalist with wide-ranging interests that include baseball, psychology, and politics. She has authored six nonfiction books, and her numerous shorter pieces have appeared in a variety of major newspapers and popular magazines. Our essay is excerpted from her latest book, Driving to Detroit *(1998). In it she describes her brief introduction to auto assembly line work and the lessons she learned from the experience.*

1   I'd toured many auto plants before, and physically this was not much different. That is, it was an assault on the senses: an enclosed, windowless world of harsh artificial light and hard concrete floors ringing with the discordant cacophony of industrial production. Metal rang on metal. Stamping presses clanked, power tools whined, pulleys groaned, hoists clanged, welding robots whooshed, sparks crackled, lasers beeped, compressed air hissed, bolts banged into place, trolleys rumbled down the aisles, and all the while, conveyor belts carrying cars in one stage or another of production, from bare metal frames to fully painted bodies, clattered and clanketed beside us and behind us and even over our heads.

2   At five in the afternoon, I started work, joining three other workers stationed around a huge rotating machine. Our job was to feed a robot.

3   Officially, we were preparing dashboard molds for foam injection. In fact, we were simply loading and unloading the machine for the robot, which injected the foam and then wiped its own nozzle as though it were wiping its nose—one of those infuriatingly human gestures that make you think, "Cute," and then hate yourself for having thought it.

4   This was one of the simplest tasks on the whole assembly line. Squirt some filler release into a hole. Lift a light plastic mold and place it on a protruding lip of the machine. Bang a board with your knee to drop three locks to hold the mold in place. Check the locks. Push a black button to bring the lip down into the right position for the next guy. Wait for the machine to rotate and present you with a new lip. And that was it. A ten-second job to be repeated ad infinitum.

5   Two hours later, I moved from one of the simplest jobs on the line to one of the most complicated: assembling the whole instrument panel. Steering wheel, indicator and wiper wands, gauges, dashboard line, the lot.

6   Audrey, the woman whose task it was to teach me this job, had a tough challenge ahead of her.

[1]Editors' title.

7   I guessed she was in her mid-thirties. Despite a mass of long brown curly hair, she had a boyish way to her, maybe because of the leather builder's apron she was wearing, its pockets so full of connectors and screws and bolts that it took me a while to realize she was six months pregnant.

8   "Is this your first?" I asked.

9   She burst out laughing. "Honey, I'm forty-three years old. And a grandmother. I married again not long ago, and"—she spread her arms wide and stared at her belly—"just look what happened. This sure is the last thing I ever expected."

10   "How long will you go on working?"

11   She laughed again. "Do you know how much kids cost? I'm staying right here till the day I pop."

12   She hadn't stopped working for a moment as we talked. She couldn't. The line was rolling, and it was either keep up or bring everything to a halt. We were standing *on* the line, a wide conveyor belt rumbling past an array of shelves piled high with parts, and beneath an overhead rack dangling power tools and bins of screws. On the line with us, every six feet or so, was a work-stand holding an empty dashboard shell, placed upside down on the stand so that it was easy to work on. Audrey's job was to make it into a complete instrument panel.

13   For the first few moments, standing on the moving belt was almost childishly fun. The world was reversed: you stood still and it went past you. Your mind knew it was you moving, not the world, but your senses told you otherwise. And all the time, the belt vibrated gently underfoot; if it weren't for the noise, it might even have been pleasantly sexy.

14   "Watch your head," Audrey said, and I ducked as a power wrench came dangling past my right ear. Followed by another. And yet another. Even though I reminded myself that it was me moving, not them, every time I looked up they seemed to be aiming for my brains with a certain inexorable malevolence.

15   I spent the first half-hour watching Audrey and figuring out how to stay out of the way. So far as I could make out, she had a total of some fifty separate procedures to complete in a logic-defying sequence of about three minutes. Each step had to be performed in perfect timing, so that the right parts and tools were at hand exactly when she needed them. And to add to the pressure, this job was what they called a "show-stopper."

16   Farther on down the line, the completed instrument panel would be lowered into the "smile joint"—a large lazy U going from side to side of the car's frame. If it didn't fit, the line would stop, and the whole plant would start running behind. "You can't go back and do it again," Audrey said. "You got to do it perfect the first time."

17   I knew I'd never be able to do this job. Yet Audrey seemed convinced that I was educable. She talked each movement out loud as she worked, with me following her around like a pet dog. Somehow, she convinced me to do a bit here and a bit there, until within an hour, I had the beginning of it down pat:

18   Walk six stands down the line, past other team members at different stages of the job, and read the manifest hanging on the dashboard shell. Pick up different parts from the shelves alongside the line, depending on whether this is to be a sedan or a wagon, an automatic or a manual shift. Jam a leather sheath over the sharp metal edge to the side of the module. Ease the parts into place. Snap-connect electrical wires: gray to the right, blue to the middle, white to the left.

19   So far so good. I was feeling quite proud of myself. Trouble was, this was only the beginning of the beginning.

20   The rest began to blur: Snap-connect a black fastener, then a yellow one. Don't delay. If you go too slow, the line will take you past the parts you need, and you'll have to start running back and forth for them. Pick up the steering shaft from a shelf

CLASSROOM ACTIVITY
Point out that unlike the other descriptive essays this one does not explore some aspect of nature. Then divide the class into small groups and have students discuss the different demands that a nature topic and a non-nature topic make on the writer. A writing assignment could follow.

and ease its thirty-pound weight down through the center of the module. Arrange the wires to run over the top of the shaft. Slip on and snap a green fastener . . .

21   Or were those last two steps the other way round? "Here," said Audrey, redoing my work.

22   Okay, now pick up two bronze-colored bolts and screws, two black bolts, a circular piece, and two silver bolts from those big bins alongside the line. Insert the silver bolts. Fine. Place the bronze-colored ones in one place, the black ones in another. Great. Pull down a power wrench from the overhead line . . .

23   I grabbed for it and missed. It began to recede from me. I stretched and yanked it down just in time to tighten the bolts. I had no idea of what I was bolting to what, or why. Neither, it turned out, did Audrey.

24   Right, you've got those bolts nice and tight. Now pick different bronze-colored bolts from another bin. No, not alongside the line—right here, hanging overhead. Fine. Insert them and tighten them by hand for now. What about the wrench? Not there yet, that comes soon. First, thread the electrical wires through the back of the module and out through this flap, then loop them over and under the shaft like so, and then . . .

25   Then what? I couldn't remember. And I was only a third of the way through the job.

26   "Don't worry," said Audrey. "It takes most people four days to learn this job. You're doing real good."

27   That was sweet of her, but it didn't feel real good to me. My attention strayed for a moment, I lost a beat, and suddenly the power tools and screw bins were bearing down on me way before I was ready for them. I worked as fast as I could, one eye on my hands, the other on the dangling wrench going past. I swore, lunged for it, and yanked at the cord as though if I pulled hard enough I could pull back the whole line and slow things down to my pace. I remembered Charlie Chaplin's desperation in *Modern Times,* and suddenly there was nothing remotely funny about it. I dropped a bolt, reached for the wrong wrench, and watched pathetically as Audrey stepped in and put everything to rights. I hadn't felt quite this incompetent since I was a kid trying to thread a sewing machine at school. I never did master that.

28   Every time I thought I had the hang of it all, another two steps somehow reversed themselves in my mind, or one slipped out of existence altogether. My ears were ringing, my mind was reeling, and my hands had never felt clumsier. I began to fumble the screws, inserting them at an angle so that they wouldn't tighten properly and had to be taken out and inserted anew. Audrey was working as hard as I was by now; we stood shoulder to shoulder, me fouling things up, her fixing them.

29   And suddenly it was ten o'clock, and there was a half-hour break for lunch. Ten at night, that is. By now, I was squinting to stop from seeing double. I was convinced that if I could just work through to the end of the shift, I'd get this job down pat. But as the line came to a halt and everything stopped moving, some remote part of my brain managed to signal a weak but just decipherable message that the pressure was getting to me. It was time to call it quits before I damaged a car, or myself, or worse still, somebody else.

30   "Don't you want some lunch before you go?" said Audrey. But I was too exhausted to even look at food. I needed fresh air. And solitude. And silence. I made my excuses, stuffed my yellow Kevlar gloves into my pocket as a memento, got lost twice trying to find the way out, and finally emerged into the parking lot.

31   Never had a parking lot seemed so beautiful: so quiet, so peaceful, so serene. Even the buzzing yellow of the sodium vapor lights seemed soothing. Behind me, the plant hummed gently, its skylights glowing into the night.

DISCUSSION QUESTIONS(p. 477)
1. The title is effective because "Assembly Line" both accurately and specifically indicates the focus of the description. In addition, "Adventure" is likely to spark interest, drawing the reader into the essay in order to determine its meaning.

2. Sight impressions occur in paragraphs 1, 3, 7, 12, 14, 16, 18, 20, 22, 24, 27, 30, and 31; sound impressions in paragraphs 1, 4, 12, 13, 28, and 31; and touch impressions in 4, 13, 18, and 28.

Mid-shift, I was the only person out here, and I had a flash of guilt mixed with giddy freedom, the kind that comes from playing hooky.

32   I found the truck, climbed in, made to start it up. Then stopped, hand in midair, and sat staring at the instrument panel. Something was wrong. I took a moment to figure it out: I'd spent the past few hours working on upside-down instrument panels, and now I was seeing this one the right way up.

33   I reached out and examined it for its component parts, thinking of the man or the woman who'd put it together, and appreciating the way it had been done. This thing I usually took so for granted that I'd never before paid a moment's attention to it, was now an astounding piece of man-made—woman-made—complexity.

34   I started the truck and drove slowly out of the lot, wondering how long I'd keep this awareness that cars are not merely machines, but things put together by human beings, products of real men and real women doing the kind of work that would drive most people crazy. Not long enough, for sure.

Discussion Questions

1. Comment on the effectiveness of the essay's title.
2. Which of the five sensory impressions does Hazleton include? Refer to specific paragraphs when answering.
3. What is the dominant impression of this essay?
4. What time signals does Hazleton use? Refer to specific paragraphs when answering.
5. This description takes the form of a narrative with the action moving forward until a turning point is reached. Where does this turning point occur?
6. Identify the conclusion of the essay and what it accomplishes.
7. After reading Hazleton's description, how do you think you would tolerate working on an assembly line as a summer job? Discuss.

Toward Key Insights

What jobs have you done or heard about that you would consider unbearable? What characteristics make them unbearable?

What jobs have you done or heard about that you would find enjoyable? What characteristics make them enjoyable?

Suggestion for Writing

Write an essay describing your introduction to some new job. Use an appropriate number of sensory details that create a dominant impression and indicate your reaction to what you learned.

E. B. White

Once More to the Lake

E. B. White (1899–1985) was born in Mount Vernon, New York, and was a graduate of Cornell University. In 1927, he joined the staff of The New Yorker, *launched just two years before, and for several decades produced a steady flow of short pieces for it. Between*

3. The dominant impression is one of noisy, unrelenting activity. Noisiness is established in the opening paragraph, and paragraphs 18–28 provide a vivid picture of repetitive, rapid-paced action.

4. The first time signal is in paragraph 2: "At five in the afternoon. . . ." Additional time signals include "Two hours later" (paragraph 5), "For the first few moments" (paragraph 13), "the first half hour" (paragraph 15), "within an hour" (paragraph 17), and "suddenly it was ten o'clock, and there was a half-hour break for lunch" (paragraph 29).

5. The turning point occurs at the end of paragraph 29 when Hazleton realizes that she's not suited for assembly-line work.

6. The conclusion consists of paragraphs 32–34. In it Hazleton reflects on the assembly-line adventure she has described. She has come to appreciate the demanding nature of this type of work and how unsuited she is for it.

7. This question should prompt some interesting responses, which might be followed by a writing assignment.

1937 and 1943, he also wrote a column, "One Man's Meat," for Harper's. *He is the author of three critically acclaimed children's books,* Stuart Little *(1945),* Charlotte's Web *(1952), and* The Trumpet of the Swan *(1970), as well as numerous adult works, including several collections of his essays and poems. In "Once More to the Lake," White creates a vivid and memorable word picture of a summer vacation that had great meaning for him and that brought him a sobering insight.*

PERSPECTIVE

Narration figures more prominently in this essay than in any of the others in this section. White presents a series of events that cover about a week's time and culminate in a turning point together with its chilling insight. On the other hand, the essay lacks dialogue and characterization of White's son.

TEACHING STRATEGIES

1. If you have students of different ages, say 10–15 years apart, ask them to discuss to what extent and why they can empathize with White's feelings and the philosophical point of the essay. Divergent views are likely.

2. Ask students why they think White ended the essay as he did rather than with actually leaving the lake at the conclusion of the trip.

3. Ask students to list the most memorable sensory details of their favorite vacation spot. The list might serve as the starting point for a descriptive essay.

1   One summer, along about 1904, my father rented a camp on a lake in Maine and took us all there for the month of August. We all got ringworm from some kittens and had to rub Pond's Extract on our arms and legs night and morning, and my father rolled over in a canoe with all his clothes on; but outside of that the vacation was a success and from then on none of us ever thought there was any place in the world like that lake in Maine. We returned summer after summer—always on August 1st for one month. I have since become a salt-water man, but sometimes in summer there are days when the restlessness of the tides and the fearful cold of the sea water and the incessant wind which blows across the afternoon and into the evening make me wish for the placidity of a lake in the woods. A few weeks ago this feeling got so strong I bought myself a couple of bass hooks and a spinner and returned to the lake where we used to go, for a week's fishing and to revisit old haunts.

2   I took along my son, who had never had any fresh water up his nose and who had seen lily pads only from train windows. On the journey over to the lake I began to wonder what it would be like. I wondered how time would have marred this unique, this holy spot—the coves and streams, the hills that the sun set behind, the camps and the paths behind the camps. I was sure the tarred road would have found it out and I wondered in what other ways it would be desolated. It is strange how much you can remember about places like that once you allow your mind to return into the grooves which lead back. You remember one thing, and that suddenly reminds you of another thing. I guess I remembered clearest of all the early mornings, when the lake was cool and motionless, remembered how the bedroom smelled of the lumber it was made of and the wet woods whose scent entered through the screen. The partitions in the camp were thin and did not extend clear to the top of the rooms, and as I was always the first up I would dress softly so as not to wake the others, and sneak out into the sweet outdoors and start out in the canoe, keeping close along the shore in the long shadows of the pines. I remembered being very careful never to rub my paddle against the gunwale for fear of disturbing the stillness of the cathedral.

3   The lake had never been what you would call a wild lake. There were cottages sprinkled around the shores, and it was in farming country although the shores of the lake were quite heavily wooded. Some of the cottages were owned by nearby farmers, and you would live at the shore and eat your meals at the farmhouse. That's what our family did. But although it wasn't wild, it was a fairly large and undisturbed lake and there were places in it which, to a child at least, seemed infinitely remote and primeval.

4   I was right about the tar: it led to within half a mile of the shore. But when I got back there, with my boy, and we settled into a camp near a farmhouse and into the kind of summertime I had known, I could tell that it was going to be pretty much the same as it had been before—I knew it, lying in bed the first morning, smelling the bedroom, and hearing the boy sneak quietly out and go off along the shore in a boat. I began to sustain the illusion that he was I, and therefore by simple transposition, that I was my father. This sensation persisted, kept cropping up

all the time we were there. It was not an entirely new feeling, but in this setting it grew much stronger. I seemed to be living a dual existence. I would be in the middle of some simple act, I would be picking up a bait box or laying down a table fork, or I would be saying something, and suddenly it would be not I but my father who was saying the words or making the gesture. It gave me a creepy sensation.

5   We went fishing the first morning. I felt the same damp moss covering the worms in the bait can, and saw the dragonfly alight on the tip of my rod as it hovered a few inches from the surface of the water. It was the arrival of this fly that convinced me beyond any doubt that everything was as it always had been, that the years were a mirage and there had been no years. The small waves were the same, chucking the rowboat under the chin as we fished at anchor, and the boat was the same boat, the same color green and the ribs broken in the same places, and under the floor-boards the same fresh-water leavings and debris—the dead hellgramite,[1] the wisps of moss, the rusty discarded fishhook, the dried blood from yesterday's catch. We stared silently at the tips of our rods, at the dragonflies that came and went. I lowered the tip of mine into the water, tentatively, pensively dislodging the fly, which darted two feet away, poised, darted two feet back, and came to rest again a little farther up the rod. There had been no years between the ducking of this dragonfly and the other one—the one that was part of memory. I looked at the boy, who was silently watching his fly, and it was my hands that held his rod, my eyes watching. I felt dizzy and didn't know which rod I was at the end of.

6   We caught two bass, hauling them in briskly as though they were mackerel, putting them over the side of the boat in a businesslike manner without any landing net, and stunning them with a blow on the back of the head. When we got back for a swim before lunch, the lake was exactly where we had left it, the same number of inches from the dock, and there was only the merest suggestion of a breeze. This seemed an utterly enchanted sea, this lake you could leave to its own devices for a few hours and come back to, and find that it had not stirred, this constant and trustworthy body of water. In the shallows, the dark, water-soaked sticks and twigs, smooth and old, were undulating in clusters on the bottom against the clean ribbed sand, and the track of the mussel was plain. A school of minnows swam by, each minnow with its small individual shadow, doubling the attendance, so clear and sharp in the sunlight. Some of the other campers were in swimming, along the shore, one of them with a cake of soap, and the water felt thin and clear and unsubstantial. Over the years there had been this person with the cake of soap, this cultist, and here he was. There had been no years.

7   Up to the farmhouse to dinner through the teeming, dusty field, the road under our sneakers was only a two-track road. The middle track was missing, the one with the marks of the hooves and the splotches of dried, flaky manure. There had always been three tracks to choose from in choosing which track to walk in; now the choice was narrowed down to two. For a moment I missed terribly the middle alternative. But the way led past the tennis court, and something about the way it lay there in the sun reassured me; the tape had loosened along the backline, the alleys were green with plantains and other weeds, and the net (installed in June and removed in September) sagged in the dry noon, and the whole place steamed with midday heat and hunger and emptiness. There was a choice of pie for dessert, and one was blueberry and one was apple, and the waitresses were the same country girls, there having been no passage of time, only the illusion of it as in a dropped curtain—the waitresses were still fifteen; their

CLASSROOM ACTIVITIES

1. Have students, working in small groups, exchange experiences that brought them an insight. Again, such a discussion might lead to a writing assignment.

2. White is a master at using emotionally evocative description. Have students, working in small groups, identify the descriptive passages that have emotional associations. The entire class could then discuss why. A writing assignment stressing emotionally evocative description could follow.

[1]Insect used as bait.

hair had been washed, that was the only difference—they had been to the movies and seen the pretty girls with the clean hair.

8   Summertime, oh summertime, pattern of life indelible, the fade-proof lake, the woods unshatterable, the pasture with the sweetfern and the juniper forever and ever, summer without end; this was the background, and the life along the shore was the design, the cottages with their innocent and tranquil design, their tiny docks with the flagpole and the American flag floating against the white clouds in the blue sky, the little paths over the roots of the trees leading from camp to camp and the paths leading back to the outhouses and the can of lime for sprinkling, and at the souvenir counters at the store the miniature birch-bark canoes and the post cards that showed things looking a little better than they looked. This was the American family at play, escaping the city heat, wondering whether the newcomers in the camp at the head of the cove were "common" or "nice," wondering whether it was true that the people who drove up for Sunday dinner at the farmhouse were turned away because there wasn't enough chicken.

9   It seemed to me, as I kept remembering all this, that those times and those summers had been infinitely precious and worth saving. There had been jollity and peace and goodness. The arriving (at the beginning of August) had been so big a business in itself, at the railway station the farm wagon drawn up, the first smell of the pine-laden air, the first glimpse of the smiling farmer, and the great importance of the trunks and your father's enormous authority in such matters, and the feel of the wagon under you for the long ten-mile haul, and at the top of the last long hill catching the first view of the lake after eleven months of not seeing this cherished body of water. The shouts and cries of the other campers when they saw you, and the trunks to be unpacked, to give up their rich burden. (Arriving was less exciting nowadays, when you sneaked up in your car and parked it under a tree near the camp and took out the bags and in five minutes it was all over, no fuss, no loud wonderful fuss about trunks.)

10   Peace and goodness and jollity. The only thing that was wrong now, really, was the sound of the place, an unfamiliar nervous sound of the outboard motors. This was the note that jarred, the one thing that would sometimes break the illusion and set the years moving. In those other summertimes all motors were inboard; and when they were at a little distance, the noise they made was a sedative, an ingredient of summer sleep. They were one-cylinder and two-cylinder engines, and some were make-and-break and some were jump-spark, but they all made a sleepy sound across the lake. The one-lungers throbbed and fluttered, and the twin-cylinder ones purred and purred, and that was a quiet sound too. But now the campers all had outboards. In the daytime, in the hot mornings, these motors made a petulant, irritable sound; at night, in the still evening when the afterglow lit the water, they whined about one's ears like mosquitoes. My boy loved our rented outboard, and his great desire was to achieve singlehanded mastery over it, and authority, and he soon learned the trick of choking it a little (but not too much), and the adjustment of the needle valve. Watching him I would remember the things you could do with the old one-cylinder engine with the heavy flywheel, how you could have it eating out of your hand if you got really close to it spiritually. Motor boats in those days didn't have clutches, and you would make a landing by shutting off the motor at the proper time and coasting in with a dead rudder. But there was a way of reversing them, if you learned the trick, by cutting the switch and putting it on again exactly on the final dying revolution of the flywheel, so that it would kick back against compression and begin reversing. Approaching a dock in a strong following breeze,

it was difficult to slow up sufficiently by the ordinary coasting method, and if a boy felt he had complete mastery over his motor, he was tempted to keep it running beyond its time and then reverse it a few feet from the dock. It took a cool nerve, because if you threw the switch a twentieth of a second too soon you would catch the flywheel when it still had speed enough to go up past center, and the boat would leap ahead, charging bull-fashion at the dock.

11   We had a good week at the camp. The bass were biting well and the sun shone endlessly, day after day. We would be tired at night and lie down in the accumulated heat of the little bedrooms after the long hot day and the breeze would stir almost imperceptibly outside and the smell of the swamp drift in through the rusty screens. Sleep would come easily and in the morning the red squirrel would be on the roof, tapping out his gay routine. I kept remembering everything, lying in bed in the mornings—the small steamboat that had a long rounded stern like the lip of a Ubangi, and how quietly she ran on the moonlight sails, when the older boys played their mandolins and the girls sang and we ate doughnuts dipped in sugar, and how sweet the music was on the water in the shining night, and what it had felt like to think about girls then. After breakfast we would go up to the store and the things were in the same place—the minnows in a bottle, the plugs and spinners disarranged and pawed over by the youngsters from the boys' camp, the fig newtons and the Beeman's gum. Outside, the road was tarred and cars stood in front of the store. Inside, all was just as it had always been, except there was more Coca-Cola and not so much Moxie and root beer and birch beer and sarsaparilla. We would walk out with a bottle of pop apiece and sometimes the pop would backfire up our noses and hurt. We explored the streams, quietly, where the turtles slid off the sunny logs and dug their way into the soft bottom; and we lay on the town wharf and fed worms to the tame bass. Everywhere we went I had trouble making out which was I, the one walking at my side, the one walking in my pants.

12   One afternoon while we were there at the lake a thunderstorm came up. It was like the revival of an old melodrama that I had seen long ago with childish awe. The second-act climax of the drama of the electrical disturbance over a lake in America had not changed in any important respect. This was the big scene, still the big scene. The whole thing was so familiar, the first feeling of oppression and heat and a general air around camp of not wanting to go very far away. In mid-afternoon (it was all the same) a curious darkening of the sky, and a lull in everything that had made life tick; and then the way the boats suddenly swung the other way at their moorings with the coming of a breeze out of the new quarter, and the premonitory rumble. Then the kettle drum, then the snare, then the bass drum and cymbals, then crackling light against the dark, and the gods grinning and licking their chops in the hills. Afterward the calm, the rain steadily rustling in the calm lake, the return of light and hope and spirits, and the campers running out in joy and relief to go swimming in the rain, their bright cries perpetuating the deathless joke about how they were getting simply drenched, and the children screaming with delight at the new sensation of bathing in the rain, and the joke about getting drenched linking the generations in a strong indestructible chain. And the comedian who waded in carrying an umbrella.

13   When the others went swimming my son said he was going in too. He pulled his dripping trunks from the line where they had hung all through the shower, and wrung them out. Languidly, and with no thought of going in, I watched him, his hard little body, skinny and bare, saw him wince slightly as he pulled up around his vitals the small, soggy, icy garment. As he buckled the swollen belt suddenly my groin felt the chill of death.

Discussion Questions

5. Older readers, particularly those who are raising or have raised children, will feel a keen sense of identity with White's sentiments. It's important to point out, however, that the author's insight is universal; time rolls on, and one generation replaces another.

6. White realizes that despite indications to the contrary, time continues moving. Someday White's son and grandson will be reliving this same experience.

1. In paragraph 4 White says that while doing or saying things "suddenly it would be not I but my father who was saying the words or making the gesture." Explain what he means.
2. White supplies relatively little information about his son except to mention that his actions resemble White's own as a child. How do you account for this brief treatment?
3. What is the significance of the missing middle track of the road (paragraph 7) and the "nervous sound of the outboard motors" (paragraph 10)?
4. Throughout the essay White spices his descriptions with precise sensory impressions of sight, hearing, touch, taste, and smell. How do these sensory details enhance his writing?
5. On what audience would this essay likely have the largest impact?
6. White's final sentence provides an indirect statement of his main point. What is the point?

Toward Key Insights

In what ways is the lake part of E. B. White's sense of personal identity?
How and to what extent can places become part of our lives?
What kinds of circumstances or events are likely to become part of our identity?

Suggestion for Writing

Write an essay describing a place you have revisited after being absent for a number of years. Indicate what was similar and what was different and describe your reactions to the changes. Appeal to at least three of the five senses.

PROCESS ANALYSIS

Reading Strategies

OVERVIEW OF PROCESS ANALYSIS ESSAYS
Three of the writers use informal diction, and one, Goldman, uses a combination of formal and informal diction. Caudren and Wald give directions for someone to carry out, one, Goldman, describes a natural process, and Wald gives readers information on how a process is carried out.

1. Determine the reason you are reading the process essay. If it is to follow instructions you will need to read in one way; if it is to understand a process, you will need to proceed differently.
2. If you are going to follow the instructions, read over the process first to get an understanding of the whole. Look for specific warnings or feedback you should consider. Get an idea of what the end result should look like. Gather any equipment you will need. Then follow the process step by step, checking after each step to make certain the results you are obtaining match those described in the process.
3. If you hope to understand the process, read first quickly to get an overview of the process. As you read through more slowly, it can be very helpful to take notes outlining the major steps of the process.

Reading Critically

1. Check to see if the process could be completed differently or more effectively. Are there any cautions that are not included in the essay that might be reasonable to observe?

2. If the writer is explaining a process, is there evidence that his account is correct? Check to see that there is good reason to believe the given account. Research could show that there are competing accounts.

Reading As a Writer

1. Observe how the writer uses verbs to indicate actions.
2. Notice how the writer gets from step to step in the process. If there is a strategy you could use, make note of it.

IAN DUNBAR

Fast Track to Perfection

Ian Dunbar is a veterinarian and behaviorist who has an international reputation for his "lure and reward" method of training animals. Born in England, he holds degrees from the Royal Veterinarian College of London University and in psychology from the University of California. He now heads the Center for Applied Animal Behavior at his California alma mater. Dunbar has written extensively about his speciality, coauthoring a series of volumes on different breeds of dog. In this selection, he shows readers how to apply his methods to training puppies.

1   Puppies mature at an astounding rate. Don't let yours fall behind on the developmental curve. Nearly everything a puppy needs to learn must be taught in 12 weeks—between the ages of 2 and 5 months. You can buy yourself time by knowing what and how to teach the puppy before you bring it home. Go to puppy classes, read behavior and training books, watch instructional videos and consult your veterinarian. Then raise your puppy perfectly by meeting these six training deadlines.

Deadline 1: Before You Bring Home a Puppy

2   Your puppy should be accustomed to a domestic environment before you bring it home—at around 8 weeks of age. Make sure it has been raised indoors and in close contact with people. It should be prepared for the clamor of everyday life—the noise of the vacuum cleaner, the hoopla surrounding sports programs on the television, children crying, adults arguing. Early exposure—before the pup's eyes and ears have fully opened—allows the puppy to gradually assimilate sights and sounds that otherwise might frighten.

3   The window for socializing begins to close by the time the pup turns 3 months of age, and its most impressionable learning period starts to fade by its fifth month.

Deadline 2: Puppy's First Day at Home

4   Misbehavior is the most common reason dogs end up in shelters. This is especially sad because owners can prevent most behavior problems. For instance, if you avoid leaving the pup unsupervised, it won't chew furniture and belongings or soil your house; while teeny accidents do little damage in themselves, they may set a precedent for habits in months to come.

5   When you cannot watch your pup, confine it to a crate or a puppy-proofed room, which should contain:

PERSPECTIVE
The many millions of dollars Americans spend on care, food, recreation, and training for their pets speak volumes about our love affair with our less-than-human friends. No surprise then that the public is quick to read virtually any type of advice that improves the quality of the owner–pet relationship.

Introduction

Warning

Notes requirements, rewards of training a perfect dog

Body: paragraphs 2–19

First step and its actions

Reason for action

Second step and its actions

Uses polite command, addressing reader as "you"

- a comfortable bed.
- a bowl of fresh water.
- a doggie toilet placed away from the bed and which simulates the outdoors. Lay down a sheet of linoleum and cover it with a disposable plastic sheet. Next lay newspaper or something absorbent. Top the three layers with dirt or sod to teach the pup to relieve itself on grass (or concrete slabs for city pups that relieve themselves curbside).
- Hollow chew toys with kibble inside to reward your puppy for chewing toys rather than furniture. During its first few weeks at home, a marvelous training ploy is to serve your puppy's food only in chew toys. After it's a chew toy-aholic—and has not had a chewing mishap for at least three months—begin to serve its dinner in a bowl.

Mini-process within process	6 At least every hour, release your puppy from its crate, quickly leash it and hurry it to its outdoor toilet area. Stand still and give the pup three minutes to produce. When it does, lavishly praise and offer *three* extra special treats. Freeze-dried liver treats work well because dogs love their strong smell.
	7 If your puppy eliminates, it may be allowed supervised exploration of the house. If it does not eliminate, lead it back to its crate or puppy-proof room and try again in half an hour.
Reason for action / **Warning**	8 Keep up the once an hour schedule until your pup is at least 3 months old to make certain it never eliminates indoors. After 3 months of age pups start to develop the bladder control necessary for longer waits between potty breaks, but you must still be vigilant. One mistake can set a bad precedent.
Reason for / **Warning**	9 Always reward your puppy for using its outdoors toilet area, but wait until it has completed its shots before taking it to public property; otherwise it can pick up other dogs' diseases. A pup must not walk or sniff where other dogs have been until it has developed sufficient immunity (between 3 and 4 months old).

Deadline 3: Puppy at 3 Months

Third step and its actions / **Warning**	10 By 3 months your pup must master socialization and basic manners. Pups that do not will have a hard time picking up these skills later in life. Unfortunately, the risk of disease means dog-to-dog socialization must wait. Meanwhile, teach your pup to be people-friendly.
Reason for action	11 As a general rule, your pup should socialize with at least 100 people before it is 3 months old. This is easier than it sounds. Invite eight friends over each Sunday to watch sports on the television. Each Monday invite eight different friends to watch *Ally McBeal* and *Dateline*. Catch up on outstanding social obligations by inviting family, friends and neighbors to weekly puppy parties. On another night, invite some neighborhood children. Socializing a puppy is great because it does wonders for *your* social life.
Reason for action / **Feedback tells reader what to expect, how to react**	12 Show your guests how to hand feed the puppy's kibble to encourage and reward it for coming, sitting and lying down. Ask your puppy to come. Praise profusely as it approaches and offer a piece of kibble when it arrives. Back up, then do it again—and again and again. Then say "Puppy, Sit" and slowly move a piece of kibble from in front of the puppy's nose to between its eyes. As the puppy raises its nose to sniff, it will lower its rear and sit. If the puppy jumps up, you're holding the food too high. When your puppy sits, say "Good dog" and offer the kibble. Now say "Puppy, Down" and lower a piece of kibble from in front of the puppy's nose to between its forepaws. As the puppy lowers its head to follow the food, it will usually lie down. If your puppy stands, hide the kibble in your palm until it lies down. Then say "Good dog" and offer the food. Coach your

guests until each can get the puppy to come, sit and lie down three times for a piece of kibble.

13   When a puppy approaches promptly and happily, it is a sign the dog is people-friendly. Sitting and lying down on request indicates respect for the person issuing instructions. If your puppy is regularly hand-fed by guests, it will learn to enjoy people's company.

Feedback explains significance of behavior

Deadline 4: Puppy at 4 1/2 Months

14   Seemingly overnight, puppies become adolescents. Enroll in a training class before yours is 14 weeks old—that is, before it starts to test your limits. A professional will teach it to stop nipping and other behavior no-no's, as well as temper its hyper-turbo energy.

Fourth step and its actions

Reason for action

15   Most puppies can start classes at 3 months. Classrooms are generally safe places; the puppies are vaccinated, the floors regularly sterilized. I advise delaying walks in public places until your puppy is 4 months old because of the risk of disease.

Reason for action

16   Puppy classes develop canine social savvy through play with other puppies in a controlled setting. Most classes are family-oriented, offering pups opportunities to socialize with all sorts of people—men, women and children. The number of behaviors your pup learns in its first training lesson will amaze you. Shy and fearful pups gain confidence. Bullies tone it down and become gentle. All dogs learn to come, sit and lie down when requested and listen to their owners and ignore distractions.

Deadline 5: Puppy at 5 Months

Fifth step and its actions

17   Take your dog everywhere—errands around town, car trips to visit friends, picnics in the park and especially to explore the neighborhood. And bring a little bag of kibble. Give a couple of pieces to each stranger who wants to meet your dog. Ask each person to offer the kibble only after your pup sits to say hello.

18   At this point, you may come to believe the canine weight-pulling record exceeds 10,000 pounds. Your dog also may begin to ignore you. A few tips:

- **Make your dog walk for its dinner**. With kibble in hand, stand still and wait for the dog to sit. Ignore everything else your dog does; it will sit eventually. When it does, say "Good dog," offer the kibble, take one giant step forward, stand still and wait for your dog to sit again. Repeat this until your dog sits each time you stop. Now take two giant steps before your stop. Then three steps, five, eight, 10, 20 and so on. *Voilà*, your dog walks calmly and attentively by your side and sits each time you stop.

Feedback tells reader what to expect, how to react

- **Take a few time-outs on each walk**. Sit down, relax and allow the dog to settle down and watch the world go by. If your pup is not the sit-still type, take along a treat-stuffed chew toy as an incentive.

- **Never take your dog's sound temperament for granted**. Outdoors can be scary and offer the occasional surprise. Give your dog a piece of kibble every time a big truck, noisy motorcycle or child on a skateboard whizzes by and your dog doesn't overreact.

Warning

- **Don't make a habit of letting your dog off-leash to run and play with other dogs;** your dog may eventually refuse to come when called. Instead, take your dog's dinner to the park and, throughout its play session, call your dog every minute or so and have it sit for a couple of pieces of kibble. It will soon get the idea and its enthusiastic response will be the talk of the park.

Warning

Feedback tells reader what to expect, how to react

<table>
<tr><td>Sixth step and its actions</td></tr>
<tr><td>Reason for action</td></tr>
<tr><td>Conclusion; indicates results to expect</td></tr>
</table>

DISCUSSION QUESTIONS

1. Several markers in the essay indicate why "Fast Track" is appropriate. Note "astounding rate," "fall behind," "must be taught in 12 weeks," and "buy yourself time" in paragraph 1; "The window for socializing begins to close . . ." in paragraph 3; "By 3 months your pup must master . . ." in paragraph 10; and "Seemingly overnight" in paragraph 14. "Perfection," while probably an exaggeration, is mentioned at the end of paragraph 1 and hinted at in paragraph 20.

2. As the pup is taken to various places, it will pull very strongly on its leash in an attempt to explore new and exciting territory, so strongly that its owner is amazed by the great force exerted.

TEACHING STRATEGIES

1. Before reading the article, have the students list ways that carbon is currently removed from the atmosphere and the implications of these processes.

2. Have students list the possible sequence of events in the future role of the krill, providing reasons for their predictions.

CLASSROOM ACTIVITIES

1. Have students work in teams to create a diagram of the krill cycle of carbon sequestration.

Deadline 6: Now and Forever

19 Continue walking your dog at least once a day and take it to a dog park several times a week. Find different walks and dog parks to meet a variety of dogs and people. If your dog always sees the same people and dogs, it may regress socially and become intolerant of strangers.

20 Now enjoy life with your good-natured, well-mannered companion. Give your dog a special bone—Good dog!—and yourself a pat on the back—Good owner!

Discussion Questions

1. Point out why Dunbar's title is appropriate. Refer to the essay when answering.
2. In paragraph 18 Dunbar states that the owner might "believe the canine weight-pulling record exceeds 10,000 pounds." Explain what he means.

Toward Key Insights

Given the choice, what animal would you prefer to train? Why? What animal would you least like to train? Why?

Suggestion for Writing

Write an essay that provides directions for training a riding horse, hunting dog, or guard dog. Be sure to include the reason for any action whose purpose is not obvious and provide cautionary warnings whenever necessary.

Caroline Goldman

Taking Carbon Down

from: Alternatives 32 no2 4 2006.

Caroline Goldman graduated with a B.A. in American Civilization and Race Relations from Brown University and earned Masters degrees in Public Administration and International Relations from Syracuse Administration. She worked for several years as a management consultant and freelance writer. She is currently the executive director for Hawkwatch International.

1 Imagine parachuting crustaceans, Millions and millions of them. This is what scientists from the British Antarctic Survey and the Centre for Coastal Studies of the University of Hull illustrated in their recent study about krill's effects on carbon sequestration.

2 Antarctic krill (Euphausia superba)—those small crustaceans that flood the Southern Ocean—have recently been recognized as a major source of carbon sinks. Scientists have known for years that krill migrate daily from the surface of the seas to the ocean's depths, but how deep they dove and how much carbon they carried with them was unknown until now.

3   Each night, krill feed on phytoplankton, algae that absorb carbon through photosynthesis. As the krill dine on the phytoplankton, the carbon is passed on to them through the food chain. Bellies full, the krill fan out their legs and parachute nearly 50 metres down through the open ocean in a vertical migration, excreting waste along the way. "The waste sinks to the ocean bottom where it gets locked up in sediment," a process known as carbon sequestration, says Dr. Geraint Tarling of the British Antarctic Survey. These dives are likely an attempt to avoid the hunting whales, seals and penguins above.

4   With 50 to 150 million, tonnes of Antarctic krill making this migration approximately three times each night, 0.02 metric gigatons of carbon per year—"an amount equivalent to the annual emissions of 35 million cars" says Tarling—is transported from earth's surface to the ocean floor, an action that helps alleviate global climate change by decreasing the atmosphere's harmful overabundance of carbon.

5   For our carbon-filled air, that's good news. The bad news is that Antarctic krill populations have seen an 80 percent decline in the past 30 years, likely due to rising temperatures that lead to declining sea ice. Sea ice serves as a breeding ground for the krill's primary food source, phytoplankton, and thus in turn attracts swarms of krill, especially the larvae. As the earth's climate rises, sea ice melts away, destroying these krill nurseries—and thus much of the krill population. The warming trend also favours salps, filter-feeding gelatinous creatures that prefer warmer waters and compete with krill for phytoplankton. Salps are also known to dine on krill larvae as they rise through the water column to reach the sea ice. Most krill-dependent feeders such as whales and penguins do not eat salps, and salps do not serve the same carbon sequestration purposes that krill perform.

6   How this dramatic krill decline will affect the crustaceans' carbon sequestration abilities is as yet unknown. "Krill are not evenly spread around the Southern Ocean," says Tarling. "It is likely that krill decreases occur in some areas to a much greater extent than in others. We are just starting to calculate how the decrease in krill affects their carbon sink capacity."

Discussion Questions

1. What is the purpose of this process account of the krill?
2. What are the steps in the process by which krill remove carbon from the atmosphere?
3. How does the writer make a technically complex process more readable for non-scientific readers?
4. How does the writer use process to explain the decrease in the krill population?
5. The writer ends with an indefinite conclusion rather than a bold and stark claim. What effect does the concluding paragraph have on likely readers?

Toward Key Insights

Often it is difficult to translate complex scientific processes into accounts that are appropriate to nonexpert readers without leaving something out or oversimplifying. To what extent does this essay seem or not seem oversimplified or incomplete? By stressing the importance of a process, it is then relatively easy to make the reader concerned about the disruption of that process. How does this writer use the positive role of krill to actually raise concerns about global warming?

2. With the assistance of a biology or chemistry teacher, provide a brief illustration of the introduction of carbon into the atmosphere or its removal. Simply burning a few twigs or some paper under a glass jar quickly demonstrates the production of carbon, which could easily be then related to burning coal for power or the burning of the Amazon Rainforest to create farmland.

DISCUSSION QUESTIONS
1. It is intended to demonstrate the essential role of the krill in removing carbon from the atmosphere and how global warming may undercut this important process.
2. a. Phytoplankton absorb carbon as part of photosynthesis. b. Krill eat the phytoplankton. c. The krill descend to escape possible predators. d. They excrete waste, which includes the carbon. e. The waste drops to the bottom of the sea floor.

3. The writer tends to use nontechnical language, defines any technical language that is essential, and uses analogies the reader will understand.

4. The writer describes how krill depend on sea ice and how the melting sea ice undercuts the phytoplankton and the krill nurseries, resulting in a decrease in the krill population.

5. The conclusion might have different effects on different readers. By not making a bold conclusion,

the writer actually adds credibility by creating an ethos of being careful and nonalarmist. It encourages the reader to think further about the possible implications of these developments.

Suggestions for Writing

With your teacher's permission, take a technical description of a process from a science textbook or science article and explain that process to less knowledgeable readers. Submit the original source with your essay.

Observe a natural process and write an account of that process to make an important point about the importance or destructiveness of that process. For example, a writer could observe erosion.

BETH WALD

Let's Get Vertical!

Beth Wald (born 1960) first felt the attraction of the mountains when, at age sixteen, she took a backpacking trip to Canada. A native of Minnesota, she studied botany and Russian at the University of Minnesota and then, in the mid-1980s, began a dual career as a free-lance writer and photographer. Her career and her love of climbing have taken her around the world. Her articles have appeared in a variety of climbing and outdoor magazines, as have her photographs, which include environmental and cultural subjects as well as sports and travel. From 1988 to 1992, she was a contributing editor for Climbing Magazine. *In our selection, Wald acquaints potential recruits with the sport of rock climbing.*

PERSPECTIVE

Wald's essay explains how a process is performed rather than providing directions for carrying it out. Therefore, instead of offering detailed instructions, it includes only a brief third-person discussion of what the process involves. Because Wald wants to attract new rock climbers, the essay's main thrust centers on matters that would concern them.

TEACHING STRATEGY

People today enjoy a considerable amount of leisure time, which allows them to engage in a wide array of recreational activities. You might develop a class discussion in which students name the steps involved in their favorite pastimes.

CLASSROOM ACTIVITY

As a follow-up to the teaching strategy, divide the class into small groups, have their members write out the steps in the processes they mentioned earlier, and then ask students to critique one another's steps to determine

1   Here I am, 400 feet up on the steep west face of Devil's Tower,[1] a tiny figure in a sea of petrified rock. I can't find enough footholds and handholds to keep climbing. My climbing partner anxiously looks up at me from his narrow ledge. I can see the silver sparkle of the climbing devices I've jammed into the crack every eight feet or so.

2   I study the last device I've placed, a half-inch aluminum wedge 12 feet below me. If I slip, it'll catch me, but only after a 24-foot fall, a real "screamer." It's too difficult to go back; I have to find a way up before my fingers get too tired. I must act quickly.

3   Finding a tiny opening in the crack, I jam two fingertips in, crimp them, pull hard, and kick my right foot onto a sloping knob, hoping it won't skid off. At the same time, I slap my right hand up to what looks like a good hold. To my horror, it's round and slippery.

4   My fingers start to slide. Panic rivets me for a second, but then a surge of adrenalin snaps me back into action. I scramble my feet higher, lunge with my left hand, and catch a wider crack. I manage to get a better grip just as my right hand pops off its slick hold. My feet find edges, and I regain my balance. Whipping a chock (wedge) off my harness, I slip it into the crack and clip my rope through a carabiner (oblong metal snaplink). After catching my breath, I start moving again, and the rest of the climb flows upward like a vertical dance.

5   **The Challenges and Rewards** I've tried many sports, but I haven't found any to match the excitement of rock climbing. It's a unique world, with its own language, communities, controversies, heroes, villains, and devoted followers. I've lived in vans, tepees, tents, and caves; worked three jobs to save money for expenses; driven 24 hours to spend a weekend at a good rock; and lived on beans

[1] A large, flat-topped rock formation, 876 feet high, in northeastern Wyoming.

and rice for months at a time—all of this to be able to climb. What is it about scrambling up rocks that inspires such a passion? The answer is, no other sport offers so many challenges and so many rewards.

6   The physical challenges are obvious. You need flexibility, balance, and strength. But climbing is also a psychological game of defeating your fear, and it demands creative thinking. It's a bit like improvising a gymnastic routine 200 feet in the air while playing a game of chess.

7   Climbers visit some of the most spectacular places on earth and see them from a unique perspective—the top! Because the sport is so intense, friendships between climbers tend to be strong and enduring.

8   **Anyone Can Climb** Kids playing in trees or on monkey bars know that climbing is a natural activity, but older people often have to relearn to trust their instincts. This isn't too hard, though. The ability to maintain self-control in difficult situations is the most important trait for a beginning climber to have. Panic is almost automatic when you run out of handholds 100 feet off the ground. The typical reaction is to freeze solid until you fall off. But with a little discipline, rational thinking, and/or distraction tactics such as babbling to yourself, humming, or even screaming, fear can change to elation as you climb out of a tough spot.

9   Contrary to popular belief, you don't have to be superhumanly strong to climb. Self-confidence, agility, a good sense of balance, and determination will get you farther up the rock than bulging biceps. Once you've learned the basics, climbing itself will gradually make you stronger, though many dedicated climbers speed up the process by training at home or in the gym.

10   Nonclimbers often ask, "How do the ropes get up there?" It's quite simple; the climbers bring them up as they climb. Most rock climbers today are "free climbers." In free climbing, the rope is used only for safety in case of a fall, *not* to help pull you up. (Climbing without a rope, called "free soloing," is a *very* dangerous activity practiced only by extremely experienced—and crazy—climbers.)

11   First, two climbers tie into opposite ends of a 150-foot-long nylon rope. Then one of them, the belayer, anchors himself or herself to a rock or tree. The other, the leader, starts to climb, occasionally stopping to jam a variety of aluminum wedges or other special gadgets, generically referred to as protection, into cracks in the rock. To each of these, he or she attaches a snaplink, called a carabiner, and clips the rope through. As the leader climbs, the belayer feeds out the rope, and it runs through the carabiners. If the leader falls, the belayer holds the rope, and the highest piece of protection catches the leader. The belayer uses special techniques and equipment to make it easy to stop falls.

12   When the leader reaches the end of a section of rock—called the pitch—and sets an anchor, he or she becomes the belayer. This person pulls up the slack of the rope as the other partner climbs and removes the protection. Once together again, they can either continue in the same manner or switch leaders. These worldwide techniques work on rock formations, cliffs, peaks, even buildings.

13   **Rocks, Rocks Everywhere** Some of the best climbing cliffs in the country are in the Shawangunk Mountains, only two hours from New York City. Seneca Rocks in West Virginia draws climbers from Washington, D.C., and Pittsburgh, Pennsylvania. Chattanooga, Tennessee, has a fine cliff within the city limits. Most states in the U.S. and provinces in Canada offer at least one or two good climbing opportunities.

14   Even if there are no large cliffs or rock formations nearby, you can climb smaller rocks to practice techniques and get stronger. This is called bouldering.

whether they are complete and presented in an effective order. A formal writing assignment could follow.

DISCUSSION QUESTIONS (p. 490)

1. The title, effective on several counts, indicates the typical position of the rock climber and also hints at Wald's passion for rock climbing. The essay certainly reinforces this attitude and involves readers by inviting them to participate in Wald's hobby: "Let's . . ." You might point out that the title is a takeoff on Olivia Newton-John's popular recording "Let's Get Physical," which celebrates the joys of physical pleasure. Because this song was popular in 1982, most students probably won't make the connection.

2. By locating herself 400 feet up Devil's Tower, Wald supplies a firsthand look at the challenges, dangers, and occasional panic associated with rock climbing, and in so doing immediately pulls her readers into the essay by grabbing their attention. In addition, by telling how she overcame the difficulty that occurred, she helps establish her qualifications for explaining the process.

3. Paragraphs 11 and 12 offer basic guidelines for rock climbing, and the introduction tells how the author handled a particular situation. The rest of the essay, however, focuses not on process per se but on related matters: the challenges and rewards of rock climbing, the physical requirements for doing it, and the locales where people can climb and lessons are available. This information provides an inducement to readers to take up the sport themselves: A paper that focused only on the rock-climbing process might well scare them off.

4. Both reasons are in paragraph 2. Wald places a wedge below herself because "If I slip, it'll catch me" (after a nasty fall). In addition, she notes that she must act quickly because "It's too difficult to go back; I have to find a way up before my fingers get too tired."

5. Paragraph 6: "flexibility, balance, and strength" and "creative thinking." Paragraph 8: "The ability to maintain self-control in difficult situations" and "a little discipline, rational thinking, and/or distraction tactics. . . ." Paragraph 9: "Self- confidence, agility, a good sense of balance, and determination. . . ." Paragraph 18: ". . . learning how to control anxiety, how to piece together a difficult sequence of moves, and how to communicate with a partner. . . ."

6. This question should prompt an interesting discussion.

Many climbers who live in cities and towns have created climbing areas out of old stone walls and buildings. Ask someone at your local outdoor shop where you can go to start climbing.

15   **Get a Helping Hand** There's no substitute for an expert teacher when it comes to learning basic techniques and safety procedures. One of the best (and least expensive) ways to learn climbing is to convince a veteran climber in your area to teach you. You can usually meet these types at the local crag or climbing shop.

16   As another option, many universities and colleges, some high schools, and some YMCAs have climbing clubs. Their main purpose is to introduce people to climbing and to teach the basics. Other clubs, such as the Appalachian Mountain Club in the eastern U.S. and the Mountaineers on the West Coast, also provide instruction. Ask at your outdoor shop for the names of clubs in your area.

17   If you live in a place completely lacking rocks and climbers, you can attend one of the fine climbing schools at the major climbing area closest to you. Magazines like *Climbing, Rock & Ice,* and *Outside* publish lists of these schools. Once you learn the basics, you're ready to get vertical.

18   In rock climbing, you can both lose yourself and find yourself. Life and all its troubles are reduced to figuring out the puzzle of the next section of cliff or forgotten in the challenge and delight of moving through vertical space. And learning how to control anxiety, how to piece together a difficult sequence of moves, and how to communicate with a partner are all skills that prove incredibly useful back on the ground!

Discussion Questions

1. Discuss the effectiveness of Wald's title.
2. At the beginning of the essay, Wald notes that she is 400 feet up one side of Devil's Tower and positioned above her climbing partner. What do you think these statements accomplish?
3. In which paragraphs does Wald detail the actual process of climbing? What do the remaining paragraphs in the body of the essay accomplish?
4. Point out two places in the first four paragraphs where Wald cites reasons for her actions.
5. What attributes does Wald believe a rock climber must have? Refer to the essay when answering.
6. After reading this essay, are you ready to begin rock climbing? Does your answer stem from Wald's content, the manner of presentation, or both? Discuss.

Toward Key Insights

What challenging activities appeal to you?
What level of risk are you willing to accept in an activity?
How do you account for your attitude about taking risks?

Suggestion for Writing

Write a process paper in which you explain the attributes required and the steps involved in one of your recreational activities.

SHARI CAUDRON

Can Generation Xers Be Trained?

Shari Caudron earned a B.A. in journalism and a master's degree in human communication. She is currently pursuing an MFA in creative nonfiction. She has been a full-time freelance journalist since 1989. In this selection she presents the procedures that many businesses have found effective in training members of "Generation X."

1   If you want to know how to reach Generation Xers, eavesdrop on a training seminar conducted by Pencom International, a Denver-based company that provides training products to such restaurant chains as Denny's and Pizza Hut. You won't hear the trainers referring to restaurant patrons as "prospective customers." Instead, they're "hot targets." The trainers don't encourage new employees to "recognize and serve customers quickly." They're told to "lock on and fire." The language isn't what you'd typically find at a corporate training seminar. But, then, Generation Xers (a term they detest) aren't typical employees.

2   "These people grew up with Sonic the Hedgehog and Atari, so training has to be attention-grabbing," says Christopher O'Donnell, vice president of Pencom. "Or as Beavis would say, 'The training can't suck.'"

3   Suck indeed. Members of Generation X, those 40 million or so Americans age 20 to 33, are forcing companies to rethink and reengineer their training programs drastically. Gen Xers' values, communication styles, and life experiences are so different from those of baby boomers that traditional training doesn't stand a chance. To connect with these young employees, forget *Father Knows Best;* bring on MTV.

4   Now, before you grumble about catering to a fringe element, here's an incentive: Training geared to the needs of Generation Xers may actually be better for training all workers.

5   "This generation is spearheading change," says O'Donnell. "They're teaching us a lot about how to manage and train everyone in the workforce."

6   Granted, not all companies experience generational differences. At Dallas-based Texas Instruments, for example, employees are hired based on certain values and characteristics. That keeps TI's corporate culture harmonious and minimizes any discrepancies between workers of different generations.

7   "We don't see generational learning differences," says Ray Gumpert, manager of training and organizational effectiveness for TI's Semiconductor Group. "We recruit a certain kind of individual, so there is great consistency among TIers."

8   In *Twentysomething: Managing and Motivating Today's New Workforce* (Master Media, 1992), Claire Raines writes that companies such as Texas Instruments are the exception, not the rule. "(Though) all generations have things in common," she says, "research on Generation Xers shows that this group typically learns very differently from those that came before them."

Who Are These People Anyway?

9   To understand why and how Xers' learning styles are so different, you have to understand the characteristics that set them apart from older workers.

10   To begin with, they are the first generation to grow up with many of their parents both working. As "latchkey kids," many learned to become self-reliant. Consequently, they tend to be independent problem solvers, who are remarkably good at getting a job done on their own.

11   Many, if not most, grew up with computers at home, in school, and at arcades on weekends, so they are amazingly technoliterate. From the Internet to CD-ROMs, familiarity with new technology is just a mouse-click away.

12   In addition, Xers have been conditioned by the American culture to expect immediate gratification. Such things as automatic teller machines, pagers, and microwave ovens have taught them that they can have what they want, when they want it. In the workplace, that can mean that they expect answers and feedback now.

13   Xers came of age in an era that began with the Watergate scandal and ended with massive corporate layoffs, so they tend to distrust institutions. They don't have to be taught that there is no such thing as lifetime employment; they never expected it. Such distrust, combined with an inherent self-reliance, means that they're more likely to regard companies as places to grow, not places to grow old.

14   So, what do all of those characteristics mean for HRD professionals? Bruce Tulgan—founder of Rainmaker, a firm in New Haven, Connecticut, that helps companies recruit, motivate, and retain Generation X workers—reminds us that in the old days, the corporate approach to training was paternalistic.

15   "It used to be 'welcome to the family,'" says Tulgan. "Companies would tell employees, 'Here is your training agenda, this is the training we'll provide, and this is what you need to know.'" That approach just doesn't work with Xers. They want to know why they must learn something, before they will take the time to learn how.

16   Says Tulgan, "I'm not saying you must change the learning objectives; you must change the process." He recommends focusing on outcomes more than techniques and on what Xers are going to be able to do, not what they need to know.

17   For example, at the Orlando-based Olive Garden restaurants, training for servers had them memorize the menu and ingredients of the dishes. Now, train-ing director Marty Fisher says that training emphasizes what servers are sup-posed to do with that information.

18   "We tell servers we want them to be tour guides for the menu," says Fisher. Through role play, servers can practice telling customers about each dish in appealing terms. That way, employees not only know why they are learning the ingredients, but they also know how to put the information to work.

19   At Chicago-based Anderson Consulting, trainers spend a lot of time upfront getting trainees' buy-in. According to Joe Kotey, a manager in the consulting education department, young employees have to see value in the training, or they aren't motivated to learn new skills. "Training results vary greatly, depend-ing on how motivated a group is to learn new skills," says Kotey. "By focusing on outcomes, we show up-front why [employees] need this information."

Pushing the Right Buttons

20   Once you have the attention of Generation Xers, keep it by making training experiences meaningful, memorable, and fun. Xers are used to being enter-tained, having been weaned on portable CD players and Game Boy™. "We can't just pour knowledge into their heads," says Fisher. "We need to combine education with entertainment."

21   One way to keep their attention is to make training experiential. As much as possible, use all six senses, role play, and simulation learning—similar to the approaches used by NASA. Astronauts aren't expected to pilot a space shuttle without having practiced. Don't expect Xers to perform without practice.

22   For example, Andersen Consulting uses CD-ROMs during training to simulate client meetings. Using audio and video clips stored on disc, trainees can interview clients, receive phone calls, obtain advice from senior consultants, and review internal memos.

23   At the end of the computerized course, trainees have an opportunity to deliver a presentation with the findings and recommendations usually delivered to a client. "We want employees to see and feel what a client call is really like," says Roberta Menconi, training manager.

24   Classroom learning can also be made experiential. Pencom's O'Donnell remembers a training session he conducted for young employees of a Denver restaurant.

25   "I was trying to communicate the importance of seating [customers] right away, but getting nowhere. When I asked employees how long [customers] could wait comfortably before being seated, their responses ranged from three minutes to several more."

26   Frustrated, O'Donnell asked the group to time him for one minute. "I acted fidgety for a full 60 seconds while they watched. That minute went on forever and drove home the point that [customers] need to be seated immediately."

27   For a generation that grew up with more remote controls than rattles, the need to control learning is important. Xers need buttons to push. They are independent, and they're used to managing their own time. Because they're accustomed to calling the shots, they tend to resent and resist efforts to force-feed them training. To give Xers a sense of control over their learning, it's wise to provide as many options as possible where and when they can participate. That means a choice of locations and times.

28   "Because this generation is stubborn, we can't be," says O'Donnell.

29   It's even better to let Xers decide how they can learn. Tulgan tells the story of a Big Six accounting firm with a series of outstanding training courses. But they were so popular that no one could get into them.

30   Says Tulgan, "I suggested that the firm put course content on videotapes, audiotapes, and interactive CDs, and in self-paced manuals and workbooks. That puts the information into employees' hands right away and makes them accountable for learning. Generation Xers like that kind of structured self-study." Given Gen Xers' penchant for technology, computers are a natural choice for delivering training. But their ability to control has to be built into the technological solutions.

31   Menconi says that Andersen tested its first CD-ROM courses with younger employees to gauge their responses. "We discovered that they click around a lot. They want control over the paths they take. They want to stop and start at will."

32   To accommodate those needs, Andersen built sophisticated navigation systems into all of its CD-ROM–based courses.

33   Gen Xers' propensity to jump around—unlike older workers who tend to go step by step—doesn't necessarily signify a lack of attention. It's more an ability to assimilate information quickly and to focus on multiple ideas at once—called, "parallel thinking."

34   "Look at MTV or commercials," says Raines, "and you'll see four or five things going on at the same time. That drives me crazy, but these kids are used to it."

35   Companies can appeal to younger workers by developing training materials that provide multiple sources of information at once. *USA Today* and *Wired* are good examples of how to present information to Xers. Those publications combine charts, photos, text, graphics, and cartoons on a single page.

36   When making your materials more eye-catching, make sure you also keep the information simple. Don't make Gen Xers have to guess what you're trying

37   to say. Raines recommends highlighting key points to make the information highly scannable.

A note of caution: Don't go overboard and be too trendy. A few years back, the Wendy's restaurant chain created a training video, "Grill Skills," that featured a rap singer in gold lamé reviewing food-grilling techniques. The video won awards. But, after a year, it lost its effectiveness; employees saw it as outdated.

Prime Targets

38   Generation Xers—more than other employee groups—tend to make job decisions based on whether training is available. So, it may be more important that you provide them with training than how you provide it.

39   Says Tulgan, "Training departments are the ace in the hole for retaining and motivating today's workforce." That's because young employees don't envision long-term relationships with their employers, he says. They know that they must keep growing in order to stay marketable. If they don't receive training, they tend to start looking around at other jobs in other companies.

40   "In today's job market, you want to train employees to leave at any time," says Tulgan. "They won't, because they'll see working for your company as an incredible opportunity to grow and develop."

41   Terri Wolfe, director of HR at Patagonia—a Ventura, California–based clothing retailer—agrees that the biggest emerging trend among younger workers is their desire for continuous education. "We have an extensive continuing education program that a majority of our younger workers take advantage of. They're taking classes not only to advance their careers, but also because they are inherently curious."

What Generation Gap

42   What is perhaps most remarkable about training Generation Xers is that the training approaches that work well with them make sense for almost everyone, regardless of age. Here are some tips for training workers of all ages.

43   **Focus** Training should emphasize end results and place learners in control. Such training helps prepare employees for challenges on the job. After all, isn't the goal of empowerment for employees to focus on business objectives and make the necessary and appropriate decisions to achieve them? Fewer managers means that all employees have to take more responsibility for their work; learner directed training is a great way to get them used to that.

44   **Be flexible** Large-scale corporate cutbacks mean that more people are overworked and are juggling multiple demands. A flexible training schedule and choice of training resources (such as CD-ROMS, videos, and so forth) help employees fit training into their work schedules.

45   **Emphasize visuals** Create eye-catching, highly scannable training materials. Most people don't have time to read through pages of materials. Like it or not, most of us have been conditioned by the media to expect a point to be made quickly.

46   **Provide continuous education** Though younger workers have never counted on cradle-to-grave employment, older employees are also getting the message that they must prepare for unexpected events. The companies that provide continuous education are in a better position to retain productive employees.

47   "If you want to see the future of work, look into the eyes of a Generation Xer," says Tulgan. "We were shaped by the same forces that have shaped the (current) workplace and economy. We're comfortable with the new workplace because we never got accustomed to the old management style."

48   But whatever you do, don't call them "Generation Xers."

Illustration **495**

Discussion Questions

1. This process essay starts by defining Generation Xers and identifying their place in the workplace. Why is this important to the purposes of the essay?
2. Instead of offering simple concrete steps in a process, how does this essay present the process of training Generation Xers? Why is this approach most likely used?
3. Identify the key elements of the process recommended by the author. Discuss whether this approach would or would not be appealing to you.
4. What is the purpose of the writer using many different businesses as examples?
5. In the end, the author identifies some specific key principles for training Generation Xers. What are the advantages of this approach?

5. The earlier part of the essay provides more complex explanations and examples. The reader may forget the main points. By providing a short list of key principles in the end, the author makes it easier for the reader to walk away with useable principles.

Toward Key Insights

To what extent are different training methods appropriate to different populations? Explore what kind of job training has been most effective for you. What were the features of that training?

Suggestion for Writing

Write a paper explaining to new employees the process of the job training they might receive at one of the places you have worked.

Select some activity you're familiar with—perhaps planning a party, programming a computer, or dieting successfully—and describe the steps involved, using appropriate comparisons and figurative language.

ILLUSTRATION

Reading Strategies

1. Read the introductory and concluding paragraphs quickly to determine the thesis for the illustration. Then read the essay quickly to get the main point of the essay. Jot down the key points of the illustration.
2. Determine, based on your own purpose for reading and the level of the essay, if it is necessary to read the essay more carefully.
3. If a more careful reading is warranted, read slowly, noticing and jotting down any key details of the illustration that make a more general point.

Reading Critically

1. Test whether the illustration really demonstrates the main point.
2. Determine whether the illustrations are typical or atypical.
3. Test the point by seeing if there are illustrations that would illuminate a different position.

OVERVIEW OF ILLUSTRATION ESSAYS
Three of the essays offer multiple examples and one (by Goodman) a single, extended example. All have a serious tone. One (by Goodman) has an unstated point, and the others have stated points. All use informal diction.

PERSPECTIVE
Binge drinking is not the only unhealthful personal practice to receive public attention: The hazards of smoking and poor eating habits have also been

widely discussed. Taken together, efforts to curb these undesirable practices reflect an unprecedented awareness of the importance of healthy lifestyles.

Reading As a Writer

1. Identify and evaluate the kinds of examples used in the illustration.
2. Notice the strategies used to link the illustrations to a main point.
3. Identify and evaluate how the illustrations were organized (as short narratives, as descriptions) and jot down any strategies you found useful.

SABRINA RUBIN ERDELY

Binge Drinking, A Campus Killer

Sabrina Rubin Erdely is an award-winning investigative journalist based in Philadelphia. She is a Senior Writer at Philadelphia *magazine, where she has been on staff since 1995, and has contributed to a wide array of other magazines. Erdely's feature writing has earned her a number of awards, including a prestigious National Magazine Award nomination. Our selection focuses on a serious and growing problem at American colleges and universities.*

Introduction: identifies serious problem, point to be illustrated

1 Pregame tailgating parties, post-exam celebrations and Friday happy hours—not to mention fraternity and sorority mixers—have long been a cornerstone of the collegiate experience. But on campuses across America, these indulgences have a more alarming side. For some of today's college students, binge drinking has become the norm.

Body: paragraphs 2–39

2 This past February I headed to the University of Wisconsin–Madison, rated the No. 2 party school in the nation by the college guide *Princeton Review,* to see the party scene for myself. On Thursday night the weekend was already getting started. At a raucous off-campus gathering, 20-year-old Tracey Middler struggled to down her beer as fist-pumping onlookers yelled, "Chug! Chug! Chug!"

End of paragraph 2, paragraphs 3 and 5: first examples support main point, as do all examples

3 In the kitchen, sophomore Jeremy Budda drained his tenth beer. "I get real wasted on weekends," he explained. Nearby, a 19-year-old estimated, "I'll end up having 17, 18 beers."

4 Swept up in the revelry, these partyers aren't thinking about the alcohol-related tragedies that have been in the news. All they're thinking about now is the next party. The keg is just about empty.

5 As the 19-year-old announces loudly, these college students have just one objective: "to get drunk!"

6 The challenge to drink to the very limits of one's endurance has become a celebrated staple of college life. In one of the most extensive reports on college drinking thus far, a 1997 Harvard School of Public Health study found that 43 percent of college students admitted binge drinking in the preceding two weeks. (Defined as four drinks in a sitting for a woman and five for a man, a drinking binge is when one drinks enough to risk health and well-being.)

7 "That's about five million students," says Henry Wechsler, who co-authored the study. "And it's certainly a cause for concern. Most of these students don't realize they're engaging in risky behavior." University of Kansas Chancellor Robert Hemenway adds, "Every year we see students harmed because of their involvement with alcohol."

Brief examples feature different students, as do all examples, providing more evidence supporting paper's point

8 Indeed, when binge drinking came to the forefront last year with a rash of alcohol-related college deaths, the nation was stunned by the loss. There was Scott Krueger, the 18-year-old fraternity pledge at the Massachusetts Institute of Technology, who died of alcohol poisoning after downing the equivalent of

Illustration   **497**

15 shots in an hour. There was Leslie Baltz, a University of Virginia senior, who died after she drank too much and fell down a flight of stairs. Lorraine Hanna, a freshman at Indiana University of Pennsylvania, was left alone to sleep off her night of New Year's Eve partying. Later that day her twin sister found her dead—with a blood-alcohol content (BAC) of 0.429 percent. (Driving with a BAC of 0.1 percent and above is illegal in all states.)

9   Experts estimate that excessive drinking is involved in thousands of student deaths a year. And the Harvard researchers found that there has been a dramatic change in why students drink: 39 percent drank "to get drunk" in 1993, but 52 percent had the same objective in 1997.

10   "What has changed is the across-the-board *acceptability* of intoxication," says Felix Savino, a psychologist at UW–Madison. "Many college students today see not just drinking but being *drunk* as their primary way of socializing."

11   The reasons for the shift are complex and not fully understood. But researchers surmise that it may have something to do with today's instant-gratification life-style—and young people tend to take it to the extreme.

12   In total, it is estimated that America's 12 million undergraduates drink the equivalent of six million gallons of beer a week. When that's combined with teenagers' need to drink secretly, it's no wonder many have a dangerous relationship with alcohol.

13   The biggest predictor of bingeing is fraternity or sorority membership. Sixty-five percent of members qualified as binge-drinkers, according to the Harvard study.

14   August 25, 1997, was meant to be a night the new Sigma Alpha Epsilon pledges at Louisiana State University in Baton Rouge would never forget, and by 8 P.M. it was certainly shaping up that way. The revelry had begun earlier with a keg party. Then they went to a bar near campus, where pledges consumed massive quantities of alcohol.

> Extended example: paragraphs 14–21

15   Among the pledges were Donald Hunt, Jr., a 21-year-old freshman and Army veteran, and his roommate, Benjamin Wynne, a 20-year-old sophomore. Friends since high school, the two gamely drank the alcoholic concoctions offered to them and everyone else.

16   Before long, many in the group began vomiting into trash cans. (Donald Hunt would later allege in a lawsuit that these "vomiting stations" were set up for that very purpose, something the defendants adamantly deny.) About 9:30, incapacitated pledges were taken back to sleep it off at the frat house.

17   The 911 call came around midnight. Paramedics were stunned at what they found: more than a dozen young men sprawled on the floor, on chairs, on couches, reeking of alcohol. The paramedics burst into action, shaking the pledges and shouting, "Hey! Can you hear me?" Four couldn't be roused, and of those, one had no vital signs: Benjamin Wynne was in cardiac arrest.

18   Checking to see that nothing was blocking Wynne's airway, the paramedics began CPR. Within minutes they'd inserted an oxygen tube into his lungs, hooked up an I.V., attached a cardiac monitor and begun shocking him with defibrillation paddles, trying to restart his heart.

19   Still not responding, Wynne was rushed by ambulance to Baton Rouge General Hospital. Lab work revealed that his blood-alcohol content was an astonishing 0.588 percent, nearly six times the legal driving limit for adults—the equivalent of taking about 21 shots in an hour.

20   Meanwhile, three other fraternity pledges were undergoing similar revival efforts. One was Donald Hunt. He would suffer severe alcohol poisoning and nearly die.

21 After working furiously on Wynne, the hospital team admitted defeat. He was pronounced dead of acute alcohol poisoning.

22 One simple fact people tend to lose sight of is that alcohol is a poison—often pleasurable, but a toxin nonetheless. And for a person with little experience processing this toxin, it can come as something of a physical shock.

23 In general, a bottle of beer has about the same alcohol content as a glass of wine or shot of liquor. And the body can remove only the equivalent of less than one drink hourly from the bloodstream.

24 Many students are not just experimenting once or twice. In the Harvard study, half of binge drinkers were "frequent binge drinkers," meaning they had binged three or more times in the previous two weeks.

25 It also is assumed by some that bingeing is a "guy thing," an activity that, like cigar smoking and watching televised sports, belongs in the realm of male bonding. Statistics, however, show that the number of heavy-drinking young women is significant. Henry Wechsler's Harvard study found that a hefty 48 percent of college men were binge drinkers, and women were right behind them at 39 percent.

Extended example: paragraphs 26–32

26 Howard Somers had always been afraid of heights. Perhaps his fear was some sort of an omen. On an August day in 1997 he helped his 18-year-old daughter, Mindy, move into her dorm at Virginia Tech. As they unloaded her things in the eighth-floor room, Somers noted with unease the position of the window. It opened inward like an oven door, its lip about level with her bed. He mentioned it, but Mindy dismissed his concern with a smile.

27 "I have gone through more guilt than you can imagine," Somers says now quietly. "Things I wish I had said or done. But I never thought this would happen. Who would?"

28 Mindy Somers knew the dangers of alcohol and tried to stay aware of her limits. She'd planned not to overdo it that Friday night, since her mother was coming in that weekend to celebrate Mindy's 19th birthday on Sunday. But it was Halloween, the campus was alive with activity, and Mindy decided to stop in at several off-campus parties.

29 When she returned to her room at 3 A.M., she was wiped out enough to fall into bed fully clothed. Mindy's bed was pushed lengthwise against the long, low window. Her roommate and two other girls, who were on the floor, all slept too soundly to notice that sometime after 4 A.M. Mindy's bed was empty.

30 When the paperboy found her facedown on the grass at 6:45 A.M., he at first thought it was a Halloween prank. Police and EMTs swarmed to the scene in minutes. Somers was pronounced dead of massive chest and abdominal injuries. She had a blood-alcohol content of 0.21 percent, equal to her having drunk about five beers in one hour.

31 Police surmised that Mindy had tried to get out of bed during the night but, disoriented, had slipped out the window, falling 75 feet to her death. "It was a strange, tragic accident," Virginia Tech Police Chief Michael Jones says.

32 A terrible irony was that the week prior to Mindy's death had been Virginia Tech's annual Alcohol Awareness Week.

33 While binge drinking isn't always lethal, it does have other, wide-ranging effects. Academics is one realm where it takes a heavy toll.

34 During my trip to Wisconsin most students told me they didn't plan on attending classes the following day. "Nah, I almost never go to class on Friday. It's no big deal," answered Greg, a sophomore. According to a survey of university administrators, 38 percent of academic problems are alcohol-related, as are 29 percent of dropouts.

DISCUSSION QUESTIONS

1. "Campus Killer" engages the reader's attention and also accurately reflects the potential consequences of binge drinking. Thus the title is effective.

2. Paragraphs 6–7 provide authoritative support for the extent of serious binge drinking, thereby estab-

Illustration   **499**

35   Perhaps because alcohol increases aggression and impairs judgment, it is also related to 25 percent of violent crimes and roughly 60 percent of vandalism on campus. According to one survey, 79 percent of students who had experienced unwanted sexual intercourse in the previous year said that they were under the influence of alcohol or other drugs at the time. "Some people believe that alcohol can provide an excuse for inappropriate behavior, including sexual aggression," says Jeanette Norris, a University of Washington researcher. Later on, those people can claim, "It wasn't me—it was the booze."

36   Faced with the many potential dangers, college campuses are scrambling for ways to reduce binge drinking. Many offer seminars on alcohol during freshman orientation. Over 50 schools provide alcohol-free living environments. At the University of Michigan's main campus in Ann Arbor, for instance, nearly 30 percent of undergrads living in university housing now choose to live in alcohol-free rooms. Nationwide several fraternities have announced that by the year 2000 their chapter houses will be alcohol-free.

37   After the University of Rhode Island topped the *Princeton Review* party list two years in a row, administrators banned alcohol at all student events on campus; this year URI didn't even crack the top ten. Some campuses respond even more severely, unleashing campus raids and encouraging police busts.

38   Researchers debate, however, if such "zero-tolerance" policies are helpful or if they might actually result in more secret, off-campus drinking. Other academics wonder if dropping the drinking age to 18 would take away the illicit thrill of alcohol and lower the number of kids drinking wildly. Others feel this would just create more drinking-related fatalities.

39   Whatever it takes, changing student behavior won't be easy. "What you've got here are people who think they are having fun," Harvard's Henry Wechsler explains. "You can't change their behavior by preaching at them or by telling them they'll get hurt."

40   Around 2 A.M. at UW–Madison a hundred kids congregate at a downtown intersection in a nightly ritual. One girl is trying to pull her roommate up off the ground. "I'm not that drunk," the one on the ground insists. "I just can't stand up."

41   Two fights break out. A police car cruises by and the crowd thins, some heading to after-hours parties. Then maybe at 3 or 4 A.M. they'll go home to get some sleep, so they will be rested for when they start to drink again. Tomorrow night.

> lishing the significance of the subject near the start of the essay. The other paragraphs elaborate on these matters as well as point out the causes of binge drinking, the nature of alcohol, and the efforts being made to combat the problem. Taken together, these paragraphs provide a broad-based picture of binge drinking.
>
> **3.** The expressions in paragraphs 2 and 3 are used orally by students who have been drinking. Rubin Erdely wants to capture the exact flavor of their language.
>
> **4.** This fragment draws attention because it is compact and it signals the frequency of binge drinking. For these reasons, it is effective.

> Conclusion: paragraphs 40–41; returns to opening example

Discussion Questions

1. Discuss the effectiveness of Rubin Erdely's title.
2. What does Rubin Erdely accomplish in paragraphs 6–7 and in paragraphs 9–13, 22–25, and 33–38?
3. How do you account for the slang expressions found in this essay: "Chug! Chug! Chug!" in paragraph 2 and "wasted" in paragraph 3?
4. Comment on the effectiveness of the two-word sentence fragment that ends the essay.

Toward Key Insights

Why would "many college students today see not just drinking but being *drunk* as their primary way of socializing"?

What can be done to counter this mind-set?

Suggestion for Writing

Write an essay illustrating some type of benefit available on campus—perhaps academic coun-seling, the campus ministry, or some ethnic or racial organization. Develop your essay with sev-eral short examples or one extended one.

MARTIN GOTTFRIED

Rambos of the Road

Martin Gottfried is a native of New York City and a writer on theatrical matters. Born in 1933, he earned an A.B. degree at Columbia University and then, after attending law school, served two years in the military intelligence branch of the U.S. Army. Following his discharge in 1959, he spent four years as a music and movie critic and since 1963 has worked as a drama critic. He has authored several books on the theater as well as magazine articles on a variety of topics. In our selection, Gottfried examines the driving behavior of all too many motorists.

PERSPECTIVE
Gottfried's essay discusses a problem that has resulted in freeway shootings in some parts of the country. In keeping with the topic, the essay maintains a serious tone throughout while shading it to reflect different emotional responses at different points of the essay. The opening four paragraphs communicate the sense of fear that Gottfried felt when chased by the driver he had passed. In paragraph 10, the finale of the bus-ramming episode, a note of incredulity creeps in as Gottfried notes that "I could not believe my eyes" at the "exercise in absurdity" that had just been played out. And in the final paragraph, he becomes indignant as he attacks the bullies who "represent an America that derides the values of decency and good manners. . . ." Shading an overall tone in this manner enhances the effectiveness of any writing.

TEACHING STRATEGY
Various writers have commented on the pressures of living in a technological society. Ask students to identify as many pressures as they

1   The car pulled up and its driver glared at us with such sullen intensity, such hatred, that I was truly afraid for our lives. Except for the Mohawk haircut he didn't have, he looked like Robert De Niro in "Taxi Driver," the sort of young man who, delirious for notoriety, might kill a president.

2   He was glaring because we had passed him and for that affront he pursued us to the next stoplight so as to express his indignation and affirm his masculinity. I was with two women and, believe it, was afraid for all three of us. It was nearly midnight and we were in a small, sleeping town with no other cars on the road.

3   When the light turned green, I raced ahead, knowing it was foolish and that I was not in a movie. He didn't merely follow, he chased, and with his headlights turned off. No matter what sudden turn I took, he followed. My passengers were silent. I knew they were alarmed, and I prayed that I wouldn't be called upon to protect them. In that cheerful frame of mind, I turned off my own lights so I couldn't be followed. It was lunacy. I was responding to a crazy *as* a crazy.

4   "I'll just drive to the police station," I finally said, and as if those were the magic words, he disappeared.

5   **Elbowing Fenders:** It seems to me that there has recently been an epidemic of auto macho—a competition perceived and expressed in driving. People fight it out over parking spaces. They bully into line at the gas pump. A toll booth becomes a signal for elbowing fenders. And beetle-eyed drivers hunch over their steering wheels, squeezing the rims, glowering, preparing the excuse of not hav-ing seen you as they muscle you off the road. Approaching a highway on an entrance ramp recently, I was strong-armed by a trailer truck so immense that its driver all but blew me away by blasting his horn. The behemoth was just inches from my hopelessly mismatched coupe when I fled for the safety of the shoulder.

6   And this is happening on city streets, too. A New York taxi driver told me that "intimidation is the name of the game. Drive as if you're deaf and blind. You don't hear the other guy's horn and you sure as hell don't see him."

7   The odd thing is that long before I was even able to drive, it seemed to me that people were at their finest and most civilized when in their cars. They

Illustration **501**

seemed so orderly and considerate, so reasonable, staying in the right-hand lane unless passing, signaling all intentions. In those days you really eased into highway traffic, and the long, neat rows of cars seemed mobile testimony to the sanity of most people. Perhaps memory fails, perhaps there were always testy drivers, perhaps—but everyone didn't give you the finger.

8   A most amazing example of driver rage occurred recently at the Manhattan end of the Lincoln Tunnel. We were four cars abreast, stopped at a traffic light. And there was no moving even when the light had changed. A bus had stopped in the cross traffic, blocking our paths: it was normal-for-New-York-City gridlock. Perhaps impatient, perhaps late for important appointments, three of us nonetheless accepted what, after all, we could not alter. One, however, would not. He would not be helpless. He would go where he was going even if he couldn't get there. A Wall Street type in suit and tie, he got out of his car and strode toward the bus, rapping smartly on its doors. When they opened, he exchanged words with the driver. The doors folded shut. He then stepped in front of the bus, took hold of one of its large windshield wipers and broke it.

9   The bus doors reopened and the driver appeared, apparently giving the fellow a good piece of his mind. If so, the lecture was wasted, for the man started his car and proceeded to drive directly *into the bus*. He rammed it. Even though the point at which he struck the bus, the folding doors, was its most vulnerable point, ramming the side of a bus with your car has to rank very high on a futility index. My first thought was that it had to be a rental car.

10   **Lane Merger:** To tell the truth, I could not believe my eyes. The bus driver opened his doors as much as they could be opened and he stepped directly onto the hood of the attacking car, jumping up and down with both his feet. He then retreated into the bus, closing the doors behind him. Obviously a man of action, the car driver backed up and rammed the bus again. How this exercise in absurdity would have been resolved none of us will ever know for at that point the traffic unclogged and the bus moved on. And the rest of us, we passives of the world, proceeded, our cars crossing a field of battle as if nothing untoward had happened.

11   It is tempting to blame such belligerent, uncivil and even neurotic behavior on the nuts of the world, but in our cars we all become a little crazy. How many of us speed up when a driver signals his intention of pulling in front of us? Are we resentful and anxious to pass him? How many of us try to squeeze in, or race along the shoulder at a lane merger? We may not jump on hoods, but driving the gantlet, we seethe, cursing not so silently in the safety of our steel bodies on wheels—fortresses for cowards.

12   What is it within us that gives birth to such antisocial behavior and why, all of a sudden, have so many drivers gone around the bend? My friend Joel Katz, a Manhattan psychiatrist, calls it, "a Rambo pattern. People are running around thinking the American way is to take the law into your own hands when anyone does anything wrong. And what constitutes 'wrong'? Anything that cramps your style."

13   It seems to me that it is a new America we see on the road now. It has the mentality of a hoodlum and the backbone of a coward. The car is its weapon and hiding place, and it is still a symbol even in this. Road Rambos no longer bespeak a self-reliant, civil people tooling around in family cruisers. In fact, there aren't families in these machines that charge headlong with their brights on in broad daylight, demanding we get out of their way. Bullies are loners, and they have perverted our liberty of the open road into drivers' license. They represent an America that derides the values of decency and good manners, then roam the highways riding shotgun and shrieking freedom. By allowing this to happen, the rest of us approve.

can and then to speculate on possible links between these pressures and the driving behavior that Gottfried illustrates.

CLASSROOM ACTIVITIES

1. Ask students, working in small groups, to list other kinds of auto macho behavior that Gottfried might have mentioned but didn't.

2. Have students, working in small groups, suggest steps that individual drivers and organizations concerned with driver safety might take to decrease auto macho behavior.

DISCUSSION QUESTIONS

1. The thesis statement is the first sentence of paragraph 5.

2. The introduction consists of the first four paragraphs. The anecdote of the driver who pursued Gottfried is designed to draw the reader into the essay. In addition, the introduction helps clarify the meaning of "auto macho" in the thesis statement.

3. One example may have been regarded as atypical.

In addition, several examples demonstrate that auto macho takes many forms.

4. Gottfried uses order of climax, as indicated by his characterization of the final example as "A most amazing example of driver rage" (paragraph 8) and by the extraordinarily ridiculous behavior of the driver.

5. Paragraph 11 points out that auto macho extends far beyond "the nuts of the world," affecting, in a milder way, everyone who drives. Paragraph 12 offers a psychiatrist's explanation for its prevalence.

6. Gottfried points out that the implications of auto macho extend beyond our highway behavior. If, as he contends, it represents "an America that derides the values of decency and good manners," then we can expect this outlook to affect other aspects of American life.

PERSPECTIVE
Gambling of all kinds enjoys widespread popularity today. But when an occasional pleasure evolves into addictive behavior, careers can be ruined and marriages and families torn apart. Small wonder then that government commissions have been created to study gambling-related problems and formulate recommendations for dealing with them.

Discussion Questions

1. Identify the thesis statement of this essay.
2. What paragraphs make up the introduction? Besides starting the essay, what function do they perform?
3. Why are several examples a better choice for this essay than one extended example?
4. In what order does Gottfried arrange his examples?
5. What does Gottfried accomplish in paragraphs 11–12?
6. What function, other than ending the essay, is served by the final paragraph?

Toward Key Insights

Do you agree with Gottfried's claim that the "new America we see on the road now . . . has the mentality of a hoodlum and the backbone of a coward"? Why or why not?
Where else have you encountered macho behavior? At athletic events? At activities that generate long lines? At political demonstrations?
What conclusions can you draw about those who engage in such behavior?

Suggestion for Writing

Write an illustration essay exploring the behavior, good or bad, that you have experienced on campus, in the workplace, or while engaged in some activity such as shopping. Use several examples, arrange them in an appropriate order, and try to account for the behavior.

MATEA GOLD AND DAVID FERRELL

Going for Broke

Matea Gold, a native of Northampton, Massachusetts, earned a BA degree from UCLA and then joined David Ferrell as a staff writer for the Los Angeles Times. *Gold earned Sacramento Press Club awards in 1994 and 1995, while Ferrell was a 1996 finalist for the Investigative Reporters and Editors Award, which recognizes outstanding investigative work. The information in this article is drawn from a seven-month nationwide investigation of legalized gambling. Its case studies offer a sobering view of the consequences of gambling addiction.*

1   Rex Coile's life is a narrow box, so dark and confining he wonders how he got trapped inside, whether he'll ever get out.

2   He never goes to the movies, never sees concerts, never lies on a sunny beach, never travels on vacation, never spends Christmas with his family. Instead, Rex shares floor space in cheap motels with other compulsive gamblers, comforting himself with delusional dreams of jackpots that will magically wipe away three decades of wreckage. He has lost his marriage, his home, his Cadillac, his clothes, his diamond ring. Not least of all, in the card clubs of Southern California, he has lost his pride.

Illustration   **503**

3   Rex no longer feels sorry for himself, not after a 29-year losing streak that has left him scrounging for table scraps to feed his habit. Still, he agonizes over what he has become at 54 and what he might have been.

4   Articulate, intellectual, he talks about existential philosophy, the writings of Camus and Sartre. He was once an editor at Random House. His mind is so jam-packed with tidbits about movies, television, baseball and history that card room regulars call him "Rex Trivia," a name he cherishes for the remnant of self-respect it gives him. "There's a lot of Rexes around these card rooms," he says in a whisper of resignation and sadness.

5   And their numbers are soaring as gambling explodes across America, from the mega-resorts of Las Vegas to the gaming parlors of Indian reservations, from the riverboats along the Mississippi to the corner mini-marts selling lottery tickets. With nearly every state in the union now sanctioning some form of legalized gambling to raise revenues, evidence is mounting that society is paying a steep price, one that some researchers say must be confronted, if not reversed.

6   Never before have bettors blown so much money—a whopping $50.9 billion last year—five times the amount lost in 1980. That's more than the public spent on movies, theme parks, recorded music and sporting events combined. A substantial share of those gambling losses—an estimated 30% to 40%—pours from the pockets and purses of chronic losers hooked on the adrenaline rush of risking their money, intoxicated by the fast action of gambling's incandescent world.

7   Studies place the total number of compulsive gamblers at about 4.4 million, about equal to the nation's ranks of hard-core drug addicts. Another 11 million, known as problem gamblers, teeter on the verge. Since 1990, the number of Gamblers Anonymous groups nationwide has doubled from about 600 to more than 1,200.

8   Compulsive gambling has been linked to child abuse, domestic violence, embezzlement, bogus insurance claims, bankruptcies, welfare fraud and a host of other social and criminal ills. The advent of Internet gambling could lure new legions into wagering beyond their means.

9   Every once in a while, a case is so egregious it makes headlines: A 10-day-old baby girl in South Carolina dies after being left for nearly seven hours in a hot car while her mother plays video poker. A suburban Chicago woman is so desperate for a bankroll to gamble that she allegedly suffocates her 7-week-old daughter 11 days after obtaining a $200,000 life-insurance policy on the baby.

10   But these tragedies that flash before the public eye are just lightning strokes of a roiling night storm. Far more often, compulsive gambling bends lives more subtly, less sensationally, over the course of years.

11   Gwen, one of the unseen masses trying to keep her head above water, sits on an easy chair in the living room of her worn Jefferson Park bungalow, watching the movie "Titanic" on an old TV. Her hair is uncombed and there are bags under her eyes. She puffs on a cigarette and shakes her foot nervously. On the screen, the great ship begins to founder.

12   "That's me," she says, tears rolling down her cheeks. "I'm sinking."

13   Gwen has just come off a three-day bender at the Hollywood Park Casino in Inglewood. She blew a paycheck, emptied out her new checking account, gambled right through her work shift. Driving home from the casino, she contemplated veering off the road, ending it all. "I just don't want to be here," she mumbles, watching Titanic's Rose and Jack struggling to hold on to a piece of driftwood in the freezing sea. "I just feel like I'm living a hopeless life. So hopeless."

TEACHING STRATEGIES

1. Ask students what types of legalized gambling they consider particularly undesirable and why. A writing assignment could follow.

2. To supplement taxes, many states use revenues from various lottery games to help fund public services. Critics charge that such games seduce the poor with false hopes of winning big. You might discuss lotteries with your class and follow up with a writing assignment.

3. Your class will probably include some students under, and some over, the age of 21. You could raise the question of whether 21 should be the minimum age to place a bet.

4. Perhaps discuss the various types of Internet gambling and what the implications are for society. The discussion could lead to a writing assignment.

CLASSROOM ACTIVITY

Ask students, working in small groups, to discuss the idea that risk taking is part of America's cultural heritage and that gambling fits within this tradition. The groups could prepare reports and present them to the class. A writing assignment might follow.

14   She's written bad checks and maxed out her credit cards. One bank closed her checking account after she put too many fake deposit slips in the ATM to withdraw cash. She lies. She tells her boss she needs a salary advance because her son is in the hospital. Late on the rent, she parks a block from the house to duck the landlord. For the last eight years, this has been her life, one so empty of joy and options that the card clubs have become her only hope of filling the hole.

15   She thinks back to that night a few years ago when, desperate to recoup her gambling losses, she pilfered several thousand dollars from the safe of a restaurant where she was working. She just needed something to get herself started, she told herself. She'd pay it back with the winnings. She blew it all in one weekend.

16   Overwhelmed by guilt, she came clean with her manager. She was booked, fingerprinted and briefly thrown behind bars. "It was the worst experience of my life," she says.

17   Gwen now makes monthly $75 restitution payments to the restaurant as part of her court-ordered probation.

18   "I have hurt so many people with my gambling," says Gwen. "I have lost best friends. After all the pain I've caused everybody, the pain I caused myself, I still have the urge to gamble. I never know what I'm going to do. I'm so afraid. I'm really afraid."

19   Science has begun to uncover clues to compulsive gambling—genetic predispositions that involve chemical receptors in the brain, the same pleasure pathways implicated in drug and alcohol addiction. But no amount of knowledge, no amount of enlightenment, makes the illness any less confounding, any less destructive. What the gamblers cannot understand about themselves is also well beyond the comprehension of family members, who struggle for normality in a world of deceit and madness.

20   Money starts vanishing: $500 here, $200 there, $800 a couple of weeks later. Where is it? The answers come back vague, nonsensical. It's in the desk at work. A friend borrowed it. It got spent on family dinners, car repairs, loans to in-laws. Exasperated spouses play the sleuth, combing through pockets, wallets, purses, searching the car. Sometimes the incriminating evidence turns up—a racing form, lottery scratchers, a map to an Indian casino. Once the secret is uncovered, spouses usually fight the problem alone, bleeding inside, because the stories are too humiliating to share.

21   "Anybody who is living with a compulsive gambler is totally overwhelmed," says Tom Tucker, president of the California Council on Problem Gambling. "They're steeped in anger, resentment, depression, confusion. None of their personal efforts will ever stop a person from their [sic] addiction. And they don't really see any hope because compulsive gambling in general is such an under-recognized illness."

22   One Los Angeles woman, whose husband's gambling was tearing at her sanity, says she slept with her fists so tightly clenched that her nails sliced into her palms. She had fantasies of death—first her own, thinking he'd feel sorry for her and stop gambling. Later, she harbored thoughts of turning her rage on her husband. She imagined getting a gun, hiding in the closet and blasting him out of her life.

23   "The hurt was so bad I think I would have pulled the trigger," she says. "There were times the pain was so much I thought being in jail, or being in the electric chair, would be less than this."

24   Five years in Gam-Anon, the 12-step support group for family and friends of compulsive gamblers, has only begun to heal her. "I don't think I'm even halfway there," she says.

Illustration **505**

25   Too often, families of gambling addicts endure more than warped finances and wrecked psyches. They have come to fear for their physical safety.

26   Trena, a 42-year-old Whittier homemaker, is among them. Several months ago, after years of agony, she filed for divorce. Her husband, a manager in an industrial plant, was making decent money and took pride in his job. He had two good children and a nice home, an airy bungalow with hardwood floors and a white-brick fireplace. Inside him, though, was a fearsome need to fulfill some glossy vision.

27   Lottery keno became the rhythmic pulse of his life. For five years, Trena says, she awoke in an empty bed every weekend. Her husband would be gone by 5:30 or 6, joining other keno regulars at the neighborhood doughnut shop, watching the numbers flash on an overhead monitor. He'd shuffle home hours later, refusing to divulge his losses.

28   Trena did what tens of thousands of spouses do: She struggled desperately to pay the bills. She hid money in Cheerios boxes, books, couch cushions, under the doormat. She drew up household budgets—hundreds of them. They became her obsession. She drafted a new one almost every day, never able to get one to work.

29   Absurd dramas were played out. On paydays, when her husband's check was directly deposited into their account, they would race each other to the bank. Trena would go to one branch, he'd head to another. She would sit at the drive-up window, jamming her withdrawal slip in the pneumatic tube the moment the bank opened. If she got the money, they could pay the utilities and keep the phone connected. If not, he'd be off to the races, the casinos or the doughnut shop.

30   Like a caged animal, she threw things—smashed a clock against the wall, broke the portable TV in the bedroom. She yelled, clawed and sometimes just sank down and cried. Trena had no money for herself, for the important personal things. She got nothing for her mom on Mother's Day.

31   Increasingly reclusive, she stopped returning calls. Chit-chatting with friends seemed a frivolous distraction when dealing with foreclosure notices, filing for bankruptcy or, worse, fending off her husband's angry demands for cash.

32   He would burst into the house shouting, "Give me my money!" Pacing, following her, tipping over plants, rifling through drawers, dumping them out to try to find it. "Don't you touch my money!"

33   Joining Gam-Anon, where Trena receives emotional support from the spouses of other gamblers, has helped her deal with her decade-long ordeal. She says she is not bitter and understands that compulsive gambling is an illness.

34   While her husband now lives with his parents, she remains in their home of 19 years, a place filled with memories as wistful as they are painful.

35   With drug or alcohol abusers, there is the hope of sobering up, an accomplishment in itself, no matter what problems may have accompanied their addictions. Compulsive gamblers often see no way to purge their urges when suffocating debts suggest only one answer: a hot streak. "They have nowhere to turn—they feel cornered," says Dr. Richard J. Rosenthal, a Beverly Hills psychiatrist who founded the California Council on Problem Gambling. "Very often they are motivated by their shame into more and more desperate attempts to avoid being found out."

36   David Phillips, a UC San Diego sociology professor, studied death records from 1982 to 1988—before legalized gambling exploded across America—and found that people in Las Vegas, Atlantic City and other gambling meccas showed significantly higher suicide rates than people in non-gambling cities.

37   Rex Trivia is not about to kill himself, but like most compulsive gamblers, he occasionally thinks about it. Looking at him, it's hard to imagine he once had a promising future as a smart young New York book editor. His pale eyes are expressionless, his hair yellowish and brittle. In his fifties, his health is failing: emphysema, three lung collapses, a bad aorta, rotting teeth.

38   His plunge has been so dizzying that at one point he agreed to aid another desperate gambler in a run of bank robberies—nine in all, throughout Los Angeles and Orange counties. When the FBI busted him in 1980, he had $50,000 in cash in a dresser drawer and $100,000 in traveler's checks in his refrigerator's vegetable crisper. Rex, who ended up doing a short stint in prison, hasn't seen that kind of money since.

39   At 11 P.M. on a Tuesday night, with a bankroll of $55—all he has—he is at a poker table in Gardena. With quick, nervous hands he stacks and unstacks his $1 chips. The stack dwindles. Down $30, he talks about leaving, getting some sleep. Midnight comes and goes. Rex starts winning. Three aces. Four threes. Chips pile up—$60, $70. "A shame to go when the cards are falling my way." He checks the time: "I'll go at 2. Win, lose or draw."

40   Fate, kismet, luck—the cards keep falling. At 2 A.M., Rex is up $97. He stands, leaves his chips on the table and goes out for a smoke. In the darkness at the edge of the parking lot, he loiters with other regulars, debating with himself whether to grab a bus and quit.

41   "I should go back in there and cash in and get out of here," he says. "That's what I should do."

42   A long pause. Crushing out his cigarette, Rex turns and heads back inside. He has made his decision.

43   "A few more hands."

Discussion Questions

1. Discuss the irony of the essay's title.
2. Why do you think Gold and Ferrell repeat "never" five times in paragraph 2?
3. Identify the essay's thesis statement.
4. By referring to specific paragraphs, point out the various illustrations that the writers use in this essay.
5. Why do you think that Gold and Ferrell cite quotations at various points?
6. What do the writers accomplish by ending the selection with a continuation of the first example?

Toward Key Insights

What factors account for the explosive growth of legalized gambling?
What benefits, if any, have resulted from this growth?
How should we address the problem of compulsive gambling?

Suggestion for Writing

Write an essay illustrating addiction to television viewing or smoking. Choose an appropriate number of examples and develop them with specific details.

Illustration **507**

ELLEN GOODMAN

The Company Man

Ellen Goodman (born 1941) is a native of Massachusetts and a 1963 graduate of Radcliffe College. A journalist since graduation, she has worked as a researcher and reporter for Newsweek *magazine as well as a writer for several major newspapers and a commentator for national radio and TV shows. She has also written articles for* MS., McCall's, *and the* Village Voice. *Book-length publications include* Turning Points *(1979),* Value Judgments *(1993), and several collections of newspaper columns. Her latest book, which she co-authored with Patricia O'Brien, is entitled* I Know Just What You Mean: The Power of Friendship in Women's Lives *(2000). She has received numerous writing awards including a 1980 Pulitzer Prize for distinguished commentary. Our selection, originally a newspaper article, depicts a workaholic whose total dedication to his job killed him.*

1   He worked himself to death, finally and precisely, at 3:00 A.M. Sunday morning.

2   The obituary didn't say that, of course. It said that he died of a coronary thrombosis—I think that was it—but everyone among his friends and acquaintances knew it instantly. He was a perfect Type A, a workaholic, a classic, they said to each other and shook their heads—and thought for five or ten minutes about the way they lived.

3   This man who worked himself to death finally and precisely at 3:00 A.M. Sunday morning—on his day off—was fifty-one years old and a vice-president. He was, however, one of six vice-presidents, and one of three who might conceivably—if the president died or retired soon enough—have moved to the top spot. Phil knew that.

4   He worked six days a week, five of them until eight or nine at night, during a time when his own company had begun the four-day week for everyone but the executives. He worked like the Important People. He had no outside "extracurricular interests," unless, of course, you think about a monthly golf game that way. To Phil, it was work. He always ate egg salad sandwiches at his desk. He was, of course, overweight, by 20 to 25 pounds. He thought it was okay, though, because he didn't smoke.

5   On Saturdays, Phil wore a sports jacket to the office instead of a suit, because it was the weekend.

6   He had a lot of people working for him, maybe sixty, and most of them liked him most of the time. Three of them will be seriously considered for his job. The obituary didn't mention that.

7   But it did list his "survivors" quite accurately. He is survived by his wife, Helen, forty-eight years old, a good woman of no particular marketable skills, who worked in an office before marrying and mothering. She had, according to her daughter, given up trying to compete with his work years ago, when the children were small. A company friend said, "I know how much you will miss him." And she answered, "I already have."

8   "Missing him all these years," she must have given up part of herself which had cared too much for the man. She would be "well taken care of."

9   His "dearly beloved" eldest of the "dearly beloved" children is a hardworking executive in a manufacturing firm down South. In the day and a half before the funeral, he went around the neighborhood researching his father, asking the neighbors what he was like. They were embarrassed.

2. By these omissions Goodman suggests that Phil could be any number of people working for any number of companies. The type she is illustrating is found in many places.

3. By illustrating the life and death of a workaholic, Goodman is sounding an alert to others caught up in the same lethal rut. Her essay is an implicit argument against workaholism.

4. By focusing on one illustration rather than several, Goodman can present a fully rounded portrait of a workaholic and the shattering impact of workaholism on its victim's family. Had Goodman used several illustrations, no such portrait would have emerged, lessening the reader's realization of the seriousness of the condition.

5. Phil spent so much time at the office and so little with his children that his son had to ask neighbors about his father's personality. Ironically the neighbors, just like Phil's family, probably didn't know him either.

6. As the headnote indicates, this essay was originally published in a newspaper column, where short paragraphs are standard fare.

10   His second child is a girl, who is twenty-four and newly married. She lives near her mother and they are close, but whenever she was alone with her father, in a car driving somewhere, they had nothing to say to each other.

11   The youngest is twenty, a boy, a high-school graduate who has spent the last couple of years, like a lot of his friends, doing enough odd jobs to stay in grass and food. He was the one who tried to grab at his father, and tried to mean enough to him to keep the man at home. He was his father's favorite. Over the last two years, Phil stayed up nights worrying about the boy.

12   The boy once said, "My father and I only board here."

13   At the funeral, the sixty-year-old company president told the forty-eight-year-old widow that the fifty-one-year-old deceased had meant much to the company and would be missed and would be hard to replace. The widow didn't look him in the eye. She was afraid he would read her bitterness and, after all, she would need him to straighten out the finances—the stock options and all that.

14   Phil was overweight and nervous and worked too hard. If he wasn't at the office, he was worried about it. Phil was a Type A, a heart-attack natural. You could have picked him out in a minute from a lineup.

15   So when he finally worked himself to death, at precisely 3:00 A.M. Sunday morning, no one was really surprised.

16   By 5:00 P.M. the afternoon of the funeral, the company president had begun, discreetly of course, with care and taste, to make inquiries about his replacement. One of three men. He asked around: "Who's been working the hardest?"

Discussion Questions

1. Goodman says that Phil was "a perfect Type A" (paragraph 2). After reflecting on her essay, explain the characteristics of this type.
2. Why do you think Goodman doesn't supply Phil's last name or the name of the company he works for?
3. What idea is Goodman trying to present?
4. Unlike the essay by Rubin Erdely, Goodman's uses one longer illustration rather than several shorter ones. Why?
5. What is the significance of Phil's oldest son going "around the neighborhood researching his father, asking the neighbors what he was like" (paragraph 9)? Why were they embarrassed?
6. How do you account for Goodman's relatively short paragraphs?

Toward Key Insights

What social values would cause individuals to work themselves to death?

In that regard, what is the significance of the company president asking "Who's been working the hardest?"

Are these values basically good, or should we make some changes in our attitudes toward work and success? If so, what kinds of changes?

Suggestion for Writing

Using one extended example, write an essay that illustrates the lifestyle of a laid-back employee or friend. Your paper need not, of course, feature a death.

CLASSIFICATION ■■ ■■ ■■ ■■ ■■ ■■

Reading Strategies

1. Identify your purpose for reading the essay and the writer's purpose for the classification. This will determine how carefully you will need to read the selection.
2. Do not lose the big picture. Identify what is being classified—types of cars, kinds of dates—and why it is being classified.
3. Notice each of the major categories and the distinctive characteristics of each category. When this material is important to you, it can be very useful to make a table that identifies each major classification and identifies the distinctive features of each category. When carefully organized, such a table can be very helpful.

Reading Critically

1. Determine if there is reasonable evidence for the classification system or if the system is arbitrary.
2. Try to come up with an alternative classification system.
3. Check to see if the categories of the classification are clear or overlap.
4. Determine whether the defining features are distinct enough to clearly apply the system.
5. Try applying the system. Does it work?

Reading As a Writer

1. Identify how the essay establishes the characteristics of the classification system.
2. Often the transition sentences in a classification essay are awkward. Examine the transition sentences and evaluate the effectiveness of the transitions.

OVERVIEW OF CLASSIFICATION ESSAYS

Two of the classification essays (by Winik and Geraci) are written informally, and two (by Sanders and Cofer) use formal–informal diction. One (by Geraci) cites expert opinion.

PERSPECTIVE

Americans define the word "friend" very broadly, including individuals such as workplace colleagues that other societies might consider acquaintances. This attitude reflects a national openness that shows itself, for example, in our practice of calling casual acquaintances or even strangers on the phone by their first names. Winik's essay therefore provides us with a memorable look at an important element of our national character.

MARION WINIK

What Are Friends For?

Marion Winik (born 1958) is a graduate of Brown University and of Brooklyn College, where she earned a master of fine arts degree in creative writing. Since graduation, she has pursued a career in education, writing, and marketing. Her writings include poems, short stories, essays, and books, and the shorter pieces have appeared in a variety of major newspapers and popular magazines. Her book, The Lunch-Box Chronicles: Notes from the Parenting Underground *(1998), discusses her experiences in raising her sons after her husband's death. In this selection, Winik takes a humorous look at the different categories of friends and the benefits derived from each one.*

1   I was thinking about how everybody can't be everything to each other, but some people can be something to each other, thank God, from the ones whose shoulder you cry on to the ones whose half-slips you borrow to the nameless ones you chat with in the grocery line.

Introduction: indicates value of friends

2   Buddies, for example, are the workhorses of the friendship world, the people out there on the front lines, defending you from loneliness and boredom. They call you up, they listen to your complaints, they celebrate your successes and curse your misfortunes, and you do the same for them in return. They hold

Body: paragraphs 2–14

First category

out through innumerable crises before concluding that the person you're dating is no good, and even then understand if you ignore their good counsel. They accompany you to a movie with subtitles or to see the diving pig at Aquarena Springs. They feed your cat when you are out of town and pick you up from the airport when you get back. They come over to help you decide what to wear on a date. Even if it is with that creep.

Second category: 3
paragraphs 3–4

What about family members? Most of them are people you just got stuck with, and though you love them, you may not have very much in common. But there is that rare exception, the Relative Friend. It is your cousin, your brother, maybe even your aunt. The two of you share the same views of the other family members. Meg never should have divorced Martin. He was the best thing that ever happened to her. You can confirm each other's memories of things that happened a long time ago. Don't you remember when Uncle Hank and Daddy had that awful fight in the middle of Thanksgiving dinner? Grandma always hated Grandpa's stamp collection; she probably left the window open during the hurricane on purpose.

4   While so many family relationships are tinged with guilt and obligation, a relationship with a Relative Friend is relatively worry-free. You don't even have to hide your vices from this delightful person. When you slip out Aunt Joan's back door for a cigarette, she is already there.

Third category:
paragraphs 5–6

5   Then there is that special guy at work. Like all the other people at the job site, at first he's just part of the scenery. But gradually he starts to stand out from the crowd. Your friendship is cemented by jokes about co-workers and thoughtful favors around the office. Did you see Ryan's hair? Want half my bagel? Soon you know the names of his turtles, what he did last Friday night, exactly which model CD player he wants for his birthday. His handwriting is as familiar to you as your own.

6   Though you invite each other to parties, you somehow don't quite fit into each other's outside lives. For this reason, the friendship may not survive a job change. Company gossip, once an infallible source of entertainment, soon awkwardly accentuates the distance between you. But wait. Like School Friends, Work Friends share certain memories which acquire a nostalgic glow after about a decade.

Fourth category: 7
paragraphs 7–9

A Faraway Friend is someone you grew up with or went to school with or lived in the same town as until one of you moved away. Without a Faraway Friend, you would never get any mail addressed in handwriting. A Faraway Friend calls late at night, invites you to her wedding, always says she is coming to visit but rarely shows up. An actual visit from a Faraway Friend is a cause for celebration and binges of all kinds. Cigarettes, Chips Ahoy, bottles of tequila.

8   Faraway Friends go through phases of intense communication, then may be out of touch for many months. Either way, the connection is always there. A conversation with your Faraway Friend always helps to put your life in perspective: when you feel you've hit a dead end, come to a confusing fork in the road, or gotten lost in some crackerbox subdivision of your life, the advice of the Faraway Friend—who has the big picture, who is so well acquainted with the route that brought you to this place—is indispensable.

9   Another useful function of the Faraway Friend is to help you remember things from a long time ago, like the name of your seventh-grade history teacher, what was in that really good stir-fry, or exactly what happened that night on the boat with the guys from Florida.

Fifth category 10

Ah, the Former Friend. A sad thing. At best a wistful memory, at worst a dangerous enemy who is in possession of many of your deepest secrets. But what was it that drove you apart? A misunderstanding, a betrayed confidence, an unrepaid loan, an ill-conceived flirtation. A poor choice of spouse can do in a friendship just like that. Going into business together can be a serious mistake. Time, money, distance, cult religions: all noted friendship killers. . . .

11   And lest we forget, there are the Friends You Love to Hate. They call at inopportune times. They say stupid things. They butt in, they boss you around, they embarrass you in public. They invite themselves over. They take advantage. You've done the best you can, but they need professional help. On top of all this, they love you to death and are convinced they're your best friend on the planet.

Sixth category: paragraphs 11–12

12   So why do you continue to be involved with these people? Why do you tolerate them? On the contrary, the real question is, What would you do without them? Without Friends You Love to Hate, there would be nothing to talk about with your other friends. Their problems and their irritating stunts provide a reliable source of conversation for everyone they know. What's more, Friends You Love to Hate make you feel good about yourself, since you are obviously in so much better shape than they are. No matter what these people do, you will never get rid of them. As much as they need you, you need them too.

13   At the other end of the spectrum are Hero Friends. These people are better than the rest of us, that's all there is to it. Their career is something you wanted to be when you grew up—painter, forest ranger, tireless doer of good. They have beautiful homes filled with special handmade things presented to them by villagers in the remote areas they have visited in their extensive travels. Yet they are modest. They never gossip. They are always helping others, especially those who have suffered a death in the family or an illness. You would think people like this would just make you sick, but somehow they don't.

Seventh category

Eighth category

14   A New Friend is a tonic unlike any other. Say you meet her at a party. In your bowling league. At a Japanese conversation class, perhaps. Wherever, whenever, there's that spark of recognition. The first time you talk, you can't believe how much you have in common. Suddenly, your life story is interesting again, your insights fresh, your opinion valued. Your various short-comings are as yet completely invisible.

Conclusion: memorable observation meshes stylistically with rest of essay

15   It's almost like falling in love.

Discussion Questions

1. Comment on the effectiveness of Winik's title.
2. Characterize the level of diction that Winik uses in her essay.
3. What elements of Winik's essay interest you the most? What elements interest you the least?

Toward Key Insights

What traits characterize the various types of friend that you have?
In what ways are these friendships mutually beneficial?

Suggestion for Writing

Write an essay classifying the various types of people that you consider undesirable. Choose an appropriate number of categories and support them with appropriate specific details.

DISCUSSION QUESTIONS
1. The title is a casual remark that we often use when friends thank us for something that we have done for them. Winik uses the remark to identify the focus on her classification. Also, the question draws readers into the essay to discover the answer.

2. The essay is informally written. Some sentences are rather long but most are quite short, and almost all are loose rather than periodic. The language is homespun and includes colloquial expressions and even slang (see "creep" at the end of

paragraph 2). There are
contractions as well as several sentence fragments.

3. These questions should
prompt an interesting discussion. A writing assignment could follow.

PERSPECTIVE
In this essay Sanders makes
a powerful case for those
who believe that power and
privilege are rooted in
social class, not gender.
Nonetheless, he also
recognizes that those who
believe that men hold the
reins of power have a
legitimate complaint:
Although women of the
privileged class enjoy lives
of comfort, even affluence,
they have only recently
begun to share power with
their male counterparts.
These considerations
suggest the complexity of
power relationships and the
need for careful thought in
addressing them.

**TEACHING
STRATEGIES**
1. You might generate a
lively discussion by asking
students the extent to
which they agree that men
have "cornered the world's
pleasures" (paragraph 9).
A writing assignment
could follow.

2. If you've already taken
up descriptive writing, ask
the class to point out where
Sanders uses description to
enrich his essay.

3. Ask students to identify
some of the distinguishing
features of Sanders's style
by referring to the essay.

4. Select a block of paragraphs from the essay and
ask students to explain
how Sanders achieves
coherence. We feel that
reinforcing the tenets of

SCOTT RUSSELL SANDERS

The Men We Carry in Our Minds

*Scott Russell Sanders was born (1945) in Memphis, Tennessee. After earning a B.A. degree
from Brown University in 1967 and a PhD from Cambridge University in 1971, he joined
the English faculty at Indiana University, where he is a full professor. Sanders is the author
of numerous books of fiction and nonfiction. These books span a wide range of genres,
including science fiction, historical novels, children's stories, folk tales, biographies, and
personal essays. He has contributed to several essay anthologies, and his articles have
appeared in literary journals and popular magazines. He has won several awards for his
writing. In this essay, Sanders, in light of what he knows about the lives of working men,
examines the view that power is rooted in gender.*

1   The first men, besides my father, I remember seeing were black convicts and
white guards, in the cottonfield across the road from our farm on the outskirts of
Memphis. I must have been three or four. The prisoners wore dingy gray-and-
black zebra suits, heavy as canvas, sodden with sweat. Hatless, stooped, they
chopped weeds in the fierce heat, row after row, breathing the acrid dust of boll-
weevil poison. The overseers wore dazzling white shirts and broad shadowy hats.
The oiled barrels of their shotguns flashed in the sunlight. Their faces in memory are utterly blank. Of course those men, white and black, have become for me
an emblem of racial hatred. But they have also come to stand for the twin poles
of my early vision of manhood—the brute toiling animal and the boss.

2   When I was a boy, the men I knew labored with their bodies. They were marginal farmers, just scraping by, or welders, steel workers, carpenters; they swept
floors, dug ditches, mined coal, or drove trucks, their forearms ropy with muscle;
they trained horses, stoked furnaces, built tires, stood on assembly lines wrestling
parts onto cars and refrigerators. They got up before light, worked all day long
whatever the weather, and when they came home at night they looked as though
somebody had been whipping them. In the evenings and on weekends they worked
on their own places, tilling gardens that were lumpy with clay, fixing broken-down
cars, hammering on houses that were always too drafty, too leaky, too small.

3   The bodies of the men I knew were twisted and maimed in ways visible and
invisible. The nails of their hands were black and split, the hands tattooed with
scars. Some had lost fingers. Heavy lifting had given many of them finicky backs
and guts weak from hernias. Racing against conveyor belts had given them ulcers.
Their ankles and knees ached from years of standing on concrete. Anyone who
had worked for long around machines was hard of hearing. They squinted, and
the skin of their faces was creased like the leather of old work gloves. There were
times, studying them, when I dreaded growing up. Most of them coughed, from
dust or cigarettes, and most of them drank cheap wine or whiskey, so their eyes
looked bloodshot and bruised. The fathers of my friends always seemed older
than the mothers. Men wore out sooner. Only women lived into old age.

4   As a boy I also knew another sort of men, who did not sweat and break down
like mules. They were soldiers, and so far as I could tell they scarcely worked at
all. During my early school years we lived on a military base, an arsenal in Ohio,
and every day I saw GIs in the guardshacks, on the stoops of barracks, at the
wheels of olive drab Chevrolets. The chief fact of their lives was boredom. Long
after I left the Arsenal I came to recognize the sour smell the soldiers gave off as

that of souls in limbo. They were all waiting—for wars, for transfers, for leaves, for promotions, for the end of their hitch—like so many braves waiting for the hunt to begin. Unlike the warriors of older tribes, however, they would have no say about when the battle would start or how it would be waged. Their waiting was broken only when they practiced for war. They fired guns at targets, drove tanks across the churned-up fields of the military reservation, set off bombs in the wrecks of old fighter planes. I knew this was all play. But I also felt certain that when the hour for killing arrived, they would kill. When the real shooting started, many of them would die. This was what soldiers were *for*, just as a hammer was for driving nails.

5   Warriors and toilers: those seemed, in my boyhood vision, to be the chief destinies for men. They weren't the only destinies, as I learned from having a few male teachers, from reading books, and from watching television. But the men on television—the politicians, the astronauts, the generals, the savvy lawyers, the philosophical doctors, the bosses who gave orders to both soldiers and laborers—seemed as remote and unreal to me as the figures in tapestries. I could no more imagine growing up to become one of these cool, potent creatures than I could imagine becoming a prince.

6   A nearer and more hopeful example was that of my father, who had escaped from a red-dirt farm to a tire factory, and from the assembly line to the front office. Eventually he dressed in a white shirt and tie. He carried himself as if he had been born to work with his mind. But his body, remembering the earlier years of slogging work, began to give out on him in his fifties, and it quit on him entirely before he turned sixty-five. Even such a partial escape from man's fate as he had accomplished did not seem possible for most of the boys I knew. They joined the Army, stood in line for jobs in the smoky plants, helped build highways. They were bound to work as their fathers had worked, killing themselves or preparing to kill others.

7   A scholarship enabled me not only to attend college, a rare enough feat in my circle, but even to study in a university meant for the children of the rich. Here I met for the first time young men who had assumed from birth that they would lead lives of comfort and power. And for the first time I met women who told me that men were guilty of having kept all the joys and privileges of the earth for themselves. I was baffled. What privileges? What joys? I thought about the maimed, dismal lives of most of the men back home. What had they stolen from their wives and daughters? The right to go five days a week, twelve months a year, for thirty or forty years to a steel mill or a coal mine? The right to drop bombs and die in war? The right to feel every leak in the roof, every gap in the fence, every cough in the engine, as a wound they must mend? The right to feel, when the layoff comes or the plant shuts down, not only afraid but ashamed?

8   I was slow to understand the deep grievances of women. This was because, as a boy, I had envied them. Before college, the only people I had ever known who were interested in art or music or literature, the only ones who read books, the only ones who ever seemed to enjoy a sense of ease and grace were the mothers and daughters. Like the menfolk, they fretted about money, they scrimped and made-do. But, when the pay stopped coming in, they were not the ones who had failed. Nor did they have to go to war, and that seemed to me a blessed fact. By comparison with the narrow, ironclad days of fathers, there was an expansiveness, I thought, in the days of mothers. They went to see neighbors, to shop in town, to run errands at school, at the library, at church. No doubt, had I looked harder at their lives, I would have envied them less. It was not my fate to become a woman, so it was easier for me to see the graces. Few of them held jobs outside the home, and those who did filled

effective writing improves student performance.
5. Discuss the extent to which students agree with the last sentence of paragraph 9. A writing assignment could follow.

CLASSROOM ACTIVITY
Divide your students into small groups and have them formulate areas of common ground or agreement between feminists and men like Sanders. The groups could then report their findings to the class. A writing assignment could follow.

DISCUSSION QUESTIONS (p. 514)
1. Sanders is concerned with presenting the images held by the feminist college students he met as well as the images he holds.
2. Sanders's childhood memory introduces, and serves as a metaphor for, two of the main categories—laborers and bosses—that he will discuss later. In addition, the paragraph introduces his extensive use of comparison.
3. The three primary categories are laborers, soldiers (warriors), and bosses. The principle of classification appears to be

degree of authority—the laborers and soldiers have no authority over others, while the bosses do.

4. Other comparisons include "they looked as though somebody had been whipping them" (paragraph 2); "The skin of their faces was creased like the leather of old work gloves" (paragraph 3); "who did not sweat and break down like mules," "the sour smell . . . as that of souls in limbo," "like so many braves waiting for the hunt to begin," and "This was what soldiers were *for*, just as a hammer was for driving nails" (paragraph 4); "as the figures in tapestries" and "than I could imagine becoming a prince" (paragraph 5); and "as a wound they must mend?" (paragraph 7). These comparisons are effective because they are vivid, accurate, and generally familiar to most readers. Students may also note that paragraphs 2–4 and 9–10 constitute longer comparisons, as does the paragraph 8 discussion of the differences in the lives led by laboring men and their wives.

5. These sentences make important points about powerful men and Sanders's attitude toward sharing power. By using short, forceful sentences, Sanders adds impact to the points he makes.

6. Because he is a man, probably the women would not believe he was an ally. Sanders would probably answer "no" to both questions.

thankless roles as clerks and waitresses. I didn't see, then, what a prison a house could be, since houses seemed to me brighter, handsomer places than any factory. I did not realize—because such things were never spoken of—how often women suffered from men's bullying. I did learn about the wretchedness of abandoned wives, single mothers, widows; but I also learned about the wretchedness of lone men. Even then I could see how exhausting it was for a mother to cater all day to the needs of young children. But if I had been asked, as a boy, to choose between tending a baby and tending a machine, I think I would have chosen the baby. (Having now tended both, I know I would choose the baby.)

9   So I was baffled when the women at college accused me and my sex of having cornered the world's pleasures. I think something like my bafflement has been felt by other boys (and by girls as well) who grew up in dirt-poor farm country, in mining country, in black ghettos, in Hispanic barrios, in the shadows of factories, in Third World nations—any place where the fate of men is as grim and bleak as the fate of women. Toilers and warriors. I realize now how ancient these identities are, how deep the tug they exert on men, the undertow of a thousand generations. The miseries I saw, as a boy, in the lives of nearly all men I continue to see in the lives of many—the body-breaking toil, the tedium, the call to be tough, the humiliating powerlessness, the battle for a living and for territory.

10   When the women I met at college thought about the joys and privileges of men, they did not carry in their minds the sort of men I had known in my childhood. They thought of their fathers, who were bankers, physicians, architects, stockbrokers, the big wheels of the big cities. These fathers rode the train to work or drove cars that cost more than any of my childhood houses. They were attended from morning to night by female helpers, wives and nurses and secretaries. They were never laid off, never short of cash at month's end, never lined up for welfare. These fathers made decisions that mattered. They ran the world.

11   The daughters of such men wanted to share in this power, this glory. So did I. They yearned for a say over their future, for jobs worthy of their abilities, for the right to live at peace, unmolested, whole. Yes, I thought, yes yes. The difference between me and these daughters was that they saw me, because of my sex, as destined from birth to become like their fathers, and therefore as an enemy to their desires. But I knew better. I wasn't an enemy, in fact or in feeling. I was an ally. If I had known, then, how to tell them so, would they have believed me? Would they now?

Discussion Questions

1. Why is the essay titled "The Men *We* Carry in *Our Minds*" rather than "The Men *I* Carry in *My Mind*"?
2. Other than starting the essay, what does paragraph 1 accomplish?
3. What primary categories of men does Sanders discuss? What principle of classification does he use?
4. Sanders uses a number of comparisons, such as "zebra suits, heavy as canvas" in paragraph 1, to enhance his writing. Point out other comparisons and comment on their effectiveness.
5. The last sentence of paragraph 10 and the second, sixth, and eighth sentences of paragraph 11 are short statements. What do you think Sanders accomplishes with these statements?
6. Judging by what Sanders writes in the essay, how do you think he would answer the questions he poses in the final two sentences of paragraph 11?

Toward Key Insights

To what extent do you believe that the views expressed in the essay by the college
    women and Sanders reflect the views of today's college women and men?
How do you account for any changes you might note?

Suggestion for Writing

*Write an essay classifying the different grade school or high school teachers that you carry in
your mind. Develop your categories with specific, informative details.*

BERNICE MCCARTHY

A Tale of Four Learners

*Bernice McCarthy, Ph.D., earned her doctorate in education and learning theory from
Northwestern University. She founded About Learning, Inc., a consulting firm on educational
theory and research. She has published a number of articles and presented workshops at major
institutions. In this essay, she classifies learners based on THE 4MAT System® she created.*

1   A young man at a midwestern middle school said of his social studies
teacher, "She doesn't label us, and she helps us do all kinds of things." That student expressed very simply my evolving understanding of style since I created the
4MAT System in 1979. The way one perceives reality and reacts to it forms a pattern over time. This pattern comes to dominate the way one integrates ideas,
skills, and information about people and the way one adapts knowledge and
forms meaning.

2   But to learn successfully, a student also needs expertise in other learning styles;
together these styles from a natural cycle of learning. That middle school teacher
apparently honored the unique style that each student brought to her classroom,
while helping each one do some stretching and master all the ways of learning.

3   Following are true stories about four types of learners. They illustrate how
students with different learning styles experience school and why we must create
opportunities for diverse learning experiences for every child.

4   Linda was in 6th grade when she hit the wall in math. She had loved school
up until then. Her teachers and classmates agreed that her poetry was quite
good, and her poems often appeared in local publications. But math was a problem. She couldn't connect it to anything—she simply could not see the patterns.
Her teachers were not pleased with her and she longed to please them.

5   Linda went on to college, and when she was a junior, a new professor arrived
on campus. The day before Linda's statistics class began, she met him in the hallway. He said, "Oh, you're Linda; I've been reading your poetry. You are going to
do very well in statistics."

6   She looked at him in amazement. "How can you say that? I have such difficulty
in all my math classes."

7   He smiled and answered, "I can tell from your poetry that you understand
symmetry. Statistics is about symmetry. As a matter of fact, statistics is the poetry

---

PERSPECTIVE
This essay offers a
classification system that
is intended to be useful
to teachers. This goal has
shaped the essay. The
different types are clearly
identified and, in each
case, have specific
defining characteristics.
Further the writer
demonstrates how this
classification system could
have an impact on
teaching. It would be
fruitful to compare this
essay with the other
classification essays.

**TEACHING
STRATEGIES**
1. Have students try to
identify their own learning
style based on the author's
classification system.
Discuss whether it works
and why or why not.

2. Have students work in
small groups to identify
the kinds of learning styles
used in classes. They may
identify different learning
styles used by different
classes (chemistry, writing,
math).

3. Is labeling good or bad?
Discuss with students
whether teachers should
or should not identify the
learning styles of students?

4. Discuss whether classes should include more learning styles or not. How could classes be changed so that they would meet the author's ideal?

CLASSROOM ACTIVITIES

1. Have students work in small groups to develop a questionnaire that would help students identify their learning styles.

2. Have students work in groups to identify a classification system of teaching styles.

of math." Linda went on to earn an A in that class. Her professor had connected statistics to her life and showed her the patterns (McCarthy 1996).

8   Linda is a Type 1 learner—the highly imaginative student who favors feeling and reflecting. These learners

9   ■ are at home with their feelings, people-oriented, outstanding observers of people, great listeners and nurturers, and committed to making the world a better place.

10   ■ prefer to learn by talking about experiences; listening and watching quietly, then responding to others and discussing ideas; asking questions; brainstorming; and examining relationships. They work well in groups or teams but also enjoy reading quietly.

11   ■ experience difficulty with long verbal explanations, with giving oral presentations, and with memorizing large chunks of abstract information. They dislike confusion or conflict, environments where mistakes are openly criticized, or where they cannot discuss their perceptions.

12   ■ have a cognitive style that puts perception before judgment, subjective knowledge before objective facts, and reflection before action. They prefer to make decisions based on feeling, are visual/auditory/kinesthetic, and experiential before conceptual.

13   As a Type 1 learner, Linda needed to connect math to her real life, to know why it was useful as a way of thinking and a way of formulating problems and solutions. She also needed her teachers to believe in her and to spend time with and nurture her.

14   Marcus was in 1st grade, and he loved school. Everything he longed for was present there—the teacher's loving interest, the thrill of deciphering the symbols that meant things, the things he could touch and feel, the addition problems that the teacher wrote on the chalkboard. He could always see the answers. His excitement was like that of the basketball player who knows that if he can just get his hands on the ball, he can sink it. Each question became an exciting foray into even more questions. And as his reading improved rapidly, he could not get enough of books. He welcomed the words and ideas of each new writer. He felt confident; he knew he belonged (McCarthy 1996).

15   Marcus is a Type 2 learner—the analytic student who favors reflecting and thinking. These learners

16   ■ have a knowledge-oriented style; are outstanding at conceptualizing material; analyze and classify their experiences and organize ideas; are highly organized and at home with details and data; are good at step-by-step tasks; are fascinated with structure; believe in their ability to understand; and are committed to making the world more lucid.

17   ■ prefer to learn through lectures and objective explanations, by working independently and systematically, and by reading and exchanging ideas.

18   ■ experience difficulty in noisy, high-activity environments, ambiguous situations, and working in groups. They also have trouble with open-ended assignments, as well as with presentations, role-playing, and nonsequential instructions. They have difficulty talking about feelings as well.

19   ■ have a cognitive style that is objective thinking, reflection before action, impersonal, auditory/visual/kinesthetic, conceptual over experiential. They tend to make judgments first, then support them with their perceptions.

20   As a Type 2 learner, Marcus found school an absolute joy. Testing, so frightening to Linda, was a tonic for him, a chance to prove he could do it. Because he

was naturally verbal and school is mostly a verbal challenge, he was—and continues to be—successful.

21   When Jimmy was in 2nd grade he did not like to read, and that made school difficult. He did enjoy having others read to him, and his younger brother, a 1st grader, read him stories every night. Jimmy did excel in math and art. He loved to work alone on projects and never wanted help. When he was asked to illustrate a story or build something to depict a math concept, he approached the task excitedly. He was happiest when he could solve a problem by creating a three-dimensional solution.

22   Unfortunately, Jimmy had a rigid teacher whose timing was always different from his own. Jimmy either finished too fast or took too long when he got really interested in a project. Once his teacher said in exasperation, "I didn't say you had to do your best work, Jimmy, just get it done!" When Jimmy's family bought a new VCR, they read the directions aloud to figure out how it worked. Jimmy stepped up and simply made it work. His reading problem continued into 3rd grade when he caught up with the others, but he never let it get him down—he was simply too busy doing other kinds of things (McCarthy 1996).

23   Jimmy is a Type 3 learner—the common-sense learner who favors thinking and doing. These learners

24   ■ are great problem solvers and are drawn to how things work. They are at home with tasks and deadlines, are productive and committed to making the world work better, and they believe in their ability to get the job done. They are also active and need opportunities to move around.

25   ■ prefer to learn through active problem solving; step-by-step procedures; touching, manipulating, and constructing; demonstrations; experimentation and tinkering; and competition.

26   ■ experience difficulty when reading is the primary means of learning and whenever they cannot physically test what they are told. They have trouble with verbal complexity, paradoxes or unclear choices, subtle relationships, and open-ended academic tasks. They also have difficulty expressing feelings.

27   ■ have a cognitive style that features objective thinking and facts over ideas, action before reflection, and judgment before perception. Their style is impersonal and kinesthetic/auditory/visual.

28   As a Type 3 learner, Jimmy needed to work things out in his own way, to create unique solutions to problems, and, most of all, to show what he learned by doing something concrete with it. His verbal skills did not kick in until well into the 3rd grade. Although this is not unusual with highly spatial learners, teachers treated it as an aberration. School was simply too regimented and too verbal for Jimmy. What saved him was his focus on his own learning.

29   When Leah was a high school freshman, she liked her new friends and some of her teachers. But she had a fierce need to learn, and school was not nearly exciting enough for her. She found so much of it deadening—memorizing endless facts that were totally irrelevant to her life. Leah had a wonderful spontaneity, and when it took hold of her, she focused so intensely that time became meaningless. Her teachers came to regard this spontaneity as a liability that was taking her away from the things she needed to know.

30   At first Leah persevered. Instead of preparing a juvenile justice report based on her social studies text, she asked to be allowed to go to juvenile court and see for herself, and then present her findings in a skit. Her teachers seldom agreed to her proposals, and after a while Leah stopped trying. She had natural leadership talent, which she expressed through her extra-curricular activities—the one

part of school she came to love. She graduated, but has believed ever since then that real learning does not happen in school (McCarthy 1996).

31   Leah is a Type 4 learner—the dynamic learner who favors creating and acting. These learners

32 ■ are proud of their subjectivity, at home with ambiguity and change, and great risk takers and entrepreneurs. They act to extend and enrich their experiences and to challenge the boundaries of their worlds for the sake of growth and renewal, and they believe in their ability to influence what happens. They initiate learning by looking for unique aspects of the information to learn and they sustain learning through trial and error.

33 ■ prefer to learn by self-discovery, talking, convincing others, looking for creative solutions to problems, and engaging in free flights of ideas. They also like to work independently and tackle open-ended academic tasks with lots of options, paradox, or subtle relationships. Their interpersonal skills are good.

34 ■ experience difficulty with rigid routines when they are not allowed to question. They also have trouble with visual complexity, methodical tasks, time management, and absolutes.

35 ■ have a cognitive style that is perception first with slight attention to judgment, subjective, relational, action-oriented, kinesthetic/auditory/visual, and experiential over conceptual.

36   Leah found learning for school's sake incomprehensible. As in Jimmy's case, doing was crucial to her approach. She preferred interviewing over reading, going to court to see for herself, exploring instead of hearing how others see things.

37   In any classroom, Linda, Marcus, Jimmy, Leah, and their many shades and varieties sit before the teacher—challenging and waiting to be challenged. The frustrating question is: why are some learners honored in our schools and others ignored, discouraged, or even frowned upon? Why did Marcus fare so well, while Linda, Jimmy, and Leah struggled to be accepted?

38   In my definition of learning, the learner makes meaning by moving through a natural cycle—a movement from feeling to reflecting to thinking and, finally, to acting. This cycle results from the interplay of two separate dimensions—perceiving and processing (Kolb 1984).

39   In perceiving, we take in what happens to us by (1) feeling, as we grasp our experience, and then by (2) thinking, as we begin to separate ourselves from the experience and name and classify it. The resulting concepts become our way of interpreting our world (Kegan 1982).

40   We also process experiences in two ways: by (1) reflecting on them, and then by (2) acting on those reflections. We also try things; we tinker.

41   The places in this cycle that we find most comfortable—where we function with natural ease and grace—are our learning preferences or styles, the "spins" we put on learning.

42   Unfortunately, schools tend to honor only one aspect of perceiving—thinking. This is very tough on kids whose approach to learning is predominately feeling. Linda and Leah, like many other Type 1 and 4 learners—both male and female—are naturals on the feeling end of experience. Jimmy and Marcus, the Type 2 and 3 learners, favor the thinking end.

43   As with feeling and thinking, reflecting and acting need to be in balance. But our schools favor reflecting. Marcus excelled at that, while both Jimmy and Leah needed to act. The lack of hands-on learning created difficulties for both of them.

44   Even as I define styles in my work, I caution that we must be wary of labels. Over time, and with experience, practice, and encouragement, students become

comfortable with learning styles that aren't naturally their own. Successful learners, in fact, develop multiple styles.

45 The 4MAT framework is designed to help students gain expertise in every learning style. We design lesson units as cycles built around core concepts, each of which incorporates experiencing (Type 1), conceptualizing (Type 2), applying (Type 3), and creating (Type 4). The styles answer the questions:

46
- Why do I need to know this? (the personal meaning of Type 1).
- What exactly is this content or skill? (the conceptual understanding of Type 2).
- How will I use this in my life? (the real-life skills of Type 3).
- If I do use this, what possibilities will it create? (the unique adaptations of Type 4).

47 Had the teachers of Linda, Marcus, Jimmy, and Leah used the entire cycle of learning styles, including those areas in which each student needed to stretch, all four students would have acquired expertise in all facets of the cycle. They would have made personal connections to the learning, examined expert knowledge, used what they were learning to solve problems, and come up with new ways to apply the learning—both personally and in the world at large. (As it happened, the students learned to do these things on their own.)

48 In addressing the various learning styles, the 4MAT System also incorporates elements of brain research—in particular, the different ways that the right and left hemispheres of the cerebral cortex process information (Benson 1985, McCarthy 1981 and 1987, Sylvester 1995, Wittrock 1985). I call these contrasting mental operations the Left and Right Modes.

49 The Left Mode is analytical and knows those things we can describe with precision. It examines cause and effect, breaks things down into parts and categorizes them, seeks and uses language and symbols, abstracts experience for comprehension, generates theory, and creates models. It is sequential and works in time.

50 The Right Mode knows more than it can tell, filling in gaps and imagining. It is intuitive. It senses feelings; forms images and mental combinations; and seeks and uses patterns, relationships, and connections. It manipulates form, distance, and space.

51 Excellence and higher-order thinking demand that we honor both sides of the brain, teaching interactively with hands-on, real-life, messy problem solving. Learners speak in words, signs, symbols, movement, and through music. The more voices students master, the more new learning they will do. Unfortunately, however, teachers persist in lecturing and using logical, sequential problem solving most of the time.

52 In assessing student performance, traditional methods work fairly well for Type 2 learners, who like to prove themselves, and Type 3 learners, who do well on tests in general. Traditional testing doesn't work as well for Types 1 and 4, however. Type 1 learners have difficulty in formal testing situations, especially when tests are timed and call for precise answers. Type 4 learners have trouble doing things by the book and with absolutes and rigid routines when they are not allowed to ask questions.

53 Further, students change roles as they move through the learning cycle. Tests that require students to recall facts obviously do not reflect the subtlety of these changes.

54 We need assessment tools that help us understand the whole person. We must assess the students' ability to picture the concept, to experiment with the idea, to combine skills in order to solve complex problems, to edit and refine

DISCUSSION QUESTIONS
1. While the author suggests that students may have a dominant learning style, she suggests students need "expertise in other learning styles." She is not contradicting herself because she is not suggesting that each student should be labeled as a type. Instead, she is arguing that teachers should offer classes that use all the learning styles.
2. The author consistently introduces an individual student and discusses his or her experience in school. This is followed by the four characteristics of learning styles: the basic orientation to the world, the preferred manner of learning, the environments that causes difficulty, and cognitive style. By following a consistent pattern, the author makes it easier to see the relationship among the different styles.
3. One of the author's key points is that schools are not usually well suited to many different learning styles. By demonstrating the problems students have, she effectively shows why teachers need to use more learning styles in their teaching.
4. The author connects learning style and the learning cycle. Learning usually has to draw on the learning cycle as a whole. The different learning styles are defined as "the places in this cycle that we find most comfortable." This is important because it shows that the learning

their work, and to adapt and integrate learning. We need to know how students are connecting information to their own experiences, how they are blending expert knowledge with their own, and how creative they are. We also need some way of measuring how students reflect on material, conceptualize, and represent what they have learned through various kinds of performances.

55   Successful learning is a continuous, cyclical, lifelong process of differentiating and integrating these personal modes of adaptation. Teachers do not need to label learners according to their style; they need to help them work for balance and wholeness. Leah needs to learn the ways of Marcus; Jimmy needs Linda's ways. And all learners need encouragement to grow.

56   Learning is both reflective and active, verbal and nonverbal, concrete and abstract, head and heart. The teacher must use many instructional methods that are personally meaningful to each student. The more students can travel the cycle, the better they can move to higher-order thinking.

57   As a final note, what became of the students I described earlier? Linda directs the management division of a major human resources consulting firm. Marcus, a former professor of statistics at a prestigious university, is now president of a research firm. Jimmy will be a senior in high school this fall. He scored 100 percent on the Illinois State Math Achievement Test and achieved cum laude in the International Latin Exam. He also had his art portfolio favorably reviewed by the Art Institute of Chicago. And Leah? Leah is a pseudonym for the author of this article.

■ References

Benson, D. F. "Language in the Left Hemisphere." *The Dual Brain: Hemispheric Specialization in Humans.* Ed. D. F. Benson and E. Zaidel. New York: Guilford, 1985.

Kegan, R. *The Evolving Self: Problems and Process in Human Development.* Cambridge, MA: Harvard UP, 1982.

Kolb, D. A. *Experiential Learning: Experience as the Source of Learning and Development.* Englewood Cliffs, NJ: Prentice-Hall, 1984.

McCarthy, B. *The 4MAT System: Teaching to Learning Styles with Right/Left Mode Techniques.* Barrington, IL: Excel, Inc., 1981, 1987.

McCarthy, B. *About Learning.* Barrington, IL: Excel, Inc., 1996.

Sylvester, R. *A Celebration of Neurons: An Educator's Guide to the Human Brain.* Alexandria, VA: ASCD, 1995.

Wittrock, M. C. "Education and Recent Neuropsychological and Cognitive Research." *The Dual Brain: Hemispheric Specialization in Humans.* Ed. D. F. Benson and E. Zaidel. New York: Guilford, 1985.

Discussion Questions

1. The author starts with an example of praise for a teacher who did not "label" her students but then goes on to classify learning styles. Is this a contradiction?
2. With each type of learning style, the author follows the same pattern. What is the pattern that she uses and is it effective?

3. In paragraphs 4, 22, and 30, the author identifies the problems three out of the four sample students had in school. Why does she do this? Is it effective?
4. After discussing the four learning styles, the author discusses in paragraphs 38–48 what she identifies as the learning cycle. What is the connection between this learning cycle and how is this important in relation to the classification system?
5. It could be easy to imagine someone who had qualities of more than one learning style. Is this a problem for the writer's classification of learning styles?
6. In the conclusion the author informs us of the successes of her four example students. How is this conclusion important to the essay?

Toward Key Insights

Try to match yourself to the four learning styles. Does one learning style seem most like you? What does this say about the classification system?
What learning styles seem to dominate in most of your classes? What effects does this seem to have on the learning success of students? Do people who have different learning styles have difficulty adjusting to the dominant learning style of educational institutions?

Suggestion for Writing

Write an essay classifying teaching styles, including the different kinds of activities involved in the classroom and the different kinds of assessment.

RON GERACI

Which Stooge Are You?

Ron Geraci became a Three Stooges *fan while watching TV reruns of their movies as a youngster in southern New Jersey. Former features editor of* Men's Health, *he has written numerous articles on men's physical and emotional health for that magazine. In our selection, Geraci contends that each of the Stooges represents a different universal personality type and that recognizing our own particular type can help us avoid its pitfalls.*

1   Men spend millions of dollars on psychotherapy trying to figure out why they're unhappy, why their kids don't respect them, why women treat them like idiots. Perhaps shrinks help some men, but for many others, it's money that would have been better spent on popcorn and videotapes. To solve many of life's problems, all you really need to do is watch the *Three Stooges.*

2   We're all variations of Moe, Larry, or Curly, and our lives are often short subjects filled with cosmic slapstick. When Moe (your boss) hits Curly (your buddy) with a corporate board and then blindsides you when you try to make it all nice, you're living a Stooge moment. Here you'll find the personality type each Stooge represents. Once you determine which Stooge you are, you'll better understand the problems you bring on yourself—and how you can be a generally happier, more successful knucklehead.

3   Everyone knows more than one Moe. These men are the insufferable know-it-alls who become driving instructors, gym teachers, and divorce attorneys. The

provide examples of each type of behavior. Then have your students, drawing on the examples, write papers depicting the behavior of an actual control freak or passive-aggressive person that they have known or a fictional one that they create.

3. Ask students to assess the personality traits associated with some other entertainment team such as the characters played by Mel Gibson and Danny Glover in the *Lethal Weapon* movies. A writing assignment could follow.

4   coach who had you do pushups in front of the team? He was a Moe. So was that boss who made you carry his golf bag.

In short, Moes are hot-tempered men who intimidate people with verbal slaps and managerial eye pokes, according to Stuart Fischoff, Ph.D., a psychologist at California State University. "Moe has a paternalistic personality, which is pretty common among men," Fischoff says. "He treats everyone like a child and bullies people to keep them off balance." Being a temperamental loudmouth also helps Moe scare off critics who might expose his little secret: He's no smarter than the saps he terrorizes. Moe himself proved that point. Although he served up most of the nose gnashings and belly bonks in 190 shorts, he always ended up back in the mud with Larry and Curly.

5   Even if you've never actually threatened to tear somebody's tonsils out, there are a few other clues that can tag you as a Moe. First, naturally, Moes are explosive hot-heads who storm through life constantly infuriated by other people. "These men suffer from classic low frustration tolerance," says Allen Elkin, Ph.D., a psychologist in New York. "This not only makes them difficult to work with, but it also gives them high blood pressure, high cholesterol, and a much greater risk of heart attack." In fact, Moes often end up seeking counseling to control their anger, usually after it costs them a job, a marriage, or a couple of good pals. "I tell them to just get away from infuriating situations quickly," says Elkin. "Remember, you don't *have* to poke Curly in the eye because he destroyed the plumbing."

6   Second, in the likely event that a Moe manages to foul things up himself, he'll find a way to blame his mistakes on other people, says Fischoff. In *Healthy, Wealthy, and Dumb* (1938), for example, Moe breaks a $5,000 vase with a 2-by-4 and screams at Larry, "Why didn't you bring me a softer board?!"

7   Your habits on the job are the most telling signs. If you're a Moe, you're probably the hardest-driving wise guy at work. "High-strung, bossy men with Moe personalities tend to live at their jobs," says Elkin. To help stop overloading themselves with work they can't possibly finish (a common Moe peccadillo), workaholic Moes should make a list of projects they *won't do* each day—and then make sure they keep their hands off those folders.

8   Moe Howard (1897–1975) had a classic Moe personality. Even offscreen, he was the fiery, short-fused leader of the trio who made all the decisions. Of course, this put a lot of worries on Moe's shoulders. "My father was an anxiety-ridden, nervous man," says Paul Howard, Moe's son. "He didn't have much patience. He always worried about his kid brother Curly, and if Larry flubbed a line, my father could become upset and criticize him almost like a director." Larry probably shaped up fast; Moe could always put some English into the next eye gouge.

9   Now, in fairness to all men with bowl cuts and bad attitudes, there are some big advantages to having a Moe personality. "If I could choose my Stooge, I'd sure as hell be a Moe," says Fischoff. Because they're usually so domineering and assertive, Moes are often able to bark their way into leadership positions quickly. (Kennedy and Nixon were Moes; Carter is a Larry.) If you crammed all the *Fortune*-100 CEOs into one Bennigan's, you'd have Moe Central with a wet bar.

10   Another Moe perk: Women flock to you like geeks to a *Star Trek* premier. Moe is an aggressive, tenacious SOB, and women are genetically programmed to find those traits sexually attractive, says Barbara Keesling, Ph.D., a Southern California sex therapist. That's because prehistoric Moes used their superior eye-poking abilities to scare off those wise-guy tigers. It's why that Moe who gave you noogies in high school went through skirts faster than J. Edgar Hoover—and why he's probably divorced now.

11   "Moes are control freaks," says Keesling. "That can be sexually exciting at first, but women get tired of it very quickly. I know—I've dated examples of all three Stooges. I'm thankful they didn't all try to sleep in my bed at once."

12   Larry is the passive, agreeable fellow who scrapes through life by taking his licks and collecting his paycheck. "Generally, things happen *to* a Larry; he doesn't make them happen," says Alan Entin, Ph.D., a psychologist with the American Psychological Association. Larry is the ubiquitous "nice guy" who commutes to his mediocre job, congenially tries to cover Curly's ass, and spends his day trying to avoid getting whacked in the nose by Moe.

13   That's right: John Q. Taxpayer is a Larry.

14   A subtle testosterone shift, though, can make all the difference in what kind of life this lovable sap leads. Give the classic Larry a little more testicularity, and you have a good-natured man who isn't a biological doormat. He'll kick a wino off your lawn but won't fink on your free cable. That makes him a perfect coworker, neighbor, and pal.

15   But subtract a little gonad power, and a Larry can be an indecisive wimp whose greatest ambition in life is to watch *Everybody Loves Raymond*. These pitiful, wishy-washy slobs constantly get clobbered for being—as Larry put it—"a victim of soicumstance," and that typically makes them passive-aggressive, says Fischoff.

16   "A Larry doesn't have the nerve to be assertive, so he protests by not doing something," Fischoff says: not securing the ladder on the triple-bunk bed, or not mentioning that the coffee is actually rat poison. Consequently, Larrys are rarely promoted. If a Larry actually does work up the courage to ask for a raise, the Moe he works for will usually give a meaningless title upgrade—or say, "Get outta here before I murder ya."

17   To determine if you're an overly passive Larry, answer these three questions.

18   *What's new?* If you're a classic Larry, nothing is new. Your answer will be the latest yarn about the office Curly who once photocopied his own butt. "Larrys live vicariously through Moes and Curlys," says Fischoff. "They don't really have a strong identity of their own."

19   *Still dream about writing a screenplay?* "Larrys don't have a life plan," says Fischoff. They bumble from one opportunity to the next while awaiting their "break"; a Moe plots his life like a war and a Curly flatly avoids challenges.

20   *Do you weasel out of big projects?* Larrys become good at deflecting responsibility. This lets them avoid the risk of failure (and success) without looking like a bum. In *Idiots Deluxe* (1945), as Curly is being attacked by a giant bear, Moe screams, "Go out there and help him!" "The bear don't need no help!" Larry yells back.

21   The chief bonus in being a Larry, of course, is that almost everyone thinks you're a swell chum. The dames eventually warm up to you, too, although it might take a few decades. Women reeling from years of turbulent relationships with Moes and Curlys often settle down with a Larry, says Keesling, because he's a stable, predictable, okeydokey guy who won't mind heading to the 7-Eleven for tampons. That makes him husband material. "I'd date Moe and Curly, but I'd marry Larry," confided several women we asked.

22   Like most Larrys, Larry Fine (1902–1975) spent his career following Moe and his free time ducking him. "Larry and Moe weren't friends," says Lyla Budnick, Larry's sister. "Their dealings were all business." Like any good Larry, he found passive-aggressive ways to make Moe fume. "My father would be at an airport hours early," says Joan Maurer, Moe's daughter, "but Larry would show up 5 minutes before the plane took off. This made my dad very upset." For Larry, making Moe sweat in a crowded airport terminal was probably a tiny payback for the daily humiliations.

23   In *The Sweet Pie and Pie* (1941), Curly tries to throw a pie at the usual gang of rich idiots but gets nailed with a pastry each time he cocks his arm. Finally he bashes himself with the pie to deprive others of the satisfaction. This illustrates Curly's strategy for life. "These men laugh at themselves so other people can't ridicule them first," says Elkin. "It comes across as funny, but this kind of defense mechanism really stems from a large reservoir of anger and resentment."

24   Curly had what's called an oral personality, and a particularly self-destructive one. Boisterous, attention-seeking men, especially those who are secretly ashamed of something, like a beer gut or a bald head, often feel that they must perform in order to be liked, says Keesling. "These guys always come in for counseling, because they experience mood swings and addiction problems. It's what killed Curly and his modern-day version, Chris Farley."

25   Men with Curly personalities are almost always fat, says Fischoff, because they live to binge. They overdose on food, booze, gambling, drugs, or sex—and sometimes on all five in one badly soiled hotel bed. Curly, a consummate binger, even outlined his plans for a utopian life in *Healthy, Wealthy, and Dumb:* "Oh boy! Pie à la mode with beer chasers three times a day!"

26   On the job, Curlys pride themselves on providing comedic relief. "A Curly senses he's no leader, so he garners attention by being a fool," says Fischoff. This nets him no respect, but it does defuse criticism. Who can fire a guy when he's down on the carpet running in circles?

27   Just like his two nitwit cohorts, Curly Howard's offscreen personality was pretty similar to that of the Stooge he portrayed. He drank heavily, overate, and smoked several cigars a day. "He would always be out carousing and drinking, and playing the spoons in nightclubs," remembers Paul Howard, his nephew.

28   "I've heard stories that my father sometimes had to pay for the damage Curly caused while drinking," says Joan Maurer, Moe's daughter. If woo-wooing was enough to get Curly belted onscreen, can you imagine what Moe dished out over a real-life antic like this?

29   Curly's lifestyle apparently made him foggy at work, too. When he barked at women or said "nyuk-nyuk-nyuk!" it was often because he had forgotten his lines. After having a series of obvious mini-strokes (he could barely grumble out his woos in 1945's *If a Body Meets a Body),* Curly had a career-ending stroke in 1946 and died in 1952 at age 48.

30   He had a hoot along the way, of course. Everybody loves a clown, so Curlys get plenty of party invites—and nightcaps with attractive women. "If each of the Stooges were to flirt with a woman, Curly would probably take her home, because his humor radiates confidence," Keesling says. (And what woman could resist an opener like "Hiya, Toots"?) But a Curly's neuroses usually shine through within a few dates, which explains why Curlys tend to have few long-term sex partners, says Keesling.

31   Curly Howard was married four times. "With the exception of his fourth marriage, his best relationship was with his dogs," says Paul Howard. Curly expressed his marital outlook pretty clearly in 1941's *An Ache in Every Stake,* as he shaved a lathered block of ice with a razor: "Are you married or happy?"

Discussion Questions

1. What is Geraci's purpose in writing this essay, and where is it stated?
2. Demonstrate your understanding of coherence by pointing out how paragraphs 3–6 are linked to one another. Refer to the essay when answering.

DISCUSSION QUESTIONS (pp. 524–525)
1. Geraci's purpose, stated in the final sentence of paragraph 2, is to help his readers identify these personality types and avoid the problems associated with them.

2. Paragraph 3, which offers examples of Moelike behavior, is linked to paragraph 4, which characterizes the Moelike personality by the summarizing phrase "In short." Paragraph 5 is in turn linked to paragraph 4 by the clause "Even if . . . tonsils out," which picks up on the "nose gnashings and belly bonks" noted in paragraph 4. Paragraph 5 then offers the first of two clues to the Moelike personality, and paragraph 6, which continues with the other, signals that fact by leading off with "Second."

3. This essay appeared in *Men's Health,* a magazine aimed at young to middle-aged males. Geraci's writing style, lively and irreverent, is perfectly suited to this audience.

4. Geraci's level of diction is highly informal. The sentences are very short, make use of numerous contractions like "they're," "it's," and "that's," and are filled with colloquial and slang expressions such as "saps" (paragraph 4), "wise guy" (paragraph 7), "noogies"

3. What audience do you think Geraci is trying to reach? Explain your answer.
4. Characterize the level of diction used in this essay. Refer to appropriate passages to support your answer.
5. Do you feel you are a rather pure version of a Moe, Larry, or Curly, somewhat of a mixture, or that you bear little resemblance to any of them?

Toward Key Insights

How do you cope with the various personality types that you encounter at school? In your social life? On the job?

Do you think it is an oversimplification to assert that "To solve many of life's problems, all you really need to do is watch the *Three Stooges*" (paragraph 1)? Why or why not?

Suggestion for Writing

Write an essay classifying three distinctive personality types. Develop your paper with relevant, specific details and write with a specific audience in mind.

COMPARISON

Reading Strategies

1. Identify your purpose for reading the comparison and the author's purpose for the comparison. Determine how carefully you need to read the comparison.
2. Identify the items that are being compared.
3. Identify the pattern of organization (point by point or block) that is used in the comparison.
4. Read carefully to establish the points of similarities and differences. When the information might be necessary for future purposes, it can be helpful to create a table that matches similarities and differences.

Reading Critically

1. Test to see if there are any biases guiding the comparison. Does the writer show any preference or prejudice?
2. Determine if the accounts of similarities and differences are accurate or whether they are exaggerated.
3. Test to see if there are other similarities or differences that can be established. Are the items more alike or more different than the author tries to suggest?

Reading As a Writer

1. Examine how the author organized the essay. Was the organization effective in guiding the reader through the essay? Note what organizational pattern was most effective.
2. Notice the sentences that the writer uses for transitions. Jot down any useful techniques.
3. Observe how much detail was used to substantiate the comparison.

(paragraph 10), and "slobs" (paragraph 15).

5. This question should prompt some interesting responses. A writing assignment could follow.

OVERVIEW OF COMPARISON ESSAYS
Three of the essays in this section are comparisons, one (by Sakamoto) is a comparison that includes an element of analogy, and one (by Waters) is solely an analogy. Two of the comparisons use the alternating pattern and two (by Sakamoto and Stephens) the block pattern. Three focus entirely on differences, and the other (by Catton), while concerned primarily with differences, devotes some attention to similarities. Like all analogies, ours calls attention to the similarities that underlie two seemingly dissimilar things. In it, the writer likens the passage of grief to the return to a house that has withstood a cruel winter. Three essays are formal–informal, one (by Stephens) is informal, and one (by Waters) uses devices like descriptive language, parallelism, and rhythmic sentences to give the writing a formal cast.

PERSPECTIVE
Catton's essay has become a classic because it deals with two well-known figures who have had considerable historical impact and who command widespread interest; it skillfully integrates both

similarities and differences; and it is clearly organized. For these reasons, it is easy to teach. (For an overview of the Comparison essays, see page 525.)

BRUCE CATTON

Grant and Lee: A Study in Contrasts

Bruce Catton (1899–1978) was a nationally recognized expert on the Civil War. Born in Petoskey, Michigan, he attended Oberlin College, then worked as a reporter for several large newspapers. Between 1942 and 1948, he held several positions in the U.S. government and then became an editor of American Heritage *magazine. His first book on the Civil War,* Mr. Lincoln's Army, *appeared in 1951 and was followed by* Glory Road *(1952) and* A Stillness at Appomattox *(1953). This last book won the Pulitzer Prize and the National Book Award and established Catton's reputation as a Civil War historian. In the years that followed, Catton continued to write books on the Civil War. In 1972 he published the auto-biographical* Waiting for the Morning Train *and in 1974* Michigan: A Bicentennial History. *In our selection, Catton points out differences as well as similarities in the two foremost adversaries of the Civil War.*

Title sets up differences

Introduction: paragraphs 1–3; background; significance of following contrasts

Body: paragraph 4 to first part, paragraph 16; alternating pattern throughout

First difference paragraphs 4–6: Lee's background, character

1   When Ulysses S. Grant and Robert E. Lee met in the parlor of a modest house at Appomattox Court House, Virginia, on April 9, 1865, to work out the terms for the surrender of Lee's Army of Northern Virginia, a great chapter in American life came to a close, and a great new chapter began.

2   These men were bringing the Civil War to its virtual finish. To be sure, other armies had yet to surrender, and for a few days the fugitive Confederate government would struggle desperately and vainly, trying to find some way to go on living now that its chief support was gone. But in effect it was all over when Grant and Lee signed the papers. And the little room where they wrote out the terms was the scene of one of the poignant, dramatic contrasts in American history.

3   They were two strong men these oddly different generals, and they represented the strengths of two conflicting currents that, through them, had come into final collision.

4   Back of Robert E. Lee was the notion that the old aristocratic concept might somehow survive and be dominant in American life.

5   Lee was tidewater Virginia, and in his background were family, culture, and tradition . . . the age of chivalry transplanted to a New World which was making its own legends and its own myths. He embodied a way of life that had come down through the age of knighthood and the English country squire. America was a land that was beginning all over again, dedicated to nothing much more complicated than the rather hazy belief that all men had equal rights and should have an equal chance in the world. In such a land Lee stood for the feeling that it was somehow of advantage to human society to have a pronounced inequality in the social structure. There should be a leisure class, backed by ownership of land; in turn, society itself should be keyed to the land as the chief source of wealth and influence. It would bring forth (according to this ideal) a class of men with a strong sense of obligation to the community; men who lived not to gain advantage for themselves, but to meet the solemn obligations which had been laid on them by the very fact that they were privileged. From them the country would get its leadership; to them it could look for the higher values—of thought, of conduct, or personal deportment—to give it strength and virtue.

6   Lee embodied the noblest elements of this aristocratic ideal. Through him, the landed nobility justified itself. For four years, the Southern states had fought a desperate war to uphold the ideals for which Lee stood. In the end, it almost seemed

as if the Confederacy fought for Lee; as if he himself was the Confederacy . . . the best thing that the way of life for which the Confederacy stood could ever have to offer. He had passed into legend before Appomattox. Thousands of tired, under-fed, poorly clothed Confederate soldiers, long since past the simple enthusiasm of the early days of the struggle, somehow considered Lee the symbol of everything for which they had been willing to die. But they could not quite put this feeling into words. If the Lost Cause, sanctified by so much heroism and so many deaths, had a living justification, its justification was General Lee.

7   Grant, the son of a tanner on the Western frontier, was everything Lee was not. He had come up the hard way and embodied nothing in particular except the eternal toughness and sinewy fiber of the men who grew up beyond the mountains. He was one of a body of men who owed reverence and obeisance to no one, who were self-reliant to a fault, who cared hardly anything for the past but who had a sharp eye for the future.

> Paragraphs 7–9: Grant's background, character

8   These frontier men were the precise opposites of the tidewater aristocrats. Back of them, in the great surge that had taken people over the Alleghenies and into the opening Western country, there was a deep, implicit dissatisfaction with a past that had settled into grooves. They stood for democracy not from any reasoned conclusion about the proper ordering of human society, but simply because they had grown up in the middle of democracy and knew how it worked. Their society might have privileges, but they would be privileges each man had won for himself. Forms and patterns meant nothing. No man was born to anything, except perhaps to a chance to show how far he could rise. Life was competition.

9   Yet along with this feeling had come a deep sense of belonging to a national community. The Westerner who developed a farm, opened a shop, or set up in business as a trader could hope to prosper only as his own community prospered—and his community ran from the Atlantic to the Pacific and from Canada down to Mexico. If the land was settled, with towns and highways and accessible markets, he could better himself. He saw his fate in terms of the nation's own destiny. As its horizons expanded, so did his. He had, in other words, an acute dollars-and-cents stake in the continued growth and development of his country.

10   And that, perhaps, is where the contrast between Grant and Lee becomes most striking. The Virginia aristocrat, inevitably, saw himself in relation to his own region. He lived in a static society which could endure almost anything except change. Instinctively, first loyalty would go to the locality in which that society existed. He would fight to the limit of endurance to defend it, because in defending it he was defending everything that gave his own life its deepest meaning.

> Second difference: Lee's loyalty

11   The Westerner, on the other hand, would fight with an equal tenacity for the broader concept of society. He fought so because everything he lived by was tied to growth, expansion, and a constantly widening horizon. What he lived by would survive or fall with the nation itself. He could not possibly stand by unmoved in the face of an attempt to destroy the Union. He would combat it with everything he had, because he could only see it as an effort to cut the ground out from under his feet.

> Grant's loyalty

12   So Grant and Lee were in complete contrast, representing two diametrically opposed elements in American life. Grant was the modern man emerging; beyond him, ready to come on the stage, was the great age of steel and machinery, of crowded cities and a restless burgeoning vitality. Lee might have ridden down from the old age of chivalry, lance in hand, silken banner fluttering over his head. Each man was the perfect champion of his cause, drawing both his strengths and his weaknesses from the people he led.

> Summary of significant differences

Transition paragraph
signals switch to
similarities

First similarity

Second similarity

Third similarity: notes
order of climax

Conclusion: significance
of the meeting

13 Yet it was not all contrast, after all. Different as they were—in background, in personality, in underlying aspiration—these two great soldiers had much in common. Under everything else, they were marvelous fighters. Furthermore, their fighting qualities were really very much alike.

14 Each man had, to begin with, the great virtue of utter tenacity and fidelity. Grant fought his way down the Mississippi Valley in spite of acute personal discouragement and profound military handicaps. Lee hung on in the trenches at Petersburg after hope itself had died. In each man there was an indomitable quality . . . the born fighter's refusal to give up as long as he can still remain on his feet and lift his two fists.

15 Daring and resourcefulness they had, too; the ability to think faster and move faster than the enemy. These were the qualities which gave Lee the dazzling campaigns of Second Manassas and Chancellorsville and won Vicksburg for Grant.

16 Lastly, and perhaps greatest of all, there was the ability, at the end, to turn quickly from war to peace once the fighting was over. Out of the way these two men behaved at Appomattox came the possibility of a peace of reconciliation. It was a possibility not wholly realized, in the years to come, but which did, in the end, help the two sections to become one nation again . . . after a war whose bitterness might have seemed to make such a reunion wholly impossible. No part of either man's life became him more than the part he played in this brief meeting in the McLean house at Appomattox. Their behavior there put all succeeding generations of Americans in their debt. Two great Americans, Grant and Lee—very different, yet under everything very much alike. Their encounter at Appomattox was one of the great moments of American history.

Discussion Questions

1. Where is Catton's thesis statement?
2. Summarize the way of life that Lee stood for, and then do the same for Grant.
3. Why do the differences between Grant and Lee receive more extended treatment than the similarities? Why are the similarities discussed last?
4. How would you characterize Catton's attitude toward the two men? Refer to specific parts of the essay when answering.

Toward Key Insights

To what extent does modern society reflect the values embodied by Grant and Lee?

How would you characterize the upper class in the United States today? Does it consist of leisured individuals who own extensive property, as Lee did, or does it have other characteristics? Are its values the same as Lee's? If not, how are they different?

If Grant was typical of the "self-reliant" non-aristocrat, how is his contemporary counterpart similar to and different from him?

Suggestion for Writing

Write an essay comparing two past or present political or military figures—perhaps Abraham Lincoln and Jefferson Davis or Dwight Eisenhower and Erwin Rommel. Try for a balanced treatment and select an appropriate organization.

DISCUSSION QUESTIONS

1. Paragraph 3 contains the thesis statement.

2. Lee stood for the aristocratic, chivalric tradition; loyalty to his locality; and a belief in a privileged leisure class destined to be leaders. Grant stood for just the opposite—democracy, self-reliance, loyalty to the nation, the chance to advance as far as ability would allow. (Catton's purpose is to contrast these two opposing outlooks.)

3. The differences between Grant and Lee (paragraphs 4–12) receive more extended treatment than the similarities because they represent the two conflicting currents that came into final collision with the outbreak of the Civil War. Similarities are discussed last because one of these similarities is the ability of both men to begin reconciliation and

NANCY MASTERSON SAKAMOTO

Conversational Ballgames

Nancy Masterson Sakamoto graduated Phi Beta Kappa from UCLA with a degree in English. Married to a Japanese artist and Buddhist priest, she lived in Japan for twenty-four years before moving with her husband and two sons to Honolulu in 1982. While in Japan, she was visiting professor at the University of Osaka. She gave in-service training to Japanese junior and senior high school English teachers and talks on intercultural topics, both in English and in Japanese, to various business, educational, and women's groups. In addition to her book, Polite Fictions: Why Japanese and Americans Seem Rude to Each Other, *still used as a textbook in Japanese universities, she coauthored a research project report sponsored by the Japanese Ministry of Education and wrote various articles for Japanese English-teaching publications. In Hawaii, she has been a speaker and seminar leader for many educational, business, and professional organizations. Her current position is professor of American Studies, Shitennoji Gakuen University (Hawaii branch). In this essay, she discusses the different conversational styles of Americans and Japanese, just one example of the many differences that distinguish different cultures.*

1   After I was married and had lived in Japan for a while, my Japanese gradually improved to the point where I could take part in simple conversations with my husband and his friends and family. And I began to notice that often, when I joined in, the others would look startled, and the conversational topic would come to a halt. After this happened several times, it became clear to me that I was doing something wrong. But for a long time, I didn't know what it was.

2   Finally, after listening carefully to many Japanese conversations, I discovered what my problem was. Even though I was speaking Japanese, I was handling the conversation in a western way.

3   Japanese-style conversations develop quite differently from western-style conversations. And the difference isn't only in the languages. I realized that just as I kept trying to hold western-style conversations even when I was speaking Japanese, so my English students kept trying to hold Japanese-style conversations even when they were speaking English. We were unconsciously playing entirely different conversational ballgames.

4   A western-style conversation between two people is like a game of tennis. If I introduce a topic, a conversational ball, I expect you to hit it back. If you agree with me, I don't expect you simply to agree and do nothing more. I expect you to add something—a reason for agreeing, another example, or an elaboration to carry the idea further. But I don't expect you always to agree. I am just as happy if you question me, or challenge me, or completely disagree with me. Whether you agree or disagree, your response will return the ball to me.

5   And then it is my turn again. I don't serve a new ball from my original starting line. I hit your ball back again from where it has bounced. I carry your idea further, or answer your questions or objections, or challenge or question you. And so the ball goes back and forth, with each of us doing our best to give it a new twist, an original spin, or a powerful smash.

6   And the more vigorous the action, the more interesting and exciting the game. Of course, if one of us gets angry, it spoils the conversation, just as it spoils a tennis game. But getting excited is not at all the same as getting angry. After all,

---

help the two sides "become one nation again."

4. Catton obviously admires, perhaps even eulogizes, the two men. Paragraphs 12 ("Each man was the perfect champion of his cause . . .") through 16 ("Their behavior there put all succeeding generations of Americans in their debt") suggest this attitude.

PERSPECTIVE
In today's global world, sensitivity to the customs of other countries and cultures is becoming increasingly important. We can hope that such mutual understanding will result in greater cooperation and fewer conflicts.

TEACHING STRATEGIES
1. In paragraphs 11, 14, and 15, Sakamoto uses "he" rather than "he or she" to refer to antecedents that are not clearly male. You might point out that since 1982, when this essay was first published, "he or she" has become common because of objections that "he" is sexist.

2. To reinforce coherence, ask several students to point out how a number of paragraphs are linked together.

3. Have students characterize Sakamoto's style by referring to several examples from the text.

CLASSROOM ACTIVITY
Since your campus almost certainly has a diverse mix of students, ask those in your class what differences

in conversational styles they have observed and how they dealt with these differences. A writing assignment could follow.

we are not trying to hit each other. We are trying to hit the ball. So long as we attack only each other's opinions, and do not attack each other personally, we don't expect anyone to get hurt. A good conversation is supposed to be interesting and exciting.

7   If there are more than two people in the conversation, then it is like doubles in tennis, or like volleyball. There's no waiting in line. Whoever is nearest and quickest hits the ball, and if you step back, someone else will hit it. No one stops the game to give you a turn. You're responsible for taking your own turn.

8   But whether it's two players or a group, everyone does his best to keep the ball going, and no one person has the ball for very long.

9   A Japanese-style conversation, however, is not at all like tennis or volleyball. It's like bowling. You wait for your turn. And you always know your place in line. It depends on such things as whether you are older or younger, a close friend or a relative stranger to the previous speaker, in a senior or junior position, and so on.

10   When your turn comes, you step up to the starting line with your bowling ball, and carefully bowl it. Everyone else stands back and watches politely, murmuring encouragement. Everyone waits until the ball has reached the end of the alley, and watches to see if it knocks down all the pins, or only some of them, or none of them. There is a pause, while everyone registers your score.

11   Then, after everyone is sure that you have completely finished your turn, the next person in line steps up to the same starting line, with a different ball. He doesn't return your ball, and he does not begin from where your ball stopped. There is no back and forth at all. All the balls run parallel. And there is always a suitable pause between turns. There is no rush, no excitement, no scramble for the ball.

12   No wonder everyone looked startled when I took part in Japanese conversations. I paid no attention to whose turn it was, and kept snatching the ball halfway down the alley and throwing it back to the bowler. Of course the conversation died. I was playing the wrong game.

13   This explains why it is almost impossible to get a Western-style conversation or discussion going with English students in Japan. I used to think that the problem was their lack of English language ability. But I finally came to realize that the biggest problem is that they, too, are playing the wrong game.

14   Whenever I serve a volleyball, everyone just stands back and watches it fall, with occasional murmurs of encouragement. No one hits it back. Everyone waits until I call on someone to take a turn. And when that person speaks, he doesn't hit my ball back. He serves a new ball. Again, everyone just watches it fall.

15   So I call on someone else. This person does not refer to what the previous speaker has said. He also serves a new ball. Nobody seems to have paid any attention to what anyone else has said. Everyone begins again from the same starting line, and all the balls run parallel. There is never any back and forth. Everyone is trying to bowl with a volleyball.

16   And if I try a simpler conversation, with only two of us, then the other person tries to bowl with my tennis ball. No wonder foreign English teachers in Japan get discouraged.

17   Now that you know about the difference in the conversational ballgames, you may think that all your troubles are over. But if you have been trained all your life to play one game, it is no simple matter to switch to another, even if you know the rules. Knowing the rules is not at all the same thing as playing the game.

18   Even now, during a conversation in Japanese I will notice a startled reaction, and belatedly realize that once again I have rudely interrupted by instinctively trying to hit back the other person's bowling ball. It is no easier for me to "just

listen" during a conversation, than it is for my Japanese students to "just relax" when speaking with foreigners. Now I can truly sympathize with how hard they must find it to try to carry on a Western-style conversation.

19   If I have not yet learned to do conversational bowling in Japanese, at least I have figured out one thing that puzzled me for a long time. After his first trip to America, my husband complained that Americans asked him so many questions and made him talk so much at the dinner table that he never had a chance to eat. When I asked him why he couldn't talk and eat at the same time, he said that Japanese do not customarily think that dinner, especially on fairly formal occasions, is a suitable time for extended conversation.

20   Since westerners think that conversation is an indispensable part of dining, and indeed would consider it impolite not to converse with one's dinner partner, I found this Japanese custom rather strange. Still, I could accept it as a cultural difference even though I didn't really understand it. But when my husband added, in explanation, that Japanese consider it extremely rude to talk with one's mouth full, I got confused. Talking with one's mouth full is certainly not an American custom. We think it very rude, too. Yet we still manage to talk a lot and eat at the same time. How do we do it?

21   For a long time, I couldn't explain it, and it bothered me. But after I discovered the conversational ballgames, I finally found the answer. Of course! In a Western-style conversation, you hit the ball, and while someone else is hitting it back, you take a bite, chew, and swallow. Then you hit the ball again, and then eat some more. The more people there are in the conversation, the more chances you have to eat. But even with only two of you talking, you still have plenty of chances to eat.

22   Maybe that's why polite conversation at the dinner table has never been a traditional part of Japanese etiquette. Your turn to talk would last so long without interruption that you'd never get a chance to eat.

Discussion Questions

1. Sakamoto notes in paragraph 1 that she "had lived in Japan for a while" and in paragraph 2 that she has listened "carefully to many Japanese conversations." Why does she note these facts at the outset of her essay?
2. What purpose is served by the first two sentences of paragraph 3?
3. Why do you think Sakamoto uses various games—tennis, volleyball, bowling— to help explain the differences between American and Japanese conversational styles?
4. Point out specific supporting details that help make this comparison successful.
5. For what audience is Sakamoto writing? Refer to the essay when answering.
6. Sakamoto ends paragraph 17 with the assertion that "Knowing the rules is not at all the same thing as playing the game." Explain what she means.

Toward Key Insights

In what ways other than conversational style might cultures exhibit pronounced differences?

What problems might these differences create, and how can we best deal with them?

DISCUSSION QUESTIONS
1. These facts, along with Sakamoto's classroom experience, qualify her to make the comparisons that follow.
2. These two sentences function as the thesis statement. The remainder of the essay supports the statements by establishing the differences between how Japanese and Western conversations develop. You might also point out that Sakamoto anticipates an obvious reader response: "The difference isn't only in the languages."
3. Sakamoto uses the familiar to help explain the unfamiliar. Most readers will know about the games; fewer will know the different conversational styles. Attempting to explain the differences without referring to the games would have been very difficult.
4. Effective supporting details are found in paragraphs 4, 5, 6, 7, 9, 10, 11, 12, 14, 15, 16, 18, 19, 20, and 21.
5. Sakamoto is writing for a broad, general audience. This is apparent from her writing style, which makes use of ordinary words, relies primarily on short sentences, most of which are loose rather than periodic, and includes contractions. The writing level is formal–informal, with a tilt toward informality.
6. The meaning can, of course, be expressed in various ways, but we suggest the following: Implementing the solution to a problem is much more difficult than merely

understanding the problem, especially when years of using a particular conversational style compound the difficulty.

Suggestion for Writing

Write a paper that discusses a problem that arose between you and someone else because of a difference in outlook or lifestyle and explain how you resolved the matter. Use either the block or alternating method of organization.

MARIFLO STEPHENS

Barbie Doesn't Live Here Anymore

Mariflo Stephens lives in Charlottesville, Virginia, where she writes essays and fiction. Her work appears in a number of major periodicals such as The Washington Post *and the* Virginia Quarterly Review. *This essay, from her memoir in progress,* Last One Home: Life After Oprah, *compares the place of the common Barbie doll in her and her daughter's lives to demonstrate the differences between two generations of women.*

PERSPECTIVE
Toys often embody our cultural attitudes. In this essay, the author lets Barbie stand for the cultural expectations of women. The author's dialogue with her daughter succinctly captures the difference between the generations. It would be worthwhile to discuss how toys change from one generation to the next. This could lead to a broader discussion of how such changes can stand for other more general changes in the culture.

TEACHING STRATEGIES
1. Before assigning this essay, have students discuss, listing on the board, their different experiences with Barbie. Get a concrete list of the things they did with the doll. Discuss how much impact Barbie and other toys had on their lives.

2. Have select students interview their parents or older faculty members about what kinds of toys were influential in their

1   I've always known there was something wrong with Barbie. She looks nice enough. And she has her own Corvette, her own band, and her own dream house. Still, I just didn't want my daughter playing with her. But how can we snub Barbie? Little girls all over Charlottesville, all over Virginia, and, yes, all over the world, seem to be spending hour after hour with her.

2   I considered relying on my own experience. When, in 1962, I was presented with my first Barbie doll, I did what all the other little girls did with their Barbies: I took her clothes off. Wow! I could hardly wait to have a pair of my very own.

3   Then I put her clothes back on. It was hard. There was a snap the size of a pinhead and Barbie hardly cooperated. I pulled the tight dress up her legs, over her hips; and it stopped right there. Had a liquid Barbie been poured into this to harden? She was stiff as stone but still smelled like new rubber. I had to put her head between my teeth to get her dress past that chest. I was exhausted. But was it ever fun, I told myself.

4   Now where were those high heels and that pair of long white gloves? I found one glove. Later my friend Jane came over to play. She took the dress off, too. We waited for something to happen. Then we went out to climb some trees. Four hours later, we told our mothers we'd had a great time playing Barbie. (This was lobbying. Jane's mother looked quizzical and noted the leaves in our hair.)

5   I was twelve in 1962, so I didn't have too many good years left for Barbie. Soon I would *be* Barbie. I was blond, wasn't I? And I would be an American teenager with no time left for playing. My time would be devoted to the serious business of dressing and dating and talking on the telephone.

6   In the months to come, I made the best of it. I spent my entire piggybank savings on Barbie clothes—sequined evening gowns, fake-fur wraps, and high heels. The outfits had themes like Barbie Goes to the Prom and Barbie Steps Out printed in a fast-moving script with exclamation marks at the end. There wasn't much to do, however, but dress and undress Barbie, and I found I had to spend most of my time looking for a lost pink high heel the size of my little fingernail.

7   Buying the clothes was the exciting part. Since I liked horses, I picked out Barbie's rodeo skirt set with white high-heeled boots and fringe. These weren't Barbie's clothes, they were mine. If I could've worn Barbie's lavender loungewear with its pink feather boa to my seventh-grade classroom, I would

have. If, that is, I could find it. Much was located under the sofa cushions, but far too late, I'm afraid.

8   Barbie retired early. I waited for my body to fill out, Barbie-style. My legs didn't grow to those proportions and neither did anything else. I got the idea that every time a teenage boy looked at me he saw only what was missing—what Barbie had that I didn't.

9   Even the blond hair didn't live up to expectations. Mine was fuzzy and its shape varied from day to day. Barbie's seemed to stay in a permanent coiffure. Evening gowns weren't even in style.

10   And not very many blondes can manage a nose that turns up that way.

11   Worst of all, Barbie doesn't do anything but lose her clothes. I had wasted a lot of money, not to mention rich fantasy time, on a false goddess.

12   When my daughter, Jane, was born, I told myself there would be no false goddesses. I didn't name her after a goddess, I named her after the girl I'd climbed trees with.

13   When relatives started to inquire about birthday gifts, I didn't say "No Barbies, please," though I wanted to. I said instead that books were very nice gifts. I mentioned there wasn't much to do with a Barbie doll except comb her hair and I was sure we'd lose those little combs.

14   Jane turned seven. She had five Barbie dolls. I didn't see her playing with them much, although every few days I would find a pink high heel somewhere. I would spot the dolls around the house—their legs splayed crazily and scarves tied around their bodies for clothes.

15   One day Jane said: "Barbies don't do anything. They don't even bend their legs when you sit them down. Their legs stick straight out." I knew she was on to something. Then we cleaned up her room. I found most of the clothes and even some of the high heels. I was pretty proud of myself. But behind me I heard Jane saying: "Let's get rid of the Barbies."

16   "Huh?"

17   "They're dumb and prissy. They clutter up everything. Let's sell them."

18   "What do you mean by 'dumb and prissy'?"

19   "They look like this," she said and raised to tiptoe and smiled maniacally. "They've got globs of blue makeup over their eyes and they can't do anything. You can't even bend their legs to sit them on a model horse."

20   I seized the moment. "What else is wrong with the Barbies?"

21   "They don't have toes. Their shoes fall off. They're always on tiptoe."

22   "That would be tiring," I said, sympathetically.

23   "They never get tired. They don't do anything."

24   "What else is wrong?"

25   "They don't wear socks or pants. Just dresses or fish-net stockings or they go barefoot. All the commercials compliment their hair, but once their hair is tangled, it never goes back."

26   "Anything else wrong?" I asked—and here she won my heart if ever there was a contest for it.

27   "They're all the same age. There are no Barbie babies and no old people."

28   "Sounds like Barbie lives in a dull world," I said.

29   "No, not dull. Dumb and prissy. Let's sell them."

30   "How much should we charge for each one?"

31   "A penny," she said disgustedly, then immediately saw her error. "No, no. A dollar."

childhood and what they remembered about these toys. Discuss the results in class.

3. Have the students list in class discussion the ways that the mother and daughter in the essay differ.

CLASSROOM ACTIVITIES

1. If possible, bring in some Barbies with accessories. Have students work in small groups to assess the doll as a possible toy for young girls.

2. Have students, working in small groups, make a list of the toys that were most important to them when they were young, the characteristics of those toys, and how those toys have changed.

DISCUSSION QUESTIONS (p. 534)

1. The mother believed she had to play with the Barbie, spent money on Barbie, and even identified with the expectations for the doll. The daughter rejected Barbie and saw the doll as "dumb and prissy." The real point of this comparison is to highlight the change in women from one generation to the next.

2. The author used a block pattern to organize her comparison. This organizational strategy allows us to see two very distinctive ways of responding to the doll.

3. The dialogue allows the author to represent the daughter's attitude toward the doll, critique the doll, and extend the critique to early images of women.

4. The conclusion emphasizes the contrast between the modern and traditional roles for women. Barbie and women have both changed. The conclusion is effective because it pulls together earlier elements of the comparison: the daughter's decision to sell her Barbies and her mother's desire to be like Barbie.

5. The image of the feather boa is used early in the essay to stand for the mother's attitude toward Barbie and then is repeated in the conclusion to help pull the essay together. The feather boa stands for the impractical desire for an artificial glamour that Barbie represented. The author writes about wanting to wear the pink feather boa to seventh grade, an image that suggests playing dress-up. In the conclusion, she links the dolls to mad women who want to know, "Who stole my feather boa?" There is a deliberate reference here to an important work of feminist literary criticism titled *The Mad Woman in the Attic*.

32   "Oh," I said, seeing my own error. Just because I considered Barbie small change didn't mean everyone else did. Six Barbies went out the back door to a secondhand shop and, in a matter of minutes, six dollars came in the front door.

33   Maybe Barbie's business suit with its one-inch briefcase inspired Jane's market wisdom.

34   After all, the new Barbies are still in stores, housed in pink boxes with bold script that seems to shout: Barbie Goes to the Office! My old dolls, with their narrow eyes and puckered lips, are upstairs like other mad women of the attic, whispering: "Who stole my feather boa?"

Discussion Questions

1. This essay compares the different reactions of mother and daughter to Barbie dolls. What are the differences in their responses? What is the real point of this comparison?
2. How does this writer organize her comparison? What is the effect of this strategy?
3. Crucial to this essay is the dialogue between mother and daughter. What does the dialogue accomplish in the essay?
4. Reread the last paragraph. What point is the author trying to make in the conclusion? Is the conclusion effective?
5. How is the image of the feather boa used in the essay? What is the meaning of the feather boa for the author? What clues in the text demonstrate this meaning?

Toward Key Insights

What role do Barbies have in the developing attitudes of girls, and is that role positive or negative?
More generally, what kinds of impacts do toys have on the developing attitudes of children?

Suggestion for Writing

Compare how a toy such as video games, or how people play with a toy, has changed over a specific period of time.

Select someone of either sex whom you know well and write an essay comparing how you and the other person, as adolescents, handled such matters as peer pressure, self-image, dating, and relationships with family members. Develop the essay with relevant supporting material.

RICHARD RODRIGUEZ

Private Language, Public Language

Richard Rodriguez (born 1944) is a native of San Francisco who is of Mexican ancestry. After learning English in the elementary grades, he went on to earn a baccalaureate degree in English at Stanford University (1967) and graduate degrees at Columbia University

PERSPECTIVE
Throughout this book we have focused on language as a means of public communication. This essay establishes the importance

(1969) and the University of California at Berkeley (1975). Rejecting job offers from several major universities, he spent the next six years writing Hunger of Memory: The Education of Richard Rodriguez *(1982), a book that traces his educational odyssey.* Days of Obligation *was published in 1992, and* Brown: The Last Discovery of America *was published in 2003. His articles have appeared in a variety of scholarly magazines. In the following essay, Rodriguez explores his contrasting childhood perceptions concerning English and his native Spanish.*

1   I remember to start with that day in Sacramento—a California now nearly thirty years past—when I first entered a classroom, able to understand some fifty stray English words.

2   The third of four children, I had been preceded to a neighborhood Roman Catholic school by an older brother and sister. But neither of them had revealed very much about their classroom experiences. Each afternoon they returned, as they left in the morning, always together, speaking in Spanish as they climbed the five steps of the porch. And their mysterious books, wrapped in shopping-bag paper, remained on the table next to the door, closed firmly behind them.

3   An accident of geography sent me to a school where all my classmates were white, many the children of doctors and lawyers and business executives. All my classmates certainly must have been uneasy on that first day of school—as most children are uneasy—to find themselves apart from their families in the first institution of their lives. But I was astonished.

4   The nun said, in a friendly but oddly impersonal voice, "Boys and girls, this is Richard Rodriguez." (I heard her sound out: *Rich-heard Road-ree-guess.*) It was the first time I had heard anyone name me in English. "Richard," the nun repeated more slowly, writing my name down in her black leather book. Quickly I turned to see my mother's face dissolve in a watery blur behind the pebbled glass door.

5   Many years later there is something called bilingual education—a scheme proposed in the late 1960s by Hispanic-American social activists, later endorsed by a congressional vote. It is a program that seeks to permit non-English-speaking children, many from lower-class homes, to use their family language as the language of school. (Such is the goal its supporters announce.) I hear them and am forced to say no: It is not possible for a child—any child—ever to use his family's language in school. Not to understand this is to misunderstand the public uses of schooling and to trivialize the nature of intimate life—a family's "language."

6   Memory teaches me what I know of these matters; the boy reminds the adult. I was a bilingual child, a certain kind—socially disadvantaged—the son of working-class parents, both Mexican immigrants.

7   In the early years of my boyhood, my parents coped very well in America. My father had steady work. My mother managed at home. They were nobody's victims. Optimism and ambition led them to a house (our home) many blocks from the Mexican south side of town. We lived among *gringos* and only a block from the biggest, whitest houses. It never occurred to my parents that they couldn't live wherever they chose. Nor was the Sacramento of the fifties bent on teaching them a contrary lesson. My mother and father were more annoyed than intimidated by those two or three neighbors who tried initially to make us unwelcome. ("Keep your brats away from my sidewalk!") But despite all they achieved, perhaps because they had so much to achieve, any deep feeling of ease, the confidence of "belonging" in public was withheld from them both. They regarded the people at work, the faces in crowds, as very distant from us. They were the others, *los gringos.*

of private language as well as its unsuitability for public use.

TEACHING STRATEGIES
1. Have students reread paragraph 5 and explain the difference between the meanings that Rodriguez and the supporters of bilingual education attach to the term "family language." Then ask students whether they agree with Rodriguez that bilingual education is impossible.

2. Paragraph 12 makes use of parallelism. Ask students to point out where it occurs and to suggest why Rodriguez uses it.

CLASSROOM ACTIVITY
Have each student list the features of his or her family's private language that set it apart from the language spoken outside the home. A writing assignment contrasting the two could follow.

That term was interchangeable in their speech with another, even more telling, *los americanos.*

8   I grew up in a house where the only regular guests were my relations. For one day, enormous families of relatives would visit and there would be so many people that the noise and the bodies would spill out to the backyard and front porch. Then, for weeks, no one came by. (It was usually a salesman who rang the doorbell.) Our house stood apart. A gaudy yellow in a row of white bungalows. We were the people with the noisy dog. The people who raised pigeons and chickens. We were the foreigners on the block. A few neighbors smiled and waved. We waved back. But no one in the family knew the names of the old couple who lived next door; until I was seven years old, I did not know the names of the kids who lived across the street.

9   In public, my father and mother spoke a hesitant, accented, not always grammatical English. And they would have to strain—their bodies tense—to catch the sense of what was rapidly said by *los gringos.* At home they spoke Spanish. The language of their Mexican past sounded in counterpoint to the English of public society. The words would come quickly, with ease. Conveyed through those sounds was the pleasing, soothing, consoling reminder of being at home.

10   During those years when I was first conscious of hearing, my mother and father addressed me only in Spanish; in Spanish I learned to reply. By contrast, English *(inglés),* rarely heard in the house, was the language I came to associate with *gringos.* I learned my first words of English overhearing my parents speak to strangers. At five years of age, I knew just enough English for my mother to trust me on errands to stores one block away. No more.

11   I was a listening child, careful to hear the very different sounds of Spanish and English. Wide-eyed with hearing, I'd listen to sounds more than words. First, there were English *(gringo)* sounds. So many words were still unknown that when the butcher or the lady at the drugstore said something to me, exotic polysyllabic sounds would bloom in the midst of their sentences. Often the speech of people in public seemed to me very loud, booming with confidence. The man behind the counter would literally ask, "What can I do for you?" But by being so firm and so clear, the sound of his voice said that he was a *gringo;* he belonged in public society.

12   I would also hear then the high nasal notes of middle-class American speech. The air stirred with sound. Sometimes, even now, when I have been traveling abroad for several weeks, I will hear what I heard as a boy. In hotel lobbies or airports, in Turkey or Brazil, some Americans will pass, and suddenly I will hear it again—the high sound of American voices. For a few seconds I will hear it with pleasure, for it is now the sound of *my* society—a reminder of home. But inevitably—already on the flight headed for home—the sound fades with repetition. I will be unable to hear it anymore.

13   When I was a boy, things were different. The accent of *los gringos* was never pleasing nor was it hard to hear. Crowds at Safeway or at bus stops would be noisy with sound. And I would be forced to edge away from the chirping chatter above me.

14   I was unable to hear my own sounds, but I knew very well that I spoke English poorly. My words would not stretch far enough to form complete thoughts. And the words I did speak I didn't know well enough to make into distinct sounds. (Listeners would usually lower their heads, better to hear what I was trying to say.) But it was one thing for *me* to speak English with difficulty. It was more troubling for me to hear my parents speak in public: their high-whining vowels and guttural consonants; their sentences that got stuck with "eh" and "ah" sounds; the confused syntax; the hesitant rhythm of sounds so different

from the way *gringos* spoke. I'd notice, moreover, that my parents' voices were softer than those of *gringos* we'd meet.

15   I am tempted now to say that none of this mattered. In adulthood I am embarrassed by childhood fears. And, in a way, it didn't matter very much that my parents could not speak English with ease. Their linguistic difficulties had no serious consequences. My mother and father made themselves understood at the county hospital clinic and at government offices. And yet, in another way, it mattered very much—it was unsettling to hear my parents struggle with English. Hearing them, I'd grow nervous, my clutching trust in their protection and power weakened.

16   There were many times like the night at a brightly lit gasoline station (a blaring white memory) when I stood uneasily, hearing my father. He was talking to a teenaged attendant. I do not recall what they were saying, but I cannot forget the sounds my father made as he spoke. At one point his words slid together to form one word—sounds as confused as the threads of blue and green oil in the puddle next to my shoes. His voice rushed through what he had left to say. And, toward the end, reached falsetto notes, appealing to his listener's understanding. I looked away to the lights of passing automobiles. I tried not to hear anymore. But I heard only too well the calm, easy tones in the attendant's reply. Shortly afterward, walking toward home with my father, I shivered when he put his hand on my shoulder. The very first chance that I got, I evaded his grasp and ran on ahead into the dark, skipping with feigned boyish exuberance.

17   But then there was Spanish. *Español:* my family's language. *Español:* the language that seemed to me a private language. I'd hear strangers on the radio and in the Mexican Catholic church across town speaking in Spanish, but I couldn't really believe that Spanish was a public language, like English. Spanish speakers, rather, seemed related to me, for I sensed that we shared—through our language—the experience of feeling apart from *los gringos*. It was thus a ghetto Spanish that I heard and I spoke. Like those whose lives are bound by a barrio, I was reminded by Spanish of my separateness from *los otros, los gringos* in power. But more intensely than for most barrio children—because I did not live in a barrio—Spanish seemed to me the language of home. (Most days it was only at home that I'd hear it.) It became the language of joyful return.

18   A family member would say something to me and I would feel myself specially recognized. My parents would say something to me and I would feel embraced by the sounds of their words. Those sounds said: *I am speaking with ease in Spanish. I am addressing you in words I never use with* los gringos. *I recognize you as someone special, close, like no one outside. You belong with us. In the family.*

19   (Ricardo.)

20   At the age of five, six, well past the time when most other children no longer easily notice the difference between sounds uttered at home and words spoken in public, I had a different experience. I lived in a world magically compounded of sounds. I remained a child longer than most; I lingered too long, poised at the edge of language—often frightened by the sounds of *los gringos*, delighted by the sounds of Spanish at home. I shared with my family a language that was startlingly different from that used in the great city around us.

21   For me there were none of the gradations between public and private society so normal to a maturing child. Outside the house was public society; inside the house was private. Just opening or closing the screen door behind me was an important experience. I'd rarely leave home all alone or without reluctance. Walking down the sidewalk, under the canopy of tall trees, I'd warily notice the—suddenly—silent neighborhood kids who stood warily watching me.

DISCUSSION QUESTIONS (p. 538–539)

1. Rodriguez establishes that when he entered school English was unfamiliar to him. He knew only about fifty English words, his brother and sister spoke only Spanish outside of class, and he had never heard the English form of his name until his teacher spoke it. Later parts of the essay explore his childhood attitudes toward English and Spanish.

2. The main point is that family language—by which Rodriguez means the language of a particular household—cannot be used in the classroom because it carries with it emotions and associations that only the members of that household can know. This point is stated in paragraph 5.

3. These paragraphs reveal that the Rodriguez family members, though accepted by their neighbors, were nevertheless outsiders—separated from those around them by unease, a different lifestyle, and, perhaps most important of all, a different language. Thus the paragraphs lead smoothly to Rodriguez's examination of his early outlook toward English and Spanish.

4. To the young Rodriguez, his parents represent security in a non-Hispanic world. When he hears them struggle to express themselves in English, he has less confidence in their "protection" and "power" (paragraph 15.)

5. Rodriguez was embarrassed by his father's rather unsuccessful attempts to communicate with the English-speaking gas-station attendant. Because he has lost confidence in his father's protective powers, he temporarily rejects his parent.

6. To build a case for the special nature of a family's language, Rodriguez must first demonstrate the family's separation from white

Nervously, I'd arrive at the grocery store to hear there the sounds of the *gringo*—foreign to me—reminding me that in this world so big, I was a foreigner. But then I'd return. Walking back toward our house, climbing the steps from the sidewalk, when the front door was open in summer, I'd hear voices beyond the screen door talking in Spanish. For a second or two, I'd stay, linger there, listening. Smiling, I'd hear my mother call out, saying in Spanish (words): "Is that you, Richard?" All the while her sounds would assure me: *You are home now; come closer; inside. With us.*

22   "*Sí,*' I'd reply.

23   Once more inside the house I would resume (assume) my place in the family. The sounds would dim, grow harder to hear. Once more at home, I would grow less aware of that fact. It required, however, no more than the blurt of the doorbell to alert me to listen to sounds all over again. The house would turn instantly still while my mother went to the door. I'd hear her hard English sounds. I'd wait to hear her voice return to soft-sounding Spanish, which assured me, as surely as did the clicking tongue of the lock on the door, that the stranger was gone.

24   Plainly, it is not healthy to hear such sounds so often. It is not healthy to distinguish public words from private words so easily. I remained cloistered by sounds, timid and shy in public, too dependent on voices at home. And yet it needs to be emphasized: I was an extremely happy child at home. I remember many nights when my father would come back from work, and I'd hear him call out to my mother in Spanish, sounding relieved. In Spanish, he'd sound light and free notes he never could manage in English. Some nights I'd jump up just at hearing his voice. With *mis hermanos* I would come running into the room where he was with my mother. Our laughing (so deep was the pleasure!) became screaming. Like others who know the pain of public alienation, we transformed the knowledge of our public separateness and made it consoling—the reminder of intimacy. Excited, we joined our voices in a celebration of sounds. *We are speaking now the way we never speak out in public. We are alone—together,* voices sounded, surrounded to tell me. Some nights, no one seemed willing to loosen the hold sounds had on us. At dinner, we invented new words. (Ours sounded Spanish, but made sense only to us.) We pieced together new words by taking, say, an English verb and giving it Spanish endings. My mother's instructions at bedtime would be lacquered with mock-urgent tones. Or a word like *sí* would become, in several notes, able to convey added measures of feeling. Tongues explored the edges of words, especially the fat vowels. And we happily sounded that military drum roll, the twirling roar of the Spanish *r*. Family language: my family's sounds. The voices of my parents and sisters and brother. Their voices insisting: *You belong here. We are family members. Related. Special to one another. Listen!* Voices singing and sighing, rising, straining, then surging, teeming with pleasure that burst syllables into fragments of laughter. At times it seemed there was steady quiet only when, from another room, the rustling whispers of my parents faded and I moved closer to sleep.

Discussion Questions

1. What does Rodriguez accomplish in his first four paragraphs? What connection do you see between these paragraphs and later parts of the essay?
2. What is Rodriguez's main point? Where is it stated?
3. Discuss the significance of paragraphs 7–9.
4. Why did his parents' difficulties with English cause Rodriguez such concern?

5. In paragraph 16 Rodriguez tells us that he "looked away to the lights of passing automobiles" and that he "ran on ahead into the dark . . . ." Explain these actions.
6. Rodriguez does not begin to develop his discussion of Spanish—the private language—until paragraph 17. Why do you think this discussion didn't occur earlier in the essay?
7. Explain why the concluding paragraph is effective.

Toward Key Insights

In what ways other than those noted by Rodriguez do children and their families create or inhabit private worlds that are separate from their public worlds? What are some of the benefits and problems that result from this dichotomy? How important is language to a person's identity and social world?

Suggestion for Writing

Write a comparison essay discussing some noteworthy difference between you, or some group you belong to, and the larger public. The difference may be one of race, ethnic background, religion, or lifestyle. Demonstrate clearly how the difference affects your relationship with that public.

HENRY JENKINS

Art Form for the Digital Age

Henry Jenkins is the John E. Burchard Professor of Humanities and Director of the Comparative Media Studies graduate program at MIT. His Column "The Digital Renaissance," from which this selection was taken, is featured in the journal Technology Review *monthly.*

Video games shape our culture. It's time we took them seriously.

1   LAST YEAR, AMERICANS BOUGHT OVER 215 million computer and video games. That's more than two games per household. The video game industry made almost as much money from gross domestic income as Hollywood.

2   So are video games a massive drain on our income, time and energy? A new form of "cultural pollution," as one U.S. senator described them? The "nightmare before Christmas," in the words of another? Are games teaching our children to kill, as countless op-ed pieces have warned?

    No. Computer games are art—a popular art, an emerging art, a largely unrecognized art, but art nevertheless.

3   Over the past 25 years, games have progressed from the primitive two-paddles-and-a-ball Pong to the sophistication of Final Fantasy, a participatory story with cinema-quality graphics that unfolds over nearly 100 hours of play. The computer game has been a killer app for the home PC, increasing consumer demand for vivid graphics, rapid processing, greater memory and better sound. The release this fall of the Sony Playstation 2, coupled with the announcement of next-generation consoles by Nintendo and Microsoft, signals a dramatic increase in the resources available to game designers.

PERSPECTIVE
Comparisons often serve as arguments. This essay argues that if video games are an art form like early cinema then they merit serious critical treatment, which, in turn, would raise the artistic standards of games. This would be an excellent opportunity to discuss how when we identify similarities or differences between things, groups, or people we are making a covert argument about how they might be treated. If a rebel group is compared with terrorists, we lose sympathy. If the treatment of some illegal immigrants is compared to the treatment of slaves, we might be morally appalled. Similarly if an essay identifies the differences between Islamic nonviolent spiritual fundamentalism and violent forms of fundamentalism, we may not be as likely to treat them as the same.

Side notes: society. Reversing the order would make the paragraphs on separation seem anticlimactic. 7. Paragraph 24 reiterates the connection between a family's language and its intimate life. Note how the tone, tender and nostalgic, reinforces the connection.

4   Games increasingly influence contemporary cinema, helping to define the frenetic pace and model the multi-directional plotting of Run Lola Run, providing the role-playing metaphor for Being John Malkovich and encouraging a fascination with the slippery line between reality and digital illusion in The Matrix. At high schools and colleges across the country, students discuss games with the same passions with which earlier generations debated the merits of the New American Cinema. Media studies programs report a growing number of their students want to be game designers rather than filmmakers.

5   The time has come to take games seriously as an important new popular art shaping the aesthetic sensibility of the 21st century. I will admit that discussing the art of video games conjures up comic images: tuxedo-clad and jewel-bedecked patrons admiring the latest Streetfighter, middle-aged academics pontificating on the impact of Cubism on Tetris, bleeps and zaps disrupting our silent contemplation at the Guggenheim. Such images tell us more about our contemporary notion of art—as arid and stuffy, as the property of an educated and economic elite, as cut off from everyday experience—than they tell us about games.

6   New York's Whitney Museum found itself at the center of controversy about digital art when it recently included Web artists in its prestigious biannual show. Critics didn't believe the computer could adequately express the human spirit. But they're misguided. The computer is simply a tool, one that offers artists new resources and opportunities for reaching the public; it is human creativity that makes art. Still, one can only imagine how the critics would have responded to the idea that something as playful, unpretentious and widely popular as a computer game might be considered art.

7   In 1925, leading literary and arts critic Gilbert Seldes took a radical approach to the aesthetics of popular culture in a treatise title *The Seven Lively Arts*. Adopting what was then a controversial position, Seldes argued that America's primary contributions to artistic expression had come through emerging forms of popular culture such as jazz, the Broadway musical, the Hollywood cinema and the comic strip. While these arts have gained cultural respectability over the past 75 years, each was disreputable when Seldes staked out his position.

8   Readers then were skeptical of Seldes' claims about cinema in particular for many of the same reasons that contemporary critics dismiss games—they were suspicious of cinema's commercial motivations and technological origins, concerned about Hollywood's appeals to violence and eroticism, and insistent that cinema had not yet produced works of lasting value. Seldes, on the other hand, argued that cinema's popularity demanded that we reassess its aesthetic qualities.

9   Cinema and other popular arts were to be celebrated, Seldes said, because they were so deeply imbedded in everyday life, because they were democratic arts embraced by average citizens. Through streamlined styling and syncopated rhythms, they captured the vitality of contemporary urban experience. They took the very machinery of the industrial age, which many felt dehumanizing, and found within it the resources for expressing individual visions, for reasserting basic human needs, desires and fantasies. And these new forms were still open to experimentation and discovery. They were, in Seldes' words, "lively arts."

10   Games represent a new lively art, one as appropriate for the digital age as those earlier media were for the machine age. They open up new aesthetic experiences and transform the computer screen into a realm of experimentation and innovation that is broadly accessible. And games have been embraced by a public that has otherwise been unimpressed by much of what passes for digital art. Much as the salon arts of the 1920s seemed sterile alongside the vitality and

inventiveness of popular culture, contemporary efforts to create interactive narrative through modernist hypertext or avant-garde installation art seem lifeless and pretentious alongside the creativity that game designers bring to their craft.

11   Much of what Seldes told us about the silent cinema seems remarkably apt for thinking about games. Silent cinema, he argued, was an art of expressive movement. He valued the speed and dynamism of D.W. Griffith's last-minute races to the rescue, the physical grace of Chaplin's pratfalls and the ingenuity of Buster Keaton's engineering feats. Games also depend upon an art of expressive movement, with characters defined through their distinctive ways of propelling themselves through space, and successful products structured around a succession of spectacular stunts and predicaments. Will future generations look back on Lara Croft doing battle with a pack of snarling wolves as the 21st-century equivalent of Lillian Gish making her way across the ice floes in *Way Down East*? The art of silent cinema was also an art of atmospheric design. To watch a silent masterpiece like Fritz Lang's *Metropolis* is to be drawn into a world where meaning is carried by the placement of shadows, the movement of machinery and the organization of space. If anything, game designers have pushed beyond cinema in terms of developing expressive and fantastic environments that convey a powerful sense of mood, provoke our curiosity and amusement, and motivate us to explore.

12   Seldes wrote at a moment when cinema was maturing as an expressive medium and filmmakers were striving to enhance the emotional experience of going to the movies—making a move from mere spectacle towards character and consequence. It remains to be seen whether games can make a similar transition. Contemporary games can pump us full of adrenaline, they can make us laugh, but they have not yet provoked us to tears. And many have argued that, since games don't have characters of human complexity or stories that stress the consequences of our actions, they cannot achieve the status of true art. Here, we must be careful not to confuse the current transitional state of an emerging medium with its full potential. As I visit game companies, I see some of the industry's best minds struggling with this question and see strong evidence that the games released over the next few years will bring us closer and closer to the quality of characterization we have come to expect from other forms of popular narrative.

13   In the March 6 issue *of Newsweek*, senior editor Jack Kroll argued that audiences will probably never be able to care as deeply about pixels on the computer screen as they care about characters in films: "Moviemakers don't have to simulate human beings; they are right there, to be recorded and orchestrated. . . . The top-heavy titillation of Tomb Raider's Lara Croft falls flat next to the face of Sharon Stone. . . . Any player who's moved to tumescence by digibimbo Lara is in big trouble." Yet countless viewers cry when Bambi's mother dies, and World War II veterans can tell you they felt real lust for *Esquire's* Vargas girls. We have learned to care as much about creatures of pigment as we care about images of real people. Why should pixels be different?

14   In the end, games may not take the same path as cinema. Game designers will almost certainly develop their own aesthetic principles as they confront the challenge of balancing our competing desires for storytelling and interactivity. It remains to be seen whether games can provide players the freedom they want and still provide an emotionally satisfying and thematically meaningful shape to the experience. Some of the best games—Tetris comes to mind—have nothing to do with storytelling. For all we know, the future art of games may look more like architecture or dance than cinema.

make a list of similarities and differences between the video game and movie clip. Have them also list the ways the video game may have influenced the form of the movie.

2. In small groups, have students identify particular video games they know well and have them list the ways the games do or do not meet the author's thesis. Discuss with the class, how they might use their examples as support for the comparison in the essay or to create an essay that contradicts this one.

DISCUSSION QUESTIONS (p. 543)
1. The author compares video games with cinema to make the point that video games should be treated as art. Just as cinema was at first not seen as an art form but later became respectable, so, he suggests, video games can be seen as a respectable art.

2. The essay has several points of comparison. Games influence the shape and form of contemporary cinema; early concerns and complaints about cinema were similar to current complaints about video games; both are "democratic arts" that use the technology of the age to produce "individual visions;" each opens up new visions; both build on the same techniques of expressive movement; both can provoke a response; both share the features at their start of being experimental forms that lack a canon or solid criticism. There seems to be some truth to this comparison but one could reasonably argue that the two forms are not as close as the author thinks. After all, video games are participatory with the goal of winning while movies are meant to be viewed as an experience.

3. By referring to an earlier critic who pointed out the value of cinema when many thought it disrespectable, the author effectively suggests that the reader might equally be premature in rejecting the idea that video games are art. In effect, it answers a possible objection by the reader that might prevent the reader from following the comparison.

4. Paragraph 11 offers a more detailed point-by-point comparison between early cinema and video games with support from specific examples. This paragraph identifies plausible structural similarities between early cinema and video games, which then adds credibility to the rest of the comparison.

5. The essay points out that games currently haven't moved from spectacle to character and consequence, don't evoke the full range of emotions that movies do currently, may not end up following the same aesthetic principles as cinema, and do not always involve storytelling. By admitting these differences and in many cases suggesting that future developments could overcome current "limitations," the author adds credibility to his comparison since he has recognized and accounted for what readers might otherwise raise as objections to his essay.

15   Such questions warrant close and passionate engagement not only within the game industry or academia, but also by the press and around the dinner table. Even Kroll's grumpy dismissal of games has sparked heated discussion and forced designers to refine their own grasp of the medium's distinctive features. Imagine what a more robust form of criticism could contribute. We need critics who know games the way Pauline Kael knew movies and who write about them with an equal degree of wit and wisdom.

16   When *The Seven Lively Arts* was published, silent cinema was still an experimental form, each work stretching the medium in new directions. Early film critics played vital functions in documenting innovations and speculating about their potential. Computer games are in a similar phase. We have not had time to codify what experienced game designers know, and we have certainly not yet established a canon of great works that might serve as exemplars. There have been real creative accomplishments in games, but we haven't really sorted out what they are and why they matter.

17   But games do matter, because they spark the imaginations of our children, taking them on epic quests to strange new worlds. Games matter because our children no longer have access to real-world play spaces at a time when we've paved over the vacant lots to make room for more condos and the streets make parents nervous. If children are going to have opportunities for exploratory play, play that encourages cognitive development and fosters problem-solving skills, they will do so in the virtual environments of games. Multi-player games create opportunities for leadership, competition, teamwork and collaboration—for nerdy kids, not just for high school football players. Games matter because they form the digital equivalent of the Head Start program, getting kids excited about what computers can do.

18   The problem with most contemporary games isn't that they are violent but that they are banal, formulaic and predictable. Thoughtful criticism can marshal support for innovation and experimentation in the industry, much as good film criticism helps focus attention on neglected independent films. Thoughtful criticism could even contribute to our debates about game violence. So far, the censors and culture warriors have gotten more or less a free ride because we almost take for granted that games are culturally worthless. We should instead look at games as an emerging art form—one that does not simply simulate violence but increasingly offers new ways to understand violence—and talk about how to strike a balance between this form of expression and social responsibility. Moreover, game criticism may provide a means of holding the game industry more accountable for its choices. In the wake of the Columbine shootings, game designers are struggling with their ethical responsibilities as never before, searching for ways of appealing to empowerment fantasies that don't require exploding heads and gushing organs. A serious public discussion of this medium might constructively influence these debates, helping identify and evaluate alternatives as they emerge.

19   As the art of games matures, progress will be driven by the most creative and forward-thinking minds in the industry, those who know that games can be more than they have been, those who recognize the potential of reaching a broader public, of having a greater cultural impact, of generating more diverse and ethically responsible content and of creating richer and more emotionally engaging stories. But without the support of an informed public and the perspective of thoughtful critics, game developers may never realize that potential.

Discussion Questions

1. What seems to be the author's main purpose in comparing video games with cinema?
2. What points of comparison does the essay make between video games and cinema? Do those points of comparison seem valid?
3. What was the rhetorical advantage of referring to Gilbert Seldes' 1925 essay in paragraph 7 and 8?
4. How is paragraph 11 organized and why is this paragraph important to the overall comparison?
5. What differences does the author point out between cinema and video games? Do these differences undercut or support his main purpose?
6. In paragraph 2, the author asks whether games teach our children to kill. Does his essay answer the question, and if it does not, does this weaken his comparison-based argument?
7. The author does not mention a lot of specific games. Why might he have made that rhetorical choice? Does it weaken his comparison?

Toward Key Insights

Often comparisons can be used to see something familiar in a new way. In this case, the author is attempting to get us to see the ways video games might be an art form. How might our idea of everyday things change if we look at advertisements as art, everyday objects as sculpture, or short messages as poetry? Are such startling comparisons appropriate or useful?

The author stresses a number of similarities between video games and cinema. That can shape our perceptions. A critical response to comparisons requires us to look for points of disagreements. In what ways may video games be significantly and forever different from cinema?

Suggestions for Writing

Write about how some other popular culture events or objects might be like art. For example, basketball could be like dance; comic books could be like visual art; extreme sports could be like ballet.

Video games such as Lara Croft have been made into movies and movies such as the Matrix *have been made into video games. Compare a specific video game with its movie counterpart.*

CAUSE AND EFFECT ▬ ▬ ▬ ▬ ▬

Reading Strategies

1. Identify the main event that is trying to be explained or the event whose effects are being studied.
2. Determine whether the writer is identifying a chain of causes that yield a result or is considering multiple causes for the same event.
3. Be careful. In more sophisticated academic writing, authors often look at several causes that they try to show are not the real explanation. Only after ruling out some key explanations do they offer the explanation that they think is most plausible.

6. The essay does not fully answer the questions in paragraph 2. However, in paragraph 19, he does suggest that an alternative way of viewing video games is that they offer "new ways to understand violence." He indicates that the issue of the effect of video games needs to be discussed within the context of recognizing them as culturally worthwhile; he also suggests that further discussion of the matter is merited. Since his main point is not about the impact of video game use, the fact that he does not fully address this question does not undermine his comparison. However, some readers may feel dissatisfied that he failed to answer what they see as a fundamental problem with video games even while he seems to praise them as a newly developing art form.

7. There are several reasons the author may not have mentioned specific video games. Many of his audience may not know the games and so simple references to the games would only confuse that audience. He also wants to focus more on the development of video games and not focus simply on the current state of the art. Finally, a more detailed focus might lose the general points of the comparison in the details of specific video games. Still, many readers might be right to object that without using examples of specific

video games, his comparison is not well supported and loses some credibility.

OVERVIEW OF CAUSE-AND-EFFECT ESSAYS
All four of the essays in this section explore both causes and effects, and all have a serious tone. One (by Luscombe and Stinchfield) is informal; the others take a formal–informal approach. Two (by Tomkins and Roiphe) cite expert opinion.

4. It can be helpful to make a diagram showing the connection between the causes and the effects.

Reading Critically

1. Evaluate the evidence the writer gives for the relationship between cause and effect. How does he or she prove that the cause(s) have the effect(s) in question?
2. Try to determine if there could be other causes or effects that the writer hasn't mentioned.
3. Writers often confuse "correlation" for causation. Just because something happens before or around another event doesn't mean that it is the cause of the event. Just because George W. Bush was president when the terrorists attacked the World Trade Centers does not mean that his presidency was in any way a cause of the attack. Does the writer confuse correlation and causation?

Reading As a Writer

1. Note how the writer organizes the causes and effects to keep them clear and distinct.
2. Observe what devices the writer uses to demonstrate the connection between the causes and the effects.
3. Examine how the writer pulls his or her ideas together in the conclusion.

RICHARD TOMKINS

Old Father Time Becomes a Terror

Richard Tomkins is consumer industries editor of the Financial Times, *where he has been a member of the editorial staff since 1983. He is currently based at the company's London headquarters, where he leads a team of journalists covering the consumer goods sector and writes about consumer trends. Previously, he was the* FT*'s marketing correspondent and, from 1993 to 1999, he was a correspondent in the newspaper's New York bureau, where he covered the consumer goods sector. Earlier positions in London included writing about the transport sector and corporate news. Tomkins was born in Walsall, England, in 1952. His formal education ended at the age of seventeen. Before becoming a journalist, he was a casual laborer, a factory worker, a truck driver, a restaurant cashier, a civil servant, and an assistant private secretary to a government minister. He left government service in 1978 to hitchhike around the world, and on returning to the U.K. in 1979, joined a local newspaper as a trainee reporter. He joined the* FT *as a subeditor four years later. In this selection, Tomkins discusses the time squeeze that many people are experiencing and offers a way to combat the problem.*

PERSPECTIVE
The time pressures of modern life have spawned many books and groups urging people to abandon their current ways of living and embrace a simpler, even agrarian, lifestyle. Extreme simplicity, however, entails time problems too. For example, growing food or sewing clothes involves many hours of work. Tomkins, it would appear, offers a more workable approach to combating time pressures.

Introduction: paragraphs 1–8; compares the leisurely 1960s (paragraphs 1–5) with the time-stressed present.

1   It's barely 6:30 A.M. and already your stress levels are rising. You're late for a breakfast meeting. Your cell-phone is ringing and your pager is beeping. You have 35 messages in your e-mail, 10 calls on your Voicemail and one question on your mind.

2   Why was it never like this for Dick Van Dyke?

3   Somehow, life seemed much simpler in the 1960s. In *The Dick Van Dyke Show,* the classic American sitcom of the era, Rob Petrie's job as a television scriptwriter

was strictly nine-to-five. It was light when he left for work and light when he got home. There was no teleconferencing during his journey from the Westchester suburbs to the TV studio in Manhattan.

4   At work, deadlines loomed, but there was plenty of time for banter around the office typewriter. There was no Internet, no Voicemail, no fax machine, no CNN. The nearest Petrie came to information overload was listening to a stream of wisecracks from his colleague Buddy Sorrell about Mel, the bald producer.

5   Meanwhile, at home, Rob's wife Laura—Mary Tyler Moore—led a life of leisure. After packing little Richie off to school, she had little to do but gossip with Millie, the next-door neighbour, and prepare the evening meal. When Rob came home, the family sat down to dinner: then it was television, and off to bed.

6   Today, this kind of life seems almost unimaginable. The demands on our time seem to grow ever heavier. Technology has made work portable, allowing it to merge with our personal lives. The nine-to-five job is extinct: in the U.S. people now talk about the 24–7 job, meaning one that requires your commitment 24 hours a day, seven days a week.

7   Home life has changed, too. Laura and Millie no longer have time for a gossip: they are vice-presidents at a bank. Richie's after-school hours are spent at karate classes and Chinese lessons. The only person at home any more is Buddy, who went freelance six months ago after being de-layered by Mel.

8   New phrases have entered the language to express the sense that we are losing control of our lives. "Time famine" describes the mismatch between things to do and hours to do them in, and "multi-tasking" the attempt to reconcile the two. If multi-tasking works, we achieve "time deepening," making better use of the time available: but usually it proves inadequate, resulting in "hurry sickness" and an increasingly desperate search for "life balance" as the sufferer moves closer to break-down.

9   It was not supposed to be this way. Technology, we thought, would make our lives easier. Machines were expected to do our work for us, leaving us with ever-increasing quantities of time to fritter away on idleness and pleasure.

10   But instead of liberating us, technology has enslaved us. Innovations are occurring at a bewildering rate: as many now arrive in a year as once arrived in a millennium. And as each invention arrives, it eats further into our time.

> Body: paragraphs 10–31

11   The motor car, for example, promised unimaginable levels of personal mobility. But now, traffic in cities moves more slowly than it did in the days of the horse-drawn carriage, and we waste our lives immobilized by congestion.

> First cause and specific effects of time stress, paragraphs 10–14: technological innovations

12   The aircraft promised new horizons, too. The trouble is, it delivered them. Its very existence created a demand for time-consuming journeys that we would never previously have dreamed of undertaking—the transatlantic shopping expedition, for example, or the trip to a convention on the other side of the world.

13   In most cases, technology has not saved time, but enabled us to do more things. In the home, washing machines promised to free women from the drudgery of the laundry. In reality, they encouraged us to change our clothes daily instead of weekly, creating seven times as much washing and ironing. Similarly, the weekly bath has been replaced by the daily shower, multiplying the hours spent on personal grooming.

14   Meanwhile, technology has not only allowed work to spread into our leisure time—the laptop-on-the-beach syndrome—but added the new burden of dealing with faxes, e-mails and Voicemails. It has also provided us with the opportunity to spend hours fixing software glitches on our personal computers or filling our heads with useless information from the Internet.

15   Technology apart, the Internet points the way to a second reason why we
feel so time-pressed: the information explosion.

16   A couple of centuries ago, nearly all the world's accumulated learning could
be contained in the heads of a few philosophers. Today, those heads could not
hope to accommodate more than a tiny fraction of the information generated in
a single day.

17   News, facts and opinions pour in from every corner of the world. The television set offers 150 channels. There are millions of Internet sites. Magazines,
books and CD-Roms proliferate.

18   "In the whole world of scholarship, there were only a handful of scientific
journals in the 18th century, and the publication of a book was an event," says
Edward Wilson, honorary curator in entomology at Harvard University's
museum of comparative zoology. "Now, I find myself subscribing to 60 or 70 journals or magazines just to keep me up with what amounts to a minute proportion
of the expanding frontiers of scholarship."

19   There is another reason for our increased stress levels, too: rising prosperity.
As ever-larger quantities of goods and services are produced, they have to be consumed. Driven on by advertising, we do our best to oblige: we buy more, travel
more and play more, but we struggle to keep up. So we suffer from what Wilson
calls discontent with super abundance—the confusion of endless choice.

20   Of course, not everyone is overstressed. "It's a convenient shorthand to say
we're all time-starved, but we have to remember that it only applies to, say, half
the population," says Michael Willmott, director of the Future Foundation, a
London research company.

21   "You've got people retiring early, you've got the unemployed, you've got
other people maybe only peripherally involved in the economy who don't have
this situation at all. If you're unemployed, your problem is that you've got too
much time, not too little."

22   Paul Edwards, chairman of the London-based Henley Centre forecasting
group, points out that the feeling of pressures can also be exaggerated, or self-
imposed. "Everyone talks about it so much that about 50 percent of unemployed
or retired people will tell you they never have enough time to get things done,"
he says. "It's almost got to the point where there's stress envy. If you're not
stressed, you're not succeeding. Everyone wants to have a little bit of this stress to
show they're an important person."

23   There is another aspect to all of this too. Hour-by-hour logs kept by thousands of volunteers over the decades have shown that, in the U.K., working hours
have risen only slightly in the last 10 years, and in the U.S., they have actually
fallen—even for those in professional and executive jobs, where the perceptions
of stress are highest.

24   In the U.S., John Robinson, professor of sociology at the University of
Maryland, and Geoffrey Godbey, professor of leisure studies at Penn State
University, both time-use experts, found that, since the mid-1960s, the average
American had gained five hours a week in free time—that is, time left after work-
ing, sleeping, commuting, caring for children and doing the chores.

25   The gains, however, were unevenly distributed. The people who benefited
the most were singles and empty-nesters. Those who gained the least—less than
an hour—were working couples with pre-school children, perhaps reflecting the
trend for parents to spend more time nurturing their offspring.

26   There is, of course, a gender issue here, too. Advances in household appliances may have encouraged women to take paying jobs: but as we have already

noted, technology did not end household chores. As a result, we see appalling inequalities in the distribution of free time between the sexes. According to the Henley Centre, working fathers in the U.K. average 48 hours of free time a week. Working mothers get 14.

27   Inequalities apart, the perception of the time famine is widespread, and has provoked a variety of reactions. One is an attempt to gain the largest possible amount of satisfaction from the smallest possible investment of time. People today want fast food, sound bytes and instant gratification. And they become upset when time is wasted.

> First general effect of time stress, paragraphs 27–28: maximizing pleasure in minimum time

28   "People talk about quality time. They want perfect moments," says the Henley Centre's Edwards. "If you take your kids to a movie and McDonald's and it's not perfect, you've wasted an afternoon, and it's a sense that you've lost something precious. If you lose some money you can earn some more, but if you waste time you can never get it back."

29   People are also trying to buy time. Anything that helps streamline our lives is a growth market. One example is what Americans call concierge services—domestic help, child care, gardening and decorating. And on-line retailers are seeing big increases in sales—though not, as yet, profits.

> Second general effect: buying time

30   A third reaction to time famine has been the growth of the work-life debate. You hear more about people taking early retirement or giving up high pressure jobs in favour of occupations with shorter working hours. And bodies such as Britain's National Work-Life Forum have sprung up, urging employers to end the long-hours culture among managers—"presenteeism"—and to adopt family-friendly working policies.

> Third general effect: re-evaluating jobs, long work hours

31   The trouble with all these reactions is that liberating time—whether by making better use of it, buying it from others or reducing the amount spent at work—is futile if the hours gained are immediately diverted to other purposes.

32   As Godbey points out, the stress we feel arises not from a shortage of time, but from the surfeit of things we try to cram into it. "It's the kid in the candy store," he says. "There's just so many good things to do. The array of choices is stunning. Our free time is increasing, but not as fast as our sense of the necessary."

> Conclusion: paragraphs 32–36; sources of time stress; author's solution to the problem

33   A more successful remedy may lie in understanding the problem rather than evading it.

34   Before the industrial revolution, people lived in small communities with limited communications. Within the confines of their village, they could reasonably expect to know everything that was to be known, see everything that was to be seen, and do everything that was to be done.

35   Today, being curious by nature, we are still trying to do the same. But the global village is a world of limitless possibilities, and we can never achieve our aim.

36   It is not more time we need: it is fewer desires. We need to switch off the cellphone and leave the children to play by themselves. We need to buy less, read less and travel less. We need to set boundaries for ourselves, or be doomed to mounting despair.

Discussion Questions

DISCUSSION QUESTIONS

1. The thesis statement is the first sentence of paragraph 10. It is positioned at this point because it allows Tomkins to first show in some detail how time stress is much greater today than in a previous era, which leads to his contention that technology has produced results the opposite to what was expected.

2. The parallel construction of this sentence emphasizes the importance of these innovations in helping create the current time bind.

1. Identify the thesis statement of this essay and suggest why it is located at this spot.
2. The following sentence appears in paragraph 4: "There is no Internet, no Voicemail, no fax machine, no CNN." What does the structure of this sentence accomplish?

3. Tomkins uses irony to indicate ways in which technology has increased rather than alleviated our time stress. Students should learn to recognize irony and perhaps sometimes use it.

4. The phrase can, of course, be explained in various ways, but we suggest something similar to the following: "Such a broad array of options is perplexing and does little to satisfy individual needs." To illustrate, consider the broad array of computers, travel options, and brands of clothing available to potential purchasers. The examples that students supply should spark a lively discussion and perhaps lead to a writing assignment.

5. Omitting this information might lead some readers to conclude that everyone is a victim of time pressure. Students should learn that key omissions can create inaccurate impressions.

3. Reread paragraph 14 and then suggest Tomkins's intention in using the word "opportunity."

4. Explain the meaning of "the confusion of endless choice" at the end of paragraph 19. Then suggest examples that illustrate this idea.

5. Why do you think Tomkins calls attention to groups that are unstressed (paragraph 21) and to studies showing the time gains for average Americans?

Toward Key Insights

Regarding the essay's final sentence, what type of boundaries do you think time-stressed individuals should set?

How can people establish these boundaries without sacrificing quality of life?

Suggestion for Writing

Write an essay discussing the causes and/or effects of some type of stress other than time stress. Possibilities might include academic or financial stress or the stress associated with personal relationships. Develop your paper with appropriate examples.

CAROLINE KNAPP

Why We Keep Stuff: If You Want to Understand People, Take a Look at What They Hang On To

Caroline Knapp, a humane and thoughtful writer, died at the age of 42 in 2002. She worked for the Phoenix newspapers as staff writer, editor, and contributing columnist. This essay is taken from The Merry Recluse: A Life in Essay—*a collection of some of the best of Knapp's writing.*

PERSPECTIVE
This is a personal reflective essay that combines the intimacy of a very personal reflection tied to the details of an individual's life and more general observations about human behaviors. Some have argued that such essays do an excellent job of showing the relationship of the individual and the universal, making general principles very personal. It is important to compare

1   Stuff, stuff, I AM surrounded by stuff. Stuff I don't need, stuff I don't use, but stuff I feel compelled to keep. Here in my office, as I write this, I am drowning in a sea of stuff.

2   There is the stuff of procrastination—piles of letters I should answer, manuscripts I should return, memos I should file away.

3   There is the stuff of daily business—interoffice communications in one heap here, this form and that form in that heap there, bills in yet another.

4   But mostly, there is the more generalized stuff, the stuff we all hold on to for inexplicable reasons—the stuff, in other words, of which stuff is made. Old catalogs of stuff I *might* want to order someday. Old magazines I *might* want to read, or reread. Unsolicited freelance articles I *might* want to publish. And even more useless stuff, stuff with no discernible purpose or future value.

5   On one corner of a shelf hangs a bunch of ribbons, saved over the years from various packages. On another, a pile of old letters from readers that I'll no doubt never open again and never answer. On my desk, a Rolodex crammed

with numbers I'll never call (the National Association of Theater Operators? The Detroit office of the National Transportation Union? *Huh?*). In one corner, I even have a pile of envelopes containing transaction slips from the automatic teller machine that date all the way back to February 1988. That's more than three years of bank slips—stuff, pure and simple.

6   Yet in an odd way, a lot of the stuff has meaning. Granted, the significance of a pile of old ribbons may be minimal, but I think the things that people choose to hang on to, and the ways they hang on to them, are quite telling—small testimonies to the ways people organize their lives on both external and internal levels. Want to understand people a little more clearly? Look through their stuff.

. . .

7   Several years ago, as I was preparing to move out of an apartment I'd lived in for four years, I undertook my first major purge of stuff, which provided an excellent lesson in the nature of the beast. Historically, I've been a relentless pack rat, the sort of person who keeps vast numbers of relics and mementos in vast numbers of boxes around the house—ticket stubs to concerts and movies; store receipts for goods and clothing I'd long ago stopped thinking about returning; letters from people I'd long ago lost track of; even old shoes. But moving out of that particular apartment was a big step—I was leaving a place where I'd lived alone (with plenty of room for stuff) and into a new apartment—and presumably, a new life—with a man (who had much less room for stuff).

8   Accordingly, the purge was more than a logistical necessity; it also had a certain psychological value. Sure, it made sense to get rid of a lot of it: I didn't really need to hang on to that broken toaster-oven, or that tattered coat I'd stopped wearing years before. I didn't need to save the letter of acceptance from the graduate school I'd long ago decided not to attend. I didn't need the three boxes of back issues of *Gourmet* magazine. But divesting myself of all that stuff meant much more than whittling down my possessions to a manageable degree.

9   At one point, I remember going through a dresser in which I kept several pairs of jeans that I'd worn during a long and protracted struggle with anorexia. They were tiny jeans in tiny, skeletal sizes, jean with bad associations, jeans with no place in the life of someone who was trying to launch into a healthier way of living. But I'd held on to them for years and, in doing so, had held on to a set of possibilities: that I might one day need those tiny, cigarette-legged jeans again; that I might one day fit into them; and accordingly, that what I felt to be my "recovery" from anorexia might be tenuous at best, false at worst.

10   The message hidden away in that dresser drawer had to do with fear, and, needless to say, throwing out the clothes from that earlier time was an enormously healthy move: it was part of an effort to say good-bye to a person I used to be.

11   And so it is with most of our stuff: the things we keep stored away in our closets and shelves often mirror the things we hold on to inside: fears, memories, dreams, false perceptions. A good deal of that stuff in my office, for example, speaks to an abiding terror of screwing up, a fear that I might actually *need* one of those articles from one of those old magazines, or one of those old phone numbers from the Rolodex, or one of those memos or letters or whatever.

12   Lurking behind the automatic-teller-machine slips? My relentless fear of finance, and the accompanying conviction that as soon as I toss them all out, the bank will call and inform me that some huge deposit I could once verify has disappeared. Even the pile of ribbons on the shelf reflects some vague anxiety, a (comparatively minor and obsessive) worry—that one of these days, I'll have a present to wrap and (gasp) there'll be no ribbon at hand to tie it up. My mother keeps a

the advantages and disadvantages of this kind of essay with a more scientific or general account that is less personal.

TEACHING STRATEGIES

1. Bring in a textbook analysis of the causes of human behavior such as kleptomania and have students identify the different values of the textbook account and the personal reflective essay.

2. In advance of having students read the essay, have students make a list of the things they keep and the reasons they don't get rid of them. Then, after students read the essay, have them compare their causes with the author's.

3. This essay uses precise personal examples to make its point. Cut out all but the most general claims and then read the edited essay. Discuss what may have been lost by such a revision.

4. In an age of experts, are our personal explanations which may not be immediately validated by scientific inquiry at all worthwhile? Discuss whether, since they have no scientific foundation, the author's thoughts on why she keeps things has any value and if so why?

CLASSROOM ACTIVITIES

1. Have the students work in groups to revise this essay so that it avoids the use of I entirely but instead reads much more like an objective essay. Discuss with the class whether the revision changes any of the major points of the essay.

2. Have students come to class with a list of things that they "keep." In pairs, have the pair partner try to determine what the "keep" list tells them about the person, if anything. Share the conclusions with the originator of the "keep" list. This can lead to a discussion of whether or not the author's causes are valid.

3. In small groups, have students generate possible alternative causes for why people do keep unnecessary things such as clothes that no longer fit, old magazines, ticket stubs, and so on. Discuss whether there are any additional causes that are not covered in the essay. If there are other possible explanations for this behavior, does this contradict the author's explanations?

DISCUSSION QUESTIONS

1. Personal reflective essays allow the writer to think through their own direction for their own life in a way that relates those experiences to broader human experience. Such essays provide readers with a different perspective on life that might help them gain a perspective on their own life. Essays, such as this one, present broader, more general themes through the specifics of an individual's experience.

2. The key thesis is that what people keep tells us a lot about what they are like. This statement is in paragraph 6.

huge basket at home filled with nothing but rubber bands, and I'm sure she holds on to it for the same reasons: it speaks to an absolute certainty on her part that the moment she throws them away, she'll find herself in desperate need of an elastic.

13 We might need it. We might miss it. It might come back in style and we might want to wear it again. If getting rid of stuff is hard, it's because it feels like cutting off options. Or sides of ourselves. Or pieces of our history. And, the actual value of holding on to stuff notwithstanding, those things can be unsettling to give up. The movie and ticket stubs I'd kept stored away for years in my old apartment, for example, reflected good times, happy moments in relationships that I didn't want to forget; the ragged coat was a piece of clothing I'd felt pretty in, a feeling I didn't want to lose; the *Gourmet* magazines held out hopes for my (then sorely lacking) kitchen skills. Even the broken toaster-oven contained a memory—I'd bought it almost a decade earlier, with a man I'd been involved with, during a very happy year we'd lived together.

14 The trick, I suppose, is to learn to manage stuff, the same way you learn to manage fears and feelings. To throw a little logic into the heaps of stuff. To think a little rationally. Would the world really come crashing down if I tossed out some crucial phone number? Would my personal history really get tossed into the trash along with my mementos? Would I die, or even suffer a mite, without all those ribbons?

15 No, probably not. But I think I'll keep holding on to those bank slips . . . just in case.

BOSTON PHOENIX
JUNE 1991

Discussion Questions

1. What is the value of a personal reflective essay such as this one for writer and reader?

2. What is the real thesis of this essay and where is it located?

3. What role do the several paragraphs detailing the kinds of clutter the author has failed to discard play in the full essay? Why did she spend so much time describing her stuff?

4. What does the author see as the dominant cause for why people fail to discard things? How does the more general cause relate to many other more specific causes?

5. In what ways does this writer sustain a personal and even intimate tone with her readers? Is this effective?

6. How do the final two paragraphs fit the essay?

Toward Key Insights

This essay provides an excellent example of a personal reflective essay. As a result, the author's discussion of why we keep certain things is not scientific. What might be the advantages of this kind of essay over a psychological study of why people retain certain items? What are some weaknesses of this kind of writing?

In the personal reflective essay, writers share with their readers more personal elements of their thoughts and lives, such as Caroline Knapp's discussion of her past struggle with anorexia. How do such intimate revelations affect readers and their relationship with the text?

Suggestion for Writing

Write a personal reflective essay to explain what you think cause some personal behaviors or emotional states, such as procrastination or impulse shopping, for readers who may share those behaviors.

ANNE ROIPHE

Why Marriages Fail

A native of New York City, Anne Roiphe was born in 1935 and earned a BA degree from Sarah Lawrence College in 1957. In a writing career spanning more than three decades, she has produced nearly a dozen works of fiction and nonfiction centering on such matters as alienation, divorce, religious tradition, children's emotional health, and the conflicts arising from the demands of family and the desire for independence. Her many periodical articles reflect these as well as similar concerns. In this essay Roiphe examines the forces leading to marital breakup.

1   These days so many marriages end in divorce that our most sacred vows no longer ring with truth. "Happily ever after" and "Till death do us part" are expressions that seem on the way to becoming obsolete. Why has it become so hard for couples to stay together? What goes wrong? What has happened to us that close to one-half of all marriages are destined for the divorce courts? How could we have created a society in which 42 percent of our children will grow up in single-parent homes? If statistics could only measure loneliness, regret, pain, loss of self-confidence and fear of the future, the numbers would be beyond quantifying.

2   Even though each broken marriage is unique, we can still find the common perils, the common causes for marital despair. Each marriage has crisis points and each marriage tests endurance, the capacity for both intimacy and change. Outside pressures such as job loss, illness, infertility, trouble with a child, care of aging parents and all the other plagues of life hit marriage the way hurricanes blast our shores. Some marriages survive these storms and others don't. Marriages fail, however, not simply because of the outside weather but because the inner climate becomes too hot or too cold, too turbulent or too stupefying.

3   When we look at how we choose our partners and what expectations exist at the tender beginnings of romance, some of the reasons for disaster become quite clear. We all select with unconscious accuracy a mate who will recreate with us the emotional patterns of our first homes. Dr. Carl A. Whitaker, a marital therapist and emeritus professor of psychiatry at the University of Wisconsin, explains, "From early childhood on, each of us carried models for marriage, femininity, masculinity, motherhood, fatherhood and all the other family roles." Each of us falls in love with a mate who has qualities of our parents, who will help us rediscover both the psychological happiness and miseries of our past lives. We may think we have found a man unlike Dad, but then he turns to drink or drugs, or loses his job over and over again or sits silently in front of the TV just the way Dad did. A man may choose a woman who doesn't like kids just like his mother or who gambles away the family savings just like his mother. Or he may choose a

---

3. The description of the things that Ms. Knapp owns accomplishes several things. It gives us a clear sense of her personality, part of the thesis of the essay. It also shows the reader that the writer probably is like most of us, making her claims more credible. It also makes it reasonable to ask why someone would keep what might seem useless things.

4. The author in paragraph 10 identifies fear as the dominant cause for our pack rat tendencies, which she extends in paragraph 11 to include memories, dreams, and false perceptions. There are many kinds of fear that the author then identifies as causes for why she keeps specific things: fear of screwing up, fear of finance, fear of cutting off options.

5. The writer uses several devices to keep the essay personal. She discusses topics that are personal such as her anorexia, the kinds of idiosyncratic things she keeps, and her admission of personal fears. She uses a confessional use of "I" as in "I didn't need to save the acceptance letter . . ." She uses informal vocabulary such as the word "stuff" and occasional short sentences that keeps the tone informal. There is more than one kind of response to this kind of writing. Some readers may feel a personal connection with the writer that they find rewarding. Others, however, may feel as if the essay forces a kind of intimacy they would rather not experience and would prefer, instead, a more formal and less personal essay.

6. The final two paragraphs serve as a logical extension of the essay. If we keep things out of fear, we can trim clutter by keeping the consequences of throwing things out in perspective. However, given the use of phrases such as "trick," "suppose," and "would the world really," it is deliberately left ambiguous whether the author will change. This can make the reader speculate a little more about the character of the writer and the likelihood of change.

PERSPECTIVE

America's high divorce rate and its accompanying problems figure strongly in the current discussion of family values. Alarmed by what's happened, some individuals have called for a tightening of current divorce laws. This approach, while keeping more couples together, would do nothing to make marriages happier. Roiphe's assessment of marriage difficulties and how to deal with them does offer the hope of better marriages—if couples, by themselves or through counseling, come to recognize and heed such advice.

TEACHING STRATEGIES

1. You might ask students whether dating relationships experience the same "crisis points" (paragraph 2) as marriages do, and if so, how to cope

4

5

6

7

8

9

10

slender wife who seems unlike his obese mother but then turns out to have other addictions that destroy their mutual happiness.

A man and a woman bring to their marriage bed a blended concoction of conscious and unconscious memories of their parents' lives together. The human way is to compulsively repeat and recreate the patterns of the past. Sigmund Freud so well described the unhappy design that many of us get trapped in: the unmet needs of childhood, the angry feelings left over from frustrations of long ago, the limits of trust and the recurrence of old fears. Once an individual senses this entrapment, there may follow a yearning to escape, and the result could be a broken, splintered marriage.

Of course people can overcome the habits and attitudes that developed in childhood. We all have hidden strengths and amazing capacities for growth and creative change. Change, however, requires work—observing your part in a rotten pattern, bringing difficulties out into the open—and work runs counter to the basic myth of marriage: "When I wed this person all my problems will be over. I will have achieved success and I will become the center of life for this other person and this person will be my center, and we will mean everything to each other forever." This myth, which every marriage relies on, is soon exposed. The coming of children, the pulls and tugs of their demands on affection and time, place a considerable strain on that basic myth of meaning everything to each other, of merging together and solving all of life's problems.

Concern and tension about money take each partner away from the other. Obligations to demanding parents or still-depended-upon parents create further strain. Couples today must also deal with all the cultural changes brought on in recent years by the women's movement and the sexual revolution. The altering of roles and the shifting of responsibilities have been extremely trying for many marriages.

These and other realities of life erode the visions of marital bliss the way sandstorms eat at rock and the ocean nibbles away at the dunes. Those euphoric, grand feelings that accompany romantic love are really self-delusions, self-hypnotic dreams that enable us to forge a relationship. Real life, failure at work, disappointments, exhaustion, bad smells, bad colds and hard times all puncture the dream and leave us stranded with our mate, with our childhood patterns pushing us this way and that, with our unfulfilled expectations.

The struggle to survive in marriage requires adaptability, flexibility, genuine love and kindness and an imagination strong enough to feel what the other is feeling. Many marriages fall apart because either partner cannot imagine what the other wants or cannot communicate what he or she needs or feels. Anger builds until it erupts into a volcanic burst that buries the marriage in ash.

It is not hard to see, therefore, how essential communication is for a good marriage. A man and a woman must be able to tell each other how they feel and why they feel the way they do; otherwise they will impose on each other roles and actions that lead to further unhappiness. In some cases, the communication patterns of childhood—of not talking, of talking too much, of not listening, of distrust and anger, of withdrawal—spill into the marriage and prevent a healthy exchange of thoughts and feelings. The answer is to set up new patterns of communication and intimacy.

At the same time, however, we must see each other as individuals. "To achieve a balance between separateness and closeness is one of the major psychological tasks of all human beings at every stage of life," says Dr. Stuart Bartle, a psychiatrist at the New York University Medical Center.

11   If we sense from our mate a need for too much intimacy, we tend to push him or her away, fearing that we may lose our identities in the merging of marriage. One partner may suffocate the other partner in a childlike dependency.

12   A good marriage means growing as a couple but also growing as individuals. This isn't easy. Richard gives up his interest in carpentry because his wife, Helen, is jealous of the time he spends away from her. Karen quits her choir group because her husband dislikes the friends she makes there. Each pair clings to each other and are angry with each other as life closes in on them. This kind of marital balance is easily thrown as one or the other pulls away and divorce follows.

13   Sometimes people pretend that a new partner will solve the old problems. Most often extramarital sex destroys a marriage because it allows an artificial split between the good and the bad—the good is projected on the new partner and the bad is dumped on the head of the old. Dishonesty, hiding and cheating create walls between men and women. Infidelity is just a symptom of trouble. It is a symbolic complaint, a weapon of revenge, as well as an unraveler of closeness. Infidelity is often that proverbial last straw that sinks the camel to the ground.

14   All right—marriage has always been difficult. Why then are we seeing so many divorces at this time? Yes, our modern social fabric is thin, and yes the permissiveness of society has created unrealistic expectations and thrown the family into chaos. But divorce is so common because people today are unwilling to exercise the self-discipline that marriage requires. They expect easy joy, like the entertainment on TV, the thrill of a good party.

15   Marriage takes some kind of sacrifice, not dreadful self-sacrifice of the soul, but some level of compromise. Some of one's fantasies, some of one's legitimate desires have to be given up for the value of the marriage itself. "While all marital partners feel shackled at times it is they who really choose to make the marital ties into confining chains or supporting bonds," says Dr. Whitaker. Marriage requires sexual, financial and emotional discipline. A man and a woman cannot follow every impulse, cannot allow themselves to stop growing or changing.

16   Divorce is not an evil act. Sometimes it provides salvation for people who have grown hopelessly apart or were frozen in patterns of pain or mutual unhappiness. Divorce can be, despite its initial devastation, like the first cut of the surgeon's knife, a step toward new health and a good life. On the other hand, if the partners can stay past the breaking up of the romantic myths into the development of real love and intimacy, they have achieved a work as amazing as the greatest cathedrals of the world. Marriages that do not fail but improve, that persist despite imperfections, are not only rare these days but offer a wondrous shelter in which the face of our mutual humanity can safely show itself.

Discussion Questions

1. State in your own words what Roiphe means when she remarks at the end of paragraph 1, "If statistics could only measure loneliness, regret, pain, loss of self-confidence and fear of the future, the numbers would be beyond quantifying."
2. In which paragraphs does Roiphe cite expert opinion? Why do you think she includes it?
3. What is accomplished by using the short sentence "This isn't easy" in paragraph 12?
4. What additional reasons can you cite for marriage failure?

with them. A writing assignment could follow.

2. Have students discuss why dating or marriage relationships succeed, and then follow the discussion with a writing assignment.

3. Ask students the extent to which they agree with the statement "The human way is to compulsively repeat and recreate the patterns of the past" (paragraph 4). A writing assignment could follow.

4. Students could discuss what is meant by achieving "a balance between separateness and closeness" (paragraph 10) and could provide concrete examples of how this might be accomplished. A writing assignment could follow.

DISCUSSION QUESTIONS

1. Possibilities might be something like "As bad as the statistics for divorce and single-parent families may be, the emotional consequences are incomparably worse" or "Statistics cannot measure the emotional consequences of family breakups." Other similar statements are, of course, possible.

2. Expert opinion, cited in paragraphs 3, 4, 10, and 15, suggests that Roiphe has researched her topic and lends an air of authority to her views. Students should understand that properly documented information obtained from their reading can provide excellent support for their ideas.

3. The short sentence contrasts markedly with the longer surrounding sentences, giving it greater force and therefore emphasizing the importance of Roiphe's comments about the challenges of marriage.

4. This question should result in an interesting discussion, which could be followed by a writing assignment.

Toward Key Insights

Which of the causes of marital breakdown do you consider most important? Why? What are the most essential things that couples can do to help lower the divorce rate?

Suggestion for Writing

Write an essay explaining why certain individuals do well (or poorly) at forming friendships. Develop your causes with relevant specific details.

BELINDA LUSCOMBE AND KATE STINCHFIELD

Why We Flirt

Often writers work together to create an article, especially in journalism but also in academic settings. Belinda Luscombe has been a Senior Editor for Time *magazine since April 1999. She started in journalism at* The Daily Telegraph *in Sidney, Australia. She joined* Time *in 1995. Her work also appears in* Sports Illustrated, Fortune, Mademoiselle, Vogue, *the* New York Times *and many other publications.*

Kate Stinchfield is a productive freelance writer who often writes for Time. *Other articles by her include "Early Bird or Night Owl? Brain Scans Show the Difference." and "The Science of Risk Taking."*

This article was published in Time *in January 2008.*

PERSPECTIVE

This essay offers a serious analysis of human behavior in a very informal and even flippant style. This is a long-standing trend in a range of periodicals that students likely encounter. It is worthwhile examining how we process information when presented in this manner rather than in a more formal language. The key question is whether the approach devalues the explanation or not.

TEACHING STRATEGIES

1. Before the students read the article, have them work in small groups to describe flirtatious behavior and offer their own explanation for why people flirt. Discuss the results as a large class. Maintain the results and then compare them with the claims of the authors.

2. Have students observe and report to class the ways FaceBook is or is not used to flirt.

3. Have students work in small groups to identify why some people, contrary to the conclusion of the

1   That smile! That glance! That rapt attention! We flirt even when we don't need to. And that can be good.

2   Contrary to widespread belief, only two very specific types of people flirt: those who are single and those who are married. Single people flirt because, well, they're single and therefore nobody is really contractually obliged to talk to them, sleep with them or scratch that difficult-to-reach part of the back. But married people, they're a tougher puzzle. They've found themselves a suitable—maybe even superior—mate, had a bit of productive fun with the old gametes and ensured that at least some of their genes are carried into the next generation. They've done their duty, evolutionarily speaking. Their genome will survive. Yay them. So for Pete's sake, why do they persist with the game?

3   And before you claim, whether single or married, that you never flirt, bear in mind that it's not just talk we're dealing with here. It's gestures, stance, eye movement. Notice how you lean forward to the person you're talking to and tip up your heels? Notice the quick little eyebrow raise you make, the sidelong glance coupled with the weak smile you give, the slightly sustained gaze you offer? If you're a woman, do you feel your head tilting to the side a bit, exposing either your soft, sensuous neck or, looking at it another way, your jugular? If you're a guy, are you keeping your body in an open, come-on-attack-me position, arms positioned to draw the eye to your impressive lower abdomen?

4   Scientists call all these little acts "contact-readiness" cues, because they indicate, nonverbally, that you're prepared for physical engagement. (More general body language is known as "nonverbal leakage." Deep in their souls, all scientists

are poets.) These cues are a crucial part of what's known in human-ethology circles as the "heterosexual relationship initiation process" and elsewhere, often on the selfsame college campuses, as "coming on to someone." In primal terms, they're physical signals that you don't intend to dominate, nor do you intend to flee—both useful messages potential mates need to send before they can proceed to that awkward talking phase. They're the opening line, so to speak, for the opening line.

5   One of the reasons we flirt in this way is that we can't help it. We're programmed to do it, whether by biology or culture. The biology part has been investigated by any number of researchers. Ethologist Irenaus Eibl Eibesfeldt, then of the Max Planck Institute in Germany, filmed African tribes in the 1960s and found that the women there did the exact same prolonged stare followed by a head tilt away with a little smile that he saw in America. (The technical name for the head movement is a "cant." Except in this case it's more like "can.")

6   Evolutionary biologists would suggest that those individuals who executed flirting maneuvers most adeptly were more successful in swiftly finding a mate and reproducing and that the behavior therefore became widespread in all humans. "A lot of people feel flirting is part of the universal language of how we communicate, especially nonverbally," says Jeffry Simpson, director of the social psychology program at the University of Minnesota.

7   Simpson is currently studying the roles that attraction and flirting play during different times of a woman's ovulation cycle. His research suggests that women who are ovulating are more attracted to flirty men. "The guys they find appealing tend to have characteristics that are attractive in the short term, which include some flirtatious behaviors," he says. He's not sure why women behave this way, but it follows that men who bed ovulating women have a greater chance of procreating and passing on those flirty genes, which means those babies will have more babies, and so on. Of course, none of this is a conscious choice, just as flirting is not always intentional. "With a lot of it, especially the nonverbal stuff, people may not be fully aware that they're doing it," says Simpson. "You don't see what you look like. People may emit flirtatious cues and not be fully aware of how powerful they are."

Flirting with Intent

8   Well, some people anyway. But then there are the rest of you. You know who you are. You're the gentleman who delivered my groceries the other day and said we had a problem because I had to be 21 to receive alcohol. You're me when I told that same man that I liked a guy who knew his way around a dolly. (Lame, I know. I was caught off guard.) You're the fifty something guy behind me on the plane before Christmas telling his fortysomething seatmate how sensual her eyes were—actually, I hope you're not, because if so, you're really skeevy. My point is, once you move into the verbal phase of flirtation, it's pretty much all intentional.

9   And there are some schools of thought that teach there's nothing wrong with that. Flirtation is a game we play, a dance for which everyone knows the moves. "People can flirt outrageously without intending anything," says independent sex researcher Timothy Perper, who has been researching flirting for 30 years. "Flirting captures the interest of the other person and says 'Would you like to play?'" And one of the most exhilarating things about the game is that the normal rules of social interaction are rubberized. Clarity is not the point. "Flirting opens a window of potential. Not yes, not no," says Perper. "So we engage ourselves in this complex game of maybe." The game is not new. The first

article, may resist flirting. Discuss as a large group what those reasons might be and whether or not the behavior of people who do not respond to flirtation needs to be explained or only flirtation.

CLASSROOM ACTIVITIES

1. Have students work in groups to write a few paragraphs as they might appear in the textbook. Discuss the ways they as readers might process the two different approaches. Which would they take as more serious? Which would they be more likely to retain the explanation? Why?

2. Have students who volunteer to act out what they see as flirtatious behavior. Have students jot down how they react to such behavior and discuss as a class.

published guide for how to flirt was written about 2,000 years ago, Perper points out, by a bloke named Ovid. As dating books go, *The Art of Love* leaves more recent publications like *The Layguide: How to Seduce Women More Beautiful Than You Ever Dreamed Possible No Matter What You Look Like or How Much You Make* in its dust. And yes, that's a real book.

10   Once we've learned the game of maybe, it becomes second nature to us. Long after we need to play it, we're still in there swinging (so to speak) because we're better at it than at other games. Flirting sometimes becomes a social fall-back position. "We all learn rules for how to behave in certain situations, and this makes it easier for people to know how to act, even when nervous," says Antonia Abbey, a psychology professor at Wayne State University. Just as we learn a kind of script for how to behave in a restaurant or at a business meeting, she suggests, we learn a script for talking to the opposite sex. "We often enact these scripts without even thinking," she says. "For some women and men, the script may be so well learned that flirting is a comfortable strategy for interacting with others." In other words, when in doubt, we flirt.

11   The thing that propels many already committed people to ply the art of woo, however, is often not doubt. It's curiosity. Flirting "is a way of testing one's mate-value and the possibility of alternatives—actually trying to see if someone might be available as an alternative," says Arthur Aron, professor of psychology at the State University of New York at Stony Brook. To evolutionary biologists, the advantages of this are clear: mates die, offspring die. Flirting is a little like taking out mating insurance.

12   If worst comes to worst and you don't still have it (and yes, I'm sure you do), the very act of flirting with someone else may bring about renewed attention from your mate, which has advantages all its own. So it's a win-win.

13   Flirting is also emotional capital to be expended in return for something else. Not usually for money, but for the intangibles—a better table, a juicier cut of meat, the ability to return an unwanted purchase without too many questions. It's a handy social lubricant, reducing the friction of everyday transactions, and closer to a strategically timed tip than a romantic overture. Have you ever met a male hairdresser who wasn't a flirt? Women go to him to look better. So the better they feel when they walk out of his salon, the happier they'll be to go back for a frequent blowout. Flirting's almost mandatory. And if the hairdresser is gay, so much the better, since the attention is much less likely to be taken as an unto-ward advance.

It's Dangerous Out There

14   But outside the hairdresser's chair, things are not so simple. Flirt the wrong way with the wrong person, and you run the risk of everything from a slap to a sexual-harassment lawsuit. And of course, the American virtue of plainspokenness is not an asset in an activity that is ambiguous by design. Wayne State's Abbey, whose research has focused on the dark side of flirting—when it transmogrifies into harassment, stalking or acquaintance rape—warns that flirting can be treacherous. "Most of the time flirtation desists when one partner doesn't respond positively," she says. "But some people just don't get the message that is being sent, and some ignore it because it isn't what they want to hear."

15   One of the most fascinating flirting laboratories is the digital world. Here's a venue that is all words and no body language; whether online or in text mes-sages, nuance is almost impossible. And since text and e-mail flirting can be

done without having to look people in the eye, and is often done with speed, it is bolder, racier and unimpeded by moments of reflection on whether the message could be misconstrued or is wise to send at all. "Flirt texting is a topic everyone finds fascinating, although not much research is out there yet," says Abbey. But one thing is clear: "People are often more willing to disclose intimate details via the Internet, so the process may escalate more quickly."

16   That's certainly the case on sites like Yahoo!'s Married and Flirting e-mail group, as well as on Marriedbutplaying.com and Married-but-flirting.com. "Flirting" in this sense appears to be a euphemism for talking dirty. A University of Florida study of 86 participants in a chat room published in *Psychology Today* in 2003 found that while nearly all those surveyed felt they were initially simply flirting with a computer, not a real person, almost a third of them eventually had a face-to-face meeting with someone they chatted with. And all but two of the couples who met went on to have an affair. Whether the people who eventually cheated went to the site with the intention of doing so or got drawn in by the fantasy of it all is unclear. Whichever, the sites sure seem like a profitable place for people like the guy behind me on the pre-Christmas flight to hang out.

17   Most people who flirt—off-line at least—are not looking for an affair. But one of the things that sets married flirting apart from single flirting is that it has a much greater degree of danger and fantasy to it. The stakes are higher and the risk is greater, even if the likelihood of anything happening is slim. But the cocktail is in some cases much headier. It is most commonly the case with affairs, therapists say, that people who cheat are not so much dissatisfied with their spouse as with themselves and the way their lives have turned out. There is little that feels more affirming and revitalizing than having someone fall in love with you. (It follows, then, that there's little that feels less affirming than being cheated on.) Flirting is a decaf affair, a way of feeling more alive, more vital, more desirable without actually endangering the happiness of anyone you love—or the balance of your bank account. So go ahead and flirt, if you can do it responsibly. You might even try it with your spouse.

A Field Guide to Flirting

Humans observed in a natural mating habitat—here, the Cock and Bull Pub in Los Angeles and Helm's Bakery in neighboring Culver City—exhibit nearly all the major flirting behaviors, whether or not they're flirting at all.

1. **Open Body Position** This come-and-get-me stance suggests the man is neither about to flee nor fight.
2. **Raised Eyebrows** Upon first seeing a potential mate, both men and women often briefly raise their eyebrows.
3. **Head Cant** Women frequently tilt their head to one side, exposing their neck, and sometimes flick their hair at the same time.
4. **Sustained Eye Contact** Men and women both hold the gaze of someone they're interested in for longer than feels quite comfortable.
5. **Leaning Forward** Both genders tend to lean in toward people they're attracted to. Sometimes they'll unconsciously point to them too, even if they're across the room.
6. **Leading Questions** A man will often ask a woman questions that allow her to show off her most attractive features.
7. **Sideways Glances** Often followed by a glance away or down and a shy smile, these coy looks are a classic flirting behavior for both sexes.

DISCUSSION QUESTIONS (p. 558)

1. Indications of readiness for physical engagement; biological programming—because those women who flirted well and men who responded to flirtation were more likely to reproduce, which supported biological basis for behavior; flirtation opens up exciting game of possibilities; flirtation is a script we have learned and have become comfortable with; flirtation tests our mate value; flirtation gains intangibles. Mostly the article offers multiple causes for flirtation but in the case of the biological causes offers a causal chain as well tied to reproduction.

2. Since the article is for an audience that will only read the article out of general interest, the writers have tried to make the topic more approachable by keeping the article personal and informal. The article uses fragments "That smile!" informal expressions, "Yay them. So for Pete's sake, . ." personal examples as in paragraph 8, and asides like ("Lame, I know. I was caught off guard"). There may be many different reactions to this style but in general readers may read the article with some interest but not take the offered explanations very seriously.

3. Since the authors use such an informal and personal style, they need to rely on experts to ensure that the explanations they are offered are viewed as credible rather than as idle guesses. The use of experts, with fairly impressive credentials, does provide much greater credibility to the explanations offered for flirtation.

4. Flirtation is a commonly used word but many may differ on its definition. Some will associate flirting with verbal behavior. As a result, the writers want to identify common physical indicators of flirtation both to establish how universal this behavior might be and to provide an agreed upon behavior for the explanations to come.

5. There is room for a disagreement here. However, it doesn't follow from the writers' explanations of why we flirt that it is good for us and that we should therefore flirt. To reach that conclusion, the writers would show that in general the effects of flirtation are indeed more likely to be positive than harmful.

Discussion Questions

1. What are the different causes the writers identify for flirting behavior? Are those causes multiple different causes, a chain of causes, or a combination?
2. This essay was written initially for *Time*, a popular news magazine. How did that affect the style of the essay, what are some examples of this style, and how does that impact on the essay?
3. The article relies heavily on the use of experts. Based on some examples from the text, why have the writers adopted this approach? What effect does it have on the credibility of the essay?
4. Why do the writers take the time in paragraph 3 to describe physical nonverbal forms of flirting?
5. In the conclusion, the writers take a stance on flirting as a behavior. Does this conclusion follow appropriately from the rest of the essay?

Toward Key Insights

This essay assumes that there are key biological and social explanations for simple human behaviors. Does this model seem to suggest that all human behaviors can be explained? Is that good or bad?

What kinds of effects might reading such an explanation of a behavior have on readers?

Suggestion for Writing

Take a common behavior such as "small talk" or "fantasy role-playing" and either with or without research write a behavior and offer an explanation for the behavior.

DEFINITION ▬ ▬ ▬ ▬ ▬ ▬ ▬ ▬

Reading Strategies

1. Clearly identify the term being defined.
2. Mark as you read the characteristics that are part of the defining characteristic of the concept. It can help to make a list of these defining characteristics.
3. Note specifically what the term being defined is *not* supposed to mean.
4. Observe any analogies, similes, or metaphors, noting specifically what the concept is suppose to be like.
5. Try to see if you can apply the concept.

OVERVIEW OF DEFINITION ESSAYS
Two of the writers in this section define abstract terms and two (Gibbs and Bercaw) define a concrete term. In developing their essays, all of the writers use brief definitions. None of the writers uses an essential definition, although one (Shames) includes a variant form that is presented as a question. All of the essays employ

Reading Critically

1. Check to see if the definition matches your intuition.
2. Determine if the definition is too narrow. If a person defines literature as works of fiction, the definition could leave out poetry.
3. Determine by applying the definition if it is too broad. If a person defines literature as works of writing, the definition would include phone books—a clearly unintended consequence of the definition.
4. Test if there are other available or possible definitions.

Reading As a Writer

1. Notice how the writer uses the introduction to explain the importance of the concept and the definition.
2. Identify the key strategies the writer uses to construct a definition—stating the defining characteristics, providing examples, indicating that to which the term does not apply.
3. Observe how the writer limits the definition so that it is not overapplied.
4. If the writer employs analogy, simile, or metaphor, determine how the device works in the context of the definition.

formal–informal diction, and all incorporate some of the other writing strategies.

LAURENCE SHAMES

The Sweet Smell of Success Isn't All That Sweet

Laurence Shames (born 1951) is a native of Newark, New Jersey, and a graduate of New York University. After completing his education, he began a career as a nonfiction writer contributing to a variety of popular magazines and to the New York Times. *Shames's book-length publications include two nonfiction works,* The Big Time: The Harvard Business School's Most Successful Class and How It Shaped America *(1986) and* The Hunger for More *(1991), which focuses on the search for values in a world of greed. He also co-authored Peter Barton's memoir* Not Fade Away *(2003). He has also authored several fictional works, with an emphasis on detective fiction.* The Naked Detective *appeared in 2000. Shames's concern for values is apparent in this selection, which attacks contemporary attitudes about success.*

PERSPECTIVE
Students, both before and after graduation, are likely to formulate personal notions about what success means to them. Today greed seems to be as much of a driving force as it was for some in the 1980s and 1990s. As a result, Shames's essay should still provide relevant reading.

1   John Milton was a failure. In writing "Paradise Lost," his stated aim was to "justify the ways of God to men." Inevitably, he fell short of accomplishing that and only wrote a monumental poem. Beethoven, whose music was conceived to transcend Fate, was a failure, as was Socrates, whose ambition was to make people happy by making them reasonable and just. The inescapable conclusion seems to be that the surest, noblest way to fail is to set one's own standards titanically high.

2   The flip-side of that proposition also seems true, and it provides the safe but dreary logic by which most of us live: The surest way to succeed is to keep one's strivings low—or at least to direct them along already charted paths. Don't set yourself the probably thankless task of making the legal system better; just shoot at becoming a partner in the firm. Don't agonize over questions about where your talents and proclivities might most fulfillingly lead you; just do a heads-up job of determining where the educational or business opportunities seem most secure.

3   After all, if "success" itself—rather than the substance of the achievements that make for success—is the criterion by which we measure ourselves and from which we derive our self-esteem, why make things more difficult by reaching for the stars?

4   What is this contemporary version of success really all about?

5   According to certain beer commercials, it consists in moving up to a premium brand that costs a dime or so more per bottle. Credit-card companies would have you believe success inheres in owning their particular piece of plastic.

Introduction: paragraphs 1–4: captures attention by ironically attacking high success standards, defending low standards

Body paragraphs 5–12

Development by examples and brief definitions

Development by effect	6

If these examples sound petty, they are. But take those petty privileges, weave them into a fabric that passes for a value system and what you've got is a national mood that has vast motivating power that can shape at least the near future of the entire country.

Development by comparison, examples, and causes	7

Under the flag of success, modern-style, liberal arts colleges are withering while business schools are burgeoning—and yet even business schools are having an increasingly hard time finding faculty members, because teaching isn't considered "successful" enough. Amid a broad consensus that there is a glut of lawyers and an epidemic of strangling litigation, record numbers of young people continue to flock to law school because, for the individual practitioner, a law degree is still considered a safe ticket.

Development by effects	8

The most sobering thought of all is that today's M.B.A.'s and lawyers are tomorrow's M.B.A.'s and lawyers: Having invested so much time and money in their training, only a tiny percentage of them will ever opt out of their early chosen fields. Decisions made in accordance with today's hothouse notions of ambition are locking people into careers that will define and also limit their activities and yearnings for virtually the rest of their lives.

Development by effects and argument	9

Many, by external standards, will be "successes." They will own homes, eat in better restaurants, dress well and, in some instances, perform socially useful work. Yet there is a deadening and dangerous flaw in their philosophy: It has little room, little sympathy and less respect for the noble failure, for the person who ventures past the limits, who aims gloriously high and falls unashamedly short.

Development by effects	10

That sort of ambition doesn't have much place in a world where success is proved by worldly reward rather than by accomplishment itself. That sort of ambition is increasingly thought of as the domain of irredeemable eccentrics, of people who haven't quite caught on—and there is great social pressure not to be one of them.

Development by effects	11

The result is that fewer people are drawn to the cutting edge of noncommercial scientific research. Fewer are taking on the sublime, unwinnable challenges of the arts. Fewer are asking questions that matter—the ones that can't be answered. Fewer are putting themselves on the line, making as much of their minds and talents as they might.

Development by effect, causes, and comparison	12

The irony is that today's success-chasers seem obsessed with the idea of *not settling*. They take advanced degrees in business because they won't settle for just a so-so job. They compete for slots at law firms and investment houses because they won't settle for any but the fastest track. They seem to regard it as axiomatic that "success" and "settling" are opposites.

Conclusion: argues against contemporary notions of success	13

Yet in doggedly pursuing the rather brittle species of success now in fashion, they are restricting themselves to a chokingly narrow swath of turf along the entire range of human possibilities. Does it ever occur to them that, frequently, success is what people settle for when they can't think of something noble enough to be worth failing at?

Discussion Questions

1. Shames notes in paragraph 3 that "'success' itself—rather than the substance of the achievements that make for success—" seems to be the touchstone by which we measure our worth. What do you think he means? Why is the distinction positioned at this point?

2. Why do you think Shames ends his essay with a rhetorical question, that is, one for which no answer is expected?

3. To what extent do you agree with Shames's idea of success? Discuss.

Toward Key Insights

What evidence do you find that not all people are consumed by the desire for money? What qualities do you consider crucial to living a "good" life? To happiness?

Suggestion for Writing

Write a definition essay explaining how the popular view of responsibility, greed, marriage, single life, friendship, or some other concept needs redefining. Use whatever writing strategies advance your purpose.

MARC ZWELLING

The Blended Economy

Marc Zwelling graduated with a BS degree in journalism from Northwestern University in 1968. After graduating, he worked for Canadian Press, the Toronto Telegram, *and as public relations official for the United Steelworkers of America. He is currently president of Vector Research and Development, Inc., and conducts opinion surveys and completes feasibility studies. He has facilitated numerous workshops and written extensively about future trends. In our selection, he examines the changing nature of the business marketplace.*

1   The traditional way to innovate is to carve a specialized niche. Some building contractors specialize in renovating nineteenth-century homes. Lawyers practice trade law, criminal law, family law, labor law, immigration, copyright, or libel. Doctors can be ear-nose-throat specialists, gerontologists, or pediatricians. Specialization is efficient; specialists do their jobs faster because they know them better than non-specialists. And a niche is usually more profitable than the mass market from which someone sliced it. The trouble with a niche is that when competitors recognize it's profitable they rush in.

2   Blending is the opposite of specialization. Instead of burrowing deeper into a field or product to specialize, blending creates a new market category. The secret in the technique is to unite different, not similar, ideas, products, or services. Minivans and sport-utility vehicles, for example, grew from blending cars and trucks, creating whole new categories of consumer vehicles.

3   Companies can continually generate new ideas by blending. Most new products today are simply extrapolations of successful products, such as a faster microprocessor, a cheaper airline ticket, a smaller camera, and so on. These innovations eventually run out of possibilities. Blending different ideas instead produces limitless new directions for innovative products.

4   A food company searching for a new product for kids might think of blending different items from a list of opposites like "frozen or unfrozen," "milk or cola," "peanut butter or peanuts," "salad or soup." Perhaps kids who love peanuts would savor them in a soup. And perhaps a cola could be frozen so it would stay

DISCUSSION QUESTIONS

1. Shames contends that we judge success not by the actual accomplishment but rather by the trappings—remium beer, credit cards, elegant meals, homes, clothing—associated with financial advancement. To highlight the distinction, Shames presents it ahead of the paragraphs that elaborate on it.

2. A rhetorical question draws the reader's attention by producing more emphasis than an assertion.

3. This question should prompt a stimulating discussion.

PERSPECTIVE

This essay presents a definition of *blending* to encourage business professionals and others to see a new way of approaching business. For that reason, many examples are chosen to show professional possibilities rather than simply recite the history of past *blends*. The essay tries to get readers thinking. In some cases it offers challenges to the reader, as in paragraph 9. It is worth discussing with students why this essay is as openended as it is and whether this approach is effective.

TEACHING STRATEGIES

1. Have students identify the features in this essay that target it to a more specific audience. Discuss with the class whether it is restricted to more specific audiences or has a more general appeal.

2. Definition by contrast with a familiar concept is a common technique. Have students review the first three paragraphs to determine how the author initiated his definition and evaluate the relative effectiveness of the approach.

3. Throughout the essay, as in paragraph 9, the author challenges the reader to think of new blends. Discuss with the class why the writer might include this technique and evaluate its relative effectiveness. Notice that many students expect essays to offer answers rather than provoke thought.

CLASSROOM ACTIVITIES

1. Working in small groups, have students identify products, types of movies, or careers that might be blends.

2. Have students, working in small groups, identify ways college courses could possibly be blended. Have the groups work to define their blended college course.

3. Blending also refers to a common linguistic strategy of combining two words such as *breakfast* and *lunch* to create a new word such as *brunch*. Have students work in small groups to create a new word by blending, such as *juit* for a *jeans suit*. Students should then define their term without using the new word or either of the composite words. The groups should offer their definitions to the class to see if the class can possibly guess the new *blend* word. For example, a meal taken in the late afternoon that may include a soup or sandwich but

5

6

6

7

8

9

10

11

12

cold longer, requiring no ice. The ideas may prove impractical, nonsensical, or just plain awful, but the point is to generate more ideas because they can lead to practical products.

Blending also operates within social and economic trends. For instance, barriers are falling between work and leisure, devastating some retail clothing chains and department stores as employees don the same outfits at home and the office.

In the job market, there is vast potential to create opportunities by combining apparently unrelated occupations. Consider the number of specialists you must work with to buy or sell a house: There is a real estate agent, the loan officer, the building inspector, an insurance agent, and the mover. One specialist hands you off to another. The blending opportunity here is for, perhaps, a "home transitions" professional who can manage all these different steps.

Some employees may have over-specialized. Specialization narrows a worker's opportunities in a slowly growing economy and causes bottlenecks in a booming economy. Blending avoids these problems.

The *New York Times* recently reported unprecedented growth in the new profession of legal nurse consultant. From none a decade ago, there are more than 4,000 in America today. Blending the skills of nurses and lawyers, legal nurse consultants help lawyers in medical-related lawsuits. Blending professions is not the same as stacking one university degree on another. The legal nurse consultant is still a nurse, not a lawyer. Nurses learn enough law in training institutes to become legal nurse consultants.

Another example of a blended career opportunity might be an ergonomic architect—a designer and engineer with special training in child development to make safer houses for families with small children.

Try mixing and matching completely dissimilar occupations, such as carpenter, receptionist, software writer, investment adviser, security guard, dentist, chemical engineer, lifeguard, teacher, embalmer, chef, hairstylist, pharmacist, actor.

A list like this may yield few blended jobs in the literal sense, but it triggers thinking about ways to add value to products and services and differentiate businesses in super-competitive markets. For instance, a funeral home could offer caskets carved by its own carpenters. A supermarket could build customer loyalty if its meat cutters demonstrate cooking techniques. A chef with pharmaceutical training or a pharmacist with cooking skills could help customers create healthier meals using herbs and other natural supplements.

Career blending is most likely to develop among entrepreneurs, as attempts to blend work in traditional settings have historically met with resistance: Unions protest that management wants to make one employee do two jobs for one worker's pay. Management says unions obstruct change and efficiency.

Indeed, most fields resist merging and consolidating because of tradition. But since nobody can predict what the market will bear, the greater the number of innovations you can generate in products, services, and careers, the greater your chance of success.

Discussion Questions

1. In the first two paragraphs, the author contrasts blending with specialization. What might be his reason for such an approach?

2. What techniques does the writer use to define blends? How effective are those approaches?

3. What examples of blends were most effective, which least effective, and why?

Toward Key Insights

Often we are trapped in our thinking by established categories. How can blending help break us out of those established categories?

Suggestion for Writing

Create a blend of your own, perhaps even creating a new word for the blend just as brunch is a blend of breakfast and lunch. Write a short paper defining your blend.

MARTI BERCAW

Krumping

Marti Bercaw is a writer and video journalist at Social, *an online journal from which this article was taken. She loves dance and frequently writes about that topic. Other articles include "Celebrate Michael Jackson's Life and Music at University City Walk!" and "The Jabbawockeez: America's 1st Best Dance Crew."*

1   On the 3rd Saturday of every month **Tommy the Clown and Debbie Allen** have a "**Battle**" that hundreds of L.A. kids join. It is a Clowning Krumping dance war of the creative kind, organized by 2 dedicated adults who love dance, love kids and understand the power of expression through dance.

2   The location is the **Debbie Allen Dance Academy** in Culver City and the stage is a quasi-boxing ring set up in a huge studio. 500 chairs and standing-room-only space is filled to capacity by the time the show starts . . . and what a show it is!

3   Tommy the Clown serves as the Master of Ceremonies and referee with a whistle. Larry the Clown is the DJ who supplies a powerful mix of music. Ani Dizon, Tommy's manager, coordinates the whole event and process. Lil Tommy, Tommy's brother, is there to help when he is not traveling the world performing Clown and Krump Dance with his crew, and he teaches Clowning classes at D.A.D.A., too.

4   On stage, two girl to girl or boy to boy dancers challenge each other in a series of rounds. One opponent sits while the other performs.

5   Individual dancers "call each other out" as well as the members of a crew but it's always one performer at a time. Dancers have been as young as 4 with no limit on the high end. Everyone, even Grandparents, are welcome to battle onstage but teenagers are in the majority.

6   The audience is made up of kids, parents, grandparents and friends. The challenging dance crew changes every month, unless there is a rematch, and goes up against the current winning crew who holds onto the gold embellished championship belt until it passes to the next winner. There are cash prizes as well. The audience votes by applause at the end of each battle. Battle scores are tallied to determine the winning crew.

7   Sometimes it's clear who has won and sometimes they have to rely on an applause meter to determine the winner. It's a tough call because all the dancers are brilliant at freestyle . . . that's what it's all about.

generally is substantial would be *dunch* for dinner/lunch or *linner* for lunch/dinner.

DISCUSSION QUESTIONS

1. There are at least two reasons for the author's approach. Since specialization will be the more familiar term for most readers, it is helpful to define the new concept, blending, by contrasting it with the familiar term. Further, the writer uses the definition as an opportunity to convince the reader of the business advantages of blending in contrast to the typical practice of specialization.

2. The author defines *blending* by contrasting it with a familiar concept, breaking down the idea to its basic and recognizable process of combining differences, and providing many examples. The examples are very helpful because they show how the process of blending can be used in different environments.

3. Some of the most successful examples are "Minivans" and "sport-utility vehicles," "the legal nurse consultant," and "meat cutters that demonstrate cooking techniques" since many of these already exist and are familiar to readers. Examples such as "peanut butter soup," "a chef with pharmaceutical training," and the "home transitions professional" might work less successfully since they will be less familiar to the reader and perhaps less credible as viable ideas.

PERSPECTIVE
Often the definition of
cultural forms, whether
Romanticism or BeBop,
requires a brief history to
identify when and how the
movement emerged and
sometimes to distinguish
how the movement is a
change from any from
which it evolved. This essay
distinguishes Krumping's
roots in Clowning. An even
fuller history could have
made this essay richer.

TEACHING STRATEGIES
1. Before the students
read this essay, have them
identify some of what they
consider contemporary
dance movements. Ask
them to define the distinctive characteristics of
those movements.

2. After students have
read the essay, have the
students either go online
to the original article or to
one of many sites with
video clips with examples
of Krumping. Have them
view some of the video
clips. Discuss which was
more helpful in under-
standing Krumping: the
article or the video clips.
Have them list what each
medium can contribute to
their understanding.

3. Have students identify
in the essay the main features that would help
them distinguishing
Krumping from other
kinds of dance. Then
have students identify
features in the article
that would apply to many
different kinds of dance.
Discuss why it is difficult
to select distinguishing
characteristics to define
something physical like
dance.

About Krump

8   "Clowning" is movement invented by Tommy the Clown who developed the strange, stilted, goofy and erratic motion to entertain audiences as a clown at parties and local events around Los Angeles from as far back as 1992. Needless to say, it caught on in a big way.

9   Street dance has an evolutionary life of its own and it's very nature demands constant adaptation and change. What was once "Clowning" evolved to "Krump Dance" or Krumping. As Tommy put it, "Krumping is the dark side of Clowning." In homage to the clown, some dancers paint designs on half their face.

10   The first time I saw "Clowning/Krumping" was five years ago. Over time, it has spread to other cities in the US, Europe and Asia. "Rize," a documentary by David Lachappelle, permanently writes "Clowning" and "Krumping" into the pop history record. It will read that this dance was born in South Central Los Angeles beginning in the last decade of the century and was performed by inner city kids who, as the third generation who's offered hip hop, were hungry for something new. They made it happen.

Krump Described

11   Krumping incorporates extreme, almost impossible freestyle body motion, coordination and rhythm. Basics include chest popping, a Charlie Chaplin-esque, comic, stumbling, staccato stride and toe dance, feet that turn out, feet that turn in, arms that go wide in a ranting wave, the body jerking up and down, prancing, the torso bent from the waist that circles around the hips 360 degrees, raised arms that wrap over and around the body, the neck and head jutting for-ward, the mouth chattering as if in a real or silent monologue. The dance is fren-zied and rapid, displaying a set of attitudes running the gamut from hostile to aggressive to seductive to comical and back again. Girls can be as good as the guys but there are fewer who compete. Their attitude can include more sexual, bump and grind elements with a flamboyant, exaggerated edge or they can have an attitude that is hard and aggressive, just like their male counterparts.

12   Krumping is not hip hop, though it uses the music and springs from the same mold. For now, it seems to stand alone as a pure urban expression.

13   It isn't pretty and it offers no apology because it tells a vivid story about being young in a hostile and dangerous world run amok. The dancer can shift from malevolent character to clown in a flash like what comes at you as you surf channels on a TV. Click, click. Life turns on a dime at the push of a button in today's world. We see the reflection in Krumping.

14   Debbie Allen and Tommy the Clown do Los Angeles a great service by providing and supporting the monthly "Battles." It is true that kids who would otherwise be involved with gangs or get into other trouble are given a creative alternative. But it is also true that these kids are already gifted, articulate about their medium and highly motivated to achieve excellence.

15   In exchange for the chance to perform, the "Clowns and Krumpers" offer every-one who cares about dance or the creation of dance form or the poetry of rap, or the embodied voice of our American culture a chance to witness art in the making.

Discussion Questions

1. What is the writer's overall purpose in writing this essay? Where is that purpose most evident?
2. Why does the author start the essay with a brief account of a specific competition?

3. What are some distinguishing features that help define Krumping?
4. The original online article had links to video clips of a Krumping competition. Where, if at all, would such video clips be helpful and why? Where would they not be needed and why?
5. In the end, the author identifies some positive features of Krumping. What impact do paragraphs 15 and 16 have on the reader?

Toward Key Insights

Increasingly, texts are being placed online where they can be supplemented by pictures as well as video and audio clips. To what extent does textual content like a definition need to stand on its own and to what extent can it depend on Web-based support material? You might want to consider the above essay as an example.

Cultural phenomenon like music and dance are especially hard to define. What are some of the challenges of defining things like Hip-Hop, Krumping, Breaking, and other similar phenomenon?

Suggestion for Writing

Take a contemporary movement such as Hip-Hop and, following the example of Marti Bercaw, write a definition paper explaining the movement.

ARGUMENT ■■■■■■■■

Reading Strategies

1. Identify the background of the author if possible. Does the author bring any expertise or experience that helps make the argument more credible?
2. Read the introduction and conclusion to gain a sense of the thesis and main points of the argument.
3. Read the argument quickly to gain an overall sense of the major points of the essay and an understanding of the organizational pattern.
4. Look for the organizational pattern of the essay and keep an eye out for transition sentences. Often an author argues by first presenting the viewpoint of several other authors, then pointing out limitations of those views, then presenting his or her own position and offering support, and finally admitting possible limitations and problems with the author's position (possibly answering these objections). This pattern often confuses readers.
5. Read carefully to identify the major claims of the argument, the reasons for the author's position, and any evidence presented for any of the claims. It can be very helpful to outline an argument, making a special note of the major reasons and evidence for the claim. Note the author's approach. Is the argument mostly deductive or inductive? Does the author try to show the negative consequences of opposing views? Does the author base the argument on authority?

Reading Critically

1. Check to see if the author demonstrates any overt bias.
2. Test to determine if the reasons given really support the author's thesis.

3. There are several important features of Krumping. 1. It is done as a form of competive, challenge dancing. 2. It uses freestyle body movements that are extreme. 3. There are a number of specific movements such as chest popping, comic stumbling, toe dance, body jerks. 4. It uses rapid changes in attitudes from aggressive to comic. 5. It can tell a vivid story.

4. Physical motions are hard to describe. Video clips could make it easier to demonstrate the physical style of the dance. Video clips could also make it easier to compare and distinguish Clowning, Krumping, and Hip-Hop. Video clips would not make it easier to explain the history of the dance or its social importance.

5. Paragraphs 14 and 15 end the essay on a positive note. They tend to have the impact of leaving a positive impression of Krumping as a social event.

3. Test to see if the evidence is adequate. Does the evidence support the claims? Is the source of the evidence trustworthy and unbiased? Is the evidence extensive or scanty? Could contrary evidence be offered?

4. Check the essay for informal fallacies.

5. Try to offer objections to the author's claims. Write objections in the margins or on a separate piece of paper.

6. See if you can formulate alternative conclusions to those proposed by the author.

7. Try to formulate reasons and concerns that the author may have neglected.

8. Read essays that present other viewpoints and compare.

Reading As a Writer

1. Note the organizational pattern of the argument. Identify how you might use the pattern in your arguments.

2. Examine how the writer connects the reasons with the major thesis.

3. Identify how the evidence is presented and connected as support.

4. Notice any effective word choice that helps cement the emotional argument.

5. Evaluate how the author establishes tone and ethos.

6. Examine how the author answers possible objections.

EZEKIEL J. EMANUEL

The Problem with Single-Payer Plans

Ezekiel J, Emanuel, M.D., Ph.D., is the Chair of the Department of Clinical Bioethics at the National Institutes of Health. He received his M.D. at Harvard's Medical School and his Ph.D. in Political Philosophy from Harvard University. Among his extensive publications is the book No Margin, No Mission: Health-Care Organizations and the Question of Ethical Excellence. *This article appeared in the January/February 2008 edition of the Hastings Center Report*

Identifies position to oppose

1   Many liberals in America dream about single-payer plans. Even if they acknowledge that a single-payer plan cannot be enacted, they still think it the best reform. Another proposal may be politically necessary to achieve universal coverage, but it would be a compromise, a fall-back. Single payer is the ideal.

Establishes assumption for argument

2   This is wrong. Even in theory, single payer is not the best reform option. Here's the problem: while it proposes the most radical reform of the health care financing system, it is conservative, even nostalgic, when it comes to the broken delivery system. It retains and solidifies the nineteenth century, fragmented, fee-for-service delivery system that provides profligate and bad quality care.

Establishes thesis and main argument

3   Reform of the American health care system needs to address problems with both the financing and the delivery systems. As proponents of single-payer systems note, the financing system is inequitable, inefficient, and unsustainable. There are now forty-seven million uninsured Americans, about 70 percent of whom are in families with full-time workers. Wealthy individuals receive much higher tax breaks than the poor, and insurance premiums are a larger percent of wages for those working at low wages and in small businesses. Many working poor and lower middle class Americans pay taxes to support Medicaid and

Builds Rogerian relationship with reader by agreeing with their concerns. Raises concerns about government role.

SCHIP, yet are excluded from these programs. The employer-based and individual market parts of the financing system are inefficient because they have huge administrative costs, especially related to insurance underwriting, sales, and marketing. The government part of the finance system is inefficient because it fails to address key policy issues, fraud, and—for Medicaid—complex determinations of eligibility. Over the last three decades, health care costs have risen 2–4 percent over growth in the overall economy. Medicaid is now the largest part of state budgets, forcing states to cut other programs.

4   But the delivery system is also fraught with problems. First, it is badly fragmented. Currently, 75 percent of physicians practice in groups of eight or less. Of the one billion office visits each year, one-third are to solo practitioners, and one-third are to groups of four or fewer physicians. On average, each year Medicare beneficiaries see seven different physicians, who are financially, clinically, and administratively uncoordinated.

> Identifies alternative problem with empirical support

5   A second problem is that the delivery system is structured for acute care, but the contemporary need is for chronic care. Over 133 million Americans have chronic conditions, and among Americans sixty-five and older, 75 percent have two or more chronic conditions, and 20 percent have five chronic conditions. Consequently, 70 percent of health care costs are devoted to patients with chronic conditions.

> Second problem with empirical support

6   Also, the care that the system delivers is of much poorer quality than Americans realize. Use of unproven, non-beneficial, marginal, or harmful services is common. The list of offending interventions that are paid for and widely used but either unproven or of marginal benefit to patients is vast—IMRT and proton beam for early prostate cancer, CT and MRI angiograms, Epogen for chemotherapy induced anemia, Erbituax and Avastin for colorectal cancer, and drug-eluting stents for coronary artery disease. Stanford researchers recently showed that between 15 and 20 percent of prescriptions are written for indications for which there is absolutely no published data supporting their use.[1] The Dartmouth studies on variation in practices demonstrate that for many interventions, more services are not better. For instance, heart attack patients in Miami receive vastly more care than similar patients in Minnesota at 2.45 times the cost, yet have slightly worse outcomes.[2]

> Identifies additional problem with delivery system using empirical support

7   In the context of reforming the American health care system, "single payer" has come to be associated with three key reforms: a single national plan for all Americans, reduced administrative costs, and negotiated prices for hospitals and physicians and perhaps for health care goods and services, such as drugs. Single-payer plans have two huge advantages.

> Identifies reasons for opponent's position

8   First, single-payer plans clearly provide for universal health care coverage. Unlike Massachusetts-style individual mandate reform proposals, single-payer plans do not achieve 95 percent or 97 percent coverage, but true 100 percent coverage for all Americans.

> Opposition reason—advantage

9   Second, single-payer plans enhance the efficiency of the health care financing system by eliminating the wasteful costs of insurance underwriting, sales, and marketing. This could save between $60 and $100 billion. Similarly, a single-payer plan with a formulary and negotiated prices would be able to reduce drug costs. McKinsey Global Institute has estimated that bringing drug costs in the United States down to those of other developed countries would save the U.S. system $57 billion.[3] This is a huge and real savings, enough to cover all the uninsured and probably expand the range of covered services to include dental care and other items.

> Second opposition reason and empirical evidence

<table>
<tr><td>Transition</td><td>10</td><td>The problem with single-payer plans is that they have an assortment of serious structural problems. To wit:</td></tr>
</table>

The problem with single-payer plans is that they have an assortment of serious structural problems. To wit:

<table>
<tr><td>Problem 1 with single payer system. Provides reasons for this problem. States criteria.</td><td>11</td></tr>
</table>

Institutionalized fee-for-service. Single-payer plans would preserve the dysfunctional delivery system. We know two things about how to reform the delivery system. First, because no one yet has the secret formula for delivering the best quality health care, a real reform of the financing system needs to foster innovation in delivery and then measure the delivery system to find out what changes improve quality. Second, while the overall contours of reform are unknown, there is a clear need for better integration and coordination of care. Integration requires three—infrastructure, information, and incentives. Better delivery of care needs an infrastructure that coordinates doctors, hospitals, home health care agencies, and other providers administratively, fiscally, and clinically. They need to share information easily. And there have to be incentives for this coordination. It will not happen spontaneously.

<table>
<tr><td>States opposition procedure and identifies negative consequences</td><td>12</td></tr>
</table>

The problem is that a single-payer approach uses fee-for-service reimbursement to entrench the existing delivery system. Retaining and institutionalizing the fee-for-service payment model would quash the ability to integrate care. Solo practitioners or small groups would have no incentive—financial or otherwise—for integration and coordination of care across providers.

<table>
<tr><td>Negative consequence of plan</td><td>13</td></tr>
</table>

Also, single-payer reform is hostile to the very organizations that have the financial and administrative capacity to build the infrastructure and information systems for the coordinated care delivery systems: insurance companies and health plans. If there is to be an infrastructure for integration of services, information-sharing, and incentives for collaboration, some organization has to develop and implement it. Call it what you will, that organization would look a lot like a health insurance company. (Some might argue that the Veterans

<table>
<tr><td>Indicates limitation of example used by opposing viewpoint</td><td></td></tr>
</table>

Affair's health system is a single-payer system that does a great job of coordinating and integrating care. True, but it covers only thirteen million people. In essence, the VA is a big health plan, like Kaiser. There is no way a single administrative body can efficiently coordinate care for three hundred million people.) In the current system, the financial incentives for health insurance companies lead to perverse behaviors, such as avoiding sick patients. But single-payer plans eliminate not only their problems, but also their potential benefits.

<table>
<tr><td>Indicates faulty assumption in opposition argument</td><td>14</td></tr>
</table>

Deceptive administrative savings. There is no doubt that a single-payer system would produce huge administrative savings, but low administrative costs should not be confused with low total health care costs.

<table>
<tr><td>Empirical evidence for above</td><td>15</td></tr>
</table>

Very low administrative costs in Medicare create an opening for fraud and abuse. The last assessment by the Inspector General of the Department of Health and Human Services occurred in 1996. At that time, the IG estimated that Medicare made about $23.2 billion in improper payments due to insufficient or absent documentation, incorrect billing, billing for excluded services, and other problems. In 1996, Medicare spent about $200 billion. Thus, fraud

<table>
<tr><td>Indicates a limitation of opposition example</td><td></td></tr>
</table>

was over 10 percent of total Medicare costs. (I leave it to you to imagine why the government has not repeated this assessment in the last decade.) True, the Canadian single-payer system does not report high levels of fraud and abuse, but Canada is not the United States. Canada's population is about one-tenth that of the United States, and Canadians believe in good government.

<table>
<tr><td>Evidence for failure in opposition assumption</td><td>16</td></tr>
</table>

Furthermore, a plan covering all Americans would be much larger than Medicare. It would have to process more than one billion physician visits, forty million hospitalizations, and 3.7 billion prescriptions each year. This would require sophisticated information technology, but that technology would be a major administrative cost, and keeping it updated could be politically difficult. As we have seen in the IRS and the FBI, there is great aversion to spending money on major IT upgrades.

17   Finally, monitoring the quality of care delivered to patients also constitutes an administrative expense. It is an administrative burden to systematically assess whether new technologies like cancer genetic fingerprints are in fact beneficial, whether new surgical procedures really lead to longer life, and whether new ways of preparing patients for surgery and handling intravenous lines reduce infections and hospital days.

> Additional reason assumption wrong

18   Nothing would absolutely prohibit single-payer plans from spending more money on administration to detect fraud, improve computerization, address payment issues, and assess quality. Nothing, that is, but a strong ideological commitment to keeping administrative expenses very, very low. The war cry for single-payer plans is very low administrative costs, but repeatedly touting this advantage creates a line in the sand. Indeed, it may exacerbate the inflexibility of a single-payer plan. Because of its size, any agency administering a single-payer plan would have a built-in tendency toward inertia. Further, striving to keep administrative costs low would translate into hiring fewer people to manage the system. Fewer people would mean less expertise for addressing problems and less time to search for creative solutions. This is a prescription for inflexibility and lack of innovation.

> Negative consequences of opposition assumption

19   **Ineffective cost-control strategies.** Efficiency savings from reduced administrative costs or cheaper drug prices should not be confused with controlling costs overall. Efficiencies, such as reducing administrative waste, are onetime savings. Controlling costs means reducing the increase in medical spending year after year. Single-payer plans use the savings from efficiencies to extend coverage to the uninsured and expand covered services without raising the total amount spent on health care. But these onetime savings do not attack the fundamental forces that drive health care cost inflation. Unless there is some mechanism to control those pressures, the onetime savings would be used up in a few years, and overall health care spending would go higher and higher. How can single-payer plans respond to this health care inflation?

> States limitation of opposition assumption

20   There are three possible approaches. One is to "constrain the supply": use the national health plan's control to constrain the introduction and deployment of technology. A single-payer plan could decide to limit the number of MRI scanners, for example. Indeed, in the Physicians' Working Group proposal, the national health plan would negotiate with hospitals on capital expansion and could easily limit how many hospitals can build facilities for MRI scanners or new specialized surgical suites.[4] This strategy creates queuing for access to the technology. As every major country trying this has learned, queuing creates huge public resentment. People on the waiting list get furious at the central administration. Americans, especially the upper middle class, are unlikely to tolerate it.

> Identifies possible negative consequence

21   Constraining supply also promotes gaming of the system and inequality. When technology is limited, patients—and physicians—try to jump the queue. Physicians are not great at creating priority lists based on medical need. Particularly when they have their own practices, their obligation is to their individual patients, not to ensuring that other physicians' patients get care and not to promoting the overall health of the population.

> Identifies possible negative consequence

22   Countries that have tried this approach have found, not surprisingly, that such gaming tends to favor well-off patients. In many facets of life, well-off people have learned how to come out on top in situations where there are limits. Limits

> Empirical evidence

on health care technology gives them one more setting in which their greater gaming skills can be deployed. A study in Winnipeg, Canada, showed that although all Canadians were legally entitled to the same services, the well-off had substantially better access to high technology services that were constrained.[5]

Negative consequence

23   A second approach, a variant of "constrain the supply," is a "low prices and fees" approach. As the only organization paying physicians, hospitals, drug companies, and other health providers, a national health plan would have a huge incentive to squeeze down on fees. This would keep costs down, and since providers would have no one else to turn to, they would have limited recourse.

Illustration of above

24   The United States government uses this low-price approach in Medicaid and Medicare. To save money, every so often Congress or the Medicare administrators roll back the fees paid to hospitals, physicians, and others. Then, just as predictably, those groups scream that they are going broke and lobby Congress to increase the fees. And so the see-saw goes on—prices rolled back and then increased after lobbying. This does not end up saving much, in part because how much is paid out depends not only on the fee or price but also on the volume—on how much is done. So one way physicians respond to lower fees is to ramp up volume; they see a lot of patients for shorter and shorter times. This is easily done because for many diseases there are no data on how often patients should be seen in the physician's office. And it is exactly how Canadian health insurance administrators kept fees low.

Empirical evidence using a single example

25   The British National Health Service used to do exactly what the Physicians' Working Group wants to do: It paid hospitals a fixed price for operating expenses and controlled capital expenditures to limit expansion and the purchase of new technologies. The result: the hospitals put off maintenance and began falling apart. They put off cleaning and became filthy. They could not buy new equipment or adapt quickly to changes in medical practice. Eventually, even the stiff-upper-lip British rebelled. The British National Health Service reversed course and recently gave hospitals the ability to make their own decisions, including decisions to raise funds or float bonds to expand or buy new technologies.

Identifies alternative assumption contrary to opposition

26   Both "constrain the supply" and "low prices and fees" are centralized, micromanaging cost control techniques. You do not have to be a die-hard capitalist to think they are bad techniques. Most left-leaning economists agree that it is better to develop incentives and let the market control costs than to have government set prices or supply.

Negative consequence

27   The third approach to cost control in a single-payer system is that adopted by Medicare in the United States: do nothing, and just pay whatever bill comes in. Let the costs go through the roof. The crisis will come later—after the current administrators and politicians are long gone. This is probably why a *New York Times* editorial said, "Even in fantasy, no one has yet come up with a way to pay for Medicare."[6]

28   These three options are what most single-payer systems in the world have done. None works, and all have long-term consequences.

Argument by analogy comparing single payer to Medicare

29   Politicized decision-making. As Michael Millenson, a health policy consultant, remarks, when single-payer advocates think about who would run the national health plan, they think of Ted Kennedy. But, he asks, what if the head were Dick Cheney? Medicare reveals what is likely to happen if we have a single-payer plan. Every Medicare decision is subject to political pressure from somewhere. When Medicare tries to lower hospital fees or equalize payments, hospitals pressure their representatives and senators for increases in payments. Patient advocacy groups lobby to have Medicare pay for their favorite technology or treatment.

Drug companies use campaign contributions—and patient advocacy groups—to prevent a Medicare formulary and forbid price negotiations that might limit their profits. The result is that Medicare decisions are made slowly, and rarely on their merits. No federal administrative agency can be completely free of political influence. But single-payer reform plans tend to ignore the importance of administrative independence.

30   The ideal reform must address not only the inequitable, inefficient, and unsustainable financing system, but also the fragmented delivery system. And it must develop a plan that creates an accountable and innovative delivery system overseen by a (relatively) independent agency that can make hard administrative choices.

■ References

[1] D. C. Radley, S. N. Finkelstein, and R. S. Stafford, "Off-Label Prescribing among Office-Based Physicians," *Archives of Internal Medicine* 166, no. 9 (2006): 1021–26.

[2] E. S. Fisher, D. E. Wennberg, T. A. Stukel, and D. J. Gottlieb, "Variations in the Longitudinal Efficiency of Academic Medical Centers." Health Affairs Web exclusive, October 7, 2004, http://content.healthaffairs.org/cgi/content/full/hlthaff.var. 19/DC3.

[3] C. Angrisano, D. Farrell, B. Kocher, M. Laboissiere, and S. Parker, "Accounting for the Cost of Health Care in the United States" (The McKinsey Global Institute, 2004), http://www.mckinsey.com/mgi/reports/pdfs/healthcare/MGI_US_HC_fullreport.pdf.

[4] "Proposal of the Physicians' Working Group for Single-Payer National Health Insurance" (Physicians for a National Health Program, 2006), http://www.pnhp.org/publications/proposal_of_the_physicians_working_group_for_singlepayer_national_health_insurance.php.

[5] D. A. Alter, A. S. Basinski, E. A. Cohen, and C. D. Naylor, "Fairness in the Coronary Angiography Queue," *Canadian Medical Association Journal* 161, no. 7 (1999): 813–17.

[6] "Talking Deficits," *New York Times* opinion, May 23, 2004.

Discussion Questions

1. In the introduction, the author clearly makes the argument political and describes the single-player plans as the dream of liberals. What is the effect of this approach? Who then is his likely audience and what is his purpose in writing this argument?
2. The author admits some of the problems with the U.S. current health care system and some advantage to single-payer systems. What effect do these admissions have on the effectiveness of the author's argument?
3. What approach does the author use to raise questions about the single-payer system? What are some strengths and weaknesses of this approach?

Criteria

PERSPECTIVE
This article serves as a sharp contrast with the next article on this topic. Rather than basing most of the argument on fact, the author raises broader concerns and issues with only some supporting facts. Even where evidence is offered, as in paragraph 22, it is less authenticated than in the next article. Still, it may be the more convincing argument. After the students read the next article, this would be a basis for a fruitful discussion about which of the two articles was more persuasive and why.

TEACHING STRATEGIES
1. Have students work in groups to make a chart of the major claims of the argument, the evidence for each claim, and the kind of credibility for the evidence. Discuss as a large group where this does and does not hurt the argument.
2. Take some of the major claims of this article. Have students work in groups to identify what answers, if any, those who support a single payer might have. Indicate what response the author would have to those answers.
3. Have students examine the article carefully to identify what the author really supports if he opposes a single-payer system. The article seems to support a marketplace approach that uses insurance companies, HMOs, and doctor's profits to result in reforms in our systems.

CLASSROOM ACTIVITIES
1. Hand out cards with sample biographies on them such as single, working mother with no health insurance at work; an employee in the health insurance industry who values his or her secure job; a small business owner who no longer feels he can afford to provide health care to his employees and still stay competitive. Discuss how they might feel about the issue if any of these were their biographies.

2. Have students interview each other to create accounts of different experiences with getting health care. Have students post the answers to their interviews without the names of the people they interviewed. Discuss what the results suggest about our current health care system.

DISCUSSION QUESTIONS (p. 571)
1. By labeling single-player plans a liberal dream, he makes the issue a political one. Since he is talking about liberals rather than to liberals, he may cause many liberals to reject his argument. As a result, his main argument seems to be conservatives must strengthen the reasons for their opposition to a single-payer plan. But in paragraph 2. he calls the single-payer plans "conservatives," which suggests his audience may have been liberals all along. This is why even when discussing a political

4. In paragraph 24, and other paragraphs, the author uses Medicaid and Medicare as examples of the possible problem with a single-payer system. Is this a fair analogy? Why?

5. In the end, the author offers no alternative solution to health care problems, except for the mention in paragraph 26 that, "it is better to develop incentives and let the market control costs than to have government set prices or supply." Does this harm the author's argument?

Toward Key Insights

One approach to any argument for a solution is to raise questions about the proposal, sometimes as a way of preserving the status quo, without offering an alternative. Is this an ethical or effective approach?

Some have said that the "perfect" is the enemy of the "better." What they mean is that everything we try to do has limitations so there can always be objections, which may make no solutions acceptable. Does this essay fall to this problem? Why or why not?

Suggestions for Writing

Based on the two articles on single-payer health care plans, and additional research if your teacher would encourage the additional research, write an argument supporting or objecting to adopting a single-payer health plan.

Focus on one specific claim of the author, such as his claim that the single-payer system has "ineffective cost-control strategies," and with additional research support or dispute his claim.

HOLLY DRESSEL

Has Canada Got the Cure?

Born in Illinois, Holly Dressel now lives in Montreal, Quebec, Canada, where she works as a researcher and writer. She has an M.A. in English from Simon Fraser University. She writes frequently for the online Yes Magazine, *the source for this article which was adapted from Ms. Dressel's book* God Save the Queen—God Save Us All: An Examination of Canadian Hospital Care via the Life and Death of Montreal's Queen Elizabeth Hospital.

Publicly funded health care has its problems, as any Canadian or Briton knows. But like democracy, it's the best answer we've come up with so far.

1   Should the United States implement a more inclusive, publicly funded health care system? That's a big debate throughout the country. But even as it rages, most Americans are unaware that the United States is the only country in the developed world that doesn't already have a fundamentally public—that is, tax-supported—health care system.

2   That means that the United States has been the unwitting control subject in a 30-year, worldwide experiment comparing the merits of private versus public health care funding. For the people living in the United States, the results of this

experiment with privately funded health care have been grim. The United States now has the most expensive health care system on earth and, despite remarkable technology, the general health of the U.S. population is lower than in most industrialized countries. Worse, Americans' mortality rates—both general and infant—are shockingly high.

Different Paths

3   Beginning in the 1930s, both the Americans and the Canadians tried to alleviate health care gaps by increasing use of employment-based insurance plans. Both countries encouraged nonprofit private insurance plans like Blue Cross, as well as for-profit insurance plans. The difference between the United States and Canada is that Americans are still doing this, ignoring decades of international statistics that show that this type of funding inevitably leads to poorer public health.

4   Meanwhile, according to author Terry Boychuk, the rest of the industrialized world, including many developing countries like Mexico, Korea, and India, viscerally understood that "private insurance would [never be able to] cover all necessary hospital procedures and services; and that even minimal protection [is] beyond the reach of the poor, the working poor, and those with the most serious health problems."[1] Today, over half the family bankruptcies filed every year in the United States are directly related to medical expenses, and a recent study shows that 75 percent of those are filed by people with health insurance.[2]

Side-by-Side: No Comparison

■ Canada   ■ U.S.

Canada and the U.S. used to be twins on public-health measurements. Here's how it looks after 35 years of Canadian universal health care.

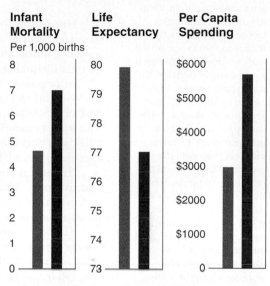

Source: World Health Organization, CIA *World Fact Book,* Centers for Disease Control

5   The United States spends far more per capita on health care than any comparable country. In fact, the gap is so enormous that a recent University of California, San Francisco, study estimates that the United States would save over $161 billion every year in paperwork alone if it switched to a single-payer system like Canada's.[3] These billions of dollars are not abstract amounts deducted from government budgets; they come directly out of the pockets of people who are sick.

6   The year 2000 marked the beginning of a crucial period, when international trade rules, economic theory, and political action had begun to fully reflect the belief in the superiority of private, as opposed to public, management, especially in the United States. By that year the U.S. health care system had undergone what has been called "the health management organization revolution." U.S. government figures show that medical care costs have spiked since 2000, with total spending on prescriptions nearly doubling.[4]

Cutting Costs, Cutting Care

7   There are two criteria used to judge a country's health care system: the overall success of creating and sustaining health in the population, and the ability to control costs while doing so. One recent study published in the *Canadian Medical Association Journal* compares mortality rates in private for-profit and nonprofit hospitals in the United States. Research on 38 million adult patients in 26,000 U.S. hospitals revealed that death rates in for-profit hospitals are significantly higher than in nonprofit hospitals: for-profit patients have a 2 percent higher chance of dying in the hospital or within 30 days of discharge. The increased death rates were clearly linked to "the corners that for-profit hospitals

issue it is advantageous to avoid political language unless it is unavoidable.

2. By admitting the existing problems and the advantages to single-player plans, the author adds credibility to his argument since he demonstrates that he understands and appreciates the concerns of those with whom he will disagree.

3. The author identifies several broad problems with our health care system that the single-payer system might not fix or might even make worse. He also suggests some structural problems with the single-payer approach, including its supposed advantage of keeping down administrative costs. There are several strengths with this approach: It suggests that even those who support a single-payer system need to rethink their support; even if readers reject one or two objections there are several more for them to consider; it provides lots of problems for the reader to think over, which makes the issue seem much more complicated and the single-payer system less worthy of support. There are some weaknesses with this approach: Because more ideas are offered with less evidence, the argument may lose credibility with some readers; since the article offers no solution, the reader might still conclude that the single-payer system is better than our current system or anything they might know; when issues become too complicated, some readers grasp at simple solutions.

4. This is a fair analogy since Medicare and Medicaid are large government-run single-payer systems. Often those arguing for a single-payer system base their support in part on these two systems.

5. The lack of a clear solution by the author does not fundamentally harm the author's argument since the objections to a single-payer system can still be valid. However, it can undercut the author's credibility with some readers who may see the author as simply a spoiler and argue back that the single-payer system may be imperfect but it is better than the alternatives. The author doesn't really address that possible response.

8   must cut in order to achieve a profit margin for investors, as well as to pay high salaries for administrators."[5]

"To ease cost pressures, administrators tend to hire less highly skilled personnel, including doctors, nurses, and pharmacists . . .," wrote P. J. Devereaux, a cardiologist at McMaster University and the lead researcher. "The U.S. statistics clearly show that when the need for profits drives hospital decisionmaking, more patients die."

The Value of Care for All

9   Historically, one of the cruelest aspects of unequal income distribution is that poor people not only experience material want all their lives, they also suffer more illness and die younger. But in Canada there is no association between income inequality and mortality rates—none whatsoever.

10   In a massive study undertaken by Statistics Canada in the early 1990s, income and mortality census data were analyzed from all Canadian provinces and all U.S. states, as well as 53 Canadian and 282 American metropolitan areas.[6] The study concluded that "the relationship between income inequality and mortality is not universal, but instead depends on social and political characteristics specific to place." In other words, government health policies have an effect.

11   "Income inequality is strongly associated with mortality in the United States and in North America as a whole," the study found, "but there is no relation within Canada at either the province or metropolitan area level—between income inequality and mortality."

12   The same study revealed that among the poorest people in the United States, even a one percent increase in income resulted in a mortality decline of nearly 22 out of 100,000.

13   What makes this study so interesting is that Canada used to have statistics that mirrored those in the United States. In 1970, U.S. and Canadian mortality rates calculated along income lines were virtually identical. But 1970 also marked the introduction of Medicare in Canada—universal, single-payer coverage. The simple explanation for how Canadians have all become equally healthy, regardless of income, most likely lies in the fact that they have a publicly funded, single-payer health system and the control group, the United States, does not.

Infant Mortality

14   Infant mortality rates, which reflect the health of the mother and her access to prenatal and postnatal care, are considered one of the most reliable measures of the general health of a population. Today, U.S. government statistics rank Canada's infant mortality rate of 4.7 per thousand 23rd out of 225 countries, in the company of the Netherlands, Luxembourg, Australia, and Denmark. The U.S. is 43rd—in the company of Croatia and Lithuania, below Taiwan and Cuba.

15   All the countries surrounding Canada or above it in the rankings have tax-supported health care systems. The countries surrounding the United States and below have mixed systems or are, in general, extremely poor in comparison to the United States and the other G8 industrial powerhouses.

16   There are no major industrialized countries near the United States in the rankings. The closest is Italy, at 5.83 infants dying per thousand, but it is still ranked five places higher.[7]

17   In the United States, infant mortality rates are 7.1 per 1,000, the highest in the industrialized world—much higher than some of the poorer states in India, for example, which have public health systems in place, at least for mothers and infants. Among the inner-city poor in the United States, more than 8 percent of mothers receive no prenatal care at all before giving birth.

Overall U.S. Mortality

18   We would have expected to see steady decreases in deaths per thousand in the mid-twentieth century, because so many new drugs and procedures were becoming available. But neither the Canadian nor the American mortality rate declined much; in fact, Canada's leveled off for an entire decade, throughout the 1960s. This was a period in which private care was increasing in Canadian hospitals, and the steady mortality rates reflect the fact that most people simply couldn't afford the new therapies that were being offered. However, beginning in 1971, the same year that Canada's Medicare was fully applied, official statistics show that death rates suddenly plummeted, maintaining a steep decline to their present rate.

19   In the United States, during the same period, overall mortality rates also dropped, reflecting medical advances. But they did not drop nearly so precipitously as those in Canada after 1971. But given that the United States is the richest country on earth, today's overall mortality rates are shockingly high, at 8.4 per thousand, compared to Canada's 6.5.

Rich and Poor

20   It has become increasingly apparent, as data accumulate, that the overall improvement in health in a society with tax-supported health care translates to better health even for the rich, the group assumed to be the main beneficiaries of the American-style private system. If we look just at the 5.7 deaths per thousand among presumably richer, white babies in the United States, Canada still does better at 4.7, even though the Canadian figure includes all ethnic groups and all income levels. Perhaps a one-per-thousand difference doesn't sound like much. But when measuring mortality, it's huge. If the U.S. infant mortality rate were the same as Canada's, almost 15,000 more babies would survive in the United States every year.

21   If we consider the statistics for the poor, which in the United States have been classified by race, we find that in 2001, infants born of black mothers were dying at a rate of 14.2 per thousand. That's a Third World figure, comparable to Russia's.[8]

22   But now that the United States has begun to do studies based on income levels instead of race, these "cultural" and genetic explanations are turning out to be baseless. Infant mortality is highest among the poor, regardless of race.

23   Vive la différence! Genetically, Canadians and Americans are quite similar. Our health habits, too, are very much alike—people in both countries eat too much and exercise too little. And, like the United States, there is plenty of inequality in Canada, too. In terms of health care, that inequality falls primarily on Canadians in isolated communities, particularly Native groups, who have poorer access to medical care and are exposed to greater environmental contamination. The only major difference between the two countries that could account for the remarkable disparity in their infant and adult mortality rates, as well as the amount they spend on health care, is how they manage their health care systems.

24   The facts are clear: Before 1971, when both countries had similar, largely privately funded health care systems, overall survival and mortality rates were almost identical. The divergence appeared with the introduction of the single-payer health system in Canada.

25   The solid statistics amassed since the 1970s point to only one conclusion: like it or not, believe it makes sense or not, publicly funded, universally available health care is simply the most powerful contributing factor to the overall health of the people who live in any country. And in the United States, we have got the bodies to prove it.

an impact on the claims of the article.

4. A single-payer system isn't socialized medicine. Distinguish before students read the essay the idea of a single-payer system and a socialized medicine or national medicine system like that in Great Britain where the doctors work for the government and hospitals are government institutions much like public schools or state colleges.

CLASSROOM ACTIVITIES
1. Have students create a table comparing the major facts about the Canadian and the United States health care systems.
2. After having read both articles, have students divide into teams on whether or not they would support a single-payer system. Allow the undecided students to be the audience. Have both sides make their case in class, preferably with additional research. In the end, have the undecided students vote for or against a single-payer system.

DISCUSSION QUESTIONS
1. The strengths of this approach: The argument seems much more factually based rather than political, the reader isn't pushed in a way that generates a negative reaction, the argument doesn't become overly long or disorganized by addressing too

[1]Terry Boychuk. *The Making and Meaning of Hospital Policy in the United States and Canada.* University of Michigan Press, Ann Arbor: 1999.

[2]David U. Himmelstein, et al. *Health Affairs,* Jan.–June 2005, http://content. healthaffairs.org/cgi/reprint/hlthaff.w5.63v1

[3]Professor James Kahn, UCSF, quoted in *Harper's Magazine,* "Harper's List," Feb. 2006.

[4]National Health Expenditure Data, www.cms.hhs.gov/NationalHealthExpendData/ downloads/tables.pdf.

[5]Devereaux, Dr. P. J., et al. "A Systematic Review and Meta-Analysis of Studies Comparing Mortality between Private For-Profit and Private Not-For-Profit Hospitals," *Canadian Medical Association Journal,* May, 2002.

[6]Nancy A. Ross et al. "Relation between Income Inequality and Mortality in Canada and in the United States: Cross Sectional Assessment Using Census Data and Vital Statistics," *Statistics Canada,* reprinted in *Health Geography,* GEOG-303, ed. Nancy Ross, McGill University, 2005, pp. 109–117.

[7]*CIA World Fact Book.* www.cia.gov/cia/publications/factbook/rankorder/2091rank.html

[8]See, among many studies blaming race, Child Health USA 2003, Health Status—Infants; HRSA, with graphs such as "Breastfeeding Rates by Race/Ethnicity, 2001"; "Very Low Birth Weight Among Infants, by Race/Ethnicity 1985–2001"; http://www. mchb.hrsa.gov/chusa03.

Discussion Questions

1. The author focuses on a comparison of the relative effectiveness of the United States and Canadian health care to make her argument rather that writing a broader and more emotional argument for a single-payer system. What are the strengths and weaknesses of this approach?
2. In paragraph 7, how does the author frame her main argument? Is this approach effective?
3. This essay depends heavily on evidence. What kinds of evidence does the writer use? How does she try to make it credible? Is it effective?
4. What strategies does the writer use in her concluding paragraphs?
5. The author's argument hinges on her suggestion that the only significant difference in the U.S. and Canadian health is a result of the differences in their health insurance systems. If we assume her statistics are correct, what other explanations might there be for such differences?

Toward Key Insights

The person who sets the terms of an argument often wins. Holly Dressel defines the key issues in the health care debate as being the cost of health care delivery and the measured health of citizens. What other issues might be equally important to consider?

There are many articles in support of a single-payer system that answer most of the criticisms of this approach. This author doesn't attempt to answer possible objections. What is the effect of her refraining from tackling a wide array of issues and sticking to the comparison as a way of formulating her argument?

Suggestion for Writing

Take one of the issues the author discusses—such as the cost of health care, the infant mortality rate, or the mortality rate in general—research the topic and write an argument either supporting or disputing the claims of the author. You will want to keep an eye on the range of alternative explanations for the statistics in question.

ALAN EHRENHALT

The Misguided Zeal of the Privacy Lobby

Alan Ehrenhalt was born in 1947 in Chicago. He received an A.B. from Brandeis University and an MS from Columbia University. He was a reporter for Congressional Quarterly *and serves as executive editor of* Governing *magazine. He has written numerous articles, editorials, and books including* The Lost City: Discovering the Forgotten Virtues of Community in the Chicago of the 1950s. *In this essay, he makes the provocative argument that there have been exaggerated and even harmful demands for privacy that overcome reasonable proposals such as the one for national identity cards.*

1   My Social Security number is 349-40-7931. I don't mind telling you that largely because I'm confident you have no interest in knowing it. You won't even write it down. Of course, you could be a secret enemy of mine, eager to use any available information to discredit me in some way. But I'm not too worried about that, either. I have my share of secrets, just like anybody else, but at the moment I can't think of a single one that's vulnerable to exposure simply upon presentation of an I.D. number.

2   But I will tell you one secret belief I have that I'm usually careful not to blurt out in polite company. It's this: I think privacy is the single most overrated issue in the entire lexicon of public policy—state, local, federal or anyplace else. Of all the dangers that this society faces as it starts the new millennium, one of the most remote is the risk that America will become an Orwellian police state, watching everything citizens do and taking down every word they say. And yet people all over the country lose a lot of sleep every night worrying about it.

3   I have great admiration for George Orwell, as a writer and thinker, and as a lifelong leftist who had the courage to expose communism for the hypocritical sham it was. But in one important way, Orwell did posterity a disservice. He depicted the surveillance methods of totalitarian society so vividly and so convincingly that an entire generation of otherwise reasonable Americans has convinced itself that Big Brother is watching them even when the truth is that Big Brother has far more important ways to spend his time.

4   "They could plug in your wire whenever they wanted to," Orwell wrote a few pages into his novel, *1984.* "You had to live—did live, from habit that became instinct—in the assumption that every sound you made was overheard, and, except in darkness, every movement scrutinized."

many issues. Weaknesses of this approach: Major objections that might be easily answered go unanswered, readers influenced by emotional appeal will not be influenced by this kind of argument, it leaves the conclusion to the reader who might reach a different decision from that of the author.

2. The author in paragraph 7 defines the criteria for a health care system as being cost and results. This seems reasonable and if readers accept these criteria, then her facts will be more persuasive. However, for those who reject her criteria or have other criteria, then her argument will be less persuasive.

3. The author almost exclusively uses statistical evidence. She helps add credibility to her evidence by indicating her sources and using fairly noncontroversial studies, including results from university studies, medical journal articles, and United States governmental statistics. As a result, the article is effective in making a credible case for its factual claims.

4. The author concisely summarizes her main argument. She also makes it seem clear that the conclusion is unavoidable by phrases such as "like it or not, believe it makes sense or no." The attempt is to make the conclusion seem more a matter of fact than personal belief.

5. While the author does briefly address this question in paragraph 23, she does not consider the issue in any depth. America is simply a much more populace country with larger cities that might create more sites for illness and place strains on health care resources. While Canada has its poor, its social system may raise their standard of living. America may have more people struggling with poverty and its health effects. America is a much more heterogeneous society with more immigrants, including illegal immigrants, who have other health care challenges. A careful study would need to look at issues like diet, health practices, stress levels, and much more.

PERSPECTIVE

Not all arguments need to be strong. Ehrenhalt is trying to open discussion and provoke thought on an issue that often has been seen as closed. It is worth discussing what an author's obligations may be, given different purposes and contexts. The fundamental questions about whether we are excessively concerned about protecting our privacy can be important. Do we really need to fear our government and if so, why? Have we already given away the privacy we claim to be protecting? What sacrifices might we be making in protecting privacy? This issue could be tied to recent invasions of privacy, such as legislation that requires librarians to report the reading habits of customers to government investigators on request.

5   I'm not a simpleton. I know there are governments in this century that have operated that way. The Stasi collected tons of data on the daily habits of ordinary East Germans and filed them away for later use. The KGB knew who the Soviet dissidents were almost from the moment they opened their mouths. I am also aware that even in a free society, horrible miscarriages of justice take place. Waco was indefensible. The police in a one-party dictatorship couldn't have acted any more irresponsibly.

6   But mature citizens in a civilized country are required to make distinctions between aberration and routine. Those of us who lay awake at night in America in 1999 worrying about the government's desire to snoop on them are mostly either (1) paranoid or (2) guilty of something. If there is a legitimate threat to our personal privacy these days, it comes from corporate capitalism, from the companies that make their living on the sale of information for commercial use. It doesn't come from the county commission, the legislature, or the U.S. Department of Health and Human Services.

7   But merely to say such a thing is to risk provoking shock and even ridicule among most members of the educated elite in this country. In the past generation, the idea that our precious privacy is under siege has transcended ideological differences, from the Cato institute on the right, which says "the history of government programs indicates privacy rights are violated routinely whenever expediency dictates," to Justice William O. Douglas on the left, who wrote near the end of his life that "we are rapidly entering the age of no privacy, where everyone is open to surveillance at all times, where there are no secrets from the government." Ask to see the evidence for these propositions, and you won't get much. But you will be branded as a naif, or a proto-Fascist, or both.

8   That is why I am so impressed with the courage of Amitai Etzioni, who dares to challenge the conventional wisdom in his new book, *The Limits of Privacy.* Etzioni is a reasonable man. He doesn't claim that our personal liberty is unimportant, or deny that the government possesses the technological capacity to invade it. He merely argues that we have gone overboard in our privacy obsession in recent years, and we need to tilt the balance back a few steps in the direction of common sense and provision for the common good.

9   And he offers convincing detail on why this is so. For reasons of privacy, for example, we fail to require HIV testing for mothers and infants, even though the information gained by such testing would save many of the infants' lives. We refuse to give law enforcement officials the tools to decipher encrypted computer messages, even though encryption makes systematic criminality easier to practice with each passing year. And on and on through a whole range of current public policy questions.

10 But of all the issues Etzioni takes up, none illustrates his point better than the controversy surrounding creation of a uniform identification process for American citizens.

11 The costs of not having such a system are hard to dispute. As Etzioni recounts, there are more than 30,000 fugitives from the federal criminal justice system running free on false identification. Each year, several thousand convicted sex offenders seek work in the child-care business alone. The use of fake identities by crooked taxpayers costs honest ones an amount estimated to be as much as $5 billion a year. Another $5 billion is thought to be owed by deadbeat parents fleeing their child-support responsibilities. At the end of 1997, the Secret Service reported that it had arrested nearly 10,000 people during the year for various financial crimes involving false or stolen identities, and placed the cost of that fraud to banks and legitimate credit-holders at $745 million.

12   There's no way such figures can be exact. Quite likely some of them have been inflated a little bit in the process of reporting. But if they are even roughly accurate, they make it quite clear that identity crime is a genuine problem in this country.

13   And it's a problem that could be solved relatively easily, by creating a card or other universal identifier proving that the person in search of a job or transferring money is in fact who he or she claims to be. We already use Social Security cards and numbers as a de facto identifier for many public purposes. It's just that they're easy to cheat on. How dangerous could it be to create a new version that liars would have to respect?

14   Not very dangerous at all, is the correct answer. But it's an answer that a privacy-obsessed American polity is stubbornly unwilling to consider. In 1993, when the Clinton administration included establishment of a medical "security card" as part of its national health care proposal, it soon discovered it had made a major tactical error. Anything that sounded remotely like a national I.D. card set the privacy lobby going full blast.

15   Of course, it doesn't take much to do that. Pick up any ordinary newspaper these days, and there's a good chance that somewhere within its pages you will find a warning that an identification system is merely the opening move in Big Brother's bid for absolute power. "Don't we remember the Nazi experience in Europe?" the editor *of Privacy Journal* asked in the *New York Times* a couple of years ago. "Don't we realize the dangers of allowing government to establish identity and legitimacy?"

16   Just last campaign season, a Nevada gubernatorial candidate offered up identity cards as a sign that America was "rushing headlong into becoming a socialist totalitarian society." Privacy zealots left and right are fond of repeating the warning of former California Senator Alan Cranston: ID cards are "a primary tool of totalitarian governments."

17   Well, yes, they are. So are whips, but they are not a cause of torture. So is tear gas. That doesn't make tear gas an emblem of totalitarianism. A little common sense would be useful here. If America starts to go down the road to Fascism, it won't be because people are carrying identification in their wallet. As Etzioni says, "Cards do not transform democratic societies into totalitarian ones."

18   In America in the 1990s, the obsession with privacy is more than just a simple overreaction to George Orwell or to horror stories about something that happened in Moscow or Beijing. It is a reflection of the hyperindividualism to which the political system has succumbed in the past generation or so, and the ways that prevents us from becoming civic grown-ups in a democratic society.

19   One trait that marks just about all of us during childhood and adolescence is an unremitting anxiety about what other people think of us. When we get older, if we are lucky, we begin to realize that, in fact, other people aren't thinking about us at all most of the time. Other people are worried about themselves. The rest of the world isn't watching us with a pair of binoculars. The sensible thing to do is figure out what we want to do and then go on and do it.

20   Of course, some people never figure this out, even in middle age. They go through life searching desperately for clues about the impressions they are creating—at home, at work, even among strangers on the street. They are convinced their friends and acquaintances are judging the most minute details of their lives, and making mental notes about their performance for use later.

21   It's not a very pleasant way to live, and it doesn't bear much resemblance to reality. As individuals, most of us manage to figure that out somewhere between adolescence and middle age. If we learned a similar lesson in our capacity as citizens, we would all be better off.

TEACHING STRATEGIES

1. Before assigning the essay, discuss with the class certain limitations on privacy currently in force including the requirement of librarians to report the reading habits of patrons on request from authorized government agencies. Are such practices harmful and if so, why?

2. Ehrenhalt's purpose is not to provide an overwhelming argument. Discuss with the class whether Ehrenhalt succeeds in the goal of getting the reader to think about an important issue.

3. Have students identify the ways the essay could be developed if it were to be transformed into a more substantial argument.

CLASSROOM ACTIVITIES

1. Have students work in small groups to identify different purposes for arguments and how that might affect expectations for the argument.

2. Have students bring in a range of argument types from movie reviews to substantial academic arguments. Have students identify the purposes and conventions of each of the arguments.

DISCUSSION QUESTIONS (p. 580)

1. The core purpose of the essay seems to be to persuade the reader that privacy is overrated and that the issue needs reconsidering. In part, the author refers the interested reader to a work that might examine the issue more fully. Since the purpose is to simply open deliberation on the issue, it is less important for the author to make a knockdown argument.

2. Ehrenhalt has several related arguments for ID cards. The notion of privacy itself is overrated. It is paranoid to think that a democracy is actually interested in placing everyone under surveillance. A number of crimes could be prevented through a national identity card. We currently have identity systems, but those systems are too easy to cheat.

3. The discussion of social security numbers has two purposes. The author can demonstrate that there is no reason to be excessively fearful on identity issues. Also the author demonstrates that we already have an identity system.

4. Ehrenhalt uses his short answer to show a flaw in the logic of his opponents' argument. The fact that a totalitarian government uses something doesn't make that item bad or even something that leads to totalitarianism. Totalitarian governments use a census and yet a requirement for a census is written into the U.S. Constitution and is arguably essential to a democracy. It is legitimate to point to flaws in the logic of an opponent's argument.

Discussion Questions

1. What seems to be the purpose of Ehrenhalt's essay? Is it essential for him to make a very strong argument?
2. What are Ehrenhalt's major arguments in favor of national identity cards?
3. What purpose does it serve for Ehrenhalt to indicate his social security number at the beginning of the article and then later indicate that we do use social security cards and numbers as forms of public identification?
4. In response to the argument that ID cards are the tools of totalitarian governments, Ehrenhalt answers that whips and tear gas are also tools of such governments. What is the point of his response? Is it an appropriate argumentative strategy?
5. What point does the author make in the concluding three paragraphs? How effective is this conclusion?

Toward Key Insights

Often we must make decisions weighing conflicting values. How important is privacy as a value compared to other values such as the protection of life and health?

Currently the government and companies have extensive amounts of information about us. There is also a scattered system of identification including driver's licenses and social security numbers. Would a national identification card actually decrease our liberty?

Suggestions for Writing

Write a paper arguing whether we as Americans are excessively concerned about privacy.

Write a paper on whether or not we should require HIV testing for mothers and infants.

BARBARA DORITY

Halt and Show Your Papers!

Barbara Dority serves as the executive director of the Washington Coalition Against Censorship. She is the president of the Humanists of Washington and edits the Secular Humanist Press. *Her columns on civil liberties appear regularly in* The Humanist Magazine. *In this selection, she argues against the use of national identity cards.*

1   The idea of a national identity (ID) card seems simple enough. Take the photographic and alphanumerical information on our birth certificates, Social Security cards, driver's licenses, and voter registration card; add a bar code, magnetic strip, fingerprint, microchip, or other biometric identifier; and display all that information (and more) on a neat plastic card no larger than a credit card. Our lives would be simplified. We'd always know for sure who we are and who everyone else really is.

2   But beneath this smooth surface lurks a complex terrain of issues and perhaps the greatest threat to personal freedom Americans have ever confronted.

3   The concept of a national ID card has been debated in the United States for over three decades. In the past, the opposition has been strong and bipartisan and has always prevailed. Extension of the Social Security number to the status of an ID card was rejected in 1971 by the Social Security Administration. In 1976, the Federal Advisory Committee on False Identification rejected the idea of a national identifier. The Carter and Reagan administrations both went on record as opposed to a national ID system.

4   In 1996, uniform national driver's license standards—which some considered tantamount to a national ID card—were enacted into law. However, their implementation was delayed, and a permanent repeal of the proposal was contained in the FY2000 Transportation Appropriations Act signed by President Clinton. In October 1999, House Majority Leader Dick Armey's website featured an article entitled "Good Riddance to the National ID Card." Armey's accompanying statement included these words:

5   This is a classic victory of freedom over "Big Brother." Because we acted quickly, no American will have to carry a National ID Card. A national driver's license with "biometric identifiers" or social security numbers is more suited to a police state than to a free country. It took three years of hard work, but we finally laid this disturbing idea to rest.

6   Not.

7   As a result of the September 11, 2001, terrorist attacks, the debate has been renewed and elevated to a higher and much more dangerous level. Just look at this sampling of headlines from recent newspaper articles around the country:

- "Support Grows for National ID Card Proposal" (*San José Mercury News,* October 16).
- "National ID Card System Failing to Attract Supporters" (*Los Angeles Times,* October 24).
- "U.S. Security Advisor: National ID Card Not Feasible" (*NewsFactor Network,* November 8).
- "National ID Card Gaining Support" (*Washington Post,* December 17).

8   Members of Congress, security experts, and high-tech executives have rushed to endorse the idea of some new form of identification system as a critical weapon in the "fight against terrorism." Unfortunately, little of this discussion has been open to the public (no surprise there), so it has been difficult to determine where the concept currently stands in the minds of the nation's decision makers.

9   George W. Bush, thankfully, has publicly stated his opposition, saying that national ID cards are unnecessary to improve security. Richard Clarke, Bush's chief of cyberspace security, agrees and does "not think it's a very smart idea." Fierce opposition comes from a wide range of privacy advocates, the American Civil Liberties Union, and even conservative organizations like the CATO Institute, Eagle Forum, and the John Birch Society.

10   And yet, as Roger Gay headlines his article in the November 29, 2001, conservative *Toogood Reports,* perhaps "It's Too Late to Stop a National I.D. Card." Marty Abrams, an information technology specialist at the law firm Hunton and Williams and a former senior credit bureau executive, summarizes the current state of the U.S. psyche well: "We're willing to accept this immense flow of data to law enforcement and their proxies to make sure we feel safe and secure. . . . The equilibrium point has shifted as a result of September 11."

5. The author draws an analogy. He wishes to suggest that the fear that others are watching our every move is a sign of personal immaturity. He wishes to argue then that as citizens we should be more mature and reject that kind of worry. The analogy, however, is weak because it isn't clear that the cases are sufficiently similar to validate the parallel.

PERSPECTIVE
The government and businesses currently have an extensive amount of information about individuals. Identity cards, some would argue, simply formalize a system that already exists. After all, the government does need information on citizens—address, driver's license, criminal record, social security number, employment history—if it is going to meet its many functions. It could be worth discussing with the class what governments need to know to conduct the necessary affairs of government and what information is simply unnecessary. This essay has some flaws. This is an opportunity to discuss with the class how even published essays can be improved.

TEACHING STRATEGIES
1. Before assigning the essay, discuss with the class what information the government does and does not have about citizens.
2. Have the students identify which of the author's

arguments are most effective and why.

3. Have students list possible positive uses of a national identity card. Discuss whether those benefits are good enough reasons to overcome the problems raised by Dority.

4. Use the essay to discuss better and worse ways of incorporating material from sources. This essay could be contrasted with other essays in the argument chapter that draw on sources, including the two essays on immigration.

CLASSROOM ACTIVITIES

1. Have students work in small groups to create a list of revisions that might improve this article.

2. Have students work in small groups to identify aspects of their lives that should remain private and why?

11   Most disturbingly, recent Pew Research Center and Harris polls show strong support for a national ID card by those polled: 70 percent and 68 percent, respectively. This preference is undoubtedly hinged on the assumption that such a system would largely prevent terrorists and other "evil-doers" from entering the country—an assumption that is, at best, extremely dubious.

12   Other ID card supporters include the Department of Defense (which already has such a system in place), Oracle CEO Larry Ellison (who has offered to provide the ID software for free and would be glad to offer his company's services to maintain the system and its massive databases—for a fee, of course), the American Association of Motor Vehicle Administrators (which sees this as an opportunity for a national driver's license system), the Air Transportation Association, the Justice Department, lawmakers in U.S.–Mexico border states, and all those in charge of immigration committees in Congress. To my absolute horror, even Bill of Rights champion Alan Dershowitz has recently endorsed the concept, claiming it would reduce racial profiling!

13   The single best overview I've found of the basic questions about national ID cards and concepts involved in their debate is contained on the objective "Frequently Asked Questions" (FAQ) page of the Privacy International website at www.privacy.org/pi/activities/idcard/idcard_faq.html. Its points are summarized below.

14   1. Who uses ID cards now? About a hundred countries currently utilize official, compulsory, national IDs for various purposes. These include Belgium, France, Germany, Greece, and Spain. Among the developed countries that don't have such a card are Australia, Canada, Ireland, New Zealand, Sweden, and the United States. Most countries that don't have a national universal card do have a health or social security card or other documents of identity.

15   2. What are the primary purposes of ID cards? Race, politics, and religion are often at the heart of older ID systems. Card systems have been instituted to control the threat of insurgents or political extremists, to facilitate religious discrimination, to enforce quota systems, and to allow for social engineering. The FAQ notes: "At the heart of such plans is a parallel increase in police powers. Even in democratic nations, police retain the right to demand ID on pain of detention."

16   3. What is the cost of an ID card system? The expense of implementing such a system has been at the forefront of both political and public opposition in a number of countries, including Australia, the Philippines, and the United Kingdom. Cost estimates to create and issue national ID cards in the United States are around $3 billion.

17   4. Can ID cards assist law enforcement? The usefulness of ID cards to law enforcement has been marginal. Little evidence has been advanced to demonstrate that they would either reduce the incidence of crime or enhance the success of prosecution. Police authorities in the Netherlands and the United Kingdom have stated their reluctance to administer a compulsory card that might erode relations with the public. Furthermore, forgeries would be inevitable. Obviously, the more an ID card is used, the greater the value placed on it and, consequently, the higher its value to criminal elements.

18   5. Can ID cards help to control illegal immigration? The impact of such cards on controlling illegal immigration has been patchy. The use of a

card for purposes of checking resident status depends on the police and other officials being given very broad powers to check identity—either a vastly increased level of constant checking of the entire population or a discriminatory checking procedure that would undoubtedly target minorities (numerous examples are included in the FAQ).

19   6. Which countries have rejected proposals for ID cards? The most celebrated campaign against a national ID card occurred just over a decade ago in Australia. In response to proposed legislation, tens of thousands of people took to the streets in opposition, and the government became dangerously split over the issue. The proposal caused such hostility that it was withdrawn in 1987. A similar proposal was presented in New Zealand a few years later and, under the leadership of the Auckland Council for Civil Liberties, an opposition campaign was formed and the proposal was abandoned.

20   In summary, the benefits of a national ID card are highly questionable, while the risks threaten the very heart of a free, democratic society. The national ACLU provides one of the most succinct summaries of the rights issues by boiling down the debate to five major reasons why a national ID card will keep us neither safe nor free:

21   Reason 1: A national ID card system won't solve the problem: it won't prevent terrorism. It wouldn't have thwarted any of the September 11 hijackers, for example, many of whom reportedly had identification documents on them and were in the country legally. Terrorists and criminals will continue to be able to obtain—by legal and illegal means—the documents needed to get a government ID, such as a birth certificate.

22   Reason 2: An ID card system will lead to a slippery slope of surveillance and monitoring of citizens. While such a system cannot protect us from terrorism it would create a system of internal passports that would significantly diminish the freedom and privacy of law-abiding citizens. Once put in place, it is exceedingly unlikely that such a system would be restricted to its original purpose. For example, the original Social Security Act contained strict prohibitions against using Social Security cards for unrelated purposes, but those strictures have been routinely ignored and steadily abandoned over the past fifty years. A national ID system would threaten the privacy that Americans have always enjoyed and gradually increase the control that government and business wields over everyday citizens.

23   Reason 3: A national ID card system would require the establishment of a database of all people in the United States. What happens then when an ID card is stolen? What proof may be used to decide who gets a card? The records of every individual would require continuous updating; would likely contain many errors, any one of which could render someone unemployable and possibly much worse until they get their "file" straightened out. And once created, the use of such a database would almost certainly expand. Law enforcement and other government agencies would soon ask to link into it, while employers, landlords, credit agencies, mortgage brokers, telemarketers, private investigators, civil litigants, and a long list of other parties would begin seeking access, further eroding the privacy that people have always expected in their personal lives. We already see this happening with a proposed airline security database of passenger profiles that would be designed to rate the security risk posed by each passenger.

24   Reason 4: ID cards would function as "internal passports" that monitor citizens' movements. Americans have long had a visceral aversion to building a

society in which the authorities could act like totalitarian sentries and demand "your papers please!" That everyday intrusiveness would be conjoined with the full power of modern computer and database technology. For example, if a police officer or security guard scans your ID card with a pocket barcode reader, would a permanent record be created of that check, including the time and your location? The end result could be a nation where citizens' movements inside their own country are monitored and recorded.

25   Reason 5: ID cards would foster new forms of discrimination and harassment. Rather than eliminating discrimination, as some have claimed, a national identity card would foster new forms of discrimination and harassment of anyone perceived as looking or sounding "foreign." That is exactly what happened after Congress passed the Employer Sanctions provision of the Immigration Reform and Control Act of 1985; it resulted in widespread discrimination against foreign-looking U.S. workers, especially Asians and Hispanics. A 1990 General Accounting Office study found almost 20 percent of employers engaged in such discriminatory practices. A national ID card would have the same effect on a massive scale, with Latinos, Asians, Arabs, and other minorities becoming subject to ceaseless status and identity checks from police, banks, merchants, and others. Failure to carry a national ID card would likely come to be viewed as a reason for search, detention, or arrest of minorities. The stigma and humiliation of constantly having to prove that they are U.S. citizens or legal immigrants would weigh heavily on such groups.

26   New York attorney Duncan Frissell writes in the *Sierra Times:* Most critics of a national ID card mention Hitler, police stops, and personal privacy to argue against the proposal. Those are certainly good reasons to oppose a national ID card, but they miss the idea's worst features. A national ID card is not really about identity. It is about authorization. A modern national ID system will:

27   ▪ Require Americans to obtain federal government authorization to travel, work, rent or buy housing, obtain medical care, use financial services, and make many purchases.

28   ▪ This federal authorization could be denied for many reasons, including database errors, a suspicious transaction profile, being a deadbeat parent, failure to pay taxes or fines, and any other social control measures Congress wishes to hang on the system.

29   ▪ The system will almost certainly create an outlaw class—as large as 10 to 20% of the population—cut off from "normal" life in America. This class will include political refuseniks, as well as those whose behavior has caused the system's software to deny their transactions. This outlaw class will sustain the underground economy for the use of future terrorists (and ordinary criminals).

30   These effects are easy to predict because they've already happened on a smaller scale.

31   Robert Ellis Smith, a lawyer and privacy specialist, says the push for a national ID card is based on the false belief that there can be a simple, high-tech solution to an immensely complex problem. "One way to predict the effectiveness of a national ID number or document is to look at environments where the true identity of all residents is known: prisons, the military, many workplaces, many college campuses," he writes in a new paper about national ID cards. "And yet these places are far from crime free."

32   Ari Schwartz, a policy analyst for the Center for Democracy and Technology, supports a national ID program that is done in a way to allow individuals to

DISCUSSION QUESTIONS (p. 585)

1. This argument is very direct. Dority indicates how ID cards were resisted in the past, why they are currently an issue, what questions and reasons can be raised in opposition to such a system, what she thinks ID cards would do, and which authorities also resist the idea.

2. Dority presents many objections. Her major objections are as follows: ID cards won't accomplish their goal of increasing security, ID cards will centralize the information the government has on individuals, ID cards could lead to increased monitoring of citizens, and ID cards could control the information held about them. But he is still concerned about the unintended consequences of a central database. "There are some measures that we should definitely be moving forward on today, and then there are some other ideas that we need to have a longer-term discussion about," he said. "This is definitely one of those longer-term ideas."

33   A similar message is offered by Peter Neumann and Lauren Weinstein, moderaters[*sic*] of the RISKS Forum (www.risks.org) and the PRIVACY Forum (www.privacyforum.org), respectively, and co-founders of People For Internet Responsibility:

34   We have noted here before that technological solutions entail risks that should be identified and understood in advance of deployment to the greatest extent possible, regardless of any panic of the moment. The purported (yet unproven) benefits of a national ID card system notwithstanding, these risks deserve to be discussed and understood in detail before any decisions regarding its adoption in any form should be made.

35   The specter of a national ID card has been cropping up in my nightmares for years. On top of the current horrifying attack on the Bill of Rights under the guise of "fighting terrorism," the potential imposition of this ultimate "Big Brother" tactic in my America leaves me in virtual despair.

36   But according to the Attorney General of the United States John Ashcroft, by writing such articles as "Invading the Bill of Rights" (*The Humanist*, November/December 2001) and this one, I'm "scaring peace-loving people with phantoms of lost liberty" and "aiding the terrorists." When I first heard this accusation, I was outraged. Upon reflection, however, I've decided I don't mind. In John Ashcroft's America, where everything is literally turned on its head, being called un-American has become the mark of a citizen who truly loves and defends the principles of the United States. (Not to mention that the company is most gratifying.)

Discussion Questions

1. What is the overall structure of the argument?
2. What are Dority's major objections to identity cards?
3. What does Dority do to demonstrate that national identity cards is a real issue? Why is this an important step in her argument?
4. Like many writers, Dority does not generate all her reasons herself but rather brings in ideas from other sources. Does the inclusion of material from the Web and ACLU weaken or strengthen the argument? How might it have been more effectively handled?
5. In paragraphs 31, 32, and 33 what is Dority's argumentative strategy? Is it effective?
6. What is the possible purpose for the conclusion? Is it effective?

Toward Key Insights

In our computerized age, the government and businesses have access to extensive amounts of information about citizens. To what extent does a national identity card pose a threat to civil liberties?

How much liberty is worth surrendering for greater security?

Marginal notes:

lead to discrimination and harassment.

3. Dority identifies newspaper articles that show support for the idea, shows that there is increased popular support for the idea, identifies those who support the idea, and identifies countries who use such a system. Many might feel that national identity cards are unlikely to find support in the United States, so the author needs to demonstrate that this issue merits our attention.

4. The actual reasons Dority draws from the sources do support her claim. Because they come from external sources, it demonstrates that this issue is a concern for more than just the author. However, the author simply drops them into her essay. Her essay would have been more effective if she had integrated the reasons into her own voice and cut any repetition.

5. Dority tries to demonstrate that even authorities who have an interest in security and might even support the idea of ID cards find problems with the concept. This is very effective since it shows that even experts in security cannot wholeheartedly embrace the idea.

6. The author anticipates and answers her critics. However, this strategy might personalize and politicize her essay and so undercut her argument.

Suggestions for Writing

Take a stance and write an essay in support of or opposed to national identity cards.

Colleges often use identification numbers and identification cards to keep track of students. Write an essay about whether such a system infringes on students.

MARTIN LUTHER KING, JR.

I Have a Dream

Martin Luther King, Jr. (1929–1968) has earned lasting fame for his part in the civil rights struggles of the 1950s and 1960s. Born in Atlanta, Georgia, he was ordained a Baptist minister in his father's church in 1947. A year later, he graduated from Morehouse College, then went on to take a Bachelor of Divinity degree at Crozier Theological Seminary (1951) and a PhD in philosophy at Boston University (1954), after which he accepted a pastorate in Montgomery, Alabama. King's involvement with civil rights grew when he organized and led a boycott that succeeded in desegregating Montgomery's bus system. In 1957, he founded and became the first president of the Southern Christian Leadership Conference and assumed a leading role in the civil rights movement. King advocated a pol- icy of nonviolent protest based on the beliefs of Thoreau and Gandhi and never veered from it despite many acts of violence directed at him. The success of King's crusade helped bring about the passage of the Civil Rights Act of 1964 and the Voting Rights Act of 1965 and won him the Nobel Peace Prize in 1964. King was assassinated on April 4, 1968, in Memphis. Since then, his birthday, January 15, has been made a national holiday. The speech "I Have a Dream" was delivered August 28, 1963, at the Lincoln Memorial in Washington, D.C., before a crowd of 200,000 people who had gathered to commemorate the centennial of the Emancipation Proclamation and to demonstrate for pending civil rights legislation. It stands as one of the most eloquent pleas ever made for racial justice.

1   I am happy to join with you today in what will go down in history as the greatest demonstration for freedom in the history of our nation.

2   Five score years ago, a great American, in whose symbolic shadow we stand today, signed the Emancipation Proclamation. This momentous decree came as a great beacon light of hope to millions of Negro slaves who had been seared in the flames of withering injustice. It came as a joyous daybreak to end the long night of their captivity.

3   But one hundred years later, the Negro still is not free; one hundred years later, the life of the Negro is still sadly crippled by the manacles of segregation and the chains of discrimination; one hundred years later, the Negro lives on a lonely island of poverty in the midst of a vast ocean of material prosperity; one hundred years later, the Negro is still languishing in the corners of American society and finds himself in exile in his own land.

4   So we've come here today to dramatize a shameful condition. In a sense we've come to our nation's capital to cash a check. When the architects of our republic wrote the magnificent words of the Constitution and the Declaration of Independence, they were signing a promissory note to which every American was to fall heir. This note was the promise that all men, yes, black men as well as

white men, would be guaranteed the unalienable rights of life, liberty, and the pursuit of happiness.

5   It is obvious today that America has defaulted on this promissory note in so far as her citizens of color are concerned. Instead of honoring this sacred obligation, America has given the Negro people a bad check; a check which has come back marked "insufficient funds." But we refuse to believe that the bank of justice is bankrupt. We refuse to believe that there are insufficient funds in the great vaults of opportunity of this nation. And so we've come to cash this check, a check that will give us upon demand the riches of freedom and the security of justice.

6   We have also come to this hallowed spot to remind America of the fierce urgency of now. This is no time to engage in the luxury of cooling off or to take the tranquilizing drug of gradualism. Now is the time to make real the promises of democracy; now is the time to rise from the dark and desolate valley of segregation to the sunlit path of racial justice; now is the time to lift our nation from the quicksands of racial injustice to the solid rock of brotherhood; now is the time to make justice a reality for all of God's children. It would be fatal for the nation to overlook the urgency of the moment. This sweltering summer of the Negro's legitimate discontent will not pass until there is an invigorating autumn of freedom and equality.

7   Nineteen sixty-three is not an end, but a beginning. And those who hope that the Negro needed to blow off steam and will now be content will have a rude awakening if the nation returns to business as usual. There will be neither rest nor tranquility in America until the Negro is granted his citizenship rights. The whirlwinds of revolt will continue to shake the foundations of our nation until the bright day of justice emerges.

8   But there is something that I must say to my people, who stand on the worn threshold which leads into the palace of justice. In the process of gaining our rightful place, we must not be guilty of wrongful deeds. Let us not seek to satisfy our thirst for freedom by drinking from the cup of bitterness and hatred. We must forever conduct our struggle on the high plain of dignity and discipline. We must not allow our creative protests to degenerate into physical violence. Again and again we must rise to the majestic heights of meeting physical force with soul force. The marvelous new militancy, which has engulfed the Negro community, must not lead us to a distrust of all white people. For many of our white brothers, as evidenced by their presence here today, have come to realize that their destiny is tied up with our destiny. And they have come to realize that their freedom is inextricably bound to our freedom. We cannot walk alone. And as we walk, we must make the pledge that we shall always march ahead. We cannot turn back.

9   There are those who are asking the devotees of Civil Rights, "When will you be satisfied?" We can never be satisfied as long as the Negro is the victim of the unspeakable horrors of police brutality; we can never be satisfied as long as our bodies, heavy with the fatigue of travel, cannot gain lodging in the motels of the highways and the hotels of the cities; we cannot be satisfied as long as the Negro's basic mobility is from a smaller ghetto to a larger one; we can never be satisfied as long as our children are stripped of their selfhood and robbed of their dignity by signs stating "For White Only"; we cannot be satisfied as long as the Negro in Mississippi cannot vote and a Negro in New York believes he has nothing for which to vote. No! No, we are not satisfied, and we will not be satisfied until "justice rolls down like waters and righteousness like a mighty stream."

10   I am not unmindful that some of you have come here out of great trials and tribulations. Some of you have come fresh from narrow jail cells. Some of you have come from areas where your quest for freedom left you battered by the

4. Ask students why King links his dream to the broader concept of the American dream.

5. Discuss whether whites, Native Americans, Mexican Americans, senior citizens, teenagers, or the handicapped are victims of injustice. Views on contemporary discrimination might lead to an argument essay on how to cope with it.

6. Throughout his campaign for civil rights, King consistently rejected the use of violence. Are there situations in which violence is justified? A discussion of this question might also lead to an argument essay.

DISCUSSION QUESTIONS (p. 589)

1. The speech was delivered as the capstone of a march to commemorate Lincoln's signing of the Emancipation Proclamation 100 years before, so it is only fitting that King begin as he does. Moreover, by mentioning Lincoln and the Emancipation Proclamation, King draws attention to the hopes that blacks experienced a century before and that are paralleled by those stirring in the blacks of his day, while reminding his listeners that the original hopes still haven't been realized.

2. King's proposition is implied. It might be stated as follows: Today, black Americans do not enjoy the rights guaranteed by the Declaration of Independence and Constitution; but if they persevere in the nonviolent struggle for civil rights, they can win these rights for themselves and their children.

3. King's immediate purpose is twofold: to inspire his followers to continue their nonviolent struggle for racial justice and to prick the consciences of white Americans. To inspire his followers, he points out the rewards that they will reap if they avoid despair and continue to persevere. To appeal to white consciences, he notes that America has not lived up to the ideal expressed in the Declaration of Independence and the Constitution (paragraph 4) and points out some of the abuses and burdens that blacks must put up with (paragraphs 9 and 10). By doing all these things King hopes to accomplish a third, less immediate purpose: to win congressional and presidential support for the civil rights legislation then being considered.

4. King's primary audience is his followers in the civil rights movement. In addition, he hopes to reach and co-opt (end of paragraph 8) white Americans, many of whom were indifferent or hostile toward his aims.

5. King's speech has four main parts. In paragraphs 3–7 he reminds his listeners of the bleak situation in which blacks find themselves and of the need for change. In paragraphs 8–10 he exhorts them to take heart and continue their struggle for justice without succumbing to bitterness and hatred. In

storms of persecution and staggered by the winds of police brutality. You have been the veterans of creative suffering. Continue to work with the faith that unearned suffering is redemptive. Go back to Mississippi. Go back to Alabama. Go back to South Carolina. Go back to Georgia. Go back to Louisiana. Go back to the slums and ghettos of our Northern cities, knowing that somehow this situation can and will be changed. Let us not wallow in the valley of despair.

11   I say to you today, my friends, that even though we face the difficulties of today and tomorrow, I still have a dream. It is a dream deeply rooted in the American dream. I have a dream that one day this nation will rise up and live out the true meaning of its creed, "We hold these truths to be self-evident, that all men are created equal." I have a dream that one day on the red hills of Georgia, sons of former slaves and the sons of former slave owners will be able to sit down together at the table of brotherhood. I have a dream that one day even the state of Mississippi, a state sweltering with the heat of injustice, sweltering with the heat of oppression, will be transformed into an oasis of freedom and justice. I have a dream that my four little children will one day live in a nation where they will not be judged by the color of their skin, but by the content of their character.

12   I HAVE A DREAM TODAY!

13   I have a dream that one day down in Alabama—with its vicious racists, with its Governor having his lips dripping with the words of interposition and nullification—one day right there in Alabama, little black boys and black girls will be able to join hands with little white boys and white girls as sisters and brothers.

14   I HAVE A DREAM TODAY!

15   I have a dream that one day every valley shall be exalted, every hill and mountain shall be made low. The rough places will be plain and the crooked places will be made straight, "and the glory of the Lord shall be revealed, and all flesh shall see it together."

16   This is our hope. This is the faith that I go back to the South with. With this faith we will be able to hew out of the mountain of despair, a stone of hope. With this faith we will be able to transform the jangling discords of our nation into a beautiful symphony of brotherhood. With this faith we will be able to work together, to pray together, to struggle together, to go to jail together, to stand up for freedom together, knowing that we will be free one day. And this will be the day. This will be the day when all of God's children will be able to sing with new meaning, "My country 'tis of thee, sweet land of liberty, of thee I sing. Land where my fathers died, land of the pilgrim's pride, from every mountain side, let freedom ring." And if America is to be a great nation, this must become true.

17   So let freedom ring from the prodigious hilltops of New Hampshire; let freedom ring from the mighty mountains of New York; let freedom ring from the heightening Alleghenies of Pennsylvania; let freedom ring from the snowcapped Rockies of Colorado; let freedom ring from the curvaceous slopes of California. But not only that. Let freedom ring from Stone Mountain of Georgia; let freedom ring from Lookout Mountain of Tennessee; let freedom ring from every hill and mole hill of Mississippi. "From every mountainside, let freedom ring."

18   And when this happens, and when we allow freedom to ring, when we let it ring from every village and every hamlet, from every state and every city, we will be able to speed up that day when all of God's children, black men and white men, Jews and Gentiles, Protestants and Catholics, will be able to join hands and sing in the words of the old Negro spiritual: "Free at last. Free at last. Thank God Almighty, we are free at last."

Discussion Questions

1. Why do you think King begins with a reference to Lincoln?
2. Does this speech have a stated or an implied proposition? What is the proposition?
3. What does King hope to accomplish by the speech? How does he go about achieving his aim(s)?
4. What is the audience for the speech?
5. How does King organize his speech? How does this organization advance his purpose?
6. Which type(s) of argumentative appeal does King use? Cite appropriate parts of the speech.
7. What kinds of stylistic devices does King use? Where do they occur? How do they increase the effectiveness of the speech?

Toward Key Insights

To what extent do people of all races relate to King's message today? Explain your answer.

Suggestion for Writing

Write an essay calling for some major social or political change. For example, you might recommend that the country enact national health insurance, institute a peacetime draft, ban smoking in all public places, amend the Constitution to ban or legalize abortions, establish federally funded day-care centers for working parents, or offer all workers a thirty-day leave of absence without pay.

WILLIAM RASPBERRY

A Journalist's View of Black Economics[1]

William Raspberry (born 1935) grew up in Okolona, Mississippi, and received his education at Indiana Central College, where he earned a Bachelor of Science degree in 1958. In college, he worked as a reporter for the Indianapolis Recorder *and following graduation continued with that publication until he entered the army. In 1962, after his military service, he began working for the* Washington Post, *an association that continues to the present. Raspberry now authors a nationally syndicated column dealing with current issues, such as criminal justice and minority concerns. In this selection Raspberry argues that black Americans should spend less time blaming their problems on racial injustice and more time creating businesses and programs to help solve these problems.*

1   I am intensely interested in the subject of the economics of black America. However, I am neither a businessman, an economist, nor a social scientist. I'm a "newspaper guy."

[1]William Raspberry, "A Journalist's View of Black Economics," © 1990, Washington Post Writers Group. Reprinted with permission.

paragraphs 11 through the first part of paragraph 16, he lays out his hopes for the future, and in the remainder of the speech he foresees victory.

6. King's speech is a masterful example of emotional and ethical appeal. Emotion is evident in every part of the speech, but perhaps most strongly in paragraph 9, which points out the injustices still suffered by blacks, and in paragraphs 16–18, which set out King's dreams for the future. In calling for racial justice, King emerges as a deeply ethical individual, an impression that is enhanced by his rejection of physical violence (paragraph 8) and his religious allusions (paragraphs 6, 15, 16, and 18).

7. King relies heavily on metaphors and repetition to accomplish his purpose. Metaphors abound throughout the speech. Brief examples include "beacon light of hope" and "flames of withering injustice" (paragraph 2); "manacles of segregation," "chains of discrimination," and "vast ocean of material prosperity" (paragraph 3); "sweltering summer . . . discontent," and "invigorating autumn of freedom" (paragraph 6); "bright day of justice" (paragraph 7); "palace of justice" and "cup of bitterness and hatred" (paragraph 8); "storms of persecution," "winds of police brutality," and "valley of despair" (paragraph 10); "table of brotherhood," "heat of

injustice, sweltering with the heat of oppression," and "oasis of freedom and justice" (paragraph 11); and "mountain of despair," "stone of hope," and "beautiful symphony of brotherhood" (paragraph 16). Paragraphs 4 and 5 constitute an extended metaphor or analogy that likens the rights guaranteed by the Constitution and Bill of Rights to a promissory note drawn on a bank. This extended metaphor includes two short metaphors: "bank of justice" and "vaults of opportunity." Repetition is likewise prominently featured in much of the speech. In paragraph 3 we have "one hundred years later," in paragraph 6 "Now is the time," in paragraph 9 "We can never be satisfied" and variations thereon, and in paragraph 10 "Go back." This technique reaches its climax with the powerful and moving repetition of "I have a dream" (paragraphs 11–15) and "Let freedom ring" (paragraphs 17 and 18). Other stylistic devices include balanced sentences "from the dark and desolate valley of segregation to the sunlit path of racial justice" and "from the quicksands of racial injustice to the solid rock of brotherhood" (paragraph 6) and similes "'until justice rolls down like waters and righteousness like a mighty stream'" (paragraph 9). Metaphors and similes add vividness to the speech, thus strengthening the listeners' grasp of the ideas presented. Repetition helps drum the points home and at the same time adds rhythm, and therefore emotional force, to the message.

2   That's not an apology. I like being a newspaper guy, and I like to think I'm a pretty good one. I point it out simply to warn you up front that what you will hear from me is neither economic analysis nor nuts-and-bolt business proposals. I like to think about things in general and my proposal is that we ought to approach this subject in this fashion.

3   **Myths About Race.** One of the things I would like us to think about is a myth: a myth that has crippled black America, sent us off on unpromising directions, and left us ill-equipped to deal with either political or economic reality.

4   That myth is that race is of overriding importance, that it is a determinant not just of opportunity but also of potential, a reliable basis for explaining political and economic realities, a reasonable way of talking about geopolitics, and the overwhelming basis on which to deal with the relationships between us.

5   When I refer to race-based explanations of the plight of black America as myth, I do not mean to suggest that all such explanations are false. My reference is to the definition of myth as a "traditional account of unknown authorship, ostensibly with a historical basis, but serving usually to explain some observed phenomenon."

6   The historical basis of our preoccupation with race is easy enough to see. America did not invent slavery. Slavery as an institution predates the Bible. But American slavery was peculiarly race-based. Since slavery is the basis for the very presence of black people in America, small wonder that race has assumed such importance in our mythology.

7   But slavery was more than just involuntary, unpaid servitude. Unlike other populations, to whom enslavement seemed a reasonable way of dealing with conquered enemies, America was never happy with the concept of one group of human beings holding another group of human beings in bondage. I suppose it was taken as a sin against God. But rather than forgo the economic benefits of slavery, American slaveholders resolved the dilemma by defining blacks not as fellow human beings but more like beasts of burden. There is nothing ungodly about a man requiring unremunerated work of an animal. Didn't God give man dominion over the animals?

8   Now it may have been that Africans were a special kind of animal: capable of thought, and human language, and even worship. But as long as whites could persuade themselves that blacks were not fully human, they could justify slavery.

9   Thus was born and reinforced the myth of inherent white superiority, which later became the basis for racial separation, for Jim Crow laws, for unequal opportunity and all sorts of evil. Nor is it just among whites that the myth survives . . . .

10   The myth that blacks cannot prevail in intellectual competition, that Chinese youngsters cannot play basketball, that Jews are specially vulnerable to guilt trips—these are negative myths whose acceptance has led to failure because they feed the assumption that failure is inevitable.

11   Objective reality is the arena in which we all must perform. But the success or failure of our performance is profoundly influenced by the attitudes—the myths—we bring to that reality.

12   Two things flow from the racism-is-all myth that we have used to account for our difficulties. The first is that it puts the solution to our difficulties outside our control. If our problems are caused by racism, and their solutions dependent on ending racism, our fate is in the hands of people who, by definition, don't love us.

13   **A Skewed Definition of Civil Rights.** The second outcome of the myth is our inclination to think of our problems in terms of a failure of racial justice. "Civil

rights," which once referred to those things whose fair distribution was a governmental responsibility, now refers to any discrepancy. Income gaps, education gaps, test-score gaps, infant-mortality gaps, life-expectancy gaps, employment gaps, business-participation gaps—all now are talked about as "civil rights" issues.

14   The problems indicated by all these gaps are real. But describing them as "civil rights" problems steers us away from possible solutions. The civil rights designation evokes a sort of central justice bank, managed by the government, whose charge is to ladle out equal portions of everything to everybody. It prompts us to think about our problems in terms of inadequate or unfair distribution. It encourages the fallacy that to attack racism as the source of our problems is the same as attacking our problems. As a result, we expend precious resources—time, energy, imagination, political capital—searching (always successfully) for evidence of racism, while our problems grow worse.

15   Maybe I can make my point clearer by reference to two other minorities. The first group consists of poor whites. There are in America not just individuals but whole pockets of white people whose situation is hardly worse than our own.

16   And yet these poor whites have their civil rights. They can vote, live where their money permits them to live, eat where their appetites and their pocketbooks dictate, work at jobs for which their skills qualify them. And yet they are in desperate straits. It doesn't seem to occur to us that the full grant and enforcement of our civil rights would leave black Americans in about the same situation that poor white people are now in. That isn't good enough for me.

17   There is another minority whose situations may be more instructive. I refer to recently arrived Asian-Americans. What is the difference between them and us? Certainly it isn't that they have managed to avoid the effects of racism. Neither the newly arrived Southeast Asians nor the earlier arriving Japanese-Americans, Chinese-Americans, and Korean-Americans are loved by white people. But these groups have spent little of their time and energy proving that white people don't love them.

18   **Opportunity Knocks: Who Answers?** The difference between them and us is our operating myths. Our myth is that racism accounts for our shortcomings. Theirs is that their own efforts can make the difference, no matter what white people think.

19   They have looked at America as children with their noses pressed to the window of a candy store: if only I could get in there, boy, could I have a good time. And when they get in there, they work and study and save and create businesses and job opportunities for their people.

20   But we, born inside the candy store, have adopted a myth that leads us to focus only on the maldistribution of the candy. Our myth leads us into becoming a race of consumers, when victories accrue to the producers.

21   Interestingly enough, this is a fairly recent phenomenon. There was a time when we, like the more recent arrivals in this country, sought only the opportunity to be productive, and we grasped that opportunity under circumstances far worse—in law, at least—than those that obtain now.

22   Free blacks and former slaves, though denied many of the rights that we take for granted today, were entrepreneurial spirits. They were artisans and inventors, shopkeepers and industrialists, financiers and bankers. The first female millionaire in America was Madame C. J. Walker. At least two companies founded at the turn of the century are now on the *Black Enterprise* list of the 100 top black firms in the country.

paragraphs 21–26, you
might note that, in
"Momma's Encounter"
(pages 464–465), Maya
Angelou mentions a store
owned by her grand-
mother.

DISCUSSION
QUESTIONS
(p. 594)
1. By establishing that he
is a journalist, Raspberry
justifies his general
approach to his topic
while providing a ration-
ale for excluding
economic analysis and
specific proposals from
his presentation.
2. Many people, including
students, regard myths as
nothing more than
straight-out lies.
Raspberry's definition not
only reveals myths to be
something very different—
sets of mistaken beliefs—
but also indicates how
those beliefs arose. Thus it
serves as a springboard for
his discussion of how the
particular myth that con-
cerns him came about.
This definition, and
Raspberry's use of it,
shows how important
it is for writers to clarify
terms that might be
misunderstood.
3. King argues in para-
graphs 5, 6, 7, 8, 9, and 11
for "justice" and specifically mentions "racial justice" in paragraph 6.
Raspberry asserts in paragraphs 13 and 14 that to
concentrate on "a failure
of racial justice" is to
"expend precious
resources . . . while our
problems grow worse."
King espouses civil rights;
Raspberry contends in
paragraph 14 that to lump
problems together under

23   Black real estate operatives transformed white Harlem into a haven for
blacks. The early 1900s saw the founding of a number of all-black towns: Mound
Bayou, Mississippi; Boley, Oklahoma; Nicodemus, Kansas; and others.

24   Boley at one time boasted a bank, twenty-five grocery stores, five hotels,
seven restaurants, a waterworks, an electricity plant, four cotton gins, three drug
stores, a bottling plant, a laundry, two newspapers, two colleges, a high school, a
grade school, four department stores, a jewelry store, two hardware stores, two
ice cream parlors, a telephone exchange, five churches, two insurance agencies,
two livery stables, an undertaker, a lumber yard, two photography studios, and an
ice plant [from J. DeSane, *Analogies and Black History: A Programmed Approach*].
Not bad for an all-black town of 4,000.

25   As Robert L. Woodson observed in his book, *On the Road to Economic Freedom*,
"The Harlem and Boley experiences, which matched aggressive black entrepreneurial activity with the self-assertion drive of the black masses, was multiplied
nationwide to the point that, in 1913, fifty years after Emancipation, black
America had accumulated a personal wealth of $700 million.

26   "As special Emancipation Day festivals and parades were held that year in
cities and towns across the country, blacks could take pride in owning 550,000
homes, 40,000 businesses, 40,000 churches, and 937,000 farms. The literacy
rate among blacks climbed to a phenomenal 70 percent—up from 5 percent
in 1863."

27   **Over-learning the Civil Rights Lesson.** What has happened since then? A lot
of things, including a good deal of success that we don't talk much about. But
among the things that have happened are two that have created problems for us.
First is the overemphasis on integration, as opposed to desegregation and
increased opportunity. Hundreds of thriving restaurants, hotels, service outlets,
and entertainment centers have gone out of business because we preferred integration to supporting our own painstakingly established institutions. Indeed,
aside from black churches and black colleges, little remains to show for that
entrepreneurial spurt of the early decades of this century.

28   The other thing that has happened is that we over-learned the lessons of the
civil rights movement. That movement, brilliantly conceived and courageously
executed, marked a proud moment in our history. The upshot was that black
Americans, for the first time in our sojourn here, enjoy the full panoply of our
civil rights.

29   Unfortunately, that period also taught us to see in civil rights terms things
that might more properly be addressed in terms of enterprise and exertion
rather than in terms of equitable distribution. Even when we speak of business
now, our focus is on distribution: on set-asides and affirmative action.

30   **Entrepreneurs and Self-Help.** Our 1960s success in making demands on
government has led us to the mistaken assumption that government can give us
what we need for the next major push toward equality. It has produced in us
what Charles Tate of the Booker T. Washington Foundation recently described
as a virtual antipathy toward capitalism.

31   Even middle-class blacks seldom talk to their children about going into business. Instead our emphasis is on a fair distribution of jobs in business created
and run by others. We ought to have a fair share of those jobs. But the emphasis,
I submit, ought to be finding ways to get more of us into business and thereby
creating for ourselves the jobs we need.

32   That is especially true with regard to the so-called black underclass who
tend to reside in areas abandoned by white businesses.

33   In addition to figuring out ways of getting our unemployed to jobs that already exist, we need to look for ways to encourage blacks in those abandoned neighborhoods to create enterprises of their own. What I have in mind are not merely the shops and Mom & Pop stores that we still patronize (but whose owners are far likelier to be Vietnamese or Koreans than blacks), but also an entrepreneurial approach to our social problems.

34   I am not suggesting that government has no role in attacking these problems. It has a major role. What I am suggesting is that we need to explore ways of creating government-backed programs that instead of merely making our problems more bearable go in the direction of solving those problems. We are forever talking about the lack of day care as an impediment to work for welfare families. But why aren't we lobbying for legislation that would relax some of the anti-entrepreneurial rules and permit some of the money now spent on public welfare to be used to establish child-care centers run by the neighbors of those who need the care? Why aren't we looking for ways to use the funds that are already being expended to create small jitney services to transport job-seekers to distant jobs?

35   **Success Is the Goal** I said at the beginning that I am not a theoretician, but I do have one little theory that may have some relevance to our subject. It is this: When people believe that their problems can be solved, they tend to get busy solving them—partly because it is the natural thing to do and partly because they would like to have the credit. When people believe that their problems are beyond solution, they tend to position themselves so as to avoid blame for their nonsolution.

36   Now none of the black leadership will tell you that they think the problems we face are beyond solution. To do so would be to forfeit their leadership positions. But their behavior, if my theory is correct, suggests their pessimism.

37   Let me offer an example of what I am talking about. Take the woeful inadequacy of education in the predominantly black central cities. Does the black leadership see the ascendancy of black teachers and school administrators and the rise of black politicians to positions of local leadership as assets to be used in improving those dreadful schools? Rarely. What you are more likely to hear are charges of white abandonment, white resistance to integration, white conspiracies to isolate black children even when the schools are officially desegregated. In short, white people are responsible for the problem.

38   But if the youngsters manage to survive those awful school systems and make their way to historically black colleges—that is, if the children begin to show signs that they are going to make it—these same leaders sing a different song. Give our black colleges a fair share of public resources, they say, and we who know and love our children will educate them.

39   The difference, I submit, is that they believe many of our high school students won't succeed, and they conspire to avoid the blame for their failure. But they believe that most of our college youngsters will make it, and they want to be in position to claim credit for their success.

40   I suspect something like that is happening in terms of our economic well-being. Many of us are succeeding, in an astonishing range of fields, and the leadership does not hesitate to point out—with perfect justification—that our success is attributable to the glorious civil rights movement: that black exertion and courage made our success possible.

41   But many of us aren't succeeding. Teenage pregnancy, dope trafficking, lawlessness, and lack of ambition make us doubt that they ever will succeed. But do our leaders suggest that the reasons have to do with the inadequacy of the civil rights movement, or with any lack of exertion and courage on the part of the

the heading of "civil rights" "steers us away from possible solutions." King, in paragraph 5, refuses to accept that the "bank of justice" is bankrupt; Raspberry, in paragraph 14, declares that thinking in terms of "a sort of central justice bank" does not address black problems. King argues for government action to protect the rights of African Americans, and states that he intends to "cash this check"—see paragraph 5—which will yield "the riches of freedom and the security of justice." Raspberry opposes a system "managed by the government, whose charge is to ladle out equal portions of everything to everybody." Students should be aware, of course, that different social circumstances prevailed at the times the two speeches were given.

4. Although an analogy never proves anything, this one helps Raspberry explain his point persuasively. Almost everybody will understand the candy store reference. Also, the analogy features significant similarities, makes its point with special force, and is not overextended.

5. Paragraphs 13 and 14 provide a flawed explanation for the existence of black problems; paragraphs 15–17 offer examples that counter this explanation. Paragraph 21 notes the productivity of earlier black generations; paragraphs 22–26 back the contention with specific examples. Paragraph 33 argues for the creation of black enterprises in blighted areas; paragraph 34 suggests some specific actions that might be taken. Paragraph 36 suggests that black leaders believe, without admitting it, that black problems can't be solved; paragraph 37 offers their failure to press for improved inner-city schools as an example of this pessimism. Students should understand the importance of clarifying their ideas with concrete, relevant examples.

6. Raspberry narrates the history of previous generations of African Americans who were very productive and entrepreneurial.

7. The conclusion, a combination of an anecdote and a recommendation phrased as a challenge, offers a forceful rationale for rejecting the myth of racism and adopting Raspberry's point of view, and therefore it is effective.

8. This question should prompt a stimulating discussion.

42 leadership? No. When we see failure among our people, and have reason to believe that the failure is permanent, our recourse is to our mainstay myth: Racism is the culprit. Mistakenly, we credit black pride for our successes and blame prejudice for our shortfalls.

42 I leave it to others to suggest the specifics by which we will move to increase the economic success of black America. I will tell you only that I believe it can be done—not only because it is being done by an encouraging number of us, but also because it has been done by earlier generations who struggled under circumstances of discrimination, deprivation, and hostility far worse than anything we now face.

43 My simple suggestion is that we stop using the plight of the black underclass as a scourge for beating up on white racists and examine both the black community and the American system for clues to how we can transform ourselves from consumers to producers.

44 I used to play a little game in which I would concede to members of the black leadership the validity of the racism explanation. "Let's say you're exactly right, that racism is the overriding reason for our situation, and that an all-out attack on racism is our most pressing priority," I'd tell them.

45 "Now let us suppose that we eventually win the fight against racism and put ourselves in the position now occupied by poor whites. What would you urge that we do next?"

46 "Pool our resources? Establish and support black businesses? Insist that our children take advantage of the opportunities that a society free of racism would offer? What should be our next step?"

47 "Well, just for the hell of it, why don't we pretend that the racist dragon has been slain already—and take that next step right now?"

Discussion Questions

1. Explain why Raspberry identifies himself as a "newspaper guy" in paragraph 1.
2. Why do you think Raspberry offers a precise definition of "myth" in paragraph 5?
3. Reread paragraphs 13 and 14 and point out specifically how Raspberry's views differ from those of Martin Luther King, Jr., in "I Have a Dream" (pages 586–588).
4. Discuss the effectiveness of the analogy Raspberry uses in paragraphs 19–20.
5. Cite three places in the essay where Raspberry states an idea and uses specific examples to clarify its meaning.
6. What writing strategy does Raspberry use to develop paragraphs 21–29?
7. Paragraphs 44–47 function as Raspberry's conclusion. Indicate why you think the conclusion is or is not effective.
8. Raspberry's and King's arguments were both delivered as speeches, King's in 1963 and Raspberry's in 1989. Which argument seems more effective? Does your answer stem from the content, effectiveness of presentation, or both?

Toward Key Insights

Raspberry makes an "entrepreneurial approach" seem like a relatively simple solution to widespread black poverty and related problems. What difficulties might such an approach face?

Is Raspberry right in suggesting that black Americans need to spend less time blaming racial injustice for their problems and more time creating businesses and enterprises? Why or why not?

Suggestion for Writing

Develop an argument that proposes how a minority group can best enhance its economic prosperity. Use whatever types of evidence seem appropriate.

NATHAN THORNBURGH

The Case for Amnesty

Nathan Thornburgh has been a Senior Editor for Time *magazine from 2000 to the present. He is author of a number of articles including "The Fallout from a Deportation" and "Dropout Nation." This article was published in* Time *in 2007.*

1   Amnesty has emerged as the pariah term of the immigration debate, disavowed even by those who believe in its goals. But what are the alternatives to letting illegals stay? Deporting millions? Devising other punishments? Doing nothing at all? Few places have struggled with these questions as much as rural Beardstown, Ill., where an April immigration raid at the town's largest employer exposed a community that is both dependent on its undocumented workers and deeply resentful of their presence. Why legalizing the illegals makes sense for Beardstown—and for America.

1. Amnesty Can Work Politically

2   One day before the June 5 Republican debate, Senator John McCain tried to preempt the coming criticism. He knew he would spend the debate flanked by nine candidates waiting to rip into the Senate compromise bill he helped write, which calls for a salve of legalization, border security and guest-worker programs. So in a Miami speech on June 4, he sought to distance himself from the *a* word. "Critics of the bill attack this as amnesty," he said. "(But) we impose fines, fees and other requirements as punishment." The bill, he said, is not amnesty.

3   Yes, it is. Whether you fine illegal aliens or stick them in English classes or make them say a hundred Hail Marys, at the end of the day, illegals would be allowed to stay and become citizens under this bill. That's amnesty. And that's a good thing for America. The estimated 12 million illegals are by their sheer numbers undeportable. More important, they are too enmeshed in a healthy U.S. economy to be extracted.

4   Yet the word *amnesty* was still used as a cudgel at the GOP debate—McCain's rivals clobbered him with the term, and he turned it on them as well, saying that doing nothing is "silent and de facto amnesty." Why are the bill's supporters so skittish about the word? If the past five years of immigration debate have taught us anything, it's that railing against the illegal invasion is easy, popular and effective. Now politicians are being roasted for conceding a reality: illegal or not, most of those 12 million are here to stay.

5   The heat extends from President George W. Bush to McCain and all the way down to the mayor of Beardstown, where a decade of intense immigration has

list such terms and discuss how they should be approached in an argument. The author embraces the term "amnesty."

3. Have the students as they read this essay list separately the arguments in support of amnesty and the arguments against certain objections to amnesty. Use this to discuss whether the weight given to answering objectives was effective.

4. This is an issue that can be very emotional for many students. Ask the students to identify their reaction to the topic. Where students have a strong emotional response, discuss the reasons for such a strong response. List with the class strategies for handling an emotional topic in a way that the issue is carefully and rationally considered. Some suggestions might be as follows: establish ground rules for discussion, remind individuals when they are getting heated, stop to recognize the emotion and the reason for the emotion, reestablish that the discussion itself does not affect the individual personally, reaffirm the importance of having a society where we can discuss emotional issues rationally with others who disagree with us.

6   turned a nearly all-white town into a place in which 72% of the prekindergarten class is Hispanic. "If I got up and said I'm gonna run each and every Mexican out of town on a donkey, the voters here would cheer me on," says Mayor Bob Walters. "But I'm not going to say that. It's not our job to deport them all, and it's not the right thing to do."

6   Many of Beardstown's white residents were pleased by the federal raid on the massive pork-processing plant at the edge of town, owned by multinational meatpacker Cargill Meat Solutions (the April 4 operation targeted a subcontractor that was cleaning the plant, not Cargill itself). The raids netted 62 people, most of whom were sent to federal detention centers that night and later deported. "It's good they got those people," Oscar Cluney, 18, told me as he hung out with his friends in the parking lot of the local Save-a-Lot store. "The whole situation here makes me kind of mad."

7   And a lot of voters are upset too—but they are deeply conflicted about the right solution. A recent Gallup poll found that 60% of people who were following the bill closely were opposed to it. But an April *USA Today/Gallup* poll found that just 14% of respondents wanted to send illegal immigrants home with no chance of returning to the U.S. The public seems confused about the definition of amnesty.

8   Politicians are tapping into the public's uncertainty. In the June 5 GOP debate, Rudy Giuliani summed up the bill's problem this way: "It's a typical Washington mess," he said. He's right, of course, but not for the reasons he thinks. Rather, the bill is a mess because it doesn't fully embrace its most important aim: amnesty. Instead, it is laden with punitive measures—designed to evoke a certain toughness—that will at most just keep illegals from participating. Amnesty, as defined by its opponents, has come to mean getting forgiveness for free. But under the Senate's current compromise, the path for illegals is not anything close to easy. Under the compromise, the 12 million would face a 13-year process including $5,000 in fines per person, benchmarks for learning English and an onerous "touchback" provision that calls for the head of each household to leave job and family behind and return to his or her home country for an indeterminate amount of time to queue up for the final green card. Nothing free about that.

9   The touchback clause is party designed to insulate the bill from criticism that amnesty would be unfair to those waiting in line to come legally. But that's a false comparison. If people are frustrated, as they should be, by the fact that some eligible immigrants have been waiting for citizenship for as many as 28 years, then by all means, fix that problem. Streamline the process for legal immigration. But don't blame that red-tape nightmare on the millions of low-wage illegals already here, who form a very different (and vastly more populous) group.

2. Amnesty Won't Depress Wages—Globalization Has Already Done That

10   Before you talk about amnesty, it makes sense to address the anger that many citizens feel. Across the U.S., Americans feel squeezed and threatened by the newcomers. Part of the anxiety is undeniably race based. Fox News's Bill O'Reilly leavened his reluctant support for the Senate bill with warnings that it "drastically alters" a country that is already "one-third minority." Others worry about language preservation. Republican Congressman Tom Tancredo of Colorado gave a breathless defense of the English language at the GOP debate, saying that bilingualism has failed other countries and that the U.S. was fast headed in that direction. Yes, it's true: Mexicans speak Spanish. Relax. Mexicans also know that English is the key to getting ahead in the U.S. When Beardstown

opened a bilingual program for all the kids in the elementary school, Hispanic parents were as worried as white parents about missing out on an English-only education. Assimilation is slow, but it is inevitable. Beardstown was settled in the 19th century by unapologetically German immigrants, but you won't hear so much as a gesundheit uttered there today. What is lacking, in Beardstown as in Washington, is faith in America's undimmed ability to metabolize immigrants from around the world, to change them more than they change the U.S.

11   Economic anxiety animates much of the resistance to amnesty, particularly from the left. Real wages have been stagnant for nearly three decades throughout the U.S., and for a place like working-class Beardstown, having to deal with a huge new influx of Spanish-speaking workers seems like adding insult to economic injury. But if times are tough in rural America, are illegal immigrants to blame? It turns out that the truly good jobs left Beardstown long before the Mexicans came. In the mid-'80s, the Cargill plant was owned by Oscar Mayer. Walters was the union representative at the plant back then, and he says it offered good jobs and good benefits, but globalization and other corporate pressures caught up with them. The company shuttered and sold the plant in 1987. Five months later, it reopened under a new owner, with lower wages and fewer benefits. "The starting wage went from $11 an hour to $7.50," says Walters. "The meatpacking industry ought to be ashamed of what they did to towns like ours."

12   The first Hispanics didn't come to work at Cargill en masse until years later. And as Cargill likes to point out, more white workers work at the factory than before. The plant has in fact grown, thanks in large part to hardworking migrants, not just from Mexico but from more than 20 other countries. The business seems robust for the time being. The workforce is unionized again. Salaries are creeping up. A new Wal-Mart Supercenter is on the way. Cargill's strength has turned Beardstown into, if not a boomtown, at least a place that investors are paying attention to. And the town is leading its pitch with the fact that it has a large Hispanic workforce, a bellwether for economic growth. "That's all I need to tell them," says Steve Twaddle, the county's director of economic development. "Businesses understand."

13   That progress, in Beardstown and in similar towns throughout the U.S., is imperiled by illegality. Cargill has long struggled to rid its rolls of illegal workers who are using false documentation. Most notably, a rumor that another raid was imminent swept through the night shift last month. Those workers who had false papers had to make a decision: stay and risk detention and deportation if the rumor were true, or leave and expose themselves as illegal workers. Cargill wouldn't comment on the incident, but locals say that dozens fled the plant that night and were fired or quit after having outed themselves by leaving.

14   It is not easy to replace them. Meatpacking is a hard job at any salary. There's plenty of new technology in the meatpacking industry, but no machine has yet been invented to take over some of the toughest positions, like the role of gut snatcher, whose sole job is to tug the offal out of each freshly killed hog that comes down the line.

15   The economics of immigration remain a mysterious science. Everyone has a pet study proving immigration suppresses wages or it builds economies. A less malleable truth is that many towns, like many companies, are faced with a stark choice in the global economy: grow or die. So Beardstown is growing, a healthy economy surrounded by dying rural towns. The U.S. is in the same situation. For all the stresses of immigration, it is the only industrialized nation with a population that is growing fast enough and skews young enough to provide the kind of

CLASSROOM ACTIVITIES (p. 598)
1. Have students work in small groups to identify what they think based on the article would be the results of an amnesty program for illegal immigrants and why.
2. Have students in some small groups attempt to identify themselves with illegal immigrants. If their parents had brought them to the United States illegally, what do they think their view of this issue would be and why? Have others identify with small business owners, and others with young high school graduates trying to find work. In each case have them identify what the issue might look like from that point of view. Then have groups switch roles. Discuss the results.

DISCUSSION
QUESTIONS (p. 599)

1. The article does man-
age to have relevance
beyond the occasion of its
writing. It does so by
addressing broader long-
term questions with exam-
ples and arguments that
are not specifically tied to
the time of its writing.

2. The topic has been and
continues to be volatile.
By admitting the heated
debate around the issue
and the concern of oppo-
nents to amnesty, the
writer gives himself credibility. By embracing the
issue of amnesty, the
writer focuses on what
often is the key issue in
much of the immigration
reform debate. Whether
the writer wins or loses the
argument, the simple
objection against
"amnesty" cannot be
raised against his immigration position.

3. Since the strongest
emotional and political
response is to reject
amnesty, any reasons for
"amnesty" are not likely to
be entertained by readers
until their objections to
the concept are answered.
For that reason, the writer
stresses the response to
common objections. The
writer uses the analogy of
the assimilation of
Germans to suggest that
Hispanic assimilation is
inevitable, used a specific
example to show that the
reduction of wages pre-
ceded illegal immigrants
entering that workforce,
suggests other areas where
lax enforcement of laws
has not harmed the gen-
eral respect for law, provides reason why amnesty
would have a positive

16 workforce that a dynamic economy needs. The illegals are part of the reason for that, and amnesty ensures that competitive advantage.

3. Amnesty Won't Undermine the Rule of Law

Google "This is a nation of laws," and you'll find a thousand online Cassandras warning that our failure to prosecute illegals is an invitation to anarchy. They are right about the U.S. being a nation of laws. But our legal system is not a house of cards, one flick away from collapse. U.S. jurisprudence has in fact always been a series of hedged bets, weighing the potential harm of a violation against the costs of enforcement. That's why people get arrested for assault but not for jaywalking. It's time to think seriously about exactly where the act of illegal immigration lies in the spectrum of criminality. Consider the complicity of U.S. employers ranging from multinational corporations to suburbanites looking for gardeners. Factor in the mixed signals that lax law enforcement sent to would-be immigrants throughout the '80s and '90s, and the crime should rank as a misdemeanor, not a felony. Even if we step up border enforcement in the future—as we should—it is true that for a long time, crossing the Rio Grande was akin more to jaywalking than breaking and entering.

17 Sure, there is a very real national-security threat in having a porous border. But a large—if unquantifiable—percentage of the people crossing that line illegally are not newcomers but rather people who have already established lives in the U.S. and would qualify for amnesty. If they were legalized and free to circulate, we could concentrate on the serious criminals and terrorists crossing the border, not a worker going back to his family.

18 In Beardstown, amnesty would also help authorities tackle crime. Right now, they spend a lot of their energy sorting out who is who in the community because illegals present local police with a bewildering maze of identities. The illegals of Beardstown work under one name and go to church under another. Parents give their kindergartners fake names to use in school. "We are absolutely unable to identify our own people," says Walters. It sounds counterintuitive, but with immigration, forgiving a crime may be the best way to restore law and order.

4. Amnesty Won't Necessarily Add to the Social-Services Burden

19 Many of the undesirable traits of illegal populations stem in large part from the simple fact that they are illegal. They use expensive emergency rooms because they lack insurance or are afraid a primary-care doctor might create a paper trail. They often don't file tax returns because of the same fear, and they turn to welfare or other social services because their illegal status consigns them to the lowest rung of the economy. We infantilize undocumented workers by relegating them to second-class status, and then we chastise them for being dependent on the nanny state.

20 "(White people) think we have it easy, that we don't pay taxes," says Fernanda, 19, whose parents were deported in the April raid. "They don't know how hard it is to get ahead here."

21 Fernanda has been in the U.S. since the eighth grade and graduated last year from Beardstown Middle/High School. Those five years of public education represent a significant investment by the U.S. government. And what's the return on that investment? Fernanda had dreams of going to college to study nursing, and Beardstown badly needs bilingual nurses. But she's illegal, and after the deportation of her parents, she has to support the entire family. So she's looking for work at local hog farms, a manual-labor job that does not make the most of her talents. "There's a great human potential in this town that doesn't see the light of day because of the legal status," says community organizer Julio Flores.

22   Some would argue that Fernanda should not have been schooled on our dime in the first place. But the reality is that Fernanda is here in the U.S. to stay. She's not going back to Mexico. Amnesty would offer millions like her a fighting chance at self-sufficiency and social mobility.

5. Amnesty Doesn't Have to Spawn Even More Illegal Immigration

23   A popular reading of recent history holds that the amnesty of 1986, which offered a path to citizenship for 3 million illegals, sparked the much larger wave of unlawful immigration that followed. According to that logic, the '86 amnesty showed would-be migrants from around the world that the U.S. was weak-willed and would eventually relent and give citizenship to its illegals. Duly encouraged, Mexicans and others stormed our borders with unprecedented vigor.

24   Illegal immigration did soar, but that's not why. Studies show that the valleys and peaks in migration have depended far less on changes in policy or policing and far more on the basic economic conditions in the U.S. and Mexico. If you want to truly tamp down illegal immigration, you could induce a recession in the U.S. A better idea might be to help Mexico create more jobs that pay better. A recent Council on Foreign Relations study found that when Mexican wages drop 10% relative to U.S. wages, attempts to cross the border illegally rise 6%. As complex and corrupt as the Mexican economy is, we ignore it at our peril.

25   While Mexico patches itself up, at least the security options are better today than in 1986. There is both the political will and the technology to make enforcement a serious part of any amnesty plan. National ID cards, real employer verification, high-tech border controls can all aid in making sure that this would be the last amnesty of this size.

26   Over fried catfish at the Riverview restaurant, Walters says he calls the feds about illegals in his town a few times a month. But he is tired of the hassle and ready for legalization. "If I could wave a magic wand, I'd rather have no Hispanics and have this town be like it was in the '50s. But that's just not going to happen," he says. "Amnesty is touchy, but we can't keep doing nothing."

27   The need for action is one thing that unites all the presidential candidates. And the coalition for immigration reform is strong enough—and wide enough—to take principled stands. The President, much of the Democratic Party, and a clutch of GOP lawmakers all support legalization. It's not too much to hope that together they could make a frank and forceful argument for amnesty and win over a conflicted nation.

effect on laws, uses an example of individual to show how legalization would increase the tax base while allowing social services to have more civic payoffs, and finally argued that other causal factors other than amnesty influence illegal immigration. Though the author's reasons and evidence is sufficient to get readers to stop and think, the evidence is neither extensive enough nor general enough to convince those fiercely opposed to amnesty.

4. The author only introduces a few positive arguments in support of amnesty. In paragraph 8 he identifies the consequences for illegal immigrants under an amnesty plan to show that they don't get off "free"; in paragraph 12 he argues that immigrants have economically strengthened Beardstown; in paragraphs 13 and 14 he argues that deportation creates hardship for business; in paragraph 18 he argues that legalization will help fight crime by allowing illegal aliens to have public identities; finally in paragraph 20 and 21 he argues that amnesty allows illegal immigrants to pay taxes

Discussion Questions

1. Like many arguments, this one is written at a particular time in relation to ongoing situations, such as the 2007–08 primary season to which this article makes mention. Does the article manage to have an impact beyond its specific context and if so how?
2. The argument starts by identifying a lot of the political difficulty surrounding the idea of amnesty for illegal immigrants and yet embraces the term and idea of amnesty. Why does the author do this? Is this approach effective?
3. Much of the argument attempts to answer common objections to amnesty. Why does the author adopt this approach? What kinds of reasons or evidence does he use to answer these objections? Is it effective?
4. The author makes few positive arguments for amnesty. Where does the writer make such supportive arguments? Are they effective? Why or why not?

and make a real contribution to American society. While the author makes good points that should get readers to stop and think, he does not present enough data to make a strong case. For example, he doesn't demonstrate how much tax revenue they would add when compared to the cost of the services they might use.

Toward Key Insights

The author approaches this issue as if it were simply a matter of measuring the benefits and harm of granting amnesty. Others approach the issue as one of principle: "we need to enforce the law or the concept of law is meaningless." Is there any way these two approaches can find common ground to carry on the discussion? Has the author achieved such a common ground?

The author attempts to assure the reader that granting "amnesty" will not result in harmful consequences. The problem of induction is that a few cases do not guarantee future results. Does he provide sufficient evidence to make this case? What would be necessary for him to make a convincing case for you as a reader?

Suggestion for Writing

Take one of the issues that the author addresses such as "amnesty won't undermine the rule of law" and argue for and against the author's position.

MARK KRIKORIAN

Not Amnesty but Attrition

Mark Krikorian is the Executive Director of the Center for Immigration Studies, a Washington D.C. think-tank that argues for stricter immigration policy. He is a regular contributor to National Review *and has also published articles in* The Washington Post, New York Times, *and* Commentary. *He is the author of* The New Case against Immigration, Both Legal and Illegal. *This article was Published in the* National Review *in March 2004.*

PERSPECTIVE
Often students and others think an effective argument needs to address all of the key issues. This article uses the effective strategy of identifying one pivotal issue and addressing that issue in more depth. By demonstrating that attrition by enforcing laws can be effective without being draconian, the writer builds on the reader's already existing concerns about amnesty and is persuasive by providing them a viable alternative.

TEACHING STRATEGIES
1. After discussing why this writer chooses to focus on one strategy, discuss how debates on other key issues could be similarly narrowed. For example, the issue over

1   The issue of what to do about illegal aliens living in the United States is often presented as a Hobson's choice: either launch mass roundups to arrest and deport 9-million-plus people, or define away the problem through legalization.

2   The second option—amnesty—is the one President Bush chose in his January 7 speech on immigration. It also underlies many congressional proposals, from the McCain-Kolbe-Flake and Hagel-Daschle bills in the Senate to the House Democratic leadership's plan unveiled in late January.

3   Few among the political elite entertain any alternative. At a recent panel discussion on the president's immigration proposal, Margaret Spellings, the president's chief domestic-policy adviser, reacted with a demure chuckle to the suggestion that we enforce the law.

4   The commentariat is more explicit. Not content to politely ignore the notion of enforcing the law, the *Wall Street Journal*, for instance, has flatly asserted that it's not possible, a "fantasy" of the "extreme," "nativist," and "restrictionist" Right. Meanwhile, the Manhattan Institute's Tamar Jacoby wrote in *The New Republic* of "futile law enforcement" and how "the migrant flow is inevitable."

5   Fortunately for America there is a third way, between the politically impossible and disruptive approach of mass roundups on one hand, and the surrender of our sovereignty by the open-borders Left and its libertarian fellow-travelers on the other. This third way is attrition, squeezing the illegal population through

consistent, across-the-board law enforcement to bring about an annual reduction in the illegal population rather than the annual increases we have seen for more than a decade. Over a few years, the number of illegal aliens would drop significantly, shrinking the problem from a crisis to a manageable nuisance.

Of Velvet Fists . . .

6   This isn't just a wonkish daydream. There is significant churn in the illegal population, which we can use to our advantage. According to a 2003 INS report, thousands of people stop being illegal aliens each year. From 1995 to 1999, an average of 165,000 a year went back home; the same number got some kind of legal status, about 50,000 were deported, and 25,000 died, for a total of more than 400,000 people each year subtracted from the resident illegal population. The problem is that the average inflow of new illegal aliens was nearly 800,000, swamping the outflow and creating an average annual increase of close to 400,000.

7   The solution, then, is to increase the number of people leaving the illegal population and to reduce the number of new illegal settlers, so that there is an annual decline in the total number. This is a measured, Burkean approach to the problem. It doesn't aspire to an immediate, magical solution to a long-brewing crisis, but rather helps us back out of an untenable situation that we helped create through our inattention to the law.

8   This begs the natural question: "But aren't we already enforcing the law?" If not, as a *Wall Street Journal* editorial has asked, "Then what is it we've been doing for 20 years now?" The answer lies in the old Soviet joke: "We pretend to work and they pretend to pay us."

9   Since 1986, Congress has passed muscular immigration laws and then made sure that they were not enforced. In that year, the Immigration Reform and Control Act (IRCA) was enacted, which traded an illegal-alien amnesty for a first-ever ban on the employment of illegal aliens. The point was to demagnetize the strong pull of good jobs—the main reason illegals come here in the first place.

10   More than 2.7 million illegals got legalized up front, with promises of tighter enforcement in the future. But the law itself was hobbled such that it became unworkable. Only if employers had a means of verifying the legal status of new hires against Social Security or INS databases could the law succeed—but Congress refused to require the INS to start developing such a system. Instead, employers were expected to do the verifying themselves, by examining a bewildering array of easily forged documents, and then they were threatened with discrimination lawsuits by the Justice Department if they looked too hard. It would be hard to imagine a system more obviously intended to fail.

11   Eventually, even this handicapped setup was sabotaged. After catching flak for workplace raids, the INS in 1998 decided to try a new approach to enforcing the hiring ban. Instead of raiding individual employers, Operation Vanguard sought to identify illegal workers at all the meatpacking plants in Nebraska through audits of personnel records. The INS then asked to interview those employees who appeared to be unauthorized—and the illegals ran off. The procedure was remarkably successful, and was meant to be repeated every two or three months until the whole industry was weaned from dependence on illegal labor.

12   Local police were very pleased with the results, but employers and politicians vociferously criticized the very idea of enforcing the immigration law. Nebraska governor Mike Johanns organized a task force to oppose the operation; the meat packers and the ranchers hired his predecessor, Ben Nelson, to lobby on their behalf; and, in Washington, Sen. Chuck Hagel made it his mission

universal health might be addressed on how everyone can be insured without changing the current system by simply extending Medicaid to the working poor or by providing tax rebates to those who need to buy their own insurance.

2. In paragraphs 17, 19, 20, and 21, the author makes a statistical argument. Place the core facts, without his conclusions, and have the class first list and then discuss all the possible explanations for the given facts.

3. In small groups and then as a class, have students identify in detail what would be required to establish any of the choke points the author suggests in paragraphs 27 and 28.

CLASSROOM ACTIVITIES

1. Have the students in small groups make a chart of the potential positive and negative consequences if the writer's suggestions are put in place and then discuss the chart as a large group.

2. Have students break up into groups. Assign identities to each group: illegal immigrants, business owners, young people looking for work, immigration officials. Have them list the feelings and concerns of each group about the attrition policy. Then switch the identities of the groups and repeat the process. Discuss the results.

in life to pressure the Justice Department to stop. The INS took the hint, and all but gave up on enforcing the hiring ban nationwide.

13   Nor is this the only example of tough-looking laws that go unenforced. In 1996 Congress passed a large immigration bill, which included a provision that sought to punish long-term illegal residence by barring illegals from future re-entry for three or ten years, depending on the length of the initial unlawful stay. Its scope was limited in any case, since it applied only to people who actually left the country and then tried to return, but it was denounced at the time by the usual suspects as "radical" and "draconian." But an examination of the law's results shows that, in its first four years, the bar prevented fewer than 12,000 people from re-entering the United States.

14   Even the expansion of border enforcement follows this pattern of ineffectuality. The Border Patrol has doubled in size since 1996, accounting for the lion's share of increased resources for enforcement. Its 10,000 agents are better equipped and doing a better job than ever before. But since, as any agent will tell you, the Border Patrol alone can't control illegal immigration, there's little danger that such increased capacity will actually curtail the flow. Again, it's a policy that appears tough, but isn't—a velvet fist in an iron glove.

Networking

15   Why does this happen? It is a manifestation of the yawning gap between public and elite opinion on immigration. The laws need to look tough, with promises of robust enforcement, to satisfy public concerns. But immigration's relatively low political importance for most people ensures that the elite preference for loose enforcement will be satisfied in the end.

16   But isn't the elite right in this case? Isn't immigration inevitable? Hardly. No one wakes up in Paraguay and decides, "Today, I will move to Sheboygan!" Immigration can take place only if there are networks of relatives, friends, and countrymen directing immigrants to a particular place. And these networks are a creation of government policy, either through proactive measures or through permitting networks to grow through non-enforcement of the law.

17   As an example, look at the Philippines and Indonesia. Both are populous, poor countries on the other side of the world, and yet the 2000 Census found about 19 times more Filipino immigrants in the United States than Indonesians, 1.4 million versus 73,000. Why? Because we ruled the Philippines for 50 years as a colony and maintained a major military presence there for another 50 years, allowing extensive networks to develop, whereas we have historically had little to do with Indonesia.

18   Granted, interrupting such networks is harder than creating them, but it is not impossible—after all, the trans-Atlantic immigration networks from the turn of the last century were successfully interrupted, and atrophied completely. And, to move beyond theory, the few times we actually tried to enforce the immigration law, it worked—until we gave up for political reasons.

19   During the first several years after the passage of the IRCA, illegal crossings from Mexico fell precipitously, as prospective illegals waited to see if we were serious. Apprehensions of aliens by the Border Patrol—an imperfect measure but the only one available—fell from more than 1.7 million in FY 1986 to under a million in 1989. But then the flow began to increase again as the deterrent effect of the hiring ban dissipated, when word got back that we were not serious about enforcement and that the system could be easily evaded through the use of inexpensive phony documents.

20   As I've written in these pages before, when we stepped up immigration enforcement against Middle Easterners (and only Middle Easterners) in the

wake of 9/11, the largest group of illegals from that part of the world, Pakistanis, fled the country in droves to avoid being caught up in the dragnet.

21   And in an inadvertent enforcement initiative, the Social Security Administration in 2002 sent out almost a million "no-match" letters to employers who filed W-2s with information that was inconsistent with SSA's records. The intention was to clear up misspellings, name changes, and other mistakes that had caused a large amount of money paid into the system to go uncredited. But, of course, most of the problem was caused by illegal aliens lying to their employers, and thousands of illegals quit or were fired when they were found out. The effort was so successful at denying work to illegals that business and immigrant-rights groups organized to stop it, and won a 90 percent reduction in the number of letters to be sent out.

War of Attrition

22   We know that when we actually enforce the law, eroding the illegal-immigration population is possible. So what would a policy of attrition look like? It would have two key components. The first would include more conventional enforcement—arrests, prosecutions, deportations, asset seizures, etc. The second would require verification of legal status at a variety of important choke points, to make it as difficult and unpleasant as possible to live here illegally.

23   As to the first, the authorities need to start taking immigration violations seriously. To use only one example, people who repeatedly sneak across the border are supposed to be prosecuted and jailed, and the Border Patrol unveiled a new digital fingerprint system in the mid '90s to make tracking of repeat crossers possible. The problem is that short-staffed U.S. attorneys' offices kept increasing the number of apprehensions needed before they would prosecute, to avoid actually having to prosecute at all.

24   It would be hard to exaggerate the demoralizing effect that such disregard for the law has on the Homeland Security Department's staff. Conversely, the morale of immigration workers would soar in the wake of a real commitment to law enforcement. We've already seen a real-world example of this, too. I met with deportation officers in a newly formed "fugitive operations team" in Southern California who, unlike other immigration personnel I have spoken with, were actually excited about their jobs. They still have gripes, but the clear political commitment to locating and deporting fugitive aliens communicates to them that their work is genuinely valued by their superiors all the way up to the White House.

25   Other measures that would facilitate enforcement include hiring more U.S. attorneys and judges in border areas, to allow for more prosecutions; passing the CLEAR Act, which would enhance cooperation between federal immigration authorities and state and local police; and seizing the assets, however modest, of apprehended illegal aliens.

26   But these and other enforcement measures will not remove most of the illegal population—the majority of illegals will have to be persuaded to deport themselves. Unlike at the visa office or the border crossing, once aliens are inside the United States, there's no physical place, no choke point at which to examine whether someone should be admitted. The solution is to create "virtual choke points"—events that are necessary for life in a modern society but are infrequent enough not to bog down the business of society.

27   This is the thinking behind the law banning the employment of illegal aliens—people have to work, so requiring proof of legal status upon starting a

DISCUSSION QUESTIONS (p. 604)

1. Many readers have reservations about amnesty. The one strong argument supporters of amnesty often depend on is the sheer impossibility of deporting all illegal immigrants. By offering an alternative to widespread deportation, the author provides an effective alternative to amnesty. This also allows the writer to focus and create a more strongly supported argument, something that can get lost when many different points are being discussed.

2. The author identifies the current debate, demonstrates how the laws have not been consistently or effectively supported, demonstrates that enforcement of laws can lead to attrition, and suggests simple ways to create choke points to produce attrition. This is a fairly simple argument, which makes it easier to follow and more convincing for many readers.

3. The author uses mostly statistical evidence to show a connection between cause and effect. For example, when the IRCA was first passed there was a decrease in apprehensions from 1.7 million to under 1 million. The repeated use of such statistics adds credibility to the writer's argument since it seems that his claims are supported by real effects.

4. The author uses the examples of Philippines and Indonesia to demonstrate that population and poverty are not the principal cause of illegal immigration but rather the networks that get established. However, the author doesn't give enough detail about these cases to help his argument. Because he doesn't consider the different possible explanations, including the different governments and different kinds of access to transportation, these examples may actually weaken his overall argument by undercutting his credibility.

5. Paragraph 29 is intended to undercut the concern that attrition would require a drastic change in American society while still holding out the need for consistent application of the law. It softens the implications of the steps the author suggests.

28   job would serve as such a virtual choke point. As discussed above, in the absence of a verification mechanism, such a system couldn't succeed. But the president signed into law at the end of last year a measure to re-authorize and expand the verification pilot programs that immigration authorities have been experimenting with since the mid 1990s.

28   Building on this fledgling system, we need to find other instances in which legal status can be verified, such as getting a driver's license, registering an automobile, opening a bank account, applying for a car loan or a mortgage, enrolling children in public schools, and getting a business or occupational license.

29   An effective strategy of immigration law enforcement requires no booby traps, no tanks, no tattoos on arms—none of the cartoonish images invoked in the objections raised routinely by the loose-borders side. The consistent application of ordinary law-enforcement tools is all we need. "Consistent," though, is the key word. Enforcement personnel—whether Border Patrol agents, airport inspectors, or plainclothes investigators—need to know that their work is valued, that their superiors actually want them to do the jobs they've been assigned, and that they will be backed up when the inevitable complaints roll in.

30   And, finally, this isn't root-canal Republicanism, bitter medicine we swallow for the greater good. Enforcement of the immigration law may not be popular among the elite, but actual voters across the political spectrum are all for it. As Alan Wolfe wrote in *One Nation, After All*, the difference between legal and illegal immigrants "is one of the most tenaciously held distinctions in middle-class America; the people with whom we spoke overwhelmingly support legal immigration and express disgust with the illegal variety."

31   If only our political leadership felt the same way.

OVERVIEW OF MIXING THE WRITING STRATEGIES ESSAYS
Although these essays combine several writing strategies, each essay has one dominant strategy assisted by other strategies.

Discussion Questions

1. Why does the author not argue directly against amnesty but rather on how a program of attrition can work?
2. What is the main organization of the author's argument? Is the argument simple or complex? How does this influence the effectiveness of the argument?
3. What kinds of evidence does the author use mostly? How does this evidence affect the credibility of the argument?
4. Why does the author use the examples of the Philippines and Indonesia? How does this strengthen and/or weaken his argument?
5. What is the function of paragraph 29 in the author's argument?

Toward Key Insights

Sullivan focuses on causes but includes definition, comparison, and classification. Tannen organizes her essay around a narrative but uses comparison and cause and effect. Sullivan's essay is

Many in creating an argument seek to tackle all of the issues in the debate. This argument focuses on one narrow aspect of the debate. What are the advantages and disadvantages in focusing on one very specific issue or option?

Whenever we argue, we make assumptions which can be questioned in turn. Since the essay focuses very specifically on attrition as a strategy to reduce the number of illegal immigrants, what objections might someone raise to this approach that don't concern the strategy in question?

Suggestion for Writing

Perhaps with some research, write an argument for/or against using a verification system such as enrolling children in public schools to serve as a choke point. Consider what steps would be necessary to make such a system work.

Identify and argue for or against one of the assumptions of the writer. For example, someone could argue that it would simply be harmful to the economy to use attrition to move out illegal immigrants who are already productive workers.

MIXING THE WRITING
STRATEGIES ■ ■ ■ ■ ■ ■ ■

Reading Strategies

1. When skimming, identify the main point the author is attempting to make.
2. To orient your reading, note in the margins the strategy the reader is using.
3. Focus on how the points fit together to develop the author's thesis.

Reading Critically

1. Test whether the claims throughout the text really support the thesis.
2. Evaluate the claims based on the critical reading strategy appropriate to the technique being used.
3. Judge whether the writer's strategies are appropriate to the point he or she is making.

Reading As a Writer

1. Identify how the writer effectively changes from strategy to strategy.
2. Look to determine how the writer connects each strategy to the main thesis.
3. Read the conclusion carefully to determine how the writer pulls a complex essay back together to make his or her main point.

Most essays mix various writing strategies for assorted purposes. This section features three examples. The discussion questions following the Sullivan and Tannen essays direct your attention to the strategies these writers use as well as other relevant aspects of the essays.

MICHAEL POLLAN

Supermarket Pastoral

Michael Pollan received an MA in English from Columbia University. He has been a contributing writer to The New York Time Magazine *since 1987. His writing has won a number of awards, including the Global Award for Environmental Journalism. He has published many articles and several books. This selection is from his 2006 book* The Omnivore's Dilemma: A Natural History of Four Meals *published by Penguin Press.*

formal, Tannen's informal mixture of formal–informal diction.

PERSPECTIVES
This selection from a full-length book offers an important insight about how language and narratives are used in our everyday life. Often it is difficult to get students to focus on language, yet it will help them be more effective writers if they become conscious of language use around them. This selection offers an excellent opportunity to begin this exploration.

TEACHING STRATEGIES
1. Before the students read the selection, have them jot down all of the things they expect from "organic" food. Write those expectations or associations on the board. Have the students discuss where they got those expectations.

2. Working in small groups, have students create two columns, one with the language used in the description of "organic" food and the other by what they suspect from the article is the reality.

3. Using the blackboard, have students identify all the points of comparison stated or implied in the text.

4. Have the students explain why the writer found the phrase "microwaveable organic TV dinners" odd. Discuss the idea of an " oxy-moron," a phrase that

seems to include an internal contradiction. Have students identify other such odd phrases.

Narrative to establish context

Illustration of claim

Comparison

Illustration

Illustration

Effect

Illustration

"Eliding" is a literary critic's term for cutting out or avoiding a word

Cause

Comparison

1   I enjoy shopping at Whole Foods nearly as much as I enjoy browsing a good bookstore, which, come to think of it, is probably no accident. Shopping at Whole Foods is a literary experience, too. That's not to take anything away from the food, which is generally of high quality, much of it "certified organic" or "humanely raised" or "free range." But right there, that's the point. It's the evocative prose as much as anything else that makes this food really special, elevating an egg or chicken breast or a bag of arugula from the realm of ordinary protein and carbohydrates into a much headier experience, one with complex aesthetic, emotional, and even political dimensions. Take the "range-fed" sirloin steak I recently eyed in the meat case. According to the brochure on the counter, it was formerly part of a steer that spent its days "living in beautiful places" ranging from "plant-diverse, high-mountain meadows to thick aspen groves and miles of sagebrush-filled flats." Now a steak like that has got to taste better than one from Safeway, where the only accompanying information comes in the form of a number: the price I mean, which you can bet will be considerably less. But I'm evidently not the only shopper willing to pay more for a good story.

2   With the growth of organics and mounting concerns about the wholesomeness of industrial food, storied food is showing up in supermarkets everywhere these days, but it is Whole Foods that consistently offers the most cutting-edge grocery lit. On a recent visit I filled my shopping cart with eggs "from cage-free vegetarian hens," milk from cows that live "free from unnecessary fear and distress," wild salmon caught by Native Americans in Yakutat, Alaska (population 833), and heirloom tomatoes from Capay Farm ($4.99 a pound), "one of the early pioneers of the organic movement." The organic broiler I picked up even had a name: Rosie, who turned out to be a "sustainably farmed" "free-range chicken" from Petaluma Poultry, a company whose "farming methods strive to create harmonious relationships in nature, sustaining the health of all creatures and the natural world." Okay, not the most mellifluous or even meaningful sentence, but at least their heart's in the right place.

3   In several corners of the store I was actually forced to choose between subtly competing stories. For example, some of the organic milk in the milk case was "ultra-pasteurized," an extra processing step that was presented as a boon to the consumer, since it extends shelf life. But then another, more local dairy boasted about the fact they had said no to ultrapasteurization, implying that their product was fresher, less processed, and therefore more organic. This was the dairy that talked about cows living free from distress, something I was beginning to feel a bit of myself by this point.

4   This particular dairy's label had a lot to say about the bovine lifestyle: Its Holsteins are provided with "an appropriate environment, including shelter and a comfortable resting area, . . . sufficient space, proper facilities and the company of their own kind." All this sounded pretty great, until I read the story of another dairy selling raw milk—completely unprocessed—whose "cows graze green pastures all year long." Which made me wonder whether the first dairy's idea of an appropriate environment for a cow included, as I had simply presumed, a pasture. All of a sudden the absence from their story of that word seemed weirdly conspicuous. As the literary critics would say, the writer seemed to be eliding the whole notion of cows and grass. Indeed, the longer I shopped in Whole Foods, the more I thought that this is a place where the skills of a literary critic might come in handy—those, and perhaps also a journalist's.

5   Wordy labels, point-of-purchase brochures, and certification schemes are supposed to make an obscure and complicated food chain more legible to the consumer. In the industrial food economy, virtually the only information that travels along the food chain linking producer and consumer is price. Just look at the

typical newspaper ad for a supermarket. The sole quality on display here is actually a quantity: tomatoes $0.69 a pound; ground chuck $1.09 a pound; eggs $0.99 a dozen—special this week. Is there any other category of product sold on such a reductive basis? The bare-bones information travels in both directions, of course, and farmers who get the message that consumers care only about price will themselves care only about yield. This is how a cheap food economy reinforces itself.

Illustration

Effect

Comparison

6   One of the key innovations of organic food was to allow some more information to pass along the food chain between the producer and the consumer— an implicit snatch of narrative along with the number. A certified organic label tells a little story about how a particular food was produced, giving the consumer a way to send a message back to the farmer that she values tomatoes produced without harmful pesticides or prefers to feed her children milk from cows that haven't been injected with growth hormones. The word "organic" has proved to be one of the most powerful words in the supermarket: Without any help from government, farmers and consumers working together in this way have built an $11 billion industry that is now the fastest growing sector of the food economy.

Illustration

Effect

7   Yet the organic label itself—like every other such label in the supermarket— is really just an imperfect substitute for direct observation of how a food is produced, a concession to the reality that most people in an industrial society haven't the time or the inclination to follow their food back to the farm, a farm which today is apt to be, on average, fifteen hundred miles away. So to bridge that space we rely on certifiers and label writers and, to a considerable extent, our imagination of what the farms that are producing our food really look like. The organic label may conjure an image of simpler agriculture, but its very existence is an industrial artifact. The question is, what about the farms themselves? How well do they match the stories told about them?

Cause

Effect

8   Taken as a whole, the story on offer in Whole Foods is a pastoral narrative in which farm animals live much as they did in the books we read as children, and our fruits and vegetables grow in well-composted soils on small farms much like Joel Salatin's. "Organic" on the label conjures up a rich narrative, even if it is the consumer who fills in most of the details, supplying the hero (American Family Farmer), the villain (Agribusinessman), and the literary genre, which I've come to think of as Supermarket Pastoral. By now we may know better than to believe this too simple story, but not much better, and the grocery store poets do everything they can to encourage us in our willing suspension of disbelief.

Definition

9   Supermarket Pastoral is a most seductive literary form, beguiling enough to survive in the face of a great many discomfiting facts. I suspect that's because it gratifies some of our deepest, oldest longings, not merely for safe food, but for a connection to the earth and to the handful of domesticated creatures we've long depended on. Whole Foods understands all this better than we do. One of the company's marketing consultants explained to me that the Whole Foods shopper feels that by buying organic he is "engaging in authentic experiences" and imaginatively enacting a "return to a utopian past with the positive aspects of modernity intact." This sounds a lot like Virgilian pastoral, which also tried to have it both ways. In *The Machine in the Garden* Leo Marx writes that Virgil's shepherd Tityrus, no primitive, "Enjoys the best of both worlds—the sophisticated order of art and the simple spontaneity of nature." In keeping with the pastoral tradition, Whole Foods offers what Marx terms "a landscape of reconciliation" between the realms of nature and culture, a place where, as the marketing consultant put it, "people will come together through organic foods to get back to the origin of things"—perhaps by sitting down to enjoy one of the microwaveable organic TV dinners (four words I never expected to see conjoined) stacked in the frozen food case. How's that for having it both ways?

Cause

Cause

Definition

Illustration

Effect

Description

Effect

Cause

Comparison

Narrative

Argument-Reason

Argument-Reason

10   Of course the trickiest contradiction Whole Foods attempts to reconcile is the one between the industrialization of the organic food industry of which it is a part and the pastoral ideals on which that industry has been built. The organic movement, as it was once called, has come a remarkably long way in the last thirty years, to the point where it now looks considerably less like a movement than a big business. Lining the walls above the sumptuously stocked produce section in my Whole Foods are full-color photographs of local organic farmers accompanied by text blocks setting forth their farming philosophies. A handful of these farms—Capay is one example—still sell their produce to Whole Foods, but most are long gone from the produce bins, if not yet the walls. That's because Whole Foods in recent years has adopted the grocery industry's standard regional distribution system, which makes supporting small farms impractical. Tremendous warehouses buy produce for dozens of stores at a time, which forces them to deal exclusively with tremendous farms. So while the posters still depict family farmers and their philosophers, the produce on sale below them come primarily from the two big corporate organic growers in California, Earthbound Farm and Grimmway Farms, which together dominate the market for organic fresh produce in America. (Earthbound alone grows 80% of the organic lettuce sold in America.)

11   As I tossed a plastic box of Earthbound prewashed spring mix salad into my Whole Foods cart, I realized that I was venturing deep into the belly of the industrial beast Joel Salatin had called "the organic empire." (Speaking of my salad mix, another small, beyond organic farmer, a friend of Joel's, had told me he "wouldn't use the stuff to make compost"—the organic purist's stock insult.) But I'm not prepared to accept the premise that industrial organic is necessarily a bad thing, not if the goal is to reform a half-trillion-dollar food system based on chain supermarkets and the consumer's expectations that food be convenient and cheap.

12   And yet to the extent that the organic movement was conceived as a critique of industrial values, surely there comes a point when the process of industrialization will cost organic its soul (to use a word still uttered by organic types without irony), when Supermarket Pastoral becomes more fiction than fact: another lie told by marketers.

13   The question is, has that point been reached, as Joel Salatin suggests? Just how well does Supermarket Pastoral hold up under close reading and journalistic scrutiny?

CLASSROOM ACTIVITIES

1. Have students bring in the language used in fast-food stores or on fast-food commercials. Working in small groups, have them identify the underlying narratives used. Discuss as part of a large group.

2. Have students research the actual reality of organic farming and bring the results to class. Working in small groups, have the students identify how they would develop the rest of a section on organic produce. Discuss the results as a large class.

Discussion Questions

1. This section of a book uses several strategies. What strategy is dominant? How does this strategy match the main point of this essay?

2. What is the effect of the author starting and returning to a narrative of his own shopping trip at Whole Foods?

3. In several places the author specifically talks about words and phrases. What are some of the words and phrases the writer discusses? Why is it important for him to talk about this language usage?

4. In paragraph 4 the author deliberately uses a sentence fragment. Is this use of a fragment effective? Why or why not?

5. This section ends in paragraph 13 with questions. Of course, the author goes on to answer these questions in the material that follows this selection. Out of context, is this conclusion effective? What do you think based on the earlier content of this text will be the answer to his questions? What evidence leads you to that conclusion?

Toward Key Insights

A large number of essays and a fair amount of college classes spend time discussing the language people use. Based on this essay, why is this discussion of language important?

In this text, the author discusses the importance of using the skills of the literary critic. Why does he think such skills are important to understanding a supermarket? Where else might the skills of the literary critic be useful?

This essay lays out the Supermarket Pastoral as one narrative used to sell food. What other narratives can you identify that are used to sell products?

Suggestions for Writing

Visit a supermarket, a toy store, a car dealership or observe several advertisements, then write an essay explaining the narrative used to sell the products.

Identify an area of life where the talk about the experience and the experience don't match and write a paper that compares the language and the reality, offering an explanation for the language and an account of the effect that the language has on those who hear or read it.

DEBORAH A. SULLIVAN

Social Bodies: Tightening the Bonds of Beauty

Deborah A. Sullivan teaches sociology at Arizona State University. She is the coauthor of Labor Pains: Modern Midwives and Home Birth, *in addition to a number of articles. The selection here is taken from the first chapter of her book* Cosmetic Surgery: The Cutting Edge of Commercial Medicine in America. *In this section she examines the reasons for and changing meanings of tattooing.*

1   Every culture has some customs that prescribe deliberately changing a body's natural appearance (Brain 1979). The methods, however, are diverse and particular to a culture at a specific period of time. Paints, for example, are used to decorate bodies in many cultures, but the pigments, patterns, permanency, and purpose of each culture's body customs vary widely. Only a nineteenth-century Bedouin woman could appreciate the eroticism of painting the whites of a man's eyes blue. While she would have regarded her own culture's customs as highly "civilized," she probably would have thought the full body designs of Aboriginal Australians, American Indians, and Africans savage. Like eighteenth-century European explorers, she might have considered the tattooing and tooth-blackening in the Pacific region bizarre, and found the deeply carved black spirals and curves on Maori faces frightening and repulsive. It is no more likely that she could have discerned the beauty intended by the African and South American tribes who create elaborate patterns of raised scars, insert large lip plates and ear and nose plugs, and file teeth to sharp points. Nor is it likely that she could have appreciated the charm of Chinese women's bound "lotus" feet,

DISCUSSION QUESTIONS (p. 608)
1. The dominant strategy is comparison. The section compares Whole Foods with traditional supermarkets and the narrative of organic produce with the reality. The main point of the essay is that those who buy organic food are buying the narrative and not necessarily the reality about their food.

2. The use of the narrative provides a concrete situation with which the reader can identify. It makes the questions the author asks seem a part of everyday life rather than something abstract. It also helps the reader identify with the author.

3. The author talks about many words and phrases including "organic," "ultrapasteurized," "an appropriate environment," "range-fed," and many other phrases. Since his main point is how we buy based on the narrative and the language rather than the reality, he can only illustrate his point by talking about the actual language that is used.

4. There is room for debate. I find it effective because it well represents the break in the author's thinking and the discordant note in recognizing his previous assumptions. Others could find it an irritating glitch in the flow of the text.

5. It is reasonable to end an essay with questions. These are good questions and do fit the topic of the essay. But it does leave us with a sense begging for more, with a feeling that instead of concluding, we should turn the page, as we are intended to do in the actual book. Much in the selection clearly indicates that the reality does not match the narrative. The author foreshadows this conclusion by indicating that while we have descriptions offered of small, local farms, the reality is that the produce comes from only two large agribusinesses.

PERSPECTIVE

This essay depends on the important insight that much of what we take to be matters of personal choice are often reflections of larger social forces. It demonstrates that what may be very personal such as the alteration of our body actually demonstrates the power of social institutions. It would be useful to discuss with the class what other personal choices may be very structured by our culture.

TEACHING STRATEGIES

1. Before assigning this essay, have the students discuss the role of tattooing and piercing in youth culture. Who gets tattoos and piercings? What kinds do they get? Are there differences in who gets which kinds? Why do people engage in these practices?

2. Admit in advance that some of this material is difficult. Have students write down as they read the essay ideas or terms that confuse them. Discuss with the class strategies to make the ideas clearer. Have students look up

Padaung women's elongated necks, or Western women's constricted waists during the Victorian era and augmented breasts in recent decades. Instead, in the implausible circumstance that a nineteenth-century Bedouin woman was exposed to such body customs, she probably would have regarded them as barbaric mutilations, much as contemporary Americans' view of female circumcision, which she might have considered normal.

The diversity of body customs has led anthropologists (e.g., Douglas 1970; Strathern 1996) to conclude that a body is both a physical and a symbolic artifact, forged by nature and by culture at a particular moment in history. Social institutions, ideology, values, beliefs, and technology transform a physical body into a social body. The resulting social body bears the imprint of the more powerful elements of its cultural context. Bodies, therefore, provide important clues to the mechanics of society.

There are many well-documented examples of the cultural construction of a social body. Although some body customs may be merely decorative, many, if not most, have social significance. Cultures in which female circumcision is common are strongly patriarchal and pronatalist. Women in these traditional cultures are believed to be weak and incapable of controlling their sexual urges. They are allowed little contact with men outside their families and are expected to hide their bodies from public view. Their social roles are circumscribed to child care and domestic functions. They receive little education and are economically dependent on men and politically powerless. They are socialized by their mothers to believe that removal of external female genitalia is a religious obligation that promotes purity, cleanliness, and fertility and that unexcised women are unattractive and beastly. Their identities as desirable women depend on the submission of their physical bodies to the dictates of social norms. The custom embodies their inferior status.

As female circumcision illustrates, the body can be a site for the expression of power in a culture. It also is used to communicate group membership, individual status, and social identity, along with associated beliefs and values. The body is often ritually modified in connection with major life transitions. In the Australian Aboriginal culture, for example, one or two front teeth are removed at puberty. Some time later boys are painted white, secluded, and circumcised to symbolize their passage into the world of men. At the end of the ceremony, they are painted red to celebrate their reentry into society as young men with all the corresponding rights and expectations of their new status. In some tribes young men undergo a subincision ceremony in which their urethra is split open before they marry and assume full adult male rights. Rites of passage between life stages in many other cultures are marked by ritualized patterns of scarification, piercing, and tattooing. These same techniques are used to proclaim more permanent kinds of social status, such as gender and social class, as are head molding and other body modifications.

Using the body to communicate power, group membership, individual status, and social identity is not limited to exotic non-Western societies. It is ubiquitous in modern societies as well. American sailors, prisoners, bikers, and other gang members have tattooed their bodies throughout most of the twentieth century. Clinton Sanders (1989) argues that they use this particular body custom, considered vulgar by most middle-class, middle-aged Americans, to proclaim their resistance to conventional social norms of appearance and behavior. Their preference for death symbols, predatory animals, insulting and salacious images further enhances their rebellious statement.

After the mid-1960s the shock value of tattoos made them popular among some younger artistic individuals looking for attention and innovative, creative modes of expression. By the 1980s they were de rigueur among heavy metal and rap performers seeking a following among adolescents and young adults based on flaunting the conventional values and beliefs of their parents and other authority figures. Punks, freaks, Goths, skinheads, stoners, tweakers, and other disaffected young adults who identified with the counterculture heroes of their generation went to shops with names like Hierarchy, Crawling Squid, and Pigments of Imagination to record their sense of alienation on their bodies.

7   The meaning of tattoos changed in the 1990s. They became a badge of youth. Professional athletes, middle-class college students, blue-collar workers, and even some suburban housewives marked their bodies with tribal patterns, Kanji lettering, and sexy butterflies and flowers. As the shock value of tattoos declined, the most alienated subgroups added other forms of body modifications to advertise their contempt for middle-class conventions. They pierced their ears, noses, eyebrows, lips, tongues, nipples, navels, and genitalia with safety pins, barbells, studs, and various rings. These cultural pioneers established Internet news groups to share information about techniques, complications, public reaction, and erotic effects. Pop singers and other media celebrities adopted less extreme versions of this new body custom to advertise their hip identity. High school girls turned nose studs and navel rings into a fashion statement, undermining their deviance value. Those seeking a body symbol of resistance capable of generating strong public revulsion experimented with more extreme forms of self-stigmatization, such as scalp implants and scarification, to proclaim their marginalized status.

8   Tattooing and piercing at the end of the twentieth century appear to have much in common with previous fashion fads that visually differentiated each young generation over the course of the twentieth century, although some cultural observers (e.g., Polhemus and Randall 1996) find deeper meaning in these trends. They suggest the practices express a yearning for continuity, community, and commitment in a fragmented postmodern culture where ritual is rare and anomie prevails. Tattooing and piercing offer more permanent ways of recording life transitions and one's place in society.

9   All body customs, whether temporary, like tweezing eyebrows and clipping nose hair, or more permanent, like tattoos and cosmetic surgery, are forms of self-creation. They are an effort to achieve a desired identity and connection with a reference group—marginal, hip, or mainstream. The process of reincarnation is universal.

10   Kim Hewitt (1997) additionally argues that body customs, particularly painful ones, can be used as part of a self-chosen health ritual. She theorizes that the physiological effects of pain can stimulate at least a temporary reprieve from numbing feelings of alienation (118). The acute awareness of feeling alive induced by pain has the potential to replace psychological fragmentation with holistic integration and a euphoric feeling of self-mastery. She claims that young women who starve and cut their bodies, like the punks and other marginalized subgroups who customize their bodies in extreme ways, are not only rebelling against societal constrictions, they also are trying to reclaim control of their bodies and establish individuality and autonomy. Other body customs, including female bodybuilding (Heywood 1998) and cosmetic surgery (Davis 1995), have been similarly interpreted as methods of psychological healing and cultural empowerment.

11   Those with a more Foucauldian perspective, such as Susan Bordo (1993, 1997), argue that such "disciplinary" body customs are outward manifestations of internalized cultural oppression. The discipline comes from an awareness of prevailing values, beliefs, norms and voluntary self-surveillance. Consequently, the

difficult terms and work to use context to explain more complicated ideas.

3. Having read the essay, list the different causes for body modification on the board. Have students list under each cause kinds of body modification that they see as a current example of this cause. Share the results. Have students identify which practices feel as if they are forced upon them and which seem acts of rebellion.

4. This selection is part of a long book on cosmetic surgery. Have students indicate, based on this selection, what they think the author's position might be on cosmetic surgery.

5. This selection offers a number of rich ideas but does not use a flashy writing style. Discuss with the students how they reacted to this selection. Would the selection be helped or harmed by a more journalistic writing style?

CLASSROOM ACTIVITIES

1. Have students bring in pictures from the Web, magazines, or books of various examples of body modification. Have the students, in small groups, divide the modifications into those that they consider common, unusual but acceptable, and unacceptable. Have them identify the cultural basis for their reactions.

2. Culture can be as invisible as the air we breathe. Have students, in small groups, identify ways that they see their culture influencing their behavior.

sense of power experienced by disciplining one's own body, whether to resist prevailing cultural dictates with tattoos and piercings or successfully conform to them with diets and cosmetic surgery, is merely a personal achievement that lacks political effect to change the culture. Instead, as Rosemary Gillespie (1996) points out, customs such as cosmetic surgery perpetuate wider social inequalities.

12   This debate raises perennial philosophical questions about the nature of social control and the extent of free will. It also raises contemporary concerns that interpreting personal behavior as victimization deprives individuals of agency and castes them as gullible cultural dupes. My own perspective is similar to that of Bordo. Respect for the right of competent adults to make decisions about their own bodies should not blind us to the impact of the larger cultural and social context in which personal choices occur. My aim is to bring the structural aspects of this context, aspects that construct cosmetic surgery, into sharper focus. This larger cultural and social context influences individual body choices, gives them social meaning, and makes some, like cosmetic surgery, common enough to be considered body customs.

■ Works Cited

Bardo, Susan. *Unbearable Weight: Feminism, Western Culture, and the Body*. Berkeley: U of California Press, 1993.

Bordo, Susan. "Braveheart, Babe, and the Body: Contemporary Images of the Body." In *Twilight Zone: The Hidden Life of Cultural Images from Plato to O.J.*, ed. Susan Bordo. Berkeley: U of California Press, 1997.

Brain, Robert. *The Decorated Body*. London: Hutchinson, 1979.

Davis, Kathy. *Reshaping the Female Body: The Dilemma of Cosmetic Surgery*. New York: Routledge, 1995.

Douglas, Mary. *Natural Symbols: Explorations in Cosmology*. New York: Pantheon, 1970.

Gillespie, Rosemary. 1996. "Women, the Body, and Brand Extension in Medicine: Cosmetic Surgery and the Paradox of Choice." *Women and Health* 24: 69–85.

Hewitt, Kim. *Mutilating the Body: Identity in Blood and Ink*. Bowling Green, Ohio: Bowling Green State U Popular Press, 1997.

Heywood, Leslie. 1998. *Bodymakers: A Cultural Anatomy of Women's Body Building*. New Brunswick, NJ: Rutgers U Press.

Polhemus, Ted, and Housk Randall. *The Customized Body*. New York: Serpent's Tale, 1996.

Sanders, Clinton. *Customizing the Body: The Art and Culture of Tatooing*. Philadelphia: Temple UP, 1989.

Strathern, Andrew. 1996. *Body Thoughts*. Ann Arbor: Michigan Press.

Discussion Questions

1. Identify the author's thesis statement. Explain as fully as possible what the author means by the thesis statement.

2. What are the advantages of the author's using many examples of body modification? How does that help make her point?

3. In the introduction, the author starts by describing the possible reaction of a nineteenth-century Bedouin woman to a variety of body modifications. What are the effects of this approach?

4. Why does the author discuss the changing meaning of tattooing?

5. This selection not only illustrates the author's thesis but does so by specifying possible causes for body modification. Identify the causes the author discusses. Do those that apply to modern tattooing seem correct to you?

6. This section from a chapter of a book draws on a variety of sources and is extensively documented. What effect does this have on the essay?

7. In the conclusion of this selection, the author raises a number of broader questions. What role do these questions play given that this selection is part of the first chapter of a book? Are they effective here where they are serving as a conclusion?

Toward Key Insights

Tattooing, piercing, and scarification are increasingly common practices. What reasons do you see for these practices?

Are those who participate in such practices "cultural dupes" who blindly follow cultural expectations or free individuals who make personal choices?

Suggestion for Writing

Write a paper that illustrates a cultural practice that you think is significant, such as the crucial role of music in the life of many college students and teens.

DEBORAH TANNEN

Gender Gap in Cyberspace[1]

Deborah Tannen (born 1945) earned a B.S. degree from the State University of New York in 1966 and a PhD from the University of California in 1979. She is now a member of the linguistics department of Georgetown University. Tannen has authored a number of books on speaking and writing as well as numerous shorter pieces that have appeared in the New York Times, Newsweek, People, *and the* Harvard Business Review. *In this selection, Tannen investigates the causes and effects of the differing male and female attitudes toward e-mail.*

1   I was a computer pioneer, but I'm still something of a novice. That paradox is telling.

2   I was the second person on my block to get a computer. The first was my colleague Ralph. It was 1980. Ralph got a Radio Shack TRS-80, I got a used Apple

---

5. There are several causes that the writer mentions: (1) social significance as a way of establishing social status, (2) expression of power, (3) mark of major life transitions, (4) establishment of group membership, (5) a health ritual. Tattooing has changed. It once was a mark of rebellion, then tattoos became a badge of youth. Currently they seem to be a mark of continuity and community. Friends go together to get tattoos.

6. The documentation adds authority to this discussion. It makes this article a part of a larger discussion. It demonstrates that there is academic validity for this work.

7. As a chapter of a book, these questions identify material to be discussed in the rest of the book. Even out of context, this can be an effective strategy. It leaves the reader with a number of important ideas to consider.

PERSPECTIVE
Because of the large and growing number of individuals actively using e-mail, differences in the ways men and women relate to and use it certainly make for an intriguing discussion. This is especially so when, as Tannen notes, these differences reflect much broader behavioral patterns.

TEACHING STRATEGIES
1. Have students reread paragraph 6 and then ask them to what extent they agree that men would never discuss their feelings

"sitting face to face."
Expect a spirited discussion between males and females. A writing assignment could follow.

2. Point out Tannen's use of parentheses (paragraphs 5, 6, 7, 8, 10, 13, and 14) and then ask the class to formulate appropriate guidelines for their use.

3. Discuss the effect of the sentence fragment that ends the essay.

CLASSROOM ACTIVITY
Divide the class into small groups and ask them to discuss how cyberspace could be used effectively in the classroom. The groups could deliver reports to the class, and a writing assignment might follow. Have students write down their own uses of computers based on the key categories specified by Tannen—general acceptance of new technology, response to problems with programs, general interest in computer technology as technology, use of e-mail. Post the results. To what extent are the results consistent with Tannen's observation, and to what extent do they diverge from her conclusions?

DISCUSSION QUESTIONS (p. 615)
1. This essay presents both causes and effects as follows: causes (paragraph 6), effects (paragraph 5 and 9), and both causes and effects (paragraphs 2, 3, 4, 7, 8, 10, 11, 12, 13, and 14).

2. Tannen uses formal-informal diction. Most of her sentences are short although some are relatively long. For the most

3   II +. He helped me get started and went on to become a maven, reading computer magazines, hungering for the new technology he read about, and buying and mastering it as quickly as he could afford. I hung on to old equipment far too long because I dislike giving up what I'm used to, fear making the wrong decision about what to buy, and resent the time it takes to install and learn a new system.

4   My first Apple came with videogames; I gave them away. Playing games on the computer didn't interest me. If I had free time I'd spend it talking on the telephone to friends.

Ralph got hooked. His wife was often annoyed by the hours he spent at his computer and the money he spent upgrading it. My marriage had no such strains—until I discovered E-mail. Then I got hooked. E-mail draws me the same way the phone does: it's a souped-up conversation.

5   E-mail deepened my friendship with Ralph. Though his office was next to mine, we rarely had extended conversations because he is shy. Face to face he mumbled so, I could barely tell he was speaking. But when we both got on E-mail, I started receiving long, self-revealing messages: we poured our hearts out to each other. A friend discovered that E-mail opened up that kind of communication with her father. He would never talk much on the phone (as her mother would), but they have become close since they both got online.

6   Why, I wondered, would some men find it easier to open up on E-mail? It's a combination of the technology (which they enjoy) and the obliqueness of the written word, just as many men will reveal feelings in dribs and drabs while riding in the car or doing something, which they'd never talk about sitting face to face. It's too intense, too bearing-down on them, and once you start you have to keep going. With a computer in between, it's safer.

7   It was on E-mail, in fact, that I described to Ralph how boys in groups often struggle to get the upper hand whereas girls tend to maintain an appearance of cooperation. And he pointed out that this explained why boys are more likely to be captivated by computers than girls are. Boys are typically motivated by a social structure that says if you don't dominate you will be dominated. Computers, by their nature, balk; you type a perfectly appropriate command and it refuses to do what it should. Many boys and men are incited by this defiance: "I'm going to whip this into line and teach it who's boss! I'll get it to do what I say!" (and if they work hard enough, they always can). Girls and women are more likely to respond, "This thing won't cooperate. Get it away from me!"

8   Although no one wants to think of herself as "typical"—how much nicer to be *sui generis*—my relationship to my computer is—gulp—fairly typical for a woman. Most women (with plenty of exceptions) aren't excited by tinkering with the technology, grappling with the challenge of eliminating bugs or getting the biggest and best computer. These dynamics appeal to many men's interest in making sure they're on the top side of the inevitable who's-up-who's-down struggle that life is for them. E-mail appeals to my view of life as a contest for connections to others. When I see that I have fifteen messages, I feel loved.

9   I once posted a technical question on a computer network for linguists and was flooded with long dispositions, some pages long. I was staggered by the generosity and the expertise, but wondered where these guys found the time—and why all the answers I got were from men.

10   Like coed classrooms and meetings, discussions on E-mail networks tend to be dominated by male voices, unless they're specifically women-only, like single-sex schools. Online, women don't have to worry about getting the floor (you just send a message when you feel like it), but, according to linguists Susan Herring and Laurel Sutton, who have studied this, they have the usual problems of having their messages ignored or attacked. The anonymity of public networks frees a small number of men to send long, vituperative, sarcastic messages that many other men either can tolerate or actually enjoy, but that turn most women off.

11   The anonymity of networks leads to another sad part of the E-mail story: there are men who deluge women with questions about their appearance and invitations to sex. On college campuses, as soon as women students log on, they are bombarded by references to sex, like going to work and finding pornographic posters adorning the walls.

12   Most women want one thing from a computer—to work. This is significant counterevidence to the claim that men want to focus on information while women are interested in rapport. That claim I found was most often true in casual conversation, in which there is no particular information to be conveyed. But with computers, it is often women who are more focused on information, because they don't respond to the challenge of getting equipment to submit.

13   Once I had learned the basics, my interest in computers waned. I use it to write books (though I never mastered having it do bibliographies or tables of contents) and write checks (but not balance my checkbook). Much as I'd like to use it to do more, I begrudge the time it would take to learn.

14   Ralph's computer expertise costs him a lot of time. Chivalry requires that he rescue novices in need, and he is called upon by damsel novices far more often than knaves. More men would rather study the instruction booklet than ask directions, as it were, from another person. "When I do help men," Ralph wrote (on E-mail, of course), "they want to be more involved. I once installed a hard drive for a guy, and he wanted to be there with me, wielding the screwdriver and giving his own advice where he could." Women, he finds, usually are not interested in what he's doing; they just want him to get the computer to the point where they can do what they want.

15   Which pretty much explains how I managed to be a pioneer without becoming an expert.

Discussion Questions

1. Does Tannen deal with causes, effects, or both? Refer to the essay when answering.
2. Characterize the level of diction in this essay.
3. Why do you think Tannen cites the two linguists in paragraph 10?
4. Point out the connecting devices that link the paragraphs in this essay.
5. What additional strategies does Tannen use?
6. Does your experience in cyberspace bear out Tannen's assertion about a gender gap? Discuss, citing specific examples.

---

part she uses everyday language although her writing does include an occasional word or expression—for example *sui generis* (paragraph 8) and "vituperative" (paragraph 10)—that might puzzle ordinary readers. Most sentences are loose rather than periodic, and there are almost no contractions or slang expressions ("dribs and drabs," paragraph 5, is one exception).

3. Citing the two linguists lends authoritative support to Tannen's comments regarding the problems women encounter online. It also shows that Tannen keeps informed about her topic helping develop reader confidence in her views.

4. Linking devices include "in fact," (paragraph 7), "Although no one . . . typical" (paragraph 8), "Like coed classrooms and meetings" (paragraph 10), "The anonymity of networks . . . story" (paragraph 11), and "Once I had learned the basics" (paragraph 13).

5. Tannen combines a number of strategies. Much of the essay highlights the differences in the ways that men and women use e-mail. She uses herself and Ralph to illustrate the main points she wants to make about gender differences.

She also uses a narrative structure that follows both her and Ralph's history with computers.

6. This question should prompt a stimulating discussion, which might be followed by a writing assignment.

Toward Key Insights

How do you account for the differences that Tannen describes? Do you believe that they are inborn or stem mainly from cultural patterns?
What steps might be taken to lessen these differences?

Suggestion for Writing

Write an essay exploring how gender affects dating done through the Internet. Support your essay with relevant, specific details.

Handbook

Handbook

Sentence Elements

Learning the parts of English sentences won't in itself improve your writing, but it will equip you to handle errors at the sentence level. Before you can identify and correct unwarranted shifts from past to present time, for example, you need to know about verbs and their tenses. Similarly, recognizing and correcting pronoun case errors require a knowledge of what pronouns are and how they are used. In this section we first cover subjects and predicates, then complements, appositives, and the parts of speech, and finally phrases and clauses.

Subjects and Predicates

The subject of a sentence tells who or what it is about. A *simple subject* consists of a noun (that is, a naming word) or a noun substitute. A *complete subject* consists of a simple subject plus any words that limit or describe it.

The predicate tells something about the subject and completes the thought of the sentence. A *simple predicate* consists of one or more verbs (words that show action or existence); a *complete predicate* includes any associated words also. In the following examples the simple subjects are underlined once and the simple predicates twice. The subjects and predicates are separated with slash marks.

> <u>William</u>/<u>laughed</u>.
>
> <u>Mary</u>/<u>has moved</u>.
>
> <u>Sarah</u>/<u>painted</u> the kitchen.
>
> The <u>student</u> over there in the corner/<u>is majoring</u> in art.

Complex subjects can be very long; it is helpful to be able to pick the simple subject out of a complex subject.

> The <u>storms</u> in March, which dropped a record rain fall in a one week time, <u>resulted</u> in fierce floods.

PERSPECTIVE
Opinions differ about whether grammar should be taught in a writing course and how it should be taught. George Hillocks, in his review of the research literature, found no connection between the teaching of grammar and improved communication skills. Sara D'Eloia concurs in her article "The Uses—and Limits—of Grammar." Why then do so many instructors continue to teach grammar? Some do it because they believe that educated people should at least know the basic structure of English. Others want to help students find and correct basic errors, and grammar instruction provides students and instructors with a common language to discuss these errors and

619

sent

A sentence can have a compound subject (two or more separate subjects), a compound predicate (two or more separate predicates), or both.

The <u>elephants</u> and their <u>trainer</u>/<u>bowed</u> to the audience and <u>left</u> the ring.

Sentences that ask questions don't follow the usual simple subject–simple predicate order. Instead, the word order may be changed slightly.

When questions use forms of the verb *be* (*is, am, are*), the verb appears before the subject while the rest of the predicate still follows the subject.

Is/<u>Angela</u>*/an experienced mountain climber?*

When the sentences include auxiliary, or helping, verbs, the auxiliary is moved in front of subject while the rest of the predicate remains in the same place.

Has/<u>a package</u>*/arrived yet for me?*

Sometimes a question word such as *when, why, who,* and *where* appears in front of the sentence with the helping verb.

When will/<u>we</u>*/be allowed to park on campus?*

Sometimes certain types of phrases and clauses can fall between the subject and the predicate. These should not be confused with the subject. They are usually easy to detect since they can be moved elsewhere in the sentence. The subject is underlined.

<u>My dog</u>/, *since he has gotten old,* simply lies around the house.

<u>My dog</u>/ simply lies around the house *since he has gotten old.*

Sometimes a phrase that is not part of the subject can introduce the sentence. This phrase can also usually be moved.

After we have repaired the rock wall,/<u>we</u>*/will begin to plant the new flowers.

<u>We</u>/will begin to plant the new flowers *after we have repaired the rock wall.*

Usage Considerations Because subjects are such important sentence elements, think carefully about each one you write so that your sentences won't be vague or misleading. Read the example below:

Our government has failed to enact a national value-added tax.

This statement can be expressed more precisely:

Congress has failed to enact a national value-added tax.

The *president* has vetoed the proposed national value-added tax.

Paying close attention to subjects lets you present your ideas more accurately and clearly.

Place a slash mark between the complete subject and the complete predicate; then underline the simple subject once and the verb(s) twice. If a subject comes between an auxiliary verb and the main verb, set it off with two slash marks. If a phrase that is not the subject comes between the subject and the predicate, set it off with two slash marks.

1. Boston is one of my favorite cities.
2. My brother built a barn for his horses.
3. The cup of coffee on the counter is mine.
4. Do you know how to design a Web page?
5. The driver of the pickup truck backed into my car and then sped away.
6. The psychology final, though it was very long, was not very hard.
7. Bulimia and anorexia are disorders that affect too many young women.
8. If you plan to make a purchase using the Internet, you should make sure that the site is secure.
9. Where can visitors to the campus park their cars?
10. The advice that we scorned in our youth may seem like wisdom in our old age.

Complements

A complement is a word or word group that forms part of the predicate and helps complete the meaning of the sentence. Anything that comes after the verb is usually a complement. There are many kinds of complement, including phrases and clauses that will be reviewed later in this chapter.

- I think *that Copland was the quintessential American composer.*
- Robert hesitated *to trap the ground hog behind his house.*
- We were late *because our car would not start.*

Four common complements of traditional grammar are direct objects, indirect objects, subject complements, and object complements.

A *direct object* names whatever receives, or results from, the action of a verb.

The millwright repaired the *lathe.* (Direct object receives action of verb *repaired.*)

Hilary painted a *picture.* (Direct object results from action of verb *painted.*)

They took *coffee* and *sandwiches* to the picnic. (Direct objects receive action of verb *took.*)

An *indirect object* identifies someone or something that receives whatever is named by the direct object.

Doris lent *me* her calculator. (Indirect object *me* receives *calculator,* the direct object.)

Will and Al bought their *boat* new sails. (Indirect object *boat* receives *sails,* the direct object.)

An indirect object can be converted to a prepositional phrase that begins with *to* or *for* and follows the direct object.

EXERCISE ANSWERS

1. Boston/is one of my favorite cities.

2. My brother/built a barn for his horses.

3. The cup of coffee on the counter/is mine.

4. Do/you/know how to design a Web page?

5. The driver of the pickup truck/backed into my car and then sped away.

6. The psychology final,/though it was very long,/was not very hard.

7. Bulimia and anorexia/are disorders that affect too many young women.

8. If you plan to make a purchase using the Internet, you/should make sure that the site is secure.

9. Where can/visitors to the campus/park their cars?

10. The advice that we scorned in our youth/may seem like wisdom in our old age.

PERSPECTIVE
Students often confuse the different types of complements. When you teach complements, it is important to stress that the four types function differently. Otherwise students may see them simply as words that follow the verb.

CLASSROOM ACTIVITIES
1. Have students complete the following sentences

with a direct object. The instructor corrected _____. The old man carried _____. For lunch, the football star ate and _____. The monkey broke _____.

2. Have students complete the following sentences with an indirect object: John sent _____ roses. The lunchroom served _____ cold mashed potatoes. The lawyer mailed _____ the contract. My brother bought _____ the latest U2 CD.

PERSPECTIVE
The use of restrictive and nonrestrictive appositives is often a sign of a student's increasing syntactical maturity and therefore should be encouraged.

CLASSROOM ACTIVITY
When introducing appositives, you might explain how to use them effectively. Use sentence-combining exercises, such as the following, that require students to join two separate sentences, employing either a restrictive or nonrestrictive appositive.
1. My brother is an avid fly fisherman. His name is David.
2. Jimmy Carter plays an important role in supervising elections in foreign countries. Jimmy Carter is a former U.S. President.
3. Charles Ives is known for writing very discordant music. Charles Ives is a famous American composer.

Doris lent her calculator *to me*.

Will and Al bought new sails *for their boat*.

A *subject complement* follows a linking verb—one that indicates existence rather than action. It renames or describes the subject.

Desmond is a *carpenter*. (Complement *carpenter* renames subject *Desmond*.)

The lights are too *bright* for Percy. (Complement *bright* describes subject *lights*.)

An *object complement* follows a direct object and renames or describes it.

The council named Donna *treasurer*. (Object complement *treasurer* renames direct object *Donna*.)

The audience thought the play *silly*. (Object complement *silly* describes direct object *play*.)

If a word is an object complement, you can form a short test sentence using *is*.

Donna is *treasurer*.

The play is *silly*.

Usage Considerations   Like subjects, direct objects can be revised for greater precision, as these examples show:

John sent *a gift*.

John sent *a giant coloring book as a birthday gift*.

Often, you can carry the revision one step further by adding an indirect object, subject complement, or other complement to the sentence.

John sent his *niece* a giant coloring book as a birthday gift. (Indirect object added.)

Appositives

An appositive is a noun or word group serving as a noun that follows another noun or noun substitute and expands its meaning. Appositives may be restrictive or nonrestrictive. Restrictive appositives distinguish whatever they modify from other items in the same class. They are written without commas.

My sister *Heidi* is a professional golfer. (Appositive *Heidi* distinguishes her from other sisters.)

I have just read a book by the novelist *Henry James*. (Appositive *Henry James* distinguishes him from other novelists.)

Nonrestrictive appositives provide more information about whatever they modify. This sort of appositive is set off by a pair of commas except at the end of a sentence; then it is preceded by a single comma.

Anatoly Karpov, *the Russian chess player*, was interviewed on TV. (Appositive names *Karpov's* occupation.)

Todd plans to major in paleontology, *the study of fossils.* (Appositive defines *paleontology.*)

noun

Usage Considerations When a brief definition is necessary, appositives can help you improve your sentences.

John Cage wrote hundreds of pieces for prepared piano.

John Cage, *a twentieth-century avant-garde composer*, wrote hundreds of pieces for prepared pianos, *instruments with odds and ends stuck between their strings to provide unusual effects.*

Don't, however, clutter your writing with appositives that provide unneeded information; the overload will impede and irritate your reader.

EXERCISE

Identify each italicized item as a direct object (DO), an indirect object (IO), a subject complement (SC), an object complement (OC), or an appositive (AP).

1. Will and Allison purchased new furniture for their *apartment.*
2. The critics considered the movie *a masterpiece.*
3. The milk tasted *rancid.*
4. Robert Heinlein, a science fiction *writer,* thought that writers should tell an interesting story.
5. Jasmine completed her research *paper* two weeks ahead of the due date.
6. John sent his wife *candy* and *flowers* for Valentine's Day.
7. Some find bad manners *unacceptable.*
8. My roommate, a terrible *procrastinator,* finally relaxed after he turned in his paper.
9. Mr. Hanley offered *me* a job.
10. Darrel is a fine young *man.*

4. Wallace Stevens worked for an insurance company. Wallace Stevens was a poet.

5. He suffered from angina. Angina is a heart condition.

Combinations

1. My brother David is an avid fly fisherman.

2. Jimmy Carter, former U.S. President, plays an important role in supervising elections in foreign countries.

3. Charles Ives, a famous American composer, is known for writing very discordant music.

4. The poet Wallace Stevens worked for an insurance company.

5. He suffered from angina, a heart condition.

EXERCISE ANSWERS

1. IO
2. OC
3. SC
4. AP
5. DO
6. DO, DO
7. OC
8. AP
9. IO
10. SC

Parts of Speech

Traditional English grammar classifies words into eight parts of speech: *nouns, pronouns, verbs, adjectives, adverbs, prepositions, conjunctions,* and *interjections.* This section discusses these categories as well as verbals, phrases, and clauses, which also serve as parts of speech.

It is important to recognize that words that may look like one part of speech can function as another part of speech. For example, the verb *swim* can function as a noun. *Swimming* is good for your health. To identify a word as a part of speech is to identify how it functions in a sentence.

Traditional grammar defined nouns as words that name persons, places, things, conditions, ideas, or qualities. Most nouns can take a plural (book, books), possessive (Andy, Andy's), or article (bench, the bench).

PERSPECTIVE
Far too often the parts of speech are glossed over as rather obvious and unremarkable elements of our language. Clearly, however, our grammatical world should not be taken for granted. Consider, for example, a language that

is less noun-centered than ours or one that is richer in adjectives. Obviously, these features would have an enormous impact on how people would conceive of the world.

CLASSROOM ACTIVITY
1. Have students describe simple, everyday events, such as sunrise, tooth-brushing, walking to class, without using nouns. The subsequent frustration should reveal the importance of nouns and be an excellent topic of discussion. In addition, the very effort to avoid nouns will, like the pink elephant an individual tries not to think about, bring them to mind.
2. Have students identify activities that a class can do as a group. For example, a class might make an average test score, produce a book with chapters written by individual students, and so on.

CLASSROOM ACTIVITIES
1. Have students write sentences in which every noun is a proper noun, and allow them to make up a proper name for each object. This exercise will help them see the difference between proper and common nouns and how common nouns contribute to our ability to think and communicate.
2. You might have students try to create their own common noun (class term) and

Proper Nouns

Some nouns, called *proper nouns*, identify one-of-a-kind items like the following and are commonly capitalized.

France	New Years
Pacific Ocean	North Dakota
Pulitzer Prize	World Series
Spirit of St. Louis	Wyandotte Corporation
Declaration of Independence	Miami-Dade Junior College

Common Nouns

Common nouns name general classes or categories of items. Some common nouns are *abstract* and name a condition, idea, or quality that we can't experience with our five senses. *Abstract nouns* often cannot accept the plural; we cannot usually say we have *envys*. *Concrete nouns* identify something that we can experience with one or more of our senses and usually have plural forms.

Abstract Nouns	**Concrete Nouns**
arrogance	man
fear	bicycle
liberalism	desk
sickness	cartoon
understanding	smoke

Count and Non-Count Nouns

Most nouns identify things we can count and such nouns usually can take the plural form: *three bananas, a book, two children*. Some nouns, including many abstract nouns, cannot accept a plural: *coffee, water, bread*.

Usage Considerations   Good writing demands precise, potent nouns. If you carefully select your nouns, you can sharpen your message. Ill-chosen nouns, on the other hand, suggest poor thinking. Note how the vague word *freedom* robs the following sentence of any specific meaning:

Our *freedom* needs to be protected.

What did the writer have in mind? Here are a few possibilities:

Our *right to own guns* needs to be protected.

Our *private behavior* needs to be protected.

Our *national sovereignty* needs to be protected.

Even when meaning does not present problems, sentences can be sharpened by careful attention to nouns. Note the greater precision of the second sentence below:

Our *dog* has a savage bite.

Our *pit bull* has a savage bite.

EXERCISE

Identify the nouns in the following sentences. Indicate if they are proper nouns (PN) or common nouns (CN), count nouns (count) non-count nouns (non-count), or collective nouns (coll). Clearly a noun can belong to more than one category.

1. Josh downloaded the new song by Rufus Wainwright from the Internet.
2. Americans want to be secure from terrorist attacks without surrendering their fundamental liberties.
3. Students quickly develop an addiction to coffee as they try to survive night-long cram sessions.
4. Our football team had an excellent season even if we didn't make it to a bowl game.
5. Math, especially algebra, is a subject that gives many students a fair amount of difficulty.
6. The water in the Gulf of Mexico can be uncomfortably warm by August.
7. Whether you agree or disagree with the views of the organization, the National Rifle Association has played an important role in the debate over how we should understand the Second Amendment.
8. Our understanding of the human genetic code has exploded in the last decade.
9. As everyone knows, Bill Clinton came from a town called *Hope*.
10. Human cloning is a very disturbing possibility for many citizens.

Pronouns

Pronouns are a special class of words that can fit the place of nouns in a sentence and sometimes can be seen as taking the place of a noun in a sentence. Pronouns can help you avoid the awkward repetition of nouns.

Personal Pronouns   Personal pronouns refer to identifiable persons or things. Personal pronouns have different cases. The subjective case is used when the pronoun serves as the subject of the sentence or clause. *I helped Steve.* The objective case is used when the pronoun is the object of a verb or preposition. *Steve helped* **me.** *We spoke about* **him.** The possessive case shows possession or ownership. *That is* **my** *briefcase. My, your, our,* and *their* always precede nouns, as in *their car. Mine, hers, ours, yours,* and *theirs* do not precede nouns, as in *That book is mine. His* and *its* may or may not precede nouns.

	Subjective	Objective	Possessive
Singular			
First person	I	me	my, mine
Second person	you	you	your, yours
Third person	he, she, it	him, her, it	his, her, hers, its
Plural			
First person	we	us	our, ours
Second person	you	you	your, yours
Third person	they	them	their, theirs

then find a definition for it. For example, a "flusterjet" might be any student who is excessively nervous just before an exam.

CLASSROOM ACTIVITY
Have students list as many nouns as possible, perhaps allowing them to refer to textbooks, then determine which are abstract and which are concrete. For example, use the nouns *arrogance* and *smoke*, pointing out that while we can see only the symptoms of arrogance, we can clearly see smoke itself.

EXERCISE ANSWERS
1. Josh (PN), song (CN, count), Rufus Wainwright (PN), Internet (PN)
2. Americans (PN), attacks (CN, count), liberties (CN, count)
3. Students (CN, count), addiction (CN, count), coffee (CN, non-count), sessions (CN, count)
4. team (CN, coll), season (CN, count), game (CN, count)
5. math (CN, non-count), algebra (CN, non-count), subject (CN, count), students (CN, count), amount (CN, count), difficulty (CN, non-count).
6. water (CN, non-count), Gulf of Mexico (PN), August (PN)
7. views (CN, count) organization (CN, count), National Rifle Association (PN), role (CN, count), debate (CN, count), Second Amendment (PN)

pro

8. understanding (CN, non-count), code (CN, count), decade (CN, count)
9. Bill Clinton (PN), town (CN, count), Hope (PN)
10. cloning (CN, non-count), possibility (CN, count), citizens (CN, count)

TEACHING STRATEGY
To help students appreciate the importance of pronouns, have them substitute the appropriate pronouns in the following passage:

The roommate John has a serious problem with John's girlfriend. John is terrified of meeting the girlfriend's family. The family members apparently don't approve of John. John's roommate tried to cheer John up by reassuring John that the girlfriend loves John, and that is what matters. John's roommate suspects that John didn't believe John's roommate. John finally went and had a terrible time. In the end, though, John and John's roommate had to laugh about the whole event. (Hint: The roommate is the writer of the passage.)

Corrected Version
My roommate John has a serious problem with his girlfriend. He is terrified of meeting her family. They apparently don't approve of him. I tried to cheer him up by reassuring him that his girlfriend loves him, and that is what matters. I suspect that he doesn't

Relative Pronouns   A relative pronoun relates a dependent clause—a word group that has a subject and a predicate but cannot function as an independent sentence—to a noun or pronoun, called an antecedent, in the main part of the sentence.

The relative pronouns include the following:

who	whose	what	whoever	whichever
whom	which	that	whomever	whatever

Who in its various forms refers to people, *which* to things, and *that* to either people or things.

Mary Beth Cartwright, *who* was arrested last week for fraud, was Evansville's "Model Citizen" two years ago. (The antecedent of *who* is *Mary Beth Cartwright.*)

He took the electric razor, *which* needed a new cutting head, to the repair shop. (The antecedent of *which* is *electric razor.*)

David Bullock is someone *whom* we should definitely hire. (The antecedent of *whom* is *someone.*)

Montreal is a city *that* I've always wanted to visit. (The antecedent of *that* is *city.*)

Which typically introduces nonrestrictive clauses, that is, clauses that provide more information about whatever they modify (see page 688).

The palace, *which* was in bad condition a century ago, is finally going to be restored. (Clause adds information about palace.)

That is typically used in other situations, especially to introduce restrictive clauses: those that distinguish the things they modify from others in the same class (see page 689).

The used car *that* I bought last week at Honest Bill's has already broken down twice. (Clause distinguishes writer's used car from others.)

Page 671 explains the use of *who* and *whom.*

Interrogative Pronouns   Interrogative pronouns introduce questions. All of the relative pronouns except *that* also function as interrogative pronouns.

who	which	whoever	whichever
whom	what	whomever	whatever
whose			

What is the matter?

Who asked you?

Whatever do you mean?

When *what, which,* and *whose* are followed by nouns, they act as adjectives, not pronouns.

Which movie should we see?

Demonstrative Pronouns   As their name suggests, demonstrative pronouns point things out. There are four such pronouns.

this	these
that	those

This and its plural *these* identify recent or nearby things.

> *This* is the play to see.
>
> *These* are the times that try men's souls.

That and its plural *those* identify less recent or more distant things.

> *That* is Mary's house across the road.
>
> *Those* were very good peaches you had for sale last week.

Reflexive and Intensive Pronouns   A reflexive pronoun is used when the pronoun refers back to a noun in the same clause. An intensive pronoun lends emphasis to a noun or pronoun. The two sets of pronouns are identical.

myself	herself	ourselves
yourself	itself	yourselves
himself	oneself	themselves

> My father cut *himself* while shaving. (reflexive pronoun)
>
> The president *himself* has asked me to undertake this mission. (intensive pronoun)

Don't substitute a reflexive pronoun for a personal pronoun.

> *Faulty*   *Jill* and *myself* are going to a movie.
>
> *Revision*   *Jill* and *I* are going to a movie.
>
> *Faulty*   *Give the tickets to John and myself.*
>
> *Revision*   *Give the tickets to John and me.*

Sometimes you'll hear people say things like "He made it *hisself*," "They're only fooling *theirself*," or "They bought *theirselves* sodas." Such forms are nonstandard. Say "himself" and "themselves" instead.

Indefinite Pronouns   These pronouns refer to unidentified persons, places, or things. One group of indefinite pronouns consistently acts as pronouns.

anybody	everything	one
anyone	nobody	somebody
anything	no one	someone
everybody	nothing	something
everyone		

A second group may function as either pronouns or adjectives.

all	any	most	few	much
another	each	either	many	neither

believe me. He finally went and had a terrible time. In the end, though, he and I had to laugh about the whole event.

PERSPECTIVE
Relative pronouns help writers formulate more complex sentences. You might introduce relative clauses through sentence-combining exercises.

CLASSROOM ACTIVITY
Have students combine the following sentences using relative pronouns:
1. He owns the Toyota Camry. The Toyota Camry has a broken headlight.
2. George Bush, Sr., was once the director of the CIA. George Bush later became president.
3. The streets are peppered with potholes. The streets will be paved this spring.
4. The word-processing program works very well. I purchased the word-processing program last year.
5. *Buddenbrooks* is a novel. I have always wanted to read *Buddenbrooks*.

Combinations
1. He owns the Toyota Camry that has a broken headlight.
2. George Bush, Sr., who was once the director of the CIA, later became president.
3. The streets that are peppered with potholes will be paved this spring. OR The streets, which are peppered with potholes, will be paved this spring.

4. The word-processing program that I purchased last year works very well.

5. *Buddenbrooks* is a novel that I have always wanted to read.

TEACHING STRATEGY
While many students are likely to be familiar with most kinds of pronouns, few use sentences that employ reciprocal pronouns. To give students practice, have them list things people might do to each other or one another and then write sentences built around these activities, using the appropriate pronouns. For example, Steve and his brother shot each other while hunting. The members of the class shook hands with one another.

EXERCISE ANSWERS
1. Anyone (indefinite)

2. himself (reflexive), my (personal, P)

3. which (interrogative) he (personal, S)

4. that (relative), mine (personal, P)

5. This (demonstrative), that (relative), I (personal, S)

6. himself (intensive), one (indefinite)

7. we (personal, S), each other (reciprocal), our (personal, P)

8. we (personal, S), you (personal, S), our (personal, P)

9. his (personal, P), us (personal, O)

10. which (relative), they (personal, S)

Here are some examples:

> *Everyone* is welcome. (indefinite pronoun)
> *Many* are called, but *few* are chosen. (indefinite pronouns)
> *Many* men but only a *few* women attend the Air Force Academy. (adjectives)

Pages 662–664 discuss indefinite pronouns as antecedents.

Reciprocal Pronouns   The two reciprocal pronouns show an interchange of action between two or more parties. *Each other* is used when two parties interact, *one another* when three or more do.

> Pam and Patty accidentally gave *each other* the same thing for Christmas. (two persons)
> The members of the football team joyfully embraced *one another* after their victory. (more than two persons)

Usage Considerations   Many students handle pronouns carelessly, damaging the clarity of their writing. Problems include letting the same pronoun stand for different nouns or using a pronoun where detailed, vivid language would be more effective. The following passage illustrates poor pronoun usage:

> My brother loves fly fishing. He thinks *it* is the only way to spend a summer weekend. In fact, whenever he's off work, he'll do *it*.

Rewritten as follows, the passage has been notably improved:

> My brother loves fly fishing. He thinks that *wading a stream and casting leisurely for trout* is the only way to spend a summer weekend. In fact, whenever he's off work, he *can be found up to his hips in water, offering his hand-tied flies to the waiting rainbows.*

EXERCISE

Identify each pronoun in the following sentences and indicate its type (personal, relative, interrogative, demonstrative, reflexive, intensive, indefinite, reciprocal). If it is a personal pronoun, indicate if it is in the subjective (S), objective (O), or possessive (P) case.

1. Anyone who wants to be successful needs to be able to use the Internet.
2. John helped himself to my copy of *The Canterbury Tales*.
3. Which fraternity did he say he was considering joining?
4. The black Subaru that is parked at the back of the lot is mine.
5. This is the kind of day that I really enjoy.
6. The president himself will teach one of the classes in political science.
7. We will all be more likely to succeed as writers if we help each other by offering our honest responses to drafts.
8. We greatly appreciate the kindness that you have shown our daughter.
9. Despite his bad back, Brian offered to help us move.
10. The prospect for manned space flights to Mars and Venus, which looked so promising in the '70s, became increasingly less likely until today they seem only a remote possibility.

Verbs

A verb indicates action or existence. Main verbs fall into two classes: *action verbs* and *linking verbs*. A very different type of verb is the *auxiliary* (or *helping*) verb, which adds specific kinds of meaning to the main verb.

Action Verbs As its name suggests, an action verb expresses action. Some action verbs are transitive, others intransitive. A *transitive* verb has a direct object that receives or results from the action and rounds out the meaning of the sentence.

> The photographer *took* the picture.

Without the direct object, this sentence would not express a complete thought. In contrast, an *intransitive* verb requires no direct object to complete the meaning of the sentence.

> Lee Ann *gasped* loudly.
> Little Tommy Tucker *sings* for his supper.

Many action verbs can play both transitive and intransitive roles, depending on the sentences they are used in.

> Kari *rode* her bicycle into town. (transitive verb)
> Karl *rode* in the front seat of the car. (intransitive verb)

Linking Verbs A linking verb shows existence or a state of affairs such as taste rather than action. Linking verbs are often followed by subject complements that reflect back on the subject of the sentence.

> Ms. Davis *is* our new director. (Complement *director* renames subject *Ms. Davis*.)
> The soup *was* lukewarm. (Complement *lukewarm* describes subject *soup*.)

The most common linking verbs are forms of the verb *to be (is, are, am, was, were, be, being, been.)* Likewise, verbs such as *seem, become, appear, remain, feel, look, smell, sound,* and *taste* function as linking verbs when they do not indicate actual physical action. In such cases, they are followed by adjectives (see pages 637–640). Here is an example:

> Harry looked *angry.*

When such verbs do indicate physical action, they function as action verbs and are followed by adverbs (see pages 640–642).

> Harry looked *angrily* at the referee.

Linking verbs can also be followed by adverb phrases of place or time.

> Your dinner is *on the table* (adverb phrase of place).
> The meeting will be *at 8:00* A.M. (adverb phrase of time).

vbs

_____ trying too hard.
Steve _____ been an
excellent employee. I
_____ trying to help
you improve. We

_____ _____

selling shoes for the last
50 years. Frank _____
probably receive a
promotion this year.

Auxiliary Verbs

Auxiliary (helping) verbs accompany action or linking verbs and provide information about time, possibility, or obligation, or establish the passive. _Have, be,_ and _do_ can function as both auxiliary and main verbs.

The auxiliary verbs _have (has, had)_ and _be (is, are, was, were)_ can provide information about time.

> Carol has repaired your computer.
>
> Carol is reformatting your hard drive.

The auxiliary verb _do_ is inserted to form the negative or a question when there is no other auxiliary.

> Ellen _did_ not resign.
>
> _Did_ Ellen resign?

Auxiliary verbs called modals show time, obligation, possibility, or ability: _shall, should, will, would, can, could, may, might._

With questions, the auxiliary verb is often moved to the front.

> _Will_ Ellen _resign?_

EXERCISE

Identify each verb or auxiliary in the following sentences and indicate whether it is a main verb (MV) or auxiliary (AUX).

1. An explosion rocked the apartment building and scattered debris in all directions.
2. We should be considering ways that we can improve the quality of our lives.
3. Americans have been buying CD players at a tremendous rate.
4. Did you ask Jennifer if she has her digital camera in her backpack?
5. With genetic screening we can identify individuals who are at higher risk for many serious diseases.
6. An espresso doesn't always taste good but it is always an eye-opener.
7. Beethoven's string quartets have stood the test of time as masterpieces that are rivaled only by Bartok's works in the genre.
8. It is almost impossible today to tune an engine yourself without the sophisticated computer equipment found in auto shops.
9. Advertisements can be an art form when they are created with imagination and aesthetic vision.
10. If yesterday's wildest dreams are today's reality, will today's wildest dreams be tomorrow's reality?

Usage Considerations

Energetic writing requires precise verbs. Don't take verbs for granted; revise them as necessary to strengthen a sentence. Note the improved precision of the second example.

> I _gave_ the maître d' a ten-dollar bill.
>
> I _slipped_ the maître d' a ten-dollar bill.

Tense

Verbs change in form to show distinctions in time. Every main verb has two basic tenses: present and past.

The *present tense* shows present condition and general or habitual action, indicates permanent truths, tells about past events in the historical present, and sometimes denotes action at some definite future time.

Verbs in the present tense must agree with their subjects. If the subject of a verb is a singular noun or pronoun (*he, she, it*), add *s* or *es* (if the word ends with an *s* or *ch* sound, as in *talks* or *teaches*). If the subject is plural or a second- person pronoun (*you*), the verb takes no ending (*talk, teach*).

Helen *looks* beautiful in her new gown. (present condition)

John *works* on the eighteenth floor. (general action)

I *brush* my teeth each morning. (habitual action)

The earth *rotates* on its axis. (permanent truth)

On November 11, 1918, the guns *fall* silent, and World War I *comes* to an end. (historical present)

Monday, I *begin* my new job. (future action)

The past tense shows that a condition existed or an action was completed in the past. This verb tense leaves the time indefinite, but surrounding words may specify it. Most verbs are regular and form the past tense by adding *-ed: talk, talked*. Some verbs are irregular and form the past by changing the vowel: *stand, stood*. A very few verbs do not change forms at all in creating the past: *set, set*.

Paul *was* angry with his noisy neighbors. (past condition, time indefinite)

Sandy *received* a long letter yesterday. (past action, time specified by *yesterday*)

Past Participle   In addition to the basic tenses, there is a *past participle* form of the main verb that is used to form the perfect form of the verb phrase and the passive voice. For most verbs, the past participle form is identical with the past tense in form.

Present	Past	Past Participle
talk	talk**ed**	talk**ed**
stand	st**oo**d	st**oo**d
set	set	set

Some verbs have different past forms and past participles. This can often lead to errors where less experienced writers often use the regular past (*He has **swam** this river before*) when the past participle form is required (*he has **swum** this river before*). Below is a table of many but not all of the irregular verbs for your reference.

Present Infinitive	Past	Past Participle	Present Infinitive	Past	Past Participle
arise	arose	arisen	blow	blew	blown
be	was, were	been	break	broke	broken
become	became	become	choose	chose	chosen
bite	bit	bitten	come	came	come
do	did	done	grow	grew	grown
draw	drew	drawn	hide	hid	hidden

vbs

following: How long have you been in this class? How long has this text been in print? How many years have you lived in this state? From what point have you been interested in your career choice?

TEACHING STRATEGY
The past perfect tense, like the present perfect, can be taught by having students convert questions into answers that use this tense, such as the following: How many times had Gary missed work before he was fired? How many home runs had Lou Gehrig hit before he retired from baseball? What other states had Mary lived in when she moved to Connecticut? How long had he been sick before he died?

TEACHING STRATEGY
If you have students write a narrative, ask them to check it for sentences where they have used the present perfect or past perfect. Ask them to read the sentences aloud or write them on the board, so the class can discuss whether each use was appropriate.

PERSPECTIVE
Students are far too inclined to use the passive voice. Sometimes they do it to imitate what they believe to be the academic style of writing. At other times, they want to avoid specifying a subject or repeating the same

Present Infinitive	Past	Past Participle	Present Infinitive	Past	Past Participle
drink	drank	drunk	know	knew	known
drive	drove	driven	ride	rode	riden
eat	ate	eaten	see	saw	seen
fall	fell	fallen	shake	shook	shaken
fly	flew	flown	slay	slew	slain
freeze	froze	frozen	speak	spoke	spoken
get	got	gotten	spring	sprang	sprung
give	gave	given	write	wrote	written

Time and Verb Forms

In addition to the tenses in English, many other forms of the verb express time.

Future Time   *Future time* is frequently indicated by the auxiliary modals *shall* or *will* with the present tense form of the verb.

> You *will feel* better after a good night's sleep. (future condition)

> I *shall attend* the concert next week. (future action)

Perfect Verb Forms   The perfect form of a verb is formed by a form of the auxiliary verb *have* and the past participle of the verb.

The *present perfect* tense is formed with *has* or *have* and the past participle of the main verb. It shows that a past condition or action, or its effect, continues until the present time.

> The players *have been* irritable since they lost the homecoming game. (Condition continues until present.)

> Juanita *has driven* a United Parcel Service truck for five years. (Action continues until present.)

> William *has repaired* the snow blower. (Effect of action continues until present although the action itself was completed in the past.)

The *past perfect* tense combines *had* and the past participle of the main verb. It refers to a past condition or action that was completed before another past condition or action.

> He *had been* in the army two years when the war ended. (Past perfect condition occurred first.)

> Vivian moved into the house that she *had built* the summer before. (Past perfect action occurred first.)

The *future perfect* tense is formed from the verbs *shall have* or *will have* plus the past participle of the main verb. It shows that a condition or an action will have been completed at some time in the future. Surrounding words specify time.

Our sales manager *will have been* with the company ten years next July. (Condition will end.)

By the end of this year, I *shall have written* the great American novel. (Action will be completed.)

Progressive Verb Forms

Each verb form, including the basic tenses, has a *progressive form* that indicates action in progress. The progressive is always indicated by some form of the verb *to be* followed by a present participle (or progressive), a verb that ends in *-ing*.

Present progressive	I am running.
Past progressive	I was running.
Future progressive	I will be running.
Present perfect progressive	I have been running.
Past perfect progressive	I had been running.
Future perfect progressive	I will have been running.

Pages 672–674 discuss unwarranted shifts in tense and their correction.

An easy way to identify the form of the verb phrase is to use the following formula.

(modal) + (have + en/ed) + (be + ing) + main verb
          Perfect   *Progressive*

Simply read the first available tense. If the modal is *will* then that designates future time. Then if *have, has,* or *had* is present, the verb phrase is *perfect*. If a form of *be* is present and the main verb ends with *ing*, then the verb phrase is progressive.

will	have	been	living
Future	*Perfect*	*Progressive*	

Usage

While most students use regular tenses and the progressive accurately, many less experienced writers do not always use the perfect verb form where appropriate. This is acceptable in informal writing; it is not acceptable for most formal writing.

Not acceptable   Jim *studied* accounting for the last three years. (This suggests that the action is over and done with.)

Acceptable   Jim *has studied* accounting for the last three years. (The present perfect verb form shows that the action comes right up to the present and may not be finished yet.)

Voice

Transitive verbs have two voices: active and passive. A verb is in the *active voice* when the subject carries out the action named by the verb.

Barry *planned* a picnic. (Subject *Barry* performs action.)

A verb is in the *passive voice* when the subject receives the action. The performer may be identified in an accompanying phrase or go unmentioned.

---

sentence construction. Encourage students to use the active voice more often and to try other ways of varying sentence structure.

TEACHING STRATEGY
Have students check their writing for sentences that use the passive voice, determine which are effective, and if necessary, recast the sentences in the active voice.

CLASSROOM ACTIVITY
Have students rewrite the following passage, using the active voice, and then compare the effectiveness of the two versions.

All grade reports should be carefully reviewed by the instructor before they are turned in to the records office. Any errors should be corrected and initialed. When a grade is not recorded, an *F* will be assigned automatically to the student. Grade changes will not be processed by this office for the first three weeks of the new term.

REVISED VERSION
Please carefully review your grade reports before you turn them in to the records office. Be sure to correct and initial any errors. When you have not recorded a grade, we will automatically assign an *F* to the student. It is essential that your report be correct and complete since we will not be able to process grade changes for the first three weeks of the new term.

A picnic *was planned* by Barry. (The phrase *by Barry* identifies the performer.)

The picnic *was canceled.* (The performer goes unmentioned.)

A passive construction always uses a form of *to be* and the past participle of an action verb. Like other constructions, the passive may show past, present, or future time.

Amy *is paid* handsomely for her investment advice. (present tense)

I *was warned* by a sound truck that a tornado was nearby. (past tense)

I *will be sent* to Ghana soon by the Peace Corps. (future tense)

I *have been awarded* a sizable research grant. (present perfect tense)

The city *had been shelled* heavily before the infantry moved in. (past perfect tense)

By the end of this month, the site for our second factory *will have been chosen.* (future perfect tense)

To convert a sentence from the passive to the active voice, make the performer the subject, the original subject the direct object, and drop the form of *to be.*

The treaty *was signed* by the general. (passive)

The general *signed* the treaty. (active)

Technical and scientific writing commonly uses the passive voice to explain processes since it focuses on the objective observation or the action rather than the agent who can vary and should be irrelevant to the result. Other kinds of writing, however, avoid the passive voice except when it is desirable to not identify the one performing the action or when the action is more significant than the actor. See pages 109–110 for more information on usage.

EXERCISE ANSWERS

1. broke (past) was thrown (past, passive)

2. has managed (present perfect)

3. is performing (present progressive)

4. will have completed (future perfect)

5. bought (past), had coveted (past perfect)

6. will be placed (future, passive), are (present)

7. has been acting (present perfect progressive), moved (past)

8. has been repaired (present perfect, passive)

9. had been consulted (past perfect, passive), was implemented (past, passive)

10. will bring (future)

EXERCISE

Identify each verb group in the following sentences, indicate its form (present, past, future, present perfect, past perfect, future perfect, and any of the progressive forms), and note any use of the passive voice.

1. Devon broke his leg when he was thrown from his horse.
2. Deidra has managed our money for the last several years.
3. The Chicago Symphony is performing Mahler's *Resurrection Symphony.*
4. We will have completed the repairs on your computer by next Friday.
5. John finally bought the used BMW convertible that he had coveted for the past year.
6. Computers will be placed in every classroom as soon as the funds are available.
7. Maria has been acting in Shakespeare plays every summer since she first moved to Michigan.
8. At last the ceiling in the McCracken Building has been repaired.
9. The faculty had been consulted before the new attendance policy was implemented.
10. The future will bring many surprising changes.

Mood   The mood of a verb shows whether the writer regards a statement as a

1. fact
2. command or request
3. wish, possibility, condition contrary to fact, or the like.

English has three moods: the indicative, imperative, and subjunctive.

A sentence in the *indicative mood* states a real or supposed fact or asks a question.

Nancy *graduates* from high school tomorrow.

We *lived* in Oakmont when Rachel was born.

He *had been* a sailor during the war.

Has Joe *asked* anyone to the prom yet?

Most verbs are used in the indicative mood.

A sentence in the *imperative mood* delivers a command or makes a request.

Leave the room immediately! (command)

Please *turn* the CD player down. (request)

The subject of a sentence in the imperative mood is always *you*. Although ordinarily unstated, the subject sometimes appears in the sentence.

You leave the room immediately!

The *subjunctive mood* is used

1. in *if, as if,* and *as though* clauses to express a wish, a possibility, or an action or a condition contrary to fact
2. in *that* clauses expressing orders, demands, requests, resolutions, proposals, or motions
3. with modal auxiliaries to express wishes, probability, possibility, permission, requirements, recommendations, suggestions, and conditions contrary to fact.

To express a present or future wish, possibility, condition or action in an *if, as if,* or *as though* clause, use *were* with any personal pronoun or noun serving as the subject of the clause.

If only Stan *were* less gullible! (present wish contrary to fact)

Even if Kay *were* to explain, Mary wouldn't believe her. (future possibility)

Arthur is behaving as if he *were* a millionaire (present condition contrary to fact)

To express a wish, possibility, or condition contrary to past facts, use *had been* or *had* plus the past participle of an action verb.

If the engine *had been lubricated*, the bearing wouldn't have burned out. (past condition contrary to fact)

Alice looked as if she *had lost* her best friend. (condition expressed in clause occurs before action of verb *looked*)

When writing *that* clauses expressing orders, demands, requests, resolutions, proposals, or motions, use *be* or the present plural form of an action verb.

I move that they *be* rewarded for their bravery.

The group proposed that Margaret *go* to the scene of the accident and *inspect* it personally.

In other *that* clauses, use the appropriate indicative form of the verb.

I know that they *were* rewarded for their bravery.

The group believed that Margaret *had gone* to the scene of the accident and *inspected* it personally.

The modal auxiliaries include the helping verbs *can, could, may, might, must, shall, will, would, should,* and *ought to.* The examples below illustrate the meanings they can express.

1. Wishes *(could, would)*
I wish I *could* shimmy like my sister Kate.
The Republicans wish the Democrats *would* go away and vice versa.

2. Probability *(should)*
Because I've studied diligently, I *should* do better on my next chemistry test.

3. Possibility *(may, might, can, could)*
Low inflation *could* cause our stock market to soar.
I *might* stay up to watch the eclipse of the moon tonight.

4. Permission *(can, may)*
The public *can* use these tennis courts every afternoon.
You *may* leave as soon as you've finished filing these folders.

5. Requirements *(must)*
The landlord has raised our rent again; we *must* find another apartment.

6. Recommendations, suggestions *(should, ought to)*
Randy *should* see a doctor about his chest pains.
All of us *ought to* exercise regularly.

7. Conditions contrary to fact *(could)*
If only I *could* live my life over!

EXERCISE ANSWERS
1. IMP
2. IND
3. SUB
4. IMP
5. IND
6. SUB
7. SUB
8. IMP
9. SUB
10. IND

For each of the following sentences, identify the mood as indicative (IND), imperative (IMP), or subjunctive (SUB):

1. See your doctor before starting a strenuous exercise program.
2. The tired runner staggered across the finish line.
3. These new cell phones should prove very popular.
4. Let me know what you think of this novel.
5. Hang gliding is a great sport for anyone unafraid of heights.
6. If you practiced more, you could become an outstanding pianist.
7. The latest unemployment figures should help calm inflation fears.

8. Stop talking right now or leave the class.
9. This movie could have been shortened by fifteen minutes without harming the story.
10. Who wants to play Scrabble this evening?

Adjectives

An adjective *modifies* a noun or pronoun by describing it, limiting it, or otherwise making its meaning more exact.

> The *brass* candlestick stood next to the *fragile* vase. (*Brass* modifies *candlestick*, and *fragile* modifies *vase*.)

> The cat is *long-haired* and *sleek*. (*Long-haired* and *sleek* modify *cat*.)

There are three general categories of adjectives: limiting, descriptive, and proper.

Limiting Adjectives   A limiting adjective identifies or points out the noun or pronoun it modifies. It may indicate number or quantity. Several categories of pronouns can serve as limiting adjectives, as can numbers and nouns.

> *Whose* briefcase is on the table? (interrogative adjective)

> The couple *whose* car was stolen called the police. (relative adjective)

> *This* restaurant has the best reputation for gourmet food. (demonstrative adjective)

> *Some* people have no social tact at all. (indefinite adjective)

> Sally swerved *her* car suddenly to avoid an oncoming truck. (possessive adjective)

> *Three* people entered the lecture hall late. (number as adjective)
> The *schoolgirl* look is fashionable this year. (noun as adjective)

Descriptive Adjectives   A descriptive adjective names a quality, characteristic, or condition of a noun or pronoun. Two or more of these adjectives, members of the largest category of adjectives, may modify the same noun or pronoun.

> The *yellow* submarine belongs to the Beatles.

> He applied *clear* lacquer to the tabletop.

> The *slim, sophisticated* model glided onto the runway.

> The child was *active, happy*, and *polite*.

Proper Adjectives   A proper adjective is derived from a proper noun and is always capitalized.

> Harwell is a *Shakespearean* actor.

Articles as Adjectives   Articles appear immediately before nouns and can therefore be considered adjectives. There are three articles in English: *a, an,* and *the. The* points to a specific item; *a* and *an* do not. *A* precedes words beginning

PERSPECTIVE
Some students avoid adjectives as though such descriptive additions might infect their writing. Others write essays that are soggy with adjectives. In discussing adjectives, you might have students assess their own use of them.

TEACHING STRATEGIES
1. Have students review several essays in the Reader to determine where adjectives have been used and to what effect. Be sure the review is not confined to narration and description essays; students need to realize that adjectives play an important role in all writing, not just "literary" essays.
2. Have students review one of their own drafts to determine where they need adjectives to help them limit their nouns and where they have used adjectives to excess.

CLASSROOM ACTIVITY
Have students identify adjectives that might limit and qualify a long list of nouns. Discuss the different effects the use of these adjectives would have. You might note that adjectives help answer the question, "What kind of _____?" Sample nouns: *dog, man, house, woman, student, child, boy, car, tire, tree, star, restaurant, potatoes*, and so on.

with consonant sounds; *an* precedes words with vowel sounds, making pronunciation easier.

> *The* right word at *the* right moment can save a friendship. (Definite articles suggest there is one right word and one right moment.)

> *A* right word can save a friendship. (Indefinite article suggests there are several right words.)

> I think I'd like *an* apple with my lunch. (No particular apple is specified.)

Sometimes the definite article refers to a class of items.

> *The* tiger is fast becoming an endangered species.

Context shows whether such a sentence refers to particular items or entire classes.

TEACHING STRATEGY
To reinforce the material on comparisons, try combining it with the section on comparison errors on pages 675–676.

Comparison with Adjectives   Adjectives can be used to show comparison. When two things are compared, shorter adjectives usually add *-er* and longer adjectives add *more*. When three or more things are compared, shorter adjectives usually add *-est* and longer ones add *most*.

> John is *taller* than Pete. (short adjective comparing two things)

> Sandra seems *more engaged* than Jill today. (long adjective comparing two things)

> John is the *tallest* of the three brothers. (short adjective comparing three things)

> Sandra is the *most engaged* student in the class. (longer adjective comparing more than three things)

Some adjectives, like the examples below, have irregular forms for comparisons.

> good—better—best

> bad—worse—worst

Don't use the *-est* form of the shorter adjective to compare just two things.

> *Faulty*   This is the *smallest* of the two castles.

Instead, use the *-er* form.

> *Revision*   This is the *smaller* of the two castles.

Position of Adjectives   Most adjectives come immediately before the words they modify. In a few set expressions (for example, heir *apparent*), the adjective immediately follows the word it modifies. Similarly, adjective pairs sometimes appear in a follow-up position for added emphasis (The rapids, *swift* and *dangerous*, soon capsized the raft). Sometimes adjectives also serve as subject complements and follow their subjects (The puppy was *friendly*).

Usage Considerations   Some students overuse adjectives, especially in descriptions, but most underuse them. Review your sentences carefully to see where adding or cutting adjectives can increase the impact of your writing.

adj

My Buick is the talk of my friends.

My *old, dilapidated, rusty, fenderless 1970* Buick is the talk of my friends.

My *rusty, fenderless 1970* Buick is the talk of my friends.

The first sentence lacks adjectives that show why the car is discussed. The second sentence overcorrects this fault by including two adjectives that repeat the information provided by the others. The final sentence strikes the proper balance.

Determiners   There is a category of words that are sometimes classified with adjectives that limit the noun or pronoun but do not name a quality or characteristic of the noun or pronoun.

Three sailboats raced around the island.

While we know how many sailboats are involved, there is no descriptive content added to the concept of sailboats.

There are many different kinds of determiners.

Determiners	**Name**
a, an	Indefinite article
the	Definite article
this, that, these, those	Demonstrative
one, two, three, four, five	Cardinal number
first, second, third, fourth	Ordinal number
my, our, your, his, her, hers, its, their	Possessive pronoun
some, any, no, every, another, enough,	Indefinite pronoun
either, neither, all, both, each, less,	Possessive noun
other, many, more, most, few, several	
Tom's, Mary's	

With the indefinite article a/an, *a* precedes words beginning with consonant sounds; *an* precedes words with a vowel sound to make pronunciation easier.

EXERCISE

Identify the adjectives and determiners in the following sentences.

1. The climbers seemed very tiny as they rappelled down the sheer cliff.
2. Janine's paper offered an insightful and well-supported argument.
3. Fresh grapefruit juice can be a tart but tasty breakfast beverage.
4. In some Medieval cathedrals there were statues representing the seven deadly sins.
5. Many expeditions to climb Mt. Everest were defeated more by the inhospitable environment than by the actual challenges of the climb.

EXERCISE ANSWERS

1. Determiners: the, the; adjectives: tiny, sheer

2. Determiners: Janine's, an; adjectives: insightful, supported

3. Determiners: a; adjectives: fresh, grapefruit, tart, tasty, breakfast

4. Determiners: some, the, seven; adjectives: Medieval, deadly

5. Determiners: many, the, the, the; adjectives: inhospitable, actual

6. Determiners: a; adjectives: good, educational, smaller

7. Determiners: the, the, the; adjectives: chilly, warm, damp, summer

8. Determiners: Cody's; adjectives: sleek, new, tight

9. Determiners: the, the, the; adjectives: black, loud, heavy, rock

10. Determiners: many; adjectives: Canadian, American

6. A good educational environment can be made better by smaller classes.
7. After the chilly air conditioning in the restaurant, Christy was grateful to step out into the warm, damp summer air.
8. Cody's sleek new convertible looked ready to fly around tight corners.
9. The black Focus seemed to pulse with the loud, heavy beat of the rock music.
10. Many Canadian writers are better known than most American critics would like to admit.

TEACHING STRATEGIES
1. To reinforce this material, try combining it with the unit on adverb errors on pages 674–676.
2. Have students identify in their writing where they have used and could use adverbs. Have them supply adverbs that improve their writing and cut adverbs that are ineffective.

Adverbs

An adverb modifies a verb, an adjective, another adverb, or a whole sentence. Adverbs generally answer questions such as "How?" "When?" "Where?" "How often?" and "To what extent?"

The floodwaters receded *very* slowly. (Adverb modifies adverb and answers the question "How?")

My sister will visit me *tomorrow*. (Adverb modifies verb and answers the question "When?")

The coach walked *away* from the bench. (Adverb modifies verb and answers the question "Where?")

The tire is *too* worn to be safe. (Adverb modifies adjective and answers the question "To what extent?")

The teller is *frequently* late for work. (Adverb modifies adjective and answers the question "How often?")

Unfortunately, the game was canceled because of rain. (The adverb modifies the whole sentence but does not answer any question.)

Formation of Adverbs

Most adverbs are formed by adding *-ly* to adjectives.

The wind is *restless*. (*Restless* is an adjective modifying *wind*.)

He walked *restlessly* around the room. (*Restlessly* is an adverb modifying *walked*.)

Many common adverbs, however (*almost, never, quite, soon, then, there,* and *too*), lack *-ly* endings.

I *soon* realized that pleasing my boss was impossible.

This movie is *too* gruesome for my taste.

Furthermore, some words such as *better, early, late, hard, little, near, only, straight,* and *wrong* do double duty as either adjectives or adverbs.

We must have taken a *wrong* turn. (*Wrong* is an adjective modifying the noun *turn*.)

Where did I go *wrong*? (*Wrong* is an adverb modifying the verb *go*.)

CLASSROOM ACTIVITY
To help students become conscious of their use of adverbs, have them complete the following sentences with effective adverbs: The instructor spoke _____.
The dorm was _____ loud. The gamekeeper raced _____ toward the lion. Steve is early to class. They _____ receive a fair amount of snow in the Rockies.
He _____ waited for the doctor.

Comparison with Adverbs   Like adjectives, adverbs can show comparison. When two things are compared, adverbs add *more*. When three or more things are compared, *most* is used.

> Harold works *more* efficiently than Don. (adverb comparing two people)
>
> Of all the people in the shop, Harold works the *most* efficiently. (adverb comparing more than two people)

Some adverbs, like some adjectives, use irregular forms for comparisons.

> well—better—best
>
> much—more—most

Position of Adverbs   Adverbs are more movable than any other part of speech. Usually, adverbs that modify adjectives and other adverbs appear next to them to avoid confusion.

> Her *especially* fine tact makes her a welcome guest at any party. (Adverb *especially* modifies adjective *fine*.)
>
> The novel was *very* badly written. (Adverb *very* modifies adverb *badly*.)

Adverbs that modify verbs, however, can often be shifted around in their sentences without causing changes in meaning.

> *Quickly*, he slipped through the doorway.
>
> He slipped *quickly* through the doorway.
>
> He slipped through the doorway *quickly*.

Usage Considerations   You can often sharpen the meaning of a sentence by adding a well-chosen adverb.

> The student squirmed in his chair.
>
> The student squirmed *anxiously* in his chair.

Including the adverb *anxiously* in the second sentence shows the mental state of the student.

Be careful, however, not to overuse adverbs because they can bog down your writing.

EXERCISE

Identify the adverbs in the following sentences:

1. Three friends slowly but steadily hiked up the mountain trail.
2. Everyone agreed that it was too hot to mow the lawn.
3. While the screenplay was exceptionally well written, the movie itself was poorly directed and badly miscast.
4. The violins entered too early but no one but the conductor really noticed.
5. We should meet tomorrow to plan our camping trip.

EXERCISE ANSWERS

1. slowly, steadily
2. too
3. exceptionally, well, poorly, badly
4. too, early really
5. tomorrow
6. strangely, unusually
7. nearer
8. fiercely
9. gradually, persistently
10. patiently, more, imaginatively

6. Some people are strangely attracted to unusually dangerous activities.
7. The two planes came nearer to each other than anyone would like.
8. Few people compete more fiercely than Phillip.
9. Gradually but persistently erosion will wear away a mountain.
10. Ms. Draco patiently explained to the class how they could approach the assignment more imaginatively.

Prepositions

A preposition links its object—a noun or noun substitute—to some other word in the sentence and shows a relationship between them. The relationship is often one of location, time, means, or reason or purpose. The word group containing the preposition and its object makes up a prepositional phrase.

The new insulation *in* the attic keeps my house much warmer now. (Preposition *in* links object *attic* to *insulation* and shows location.)

We have postponed the meeting *until* tomorrow. (Preposition *until* links object *tomorrow* to *postponed* and shows time.)

The tourists traveled *by* automobile. (Preposition *by* links object *automobile* to *traveled* and shows means.)

Warren swims *for* exercise. (Preposition *for* links object *exercise* to *swims* and shows reason or purpose.)

The following list includes the most common prepositions, some of which consist of two or more words:

about	before	except	on
above	behind	for	onto
across	below	from	out of
after	beside	in	over
against	between	instead of	since
along with	by	into	through
among	by reason of	like	to
around	contrary to	near	toward
at	down	next to	under
because of	during	of	with
			without

Many of these combine to form additional prepositions: *except for, in front of, by way of, on top of,* and the like.

Some words that are usually used as prepositions such as *up, on,* and *in* can also function as a different part of speech called a *verb particle.* Here are two examples.

The instructor let Jeff make *up* the test.

The officer turned *in* his best friend.

The verb particle is closely associated with the verb and is a part of its meaning. If a word is a verb particle, it can usually be moved after the noun.

The instructor let Jeff make the test *up.*

The officer turned his best friend *in.*

Usage Considerations   It is easy to use a small group of prepositions over and over in your writing. This habit often results in imprecise or misleading sentences. To avoid this problem, think carefully about your choice of prepositions as you revise. Read the following example:

> He walked *by* the railroad tracks on his way home.

Note that two interpretations are possible.

> He walked *along* the railroad tracks on his way home.

> He walked *past* the railroad tracks on his way home.

Clearly you would use the preposition that conveys your intended meaning.

EXERCISE

Identify the prepositions (P) and their objects (O) in the following sentences:

1. Angela searched her house for a book of poems by Rilke.
2. Dave and Silvia traveled across America on a motorcycle.
3. Because of the hurricane, the causeway from the Florida Keys was closed.
4. Contrary to everyone's expectation, Barry decided to go into advertising instead of theater.
5. Before her first class, Carrie likes to swim twenty-five laps in the school's pool.
6. The two boys hid for several hours in the woods behind their house.
7. In his paper on cloning, James cut through the confusion about the topic and clearly presented the arguments for each side of the issue.
8. Almost out of gas, Janine's car raced across the finish line in first place.
9. A good listener sometimes needs to hear the message behind the words.
10. I always hated it when trapeze artists flew through the air without a net beneath them.

Conjunctions

Conjunctions serve as connectors, linking parts of sentences or whole sentences. These connectors fall into three groups: coordinating conjunctions, subordinating conjunctions, and conjunctive adverbs.

Coordinating Conjunctions   Coordinating conjunctions connect terms of equal grammatical importance: words, word groups, and simple sentences. These conjunctions can occur singly *(and, but, or, nor, for, yet, so)* or in pairs called correlative conjunctions *(either—or, neither—nor, both—and,* and *not only—but also).* The elements that follow correlative conjunctions must be parallel, that is, have the same grammatical form.

> Tom *and* his cousin are opening a coffee shop. (Coordinating conjunction connects nouns.)

> Shall I serve the tea in the living room *or* on the veranda? (Coordinating conjunction connects phrases.)

con

CLASSROOM ACTIVITY
Have students use as many coordinating conjunctions as they can to combine the following sentences:
Silvia likes my brother. Silvia likes me.

Jason is not interested in history. Jason is not interested in geography.

You may take chemistry. You may take physics.

We had wanted to go trout fishing. We drove up to the Au Sable river. We had forgotten our fishing gear.

He is in ill health. He still works 15 hours a day.

CLASSROOM ACTIVITY
Have students combine the following sets of sentences with the appropriate subordinating conjunctions:

Some former Soviet republics have moved to a more democratic form of government. The United States has had to change its foreign policy.

They turn down the heat on the weekends. The university can save on fuel bills.

He had studied for two days. He did poorly on the chemistry final.

I am going to Europe this summer, *but* Marjorie is staying home. (Coordinating conjunction connects simple sentences.)

Amy *not only* teaches English *but also* writes novels. (Correlative conjunctions connect parallel predicates.)

You can study nursing *either* at Ferris State University *or* at DeWitt College. (Correlative conjunctions connect parallel phrases.)

Friendship is *both* pleasure *and* pain. (Correlative conjunctions connect parallel nouns.)

Subordinating Conjunctions

Like relative pronouns, subordinating conjunctions introduce subordinate clauses, relating them to independent clauses, which can stand alone as complete sentences. Examples of subordinating conjunctions include *because, as if, even though, since, so that, whereas,* and *whenever* (see page 100 for a more comprehensive list).

I enjoyed the TV program *because* it was so well acted. (Conjunction connects *it was so well acted* to rest of sentence.)

Whenever you're ready, we can begin dinner. (Conjunction connects *you're ready* to rest of sentence.)

Conjunctive Adverbs

These connectors resemble both conjunctions and adverbs. Like conjunctions, they serve as linking devices between elements of equal rank. Like adverbs, they function as modifiers, showing such things as similarity, contrast, result or effect, addition, emphasis, time, and example.

The job will require you to travel a great deal; *however*, the salary is excellent.

Sean cares nothing for clothes; *in fact*, all of his socks have holes in their toes.

The following list groups the most common conjunctive adverbs according to function:

Similarity: likewise, similarly

Contrast: however, nevertheless, on the contrary, on the other hand, otherwise

Result or effect: accordingly, as a result, consequently, hence, therefore, thus

Addition: also, furthermore, in addition, in the first place, moreover

Emphasis or clarity: in fact, in other words, indeed, that is

Time: afterward, later, meanwhile, subsequently

Example: for example, for instance, to illustrate

Conjunctive adverbs should not be confused with coordinating conjunctions. Unlike conjunctions and more like adverbs, conjunctive adverbs can move, often to create a specific emphasis.

The job will require you to travel a great deal; the salary, *however*, is excellent.

The job will require you to travel a great deal; *however*, the salary is excellent.

Sean cares nothing for clothes; all of his socks, *in fact*, have holes in their toes.

Sean cares nothing for clothes; *in fact*, all of his socks have holes in them.

Because conjunctive adverbs can move, the second independent clause must be treated as a complete sentence and either be joined to the previous independent clause with a semicolon or be separated by a period.

Usage Considerations   You can add variety and precision to your writing by varying the conjunctions you use. If you consistently rely on the conjunction *because*, try substituting *as* or *since*. Likewise, you may periodically replace *if* with *provided that*. The right conjunction shows the realtionship among ideas.

When you have choppy sentences, try combining them by using a conjunction.

You can buy smoked salmon at Sally's Seafoods. You can buy it at Daane's Thriftland as well.

You can buy smoked salmon *either* at Sally's Seafoods *or* at Daane's Thriftland.

The revision is much smoother than the original sentence pair.

Interjections

An interjection is an exclamatory word used to gain attention or to express strong feeling. It has no grammatical connection to the rest of the sentence. An interjection is followed by an exclamation point or a comma.

Hey! Watch how you're driving! (strong interjection)

Oh, is the party over already? (mild interjection)

EXERCISE

Identify the coordinating conjunctions (CC), subordinating conjunctions (SC), conjunctive adverbs (CA), and interjections (I) in the following sentences:

1. There is evidence that the polar ice caps are receding; however, scientists do not yet know the probable impact of this event.
2. Neither term limits nor campaign reform will take money out of politics.
3. Since there has been an increase in the alligator population, some lawmakers think the ban on alligator hide products should be lifted.
4. Rats! My computer ate my report.
5. Most companies work hard to secure their Internet sites, but hackers can usually find their way around these safeguards.
6. Extensive resources have been committed to the war on drugs; nevertheless, illegal narcotics continue to flow into this country.
7. After Barbara got the promotion, she took all her coworkers out to celebrate.
8. Basketball and racquetball are both excellent aerobic activities.
9. You can either enjoy a brisk game of tennis or relax in the hot tub.
10. Most people like to snack while they watch television.

EXERCISE ANSWERS
1. however (CA)
2. neither . . . nor (CC)
3. since (SC)
4. rats (I)
5. but (CC)
6. nevertheless (CA)
7. After (SC)
8. and (CC)
9. either . . . or (CC)
10. while (SC)

Phrases and Clauses

Phrases

A phrase is a group of words that lacks a subject and a predicate and serves as a single part of speech. This section discusses four basic kinds of phrase: *prepositional, participial, gerund,* and *infinitive*. The last three are based on participles, gerunds, and infinitives, verb forms known as verbals. A fifth type of phrase, the verb phrase, consists of sets of two or more verbs (*has fixed, had been sick, will have been selected,* and the like).

Prepositional Phrases   A prepositional phrase consists of a preposition, one or more objects, and any associated words. These phrases serve as adjectives or adverbs.

The picture *over the mantel* was my mother's. (prepositional phrase as adjective)

He bought ice skates *for himself.* (prepositional phrase as adverb modifying verb)

The toddler was afraid *of the dog.* (prepositional phrase as adverb modifying adjective)

Our visitors arrived late *in the day.* (prepositional phrase as adverb modifying another adverb)

Frequently, prepositional phrases occur in series. Sometimes they form chains in which each phrase modifies the object of the preceding phrase. At other times some or all of the phrases may modify the verb or verb phrase.

John works *in a clothing store/ on Main Street/ during the summer.*

Here the first and third phrases serve as adverbs modifying the verb *works* and answering the questions "Where?" and "When?" while the second phrase serves as an adjective modifying *store* and answering the question "Where?"

On occasion, especially in questions, a preposition may be separated from its object, making the phrase difficult to find.

Dr. Perry is the person *whom* I've been looking *for.*

What are you shouting *about?*

Participial Phrases   A participial phrase consists of a participle plus associated words. Participles are verb forms that, when used in participial phrases, function as adjectives or adverbs. A present participle ends in *-ing* and indicates an action currently being carried out. A past participle ends in *-ed, -en,-e, -n, -d,* or *-t* and indicates some past action.

The chef *preparing dinner* trained in France. (present participial phrase as adjective)

The background, *sketched in lightly,* accented the features of the woman in the painting. (past participial phrase as adjective)

She left *whistling a jolly melody.* (present participial phrase as adverb)

A perfect participial phrase consists of *having* or *having been* plus a past participle and any associated words. Like a past participial phrase, it indicates a past action.

Having alerted the townspeople about the tornado, the sound truck returned to the city garage. (perfect participial phrase)

Having been alerted to the tornado, the townspeople sought shelter in their basements. (perfect participial phrase)

Some participial phrases that modify persons or things distinguish them from others in the same class. These phrases are written without commas. Other phrases provide more information about the persons or things they modify and are set off with commas.

The man *fixing my car* is a master mechanic. (Phrase distinguishes man fixing car from others.)

Mr. Welsh, *fatigued by the tennis game,* rested in the shade. (Phrase provides more information about Mr. Welsh.)

Gerund Phrases   A gerund phrase consists of a gerund and the words associated with it. Like present participles, gerunds are verb forms that end in *-ing.* Unlike participles, though, they function as nouns rather than as adjectives or adverbs.

Kathryn's hobby is *collecting stamps.* (gerund phrase as subject complement)

Kathryn's hobby, *collecting stamps,* has made her many friends. (gerund phrase as appositive)

He devoted every spare moment to *overhauling the car.* (gerund phrase as object of preposition.)

Infinitive Phrases   An infinitive phrase consists of the present principal part of a verb preceded by *to (to fix, to eat),* together with any accompanying words. These phrases serve as adjectives, adverbs, and nouns.

This looks like a good place *to plant the shrub.* (infinitive phrase as adjective)

Lenore worked *to earn money for college.* (infinitive phrase as adverb)

My goal is *to have my own business some day.* (infinitive phrase as noun)

Gerunds can often be substituted for infinitives and vice versa.

To repair this fender will cost two hundred dollars. (infinitive phrase as subject)

Repairing this fender will cost two hundred dollars. (gerund phrase as subject)

At times the *to* in an infinitive is omitted following verbs such as *make, dare, let,* and *help.*

Kristin didn't dare *(to) move* a muscle.

The psychiatrist helped me *(to) overcome* my fear of flying.

Verbals Not in Phrases   Participles, gerunds, and infinitives can function as nouns, adjectives, or adverbs, even when they are not parts of phrases.

(margin note)

spare moment to _____. _____ occupied most of my weekend _____. Politicians seem to enjoy _____. _____ has helped me invest my money wisely. *Infinitive phrases:* My goal is _____. He worked very hard _____. The library is not a good place _____. Sally decided _____.

phr

That *sunbathing* woman is a well-known model. (participle as adjective)
Dancing is fine exercise. (gerund)
The children want *to play*. (infinitive as noun)
If you're looking for a job, Sally is the person *to see*. (infinitive as adjective)
I'm prepared *to resign*. (infinitive as adverb)

Usage Considerations   Phrases can often clarify or develop the information in a sentence or combine choppy sentences.

Original	My brother is fishing.
Revision	My brother is fishing *for trout just below Barnes Dam on Sidewinder Creek.* (prepositional phrases added)
Original	The boat barely made shore.
Revision	The boat, *listing heavily and leaking badly*, barely made shore. (participial phrases added)

To avoid ponderous sentences, don't, however, weigh them down with phrases, as in the following example:

My brother is fishing for trout just below Barnes Dam on Sidewinder Creek *near Perry Pass in the mountains of Central Colorado.*

Testing a Phrase's Function

To determine whether a phrase is functioning as noun, adjective, or adverb, try a substitution test; if a common noun (something, someone, or it), adjective or adjective phrase, or adverb fits, that demonstrates the function of the phrase.

Walking at a brisk pace is excellent exercise. (gerund phrase)
Something is excellent exercise. (noun phrase)
I am prepared *to finish the job.* (infinitive phrase)
I am prepared *completely.* (adverb phrase)
He was a man *of unusual craftiness.* (prepositional phrase)
He was a *crafty* man. (adjective phrase)

EXERCISE

Identify the italicized phrases as prepositional, participial, gerund, or infinitive and indicate whether each is used as a noun, an adjective, or an adverb.

1. *Sleeping in late* can be one of the great pleasures of a holiday.
2. The students waited *for ten minutes* before they left.
3. *Racing around the corner*, Tim crashed into another student and sent her sprawling.
4. The employees were afraid that there was a plan *to lay off a third of the workforce.*
5. The grass *in the backyard* had grown so long that it was impossible to cut with a lawnmower.

cl

6. The company has decided *to go forward* with the direct marketing campaign.
7. Our guest speaker has written a book about *kayaking around New Zealand*.
8. Most high school students cannot wait *to graduate*.
9. David broke his leg *skiing in Colorado*.
10. We cheered as Joan, *panting with exhaustion*, crossed the finish line.

Clauses

A clause is a word group that includes a subject and a predicate. An *independent clause*, sometimes called a main clause, expresses a complete thought and can function as a simple sentence. A *subordinate clause*, or dependent clause, cannot stand by itself. Subordinate clauses may serve as nouns, adjectives, or adverbs.

Noun Clauses   A noun clause can serve in any of the ways that ordinary nouns can.

> *What the neighbor told John* proved to be incorrect. (noun clause as subject)

> The woman asked *when the bus left for Spokane*. (noun clause as direct object)

> I'll give a reward to *whoever returns my billfold*. (noun clause as object of preposition *to*)

Noun clauses normally begin with one of the following words:

Relative Pronouns		**Interrogative Pronouns**
who	whoever	when
whom	whomever	why
whose	that	where
what	whatever	how
which	whichever	whether

The complementizer *that* is sometimes omitted from the beginning of a clause that acts as a direct object.

> Dr. Kant thinks *(that) he knows everything*.

If a clause is serving as a noun, you can replace it with the word *something* or *someone*, and the sentence will still make sense.

> Dr. Kant thinks *something*.

If the clause is serving as an adjective or an adverb, making the substitution turns the sentence into nonsense.

> The person *who wins the lottery* will receive two million dollars.

> The person *someone* will receive two million dollars.

Adjective Clauses   Like ordinary adjectives, adjective clauses, often called *relative clauses*, modify nouns and noun substitutes.

cl

Give me one reason *why you feel the way you do.* (Adjective clause modifies noun.)

I'll hire anyone *that Dr. Stone recommends.* (Adjective clause modifies pronoun.)

Generally, adjective clauses begin with one of the following words:

Relative Pronouns	Relative Adverbs
who	when
whom	where
whose	why
what	after
which	before
that	

Sometimes the word that introduces the clause can be omitted.

The chair *(that) we ordered last month* has just arrived. (pronoun *that* omitted but understood)

The man *(whom) we were talking to* is a movie producer. (pronoun *whom* omitted but understood)

Sometimes, too, a preposition comes ahead of the introductory pronoun.

The grace *with which Nelson danced* made the onlookers envious.

An adjective clause may be restrictive and distinguish whatever it modifies from others in the same class, or it may be nonrestrictive and provide more information about whatever it modifies.

Flora wiped up the cereal *that the baby had spilled.* (restrictive clause)

Harriet Thomas, *who was born in Alaska,* now lives in Hawaii. (nonrestrictive clause)

As these examples show, restrictive clauses are not set off with commas, but nonrestrictive clauses are. See pages 688–689 for further information.

Adverb Clauses These clauses modify verbs, adjectives, adverbs, and sentences, answering the same questions that ordinary adverbs do.

You may go *whenever you wish.* (Adverb clause modifies verb.)

Sandra looked paler *than I had ever seen her look.* (Adverb clause modifies adjective.)

Darryl shouted loudly *so that the rescue party could hear him.* (Adverb clause modifies adverb.)

Unless everyone cooperates, this plan will never succeed. (Adverb clause modifies whole sentence.)

The word or word group that introduces an adverb clause is always a subordinating conjunction. Here are the most common of these conjunctions, grouped according to the questions they answer.

When? after, as, as soon as, before, since, until, when, whenever, while
Where? where, wherever
How? as if, as though
Why? as, because, now that, since, so that
Under what conditions? although, if, once, provided that, though, unless
To what extent? than

Occasionally in an adverb clause, the omission of one or more words won't hurt its meaning. Such a construction is called an *elliptical clause*.

While (he was) making a sandwich, Garth hummed softly. (*he was* omitted but understood)

Unlike noun and adjective clauses, adverb clauses can often be moved about in their sentences.

Garth hummed softly *while (he was) making a sandwich.*

Usage Considerations   Like phrases, clauses can help develop sentences as well as smooth out choppiness.

Original	The old grandfather clock ticked loudly through the night.
Revision	The old grandfather clock *that my great-aunt gave me before she died* ticked loudly through the night. (Clause adds information.)
Original	The chemistry professor insisted on lab safety. He had been hurt in a lab explosion the previous year.
Revision	The chemistry professor, *who had been hurt in a lab explosion the previous year,* insisted on lab safety. (Clause adds smoothness.)

To avoid clumsiness, avoid overloaded sentences like the one below:

The old grandfather clock that my great-aunt gave me before she died *and that I took with me to England when my company transferred me there for two years* ticked loudly through the night.

EXERCISE

Identify the italicized clauses as noun, adjective, or adverb.

1. Brad pulled a muscle in his back *while he was lifting weights.*
2. The astronauts *who landed on the moon* should still be household names.
3. Some astronomers suggested *that Pluto should not be considered a planet.*
4. Jody Singleton was touched by the cards *her students sent her.*
5. *Although coffee shops would seem like the quintessential small business,* some companies have turned America's coffee habit into multimillion dollar chains.
6. *Whoever decorated this house* has an excellent eye.
7. Andrea was pleased to find out that her new employer used the kind of accounting software *on which she had been trained.*

EXERCISE ANSWERS
1. adverb
2. adjective
3. noun
4. adjective
5. adverb
6. noun
7. adjective
8. adjective
9. adverb
10. noun

8. The Concorde, *which offers supersonic trips across the Atlantic,* has been much less popular than was originally expected.
9. *While she was waiting at the check-in counter of the airport,* Jasmine was able to read two chapters in her history text.
10. Many companies like to go *where the labor costs and taxes are lowest.*

Coordination and Subordination

Coordination and subordination are ways to rank ideas in sentences. Coordination makes ideas equal; subordination makes them unequal. To understand coordination and subordination, you need to know about four kinds of sentences: simple, compound, complex, and compound–complex.

Simple Sentences   A simple sentence has one subject and one predicate. Some simple sentences consist merely of a single noun and a single verb.

> Millicent shouted.

Others include elements such as compound subjects, compound verbs, direct objects, indirect objects, and subject complements.

> Jim and Sue have bought a car. *(compound subject, direct object)*

> Lucretia Borgia smiled and mixed her guests a cocktail. *(compound verb, indirect object, direct object)*

> Autumn is a sad season. *(subject, complement)*

Compound Sentences   A compound sentence contains two or more independent clauses, each holding the same (coordinate) rank. As a result, the idea in the first clause receives the same emphasis as the idea in the second.

In some cases, a comma and a coordinating conjunction *(and, but, or, nor, for, yet, so)* link successive clauses.

> Name the baby Huey, *or* I'll cut you out of my will.

> The audience was young, friendly, and responsive, *so* it cheered for each speaker.

In others, a semicolon and a conjunctive adverb *(for example, however, in fact, likewise, meanwhile, instead,* and the like) furnish the connection.

> Tod wants to see the play; *in fact,* he's talked about it for weeks.

> Today, many young women do not rush into marriage and motherhood; *instead,* they spend several years establishing careers.

Finally, a writer may omit any connecting word and separate the clauses with a semicolon.

> The sky grew pitch black; the wind died; an ominous quiet hung over the whole city.

> Be sure to read this Hemingway novel; it suggests how to cope gracefully with pressure.

As the preceding sentences show, compound sentences allow writers to express simple relationships among simple ideas. However, such sentences have one important limitation: It is impossible to highlight one particular idea. To do this, we need complex sentences.

Complex Sentences

A complex sentence has one independent clause and one or more dependent clauses. Relegating an idea to a dependent clause shows that the writer wishes it to receive less emphasis than the idea in the main clause. In the following examples the dependent clauses are italicized.

Because the young, friendly audience was responsive, it cheered for each speaker.

After the dance was over, Arthur collapsed on the sofa.

Once they had reached the lakeshore, the campers found a level spot *where they could pitch their tent*.

Unlike compound sentences, complex ones allow writers to vary the emphasis of ideas.

While I watered the grass, I discussed stock options with Liz.

I watered the grass *while I discussed stock options with Liz*.

The first sentence emphasizes the talk with Liz, the second watering the lawn.

Compound–Complex Sentences

This type of sentence features two or more independent clauses and one or more dependent clauses. Here are two examples with the dependent clauses italicized:

Ms. Harris works as an investment manager, and Mr. Williams, *who lives next door to her*, owns a jewelry store.

If you are to communicate properly, your thoughts must be clear and correct; thoughts are wasted *when language is muddled*.

EXERCISE

Label the independent and dependent clauses in the sentences below. Then identify each sentence as simple, compound, complex, or compound–complex.

1. A career in broadcasting requires good verbal skills, an extensive wardrobe, and a pleasant smile.
2. Because its bag was too full, the vacuum cleaner backfired, leaving the room dirtier than it had been.
3. Leave your boots in the back hall, please.
4. When Tom arrived home, his roommate asked him where he had really gone; six hours seemed too long a time to spend in the library.
5. My orange tree blossomed last week; however, the grapefruit trees have withered, probably because of the freeze last month.

"I know," and the second consists of everything following the colon. The dependent clause is "why he moved here." (Note: Some instructors would classify this sentence as compound because the dependent clause serves as a direct object of "I know.")

9. This is a simple sentence and so has one independent clause.

10. This is a compound sentence. The first independent clause precedes the semicolon; the second one follows it.

6. Kites make good gifts for children; even if a child already has a kite, a second one will come in handy if the first one becomes tangled in a tree.

7. It's risky to confide in a coworker because one can never be sure that the confidence will be kept.

8. I know why he moved here: He likes having the only dental practice in this part of the state.

9. The pencil and the stapler are on the table next to the window in Mr. Brigg's office.

10. Don't add bleach to your load of colored shirts; the colors will fade and the fibers weaken.

Editing to Correct Sentence Errors

Accepted usage improves the smoothness of your prose, makes your writing easier to understand, and demonstrates that you are a careful communicator. These assets, in turn, increase the likelihood that the reader will accept your ideas.

When you've finished revising the first draft of a piece of writing, edit it with a critic's eye to ensure that you eliminate errors. Circle sentences or parts of them that are faulty or suspect. Then check your circled items against this section of the Handbook, which deals with the most common errors in college writing.

Revising Sentence Fragments

A sentence fragment is a group of words that fails to qualify as a sentence but is capitalized and punctuated as if it were a sentence. To be a sentence, a word group must (1) have a subject and a verb and (2) make sense by itself. The first of the following examples has a subject and a verb; the second does not. Neither makes sense by itself.

> If you want to remain.
> His answer to the question.

Methods of Revision   Eliminating a sentence fragment is not hard. Careful reading often shows that the fragment goes with the sentence that comes just before or just after it. And sometimes two successive fragments can be joined. Note how we've corrected the fragments (italicized) in the following pairs:

Faulty	*Having been warned about the storm.* We decided to stay home.
Revision	Having been warned about the storm, we decided to stay home.
Faulty	*After eating.* The dog took a nap.
Revision	After eating, the dog took a nap.
Faulty	Sally went to work. *Although she felt sick.*
Revision	Sally went to work although she felt sick.
Faulty	Dave bought a new suit. *Over at Bentley's.*
Revision	Dave bought a new suit over at Bentley's.

PERSPECTIVE
Students commit sentence errors for a variety of reasons. Some, despite knowing the rules, simply make mistakes. Others have a poor grasp of the rules or misconstrue a particular one. Still others write as their community speaks, sometimes contrary to standard written grammar. Some students improve markedly when told they'll lose points for grammatical errors; others improve when you make them proofread their drafts several times. Still others need a review of the rules. Depending upon your students and personal preference, you can handle errors as they occur in student papers or set aside ten minutes of a class period to review a type of error.

PERSPECTIVE
Usually sentence fragments result because students place periods where they pause or where they signal phrase and

655

clause breaks. As a result, many fragments are nothing more than isolated phrases and clauses.

Faulty — *That bronze clock on the mantel. Once belonged to my grandmother.*
Revision — That bronze clock on the mantel once belonged to my grandmother.

Joining a fragment to a sentence or to another fragment works only if the problem is simply one of mispunctuation. If the fragment stems from an improperly developed thought, revise the thought into correct sentence form.

Punctuating Your Corrections When you join a fragment to the following sentence, you need not place a comma between the two unless the fragment has six or more words or if omitting a comma might cause a misreading. When joining a fragment to the preceding sentence, omit a comma unless there is a distinct pause between the two items. The preceding examples illustrate these points.

Intentional Fragments Fragments are commonly used in conversation and the writing that reproduces it. Professional writers also use fragments to gain special emphasis or create special effects. Pages 101–102 discuss these applications.

Connected Discourse Exercise

Identify and correct the sentence fragments in the following letter:

Dear Phone Company:

Recently I received a phone bill for over $500. While I do use the phone fairly extensively. Most of the calls I make are local ones. In this case, many of the calls on my bill were to other countries. Including a phone call to New Delhi, India. I can hardly be held responsible for these calls. Especially since I don't know anyone who lives overseas. Since the only long-distance call I made was to Kalamazoo, Michigan. I have deducted the charges for all the other long-distance calls from my bill and am sending you the balance. In order to prevent this type of error from happening again. Would you please have a representative determine why these charges appeared on my bill?

Sincerely,

Desperate

Ten main clauses paired with fragments are shown below. In each case identify the sentence (S) and the fragment (F) and then eliminate the fragment.

1. I would like you to meet Janine Lee. One of my good friends from high school.
2. Jason and Steve bought several posters. To spruce up their dorm room walls.
3. In order to get tickets to the concert. We had to stand in line for hours.
4. After we finish studying for our math test. We plan to go out for pizza.

TEACHING STRATEGIES

1. Students sometimes have problems proofreading for sentence fragments because they unconsciously leap across the period to read the complete sentence. You might show them how to check any suspicious sentence by reading it aloud and seeing whether it is complete. Be careful what you say. If you tell students they should check for the presence of a subject and a verb, they might mistake subordinate clauses for sentences.

2. Sometimes students recognize a sentence fragment only when you make them see how it leaves them waiting for the other shoe to drop. Present them with a series of fragments such as the following and ask whether they are satisfied or believe more is needed: The people who live next door. Since I have to read a paper at the conference next week. Although many of you wrote fairly good papers. Since this is a college class. During the last week of September.

5. The road to Cedar Lake will be closed for months. Because the flood has washed away the bridge over the Rouge River.
6. Carol bought the new computer. That she had wanted for months.
7. If the debate team lives up to its potential. We are sure to win the state finals.
8. There are several ways for companies to save on energy costs. One of them energy recycling.
9. Kristen first searched the library for information for her report. And then turned to the Internet for additional material.
10. Pleased by the amount of the painting he had already completed. John allowed himself a two-hour break to watch the football game.

EXERCISE ANSWER

Dear Phone Company:

Recently I received a phone bill for over $500. While I do use the phone fairly extensively, most of the calls I make are local ones. In this case, many of the calls on my bill were to other countries, including

ro cs

Revising Run-On Sentences and Comma Splices

A run-on, or fused, sentence occurs when one sentence runs into another without anything to mark their junction. A comma splice occurs when only a comma marks the junction. These errors lead your readers to think that you are hasty or careless. Here are several examples:

a phone call to New Delhi, India. I can hardly be held responsible for these calls, especially since I don't know anyone who lives overseas. Since the only long-distance call I made was to Kalamazoo, Michigan, I have deducted the charges for all the other long-distance calls from my bill and am sending you the balance. In order to prevent this type of error from happening again, would you please have a representative determine why these charges appeared on my bill?

Sincerely,
Desperate

Run-on sentence	Laura failed to set her alarm she was late for work.
Comma splice	Violets are blooming now, my lawn is covered with them.
Run-on sentence	Rick refused to attend the movie he said he hated horror shows.
Comma splice	Perry watched the road carefully, he still missed his turn.
Run-on sentence	Janet worked on her term paper her friend studied for a calculus test.
Comma splice	Janet worked on her term paper, her friend studied for a calculus test.

EXERCISE ANSWERS
1. S, F (Lee, one)
2. S, F (posters to)
3. F, S (concert, we)
4. F, S (test, we)
5. S, F (months because)
6. S, F (computer that)
7. F, S (potential, we)
8. S, F (costs, one)
9. S, F (report and)
10. F, S (completed, John)

Testing for Errors To check out a possible comma splice or fused sentence, read what precedes and follows the comma or suspected junction and see whether the two parts can stand alone as sentences. If *both parts* can stand alone, there is an error. Otherwise, there is not.

Darryl is a real troublemaker, someday he'll find himself in serious difficulty.

Examination of the parts preceding and following the comma shows that each is a complete sentence:

Darryl is a real troublemaker.

Someday he'll find himself in serious difficulty.

The writer has therefore committed a comma splice that needs correction.

ro cs

Methods of Revision   You can correct run-on sentences and comma splices in several ways.

1. Create two separate sentences.

   Revision   Violets are blooming now. My lawn is covered with them.

   Revision   Rick refused to attend the movie. He said he hated horror shows.

2. Join the sentences with a semicolon.

   Revision   Violets are blooming now; my yard is covered with them.

   Revision   Rick refused to attend the movie; he said he hated horror shows.

3. Join the sentences with a comma and a coordinating conjunction (*and, but, or, nor, for, yet, so*).

   Revision   Laura failed to set her alarm, *so* she was late for work.

   Revision   Perry watched the road carefully, *but* he still missed his turn.

4. Join the sentences with a semicolon and a conjunctive adverb (see page 644).

   Revision   Laura failed to set her alarm; *consequently*, she was late for work.

   Revision   Violets are blooming now; *in fact*, my yard is covered with them.

5. Introduce one of the sentences with a subordinating conjunction (see pages 646, 650–651).

   Revision   *Because* Laura failed to set her alarm, she was late for work.

   Revision   Janet worked on her term paper *while* her friend studied for a calculus test.

As our examples show, you can often correct an error in several ways.

Connected Discourse Exercise

Identify and correct the comma splices and run-on sentences in the following letter:

Dear Desperate:

We are sorry to hear that you are having difficulty paying your bill, it is, however, your responsibility. Unfortunately we have no way to prevent you from making overseas calls, you have to curb your own tendency to reach out and touch your friends. Following your instructions, we are sending a technician to remove your phone. Please be home this Friday morning he will arrive then. Even though we will remove your phone, you are still responsible for the unpaid portion of your bill, it is your financial obligation. We would dislike referring this matter to a collection agency, it could ruin your credit rating.

Sincerely,

Your friendly phone representative

morning, for he will arrive then. Even though we will remove your phone, you are still responsible for the unpaid portion of your bill. It is your financial obligation. We would dislike referring this matter to a collection agency since it could ruin your credit rating.
Sincerely,
Your friendly phone representative

Indicate whether each item is correct (C), is a run-on sentence (RO), or contains a comma splice (CS) and then correct the faulty items.

1. Our company's Internet-based sales are up twenty percent; however, our store sales are down thirty percent.
2. Our computer assistants have only had three weeks of training, you cannot expect them to know the answer to every technical question.
3. Ellen worked very hard on her report she really earned her A.
4. The research on the effect of T.V. violence on children remains inconclusive, but still most of us would think that excessive exposure to images of violence would be harmful.
5. Alternative forms of punishment such as home incarceration have proven very effective, nevertheless prison is still the standard punishment for most nonviolent crimes.
6. The photographer accidentally exposed his film to the light as a result all our wedding pictures were ruined.
7. Jason got a terrific tan, he spent the winter break in Florida.
8. While tuberculosis is a terrible disease, it is rare and usually can be treated with antibiotics.
9. Many doctors' offices want to decrease costs they increasingly use physician assistants.
10. We have carefully reviewed your proposal for flexible work hours, we think it would improve employee satisfaction.

EXERCISE ANSWERS
1. C.
2. CS. training, so you / training; therefore, you / training. You
3. RO. report; she / report. She
4. C.
5. CS. effective; nevertheless,/ effective. Nevertheless,
6. RO. light; as a result, / light. As a result,
7. CS. tan because he / tan. He
8. C.
9. RO. costs, so / costs; therefore,
10. CS. hours, and / hours. We / hours; we

Creating Subject–Verb Agreement

A verb should agree in number with its subject. Singular verbs should have singular subjects, and plural verbs should have plural subjects.

Correct	My *boss* **is** a grouch. (singular subject and verb)
Correct	The *apartments* **have** two bedrooms. (plural subject and verb)

Ordinarily, matching subjects and verbs causes no problems. The following special situations, however, can create difficulties.

Subject and Verb Separated by a Word Group   Sometimes a word group that includes one or more nouns comes between the subject and the verb. When this happens, match the verb with its subject, not a noun in the word group.

PERSPECTIVE
Errors in subject–verb agreement rarely occur because students misunderstand the rules. In most cases, errors happen because students lose track of the subject.

Correct　　Our *basket* of sandwiches *is* missing.

Correct　　Several *books* required for my paper *are* not in the library.

Correct　　Mr. *Schmidt*, along with his daughters, *runs* a furniture store.

Correct　　The old *bus*, crammed with passengers, *was* unable to reach the top of the hill.

Two Singular Subjects　Most singular subjects joined by *and* take a plural verb.

Correct　　The *couch* and *chair were* upholstered in blue velvet.

Sentences like the one above almost never cause problems. With subjects like *restoring cars* and *racing motorcycles*, however, singular verbs are often mistakenly used.

Faulty　　*Restoring cars* and *racing motorcycles consumes* most of Frank's time.

Revision　　*Restoring cars* and *racing motorcycles consume* most of Frank's time.

When *each* or *every* precedes the subjects, use a *singular* verb in place of a plural.

Correct　　Every *book* and *magazine was* badly water-stained.

Singular subjects joined by *or, either—or,* or *neither—nor* also take singular verbs.

Correct　　A *pear* or an *apple is* a good afternoon snack.

Correct　　Neither *rain* nor *snow slows* our letter carrier.

Finally, use a singular verb when two singular subjects joined by *and* name the same person, place, or thing.

Correct　　My *cousin* and business *partner* is retiring next month.

Cousin and *partner* refer to the same person.

One Singular and One Plural Subject　When one singular subject and one plural subject are joined by *or, either—or,* or *neither—nor,* match the verb with the closer of the two.

Correct　　Neither *John* nor his *parents were* at home.

Correct　　Neither his *parents* nor *John was* at home.

As these examples show, the sentences are usually smoother when the plural subject follows the singular.

Collective Nouns As Subjects　Collective nouns (*assembly, class, committee, family, herd, majority, tribe,* and the like) are singular in form but stand for groups

or collections of people or things. Ordinarily, collective nouns are considered to be singular and therefore take singular verbs.

Correct   The *class* is writing a test.

Correct   The *herd was* clustered around the water hole.

Sometimes, though, a collective noun refers to the separate individuals making up the grouping, and then it requires a plural verb.

Correct   The *jury are* in dispute about the verdict.

Sentences in Which the Verb Comes Ahead of the Subject   Sentences

that begin with words such as *here, there, how, what,* and *where* fall into this category. With such sentences, the verb must agree with the subject that follows it.

Correct   Here *is* my *house.*

Correct   Where *are* my *shoes?*

Correct   There *is* just one *way* to solve this problem.

Correct   There *go* my *chances* for a promotion.

Connected Discourse Exercise

Identify and correct the subject–verb agreement errors in the following letter:

Regional Accounts Manager:

One of your area phone representatives have seriously misread a letter I submitted with my bill. I refused to pay for long-distance overseas calls since neither I nor my roommate know anyone who lives overseas. Instead of deducting the calls from my bill, she sent someone to remove my phone. Now my phone, along with many of my valuable possessions, have been removed. Unfortunately the technician, whom I allowed into my apartment only after carefully checking his credentials, were a thief. He locked me in a closet and cleared out the apartment. I have called the police, but I also expect the phone company to reimburse me for my losses. There is only two choices. Either the stolen items or a check covering the loss need to be sent to me immediately. Otherwise I am afraid I will be forced to sue. A jury are sure to rule in my favor. In addition, I expect to find that those overseas calls has been deducted from my bill.

Sincerely,

Desperately Desperate

EXERCISE ANSWER

Regional Accouns Manager:

One of your area phone representatives has seriously misread a letter I submitted with my bill. I refused to pay for long-distance overseas calls since neither I nor my roommate knows anyone who lives overseas. Instead of deducting the calls from my bill, she sent someone to remove my phone. Now my phone, along with many of my valuable possessions, has been removed. Unfortunately the technician, whom I allowed into my apartment only after carefully checking his credentials, was a thief. He locked me in a closet and cleared out the apartment. I have called the police, but I also expect the phone company to reimburse me for my losses. There are only two choices. Either the stolen items or a check covering the loss needs to be sent to me immediately. Otherwise I am afraid I will be forced to sue. A jury is sure to rule in my favor. In addition, I expect to find that those overseas calls have been deducted from my bill.

Sincerely,

Desperately Desperate

Choose the correct verb form from the pair in parentheses.

1. The library, along with many of the books, (*was, were*) severely damaged by the storm.
2. Congress (*retains, retain*) the right to control the country's purse strings.
3. A house with two baths and four bedrooms (*is, are*) for sale in my neighborhood.
4. What (*does, do*) these new printers cost?
5. A van or three cars (*is, are*) needed to drive the wrestling team to the meet.
6. Each of these suggestions (*has, have*) a lot of merit.
7. John Finch and his assistant (*plans, plan*) to review the contract with you next Friday.
8. There (*is, are*) a few advantages to carefully planning your work schedule.
9. Every piece of clothing and bedding (*has, have*) to be washed in scalding water.
10. Each of our employees (*knows, know*) the answer to the most common questions about our product.

Achieving Pronoun–Antecedent Agreement

The antecedent of a pronoun is the noun or pronoun to which it refers. Just as subjects should agree with their verbs, pronouns should agree with their antecedents: singular antecedents require singular pronouns, and plural antecedents require plural pronouns. Ordinarily, you will have no trouble matching antecedents and pronouns. The situations below, however, can cause problems.

Indefinite Pronouns As Antecedents   Indefinite pronouns include words like *each, either, neither, any, everybody, somebody,* and *nobody.* Whenever an indefinite pronoun is used as an antecedent, the pronoun that refers to it should be singular.

> *Faulty*   *Neither* of the actors had learned *their* lines.

> *Revision*   *Neither* of the actors had learned *his* lines.

As the revised example shows, this rule applies even when the pronoun is followed by a plural noun.

When the gender of the antecedent is unknown, you may follow it with *his or her*, or if this results in awkwardness, rewrite the sentence in the plural.

> *Correct* *Anyone* who has studied *his or her* assignments properly should do well on the test.

> *Correct* *Those* who have studied *their* assignments properly should do well on the test.

Occasionally, a ridiculous result occurs when a singular pronoun refers to an indefinite pronoun that is obviously plural in meaning. When this happens, rewrite the sentence to eliminate the problem.

Faulty   *Everybody* complained that the graduation ceremony had lasted too long, but I didn't believe *him.*

Revision   Everybody complained that the graduation ceremony had lasted too long, but I didn't agree.

Two Singular Antecedents
Two or more antecedents joined by *and* ordinarily call for a plural pronoun.

Correct   Her briefcase and umbrella were missing from *their* usual place on the hall table.

When *each* or *every* precedes the antecedent, use a singular pronoun.

Incorrect Every college and university must do *their* best to provide adequate student counseling.

Correct   Every college and university must do *its* best to provide adequate student counseling.

Singular antecedents joined by *or, either—or,* or *neither—nor* call for singular pronouns.

Correct   Neither Carol nor Irene had paid *her* rent for the month.

Applying this rule can sometimes yield an awkward or foolish sentence. When this happens, rewrite the sentence to avoid the problem.

Faulty   Neither James nor Sally has finished *his or her* term project.

Revision   James and Sally have not finished *their* term projects.

Singular antecedents joined by *and* that refer to the same person, place, or thing use a singular pronoun.

Correct   My *cousin* and business *partner is* retiring to *her* condo in Florida next month.

Singular and Plural Antecedents
If one singular and one plural antecedent are joined by *or, either—or,* or *neither—nor,* the pronoun agrees with the closer one.

Correct   Either Terrence James or the Parkinsons will let us use *their* lawn mower.

Correct   Either the Parkinsons or Terrence James will let us use *his* lawn mower.

Sentences of this sort are generally smoother when the plural subject follows the singular.

Collective Nouns As Antecedents
When a collective noun is considered a single unit, the pronoun that refers to it should be singular.

Correct   The *troop* of scouts made *its* way slowly through the woods.

TEACHING STRATEGIES
1. Some students balk at the idea that *everybody* and other indefinite pronouns actually are singular. To set matters straight, ask everybody to raise his or her hand and then point out that one hand was raised per individual. Seeing indefinite pronouns as consisting of two words—*any one, every body,* and the like—also emphasizes that they are singular.

2. Because the rules and problem areas for pronoun–antecedent agreement are the same as those for subject–verb agreement, you might point out the similarities. This approach will reinforce the material in both sections.

3. Although the rules for agreement are not difficult, students often have trouble proofreading their own papers. Since they are unaccustomed to going back and checking for agreement, their attention tends to push forward. To help them overcome this tendency, have them read their most recent draft, identify the pronouns, and then draw an arrow back to each antecedent to determine whether there is agreement. Now is also a good time to have students see whether they are using too many pronouns.

pa agr

When the collective noun refers to the separate individuals in the group, use a plural pronoun.

Correct   The *staff* lost *their* jobs when the factory closed.

Connected Discourse Exercise

Identify and correct the pronoun–antecedent agreement errors in the following letter:

Dear Desperately Desperate:

We were sorry to hear about the theft from your apartment. Apparently a gang of con artists recently had their base of operations in your city. It posed as repair technicians and presented false credentials to anyone expecting their phone to be repaired. Someone also must have intercepted your mail and written their own response since we have no record of any previous letter from you. Clearly neither the representative you mentioned nor the phony phone technician could have held their position with our company. Every one of our technicians must provide us with their fingerprints and take periodic lie detector tests. Further, none of our representatives will answer correspondence since it is not a part of their job description. For these reasons, we do not believe we are responsible for your losses. However, a review of our records shows that you owe $500; we have included a copy of the bill in case you have misplaced the original.

Sincerely,

Accounts Manager

Choose the right pronoun from the pair in parentheses.

1. Company rules require every memo and letter to receive (*its, their*) correct authorization number.
2. Neither the Grangers nor Tom Cauldwell knew (*his, their*) lines by opening night.
3. After weeks of deliberation, the jury finally reached (*its, their*) decision.
4. Maria and Tim completed (*his or her, their*) project by the deadline.
5. Either Roderick or Shannon will present (*his or her, their*) personalized invitation to our special sale.
6. Either Sally or the Randalls will lend us (*her, their*) punch bowl for our party.
7. The class rushed into the computer room and took (*his or her, their*) seats.
8. Everybody has been assigned (*his or her, their*) own log-on name and password.
9. Every one of the women in our police force has proved that (*she, they*) can handle the duties of an officer.
10. Either Richard or Frank will be able to offer you (*his, their*) help in planning the science fiction film festival.

Using Effective Pronoun Reference

Any pronoun except an indefinite pronoun should refer to just one noun or noun substitute—its antecedent. Reference problems result when the pronoun has two or more antecedents, a hidden antecedent, or no antecedent. These errors can cause mixups in meaning as well as ridiculous sentences.

More Than One Antecedent   The following sentences lack clarity because their pronouns have two possible antecedents rather than just one:

Faulty   Take the screens off the windows and wash *them.*

Faulty   Harry told Will that *he* was putting on weight.

The reader can't tell whether the screens or the windows should be washed or who is putting on weight.

Sometimes we see a sentence like this one:

Faulty   If the boys don't eat all the Popsicles, put *them* in the freezer.

In this case, we know it's the Popsicles that should be stored, but the use of *them* creates an amusing sentence.

Correct these faults by replacing the pronoun with a noun or by rephrasing the sentence.

Revision   Wash the windows after you have taken off the screens.

Revision   Take off the screens so that you can wash the windows.

Revision   Harry told Will, "I am (you are) putting on weight."

Revision   Put any uneaten Popsicles in the freezer.

Hidden Antecedent   An antecedent is hidden if it takes the form of an adjective rather than a noun.

Faulty   The movie theater is closed today, so we can't see *one.*

Faulty   As I passed the tiger's cage, it lunged at me.

To correct this fault, replace the pronoun with the noun used as an adjective or switch the positions of the pronoun and the noun and make any needed changes in their forms.

Revision   The theater is closed today, so we can't see a movie.

Revision   As I passed its cage, the tiger lunged at me.

No Antecedent   A no-antecedent sentence lacks any noun to which the pronoun can refer. Sentences of this sort occur frequently in everyday conversation but should be avoided in formal writing. The examples below illustrate this error:

Faulty   The lecture was boring, but *they* took notes anyway.

Faulty   On the news program, *it* told about a new crisis in the Persian Gulf.

5. his or her
6. their
7. their
8. his or her
9. she
10. his

pr ref

TEACHING STRATEGY
This section can easily be combined with the section on pronoun–antecedent agreement. As students check their drafts for pronoun agreement, they might also determine whether the pronouns have appropriate and clear antecedents.

To set matters right, substitute a suitable noun for the pronoun or reword the sentence.

Revision   The lecture was boring, but the students took notes anyway.

Revision   The news program told about a new crisis in the Persian Gulf.

Sometimes *this, that, it,* or *which* will refer to a whole idea rather than a single noun. This usage is acceptable provided the writer's meaning is obvious, as in this example:

Correct   The instructor spoke very softly, *which* meant we had difficulty hearing him.

Problems occur, however, when the reader can't figure out which of two or more ideas the pronoun refers to.

Faulty   Ginny called Sally two hours after the agreed-upon time and postponed their shopping trip one day. *This* irritated Sally very much.

What caused Sally to be irritated—the late call, the postponement of the trip, or both? Again, rewording or adding a clarifying word will correct the problem.

Revision   Ginny called Sally two hours after the agreed-upon time and postponed their shopping trip one day. *This tardiness* irritated Sally very much.

Revision   Ginny called Sally two hours after the agreed-upon time and postponed their shopping trip one day. Ginny's *change of plans* irritated Sally very much.

The first of these examples illustrates the addition of a clarifying word; the second illustrates rewriting.

Connected Discourse Exercise

Identify and correct any faulty pronoun references in the following memorandum:

To: Director of Food Services, Groan University

From: Vice President of College Services

Date: February 19, 20__ __

Subject: Student Complaints about Cafeteria

Complaints about food quality and cafeteria hours are common but easily resolved. They can be extended by simply installing vending machines. It might not make for a nutritious meal, but it certainly will undercut some of the dissatisfaction. Of course, no matter how good the food, they will complain. Still, you can partially defuse those complaints by having

---

pr ref

EXERCISE ANSWER

TO: Director of Food Services, Groan University

FROM: Vice President of College Services

DATE: February 19, 20__

SUBJECT: Student Complaints about Cafeteria

Complaints about food quality and cafeteria hours are common but easily resolved. The cafeteria hours can be extended by simply installing vending machines. Snack food might not make for a nutritious meal, but it certainly will undercut some of the dissatisfaction. Of course, no matter how good the food, students will complain. Still, you can partially defuse those complaints by having students list their major concerns and then meeting the common objections. Of course, you can always increase student satisfaction by purchasing a soft ice cream machine and offering ice cream cones for dessert.

students list their major concerns and then meeting them. Of course, you can always increase student satisfaction by purchasing a soft ice cream machine and offering it for dessert.

Indicate whether each sentence is correct (C) or contains a faulty pronoun reference (F) and then correct the faulty sentences.

1. When Al accidentally slammed down on his car's accelerator instead of the brake, it roared forward into the intersection.
2. They have informed me that we have seen a 15 percent increase in sales this month.
3. When the supervisor walked by the water cooler, they stopped talking.
4. I like trout fishing because it is very relaxing.
5. Since I knew that our employees found their chairs uncomfortable, I replaced them with new ones.
6. In the report, it suggested that we needed to be more attentive to employee suggestions.
7. Because the batting cap hurt his head, Fred removed it.
8. Frank told his best friend that his wife wanted to spend more time with him.
9. At Electronic City, they sell many brands of computers.
10. Janine asked Caroline if she could rewrite her paper for her English class.

Managing Shifts in Person

Pronouns can be in the first person, second person, or third person. *First-person* pronouns identify people who are talking or writing about themselves, *second-person* pronouns identify people being addressed directly, and *third-person* pronouns identify persons or things that are being written or spoken about. The following table sorts pronouns according to person:

First Person	Second Person	Third Person
I	you	he
me	your	she
my	yours	it
mine	yourself	his
we	yourselves	her
us		hers
our		its
ours		one
ourselves		they
		their
		theirs
		indefinite pronouns

All nouns are in the third person. As you revise, be alert for unwarranted shifts from one person to another.

shft

PERSPECTIVE
When students shift paragraphs, they sometimes lose track of the form of address they are using and shift person as well. Shifts are especially likely when students are uncertain whether they will adopt a formal or informal tone.

TEACHING STRATEGY
As students review for pronoun-agreement errors, have them check for unwarranted shifts in person. These are especially likely to occur if students are not sure whether to use *one* or *you*.

EXERCISE ANSWER
Good health is clearly important to you. But it is your responsibility to ensure your own good health. You can start with simple exercises. We would like to provide you with a low-impact aerobics DVD for only $15. We guarantee that the more out of shape you are, the quicker you will notice the benefits. The way your body feels affects the quality of your life. Let our tape help you to a better life.

EXERCISE ANSWER
1. S. collected our essays, she told us / After the teacher collected the essays,
2. S. To be successful
3. C.
4. S. of the stadium, many of us felt we
5. C.

Faulty	I liked *my* British vacation better than *my* vacation in France and Italy because *you* didn't have language problems.
Revision	I liked *my* British vacation better than *my* vacation in France and Italy because *I* didn't have language problems.
Faulty	Holidays are important to *everyone*. They boost *your* spirits and provide a break from *our* daily routine.
Revision	Holidays are important to *everyone*. They boost *one's* spirits and provide a break from *one's* daily routine.
Faulty	The taller the *golfer*, the more club speed *you* will have with a normally paced swing.
Revision	The taller the *golfer*, the more club speed *he* or *she* will have with a normally paced swing.

As these examples show, the shift can occur within a single sentence or when the writer moves from one sentence to another.

Some shifts in person, however, are warranted. Read the following correct sentence:

Correct	*I* want *you* to deliver these flowers to Ms. Willoughby by three o'clock. *She* needs them for a party.

Here the speaker identifies himself or herself (*I*) while speaking directly to a listener *(you)* about someone else *(she)*. In this case, shifts are needed to get the message across.

Connected Discourse Exercise

Identify and correct the unwarranted shifts in person in the following paragraph:

Good health is clearly important to you. But it is one's responsibility to ensure our own good health. You can start with simple exercises. We would like to provide you with a low impact aerobics DVD for only $15. We guarantee that the more out of shape the customer, the quicker you will notice the benefits. The way our bodies feel affects the quality of one's lives. Let our tape help you to a better life.

Indicate whether the sentence is correct (C) or contains an unwarranted shift in person (S). Correct faulty sentences.

1. After the teacher collected our essays, she told the students that she would return the graded papers on Wednesday.

2. For someone to be successful in today's marketplace, you need to have adequate technical skills.
3. If you each will bring the results of your assigned research to the next meeting, we will be ready to begin working on our collaborative report.
4. Because our tickets were in the nosebleed section of the stadium, many of the fans felt they would have been better off watching the football game on TV.
5. If you want theater tickets, I will be glad to purchase them on my way home from work.
6. Anyone who would like to purchase the discounted Caribbean cruise tickets should place your order by May 15.
7. We enjoy living in the Grand Rapids area very much; you have access to theater, sporting events, and fine dining.
8. On major holidays, most Americans travel long distances, often at great inconvenience, to visit our relatives.
9. If you would like to learn to kayak, novices can usually get free lessons from the people who sell kayaks.
10. In our attempt to determine whether there has been an increase in tornado activity over the last twenty years, the researchers collected data on storm sightings and damage reports.

6. S. place his or her order by May 15. / If you would like . . . , you should place
7. S. we have access
8. S. to visit their relatives./ On major holidays, most of us travel
9. S. you can usually

case

10. S. In our attempt . . . , we collected / In an attempt . . . , the researchers.

Using the Right Pronoun Case

Case means the changes in form that a personal pronoun (see page 625) undergoes to show its function in a sentence. English has three cases: the *subjective*, the *nonsubjective* (objective), and the *possessive*. The following chart shows the different forms:

Subjective Form	Nonsubjective Form	Possessive Form
I	me	my, mine
he	him	his
she	her	her, hers
we	us	our, ours
you	you	your, yours
they	them	their, theirs
who	whom	whose

The subjective case is used for subjects and subject complements, the nonsubjective for direct objects, indirect objects, and objects of prepositions. The possessive case shows ownership and is also used with gerunds.

The following pointers will help you select the proper pronoun as you revise.

We and *Us* Preceding Nouns
Nouns that serve as subjects take the pronoun *we.* Other nouns take the pronoun *us.*

Correct   *We* tourists will fly home tomorrow. (*We* accompanies the subject.)

Correct   The guide showed *us* tourists through the cathedral. (*Us* accompanies a nonsubject.)

PERSPECTIVE
Students often make mistakes in selecting a pronoun case because they have internalized a faulty set of rules. It is not unusual for students to object to the correct form because it sounds odd to them. In some cases, of course, the rules are changing. For instance, some linguists suggest that the *who/whom* distinction will soon disappear. Still, until this change is definitely established, it is not difficult for students to learn this distinction. After all, whom could it hurt?

TEACHING STRATEGY
To counteract the effects of faulty rules, have students repeat the correct form until it seems less odd.

case

1. That man stole my jacket. The man is heading toward us.
2. I am studying chemistry with the professor. The professor won a Nobel Prize.
3. Miss Jenkins is a dean. Very few people know Miss Jenkins.
4. Dick Pulaski enjoys the company of students. Students like to discuss ideas.

Combinations
1. The man who stole my jacket is heading toward us.
2. The professor with whom I am studying chemistry won a Nobel Prize./I am studying chemistry with the professor who . . .
3. Miss Jenkins is a dean whom very few people know.
4. Dick Pulaski enjoys the company of students who like to discuss ideas.

If you can't decide which pronoun is right, mentally omit the noun and read the sentence to yourself, first with one pronoun and then with the other. Your ear will indicate the correct form.

My mother made (*we, us*) children vanilla pudding for dessert.

Omitting *children* shows immediately that *us* is the right choice.

Correct   My mother made *us* children vanilla pudding for dessert.

Pronouns Paired with Nouns   When such a combination serves as the subject of a sentence or accompanies the subject, use the subject form of the pronoun. When the combination plays a nonsubject role, use the nonsubject form of the pronoun.

Correct   Arlene and *I* plan to join the Peace Corps. (*I* is part of the compound subject.)

Correct   Two people, Mary and *I*, will represent our school at the meeting. (*I* is part of a compound element accompanying the subject.)

Correct   The superintendent told Kevin and *him* that they would be promoted soon. (*Him* is part of a compound nonsubject.)

Correct   The project was difficult for Jeffrey and *him* to complete. (*Him* is part of a compound nonsubject.)

Again, mentally omitting the noun from the combination will tell you which pronoun is correct.

Who and Whom in Dependent Clauses   Use *who* for the subjects of dependent clauses; otherwise use *whom*.

Correct   The Mallarys prefer friends *who are interested in the theater.* (*Who* is the subject of the clause.)

Correct   Barton is a man *whom very few people like.* (*Whom* is not the subject of the clause.)

A simple test will help you decide between *who* and *whom*. First, mentally isolate the dependent clause. Next, block out the pronoun in question and then insert *he* (or *she*) and *him* (or *her*) at the appropriate spot in the remaining part of the clause. If *he* (or *she*) sounds better, *who* is right. If *him* (or *her*) sounds better, *whom* is right. Let's use this test on the sentence below:

The woman *who(m) Scott is dating* works as a mechanical engineer. Scott is dating (*she, her*).

Clearly *her* is correct; therefore, *whom* is the proper form.

Correct   The woman *whom Scott is dating* works as a mechanical engineer.

Pronouns As Subject Complements   In formal writing, pronouns that serve as subject complements (see page 622) always take the subject form.

> *Correct*   It is *I*.
>
> *Correct*   It was *she* who bought the old Parker mansion.

This rule, however, is often ignored in informal writing.

> It's *her*.
>
> That's *him* standing over by the door.

Comparisons Using *than* or *as . . . as*   Comparisons of this kind often make no direct statement about the second item of comparison. When the second naming word is a pronoun, you may have trouble choosing the right one.

> Harriet is less outgoing than (*they, them*).
>
> My parents' divorce saddened my sister as much as (*I, me*).

Not to worry. Expand the sentence by mentally supplying the missing material. Then try the sentence with each pronoun and see which sounds right.

> Harriet is less outgoing than (*they, them*) are.
>
> My parents' divorce saddened my sister as much as it did (*I, me*).

Obviously *they* is the right choice for the first sentence, and *me* is the right choice for the second one.

> *Correct*   Harriet is less outgoing than *they* are.
>
> *Correct*   My parents' divorce saddened my sister as much as it did *me*.

Pronouns Preceding Gerunds   Use the possessive form of a pronoun that precedes a gerund (see page 647).

> I dislike *their* leaving without saying goodbye.
>
> Ted can't understand *her* quitting such a good job.

This usage emphasizes the action named by the gerund instead of the person or persons performing it. Thus, in the above sentences, the possessive form of the pronoun signals that it's the *leaving* the writer dislikes and the *quitting* that Ted can't understand. The persons involved are secondary.

When the pronoun precedes a participle (see pages 645–648), it should be in the nonsubject case. The emphasis is then on the actor rather than the action.

> Jennifer caught *them* listening to records instead of studying.

In this example, Jennifer caught the listeners, not the listening.

If you have trouble deciding between the nonsubject and possessive forms of a pronoun, ask yourself whether you want to emphasize the action or the actor; then proceed accordingly.

Connected Discourse Exercise

Identify and correct the pronoun case errors in the following paragraph:

Between my brother and I, we are always able to pull at least five good-sized trout a day from the creek behind our house. Us rural trout fishermen just seem to have the knack. Of course, those city fishermen whom insist on employing artificial flies won't appreciate our methods even if they can't do as well as us. We just let our bait, usually a juicy worm, float downstream to the waiting trout. Of course, my brother won't let the fishing interfere with him sleeping. In fact, it was him that developed the idea of looping the line around his toe so that he would wake up when a trout took the bait. Others have told my brother and I that this method is dangerous, but neither of us has lost a toe yet. Of course, the people who we invite to dinner don't complain about our methods, and they seem to enjoy the fish.

Choose the right form of the pronoun for each of the following sentences. For the purpose of this exercise, assume that there would have been the appropriate pronoun antecedent in the sentence preceding the one that is shown.

1. No one is as pleased as (*I, me*) by John's recent promotion to assistant vice president.
2. There is no excuse for (*him, his*) yelling at us in public.
3. The newspaper's editor praised Marge and (*I, me*) for our coauthored article on women in the military.
4. Randy has a better grasp of European history than (*I, me*).
5. Megan is one student (*who, whom*) I believe really understands the importance of writing well.
6. (*We, Us*) Americans pride ourselves on our individuality.
7. The conductor decided that Marie and (*I, me*) should sing a duet at the next recital.
8. Rilke is the poet (*who, whom*) I like best.
9. The judge told (*we, us*) contestants that we would be called when it was our turn.
10. The manager of the movie theater gave Tom and (*I, me*) four free passes.

Creating Consistency in Showing Time

Inconsistencies occur when a writer shifts from the past tense to the present or vice versa without a corresponding shift in the time of the events being described. The following paragraph contains an uncalled-for shift from the present tense to the past:

> As *The Most Dangerous Game* opens, Sanger Rainsford, a famous hunter and author, and his old friend Whitney are standing on the deck of a yacht and

discussing a mysterious island as the ship passes near it. Then, after everyone else has gone to bed, Rainsford manages to fall overboard. He swims to the island and ends up at a chateau owned by General Zaroff, a refugee from the Communist takeover in Russia. Zaroff, bored with hunting animals, has turned to hunting humans on his desert island. Inevitably, Rainsford is turned out into the jungle to be hunted down. There were [shift to past tense] actually four hunts over a three-day period, and at the end of the last one, Rainsford jumped into the sea, swam across a cove to the chateau, and killed Zaroff in the general's own bedroom. Afterward he sleeps [shift back to present tense] and decides "he had never slept in a better bed."

The sentence with the unwarranted shift in tense should read as follows:

> There are actually four hunts over a three-day period, and at the end of the last one, Rainsford jumps into the sea, swims across a cove to the chateau, and kills Zaroff in the general's own bedroom.

The time shift in the quotation part of the final sentence is justified because the sleeping has occurred before Rainsford's thoughts about it.

A second kind of inconsistency results when a writer fails to distinguish the immediate past from the less immediate past. The following sentence illustrates this error:

Faulty   Mary *answered* all thirty test questions when the class ended.

This sentence indicates that Mary completed all thirty test questions during the final instant of the class, an impossibility. When you detect this type of error in your writing, determine which action occurred first and then correct the error by adding *had* to the verb. In this case, the first verb needs correcting:

Revision   Mary *had answered* all thirty test questions when the class ended.

Besides adding *had*, you may sometimes need to alter the verb form.

Faulty   Before he turned twenty, John *wrote* two novels.

Revision   Before he turned twenty, John *had written* two novels.

Connected Discourse Exercise

Identify and correct any inconsistencies in showing time in the following passage:

There is no better time to go swimming than at night. The summer after I had graduated from high school, I worked for a landscaping company. After a sweaty day mowing lawns and digging up gardens, all of us who worked there would jump into the back of Dick's old pickup and rattle out to Woods Lake. It is just dark as we arrive. The moon is beautiful, reflected in that black and digging up gardens, all of us who worked there would jump into the back of Dick's old pickup and rattle out to Woods Lake. It would be just dark as we arrived. The moon would be beautiful, reflected in that black mirror set in a frame of hills. We would

mirror set in a frame of hills. We stumble down a small, sandy hill to the beach, where we strip off our dusty jeans and sweaty shirts before plunging into the cool reflection of stars.

EXERCISE

Indicate whether each sentence is correct (C) or contains an unwarranted shift (S) in tense. Then correct the faulty sentences.

1. A thin wisp of smoke drifts from under the hood, and then the engine burst into flames.
2. After Kyra finishes checking the computers for viruses, she will load the new software.
3. Jason took on many projects but finishes few of them.
4. After I finished preparing dinner, I went for a long walk.
5. As Charlie laid pieces of the model on the table, his wife picks them up.
6. As soon as the snow falls, we break out our cross-country skis.
7. David is building his own house but found it harder work than he anticipated.
8. While Robert applies the adhesive, David carefully positioned the floor tiles.
9. Tonya stood in line for the movie tickets while Doug searches for a parking space.
10. Although it started to rain heavily, Debbie continues to mow the lawn.

mis adj/adv

stumble down a small, sandy hill to the beach, where we would strip off our dusty jeans and sweaty shirts before plunging into the cool reflection of stars.

EXERCISE ANSWERS

1. S. drifted
2. C.
3. S. takes / finished
4. S. had finished
5. S. lays / picked
6. C.
7. S. built / finds
8. S. applied / positions
9. S. searched
10. S. continued

PERSPECTIVE

Confusion of adjectives and adverbs tends to be based on deeply ingrained habits of speech. Few students can easily overcome them. Instead, they need to develop gradually an ear for the correct usage and in the meantime to check their drafts consistently for any of the commonly confused adjective–adverb pairs.

Using Adjectives and Adverbs Effectively

Inexperienced writers often use adjectives when they should use adverbs and also confuse the comparative and superlative forms of these parts of speech when making comparisons.

Misusing Adjectives for Adverbs   Although most adjectives can be misused as adverbs, the following seven, listed with the corresponding adverbs, cause the most difficulty.

Adjectives	Adverbs
awful	awfully
bad	badly
considerable	considerably
good	well
most	almost
real	really
sure	surely

The following sentences show typical errors:

Faulty   Bryan did *good* in his first golf lesson. (*good* mistakenly used to modify verb *did*)

Faulty   *Most* every graduate from our auto service program receives several job offers. (*most* mistakenly used to modify adjective *every*)

Faulty   The speech was delivered *real* well. (*real* mistakenly used to modify adverb *well*)

Because adverbs modify verbs, adjectives, and other adverbs (see page 640), and adjectives modify nouns and noun substitutes (see page 637), the above sentences clearly require adverbs.

Revision   Bryan did *well* in his first golf lesson.

Revision   *Almost* every graduate from our auto service program receives several job offers.

Revision   The speech was delivered *really* well.

In one notable case, an adverb is commonly misused as an adjective.

Faulty   I feel *badly* about providing the wrong phone number. (*Badly* is mistakenly used as a subject complement.)

Revision   I feel *bad* about providing the wrong phone number.

If you can't decide whether a sentence requires an adjective or an adverb, determine the part of speech of the word being modified and proceed accordingly.

Confusing the Comparative and Superlative Forms in Comparisons The comparative form of adjectives and adverbs is used to compare two things, the superlative form to compare three or more things. Adjectives with fewer than three syllables generally add *-er* to make the comparative form and *-est* to make the superlative form (tall, tall*er*, tall*est*). Adjectives with three or more syllables generally add *more* to make the comparative and *most* to make the superlative (enchanting, *more* enchanting, *most* enchanting), as do most adverbs of two or more syllables (loudly, *more* loudly, *most* loudly).

When making comparisons, beginning writers sometimes mistakenly use double comparatives or double superlatives.

Faulty   Harry is *more taller* than James. (double comparative)

Faulty   The Chrysler Building has the *most splendidest* lobby I've ever seen. (double superlative)

The correct versions read as follows:

Revision   Harry is *taller* than James.

Revision   The Chrysler Building has the *most splendid* lobby I've ever seen.

In addition, writers may erroneously use the superlative form, rather than the comparative form, to compare two things.

Faulty   Barry is the *richest* of the two brothers.

Faulty   Jeremy is the *most talented* of those two singers.

TEACHING STRATEGIES
1. Some devices help students decide which form to use. If they can use *very* instead of *really*, then they can be sure they need the adverb form. For *good/well*, it sometimes helps students to try substituting words like *wonderfully*; for some reason, they are less likely to make mistakes with multisyllabic words. Similarly, students might want to check *bad/ badly* with words like *terrible*. Of course, it is best if students can identify what word is being modified and then decide whether the word is an adjective or an adverb.

2. When students have extreme difficulty with adjectives and adverbs, have them construct, and say aloud, sentences that use the appropriate forms. Some students have an aversion to expressions like "He plays football really well," which they regard as "uppity." When such feelings surface, you might discuss dialects. Whatever their feelings, students need to recognize that edited American English is the common currency of the professions.

EXERCISE ANSWER
This year our football team is outstanding. Spike Jones, our quarterback, has been playing really well this past season. Stan Blunder, the more talented of our two ends, hasn't dropped a pass all season. The team can

almost always count on Stan to catch the crucial first-down pass. Of course, the team wouldn't be where it is today without John Schoolyard's good coaching. He has made this team much better than it was even a year ago. Only the kicking

team has done badly this season. Of course, with this wonderful offense, the defensive players haven't gotten much practice. The good news is, then, that we can surely expect to watch some terrific college football for years to come.

EXERCISE ANSWERS

1. bad
2. really
3. well
4. prettiest
5. quietest
6. badly
7. less
8. Almost
9. really
10. strongest

PERSPECTIVE
Don't be surprised if students actually produce more misplaced and dangling modifiers after you teach these units. In part, this happens because stressing modifiers can stimulate students to use more of them. When errors do increase, direct students to restructure their sentences so that their modifiers are more effective.

Here are the sentences correctly written:

Revision	Barry is the *richer* of the two brothers.
Revision	Jeremy is the *more talented* of those two singers.

Reserve the superlative form for comparing three or more items.

Correct	Barry is the *richest* of the three brothers.
Correct	Jeremy is the *most talented* of those four singers.

Connected Discourse Exercise

Identify and correct the adjective–adverb errors in the following paragraph:

    This year our football team is outstanding. Spike Jones, our quarterback, has been playing real good this past season. Stan Blunder, the most talented of our two ends, hasn't dropped a pass all season. The team can most always count on Stan to catch the crucial first-down pass. Of course, the team wouldn't be where it is today without John Schoolyard's good coaching. He has made this team much more better than it was even a year ago. Only the kicking team has done bad this season. Of course, with this most wonderfulest offense, the defensive players haven't gotten much practice. The good news is, then, that we can sure expect to watch some terrific college football for years to come.

For each of the following sentences, choose the proper word from the pair in parentheses:

1. The milk in the refrigerator tastes (*bad, badly*).
2. Old science fiction movies can be (*real, really*) funny to watch because of the clumsy special effects and stilted dialogue.
3. Steve did (*good, well*) on his history project.
4. The Vandorns have the (*prettiest, most prettiest*) house in the development.
5. Dana is the (*quieter, quietest*) of our three children.
6. Terry hurt his knees (*bad, badly*) playing football.
7. The Mustang is the (*less, least*) expensive of the two sports cars you are considering.
8. (*Most, Almost*) all of our employees make use of the day care facility we provide on the premises.
9. It is (*real, really*) important to read the entire manual.
10. The Powermax is the (*stronger, strongest*) of the three kinds of garage door openers we sell.

Placing Modifiers Correctly

A misplaced modifier is a word or word group that is improperly separated from the word it modifies. When separation of this type occurs, the sentence often sounds awkward, ridiculous, or confusing.

Usually, you can correct this error by moving the modifier next to the word it is intended to modify. Occasionally, you'll also need to alter some of the phrasing.

Faulty	There is a bicycle in the basement *with chrome fenders.* (The basement appears to have chrome fenders.)
Faulty	David received a phone call from his uncle *that infuriated him.* (The uncle appears to have infuriated David.)
Revision	There is a bicycle *with chrome fenders* in the basement.
Revision	David received an *infuriating* phone call from his uncle. (Note the change in wording.)

In shifting the modifier, don't inadvertently create another faulty sentence.

Faulty	Fritz bought a magazine with an article about Michael Jackson *at the corner newsstand.* (The article appears to tell about Jackson's visit to the corner newsstand.)
Faulty	Fritz bought a magazine *at the corner newsstand* with an article about Michael Jackson. (The corner newsstand appears to have an article about Jackson.)
Revision	*At the corner newsstand,* Fritz bought a magazine with an article about Michael Jackson.

As you revise, watch also for *squinting modifiers*—that is, modifiers positioned so that the reader doesn't know whether they are supposed to modify what comes ahead of them or what follows them.

Faulty	The man who was rowing the boat *frantically* waved toward the onlookers on the beach.

Is the man rowing frantically or waving frantically? Correct this kind of error by repositioning the modifier so that the ambiguity disappears.

Revision	The man who was *frantically* rowing the boat waved toward the onlookers on the beach.
Revision	The man who was rowing the boat waved *frantically* toward the onlookers on the beach.

EXERCISE

Indicate whether each sentence is correct (C) or contains a misplaced modifier (MM). Correct faulty sentences.

1. Jason handed his report to his teacher neatly tucked into a binder.
2. The girl driving past the school wildly waved at her friends.
3. The dancers practiced Swan Lake for a month before the performance.
4. I tossed the rainbow trout to my brother still hooked firmly in the mouth.
5. Most companies do not like placing managers in charge of employees who are inexperienced.
6. There is a computer in our classroom that beeps loudly at the most unexpected times.
7. You can learn about recent volcanic eruptions at your local library.
8. Steve devoured greasy barbecued spareribs wearing a new suit.
9. The instructor reminded students on the last day of classes to turn in their twenty-page paper.
10. Stacey found beautiful and inexpensive macramé wall hangings for her dorm room in the Bahamas.

Revising Dangling Modifiers

A dangling modifier is a phrase or clause that lacks clear connection to the word or words it is intended to modify. As a result, sentences are inaccurate, often comical. Typically, the modifier leads off the sentence, although it can also come at the end.

Sometimes the error occurs because the sentence fails to specify who or what is modified. At other times, the separation is too great between the modifier and what it modifies.

Faulty   *Walking in the meadow*, wildflowers surrounded us. (The wildflowers appear to be walking in the meadow.)

Faulty   Dinner was served *after saying grace*. (The dinner appears to have said grace.)

Faulty   *Fatigued by the violent exercise*, the cool shower was very relaxing. (The cool shower appears to have been fatigued.)

The first of these sentences is faulty because the modifier is positioned too far away from *us*. The other two are faulty because they do not identify who said grace or found the shower relaxing.

You can correct dangling modifiers in two basic ways. First, leave the modifier unchanged and rewrite the main part of the sentence so that it begins with the term actually modified. Second, rewrite the modifier so that it has its own subject and verb, thereby eliminating the inaccuracy.

Revision   *Walking in the meadow*, we were surrounded by wildflowers. (The main part of the sentence has been rewritten.)

Revision   *As we walked in the meadow*, wildflowers surrounded us. (The modifier has been rewritten.)

Revision   Dinner was served *after we had said grace*. (The modifier has been rewritten.)

Revision   *Fatigued by the violent exercise,* Ted found the cool shower very relaxing. (The main part of the sentence has been rewritten.)

Revision   *Because Ted was fatigued by the violent exercise,* the cool shower was very relaxing. (The modifier has been rewritten.)

Ordinarily, either part of the sentence can be rewritten, but sometimes only one part can.

Indicate whether each sentence is correct (C) or contains a dangling modifier (DM). Correct faulty sentences.

1. After listening to a tape of Orson Welles' radio broadcast of *The War of the Worlds*, I understood why many who tuned into the middle of the broadcast panicked.
2. The baseball game will start after singing *The Star-Spangled Banner*.
3. Looking at the night sky, a million stars seemed to smile down on us.
4. Driving with his emergency brake on, Matt wore down the brake pads.
5. Having scored 100 percent on the pretest, the teacher placed two students in the next level math class.
6. Picasso was known to leave customers waiting for several days, painting furiously.
7. John cataloged his CD collection, listing each CD in a database.
8. Sitting on the back porch, a black bear shuffled across the lawn to raid our garbage cans.
9. Please send an e-mail to the project head listing your concerns.
10. Rushing over the banks, Main Street was soon under three feet of water.

Maintaining Parallelism

Nonparallelism results when equivalent ideas follow different grammatical forms. One common kind of nonparallelism occurs with words or word groups in pairs or in a series.

Faulty   Althea enjoys *jogging, biking,* and *to swim.*

Faulty   The superintendent praised the workers *for their productivity* and *because they had an excellent safety record.*

Faulty   The banner was *old, faded,* and *it had a rip.*

Note how rewriting the sentences in parallel form improves their smoothness.

Revision   Althea enjoys *jogging, biking,* and *swimming.*

Revision   The superintendent praised the workers for *their productivity* and *their excellent safety record.*

Revision   The banner was *old, faded,* and *ripped.*

Nonparallelism also occurs when correlative conjunctions *(either—or, neither—nor, both—and,* and *not only—but also)* are followed by unlike elements.

Faulty   That sound *either* <u>was a thunderclap</u> *or* <u>an explosion</u>.

Faulty   The basement was *not only* <u>poorly lighted</u> *but also* <u>it had a foul smell</u>.

Ordinarily, repositioning one of the correlative conjunctions will solve the problem. Sometimes, however, one of the grammatical elements must be rewritten.

Revision   That sound was *either* <u>a thunderclap</u> *or* <u>an explosion</u>. (*Either* has been repositioned.)

Revision   The basement was *not only* <u>poorly lighted</u> *but also* <u>foul smelling</u>. (The element following *but also* has been rewritten.)

EXERCISE

Indicate whether each sentence is correct (C) or nonparallel (NP). Correct faulty sentences.

1. The cause of the fire either was faulty wiring or an overloaded outlet.
2. After graduation, Marci will be moving to Chicago and work for a large public relations firm.
3. For spring break, Steve and his friends plan to visit either New Orleans or Orlando.
4. A good candidate for social work enjoys talking with people, helps solve problems, and seeing projects through to their conclusion.
5. This course will involve reading a number of short stories, and you will need to turn in weekly journal responses.
6. Although he was an excellent auto mechanic, Andy could neither repair air conditioning units nor car stereos.
7. Canton chicken balls are sweet, tangy, and satisfying.
8. In my spare time, I enjoy reading, canoeing, and to play the piano.
9. As stage manger, Susan had to design, construct, and maintain the set for the school play.
10. As a reference librarian, Colin is responsible for instructing students in how to perform database searches, helping researchers find the material they need, maintaining the reference section, and he also manages the patent collection.

Revising Faulty Comparisons

A faulty comparison results if you (1) mention one of the items being compared but not the other, (2) omit words needed to clarify the relationship, or (3) compare different sorts of items. Advertisers often offend in the first way.

Faulty   Irish tape has better adhesion.

With what other tape is Irish tape being compared? Scotch tape? All other transparent tape? Mentioning the second term of a comparison eliminates reader guesswork.

Revision   Irish tape has better adhesion than any other transparent tape.

Two clarifying words, *other* and *else*, are frequently omitted from comparisons, creating illogical sentences.

Faulty   Sergeant McNabb is more conscientious than any officer in his precinct.

Faulty   Stretch French is taller than anyone on his basketball team.

The first sentence is illogical because McNabb is one of the officers in his precinct and therefore cannot be more conscientious than any officer in the precinct. Similarly, because French is a member of his basketball team, he can't be taller than anyone on his team. Adding *other* to the first sentence and *else* to the second corrects matters.

Revision   Sergeant McNabb is more conscientious than any *other* officer in his precinct.

Revision   Stretch French is taller than anyone *else* on his basketball team.

Comparing unlike items is perhaps the most common kind of comparison error. Here are two examples:

Faulty   The cities in California are larger than North Dakota.

Faulty   The cover of this book is much more durable than the other book.

The first sentence compares the cities of California with a state, while the second compares the cover of a book with a whole book. Correction consists of rewriting each sentence so that it compares like items.

Revision   The cities in California are larger than *those in* North Dakota.

Revision   The cover of this book is much more durable than *that of* the other book.

Connected Discourse Exercise

Identify and correct the misplaced modifiers, dangling modifiers, nonparallelism, and faulty comparisons in the following memorandum:

TO: All Residence Hall Advisors in Knuckles Hall

FROM: John Knells, Residency Hall Director

DATE: March 13, 20___ __

SUBJECT: Noise in Residence Hall

Recently I received a report from a student that deeply disturbed me.

Apparently, after quiet hours students still have visitors in their rooms, are playing their stereos loudly, and are even staging boxing matches in the halls. The student who wrote me desperately tries to study. However, he is

---

comp

EXERCISE ANSWER

TO: All Residence-Hall Advisors in Knuckles Hall

FROM: John Knells, Residency Hall Director

DATE: March 13, 20_ _

SUBJECT: Noise in Residence Hall

Recently I received a deeply disturbing report from a student. Apparently, after quiet hours students still have visitors in their rooms, play their stereos loudly, and even stage boxing matches in the halls. The student who wrote me tries desperately to study. However, disturbed by the noise, he is often forced to leave his room. He was not the only one to complain. You should know that we have had more complaints about Knuckles Hall than about any other dorm on campus. Since I discussed this problem with you at the last staff meeting, things haven't seemed to get any better. The rules are not only poorly enforced but also completely ignored. Your job performance is worse than the students' behavior. If you don't improve immediately, I will be forced to dismiss you.

EXERCISE ANSWERS

1. FC. any other American play.
2. FC. greater than that of the
3. FC. profits than last quarter's. / than those of our competitors.

frag

4. FC. than that at the Eatery. / than the brunch at the Eatery.
5. C.
6. FC. mine usually gets
7. FC. than those in Maine. / than the winters in Maine.
8. FC. more flavors than our competitor's shop. / more flavors than our previous shop.
9. FC. lighter than that on the back. / than the paint on the back.
10. C.

often forced to leave his room disturbed by the noise. He was not the only one to complain. You should know that we have had more complaints about Knuckles Hall than any dorm on campus. Since discussing this problem with you at the last staff meeting, things haven't seemed to get any better. The rules are not only poorly enforced but also they are completely ignored. Your job performance is worse than the students. If you don't improve immediately, I will be forced to dismiss you.

EXERCISE

Indicate whether each sentence is correct (C) or contains a faulty comparison (FC). Correct the faulty comparison.

1. *Death of a Salesman* is performed more often than any American play.
2. The power of today's laptop computers is much greater than the large defense department mainframes of the 1950s.
3. This quarter's earning report shows significantly greater net profits.
4. The Sunday brunch at the 1913 room is much more elegant than the Eatery.
5. Of the two quarterbacks, Allen has a stronger throwing arm than Tom.
6. In contrast to your car, I usually get 40 miles to the gallon.
7. The winters in North Dakota are much worse than Maine.
8. Our new ice cream shop offers many more flavors.
9. The paint on the front of the house is much lighter than the back.
10. Professor Hinkley has published many more articles than the other members of his department.

Editing to Correct Faulty Punctuation and Mechanics

Punctuation marks indicate relationships among different sentence elements. As a result, these marks help clarify the meaning of written material. Similarly, a knowledge of mechanics—capitalization, abbreviations, numbers, and italics—helps you avoid distracting inconsistencies.

This part of the Handbook covers the fundamentals of punctuation and mechanics. Review it carefully when you edit your final draft.

Apostrophes

Apostrophes (') show possession, mark contractions, and indicate plurals that are singled out for special attention.

Possession   Possessive apostrophes usually show ownership *(Mary's cat)*. Sometimes, though, they identify the works of creative people *(Hemingway's novels)* or indicate an extent of time or distance *(one hour's time, one mile's distance)*.

Possessive apostrophes are used with nouns and with pronouns like *someone, no one, everybody, each other,* and *one another*. The possessive form is easily recognized because it can be converted to a prepositional phrase beginning with *of*.

The collar of the dog

The whistle of the wind

The intention of the corporation

The birthday of Scott

To show possession with pronouns like those above, singular nouns, and plural nouns that do not end in an *s*, add an apostrophe followed by an *s*.

Someone's car is blocking our drive. (possessive of pronoun *someone*)

The *manager's* reorganization plan will take effect next week. (possessive of singular noun *manager*)

The *women's* lounge is being redecorated. (possessive of plural noun *women*)

PERSPECTIVE
Although students have been told to use their speech patterns as clues to correct punctuation, this advice often creates more trouble than it is worth, as speech patterns can vary. Punctuation is best viewed as related to the structure of our language; it helps us make sense of the written word.

PERSPECTIVE
It is common for students to confuse plurals and possessives. Often, after studying possessive apostrophes, students who have not been using possessives will overcompensate by placing an apostrophe next to every *s* that concludes a word.

TEACHING STRATEGY
Introduce possessives in direct contrast to plurals so that students will have to determine whether an apostrophe is actually needed. Try using the following sentence pairs:

The managers are meeting in the next room. The managers' reorganization plan will take effect next week.

All the workers' lockers were moved. All the workers checked their paychecks.

The teachers' lounge is being redecorated. The teachers insisted upon the redecoration.

Sentences that make comparisons sometimes include two possessives, the second coming at the very end. In such cases, be sure to use an apostrophe with the second possessive.

Birmingham's football team is much better than *Central's.*

With singular nouns that end in *s*, the possessive is sometimes formed by merely adding an apostrophe at the end *(James' helmet).* The preferred usage, however, is *'s (James's helmet)* unless the addition of the *s* would make it awkward to pronounce the word.

Moses's followers entered the Promised Land. (awkward pronunciation of *Moses's)*

Moses' followers entered the Promised Land. (nonawkward pronunciation of *Moses')*

Plural nouns ending in *s* form the possessive by adding only an apostrophe at the end.

All the *ladies'* coats are on sale today. (possessive of plural noun *ladies)*

The *workers'* lockers were moved. (possessive of plural noun *workers)*

To show joint ownership by two or more persons, use the possessive form for the last-named person only. To show individual ownership, use the possessive form for each person's name.

Ronald and *Joan's* boat badly needed overhauling. (joint ownership)
Laura's and *Alice's* term projects are almost completed. (individual ownership)

Hyphenated nouns form the possessive by adding *'s* to the last word.

My *mother-in-law's* house is next to mine.

Never use an apostrophe with the possessive pronouns *his, hers, whose, its, ours, yours, theirs.*

This desk is *his;* the other one is *hers.* (no apostrophes needed)

Contractions Contractions of words or numbers omit one or more letters or numerals. An apostrophe shows exactly where the omission occurs.

Wasn't that a disappointing concert? (contraction of *was not)*

Around here, people still talk about the blizzard of *'79.* (contraction of *1979)*

Don't confuse the contraction *it's,* meaning *it is* or *it has,* with the possessive pronoun *its,* which should never have an apostrophe. If you're puzzled by an *its* that you've written, try this test. Expand the *its* to *it is* or *it has* and see whether the sentence still makes sense. If it does, the *its* is a contraction and needs the apostrophe. If the result is nonsense, the *its* is a possessive pronoun and does not get an apostrophe. Here are some examples:

Its awfully muggy today.

Its been an exciting trip.

Every dog has *its* day.

The first example makes sense when the *its* is expanded to *it is*.

It is awfully muggy today.

The second makes sense when the *its* is expanded to *it has*.

It has been an exciting trip.

Both of these sentences therefore require apostrophes.

It's awfully muggy today.

It's been an exciting trip.

The last sentence, however, turns into nonsense when the *its* is expanded.

Every dog has *it is* day.

Every dog has *it has* day.

In this case, the *its* is a possessive pronoun and requires no apostrophe.

Every dog has *its* day.

Plurals   To improve clarity, the plurals of letters, numbers, symbols, and words being singled out for special attention are written with apostrophes.

Mind your *p*'s and *q*'s. (plurals of letters)

Your *5*'s and *6*'s are hard to tell apart. (plurals of numbers)

The formula was sprinkled with [Φ]'s and [σ]'s. (plurals of symbols)

Don't use so many *however*'s and *therefore*'s in your writing. (plurals of words)

Apostrophes can be used, though they are not needed, to form the plurals of abbreviations.

How many *CD*'s (or *CDs*) do you own? (plurals of abbreviation for *compact discs*)

When no danger of confusion exists, an *s* alone will suffice.

During the late *1960s,* many university students demanded changes in academic life.

comma

Connected Discourse Exercise

Supply, delete, or relocate apostrophes as necessary in the following memorandum:

TO: The Records Office Staff
FROM: The Assistant Registrar
DATE: January 27, 20__ __
SUBJECT: Faulty Student Transcripts
Recently, we have had too many student complaints' about handwritten transcripts. Apparently its hard to tell the B's and D's apart. One staff members' handwriting is totally illegible. This staffs carelessness is unacceptable. Someone's even gone so far as to write grade change's in pencil, which allows students to make changes. This can't continue. In a short time, John and Mary's student assistants will be typing the past transcripts into our new computer system. Once grades are entered, the computers ability to generate grade reports will solve this problem. Until that time, lets make an effort to produce clear and professional-looking transcripts.

Supply apostrophes where necessary to correct the following sentences:

1. This years winter promises to be significantly more severe than last years.
2. Everyones office will be furnished with the newest ergonomic chairs and work spaces.
3. Were attempting to determine how our students needs can best be met.
4. When you are writing numbers quickly by hand, its important to keep your *7s* and *1s* very distinct.
5. Somebodys purse was left in Dean Smiths office.
6. Once everybodys research has been presented, well be better able to reach a decision.
7. Cindys computer program was much more efficient than her peers programs.
8. There are two *Rs* and two *Ss* in the word "embarrassment."
9. Lets determine what caused the schools mainframe computer to fail before we panic.
10. Every city has its own charms that are available for the informed visitors delight.

Commas

Since commas (,) occur more frequently than any other mark of punctuation, it's vital that you learn to use them correctly. When you do, your sentence structure is clearer, and your reader grasps your meaning without having to reread.

Commas separate or set off independent clauses, items in a series, coordinate adjectives, introductory elements, places and dates, nonrestrictive expressions, and parenthetical expressions.

Independent Clauses   When you link two independent clauses with a coordinating conjunction (*and, but, or, nor, for, yet,* or *so*), put a comma in front of the conjunction.

> Arthur is majoring in engineering, *but* he has decided to work for a clothing store following graduation.

> The water looked inviting, *so* Darlene decided to go for a swim.

Don't confuse a sentence that has a compound predicate (see page 619) with a sentence that consists of two independent clauses.

> Tom watered the garden and mowed the lawn. (single sentence with compound predicate)

> Tom watered the garden, *and* Betty mowed the lawn. (sentence with two independent clauses)

Here's a simple test. Read what follows the comma. Unless that part can stand alone as a sentence, don't use a comma.

Items in a Series   A series consists of three or more words, phrases, or clauses following on one another's heels. Whenever you write a series, separate its items with commas.

> *Sarah, Paul,* and *Mary* are earning *A's* in advanced algebra. (words in a series)

> Nancy strode *across the parking lot, through the revolving door,* and *into the elevator.* (phrases in a series)

> The stockholders' report said *that the company had enjoyed record profits during the last year, that it had expanded its work force by 20 percent,* and *that it would soon start marketing several new products.* (clauses in a series)

Coordinate Adjectives   Use commas to separate coordinate adjectives—those that modify the same noun or noun substitute and can be reversed without altering the meaning of the sentence.

> Andrea proved to be an efficient, cooperative employee.

> Andrea proved to be a cooperative, efficient employee.

When reversing the word order wrecks the meaning of the sentence, the adjectives are not coordinate and should be written without a comma.

> Many new brands of videocassette recorders have come on the market lately.

Reversing the adjectives *many* and *new* would turn this sentence into nonsense. Therefore, no comma should be used.

Introductory Elements   Use commas to separate introductory elements—words, phrases, and clauses—from the rest of the sentence. When an introductory element is short and the sentence will not be misread, you can omit the comma.

---

over the conjunction and see whether the word group on either side can stand as an independent sentence. If both can, the student should use a comma. Some students, however, will probably still not see the point. Often, they are confused because they have trouble understanding that a pronoun can be the subject of an independent clause, something you probably will have to reexplain to them.

PERSPECTIVE
Some students have learned that a comma should not be used before the last item in a series. Although the popular press often omits the final

comma

comma, many businesses still prefer its inclusion. You might explain this variation to your students.

TEACHING STRATEGY
Have students test for coordinate adjectives by mentally inserting an *and* between the pair in question. If the meaning does not change, the adjectives are coordinate, and a comma is required.

TEACHING STRATEGIES
1. Sometimes students suspect that a sentence has an introductory element, but they don't know for sure. When this happens, have them reposition the suspected element at the end of the sentence. If it is indeed an introductory element, the meaning of

the sentence will not be materially altered. Note that the preceding sentence passes this test.

2. Students sometimes mistake complete subjects for introductory phrases: Studying late at night, isn't always the best strategy. (incorrect) Studying late at night isn't always the best strategy. (correct) In most cases, the "move" test will reveal the error. "Isn't always the best strategy, studying late at night" just doesn't make sense, even to an undiscriminating eye.

TEACHING STRATEGY
Because students often fail to put needed commas after names of places and dates, ask them to proofread with this oversight in mind.

comma

TEACHING STRATEGY
You might combine this unit with the earlier one on relative pronouns (page 626), where supplementary sentence-combining exercises are provided. Students can best learn how such expressions work, and especially the difference between restrictive and nonrestrictive expressions, by constructing some themselves. A few more sentence-combining pairs follow:
James Johnson has been arrested for embezzlement. James Johnson was our head accountant.
Anybody has a toothache. Anybody should go to the dentist.

Correct	After bathing, Jack felt refreshed.
Correct	Soon I will be changing jobs.
Correct	Soon, I will be changing jobs.
Correct	When Sarah smiles her ears wiggle.
Correct	When Sarah smiles, her ears wiggle.

The first example needs a comma; otherwise, the reader might become temporarily confused.

After bathing Jack . . .

Always use commas after introductory elements of six or more words.

Correct	Whenever I hear the opening measure of Beethoven's *Fifth Symphony*, I get goose bumps.

Places and Dates   Places include mailing addresses and geographical locations. The following sentences show where commas are used:

Sherry Delaney lives at 651 Daniel Street, Memphis, Tennessee 38118.

I will go to Calais, France, next week.

Morristown, Oklahoma, is my birthplace.

Note that commas appear after the street designation and the names of cities, countries, and states, except when the name of the state is followed by a zip code.

Dates are punctuated as shown in the following example:

On Sunday, June 9, 1991, Elaine received a degree in environmental science.

Here, commas follow the day of the week, the day of the month, and the year.

With dates that include only the month and the year, commas are optional.

Correct	In July 1989 James played chess for the first time.
Correct	In July, 1989, James played chess for the first time.

Nonrestrictive Expressions   A nonrestrictive expression supplies added information about whatever it modifies. This information, however, is *nonessential* and does not affect the basic meaning of the sentence. The two sentences below include nonrestrictive expressions:

Senator Conwell, *the senior senator from this state*, faces a tough campaign for reelection.

My dog, *frightened by the thunder*, hid under my bed while the storm raged.

If we delete the phrase *the senior senator from this state* from the first sentence, we still know that Senator Conwell faces a tough reelection battle. Likewise, if we delete *frightened by the thunder* from the second sentence, we still know that the dog hid during the storm.

Restrictive expressions, which are written *without commas*, distinguish whatever they modify from other persons, places, or things in the same category. Unlike nonrestrictive expressions, they are almost always *essential* sentence elements. Omitting a restrictive expression alters the meaning of the sentence, and the result is often nonsense.

Any person *caught stealing from this store* will be prosecuted.

Dropping the italicized part of this sentence leaves us with the absurd statement that any person, not just those caught stealing, faces prosecution.

Parenthetical Expressions   A parenthetical expression is a word or a word group that links one sentence to another or adds information or emphasis to the sentence in which it appears. Parenthetical expressions include the following:

Clarifying phrases

Names and titles of people being addressed directly

Abbreviations of degree titles

Echo questions

"Not" phrases

Adjectives that come after, rather than before, the words they modify

The examples that follow show the uses of commas:

All of Joe's spare time seems to center around reading. Kevin, *on the other hand*, enjoys a variety of activities. (phrase linking two sentences)

Myra Hobbes, *our representative in Seattle*, is being transferred to Spokane next month. (clarifying phrase)

I think, *Jill*, that you'd make a wonderful teacher. (name of person addressed directly)

Tell me, *Captain*, when the cruise ship is scheduled to sail. (title of person addressed directly)

Harley Kendall, *Ph.D.*, will be this year's commencement speaker. (degree title following name)

Alvin realizes, *doesn't he*, that he stands almost no chance of being accepted at West Point? (echo question)

Mathematics, *not home economics*, was Tammy's favorite high school subject. ("not" phrase)

The road, *muddy and rutted*, proved impassable. (adjectives following word they modify)

Punctuating Conjunctive Adverbs   Writers often mistakenly punctuate conjunctive adverbs with commas and create, as a result, a comma splice.

Floridians do not have the heating bills of their Northern neighbors, however, they do have extensive air-conditioning bills.

A man has a broken leg. A man should not go skiing. Marsha Ames is the new president of our company. Marsha Ames was once the head of the accounting department.

Combined Sentences

James Johnson, our head accountant, has been arrested for embezzlement.

Anybody who has a toothache should go to the dentist.

A man who has a broken leg should not go skiing.

Marsha Ames, once the head of the accounting department, is the new president of our company.

comma

comma

Conjunctive adverbs actually do not join sentences and can actually be moved, revealing the underlying comma splice.

Floridians do not have the heating bills of their Northern neighbors, they do, however, have extensive air-conditioning bills.

To fix such comma splices, join the sentences with a semicolon or punctuate with a period and start a new sentence.

Floridians do not have the heating bills of their Northern neighbors; however, they do have extensive air-conditioning bills.

Floridians do not have the heating bills of their Northern neighbors. However, they do have extensive air-conditioning bills.

Connected Discourse Exercise

Add or delete commas as necessary in the following letter:

Dear Loy Norrix Knight:

While we know you will be busy this summer we hope you will take time to join us for the twenty-five-year reunion of the graduating class of 1987. The reunion will include a cocktail hour a buffet dinner and a dance. For your entertainment we are going to bring in a professional band and a band starring some of your good, old high school chums. John Mcleary who is now a well-known professional nightclub performer will serve as the emcee. Do you remember him hosting our senior-year assemblies?

Yes many of your former, hardworking teachers will be at the reunion. You can thank them for the difference they made in your life or you can tell them what you've thought of them all these years. This reunion will also be your opportunity to catch up on the lives of your former friends find out what that old flame now looks like and brag a little about your own successes. And if you are really lucky you might even be able to sneak a dance with your high school prom partner.

We hope you will make plans, to join us here at the Kalamazoo Hilton on July 28, 2002, at 7 P.M. Wear your best 1980s-style clothes. Remember revisiting the past can be fun.

Sincerely,
The Reunion Committee

Supply commas as necessary to correct the following sentences:

1. Let us know Ms. Granger when you would like to enjoy your free stay at Rolling Hills Resort.
2. The landscapers killed the existing grass rototilled the ground added new topsoil and sprayed the prepared ground with hydroseed.
3. If you are interested in making a tax-deductible donation to the Stratford Festival please write Carla Darma treasurer at 165 University Avenue Suite 700 Toronto Ontario Canada M5H 3B8.
4. The day was unusually beautiful so Mr. Collins decided to hold his class on the Romantic poets outside.
5. Standing in the long winding line for hours on a hot muggy New York summer day Tom was able to get discount tickets to one of the most popular musicals.
6. Mr. Carlin was hired by our New York office on March 25 1997 and was supposed to report to work in our Nome Alaska office three months after his hiring date.
7. Before eating raccoons carefully wash their paws.
8. Despite the many kinds of electronic entertainment available today many people continue to prefer to read a good book.
9. Your fireplace which is cracked in several places will need to be repaired before you can use it.
10. When it is performed well *Waiting for Godot* considered by many to be a masterpiece of existential theater is actually quite humorous.

EXERCISE ANSWERS

1. know, Granger,
2. grass, ground, topsoil,
3. Festival, Darma, treasurer, Avenue, 700, Toronto, Ontario,
4. beautiful,
5. long, hot, day,
6. March 25, 1997, Nome, Alaska,
7. eating,
8. today,
9. fireplace, places,
10. well, *Godot*, theater,

Semicolons

The main use of the semicolon (;) is to separate independent clauses, which may or may not be connected with a conjunctive adverb (see pages 644–645). Other uses include separating

> two or more series of items
>
> items containing commas in a single series
>
> independent clauses that contain commas and are connected with a coordinating conjunction.

Independent Clauses   The examples that follow show the use of semicolons to separate independent clauses.

> The fabric in this dress is terrible; its designer must have been asleep at the swatch. (no conjunctive adverb)
>
> Steve refused to write a term paper; *therefore*, he failed the course. (conjunctive adverb *therefore* joining independent clauses)

Conjunctive adverbs can occur within, rather than between, independent clauses. When they do, set them off with commas.

> Marsha felt very confident. Jane, *on the other hand*, was nervous and uncertain. (conjunctive adverb within independent clause)

To determine whether a pair of commas or a semicolon and comma are required, read what comes before and after the conjunctive adverb. Unless both sets of words can stand alone as sentences, use commas.

PERSPECTIVE

As they do with other punctuation marks, students tend to overuse the semicolon once they have learned its applications. For many inexperienced writers, semicolons seem like a bargain, providing the force of the period and the continuity of the comma, making it possible to avoid comma splices forever. Warn students about excessive semicolons in their writing. Students need to realize that semicolons are a specialized punctuation mark, not simply a way of avoiding subordinating conjunctions, coordinating conjunctions, and periods; and when used excessively, they can result in an artificially formal style.

Two or More Series of Items   With sentences that have two or more series of items, writers often separate the series with semicolons in order to lessen the chances of misreading.

> My duties as secretary include typing letters, memos, and purchase orders; sorting, opening, and delivering mail; and making plane and hotel reservations for traveling executives.

The semicolons provide greater clarity than commas would.

Comma-Containing Items within a Series   When commas accompany one or more of the items in a series, it's often better to separate the items with semicolons instead of commas.

> The meal included veal, which was cooked to perfection; asparagus, my favorite vegetable; and brown rice, prepared with a touch of curry.

Once again, semicolons provide greater clarity than additional commas.

Independent Clauses With Commas and a Coordinating Conjunction
Ordinarily, a comma is used to separate independent clauses joined by a coordinating conjunction. When one or more of the clauses have commas, however, a semicolon provides clearer separation.

> The long black limousine pulled up to the curb; and Jerry, shaking with excitement, watched the President alight from it.

The semicolon makes it easier to see the two main clauses.

Connected Discourse Exercise

Add and delete semicolons as appropriate in the following letter. You may have to substitute semicolons for commas.

Dear Student:

Our college, as you are well aware, has been going through a number of changes, and these developments, both in the registration system and the curriculum, will continue next year. In the end these improvements will only benefit you; but we know that many of you have been anxious about the exact nature of the changes. To answer your questions, we have arranged an open forum with Linda Peters, president of the college, Drake Stevens, the registrar, and Jerry Mash, vice-president of academic affairs. The meeting will be held in Johnston Hall; 2 P.M.; March 23. Please come with your questions, this is your opportunity to put your fears to rest.

Sincerely,

John X. Pelle

Dean of Students

EXERCISE

Supply semicolons wherever they are necessary or desirable in the following sentences. You may have to substitute semicolons for commas. If a sentence is correct, write C.

1. When he visits the main office, Mr. Harmon would like to meet with the vice president of marketing, Carol Chaffe, the personnel director, Carl Hart, and the vice president of finance, Mary Angelo.
2. Donald Nathanson, a clinical psychologist, has written an insightful book on shame, and other psychologists, who at first were very critical of his work, have begun to use his ideas in their practice.
3. E-mail is a crucial part of most businesses; in fact, some companies have replaced all memos with electronic communication.
4. This year a number of new musicals have opened on Broadway, it promises to be an exciting theater season.
5. The reading for the course was eclectic, including *The Invisible Man*, a science fiction novel, *Shane*, a western, and *Antigone*, a classic Greek play.
6. Computers can crash at any time, therefore, it is important to back up your data frequently.
7. Sales have decreased significantly this past year, we are likely to see an equivalent drop in our profits.
8. The landscaper planted carpet juniper, canby pachistima, and English ivy for ground cover, rhododendron, pyracantha, and pieris for shrubs, and a blue spruce, a Japanese black pine, and a maple for trees.
9. Chess, a game played by millions, can sharpen your mind, and now there are computer programs, most very inexpensive, that can help you learn the game.
10. We will offer sales training this summer in Lansing, Michigan, Ames, Iowa, and Minneapolis, Minnesota.

Periods, Question Marks, and Exclamation Points

Since periods, question marks, and exclamation points signal the ends of sentences, they are sometimes called *end marks*. In addition, periods and question marks function in several other ways.

Periods   Periods (.) end sentences that state facts or opinions, give instructions, make requests that are not in the form of questions, and ask indirect questions—those that have been rephrased in the form of a statement.

Linda works as a hotel manager. (Sentence states fact.)

Dean Harris is a competent administrator. (Sentence states opinion.)

Clean off your lab bench before you leave. (Sentence gives instruction.)

Please move away from the door. (Sentence makes request.)

I wonder whether Ruthie will be at the theater tonight. (Sentence asks indirect question.)

The hospitals would be jammed to overflowing with victims of heat prostration.

EXERCISE ANSWER

Dear Student:

Our college, as you are well aware, has been going through a number of changes; and these developments, both in the registration system and the curriculum, will continue next year. In the end these improvements will only benefit you, but we know that many of you have been anxious about the exact nature of the changes. To answer your questions, we have arranged an open forum with Linda Peters, president of the college; Drake

.?!

Stevens, the registrar; and Jerry Mash, vice-president of academic affairs. The meeting will be held in Johnston Hall, 2 P.M., March 23. Please come with your questions; this is your opportunity to put your fears to rest.

Sincerely,

John X. Pelle

Dean of Students

EXERCISE ANSWERS

1. Chaffe; Hart;
2. shame;
3. C.
4. Broadway;

5. novel; western;
6. time;
7. year;
8. cover; shrubs;
9. mind;
10. Michigan; Iowa;

PERSPECTIVE
In some ways, you have been teaching end marks throughout this Handbook. Whether you are helping students to identify sentences or to avoid comma splices, you need to refer to end marks. Although most college instructors would like to take these marks for granted, many students have problems with them. Inexperienced writers sometimes fail to use them. Why? Mina

.?!

Shaughnessy has suggested that these writers see the period as ending a thought, something they don't like to do since it seems so hard for them to get started again. Furthermore, students usually don't construct sentences one at a time. Halfway through one sentence, they are already thinking of the next. As a result, they may link everything together with commas.

TEACHING STRATEGIES
1. Usually students who avoid end marks do include some punctuation marks at the sentence breaks. Have students review their writing to

Periods also follow common abbreviations as well as a person's initials.

Mr.	Sr.	P.M.
Mrs.	B.C.	lb.
Jr.	A.D.	St.
Dr.	A.M.	Corp.

Mark J. Valentini, Ph.D., has consented to head the new commission on traffic safety.

Writers today often omit periods after abbreviations for the names of organizations or government agencies, as the following examples show:

ABC	FBI	IRS
ACLU	FHA	NAM
AFL-CIO	GM	USAF

An up-to-date college dictionary will indicate whether a certain abbreviation should be written without periods.

Periods also precede decimal fractions and separate numerals standing for dollars and cents.

0.81 percent	$5.29
3.79 percent	$0.88

Question Marks   A question mark (?) ends a whole or a partial sentence that asks a direct question (one that repeats the exact words of the person who asked it).

Do you know how to operate this movie projector? (whole sentence asking a direct question)

Has Cinderella scrubbed the floor? Swept the hearth? Washed the dishes? (sentence and sentence parts asking direct questions)

Dr. Baker—wasn't she your boss once?—has just received a promotion to sales manager. (interrupting element asking a direct question)

The minister inquired, "Do you take this woman to be your lawful wedded wife?" (quotation asking a direct question)

A question mark may be used to indicate uncertainty.

Jane Seymour (1509?–1537), third wife of Henry VIII, was a lady in waiting to his first two wives.

Exclamation Points   Exclamation points (!) are used to express strong emotion or especially forceful commands.

Darcy! I never expected to see you again!
Sam! Turn that radio down immediately!
Help! Save me!

Use exclamation points sparingly; otherwise, they will quickly lose their force.

Connected Discourse Exercise

Add, change, or remove end marks as necessary. You may want to do some slight rewording.

It was horrifying, the mob of screaming fans grabbed Jack Slitherhips as he left the concert hall. Soon all I could see were his arms reaching for help. But it never came. Why do fans act this way. I am left wondering whether they love or hate their idols? They tore the clothes off Slitherhips, they tore out patches of his hair, someone even snatched his false teeth. Is this any way to treat a fading rock star. Jack is now in the hospital in a complete body cast; when I finally got to see him, he mumbled that he was giving up show business, he plans to settle down on a small farm. Who can blame him?

EXERCISE

Supply periods, question marks, or exclamation points wherever they are necessary. You may have to change existing punctuation marks. If a sentence is correct, write C.

1. Be sure to proofread your paper before you submit it for a grade.
2. Sigmund Freud—isn't he now generally dismissed by many psychologists—really established the concept of the unconscious.
3. The sales tax in our state was raised to 65 percent.
4. Great we will have to buy another candle.
5. Carla used to study until 2 A.M. every night.
6. When you shopped for a new computer, did you consider what programs you wanted to run, set a budget for yourself, check the reliability of the different brands.
7. The engineer wanted to know how much stress would be placed on the beams.
8. Has Dr Stevens read the research on the most recent anti-clotting medication.
9. Run for your life, the tiger has escaped from the zoo.
10. Be sure to check your e-mail as soon as you start work.

Colons, Dashes, Parentheses, and Brackets

Colons, dashes, parentheses, and brackets separate and enclose, thereby clarifying relationships among the various parts of a sentence.

Colon   Colons (:) introduce explanations and anticipated lists following words that could stand alone as a complete sentence.

His aim in life is grandiose: to corner the market in wheat. (explanation)

Three students have been selected to attend the conference: Lucille Perkins, Dan Blakely, and Frank Napolis. (list)

identify places where they need end marks. Often, checking for comma splices and run-ons will solve the end mark problem. However, to avoid the danger that inexperienced writers will become obsessive about using periods and produce a series of short, choppy sentences, this check should be made during proofreading.
2. Teaching end marks allows you to explore matters of style. Have students read over their drafts, note where end marks are used, and then consider their findings in light of questions like these: Are my sentences too short and choppy? Have I supplied needed question

`:—() []`

marks? Used any unnecessarily? Should I combine certain sentences by substituting a semicolon, conjunctive adverb, or some other form of conjunction for the period? Have I overused exclamation points?

EXERCISE ANSWER
(There is more than one way to punctuate this passage.)
It was horrifying. The mob of screaming fans grabbed Jack Slitherhips as he left the concert hall. Soon all I could see were his arms reaching for help—but it never came. Why do fans act this way? I am left wondering whether they

: – () []

Three factors can cause financial problems for farmers: (1) high interest rates, (2) falling land values, and (3) a strong dollar, which makes it difficult to sell crops abroad. (numbered list)

The first of the following sentences is incorrect because the words preceding the colon can't stand alone as a sentence:

Faulty The tools needed for this job include: a hacksaw, a file, and a drill.

Revision The tools needed for this job include a hacksaw, a file, and a drill.

Colons also frequently introduce formal quotations that extend beyond a single sentence.

The speaker stepped to the lectern and said: "I am here to ask for your assistance. Today several African nations face a food crisis because drought has ruined their harvests. Unless we provide help quickly, thousands of people will die of starvation."

In such situations, the material preceding the quotation need not be a complete sentence.

Colons also separate hours from minutes (8:20 A.M.), salutations of business letters from the body of the letters (Dear Ms. Stanley:), titles of publications from subtitles (*The Careful Writer: A Guide to English Usage*), numbers indicating ratios (a 3:2:2 ratio), and chapter from verse in biblical references (Luke 6:20–49).

Dashes Like colons, dashes (—) set off appositives, lists, and explanations but are used in less formal writing. A dash emphasizes the material it sets off.

Only one candidate showed up at the political rally—Jerry Manders. (appositive)

The closet held only three garments—an out-at-the-elbows sports coat, a pair of blue jeans, and a tattered shirt. (list)

I know what little Billy's problem is—a soiled diaper. (explanation)

Dashes set off material that interrupts the flow of thought within a sentence.

Her new car—didn't she get it just three months ago?—has broken down twice.

Similarly, dashes are used to mark an interrupted segment of dialogue.

"I'd like to live in England when I retire."

"In England? But what will your wife—?"

"My wife likes the idea and can hardly wait for us to make the move."

Dashes set off parenthetical elements containing commas, and a dash can set off comments that follow a list.

The comedian—short, fat, and squeaky-voiced—soon had everyone roaring with laughter. (parenthetical element with commas)

A brag, a blow, a tank of air—that's what Senator Conwell is. (comment following a list)

Type a dash as two unspaced hyphens and leave no space between it and the words on either side of it.

Parentheses   Parentheses () are used to enclose numbers or letters that designate the items in a formal list and to set off incidental material within sentences. Except in the kind of list shown in the first example below, a comma does not usually precede a parenthesis.

Each paper should contain (1) an introduction, (2) several paragraphs developing the thesis statement, and (3) a conclusion.

Some occupations (computer programming, for example) may be overcrowded in ten years.

If the material in parentheses appears within a sentence, don't use a capital letter or period, even if the material is itself a complete sentence.

The growth of genetic engineering (one cannot foresee its consequences) worries some people today.

If the material in parentheses is written as a separate sentence, however, then punctuate it as you would a separate sentence.

Paula's angry outburst surprised everyone. (She had seemed such a placid person.)

If the material in parentheses comes at the end of a sentence, put the final punctuation after the closing parenthesis.

This company was founded by Willard Manley (1876–1951).

In contrast to dashes, parentheses de-emphasize the material they enclose.

Brackets   In quoted material, brackets [] enclose words or phrases that have been added to make the message clearer. They are also used with the word *sic* (Latin for "thus") to point out errors in quoted material.

"This particular company [Zorn Enterprises, Inc.] pioneered in the safe disposal of toxic wastes," the report noted. (The bracketed name is added to the original.)

"[John Chafin's] expertise in science has made him a popular figure on the lecture circuit," his friend stated. (The bracketed name replaces *his* in the original.)

"The principle [sic] cause of lung cancer is cigarette smoking," the article declared. (the word *principal* is misspelled "principle" in the original.)

To call attention to an error, follow it immediately with the bracketed *sic*. The reader will then know that the blame rests with the original writer, not with you.

TEACHING STRATEGIES
1. You can simplify the rule for colons by treating an explanation that follows an independent clause as a list.
2. Have students generate sentences that use a colon, employing the following questions as prompts: What are the three basic reasons students skip classes? What are four subjects required in high school? What is the one quality essential to success? What are the four basic food groups?

TEACHING STRATEGY
Have students combine the following sentence pairs by using the dash: They offer only one thing for breakfast. That is cold oatmeal.

`: – () []`

It frequently takes students five years to earn a college diploma. Wasn't it supposed to take four years?
The movie star had the politicians completely captivated. The movie star was beautiful, charming, and witty.
He certainly made a spectacle of himself. He was blowing her kisses, waving his handkerchief, and yelling out her name.

Combinations
They offer only one thing for breakfast—cold oatmeal.
It frequently takes students five years—wasn't it supposed to take four?—to earn a college diploma.
The movie star—beautiful, charming, and witty—had the politicians completely captivated.

He certainly made a spectacle of himself—blowing her kisses, waving his handkerchief, and yelling out her name.

PERSPECTIVE
Students are often confused about when to use parentheses, when commas, and when dashes. In some cases, the difference is really a matter of style; however, these punctuation marks do produce different effects. While commas tend to incorporate the set-off material into the sentence, parentheses tend to exclude it. Dashes, if anything, tend to draw attention to the material.

: – ( ) [ ]

CLASSROOM ACTIVITY
Have students compare the following sets of punctuation to determine the different effects that they produce:
It frequently takes a college student five years, instead of four, to earn a diploma. It frequently takes a college student five years (instead of four) to earn a diploma. It frequently takes a college student five years— instead of four—to earn a diploma.
Mitch Data, our computer programmer, has trouble with basic math. Mitch Data (our computer programmer) has trouble with basic math. Mitch Data—our computer programmer—has trouble with basic math.

Connected Discourse Exercise

Supply any necessary or appropriate colons, dashes, parentheses, and brackets in the following letter:

Wayout Auto Company

We at Oldfield Sales a subsidiary of Jip, Inc., have had a serious problem with the cars we ordered from your company for leasing to our customers who will probably never return to us again. Two major parts fell off while the cars were sitting in the customers' driveways the exhaust system and the transmission. If this had happened while they were driving thank goodness it didn't, our customers could have been killed. Just imagine what that especially once it got into the newspapers would have done to our business. We must hold you to your claim that "while our cars are the cheepest sic on the market, we garuntee sic every car we sell." We expect immediate reimbursement for all the cars we purchased from you plus one million dollars to cover the damage to our reputation. A menace, a rip-off, a bad business deal, that's what your cars are. If you don't issue a formal recall for all your vehicles by 5:30 P.M., Friday, July 23, we will be forced to forward this matter to the federal government.

> Sincerely,
> Ken Swindelle
> Service Manager

Supply colons, dashes, parentheses, and brackets wherever they are necessary.

1. Many former Presidents Millard Fillmore, for example have been largely forgotten by most Americans.
2. Our international sales have outperformed domestic sales by an 83 ratio.
3. The newspaper headline read, "Piece sic deal broken."
4. Among our social ills, one condition seems to be the source of many other problems poverty.
5. The new library better considered an information center will have over fifty computers with full Internet capability.
6. Our city area offers many advantages to businesses a skilled workforce, a well-developed infrastructure, and low taxes.
7. His Friedrich Nietzsche's *Thus Spoke Zarathustra* should be very familiar to anyone interested in the history of ideas.
8. In early June every elementary school student's thoughts turn to one thing summer vacation.
9. Mozart, Miles Davis, The Talking Heads his tastes certainly are eclectic.
10. The activities at the Pine Tree Resort include horseback riding, kayaking, swimming, water skiing, and much more.

Quotation Marks

Quotation marks (" ") set off direct quotations, titles of short written or broadcast works, subdivisions of books, and expressions singled out for special attention.

Direct Quotations   A direct quotation repeats a speaker's or writer's exact words.

"Tell me about the movie," said Debbie. "If you liked it, I may go myself."

The placement director said, "The recruiter for Procter and Gamble will be on campus next Thursday to interview students for marketing jobs." (spoken comment)

"The U.S. trade deficit is expected to reach record levels this year," the *Wall Street Journal* noted. (written comment)

Jackie said the party was "a total flop."

As these sentences show, a comma or period that follows a direct quotation goes inside the quotation marks. When a quotation is a sentence fragment, the comma preceding it is omitted.

When an expression like "he said" interrupts a quoted sentence, use commas to set off the expression. When the expression comes between two complete quoted sentences, use a period after the expression and capitalize the first word of the second sentence.

"Hop in," said Jim. "Let me give you a ride to school."

"Thank you," replied Kelly, opening the car door and sliding into the front seat.

"I can't remember," said Jim, "when we've had a worse winter."

Titles of Short Works and Subdivisions of Books   These short works include magazine articles, essays, short stories, chapters of books, one-act plays, short poems, songs, and television and radio episodes.

The article was titled "The Real Conservatism." (article)

Last night I read John Cheever's "The Enormous Radio," "Torch Song," and "The Swimmer." (short stories)

Many John Denver fans consider "Take Me Home, Country Roads" to be his greatest piece of music. (song)

The unsuccessful TV show *Pursued* ended its brief run with a segment titled "Checkmate." (TV episode)

Here, as with direct quotations, a comma or period that follows a title goes inside the quotation marks.

Expressions Singled Out for Special Attention   Writers who wish to call the reader's attention to a word or symbol sometimes put it within quotation marks.

The algebraic formula included a "π," a "Θ," and a "Δ."

"Bonnets" and "lifts" are British terms for car hoods and elevators.

More frequently, however, these expressions are printed in italics (page 710).

Again, any commas and periods that follow expressions set off by quotation marks go inside the marks.

Quotation Marks Within **Quotation Marks** When a direct quotation or the title of a shorter work appears within a direct quotation, use single quotation marks (' ').

"I heard the boss telling the foreman, 'Everyone will receive a Christmas bonus,'" John said.

The instructor told the class, "For tomorrow, read Ernest Hemingway's 'The Killers.'"

Note that the period goes inside of both the single and double quotation marks.

Positioning of Semicolons, Colons, and Question Marks Position semicolons and colons that come at the end of quoted material after, not before, the quotation marks.

Marcia calls Francine "that greasy grind"; however, I think Marcia is simply jealous of Francine's abilities.

There are two reasons why I like "Babylon Revisited": the characters are interesting and the writing is excellent.

When a question mark accompanies a quotation, put it outside the quotation marks if the whole sentence rather than the quotation asks the question.

Why did Cedric suddenly shout, "This party is a big bore"?

Put the question mark inside the quotation marks if the quotation, but not the whole sentence, asks a question or if the quotation asks one question and the whole sentence asks another.

Marie asked, "What college is your brother planning to attend?" (The quoted material, not the whole sentence, asks the question.)

Whatever possessed him to ask, "What is the most shameful thing you ever did?" (The whole sentence and the quoted material ask separate questions.)

Connected Discourse Exercise

Use quotation marks correctly in the following paragraph:

Mr. Silver recently lectured our class on Stephen Crane's The Bride Comes to Yellow Sky. One thing we shouldn't forget, Mr. Silver insisted, is that the town is deliberately named Yellow Sky. What is the significance of

Crane's choice of the words Yellow Sky? Mr. Silver pointed out a number of possible associations, including cowardice, the setting sun, the open expanse of the West, freedom, the sand in the concluding passage. The story, Mr. Silver stated, is drenched in color words. For example, he pointed out, in the first three paragraphs alone Crane mentions vast flats of green grass, brick-colored hands, new black clothes, and a dress of blue cashmere.

Supply properly positioned quotation marks wherever they are necessary.

1. Some linguists think that the quintessential American ok may have come from the African waka.
2. My favorite piece of jazz music is St. James Infirmary.
3. What did Yeats mean by the line in his famous poem The Second Coming, Things fall apart, the center cannot hold?
4. Carl Thomas described the performance as extremely intense.
5. I managed to read Faulkner's short story The Bear, Jennifer sighed, but I don't really know what I want to say about it in my paper for English.
6. Why do so many student writers consistently confuse effect with affect?
7. In response to the Great Depression, Franklin Roosevelt declared The only thing we have to fear is fear itself; however, many families who had lost their homes and couldn't even earn enough for food really did have something to fear.
8. Yiddish words like mishugana and kibitz have come to be used outside the Jewish community.
9. In his closing argument, the defense attorney asked the jury, How would any one of us act if accused of a crime we knew we didn't commit?
10. Henry Ford supposedly called history bunk.

Hyphens

Hyphens (-) are used to join compound adjectives and nouns, compound numbers and word-number combinations, and certain prefixes and suffixes to the words with which they appear. In addition, hyphens help prevent misreadings and awkward combinations of letters or syllables and are used to split words between two lines.

Compound Adjectives

Hyphens are often used to join separate words that function as single adjectives and come before nouns. Typical examples follow:

Howard is a very *self-contained* person.

The *greenish-yellow* cloud of chlorine gas drifted toward the village.

Betty's *devil-may-care* attitude will land her in trouble someday.

When the first word of the compound is an adverb ending in *-ly* or when the compound adjective follows the noun it modifies, no hyphen is used.

The *badly* burned crash victim was rushed to the hospital.

The color of the chlorine gas was *greenish yellow.*

When two or more compound adjectives modify the same last term, the sentence will flow more smoothly if that term appears just once, after the last item in the series. The hyphens accompanying the earlier terms in the series are kept, however.

Many seventeenth-, eighteenth-, and nineteenth-century costumes are on display in this museum.

Compound Nouns   Hyphenated nouns include such expressions as the following:

secretary-treasurer	good-for-nothing
sister-in-law	man-about-town

Here is a sentence with hyphenated nouns:

Denton is *editor-in-chief* of the largest newspaper in this state.

Compound Numbers and Word–Number Combinations   Hyphens are used to separate two-word numbers from twenty-one to ninety-nine and fractions that have been written out.

Marcy has worked *twenty-one* years for this company.

One-fourth of my income goes for rent.

Similarly, hyphens are used to separate numerals from units of measurement that follow them.

This chemical is shipped in *50-gallon* drums.

Prefixes and Suffixes   A prefix is a word or set of letters that precedes a word and alters its meaning. A suffix is similar but comes at the end of the word. Although most prefixes are not hyphenated, the prefixes *self-* and *all-* do get hyphens, as does the suffix *-elect.* Also the prefix *ex-* is hyphenated when it accompanies a noun.

This stove has a *self-cleaning* oven.

Let Claire Voyant, the *all-knowing* soothsayer, read your future in her crystal ball.

Ethel is the *chairperson-elect* of the club.

Several *ex-teachers* work in this department.

A prefix used before a capitalized term is always hyphenated.

The *ex-FBI* agent gave an interesting talk on the operations of that agency.

Preventing Misreadings and Awkward Combinations of Letters and Syllables   Hyphens help prevent misreadings of certain words and also break up awkward combinations of letters and syllables between certain prefixes and suffixes and their core words.

> The doctor *re-treated* the wound with a new antibiotic. (The hyphen prevents the misreading *retreated*.)

> The company plans to *de-emphasize* sales of agricultural chemicals. (The hyphen prevents the awkward repetition of the letter *e* in *deemphasize*.)

Between Syllables   Whenever you have to split a word between two lines, place a hyphen at the end of the first line to show the division. The word is always broken, and the hyphen inserted, between syllables. (Any good dictionary shows the syllable divisions of each word it includes.) Never divide a one-syllable word or leave two letters to be placed on the second line, even if those two letters constitute a syllable.

Supply hyphens wherever they are necessary. If the sentence is correct, write C.

1. The piece of music ended with bird like sounds made by the entire woodwind section.
2. In this brokerage firm we follow sound investment strategies rather than chase after will o' the wisp schemes.
3. It can be sobering for the president elect to learn the full requirements of the job.
4. The union negotiators were forced to retreat from their initial demands.
5. One fifth of the shipment of fresh tomatoes turned out to be spoiled.
6. The classical radio station can be received by anyone within a 100 mile radius of its broadcasting tower.
7. In this class, we will study nineteenth and twentieth century American authors.
8. Emerson thought that it was important for people to be self reliant.
9. Once the power came back on, I had to recreate the file.
10. The Gundersons have been married for thirty five years.

Capitalization

Capitalize the first word in any sentence, the pronoun *I*, proper nouns and adjectives, titles used with names, and the significant words in literary and artistic titles.

Proper Nouns   A proper noun names one particular person, group of persons, place, or thing. Such nouns include the following:

> Persons
>
> Organizations
>
> Racial, political, and religious groups

Countries, states, cities, and streets

Companies and buildings

Geographical locations and features

Days, months, and holidays

Trademarks

Languages

Ships and aircraft

Abbreviations for academic degrees

Sacred writings and pronouns standing for God and Jesus

Titles used in place of names

The sentences below show the capitalization of proper nouns:

Sigmund works for the *National Psychoanalytical Institute,* an organization that has done much to advance the science of psychiatry.

How much does this roll of *Saran Wrap* cost?

Gwen Greene moved to *Paris, France,* when her father became the consul there.

On *Friday, December* 10, 1993, *Michael Jordan* visited our city.

Larry has a master of arts degree, and his sister has a *Ph.D.*

My father works for the *Ford Motor Company,* but I work for *Daimler Chrysler.*

Do not capitalize words like *institute, college, company,* or *avenue* unless they form part of a proper name. Likewise, do not capitalize the names of courses unless they start a sentence, are accompanied by a course number, or designate a language.

I have a 95 average in *Economics* 112 but only a 73 average in sociology.

Harry plans to take intermediate *German* in his junior year.

Do you plan to attend *Drew College* or some other college?

Proper Adjectives   Adjectives created from proper nouns are called proper adjectives. Like the nouns themselves, they should be capitalized.

Lolita Martinez, our class valedictorian, is of *Mexican* ancestry. (*Mexican* is derived from the proper noun *Mexico.*)

Abbreviations   As a general rule, capitalize abbreviations only if the words they stand for are capitalized.

Milton DeWitt works for the *IRS.* (*IRS* is capitalized because *Internal Revenue Service* would be.)

The flask holds 1,500 *ml* of liquid. (The abbreviation *ml* is not capitalized because *milliliters* would not be.)

cap

A few abbreviations are capitalized even though all or some of the words they stand for aren't. Examples include TV (television) and VCR (videocassette recorder). Others are shown on page 694.

Personal Titles   Capitalize a personal title if it precedes a name or is used in place of a name. Otherwise, do not capitalize.

The division is under the command of *General* Arnold Schafer.

Tell me, *Doctor*, do I need an operation?

The *dean* of our engineering division is Dr. Alma Haskins.

Many writers capitalize titles of high rank when they are used in place of names.

The *President* will sign this bill tomorrow.

The *president* will sign this bill tomorrow.

Either usage is acceptable.

Titles of Literary and Artistic Works   When citing the titles of publications, pieces of writing, movies, television programs, paintings, sculptures, and the like, capitalize the first and last words and all other words except *a, an, the*, coordinating conjunctions, and one-syllable prepositions.

Last week I played *Gone with the Wind* on my VCR and read Christopher Isherwood's *Goodbye to Berlin*. (the preposition *with*, the article *the*, and the preposition *to* are not capitalized.)

John is reading a book called *The Movies of Abbott and Costello*. (The preposition *of* and the coordinating conjunction *and* are not capitalized. *The* is capitalized because it is the first word of the title.)

Although I'm no TV addict, I used to watch every episode of *Murder, She Wrote*. (All of the words in the title are capitalized.)

Note that the titles of literary and artistic works are italicized.

Identify any word or abbreviation that should be capitalized in the following sentences:

1. Every friday at 1:00 P.M. the computer support team meets to review the problems that occurred during the previous week.
2. Any student of mexican history will soon see how radically different that history has been from american history.
3. Though many consider it a liberal organization, the aclu has actually protected the right to free speech of many extremely conservative groups.
4. Many students in the rotc choose to take history 321: american military history to satisfy their humanities requirement.
5. A student has a right to be proud upon earning an a.a.s. or a b.s. degree.

cap

EXERCISE ANSWERS
1. Friday
2. Mexican history, American history.
3. ACLU
4. ROTC, History 321: American Military History
5. A.A.S. or a B.S.
6. Dean Styron by October 1.
7. Latin
8. Professor
9. Roman, Ovid's *Metamorphoses*.
10. Dr. . . . U.S. submarine *Eel*.

6. All requests for sabbatical leave must be submitted to dean Styron by october 1.

7. Though many consider latin a dead language, others continue to study it since so many great classical works were written in that language.

8. Your request for a leave of absence cannot be approved by professor Murphy.

9. Students of roman literature should be familiar with ovid's *metamorphoses.*

10. During World War II, dr. Johnson served on the u.s. submarine eel.

ab

Abbreviations

Items that are abbreviated include certain personal titles, names of organizations and agencies, Latin terms, and specific and technical terms.

Personal Titles Abbreviate *Mister, Doctor,* and similar titles when they come just ahead of a name, and *Junior, Senior,* and degree titles when they follow names.

> Will *Mr.* Harry Babbitt please come to the front desk?

> Arthur Compton, *Sr.,* is a well-known historian; his son, Arthur Compton, *Jr.,* is a television producer.

> This article on marital discord was written by Irma Quarles, *Ph.D.*

Names of Organizations and Agencies Many organizations and agencies are known primarily by their initials rather than their full names. Several examples follow:

AAA	FBI	NBC
CARE	FHA	NATO
CIA	IBM	UNESCO

Latin Terms Certain Latin terms are always abbreviated; others are abbreviated when used with dates or times.

> e.g. (*exempli gratia:* for example)

> i.e. (*id est:* that is)

> etc. (*et cetera:* and [the] others)

> vs. or v. (*versus:* against)

> A.D. (*anno Domini:* in the year of our Lord)

> A.M. or a.m. (*ante meridiem:* before noon)

> P.M. or p.m. (*post meridiem:* after noon)

> The play starts at 8 P.M.

> Many writers (*e.g.,* Dylan Thomas and Truman Capote) have had serious problems with alcohol.

For consistency with A.D., the term "before Christ" is abbreviated as B.C.

Scientific and Technical Terms   For brevity's sake, scientists and technicians abbreviate terms of measurement that repeatedly occur. Terms that the reader would not know are written out the first time they are used, and they are accompanied by their abbreviation in parentheses. Unfamiliar organizations and agencies that are mentioned repeatedly are handled in like manner.

The viscosity of the fluid measured 15 centistokes (cs) at room temperature. Common practice calls for writing such abbreviations without periods unless they duplicate the spelling of some word.

Standard dictionaries list common abbreviations. When you don't recognize one, look it up. Use abbreviations sparingly in essays. If you're unsure about what is appropriate, don't abbreviate.

EXERCISE

Supply abbreviations wherever they are necessary or are customarily used.

1. Despite extensive competition, International Business Machines continues to be a major player in the computer industry.
2. We are pleased that Mister Jones has decided to join our firm.
3. Dissolve 1 gram of NaCl in 20 milliliters of water.
4. The freezing point of water at sea level is 32° Fahrenheit (0° Celsius).
5. Since its start, the National Broadcasting Company has been strongly committed to its news programming.
6. Doctor Baxter has been doing extensive research on nanotechnology, supported by a National Science Foundation grant.
7. Carl Thorton, Junior, will offer a workshop on how to save for retirement.
8. Many composers who are now seen as giants of classical music (*exempli gratia*, Mozart and Beethoven) died paupers.
9. After Friday's performance of Shakespeare's *Midsummer Night's Dream*, Carol Brice, Doctor of Philosophy, will discuss the use of nature imagery in the play.
10. Crimes that cross state boundaries are often investigated by the Federal Bureau of Investigation.

EXERCISE ANSWERS

1. IBM
2. Mr. Jones
3. 1 g, 20 ml
4. 32°F (0°C).
5. NBC (no "the" before abbreviation)
6. Dr. Baxter, NSF grant.
7. Carl Thorton, Jr.,
8. (e.g., . . .)
9. Brice, Ph.D.
10. FBI.

num

Numbers

Some instructors ask their students to use figures for numbers larger than ninety-nine and to spell out smaller numbers.

Boise is *100* miles from here.

Boise is *ninety-nine* miles from here.

Other instructors prefer that students switch to figures beginning with the number ten.

My son will be *nine* years old on his next birthday.

My son will be *10* years old on his next birthday.

With either practice, the following exceptions apply.

Numbers in a Series   Write all numbers in a series the same way regardless of their size.

Gatsby has *64* suits, *110* shirts, and *214* ties.

In just one hour the emergency room personnel handled *two* stabbings, *five* shootings, and *sixteen* fractures.

We have *150* salespeople, *51* engineers, and *7* laboratory technicians.

Dates   Use figures for dates that include the year.

February *14, 1985* or 14 February 1935 (not February 14th, 1985)

When the date includes the day but not the year, you may use figures or spell out the number.

June 9

June ninth

the ninth of June

Page Numbers and Addresses   Use figures for page numbers and street numbers in addresses.

Check the graph on page *415*.

I live at *111* Cornelia Street, and my office is at *620* Fifth Avenue.

Numbers Beginning Sentences   Spell out any number that begins a sentence. If this requires three or more words, rephrase the sentence so that the number comes after the opening and numerals can be used.

The year *1989* was a good year for this wine.

Sixty thousand fans jammed the stadium.

An army of *265,000* troops assaulted the city. (If this number began the sentence, five words—an excessive number—would be needed to write it out.)

Decimals, Percentages, Times   Use figures for decimals and percentages as well as for expressions of time that are accompanied by A.M. or P.M.

The shaft has a *0.37*-inch diameter.

Last year the value of my house jumped *25* percent.

The plane leaves here at *9:50* A.M. and reaches New Orleans at *2:30* P.M.

One Number Following Another   When a number-containing term that denotes a unit of weight or measurement comes immediately after another number, spell out the first number, if smaller than 100, and use numerals for the second one. If the first number is larger than 100, use numerals for it and spell out the second one.

We ordered *six 30-*gallon drums of solvent for the project.

The supplier shipped us *600 thirty-*gallon drums by mistake.

Identify any miswriting of numbers in the following sentences and rewrite these numbers correctly:

1. The supermarket ordered five hundred five-pound bags of sugar.
2. The Whitney Museum of American Art is at Nine Hundred and Forty-Five Madison Avenue, New York City.
3. The holes that the automated system drilled in the brackets were off by two hundredths of an inch.
4. The first memo warning the company of the problem was dated May fifteenth, 1993.
5. There will be a meeting at three-thirty P.M., May fifth, to discuss our new marketing plan.
6. Our local library has 658 CDs, 132 videocassettes, and sixty-three computer programs.
7. 8,000 people usually subscribe to our symphony orchestra series.
8. There are a number of serious editing errors on page thirty-nine of the report.
9. Over the last year, sales have increased by twenty-three percent.
10. We found that only 3 computers needed to be upgraded.

EXERCISE ANSWERS

1. 500 five-pound bags of sugar.
2. 945 Madison Avenue, New York City.
3. .02 inch.
4. May 15, 1993.
5. 3:30 P.M.
6. 63 computer programs.
7. Eight thousand people
8. page 39 of the report.
9. 23 percent.
10. only three computers

ital

Italics

Italics are used for the titles of longer publications, the names of vehicles and vessels, foreign words and phrases, and expressions singled out for special attention. Use underlining to represent italics when hand writing or typing papers.

Titles of Longer Publications and Artistic Works These items may include the following:

books	record albums	long musical works and poems
magazines	paintings	plays
newspapers	movies	sculptures

As noted on page 699, quotation marks are used for the titles of articles, short stories, short poems, one-act plays, and other brief pieces of writing.

Last night I finished F. Scott Fitzgerald's *The Great Gatsby* and read two articles in *The New Yorker.* (book, magazine)

Michelangelo's *David* is surely one of the world's greatest sculptures. (sculpture)

The *Detroit Free Press* had praise for the revival of Tennessee Williams's play *The Glass Menagerie.* (newspaper, play)

Stephen Vincent Benét's poem *John Brown's Body* won a Pulitzer Prize in 1929. (book-length poem)

Do not use italics when naming the Bible and its parts or other religious works such as the Torah and Koran.

Joanna's favorite book of the Bible is the Book of Ecclesiastes, part of the Old Testament.

Names of Vehicles and Vessels   Names of particular airplanes, ships, trains, and spacecraft are italicized.

The plane in which Charles Lindbergh flew over the Atlantic Ocean was named *The Spirit of St. Louis.*

Foreign Expressions   Use italics to identify foreign words and phrases that have not yet made their way into the English language.

The writer has a terribly pessimistic *weltanschauung.* (philosophy of life)

This season, long skirts are the *dernier cri.* (the latest thing)

When such expressions become completely assimilated, the italics are dropped. Most dictionaries use an asterisk (*), a dagger (†), or other symbol to identify expressions that need italicizing.

Expressions Singled Out for Special Attention   These include words, letters, numerals, and symbols.

The Greek letter *pi* is written π.

I can't tell whether this letter is meant to be an *a* or an *o* or this number a *7* or a *9.*

In England, the word *lorry* means truck.

As noted on pages 700–701, quotation marks sometimes replace italics for this purpose.

Connected Discourse Exercise

Use hyphens, capitalization, abbreviations, numbers, and italics properly in the following passage:

Because I can speak Russian fluently, I was recruited by the central intelligence while still at Boston college. I suspected that it was professor Hogsbottom, a Political Science teacher, who had suggested that they consider me. After all, he had been a General during World War II and still had connections with the intelligence community. It turned out that my brother in law was responsible; he was an ex FBI agent. Soon I was an american spy

EXERCISE ANSWERS
Because I can speak Russian fluently, I was recruited by the CIA while still at Boston College. I suspected that it was Professor Hogsbottom, a political science teacher, who had suggested that they consider me. After all, he had been a general during World War II and still had connections with the intelligence community. It turned out that my brother-in-law was responsible: He was an ex-FBI agent. Soon I was an American spy located, of all places, in England. Who would suspect that we had to spy on the English? For three years I posed as a British aristocrat who was a general *bon vivant* and man-about-town. I went by the alias of Mr. Henry Higgins, Jr. Everyone, of course, wanted to know if I had seen *My Fair Lady.* Personally I thought the whole thing was a Monty Python type of joke until I found a position in the

located, of all places, in England. Who would suspect that we had to spy on the english? For 3 years I posed as a british aristocrat who was a general bon vivant and man about town. I went by the alias of Mister Henry Higgins, Junior. Everyone, of course, wanted to know if I had seen My Fair Lady. Personally I thought the whole thing was a monty python type of joke until I found a position in the british secret service. Who could have believed the british kept so many secrets from their american allies? For twenty one years I spied on the british without anyone suspecting that I was an all american boy. I did find out recently, however, that because of my fluent russian they had suspected me of being a russian spy and had been feeding me false information all along.

British secret service. Who could have believed the British kept so many secrets from their American allies? For twenty-one years I spied on the British without anyone suspecting that I was an all-American boy. I did find out recently, however, that because of my fluent Russian they had suspected me of being a Russian spy and had been feeding me false information all along.

EXERCISE

Supply italics wherever they are necessary.

1. The British often use the word lift to refer to an elevator.
2. Arthur Miller's Death of a Salesman is considered by many critics to be the great American tragedy.
3. Linguists consider b to be voiced and p to be unvoiced.
4. Given the quality of the movie version, it takes a considerable amount of courage to produce a stage version of the musical West Side Story.
5. The delight many people take in the discomfort of characters in situation comedies suggests that all of us may be subject to some schadenfreude.
6. The USS Enterprise was the first nuclear aircraft carrier.
7. I have always fantasized about taking a ride on the Orient Express, which figured so prominently in a mystery by Agatha Christie.
8. There are few artistic statements against war that are stronger than Picasso's Guernica.
9. There has been a very conscious effort to make Scientific American available to a larger segment of the reading public.
10. It is a shame that so few students read Dostoevsky's Crime and Punishment as part of their education.

ital

EXERCISE ANSWERS
1. *lift*
2. *Death of a Salesman*
3. *b, p*
4. *West Side Story*
5. *schadenfreude*
6. *Enterprise*
7. *Orient Express*
8. *Guernica*
9. *Scientific American*
10. *Crime and Punishment*

Spelling

1. Some students rarely commit spelling errors, while others misspell the most common words. It is essential to teach weaker spellers how they can improve. One way to help them is to make them responsible for their misspelled words, for example, by deducting points for errors. To regain the lost points, a student should have to turn in a sheet listing each misspelled word, its correct spelling, the likely reason for its misspelling, and some kind of mnemonic device to help him or her remember the correct spelling. The student should also be held responsible for spelling the word correctly in the future.

2. It is helpful to observe the pattern of a weak speller's errors. Once you begin to grasp the pattern, you can be more effective in helping. Here are some common kinds of errors:
(a) Errors of haste.

sp

"Why the big deal about accurate spelling?"

"Does it really make that much difference if I have an *i* and an *e* turned around or if I omit a letter when spelling a word?"

Students frequently question the importance of proper spelling. Perhaps the answer is suggested by the following sentence, taken from a student essay:

I spent over seven hours *studing* one day last week.

The omission of a *y* in *studing* changes the person from one who is studious to one who is a dreamer. Not only does inaccurate spelling smack of carelessness, but also it sometimes drastically alters meaning.

Although there is no sure-fire way of becoming a good speller, you can minimize the difficulties by learning basic spelling rules, applying helpful spelling tips, and memorizing the proper spelling of troublesome words.

Spelling Rules

The following four rules should ease spelling pains.

Rule 1   If a word has the double vowels* *ie* or *ei* and the combination has a long *e* sound (as in *me*), use *ie* except after *c*. If the combination has an *a* sound, use *ei*.

ie (as long *e*)	*ei* after *c*	*ei* (as long *a*)
relieve	deceive	freight
belief	receive	neighbor
grieve	receipt	reign
piece	perceive	weigh

The main exceptions to this rule include *either, financier, leisure, neither, seize, species,* and *weird.*

Rule 2   If a one-syllable word (example: *sin*) ends in a single consonant preceded by a single vowel, double the consonant before adding a suffix

---

*The vowels are *a, e, i, o,* and *u.* The consonants are the remaining letters of the alphabet.

"Dear Mom. Wud you belive I lost my job at the offise today? I gess sumwun thair doesnt like me."

From Recess Time, The Best Cartoons from The Kappan, edited by Kristin Herzog. ©1983 Bardulf Ueland. Reprinted by permission of the Estate of Bardulf Ueland.

(see page 702) that starts with a vowel. Apply the same rule with a word of two or more syllables (example: *admit*) if the final syllable is accented and ends with a single consonant preceded by a vowel.

Words with Single Syllables	Words with Two or More Syllables
rig—rigged	admit—admittance
sin—sinned	control—controller
stop—stopping	equip—equipped

If the accent does not fall on the last syllable, do not double the final consonant.

audit—audited	chatter—chattered
counsel—counselor	simmer—simmering

Rule 3   If a word ends in *y* preceded by a single consonant, change the *y* to an *i* unless you are adding the suffix *-ing*.

y changed to *i*	*y* retained
beauty—beautiful	copy—copying
fury—furious	defy—defying
easy—easily	dry—drying
vary—various	vary—varying

Some students have learned phonics too well and attempt to spell words as they sound. When they do, the same letter group may be represented differently in the same paper. For example, the words *though, through,* and *tough* may be written as "tho," "throo," and "tuff." In such cases, students need to be familiarized with the morphological features of English so that they can understand the "meaningful" regularities among words. (c) Misspellings resulting from poor pronunciation. Students who say "bafroom" may not hear the *th* in *bathroom*. If you see errors of this sort, help students by teaching them the right pronunciation. (d) Confusion of homophones. Some students consistently confuse words like *know* and *no*. When this is the source of the misspelling, bring the homophones to the student's attention. (e) Difficulty in seeing the structure of words. Some students blur syllables or even omit some. As a result, "parallel" becomes "parall." Such students must first learn how to

sp

sound out the word, then how to break it into its syllables. (f) Poor visual memory. Some students are poor readers and have little visual memory. Have such students copy the correctly spelled word in different colored ink, break it into its key parts, and compare the copy to the original. Some students even benefit from writing a word in the air with their hands while they say it.

3. Mina Shaughnessy's book *Errors and Expectations* has such important suggestions about approaching extremely weak spellers that they are worth repeating here: (a) "Assume at the outset that the misspellings of young adults can be brought under control" (175). (b) "Begin by teaching the student to observe himself as a speller" (175). (c) "Before attempting to work on

individual errors, make certain the student understands certain terms and operations" (177). (d) "If possible start to work on misspellings that can be controlled by the application of rules" (177). (e) "Develop an awareness of the main discrepancies between the student's pronunciation of words and the models of pronunciation upon which the spelling system is based" (179). (f) "Develop an awareness of the ways in which pronunciation

sp

helps the speller" (179). (g) "Develop the student's ability to discriminate among graphemic options" (181). (h) "Teach the use of the dictionary" (185).

4. The term *dyslexia* should be reserved for a very specific neurological condition that causes students to have problems processing what they hear

Rule 4 If a word ends in a silent *e*, the *e* is usually dropped when a suffix starting with a vowel is added.

blue—bluish   fame—famous
dense—density   grieve—grievous

In a few cases, the *e* is retained to avoid pronunciation difficulties or confusion with other words.

dye—dyeing (not dying)   singe—singeing (not singing)
shoe—shoeing (not shoing)

The *e* is also retained when it is preceded by a soft *c* sound (pronounced like the letter *s*) or a soft *g* sound (pronounced like the letter *j*) and the suffix being added starts with an *a* or an *o*.

peace—peaceable   courage—courageous
change—changeable   manage—manageable

Helpful Spelling Tips

Here are some tips that can further improve your spelling:

1. Examine each problem word carefully, especially prefixes (*au*dience, *au*dible), suffixes (superintend*ent*, descend*ant*), and double consonants (sate*ll*ite, roo*mm*ate, and co*ll*apsible).

2. Sound out each syllable carefully, noting its pronunciation. Words like *height, governor,* and *candidate* are often misspelled because of improper pronunciation.

3. Make a list of your problem words and review them periodically. Concentrate on each syllable and any unusual features (ar*c*tic, ambig*uous*).

4. Use any crutches that will help: there is *gain* in *bargain;* to *breakfast* is to *break a fast;* a disease causes *dis-ease.*

5. When you copy anything from the blackboard or a textbook, copy it carefully. Writing a word correctly helps you to spell it correctly the next time.

6. Buy a good collegiate dictionary and look up the words you don't know how to spell. (See pages 115–116 for more information on dictionaries.)

7. If you have a word processor that has a spell checker, use it. But a word of caution: Don't rely exclusively on this tool. Your spell checker may not distinguish between *to* and *too, their* and *there,* and similar sound-alike words. The ultimate spell checker is you.

List of Troublesome Words

Students frequently misspell the words in the following list. Study these words carefully until the correct spelling becomes automatic. Then have a friend read them to you while you write them down. Tag the ones you misspell and whenever you revise a paper, check especially for these words.

abandoned	allotted	barbiturate	commit
abbreviate	allowed	beautiful	commitment
absence	all right	beggar	committed
absorb	already	believe	committee
absorption	although	beneficial	committing
absurd	altogether	benefit	comparatively
academy	always	benefited	competent
accelerate	amateur	biscuit	competition
accept	ambiguous	boundary	concede
access	among	bourgeois	conceive
accessible	analysis (analyses)	breathe	condemn
accident	analyze	Britain	condescend
accidentally	anonymous	bulletin	confident
accommodate	anxiety	bureau	congratulations
accomplish	apartment	bureaucracy	connoisseur
accumulate	apparent	business	conqueror
accustom	appearance	cafeteria	conscience
achieve	appreciate	calendar	conscientious
achievement	appropriate	camouflage	conscious
acknowledge	architecture	campaign	consistency
acknowledgment	arctic	candidate	consistent
acquaintance	argue	carburetor	conspicuous
acquire	arguing	carriage	contemptible
acquit	argument	carrying	continuous
acquitted	arithmetic	casual	controversy
address	ascent	category	convenience
advice	assassin	causal	convenient
advise	assent	ceiling	coolly
aerial	assistance	cellar	cooperate
aggravate	assistant	cemetery	corollary
aggravated	athlete	changeable	corps
aggression	athletics	changing	corpse
aggressive	attempt	characteristic	correlate
aging	attendance	chauffeur	counterfeit
alcohol	average	chief	courteous
allege	bachelor	colloquial	criticism
alleviate	balance	colonel	criticize
alley(s)	balloon	column	cruelty
allot	barbarous	commission	curiosity

and see. Usually a student with dyslexia will show pronounced reversals of letters or even confuse letters like *d's* and *b's*. Some students will wrongly identify themselves as dyslexic to explain their spelling problems. When a student seems to have excessive problems mastering spelling and you suspect a learning difficulty, refer him or her to your school's testing service or office of student developmental services. Even students with mild dyslexia can be helped. A student's learning disability should not be a call to surrender but rather a challenge to be overcome.

sp

curriculum	enthusiastic	heroes	manual
dealt	environment	hindrance	marriage
deceit	equal	hygiene	mathematics
deceive	equip	hypocrisy	mattress
decent	equipment	hysterical	meant
decision	equipped	illiterate	medicine
defendant	equivalent	illogical	medieval
defense	especially	illusion	mediocre
definite	exaggerate	immediate	melancholy
definitely	exceed	implement	miniature
dependent	excellent	impromptu	minute
descendant	except	inadequate	miscellaneous
descent	excerpt	incident	mischievous
describe	excess	incidentally	misspell
description	excitement	independent	modifies
desert	exercise	indict	modify
desirable	existence	indispensable	modifying
despair	experience	individual	moral
desperate	extraordinary	inevitable	morale
dessert	extremely	infinitely	mortgage
develop	fallacy	ingenious	mosquitoes
development	familiar	ingenuous	muscle
difference	fascinate	innocent	mysterious
dilemma	fascist	intelligent	necessary
disappear	February	interest	neither
disastrous	fiery	interfere	nevertheless
discernible	finally	irresistible	niece
disciple	financier	irresponsible	noticeable
discipline	foreign	jeopardy	obedience
discussion	foreword	judgment	occasion
disease	forfeit	judicial	occasionally
dissatisfied	forward	knowledge	occur
dissipate	friend	knowledgeable	occurred
dominant	fulfill	laboratory	occurrence
drunkenness	gaiety	legitimate	occurring
echoes	gases	leisure	official
ecstasy	gauge or gage	library	omission
efficiency	genius	license	omit
efficient	genuine	lightning	omitted
eighth	government	loneliness	omitting
eligible	grammar	loose	opinion
eliminate	guarantee	lose	opponent
embarrass	guard	magnificent	opportunity
emphasis	handkerchief	maintain	optimistic
employee	harass	maintenance	original
engineer	height	maneuver	outrageous

pamphlet
parallel
paralysis
parliament
particularly
pastime
patent
peaceable
perceive
perfectible
perform
permanent
permissible
perseverance
persuade
physical
physician
picnic
picnicked
playwright
pleasant
pleasurable
politician
possess
possession
possible
potatoes
practice
precede
precedent
precious
predominant
preference
preferred
prejudice
preparation
privilege
probably
procedure
proceed
professor
prominent
pronounce
pronunciation
propaganda
propagate

propeller
prophecy
prophesy
prostate
prostrate
protein
psychiatry
psychology
pursue
pursuit
quantity
questionnaire
quiet
quite
quiz
quizzes
realize
receipt
receive
recipe
recognizable
recommend
refer
reference
referring
reign
relevant
relieve
religious
remembrance
reminisce
reminiscence
reminiscent
rendezvous
repellent
repentance
repetition
representative
resemblance
resistance
restaurant
rhetoric
rhyme
rhythm
roommate
sacrifice

sacrilege
sacrilegious
safety
salary
sandwich
scarcely
scene
scenic
schedule
science
secretary
seize
sensible
separate
sergeant
severely
siege
similar
simultaneous
sincerely
skeptical
skiing
skillful
skis
society
sophomore
source
specifically
specimen
sponsor
spontaneous
statistics
steely
strategy
studying
subtle
subtlety
subtly
succeed
success
successful
succinct
suffrage
superintendent
supersede
suppose

suppress
surprise
syllable
symmetry
sympathize
synonym
synonymous
tangible
tariff
technical
technique
temperament
temperature
temporary
tenant
tendency
thorough
thought
through
traffic
trafficking
tragedy
tranquillity or
  tranquility
transcendent
transcendental
transfer
transferred
transferring
translate
tries
truly
twelfth
tyrannical
tyranny
unanimous
unconscious
undoubtedly
unmistakable
unnecessary
until
unwieldy
urban
urbane
usage
useful

sp

using	vengeance	Wednesday	worshiped or
usual	victorious	weird	worshipped
usually	village	whether	wreak
vacancy	villain	whole	wreck
vacillate	waive	wholly	writing
vacuum	warrant	wield	written
valuable	warring	wintry	yield
vegetable	weather	wiry	

Glossary of Word Usage

The English language has many words and expressions that confuse writers and thereby lessen the precision and effectiveness of their writing. These troublesome items include the following:

Word pairs that sound alike or almost alike but are spelled differently and have different meanings

Word pairs that do not sound alike but still are often confused

Words or phrases that are unacceptable in formal writing

The following glossary identifies the most common of these troublemakers. Familiarize yourself with its contents. Then consult it as you revise your writing if you have even the slightest doubt about the proper use of a word, phrase, or expression.

a, an Use *a* with words beginning with a consonant sound (even if the first written letter is a vowel); use *an* with words beginning with a vowel or a vowel sound.

a brush, *a* student, *a* wheel, *a* risky situation, *a* once-in-a-lifetime opportunity

an architect, *an* apple, *an* unworthy participant, *an* interesting proposal, *an* honest politician

accept, except *Accept* is a verb meaning "to receive" or "to approve." *Except* is used as a verb or a preposition. As a verb, *except* means "to take out, exclude, or omit." As a preposition, it means "excluding," "other than," or "but not."

She *accepted* the bouquet of flowers.

Linda excepted Sally from the list of guests. (verb)

All of Linda's friends *except* Sally came to the party. (preposition)

access, excess *Access* is a noun meaning "means or right to enter, approach, or use." In the computer field it is a verb meaning "gain entrance to." *Excess* is an adjective meaning "too much; more than needed; lack of moderation."

I have *access* to a summer cottage this weekend.

The code permits users to *access* the computer.

The airline booked an *excess* number of passengers on that flight.

adapt, adopt To *adapt* is "to adjust," often by modification. To *adopt* is "to take as one's own."

He *adapted* to the higher elevations of the Rocky Mountains.

She *adopted* the new doctrine expounded by the prophet.

Basic Writing 1 (1977): 1–20. Argues that instruction in formal grammar does little to improve student writing and that it is more effective to place our instruction within the context of student writing.

Dobie, A. B. "Orthographical Theory and Practice, or How to Teach Spelling." *Journal of Basic Writing* 5 (1986): 41–48. Shows how the differences between orthography and pronunciation can result in very specific practices for the teaching of spelling.

Kolln, M. "Closing the Books on Alchemy." *College Composition and Communication* 32 (1981): 139–51. Argues that we should still teach grammar to ensure a shared vocabulary and conceptual framework.

Kroll, B., and J. Schafer. "Error Analysis and the Teaching of Composition." *College Composition and Communication* 29 (1978): 242–48. Explains how we can effectively observe the pattern in student errors, determine the source of those errors, and then provide the most effective instruction.

Shaughnessy, M. P. *Errors and Expectations: A Guide for the Teacher of Basic Writing.* New York: Oxford UP, 1977. If there is any one work

adverse, averse   *Adverse* is an adjective meaning "unfavorable." *Averse* is an adjective meaning "disinclined" or "feeling distaste for."

Adverse circumstances caused the ceremony to be postponed.

Martha was *averse* to naming all the guilty children.

advice, advise   *Advice* is a noun meaning "a recommendation about how to deal with a situation or problem." *Advise* is a verb meaning "to recommend or warn."

The young man followed his sister's *advice.*

Mr. Smith *advised* John to buy 10,000 shares of the stock.

affect, effect   Although both words may function as nouns and verbs, usually *affect* is a verb and *effect* is a noun. The verb *affect* means "to influence, cause a change in, or arouse the emotions of." The noun *affect* is a technical term in psychology and refers to feeling. The noun *effect* means "result or outcome." The verb *effect* means "to bring about or achieve."

His speech *affected* me greatly. (verb)

The *effect* of the announcement was felt immediately. (noun)

The doctor was soon able to *effect* a cure. (verb)

aggravate   *Aggravate* is a verb meaning "to intensify or make worse" an existing situation. The use of *aggravate* to mean "annoy" or "anger" is colloquial.

Colloquial	Susan's behavior at the dance really *aggravated* me.
Standard	Marcy's interference only *aggravated* the conflict between Bill and Nadine.

ain't   This nonstandard term for *isn't, aren't, hasn't,* or *haven't* is unacceptable in college writing.

all ready, already   *All ready* means "completely prepared" or "everyone is ready." *Already* means "previously, even now, even then."

The scouts are *all ready* for the camp out.

When we arrived we found he had *already* gone.

The report is *already* a week overdue.

all right, alright   *Alright* is a nonstandard spelling of *all right* and is not acceptable in college writing.

all together, altogether   *All together* means "all in one place" or "in unison." *Altogether* is an adverb meaning "completely, entirely."

The family was *all together* at the wedding.

All together, men, push!

Mr. Doe is *altogether* at fault for writing the letter.

allusion, delusion, illusion   An *allusion* is an indirect reference. A *delusion* is a mistaken belief, often part of a psychological condition. An *illusion* is a deceptive appearance presented to the sight or created by the imagination.

In his sermon, the minister made many *allusions* to the New Testament.

He suffers from the *delusion* that he is a millionaire.

They wore makeup to give the *illusion* of beauty.

a lot, alot   *Alot* is an erroneous spelling of the two words *a lot*. The phrase *a lot* is usually colloquial; in formal writing replace it with "many."

already   See *all ready, already.*

alright   See *all right, alright.*

alternately, alternatively   *Alternately* means "occurring by turns, one after the other." *Alternatively* means "providing a choice between two items."

> The U.S. flag has seven red and six white stripes, arranged *alternately.*

> Highway 44 offers the most direct route to Junction City. *Alternatively,* Highway 88 is much more scenic.

altogether   See *all together, altogether.*

among,   between   Use *between* when referring to two things and *among* when referring to more than two.

> He divided the candy *between* Allan and Stephanie.

> He divided the candy *among* the five children.

amoral, immoral   *Amoral* means "neither moral nor immoral; morally neutral." *Immoral* means "contrary to the moral code."

> The movie, which takes no clear position on the behavior it depicts, seems curiously *amoral.*

> Murder is an *immoral* act.

amount, number   *Amount* refers to total quantities, things in bulk, or weight. *Number* refers to countable things. Never use *amount* when referring to people.

> Cassandra inherited a large *amount* of money.

> Cassandra now has a large *number* of friends.

an, a   See *a, an.*

and/or   Although often used in commercial and legal documents, this combination should be avoided in other writing.

angry, mad   *Mad* means "insane," although it is often used colloquially to mean "annoyed" or "angry." To be precise, use *mad* only to mean insane.

> *Colloquial*   I was *mad* at Debbie.

> *Standard*   I was *angry* with Debbie.

any, any other   Do not use *any* when you mean *any other.* Using *any* in the following example would mean that Theresa is more qualified than herself:

> Theresa is more qualified than *any other* candidate.

anyone, any one   *Anyone* means "any person." *Any one* means "any single person or thing."

> I can whip *anyone* in this room.

> I saw three movies last week but didn't like *any one* of them.

appraise, apprise   *Appraise* means "to determine the value of something." *Apprise* means "to notify" or "to tell."

that today's writing teacher must read, this is it. Shaughnessy provides a careful analysis of the reasons weaker students have problems with grammar, punctuation, spelling, and vocabulary and offers very specific, carefully considered, and tested teaching methods.

Williams, J. M. *Style: Ten Lessons in Clarity and Grace.* 2nd ed. Glenview, IL: Scott, 1985. Helps to connect issues of grammar and error to issues of style.

usage

The jeweler *appraised* the gold brooch at $1,500.

Having been *apprised* of the situation, the family priest was able to reconcile the parents and the children.

apt, liable, likely   Both *apt* and *liable* express a tendency or inclination. *Liable* suggests something unpleasant or likely to result in legal action. It should be used only when the event may have unpleasant consequences.

We are *liable* to miss the train.

My lawyer said that I was *liable* for the damage my car had caused.

If the probable consequences are not unpleasant, *apt* is the better word.

I am *apt* to buy books if we go to the shopping center.

Likely merely implies strong probability.

Sandra is *likely* to pass this course without difficulty.

around   *Around* is colloquial use for "approximately" or "about."

Colloquial	She arrived *around* 10:00 P.M. The blouse cost *around* $15.
Standard	She arrived at *approximately* 10:00 P.M. The blouse cost *about* $15.

as   *As* is frequently used as a weak substitute for *because, since, when,* and *while.*

Weak	She ran out of the house *as* it was on fire.
Better	She ran out of the house *because* it was on fire.

As should not be used in place of *whether* or *that.*

Nonstandard	I don't know *as* I like her.
Standard	I don't know *that* I like her. I don't know *whether* I like her.

as, like   *As* may be used as a conjunction that introduces an adverb clause, but *like* should not be used this way.

Unacceptable	*Like* my father always said, "You can fool some of the people all of the time."
Standard	*As* my father always said, "You can fool some of the people all of the time."

Like may, however, be used as a preposition.

In times *like* this, it's hard not to despair.

Any woman *like* Sally can expect a successful career in business.

assure, ensure, insure   To *assure* is "to make safe from risk, to guarantee" or "to convince." *Ensure* and *insure* can be variant spellings meaning "to make certain." *Insure,* however, is now generally associated with the business of insurance.

The counselor tried to *assure* the students that they had made a wise choice.

The captain *assured* them that they would be rescued.

The father, wanting to *ensure* his son's college education, applied for a federally *insured* loan.

usage

averse   See *adverse, averse*.

awful, awfully   In everyday speech, *awful* is used to describe things disagreeable or objectionable: "an *awful* movie," "an *awful* character." *Awfully* is used colloquially as an intensifier: "*awfully* nice," "*awfully* bad." Unless they are used to mean "solemnly impressive," however, both words should be avoided in formal writing.

The *awful* majesty of the cathedral silenced the chattering tourists.

awhile, a while   *A while*, consisting of the noun *while* and the article *a*, means "a period of time." *Awhile* is an adverb meaning "for a short time."

Dinner will be served in *a while*.

Sit *awhile* and tell me the latest gossip.

bad, badly   *Bad* is an adjective. *Badly* is an adverb. *Badly* is colloquial when used to mean "very much."

Unacceptable	She feels *badly* about her mistake.
	Tom behaved *bad* at the circus.
Colloquial	I want a new car *badly*.
Standard	She feels *bad* about her mistake. (adjective as subject complement)
	Tom behaved *badly* at the circus. (adverb)
	I want a new car *very much*.

being as, being that   When used as substitutes for *because* or *since*, these expressions are nonstandard.

Nonstandard	*Being that* I was the first in line, I was able to purchase choice tickets.
Standard	*Because* I was first in line, I was able to purchase choice tickets.

beside, besides   Both words are prepositions, but they have different meanings. *Beside* means "at the side of," and *besides* means "in addition to."

Sheila and Bill sat *beside* the trailer to eat their lunch.

Besides Harvey, Seymour is coming to dinner.

between   See *among, between*.

breath, breathe   *Breath* is a noun and *breathe* is its verb counterpart.

Nicole stepped outside the stuffy cabin for a *breath* of fresh air.

The cabin was so stuffy that Nicole could hardly *breathe*.

broke   *Broke*, when used to mean "without money," is colloquial.

Colloquial	Because Shelley was *broke*, she had to miss the movie.
Standard	Because Shelley *had no money*, she had to miss the movie.

can, may   *Can* refers both to permission and to the ability to do something, while *may* refers to permission only.

I think I *can* pass the exam on Friday. (ability)

My mother says I *can* go to the movies. (permission)

May I take the test next Monday? (permission)

When used to denote permission, *can* lends a less formal air to writing than does *may*.

cannot, can not   The use of *cannot* is preferred unless the writer wishes to italicize the *not* for emphasis.

> You *cannot* expect a raise this year.

> No, you can *not* expect a raise this year.

can't hardly   This nonstandard form for *cannot, can't,* or *can hardly* is unacceptable in college writing.

can't help but   In college writing, this colloquial phrase should be revised to the simpler *I can't help* or *I cannot help.*

> *Colloquial*   I *can't help but* wish that I were going to the concert.

> *Standard*   I *can't help* wishing that I were going to the concert.

capital, capitol   *Capital* means "a city that serves as a seat of government." *Capitol* means "a building in which a state legislature meets" or "the building in which Congress meets."

> Dover is the *capital* of Delaware.

> The *capitol* in Dover is popular with visitors.

Capital can also refer to wealth or assets, to an offense punishable by death, or to something excellent or first-rate.

> My *capital* consists entirely of stocks and bonds.

> Murder is a *capital* crime in this state.

> That's a *capital* suggestion!

censor, censure   To *censor* is "to judge"—literature, movies, letters, and the like—and to decide what material is unfit to be read or seen. To *censure* is "to judge harshly" or "find fault with."

> The warden *censored* all the prisoners' mail.

> The judge *censured* Clyde's criminal behavior.

childish, childlike   Both of these terms mean "like a child." *Childish*, however, has a negative connotation.

> He is fifty-two years old, but he behaves in a *childish* manner.

> Jon's face has a *childlike* quality that everyone likes immediately.

cite, sight, site   *Cite* means "to mention or quote as an example," *sight* means "to see" or "a view," and *site* means "a location."

> Cheryl *cited* Abraham Lincoln's Emancipation Proclamation in her talk.

> He was able to *sight* the enemy destroyers through the periscope.

> The building *site* is a woody area south of town.

climactic, climatic   *Climactic* is an adjective that means "of, being, or relating to a climax." *Climatic* is an adjective meaning "of or relating to a climate."

> Riding the roller coaster was the *climactic* event of Alice's day.

> The *climatic* features of Arizona are desirable to many people.

complement, compliment   Both words can act as nouns or verbs. As a noun, *complement* means "something that completes or makes up the whole." As a verb, it means "to complete or perfect." As a noun, *compliment* means "a flattering or praising remark." As a verb, it means "to flatter or praise."

> A *complement* of navy personnel boarded the foreign freighter. (noun)

> This fruit will *complement* the meal nicely. (verb)

> Scott paid Sara Jane a lovely *compliment* at the time of her graduation. (noun)

> Mother *complimented* me for cleaning my room. (verb)

conscience, conscious   *Conscience* refers to the sense of moral right or wrong. *Conscious* refers to the awareness of one's feelings or thoughts.

> Edgar's *conscience* forced him to return the money.

> Basil was not *conscious* of his angry feelings.

Do not confuse *conscious* with *aware;* although these words are similar in meaning, one is *conscious* of feelings or actions but *aware* of events.

contemptible, contemptuous   *Contemptible* means "deserving of contempt." *Contemptuous* means "displaying contempt."

> Peter's drunkenness is *contemptible.*

> Mary is *contemptuous* of Peter's drunkenness.

continual, continuous   *Continual* means "frequently or regularly repeated." *Continuous* means "uninterrupted."

> The telephone's *continual* ringing made the morning a nightmare.

> His wound caused him *continuous* pain for a week.

could have, could of   *Could of* is an unacceptable substitute for *could have* because a preposition cannot substitute for a verb.

> *Nonstandard*   I *could of* gone with my parents to Portugal.

> *Standard*   I *could have* gone with my parents to Portugal.

council, counsel   A *council* is a group of people that governs or advises. *Counsel* can be used as both a noun and a verb. The noun means "advice," and the verb means "to advise."

> The city *council* meets on the second Tuesday of every month.

> The lawyer's *counsel* was sound. (noun)

> The psychologist *counsels* many abused children. (verb)

couple   *Couple* denotes two things and should not be used to refer to more than that number.

criteria, criterion   *Criterion* is always singular; *criteria* always plural.

> The primary *criterion* for performing this job is manual dexterity.

> Manual dexterity is but one of many *criteria* on which you will be judged.

cute   *Cute*, an overused colloquialism, should be avoided; it has too many connotations to be used precisely in writing.

usage

data *Data* is the plural of *datum*. Although *data* is sometimes used with a singular verb, this use is considered incorrect.

> *Standard* These *data* are incorrect.
>
> *Unacceptable* This *data* is incorrect.

definite, very definite Since *definite* means "precise" or "unmistakable," *very definite* is repetitive. One really cannot be more definite than *definite*.

delusion See *allusion, delusion, illusion*.

desert, deserts, dessert *Desert* is land that is arid. With the accent on the last syllable, it is a verb meaning "to abandon." *Deserts* means "that which is deserved." *Dessert* is food served after dinner.

> The Sonoran *desert* is full of plant life.
>
> You'll get your just *deserts* if you *desert* me now.
>
> They had cheesecake for *dessert* every Thursday night.

device, devise *Device* is a noun meaning "a mechanical contrivance, gadget, or tool." *Devise* is a verb meaning "to plan or invent."

> This new *device* gives us better gas mileage.
>
> We must *devise* a new approach to our problem.

different from, different than *Different from* is preferred over *different than*.

> His ideas on marriage were *different from* those of his wife.

Different than is accepted, however, when a clause follows and the *from* construction would be wordy.

> *Acceptable* Susan looks *different than* she did last summer.
>
> *Wordy* Susan looks *different from* the way she looked last summer.

discreet, discrete To be *discreet* means to be "prudent, tactful, or careful of one's actions." *Discrete* means "distinct or separate."

> Jack was always *discreet* when he talked to his grandparents.
>
> When two atoms of hydrogen combine with one atom of oxygen, they are no longer *discrete* entities.

disinterested, uninterested A person who is *disinterested* is impartial or unbiased. A person who is *uninterested* is indifferent or not interested.

> We need a *disinterested* judge to settle the dispute.
>
> Joe is completely *uninterested* in sports.

don't This contraction for *do not* should never be used with singular subjects such as *he, she,* or *it*. Instead, use *doesn't*, the contraction for *does not*, with singular subjects.

> *Nonstandard* *Don't* he know how to spell?
> That mistake *don't* help your image.
> She *don't* think of anyone except herself.
>
> *Standard* *Doesn't* he know how to spell? That mistake *doesn't* help your image.
> She *doesn't* think of anyone except herself.

due to *Due to* has always been acceptable following a linking verb.

> Her success was *due to* hard work.

Purists, however, object to *due to* when it is used in other situations, especially in introductory phrases.

> *Due to* the many requests we have had, not everyone who wishes tickets will receive them.

In such cases, you may wish to recast the sentence.

> *Because* we have had so many requests, not everyone who wishes tickets will receive them.

effect See *affect, effect.*

e.g. This abbreviation, from the Latin *exempli gratia,* means "for example." Avoid using it except in comments in parentheses and in footnotes, and always follow it with a comma.

elicit, illicit *Elicit* is a verb that means "to draw forth." *Illicit* is an adjective meaning "not permitted."

> A good professor can always *elicit* responses from students.

> He was engaged in many types of *illicit* activities.

emigrate, immigrate When people *emigrate,* they move out of a country. When people *immigrate,* they move into a country.

> The family *emigrated* from Poland.

> Many Russians *immigrated* to America.

eminent, imminent *Eminent* means "prominent," whereas *imminent* means "about to happen."

> Niels Bohr was an *eminent* physicist.

> Our instruments show that an earthquake is *imminent.*

ensure See *assure, ensure, insure.*

enthused, enthusiastic *Enthused* is a colloquial word and should not be used in place of *enthusiastic.*

> *Colloquial*   John was *enthused* about the prospects for jobs in his hometown.

> *Standard*   John was *enthusiastic* about the prospects for jobs in his hometown.

especially, specially The term *especially* means "particularly, notably." *Specially* means "for a specific purpose."

> He is an *especially* talented pianist.

> He was *specially* chosen to represent his group.

et al. This expression, from the Latin *et alia,* means "and others," referring to people. Ordinarily, the abbreviation should be used only in footnotes and bibliographic entries.

etc. This abbreviation, from the Latin *et cetera,* means "and other things" and is used in reference to objects rather than people. It should be avoided except in comments in parentheses or in footnotes. It should never be preceded by *and.*

everyone, every one *Everyone* means "every person." *Every one* means "every particular person or thing."

usage

Everyone who wants to go to the ball game should let me know today.

If you carefully check *every one* of your paragraphs, you can improve your writing.

except See *accept, except.*

excess See *access, excess.*

explicit, implicit *Explicit* means "clearly expressed" or "straightforward." *Implicit* means "implied" or "understood without direct statement."

You must state your needs *explicitly* if you want them fulfilled.

When I took on the project, I made an *implicit* commitment to see it through.

extant, extent *Extant* is an adjective meaning "still existing." *Extent* is a noun meaning "scope, size, range, limit."

The dodo bird is no longer *extant.*

From Nevada to Colorado is the *extent* of my travels.

farther, further The traditional distinction is that *farther* refers to physical distance and *further* to distance in time. Only *further* should be used to mean "additional" or "additionally."

In the race for the Muscular Dystrophy Association, Janet ran *farther* than Cindy.

If you think *further* on the matter, I am certain we can reach an agreement.

Let me make one *further* point.

fewer, less *Fewer* refers to countable items. *Less* refers to quantity or degree.

Mrs. Smith has *fewer* dogs than cats.

There is *less* money in Joan's checking account than in Stanley's.

Jack was *less* ambitious in his later years.

Never use *less* to refer to people.

Nonstandard   *Less* people were there than I expected.

Standard   *Fewer* people were there than I expected.

flaunt, flout To *flaunt* is "to display in a showy way." To *flout* is "to express contempt" or "to show scorn."

Jay *flaunted* his handsome physique before all his friends.

Jerrold *flouted* the convention of dressing for dinner by arriving in tennis shoes.

formally, formerly *Formally* means "according to established forms, conventions, and rules; ceremoniously." *Formerly* means "in the past."

The ambassador *formally* greeted his dinner guests.

Formerly, smallpox was one of our most serious diseases.

funny *Funny* refers to something that is amusing. In college writing it should not be used to mean "odd" or "unusual."

Colloquial   I felt *funny* visiting my old fourth-grade classroom.

Standard   I felt *odd* visiting my old fourth-grade classroom.

usage

further See *farther, further.*

get *Get*, in any of its many colloquial senses, should not be used in writing.

> *Colloquial*   Her way of looking at a man really *gets* me.
> I'll *get* him if it's the last thing I do.
>
> *Standard*   Beth will *get* at least a *B* in this course.

good and Replace this colloquial phrase with *very*.

> *Colloquial*   She is *good and* tired of the cafeteria food.
>
> *Standard*   She is *very* tired of the cafeteria food.

good, well Do not mistakenly use *good* as an adverb when an adjective is required.

> *Unacceptable*   John did *good* on his first test.
>
> *Standard*   John is making *good* progress on his report.
> John is a *good* student.

Well can be used as an adjective meaning "in good health." Otherwise it should always be used as an adverb.

> Last week I had a bad cold, but now I am *well.* (adjective)

> John did *well* on his first test. (adverb)

got, gotten Both are acceptable past-participle forms of the verb *to get.*

had ought, hadn't ought Both are incorrect in formal writing. The correct forms are *ought* and *ought not.*

> I *ought* to start studying.

> You *ought not* to cut class again.

hanged, hung People may be *hanged.* Objects may be *hung.*

> The prisoner was *hanged* at noon.

> Mavis *hung* the picture in the dining room.

hisself, theirself, theirselves These are nonstandard forms of *himself* and *themselves.*

hopefully *Hopefully* means "in a hopeful manner." In informal speaking, it is used to mean "it is hoped" or "I hope," but this usage is not correct in formal writing. (Compare this with *carefully*, which means "in a careful manner"; no one uses *carefully* to mean "it is cared.")

> *Colloquial*   *Hopefully*, it will not rain during the class picnic.
>
> *Standard*   Sally walked *hopefully* into the boss's office to ask for a raise.

hung See *hanged, hung.*

i.e. This abbreviation, meaning "that is," comes from the Latin *id est.* Avoid using it except in comments in parentheses or footnotes, and always follow it with a comma.

usage

if, whether   *If* is used to introduce adverb clauses, where it means "assuming that."

If I finish my report on time, I'll attend the concert with you.

If and *whether* are often used interchangeably to introduce noun clauses that follow verbs such as *ask, say, doubt, know,* and *wonder.* In formal writing, however, *whether* is preferred.

> *Less Desirable*   I don't know *if* we'll be able to see the North Star tonight.

> *More Desirable*   I don't know *whether* we'll be able to see the North Star tonight.

illicit   See *elicit, illicit.*

illusion   See *allusion, delusion, illusion.*

immigrate   See *emigrate, immigrate.*

imminent   See *eminent, imminent.*

immoral   See *amoral, immoral.*

impact   Although *impact* is sometimes used in colloquial speech as a verb meaning "affect," this use is unacceptable in college writing.

> *Colloquial*   This new law will greatly *impact* political campaigning.

> *Standard*   This new law will greatly *affect* political campaigning.

implicit   See *explicit, implicit.*

imply, infer   To *imply* is "to indicate indirectly or give implication." To *infer* is "to conclude from facts, evidence, or indirect suggestions."

Jack *implied* that he wanted a divorce when he told his wife that all marriages come to an end.

Doris *inferred* that Jack wanted a divorce when he told her all marriages come to an end.

As these examples indicate, speakers and writers imply; listeners and readers infer.

incidence, incidents   *Incidents* are separate, countable experiences. *Incidence* refers to the rate at which something occurs.

Two *incidents* during childhood led to her reclusiveness.

The *incidence* of cancer in Japan is less than that in the United States.

incredible, incredulous   *Incredible* means "fantastic, unbelievable." *Incredulous* means "skeptical, disbelieving."

That she could run so fast seemed *incredible.*

Why is Bill wearing that *incredulous* look?

infer   See *imply, infer.*

ingenious, ingenuous   *Ingenious* means "clever and inventive." *Ingenuous* means "unsophisticated and innocent."

Sue presented an *ingenious* solution to our problem.

Mary's *ingenuous* comments amused everyone in the room.

in regards to   This is an incorrect use of *in regard to.*

insure   See *assure, ensure, insure.*

usage

inter-, intra-   *Inter-* means "between or among." *Intra-* means "within."

>From Chicago to Milwaukee is an *interstate* drive of approximately ninety miles.

>From San Francisco to Los Angeles is an *intrastate* drive of about 400 miles.

in terms of   Avoid this vague, overused expression.

> *Vague*   *In terms of* the price he is asking, I would not recommend purchasing Tom's car.

> *Preferred*   *Because* of the price he is asking, I would not recommend purchasing Tom's car.

irregardless   This nonstandard form of *regardless* includes the repetitive elements of *ir* and *less*, both of which mean "without."

is when, is where   *Is when* properly refers only to time.

> April *is when* our lilac bush blooms.

Is where properly refers only to place.

> Athens *is where* I met him.

The following sentences are *faulty* because of poorly phrased predicates which indicate that muckraking is a place and an abscess is a time:

> Muckraking *is where* someone investigates corporate or governmental abuses of power.

> An abscess *is when* some spot in body tissue fills with pus.

These sentences should be rephrased to eliminate the faulty assertion.

> Muckraking is the investigation of corporate or governmental abuses of power.

> An abscess occurs when some spot in body tissue fills with pus.

its, it's, its'   *Its* is a possessive pronoun. *It's* is a contraction of *it is* or *it has*.

> The gold chair was ruined, for someone had torn *its* seat.

> *It's* all I have to offer. (It is all I have to offer.)

> *It's* been a difficult day. (It has been a difficult day.)

> There is no correct use for *its'*.

kind of, sort of   In college writing, these are unacceptable substitutes for *somewhat*, *rather*, or *slightly*.

> *Colloquial*   She is *sort of* angry.
> I am *kind of* glad she went away.

> *Standard*   She is *somewhat* angry.
> I am *rather* glad she went away.

When *kind* and *sort* refer to a type, use them with singular nouns and verbs. With their plural forms, *kinds* and *sorts*, use plural nouns and verbs.

> *Unacceptable*   These *kind* of exams are difficult.

> *Standard*   This *kind* of exam is difficult.
> These *kinds* of exams are difficult.

usage

In such constructions, be certain that *kind of* or *sort of* is essential to your meaning. Otherwise, these phrases are unnecessary.

later, latter   *Later* refers to time; *latter* points out the second of two items. If more than two items are listed, use *last* to refer to the final one.

> He arrived at the party *later* than he was expected.

> Although Professors Stein and Patterson both lectured during the course, only the *latter* graded the final exam.

> Of my three cats, Sheba, Tiger, and Spot, only the *last* still needs the vaccination.

lay, lie   *Lie* means "to recline" or "to remain in a particular position." It never takes a direct object. *Lay* means "to place" and always takes a direct object. These verbs are often confused, in part because the past tense of *lie* is *lay*. (The past tense of *lay* is *laid*.)

> If I *lie* here a minute, I shall feel better.

> *Lay* the book on the table, please.

> As I *lay* asleep, a robber entered my apartment and stole my stereo.

> He *laid* a hand on her shoulder.

leave, let   *Leave* means "to depart," and *let* means "to allow." Never use *leave* when *let* is meant.

> *Nonstandard*   *Leave* him figure it out alone.

> *Standard*   *Let* him figure it out alone.

lend, loan   Traditionally, *loan* has been classed as a noun and *lend* as a verb. Today, the use of *loan* as a verb is so commonplace that it is accepted as colloquial English.

> *Standard*   I have applied for a *loan* so that I can buy a car. (noun)
>
> Please *lend* me your class notes. (verb)

> *Colloquial*   Please *loan* me your class notes. (verb)

less   See *fewer, less*.

let   See *leave, let*.

liable   See *apt, liable, likely*.

lie   See *lay, lie*.

like   See *as, like*.

likely   See *apt, liable, likely*.

literally   The word *literally* means "restricted to the exact, stated meaning." In formal writing, use *literally* only to designate factual statements.

> *Colloquial*   It was 65°, but I was *literally* freezing.

> *Standard*   Our dog was *literally* foaming at the mouth.
>
> It was 65°, but I was *very* cold.

loan   See *lend, loan*.

loose, loosen, lose   *Loose* can be used as both a verb and an adjective. As a verb, it means "untie or unfasten"; as an adjective, it means "unattached, unrestrained, not confined." *Loosen* is a verb meaning "undo or ease." *Lose* can be used only as a verb meaning "mislay, fail to win, unable to maintain."

> He *loosed* the restraints on the tiger. (verb)
>
> One should wear *loose* clothing when bowling. (adjective)
>
> When will Mrs. Brady *loosen* her control over young Tom? (verb)
>
> You would *lose* your nose if it were not attached to your face. (verb)

lots, lots of *Lots* and *lots of* colloquially mean "many, much, a large amount, or a great amount." Avoid these expressions in college writing.

> *Colloquial* I've spent *lots of* money in my life.
>
> *Standard* I have spent *much* money in my life.

mad See *angry, mad*.

many, much *Many* is used when referring to countable items; *much* is used when referring to an indefinite amount or to abstract concepts.

> There are *many* students in the biology class.
>
> How did Betty learn so *much* in so little time?

may See *can, may*.

may be, maybe *May be* is always used as a verb phrase. *Maybe* is an adverb meaning "perhaps."

> I *may be* chairman of the board by next June.
>
> *Maybe* we will see Jim at home.

medium, media *Medium* is the singular form of this word; *media* is the plural.

> Television is the *medium* I use most to get the news.
>
> The *media* have given extensive coverage to the brain transplant story.

much See *many, much*.

myself *Myself* is an intensive and a reflexive pronoun; it cannot substitute for a personal pronoun such as *I* or *me*.

> *Unacceptable* Four other students and *myself* founded the club.
>
> *Standard* Four other students and *I* founded the club.

nice *Nice* is an adjective suggesting delicacy, precision, subtlety, accuracy, the ability to discriminate, or the need for great care.

> These two seemingly identical proposals actually have several *nice* differences.
>
> This author's short stories have a *nice* touch.

Nice as a term of approval meaning "pleasing, enjoyable, attractive" is too generalized for use in college writing.

not hardly This is a nonstandard variation of *hardly* and is inappropriate in college writing.

number See *amount, number*.

usage

of between, of from, off of   Eliminate the unnecessary *of* from these colloquial phrases.

Colloquial	There was a crowd *of between* three and four thousand people at the contest. Get *off of* my property!
Standard	The crowd at the contest numbered *between* three and four thousand people. Get *off* my property!

on account of   When used to begin an adverb clause (see pages 648–649), this is a nonstandard substitute for *because*.

Nonstandard	The team was unable to practice *on account of* everyone was still upset over Tuesday's loss.
Standard	The team was unable to practice *because* everyone was still upset over Tuesday's loss.

When *on account of* precedes a single word or a phrase, it is considered colloquial.

Colloquial	The game was called *on account of* rain.

over, more than   *Over* should not be substituted for *more than;* if *more than* fits the phrase, use it.

Nonstandard	My brother likes ice cream *over* cake.
Standard	My brother likes ice cream *more than* cake.

passed, past   *Passed* is a verb designating activity that has taken place. *Past* is a noun or an adjective designating a former time.

The parade *passed* the reviewing stand at 10:30 A.M.

In the *past*, few people were concerned about the environmental effects of pesticides.

This *past* summer, I visited France.

patience, patients   *Patience* means "the ability to wait or endure without complaining." *Patients* are "people being treated by health-care professionals."

Thad's *patience* was exhausted by the slow service in the restaurant.

Following the tornado, doctors in the emergency room treated over sixty *patients*.

persecute, prosecute   *Persecute* means "to harass persistently because of race, religion, or belief." *Prosecute* means "to bring legal suit against."

Ethnic groups are often *persecuted*.

The company will *prosecute* anyone caught stealing.

personal, personnel   *Personal* is an adjective meaning "private, individual." *Personnel* are the people working in an organization.

Religious preference is a *personal* matter that you do not have to reveal during a job interview.

The *personnel* of the sanitation department will not be involved in the city workers' strike.

plenty   When used as an adverb, *plenty* should be replaced by *very*.

    Colloquial   That geology exam was *plenty* hard.

    Standard   That geology exam was *very* hard.

precede, proceed   *Precede* means "to go before or ahead of." *Proceed* means "to go on" or "to go forward."

The ritual of sharpening his pencils always *preceded* doing his homework.

The guide then said, "If you will *proceed,* I will show you the paintings by da Vinci."

predominant, predominate   *Predominant* is an adjective meaning "chief, main, most frequent." *Predominate* is a verb meaning "to have authority over others."

The *predominant* European influence on South American culture was Spanish.

In America, the will of the people should *predominate.*

presently   *Presently* means "soon" rather than "at the present time." *Currently* is correct for the second meaning.

I will be there *presently.*

Currently, I am otherwise engaged.

principal, principle   *Principal,* which means "chief," "most important," or "the amount of money on which interest is computed," is used as both a noun and an adjective. *Principle* is used only as a noun and means "truths, beliefs, or rules generally dealing with moral conduct."

The *principal* suspect in the case was arrested last Friday by the police.

The *principal* of Lewiston High School is Alison Cooperstein.

At this interest rate, your *principal* will double in ten years.

His *principles* are unconventional.

proceed   See *precede, proceed.*

prosecute   See *persecute, prosecute.*

quiet, quite   *Quiet* is an adjective meaning "silent, motionless, calm." *Quite* is an adverb meaning "entirely" or "to a considerable extent or degree."

The class grew *quiet* when the teacher walked in.

He is *quite* wrong.

The movie was *quite* good.

raise, rise   *Raise* is a transitive verb and therefore requires a direct object. *Rise,* its intransitive counterpart, takes no direct object.

We plan to *raise* horses on our new farm.

The temperature is expected to *rise* to 75°F tomorrow.

Raise can also be a noun meaning "an increase in pay."

Tammy received a 25 percent *raise* last week.

real, really   *Real* is an adjective; *really* is an adverb.

She had *real* plants decorating the bedroom.

usage

When used as an adverb, *real* is a colloquialism and should be replaced with *really.*

| Colloquial | We had a *real* good time at the party. |
| Standard | We had a *really* good time at the party. |

reason is because, reason is that   The *reason is because* is colloquial and unacceptable in formal writing; the *reason is that* is the correct usage.

| Colloquial | The *reason is because* I love her. |
| Standard | The *reason is that* I love her. |

respectfully, respectively   *Respectfully* means "with respect." *Respectively* indicates that the items in one series are related to those in a second series in the order given.

Joseph should treat his parents *respectfully.*

Tom, Anna, and Susan were assigned *Bleak House, Great Expectations,* and *Dombey and Son, respectively,* for their reports.

rise   See *raise, rise.*

sensual, sensuous   *Sensual* refers to bodily or sexual sensations. *Sensuous* refers to impressions experienced through the five senses.

Singles bars offered *sensual* pleasures without emotional commitments.

The Tivoli Garden provides many *sensuous* delights for visitors.

set, sit   Generally, *set* means "to place" and takes a direct object. *Sit* means "to be seated" and does not take a direct object.

Alice *set* her glass on the mantel.

May I *sit* in this chair?

When it refers to the sun, however, *set* is used without a direct object.

As the sun *set,* we turned homeward.

shall, will   *Shall* is used in first-person (see page 667) questions and in specialized forms of writing such as military orders and laws. Otherwise, *will* is generally used.

Shall we go to the movies tonight?

The company *shall* fall into formation at precisely twelve noon.

No family home *shall* be assessed at more than 50 percent of its actual value.

should have, should of   *Should of* is an unacceptable substitute for *should have* because a preposition cannot substitute for a verb.

| Nonstandard | I *should of* gone to the lake. |
| Standard | I *should have* gone to the lake. |

[sic]   This Latin word, always enclosed in brackets, follows quoted errors in grammar, spelling, or information. Inclusion of [sic] indicates that the error appeared in the original, which is being quoted exactly.

sight   See *cite, sight, site.*

sit   See *set, sit.*

usage

site   See *cite, sight, site.*

so   *So* is an acceptable coordinating conjunction but tends to add an informal effect to writing and should therefore be used sparingly. For example, "Tom said he was divorcing me, *so* I began to cry" would be more effective if restated as follows: "When Tom said he was divorcing me, I began to cry." Do not use *so* as a substitute for *extremely* or *very* except with adverb clauses beginning with *that.*

Colloquial	You are *so* careless in what you say.
	The discussion was *so* informative that I took many notes.
Standard	You are *very* careless in what you say.
	The discussion was *extremely* informative.

some   *Some* is colloquial and unacceptable in writing when used as an intensifier (We had *some* time of it!) or an adverb (He'll probably pout *some* after you leave).

sometime, some time, sometimes   *Sometime* means "at a future unspecified time," *some time* means "a span of time," and *sometimes* means "occasionally."

We should get together *sometime* and play bridge.

The weather has been hot for *some time.*

Sometimes I go to dinner with Ethel.

sort of   See *kind of, sort of.*

specially   See *especially, specially.*

stationary, stationery   *Stationary* means "not moving" or "fixed." *Stationery* means "paper for writing letters."

The circular part in the center must remain *stationary,* or the machine will not function.

Sue always writes on scented *stationery.*

such, such . . . that   The use of *such* when it means "very" or "extremely" is unacceptable unless it is followed by a *that* clause completing the thought.

Colloquial	They were *such* good cookies.
Standard	They were *such* good cookies *that* I asked Steve for his recipe.

suppose to, supposed to   *Suppose to* is the nonstandard form of *supposed to.* In speech, it is difficult to hear the final *d* on *supposed,* and one may say *suppose to* without being detected; however, the correct written form is always *supposed to.*

sure, surely   *Sure* is colloquial for the adverb *surely.*

Colloquial	You *sure* know how to make good coffee, Mrs. Olsen.
Standard	You *surely* know how to make good coffee, Mrs. Olsen.

Although *surely* is correct, it may sound too formal and insincere. Therefore, *certainly* is often a better word to use.

take and, try and   Avoid these expressions. Simply eliminate them from the sentence or substitute *try to* for *try and.*

usage

Unacceptable	If you *take and* cover the tomato plants, they probably won't freeze. I think you should *try and* settle your differences.
Standard	If you cover the tomato plants, they probably won't freeze. I think you should *try to* settle your differences.

than, then   *Than* is used to make comparisons; *then* means "at that time, in that case," or "after that."

Jill is taller *than* her brother.

First we will eat, and *then* we will discuss business.

that, which   These two words have the same meaning. *That* may refer both to things and groups of people; *which*, only to things. When referring to things, *that* is generally used with clauses that distinguish the things they modify from others in the same class (restrictive clauses). *Which* is generally used with clauses that add information about the things they modify (nonrestrictive clauses). Note that clauses starting with *which*, unlike those starting with *that*, are generally preceded by a comma.

Any book *that* she likes is certain to be trashy. (restrictive clause)

The Winthrop Building, *which* cost two million dollars to construct, could not now be duplicated for ten times that much. (nonrestrictive clause)

See pages 688–689 of the Handbook for a more comprehensive explanation of restrictive and nonrestrictive expressions.

their, there, they're   These three separate words are often confused because they sound alike. *Their* is the possessive form of *they*. *There* is an expletive that appears at the beginning of a sentence and introduces the real subject, or it is an adverb meaning "in or at that place, at that point." *They're* is a contraction of *they are*.

It is *their* basketball.

There are many reasons why I cannot come.

Put the sofa down *there*.

They're going to be here soon.

theirself, theirselves   See *hisself, theirself, theirselves*.

then   See *than, then*.

there   See *their, there, they're*.

thorough, through   *Thorough* means "careful, complete, exact, painstaking." *Through* means "in one side and out the other, from end to end, from start to finish, over the whole extent of, finished."

Brenda has done a *thorough* job.

Let's run *through* the plan again.

thusly   *Thusly* is a nonstandard form of *thus*.

to, too, two   *To* is a preposition meaning "as far as, toward, until, onto." *Too* is an adverb meaning "excessively" or "also." *Two* is a number.

I'm going *to* the store.

Are you going *too*?

This car is *too* expensive for me.

There are *two* characters in the play.

toward, towards   Both forms are correct. *Toward* generally is used in the United States and *towards* in England.

try and   See *take and, try and*.

two   See *to, too, two*.

uninterested   See *disinterested, uninterested*.

unique   *Unique* means "without an equal" or "extremely unusual" and thus should not be modified by an adverb such as *very*.

use to, used to   *Use to* is the nonstandard form of *used to*. In speech it is difficult to hear the *d* on *used*, and one may say *use to* without being detected; however, the correct written form is always *used to*.

used to could   This phrase is nonstandard for *used to be able to*.

Nonstandard	I *used to could* run ten miles.
Standard	I *used to be able to* run ten miles.

very definite   See *definite, very definite*.

wander, wonder   *Wander* is a verb meaning "to move about without a plan or set destination." *Wonder* is a noun meaning "something causing surprise, admiration, or awe" or a verb meaning "to be curious about."

Some people like to *wander* through shopping malls for recreation.

That child is a *wonder* at mathematics.

I *wonder* whether I have received an *A* on that test.

way, ways   *Ways* may be used to refer to two or more means or methods but not to time or distance.

Unacceptable	Timbuktu is a long *ways* from the United States.
Standard	There are two *ways* of thinking about that issue.
	Timbuktu is a long *way* from the United States.

well   See *good, well*.

were, where   *Were* is the past form of the verb *to be*. *Where* is an adverb or a pronoun meaning "in, at, to, from a particular place or situation" or "which or what place."

I'm sorry that you *were* ill yesterday.

Mr. Morris will show you *where* to register.

where . . . at, to, from   *At, to,* and *from* are unnecessary after *where*.

Wordy	*Where* are you taking the car *to*?
	Where does she live *at*?
	Where did you get the book *from*?
Standard	*Where* are you taking the car?
	Where does she live?
	Where did you get the book?

usage

whether See *if, whether.*

which See *that, which.*

who, whom In formal writing, *who* should be used only as a subject in clauses and sentences and *whom* only as an object.

Unacceptable	*Who* are you taking to dinner on Friday?
	I know *who* the boss will promote.
	John is the candidate *whom* I think will be elected.
Standard	*Whom* are you taking to dinner on Friday?
	I know *whom* the boss will promote.
	John is the candidate *who* I think will be elected.

See page 670 of the Handbook for a fuller discussion of *who* and *whom.*

who's, whose *Who's* is a contraction of *who is* or *who has,* and *whose* is the possessive form of *who.*

Who's coming to see us tonight?

I would like to know *who's* been dumping trash in my yard.

Whose book is that?

will See *shall, will.*

wise Do not randomly add *wise* to the ends of nouns. Such word coinings are ineffective.

Ineffective	Personality *wise,* Sheila is ideal for the job.
Standard	Sheila has an *ideal personality* for the job.

wonder See *wander, wonder.*

would have, would of *Would of* is an unacceptable substitute for *would have.* A preposition cannot substitute for a verb.

Nonstandard	I *would of* enjoyed seeing the Picasso exhibit.
Standard	I *would have* enjoyed seeing the Picasso exhibit.

would have been, had been When *would* occurs in the main part of a sentence, use *had been* (not *would have been*) in an "if" clause.

Nonstandard	If the engine *would have been* lubricated, the bearing *would not have* burned out.
Standard	If the engine *had been* lubricated, the bearing *would not have* burned out.

your, you're *Your* is a possessive form of *you; you're* is a contraction of *you are.*

Where is *your* history book?

Tell me when *you're* ready to leave.

Credits

Bonnie Angelo, "Those Good Ole Boys," *Time,* Sept. 27, 1976, p. 47.

Maya Angelou, "Mamma's Encounter," from *I Know Why the Caged Bird Sings.* Copyright © 1969 by Maya Angelou. Used by permission of Random House, Inc.

"Antigen," *Encyclopaedia Britannica,* 1974, I, 417.

Marti Bercaw, "Krumping." Marti Bercaw, Socal.com Writer. Reprinted by permission of the author.

Ray Allen Billington, "The Frontier Disappears," *The American Story,* ed. Earl Schenck Miers (Great Neck, NY: Channel, 1956).

"The Brink of a Disaster," *America,* March 31, 1979, p. 247.

Gladys Hasty Carroll, *Sing Out the Glory* (Boston: Little Brown, and Co., 1958).

Rachel Carson, *Silent Spring* (Boston: Houghton Mifflin, 1962).

Bruce Catton, "Grant and Lee: A Study in Contrasts," from *The American Story,* ed. Earl Schenck Miers. Reprinted by permission of U.S. Capital Historical Society.

Shari Caudron, "Can Generation X Be Trained?" *Training and Development Magazine,* v. 51, March 1997, pp. 20–4. Copyright © 1997 from T&D by Shari Caudron. Reprinted with permission of American Society for Training and Development.

Robert Claiborne, "Future Schlock," *The Nation, Jan.* 25, 1971, p. 117.

Cecil Clutton and John Stanford, *The Vintage Motor-car* (New York: Charles Scribner's Sons, 1955), p. 135.

Joseph Conrad, *Lord Jim* (New York: Holt, Rinehart and Winston, 1957), p. 13.

"Controlling Phobias Through Behavior Modification." *USA Today,* August 1978.

Countee Cullen, "Yet Do I Marvel" Copyrights held by the Amistad Research Center, Tulane University, New Orleans, Louisiana. Administered by JJKR Associates, New York, NY.

Lester del Ray, *The Mysterious Shy* (New York: Chilton Book Company, 1964).

Magda Denes, *In Necessity and Sorrow: Life and Death in an Abortion Hospital* (New York: Basic Books, 1976), p. xiv.

Robert Dick-Read, *Sanamu: Adventures in Search of African Art* (New York: E. P. Dutton, 1964), pp. 228–29.

Joan Didion, "On Self-Respect," in *Slouching Toward Bethlehem* (New York: Farrar, Straus and Giroux, 1968), pp. 143–44.

Barbara Dority, "Halt and Show Your Papers!," from *The Humanist,* v. 62 no. 2 (Mar.–Apr. 2002), pp. 10–13. Reprinted by permission.

Michael Dorris, excerpt from *A Yellow Raft in Blue Water* (New York: Henry Holt and Co., Inc.), 1987.

Holly Dressel, "Has Canada Got the Cure?" Reprinted from "Health Care For All" the Fall 2006 issue of *Yes! Magazine. Yes!* is a non-profit, ad-free national publication that offers positive solutions for creating a just and sustainable world.

Ian Dunbar, "Fast Track to Perfection." *Dog Fancy* Magazine, April 1999, reprinted by permission of the author.

Leo Durocher, *Nice Guys Finish Last* (New York: Simon & Schuster, 1975), p. 54.

Wayne Dyer, *What Do You Really Want for Your Children?* (New York: William Morrow, Inc., 1985).

Alan Ehrenhalt, "The Misguided Zeal of the Privacy Lobby," from *Governing,* v. 12 no. 8 (May 1999), pp. 7–8. Reprinted by permission.

Loren Eiseley, "The Judgment of the Birds," in *The Immense Journey* (New York: Random House, 1956), pp. 174–75.

Mark Krikorian, "Not Amnesty, but Attrition." From *National Review* 56 no5 38-41 Mr 22 2004. Reprinted by permission.

Marilyn Kluger, "A Time of Plenty," *Gourmet*, Nov. 1976, p. 22.

Caroline Knapp, "Why We Keep Stuff: If You Want to Understand People, Take a Look at What They Hang On To" from *The Merry Recluse* (New York: Counterpoint, 2004), pp. 195–198. Copyright held by author.

Library catalog screens reprinted by permission of Innovative Interfaces, Inc.

John Lovesey, "A Myth Is as Good as a Mile," *Sports Illustrated*, Nov. 9, 1964.

Belinda Luscombe / Kate Stinchfield, "Why We Flirt." *Time* 171 no 4 62-5 Ja 28 2008. Copyright © Time Inc., 2005. All rights reserved. No part of this material may be duplicated or redisseminated without permission

Marilyn Machlowitz, "Workaholism: What's Wrong with Being Married to Your Work?" *Working Woman*, May 1978, p. 51.

Malcolm X, *The Autobiography of Malcolm X* (New York: Ballantine Books, 1964), p. 171.

Marshall Mandell, "Are You Allergic to Your House?" *Prevention*, Sept. 1979, p. 101.

Marya Mannes, "Wasteland," in *More in Anger* (Philadelphia: J. B. Lippincott, 1958), p. 40.

Bernice McCarthy, "A Tale of Four Learners," from *Educational Leadership*, v. 54, March 1997, pp. 46–51.

H. L. Mencken, "The Libido for the Ugly," Copyright 1927 by Alfred A. Knopf, Inc., and renewed 1955 by H. L. Mencken. Reprinted from *A Mencken Chrestomathy*, edited and annotated by H. L. Mencken, by permission of the publisher.

Thomas H. Middleton, "The Magic Power of Words," *Saturday Review*, Dec. 11, 1976, p. 90.

Don Ethan Miller, "A State of Grace: Understanding the Martial Arts," *Atlantic Monthly*, Sept. 1980. Copyright © 1980 by Don Ethan Miller.

George Orwell, excerpt from "Shooting an Elephant," in *Shooting an Elephant and Other Essays*, copyright © 1950 by Sonia Brownell Orwell; renewed 1978 by Sonia Pitl-Rivers. Reprinted by permission of Harcourt, Inc.

Jo Goodwin Parker, "What Is Poverty?" in George Henderson, *America's Other Children: Public Schools Outside Suburbia* (University of Oklahoma Press, 1971).

Nancy Perry, "Saving the Schools: How Business Can Help," from *Fortune*, Nov. 7, 1988.

David Pilgrim, "What Was Jim Crow?" Jim Crow Museum of Racist Memorabilia, Sept. 2000, pp. 1–8. Mar 2006. http://www.ferris.edu/jimcrow/what.htm.

Michael Pollan, "Supermarket Pastoral." From *The Omnivore's Dilemma: A Natural History of Four Meals*. New York: Penguin Books, 2006. pp. 134-139. Reprinted by permission.

J. Winston Porter, "We'll Trash *U.S.A. Today* Too," from *U.S.A. Today*, July 11, 1988. All rights reserved.

William Raspberry, "A Journalist's View of Black Economics," copyright © 1990, Washington Post Writers Group. Reprinted with permission.

Excerpt from *Reader's Guide to Periodical Literature*, May, 1984. Copyright © 1984 by The H.W. Wilson Company. Material reprinted with permission of the publisher.

Lord Richie-Calder, "The Doctor's Dilemma," *The Center Magazine*, Sept.–Oct. 1971.

Richard Rodriguez, "Private Language, Public Language." From *Aria: A Memoir of a Bilingual Childhood* by Richard Rodriguez. Copyright © 1980 by Richard Rodriguez. Reprinted by permission of Georges Borchardt, Inc., for the author: Originally appeared in *American Scholar*.

Mark Peter Roget, Formlessness excerpt from Roget's International Thesaurus, 5th edition by Peter Mark Roget. Copyright © 1992 by HarperCollins Publishers, Inc. Reprinted by permission of HarperCollins Publishers, Inc.

Anne Roiphe, "Why Marriages Fail," from *Family Weekly*, Feb. 27, 1983. Permission granted by International Creative Management, Inc. Copyright © 1983 by Anne Roiphe.

Bertrand Russell, *The ABC of Relativity* (London: Allen and Unwin, 1965), pp. 46–47.

Nancy Masterson Sakamoto, "Conversational Ballgames." From Kinsiedo, Ltd., 1982. Reprinted by permission of Nancy Masterson Sakamoto. All rights reserved.

Marta Salinas, "The Scholarship Jacket" from *Nosotras: Latina Literature Today* by Maria del Carmen Boza, Beverly Silva, and Carmen Valle, editors. Bilingual Press/Editorial Bilingue, 1986. Tempe, Arizona. Originally from *Cuentos Chicanos: A Short Story Anthology*, Eds. Rudolfo A. Anaya and Antonio Márquez. Reprinted by permission of Bilingual Press/Editorial Bilingüe.

Robert J. Samuelson, "Getting Serious," *Newsweek*, Sept. 18, 1995, pp. 40–44.

Scott Russell Sanders, "The Men We Carry in Our Minds," copyright © 1984 by Scott Russell Sanders; first appeared in *Milkweed Chronicle;* reprinted by permission of the author and Virginia Kidd Agency, Inc.

Mark Schapiro, "Children of a Lesser God," *Harper's Bazaar*, April 1996, pp. 205–18.

Laurence Shames, "The Sweet Smell of Success Isn't All That Sweet." Copyright © 1986 by Lawrence Shames. Reprinted by permission of the author.

Gideon Sjoberg, "The Origin and Development of Cities," *Scientific American*, Sept. 1965, p. 55.

Elliott L. Smith and Andrew W. Hart, *The Short Story: A Contemporary Looking Glass* (New York: Random House, 1981).

Mariflo Stephens, "Barbie Doesn't Live Here Anymore." Reprinted with permission of Simon & Schuster Adult Publishing Group, from *The Barbie Chronicles*, edited by Yona Zeldis McDonough. Copyright © 1999 by Mariflo Stephens. Copyright © 1999 by Yona Zeldis McDonough. Barbie™ is a registered trademark of Mattel, Inc.

Deborah Sullivan, "Cosmetic Surgery: The Cutting Edge of Commercial Medicine in America," copyright © 2001 by Deborah A. Sullivan. Reprinted by permission of Rutgers University Press.

Joyce Susskind, "Surprises in a Woman's Life," *Vogue*, Feb. 1979, p. 252.

Deborah Tannen, "Gender Gap in Cyberspace," from *Newsweek* (April 16, 1994) © Newsweek, Inc. All rights reserved. Reprinted by permission.

Deems Taylor, "The Monster" in *Of Mice and Music* (New York: Simon & Schuster, 1965).

James Alexander Thom, "The Perfect Picture," reprinted with permission from the Aug. 1976 *Reader's Digest*. Copyright © 1976 by The Reader's Digest Association, Inc.

Lewis Thomas, excerpt from "Societies as Organisms," in *The Lives of a Cell* by Lewis Thomas. Copyright © 1971 by The Massachusetts Medical Society.

Nathan Thornburgh, "The Case for Amnesty." *Time* 169 no. 25, 38-9, 41-2, Je 18 2007. Copyright © Time, Inc. 2005. All rights reserved. No part of this material may be duplicated or disseminated without permission.

Richard Tomkins, "Old Father Time Becomes a Terror," from *Financial Times*, March 20, 1999. Reprinted by permission.

Rafael Vglesias, excerpt from *Fearless* (New York: Warner Books, 1993).

Beth Wald, "Let's Get Vertical!" from *Listen: Journal of Better Living*, June 1989. Reprinted by permission.

Eudora Welty, "A Visit of Charity," from *A Curtain of Green and Other Stories* (New York: Harcourt, 1941, 1969).

E. B. White, "Once More to the Lake," from *One Man's Meal*, text copyright © 1941 by E. B. White. Reprinted by permission of Tilbury House of Publishers, Gardiner, Maine.

Marion Winik, "What Are Friends For?" From *Telling* by Marion Winik, copyright © 1994 by Marion Winik. Used by permission of Villard Books, a division of Random House, Inc.

Tom Wolfe, *The Pump House Gang* (New York: World Journal Tribune, 1966), p. 293.

John V. Young. "When the Full Moon Shines Its Magic over Monument Valley," *New York Times*, March 16, 1969. Section 10, p. 1. Copyright © 1969 by John V. Young.

David Zimmerman, "Arc Test-Tube Babies the Answer for the Childless?" *Woman's Day*, May 1979, p. 26.

Marc Zwelling, "The Blended Economy," from *The Futurist*, v. 36 no. 1 (Jan.–Feb. 2002), pp. 12–13. Reprinted by permission.

Index

All page references marked with an "E" refer to the chapter on business communication available at www.mycomplab.com.

A

Abbreviations, 706–7
  in business letter
    for inside address, E–3
    two-letter state, E–3
  capitalization of, 704–5
  of Latin terms, 706
  of names of organizations
    and agencies, 706
  periods after, 694
  of personal titles, 706
  of scientific and technical
    terms, 707
Abstract nouns, 624
Abstracts for professional
    essays, 16
Abstract terms, 242
Accept/except, 114
Action, role of, in narration,
    138–39
Action verbs, 629
Active voice, 110, 633
Addresses, 708
Adjective clauses, 649–51
Adjectives, 637–39
  articles as, 637–38
  comparison with, 638
  compound, 701–2
  demonstrative, 92–93
  descriptive, 637
  determiners as, 639
  effective uses of, 674–76
  limiting, 637
  misusing, 674–75
  position of, 638
  proper, 637, 704
Advanced search, 359–62
Adverb clauses, 650–51
Adverbs, 640–41
  comparison with, 641
  conjunctive, 644, 652,
    689–90
  effective uses of, 674–76

formation of, 640
misusing, 674–75
position of, 641
Agency names, abbreviations
  of, 706
Agreement
  pronoun-antecedent,
    662–64
  subject-verb, 659–61
Alternating pattern in organizing comparison,
    214–15
*The American Heritage
    Dictionary,* 118–19
American Psychological
    Association (APA)
    system, 407,
    416–17
  for authors identified
    in text, 431
  for authors with same
    last name, 427
  for citing quotations,
    429–30
  for indirect citations, 431
  for in-text citations, 425–27
  for preparing papers,
    380–81
  for separate works of, by
    same author, 428
  for two sources for same
    citation, 428
  for unsigned references
    and, 429
Analogy
  in argument, 267–68
  in comparison, 215–16
Anecdotes in introduction, 93
Angelou, Maya, 10
Antecedents, 626
  collective nouns as, 663–64
  hidden, 665
  indefinite pronouns as,
    662–63

more than one, 665
no, 665–66
Apostrophes, 683–85
  in contractions, 684–85
  in plurals, 685
  in showing possession,
    683–84
Appeal
  to the crowd, 272
  emotional, 268–69
  rational, 258–62
*Applied Science and Technology
    Index,* 361
Appositives, 622–23
  dashes to set off, 696–97
  nonrestrictive, 622
  restrictive, 622
Arguing off the point, 272
Argument ad hominem, 272
Argument paper, 341
Arguments, 257–91
  analogy in, 267–68
  defined, 257
  for different purposes,
    277–78
  directing, to readers, 278
  emotional appeal in,
    268–69
  ethical appeal in, 269–70
  exploratory, 279–80
  organization and, 87
  planning and drafting,
    275–82
  rational appeal in, 258–62
    established truth in, 259
    evaluation of evidence
      in, 261–62
    opinions of authorities,
      259–60
    personal experience
      in, 261
    primary source
      information
      in, 260

statistical findings in,
    260–61
reasoning strategies, 263–68
  analogy in argument in,
    267–68
  deduction in, 264–67
  induction in, 263–64
  revising, 282–83
  Rogerian, 279
  student essay of, 283–88
Articles, obtaining, for
    research paper,
    362–63
Articles (a, an, the) as
    adjectives, 637–38
Assignments
  reading carefully, 20–21
  understanding, in writing
    process, 31–32
The Atlantic Monthly, 369, 370
Attitude, importance of, in
    revision, 55
Audience
  development of profile, 7
  identifying, 38–39
  for writing, 6–10
Audiovisual media
  APA style for, 420
  MLA style for, 412–13
Author, expertise of, in
    evaluating sources,
    369, 370
Authorities, opinions of, in
    arguments, 259–60
Auxiliaries, modal, 636
Auxiliary verbs, 620, 630

B

Backup copy, importance of
    keeping, 73
Balanced sentences, 109–10
Bar graphs, 398
Begging question, 271

745

Editing Symbols

Symbol	Problem	Page	Symbol	Problem	Page
ab	improper abbreviation	706–707	*no*	new paragraph not needed	
agr pa	faulty agreement of pronoun and antecedent	662-664	⊙	period needed	693–696
			// or para	nonparallelism	679–680
agr sv	faulty agreement of subject and verb	659–662	*? or ques*	missing or misused question mark	694
V or apos	missing or misused apostrophe	683–686	*" / " or quot*	missing or misused quotation marks	699–701
awk	awkward phrasing		*ref*	unclear reference of pronoun to antecedent	665–667
bib	faulty bibliographic form	408–425			
cap	capital letter needed	703–706	*ro*	run-on sentence	657–659
case	wrong case	669–672	*; or sem*	missing or misused semicolon	691–693
cl	cliché	133			
⌃ or com	missing or misused comma	686–691	*sp*	spelling error	712–718
cs	comma splice	657–659	*shift p*	shift in person	667–669
comp	faulty comparison	680–682	*shift t*	shift in tense	672–674
dm	dangling modifier	678–679	*sq*	squinting modifier	677
... or ellip	missing or misused ellipsis	373–375	*t or tense*	wrong tense	632–634
frag	sentence fragment	655–657	*trans*	poor transition	
ital	missing or misused italics	709–711	*vb*	wrong verb form	
lc	lowercase (small) letter needed	703–706	*wdy*	wordiness	132–133
// or lev	wrong level of usage	120–124	*ww*	wrong word	
log	faulty logic		⸓	delete (omit)	
mm	misplaced modifier	677–678	⌃	material omitted	
num	use numerals	707–709	⑦	meaning unclear or word illegible	
nsu	nonstandard usage new paragraph needed				